NORTH CAROLINA

PRENTICE HALL
LITERATURE

PENGUIN EDITION

PEARSON

Prentice
Hall

Upper Saddle River, New Jersey
Boston, Massachusetts

ISBN 0-13-131717-2

2 3 4 5 6 7 8 9 10   09 08 07 06 05

Cover: *Play It Pretty for the People*, collage, Phoebe Beasley/Omni-Photo Communications, Inc.

ACKNOWLEDGMENTS

Grateful acknowledgment is made to the following for copyrighted material:

Alumni Association of the University of British Columbia "The Jade Peony" by Wayson Choy from *Ubc Alumni Chronicle*, Vol. 34, No. 4, Winter 1979.

Arte Público Press "A Voice" by Pat Mora from *Communion*. Copyright © 1991 by Pat Mora.

Ballantine Books "New Road Chicken Pies from The Book Lover's Cookbook" by Shaunda Kennedy Wenger and Janet Kay Jensen from *The Book Lover's Cookbook: Recipes Inspired By Celebrated Works Of Literature And The Passages That Feature Them*. Copyright © 2003 by Shaunda Kennedy Wenger and Janet Jensen. All rights reserved.

Susan Bergholz Literary Services "My English" by Julia Alvarez from *Something To Declare*. Copyright © Julia Alvarez, 1998. "A Celebration of Grandfathers" by Rudolfo Anaya. Copyright © 1983 by Rudolfo Anaya. First published in *New Mexico Magazine*, March 1983. Reprinted by permission of Susan Bergholz Literary Services, New York. All rights reserved.

Gary L. Blackwood "The Shakespeare Stealer" by Gary L. Blackwood from *The Shakespeare Stealer*. Copyright © 2003 by Gary L. Blackwood. Used by permission.

Brandt & Hochman Literary Agents, Inc. "Sonata For Harp and Bicycle" from *The Green Flash and Other Tales of Horror* by Joan Aiken. Copyright © 1957, 1958, 1959, 1960, 1965, 1968, 1969, 1971 by Joan Aiken. "The Most Dangerous Game" by Richard Connell from *The Most Dangerous Game*. Copyright © 1924 by Richard Connell. Copyright renewed © 1952 by Louise Fox Connell. Reprinted by permission of Brandt & Hochman Literary Agents, Inc.

Jonathan Clowes Ltd. on behalf of Andrea Plunket "The Red-headed League" from *The Adventures Of Sherlock Holmes* by Sir Arthur Conan Doyle. Copyright © 1996 Sir Arthur Conan Doyle Copyright Holders. Reprinted by kind permission of Jonathan Clowes Ltd., London, on behalf of Andrea Plunket, the Administrator of the Sir Arthur Conan Doyle Copyrights.

Catherine Costello "There is No Word for Goodbye" by Mary Tall Mountain from *There Is No Word For Goodbye: Poems By Mary Tall Mountain*. Copyright © 1994 by Tall Mountain Estate. All rights reserved.

Coffee House Press "Problems With Hurricanes" by Victor Hernandez Cruz, from *Red Beans*. Copyright © 1991 by Victor Hernandez Cruz. Reprinted by permission of Coffee House Press.

Don Congdon Associates, Inc. "The Golden Kite, the Silver Wind" by Ray Bradbury from *Epoch, February 1953*. Reprinted by permission of Don Congdon Associates, Inc. Copyright © 1953 by Epoch Associates; renewed 1981 by Ray Bradbury.

Farrar, Straus & Giroux, LLC "The Washwoman" from *A Day of Pleasure* by Isaac Bachevis Singer. Copyright © 1969 by Isaac Bashevis Singer. "Prologue and Epilogue from The Odyssey" from *The Odyssey: A Stage Version* by Derek Walcott. Copyright © 1993 by Derek Walcott. "The Odyssey, Part 1: The Adventure of Odysseus; Part 2: The Return of Odysseus" from *The Odyssey* by Homer, translated by R. Fitzgerald. Copyright © 1961, 1963 by Robert Fitzgerald and renewed 1989 by Benedict R. C. Fitzgerald. "The Serenade in Nine Innings" by Judith Ortiz Cofer from *The Meaning Of Consuelo*. Copyright © 2003 by Judith Ortiz Cofer. All rights reserved.

Graywolf Press "Fifteen" from *The Way It Is: New and Selected Poems* by William Stafford. Copyright © 1966, 1998 by the Estate of William Stafford. Reprinted from The Way It Is: New and Selected Poems with the permission of Graywolf Press, Saint Paul, MN.

Scovil Chichak Galen Literary Agency, Inc. "If I Forget Thee, Oh Earth . . ." from *Expedition To Earth* by Arthur C. Clarke. Copyright © 1953, 1970 by Arthur C. Clarke; Copyright © 1951 by Columbia Publications, Inc. Used by permission.

Professor Anthony L. Gooch "Cassell's Spanish-English English-Spanish Dictionary" by Anthony Gooch and Angel Garcia de Paredes from *Cassell's Spanish-English English-Spanish Dictionary*. Copyright © 1978 by Macmillan Publishing Company, a division of Macmillan, Inc. All rights reserved.

(Continued on page R68, which is hereby considered an extension of this copyright page.)

CONTRIBUTING AUTHORS

The contributing authors guided the direction and philosophy of *Prentice Hall Literature: Penguin Edition.* Working with the development team, they helped to build the pedagogical integrity of the program and to ensure its relevance for today's teachers and students.

Kevin Feldman

Kevin Feldman, Ed.D. is the Director of Reading and Intervention for the Sonoma County Office of Education and an independent educational consultant. He publishes and provides consultancy and training nationally, focusing upon improving school-wide literacy skills as well as targeted interventions for struggling readers, special needs students, and second language learners. Dr. Feldman is the co-author of the California Special Education Reading Task Force report and the lead program author for the 2002 Prentice Hall secondary language arts program *Timeless Voices, Timeless Themes.* He serves as technical consultant to the California Reading and Literature Project and the CalSTAT State Special Education Improvement Project. Dr. Feldman has taught for nineteen years at the university level in Special Education and Masters' level programs for University of California, Riverside, and Sonoma State University.

Dr. Feldman earned his undergraduate degree in Psychology from Washington State University and has a Master's Degree from UC Riverside in Special Education, Learning Disabilities, and Instructional Design. He has an Ed.D. from the University of San Francisco in Curriculum and Instruction.

Sharon Vaughan

Sharon Vaughn, Ph.D., is the H.E. Hartfelder/The Southland Corporation Regents Professor at the University of Texas and also director of the Vaughn Gross Center for Reading and Language Arts at the University of Texas (VGCRLA). As director of the VGCRLA, she leads more than five major initiatives, including The Central Regional Reading First Technical Assistance Center; the Three-Tier Reading Research Project; a bilingual-biliteracy (English/Spanish) intervention research study; the first through fourth grade Teacher Reading Academies that have been used for teacher education throughout Texas and the nation; and the creation of online professional development in reading for teachers and other interested professionals.

Dr. Vaughn has published more than ten books and over one hundred research articles. She is Editor in Chief of the *Journal of Learning Disabilities* and serves on the editorial board of more than ten research journals, including the *Journal of Educational Psychology,* the *American Educational Research Journal,* and the *Journal of Special Education.*

Kate Kinsella

Kate Kinsella, Ed.D. is a teacher educator in the Department of Secondary Education at San Francisco State University. She teaches coursework addressing academic language and literacy development in linguistically and culturally diverse classrooms. She maintains secondary classroom involvement by teaching an academic literacy class for adolescent English learners through the University's Step to College Program. She publishes and provides consultancy and training nationally, focusing upon responsible instructional practices that provide second language learners and less proficient readers in grades 4–12 with the language and literacy skills vital to educational mobility.

Dr. Kinsella is the program author for *Reading in the Content Areas: Strategies for Reading Success,* published by Pearson Learning, and the lead program author for the 2002 Prentice Hall secondary language arts program *Timeless Voices, Timeless Themes.* She is the co-editor of the *CATESOL Journal* (CA Assn. of Teachers of ESL) and serves on the editorial board for the *California Reader.* A former Fulbright scholar, Dr. Kinsella has received numerous awards, including the prestigious Marcus Foster Memorial Reading Award, offered by the California Reading Association in 2002 to a California educator who has made a significant statewide impact on both policy and pedagogy in the area of literacy.

Differentiated Instruction Advisor
Don Deshler

Don Deshler, Ph.D, is the Director of the Center for Research on Learning (CRL) at the University of Kansas. Dr. Deshler's expertise centers on adolescent literacy, learning strategic instruction, and instructional strategies for teaching content area classes to academically diverse classes. He is the author of *Teaching Content to All: Evidence-Based Inclusive Practices in Middle and Secondary Schools,* a text which presents the instructional practices that have been tested and validated through his research at CRL.

UNIT AUTHORS

An award-winning contemporary author hosts each unit in each level of Prentice Hall Literature. *Serving as a guide for your students, these authors introduce literary concepts, answer questions about their work, and discuss their own writing processes, using their works as models. Following are the featured unit authors for Grade 9.*

Elizabeth **McCracken** (b. 1966)

Unit 1: Fiction and Nonfiction Elizabeth McCracken is highly qualified as a guide for this unit, having written prize-winning fiction and nonfiction. Her first novel, *The Giant's House*, was a finalist for the National Book Award. Her non-fiction includes pieces on Charles Dickens's *Bleak House* and Victor Hugo's *The Hunchback of Notre Dame* and the personal essay "Desiderata." In both genres, she creates a lively and engaging voice.

Wayson **Choy** (b. 1939)

Unit 2: Short Stories Known for his novel *The Jade Peony*, which won Canada's Trillium Book Award, and for its sequel, *All That Matters*, Wayson Choy is also devoted to the short-story form. The seed for *The Jade Peony* was a much-anthologized short story of the same name, and another story received the Best American Short Stories Award. His writing has been praised by *Maclean's* magazine for its "exquisite grace."

Rebecca **Walker** (b. 1969)

Unit 3: Types of Nonfiction Rebecca Walker is the ideal guide for the nonfiction unit. Her essays and articles have appeared in many magazines and publications, and her books are taught in high schools and colleges in the U.S. and Canada. When she was twenty-five, Ms. Walker was named by *Time* magazine as one of fifty influential American leaders under the age of forty. She has received awards for both her writing and her work as an advocate for young women.

Pat **Mora** (b. 1942)

Unit 4: Poetry Pat Mora, the guide for the poetry unit, has won acclaim for both writing and teaching poetry. Her many verse collections include *Agua Santa: Holy Water, Borders, Chants, Communion,* and *My Own True Name: New and Selected Poems for Young Adults.* Among the prizes given to her verse are the Southwest Book Award and the Pellicer-Frost Bi-national Poetry Award.

Gary L. **Blackwood** (b. 1945)

Unit 5: Drama Though famous for his award-winning fiction and nonfiction for young adults, Gary L. Blackwood is a perfect guide for the drama unit. He has had half a dozen stage plays produced, including his dramatization of his novel *The Shakespeare Stealer,* performed at the Kennedy Center in Washington, D.C., and at other well-known theaters. Mr. Blackwood has also taught classes and workshops in playwriting.

Coach Dean **Smith** (b. 1931) and John **Kilgo** (b. 1935)

Unit 6: Themes in Literature:
Heroism Coach Dean Smith is ideally suited as a guide for this unit on heroism. Throughout his career with the University of North Carolina basketball team, he was known as much for developing the character of his players as he was for his 879 career victories. With John Kilgo, a distinguished sportswriter, Smith wrote about his philosophy in *The Carolina Way.*

State of North Carolina
Program Advisors

Shanita Anderson
Grays Creek Middle School
Hope Hills, NC

Michael D. Blas
Lowe's Grove Middle School
Durham, NC

Karen C. Lilly-Bowyer
Winston-Salem/Forsyth County Schools
Winston-Salem, North Carolina

Amanda Grose
Lufkin Road Middle School
Apex, NC

Stephanie S. Kestner
Providence High School
Charlotte, NC

Mark Kozlowski
Winston-Salem/Forsyth County Schools
Winston-Salem, NC

Erin McDermott
Brogden Middle School
Durham, NC

Suzanne V. Micallef
John T. Hoggard High School
Wilmington, NC

Donna H. Morris
South Mecklenburg High School
Charlotte, North Carolina

Melaine Rickard
Alamance-Burlington Schools
Burlington, NC

Andrea Rumley
Alamance-Burlington Schools
Graham, NC

Tara Alexandra Thomas
South Mecklenburg High School
Charlotte, North Carolina

Betty S. Tunks
North Rowan High School
Spencer, North Carolina

Stephanie J. Wallace
East Forsyth High School
Kernersville, NC

Harriett Wilson
Vance High School,
Charlotte-Mecklenberg Schools
Charlotte, NC

Susanna Quick Winton
Lufkin Road Middle School
Apex, NC

North Carolina
Academic Achievement Handbook

NC ***All selections and workshops in this unit support your***
North Carolina standards.

Part Two
Reading Skills Focus: Author's Purpose

Unit 2 Short Stories

From the Author's Desk

Wayson Choy

Part One
Reading Skills Focus: Make Inferences

Reading Informational Material: Evaluate Visual Aids

Comparing Literary Works

> **NC** *All selections and workshops in this unit support your North Carolina standards.*

Part Two
Reading Skills Focus: Cause and Effect

All selections and workshops in this unit support your North Carolina standards.

Part Two
Reading Skills Focus: Analyze Persuasive Texts

Unit 4 Poetry

 All selections and workshops in this unit support your North Carolina standards.

Part Two
Reading Skills Focus: Paraphrase

Unit 5 Drama

Part One
Reading Skills Focus: Summarize

NC   *All selections and workshops in this unit support your North Carolina standards.*

Part Two
Reading Skills Focus: Draw Conclusions

Unit 6

Themes in Literature
Heroes and Dreamers

From the Author's Desk

Dean Smith

Part One
Reading Skills Focus: Cultural and Historical Context

Reading Informational Material: Follow Directions

Comparing Literary Works

All selections and workshops in this unit support your North Carolina standards.

Part Two
Reading Skills Focus: Compare and Contrast

RESOURCES

SELECTIONS BY READING SKILL

Unit Three

Unit Four

(Continued on next page)

SELECTIONS BY THEME

▮ Spine Tinglers

▮ Challenges and Choices

Moments of Discovery

The Lighter Side

■ Reflections on the Past, Visions of the Future

■ Hope and Aspiration

INFORMATIONAL TEXTS AND OTHER NONFICTION

■ Reading Informational Materials—Instructional Workshops

■ Additional Nonfiction—Selections by Type

■ Literature in Context—Reading in the Content Areas

A wealth of expository nonfiction is found throughout this program. Nonfiction texts are highlighted in red in the Index.

COMPARING LITERARY WORKS

WORKSHOPS

Writing Workshops

Spelling Workshops

Communications Workshops

Your Guide to North Carolina Standards and Testing

What's a GLC?

Grade Level Competencies (GLCs) are part of the North Carolina Standard Course of Study. Your teachers are responsible helping you master all of the GLCs for language arts. Here is a sample GLC for ninth grade as well as a question that tests your understanding of the standard.

Standards Groupings

To help you better understand the GLCs, we've assigned them names and abbreviations that relate to what they cover. For example, Competency Goal 2 covers the area of reading for information, so we've assigned the name **Informational Reading** or **IR** to make it a bit clearer.

SAMPLE GLC

IR-2.01.4 Demonstrate the ability to read, listen to and view a variety of increasingly complex print and non-print information appropriate to grade level and course literary focus by demonstrating comprehension of main idea and supporting details.

SAMPLE QUESTION

1. Based on the selection, which of the following statements about green tea is true?

   A It is a medicine.

   B It is consumed only in East Asian countries.

   C It decreases alertness.

   D It provides many health benefits.

As a student in North Carolina, your reading skills will be tested each year from grades 3 to 8. North Carolina's reading test is called the **End-of-Course (EOC) Test.** You will also be required to take the **North Carolina Writing Assessment** in grade 10. This exam requires you to write an informational composition.

View of North Carolina Mountains from Round Bald, Roan Mountain, NC

Standard Course of Study

English I

The following section lays out the North Carolina English I Standard Course of Study, which specifies what you are expected to learn this year in language arts class.

Competency Goal 1: The learner will express reflections and reactions to print and non-print text and personal experiences.

WL Written
    Language

WL-1.01 Narrate personal experiences that offer an audience:

WL-1.01.1 scenes and incidents located effectively in time and place.

WL-1.01.2 vivid impressions of being in a setting and a sense of engagement in the events occurring.

WL-1.01.3 appreciation for the significance of the account.

WL-1.01.4 a sense of the narrator's personal voice.

WL-1.02 Respond reflectively (individually and in groups) to a variety of expressive texts in a way that offers an audience:

WL-1.02.1 an understanding of the student's personal reaction to the text.

WL-1.02.2 a sense of how the reaction results from a careful consideration of the text.

WL-1.02.3 an awareness of how personal and cultural influences affect the response.

WL-1.03 Demonstrate the ability to read, listen to and view a variety of increasingly complex print and non-print expressive texts appropriate to grade level and course literary focus, by:

WL-1.03.1 selecting, monitoring, and modifying as necessary reading strategies appropriate to readers' purpose.

WL-1.03.2 identifying and analyzing text components and evaluating their impact on the text.

WL-1.03.3 providing textual evidence to support understanding of and reader's response to text.

WL-1.03.4 summarizing key events and/or points from text.

WL-1.03.5 making inferences, predicting, and drawing conclusions based on text.

WL-1.03.6 identifying and analyzing personal, social, historical or cultural influences, contexts, or biases.

WL-1.03.7 making connections between works, self and related topics.

WL-1.03.8 analyzing and evaluating the effects of author's craft and style.

WL-1.03.9 analyzing and evaluating the connections or relationships between and among ideas, concepts, characters and/or experience.

WL-1.03.10 identifying and analyzing elements of expressive environment found in text in light of purpose, audience, and context.

Key to Standard Codes

WL	Written Language
IR	Informational Reading
FA	Foundations of Argument
CT	Critical Thinking
LT	Literature
GU	Grammar and Usage

Standards in green type are assessed

NORTH CAROLINA

Competency Goal 2: The learner will explain meaning, describe processes, and answer research questions to inform an audience.

IR   Informational Reading

IR-2.01	**Demonstrate the ability to read, listen to and view a variety of increasingly complex print and non-print informational texts appropriate to grade level and course literary focus, by:**
IR-2.01.1	selecting, monitoring, and modifying as necessary reading strategies appropriate to readers' purpose.
IR-2.01.2	identifying and analyzing text components (such as organizational structures, story elements, organizational features) and evaluating their impact on the text.
IR-2.01.3	providing textual evidence to support understanding of and reader's response to text.
IR-2.01.4	demonstrating comprehension of main idea and supporting details.
IR-2.01.5	summarizing key events and/or points from text.
IR-2.01.6	making inferences, predicting, and drawing conclusions based on text.
IR-2.01.7	identifying and analyzing personal, social, historical or cultural influences, contexts, or biases.
IR-2.01.8	making connections between works, self and related topics.
IR-2.01.9	analyzing and evaluating the effects of author's craft and style.
IR-2.01.10	analyzing and evaluating the connections or relationships between and among ideas, concepts, characters and/or experiences.
IR-2.01.11	identifying and analyzing elements of informational environment found in text in light of purpose, audience, and context.

IR-2.02	**Explain commonly used terms and concepts by:**
IR-2.02.1	clearly stating the subject to be defined.
IR-2.02.2	classifying the terms and identifying distinguishing characteristics.
IR-2.02.3	organizing ideas and details effectively.
IR-2.02.4	using description, comparison, figurative language, and other appropriate strategies purposefully to elaborate ideas.
IR-2.02.5	demonstrating a clear sense of audience and purpose.

IR-2.03	**Instruct an audience in how to perform specific operations or procedures by:**
IR-2.03.1	considering the audience's degree of knowledge or understanding.
IR-2.03.2	providing complete and accurate information.
IR-2.03.3	using visuals and media to make presentations/products effective.
IR-2.03.4	using layout and design elements to enhance presentation/product.

IR-2.04	**Form and refine a question for investigation, using a topic of personal choice, and answer that question by:**
IR-2.04.1	deciding upon and using appropriate methods such as interviews with experts, observations, finding print and non-print sources, and using interactive technology or media.
IR-2.04.2	prioritizing and organizing the information.
IR-2.04.3	incorporating effective media and technology to inform or explain.
IR-2.04.4	reporting (in written and/or presentational form) the research in an appropriate form for a specified audience.

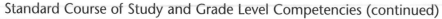

Competency Goal 3: The learner will examine argumentation and develop informed opinions.

FA Foundations of Argument

FA-3.01   Study argument by:

FA-3.01.1   examining relevant reasons and evidence.

FA-3.01.2   noting the progression of ideas that substantiate the proposal.

FA-3.01.3   analyzing style, tone, and use of language for a particular effect.

FA-3.01.4   identifying and analyzing personal, social, historical, or cultural influences, contexts, or biases.

FA-3.02   Express an informed opinion that:

FA-3.02.1   states clearly a personal view that is logical and coherent.

FA-3.02.2   engages the reader's interest or curiosity.

FA-3.03   Support that informed opinion by:

FA-3.03.1   providing relevant and convincing reasons.

FA-3.03.2   using various types of evidence, such as experience or facts.

FA-3.03.3   using appropriate and effective language, reasons, and organizational structure for the audience and purpose.

FA-3.04   Demonstrate the ability to read, listen to and view a variety of increasingly complex print and non-print argumentative texts appropriate to grade level and course literary focus, by:

FA-3.04.1   selecting, monitoring, and modifying as necessary reading strategies appropriate to readers' purpose.

FA-3.04.2   identifying and analyzing text components (such as organizational structures, story elements, organizational features) and evaluating their impact on the text.

FA-3.04.3   providing textual evidence to support understanding of and reader's response to text.

FA-3.04.4   demonstrating comprehension of main idea and supporting details.

FA-3.04.5   summarizing key events and/or points from text.

FA-3.04.6   making inferences, predicting, and drawing conclusions based on text.

FA-3.04.7   identifying and analyzing personal, social, historical or cultural influences, contexts, or biases.

FA-3.04.8   making connections between works, self and related topics.

FA-3.04.9   analyzing and evaluating the effects of author's craft and style.

FA-3.04.10   analyzing and evaluating the connections or relationships between and among ideas, concepts, characters and/or experiences.

FA-3.04.11   identifying and analyzing elements of argumentative environment found in text in light of purpose, audience, and context.

Key to Standard Codes

WL	Written Language
IR	Informational Reading
FA	Foundations of Argument
CT	Critical Thinking
LT	Literature
GU	Grammar and Usage

Standards in green type are assessed

Competency Goal 4: The learner will create and use standards to critique communication.

CT   Critical Thinking

CT-4.01   Evaluate the effectiveness of communication by:

CT-4.01.1   examining the use of strategies in a presentation/product.

CT-4.01.2   applying a set of predetermined standards.

CT-4.01.3   creating an additional set of standards and applying them to the presentation/product.

CT-4.01.4   comparing effective strategies used in different presentations/ products.

NORTH CAROLINA

CT-4.02	**Read and critique various genres by:**
CT-4.02.1	using preparation, engagement, and reflection strategies appropriate for the text.
CT-4.02.2	identifying and using standards to evaluate aspects of the work or the work as a whole
CT-4.02.3	judging the impact of different stylistic and literary devices on the work.

CT-4.03	**Demonstrate the ability to read, listen to and view a variety of increasingly complex print and non-print critical texts appropriate to grade level and course literary focus, by:**
CT-4.03.1	selecting, monitoring, and modifying as necessary reading strategies appropriate to readers' purpose.
CT-4.03.2	identifying and analyzing text components and evaluating their impact on the text.
CT-4.03.3	providing textual evidence to support understanding of and reader's response to text.
CT-4.03.4	demonstrating comprehension of main idea and supporting details.
CT-4.03.5	summarizing key events and/or points from text.
CT-4.03.6	making inferences, predicting, and drawing conclusions based on text.
CT-4.03.7	identifying and analyzing personal, social, historical or cultural influences, contexts, or biases.
CT-4.03.8	making connections between works, self and related topics.
CT-4.03.9	analyzing and evaluating the effects of author's craft and style.
CT-4.03.10	analyzing and evaluating the connections or relationships between and among ideas, concepts, characters and/or experiences.
CT-4.03.11	identifying and analyzing elements of critical environment found in text in light of purpose, audience, and context.

Competency Goal 5: The learner will demonstrate understanding of various literary genres, concepts, elements, and terms.

LT Literature

LT-5.01	**Read and analyze various literary works by:**
LT-5.01.1	using effective reading strategies for preparation, engagement, reflection.
LT-5.01.2	recognizing and analyzing the characteristics of literary genres, including fiction and drama.
LT-5.01.3	interpreting literary devices such as allusion, symbolism, figurative language, flashback, dramatic irony, dialogue, diction, and imagery.
LT-5.01.4	understanding the importance of tone, mood, diction, and style.
LT-5.01.5	explaining and interpreting archetypal characters, themes, settings.
LT-5.01.6	explaining how point of view is developed and its effect on literary texts.
LT-5.01.7	determining a character's traits from his/her actions, speech, appearance, or what others say about him or her.
LT-5.01.8	explaining how the writer creates character, setting, motif, theme, and other elements.
LT-5.01.9	making thematic connections among literary texts and media and contemporary issues.
LT-5.01.10	understanding the importance of cultural and historical impact on literary texts.
LT-5.01.11	producing creative responses that follow the conventions of a specific genre and using appropriate literary devices for that genre.

LT-5.02 **Demonstrating increasing comprehension and ability to respond personally to texts by selecting and exploring a wide range of genres.**

LT-5.03 **Demonstrate the ability to read, listen to and view a variety of increasingly complex print and non-print critical texts appropriate to grade level and course literary focus, by:**

LT-5.03.1 selecting, monitoring, and modifying as necessary reading strategies appropriate to readers' purpose.

LT-5.03.2 identifying and analyzing text components and evaluating their impact on the text.

LT-5.03.3 providing textual evidence to support understanding of and reader's response to text.

LT-5.03.4 demonstrating comprehension of main idea and supporting details.

LT-5.03.5 summarizing key events and/or points from text.

LT-5.03.6 making inferences, predicting, and drawing conclusions based on text.

LT-5.03.7 identifying and analyzing personal, social, historical or cultural influences, contexts, or biases.

LT-5.03.8 making connections between works, self and related topics.

LT-5.03.9 analyzing and evaluating the effects of author's craft and style.

LT-5.03.10 analyzing and evaluating the connections or relationships between and among ideas, concepts, characters and/or experiences.

LT-5.03.11 identifying and analyzing elements of literary environment found in text in light of purpose, audience, and context.

Competency Goal 6: The learner will apply conventions of grammar and language usage.

GU-6.01 **Demonstrate an understanding of conventional written and spoken expression that:**

GU-6.01.1 uses varying sentence types purposefully, correctly, and for specific effect.

GU-6.01.2 selects verb tense to show an appropriate sense of time.

GU-6.01.3 applies parts of speech to clarify and edit language.

GU-6.01.4 addresses clarity and style through such strategies as parallelism; appropriate coordination and subordination; variety and details; appropriate and exact words; and conciseness.

GU-6.01.5 analyzes the place and role of dialects and standard/nonstandard English.

GU-6.01.6 uses vocabulary strategies such as roots and affixes, word maps, and context clues to discern the meanings of words.

GU-6.02 **Discern and correct errors in spoken and written English by:**

GU-6.02.1 avoiding fragments, run-ons, and comma splices.

GU-6.02.2 selecting correct subject-verb agreement, consistent verb tense, and appropriate verbs.

GU-6.02.3 using and placing modifiers correctly.

GU-6.02.4 editing for spelling and mechanics (punctuation and capitalization).

Key to Standard Codes

WL Written Language

IR Informational Reading

FA Foundations of Argument

CT Critical Thinking

LT Literature

GU Grammar and Usage

Standards in green type are assessed

GU Grammar and Usage

Writing Assessment
Scoring Model

The following rubrics are similar to those used to score your response on the North Carolina Writing Assessment, which you are required to take in grade 10. The Conventions Rubric is used to assign a score for form—how well your writing conforms to the conventions of English grammar. The Composing Rubric is used to assign a score for the content of what you write—how well you express and organize your ideas.

> **Find the Formative Rubric with the Unit Writing Workshops**

Conventions Rubric

Points	Description
2	**Exhibits reasonable control of grammatical conventions appropriate to the writing task** • Exhibits reasonable control of sentence formation • Exhibits reasonable control of standard usage including agreement, tense, and case • Exhibits reasonable control of mechanics including use of capitalization, punctuation, and spelling
1	**Exhibits minimal control of grammatical conventions appropriate to the writing task** • Exhibits minimal control of sentence formation • Exhibits minimal control of standard usage including agreement, tense, and case • Exhibits minimal control of mechanics including use of capitalization, punctuation, and spelling
0	**Lacks control of grammatical conventions appropriate to the writing task** • Lacks control of sentence formation • Lacks control of standard usage including agreement, tense, and case • Lacks control of mechanics including use of capitalization, punctuation, and spelling

Composing Rubric

Points	Description
4	• Topic/subject is clear, though it may or may not be explicitly stated • Maintains focus on topic/subject throughout the response • Organizational structure establishes relationships between and among ideas and/or events • Consists of a logical progression of ideas and/or events and is unified and complete • Support and elaboration are related to and supportive of the topic/subject • Consists of specific, developed details • Exhibits skillful use of vocabulary that is precise and purposeful • Demonstrates skillful use of sentence fluency
3	• Topic/subject is generally clear, though it may or may not be explicitly stated • May exhibit minor lapses in focus on topic/subject • Organizational structure establishes relationships between and among ideas and/or events, although minor lapses may be present • Consists of a logical progression of ideas and/or events and is reasonably complete, although minor lapses may be present • Support and elaboration may have minor weaknesses in relatedness to and support of the topic/subject • Consists of some specific details • Exhibits reasonable use of vocabulary that is precise and purposeful • Demonstrates reasonable use of sentence fluency
2	• Topic/subject may be vague • May lose or may exhibit major lapses in focus on topic/subject • Organizational structure may establish little relationship between and among ideas and/or events • May have major lapses in the logical progression of ideas and/or events and is minimally complete • Support and elaboration may have major weaknesses in relatedness to and support of the topic/subject • Consists of general and/or undeveloped details, which may be presented in a list-like fashion • Exhibits minimal use of vocabulary that is precise and purposeful • Demonstrates minimal use of sentence fluency
1	• Topic/subject is unclear or confusing • May fail to establish focus on topic/subject • Organizational structure may not establish connection between and among ideas and/or events • May consist of ideas and/or events that are presented in a random fashion and is incomplete or confusing • Support and elaboration attempts to support the topic/subject but may be unrelated or confusing • Consists of sparse details • Lacks use of vocabulary that is precise and purposeful • May not demonstrate sentence fluency
NS	This code may be used for compositions that are entirely illegible or otherwise unscorable: blank responses, responses written in a foreign language, restatements of the prompt, and responses that are off-topic or incoherent.

Writing Assessment Practice

In grade 10, students are required to take the North Carolina Writing Assessment. For the grade 10 test, you will have to write an informational composition in response to a prompt. Below is a sample prompt. Use the prompt to practice writing in the test format. Then use the North Carolina Scoring Model to evaluate how well you did.

Sample Writing Prompt

Read the following quotations about honesty, which is fairness and straightforwardness of conduct; adherence to the facts.

"If you tell the truth you don't have to remember anything."

Mark Twain (1835–1910)

"An honest man can feel no pleasure in the exercise of power over his fellow citizens."

Thomas Jefferson (1743–1826), letter to John Melish, January 13, 1813

"No legacy is so rich as honesty."

William Shakespeare (1564–1616), "*All's Well that Ends Well*", Act 3 scene 5

"Our lives improve only when we take chances — and the first and most difficult risk we can take is to be honest with ourselves."

Walter Anderson

Write a letter to a good friend on the meaning of honesty. You may use the ideas presented above, your own experiences, observations, and/or readings.

As you write, remember to:

- Focus on the meaning of imagination.
- Consider the audience, purpose and context of your writing.
- Organize the ideas and details effectively.
- Include specific examples that clearly develop your writing.
- Edit your writing for standard grammar, spelling and punctuation.

Countdown to the Test

Practice for the End-of-Course Reading Comprehension Test

Your mastery of the Standard Course of Study for English language arts is measured by the End-of-Course Test and the North Carolina Writing Assessment. To do well on these exams, you'll need to practice.

Countdown to the Test provides six short tests with questions that look like those you'll encounter on the EOC Test. Your teacher will set the pace for the countdown. As you work through the material, note the Skill Focus for each test and the types of questions that pose a struggle for you.

The Countdown

Test	Use After	Skill Focus Unit	Skill Review (text pages)
1	1	Make Predictions Fact and Opinion	1–92 93–169
2	2	Make Inferences Draw Conclusions	180–288 289–380
3	3	Author's Purpose Main Idea	384–470 471–544
4	4	Context Clues Paraphrase	548–624 625–696
5	5	Summarize Compare and Contrast	700–878 879–928
6	6	Cause and Effect Purpose for Reading	932–1044 1045–1142

A Note to Parents

The North Carolina Standard Course of Study outlines the knowledge that your child needs to pass the North Carolina End-of-Course Test and Writing Assessment. Using the chart to the left, you can help your child review the skills covered in the textbook and monitor your child's progress in mastering these concepts.

EOC Test Practice

Read this selection from an autobiography and answer the questions that follow.

The Story of My Life

by Helen Keller

One brief spring, musical with the song of robin and mocking-bird, one summer rich in fruit and roses, one autumn of gold and crimson sped by and left their gifts at the feet of an eager, delighted child. Then, in the dreary month of February, came the illness which closed my eyes and ears and plunged me into the unconsciousness of a new-born baby. They called it acute congestion of the stomach and brain. The doctor thought I could not live. Early one morning, however, the fever left me as suddenly and mysteriously as it had come. There was great rejoicing in the family that morning, but no one, not even the doctor, knew that I should never see or hear again.

1. Why did the author *most likely* describe the four seasons?

  A to exaggerate Helen's love of nature

  B to reveal winter as a symbol for loss

  C to explain which season was Helen's favorite

  D to portray Helen's fascination with birds

2. What is the author's *main* purpose in writing this selection?

  A to debate

  B to persuade

  C to instruct

  D to explain

3. Based on the selection, what will the author *most likely* discuss next?

  A another memorable experience from her childhood

  B how the sight and hearing loss continued to affect her

  C the time before she became ill

  D how she became a writer

4. What is the tone of the selection?

  A anxious

  B playful

  C reflective

  D disappointed

5. Based on the selection, what is the meaning of *acute*?

  A temporary

  B severe

  C unusual

  D unexplainable

6. What is the main idea of the passage?

  A The author does not understand why she became ill.

  B The author's doctor did not think she would live.

  C The author's childhood was altered by an illness.

  D The author's family rejoiced when the fever left her.

 EOC Test Question Categories

Cognition: Questions 2, 5, 6

Interpretation: Questions 1, 3, 4

EOC Test Practice

Read this selection from a short story and answer the questions that follow.

The Cask of Amontillado
by Edgar Allan Poe

It was in vain that Fortunato, uplifting his dull torch, endeavoured to pry into the depth of the recess. Its termination the feeble light did not enable us to see. "Proceed," I said; "herein is the Amontillado. As for Luchesi--"

"He is an ignoramus," interrupted my friend, as he stepped unsteadily forward, while I followed immediately at his heels. In an instant he had reached the extremity of the niche, and finding his progress arrested by the rock, stood stupidly bewildered. A moment more and I had fettered him to the granite. In its surface were two iron staples, distant from each other about two feet, horizontally. From one of these depended a short chain, from the other a padlock. Throwing the links about his waist, it was but the work of a few seconds to secure it. He was too much astounded to resist. Withdrawing the key I stepped back from the recess.

1. Which of the following is *best* supported by the selection?

- **A** Fortunato is easily misled.
- **B** Fortunato has never had many friends.
- **C** Fortunato is a well-educated man.
- **D** Fortunato likes to deceive people.

2. Which of the following relationships is *most similar* to the relationship below?
fettered : released

- **A** astounded : bewildered
- **B** allowed : forbade
- **C** anger : violence
- **D** termination : stop

3. What is the narrator's attitude toward Fortunato?

- **A** curious
- **B** jealous
- **C** suspicious
- **D** unsympathetic

4. Which of the following is an example of irony?

- **A** Fortunato called Luchesi an "ignoramus," but was caught himself.
- **B** The narrator chose not to enter the recess first.
- **C** It was too dark in the recess to see anything.
- **D** The narrator encouraged Fortunato to find the Amontillado.

5. Based on the selection, what will the narrator *most likely* do next?

- **A** apologize to Fortunato
- **B** leave Fortunato
- **C** enter the recess himself
- **D** search somewhere else for the Amontillado

6. What is the main idea of the selection?

- **A** Friends can always be counted on.
- **B** Be careful what you wish for.
- **C** It may be difficult to recognize a villain.
- **D** Some people are doomed to fail.

(NC) EOC Test Question Categories

Cognition: Question 4   *Critical Stance:* Question 4
Interpretation: Questions 1, 3, 5, 6   *Connection:* Question 2

EOC Test Practice

Read this selection from an essay and answer the questions that follow.

The Benefits of Green Tea

The Chinese have enjoyed the benefits of green tea for over 2,000 years. Green tea, which is consumed in many East Asian countries, is a staple element of Chinese culture and medicine. Although not technically a medicine, green tea has been shown to aid health in a variety of ways.

All tea (both green and black) is made from the leaves of the Camellia synthesis plant, which is native to Southern China. The leaves contain natural antioxidants, which are substances that help maintain health by slowing destruction of cell molecules. In general, green tea produces a feeling of well-being by decreasing sleepiness and increasing alertness.

1. What is the author's *main* purpose in writing this selection?

A to entertain   **C** to persuade

B to debate   **D** to inform

2. Based on the selection, what is the meaning of *staple*?

A needless   **C** important

B unusual   **D** newfound

3. Why does the author *most likely* mention the origin of green tea?

A to introduce the reader to Chinese culture

B to explain why the Chinese are so healthy

C to show that green tea is an ancient remedy

D to entertain the reader with unusual facts

4. Based on the selection, which of the following statements about green tea is true?

A It is a medicine.

B It is consumed only in East Asian countries.

C It decreases alertness.

D It provides many health benefits.

5. Which of the following relationships is *most similar* to the relationships below?

green tea : health

A China : medicine

B alertness : fatigue

C exercise : performance

D improve : enhance

6. Which element of nonfiction does this selection have?

A argument and rebuttal

B fact and opinion

C comparison and contrast

D supporting details

 EOC Test Question Categories

Cognition: Questions 1, 2, 4, 6   *Connection:* Question 5
Critical Stance: Question 3

EOC Test Practice

The first and last stanzas of a poem are included below. Read the selection and answer the questions that follow.

I Wandered Lonely as a Cloud
by William Wordsworth

I wandered lonely as a cloud
That floats on high o'er vales and hills,
When all at once I saw a crowd,
A host, of golden daffodils;
Beside the lake, beneath the trees
Fluttering and dancing in the breeze . . .

. . . For oft, when on my couch I lie
In vacant or in pensive mood,
They flash upon that inward eye
Which is the bliss of solitude;
And then my heart with pleasure fills,
And dances with the daffodils.

1. In this selection, which of the following is an example of a simile?

   A lonely as a cloud

   B my heart with pleasure fills

   C flash upon that inward eye

   D dances with the daffodils

2. In the first stanza, what is dancing in the breeze?

   A a crowd   C trees

   B daffodils   D the lake

3. Based on the selection, what is the meaning of *pensive*?

   A excited   C ignorant

   B thoughtful   D frightened

4. In the last stanza, what is the meaning of the phrase, "They flash upon that inward eye"?

   A The speaker is easily distracted.

   B The speaker's eyes have become weak.

   C The speaker is about to fall asleep.

   D The speaker recalls an image from the past.

5. Which describes the type of rhyme in this selection?

   A slant rhyme   C internal rhyme

   B end rhyme   D beginning rhyme

6. In this selection, how does the speaker feel about being alone?

   A depressed   C confused

   B satisfied   D remorseful

 EOC Test Question Categories

Cognition: Questions 1, 2, 3, 5

Interpretation: Questions 4, 6

EOC Test Practice

Read this selection from an translation of a tragedy by Sophocles. Then answer the questions that follow.

Antigone

translated by Ian Johnston

ANTIGONE: Look—what's Creon doing with our two brothers? He's honouring one with a full funeral and treating the other one disgracefully! Eteocles, they say, has had his burial according to our customary rites, to win him honour with the dead below. But as for Polyneices, who perished so miserably, an order has gone out throughout the city—that's what people say. He's to have no funeral or lament, but to be left unburied and unwept, a sweet treasure for the birds to look at, for them to feed on to their heart's content. That's what people say the noble Creon has announced to you and me—I mean to me—and now he's coming to proclaim the fact, to state it clearly to those who have not heard. For Creon this matter's really serious. Anyone who acts against the order will be stoned to death before the city. Now you know, and you'll quickly demonstrate whether you are nobly born, or else a girl unworthy of her splendid ancestors.

ISMENE: Oh my poor sister, if that's what's happening, what can I say that would be any help to ease the situation or resolve it?

ANTIGONE: Think whether you will work with me in this and act together.

1. Based on the selection, what is the meaning of *lament*?

   A time of mourning   C disgrace
   B denial   D special order

2. What is the author's *main* purpose in writing this selection?

   A to entertain   C to explain
   B to instruct   D to debate

3. Which statement *best* summarizes this selection?

   A Antigone is upset that her brothers have died.
   B Creon has vowed to stone anyone who acts against his order.
   C Creon is honoring Etocles and treating Polyneices shamefully.
   D Ismene is unsure of how to help her sister.

4. What does the author mean when he writes, "You'll demonstrate whether you are nobly born, or else a girl unworthy . . ."?

   A One should be willing to fight for honor.
   B One deserves time to mourn.
   C One's family history should be forgotten.
   D One should not follow one's heart.

5. Based on the selection, what will Antigone *most likely* do next?

   A act against the king's orders
   B leave the kingdom
   C obey the king's orders
   D forget the situation entirely

6. Based on the selection, how does Antigone view Creon?

   A with sympathy   C with jealousy
   B with admiration   D with disdain

NC **EOC Test Question Categories**

Cognition: Questions 1, 2, 3

Interpretation: Questions 4, 5, 6

EOC Test Practice

Read this selection from an adaptation of an epic poem and answer the questions that follow.

Beowulf

Higelac's man am I," answered the leader. "Ecgtheow, my sire; my name, Beowulf. Lead me, I pray thee, to thy lord, for I have come over seas to free him forever from his secret foe, and to lift the cloud that hangs over the stately mead-hall."

Over the stone-paved streets the officer led the warriors, their armor clanking, their boar-tipped helmets sparkling, to the goodly hall, Heorot. There were they warmly welcomed, for Hrothgar had known Beowulf's king; the fame of the young man's strength had also reached him, and he trusted that in his strong grasp Grendel should die . . .

. . . But Hunferd sat at the banquet, and envious of Beowulf's fame, taunted him with his swimming match with Breca. "Seven days and nights thou didst swim with Breca; but he was stronger, and he won. Worse will happen to thee, if thou dare this night to await Grendel!"

"Easy it is to brag of Breca's deeds when drunk with beer, friend Hunferd!" replied Beowulf. "Seven days and nights I swam through the sea-water, slaying the monsters of the deep. Rough was the wave, terrible were the water beasts; but I reached the Finnish land. Wert thou as brave as thou claim'st to be, Grendel would ne'er have caused such chaos in thy monarch's land."

---

1. Who is the antagonist of the selection?
   A Beowulf
   B Grendel
   C Breca
   D Hrothgar

2. In this selection what is the **best** indication of the cultural setting?
   A the rule of a monarchy
   B the inclusion of a hero
   C elements of fantasy
   D mention of a swimming match

3. Based on the selection, what is the meaning of *stately*?
   A grand
   B evil
   C modest
   D unworthy

4. Which **best** describes the difference between Beowulf and Hunferd?
   A Beowulf seems foolish whereas Hunferd seems sensible.
   B Hunferd seems critical whereas Beowulf seems accepting.
   C Beowulf seems confident whereas Hunferd seems insecure.
   D Hunferd seems angry whereas Beowulf seems calm.

5. Which **best** describes the hero in this selection?
   A a weak character who shows unexpected bravery
   B a foolish character who is mistaken for a warrior
   C a well-meaning character with a major flaw
   D a larger-than-life character who is capable of great deeds

6. What does the author mean when he writes, ". . . to lift the cloud that hangs over the stately mead-hall"?
   A to bring light back to the kingdom
   B to restore peace of mind in the kingdom
   C to improve the appearance of the mead-hall
   D to open the mead-hall to outsiders

 EOC Test Question Categories

Cognition: Questions 1, 3   *Connection:* Question 2
Interpretation: Questions 4, 5, 6

Fiction and Nonfiction

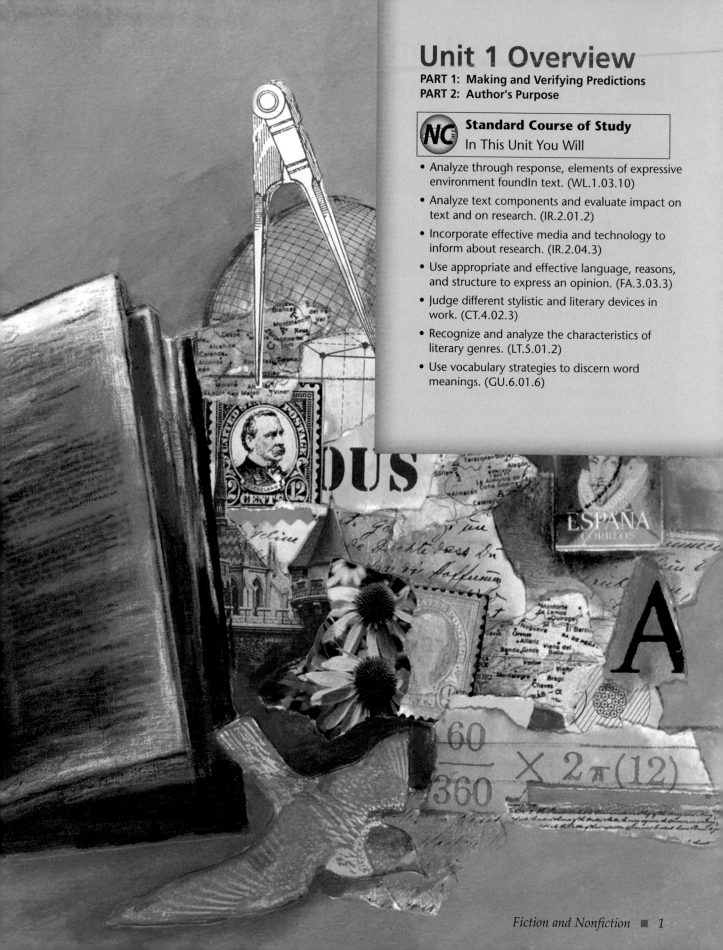

Unit 1 Overview

PART 1: Making and Verifying Predictions
PART 2: Author's Purpose

NC | **Standard Course of Study**
In This Unit You Will

- Analyze through response, elements of expressive environment foundIn text. (WL.1.03.10)
- Analyze text components and evaluate impact on text and on research. (IR.2.01.2)
- Incorporate effective media and technology to inform about research. (IR.2.04.3)
- Use appropriate and effective language, reasons, and structure to express an opinion. (FA.3.03.3)
- Judge different stylistic and literary devices in work. (CT.4.02.3)
- Recognize and analyze the characteristics of literary genres. (LT.5.01.2)
- Use vocabulary strategies to discern word meanings. (GU.6.01.6)

Introduction
Fiction and Nonfiction

From the Author's Desk

Elizabeth McCracken
Talks About the Forms

Elizabeth McCracken

▲ **Elizabeth McCracken** has written short stories and novels about unusual and unforgettable characters.

This is how I learned the difference between fiction and nonfiction.

On my 15th birthday I walked into the local public library and demanded a job and wonder of wonders they gave me one. Good thing: most of the jobs my friends had (waitress, camp counselor, ice cream scooper) required eye contact and good balance. I had a terrific knowledge of the alphabet, and a need *not* to look people in the eye. In other words, I was a born shelver.

On-the-Job Training

Fiction is prose writing that tells about imaginary characters and events; **nonfiction** is prose writing that presents information and ideas about real people, places, events, or objects.

My beat was Fiction A–SM, which was in the hallway leading from the circulation desk to the reference room. The library building was old and weird and made of lots of little rooms. Books had to be shelved where they could. Fiction SM–Z, for instance, was in the front room. The majority of shelf space was devoted to nonfiction, the way it is in most libraries.

◄ **Critical Viewing** This image seems to show a child learning to write. Do you think it is easier to learn to write fiction or nonfiction? Why?

"Nonfiction was bossy"

At first I wasn't interested in nonfiction. Nonfiction was bossy. Cookbooks, history books, and auto repair manuals told you what happened or they told you what to do. You had to believe it because it was true. How could that compare to my beloved Fiction A–SM?

Let's face it: I wasn't even interested in Fiction SM–Z. I shelved novels and short story collections, books with black and white skulls on the spine (mysteries) or yellow and red Young Adult stickers.

Fiction is a piece of truth that turns lies to meaning.
from *Skin*
—Dorothy Allison

I was very slow because I kept stopping to read. Somewhere in there, I decided to write a book myself, a novel that one day would be shelved in Fiction A–SM. The only problem was what to write about: I'd had a dull, happy life.

After a while I got faster, and they gave me an additional section to shelve: New Nonfiction. It turned out that I *liked* history books (the 900s), collections of essays (800s), biographies (shelved according to subject), even cookbooks (600s).

Fictional Characters With Nonfictional Cars

These books made me want to write, too. I could make up characters and then look up what kind of cars they'd drive, what kind of food they'd eat, what kind of clothes they'd wear. Even now, the first thing I do when I start a short story or a novel is to read a nonfiction book on the same subject.

More About Elizabeth McCracken

Elizabeth McCracken (b. 1966), who was a librarian before she became a full-time writer, says she misses working in the library. Her dual identity as novelist and librarian serves her well in her first novel, *The Giant's House* (1996), which depicts a relationship between a librarian and the world's tallest teenager. In explaining her fascination with eccentric characters, she has said, "I believe that most people are extraordinary."

Fast Facts

▶ McCracken was influenced at an early age by "a lot of relatives who were very serious about telling stories."

▶ She confesses that "there are probably more times than I care to admit when I giggle happily at something I've written."

Exploring Fiction and Nonfiction

Characteristics of Fiction

All works of fiction, no matter how long, short, simple, or complex, share certain elements.

- Fiction features **characters,** invented people who experience a series of events, called the **plot.** Characters always face a **conflict,** or problem, that sets the plot in motion.
- It occurs in a time and place, or **setting.** The setting may be real or imaginary.
- Fiction is told, or narrated, from the **point of view** of a character who may or may not be part of the story.
- It includes a **theme,** a message or an insight about life.

Types of Fiction

Works of fiction can be categorized by length and complexity.

- A **novel** is a long work of fiction that is usually presented in segments called **chapters.** Novels often feature several characters, take place in multiple settings, and concern more than one conflict. In addition to the main plot, a novel may contain subplots, or separate, related stories.
- A **novella** is a work of fiction that is longer than a short story but shorter than a novel.
- A **short story** is a work of fiction that is brief enough to be read in one sitting. Short stories usually focus on one main plot that is driven by a single conflict.

▶ **Critical Viewing** How does the physical appearance of these books compare to the imaginative possibilities they hold? [**Compare and Contrast**]

Characteristics of Nonfiction

Works of nonfiction differ from works of fiction in several ways.

- The people, events, places, and ideas presented in nonfiction are real, not invented.
- Nonfiction is narrated by an author who is a real person.
- It presents facts, describes true-life experiences, or discusses ideas.
- Nonfiction is written for a specific **audience,** or group of readers. In addition, it addresses a clear **purpose,** or reason for writing. The audience and purpose influence the type of information a writer includes.
- **Tone,** the author's attitude toward the subject or reader, is displayed through the writer's word choice and style.

Types of Nonfiction

There are four main types, or modes, of nonfiction that are defined by their purposes.

- **Narrative** nonfiction tells stories of real-life events. Examples include autobiographies and memoirs. Some narrative nonfiction is **reflective writing,** which shares the writer's thoughts and feelings about a personal experience, an idea, or a concern. Examples include reflective essays, personal essays, and journals.
- **Expository** nonfiction informs or explains. Examples include analytical essays and research reports.
- **Persuasive** nonfiction presents reasons and evidence to convince the reader to act or think in a certain way. Examples include editorials and political speeches.
- **Descriptive** nonfiction uses details related to the senses to create mental images for the reader. Examples include character sketches and scientific observations.

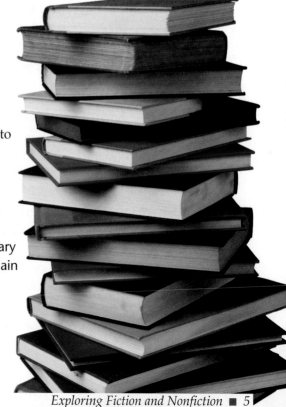

Check Your Understanding

For each of the following items, indicate whether the literary work being described is more likely fiction or nonfiction. Explain your response.

1. a book about the training routine of a champion athlete
2. a politician's memories of her childhood
3. a story set on another planet in the distant future
4. an essay about a social issue

My fiction often starts with a photograph: I stare, I get obsessed, I start to make things up.

Inspired by *The Guinness Book of World Records*

My favorite book when I was a kid was *The Guinness Book of World Records,* and every year the same picture appeared in the front: the world's tallest man, Robert Pershing Wadlow, who grew to be 8'11". The picture showed him with his father and little brother; Robert Wadlow's hair brushed the ceiling of their house.

Other than being enormous, he was ordinary looking. He wore glasses and a suit. His ears stuck out a little. There was a little chart of his ages and heights. For instance, when he was in kindergarten he was more than six feet tall.

Maybe that picture meant something to me because I was always the shortest kid in school, and that seemed something like being the tallest, but mostly I liked how ordinary it was. If you were that tall, you'd have to work hard to be ordinary. People wouldn't want to let you be normal. No matter what your real personality was, all people would see would be *tall*. They'd keep telling you that you *weren't* normal, and soon you might think the same thing.

My Main Characters and Their Conflicts

I did a little research on Robert Wadlow when I started *The Giant's House,* but mostly I wanted to make things up, to get to know *my* **characters**: James Carlson Sweatt, the World's Tallest Man, and the people who knew him.

I decided to tell the story from the **point of view** of Peggy, the town librarian, because I needed someone who would always be struggling to see both sides of James—the enormous body that needed a lot of help to get through the ordinary-sized world, and the regular, teenaged-sized personality that needed conversation and music and company.

That's the narrator's **conflict** in the book, just as James's struggle is simply to live as best as he can, considering his size.

from
The Giant's House

Elizabeth McCracken

James took out books on astronomy, ornithology:[1] sciences at once about tininess and height. He approached the desk with books he'd liked and asked for more—he knew it was easier to find more books with a good example in hand.

Then one day, in the first months of 1955—I remember looking over his head at some awful persistent Christmas decoration Astoria had stuck to the ceiling—he came to me without books. His height had become unwieldy; he reached out to touch walls as he walked, sometimes leaving marks way above where the other teenage boys smudged their hands. "I want books about people like me," he said.

I thought I knew what he was talking about, but I wanted to be cautious. "What exactly about you?" I asked. I made myself think of all the things he could have meant: Boy Scouts, basketball players. Never jump to conclusions when trying to answer a reference question. Interview the patron.

---

1. astronomy, ornithology Astronomy is the study of the stars and planets. Ornithology is the study of birds.

Fiction
Setting McCracken quickly establishes the time setting of her narrative—early 1955.

Reading Check

What kind of books does James ask the librarian to find?

"Tall people," he said.

"Tall people? Just tall people in general?"

"Very tall people. Like *me*," he said, clearly exasperated with my playing dumb. "What they do."

"Okay," I told him. "Try the card catalog. Look in the big books on the table—see those books?" I pointed. "Those are books of subject headings for the card catalog. Look under words that you think describe your topic." James was used to me doing this: I gave directions but would not pull the books off the shelf for him. My job was to show people—even people I liked—how to use the library, not to use it for them. "Dig around," I said. "Try height, try stature. Then look in the catalog for books."

He nodded, leaned on the desk, and pushed off.

An hour later he headed out the door.

▼ **Critical Viewing** Does this library seem like the "small-town" place Peggy describes on page 9? Explain. **[Connect]**

Elizabeth McCracken
Author's Insight
Card catalogs have been replaced by computer catalogs. I miss them, even though computers are more efficient in almost every way.

"Did you find what you needed?" I asked.

"There isn't anything," he said. "There was one book that sort of was about it, but I couldn't find it on the shelf."

"There's something," I told him. "Come back. We'll look for it together."

That night after closing, I hunted around myself. The only thing under *stature* was a book about growth and nutrition. I tried our two encyclopedias under height and found passing references. Not much.

In truth, my library was a small-town place, and this was a specialized topic. Still, I was certain I could find more. I got that familiar mania—there is information somewhere here, and I can find it, I have to. A good librarian is not so different from a prospector, her whole brain a divining rod. She walks to books and stands and wonders: here? Is the answer here? The same blind faith in finding, even when hopeless. If someone caught me when I was in the throes of tracking something <u>elusive</u>, I would have told them: but it's out there. I can feel it. God *wants* me to find it.

That night I wandered the reference department, eyed the bindings of the encyclopedias, dictionaries, atlases. James was so big I almost expected to locate him in the gazetteer.[2] I set my hands upon our little card catalog, curled my fingers in the curved handles of the drawers. Then I went to the big volumes of subject headings.

Looking under *height* and *stature* turned up nothing; *anthropometry* was not quite right. Then I realized the word I was looking for: *Giant*.

Giant described him. *Giant*, I knew, would lead me to countless things—not just the word, located in indexes and catalogs and encyclopedias, but the idea of Giant, the knowledge that the people that James wanted to read about, people who could be described as like him, were not just tall but giants. I sat in a spindle-backed chair in the reference room, waiting for a minute. Then I checked the volume of the Library of Congress headings. *Giants. See also: dwarfs.*

We did not have a book, but I found several encyclopedia entries. Nowadays I could just photocopy; but that night I wrote down the page and volume numbers, thinking I could not bear to tell him the word to look under. Most of the very tall people mentioned in the encyclopedia had worked in the circus as professional giants, so I went to our books on the circus.

The photographs showed enormous people. Not just tall, though of course they were that, often with an ordinary person posed

---

2. gazetteer (gaz´ ə tir´) *n.* dictionary or index of geographical names.

Vocabulary Builder
elusive (ē loo´ siv) *adj.* hard to grasp or retain mentally

Elizabeth McCracken
Author's Insight
I love the word *anthropometry*, which means the measuring of human beings.

Reading Check

What word does the librarian use to direct her search?

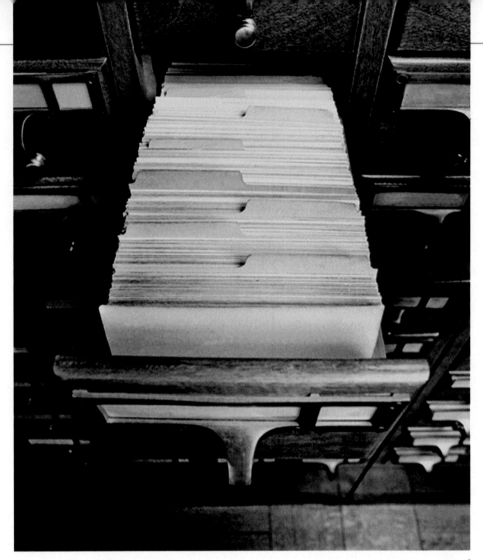

◄ **Critical Viewing**
Why might a card
catalog like the one
shown seem rich with
possibility to a
librarian like Peggy?
[Speculate]

beside them. The tall people looked twice as big as the ambassador from the normal-sized, as if they were an entirely different race. The books described weak stomachs and legs and bones. Sometimes what made them tall showed in their faces: each feature looked like something disturbed in an avalanche, separate from the others, in danger of slipping off.

Anna Swann, the Nova Scotia Giantess, married Captain Bates, the Kentucky Giant. As a young woman at Barnum's Dime Museum in New York, Miss Swann had been in two fires; in the second she had to be lifted out by a crane. No ordinary over-the-shoulder res-cue for a woman better than seven feet tall. She and her husband retired to Ohio, to a specially made house. Their church installed an extra-large pew.

Byrne, the Irish Giant, lived in fear of a certain doctor who lusted after his skeleton; he imagined the doctor's giant kettle ready to boil his bones.

Fiction
Characters Real-life
details about Anna
Swann, Byrne, and
Jack Earle make these
characters more vivid.

Jack Earle was over seven feet tall, traveled with the circus for years; after his retirement he wrote poetry.

I took comfort in Anna Swann and her husband. They were solid-looking people. Respectable. They'd had two children, though neither survived. The book described them as *in love*, and you could believe that from the pictures: their complementary heights were just a lovely coincidence to their love affair. I found myself that late night a little jealous of Anna Swann and her handsome, bearded captain.

The books said that giants tended to exaggerate their heights for exhibition purposes. I did not know it then, but every person I read about was shorter than James grew to be.

The worst book was called *Medical Curiosities*. I say worst now. That is hindsight. The night I looked, I thought, in fact, that it was the best book—not because it was good or even accurate, but because it had the most pages on the subject I was researching. I found it under the subject heading *Abnormalities, human*. A terrible phrase, and one I knew I could not repeat to James. It was a late-nineteenth-century medical book, described two-headed people and parasitic twins and dwarfs. And giants. Not exactly information, but interesting: giants who had enormous or usual appetites; ones who grew throughout their lives or only after adolescence; professional giants and private citizens.

Elizabeth McCracken
Author's Insight
I can't remember whether I've seen this book or I made it up. There are definitely books with this title, but did I have one in mind? Who knows!

So I took that book, and the circus books, marked the <u>pertinent</u> places with the old catalog cards I used for scrap, and set them aside. Ready for him, so that he did not have to look in the index, or wander through the pages at all.

Vocabulary Builder
pertinent (pʉrt´'n ənt) *adj.* relevant; having a connection to the matter at hand

"Your tall friend is here," Astoria said to me the next week. I was in my office, reading reviews. "He's looking for you."

James waited for me at the circ desk. "You said we could—"

"I looked," I said. I'd stowed the books beneath the shelf. "Try these out."

He took them to the big table in the front room. Read them.

Reading Check
Under what subject heading does the librarian finally find information that will be useful to James?

He made the sturdy chair, the same chair I'd sat in the night before, seem tiny.

Afterward he came up to me.

"How were they?" I asked. "Would you like to take them home?"

He shook his head.

"No," he said. "Thanks."

"Nothing useful here at all?"

"No," he said.

I tried to catch his eye. "Close?"

"Close. I guess." He pointed at *Medical Curiosities.* "I guess that's close."

I picked up the book and opened it to where the marker was, but he'd moved it to another page. A line drawing of a double-bodied baby looked up at me. Horrible. I snapped the book shut.

"I meant medical books," he said. "But new ones. Ones that say what goes wrong. How to cure it."

"Cures," I said. "Oh." Cures for giants? No such thing. No cure for height. Only preventive medicine. I said it as a question. "Cures? For tall people?"

"Yes," he said.

All I wanted was for him to explain it to me. It seemed presumptuous to come to any conclusions myself. I knew what he was talking about. I did. But what he wanted, I couldn't help him with.

Darla, the shelver, came rattling up with her metal cart. "Shelve these?" she said, pointing at the books. The catalog cards I'd used stuck out from the pages; James had lined them up, like a pack of cards he'd shuffled into them. "Hi, Jim," she said.

"Hi." He squinted down at her.

She stared at me; I waited for her to get back to shelving.

"Peggy. Shelve them, or not?"

"Not yet," I said. She sighed and pushed the cart off.

James stood in silence on the other side of the desk. He looked ready to leave.

"You mean how to stop growing," I said.

"Yes." Now he looked at me. "Medicine, or operations, or something."

"I'm not sure we have anything here," I said. That was a lie. I knew we didn't. "A medical library somewhere, perhaps. Or a university library. But really—" I started pulling the bookmarks from the books. I tried to sound gentle. "Really, you should ask your doctor."

"I have," he said. "I've asked a lot of doctors."

Fiction
Plot Peggy's attempts at research finally cause James to reveal his real quest.

Elizabeth McCracken
Author's Insight Earlier in the book, James comes to the library to learn how to do card and other magic tricks.

Q. How did you decide on the details to suggest James's height, such as his reaching "out to touch walls as he walked"?

A. I had a brown paper, life-sized cutout of James on a wall of my apartment while I wrote *The Giant's House.* When I wanted to really think about what it would mean to be that tall, I got out of my chair and stood next to it. It was a very strange experience: My head came up to his waist. Most of the details came out of that.

Q. To what extent is the narrator acting as more than a helpful librarian?

A. Peggy is a good person, and a good librarian, but she's also lonely, needy, grasping. She needs every patron desperately, and James most of all. To get close to people she tries to be extra-helpful.

Q. Did you want the failure of James's library search to be symbolic?

A. I wanted to demonstrate to two characters who believed that books could solve all problems that even books can fall short, and you have to look for answers from actual people—which is, I guess, symbolic!

StudentCorner

Q. Why didn't you use James as a narrator? Wouldn't he be more effective in conveying his own thoughts?
—Maria Seger, Bethel Park, Pennsylvania

A. One of the things I was interested in when I started the book was how who James was physically changed the people around him. Some people would be able to ignore his height and see the person inside, and others wouldn't. I didn't think I could do that in his voice. Then, once I found Peggy's voice, I got as interested in *her* thoughts as I was in his.

Writing Workshop: *Work in Progress*

Autobiographical Narrative

For an autobiographical narrative you may write, list three vivid memories. Describe the visual picture you see in your mind for each of these memories. Save this Memory List in your writing portfolio.

I write fiction naturally, but most of my nonfiction comes out of an assignment. In the case of "Desiderata," someone at my publishing house was putting together a Web site and asked me to write a **personal essay,** with an **informal tone.** My **audience,** of course, would be anyone who visited the site, and my **purpose** was to make them want to read my novel *The Giant's House.*

How to Find Subjects for Writing: Be a Snoop!

Personally, I find myself boring, but other people interest me. In other words, I'm a snoop. I like to read through other people's mail, flip through other people's photo albums, eavesdrop on other people's phone conversations. Best of all: my family's mail, my family's conversations.

I'm the youngest in my family, and it shows: I'm a bratty kid sister, always sneaking in places, always wondering what happened before I showed up. My parents were married for thirteen years before I was born! My brother was alive for two and a half years! No fair! I want to know everything, and what I don't know I'll make up.

Finding Inspiration in a Shopping List

I couldn't figure out exactly what to write about for the Web site until I looked at my grandmother's shopping list, which was taped to my computer screen. So that's what I decided to write about.

My nosiness is probably what made me a writer. I was lucky enough to have been born into a family of sentimental packrats, and before I could even read, my relatives were showing me photographs and telling me stories. I liked to hear *The Little Engine That Could,* but even better I liked to hear the story of my mother and her twin sister and their first exchange of birthday presents. They gave each other an American flag and a balloon on a stick.

The essay itself was my way of getting all that ephemera—stuff that's doomed to disappear or degrade, things that were never meant to last—in some kind of order.

DESIDERATA

Elizabeth McCracken

Desiderata, I learned in library science school, were the items you needed for an archive to make it useful. Useful, not complete, because there is no such thing as a complete archive. There's always a letter out there you want and need, either in someone else's collection or in an attic or just unfound. You need and want things you don't even know exist. That's how collections work.

I come from a family strong on documents. I have a small archive myself. My grandfather McCracken was a genealogist—I have his history of the McCrackens, a lovely compilation of research on early ancestors and personal remembrances of his own relatives. His wife, my grandmother, wrote stories and poems; I have copies of those, and remember once opening a drawer full of letters she wrote to God, part prayer and part daily correspondence to Someone dear. I have my grandmother Jacobson's collection of family letters; she had 11 brothers and sisters, some who wrote often and some just now and then. I have diplomas of relatives I never met. I have diaries and laundry lists. I love anything written by a relative, any evidence of what they really thought.

Elizabeth McCracken
Author's Insight
The minute I heard the word "desiderata" I knew I would try to use it in my writing. It appears in *The Giant's House,* too.

Elizabeth McCracken
Author's Insight
My grandfather edited a magazine called *The American Genealogist* for years.

And I read these documents fairly regularly. Besides letters from her family, my grandmother also saved letters from Martha, her children's nanny. My mother, who says she had the happiest childhood on record, remembers Martha and her letters as lovely and slightly daffy. Her twin sister, my aunt Carolyn, remembers the letters and the woman as dark and Dickensian[1], longing for a time that never really existed. I'd always assumed that the truth was somewhere in the middle, but I have the letters and now know that Martha was, at best, weird. She wrote to my travelling grandmother that the twins—The Dollies, she called them—didn't miss her at all. She reported that she took them out to her mother's farm, and couldn't understand why the girls were so upset to be served for dinner the chicken they'd met earlier. She reported on The Dollies' toilet training as if it were grand opera, and the Dollies heroines who wanted only, desperately, to triumph.

I'm glad to know this, I think. Certainly, it's a whole different Martha than the one I knew from my mother's stories. I know Martha now because of all that she reveals of herself, not knowing she was doing it, in her letters.

Still, there are many frustrations to family papers. First of all, you may learn things you don't want to know. For instance: some of my grandmother's sisters wanted to sue the widow of one of their brothers. Even in letters from the litigious[2] sisters themselves, this comes across as merely petty and <u>vindictive</u>. There are letters that can break your heart: my Aunt Edna, writing to my grandmother, lamented how poor her health was, how the doctors told her to slow down; I know from the dates that Edna died two weeks later, of a heart attack.

But the major frustration is how incomplete everything is, how incomplete *people* are if you try to meet them this way. The great-aunt who wanted to sue only happened to write it down; maybe she gave up the idea. Maybe she was suffering otherwise—her life was continually tragic in small ways, I know that. Some of the great-aunts I barely know, because they barely wrote. Or rather, I *think* they barely wrote—my grandmother saved every letter some years, and selected letters others. Perhaps those great-aunts simply never made it into the collection.

And then there's my grandmother Jacobson herself. She was a wonderful and complex woman, an attorney and small

Vocabulary Builder
vindictive (vin dik′tiv) *adj.* revengeful; inclined to seek vengeance

---

1. Dickensian of or relating to English novelist Charles Dickens (1812–1880).
2. litigious (li tij′ əs) *adj.* given to carrying out lawsuits; quarrelsome.

businessperson who died at home at the age of 90. The pieces of paper I have from her don't conjure her up at all. Her diary (which I don't own but have read) is a very careful record of daily events, nothing more. She doesn't detail worries or doubts, and the fact is she was a worried and somewhat doubtful person. I think she knew that we'd read it, eventually, and didn't want to tell us in her diary anything she hadn't told us already.

One piece of paper I do have: a post-it note from late in her life, which she used to mark a recipe in *The Jewish Cookbook*. It says:

coffee
bananas
bread
milk
wax beans?

and then, in the corner, written diagonally and underlined,

lottery ticket.

I know that this dates to a time when she was both worried about money and had become very serious about luck. I don't know how superstitious she'd previously been, but about two years before she died, she began to see luck good and bad, in everything: she read her horoscope, her children's horoscope, the horoscope of everyone who might touch her life that day. She believed in fortune cookies. She told her own fortune playing solitaire. And she bought lottery tickets, not so much because she believed she might win but because not playing meant she did not believe that sudden good things could happen. She was a businessperson, after all: she knew what a bad investment that weekly dollar was.

I love that little green piece of paper. *Desideratum* to me, though less than ephemera[3] to anyone else.

I could tell dozens of other stories from the pages of family papers: my aunt Blanche's pell-mell record of taking care of her favorite sister, Elizabeth, who was dying of Alzheimer's; Blanche has that disease herself now, and you can see the early signs in these notes. My great-uncles' cheery letters from Europe during World War II. A letter my brother wrote to my grandmother when I was four and he was six, thanking her for a gift and then recording that I was resisting writing a thank-you note myself.

---

3. **ephemera** (e fem′ ər ə) *n.* something, often printed material, meant to last for only a short time.

Nonfiction
Exposition The actual text from her grandmother's note helps the author show the kinds of pieces she has collected. Later, she explains how she finds meaning in them.

Elizabeth McCracken
Author's Insight Four of my grandmother's brothers served overseas. Their mother died five hours after the last, my great-uncle Gerald, came back to the family house.

Reading Check

What is the author's major frustration in regard to her collection of family papers?

Here's a last story. My father's parents were, when I knew them, quiet people. I know now that my version of them is different from anyone else's, but they were my grandparents and I never questioned who I understood them to be. After their deaths, I inherited a cherry chest-of-drawers from their house. I owned this imposing piece of furniture for a few years before I lifted some paper lining from one of the drawers and found a letter. Part of a letter, actually, written by my grandfather to my grandmother before their marriage.

It was one of the most beautiful love letters I've ever read, full of delight for her person and for their love together. It was passionate and thrilled and almost disbelieving of his great fortune, to have found her. I never imagined my grandfather, my quiet careful grandfather, was the sort of man who'd write any kind of love letter, never mind this kind. Wrong again. And my grandmother had saved it for more than fifty years. I wondered whether she took it out and reread it from time to time, or whether she'd forgotten where she'd put it.

My parents were out of town that weekend, and as it happened I'd agreed to pick them up at the airport. I brought the letter to give to my father—if it meant that much to me, I couldn't imagine what it would mean to him. And so, sitting on a bench in Logan,[4] I gave it to him. "Look what I found," I said.

"Oh," he said, perfectly pleased but not surprised. "Another letter. I'll put it with the others."

Turns out there were many more—my grandparents had written each other several times a day during their courtship. Which makes it, of course, a happier story.

My question is: was that letter more a *desideratum* for me, or my father? He had the collection, I didn't. Sometimes I regret giving it to him. I've forgotten the exact words my grandfather used, but it doesn't seem right to ask for someone else's love letter back. Someday I'll see it again, I know. Meanwhile, I need it and desire it. I need and desire everything that belongs to my family, and in some ways, I think, that's what I do with my days, writing fiction. I am writing love letters to diaries and post-it notes and telegrams and birthday cards. I am writing love letters to love letters.

▲ Critical Viewing
Are letters and photos like these meaningful to society as a whole or just to individuals and families? Explain. **[Make a Judgment]**

---

4. **Logan** Boston's Logan International Airport, named for General Edward Lawrence Logan.

Q. What audience did you have in mind for this article?

A. I was asked to write an essay for my publisher's Web site when *The Giant's House* came out, and I hadn't really written nonfiction. I knew it would have to be a relatively short essay, and I knew I wanted it to be something that would (I hoped) make people want to read the novel itself. But I didn't imagine one particular person reading it. Mostly, I'm my own audience when I write (and a demanding, judgmental one at that).

Q. How did members of your family react to this article?

A. They liked it, I think. I say *I think* because while I try my best never to write something that would upset my family, I try hard not to worry too much about exactly what they'll think about my work—I love them and want to write about them, but if I imagined, say, my parents reading everything I wrote, I'd never write anything!

Q. Why is writing fiction like "writing love letters to love letters"?

A. All of those family love letters and photographs and diaries are what made me want to be a writer: I wanted to think about the family stories and do them justice. I'm grateful that my relatives are such packrats. It's been a real help to have the family documents as inspiration.

StudentCorner

Q. Was it hard to leave your grandfather's letter with your father, risking the possibility that you might not ever see it again?
                                                —Meredith Kern, Oakland, New Jersey

A. It was extremely hard! Still, I know it was the right thing to do. That letter belonged with the other letters.

 Writing Workshop: *Work in Progress*

Autobiographical Narrative
Choose one item from the Memory List in your writing portfolio. Build the scene you see in your mind by adding details related to other senses. Include what you heard, smelled, and felt. Save this expanded Memory List in your writing portfolio.

Apply the Skills

Fiction and Nonfiction

Thinking About the Selections

1. **Respond:** Do you feel sympathy for James in *The Giant's House*? Explain.

2. **(a) Recall:** What information about his condition does James hope to find? **(b) Infer:** What actions has he already taken to get this information? **(c) Describe:** Using details from the text, describe James's attitude toward his plight.

3. **(a) Recall:** Note two points at which the narrator, Peggy, refers to her training as a librarian. **(b) Analyze:** Do Peggy's efforts for James meet her criteria for being a good librarian? Explain.

4. **(a) Speculate:** Imagine that *The Giant's House* is set in the present day. Complete a chart like the one shown to list specific research sources, including the Internet and the library, that James could use to find information about his condition. **(b) Evaluate:** Discuss your chart with a classmate to identify the most valuable resource. Share your ideas with the class.

Research Question	Possible Source

5. **(a) Recall:** In "Desiderata," what are some of the frustrations McCracken experiences in "meeting" people through family papers? **(b) Speculate:** Based on this essay, why do you think McCracken became a writer of **fiction**?

Fiction and Nonfiction Review

6. How does the **setting** of *The Giant's House* affect James's problem?

7. In her **nonfiction** essay "Desiderata," is McCracken's primary purpose to persuade, to inform, or to reflect? Explain.

Research the Author

Elizabeth McCracken was a librarian before she became a writer. Using the Internet and library resources, identify other McCracken works that reveal her interest in libraries, documents, and research. Present your findings to the class in an **oral report.**

- Prepare summaries of McCracken works that touch on library work, archives, and research.
- Include quotes from McCracken's writings.

QuickReview

Selections at a Glance

In *The Giant's House,* a young man searches for information in a small-town library.

"**Desiderata**" describes the power of ordinary writings to preserve family history.

Go Online
Assessment
For: Self-test
Visit: www.PHSchool.com
Web Code: epa-6101

Fiction: literary narratives about imagined people and events

Nonfiction: literary works that present information about real people, events, or ideas

Setting: the time and place in which a story takes place

Skills You Will Learn

Literary Analysis: *Narrative Essay*
Reading Skill: *Ask Questions to Make Predictions*

Reading Skill: *Read to Perform a Task*

Literary Analysis: *Plot, Foreshadowing, and Suspense*
Reading Skill: *Read On to Verify Predictions*

Literary Analysis: *First-Person and Third-Person Omniscient Point of View*

Literature You Will Read

Reading and Vocabulary Skills Preview

Reading: Make Predictions

Standard Course of Study

- Select, monitor, and modify reading strategies appropriate to argumentative texts. (FA.3.04.1)

- Recognize and analyze the characteristics of literary genres. (LT.5.01.2)

▶ A **prediction** is a logical assumption about what will happen next.

Skills and Strategies You Will Learn in Part 1

In Part 1 you will learn

- to **ask questions** and **make meaningful predictions** (p. 22)
- to **read ahead** to **verify,** and **evaluate** and **revise predictions** (p. 46)
- to **use predictions** when you **read to perform a task** (p. 42)

Using the Skills and Strategies in Part 1

In Part 1, you will learn to **ask questions** that identify details that clarify your expectations and help you make predictions. You will also learn to check your predictions as you continue reading and to look back at clues you may have missed when your predictions need to be revised. **Making, verifying, and revising predictions** helps you recognize and understand the reasons for, and connections between, events and actions.

The chart models the skills and strategies you will learn in Part 1.

Story Details
The character is in the building and all the doors are locked.

Question
Is the character going to get out?

Prediction
The character will not escape from the building.

→

Read Ahead
The character sees a window.

→

Evaluate Prediction
My first prediction was logical but new information changes my thinking.

→

Revise Prediction
The character will escape through the window.

Academic Vocabulary: Words for Responding to Literature

The following words will help you write and talk about the selections in Part 1.

Word	Definition	Example Sentence
contemporary *adj.*	recent or current; living or happening at the same time	The setting is a *contemporary* American town.
involve *v.*	to include, to require	The author's recollections of childhood *involve* many humorous memories.
specific *adj.*	precise, or definite	The details establish a *specific* setting.
participate *v.*	to take part in, to join	Several characters *participate* in the conflict over the farm.
contribute *v.*	give, add, provide	Details *contribute* to a story's mood.

Vocabulary Skill: Word Roots

▶ A **word root** is the basic unit of meaning in a word.

In Part 1 you will learn

- Latin root *-tempor-* (p. 70)
- Latin root *-spec-* (p. 70)
- Latin root *-volve-* (p. 40)
- Latin root *-part-* (p. 40)

Many English words are built upon **Latin or Greek roots.** Knowing roots can help you determine the meanings of words. Dictionaries provide information on the meaning and history of each word part.

The word is usually used as an adjective.　　　　The parts of the words are shown with their history.

con•tem•po•rary (kən tem′ pə rer′ ē) **adj.** [< L *com-*, with + L temporarium< tempus,time: see **TEMPER**] **1.** living or happening at the same period of time **2.** of about the same age **3.** of or in the same style of the present or recent times; modern. *n. pl.* rar′ies **1.** a person living in the same period as another...

The word can also be used as a noun. The entry shows the changes for the plural form of the noun.

Activity Arrange the words into three pairs according to the root they share: *involve, species, extemporaneous, revolve, inspect, contemporary.* Explain why you pair the words as you do.

Practice these skills with either "The Washwoman" (p. 26) or "New Directions" (p. 35).

Literary Analysis

A **narrative essay** is a short piece of nonfiction that tells a story about a real person or event. In a narrative essay, the author chooses to include **significant details** that help move the story forward or that help to make his or her point about the subject. For example, if an author writing about a famous singer wants to stress that the singer comes from a musical family, the essay might mention that the singer's father plays guitar. The essay probably wouldn't mention that the singer's father collects stamps. As you read, notice how the author's choice of significant details influences your impressions of the people and events he or she describes.

Reading Skill

A **prediction** is an informed idea about what might happen later in a narrative. Predictions are based on details in the text and your own experience. When you **verify predictions,** you read on to see if the prediction is correct.

Pause periodically while reading and **ask questions** about text details and events.

- Why does the author mention this detail?
- How might it become important later on?

Look for the answers as you read ahead. Use a chart like this to record your predictions and whether or not they are accurate.

NC **Standard Course of Study**

- Make inferences and draw conclusions in response based on text. (WL.1.03.5)
- Provide textual evidence to support understanding of and response to text in answering questions. (IR.2.01.3)
- Demonstrate comprehension of main idea and supporting details in literary texts. (LT.5.03.5)

Detail
". . . she could 'mix groceries well enough to scare hungry away.'"

Question
Why does the author mention this detail?

Prediction
The character might sell food to support her family.

Verification?

Vocabulary Builder

The Washwoman

- **forebears** (fôr´ berz) *n.* ancestors (p. 27) *His* <u>forebears</u> *started the family business.*
- **rancor** (raŋ´kər) *n.* bitter hate (p. 28) *The rivals fumed with* <u>rancor</u> *for each other.*
- **atonement** (ə tōn´ mənt) *n.* act of making up for a wrongdoing or injury (p. 28) *He volunteered at a nursing home as* <u>atonement</u> *for his misbehavior.*
- **obstinacy** (äb´ stə nə sē) *n.* stubbornness (p. 30) *The child refused to clean up, and she was punished for her* <u>obstinacy</u>.

New Directions

- **amicably** (am´ i kə blē) *adv.* in a friendly way (p. 36) *They settled their disagreements* <u>amicably</u>.
- **meticulously** (mə tik´ yo͞o ləs lē) *adv.* very carefully and precisely (p. 36) *She* <u>meticulously</u> *applied her makeup.*
- **ominous** (äm´ ə nəs) *adj.* threatening (p. 37) *The sound of the thunder seemed* <u>ominous</u>.
- **unpalatable** (un pal´ it ə bəl) *adj.* distasteful; unpleasant (p. 37) *She thought changing diapers was her most* <u>unpalatable</u> *chore.*

Build Understanding • *The Washwoman*

Background

Jews in Poland "The Washwoman" takes place in the early twentieth century in what is now Poland. Centuries earlier, many Jewish people had settled there, drawn by the promise of religious tolerance. By Singer's time, Poland had been conquered by other countries. Yet, Poland's Jews held on to their traditions, continuing to speak Yiddish, a language blending German with Hebrew and other languages.

Connecting to the Literature

Reading/Writing Connection In "The Washwoman," a woman struggles in the bitter cold to complete a chore. Write three or four reasons people might have for sticking to a difficult task. Use at least three of the following words: *accomplish, demonstrate, justify, confront.*

READ MORE

by
Isaac Bashevis Singer
*Gimpel the Fool
and Other Stories
In My Father's Court*

Meet the Author

Isaac Bashevis **Singer** (1904–1991)

Storytelling always had an important place in Isaac Bashevis Singer's life. He grew up in the city of Warsaw in what now is Poland. Singer's father was a rabbi, a teacher of the Jewish faith and laws. Advice-seekers streamed through the family home, telling their stories as the fascinated young Singer listened and observed.

"Life Itself Is a Story" Fleeing persecution against Jews, Singer left Poland for New York City in 1935. In New York, Singer began to make a name for himself as a writer. He set many of his tales in the world of European Jewry he had left. Ironically, as he wrote, World War II devastated that world. Villages like the one of his birth were wiped off the face of the earth even as Singer brought them to life on the page.

Fast Facts

▶ Singer wrote in Yiddish throughout his life, and he often translated his own work into English.
▶ In 1978, Singer won the Nobel Prize for Literature.

Go **Online**
Author Link

For: More about the author
Visit: www.PHSchool.com
Web Code: epe-9102

The Washwoman

Isaac Bashevis Singer

Our home had little contact with Gentiles.[1] The only Gentile in the building was the janitor. Fridays he would come for a tip, his "Friday money." He remained standing at the door, took off his hat, and my mother gave him six groschen.[2]

Besides the janitor there were also the Gentile washwomen who came to the house to fetch our laundry. My story is about one of these.

She was a small woman, old and wrinkled. When she started washing for us, she was already past seventy. Most Jewish women of her age were sickly, weak, broken in body. All the old women in our street had bent backs and leaned on sticks when they walked. But this washwoman, small and thin as she was, possessed a strength that came from generations of peasant <u>forebears</u>. Mother would count out to her a bundle of laundry that had accumulated over several weeks. She would lift the unwieldy pack, load it on her narrow shoulders, and carry it the long way home. She lived on Krochmalna Street too, but at the other end, near the Wola section. It must have been a walk of an hour and a half.

She would bring the laundry back about two weeks later. My mother had never been so pleased with any washwoman. Every piece of linen sparkled like polished silver. Every piece was neatly ironed. Yet she charged no more than the others. She was a real find. Mother always had her money ready, because it was too far for the old woman to come a second time.

Laundering was not easy in those days. The old woman had no faucet where she lived but had to bring in the water from a pump. For the linens to come out so clean, they had to be scrubbed thoroughly in a washtub, rinsed with washing soda, soaked, boiled in an enormous pot, starched, then ironed. Every piece was handled ten times or more. And the drying! It could not be done outside because thieves would steal the laundry. The wrung-out wash had to be carried up to the attic and hung on clotheslines. In the winter it would become as brittle as glass and almost break when touched. And there was always a to-do with other housewives and washwomen who wanted the attic clothesline for their own use. Only God knows all the old woman had to endure each time she did a wash!

---

1. **Gentiles** any persons not Jewish; here, specifically Christians.
2. **groschen** (grō´ shen) Austrian cent or penny.

Literary Analysis
Narrative Essay
Which detail in this paragraph helps you identify this as a narrative essay?

Vocabulary Builder
forebears (fôr´ berz´) *n.* ancestors

Reading Check
According to Singer, what is the washwoman's physical appearance?

She could have begged at the church door or entered a home for the penniless and aged. But there was in her a certain pride and love of labor with which many Gentiles have been blessed. The old woman did not want to become a burden, and so she bore her burden.

My mother spoke a little Polish, and the old woman would talk with her about many things. She was especially fond of me and used to say I looked like Jesus. She repeated this every time she came, and Mother would frown and whisper to herself, her lips barely moving, "May her words be scattered in the wilderness."

The woman had a son who was rich. I no longer remember what sort of business he had. He was ashamed of his mother, the wash-woman, and never came to see her. Nor did he ever give her a groschen. The old woman told this without <u>rancor</u>. One day the son was married. It seemed that he had made a good match. The wedding took place in a church. The son had not invited the old mother to his wedding, but she went to the church and waited at the steps to see her son lead the "young lady" to the altar.

The story of the faithless son left a deep impression on my mother. She talked about it for weeks and months. It was an affront not only to the old woman but to the entire institution of mother-hood. Mother would argue, "Nu, does it pay to make sacrifices for children? The mother uses up her last strength, and he does not even know the meaning of loyalty."

And she would drop dark hints to the effect that she was not certain of her own children: Who knows what they would do some day? This, however, did not prevent her from dedicating her life to us. If there was any delicacy in the house, she would put it aside for the children and invent all sorts of excuses and reasons why she herself did not want to taste it. She knew charms that went back to ancient times, and she used expressions she had inherited from generations of devoted mothers and grandmothers. If one of the children complained of a pain, she would say, "May I be your ransom and may you outlive my bones!" Or she would say, "May I be the <u>atonement</u> for the least of your fingernails." When we ate she used to say, "Health and marrow in your bones!" The day before the new moon she gave us a kind of candy that was said to prevent parasitic worms. If one of us had something in his eye, Mother would lick the eye clean with her tongue. She also fed us rock candy against coughs, and from time to time she would take us to be blessed against the evil eye. This did not prevent her from studying *The Duties of the Heart*, *The Book of the Covenant*, and other serious philosophic works.

◀ **Critical Viewing**
How does this depiction of a neighborhood in Poland compare with Singer's description of his community? **[Compare]**

But to return to the washwoman. That winter was a harsh one. The streets were in the grip of a bitter cold. No matter how much we heated our stove, the windows were covered with frostwork and decorated with icicles. The newspapers reported that people were dying of the cold. Coal became dear. The winter had become so severe that parents stopped sending children to cheder,[3] and even the Polish schools were closed.

On one such day the washwoman, now nearly eighty years old, came to our house. A good deal of laundry had accumulated during the past weeks. Mother gave her a pot of tea to warm herself, as well as some bread. The old woman sat on a kitchen chair trembling and shaking, and warmed her hands against the teapot. Her fingers were gnarled from work, and perhaps from arthritis too. Her finger-nails were strangely white. These hands spoke of the stubbornness of mankind, of the will to work not only as one's strength permits but beyond the limits of one's power. Mother counted and wrote down the list: men's undershirts, women's vests, long-legged drawers, bloomers, petticoats, shifts, featherbed covers, pillowcases, sheets, and the men's fringed garments. Yes, the Gentile woman washed these holy garments as well.

✓ **Reading Check**

Why does the washwoman do other people's laundry?

---

3. cheder (khā´ dər) *n.* religious school.

The bundle was big, bigger than usual. When the woman placed it on her shoulders, it covered her completely. At first she swayed, as though she were about to fall under the load. But an inner <u>obstinacy</u> seemed to call out: No, you may not fall. A donkey may permit himself to fall under his burden, but not a human being, the crown of creation.

It was fearful to watch the old woman staggering out with the enormous pack, out into the frost, where the snow was dry as salt and the air was filled with dusty white whirlwinds, like goblins dancing in the cold. Would the old woman ever reach Wola?

She disappeared, and Mother sighed and prayed for her.

Usually the woman brought back the wash after two or, at the most, three weeks. But three weeks passed, then four and five, and nothing was heard of the old woman. We remained without linens. The cold had become even more intense. The telephone wires were now as thick as ropes. The branches of the trees looked like glass. So much snow had fallen that the streets had become uneven, and sleds were able to glide down many streets as on the slopes of a hill. Kindhearted people lit fires in the streets for vagrants[4] to warm themselves and roast potatoes in, if they had any to roast.

For us the washwoman's absence was a catastrophe. We needed the laundry. We did not even know the woman's address. It seemed certain that she had collapsed, died. Mother declared she had had a premonition, as the old woman left our house that last time, that we would never see our things again. She found some old torn shirts and washed and mended them. We mourned, both for the laundry and for the old, toil-worn woman who had grown close to us through the years she had served us so faithfully.

More than two months passed. The frost had subsided, and then a new frost had come, a new wave of cold. One evening, while Mother was sitting near the kerosene lamp mending a shirt, the door opened and a small puff of steam, followed by a gigantic bundle, entered. Under the bundle tottered the old woman, her face as white as a linen sheet. A few wisps of white hair straggled out from beneath her shawl. Mother uttered a half-choked cry. It was as though a corpse had entered the room. I ran toward the old woman and helped her unload her pack. She was even thinner now, more bent. Her face had become more gaunt, and her head shook from side to side as though she were saying no. She could not utter a clear word, but mumbled something with her sunken mouth and pale lips.

4. **vagrants** (vā′ grənts) *n.* people who wander from place to place, especially those without regular jobs.

Vocabulary Builder
obstinacy (äb′ stə nə sē) *n.* stubbornness

Reading Skill
Making and Verifying Predictions What prediction do you make based on these details about the cold and the washwoman's absence?

After the old woman had recovered somewhat, she told us that she had been ill, very ill. Just what her illness was, I cannot remember. She had been so sick that someone had called a doctor, and the doctor had sent for a priest. Someone had informed the son, and he had contributed money for a coffin and for the funeral. But the Almighty had not yet wanted to take this pain-racked soul to Himself. She began to feel better, she became well, and as soon as she was able to stand on her feet once more, she resumed her washing. Not just ours, but the wash of several other families too.

"I could not rest easy in my bed because of the wash," the old woman explained. "The wash would not let me die."

"With the help of God you will live to be a hundred and twenty," said my mother, as a benediction.

"God forbid! What good would such a long life be? The work becomes harder and harder . . . my strength is leaving me . . . I do not want to be a burden on anyone!" The old woman muttered and crossed herself, and raised her eyes toward heaven.

Fortunately there was some money in the house and Mother counted out what she owed. I had a strange feeling: the coins in the old woman's washed-out hands seemed to become as worn and clean and pious as she herself was. She blew on the coins and tied them in a kerchief. Then she left, promising to return in a few weeks for a new load of wash.

But she never came back. The wash she had returned was her last effort on this earth. She had been driven by an indomitable will to return the property to its rightful owners, to fulfill the task she had undertaken.

And now at last her body, which had long been no more than a shard[5] supported only by the force of honesty and duty, had fallen. Her soul passed into those spheres where all holy souls meet, regardless of the roles they played on this earth, in whatever tongue, of whatever creed. I cannot imagine paradise without this Gentile washwoman. I cannot even conceive of a world where there is no recompense for such effort.

Reading Skill
Making and Verifying Predictions Was your earlier prediction about the old woman accurate? Why or why not?

▲ **Critical Viewing** What do you think it would be like to wash clothes using a washboard and tub like these? **[Speculate]**

---

5. **shard** (shärd) *n.* fragment or broken piece.

Apply the Skills

The Washwoman

Thinking About the Selection

1. **Respond:** Why do you think the washwoman gives so much and asks so little in return?
2. **(a) Recall:** Which job does the washwoman perform for Singer's family? **(b) Connect:** Which laborious obstacles to doing the job well does Singer describe?
3. **(a) Recall:** What prevents the washwoman from returning to the family for several months? **(b) Draw Conclusions:** What does the washwoman's eventual return tell you about her character?
4. **(a) Recall:** What specific information about the washwoman's personal life does the author include? **(b) Speculate:** What other kinds of information about the washwoman might the author have chosen to include but left out? **(c) Assess:** Based on this essay, explain why an author might choose to include some details and omit others.

Literary Analysis

5. **(a)** In this **narrative essay,** what difficulties does the washwoman face? **(b)** How does she respond to those challenges? **(c)** What inspirational lesson does the author take away from the story of the washwoman's life?
6. **(a)** Use a chart like the one shown to record three **significant details** that Singer uses to describe the washwoman and her son.

The Washwoman	The Washwoman's Son

    (b) What impression of each character does each detail create?
7. **(a)** What point does Isaac Bashevis Singer make in this narrative essay? **(b)** Which details in the essay best support this point?

Reading Skill

8. Write down three **predictions** that you made while reading "The Washwoman." Then, trade papers with a partner and discuss the accuracy of your predictions and the details you used to make them. Finally, explain how your method of making and verifying predictions has or has not changed as a result of your discussion.

Vocabulary Builder

Practice Use a word from the vocabulary list for "The Washwoman" on page 24 to replace each underlined word with its opposite.

1. The former enemies have put their old <u>friendship</u> behind them.
2. The actor's <u>flexibility</u> made him difficult to direct.
3. She inherited the family trade from her <u>children</u>.
4. Running extra laps was his <u>reward</u> for being late to practice.

Adding Words to Your Vocabulary A **synonym** is a word that has the same or similar meaning as another word. Using a thesaurus, find a synonym for each word in the vocabulary list for "The Washwoman" on page 24. Use each synonym in a sentence that makes the meaning of the word clear. (For help with reference materials, see page R7.)

Writing

Using "The Washwoman" as a model, write an **anecdote**, a brief narrative, about a person whom you know and admire. For example, you might describe something admirable that the person did and what you learned from it.

- Before you draft, note what you admire about the person.
- Describe a specific event that illustrates the characteristics you admire in your subject.

For *Grammar, Vocabulary,* and *Assessment,* see **Build Language Skills,** pages 40–41.

Extend Your Learning

Listening and Speaking Conduct an **interview** with an older person whom you admire. Before you begin, list questions about the person's life. Speak with confidence and poise as you ask your questions, and listen carefully to the answers. Ask follow-up questions when appropriate. Record the person's answers and share your findings with the class.

Research and Technology With classmates, use Internet and library resources to find information about Singer's native Poland, including its history of shifting borders. Share your findings with the class in an **oral presentation**.

- Divide the presentation so that each of you delivers part of it.
- Use visual aids in your presentation, including maps.

Narrative Essay

Background

Limited Options In the early 1900s, job opportunities were unavailable to many Americans—particularly African Americans like Annie Johnson in "New Directions." At that time, the most common jobs available for African American women were cleaning, childcare, and general household labor. For women who had families, caring for someone else's household was an extra burden.

Connecting to the Literature

Reading/Writing Connection In "New Directions," an African American woman decides to make a major change in her life at a time when many choices were closed to her. List some of the character traits one might need to succeed in a new venture. Use at least three of these words: *analyze, establish, initiate, transform.*

Review

For **Literary Analysis, Reading Skill,** and **Vocabulary Builder,** see page 24.

READ MORE

by Maya Angelou
The Complete Collected Poems of Maya Angelou

Meet the Author

Maya **Angelou** (b.1928)

Maya Angelou's life is a story of overcoming hardships and succeeding. She was raised in rural, segregated Arkansas. In 1940, she moved to San Francisco, where she worked as a waitress, cook, and dancer. In the 1950s, Angelou went to New York, where she discovered her talents as a writer.

"I am human, and nothing human can be alien to me." Angelou wrote these words, and she lives by them. She went on to become an author, a poet, a playwright, an editor, an actress, a director, and a teacher. Her many literary honors include a nomination for a Pulitzer Prize. She also read one of her poems at President Bill Clinton's inauguration.

Fast Facts

▶ Angelou's first name is Marguerite. Her brother gave her the nickname *Maya* when she was a child.
▶ The feature film *Georgia, Georgia* was adapted from one of her stories.

Go **Online**
Author Link

For: More about the author
Visit: www.PHSchool.com
Web Code: epe-9103

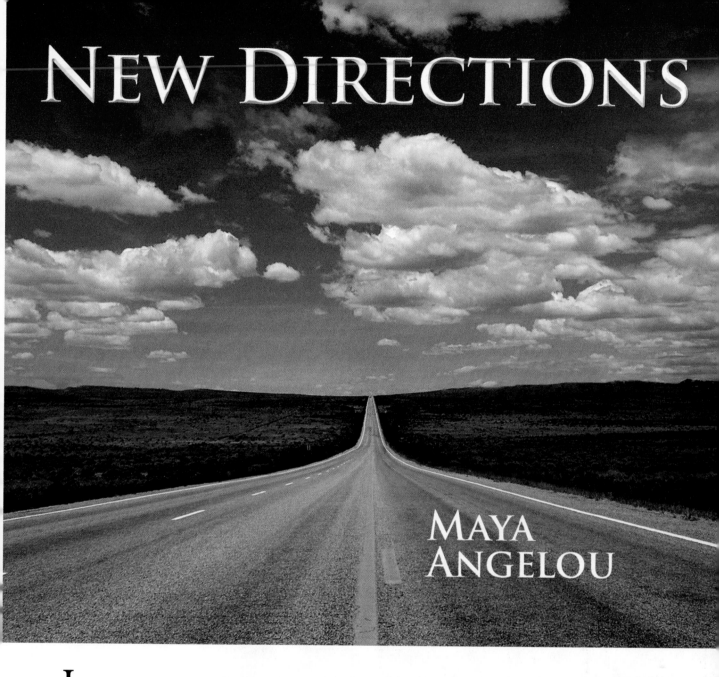

NEW DIRECTIONS

MAYA ANGELOU

In 1903 the late Mrs. Annie Johnson of Arkansas found herself
with two toddling sons, very little money, a slight ability to read and
add simple numbers. To this picture add a disastrous marriage and
the burdensome fact that Mrs. Johnson was a Negro.

When she told her husband, Mr. William Johnson, of her dissatis-
faction with their marriage, he conceded that he too found it to be
less than he expected, and had been secretly hoping to leave and
study religion. He added that he thought God was calling him not
only to preach but to do so in Enid, Oklahoma. He did not tell her
that he knew a minister in Enid with whom he could study and who
had a friendly, unmarried daughter. They parted <u>amicably</u>, Annie

Vocabulary Builder
amicably (am´ i kə
blē) *adv.* in a friendly
way

keeping the one-room house and William taking most of the cash to carry himself to Oklahoma.

Annie, over six feet tall, big-boned, decided that she would not go to work as a domestic and leave her "precious babes" to anyone else's care. There was no possibility of being hired at the town's cotton gin or lumber mill, but maybe there was a way to make the two factories work for her. In her words, "I looked up the road I was going and back the way I come, and since I wasn't satisfied, I decided to step off the road and cut me a new path." She told herself that she wasn't a fancy cook but that she could "mix groceries well enough to scare hungry away and from starving a man."

She made her plans <u>meticulously</u> and in secret. One early evening to see if she was ready, she placed stones in two five-gallon pails and carried them three miles to the cotton gin. She rested a little, and then, discarding some rocks, she walked in the darkness to the saw mill five miles farther along the dirt road. On her way back to her little house and her babies, she dumped the remaining rocks along the path.

That same night she worked into the early hours boiling chicken and frying ham. She made dough and filled the rolled-out pastry with meat. At last she went to sleep.

Vocabulary Builder
meticulously (mə tik´ yoo ləs lē) *adv.* very carefully and precisely

Reading Skill
Making and Verifying Predictions What prediction do you make about Annie's plans? Why?

◄ **Critical Viewing** Judging from this photograph, why do you think Annie Johnson felt that lumber workers would want to buy her pies? **[Draw Conclusions]**

The next morning she left her house carrying the meat pies, lard, an iron brazier, and coals for a fire. Just before lunch she appeared in an empty lot behind the cotton gin. As the dinner noon bell rang, she dropped the savors into boiling fat and the aroma rose and floated over to the workers who spilled out of the gin, covered with white lint, looking like specters.

Most workers had brought their lunches of pinto beans and biscuits or crackers, onions and cans of sardines, but they were tempted by the hot meat pies which Annie ladled out of the fat. She wrapped them in newspapers, which soaked up the grease, and offered them for sale at a nickel each. Although business was slow, those first days Annie was determined. She balanced her appearances between the two hours of activity.

So, on Monday if she offered hot fresh pies at the cotton gin and sold the remaining cooled-down pies at the lumber mill for three cents, then on Tuesday she went first to the lumber mill presenting fresh, just-cooked pies as the lumbermen covered in sawdust emerged from the mill.

For the next few years, on balmy spring days, blistering summer noons, and cold, wet, and wintry middays, Annie never disappointed her customers, who could count on seeing the tall, brown-skin woman bent over her brazier, carefully turning the meat pies. When she felt certain that the workers had become dependent on her, she built a stall between the two hives of industry and let the men run to her for their lunchtime provisions.

She had indeed stepped from the road which seemed to have been chosen for her and cut herself a brand-new path. In years that stall became a store where customers could buy cheese, meal, syrup, cookies, candy, writing tablets, pickles, canned goods, fresh fruit, soft drinks, coal, oil, and leather soles for worn-out shoes.

Each of us has the right and the responsibility to assess the roads which lie ahead, and those over which we have traveled, and if the future road looms <u>ominous</u> or unpromising, and the roads back uninviting, then we need to gather our resolve and, carrying only the necessary baggage, step off that road into another direction. If the new choice is also <u>unpalatable</u>, without embarrassment, we must be ready to change that as well.

Literature in Context

Culture Connection

Iron Braziers Annie Johnson uses an iron brazier (brā´ zhər) to cook her meat pies. A brazier is a pan or bowl that holds burning coals or charcoal as a heat source for cooking. In some braziers, food is placed on a grill directly over the flames. Johnson uses hers to heat a pot of boiling fat so that she can deep-fry her pies.

An iron brazier would have been heavy and difficult to carry, especially along with the other supplies needed to cook the pies.

Johnson's process for cooking and selling her pies was laborious, but she made the best use of the means available to her.

Connect to the Literature

What does Johnson's willingness to endure the work involved in using an iron brazier suggest about her character?

Apply the Skills

New Directions

Thinking About the Selection

1. **Respond:** What do you admire about Annie Johnson? Explain.
2. **(a) Recall:** Why does Annie Johnson have to find a source of income? **(b) Recall:** Why does she decide against a job as a domestic? **(c) Infer:** What does Annie Johnson's decision suggest about the kind of mother she is?
3. **(a) Recall:** What does Annie Johnson decide to do to earn a living? **(b) Evaluate:** How would you describe Annie Johnson's abilities as a businessperson? Explain.
4. **(a) Recall:** In what ways does Annie Johnson's business grow? **(b) Draw Conclusions:** What does her achievement suggest about the human spirit in general?
5. **Make a Judgment:** Do you think taking a "new direction" in life is worth the risk of failure? Explain.

Literary Analysis

6. **(a)** In this **narrative essay,** what problem sets the story in motion? **(b)** How is the problem overcome?
7. **(a)** Use a chart like the one shown to record three **significant details** that Angelou uses to describe Annie Johnson and her husband.

Annie Johnson	Annie Johnson's Husband

   (b) What impression of each character does each of these details create?
8. **(a)** What point do you think Maya Angelou makes in this narrative essay? **(b)** Which details in the essay best support this point?

Reading Skill

9. Write down three **predictions** that you made while reading "New Directions." Then, trade papers with a partner and discuss the accuracy of your predictions and the details you used to make them. Finally, explain how your method of making and verifying predictions has or has not changed as a result of your discussion.

QuickReview

Essay at a Glance
The author finds inspiration in the tale of a young mother who starts a business to support her family.

Go Online
Assessment
For: Self-test
Visit: www.PHSchool.com
Web Code: epa-6104

Narrative Essay: an essay that tells a story about real people or events

Significant Details: key pieces of information in a literary work

Prediction: an informed idea about what might happen later

Vocabulary Builder

Practice Use a word from the "New Directions" vocabulary list on page 24 to replace each underlined word with its opposite.

1. When people act in a friendly manner, they behave <u>viciously</u>.
2. Some people think that spinach is <u>delicious</u>.
3. The rumble of a volcano is an <u>encouraging</u> sound.
4. You can avoid mistakes on tests by checking your work <u>carelessly</u>.

Adding Words to Your Vocabulary A synonym is a word that has the same or similar meaning as another word. Using a thesaurus, find a synonym for each word in the vocabulary list for "New Directions" on page 24. Use each synonym in a sentence that makes the meaning of the word clear. (For help with reference materials, see page R7.)

Writing

Using "New Directions" as a model, write an **anecdote,** a brief narrative, about a person whom you know and admire. For example, you might describe something admirable that the person did and what you learned from it.

- Before you draft, note what you admire about the person.
- Describe a specific event that illustrates the characteristics you admire in your subject.

For *Grammar, Vocabulary,* and *Assessment,* see **Build Language Skills,** pages 40–41.

Extend Your Learning

Listening and Speaking With another student, role-play an **interview** between Annie Johnson and a potential employer. Listen carefully to what your partner says in the interview, and respond with appropriate questions or answers. Speak with confidence and poise. After the role play, give each other feedback on your work.

Research and Technology With classmates, follow Johnson's example and identify a business opportunity in your community. Deliver an **oral presentation** on your idea in class.

- Divide the presentation so that each of you delivers part of it.
- Incorporate maps and other visual aids into your presentation.

Build Language Skills

Vocabulary Skill

Word Roots When you *participate* in an activity, you *involve* yourself in it. Both *participate* and *involve* have Latin roots. The word *participate* has the **Latin root -part-,** meaning "portion or part of." To *participate* is to "take part." Other cognates of *-part-* will be related to "portion, part." *Involve* has the **Latin root -volve-,** meaning "roll." *Involve* means "roll in," or "include." The root *-volve-* is closely related to the root *-volut-,* which also means "roll."

Practice Explain how one of the roots *-volve-, -volut-,* or *-part-* contributes to the meaning of the underlined word in each sentence. If necessary, use a dictionary for help. Then write a new sentence using the underlined word.

1. Understanding the work <u>involves</u> studying the characters.
2. Your <u>participation</u> in the discussion is important.
3. Seasons are the result of the Earth's <u>revolution</u> around the sun.
4. The <u>partition</u> divides the two sides of the room.
5. The plot <u>revolves</u> around a conflict.

Grammar Lesson

Common Nouns and Proper Nouns A **common noun** names any one of a class of people, places, or things. A **proper noun** names a specific person, place, or thing and begins with a capital letter.

Type	Common Noun	Proper Noun
person	student	Deana Johnson
place	city	Raleigh-Durham
thing	novel	*A Separate Peace*

MorePractice

For more practice with common and proper nouns, see p. R40.

Practice Copy each of the following sentences. Draw one line under each common noun and two lines under each proper noun.

1. Astronauts reached the moon in July of the year my mother was born.
2. Millions of people around the world watched Neil Armstrong become the first person to walk on the moon.
3. Americans were filled with pride.
4. The president awarded the crew medals.
5. They were honored with a parade in New York City.

Prentice Hall Writing and Grammar Connection: Chapter 16, Section 2.

Reading: Make Predictions

Directions: *Read the selection. Then, answer the questions.*

Lance pulled on his helmet, and checked his skates one last time. He was a little nervous inside, but confident, as well. He had been speed racing for three years and had won the finals the past two years. Now he felt he was ready to make it three years in a row.

Lance knew that even though he had won the past two years, he could not take anything for granted. He had trained every day for weeks, harder than in past years. Now he took his place in the line, waiting for the starting gun. He glanced at the racer next to him and saw fear in his eyes.

Standards Assessed

• IR.2.04.1
• IR.2.04.4
• LT.5.03.8

1. Which of the following would not help you make a prediction?
   A Lance had been racing for three years.
   B He had won the past two years.
   C He had trained harder than in past years.
   D The gun sounded and the race was on.

2. What is a prediction about the race's end?
   A The boy next to Lance will win the race.
   B Lance will be disqualified for not wearing a helmet.
   C Lance will win the race.
   D Lance will become exhausted during the race and drop out.

3. Which of the following details make that a logical prediction?
   A Lance glanced at the racer next to him.
   B Lance had to check his kneepads and skates.
   C Lance was nervous and seemed worried.
   D Lance had won before, and had trained hard.

4. What detail in a future paragraph would make you revise your prediction?
   A Lance paces himself well.
   B The racer in front of Lance falls.
   C Lance feels that the training paid off.
   D Lance sets the pace at the beginning of the race.

Timed Writing: Narration [Critical Stance]

Write a brief narrative about a person who refused to give up and who eventually succeeded in spite of difficult odds. Base your story on actual events, and identify the challenges your subject faced. **(20 minutes)**

 Writing Workshop: *Work in Progress*

Autobiographical Narrative

Choose one item from the Memory List saved in your writing portfolio. Build the scene in your mind by adding other senses. Include what you heard, how warm or cold it was and how it felt. Save your Memory List in your writing portfolio.

Reading Informational Materials

Instructions: Recipes

In Part 1, you are learning how to make predictions while reading literature. Predicting is also useful when you read instructions. Predictions allow you to anticipate when you will need certain materials and how you will use them. The instructions that follow are for a recipe. If you read "New Directions" by Maya Angelou, you will notice that Annie Johnson may have used a similar recipe to bake the meat pies she sold.

About Instructions: Recipes

Instructions provide a step-by-step guide to performing a specific task. A recipe is a form of instruction that tells you how to prepare something to eat. Recipes usually include the following elements:

- A list of all the <u>ingredients</u> you will need
- The exact <u>quantity</u> of each ingredient
- The <u>order</u> in which the ingredients should be combined
- The <u>methods</u> for combining the ingredients (such as mixing, blending, melting)
- The <u>time</u> required for cooking, baking, chilling, freezing, etc.
- The number of <u>servings</u> the recipe will make

Reading Skill

Like most instructions, recipes present a series of specific steps you must follow to complete a larger task. When **reading to perform a task,** pay attention to the order of the required steps. Check off each step as you complete it or use a bookmark to keep your place on the page. Be sure to finish each step before going on to the next one, until your task is complete.

When you read a recipe, pay close attention to words that signal important details, especially words of quantity and adverbs that tell how to perform tasks. The chart shown here identifies signal words.

Recipe Instruction	Signal Word
Gradually add the broth and milk . . .	Gradually
Cook over *medium* heat . . .	medium
. . . on a *lightly* floured surface.	lightly
Put a *spoonful* of filling in center . . .	spoonful

- Make connections between works, self and related topics in communication. (CT.4.03.8)
- Understand the importance of cultural and historical impact on texts. (LT.5.01.10)

from **The Book Lover's Cookbook**

New Road Chicken Pies

by Shaunda Kennedy Wenger and Janet Kay Jensen

Oliver Twist's request for more gruel starts a riot, and Ma Joad agonizes over not being able to fill the bellies of hungry children who watch her family eat stew. When characters deal with food, whether they're eating, cooking, dreaming, manipulating, or suffering, they step off the page and connect with the reader.

Food scenes offer a universal platform that can foster connections between the reader and the character. Some food scenes bring such strong feelings of nostalgia, the experience between the fiction of the story, the reality of the present, and the memories of the past blur to the point where we question, *Could I have known this author? Could I have known this character?*

This recipe links the real-life experience of preparing and eating delicious meat-pies to the characters and events in Maya Angelou's story "New Directions."

> The introduction describes the way in which a recipe can connect readers to literary characters.

New Road Chicken Pies (a.k.a. Turnovers)

FILLING:
1/2 cup potatoes, diced
1/4 cup carrots, diced
3 tablespoons celery, chopped
1 teaspoon onion, minced
1 tablespoon butter or margarine
3 tablespoons all-purpose flour
Salt and pepper to taste
1 cup chicken broth
1/3 cup milk
1 teaspoon fresh parsley, minced
1/4 cup frozen peas, thawed
1 1/2 cups chicken, cooked & diced

PASTRY DOUGH:
2/3 cup shortening or margarine
2 cups all-purpose flour
1/2 teaspoon salt
5 to 7 tablespoons water
1 egg white
1 teaspoon water

> The recipe begins with a complete list of every ingredient needed and the exact amounts required. Some items must be *diced, chopped, minced,* or *thawed* before the mixing of ingredients begins.

(continued)

Reading Informational Materials

New Road Chicken Pies (continued)

Boil the potatoes, carrots, celery, and onions until tender, about 6 to 8 minutes. Drain and set aside. In a separate saucepan, melt the butter or margarine over medium heat. Whisk in the flour, salt, and pepper. Gradually add the broth and milk, whisking continually to keep sauce smooth. Cook over medium heat until thickened. Stir in the cooked vegetables, parsley, peas, and chicken and continue cooking until warmed through.

Prepare pastry by mixing the shortening or margarine, sugar, flour, and salt in a bowl with a fork or pastry blender until the mixture is crumbly. Add water 1 tablespoon at a time until dough is pliable. Work dough into a ball with hands after last tablespoon of water is added.

> The writers of most recipes assume that you will have all the necessary utensils. The writer of this recipe assumes that users will have a whisk.

With a rolling pin, roll the pastry dough out to a 1/4-inch thickness on a lightly floured surface. Cut 4-inch or 5-inch-diameter circles from the dough. Put a spoonful of filling in center of each circle. Fold to a half-moon shape. Press edges together to make a seam. Crimp edges with a fork, dipping tines in flour as needed to keep from sticking to dough.

In a small bowl, whisk together egg white and 1 teaspoon water. Brush egg white mixture onto the tops of the turnovers with a pastry brush. Cut a small slit in the top of each turnover. Bake on ungreased cookie sheet at 375° for 15 to 20 minutes or until golden brown.

(MAKES 8 TO 10 TURNOVERS)

> The last line provides the number of servings the recipe makes. If you want to make 16–20 turnovers, you would double the quantities of the ingredients.

EOC **Test Practice**

Reading: Read to Perform a Task

Directions: *Choose the letter of the best answer to each question.*

Standards Assessed
- FA.3.03.3
- LT.5.01.11
- LT.5.03.1

1. For eight to ten turnovers, how much celery do you use?
   A 1/4 cup
   B 3 teaspoons
   C 3 tablespoons
   D 5 to 7 stalks

2. When you add the broth and milk, how often should you whisk the sauce?
   A never
   B continually
   C three or four times
   D until the vegetables are cooked

3. Which of the following tasks do you perform just before baking?
   A slit the top of each turnover
   B dice the carrots
   C fold the dough into half-moon shapes
   D add the cooked vegetables to the sauce

Reading: Comprehension and Interpretation

Directions: *Write your answers on a separate piece of paper.*

4. What is the shape of the finished turnovers? [**Knowledge**]
5. Why might you need to dip the tines of the fork in flour when crimping the edges of the dough? [**Generating**]
6. Compare a section of the recipe that gives specific instructions or measurements to a part of the instructions that is more open-ended. Explain the possible reasons for the difference. [**Organizing**]

Timed Writing: Explanation [Cognitive]

Describe a process you know well, such as how to cook something, how to make something, or how to assemble something. Remember to identify all the ingredients, materials, or tools needed. Explain each step clearly and precisely, and be sure the steps follow a logical order. Include signal words that will help readers understand the steps in the process.**(20 minutes)**

Practice these skills with either "Sonata for Harp and Bicycle" (p. 48) or "The Cask of Amontillado" (p. 61).

NC **Standard Course of Study**

- Provide evidence to support understanding of response to text. (WL.1.03.3)
- Make inferences and draw conclusions based on text to answer research questions. (IR.2.01.6)
- Explain how the writer creates literary elements. (LT.5.01.8)

Literary Analysis

Plot is the sequence of events in a narrative. It is structured around a **conflict,** or problem, and it can be divided into the following parts:

- **Rising Action:** central conflict is introduced
- **Climax:** high point of intensity in the conflict is reached
- **Falling Action:** conflict's intensity lessens
- **Resolution:** conflict concludes and loose ends are tied up

Writers use a variety of techniques to keep readers interested in the plot. One of these, **foreshadowing,** is the use of clues to hint at events that will happen later in a story. Authors use this technique to create **suspense,** a feeling of tension that keeps readers wondering what will happen next.

Reading Skill

A **prediction** is an informed guess about what will happen later in a narrative. Notice details that may foreshadow future events. Make predictions based on those details, and then **read on to verify your predictions.** If a prediction turns out to be wrong, evaluate your reasoning.

- Did you misread details?
- Did the author purposely create false expectations in order to surprise you later in the story?

Revise, or change, your prediction based on your evaluation. Use a chart like the one shown to record your predictions and evaluate their accuracy. Analyze any inaccurate predictions to determine why they were incorrect.

Prediction
The butler will be exposed as the criminal.

Outcome
The gardener is exposed as the criminal.

Analysis of Prediction
The author created a surprise ending by misleading readers.

Vocabulary Builder

Sonata for Harp and Bicycle

- **tantalizingly** (tan´ tə līz´ iŋ lē) *adv.* in a teasing way (p. 50) *He held the ball tantalizingly out of reach.*
- **furtive** (fur´ tiv) *adj.* sneaky (p. 52) *With a furtive wink, he let his friend in on the joke.*
- **reciprocate** (ri sip´ rə kāt´) *v.* return (p. 54) *She refused to reciprocate his anger.*

The Cask of Amontillado

- **precluded** (prē klo̅o̅d´ id) *v.* prevented (p. 61) *His injury precluded any hope of victory.*
- **retribution** (re´ trə byo̅o̅´shən) *n.* payback; punishment for a misdeed (p. 61) *He wanted retribution for the insult he had received.*
- **explicit** (eks plis´ it) *adj.* clearly stated (p. 63) *I could not ignore her explicit refusal.*

Background

Sonatas A sonata (sə nät´ ə) is a musical composition in several movements, or parts. Sonatas are often written for solo piano or for piano and another instrument. In titling her story "Sonata for Harp and Bicycle," Joan Aiken playfully suggests a musical structure that will, like a sequence of chords, be resolved harmoniously at the end.

Connecting to the Literature

Reading/Writing Connection This story features a character who strives to solve a mystery. Many people, such as detectives and reporters, seek out the truth every day as part of their jobs. Write a few sentences describing the qualities a person would need for this type of work. Use at least three of these words: *anticipate, comprehend, confirm, eliminate, expose.*

READ MORE

**by
Joan Aiken**
*Midnight Is a Place
Night Fall*

Meet the Author

Joan **Aiken** (b. 1924)

The daughter of an American poet, Conrad Aiken, and a Canadian mother, Jessie MacDonald, Joan Aiken was born and grew up in England. She lived with her family in an eerie old house, an experience that helped foster her fascination with mystery and the unexplained. Her mother's second husband was another writer, Martin Armstrong. Not surprisingly, Aiken knew when she was very young that she would become a writer someday.

The "Family Trade" Aiken began writing when she was five and published her first story at sixteen. After spending some time working in London for a magazine, an advertising agency, and the United Nations, she decided to pursue what she has called "the family trade." Her many literary works include novels, poems, plays, and stories for both children and adults.

Fast Facts

▶ Aiken did not attend a school until she was twelve. Before then, she was taught at home by her mother.
▶ Aiken once worked as an advertising copywriter, as does her main character in "Sonata for Harp and Bicycle."

For: More about the author
Visit: www.PHSchool.com
Author Link Web Code: epe-9104

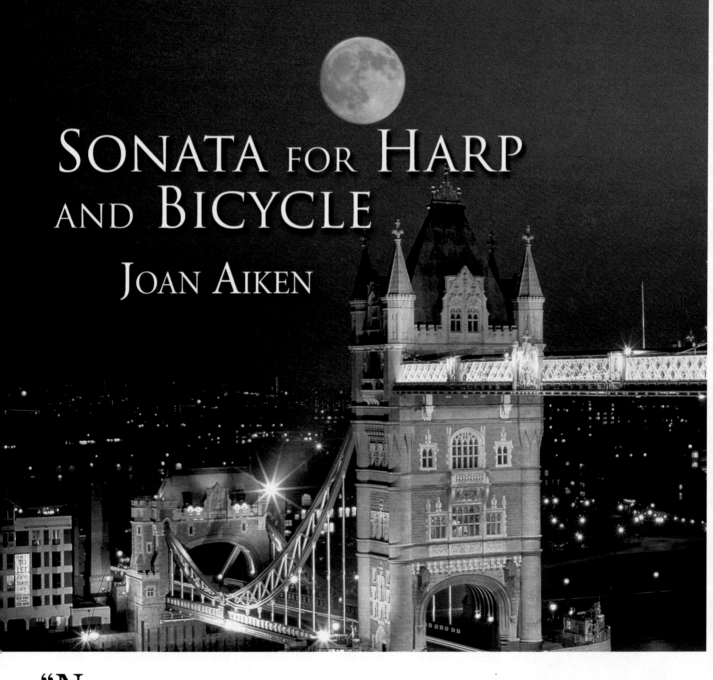

SONATA FOR HARP AND BICYCLE

JOAN AIKEN

"**N**o one is allowed to remain in the building after five o'clock," Mr. Manaby told his new assistant, showing him into the little room that was like the inside of a parcel.

"Why not?"

"Directorial policy," said Mr. Manaby. But that was not the real reason.

Gaunt and sooty, Grimes Buildings lurched up the side of a hill toward Clerkenwell.[1] Every little office within its dim and crumbling exterior owned one tiny crumb of light—such was the proud

---

1. Clerkenwell district of London.

boast of the architect—but toward evening the crumbs were collected as by an immense vacuum cleaner, absorbed and demolished, yielding to an uncontrollable mass of dark that came tumbling in through windows and doors to take their place. Darkness infested the building like a flight of bats returning willingly to roost.

"Wash hands, please. Wash hands, please," the intercom began to bawl in the passages at a quarter to five. Without much need of prompting, the staff hustled like lemmings along the corridors to green- and blue-tiled washrooms that mocked with an illusion of cheerfulness the encroaching dusk.

Reading Check

What is the new assistant told about being in the building after five o'clock?

"All papers into cases, please," the voice warned, five minutes later. "Look at your desks, ladies and gentlemen. Any documents left lying about? Kindly put them away. Desks must be left clear and tidy. Drawers must be shut."

A multitudinous shuffling, a rustling as of innumerable bluebottle flies might have been heard by the attentive ear after this injunction, as the employees of Moreton Wold and Company thrust their papers into cases, hurried letters and invoices into drawers, clipped statistical abstracts together and slammed them into filing cabinets, dropped discarded copy into wastepaper baskets. Two minutes later, and not a desk throughout Grimes Buildings bore more than its customary coating of dust.

"Hats and coats on, please. Hats and coats on, please. Did you bring an umbrella? Have you left any shopping on the floor?" At three minutes to five the homegoing throng was in the lifts[2] and on the stairs; a clattering, staccato-voiced flood darkened momentarily the great double doors of the building, and then as the first faint notes of St. Paul's[3] came echoing faintly on the frosty air, to be picked up near at hand by the louder chimes of St. Biddulph's-on-the-Wall, the entire premises of Moreton Wold stood empty.

"But why is it?" Jason Ashgrove, the new copywriter, asked his secretary one day. "Why are the staff herded out so fast? Not that I'm against it, mind you; I think it's an admirable idea in many ways, but there is the liberty of the individual to be considered, don't you think?"

"Hush!" Miss Golden, the secretary, gazed at him with large and terrified eyes. "You mustn't ask that sort of question. When you are taken onto the Established Staff you'll be told. Not before."

"But I want to know now," Jason said in discontent. "Do you know?"

"Yes, I do," Miss Golden answered <u>tantalizingly</u>. "Come on, or we shan't have finished the Oat Crisp layout by a quarter to." And she stared firmly down at the copy in front of her, lips folded, candyfloss hair falling over her face, lashes hiding eyes like peridots,[4] a girl with a secret.

Jason was annoyed. He rapped out a couple of rude and witty rhymes which Miss Golden let pass in a withering silence.

"What do you want for your birthday, Miss Golden? Sherry? Fudge? Bubble bath?"

2. **lifts** *n.* British term for elevators.
3. **St. Paul's** famous church in London.
4. **peridots** (per´ i däts´) *n.* yellowish-green gems.

Literary Analysis
Plot and Foreshadowing
What problem for Jason is introduced in his conversation with Miss Golden?

Vocabulary Builder
tantalizingly (tan´ tə līz´ iŋ lē) *adv.* in a teasing way

"I want to go away with a clear conscience about Oat Crisps," Miss Golden retorted. It was not true; what she chiefly wanted was Mr. Jason Ashgrove, but he had not realized this yet.

"Come on, don't tease! I'm sure you haven't been on the Established Staff all that long," he coaxed her. "What happens when one is taken on, anyway? Does the Managing Director have us up for a confidential chat? Or are we given a little book called *The Awful Secret of Grimes Buildings*?"

Miss Golden wasn't telling. She opened her drawer and took out a white towel and a cake of rosy soap.

"Wash hands, please! Wash hands, please!"

Jason was frustrated. "You'll be sorry," he said. "I shall do something desperate."

"Oh no, you mustn't!" Her eyes were large with fright. She ran from the room and was back within a couple of moments, still drying her hands.

"If I took you out for a coffee, couldn't you give me just a tiny hint?"

Side by side Miss Golden and Mr. Ashgrove ran along the green-floored passages, battled down the white marble stairs among the hundred other employees from the tenth floor, the nine hundred from the floors below.

He saw her lips move as she said something, but in the clatter of two thousand feet the words were lost.

"—fire escape," he heard, as they came into the momentary hush of the carpeted entrance hall. And "—it's to do with a bicycle. A bicycle and a harp."

"I don't understand."

Now they were in the street, chilly with the winter dusk smells of celery on carts, of swept-up leaves heaped in faraway parks, and cold layers of dew sinking among the withered evening primroses in the bombed areas. London lay about them wreathed in twilit mystery and fading against the barred and smoky sky. Like a ninth wave the sound of traffic overtook and swallowed them.

"Please tell me!"

But, shaking her head, she stepped onto a scarlet homebound bus and was borne away from him.

Jason stood undecided on the pavement, with the crowds dividing around him as around the pier of a bridge. He scratched his head, looked about him for guidance.

An ambulance clanged, a taxi hooted, a drill stuttered, a siren wailed on the river, a door slammed, a brake squealed, and close beside his ear a bicycle bell tinkled its tiny warning.

A bicycle, she had said. A bicycle and a harp.

Reading Skill

Making and Verifying Predictions Which text clue leads you to predict that a romance will develop between Jason and Miss Golden? Explain.

Reading Check

What question does Jason Ashgrove want answered by Miss Golden?

Jason turned and stared at Grimes Buildings.

Somewhere, he knew, there was a back way in, a service entrance. He walked slowly past the main doors, with their tubs of snowy chrysanthemums, and up Glass Street. A tiny <u>furtive</u> wedge of darkness beckoned him, a snicket, a hacket, an alley carved into the thickness of the building. It was so narrow that at any moment, it seemed, the overtopping walls would come together and squeeze it out of existence.

Walking as softly as an Indian, Jason passed through it, slid by a file of dustbins,[5] and found the foot of the fire escape. Iron treads rose into the mist, like an illustration to a Gothic[6] fairy tale.

He began to climb.

When he had mounted to the ninth story he paused for breath. It was a lonely place. The lighting consisted of a dim bulb at the foot of every flight. A well of gloom sank beneath him. The cold fingers of the wind nagged and fluttered at the tails of his jacket, and he pulled the string of the fire door and edged inside.

Grimes Buildings were triangular, with the street forming the base of the triangle, and the fire escape the point. Jason could see two long passages coming toward him, meeting at an acute angle where he stood. He started down the left-hand one, tiptoeing in the cavelike silence. Nowhere was there any sound, except for the far-away drip of a tap. No night watchman would stay in the building; none was needed. Burglars gave the place a wide berth.

Jason opened a door at random; then another. Offices lay everywhere about him, empty and forbidding. Some held lipstick-stained tissues, spilled powder, and orange peels; others were still foggy with cigarette smoke. Here was a Director's suite of rooms—a desk like half an acre of frozen lake, inch-thick carpet, roses, and the smell of cigars. Here was a conference room with scattered squares of doodled blotting paper. All equally empty.

He was not sure when he first began to notice the bell. Telephone, he thought at first, and then he remembered that all the outside lines were disconnected at five. And this bell, anyway, had not the regularity of a telephone's double ring: there was a tinkle, and then silence; a long ring, and then silence; a whole volley of rings together, and then silence.

Jason stood listening, and fear knocked against his ribs and shortened his breath. He knew that he must move or be paralyzed by it. He ran up a flight of stairs and found himself with two more endless green corridors beckoning him like a pair of dividers.

---

5. dustbins British term for garbage cans.
6. Gothic *adj.* mysterious.

Vocabulary Builder
furtive (fur´ tiv) *adj.*
sneaky

Literary Analysis
Plot and Suspense
How do Jason's actions increase the suspense of the narrative?

▶ **Critical Viewing**
Based on this photo of Big Ben, a clock tower in London, England, why is an old London building at night an appropriate setting for a frightening story?
[Analyze]

Another sound now: a waft of ice-thin notes, riffling up an arpeggio[7] like a flurry of snowflakes. Far away down the passage it echoed. Jason ran in pursuit, but as he ran the music receded. He circled the building, but it always outdistanced him, and when he came back to the stairs he heard it fading away to the story below.

He hesitated, and as he did so heard again the bell; the bicycle bell. It was approaching him fast, bearing down on him, urgent, menacing. He could hear the pedals, almost see the shimmer of an invisible wheel. Absurdly, he was reminded of the insistent clamor of an ice-cream vendor, summoning children on a sultry Sunday afternoon.

There was a little fireman's alcove beside him, with buckets and pumps. He hurled himself into it. The bell stopped beside him, and then there was a moment while his heart tried to shake itself loose in his chest. He was looking into two eyes carved out of expressionless air; he was held by two hands knotted together out of the width of dark.

"Daisy, Daisy?" came the whisper. "Is that you, Daisy? Have you come to give me your answer?"

Jason tried to speak, but no words came.

"It's not Daisy! Who are you?" The sibilants[8] were full of threat. "You can't stay here. This is private property."

He was thrust along the corridor. It was like being pushed by a whirlwind—the fire door opened ahead of him without a touch, and he was on the openwork platform, clutching the slender railing. Still the hands would not let him go.

"How about it?" the whisper mocked him. "How about jumping? It's an easy death compared with some."

Jason looked down into the smoky void. The darkness nodded to him like a familiar.[9]

"You wouldn't be much loss, would you? What have you got to live for?"

Miss Golden, Jason thought. She would miss me. And the syllables Berenice Golden lingered in the air like a chime. Drawing on some unknown

---

7. arpeggio (är pej´ ō) *n.* notes of a chord played one after the other instead of together.
8. sibilants (sib´ əl əntz) *n.* hissing sounds.
9. a familiar a spirit.

Literary Analysis
Plot and Foreshadowing What earlier details foreshadowed this mysterious ringing?

Reading Check

What makes the ringing sound that Jason hears inside the Grimes Buildings?

deposit of courage he shook himself loose from the holding hands and ran down the fire escape without looking back.

Next morning when Miss Golden, crisp, fragrant, and punctual, shut the door of Room 492 behind her, she stopped short of the hat-pegs with a horrified gasp.

"Mr. Ashgrove, your hair!"

"It makes me look more distinguished, don't you think?" he said.

It had indeed this effect, for his impeccable dark cut had turned to a stippled silver which might have been envied by many a diplomat.

"How did it happen? You've not—" her voice sank to a whisper—"*you've not been in Grimes Buildings after dark?*"

"Miss Golden—Berenice," he said earnestly. "Who was Daisy? Plainly you know. Tell me the story."

"Did you see him?" she asked faintly.

"Him?"

"William Heron—The Wailing Watchman. Oh," she exclaimed in terror, "I can see you did. Then you are doomed—doomed!"

"If I'm doomed," said Jason, "let's have coffee, and you tell me the story quickly."

"It all happened over fifty years ago," said Berenice, as she spooned out coffee powder with distracted extravagance. "Heron was the night watchman in this building, patrolling the corridors from dusk to dawn every night on his bicycle. He fell in love with a Miss Bell who taught the harp. She rented a room—this room—and gave lessons in it. She began to <u>reciprocate</u> his love, and they used to share a picnic supper every night at eleven, and she'd stay on a while to keep him company. It was an idyll,[10] among the fire buckets and the furnace pipes.

"On Halloween he had summoned up the courage to propose to her. The day before he had told her he was going to ask her a very important question, and he came to the Buildings with a huge bunch of roses and a bottle of wine. But Miss Bell never turned up.

"The explanation was simple. Miss Bell, of course, had been losing a lot of sleep through her nocturnal romance, and so she used to take a nap in her music room between seven and ten, to save going home. In order to make sure that she would wake up, she persuaded her father, a distant relative of Graham Bell,[11] to attach an alarm-waking fixture to her telephone which called her every night at ten. She was too modest and shy to let Heron know that

▼ Critical Viewing
Describe the sound you think this harp would make. **[Speculate]**

Vocabulary Builder
reciprocate (ri sip′ rə kāt′) *v.* return

---

10. **idyll** (ī′ dəl) *n.* romantic scene, usually in the country.
11. **Graham Bell** Alexander Graham Bell (1847–1922), the inventor of the telephone.

she spent those hours in the building, and to give him the pleasure of waking her himself.

"Alas! On this important evening the line failed, and she never woke up. The telephone was in its infancy at that time, you must remember.

"Heron waited and waited. At last, mad with grief and jealousy, having called her home and discovered that she was not there, he concluded that she had betrayed him; he ran to the fire escape, and cast himself off it, holding the roses and the bottle of wine.

"Daisy did not long survive him but pined away soon after. Since that day their ghosts have haunted Grimes Buildings, he vainly patrolling the corridors on his bicycle, she playing her harp in the room she rented. But they never meet. And anyone who meets the ghost of William Heron will himself, within five days, leap down from the same fatal fire escape."

She gazed at him with tragic eyes.

"In that case we must lose no time," said Jason, and he enveloped her in an embrace as prompt as it was ardent. Looking down at the gossamer hair sprayed across his pin-stripe, he added, "Just the same it is a preposterous situation. Firstly, I have no intention of jumping off the fire escape—" here, however, he repressed a shudder as he remembered the cold, clutching hands of the evening before—"and secondly, I find it quite nonsensical that those two inefficient ghosts have spent fifty years in this building without coming across each other. We must remedy the matter, Berenice. We must not begrudge our new-found happiness to others."

He gave her another kiss so impassioned that the electric typewriter against which they were leaning began chattering to itself in a frenzy of enthusiasm.

"This very evening," he went on, looking at his watch, "we will put matters right for that unhappy couple and then, if I really have only five more days to live, which I don't for one moment believe, we will proceed to spend them together, my bewitching Berenice, in the most advantageous manner possible."

She nodded, spellbound.

"Can you work a switchboard?" he added. She nodded again. "My love, you are perfection itself. Meet me in the switchboard room then, at ten this evening. I would say, have dinner with me, but I shall need to make one or two purchases and see an old R.A.F.[12] friend. You will be safe from Heron's curse in the switchboard room if he always keeps to the corridors."

"I would rather meet him and die with you," she murmured.

---

12. **R.A.F.** Royal Air Force.

Literary Analysis
Plot and Foreshadowing How does this new information increase the suspense of the narrative?

Reading Skill
Making and Verifying Predictions What do you think Jason might do to "remedy the matter"?

Reading Check

According to Berenice, what happens to anyone who meets the ghost of William Heron?

"My angel, I hope that won't be necessary. Now," he said, sighing, "I suppose we should get down to our day's work."

Strangely enough the copy they wrote that day, although engendered from such agitated minds, sold more packets of Oat Crisps than any other advertising matter before or since.

That evening when Jason entered Grimes Buildings he was carrying two bottles of wine, two bunches of red roses, and a large canvas-covered bundle. Miss Golden, who had concealed herself in the switchboard room before the offices closed for the night, eyed these things with surprise.

"Now," said Jason, after he had greeted her, "I want you first to ring our own extension."

"No one will reply, surely?"

"I think she will reply."

Sure enough, when Berenice rang Extension 170 a faint, sleepy voice, distant and yet clear, whispered, "Hullo?"

"Is that Miss Bell?"

"Yes."

Berenice went a little pale. Her eyes sought Jason's and, prompted by him, she said formally, "Switchboard here, Miss Bell. Your ten o'clock call."

"Thank you," the faint voice said. There was a click and the line went blank.

"Excellent," Jason remarked. He unfastened his package and slipped its straps over his shoulders. "Now plug into the intercom."

Berenice did so, and then said, loudly and clearly, "Attention. Night watchman on duty, please. Night watchman on duty. You have an urgent summons to Room 492. You have an urgent summons to Room 492." The intercom echoed and reverberated through the empty corridors, then coughed itself to silence.

"Now we must run. You take the roses, sweetheart, and I'll carry the bottles."

Together they raced up eight flights of stairs and along the passages to Room 492. As they neared the door a burst of music met them—harp music swelling out, sweet and triumphant. Jason took a bunch of roses from Berenice, opened the door a little way, and gently deposited them, with a bottle, inside the door. As he closed it again Berenice said breathlessly, "Did you see anyone?"

"No," he said. "The room was too full of music." She saw that his eyes were shining.

They stood hand in hand, reluctant to move away, waiting for they hardly knew what. Suddenly the door opened again. Neither

Reading Skill
Making and Verifying Predictions What do you predict Jason will do with the two bunches of roses? Why?

Berenice nor Jason, afterward, would speak of what they saw but each was left with a memory, bright as the picture on a Salvador Dali[13] calendar, of a bicycle bearing on its saddle a harp, a bottle of wine, and a bouquet of red roses, sweeping improbably down the corridor and far, far away.

"We can go now," Jason said.

He led Berenice to the fire door, tucking the bottle of Médoc in his jacket pocket. A black wind from the north whistled beneath them as they stood on the openwork platform, looking down.

"We don't want our evening to be spoiled by the thought of a curse hanging over us," he said, "so this is the practical thing to do. Hang onto the roses." And holding his love firmly, Jason pulled the rip cord of his R.A.F. friend's parachute and leaped off the fire escape.

A bridal shower of rose petals adorned the descent of Miss Golden, who was possibly the only girl to be kissed in midair in the district of Clerkenwell at ten minutes to midnight on Halloween.

Reading Skill
Making and Verifying Predictions Do the events at the end of the story verify your predictions? Why or why not?

---

13. **Salvador Dali** (sal´ və dôr´ dä´ lē) modern artist (1904–1989) famous for his unusual pictures.

▼ **Critical Viewing** What advantages would patrolling corridors on bicycle offer as opposed to patrolling on foot? **[Evaluate]**

Apply the Skills

Sonata for Harp and Bicycle

Thinking About the Selection

1. **Respond:** If you were Jason, would you try to solve the mystery of the Grimes Buildings? Explain.
2. **(a) Recall:** What three important objects does Miss Golden mention to Jason as they leave the Grimes Buildings at five P.M.? **(b) Connect:** How does he use this information?
3. **(a) Recall:** What physical change has happened to Jason when he sees Miss Golden the next day? **(b) Analyze:** What evidence suggests that his encounter in the closed building has caused the change?
4. **(a) Recall:** What actions does Jason take to avoid the curse that awaits those who see Heron's ghost? **(b) Infer:** Who is more concerned about the curse—Jason or Miss Golden? Explain.
5. **Generalize:** What lesson do the circumstances of William Heron's death teach about the danger of making rash decisions?

Literary Analysis

6. Using a chart like the one shown, identify two key events in the **rising action,** one event in the **falling action,** and the event that marks the **climax.** Then, trade charts with a partner and discuss the reasons why you chose the events that you did. Finally, explain to your partner how your understanding of the story has or has not changed as a result of the discussion.

7. **(a)** Identify a statement or event that **foreshadows** Jason's decision to enter the Grimes Buildings after closing hours. **(b)** How does the use of foreshadowing increase the story's **suspense**? Explain.

Reading Skill

8. **(a)** What **prediction** did you make when Jason entered the Grimes Buildings after closing and heard a bicycle bell? **(b)** On what details did you base your prediction?
9. Was your prediction **verified** by later story events? Explain.

QuickReview

Story at a Glance
Jason Ashgrove solves the mystery of the haunted Grimes Buildings.

—Assessment

For: Self-test
Visit: www.PHSchool.com
Web Code: epa-6105

Plot: the sequence of events in a narrative. Elements include *rising action, climax, falling action,* and *resolution.*

Foreshadowing: a hint or clue about events that will happen later in a story

Suspense: a feeling of tension caused by anticipation of what might happen later

Prediction: an informed idea about what might happen later

Vocabulary Builder

Practice Analogies show the relationships between pairs of words. Use a word from the "Sonata for Harp and Bicycle" vocabulary list on page 46 to complete each analogy. For each case, your choice should create a word pair that matches the relationship between the first two words.

1. angry : shout :: _____ : whisper
2. steal : take :: _____ : give
3. hopelessly : far :: _____ : near

Adding Words to Your Vocabulary *Furtive* can be defined by its synonym *sneaky.* A **synonym** is a word that has the same or nearly the same definition as another word. Other synonyms for *furtive* include *stealthy, covert,* and *surreptitious.* These words are synonyms, but they do not mean exactly the same thing. Look up each word in a dictionary, and for each word, write a sentence that reflects its specific meaning. (For help with reference materials, see page R6.)

Writing

Joan Aiken has said, "A flat or unsatisfactory ending is the worst sin a writer can commit." Write a **critique** evaluating the ending of "Sonata for Harp and Bicycle," and state whether you find it satisfactory.

- Before writing, make a list of qualities that create satisfactory endings. Check off those qualities that appear in Aiken's story.
- Use the checklist as evidence in your critique.

For *Grammar, Vocabulary,* and *Assessment,* see **Build Language Skills,** pages 70–71.

Extend Your Learning

Listening and Speaking Present a **retelling** of "Sonata for Harp and Bicycle" from the ghosts' point of view. As you speak, use facial expressions and body movements to give personality to Heron and Miss Bell.

Research and Technology Work with classmates to create a **storyboard** for a movie version of "Sonata for Harp and Bicycle."

- Use Internet and library resources to find other storyboards that can serve as guides for your own.
- Decide as a group which story events to depict. Draw those scenes in comic book style, and write a brief description for each frame.

Build Understanding • *The Cask of Amontillado*

Background

Catacombs Much of the action in this story takes place in cata-combs—underground tunnels that house tombs. These long, often complex passageways stretch out like cities of the dead. In past centuries, some wealthy European families held funerals in catacombs beneath the family manor. The dead were laid to rest surrounded by the bones of their ancestors.

Connecting to the Literature

Reading/Writing Connection Write a short paragraph explaining why you think people enjoy reading stories set in scary places like catacombs. Use at least three of the following words: *interpret, participate, contribute, elevate.*

Review

For **Literary Analysis, Reading Skill,** and **Vocabulary Builder,** see page 46.

READ MORE

by Edgar Allan Poe
"The Fall of the House of Usher"
"The Tell-Tale Heart"

Meet the Author

Edgar Allan **Poe** (1809–1849)

One of the first great American storytellers, Edgar Allan Poe made the most of a short, tragic life. Orphaned at the age of three, Poe was raised by foster parents, the Allans, from whom he took his middle name. The Allans were good to Poe and gave him an education, but he had to leave college when his foster father refused to pay Poe's gambling debts. Poe found some happiness when he married Virginia Clemm. Her death from tuberculosis in 1847 caused Poe to become increasingly antisocial. In 1849, he was discovered in a delirious condition on a Baltimore street, and three days later he was dead.

An Inspiration to Later Generations Like few others, Poe blazed trails for future writers. His work helped to define the short story, and his dark imagination helped establish the genre of horror literature now popularized by writers like Stephen King.

Fast Facts

▶ Poe invented the genre of the detective story with his tale "The Murders in the Rue Morgue."

▶ Poe's first book, *Tamerlane and Other Poems,* was a failure. Recently, an original copy sold for $150,000.

Go Online
Author Link

For: More about the author
Visit: www.PHSchool.com
Web Code: epe-9105

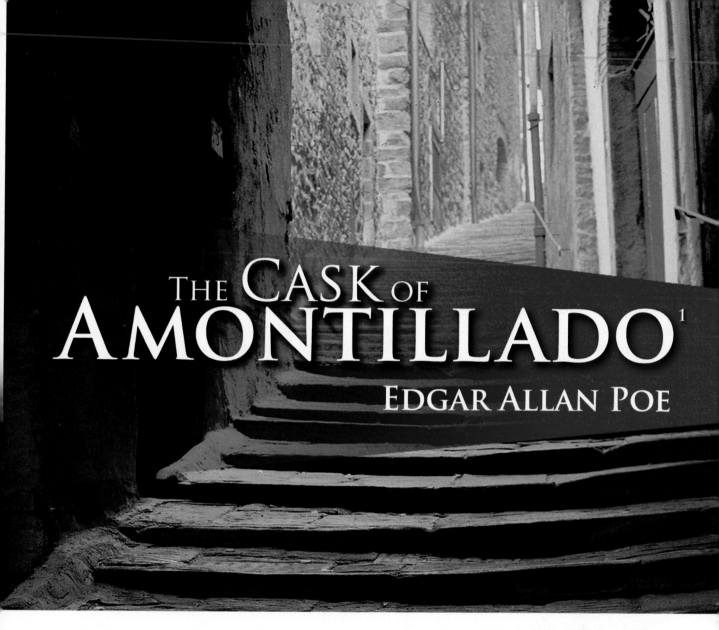

THE CASK OF AMONTILLADO[1]

EDGAR ALLAN POE

The thousand injuries of Fortunato I had borne as I best could, but when he ventured upon insult I vowed revenge. You, who so well know the nature of my soul, will not suppose, however, that I gave utterance to a threat. At *length* I would be avenged; this was a point definitely settled—but the very definitiveness with which it was resolved <u>precluded</u> the idea of risk. I must not only punish but punish with impunity.[2] A wrong is unredressed when <u>retribution</u> overtakes its redresser. It is equally unredressed when the avenger fails to make himself felt as such to him who has done the wrong.

It must be understood that neither by word nor deed had I given Fortunato cause to doubt my good will. I continued, as was my

---

1. Amontillado (ə män′ tə ya′ dō) *n.* a pale, dry sherry.
2. impunity (im pyōō′ nə tē′) *n.* freedom from consequences.

Vocabulary Builder
precluded (prē klōōd′ id) *v.* prevented

retribution (re′ trə byōō′ shən) *n.* payback; punishment for a misdeed

Reading Check

Why does the narrator vow revenge on Fortunato?

wont, to smile in his face, and he did not perceive that my smile *now* was at the thought of his immolation.[3]

He had a weak point—this Fortunato—although in other regards he was a man to be respected and even feared. He prided himself on his connoisseurship[4] in wine. Few Italians have the true virtuoso[5] spirit. For the most part their enthusiasm is adopted to suit the time and opportunity, to practice imposture upon the British and Austrian millionaires. In painting and gemmary, Fortunato, like his countrymen, was a quack, but in the matter of old wines he was sincere. In this respect I did not differ from him materially; I was skillful in the Italian vintages myself, and bought largely whenever I could.

It was about dusk, one evening during the supreme madness of the carnival season, that I encountered my friend. He accosted me with excessive warmth, for he had been drinking much. The man wore motley.[6] He had on a tight-fitting parti-striped dress, and his head was surmounted by the conical cap and bells. I was so pleased to see him that I thought I should never have done wringing his hand.

I said to him, "My dear Fortunato, you are luckily met. How remarkably well you are looking today. But I have received a pipe[7] of what passes for Amontillado, and I have my doubts."

"How?" said he. "Amontillado? A pipe? Impossible! And in the middle of the carnival!"

"I have my doubts," I replied: "and I was silly enough to pay the full Amontillado price without consulting you in the matter. You were not to be found, and I was fearful of losing a bargain."

"Amontillado!"

"I have my doubts."

"Amontillado!"

"And I must satisfy them."

"Amontillado!"

"As you are engaged, I am on my way to Luchesi. If any one has a critical turn it is he. He will tell me—"

"Luchesi cannot tell Amontillado from sherry."

"And yet some fools will have it that his taste is a match for your own."

"Come, let us go."

"Whither?"

"To your vaults."

Reading Skill
Making and Verifying Predictions What role do you predict Fortunato's "weak point" will play in the narrator's revenge?

---

3. **immolation** (im′ ə lā′ shən) *n.* destruction.
4. **connoisseurship** (kän′ ə sʉr′ ship) *n.* expert judgment.
5. **virtuoso** (vʉr′ choō ō′ sō) *adj.* masterly skill in a particular field.
6. **motley** (mät′ lē) *n.* a clown's multicolored costume.
7. **pipe** (pīp) *n.* large barrel, holding approximately 126 gallons.

"My friend, no; I will not impose upon your good nature. I perceive you have an engagement. Luchesi—"

"I have no engagement—come."

"My friend, no. It is not the engagement, but the severe cold with which I perceive you are afflicted. The vaults are insufferably damp. They are encrusted with niter."

"Let us go, nevertheless. The cold is merely nothing. Amontillado! You have been imposed upon. And as for Luchesi, he cannot distinguish sherry from Amontillado."

Thus speaking, Fortunato possessed himself of my arm; and putting on a mask of black silk and drawing a *roquelaure*[8] closely about my person, I suffered him to hurry me to my palazzo.

There were no attendants at home; they had absconded to make merry in honor of the time. I had told them that I should not return until the morning, and had given them <u>explicit</u> orders not to stir from the house. These orders were sufficient, I well knew, to insure their immediate disappearance, one and all, as soon as my back was turned.

I took from their sconces two flambeaux, and giving one to Fortunato, bowed him through several suites of rooms to the archway that led into the vaults. I passed down a long and winding staircase, requesting him to be cautious as he followed. We came at length to the foot of the descent, and stood together upon the damp ground of the catacombs of the Montresors.

The gait of my friend was unsteady, and the bells upon his cap jingled as he strode.

"The pipe," he said.

"It is farther on," said I; "but observe the white webwork which gleams from these cavern walls."

He turned towards me, and looked into my eyes with two filmy orbs that distilled the rheum of intoxication.

"Niter?" he asked, at length.

"Niter," I replied. "How long have you had that cough?"

A Critical Viewing
How does this costume compare with your image of Fortunato's costume? **[Compare and Contrast]**

Vocabulary Builder
explicit (eks plis′ it) *adj.* clearly stated

Reading Check

What common interest does the narrator share with Fortunato?

---

8. *roquelaure* (räk′ ə lôr) *n.* knee-length cloak.

"Ugh! ugh! ugh!—ugh! ugh! ugh!—ugh! ugh! ugh!—ugh! ugh! ugh!—ugh! ugh! ugh!"

My poor friend found it impossible to reply for many minutes.

"It is nothing," he said, at last.

"Come," I said, with decision, "we will go back; your health is precious. You are rich, respected, admired, beloved; you are happy, as once I was. You are a man to be missed. For me it is no matter. We will go back; you will be ill, and I cannot be responsible. Besides, there is Luchesi—"

"Enough," he said; "the cough is a mere nothing; it will not kill me. I shall not die of a cough."

"True—true," I replied; "and, indeed, I had no intention of alarming you unnecessarily—but you should use all proper caution. A draft of this Médoc will defend us from the damps."

Here I knocked off the neck of a bottle which I drew from a long row of its fellows that lay upon the mold.

"Drink," I said, presenting him the wine.

He raised it to his lips with a leer. He paused and nodded to me familiarly, while his bells jingled.

"I drink," he said "to the buried that repose around us."

"And I to your long life."

He again took my arm, and we proceeded.

"These vaults," he said, "are extensive."

"The Montresors," I replied, "were a great and numerous family."

"I forget your arms."

"A huge human foot d'or, in a field azure; the foot crushes a serpent rampant whose fangs are imbedded in the heel."

"And the motto?"

"*Nemo me impune lacessit.*"[9]

"Good!" he said.

The wine sparkled in his eyes and the bells jingled. My own fancy grew warm with the Médoc. We had passed through long walls of piled skeletons, with casks and puncheons[10] intermingling, into the inmost recesses of the catacombs. I paused again, and this time I made bold to seize Fortunato by an arm above the elbow.

"The niter!" I said; "see, it increases. It hangs like moss upon the vaults. We are below the river's bed. The drops of moisture trickle among the bones. Come, we will go back ere it is too late. Your cough—"

"It is nothing," he said; "let us go on. But first, another draft of the Médoc."

Literary Analysis
Plot and Foreshadowing
What fate does this conversation foreshadow for Fortunato?

---

9. *Nemo me impune lacessit* Latin for "No one attacks me with impunity."
10. puncheons (pun´ chənz) *n.* large barrels.

I broke and reached him a flagon of De Grâve. He emptied it at a breath. His eyes flashed with a fierce light. He laughed and threw the bottle upwards with a gesticulation I did not understand.

I looked at him in surprise. He repeated the movement—a grotesque one.

"You do not comprehend?" he said.

"Not I," I replied.

"Then you are not of the brotherhood."

"How?"

"You are not of the masons."[11]

"Yes, yes," I said; "yes, yes."

"You? Impossible! A mason?"

"A mason," I replied.

"A sign," he said, "a sign."

"It is this," I answered, producing from beneath the folds of my *roquelaure* a trowel.

"You jest," he exclaimed, recoiling a few paces. "But let us proceed to the Amontillado."

"Be it so," I said, replacing the tool beneath the cloak and again offering him my arm. He leaned upon it heavily. We continued our route in search of the Amontillado. We passed through a range of low arches, descended, passed on, and descending again, arrived at a deep crypt, in which the foulness of the air caused our flambeaux rather to glow than flame.

At the most remote end of the crypt there appeared another less spacious. Its walls had been lined with human remains, piled to the vault overhead, in the fashion of the great catacombs of Paris. Three sides of this interior crypt were still ornamented in this manner. From the fourth side the bones had been thrown down, and lay promiscuously upon the earth, forming at one point a mound of some size. Within the wall thus exposed by the displacing of the bones, we perceived a still interior crypt or recess, in depth about four feet, in width three, in height six or seven. It seemed to have been constructed for no especial use within itself, but formed merely the

---

11. **masons** the Freemasons, an international secret society.

Literature in Context

Literature Connection

Poe and the Gothic Tradition The literary genre known as gothic fiction emerged in England in the late 1700s in works like *Castle of Otranto* (1765) by Horace Walpole and *The Mysteries of Udolpho* (1794) by Ann Radcliffe. The word *gothic* was originally used to describe a style of building that was common in the late Middle Ages. To writers in the eighteenth century, the cold chambers and secret passages of such buildings suggested mystery and dark tales of vengeance and passion.

Edgar Allan Poe translated the imagery and atmosphere of British gothic fiction to an American landscape, pioneering an American gothic tradition. Contemporary writers like Stephen King and Anne Rice, as well as countless filmmakers, carry on that tradition today.

Connect to the Literature

What qualities of gothic fiction do you find in "The Cask of Amontillado"? Explain.

Reading Check

Where does Montresor bring Fortunato?

interval between two of the colossal supports of the roof of the catacombs, and was backed by one of their circumscribing walls of solid granite.

It was in vain that Fortunato, uplifting his dull torch, endeavored to pry into the depth of the recess. Its termination the feeble light did not enable us to see.

"Proceed," I said: "herein is the Amontillado. As for Luchesi—"

"He is an ignoramus," interrupted my friend, as he stepped unsteadily forward, while I followed immediately at his heels. In an instant he had reached the extremity of the niche, and finding his progress arrested by the rock, stood stupidly bewildered. A moment more and I had fettered him to the granite. In its surface were two iron staples, distant from each other about two feet, horizontally. From one of these depended a short chain, from the other a padlock. Throwing the links about his waist, it was but the work of a few seconds to secure it. He was too much astounded to resist. Withdrawing the key I stepped back from the recess.

"Pass your hand," I said, "over the wall; you cannot help feeling the niter. Indeed, it is very damp. Once more let me implore you to return. No? Then I must positively leave you. But I must first render you all the little attentions in my power."

"The Amontillado!" ejaculated my friend, not yet recovered from his astonishment.

"True," I replied; "the Amontillado."

As I said these words I busied myself among the pile of bones of which I have before spoken. Throwing them aside, I soon uncovered a quantity of building stone and mortar. With these materials and with the aid of my trowel, I began vigorously to wall up the entrance of the niche.

I had scarcely laid the first tier of the masonry when I discovered that the intoxication of Fortunato had in a great measure worn off. The earliest indication I had of this was a low moaning cry from the depth of the recess. It was not the cry of a drunken man. There was then a long and obstinate silence. I laid the second tier, and the third, and the fourth; and then I heard the furious vibrations of the chain. The noise lasted for several minutes, during which, that I might hearken to it with the more satisfaction, I ceased my labors and sat down upon the bones. When at last the clanking subsided, I resumed the trowel, and finished without

▲ **Critical Viewing** Explain how the context of a story might make festive masks like these seem sinister. **[Interpret]**

interruption the fifth, the sixth, and the seventh tier. The wall was now nearly upon a level with my breast. I again paused, and holding the flambeaux over the masonwork, threw a few feeble rays upon the figure within.

A succession of loud and shrill screams, bursting suddenly from the throat of the chained form, seemed to thrust me violently back. For a brief moment I hesitated, I trembled. Unsheathing my rapier, I began to grope with it about the recess; but the thought of an instant reassured me. I placed my hand upon the solid fabric of the catacombs, and felt satisfied. I reapproached the wall; I replied to the yells of him who clamored. I reechoed, I aided, I surpassed them in volume and in strength. I did this, and the clamorer grew still.

It was now midnight, and my task was drawing to a close. I had completed the eighth, the ninth, and the tenth tier. I had finished a portion of the last and the eleventh; there remained but a single stone to be fitted and plastered in. I struggled with its weight; I placed it partially in its destined position. But now there came from out the niche a low laugh that erected the hairs upon my head. It was succeeded by a sad voice, which I had difficulty in recognizing as that of the noble Fortunato. The voice said—

"Ha! ha! ha!—he! he! he!—a very good joke, indeed—an excellent jest. We will have many a rich laugh about it at the palazzo—he! he! he!—over our wine—he! he! he!"

"The Amontillado!" I said.

"He! he! he!—he! he! he!—yes, the Amontillado. But is it not getting late? Will not they be awaiting us at the palazzo, the Lady Fortunato and the rest? Let us be gone."

"Yes," I said, "let us be gone."

"For the love of God, Montresor!"

"Yes," I said, "for the love of God!"

But to these words I hearkened in vain for a reply. I grew impatient. I called aloud—

"Fortunato!"

No answer. I called again—

"Fortunato!"

No answer still. I thrust a torch through the remaining aperture and let it fall within. There came forth in return only a jingling of the bells. My heart grew sick; it was the dampness of the catacombs that made it so. I hastened to make an end of my labor. I forced the last stone into its position; I plastered it up. Against the new masonry I reerected the old rampart of bones. For the half of a century no mortal has disturbed them. *In pace requiescat!*[12]

---

12. *In pace requiescat!* Latin for "May he rest in peace!"

Reading Skill
Making and Verifying Predictions Does this scene in which Montresor imprisons Fortunato verify your earlier predictions? Explain.

Apply the Skills

The Cask of Amontillado

Thinking About the Selection

1. **Respond:** At what point in the story do you find Montresor most disturbing? Explain.
2. **(a) Recall:** How does Montresor describe Fortunato's strengths and weaknesses early in the story? **(b) Analyze:** Which character traits make Fortunato easy prey for Montresor?
3. **(a) Recall:** What specific steps does Montresor take to ensure that his plan works? **(b) Interpret:** Why does Montresor keep urging Fortunato to turn back?
4. **(a) Recall:** Why does Montresor hate Fortunato? **(b) Support:** Why does Montresor feel he has the right to punish Fortunato? **(c) Assess:** Does Montresor express any regret or ever question whether this punishment is just or rational?
5. **Evaluate:** Montresor acts as both judge and executioner in this story. Explain whether you think individuals are ever justified in taking justice into their own hands.

Literary Analysis

6. Using a chart like the one shown, identify two key events in the **rising action**, one event in the **falling action**, and the event that marks the **climax.** Then, trade charts with a partner and discuss the reasons why you chose the events that you did. Finally, explain to your partner how your understanding of the story has or has not changed as a result of the discussion.

7. **(a)** Identify a statement or an event that **foreshadows** Fortunato's fate. **(b)** How does foreshadowing add to the **suspense**? Explain.

Reading Skill

8. **(a)** What **prediction** did you make after reading about Montresor's and Fortunato's shared interest in wine? **(b)** On what details did you base your prediction?
9. Was your prediction **verified** by later story events? Explain.

Vocabulary Builder

Practice **Analogies** show the relationships between pairs of words. Use a word from the vocabulary list for "The Cask of Amontillado" on page 46 to complete each analogy. For each case, your choice should create a word pair that matches the relationship between the first two words.

1. conversation: dialogue :: _____ : revenge

2. harmed : helped :: _____ : allowed

3. delicious : food :: _____ : instructions

Adding Words to Your Vocabulary *Precluded* can be defined by the synonym *prevented*. A **synonym** is a word that has the same or nearly the same definition as another word. Other synonyms for *precluded* include *hindered, deterred,* and *stopped.* These words are synonyms, but they do not mean exactly the same thing. Look up each word in a dictionary, and for each word, write a sentence that reflects its specific meaning. (For help with reference materials, see page R6.)

Writing

In writing "The Cask of Amontillado," Poe clearly intended to keep readers on the edge of their seats. Did he succeed? Write a **critique** in which you evaluate "The Cask of Amontillado" as a suspenseful story.

- Before writing, make a list of qualities a suspenseful story should have. Check off those qualities that appear in Poe's story.
- Consult your checklist as you write, and use it as evidence to support your argument.

For *Grammar, Vocabulary,* and *Assessment,* see **Build Language Skills,** pages 70–71.

Extend Your Learning

Listening and Speaking Present a **retelling** of Poe's story from Fortunato's point of view. As you speak, use facial expressions and body movements effectively to convey Fortunato's personality.

Research and Technology Work with classmates to create a **storyboard** for a movie version of "The Cask of Amontillado."

- Use Internet and library resources to find other storyboards that can serve as guides for your own.
- Decide as a group which events to depict. Draw those scenes in comic book style and write a brief description for each frame.

Build Language Skills

Vocabulary Skill

Word Roots *Contemporary*, which means "of the current time," contains the **Latin root** *-tempor-*, which means "of time." *Specific* also contains a **Latin root**: *-spec-*, which means to "see." When you make something *specific*, you make it able to be seen and known. Knowing these roots will help you understand and remember the meaning of words that contain them.

Practice Each of the following words is based on either *-tempor-* or *-spec-*. Explain how the meaning of the root can help you remember the meaning of the word. Then, write a synonym for each of the words.

1. temporary
2. specify
3. extemporaneous
4. tempo
5. specification

Grammar Lesson

Abstract and Concrete Nouns Nouns that name people, places, or things that can be seen or recognized through any of the five senses are called **concrete nouns.** Nouns that name ideas, actions, conditions, and qualities—things that cannot be recognized through the senses—are called **abstract nouns.**

More**Practice**

For more practice with common and proper nouns, see Grammar Handbook, p. R40.

Abstract Noun	Concrete Noun
Fortunato discovered Montresor's *intention,* but it was too late.	William Heron patrolled the halls on a *bicycle.*

Practice Copy the following sentences. Underline the concrete nouns once and the abstract nouns twice. Then, choose three concrete nouns and three abstract nouns and use them to write your own sentences.

1. Dreams are thought to be about events in your day.
2. Some psychologists believe that everything you do is recorded in your brain.
3. The thought of so much information being stored in your memory is amazing.
4. According to some, your brain sorts out your fears, thoughts, and hopes while you sleep.
5. Daydreams are different from the dreams you have when you sleep.

W͓G Prentice Hall Writing and Grammar Connection: Chapter 16, Section 1.

Reading: Make Predictions

Standards Assessed

- WL.1.01.2
- CT.4.03.2
- CT.4.03.9

Directions: *Read the selection. Then, answer the questions.*

And when finally they did meet up again, neither offered a clue to the other that he, or she, had been the object of obsessive thought for weeks. She spotted him as soon as she came into the store, but she kept her eyes strictly in front of her as she pulled out a cart and wheeled it toward the produce. And he, too, knew the instant she came through the door—though the orange bow was gone, replaced by a small but bright yellow flower instead—and he never once turned his head in her direction but watched her from the corner of his vision as he tried to swallow back the fear in his throat.

—from "Checkouts" by Cynthia Rylant

1. Which of the following details is least useful in making a prediction about what will happen?
   A He, or she, had been the object of obsessive thought for weeks.
   B She spotted him as soon as she came into the store.
   C He knew the instant she came through the door.
   D The orange bow was gone.

2. Which further detail is most relevant to a prediction made from the information in this passage?
   A "The girl hated herself for not checking out at the boy's line."
   B "This is often the way of children, when they truly want a thing."

   C "And perhaps cats, who have been known to react in the same way.."
   D "the bag boy grew so bored with his job . . ."

3. Which detail would verify a prediction that the boy and the girl will never reveal their feelings to each other?
   A "The girl hated herself for not checking out at the boy's line."
   B "This is often the way of children, when they truly want a thing."
   C "And the bag boy let her leave the store, pretending to take no notice of her."
   D "Strange, how attractive clumsiness can be."

Timed Writing: Explanation [Critical Stance]

Review "Sonato for Harp and Bicycle" or "The Cask of Amontillado." Write a brief explanation of how the author creates the mood of the story. **(20 minutes)**

 Writing Workshop: *Work in Progress*

Autobiographical Narrative

Use the scene description from the Memory List in your writing portfolio. Next to each person's description jot down how you reacted to what they were doing. Save this work in your writing portfolio.

Point of View

Point of view is the perspective from which a story is narrated, or told.

- **First-person point of view:** The narrator is a character who participates in the action of the story and uses the first-person pronouns *I* and *me* to describe himself or herself.
- **Third-person point of view:** The narrator is not a character in the story but is a voice outside the action. The narrator uses the third-person pronouns *he, she, him, her, they,* and *them* to refer to all characters. There are two kinds of third-person point of view. In the **third-person omniscient** point of view, the narrator knows everything, including the thoughts and feelings of all the characters. In the **third-person limited point of view,** the narrator sees things through one character's eyes and reveals that character's feeling and thoughts. The narrator can describe what other characters do or say but not what they feel or think.

Standard Course of Study

- Judge different stylistic and literary devices in work. (CT.4.02.3)
- Explain how the writer creates literary elements. (LT.5.01.8)

Comparing Points of View

Point of view affects the type of information a reader receives.

- The first-person point of view in "The Girl Who Can" allows the reader to know all of the narrator's inner thoughts. Her sense of the world shapes the reader's experience of the story.
- By contrast, the omniscient point of view used in "Checkouts" lets the reader see opportunities the main characters do not even know they have.

Compare the effects of these two different points of view in these selections by using a Venn diagram like the one shown.

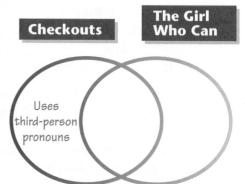

Vocabulary Builder

Checkouts

- **reverie** (rev´ ə rē) *n.* dreamy thought of pleasant things (p. 79) *Lost in a <u>reverie</u>, she did not hear the bell.*

- **dishevelment** (di shev´ əl ment) *n.* disorder; messiness (p. 80) *The wind left her hair in a state of <u>dishevelment</u>.*

- **perverse** (pər vurs´) *adj.* deviating from what is considered right or reasonable (p. 81) *He took <u>perverse</u> pleasure in arriving late.*

The Girl Who Can

- **fertile** (furt´'l) *adj.* able to make plants grow (p. 83) *They bought a farm with <u>fertile</u> soil.*

- **comprehension** (käm´ prē hen´ shen) *n.* understanding (p. 84) *The reason for his anger is beyond my <u>comprehension</u>.*

- **humble** (hum´ bəl) *adj.* modest; having humility (p. 85) *Although he won the race, he remained <u>humble</u> with his teammates.*

Build Understanding

Reading/Writing Connection

The main characters in these stories have the chance to reach for opportunities, but they must balance goals against risk. Write a few sentences to explain how you might decide whether to take a chance at something you value. Use at least three of the following words in your response: *impact, display, reveal, emerge, signify.*

Meet the Authors

Cynthia **Rylant** (b. 1954)

Cynthia Rylant spent four years as a child living with her grandparents in a small town in West Virginia. With no public library and very little money to buy books, she started reading comic books. Once in college, she discovered great literature, but she did not consider becoming a writer until she took a job as a librarian and began reading children's books.

Writing About Her Life In her writing, Rylant draws upon her experiences as both a child and young adult. "The best writing," she says, "is that which is most personal, most revealing." She has written numerous award-winning stories, poems, and novels.

Ama Ata **Aidoo** (b. 1942)

Ama Ata Aidoo was born in Ghana, Africa, where her father was a village chief. He wanted his daughter to have a Western education and sent her to a university in Cape Coast, Ghana. Aidoo earned her bachelor's degree in English and later taught at universities in Ghana and the United States.

Works and Themes Aidoo has written plays, short stories, poetry, and novels. Her fiction, written in English, often explores the conflicts between Western and African cultures and the roles of women in modern society.

Go Online
Author Link

For: More about the authors
Visit: www.PHSchool.com
Web Code: epe-9106

Checkouts

Cynthia Rylant

Her parents had moved her to Cincinnati, to a large house with beveled glass[1] windows and several porches and the history her mother liked to emphasize. You'll love the house, they said. You'll be lonely at first, they admitted, but you're so nice you'll make friends fast. And as an impulse tore at her to lie on the floor, to hold to their ankles and tell them she felt she was dying, to offer anything, anything at all, so they might allow her to finish growing up in the town of her childhood, they firmed their mouths and spoke from their chests and they said, It's decided.

▲ **Critical Viewing**
Which features of a supermarket might help people take their minds off their troubles? **[Analyze]**

---

1. beveled (bev´ əld) **glass** *n.* glass having angled or slanted edges.

They moved her to Cincinnati, where for a month she spent the greater part of every day in a room full of beveled glass windows, sifting through photographs of the life she'd lived and left behind. But it is difficult work, suffering, and in its own way a kind of art, and finally she didn't have the energy for it anymore, so she emerged from the beautiful house and fell in love with a bag boy at the supermarket. Of course, this didn't happen all at once, just like that, but in the sequence of things that's exactly the way it happened.

She liked to grocery shop. She loved it in the way some people love to drive long country roads, because doing it she could think and relax and wander. Her parents wrote up the list and handed it to her and off she went without complaint to perform what they regarded as a great sacrifice of her time and a sign that she was indeed a very nice girl. She had never told them how much she loved grocery shopping, only that she was "willing" to do it. She had an intuition which told her that her parents were not safe for sharing such strong, important facts about herself. Let them think they knew her.

Once inside the supermarket, her hands firmly around the handle of the cart, she would lapse into a kind of <u>reverie</u> and wheel toward the produce. Like a Tibetan monk in solitary meditation, she calmed to a point of deep, deep happiness; this feeling came to her, reliably, if strangely, only in the supermarket.

Then one day the bag boy dropped her jar of mayonnaise and that is how she fell in love.

He was nervous—first day on the job—and along had come this fascinating girl, standing in the checkout line with the unfocused stare one often sees in young children, her face turned enough away that he might take several full looks at her as he packed sturdy bags full of food and the goods of modern life. She interested him because her hair was red and thick, and in it she had placed a huge orange bow, nearly the size of a small hat. That was enough to distract him, and when finally it was her groceries he was packing, she looked at him and smiled and he could respond only by busting her jar of mayonnaise on the floor, shards of glass and oozing cream decorating the area around his feet.

She loved him at exactly that moment, and if he'd known this perhaps he wouldn't have fallen into the brown depression he fell into, which lasted the rest of his shift. He believed he must have looked the fool in her eyes, and he envied the sureness of everyone around him: the cocky cashier at the register, the grim and harried store manager, the bland butcher, and the brazen bag boys who smoked in the warehouse on their breaks. He wanted a second chance. Another chance to be confident and say witty things to her

Vocabulary Builder
reverie (rev´ ə rē) *n.* dreamy thought of pleasant things

Literary Analysis
Point of View Whose thoughts and feelings are expressed in this paragraph?

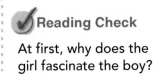

Reading Check

At first, why does the girl fascinate the boy?

as he threw tin cans into her bags, persuading her to allow him to help her to her car so he might learn just a little about her, check out the floor of the car for signs of hobbies or fetishes and the bumpers for clues as to beliefs and loyalties.

But he busted her jar of mayonnaise and nothing else worked out for the rest of the day.

Strange, how attractive clumsiness can be. She left the supermarket with stars in her eyes, for she had loved the way his long nervous fingers moved from the conveyor belt to the bags, how deftly (until the mayonnaise) they had picked up her items and placed them in her bags. She had loved the way the hair kept falling into his eyes as he leaned over to grab a box or a tin. And the tattered brown shoes he wore with no socks. And the left side of his collar turned in rather than out.

The bag boy seemed a wonderful contrast to the perfectly beautiful house she had been forced to accept as her home, to the history she hated, to the loneliness she had become used to, and she couldn't wait to come back for more of his awkwardness and <u>dishevelment</u>.

Incredibly, it was another four weeks before they saw each other again. As fate would have it, her visits to the supermarket never coincided with his schedule to bag. Each time she went to the store, her eyes scanned the checkouts at once, her heart in her mouth. And each hour he worked, the bag boy kept one eye on the door, watching for the red-haired girl with the big orange bow.

Yet in their disappointment these weeks there was a kind of ecstasy. It is reason enough to be alive, the hope you may see again some face which has meant something to you. The anticipation of meeting the bag boy eased the girl's painful transition into her new and jarring life in Cincinnati. It provided for her an anchor amid all that was impersonal and unfamiliar, and she spent less time on thoughts of what she had left behind as she concentrated on what might lie ahead. And for the boy, the long and often tedious hours at the supermarket which provided no challenge other than that of showing up the following workday . . . these hours became possibilities of mystery and romance for him as he watched the electric doors for the girl in the orange bow.

And when finally they did meet up again, neither offered a clue to the other that he, or she, had been the object of obsessive thought for weeks. She spotted him as soon as she came into the store, but she kept her eyes strictly in front of her as she pulled out a cart and wheeled it toward the produce. And he, too, knew the instant she came through the door—though the orange bow was gone, replaced by a small but bright yellow flower instead—and he never once

Literary Analysis
Point of View What does the narrator reveal about the boy's regrets?

Vocabulary Builder
dishevelment (di shev´ əl ment) *n.* disorder; messiness

Literary Analysis
Point of View Which details here suggest the story is told from the omniscient point of view? Explain.

turned his head in her direction but watched her from the corner of his vision as he tried to swallow back the fear in his throat.

It is odd how we sometimes deny ourselves the very pleasure we have longed for and which is finally within our reach. For some <u>perverse</u> reason she would not have been able to articulate, the girl did not bring her cart up to the bag boy's checkout when her shopping was done. And the bag boy let her leave the store, pretending no notice of her.

This is often the way of children, when they truly want a thing, to pretend that they don't. And then they grow angry when no one tried harder to give them this thing they so casually rejected, and they soon find themselves in a rage simply because they cannot say yes when they mean yes. Humans are very complicated. (And perhaps cats, who have been known to react in the same way, though the resulting rage can only be guessed at.)

The girl hated herself for not checking out at the boy's line, and the boy hated himself for not catching her eye and saying hello, and they most sincerely hated each other without having ever exchanged even two minutes of conversation.

Eventually—in fact, within the week—a kind and intelligent boy who lived very near her beautiful house asked the girl to a movie and she gave up her fancy for the bag boy at the supermarket. And the bag boy himself grew so bored with his job that he made a desperate search for something better and ended up in a bookstore where scores of fascinating girls lingered like honeybees about a hive. Some months later the bag boy and the girl with the orange bow again crossed paths, standing in line with their dates at a movie theater, and, glancing toward the other, each smiled slightly, then looked away, as strangers on public buses often do, when one is moving off the bus and the other is moving on.

Vocabulary Builder
perverse (pər vurs´)
adj. deviating from what is considered right or reasonable

Literary Analysis
Point of View Which details in this paragraph might be omitted if the story were told from the third-person limited point of view? Explain.

Thinking About the Selection

1. **Respond:** Were you disappointed that the girl and boy did not get together? Explain.

2. **(a) Recall:** What do the boy and girl think about while they are apart? **(b) Speculate:** How do you think the two characters feel when they see each other at the movie theater?

3. **Draw Conclusions:** Does the experience described in the story seem like a missed opportunity or a necessary outcome? Explain.

4. **(a) Summarize:** Why do the boy and girl never act on their feelings? **(b) Make a Judgment:** Do you agree with the narrator that "humans are very complicated"? Explain.

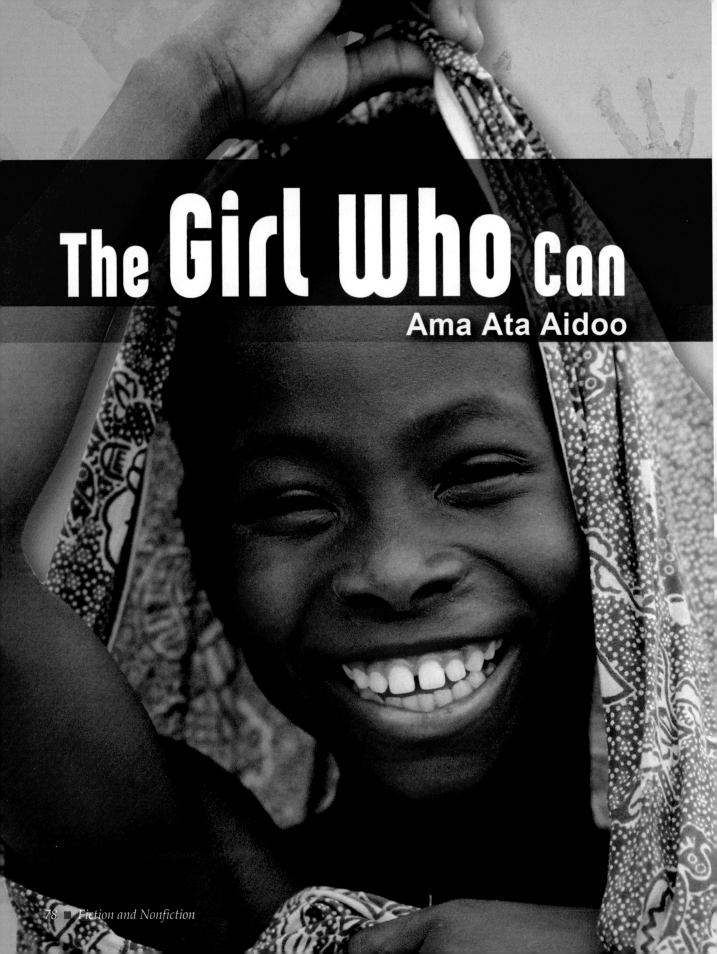

The Girl Who Can

Ama Ata Aidoo

They say that I was born in Hasodzi; and it is a very big village in the central region of our country, Ghana. They also say that when all of Africa is not choking under a drought, Hasodzi lies in a very <u>fertile</u> lowland in a district known for its good soil. Maybe that is why any time I don't finish eating my food, Nana says, "You Adjoa, you don't know what life is about . . . you don't know what problems there are in this life . . ."

As far as I could see, there was only one problem. And it had nothing to do with what I knew Nana considered as 'problems,' or what Maami thinks of as 'the problem.' Maami is my mother. Nana is my mother's mother. And they say I am seven years old. And my problem is that at this seven years of age, there are things I can think in my head, but which, maybe, I do not have the proper language to speak them out with. And that, I think, is a very serious problem because it is always difficult to decide whether to keep quiet and not say any of the things that come into my head, or say them and get laughed at. Not that it is easy to get any grown-up to listen to you, even when you decide to take the risk and say something serious to them.

Take Nana. First, I have to struggle to catch her attention. Then I tell her something I had taken a long time to figure out. And then you know what always happens? She would at once stop whatever she is doing and, mouth open, stare at me for a very long time. Then, bending and turning her head slightly, so that one ear comes down towards me, she'll say in that voice: "Adjoa, you say what?" After I have repeated whatever I had said, she would either, still in that voice, ask me "never, never, but NEVER to repeat THAT," or she would immediately burst out laughing. She would laugh and laugh and laugh, until tears run down her cheeks and she would stop whatever she is doing and wipe away the tears with the hanging edges of her cloth. And she would continue laughing until she is completely tired. But then, as soon as another person comes by, just to make sure she doesn't forget whatever it was I had said, she would repeat it to her. And then, of course, there would be two old people laughing and screaming with tears running down their faces. Sometimes this show continues until there are three, four or even more of such laughing and screaming tear-faced grownups. And all that performance for whatever I'd said? I find something quite confusing in all this. That is, no one ever explains to me why sometimes I shouldn't repeat some things I say; while at other times, some other things I say would not only be all right, but would be considered so funny they would be repeated so many times for so many people's enjoyment. You see how neither way of hearing me out can encourage me to express my thoughts too often?

◀ **Critical Viewing**
Describe the feelings the girl in the photograph expresses. **[Speculate]**

Vocabulary Builder
fertile (furt´´l) *adj.* able to make plants grow

Literary Analysis
Point of View Which pronouns in this paragraph show that this story is being told from the first-person point of view?

Reading Check
What does the narrator say is her problem?

The Girl Who Can ■ 79

Like all this business to do with my legs. I have always wanted to tell them not to worry. I mean Nana and my mother. It did not have to be an issue for my two favorite people to fight over. I didn't want to be told not to repeat it or for it to be considered so funny that anyone would laugh at me until they cried. After all, they were my legs . . . When I think back on it now, those two, Nana and my mother must have been discussing my legs from the day I was born. What I am sure of is that when I came out of the land of sweet, soft silence into the world of noise and <u>comprehension</u>, the first topic I met was my legs.

That discussion was repeated very regularly.

Nana: "Ah, ah, you know, Kaya, I thank my God that your very first child is female. But Kaya, I am not sure about her legs. Hm . . . hm . . . hm . . ."

And Nana would shake her head.

Maami: "Mother, why are you always complaining about Adjoa's legs? If you ask me . . ."

Nana: "They are too thin. And I am not asking you!"

Nana has many voices. There is a special one she uses to shut everyone up.

"Some people have no legs at all," my mother would try again with all her small courage.

"But Adjoa has legs," Nana would insist; "except that they are too thin. And also too long for a woman. Kaya, listen. Once in a while, but only once in a very long while, somebody decides — nature, a child's spirit mother, an accident happens, and somebody gets born without arms, or legs, or both sets of limbs. And then let me touch wood; it is a sad business. And you know, such things are not for talking about everyday. But if any female child decides to come into this world with legs, then they might as well be legs."

"What kind of legs?" And always at that point, I knew from her voice that my mother was weeping inside. Nana never heard such inside weeping.

▼ **Critical Viewing**
Might these mothers and children have relationships similar to those between Adjoa and her elders? Explain. **[Connect]**

Not that it would have stopped Nana even if she had heard it. Which always surprised me. Because, about almost everything else apart from my legs, Nana is such a good grown-up. In any case, what do I know about good grown-ups and bad grown-ups? How could Nana be a good grown-up when she carried on so about my legs? All I want to say is that I really liked Nana except for that.

Nana: "As I keep saying, if any woman decides to come into this world with her two legs, then she should select legs that have meat on them: with good calves. Because you are sure such legs would support solid hips. And a woman must have solid hips to be able to have children."

"Oh, Mother." That's how my mother would answer. Very, very quietly. And the discussion would end or they would move on to something else.

Sometimes, Nana would pull in something about my father:

How, "Looking at such a man, we have to be <u>humble</u> and admit that after all, God's children are many . . ."

How, "After one's only daughter had insisted on marrying a man like that, you still have to thank your God that the biggest problem you got later was having a granddaughter with spindly legs that are too long for a woman, and too thin to be of any use."

The way she always added that bit about my father under her breath, she probably thought I didn't hear it. But I always heard it. Plus, that is what always shut my mother up for good, so that even if I had not actually heard the words, once my mother looked like even her little courage was finished, I could always guess what Nana had added to the argument.

"Legs that have meat on them with good calves to support solid hips . . . to be able to have children."

So I wished that one day I would see, for myself, the legs of any woman who had had children. But in our village, that is not easy. The older women wear long wrap-arounds[1] all the time. Perhaps if they let me go bathe in the river in the evening, I could have checked. But I never had the chance. It took a lot of begging just to get my mother and Nana to let me go splash around in the shallow end of the river with my friends, who were other little girls like me. For proper baths, we used the small bathhouse behind our hut. Therefore, the only naked female legs I have ever really seen are those of other little girls like me, or older girls in the school. And those of my mother and Nana: two pairs of legs which must surely belong to the approved kind; because Nana gave birth to my mother and my mother gave birth to me. In my eyes, all my friends have got

---

1. **wrap-arounds** (rap´ ə rɒundz´) *n.* a type of garment that is open down the side and is wrapped around the body.

legs that look like legs, but whether the legs have got meat on them to support the kind of hips that . . . that I don't know.

According to the older boys and girls, the distance between our little village and the small town is about five kilometers. I don't know what five kilometers mean. They always complain about how long it is to walk to school and back. But to me, we live in our village, and walking those kilometers didn't matter. School is nice. School is another thing Nana and my mother discussed often and appeared to have different ideas about. Nana thought it would be a waste of time. I never understood what she meant. My mother seemed to know—and disagreed. She kept telling Nana that she— that is, my mother—felt she was locked into some kind of darkness because she didn't go to school. So that if I, her daughter, could learn to write and read my own name and a little besides—perhaps be able to calculate some things on paper—that would be good. I could always marry later and maybe . . .

Nana would just laugh. "Ah, maybe with legs like hers, she might as well go to school."

Running with our classmates on our small sports field and winning first place each time never seemed to me to be anything about which to tell anyone at home. This time it was different. I don't know how the teachers decided to let me run for the junior section of our school in the district games. But they did.

When I went home to tell my mother and Nana, they had not believed it at first. So Nana had taken it upon herself to go and "ask into it properly". She came home to tell my mother that it was really true. I was one of my school's runners.

"Is that so?" exclaimed my mother. I know her. Her mouth moved as though she was going to tell Nana, that, after all, there was a secret about me she couldn't be expected to share with anyone. But then Nana herself looked so pleased, out of surprise, my mother shut her mouth up. In any case, since the first time they heard the news, I have often caught Nana staring at my legs with a strange look on her face, but still

▼ **Critical Viewing**
How does your view of the narrator compare to the girls in this image? **[Compare]**

Country Profile: Ghana

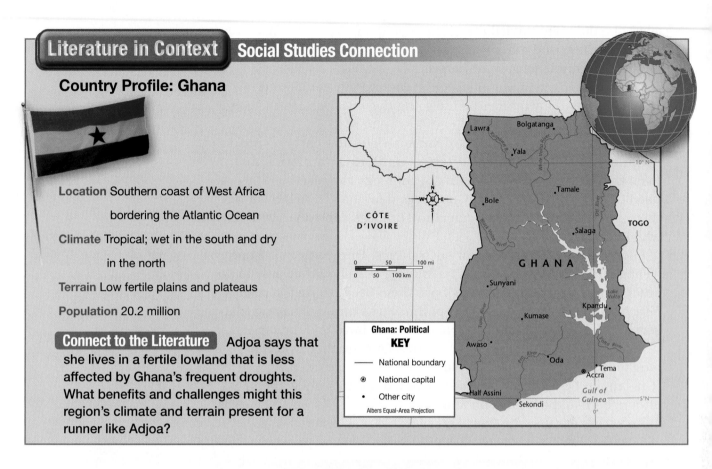

Location Southern coast of West Africa
bordering the Atlantic Ocean

Climate Tropical; wet in the south and dry
in the north

Terrain Low fertile plains and plateaus

Population 20.2 million

Connect to the Literature Adjoa says that she lives in a fertile lowland that is less affected by Ghana's frequent droughts. What benefits and challenges might this region's climate and terrain present for a runner like Adjoa?

pretending like she was not looking. All this week, she has been washing my school uniform herself. That is a big surprise. And she didn't stop at that, she even went to Mr. Mensah's house and borrowed his charcoal pressing iron. Each time she came back home with it and ironed and ironed and ironed the uniform, until, if I had been the uniform, I would have said aloud that I had had enough.

Wearing my school uniform this week has been very nice. At the parade, on the first afternoon, its sheen caught the rays of the sun and shone brighter than anybody else's uniform. I'm sure Nana saw that too, and must have liked it. Yes, she has been coming into town with us every afternoon of this district sports week. Each afternoon, she has pulled one set of fresh old cloth from the big brass bowl to wear. And those old clothes are always so stiffly starched, you can hear the cloth creak when she passes by. But she walks way behind us schoolchildren. As though she was on her own way to some place else.

Yes, I have won every race I ran for my school, and I have won the cup for the best all-round junior athlete. Yes, Nana said that she didn't care if such things are not done. She would do it. You know

Reading Check

After learning about her running talent, what does Nana do with the narrator's uniform?

The Girl Who Can ■ 83

what she did? She carried the gleaming cup on her back. Like they do with babies, and other very precious things. And this time, not taking the trouble to walk by herself.

When we arrived in our village, she entered our compound to show the cup to my mother before going to give it back to the head-master.

Oh, grown-ups are so strange. Nana is right now carrying me on her knee, and crying softly. Muttering, muttering, muttering that: "saa, thin legs can also be useful . . . thin legs can also be useful . . ." that "even though some legs don't have much meat on them, to carry hips . . . they can run. Thin legs can run . . . then who knows? . . ."

I don't know too much about such things. But that's how I was feeling and thinking all along. That surely, one should be able to do other things with legs as well as have them because they can support hips that make babies. Except that I was afraid of saying that sort of thing aloud. Because someone would have told me never, never, but NEVER to repeat such words. Or else, they would have laughed so much at what I'd said, they would have cried.

It's much better this way. To have acted it out to show them, although I could not have planned it.

As for my mother, she has been speechless as usual.

Thinking About the Selection

1. **Respond:** What was the most surprising part of this story to you? Explain.

2. **(a) Recall:** What criticism does Nana make about the narrator's legs? **(b) Draw Conclusions:** In what ways does this criticism show that Nana fears for Adjoa's future? Explain. **(c) Make Generalizations:** Based on these details, what kinds of lives do you think many women in Ghana are expected to lead?

3. **(a) Recall:** What are Nana's feelings about the narrator going to school? **(b) Compare and Contrast:** How do the mother's feelings about school differ from Nana's?

4. **(a) Infer:** After Adjoa is chosen for the district games, why does Nana keep staring at her legs? **(b) Draw Conclusions:** Why does Nana iron Adjoa's school uniform so carefully?

5. **(a) Analyze:** At the end of the story, Adjoa says it was much better to "have acted it out to show them." What has she "acted out"? **(b) Evaluate:** Was it "better," as Adjoa says? Explain.

Apply the Skills

Checkouts • The Girl Who Can

Comparing Points of View

1. Use a chart like the one shown to note the actions, thoughts, and feelings of the listed characters in both stories.

Checkouts	Actions	Thoughts	Feelings
Girl			
Boy			

The Girl Who Can	Actions	Thoughts	Feelings
Nana			
Adjoa			

2. How does **point of view** affect what you know about the boy's feelings and thoughts compared to what you know about Nana's feelings and thoughts?

3. **(a)** Which details from your chart show that the **third-person omniscient point of view** in "Checkouts" gives readers insight into the inner lives of all the characters? Explain. **(b)** Which details show that the **first-person point of view** in "The Girl Who Can" lets the reader understand the narrator best of all? Explain.

Writing to Compare Literary Works

Compare and contrast the girl in "Checkouts" and the narrator in "The Girl Who Can." In an essay, explain how point of view affected your attitude toward the girls. Use these questions to get started:
- Who are the narrators in the two stories?
- How do you know what each girl is thinking?
- How do other characters react to each girl?

Vocabulary Builder

Practice For each item, write a new sentence that uses a word from the vocabulary list on page 72 and expresses a similar idea.

1. He laughed cruelly at himself.
2. She felt she did not deserve an award.
3. I finally grasp what you mean.
4. That soil is rich.
5. She became lost in thought.
6. He changed his untidy clothes.

Reading: Make Predictions

Directions: *Questions 1–5 are based on the following questions*

There are times when one decides to go in a different direction, not because it is better for oneself, but because it is obviously better for one's family. That is how my grandmother ended up "somewhere else."

She and her husband had been planning on going with the California gold rush crowd. They weren't going, like most of the rest, to pan for gold. My grandmother was smart, ambitious, and too practical to believe that riches just fell into your hands. But they figured there were enough fools who were going to follow gold fantasies that there would be plenty of business opportunities. And, though they worked hard, in the little town in which they lived there were all too few business opportunities.

1. What prior knowledge would help you make predictions based on this passage?
   A   the history of working women
   B   political history of the West
   C   History of California
   D   economic history of the South

2. According to the passage, the grandmother
   A   will become a farmer in California.
   B   will start a business in California.
   C   will go to college in California.
   D   will pan for gold in California.

3. What can you predict about the grandmother's success based on the details given about her character?
   A   She is going to be easily fooled and led astray.
   B   She will be unsuccessful and return to the South.
   C   She will be a practical and successful businesswoman.
   D   She will let her husband do all the work.

4. If this is the introduction to a written work you can predict that the rest of the story will focus on
   A   the family and the South.
   B   the history of the family.
   C   the narrator's grandmother.
   D   the grandmother's ancestors.

5. What kind of details in the rest of the story would verify a prediction that grandmother was successful in her new life?
   A   Grandmother refuses to talk about her years in California.
   B   Grandmother writes sad letters home to her friends in the South.
   C   Grandmother sells her family's belongings to raise funds.
   D   Grandmother buys a large house in California.

Standards Assessed

• GU.6.01.6
• IR.2.02.5
• WL.1.03.5

Directions: *Choose the definition that best fits the underlined word as it is used in the sentence.*

6. The <u>specific</u> requirements for this project are posted on the school's Web site.
   A expanded
   B exact
   C design
   D general

7. Isn't it strange that the same two people were <u>involved</u> in both accidents?
   A required
   B elaborated
   C cited
   D included

8. He looks so old and tired; it is difficult to believe that he is my <u>contemporary</u>
   A about the same age
   B living in the same time
   C part of the modern world
   D antebellum

9. I understand that he is a major <u>contributor</u> to the Red Cross and will be honored for his generosity.
   A one who gives to
   B one who works with
   C one who writes for
   D one who is responsible for

10. We wrote a letter to the members of the Olympic track team asking them to <u>participate</u> in our fundraiser.
    A to take part
    B to share
    C to acknowledge
    D to refer

11. The coach will <u>inspect</u> the field before we play.
    A to pass or fail
    B to decide on authenticity
    C to look carefully at
    D to maintain vigilance

12. The demolition of the building was quite a <u>spectacle</u>.
    A unusual sight
    B revolving activity
    C disappointment
    D concern

13. Some leaves have <u>revolute</u> edges.
    A move in an upward direction
    B change governments
    C rolled backward or downward
    D start a change

14. The <u>revolving</u> Ferris Wheel made me dizzy.
    A to change, or improve, considerably
    B to divide in several parts
    C to start, or begin, several times
    D to turn, or roll, over

15. That is a <u>temporal</u> concern.
    A lasting only for a time
    B something that is of government
    C without a known end
    D something that is imposed

Narration: Autobiographical Narrative

Some of the best stories you may read are not imaginary—they describe real events in the writer's life and share the lessons or wisdom the writer gained from the experiences. Such stories are called **autobiographical narratives.** Follow the steps outlined in this workshop to write your own autobiographical narrative.

Assignment Write an autobiographical narrative about an event that taught you a valuable lesson.

What to Include Your autobiographical narrative should feature:
- A sequence of events involving you, the writer
- A problem, or conflict, and a lesson you learned from it
- Details that locate scenes and incidents in specific places
- Your personal thoughts, feelings, or views about the events
- Error-free grammar, including correct use of possessive nouns

To preview the criteria on which your autobiographical narrative may be judged, see the rubric on page 92.

Prewriting

Choosing Your Topic

Write your narrative about a topic that matters to you.

Blueprinting First, sketch a blueprint, or map, of a place you know well. Label each room or area. Then, jot down words or phrases you associate with each area. Choose one of these ideas as your topic.

Gathering Details

Structure the sequence. Create a detailed record of events by making a timeline. Write down the first incident related to your subject and record subsequent incidents in the order in which they occurred.

Standard Course of Study

- Apply parts of speech to clarify and edit language. (GU.6.01.3)
- Understand the importance of tone, mood, diction, and style. (LT.5.01.4)
- Analyze elements of literary environment found in text. (LT.5.03.12)

Using the Form

You may use elements of this form in these types of writing:
- letters and journals
- reflective essays
- persuasive essays

Reading | Writing Connection

To get a feel for autobiographical narratives, read "My English" by Julia Alvarez on page 107.

Timeline

Event 2: Dad took off training wheels.

Event 4: Improved riding. Tried other activities.

Event 1: Dreamed of riding bike with no training wheels.

Event 3: Rode two-wheeled bike and fell.

Work in Progress
Review the work you did on pages 13, 19, 41 and 71.

Drafting

Shaping Your Writing

Identify your main point. As you draft, think about why this story matters to you. To do so, clearly state the main problem you experienced and what you learned from it. Organize your details to highlight the importance of that main point.

Pace the action. Details and description add substance to your essay, but too much can slow the pace, or flow, of the story. To maintain interest, use details to accomplish these goals:
- Emphasize the central conflict that sets the story in motion.
- Reveal some details up front, but delay others.

Providing Elaboration

Choose vivid details. As you write, do not just list events. Instead, use details to show readers what happened and how it felt. Add life to your story with precise descriptions of places, people, and events. The chart shown here provides some tips to help you elaborate further on an idea.

Story Element	Elaboration Tip
Experience	Explain its main effect on you.
Time and Place	Describe impressions using sensory details.
Suspense	Add details that raise the tension and heighten the story's problem.
Main events of story	Include thoughts or feelings that occurred to you at the time of the events.
Story outcome	Consider other possible outcomes of events.

Revising

Revising Your Sentences

Vary your sentence beginnings. Even though your narrative is about an event that happened to you, avoid beginning every sentence with *I*. Look closely at the sentences in your draft and vary sentence beginnings to make your story more interesting.

Reading Writing Connection

To read the complete student model, see page 91.

Student Model: Revising to Vary Sentence Beginnings

~~I was~~ **My sister and I were** packing for an upcoming trip to youth camp one late Thursday night in July. **This was my first time attending** ~~I was with my sister.~~ I had ~~never attended~~ the camp, but it would be my older sister Phoebe's third experience.

A variety of sentence beginnings makes the essay more interesting.

Integrating Grammar Skills

Revising to Correct Use of Possessive Nouns

Possessive nouns show to whom places or things belong. A possessive noun is most often formed by adding an apostrophe or an apostrophe and an *s* to a noun.

Prentice Hall Writing and Grammar Connection: Chapter 29, Section 6

Noun	Possessive Noun
the homework of the *student*	the *student's* homework

Because they modify other nouns, possessive nouns function in sentences as adjectives.

Forming Possessive Nouns Correctly
Singular Nouns

- Add an apostrophe and an *s* to show the possessive case of most singular nouns.

      the radiator of the car ⟶ the car's radiator

- When a singular noun ends in *s,* you may still be able to add an apostrophe and *s*. However, if the apostrophe and *s* make the word difficult to pronounce, the apostrophe may be used alone.

      the sleeve of the dress ⟶ the dress's sleeve

      the poetry of Burns ⟶ Burns' poetry

Plural Nouns

- Add an apostrophe to show the possessive case of plural nouns ending in *s* or *es:* the *representatives'* decision.
- Add an apostrophe and *s* to show the possessive case of plural nouns that do not end in *s* or *es:* the *men's* books.

Compound Nouns

- Add an apostrophe and *s* to the last word of a compound noun: the Prime Minister's visit.
- Add only an apostrophe if the last word of a compound noun ends in *s:* the Organization of Countess' work.

Apply It to Your Editing

Review the draft of your autobiographical narrative, highlighting all the possessive nouns. Check that you have used a singular possessive when you meant singular, and a plural possessive when you meant plural. Correct any errors you find.

Student Model: Jonathan Chan
Royersford, PA

True Friend

Late one Thursday night in July, my sister and I were packing for our upcoming trip to youth camp. This was my first time attending the camp, but it would be my older sister Phoebe's third experience. Everything was running smoothly until my mother called from downstairs, "Don't forget to grab a sleeping bag from my closet!" Our mother never dreamed such a simple statement would start a desperate dash by both of us to seize the most coveted sleeping bag in our household.

The night-sky blue, extra long, brand new, one hundred percent fleece sleeping bag with a built-in pillow was one-of-a-kind. By comparison, the old sleeping bag, with a broken zipper and a small hole forming at the bottom, looked even worse. Phoebe and I reached for the beautiful new bag at the exact same moment. Insulting remarks sailed from our lips as we each grabbed it. Our stomps and yells attracted our parents to the fight scene. I began to argue that I had reached the bag first, when my sister simply let go, returned to her room, and slammed the door. She was so thoroughly angry, we did not speak again that night.

As the weekend progressed, our relationship did not improve. Even worse, she had shared the story with her friends. Phoebe's words were so moving, they convinced her friends to embark on a personal voyage to "get me." As a result, I spent the getaway with a target on my back.

As the skinny new kid at the camp, terror struck my heart when I heard a rumor about the plot against me. By Sunday morning, the plan, "Operation Little Brother," was all set. My sister's friends were on a mission.

I was shooting hoops in the gym that morning when my sister's friends appeared. I looked frantically for an escape but was quickly surrounded. The assailants closed to within inches of me when a familiar voice echoed through the emptiness of the open gymnasium. My sister walked calmly between her friends and me and said, "Do not bother him or you will feel the wrath of Phoebe." I was in awe. With this statement, "Operation Little Brother" came to an abrupt end. The sister I was feuding with had just saved me. Her friends never bothered me again.

On the trip home I asked her to explain her unlikely action. She simply replied, "I still don't like you, but I would dislike myself even more if I ever abandoned a friend in trouble." Since then, I have often modeled my actions to emulate my sister's behavior that day. I have learned that even when I am angry, I must stand up for my friends. My sister has taught me many things, but the most important lesson is how to be a true friend.

The author's use of dialogue helps to make this opening scene more real and vivid.

The detailed description of the sleeping bag helps to establish the conflict.

Here, the conflict intensifies.

The author uses specific details to paint a picture of the problem he faces.

The use of dialogue and description help to convey the drama of the moment and make it seem real.

The author concludes by drawing an important lesson from his experience.

Writing Workshop

Editing and Proofreading

Check your draft for errors in grammar, spelling, and punctuation.
Focus on Dates and Facts: Review your manuscript and make sure you have provided accurate factual information. Capitalize the proper names of people or places and use correct punctuation when including dates.

Prentice Hall Writing and Grammar Connection:
Chapter 29, Section 6

Publishing and Presenting

Consider one of the following ways to share your writing:
Present an oral narrative. Mark up a copy of your autobiographical narrative, underlining any thoughts or conversations that you believe your audience would enjoy. As you present to your classmates, emphasize those passages. When you are done, gracefully accept your classmates' applause and praise.
Post your essay. Create a bulletin board display of the narratives written by you and your classmates. Have each writer supply a short comment about the event or idea that inspired his or her writing.

Reflecting on Your Writing

Writer's Journal Jot down your thoughts on writing an autobiographical narrative. Begin by answering these questions:
- How does the use of details help to make a narrative clearer and more vivid?
- What did you learn about yourself as you wrote?

Rubric for Self-Assessment

To assess your autobiographical narrative, use the following rubric.

Criteria	Rating Scale
	Not very *Very*
Focus: How central are you to the action of the story?	1 2 3 4 5
Organization: How clearly organized is the sequence of events?	1 2 3 4 5
Support/Elaboration: How powerfully are sensory details used to locate scenes in specific places?	1 2 3 4 5
Style: How clearly do you convey your insights, thoughts, and feelings?	1 2 3 4 5
Conventions: How correct is your grammar, especially your use of possessive nouns?	1 2 3 4 5

Unit 1
Part 2
Author's Purpose

Skills You Will Learn

Literary Analysis: *Autobiographical Writing and Author's Voice*

Reading Skill: *Preview a Work to Identify the Author's Purpose*

Reading Skill: *Recognize the Organizational Features of a Text*

Literary Analysis: *Character*
Reading Skill: *Reflect on a Work*

Literary Analysis: *Theme*

Literature You Will Read

Reading: Author's Purpose

**Standard Course
of Study**

• Analyze text components
and evaluating impact on
argumentative text.
(FA.3.04.2)

> ▶ An **author's purpose** is his or her reason for writing. There are four
> general purposes for writing—to entertain, to inform, to describe,
> and to persuade.

Skills and Strategies You Will Learn in Part 2

In Part 2 you will learn
- to **preview** a work to **determine the author's general purpose** (p. 96)
- to **reflect** on a work to **determine the author's specific purpose** (p. 126)
- to **recognize organizational features of a text** and how organization is utilized to implement the **author's purpose** (p. 118)

Using the Skills and Strategies in Part 2

In Part 2, you will learn to focus your reading by previewing the work to identify the author's purpose. You will also learn to reflect on and refine your concept of purpose while you continue to read. Previewing, identifying the author's purpose, and then reflecting on that purpose while you read helps you to read intelligently.

This chart shows how you can apply the skills and strategies you will learn in Part 2.

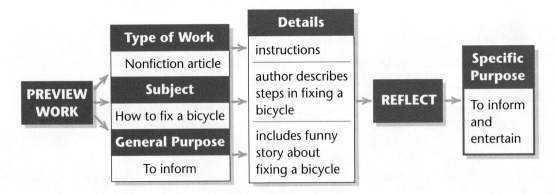

Academic Vocabulary: Words for Evaluating Literature

The following words will help you write and talk about an author's purpose.

Word	Definition	Example Sentence
vital *adj.*	necessary	Sensory details are *vital* to a novel.
appreciate *v.*	to recognize; to understand and be grateful for	We seldom *appreciate* the precise use of language in a poem.
trivial *v.*	of little or no importance	The story has too many *trival* details.
display *v.*	to exhibit; to show	The character *displays* benevolent characteristics.
detect *v.*	to discover	*Detecting* shifts of tone and mood in a work takes practice.

Vocabulary Skills you will learn in Part 2

▶ The origin of a word is the language it came from.

In Part 2 you will learn
- Latin root *-vit-* (p. 144)
- Latin root *-via-* (p. 95)
- Latin root *-tri-* (p. 116)

The English language is made up words, that come from many different languages. Many words have the same root. The chart shows a dictionary entry and the changes this root has gone through.

via (vī′ə) [L. abl. sing. of via, a way < IE base wei-, to go strive toward> Gr *ienai*, to go, OE *wath*, a hunt, chase]

viable
tri**via**l
viaduct
tri**via**

Activity Fill in the roots *via, tri,* or *vit* to complete the word that goes with each clue.

1. necessary to life _____al
2. to change direction de_____te
3. able to live _____ble
4. a brief autobiography _____ae
5. a three pronged spear _____dent

Build Skills from *A White House Diary* • *My English*

Practice these skills with either the excerpt from *A White House Diary* (p. 98) or "My English" (p. 107).

Standard Course of Study

- Identify and analyze elements of argument. (FA.3.04.11)
- Use preparation, engagement, and reflection appropriate to critique text. (CT.4.02.1)
- Use reading strategies for preparation, engagement, reflection. (LT.5.01.1)

Literary Analysis

Voice is the way a writer sounds on the page. For example, the writer's voice in a work can be *smooth and sophisticated, choppy and blunt,* or *breathless and full of wonder.* Voice is a result of several elements:

- *Word Choice:* the kinds of words the writer uses
- *Attitude:* the way the writer feels about his or her subject
- *Sentence Structure:* the arrangement of words in sentences

In **autobiographical writing,** the author tells all or part of his or her own life's story. The kind of details that are included show what the writer notices, thinks, and feels about events. The voice of autobiographical writing usually reflects the writer's own personality and way of speaking.

Text Feature	Insight About Purpose

Reading Skill

An **author's purpose** is his or her main reason for writing. An author writes for a general purpose, such as to inform, to entertain, or to persuade. He or she also writes for a specific purpose, such as to expose a particular problem in society. Before you read, **preview to look for an author's purpose.**

- Notice information or ideas conveyed in the title.
- Look for any organizing features, like subheads.
- Identify the subject of photos, illustrations, or diagrams.

As you preview, use an organizer like the one shown to jot down ideas about the author's specific purpose. Later, as you read the full text, confirm whether your ideas are correct.

Vocabulary Builder

from *A White House Diary*

- **tumultuous** (tōō mulʹchōō əs) *adj.* greatly disturbed; in an uproar (p. 101) *The year we moved cross-country was a <u>tumultuous</u> one.*

- **implications** (imʹpli kāʹshənz) *n.* indirect results (p. 102) *He did not think about the <u>implications</u> of his decision to change jobs.*

- **poignant** (poinʹyənt) *adj.* emotionally touching (p. 103) *The moment of farewell is often very <u>poignant</u>.*

My English

- **bilingual** (bī liŋʹgwəl) *adj.* using two languages (p. 107) *The <u>bilingual</u> student speaks both Japanese and English.*

- **countenance** (kounʹtə nəns) *n.* face (p. 109) *The child's overjoyed <u>countenance</u> showed her relief at being home.*

- **interminably** (in turʹmi nə blē) *adv.* endlessly. (p. 113) *To the tired, hungry audience, the speaker went on <u>interminably</u>.*

Autobiography

Background

The Assassination of JFK President John F. Kennedy was a young, vibrant, and popular leader who had been elected in 1960. His assassination on November 22, 1963, was a stunning and unforgettable event. As the news media reported the tragedy, people wept openly in the streets. A mournful nation agreed with Lyndon B. Johnson, JFK's successor, when he said, "We have suffered a loss that cannot be weighed."

Connecting to the Literature

Reading/Writing Connection For many Americans, the speeches of John F. Kennedy remain a source of inspiration and hope. Write a brief paragraph about a person whose actions or ideas you find inspiring. Use at least three of these words: *evoke, invoke, embody, motivate, illustrate.*

Meet the Author

Lady Bird **Johnson** (b. 1912)

Texas-born Claudia Alta Taylor received her nickname when a nurse said the two-year-old was as pretty as a "lady bird." A graduate of the University of Texas, Lady Bird met and married Lyndon Johnson, then a young Congressional aide, in 1934. Even though she was a shy woman, Lady Bird was a most valued advisor and effective campaigner for her husband, who said that voters "would happily have elected her over me."

Living History When President Kennedy was assassinated, Vice President Lyndon Johnson became president, and Lady Bird became First Lady of the United States. In this role, she made many contributions to her husband's agenda, including the launch of Head Start, a project that makes early childhood education available to all children.

Fast Facts

▶ In 1982, Lady Bird Johnson founded the National Wildflower Research Center in Austin, Texas.

▶ *A White House Diary* was published in 1970, shortly after the Johnsons returned to Texas, where Mrs. Johnson still lives.

Go Online
Author Link
For: More about the author
Visit: www.PHSchool.com
Web Code: epe-9108

FROM

A WHITE HOUSE
DIARY

LADY BIRD JOHNSON

DALLAS, FRIDAY, NOVEMBER 22, 1963

It all began so beautifully. After a drizzle in the morning, the sun came out bright and clear. We were driving into Dallas. In the lead car were President and Mrs. Kennedy, John and Nellie Connally,[1] a Secret Service[2] car full of men, and then our car with Lyndon and me and Senator Ralph Yarborough.

The streets were lined with people—lots and lots of people—the children all smiling, placards, confetti, people waving from windows. One last happy moment I had was looking up and seeing Mary Griffith leaning out of a window waving at me. (Mary for many years had been in charge of altering the clothes which I purchased at Neiman-Marcus.)

Then, almost at the edge of town, on our way to the Trade Mart for the Presidential luncheon, we were rounding a curve, going down a hill, and suddenly there was a sharp, loud report. It sounded like a shot. The sound seemed to me to come from a building on the right above my shoulder. A moment passed, and then two more shots rang out in rapid succession. There had been such a gala air about the day that I thought the noise must come from firecrackers—part of the celebration. Then the Secret Service men were suddenly down in the lead car. Over the car radio system, I heard "Let's get out of here!" and our Secret Service man, Rufus Youngblood, vaulted over the front seat on top of Lyndon, threw him to the floor, and said, "Get down."

Senator Yarborough and I ducked our heads. The car accelerated terrifically—faster and faster. Then, suddenly, the brakes were put on so hard that I wondered if we were going to make it as we wheeled left and went around the corner. We pulled up to a building. I looked up and saw a sign, "HOSPITAL." Only then did I believe that this might be what it was. Senator Yarborough kept saying in an excited voice, "Have they shot the President? Have they shot the President?" I said something like, "No, it can't be."

As we ground to a halt—we were still the third car—Secret Service men began to pull, lead, guide, and hustle us out. I cast one last look over my shoulder and saw in the President's car a bundle of pink, just like a drift of blossoms, lying on the back seat. It was Mrs. Kennedy lying over the President's body.

---

1. **John and Nellie Connally** John Connally, then Governor of Texas, and his wife, Nellie.
2. **Secret Service** division of the U.S. Treasury Department, responsible for protecting the president.

◄ **Critical Viewing** What does this photograph reveal about the mood in the moments leading up to the assassination of President Kennedy? **[Infer]**

Reading Skill
Author's Purpose
What would previewing this subhead suggest to you about the author's purpose in this part of her diary?

Literary Analysis
Voice and Autobiographical Writing What do the details about firecrackers tell you about the writer's attitude toward the events she describes?

Reading Check

Where are the Johnsons taken after shots are fired?

The Secret Service men rushed us to the right, then to the left, and then onward into a quiet room in the hospital—a very small room. It was lined with white sheets, I believe.

People came and went—Kenny O'Donnell, the President's top aide, Congressman Homer Thornberry, Congressman Jack Brooks. Always there was Rufe right there and other Secret Service agents—Emory Roberts, Jerry Kivett, Lem Johns, and Woody Taylor. People spoke of how widespread this might be. There was talk about where we would go—to the plane, to our house, back to Washington.

Through it all Lyndon was remarkably calm and quiet. He suggested that the Presidential plane ought to be moved to another part of the field. He spoke of going back out to the plane in unmarked black cars. Every face that came in, you searched for the answer. I think the face I kept seeing the answer on was the face of Kenny O'Donnell, who loved President Kennedy so much.

It was Lyndon who spoke of it first, although I knew I would not leave without doing it. He said, "You had better try to see Jackie and Nellie." We didn't know what had happened to John.

I asked the Secret Service if I could be taken to them. They began to lead me up one corridor and down another. Suddenly I

Literature in Context   **History Connection**

The Legacy of JFK

At the age of 43, John Fitzgerald Kennedy became the youngest president in American history. He brought to the White House a new energy, optimism, and hope for the future. The initiatives he sought changed America.

▲ Kennedy, shown here with astronaut John Glenn, committed the nation to space exploration.

Kennedy established the Peace Corps in 1961. To date, 170,000 volunteers have served in 137 countries.
▼

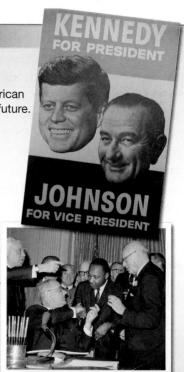

Kennedy ▶ initiated the Civil Rights Act. Johnson, with Dr. Martin Luther King Jr., at his side, signed it into law in 1965.

Connect to the Literature   How does information about President Kennedy's ideas help explain the intense grief most Americans felt over his death?

◀ **Critical Viewing**
What do these peoples' facial expressions reveal about their feelings following the assassination? **[Interpret]**

found myself face to face with Jackie in a small hallway. I believe it was right outside the operating room. You always think of someone like her as being insulated, protected. She was quite alone. I don't think I ever saw anyone so much alone in my life. I went up to her, put my arms around her, and said something to her. I'm sure it was something like "God, help us all," because my feelings for her were too <u>tumultuous</u> to put into words.

And then I went to see Nellie. There it was different, because Nellie and I have gone through so many things together since 1938. I hugged her tight and we both cried and I said, "Nellie, John's going to be all right." And Nellie said, "Yes, John's going to be all right." Among her many other fine qualities, she is also strong.

I turned and went back to the small white room where Lyndon was. Mac Kilduff, the President's press man on this trip, and Kenny O'Donnell were coming and going. I think it was from Kenny's face that I first knew the truth and from Kenny's voice that I first heard the words "The President is dead." Mr. Kilduff entered and said to Lyndon, "Mr. President."

It was decided that we would go immediately to the airport. Hurried plans were made about how we should get to the cars and who was to ride in which car. Our departure from the hospital and approach to the cars was one of the swiftest walks I have ever made.

We got in. Lyndon told the agents to stop the sirens. We drove along as fast as we could. I looked up at a building and there, already, was a flag at half-mast. I think that was when the enormity of what had happened first struck me.

Vocabulary Builder
tumultuous (too mul´ choo əs) *adj.* greatly disturbed; in an uproar

 Reading Check

How did Mrs. Johnson first know that the president was dead?

When we got to the field, we entered *Air Force One*[3] for the first time. There was a TV set on and the commentator was saying, "Lyndon B. Johnson, now President of the United States." The news commentator was saying the President had been shot with a 30-30 rifle. The police had a suspect. They were not sure he was the assassin.

On the plane, all the shades were lowered. We heard that we were going to wait for Mrs. Kennedy and the coffin. There was a telephone call to Washington—I believe to the Attorney General.[4]

It was decided that Lyndon should be sworn in here as quickly as possible, because of national and world <u>implications</u>, and because we did not know how widespread this was as to intended victims. Judge Sarah Hughes, a Federal Judge in Dallas—and I am glad it was she—was called and asked to come in a hurry to administer the oath.

Mrs. Kennedy had arrived by this time, as had the coffin. There, in the very narrow confines of the plane—with Jackie standing by Lyndon, her hair falling in her face but very composed, with me beside him, Judge Hughes in front of him, and a cluster of Secret Service people, staff, and Congressmen we had known for a long time around him—Lyndon took the oath of office.

---

3. *Air Force One* name of the airplane officially assigned to transport the president of the United States.
4. **Attorney General** chief law officer of the nation, head of the U.S. Department of Justice; at the time, the position was held by Robert Kennedy, the president's brother.

▲ Critical Viewing
This photograph shows Lyndon Johnson assuming his duties as president. How do you think he felt at that moment? Why? **[Analyze]**

Vocabulary Builder
implications (im′ pli kā′ shənz) *n.* indirect results

It's odd the little things that come to your mind at times of utmost stress, the flashes of deep compassion you feel for people who are really not at the center of the tragedy. I heard a Secret Service man say in the most desolate voice—and I hurt for him: "We never lost a President in the Service." Then, Police Chief Curry of Dallas came on the plane and said, "Mrs. Kennedy, believe me, we did everything we possibly could." That must have been an agonizing moment for him.

We all sat around the plane. The casket was in the corridor. I went in the small private room to see Mrs. Kennedy, and though it was a very hard thing to do, she made it as easy as possible. She said things like, "Oh, Lady Bird, we've liked you two so much. . . . Oh, what if I had not been there. I'm so glad I was there."

I looked at her. Mrs. Kennedy's dress was stained with blood. One leg was almost entirely covered with it and her right glove was caked, it was caked with blood—her husband's blood. Somehow that was one of the most poignant sights—that immaculate woman exquisitely dressed, and caked in blood.

I asked her if I couldn't get someone in to help her change and she said, "Oh, no. Perhaps later I'll ask Mary Gallagher but not right now." And then with almost an element of fierceness—if a person that gentle, that dignified, can be said to have such a quality—she said, "I want them to see what they have done to Jack."

I tried to express how we felt. I said, "Oh, Mrs. Kennedy, you know we never even wanted to be Vice President and now, dear God, it's come to this." I would have done anything to help her, but there was nothing I could do, so rather quickly I left and went back to the main part of the airplane where everyone was seated.

The flight to Washington was silent, each sitting with his own thoughts. One of mine was a recollection of what I had said about Lyndon a long time ago—he's a good man in a tight spot. I remembered one little thing he had said in that hospital room—"Tell the children to get a Secret Service man with them."

Finally we got to Washington, with a cluster of people waiting and many bright lights. The casket went off first, then Mrs. Kennedy, and then we followed. The family had come to join her. Lyndon made a very simple, very brief, and, I think, strong statement to the people there. Only about four sentences. We got in helicopters, dropped him off at the White House, and I came home in a car with Liz Carpenter.[5]

---

5. **Liz Carpenter** Mrs. Johnson's press secretary.

Reading Skill
Author's Purpose
What is the writer's purpose in including the comments of the Secret Service man?

Vocabulary Builder
poignant (poin´ yənt)
adj. emotionally touching

Literary Analysis
Voice and Autobiographical Writing What does this passage reveal about Mrs. Johnson's attitude toward Mrs. Kennedy?

Apply the Skills

from *A White House Diary*

Thinking About the Selection

1. **Respond:** What do you admire most about Mrs. Johnson? Explain.
2. **(a) Recall:** What does Mrs. Kennedy say when Mrs. Johnson offers to find someone to help her change her clothes? **(b) Interpret:** What does Mrs. Kennedy mean? **(c) Analyze:** Why do you think Mrs. Johnson reported this detail?
3. **(a) Recall:** What comment about her husband does Mrs. Johnson recall on the flight back to Washington? **(b) Interpret:** What character traits does this comment suggest President Johnson possessed? Explain. **(c) Support:** Which details from the selection show that Mrs. Johnson possesses similar character traits?
4. **Evaluate:** Do you think Mrs. Johnson effectively expresses what it felt like to live through this historic incident? Explain.

Literary Analysis

5. **(a)** Complete a chart like the one shown to find examples of Johnson's **word choice, attitude,** and **sentence structure.**

VOICE		
Word Choice	**Attitude**	**Sentence Structure**

   (b) Using examples from your chart, describe Johnson's **voice** in this work.
6. **(a)** What details about Lyndon Johnson are emphasized in Lady Bird Johnson's **autobiographical writing? (b)** Why would Lady Bird Johnson notice these details more than someone else might? **(c)** What are two other details about feelings and incidents that reflect Mrs. Johnson's unique perspective on events?

Reading Skill

7. Review the notes you made in your **preview** of the excerpt. Which of your ideas about the **author's purpose** were confirmed as you read the selection? Which were not? Explain.
8. **(a)** What general purpose do you think Mrs. Johnson had in writing this portion of *A White House Diary*? Explain. **(b)** What more specific purpose(s) do you think she had for writing? Support your answer with details from the diary.

Vocabulary Builder

Practice **Analogies** show the relationships between pairs of words. To complete each analogy, use a word from the vocabulary list for the excerpt from *A White House Diary* on page 96. For each case, your choice should create a word pair that matches the relationship between the first two words given.

1. weak : strong :: calm : _____
2. rain : flood :: choice : _____
3. laughter : humorous :: sadness : _____

Adding Words to Your Vocabulary A word's **denotation** is its direct, literal meaning. A word's **connotations** are the ideas associated with it. For example, *stirring* and *poignant* share a similar denotative meaning. However, their connotative meanings are very different. Using a dictionary and a thesaurus, investigate the connotations of each word. Then, use each word in a sentence that illustrates its specific connotation. (For more on using a dictionary and a thesaurus, see pages R6–7.)

Writing

Using the excerpt from *A White House Diary* as inspiration, write a **journal entry** of your own in which you describe and react to an event of local, national, or global significance. As you prepare to write, consider the following questions:

- Who was affected by this event and in what way?
- What specific words or images does this event call to mind?

For *Grammar, Vocabulary,* and *Assessment,* see **Build Language Skills,** pages 116–117.

Extend Your Learning

Listening and Speaking With three or four classmates, enact a **radio broadcast** of a news bulletin about the Kennedy assassination.

- As you work together to write a script, evaluate your word choices to make sure they suit your audience and purpose.
- Use appropriate vocal inflection to convey the gravity of the news.

Research and Technology Using presentation software, prepare a list of at least three main points and an **introduction for a multimedia presentation** about First Ladies in American history. Discuss how the role of the First Lady has changed over time.

Autobiographical Essay

Background

Alvarez's Two Nationalities Julia Alvarez, the author of "My English," was born in New York but grew up in the Dominican Republic, a small Caribbean nation. An independent state since 1844, the Dominican Republic has often struggled with foreign conquest, political unrest, and dictatorship. Alvarez's family was forced to return to New York in 1960 because her father had participated in a movement against the brutal Dominican dictator Raphael Trujillo.

Connecting to the Literature

Reading/Writing Connection Julia Alvarez has experienced both dictatorship and democracy. Write three statements contrasting these two forms of government. Use at least three of the following words: *debate, demonstrate, deprive, dictate, rebel.*

Review

For **Literary Analysis, Reading Skill,** and **Vocabulary Builder,** see page 96.

READ MORE

by Julia Alvarez
How the Garcia Girls Lost Their Accents

Meet the Author

Julia **Alvarez** (b. 1950)

When her family fled the Dominican Republic and returned to New York, Julia Alvarez was ten years old, and Spanish was her primary language. Painfully aware of not fitting in, Julia took refuge in reading and making up stories. She says, "I landed, not in the United States, but in the English language. That became my new home."

"I Write to Find Out Who I Am." Alvarez attended Middlebury College, where she won several poetry awards. She later earned a master's degree in creative writing from Syracuse University. Alvarez says that writing is "a way to understand yourself." Her writing has been praised for its humor, sensitivity, and insight.

Fast Facts

▶ Julia Alvarez has established a farm in the Dominican Republic called Alta Gracia. The farm includes a school and its own line of coffee.

▶ One of her books, *In the Time of the Butterflies,* was made into a film starring Salma Hayek.

For: More about the author
Visit: www.PHSchool.com
Web Code: epe-9109

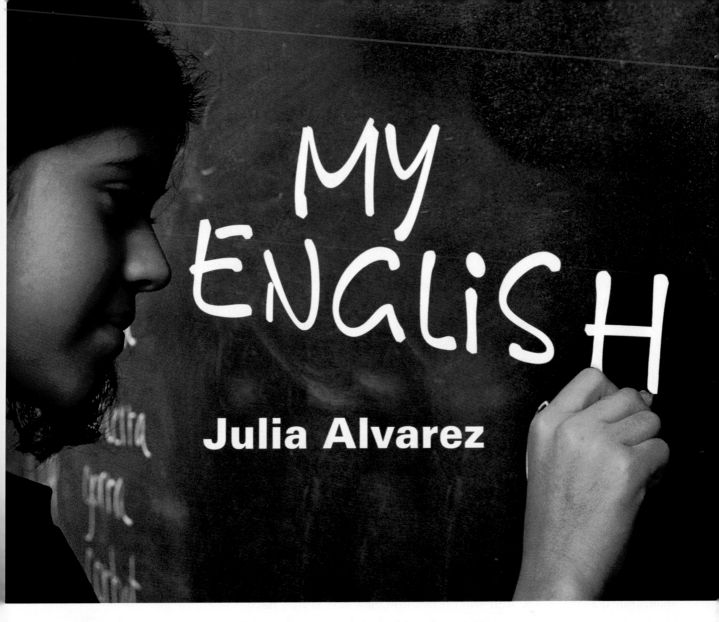

MY ENGLISH

Julia Alvarez

Mami and Papi used to speak it when they had a secret they wanted to keep from us children. We lived then in the Dominican Republic, and the family as a whole spoke only Spanish at home, until my sisters and I started attending the Carol Morgan School, and we became a <u>bilingual</u> family. Spanish had its many tongues as well. There was the castellano[1] of Padre[2] Joaquín from Spain, whose lisp we all loved to imitate. Then the educated español my parents' families spoke, aunts and uncles who were always correcting us children, for we spent most of the day with the maids and so had picked up their "bad Spanish." Campesinas,[3] they spoke a lilting,

Vocabulary Builder
bilingual (bī lin´ gwəl)
adj. using two
languages

---

1. castellano (cä´ stä yä´ nō) Spanish for "Castilian," the most widely spoken dialect of the Spanish language.
2. Padre (pä´ drä) "Father" (Spanish), a form of address for a Roman Catholic priest.
3. Campesinas (cäm pä sē´ näs) "simple rural women; peasant women" (Spanish).

animated campuno,[4] ss swallowed, endings chopped off, funny turns of phrases. This campuno was my true mother tongue, not the Spanish of Calderón de la Barca or Cervantes or even Neruda,[5] but of Chucha and Iluminada and Gladys and Ursulina from Juncalito and Licey and Boca de Yuma and San Juan de la Maguana.[6] Those women yakked as they cooked, they storytold, they gossiped, they sang—boleros, merengues, canciones, salves.[7] Theirs were the voices that belonged to the rain and the wind and the teeny, teeny stars even a small child could blot out with her thumb.

Besides all these versions of Spanish, every once in a while another strange tongue emerged from my papi's mouth or my mami's lips. What I first recognized was not a language, but a tone of voice, serious, urgent, something important and top secret being said, some uncle in trouble, someone divorcing, someone dead. *Say it in English so the children won't understand.* I would listen, straining to understand, thinking that this was not a different language but just another and harder version of Spanish. *Say it in English so the children won't understand.* From the beginning, English was the sound of worry and secrets, the sound of being left out.

I could make no sense of this "harder Spanish," and so I tried by other means to find out what was going on. I knew my mother's face by heart. When the little lines on the corners of her eyes crinkled, she was amused. When her nostrils flared and she bit her lips, she was trying hard not to laugh. She held her head down, eyes glancing up, when she thought I was lying. Whenever she spoke that gibberish English, I translated the general content by watching the Spanish expressions on her face.

Soon, I began to learn more English, at the Carol Morgan School. That is, when I had stopped gawking. The teacher and some of the American children had the strangest coloration: light hair, light eyes, light skin, as if Ursulina had soaked them in bleach too long,

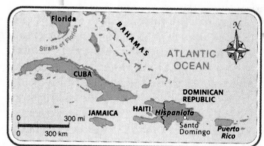
---

4. **campuno** (căm pōō´nō) Spanish dialect spoken in rural areas of the Dominican Republic.
5. **Calderón de la Barca** (căl de rôn´ dā lä bär´ cä) . . . **Cervantes** (ser vän´ tes) . . . **Neruda** (nā rōō´ dä) important literary figures.
6. **Juncalito** (hōōn cä lē´ tō) . . . **Licey** . . . **Boca de Yuma** (bō´ cä dā yōō´ mä) . . . **San Juan de la Maguana** (sän hwän´ dā lä mä gwä´ nä) small rural villages in the Dominican Republic.
7. **boleros** (bō ler´ ōs) . . . **merengues** (mə ren´ gās) . . . **canciones** (căn sē ō´ nes) . . . **salves** (säl´ ves) Spanish and Latin American songs and dances.

to' deteñío.[8] I did have some blond cousins, but they had deeply tanned skin, and as they grew older, their hair darkened, so their earlier paleness seemed a phase of their acquiring normal color. Just as strange was the little girl in my reader who had a *cat* and a *dog*, that looked just like un gatito y un perrito. Her mami was *Mother* and her papi *Father*. Why have a whole new language for school and for books with a teacher who could speak it teaching you double the amount of words you really needed?

Butter, butter, butter, butter. All day, one English word that had particularly struck me would go round and round in my mouth and weave through all the Spanish in my head until by the end of the day, the word did sound like just another Spanish word. And so I would say, "Mami, please pass la mantequilla." She would scowl and say in English, "I'm sorry, I don't understand. But would you be needing some butter on your bread?"

Why my parents didn't first educate us in our native language by enrolling us in a Dominican school, I don't know. Part of it was that Mami's family had a tradition of sending the boys to the States to boarding school and college, and she had been one of the first girls to be allowed to join her brothers. At Abbot Academy,[9] whose school song was our lullaby as babies ("Although Columbus and Cabot[10] never heard of Abbot, it's quite the place for you and me"), she had become quite Americanized. It was very important, she kept saying, that we learn our English. She always used the possessive pronoun: *your* English, an inheritance we had come into and must wisely use. Unfortunately, my English became all mixed up with our Spanish.

Mix-up, or what's now called Spanglish, was the language we spoke for several years. There wasn't sentence that wasn't colonized by an English word. At school, a Spanish word would suddenly slide into my English like someone butting into line. Teacher, whose face I was learning to read as minutely as my mother's, would scowl but no smile played on her lips. Her pale skin made her strange <u>countenance</u> hard to read, so that I often misjudged how much I could get away with. Whenever I made a mistake, Teacher would shake her head slowly, "In English, YU-LEE-AH, there's no such word as *columpio*. Do you mean a *swing?*"

I would bow my head, humiliated by the smiles and snickers of the American children around me. I grew insecure about Spanish. My native tongue was not quite as good as English, as if words like

---

8. to' deteñío (tō dā tān yē´ ō) "all washed out" or "completely colorless" (Spanish).
9. Abbot Academy boarding school for girls in Andover, Massachusetts; merged in 1973 with the neighboring boys' school, Phillips Academy.
10. Cabot (1450?–1498?) (kab´ ət) John Cabot, Italian explorer who sailed in the service of England and discovered the coast of North America in 1497.

Literary Analysis
Voice and Autobiographical Writing Which words and phrases here convey the writer's uncertainty and unwillingness about learning English?

Vocabulary Builder
countenance (kount´'n əns) *n.* face

Reading Check

Which language did Alvarez learn to speak first—English or Spanish?

columpio were illegal immigrants trying to cross a border into another language. But Teacher's discerning grammar-and-vocabulary-patrol ears could tell and send them back.

Soon, I was talking up an English storm. "Did you eat English parrot?" my grandfather asked one Sunday. I had just enlisted yet one more patient servant to listen to my rendition of "Peter Piper picked a peck of pickled peppers" at breakneck pace. "Huh?" I asked impolitely in English, putting him in his place. *Cat got your tongue? No big deal! So there! Take that! Holy Toledo!* (Our teacher's favorite "curse word.") *Go jump in the lake! Really dumb. Golly. Gosh.* Slang, clichés, sayings, hotshot language that our teacher called, ponderously, idiomatic expressions. Riddles, jokes, puns, conundrums. *What is yellow and goes click-click? Why did the chicken cross the road? See you later, alligator.* How wonderful to call someone an alligator and not be scolded for being disrespectful. In fact, they were supposed to say back, *In a while, crocodile.*

There was also a neat little trick I wanted to try on an English-speaking adult at home. I had learned it from Elizabeth, my smart-alecky friend in fourth grade, whom I alternately worshiped and resented. I'd ask her a question that required an explanation, and she'd answer, "Because . . ." "Elizabeth, how come you didn't go to Isabel's birthday party?" "Because . . ." "Why didn't you put your name in your reader?" "Because . . ." I thought that such a cool way to get around having to come up with answers. So, I practiced saying it under my breath, planning for the day I could use it on an unsuspecting English-speaking adult.

One Sunday at our extended family dinner, my grandfather sat down at the children's table to chat with us. He was famous, in fact, for the way he could carry on adult conversations with his grandchildren. He often spoke to us in English so that we could practice speaking it outside the classroom. He was a Cornell[11] man, a United Nations representative from our country. He gave speeches in English. Perfect English, my mother's phrase. That Sunday, he asked me a question. I can't even remember what it was because I wasn't really listening but lying in wait for my chance. "Because . . .," I answered him. Papito waited a second for the rest of my sentence and then gave me a thumbnail grammar lesson, "*Because* has to be followed by a clause."

"Why's that?" I asked, nonplussed.[12]

"Because," he winked, "Just because."

---

11. **Cornell** Cornell University in Ithaca, New York.
12. **nonplussed** (nän plüst´) *v.* confused; baffled

Literary Analysis
Voice and Autobiographical Writing How would you describe the author's voice based on her examples of idiomatic expressions?

▶ **Critical Viewing** How do you think Julia Alvarez would have felt encountering a bustling crowd like this one for the first time? **[Speculate]**

A beginning wordsmith, I had so much left to learn; sometimes it was disheartening. Once Tío[13] Gus, the family intellectual, put a speck of salt on my grandparents' big dining table during Sunday dinner. He said, "Imagine this whole table is the human brain. Then this teensy grain is all we ever use of our intelligence!" He enumerated geniuses who had perhaps used two grains, maybe three: Einstein, Michelangelo, da Vinci, Beethoven. We children believed him. It was the kind of impossible fact we thrived on, proving as it did that the world out there was not drastically different from the one we were making up in our heads.

Later, at home, Mami said that you had to take what her younger brother said "with a grain of salt." I thought she was still referring to Tío Gus's demonstration, and I tried to puzzle out what she was saying. Finally, I asked what she meant. "Taking what someone says with a grain of salt is an idiomatic expression in English," she explained. It was pure voodoo is what it was—what later I learned poetry could also do: a grain of salt could symbolize both the human brain and a condiment for human nonsense. And it could be itself, too: a grain of salt to flavor a bland plate of American food.

When we arrived in New York, I was shocked. A country where everyone spoke English! These people must be smarter, I thought. Maids, waiters, taxi drivers, doormen, bums on the street, all spoke this difficult language. It took some time before I understood that Americans were not necessarily a smarter, superior race. It was as

---

13. Tío (tē′ ō) "Uncle" (Spanish).

Reading Skill
Author's Purpose
Why do you think the writer includes these details about Mami's comments?

✔ **Reading Check**

To what city does Alvarez's family relocate?

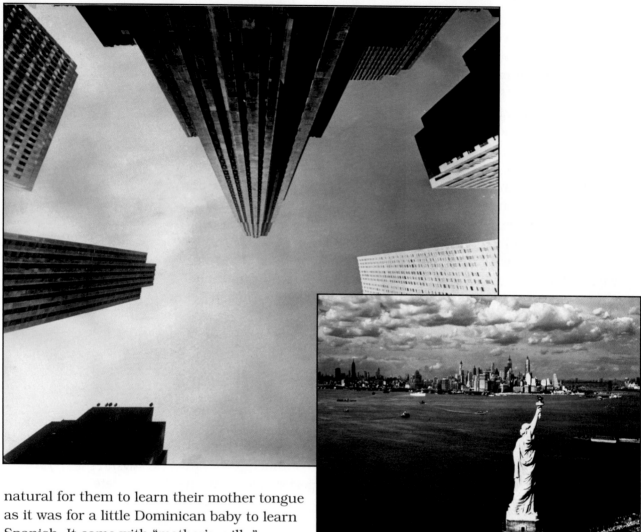

natural for them to learn their mother tongue as it was for a little Dominican baby to learn Spanish. It came with "mother's milk," my mother explained, and for a while I thought a mother tongue was a mother tongue because you got it from your mother's milk along with proteins and vitamins.

Soon it wasn't so strange that everyone was speaking in English instead of Spanish. I learned not to hear it as English, but as sense. I no longer strained to understand, I understood. I relaxed in this second language. Only when someone with a heavy southern or British accent spoke in a movie, or at church when the priest droned his sermon—only then did I experience that little catch of anxiety. I worried that I would not be able to understand, that I wouldn't be able to "keep up" with the voice speaking in this acquired language. I would be like those people from the Bible we had studied in religion class, whom I imagined standing at the foot of an enormous tower[14] that looked just like the skyscrapers

▲ **Critical Viewing**
Based on these photographs, why do you think Alvarez might have found New York to be both intimidating and exciting? **[Analyze]**

---

14. enormous tower a reference to the Tower of Babel in Genesis 11:1–9. According to Genesis, early Babylonians tried to build a tower to heaven, but they were thwarted when God caused them to speak many languages rather than one.

around me. They had been punished for their pride by being made to speak different languages so that they didn't understand what anyone was saying.

But at the foot of those towering New York skyscrapers, I began to understand more and more—not less and less—English. In sixth grade, I had one of the first in a lucky line of great English teachers who began to nurture in me a love of language, a love that had been there since my childhood of listening closely to words. Sister Maria Generosa did not make our class <u>interminably</u> diagram sentences from a workbook or learn a catechism[15] of grammar rules. Instead, she asked us to write little stories imagining we were snowflakes, birds, pianos, a stone in the pavement, a star in the sky. What would it feel like to be a flower with roots in the ground? If the clouds could talk, what would they say? She had an expressive, dreamy look that was accentuated by the wimple[16] that framed her face.

Supposing, just supposing . . . My mind would take off, soaring into possibilities, a flower with roots, a star in the sky, a cloud full of sad, sad tears, a piano crying out each time its back was tapped, music only to our ears.

Sister Maria stood at the chalkboard. Her chalk was always snapping in two because she wrote with such energy, her whole habit[17] shaking with the swing of her arm, her hand tap-tap-tapping on the board. "Here's a simple sentence: 'The snow fell.'" Sister pointed with her chalk, her eyebrows lifted, her wimple poked up. Sometimes I could see wisps of gray hair that strayed from under her headdress. "But watch what happens if we put an adverb at the beginning and a prepositional phrase at the end: 'Gently, the snow fell on the bare hills.'"

I thought about the snow. I saw how it might fall on the hills, tapping lightly on the bare branches of trees. Softly, it would fall on the cold, bare fields. On toys children had left out in the yard, and on cars and on little birds and on people out late walking on the streets. Sister Marie filled the chalkboard with snowy print, on and on, handling and shaping and moving the language, scribbling all over the board until English, those verbal gadgets, those tricks and turns of phrases, those little fixed units and counters, became a charged, fluid mass that carried me in its great fluent waves, rolling and moving onward, to deposit me on the shores of my new homeland. I was no longer a foreigner with no ground to stand on. I had landed in the English language.

Vocabulary Builder
interminably (in tʉr′ mi nə blē) *adv.* endlessly

Literary Analysis
Voice and Autobiographical Writing Which words and phrases in this paragraph give the author's voice a poetic quality?

---

15. catechism (kat′ə kiz′ əm) *n.* short book written in question-and-answer format.
16. wimple (wim′ pəl) *n.* cloth worn around the head, neck, and chin by some nuns.
17. habit (hab′ it) *n.* robe or dress worn by some nuns.

Apply the Skills

My English

Thinking About the Selection

1. **Respond:** After reading her account of her early life, what question would you like to ask Julia Alvarez? Explain.
2. **(a) Recall:** When Alvarez was young, at what times did her parents speak English at home? **(b) Infer:** Why do you think Alvarez says that English was the "sound of being left out"?
3. **(a) Recall:** What method did Sister Maria Generosa use to teach English? **(b) Compare and Contrast:** How does this method differ from the way Alvarez was taught at the Carol Morgan School? **(c) Assess:** Which method does Alvarez prefer? Why?
4. **Evaluate:** How well do you think Alvarez succeeds in portraying the evolution of her relationship with the English language? Explain.

Literary Analysis

5. **(a)** Complete a chart like the one shown to find examples of Alvarez's **word choice**, **attitude**, and **sentence structure**.

VOICE		
Word Choice	**Attitude**	**Sentence Structure**

   (b) Using examples from your chart, describe Alvarez's **voice** in this work of nonfiction.
6. **(a)** What details about learning English are emphasized in Julia Alvarez's **autobiographical writing? (b)** Why would Alvarez notice these details more than someone else might? **(c)** What are two other details that reflect Alvarez's individual perspective on the English language?

Reading Skill

7. Review the notes you made in your **preview** of "My English." Which of your ideas about the **author's purpose** were confirmed as you read the selection? Which were not? Explain.
8. **(a)** What general purpose do you think Alvarez had in writing this essay? Explain. **(b)** What more specific purpose or purposes do you think she had for writing? Support your answer with details from the essay.

QuickReview

Essay at a Glance
Julia Alvarez reflects on her changing relationship with the English language.

Go Online
Assessment
For: Self-test
Visit: www.PHSchool.com
Web Code: epa-6109

Autobiographical Writing: literary works in which an author tells all or part of his or her life's story

Voice: the way a writer "sounds" or "speaks" on the page

Author's Purpose: a writer's main reason for writing a literary work

Vocabulary Builder

Practice **Analogies** show the relationships between pairs of words. To complete each analogy, use a word from the "My English" vocabulary list on page 96. For each case, your choice should create a word pair that matches the relationship between the first two words.

1. happily : sadly :: _____ : quickly
2. bipartisan : party :: _____ : language
3. frame : photograph :: _____ : expression

Adding Words to Your Vocabulary A word's **denotation** is its direct, literal meaning. A word's **connotations** are the ideas associated with it. For example, *eternally* and *interminably* share a similar denotative meaning. However, their connotative meanings are very different. Using a dictionary and a thesaurus, investigate the connotations of each word. Then, use each word in a sentence that illustrates its specific connotation. (For more on using a dictionary and a thesaurus, see pages R6–7.)

Writing

In "My English," Julia Alvarez writes about her experience with the English language—a subject of great importance to her. Using her work as inspiration, write a **journal entry** on a subject of importance to you. As you prepare to write, consider the following questions:

- Has this subject always been important to you? Why or why not?
- How does this subject influence your outlook on the world?

For *Grammar, Vocabulary,* and *Assessment,* see **Build Language Skills,** pages 116–117

Extend Your Learning

Listening and Speaking With three or four classmates, deliver a **radio broadcast** that advertises a foreign-language school. Use Alvarez's experience with English to guide your shaping of the school's message.

- As you work together to write a script, evaluate your word choices to make sure they suit your audience and purpose.
- Speak in an enthusiastic tone that generates interest in the school.

Research and Technology Prepare a list of at least three key points and the **introduction for a multimedia presentation** on immigration to the United States since 1800. Discuss the reasons people left their home countries and what they sought in America.

Build Language Skills

Vocabulary Skill

Word Origins The etymology of a word is both its origin and the history of how the word has changed. Words from other languages were adapted to fit the English-speaking culture, often by adding to the root as new inventions and ways of life demanded. For example, the Latin root *-tri-* meant "three" *or* "the crossroads or common place." Over the years, the word *trivial* has changed to mean "not important—common."

Practice Explain the origin of the underlined words.

1. Would you please submit that request in <u>triplicate</u>?

2. The plays were written as a <u>trilogy</u>.

3. The term <u>Triple</u> Alliance is used several times in history.

4. We are going to the West <u>via</u> Chicago.

5. We need to discuss a matter of <u>vital</u> importance.

Grammar Lesson

Personal and Reflexive Pronouns A **pronoun** is a word that stands for a noun or for a word that takes the place of a noun. A **personal pronoun** refers to the person speaking (first person), the person spoken to (second person), or the person, or thing spoken about (third person). **Reflexive pronouns** end in *-self* or *-selves* and are used to indicate that someone or something performs an action to, for, or upon itself.

MorePractice

For more practice with personal and reflexive pronouns, see the Grammar Handbook, p. R40.

	First Person	**Second Person**	**Third Person**
Personal Pronouns	**Singular:** I, me, my, mine **Plural:** we, us, our, ours	**Singular:** you, your, yours **Plural:** you, your, yours	**Singular:** he, she, him, her, his, hers, it, its **Plural:** they, them, their, theirs
Reflexive Pronouns	**Singular:** myself **Plural:** ourselves	**Singular:** yourself **Plural:** yourselves	**Singular:** himself, herself, itself **Plural:** themselves

Practice Identify the pronouns in each of the following items, indicate whether each pronoun is personal or reflexive. Recast the sentence without the reflexive pronoun.

1. You will have to learn the new system yourself.

2. They found themselves amused by the speaker's anecdotes.

3. Some fish feed themselves through a long tube.

4. We went to the library to study by ourselves.

5. He busied himself in the garden.

Prentice Hall Writing and Grammar Connection: Chapter 16, Section 2.

Reading Skill: Author's Purpose

Standards Assessed

• WL.1.02.1
• IR.2.03.3
• IR.2.04.3

Directions: *Read about Lincoln. Then answer the questions.*

Between the days in which he crawled as a baby on the dirt floor of a Kentucky cabin, and the time when he gave his final breath in Washington, he packed a rich life with work, thought, laughter, tears, hate, love.

With vast reservoirs of the comic and the droll, and notwithstanding a mastery of mirth and nonsense, he delivered a volume of addresses and letters of terrible and serious appeal, with import beyond his own day....

Perhaps no human clay pot has held more laughter and tears.

—from *A Lincoln Preface* by Carl Sandburg

1. What is the purpose of the passage?
   A persuade readers that Lincoln did not deserve his reputation.
   B make readers admire Lincoln's humor.
   C win favor with President Lincoln.
   D make readers see Lincoln as both human and remarkable.

2. Sandburg's likely purpose for including the phrase "filled with laughter and tears" is to
   A make readers pity Lincoln.
   B comment on the tragedy of the Civil War.
   C emphasize Lincoln's outstanding qualities.
   D contrast Lincoln with other leaders.

3. What is a possible reason that Sandburg uses contrasting phrases?

   A as contrast to Lincoln's personality.
   B to phrases contradict the author's personality.
   C to phrases emphasize Lincoln's sense of humor.
   D to phrases reinforce the contrasts in Lincoln's life.

4. The line containing "he delivered a volume . . ." serves to
   A remind the reader that Lincoln was an educated person.
   B remind the reader that Lincoln's ideas impacted the future.
   C reassure the reader that this is the Lincoln who gave the Gettysburg address.
   D assure the reader that the work is serious.

Timed Writing: Explanation [Critical Stance]

Review "The White House Diary" or "My English." Write an explanation of the values that the author reveals in their work. Use specifics from the text to support your points. **(20 minutes)**

 ## Writing Workshop: *Work in Progress*

Problem-Solution Essay

Think of issues that concern people in your school or community. Jot down five problems you think can be solved. Choose one problem and write a statement of a possible solution. Put these notes in your writing folder.

Reading Informational Materials

Spanish/English Dictionaries

In Part 2, you are learning how to determine the author's purpose while reading literature. This skill is also useful when reading informational texts, such as product user guides and dictionaries. In these types of texts, organizational features are designed for various purposes, such as calling attention to important text elements. If you read *My English* by Julia Alvarez, you may have wanted to use a Spanish/English dictionary.

Standard Course of Study

- Select, monitor, and modify reading strategies appropriate to critiquing work. (CT.4.03.1)
- Address clarity and style through grammar and usage. (GU.6.01.4)

About Spanish/English Dictionaries

Spanish/English dictionaries provide detailed information that can help you translate information from one language into the other. Like other bilingual dictionaries, Spanish/English dictionaries often include these features:

- Word definitions in both languages
- Parts of speech
- Gender forms
- Examples of how the word is used
- Examples of idioms, expressions like "hit the nail on the head" whose meanings differ from the meanings of the individual words
- Pronunciation key

Reading Skill

Before using a bilingual dictionary, you may want to review the user guide in the front of the book. The user guide will help you **recognize the organizational features of the text**, including headings, keywords, labels, and special notes to readers. Organizational features identify and emphasize specific pieces of information. The questions in the box shown can help you locate and understand labels and features of the user guide.

Questions to Ask About Organizational Features

- ❑ What are the main headings on the page?
- ❑ How is certain information labeled or highlighted?
- ❑ What features have been pointed out? Why?
- ❑ What information is provided in the key?
- ❑ Are there special notes on the page?

Spanish-English Dictionary User Guide

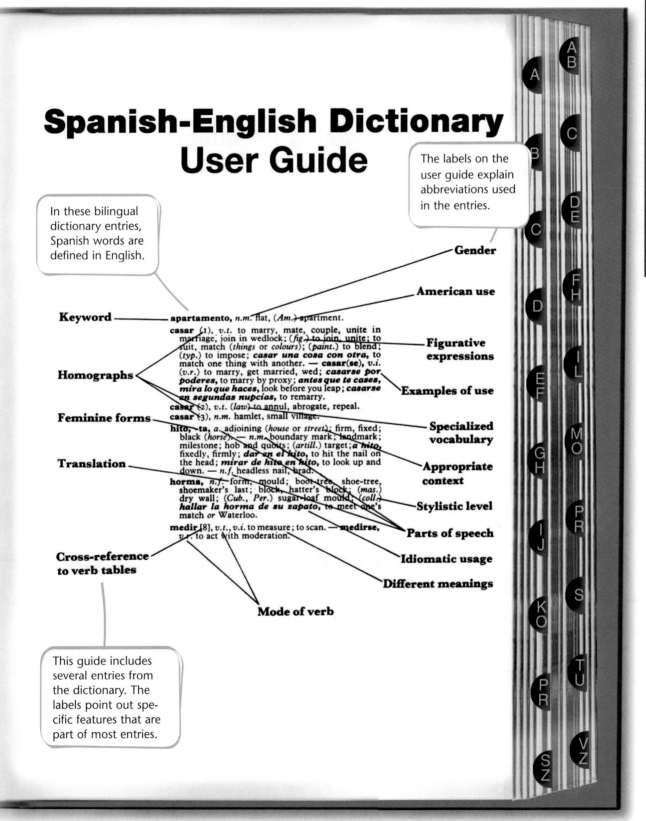

The labels on the user guide explain abbreviations used in the entries.

In these bilingual dictionary entries, Spanish words are defined in English.

Gender

American use

Keyword — **apartamento,** *n.m.* flat, (*Am.*) apartment.

casar (1), *v.t.* to marry, mate, couple, unite in marriage; join in wedlock; (*fig.*) to join, unite; to suit, match (*things* or *colours*); (*paint.*) to blend; (*typ.*) to impose; **casar una cosa con otra,** to match one thing with another. — **casar(se),** *v.i.* (*v.r.*) to marry, get married, wed; **casarse por poderes,** to marry by proxy; **antes que te cases, mira lo que haces,** look before you leap; **casarse en segundas nupcias,** to remarry.

Homographs

casar (2), *v.t.* (*law*) to annul, abrogate, repeal.

Feminine forms — **casar** (3), *n.m.* hamlet, small village.

hito, -ta, *a.* adjoining (*house* or *street*); firm, fixed; black (*horse*). — *n.m.* boundary mark; landmark; milestone; hob and quoits; (*artill.*) target; **a hito,** fixedly, firmly; **dar en el hito,** to hit the nail on the head; **mirar de hito en hito,** to look up and down. — *n.f.* headless nail, brad.

Translation

horma, *n.f.* form, mould; boot-tree, shoe-tree, shoemaker's last; block, hatter's block; (*mas.*) dry wall; (*Cub., Per.*) sugar-loaf mould; (*coll.*) **hallar la horma de su zapato,** to meet one's match *or* Waterloo.

medir [8], *v.t., v.i.* to measure; to scan. — **medirse,** *v.r.* to act with moderation.

Cross-reference to verb tables

Figurative expressions

Examples of use

Specialized vocabulary

Appropriate context

Stylistic level

Parts of speech

Idiomatic usage

Different meanings

Mode of verb

This guide includes several entries from the dictionary. The labels point out specific features that are part of most entries.

Key to Spanish Pronunciation

This guide explains how letters are pronounced in Spanish.

Vowels

i	*seen*
e	*late*
a	*past* (Northern English)
o	*soldier*
u	*boot*

Diphthongs

ie	*Yale*
ei	*paying*
eu	*pear, July; e-u* run together
ai, ay	*sky*
au	*cow*
oi, oy	*boy*
ue	*way*

Consonants

b, v (*initial*)	*best*
b, v (*intervocalic*)	like *b* without lips touching
c (*before a, o, u or consonant*), k, qu	*kind*
c (*before e or i*), z	*think*
ch	*choose*
d (*initial*)	*dear*
d (*intervocalic*)	*there*
f	*find*
g (*before a, o, u or consonant*)	*gain*

g (*before e or i*), j	*loch* (Scots)
h	*honour*
l	*long*
ll	*million*
m	*mice*
n	*banner*
ñ	*onion*
p	*copper*
r	*large* (Scots)
rr	*round* (Scots)
s	*goose*
t	*tank*
w	like Spanish b, v
x (*intervocalic*)	*axe* or *pigskin* or *eggs*
x (*before consonant*)	*extreme* or *paste*
y	*yellow*

American Spanish

The following are the main features which distinguish the pronunciation of American from that of Castilian Spanish; they also occur in Southern Spain

c (*before e or i*), z	*goose*
ll (*in many regions of Spain and of Spanish America*)	
ll (*Argentina, Uruguay*)	*yellow* *pleasure*
s (*at end of word or before a consonant; in parts of Southern Spain and America*)	

The pronunciation of Spanish spoken in Spain differs from the Spanish spoken in Latin America. These notes point out key distinctions.

Note on Spanish Gender

Most nouns in English do not have a gender. In Spanish, most nouns have either a masculine or feminine form. This note explains how the dictionary indicates the gender.

As a general rule, nouns ending in *-a, -ción, -gión, -sión, -tión, -xión, -dad, -tad, -tud, -ez* and *-umbre* are feminine; all other nouns are masculine. In the body of the text genders are given only where this rule does not apply or in order to clarify its application.

Reading: Recognizing Organizational Features of Printed Text

Standards Assessed

• GU.6.01.6
• LT.5.03.2
• WL.1.03.3

Directions: *Choose the letter of the best answer to each question.*

1. Which feature would guide you to a specific entry in a dictionary?

   A keyword

   B feminine forms

   C homograph

   D mode of verb

2. Under which heading would you look to find the pronunciation of the *e* in the Spanish word *medir*?

   A Vowels

   B Diphthongs

   C Consonants

   D American Spanish

3. Where can you look to confirm whether a word ending in *-tad* is masculine or feminine?

   A in the Key to Spanish Pronunciation

   B in the entry for the word

   C in the Note on Spanish Gender

   D under the "Diphthongs" heading

Reading: Comprehension and Interpretation

Directions: *Write your answers on a separate sheet of paper.*

4. Based on the entry for *hito,* why would it be important to use the correct gender of a noun in Spanish? **[Applying]**

5. Explain how you would find the part of speech of a Spanish word. **[Generating]**

6. **(a)** What idiomatic usages are included for the word *casar*?
   (b) Why would someone wishing to speak another language find information on idioms useful?

Timed Writing: Exposition [Critical Stance]

Write a brief expository essay to explain the purpose and usefulness of a bilingual dictionary. In your answer, explain who would benefit from such a dictionary, and identify two situations in which a bilingual dictionary would be helpful. **(20 minutes)**

Practice these skills with either "The Secret Life of Walter Mitty" (p. 124) or "Uncle Marcos" (p. 133).

Literary Analysis

A **character** is a person or an animal who takes part in the action of a literary work.

- A **round character** is complex, showing many different qualities—revealing faults as well as virtues. A **flat character** is one-dimensional, showing a single trait.
- A **dynamic character** develops, changes, and learns something during the course of a story—unlike a **static character,** who remains the same.

The main character of a story tends to be a round character and usually a dynamic one. The main character's development and growth are often central to a story's plot and theme. As you read, consider the traits that make characters seem round or flat, dynamic or static.

Reading Skill

An **author's purpose** is his or her main reason for writing. In fiction, the specific purpose is often conveyed through the story's theme, message, or insight. Pause periodically while reading and **reflect** on the story's details and events to determine the author's purpose. Ask questions such as the following:

- *What significance might this event have?*
- *Why does the author include this detail?*

Based on your reflections, formulate ideas about what the author's purpose might be. Use a chart like the one shown to organize your thoughts.

Story Event or Detail

↓

Possible Significance

↓

Author's Purpose?

Vocabulary Builder

The Secret Life of Walter Mitty

- **distraught** (di strôt´) *adj.* troubled or confused (p. 126) *She was distraught over losing her wallet.*
- **insolent** (in´ sə lənt) *adj.* boldly disrespectful (p. 126) *Her insolent words offended the guests.*
- **inscrutable** (in skro͞ot´ ə bəl) *adj.* baffling; mysterious (p. 129) *No one has ever solved the puzzle of his inscrutable personality.*

Uncle Marcos

- **pallid** (pal´ id) *adj.* pale (p. 133) *The flu gave him a weak and pallid appearance.*
- **disconsolately** (dis kän´ sə lit lē) *adv.* very unhappily (p. 138) *He gazed disconsolately as his friends drove to the game without him.*
- **unrequited** (un ri kwīt´ id) *adj.* not returned or repaid (p. 140) *Romance novels sometimes describe the sadness of unrequited love.*

Background

Reality and Imagination Psychologists say that a person's thoughts are often a series of seemingly unconnected reflections. An event in the real world can prompt unpredictable mental responses, such as memories, snippets of songs, or daydreams. In Thurber's story, random events cause Walter Mitty's thoughts to jump back and forth between his exciting "secret" life and his humdrum everyday existence.

Connecting to the Literature

Reading/Writing Connection "The Secret Life of Walter Mitty" is about a man whose daydreams are more real and interesting to him than the workaday world that triggers them. Write down one ordinary event and one amazing daydream that it could prompt. Use at least three of these words: *derive, enhance, manifest, project.*

READ MORE

by James Thurber
*My World—
and Welcome to It*

Meet the Author

James **Thurber** (1894–1961)

James Thurber was a rare writer who expressed his comic genius in both words and pictures. He wrote stories, plays, essays, and poems, and he was also a great cartoonist. Born in Ohio, he joined the staff of *The New Yorker* magazine in 1927. "The Secret Life of Walter Mitty" was published in that magazine in 1939, becoming an instant success.

Humor and Anxiety Many of Thurber's stories and sketches grew directly out of his own life. As he put it, "Humor is a kind of emotional chaos told about calmly and quietly in retrospect." Thurber's characters try to stand up to the surprises of the modern world. Whether they succeed or fail, they always strike readers as authentic and very funny.

Fast Facts

▶ Thurber's cartoon characters included strangely shaped dogs who seemed to have human expressions.

▶ Thurber offered a Hollywood producer $10,000 *not* to make a movie about Walter Mitty. The movie was made anyway in 1947.

 For: More about the author
Author Link **Visit:** www.PHSchool.com
Web Code: epe-9110

The Secret Life of Walter Mitty

James Thurber

The Man with Three Masks, John Rush, Courtesy of the artist

▲ **Critical Viewing** Why might the man hold one mask up to his face and have other masks nearby? **[Analyze]**

We're going through!" The Commander's voice was like thin ice breaking. He wore his full-dress uniform, with the heavily braided white cap pulled down rakishly over one cold gray eye. "We can't make it, sir. It's spoiling for a hurricane, if you ask me." "I'm not asking you, Lieutenant Berg," said the Commander. "Throw on the power lights! Rev her up to 8,500! We're going through!" The pounding of the cylinders increased: ta-pocketa-pocketa-pocketa-*pocketa-pocketa*. The Commander stared at the ice forming on the pilot window. He walked over and twisted a row of complicated dials. "Switch on No. 8 auxiliary!" he shouted. "Switch on No. 8 auxiliary!" repeated Lieutenant Berg. "Full strength in No. 3 turret!" shouted the Commander. "Full strength in No. 3 turret!" The crew, bending to their various tasks in the huge, hurtling eight-engined Navy hydroplane,[1] looked at each other and grinned. "The Old Man'll get us through," they said to one another. "The Old Man ain't afraid of Hell!" . . .

"Not so fast! You're driving too fast!" said Mrs. Mitty. "What are you driving so fast for?"

"Hmm?" said Walter Mitty. He looked at his wife, in the seat beside him, with shocked astonishment. She seemed grossly unfamiliar, like a strange woman who had yelled at him in a crowd. "You were up to fifty-five," she said. "You know I don't like to go more than forty. You were up to fifty-five." Walter Mitty drove on toward Waterbury in silence, the roaring of the SN202 through the worst storm in twenty years of Navy flying fading in the remote, intimate airways of his mind. "You're tensed up again," said Mrs. Mitty. "It's one of your days. I wish you'd let Dr. Renshaw look you over."

Walter Mitty stopped the car in front of the building where his wife went to have her hair done. "Remember to get those overshoes while I'm having my hair done," she said. "I don't need overshoes," said Mitty. She put her mirror back into her bag. "We've been all through that," she said, getting out of the car. "You're not a young man any longer." He raced the engine a little. "Why don't you wear your gloves? Have you lost your gloves?" Walter Mitty reached in a pocket and brought out the gloves. He put them on, but after she had turned and gone into the building and he had driven on to a red light, he took them off again. "Pick it up, brother!" snapped a cop as the light changed, and Mitty hastily pulled on his gloves and lurched ahead. He drove around the streets aimlessly for a time, and then he drove past the hospital on his way to the parking lot.

. . . "It's the millionaire banker, Wellington McMillan," said the pretty nurse. "Yes?" said Walter Mitty, removing his gloves slowly.

Reading Skill
Author's Purpose
Pause to reflect. What does the phrase "intimate airways of his mind" suggest about the author's purpose in writing this story?

✓ **Reading Check**
Why is Mrs. Mitty upset?

---

1. hydroplane (hī′ drō plān′) *n.* seaplane.

"Who has the case?" "Dr. Renshaw and Dr. Benbow, but there are two specialists here, Dr. Remington from New York and Mr. Pritchard-Mitford from London. He flew over." A door opened down a long, cool corridor and Dr. Renshaw came out. He looked distraught and haggard. "Hello, Mitty," he said. "We're having the devil's own time with McMillan, the millionaire banker and close personal friend of Roosevelt. Obstreosis of the ductal tract.[2] Tertiary. Wish you'd take a look at him." "Glad to," said Mitty.

In the operating room there were whispered introductions: "Dr. Remington, Dr. Mitty. Mr. Pritchard-Mitford, Dr. Mitty." "I've read your book on streptothricosis," said Pritchard-Mitford, shaking hands. "A brilliant performance, sir." "Thank you," said Walter Mitty. "Didn't know you were in the States, Mitty," grumbled Remington. "Coals to Newcastle,[3] bringing Mitford and me up here for tertiary." "You are very kind," said Mitty. A huge, complicated machine, connected to the operating table, with many tubes and wires, began at this moment to go pocketa-pocketa-pocketa. "The new anesthetizer is giving way!" shouted an intern. "There is no one in the East who knows how to fix it!" "Quiet, man!" said Mitty, in a low, cool voice. He sprang to the machine, which was now going pocketa-pocketa-queep-pocketa-queep. He began fingering delicately a row of glistening dials. "Give me a fountain pen!" he snapped. Someone handed him a fountain pen. He pulled a faulty piston out of the machine and inserted the pen in its place. "That will hold for ten minutes," he said. "Get on with the operation." A nurse hurried over and whispered to Renshaw, and Mitty saw the man turn pale. "Coreopsis has set in," said Renshaw nervously. "If you would take over, Mitty?" Mitty looked at him and at the craven figure of Benbow, who drank, and at the grave, uncertain faces of the two great specialists. "If you wish," he said. They slipped a white gown on him; he adjusted a mask and drew on thin gloves; nurses handed him shining . . .

"Back it up, Mac! Look out for that Buick!" Walter Mitty jammed on the brakes. "Wrong lane, Mac," said the parking-lot attendant, looking at Mitty closely. "Gee. Yeh," muttered Mitty. He began cautiously to back out of the lane marked "Exit Only." "Leave her sit there," said the attendant. "I'll put her away." Mitty got out of the car. "Hey, better leave the key." "Oh," said Mitty, handing the man the ignition key. The attendant vaulted into the car, backed it up with insolent skill, and put it where it belonged.

They're so cocky, thought Walter Mitty, walking along Main Street; they think they know everything. Once he had tried to take

---

2. **obstreosis of the ductal tract** Thurber has invented this and other medical terms.
3. **coals to Newcastle** The proverb "bringing coals to Newcastle" means bringing things to a place unnecessarily—Newcastle, England, was a coal center and so did not need coal brought to it.

Vocabulary Builder
distraught (di strôt´) *adj.* troubled or confused

Literary Analysis
Character How does this shift in scenes show that Walter Mitty is a multidimensional character?

Vocabulary Builder
insolent (in´ sə lənt) *adj.* boldly disrespectful

his chains off, outside New Milford, and he had got them wound around the axles. A man had had to come out in a wrecking car and unwind them, a young, grinning garageman. Since then Mrs. Mitty always made him drive to a garage to have the chains taken off. The next time, he thought, I'll wear my right arm in a sling; they won't grin at me then. I'll have my right arm in a sling and they'll see I couldn't possibly take the chains off myself. He kicked at the slush on the sidewalk. "Overshoes," he said to himself, and he began looking for a shoe store.

When he came out into the street again, with the overshoes in a box under his arm, Walter Mitty began to wonder what the other thing was his wife had told him to get. She had told him, twice, before they set out from their house for Waterbury. In a way he hated these weekly trips to town— he was always getting something wrong. Kleenex, he thought, Squibb's, razor blades? No. Toothpaste, toothbrush, bicarbonate, carborundum, initiative and referendum?[4] He gave it up. But she would remember it. "Where's the what's-its-name?" she would ask. "Don't tell me you forgot the what's-its-name." A newsboy went by shouting something about the Waterbury trial.

. . . "Perhaps this will refresh your memory." The District Attorney suddenly thrust a heavy automatic at the quiet figure on the witness stand. "Have you ever seen this before?" Walter Mitty took the gun and examined it expertly. "This is my Webley-Vickers 50.80," he said calmly. An excited buzz ran around the courtroom. The Judge rapped for order. "You are a crack shot with any sort of firearms, I believe?" said the District Attorney, insinuatingly. "Objection!" shouted Mitty's attorney. "We have shown that the defendant could not have fired the shot. We have shown that he wore his right arm in a sling on the night of the fourteenth of July." Walter Mitty

New Orleans Fantasy, 1985 (detail) Max Papart Lithograph, Courtesy of Nahan Galleries, New York

▲ **Critical Viewing**
Describe a situation that might make Walter Mitty daydream about being a circus performer like the one shown. **[Hypothesize]**

Reading Check
Why does Mitty say that next time he will wear his arm in a sling?

---

4. **carborundum** (kär′ bə run′ dəm), **initiative** (i nish′ ē ə tiv) **and referendum** (ref′ ə ren′ dəm) Thurber is purposely making a nonsense list; *carborundum* is a hard substance used for scraping, *initiative* is the right of citizens to introduce ideas for laws, and *referendum* is the right of citizens to vote on laws.

The Secret Life of Walter Mitty ■ 127

raised his hand briefly and the bickering attorneys were stilled. "With any known make of gun," he said evenly, "I could have killed Gregory Fitzhurst at three hundred *feet with my left hand.*" Pandemonium broke loose in the courtroom. A woman's scream rose above the bedlam and suddenly a lovely, dark-haired girl was in Walter Mitty's arms. The District Attorney struck at her savagely. Without rising from his chair, Mitty let the man have it on the point of the chin. "You miserable cur!" . . .

"Puppy biscuit," said Walter Mitty. He stopped walking and the buildings of Waterbury rose up out of the misty courtroom and surrounded him again. A woman who was passing laughed. "He said 'Puppy biscuit,'" she said to her companion. "That man said 'Puppy biscuit' to himself." Walter Mitty hurried on. He went into an A. & P., not the first one he came to but a smaller one farther up the street. "I want some biscuit for small, young dogs," he said to the clerk. "Any special brand, sir?" The greatest pistol shot in the world thought a moment. "It says 'Puppies Bark for It' on the box," said Walter Mitty.

His wife would be through at the hairdresser's in fifteen minutes, Mitty saw in looking at his watch, unless they had trouble drying it; sometimes they had trouble drying it. She didn't like to get to the hotel first; she would want him to be there waiting for her as usual. He found a big leather chair in the lobby, facing a window, and he put the overshoes and the puppy biscuit on the floor beside it. He picked up an old copy of *Liberty* and sank down into the chair. "Can Germany Conquer the World Through the Air?" Walter Mitty looked at the pictures of bombing planes and of ruined streets.

. . . "The cannonading has got the wind up in young Raleigh,[5] sir," said the sergeant. Captain Mitty looked up at him through tousled hair. "Get him to bed," he said wearily. "With the others. I'll fly alone." "But you can't, sir," said the sergeant anxiously. "It takes two men to handle that bomber and the Archies[6] are pounding hell

---

5. **has got the wind up in young Raleigh** has made young Raleigh nervous.
6. **Archies** slang term for antiaircraft guns.

Social Studies Connection

The Royal Air Force Although he is American, Mitty fantasizes about being a brave and handsome English officer, a bomber pilot in the Royal Air Force (RAF). The RAF was officially formed in 1918 and distinguished itself in numerous air battles during World War I. RAF pilots would earn even greater distinction in the Battle of Britain during World War II. The reference to "Von Richtman's circus" recalls one of the RAF's finest moments—the shooting down in 1918 of Baron Manfred von Richtofen, also known as "The Red Baron," who was Germany's greatest fighter pilot.

Connect to the Literature

What elements of life in the RAF would Mitty enjoy?

out of the air. Von Richtman's circus[7] is between here and Saulier." "Somebody's got to get that ammunition dump," said Mitty. "I'm going over. Spot of brandy?" He poured a drink for the sergeant and one for himself. War thundered and whined around the dugout and battered at the door. There was a rending of wood and splinters flew through the room. "A bit of a near thing," said Captain Mitty carelessly. "The box barrage is closing in," said the sergeant. "We only live once, Sergeant," said Mitty, with his faint, fleeting smile. "Or do we?" He poured another brandy and tossed it off. "I never see a man could hold his brandy like you, sir," said the sergeant. "Begging your pardon, sir." Captain Mitty stood up and strapped on his huge Webley-Vickers automatic. "It's forty kilometers through hell, sir," said the sergeant. Mitty finished one last brandy. "After all," he said softly, "what isn't?" The pounding of the cannon increased; there was the rat-tat-tatting of machine guns, and from somewhere came the menacing pocketa-pocketa-pocketa of the new flame-throwers. Walter Mitty walked to the door of the dugout humming "Après de Ma Blonde."[8] He turned and waved to the sergeant. "Cheerio!" he said. . . .

Something struck his shoulder. "I've been looking all over this hotel for you," said Mrs. Mitty. "Why do you have to hide in this old chair? How did you expect me to find you?" "Things close in," said Walter Mitty vaguely. "What?" Mrs. Mitty said. "Did you get the what's-its-name? The puppy biscuit? What's in that box?" "Overshoes," said Mitty. "Couldn't you have put them on in the store?" "I was thinking," said Walter Mitty. "Does it ever occur to you that I am sometimes thinking?" She looked at him. "I'm going to take your temperature when I get you home," she said.

They went out through the revolving doors that made a faintly derisive whistling sound when you pushed them. It was two blocks to the parking lot. At the drugstore on the corner she said, "Wait here for me. I forgot something. I won't be a minute." She was more than a minute. Walter Mitty lighted a cigarette. It began to rain, rain with sleet in it. He stood up against the wall of the drugstore, smoking. . . . He put his shoulders back and his heels together. "To hell with the handkerchief," said Walter Mitty scornfully. He took one last drag on his cigarette and snapped it away. Then, with that faint, fleeting smile playing about his lips, he faced the firing squad; erect and motionless, proud and disdainful, Walter Mitty the Undefeated, <u>inscrutable</u> to the last.

---

7. **Von Richtman's circus** German airplane squadron.
8. **"Après de Ma Blonde"** (ō prä′ də mä mä blôn′ də) "Next to My Blonde," a popular French song.

Literary Analysis
Character How do Walter Mitty's responses in this paragraph indicate that he is a complex character?

Vocabulary Builder
inscrutable (in skrōōt′ ə bəl) *adj.* baffling; mysterious

Apply the Skills

The Secret Life of Walter Mitty

Thinking About the Selection

1. **Respond:** Do you feel sorry for Walter Mitty? Why or why not?
2. **(a) Recall:** What distraction jars Mitty out of his first daydream? **(b) Compare and Contrast:** Explain how Mitty's behavior in this daydream differs from his behavior in real life.
3. **(a) Recall:** In the "real world," what tasks are Mitty and his wife carrying out? **(b) Infer:** What deeds is Mitty attempting to accomplish in his fantasy life? **(c) Compare and Contrast:** How do the tasks of his daily life compare to those of his fantasy life?
4. **(a) Infer:** Which aspects of Mitty's personality trigger his final daydream? **(b) Draw Conclusions:** In what ways is this daydream a comment on his fate in real life?
5. **(a) Evaluate:** Do Mitty's daydreams help him in any way or do they hurt him? Write down three details from the story that support your evaluation. **(b) Discuss:** Share your responses with a small group and discuss the differences and similarities among them. **(c) Reflect:** How has your evaluation grown or changed as a result of this discussion?

Literary Analysis

6. Mitty wants to be like the heroes in his daydreams. **(a)** Using a chart like the one shown, identify one detail from each of Mitty's daydreams and the quality that each detail reveals.

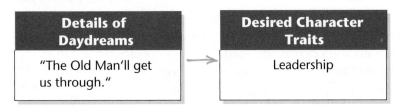

Details of Daydreams		Desired Character Traits
"The Old Man'll get us through."	→	Leadership

   (b) In a few sentences, summarize the **character** of the man Mitty wants to be.
7. Review the characters of Walter and Mrs. Mitty. **(a)** Determine whether each character is **round** or **flat**. Explain. **(b)** Determine whether each character is **static** or **dynamic**. Explain.

Reading Skill

8. **(a)** What specific **purpose** might James Thurber have had for creating the character of Walter Mitty? **(b)** Identify three details from the story and explain how **reflecting** on them helped you determine Thurber's purpose.

QuickReview

Story at a Glance
A meek man daydreams to escape his humdrum life.

Go Online
Assessment
For: Self-test
Visit: www.PHSchool.com
Web Code: epa-6110

Character: a person or an animal who takes part in the action of a literary work. Characters can be *round* or *flat*, *dynamic* or *static*.

Author's Purpose: a writer's main reason for writing a literary work

Vocabulary Builder

Practice Review the vocabulary list for "The Secret Life of Walter Mitty" on page 122. Then, decide whether each of the following statements below is true or false. Explain your answers.

1. Someone who is *distraught* is likely to behave in a calm manner.

2. Coaches encourage their players to be *insolent.*

3. *Inscrutable* handwriting is difficult to interpret.

Adding Words to Your Vocabulary Using a dictionary or a thesaurus, find an **antonym,** a word that has the opposite meaning, for each italicized word from the vocabulary list. Then, use each antonym correctly in a sentence. (For more on using a dictionary and a thesaurus, see pages R6–7.)

Writing

Write a **character profile** of one of the heroic personalities in Walter Mitty's daydreams.

- Begin by jotting down details that capture the character's appearance, personality, and achievements.
- Decide on a single impression to convey about the character.
- Organize and present details so that they all contribute to that one impression.

For *Grammar, Vocabulary,* and *Assessment,* see **Build Language Skills,** pages 144–145.

Extend Your Learning

Listening and Speaking Write and perform a comic **scene** based on one of Walter Mitty's daydreams.

- Choose the daydream you find most appealing.
- Write a script for the scene.
- Cast the scene, and briefly rehearse.

Perform the scene for the class.

Research and Technology Use a variety of sources, including the library and the Internet, to research scientific facts and theories about daydreams. Record your research in a **learning log,** a written record of information you discover about the topic. Analyze the information by discussing it with classmates and by comparing your findings to Thurber's story.

Short Story

Background

Magical Realism Imagine a world in which people float in the air and rain falls continuously for years. Such fantastic details fill stories and novels by a group of writers, including Isabel Allende, who are called magical realists. Works of magical realism blend fantastic details with realistic ones to stretch the boundaries of readers' imaginations.

Connecting to the Literature

Reading/Writing Connection Some of the incidents in "Uncle Marcos" seem magical and mysterious. Write a brief description of an event that now seems magical or mysterious because it has been exaggerated over time with retelling. Use at least three of these words: *enhance, alter, distort, evolve, generate.*

Review

For **Literary Analysis, Reading Skill,** and **Vocabulary Builder,** see page 122.

by Isabel Allende
The Stories of Eva Luna
My Invented Country

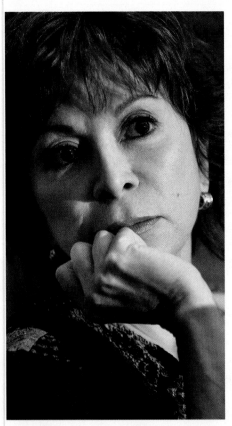

Meet the Author

Isabel **Allende** (b. 1942)

The daughter of diplomats, Isabel Allende grew up in the South American country of Chile. Her uncle was the Chilean president Salvador Allende. When his government was overthrown in 1973, Isabel Allende fled to Venezuela. She lived there in exile until 1988, when she moved to California.

Family and Fiction "Uncle Marcos" is excerpted from Allende's first novel, *The House of the Spirits,* which was inspired by her own remarkable family. Allende's family stories, however, are usually told with large helpings of imagination. She delights in blending the real and the imaginary. Allende once summed up her profession by quoting her granddaughter. Asked what it means to have a great imagination, the child replied, "You can remember what never happened."

Fast Facts

▶ Allende's first novel, *The House of the Spirits,* began as a letter to her 100-year-old grandfather.

▶ Allende spends ten to twelve hours writing each day. She says the storytelling is the fun part but the writing "is a lot of work!"

For: More about the author
Visit: www.PHSchool.com
Web Code: epe-9111

Uncle Marcos

from *The House of the Spirits*

Isabel Allende

. . . It had been two years since Clara had last seen her Uncle Marcos, but she remembered him very well. His was the only perfectly clear image she retained from her whole childhood, and in order to describe him she did not need to consult the daguerreotype[1] in the drawing room that showed him dressed as an explorer leaning on an old-fashioned double-barreled rifle with his right foot on the neck of a Malaysian tiger, the same triumphant position in which she had seen the Virgin standing between plaster clouds and <u>pallid</u> angels at the main altar, one foot on the vanquished devil. All Clara had to do to see her uncle was close her

Vocabulary Builder
pallid (pal´ id) *adj.*
pale

---

1. **daguerreotype** (də ger´ ō tīp´) *n.* early type of photograph.

eyes and there he was, weather-beaten and thin, with a pirate's mustache through which his strange, sharklike smile peered out at her. It seemed impossible that he could be inside that long black box that was lying in the middle of the courtyard.

Each time Uncle Marcos had visited his sister Nivea's home, he had stayed for several months, to the immense joy of his nieces and nephews, particularly Clara, causing a storm in which the sharp lines of domestic order blurred. The house became a clutter of trunks, of animals in jars of formaldehyde,[2] of Indian lances and sailor's bundles. In every part of the house people kept tripping over his equipment, and all sorts of unfamiliar animals appeared that had traveled from remote lands only to meet their death beneath Nana's irate broom in the farthest corners of the house. Uncle Marcos's manners were those of a cannibal, as Severo put it. He spent the whole night making incomprehensible movements in the drawing room; later they turned out to be exercises designed to perfect the mind's control over the body and to improve digestion. He performed alchemy[3] experiments in the kitchen, filling the house with fetid smoke and ruining pots and pans with solid substances that stuck to their bottoms and were impossible to remove. While the rest of the household tried to sleep, he dragged his suitcases up and down the halls, practiced making strange, high-pitched sounds on savage instruments, and taught Spanish to a parrot whose native language was an Amazonic dialect. During the day, he slept in a hammock that he had strung between two columns in the hall, wearing only a loincloth that put Severo in a terrible mood but that Nivea forgave because Marcos had convinced her that it was the same costume in which Jesus of Nazareth had preached. Clara remembered perfectly, even though she had been only a tiny child, the first time her Uncle Marcos came to the house after one of his voyages. He settled in as if he planned to stay forever. After a short time, bored with having to appear at ladies' gatherings where the mistress of the house played the piano, with playing cards, and with dodging all his relatives' pressures to pull himself together and take a job as a clerk in Severo del Valle's law practice, he bought a barrel organ and took to the streets with the hope of seducing his Cousin Antonieta and entertaining the public in the bargain. The machine was just a rusty box with wheels, but he painted it with seafaring designs and gave it

▲ **Critical Viewing**
In this story, a man builds a flying machine. Which character traits might you find in someone who would try to do this? **[Speculate]**

---

2. formaldehyde (fôr mal′ də hīd′) *n.* solution used as a preservative.
3. alchemy (al′ kə mē) *adj.* early form of chemistry, with philosophic and magical associations.

a fake ship's smokestack. It ended up looking like a coal stove. The organ played either a military march or a waltz, and in between turns of the handle the parrot, who had managed to learn Spanish although he had not lost his foreign accent, would draw a crowd with his piercing shrieks. He also plucked slips of paper from a box with his beak, by way of selling fortunes to the curious. The little pink, green, and blue papers were so clever that they always divulged the exact secret wishes of the customers. Besides fortunes there were little balls of sawdust to amuse the children. The idea of the organ was a last desperate attempt to win the hand of Cousin Antonieta after more conventional means of courting her had failed. Marcos thought no woman in her right mind could remain impassive before a barrel-organ serenade. He stood beneath her window one evening and played his military march and his waltz just as she was taking tea with a group of female friends. Antonieta did not realize the music was meant for her until the parrot called her by her full name, at which point she appeared in the window. Her reaction was not what her suitor had hoped for. Her friends offered to spread the news to every salon[4] in the city, and the next day people thronged the downtown streets hoping to see Severo del Valle's brother-in-law playing the organ and selling little sawdust balls with a motheaten parrot, for the sheer pleasure of proving that even in the best of families there could be good reason for embarrassment. In the face of this stain to the family reputation, Marcos was forced to give up organ grinding and resort to less conspicuous ways of winning over his Cousin Antonieta, but he did not renounce his goal. In any case, he did not succeed, because from one day to the next the young lady married a diplomat who was twenty years her senior; he took her to live in a tropical country whose name no one could recall, except that it suggested negritude,[5] bananas, and palm trees, where she managed to recover from the memory of that suitor who had ruined her seventeenth year with his military march and his waltz. Marcos sank into a deep depression that lasted two or three days, at the end of which he announced that he would never marry and that he was embarking on a trip around the world. He sold his organ to a blind man and left the parrot to Clara, but Nana secretly poisoned it with an overdose of cod-liver oil, because no one could stand its lusty

---

4. **salon** (sə län´) *n.* regular gathering of distinguished guests that meets in a private home.
5. **negritude** (neg´ rə to͞od´) *n.* blacks and their cultural heritage.

Literary Analysis
Character In what way does Uncle Marcos's behavior suggest that he is a multidimensional character?

Reading Check

What does Uncle Marcos do with the barrel organ?

glance, its fleas, and its harsh, tuneless hawking of paper fortunes and sawdust balls.

That was Marcos's longest trip. He returned with a shipment of enormous boxes that were piled in the far courtyard, between the chicken coop and the woodshed, until the winter was over. At the first signs of spring he had them transferred to the parade grounds, a huge park where people would gather to watch the soldiers file by on Independence Day, with the goosestep they had learned from the Prussians. When the crates were opened, they were found to contain loose bits of wood, metal, and painted cloth. Marcos spent two weeks assembling the contents according to an instruction manual written in English, which he was able to decipher thanks to his invincible imagination and a small dictionary. When the job was finished, it turned out to be a bird of prehistoric dimensions, with the face of a furious eagle, wings that moved, and a propeller on its back. It caused an uproar. The families of the oligarchy[6] forgot all about the barrel organ, and Marcos became the star attraction of the season. People took Sunday outings to see the bird; souvenir vendors and strolling photographers made a fortune. Nonetheless, the public's interest quickly waned. But then Marcos announced that as soon as the weather cleared he planned to take off in his bird and cross the mountain range. The news spread, making this the most talked-about event of the year. The contraption lay with its stomach on terra firma,[7] heavy and sluggish and looking more like a wounded duck than like one of those newfangled airplanes they were starting to produce in the United States. There was nothing in its appearance to suggest that it could move, much less take flight across the snowy peaks. Journalists and the curious flocked to see it. Marcos smiled his immutable[8] smile before the avalanche of questions and posed for photographers without offering the least technical or scientific explanation of how he hoped to carry out his plan. People came from the provinces to see the sight. Forty years later his great-nephew Nicolás, whom Marcos did not live to see, unearthed the desire to fly that had always existed in the men of his lineage. Nicolás was interested in doing it for commercial reasons, in a gigantic hot-air sausage on which would be printed an advertisement for carbonated drinks. But when Marcos announced his plane trip, no one believed that his contraption could be put to any practical use. The appointed day dawned full of clouds, but so many people had turned out that Marcos did not want to

▼ **Critical Viewing**
This sketch of a helicopter by Leonardo da Vinci predates the first working helicopters by about 450 years. What do you think Uncle Marcos would have thought of da Vinci? **[Speculate]**

---

6. oligarchy (äl′ i gär′ kē) *n.* government ruled by a few.
7. terra firma (ter′ a fur′ ma) *n.* Latin term meaning "firm earth; solid ground."
8. immutable (im myoōt′ ə bəl) *adj.* never changing.

disappoint them. He showed up punctually at the appointed spot and did not once look up at the sky, which was growing darker and darker with thick gray clouds. The astonished crowd filled all the nearby streets, perching on rooftops and the balconies of the nearest houses and squeezing into the park. No political gathering managed to attract so many people until half a century later, when the first Marxist candidate attempted, through strictly democratic channels, to become President. Clara would remember this holiday as long as she lived. People dressed in their spring best, thereby getting a step ahead of the official opening of the season, the men in white linen suits and the ladies in the Italian straw hats that were all the rage that year. Groups of elementary-school children paraded with their teachers, clutching flowers for the hero. Marcos accepted their bouquets and joked that they might as well hold on to them and wait for him to crash, so they could take them directly to his funeral. The bishop himself, accompanied by two incense bearers, appeared to bless the bird without having been asked, and the police band played happy, unpretentious music that pleased everyone. The police, on horseback and carrying lances, had trouble keeping the crowds far enough away from the center of the park, where Marcos waited dressed in mechanic's overalls, with huge racer's goggles and an explorer's helmet. He was also equipped with a compass, a telescope, and several strange maps that he had traced himself based on various theories of Leonardo da Vinci and on the polar knowledge of the Incas.[9] Against all logic, on the second try the bird lifted off without mishap and with a certain elegance, accompanied by the creaking of its skeleton and the roar of its motor. It rose flapping its wings and disappeared into the clouds, to a send-off of applause, whistlings, handkerchiefs, drumrolls, and the sprinkling of holy water. All that remained on earth were the comments of the amazed crowd below and a multitude of experts, who attempted to provide a reasonable explanation of the miracle. Clara continued to stare at the sky long after her uncle had become invisible. She thought she saw him ten minutes later, but it was only a migrating sparrow. After three days the initial euphoria that had accompanied the first airplane flight in the country died down and no one gave the episode another thought, except for Clara, who continued to peer at the horizon.

After a week with no word from the flying uncle, people began to speculate that he had gone so high that he had disappeared into outer space, and the ignorant suggested he would reach the moon. With a mixture of sadness and relief, Severo decided that his

---

9. Leonardo da Vinci (lḗ ə när′ dō də vin′ chē) **. . . Incas** Leonardo da Vinci (1452–1519) was an Italian painter, sculptor, architect, and scientist. The Incas were Native Americans who dominated ancient Peru until the Spanish conquest.

Reading Skill
Author's Purpose
What does the statement "Clara would remember this holiday as long as she lived suggest about the author's purpose in this story?

Reading Check

Where does Uncle Marcos plan to fly in his flying machine?

brother-in-law and his machine must have fallen into some hidden crevice of the cordillera,[10] where they would never be found. Nivea wept <u>disconsolately</u> and lit candles to San Antonio, patron of lost objects. Severo opposed the idea of having masses said, because he did not believe in them as a way of getting into heaven, much less of returning to earth, and he maintained that masses and religious vows, like the selling of indulgences, images, and scapulars,[11] were a dishonest business. Because of his attitude, Nivea and Nana had the children say the rosary,[12] behind their father's back for nine days. Meanwhile, groups of volunteer explorers and mountain climbers tirelessly searched peaks and passes, combing every accessible stretch of land until they finally returned in triumph to hand the family the mortal remains of the deceased in a sealed black coffin. The intrepid traveler was laid to rest in a grandiose funeral. His death made him a hero and his name was on the front page of all the papers for several days. The same multitude that had gathered to see him off the day he flew away in his bird paraded past his coffin. The entire family wept as befit the occasion, except for Clara, who continued to watch the sky with the patience of an astronomer. One week after he had been buried, Uncle Marcos, a bright smile playing behind his pirate's mustache, appeared in person in the doorway of Nivea and Severo del Valle's house. Thanks to the surreptitious[13] prayers of the women and children, as he himself admitted, he was alive and well and in full possession of his faculties, including his sense of humor. Despite the noble lineage of his aerial maps, the flight had been a failure. He had lost his airplane and had to return on foot, but he had not broken any bones and his adventurous spirit was intact. This confirmed the family's eternal devotion to San Antonio, but was not taken as a warning by future generations, who also tried to fly, although by different means. Legally, however, Marcos was a corpse. Severo del Valle was obliged to use all his legal ingenuity to bring his brother-in-law back to life and the full rights of citizenship. When the coffin was pried open in the presence of the appropriate authorities, it was found to contain a bag of sand. This discovery ruined the reputation, up till then untarnished, of the volunteer explorers and mountain climbers, who from that day on were considered little better than a pack of bandits.

Marcos's heroic resurrection made everyone forget about his barrel-organ phase. Once again he was a sought-after guest in all

Vocabulary Builder
disconsolately (dis kän´ sə lit lē) *adv.* very unhappily

Reading Skill
Author's Purpose
What do the narrator's observations about Marcos suggest about the author's purpose?

Literary Analysis
Character Which details in this passage indicate that Marcos has changed since the beginning of the story?

---

10. cordillera (kôr´ dil yer´ə) *n.* system or chain of mountains.
11. indulgences, images, and scapulars (skap´ yə lərz) Indulgences are pardons for sins; images are pictures or sculptures of religious figures; and scapulars are garments worn by Roman Catholics as tokens of religious devotion.
12. say the rosary use a set of beads to say prayers.
13. surreptitious (sur´ əp tish´ əs) *adj.* secretive.

the city's salons and, at least for a while, his name was cleared. Marcos stayed in his sister's house for several months. One night he left without saying goodbye, leaving behind his trunks, his books, his weapons, his boots, and all his belongings. Severo, and even Nivea herself, breathed a sigh of relief. His visit had gone on too long. But Clara was so upset that she spent a week walking in her sleep and sucking her thumb. The little girl, who was only seven at the time, had learned to read from her uncle's storybooks and been closer to him than any other member of the family because of her prophesying powers. Marcos maintained that his niece's gift could be a source of income and a good opportunity for him to cultivate his own clairvoyance.[14] He believed that all human beings possessed this ability, particularly his own family, and that if it did not function well it was simply due to a lack of training. He bought a crystal ball in the Persian bazaar, insisting that it had magic powers and was from the East (although it was later found to be part of a buoy from a fishing boat), set it down on a background of black velvet, and announced that he could tell people's fortunes, cure the evil eye, and improve the quality of dreams, all for the modest sum of five centavos.[15] His first customers were the maids from around the neighborhood. One of them had been accused of stealing, because her employer had misplaced a valuable ring. The crystal ball revealed the exact location of the object in question: it had rolled beneath a wardrobe. The next day there was a line outside the front door of the house. There were coachmen, storekeepers, and milkmen; later a few municipal employees and distinguished ladies made a discreet appearance, slinking along the side walls of the house to keep from being recognized. The customers were received by Nana, who ushered them into the waiting room and collected their fees. This task kept her busy throughout the day and demanded so much of her time that the family began to complain that all there ever was for dinner was old string beans and jellied quince.[16] Marcos decorated the carriage house with some frayed curtains that had once belonged in the drawing room but that neglect and age had turned to dusty rags. There he and Clara received the customers. The two divines wore tunics "color of the men of light," as Marcos called the color yellow. Nana had dyed them with saffron powder, boiling them in pots usually reserved for rice and pasta. In addition to his tunic, Marcos wore a turban around his head and an Egyptian amulet around his neck. He had

▲ **Critical Viewing**
What qualities of a crystal ball make it appear to have "magic powers"? **[Analyze]**

Reading Check

What power does Marcos believe Clara holds?

---

14. clairvoyance (kler voi´ əns) *n.* supposed ability to perceive unseen things.
15. centavos (sen tä´ vōs) *n.* coins equal to 1/100 of a cruzeiro, the basic monetary unit of Brazil.
16. quince (kwins) golden or greenish-yellow, hard, apple-shaped fruit.

grown a beard and let his hair grow long and he was thinner than ever before. Marcos and Clara were utterly convincing, especially because the child had no need to look into the crystal ball to guess what her clients wanted to hear. She would whisper in her Uncle Marcos's ear, and he in turn would transmit the message to the client, along with any improvisations of his own that he thought pertinent. Thus their fame spread, because all those who arrived sad and bedraggled at the consulting room left filled with hope.

<u>Unrequited</u> lovers were told how to win over indifferent hearts, and the poor left with foolproof tips on how to place their money at the dog tracks. Business grew so prosperous that the waiting room was always packed with people, and Nana began to suffer dizzy spells from being on her feet so many hours a day. This time Severo had no need to intervene to put a stop to his brother-in-law's venture, for both Marcos and Clara, realizing that their unerring guesses could alter the fate of their clients, who always followed their advice to the letter, became frightened and decided that this was a job for swindlers. They abandoned their carriage-house oracle and split the profits, even though the only one who had cared about the material side of things had been Nana.

Of all the del Valle children, Clara was the one with the greatest interest in and stamina for her uncle's stories. She could repeat each and every one of them. She knew by heart words from several dialects of the Indians, was acquainted with their customs, and could describe the exact way in which they pierced their lips and earlobes with wooden shafts, their initiation rites, the names of the most poisonous snakes, and the appropriate antidotes for each. Her uncle was so eloquent that the child could feel in her own skin the burning sting of snakebites, see reptiles slide across the carpet between the legs of the jacaranda[17] room divider, and hear the shrieks of macaws behind the drawing-room drapes. She did not hesitate as she recalled Lope de Aguirre's search for El Dorado,[18] or the unpronounceable names of the flora and fauna her extraordinary uncle had seen; she knew about the lamas who take salt tea with yak lard and she could give detailed descriptions of the opulent women of Tahiti, the rice fields of China, or the white prairies of the North, where the eternal ice kills animals and men who lose their way, turning them to stone in seconds. Marcos had various travel journals in which he recorded his excursions and impressions, as well as a collection of maps and books of stories and fairy tales that he kept in the trunks he stored in the junk room at the far end of

Vocabulary Builder
unrequited (un ri kwit´ id) *adj.* not returned or repaid

Literary Analysis
Character Which details in this paragraph indicate that Clara, like Marcos, is a complex character?

---

17. **jacaranda** (jak´ ə ran´ də) type of tropical American tree.
18. **Lope de Aguirre's** (lō´ pā dā ä gēr´ rās) . . . **El Dorado** Lope de Aguirre was a Spanish adventurer (1510–1561) in colonial South America who searched for a legendary country called El Dorado, which was supposedly rich in gold.

the third courtyard. From there they were hauled out to inhabit the dreams of his descendants, until they were mistakenly burned half a century later on an infamous pyre.

Now Marcos had returned from his last journey in a coffin. He had died of a mysterious African plague that had turned him as yellow and wrinkled as a piece of parchment. When he realized he was ill, he set out for home with the hope that his sister's ministrations and Dr. Cuevas's knowledge would restore his health and youth, but he was unable to withstand the sixty days on ship and died at the latitude of Guayaquil,[19] ravaged by fever and hallucinating about musky women and hidden treasure. The captain of the ship, an Englishman by the name of Longfellow, was about to throw him overboard wrapped in a flag, but Marcos, despite his savage appearance and his delirium, had made so many friends on board and seduced so many women that the passengers prevented him from doing so, and Longfellow was obliged to store the body side by side with the vegetables of the Chinese cook, to preserve it from the heat and mosquitoes of the tropics until the ship's carpenter had time to improvise a coffin. At El Callao[20] they obtained a more appropriate container, and several days later the captain, furious at all the troubles this passenger had caused the shipping company and himself personally, unloaded him without a backward glance, surprised that not a soul was there to receive the body or cover the expenses he had incurred. Later he learned that the post office in these latitudes was not as reliable as that of far-off England, and that all his telegrams had vaporized en route. Fortunately for Longfellow, a customs lawyer who was a friend of the del Valle family appeared and offered to take charge, placing Marcos and all his paraphernalia in a freight car, which he shipped to the capital to the only known address of the deceased: his sister's house. . . .

Literature in Context

Humanities Connection

Magical Realists The literary movement known as Magical Realism is most closely associated with the wonder-filled novels and short stories of a group of twentieth-century Latin American authors. Isabel Allende is an important writer in this group. The great Argentinian writer Jorge Luis Borges is another. His style often combines realistic characters and events with details that seem to come out of dreams and myths. Gabriel García Márquez of Colombia is often considered the central figure of the movement. His works chronicle the lives of passionate and sympathetic characters who experience miraculous happenings and strange, unearthly events.

Connect to the Literature

What elements of "Uncle Marcos" confirm that it belongs to the literary movement known as Magical Realism?

---

19. **Guayaquil** (gwī ä kēl') seaport in western Ecuador.
20. **El Callao** (kə yä' ō) seaport in western Peru.

Apply the Skills

Uncle Marcos

Thinking About the Selection

1. **Respond:** Which of Uncle Marcos's adventures would you most like to share with him? Why?
2. **(a) Recall:** What does Uncle Marcos do to try to win the hand of Cousin Antonieta? **(b) Connect:** Is her reaction what Uncle Marcos expects? Explain. **(c) Compare and Contrast:** How do the actions that each character takes after the courtship differ?
3. **(a) Recall:** What does Uncle Marcos make from the materials he brings back in "enormous boxes"? **(b) Infer:** What do you think motivates Uncle Marcos to undertake this project?
4. **(a) Compare and Contrast:** Compare and contrast Clara's reaction to her uncle's disappearance with those of the others. **(b) Interpret:** What does Clara's reaction show about her personality and her relationship to Uncle Marcos? Explain.
5. **(a) Draw Conclusions:** What life lessons can people learn from the character of Uncle Marcos? **(b) Discuss:** Share your responses with a small group and discuss the differences and similarities among them. **(c) Reflect:** How has your response grown or changed as a result of this discussion?

Literary Analysis

6. **(a)** Using a chart like the one shown, list at least three of Uncle Marcos's projects or adventures. Then, identify a quality that each project or adventure reveals.

Projects or Adventures		Character Traits
shoots tiger	→	courage

   (b) Based on his projects and adventures, summarize the **character** of Uncle Marcos in a few sentences.
7. Review the characters of Clara and Uncle Marcos. **(a)** Determine whether each character is **round** or **flat**. Explain. **(b)** Determine whether each character is **static** or **dynamic**. Explain.

Reading Skill

8. **(a)** What specific **purpose** might Isabel Allende have had for creating the character of Uncle Marcos? **(b)** Identify three details from the story and explain how **reflecting** on them helped you determine Allende's purpose.

QuickReview

Story at a Glance
An eccentric man makes a lasting impression on his niece.

Go **O**nline
Assessment
For: Self-test
Visit: www.PHSchool.com
Web Code: epa-6111

Character: a person or an animal who takes part in the action of a literary work. Characters can be *round* or *flat*, *dynamic* or *static*.

Author's Purpose: a writer's main reason for writing a literary work

Vocabulary Builder

Practice Review the vocabulary list for "Uncle Marcos" on page 122. Then, decide whether each of the following statements is true or false. Explain your answers.

1. Something that looks *pallid* is full of color.

2. Sighing *disconsolately* is a good way to express enthusiasm.

3. *Unrequited* love is symbolized by a wedding.

Adding Words to Your Vocabulary Using a dictionary or a thesaurus, find an **antonym**, a word that has the opposite meaning, for each italicized word from the vocabulary list. Then, use each antonym correctly in a sentence. (For more on using a dictionary and a thesaurus, see pages R6–7.)

Writing

Write a **character profile** of Uncle Marcos.
- Begin by jotting down details that capture the character's appearance, personality, and achievements.
- Decide on a single impression to convey about the character.
- Organize and present details so that they all contribute to that one impression.

For *Grammar, Vocabulary,* and *Assessment,* see **Build Language Skills,** pages 144–145.

Extend Your Learning

Listening and Speaking Write and perform a **scene** based on the passage in which Uncle Marcos makes his flight across the mountains.
- Write a script for the scene.
- Cast the scene, and briefly rehearse.

Perform the scene for the class.

Research and Technology Use a variety of sources, including the library and the Internet, to research the history of human flight. Record your research in a **learning log,** a written record of information you discover about the topic. Analyze the information by discussing it with classmates and by comparing your findings to Uncle Marcos's adventure with flight. In your discussions, decide if that aspect of the story is realistic or fantastic.

Build Language Skills

The Secret Life of Walter Mitty • Uncle Marcos

Vocabulary Skill

Word Origins Words from Latin and Greek roots form the core of the English language. Numerous English words that have been invented, or coined, use a combination of roots from different languages. In 1913, C. Funk, a Polish biochemist, coined the word -vitamin- from the Latin -vit-, meaning "life," and the German root-amin-, for he believed that vitamins were essential to life.

Practice Next to each word or compound word, write the root that it came from. Then, write down what has been added to the root as the word evolved.

1. viable   3. vital signs   5. triad
2. revolve   4. triathlon

Grammar Lesson

Pronouns: Relative, Interrogative, and Indefinite Pronouns are words that stand for nouns.

- A **relative pronoun** begins a subordinate clause and connects it to another idea in the sentence. The five relative pronouns are *that, which, who, whom,* and *whose.*

- An **interrogative pronoun** is used to begin a question. The five interrogative pronouns are *what, which, who, whom,* and *whose.*

- **Indefinite pronouns** refer to people, places, or things, often without specifying which ones.

MorePractice

For more practice with pronouns, see the Grammar Handbook, p. R40.

INDEFINITE PRONOUNS						
Singular				**Plural**	**Singular or Plural**	
another	either	much	one	both	all	most
anybody	everybody	neither	other	few	any	none
anyone	everyone	nobody	somebody	many	more	some
anything	everything	no one	someone	others		
each	little	nothing	something	several		

Practice Identify the pronouns in each sentence and tell whether each is relative, interrogative, or indefinite.

1. Some of the pies looked delicious.
2. Whose do you want to take?
3. Andrew is the sprinter who always wins.
4. We met Lori's Dad, whose hair is red.

WG Prentice Hall Writing and Grammar Connection: Chapter 16, Section 2.

Reading Skill: Author's Purpose

Directions: *Read the selection. Then answer the questions.*

She had no proper wardrobe, no jewels, nothing. . . . She would have so loved to charm, to be envied, to be admired and sought after.

She had a rich friend, a schoolmate from the convent she had attended, but she didn't like to visit her because it always made her so miserable when she got home again. She would weep for whole days at a time from sorrow, regret, despair, and distress. . . .

She danced enraptured—carried away, intoxicated with pleasure, forgetting everything in this triumph of her beauty and the glory of her success, floating in a cloud of happiness . . . .

     —from "The Necklace" by Guy de Maupassant

Standards Assessed
- WL.1.01.2
- IR.2.01.7
- LT.5.01.7

1. The emphasis on the character indicates that author is highlighting
   A a trait of society.
   B a political insight.
   C a human trait.
   D a trend of the future.

2. From the passage the reader can speculate that the author's purpose is
   A to impart a lesson about possessions.
   B to impart a lesson about quickly changing emotions.
   C to impart a lesson about music's power.
   D to demonstrate the joy of wealth.

3. What is the best description of the author's purpose?
   A to entertain
   B to inform
   C to describe
   D to persuade

4. What would previewing this work tell the reader?
   A This is a text to skim and scan.
   B This is a text to read normally.
   C Notes should be taken as you read.
   D Notes should be taken after you reflect on the text.

Timed Writing: Explanation

Review "The Secret Life of Walter Mitty" or "Uncle Marcos." Write an explanation of why, in your opinion, people long for adventure. Use specifics from the text to support your explanation. **(20 minutes)**

 ## Writing Workshop: *Work in Progress*

Problem-Solution Essay
Build on the Problem/Solution Notes you created. List three specific examples of the problem. Then, list three examples of how your solution would work. Put these notes in your writing portfolio.

Theme

Theme is the central message or insight about life that is conveyed through a short story, an essay, or other literary work. Sometimes, the theme is stated directly. More often, it is suggested indirectly through the words and experiences of the characters or through the events of a story.

Comparing Themes

The development of theme depends in part on the genre, or form, of the work.

- **Nonfiction:** In nonfiction literature, such as essays, the theme is usually stated directly as a main idea. Because the *structure*, or organization, of nonfiction writing varies, the theme may be stated in the beginning, the middle, or the end of a work. The writer supports, or proves, the idea with facts, details, and examples.
- **Fiction and poetry:** In most short stories, novels, poetry, and plays, the theme is implied, or suggested. Readers must figure out the theme by looking at the ideas expressed through story events, characters' statements and actions, or patterns of related images and ideas called *motifs*.

Both of the following selections address the topics of the environment. However, the selections are different genres. "If I Forget Thee, Oh Earth" is a short story, and the excerpt from *Silent Spring* is a work of nonfiction. As you read, use a Venn diagram like the one shown to compare the themes and the ways in which each author develops them.

Standard Course of Study

- Judge different stylistic and literary devices in work. (CT.4.02.3)
- Interpret literary devices. (LT.5.01.3)
- Produce responses that follow the conventions of a specific genre. (LT.5.01.11)

If I Forget Thee, Oh Earth   **Silent Spring**

Deals with environmental issues.

Vocabulary Builder

If I Forget Thee, Oh Earth. . .

- **purged** (pɝjd) *v.* cleansed (p. 148) *The ointment purged the wound of infection.*
- **perennial** (pə ren´ ē əl) *adj.* happening over and over; perpetual (p. 151) *The perennial floods wore down the rocks.*

from Silent Spring

- **blight** (blīt) *n.* something that destroys or prevents growth (p. 154) *A terrible blight killed all their crops.*
- **maladies** (mal´ ə dēz) *n.* diseases (p. 154) *They became sick from various maladies.*
- **moribund** (môr´ i bund´) *adj.* dying (p. 155) *Due to the drought, my garden is moribund.*

Build Understanding

Connecting to the Literature

Reading/Writing Connection Both of these stories present a grim vision of the future that encourages readers to take action to protect Earth. Explain your vision of the future and what you think humans might do to preserve the Earth. Use at least three of the following words in your response: *adapt, challenge, communicate, distribute, maximize.*

Meet the Authors

Arthur C. **Clarke** (b. 1917)

Born in England, Arthur C. Clarke is both a writer and a scientist. He wrote his first science fiction stories during his teens, and he has since published more than fifty works of fiction and nonfiction.

A True Scientist Although best known for his science fiction, Clarke is a serious scientist as well. In 1945, he published a technical article called "Extra-Terrestrial Relays" in which he established the principles of the satellite communications system we have today.

Rachel **Carson** (1907–1964)

Even as a young girl, Rachel Carson thought of herself as a writer, and she entered college to pursue that goal. Once there, she renewed an interest in nature and switched her major to marine biology. She later earned a master's degree in zoology.

Environmental Activist Carson had long been worried about the overuse of pesticides. "Everything which meant most to me as a naturalist was being threatened," she said, and she felt that the most important thing she could do was publicize the facts. *Silent Spring* became one of the most influential environmental books ever written. Carson died of cancer before she witnessed the major impact of her book.

For: More about the authors
Visit: www.PHSchool.com
Web Code: epe-9113

"If I Forget Thee, Oh Earth..."

Arthur C. Clarke

When Marvin was ten years old, his father took him through the long, echoing corridors that led up through Administration and Power, until at last they came to the uppermost levels of all and were among the swiftly growing vegetation of the Farmlands. Marvin liked it here: it was fun watching the great, slender plants creeping with almost visible eagerness toward the sunlight as it filtered down through the plastic domes to meet them. The smell of life was everywhere, awakening inexpressible longings in his heart: no longer was he breathing the dry, cool air of the residential levels, <u>purged</u> of all smells but the faint tang of ozone.[1] He wished he could stay here for a little while, but Father would not let him. They went onward until they had reached the entrance to the Observatory, which he had never visited: but they did not stop, and Marvin knew with a sense of rising excitement that there could be only one goal left. For the first time in his life, he was going Outside.

---

1. ozone (ō´ zōn´) *n.* form of oxygen with a sharp odor.

Literary Analysis
Theme What information about Marvin's environment appears in this description of the Farmlands?

Vocabulary Builder
purged (pʉrjd) *v.* cleansed

There were a dozen of the surface vehicles, with their wide balloon tires and pressurized cabins, in the great servicing chamber. His father must have been expected, for they were led at once to the little scout car waiting by the huge circular door of the airlock. Tense with expectancy, Marvin settled himself down in the cramped cabin while his father started the motor and checked the controls. The inner door of the lock slid open and then closed behind them: he heard the roar of the great air pumps fade slowly away as the pressure dropped to zero. Then the "Vacuum" sign flashed on, the outer door parted, and before Marvin lay the land which he had never yet entered.

He had seen it in photographs, of course: he had watched it imaged on television screens a hundred times. But now it was lying all around him, burning beneath the fierce sun that crawled so slowly across the jet-black sky. He stared into the west, away from the blinding splendor of the sun—and there were the stars, as he had been told but had never quite believed. He gazed at them for a long time, marveling that anything could be so bright and yet so tiny. They were intense unscintillating points, and suddenly he remembered a rhyme he had once read in one of his father's books:

Twinkle, twinkle, little star,
How I wonder what you are.

Well, he knew what the stars were. Whoever asked that question must have been very stupid. And what did they mean by "twinkle"? You could see at a glance that all the stars shone with the same steady, unwavering light. He abandoned the puzzle and turned his attention to the landscape around him.

They were racing across a level plain at almost a hundred miles an hour, the great balloon tires sending up little spurts of dust behind them. There was no sign of the Colony: in the few minutes while he had been gazing at the stars, its domes and radio towers had fallen below the horizon. Yet there were other indications of man's presence, for about a mile ahead Marvin could see the curiously shaped structures clustering round the head of a mine. Now and then a puff of vapor would emerge from a squat smokestack and would instantly disperse.

They were past the mine in a moment: Father was driving with a reckless and exhilarating skill as if—it was a strange thought to come into a child's mind—he were trying to escape from something. In a few minutes they had reached the edge of the plateau on which the Colony had been built. The ground fell sharply away beneath them in a dizzying slope whose lower stretches were lost in shadow. Ahead, as far as the eye could reach, was a jumbled wasteland of

Literary Analysis
Theme What do the words "burning beneath the fierce sun" suggest about what Marvin is observing?

Reading Check

What astronomical bodies does Marvin see for the first time?

craters, mountain ranges, and ravines. The crests of the mountains, catching the low sun, burned like islands of fire in a sea of darkness: and above them the stars still shone as steadfastly as ever.

There could be no way forward—yet there was. Marvin clenched his fists as the car edged over the slope and started the long descent. Then he saw the barely visible track leading down the mountainside, and relaxed a little. Other men, it seemed, had gone this way before.

Night fell with a shocking abruptness as they crossed the shadow line and the sun dropped below the crest of the plateau. The twin searchlights sprang into life, casting blue-white bands on the rocks ahead, so that there was scarcely need to check their speed. For hours they drove through valleys and past the foot of mountains whose peaks seemed to comb the stars, and sometimes they emerged for a moment into the sunlight as they climbed over higher ground.

And now on the right was a wrinkled, dusty plain, and on the left, its ramparts and terraces rising mile after mile into the sky, was a wall of mountains that marched into the distance until its peaks sank from sight below the rim of the world. There was no sign that men had ever explored this land, but once they passed the skeleton of a crashed rocket, and beside it a stone cairn[2] surmounted by a metal cross.

It seemed to Marvin that the mountains stretched on forever: but at last, many hours later, the range ended in a towering, precipitous headland[3] that rose steeply from a cluster of little hills. They drove down into a shallow valley that curved in a great arc toward the far side of the mountains: and as they did so, Marvin slowly realized that something very strange was happening in the land ahead.

The sun was now low behind the hills on the right: the valley before them should be in total darkness. Yet it was awash with a cold white radiance that came spilling over the crags beneath which

---

2. **cairn** (kern) *n.* a cone-shaped pile of stones built as a monument.
3. **precipitous headland** (prē sip´ ə təs hed´ land´) *n.* steep cliff that juts out over water.

they were driving. Then, suddenly, they were out in the open plain, and the source of the light lay before them in all its glory.

It was very quiet in the little cabin now that the motors had stopped. The only sound was the faint whisper of the oxygen feed and an occasional metallic crepitation as the outer walls of the vehicle radiated away their heat. For no warmth at all came from the great silver crescent that floated low above the far horizon and flooded all this land with pearly light. It was so brilliant that minutes passed before Marvin could accept its challenge and look steadfastly into its glare, but at last he could discern the outlines of continents, the hazy border of the atmosphere, and the white islands of cloud. And even at this distance, he could see the glitter of sunlight on the polar ice.

It was beautiful, and it called to his heart across the abyss of space. There in that shining crescent were all the wonders that he had never known—the hues of sunset skies, the moaning of the sea on pebbled shores, the patter of falling rain, the unhurried benison of snow. These and a thousand others should have been his rightful heritage, but he knew them only from the books and ancient records, and the thought filled him with the anguish of exile.

Why could they not return? It seemed so peaceful beneath those lines of marching cloud. Then Marvin, his eyes no longer blinded by the glare, saw that the portion of the disk that should have been in darkness was gleaming faintly with an evil phosphorescence[4] and he remembered. He was looking upon the funeral pyre of a world— upon the radioactive aftermath of Armageddon[5]. Across a quarter of a million miles of space, the glow of dying atoms was still visible, a <u>perennial</u> reminder of the ruinous past. It would be centuries yet before that deadly glow died from the rocks and life could return again to fill that silent, empty world.

And now Father began to speak, telling Marvin the story which until this moment had meant no more to him than the fairy tales he had once been told. There were many things he could not understand: it was impossible for him to picture the glowing, multicolored pattern of life on the planet he had never seen. Nor could he comprehend the forces that had destroyed it in the end, leaving the Colony, preserved by its isolation, as the sole survivor. Yet he could share the agony of those final days, when the Colony had learned at last that never again would the supply ships come flaming down through the stars with gifts from home. One by one

---

4. **phosphorescence** (fäs´ fə res´ əns) n. emission of light resulting from exposure to radiation.
5. **Armageddon** (är´ mə ged´ 'n) n. in the Bible, the place where the final battle between good and evil is to be fought.

Literary Analysis
Theme Which details in these paragraphs provide an insight into what Marvin, and others in his colony, have lost?

Vocabulary Builder
perennial (pə ren´ ē əl) adj. happening over and over; perpetual

Reading Check
What does Marvin notice in a portion of the disk?

the radio stations had ceased to call: on the shadowed globe the lights of the cities had dimmed and died, and they were alone at last, as no men had ever been alone before, carrying in their hands the future of the race.

Then had followed the years of despair, and the long-drawn battle for survival in their fierce and hostile world. That battle had been won, though barely: this little oasis of life was safe against the worst that Nature could do. But unless there was a goal, a future toward which it could work, the Colony would lose the will to live, and neither machines nor skill nor science could save it then.

So, at last, Marvin understood the purpose of this pilgrimage. He would never walk beside the rivers of that lost and legendary world, or listen to the thunder raging above its softly rounded hills. Yet one day—how far ahead?—his children's children would return to claim their heritage. The winds and the rains would scour the poisons from the burning lands and carry them to the sea, and in the depths of the sea they would waste their venom until they could harm no living things. Then the great ships that were still waiting here on the silent, dusty plains could lift once more into space, along the road that led to home.

That was the dream: and one day, Marvin knew with a sudden flash of insight, he would pass it on to his own son, here at this same spot with the mountains behind him and the silver light from the sky streaming into his face.

He did not look back as they began the homeward journey. He could not bear to see the cold glory of the crescent Earth fade from the rocks around him, as he went to rejoin his people in their long exile.

Literary Analysis
Theme What message about the future is conveyed through the details in this paragraph?

Thinking About the Selection

1. **Respond:** How do you think you would handle Marvin's situation? Explain.

2. **(a) Infer:** What evidence indicates that the story is set on the moon? **(b) Analyze:** How does the choice of setting make the story more realistic?

3. **(a) Recall:** At the end of the story, what does Marvin decide to do? **(b) Draw Conclusions:** What was the purpose of Marvin's trip with his father?

4. **(a) Infer:** How did Earth come to be destroyed? **(b) Speculate:** What suggestions do you think Clarke would offer today to prevent a situation like the one in the story from occurring?

Silent Spring

Rachel Carson

There was once a town in the heart of America where all life seemed to live in harmony with its surroundings. The town lay in the midst of a checkerboard of prosperous farms, with fields of grain and hillsides of orchards where, in spring, white clouds of bloom drifted above the green fields. In autumn, oak and maple and birch set up a blaze of color that flamed and flickered across a backdrop of pines. Then foxes barked in the hills and deer silently crossed the fields, half hidden in the mists of the fall mornings.

Literary Analysis
Theme Which details in this paragraph paint a picture of the beauty and energy of nature? Explain.

Along the roads, laurel, viburnum and alder, great ferns and wildflowers delighted the traveler's eye through much of the year. Even in winter the roadsides were places of beauty, where countless birds came to feed on the berries and on the seed heads of the dried weeds rising above the snow. The countryside was, in fact, famous for the abundance and variety of its bird life, and when the flood of migrants was pouring through in spring and fall people traveled from great distances to observe them. Others came to fish the streams, which flowed clear and cold out of the hills and contained shady pools where trout lay. So it had been from the days many years ago when the first settlers raised their houses, sank their wells, and built their barns.

Then a strange <u>blight</u> crept over the area and everything began to change. Some evil spell had settled on the community: mysterious <u>maladies</u> swept the flocks of chickens; the cattle and sheep sickened and died. Everywhere was a shadow of death. The farmers

▼ **Critical Viewing** What might the author think about the aerial spraying of crops with chemicals that kill pests? **[Connect]**

spoke of much illness among their families. In the town the doctors had become more and more puzzled by new kinds of sickness appearing among their patients. There had been several sudden and unexplained deaths, not only among adults but even among children, who would be stricken suddenly while at play and die within a few hours.

There was a strange stillness. The birds, for example—where had they gone? Many people spoke of them, puzzled and disturbed. The feeding stations in the backyards were deserted. The few birds seen anywhere were <u>moribund</u>; they trembled violently and could not fly. It was a spring without voices. On the mornings that had once throbbed with the dawn chorus of robins, catbirds, doves, jays, wrens, and scores of other bird voices there was now no sound; only silence lay over the fields and woods and marsh.

On the farms the hens brooded, but no chicks hatched. The farmers complained that they were unable to raise any pigs—the

Vocabulary Builder
moribund (môr´ i bund´) *adj.* dying

✓Reading Check

What changes does the "strange blight" cause?

litters were small and the young survived only a few days. The apple trees were coming into bloom but no bees droned among the blossoms, so there was no pollination and there would be no fruit.

The roadsides, once so attractive, were now lined with browned and withered vegetation as though swept by fire. These, too, were silent, deserted by all living things. Even the streams were now lifeless. Anglers[1] no longer visited them, for all the fish had died.

In the gutters under the eaves and between the shingles of the roofs, a white granular powder still showed a few patches; some weeks before it had fallen like snow upon the roofs and the lawns, the fields and streams.

No witchcraft, no enemy action had silenced the rebirth of new life in this stricken world. The people had done it themselves.

This town does not actually exist, but it might easily have a thousand counterparts in America or elsewhere in the world. I know of no community that has experienced all the misfortunes I describe. Yet every one of these disasters has actually happened somewhere, and many real communities have already suffered a substantial number of them. A grim specter has crept upon us almost unnoticed, and this imagined tragedy may easily become a stark reality we all shall know.

---

1. **anglers** (aŋ´ glərz) *n.* people who fish with a line and hook.

Literary Analysis
Theme How do you react to this description of a sudden change? What message is the author suggesting?

Literary Analysis
Theme Is the theme stated directly here or is it implied? Explain.

Thinking About the Selection

1. **Respond:** What do you find most troubling about the environmental problems described in this excerpt? Explain.

2. **(a) Recall:** What is the condition of life at the beginning of this excerpt? **(b) Compare and Contrast:** How does the condition of life change as the narrative continues?

3. **(a) Recall:** What happens to the farm animals and the vegetation? **(b) Infer:** What causes this sudden change?

4. **(a) Recall:** What information about the town does Carson reveal at the end of the excerpt? **(b) Speculate:** Would the narrative be more effective if the town was real? Why or why not?

5. **(a) Recall:** According to Carson, who caused the environmental problems? **(b) Speculate:** What suggestions do you think Carson would make to people today?

Apply the Skills

If I Forget Thee, Oh Earth. . . • from *Silent Spring*

Comparing Themes

1. Use a chart like the one shown to analyze the themes expressed in "If I Forget Thee, Oh Earth. . ." and the excerpt from Silent Spring. List important details from each selection, what you think the details mean, and the theme of the selection.

Details from "If I Forget Thee, Oh Earth. . ."	What They Mean	Theme
Details from *Silent Spring*	What They Mean	Theme

2. **(a)** Using details from the chart, explain how the themes in the two selections are similar. **(b)** How is the theme expressed differently in each?

Writing to Compare Literary Works

Write an essay in which you compare your reactions to "If I Forget Thee, Oh Earth. . ." and the excerpt from *Silent Spring*. In your response, consider how the author's choice to write fiction or nonfiction affects your reading experience. Use the following questions to get started.

- Do you feel more affected by the experiences of the fictional character Marvin or by the words of Rachel Carson, the author of *Silent Spring*?
- Do you find fiction or nonfiction more effective in expressing a theme?
- Why do you think an author would choose one genre over another when conveying a theme?

Vocabulary Builder

Practice For each item, write a sentence in which you use the word pair correctly.

1. purged; weeds
2. perennial; campaign
3. blight; garden
4. maladies; doctor
5. moribund; sadness

QuickReview

Theme: the central message or insight about life that is conveyed through a literary work

Go Online
Assessment
For: Self-test
Visit: www.PHSchool.com
Web Code: epa-6112

Reading: Author's Purpose

Directions: *Questions 1–5 are based on the following selection.*

Selection 1

The streets weren't always this clean in our little town, the trees weren't always as green, and the quiet peaceful cadence of crickets and birds did not always ring in the woods. The effort that it took to reclaim our town was tremendous and we are in danger of losing what we fought so hard to achieve.

Selection 2

It was the town I grew up in, one of those small towns that seem to float peacefully on, no issues that aren't solved in town meetings, no crime that is not petty, no problems. Of course, the town did contain one Mrs. Funk. Mrs. Funk was eccentric in the way only old women who have lived someplace all of their lives can be eccentric. It wasn't her 15 cats, or her propensity to call everyone sir, or even her purple shutters that resulted in this distinction. It was her immensely amusing schedule, one an army general would value.

1. The details in Selection 1 suggest which of the following?
   A The author is writing a scientific article.
   B The author is familiar with the place.
   C The author is writing an informative article.
   D The author has a specific opinion.

2. Details in Selection 1 show that the author's purpose is probably
   A to entertain.
   B to persuade.
   C to inform.
   D to describe.

3. Selection 2 suggests that the author's purpose is
   A to entertain.
   B to persuade.
   C to inform.
   D to describe.

4. Which of the following would be most useful in evaluating the author's purpose for Selection 1?
   A A biography of the author.
   B A review of the book.
   C Details of the entire selection.
   D Comments on the author's web site.

5. The third sentence in Passage 2 helps the reader
   A reevaluate the author's purpose.
   B confirm that this is written to entertain.
   C evaluate the position the author will take.
   D confirm that this is written to inform.

A. Directions: *Choose the word that best completes the sentence.*

Standards
Assessed

• CT.4.02.1
• WL.1.03.10
• WL.1.03.2

6. Conditioning is considered _____ to becoming a competent athlete.
   A unnecessary
   B vital
   C trivial
   D likely

7. Following directions exactly is not _____; it is important in any experiment.
   A possible
   B vital
   C trivial
   D appreciated

8. We choose not to _____ graphic pictures of the war.
   A appreciate
   B detect
   C display
   D vitalize

9. Animals can _____ odors of which humans are unaware.
   A detect
   B trivialize
   C capture
   D appreciate

10. Those who are trying to concentrate rarely _____ hearing loud music.
    A detect
    B trivialize
    C capture
    D appreciate

11. Swimming, running and bicycling are all part of a _____.
    A viaticum
    B vitality
    C triathlon
    D vitate

12. Ancient Romans called traveling expenses _____.
    A viaticum
    B vitality
    C triathlon
    D vitate

13. The power to go on living is also referred to as _____.
    A viaticum
    B vitality
    C triathlon
    D vitate

14. An accurate name for a combination of three herbal products is _____.
    A vitamin
    B triherbal
    C viaherbal
    D triamin

15. A curriculum vita is a list of important accomplishments in _____.
    A life
    B the first third of one's career
    C the last third of one's career
    D a specific job

Spelling Workshop

Content Area Words

Content area words are those that come from science, history, literature, and other subject areas that you may study.

NC Standard Course of Study

• Edit for spelling and mechanics. (GU.6.02.4)

An **Isthmus** or an **Island?** *Isthmus* and *island* are two examples of frequently misspelled content area words. While content area words are not necessarily difficult, they may have letters that are silent, like the *th* in *isthmus* or the *s* in *island,* or other challenging letter patterns. Focus on the words you may spell wrong and learn their correct spellings.

I hope this is an Isthmus and not an Island.

Practice Read the clues. Then, on a separate piece of paper, write the word from the word list that is indicated by the clue.

1. the opposite of comedy
2. fractions, algebra, geometry
3. very cold region
4. two lines that never come together
5. important body parts
6. comparison between two unlike things
7. study of the mind
8. the world all around us
9. leave one's country to live elsewhere
10. water and steam rising from the earth

Word List
environment
emigrate
muscles
geyser
arctic
tragedy
psychology
parallel
mathematics
metaphor

EOC **Test Practice**

A. Directions: *Choose the letter of the sentence in which the underlined word is spelled correctly.*

Standards Assessed

• GU.6.02.4

1. **A** Our class read a Greek <u>tradgedy</u>.
   B The main character had to <u>emigrate</u> from his homeland.
   C It seemed that every speech contained a <u>metephor</u>.
   D The play showed that people can overcome a bad <u>envirament</u>.

   A I have never been good at <u>mathamatics</u>.
   B I can't even draw <u>parralel</u> lines.
   C I get nervous and my <u>mussles</u> start to twitch.
   D Should I see a <u>psychology</u> specialist?

   A In an Ice Age, <u>artic</u> conditions would be widespread.
   B Every <u>giser</u> would freeze.

   C People would try to <u>emmigrate</u> to warmer areas.
   D They would look for a better <u>environment</u>.

   A The science fiction story was set in a <u>parrellel</u> universe.
   B People sat and studied <u>mathematicks</u> all day.
   C Everyone's <u>muscles</u> got weak from not being used.
   D The story ended in <u>tradegy</u>.

B. Directions: *Write the letter of the word that would be the correct spelling to fill in the blank.*

1. "The road was a ribbon" is a _____.
   A metephor
   B metaphor
   C metafore
   D metefor

2. Old Faithful is a famous _____.
   A geiser
   B giser
   C geyser
   D gyser

3. You can sometimes use _____ to train a pet.
   A sychology
   B sycholigy
   C phsychology
   D psychology

4. Penguins do not live in the _____ region.
   A artic
   B arctic
   C arctick
   D artick

5. This exercise will stretch your leg _____.
   A mussles
   B musels
   C musles
   D muscles

6. That factory pollutes the _____.
   A environment
   B enviroment
   C envirament
   D envirinment

Writing Workshop

Exposition: Problem-and-Solution Essay

Some forms of expository writing engage us in the struggles and resolutions of our daily lives. In a **problem-and-solution essay,** an author identifies and explains a problem and then proposes a practical solution. Follow the steps in this workshop to write your own problem-and-solution essay.

Assignment Write a problem-and-solution essay about an issue that confronts your school or community.

What to Include Your problem-and-solution essay should feature the following elements:
- a statement of the problem and a suggested solution
- facts, statistics, and details that show the problem's scope and indicate how it can be solved
- language appropriate to the level of knowledge of your audience
- a logical organization
- error-free grammar, including correct use of pronouns

To preview the criteria on which your problem-and-solution essay may be assessed, see the rubric on page 169.

NC **Standard Course of Study**

- Use description, comparison, figurative language to elaborate ideas to inform audience (IR.2.02.4)
- Recognize and analyze the characteristics of literary genres. (LT.5.01.2)

Using the Form
You may use elements of this form in these types of writing:
- letters and memos
- proposals
- editorials

Writing Workshop: *Work in Progress*

If you have completed the Work-in-Progress assignments, you have several ideas in your portfolio that you might wish to pursue in your problem-and-solution essay. Continue to develop these ideas, or explore a new idea as you complete this Writing Workshop.

Reading Writing Connection

To get a feel for the use of problem-and-solution structure in a speech, read "First Inaugural Address" by Franklin Delano Roosevelt on page 503.

Prewriting

Choosing Your Topic

To select a topic for your problem-and-solution essay, use one of the following strategies:

- **Media Scan** Review local newspapers and television news programs for items about issues and problems in your community. List problems for which you can imagine practical solutions, and select one as your topic.

- **Sentence Starters** Complete the following sentence starters and jot down any associated ideas that come to mind. Then, choose one of the issues generated by the sentence starters as your topic.

  One thing that really annoys me is . . .
  The biggest problem people my age face is . . .
  Life would be better in my community if . . .
  The world would be a much better place if . . .

Narrowing Your Topic

Create a problem profile. Once you have chosen a topic, create a profile to help you focus your essay on a specific aspect of the problem. Answer the following questions about the problem:

- Who is affected by the problem?
- What causes the problem to occur?
- Is there more than one cause of the problem?
- What are some possible solutions to the problem?

Gathering Details

Consider your audience. Once you have clearly defined the problem, collect the details and information you will need to start your draft. Assess all possible solutions and weed out the less practical ones. Then, determine whom you want to reach with your essay and which aspects of the problem affect them most. For example, if you are trying to reach community leaders, you may shape your message differently than if you are trying to reach a peer group. As you narrow your focus, identify the ideas that will have the strongest impact on your target audience.

Work in Progress
Review the work you did on pages 117 and 145.

Problem Profile

Problem: Litter is creating an unsafe and unsightly environment.

Who is affected? Everyone on Earth

What causes the problem?
Lack of:
- responsibility
- environmental education
- sense of ownership

What are the possible solutions? Stiffer fines, more policing, more environmental education, volunteer trash pickup

---

Drafting

Shaping Your Writing

Engage your audience immediately. To make the problem real to your audience, consider one of these strategies for starting your essay:

- **Personal example:** Provide a detail from your own experience.

- **Anecdote:** Give a factual account of how the problem has already affected others.

- **Scenario:** Present a hypothetical but realistic picture of future consequences if the problem is not addressed.

Outline the problem clearly. Use a sunburst organizer to display aspects of the central problem, including likely causes. Then, select and develop only those details that will make the problem clear, significant, and urgent to your audience.

Providing Elaboration

Select convincing details. You cannot "prove" your solution in advance, but you can persuade the audience that your proposal is likely to work by using the following types of evidence:

- **Statistics:** Provide relevant numerical data.

- **Expert opinions:** Include the advice of those who have training or experience related to your topic problem.

- **Comparable situations:** Describe other real-life difficulties that were resolved by actions similar to the ones you propose.

Make sure that you establish clear connections among the various types of evidence you use.

Address readers' concerns. Include one or two skeptical questions. Then, provide well-supported answers that show why your solution is best.

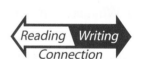

To read the complete student model, see p. 168.

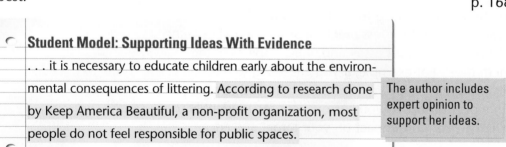

Student Model: Supporting Ideas With Evidence

. . . it is necessary to educate children early about the environmental consequences of littering. According to research done by Keep America Beautiful, a non-profit organization, most people do not feel responsible for public spaces.

The author includes expert opinion to support her ideas.

From the Author's Desk

Elizabeth McCracken

On Word Choice

Elizabeth McCracken

One of the best things about writing my novel *Niagara Falls All Over Again,* which tells the story of a comedy team, was that I could watch videotapes of old TV shows and movies, and claim that I was working. My favorites tapes were old episodes of a show that my beloved comic duo Abbott and Costello hosted once a month. This passage is basically just a description of what I saw when I was "working," watching *The Colgate Comedy Hour.*

"Write about your most beloved obsessions."

——Elizabeth McCracken

Professional Model:

from *Niagara Falls All Over Again*

We broke into television as the once-a-month hosts of a weekly hour-long live variety show. By 1951, our movie career was mostly over, and we were back where we'd begun, except famous, rich, and middle-aged: a thin man and a fat man on a stage, willing to do anything for a laugh. We were shameless. We insulted the band leader, we knocked down scenery on purpose, we tried to crack each other up. We broke props we'd need later, just so we could improvise first about the breakage, and then about the lack of props. Our old wheezing vaudeville jokes were new again, thanks to the postwar baby boom: the country was full of brand-new people with blissfully unsophisticated senses of humor. You could see Rocky search for the red light that told us which camera was paying attention, doing a slow burn and then saying, "Watch me, camera two," and tipping his hat. . . .

I have a weakness for repetition, both straight repeats (like all the We's) and slight variations, like *break, broke.*

Some writers say, Avoid adverbs. It's true that some people use adverbs to do the work that verbs and adjectives should do, but I use *blissfully* here as a joke—most people wouldn't see a lack of sophistication as *blissful.*

He's wearing a bowler hat. I draw my characters' clothing when I write (though I'm a very poor artist). I know them better if I know what they wear.

Writing Workshop

Revising

Revising Your Paragraphs

Support your generalizations. Look at each paragraph to be sure that the details support or explain the main idea of its topic sentence. Use the following strategy:

1. Highlight your topic sentence, the general statement in which you summarize the main idea of the paragraph.

2. Underline the supporting sentences that develop this idea.

3. Eliminate any sentences that do not support the main idea or that simply restate it.

Student Model: Revising to Support Generalizations

Litter is harmful for many reasons. For one, roadside litter is eventually washed into our waterways and oceans— water we use for drinking and recreation. Also, animals might entangle themselves or mistake trash for food and swallow it. ~~Air pollution is also a serious problem.~~

Eliminating sentences that do not support the main idea makes the paragraph clearer and stronger.

Revising Your Word Choice

Evaluate your vocabulary. Review your draft as if you were a member of your target audience. Find specialized terms that need to be defined or vocabulary that seems too difficult or easy for your readers. Then, adjust your language accordingly.

General audience: Another way to fight fatigue is to exercise.

Target audience of experts: Another way to raise low levels of blood sugar is to get more exercise.

Peer Review: Exchange drafts with a partner. Review each other's work, circling words that are either too specialized and technical or too simple and basic for your target audiences. Then, revise your draft, replacing inappropriate terms with language that better suits your readers' experience and knowledge levels. Discuss your decisions with your partner.

Integrating Grammar Skills

Revising Faulty Pronoun-Antecedent Agreement

Prentice Hall Writing and Grammar Connection: Chapter 25, Section 2

Pronouns are words that take the place of nouns. Antecedents are the nouns for which pronouns stand.

Identifying Errors in Pronoun-Antecedent Agreement Pronouns "disagree" with their antecedents when they are mismatched in number, person, or gender. A pronoun should agree with its antecedent in number:

Incorrect: *Anne and Natasha* reminded *her* parents.
Correct: *Anne and Natasha* reminded *their* parents. (plural)
Incorrect: *Neither Carl nor Jeff* remember *their* ID number.
Correct: *Neither Carl nor Jeff* remembers *his* ID number. (singular)

A pronoun should agree with its antecedent in person:

Incorrect: When a *person* hurries, *you* often make mistakes.
Correct: When *a person* hurries, *he or she* often makes mistakes. (third-person singular)
Correct: When *people* hurry, *they* often make mistakes. (third-person plural)

Fixing Errors in Pronoun-Antecedent Agreement To correct pronoun-antecedent errors, first identify the antecedent of each pronoun. As you work through each paragraph of your draft, consider the following:

1. **For compound antecedents joined by *and*, use a plural personal pronoun.**
2. **For singular antecedents joined by *or* or *nor*, use a singular personal pronoun.**
3. **Check every occurrence of the pronoun *you* to make sure that you have not made a shift in person.**

Gender of Third-Person Singular Pronouns		
Masculine	**Feminine**	**Neuter**
he, him, his, himself	she, her, hers, herself	it, its, itself

Apply It to Your Editing

Review the first and last paragraphs in your draft. Underline each antecedent and circle each pronoun. Check the marked words for pronoun-antecedent agreement and fix any errors.

Student Model: Naomi Barrowclough
Maplewood, NJ

Environmental Un-Consciousness

During a recent Earth Day cleanup, I became disgusted by the amount of trash I picked up within a two-hour period. People had thrown little papers, bits of plastic, and candy wrappers until the mess formed a multicolored carpet over the green grass. Those who litter may not realize that litter creates serious environmental problems.

> In the opening paragraph, Naomi provides a general statement of the problem.

We've all been told not to litter, but it does not seem to sink in. One person may think his or her contribution is only a microscopic addition when viewed against the whole. But if every person shared this sense of irresponsibility, Earth would soon be overwhelmed by pollution.

> Here, the author provides greater detail to explain the problem more fully.

Litter is harmful for many reasons. For one, roadside litter eventually washes into waterways and oceans—water we use for drinking and recreation. Also, animals might entangle themselves or mistake trash for food and swallow it. In our public spaces, children spend a great deal of time in areas where they could be physically harmed by the pollution caused by litter.

There is no simple solution to the problem of litter, only an array of possible solutions with one strategy in common: Create a feeling of ownership over public spaces. Some of the most popular sites for litter are beaches and parks because people feel no sense of ownership over these places. These same people would never litter in their own homes.

> Naomi introduces a general solution here.

To create a feeling of ownership, it is necessary to educate children early about the environmental consequences of littering. According to research done by Keep America Beautiful, a non-profit organization, most people do not feel responsible for public spaces. They think "someone else" will clean up. To change this attitude, schools could lead field trips to local beaches or parks where students pick up trash and test water quality. If kids have to fish two shopping carts from the side of a stream, as I did, they might think twice about throwing something else on the ground. If they see that contaminated water is harmful to both humans and wildlife, they might stop someone they see littering.

> In this paragraph, specific strategies for achieving the solution are introduced.

There is no easy way to stop littering. Fines and policing alone will not do the trick because people will just look before they litter. Until people understand that littering is irresponsible and has devastating environmental consequences, they will continue to litter. The solution lies in education and creating a sense of ownership about our public spaces.

> In the final paragraph, Naomi addresses a potential concern and then restates her solution.

Editing and Proofreading

Check your draft for errors in spelling, grammar, and punctuation.
Focus on Spelling: As you proofread, circle words that you are not sure how to spell, frequently misspell, or seldom use. Then, use reference resources to confirm the correct spelling of the circled words.

Publishing and Presenting

To make the best use of your problem-and-solution essay, share it with people who can help you make a difference.
Send a letter. Send your essay to the appropriate government official, agency, or organization. When you receive a response, share it with your classmates in a presentation. Save both the essay and response in your portfolio.
Make a speech. Deliver your essay as a speech to a group within your school or community that shares your concerns about the problem. Afterward, lead a question-and-answer session. Be sure to modify or restate your answers if the audience seems confused. Report any consequences of your speech to your classmates.

Reflecting on Your Writing

Writer's Journal Jot down your thoughts on writing a problem-and-solution essay. Begin by answering these questions:
  • Which prewriting and drafting strategies were most useful to you?
  • What new insights or techniques may help you analyze and respond to a problem in the future?

Rubric for Self-Assessment

To assess your problem-and-solution essay, use the following rubric.

NC Criteria	Rating Scale				
	not very				very
Focus: How adequately do you explore the problem in the essay?	1	2	3	4	5
Organization: How well do you organize the steps of the solution?	1	2	3	4	5
Support/Elaboration: How convincing are your facts, details, and reasons?	1	2	3	4	5
Style: How appropriate is the language for the audience's knowledge level?	1	2	3	4	5
Conventions: How correct is your grammar, especially your use of pronouns?	1	2	3	4	5

Analyzing Broadcast Media Presentations

While television, radio, the Internet, and other media sources can provide valuable information, you should analyze information critically and evaluate its reliability.

Determine purpose

Media presentations may be intended to entertain, to inform, to persuade, or to achieve a combination of purposes. Knowing the purpose of a presentation will help you establish expectations and evaluate the presentation.

Evaluating the Content

Evaluate evidence and opinions included in the presentation. Determine whether what is presented meets the following criteria.

- **Relevance:** Statements should be related to the point being made. Watch for statements that are included for their shock value only.

- **Reliability:** Facts should come from reliable, verifiable, sources. Opinions should come from experts, individuals, or groups who have experience and knowledge. Propaganda often uses "facts" which have no basis.

- **Consistency:** Statements should be consistent. Watch for statements that are inconsistent and geared to sway and audience.

Evaluating the Methods

Think about the methods used to present the information.

- **Charged Language** Listen for words and phrases that are meant to manipulate, or affect your emotions.

- **Charged Images** Images can also affect emotions. The use of an unflattering image of someone will usually make you think negatively about that person.

- **Use of Stereotypes** Stereotypes are simplified and often negative depictions of groups of people. They are a type of charged, or emotionally laden, content and should not be present in reliable broadcasts.

Activity > *Prepare and Deliver a Speech* > Analyze a television news program or talk show using the Feedback Form as a guide. Share your conclusions in a class discussion.

Standard Course of Study

- Analyze text components and evaluate impact on text and on research. (IR.2.01.2)
- Use visuals and media to make presentations effective in explaining procedures. (IR.2.03.3)

Media Presentation Feedback Form

Rating System
Poor 1 2 3 4 5 Excellent

Use of Facts
____ Relevant Facts
____ Reliable Support
____ Complete Support

Presentation
____ Sets
____ Graphics
____ Speaker's tone
____ Speaker's Clarity

Does the presentation include charged language?

Does it include charged images?

Does it present stereotypes?

Conclusions
Was the presentation objective?

Was the presentation reliable?

A Pocketful of Rye

Agatha Christie
Signet, 2000

Mystery Elderly Miss Jane Marple may not look like a detective, but her keen mind and profound understanding of human nature helps her unravel many mysteries that puzzle England's police. Here, she helps solve the murder of a rich businessman whose unpleasant family falls under suspicion for the crime.

Great Expectations

Charles Dickens
Pearson Prentice Hall, 2000

Novel This justly famous nineteenth-century novel follows the adventures of Pip, a poor young man, who finds his life changed irrevocably when a mysterious benefactor bestows "great expectations" on him.

A Separate Peace

John Knowles
Bantam Books, 1959

Novel Gene and Phineas share a room at Devon, an exclusive New England prep school, during the summer prior to World War II. The boys form a complex bond of friendship that draws out both their best and worst characteristics and ultimately leads to violence, a confession, and the betrayal of trust.

Rosa Parks: My Story

Rosa Parks with Jim Haskins
Puffin Books, 1992

Autobiography Rosa Parks describes her role in the civil rights movement. Her involvement began in 1955 on a bus in Montgomery, Alabama, and continued through the historic Supreme Court decision on segregation in 1956. This is a story of how one person's courage changed the course of the United States.

These titles are available in the Penguin/Prentice Hall Literature Library.
Consult your teacher before choosing one.

Think About It Most people associate comics with superheroes, humorous animals, and amusing people who have exaggerated facial features. As you read this excerpt from *Understanding Comics,* consider how much the writer/ illustrator changes your impressions and ideas about a typical comic strip.

excerpt from

Understanding Comics

Scott McCloud

IN LESS THAN A *YEAR*, I BECAME *TOTALLY OBSESSED* WITH COMICS! I DECIDED TO BECOME A *COMICS ARTIST* IN *10th GRADE* AND BEGAN TO *PRACTICE, PRACTICE, PRACTICE!*

I FELT THAT THERE WAS SOMETHING *LURKING* IN COMICS... SOMETHING THAT HAD *NEVER BEEN DONE.*

SOME KIND OF *HIDDEN POWER!*

BUT WHENEVER I TRIED TO *EXPLAIN* MY FEELING, I FAILED *MISERABLY.*

COMIC BOOKS?! HA! HA! HA!

BUT IT- BUT IT'S- BUH...

SURE, I REALIZED THAT COMIC BOOKS WERE USUALLY *CRUDE, POORLY-DRAWN, SEMILITERATE, CHEAP, DISPOSABLE KIDDIE FARE--*

--*BUT*--

THEY DON'T *HAVE* TO BE!

THE *PROBLEM* WAS THAT FOR *MOST PEOPLE,* THAT WAS WHAT *"COMIC BOOK" MEANT!*

DON'T GIMME THAT *COMIC BOOK* TALK, BARNEY!

IF PEOPLE FAILED TO *UNDERSTAND* COMICS, IT WAS BECAUSE THEY DEFINED WHAT COMICS COULD BE *TOO NARROWLY!*

A *PROPER DEFINITION,* IF WE COULD *FIND* ONE, MIGHT GIVE *LIE* TO THE STEREOTYPES--

--AND SHOW THAT THE *POTENTIAL* OF COMICS IS *LIMITLESS* AND *EXCITING!*

THIS IS WHERE OUR JOURNEY *BEGINS.*

from *Understanding Comics* ■ 173

THE WORLD OF COMICS IS A **HUGE** AND **VARIED** ONE. OUR DEFINITION MUST ENCOMPASS ALL THESE TYPES--

--WHILE NOT BEING **SO** BROAD AS TO INCLUDE ANYTHING WHICH IS CLEARLY **NOT** COMICS.

"**COMICS**" IS THE WORD WORTH DEFINING, AS IT REFERS TO THE MEDIUM **ITSELF**, NOT A SPECIFIC **OBJECT** AS "COMIC BOOK" OR "COMIC STRIP" DO.

WE CAN ALL VISUALIZE **A** COMIC.

BUT WHAT--

--IS--

--COMICS?

THE ARTFORM -- THE *MEDIUM* -- KNOWN AS COMICS IS A *VESSEL* WHICH CAN HOLD ANY *NUMBER* OF *IDEAS* AND *IMAGES*.

COMICS
Writers
ARTISTS
Trends
GENRES
STYLES
subject matter
THEMES

THE *"CONTENT"* OF THOSE IMAGES AND IDEAS IS, OF COURSE, UP TO *CREATORS*, AND WE ALL HAVE DIFFERENT *TASTES*.

~GLUG~
~GLUG~

PTU!!!

~GAAK~
~WHEEEEZ~
~KAF! KAF!~
GLUGH-GGH...

~ahem~

THE *TRICK* IS TO NEVER MISTAKE THE *MESSAGE* --

-- FOR THE *MESSENGER*.

COMICS

AT ONE TIME OR ANOTHER VIRTUALLY *ALL* THE GREAT MEDIA HAVE RECEIVED *CRITICAL EXAMINATION*, IN AND OF *THEMSELVES*.

WRITTEN WORD

MUSIC

VIDEO

THEATRE

VISUAL ART

FILM

BUT FOR *COMICS*, THIS ATTENTION HAS BEEN *RARE*. *

LET'S SEE IF WE CAN HELP *RECTIFY* THE SITUATION.

EISNER'S TERM SEEMS LIKE A GOOD PLACE TO *START.*

LET'S SEE IF WE CAN EXPAND IT TO A PROPER DICTIONARY-STYLE DEFINITION.

ANY *IDEAS?*

SEQUENTIAL ART

THERE ARE A LOT OF DIFFERENT *KINDS* OF ART. HOW ABOUT SOMETHING A LITTLE MORE *SPECIFIC?*

OKAY.

HOW'S *THIS?*

SEQUENTIAL *VISUAL* ART

HEY, WHAT ABOUT *ANIMATION?!*

BEG PARDON?

SEQUENTIAL VISUAL ART

ISN'T ANIMATED FILM JUST *VISUAL ART IN SEQUENCE?*

HMM... GOOD POINT.

I GUESS THE BASIC DIFFERENCE IS THAT ANIMATION IS SEQUENTIAL IN *TIME* BUT NOT SPATIALLY *JUXTAPOSED** AS COMICS ARE.

EACH SUCCESSIVE FRAME OF A *MOVIE* IS PROJECTED ON EXACTLY THE *SAME* SPACE -- THE *SCREEN* -- WHILE EACH FRAME OF *COMICS* MUST OCCUPY A *DIFFERENT* SPACE.

SPACE DOES FOR *COMICS* WHAT *TIME* DOES FOR *FILM!*

WHRRRR RRRR

Meet the Author

Scott McCloud started drawing comics at age twelve. After graduating from college, he began his career as a cartoonist. He has since published an award-winning comic book series called *Zot!* as well as *Destroy!*, a parody of superhero comics.

Readings in Media
Talk About It

Use these questions to guide a discussion of this selection.

1. Do you accept McCloud's final definition of comics?
2. McCloud compares comics to art forms such as film, music, and theater. Choose one of the following items to discuss with a group.
   - Do you think the same level of skill, imagination, and effort used to create other art forms is needed to create comics? Explain.
   - Government funding is sometimes given to support the arts. Do you think funding should be given to comic writers? Why or why not?

   Choose a point person to share your ideas with the class.

Unit
2

Short Stories

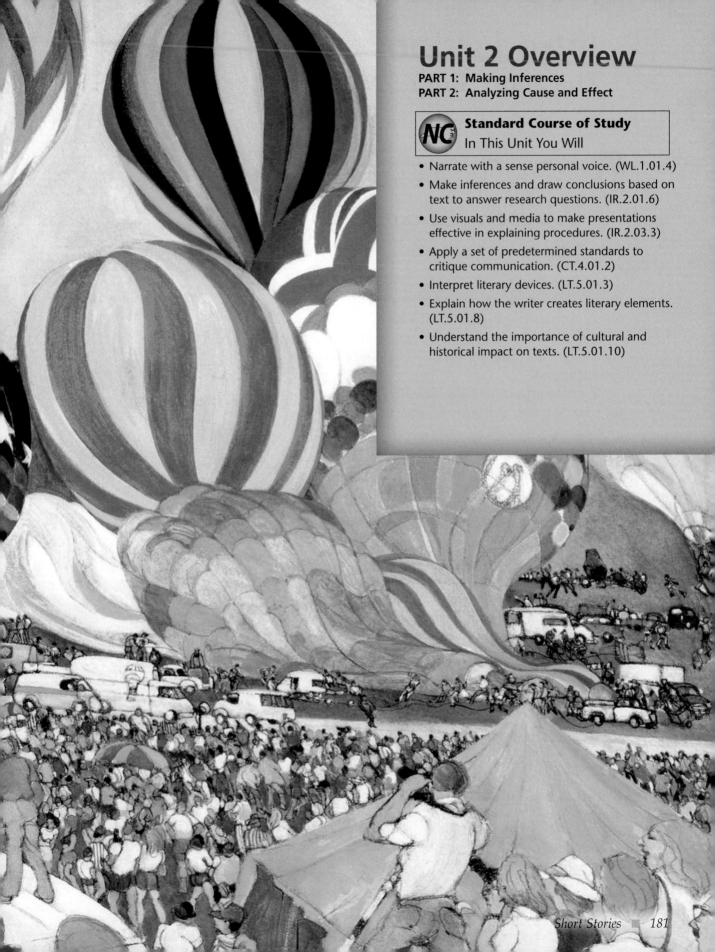

Unit 2 Overview

PART 1: Making Inferences
PART 2: Analyzing Cause and Effect

> ### Standard Course of Study
> In This Unit You Will

- Narrate with a sense personal voice. (WL.1.01.4)
- Make inferences and draw conclusions based on text to answer research questions. (IR.2.01.6)
- Use visuals and media to make presentations effective in explaining procedures. (IR.2.03.3)
- Apply a set of predetermined standards to critique communication. (CT.4.01.2)
- Interpret literary devices. (LT.5.01.3)
- Explain how the writer creates literary elements. (LT.5.01.8)
- Understand the importance of cultural and historical impact on texts. (LT.5.01.10)

Introduction:
The Short Story

Wayson Choy

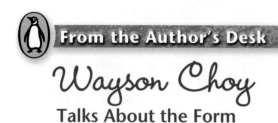

From the Author's Desk

Wayson Choy
Talks About the Form

Your life, like mine, is surrounded by all kinds of stories. We collect them, and we tell them. Think how you are always hungry for stories that inspire or scare you, that make you thoughtful about important things, or remind you, in fresh ways, of your present or past.

In fact, everyone's life is an assemblage of short stories—like the kind that writers create to enhance our understanding of our own decisive moments and revelations.

▲ **Wayson Choy** draws on his own boyhood memories of Vancouver's Chinatown to re-create the experiences of Chinese Canadians who lived more than half a century ago.

Short Stories Deepen Our Awareness

More than just entertainment, a fine **short story** will always focus on a fragment of truth that matters to you. Such a story often relates a brief incident, to create a unity—a harmony of details—that will expose you to a deeper experience of life. The climax of a good short story can flash inside you like a bolt of lightning or gently glow like a candle. In fact, the light a fine story gives to you can linger for a lifetime.

For example, when I first read Shirley Jackson's "The Lottery," I came to realize that ordinary people—like you or me—can willfully take part in chilling,

▶ **Critical Viewing** Choy describes how important a short story can be for a reader. How does this illustration dramatize that importance? **[Interpret]**

horrific events. And when I first read Truman Capote's "A Christmas Memory," his story made me think in new ways about a family member who loved me when I was very young, and who was now gone. Like me, you may discover that short stories can powerfully disturb and awaken you.

The Best Stories Say, *"You Are Not Alone"*

But what makes a short story a good one? The passage here by the famous writer Somerset Maugham recalls Edgar Allan Poe's idea that a good story—like those collected in this unit—will "sparkle, excite or impress." Isn't that what your own favorite stories do for you?

The short story is a work of fiction created from the writer's imagination and personal vision. If you surrender to the writer's **narrative voice**—that enchanted moment when you begin to *hear* a storytelling voice—you will be transported into another world. And always, the best short stories will say to the deepest part of you . . . *You are not alone.*

> *It is not hard to state what Poe meant by a good short story: it is a piece of fiction, dealing with a single incident, material or spiritual, that can be read at a sitting; it is original, it must sparkle, excite or impress; and it must have a unity of effect or impression.*
>
> **from "Credo of a Storyteller"**
> —W. Somerset Maugham

More About Wayson Choy

In his books, Wayson Choy (b. 1939) deals with a theme arising from the immigrant experience—the conflicts between generations and cultures. In *The Jade Peony*, he tells how members of the Chen family must balance their allegiance to the past and their dreams for the future in order to form their own identities. Choy published this novel, his first, when he was in his late fifties. He taught for many years at Humber College, Toronto, Canada.

Fast Facts

▶ Late in life, Choy learned from a former babysitter that he had been adopted.

▶ Choy, who believes in luck, bought seven lottery tickets (he considers seven a lucky number) and won a large prize!

Exploring Short Stories

Elements of Short Stories

A **short story** is a brief work of fiction meant to be read in one sitting. Due to the length of a short story (usually between 500 and 10,000 words), it must be crafted in a concise, compact manner that accomplishes its purpose in relatively few words.

The following are some of the key elements of a short story.

Plot A short story's **plot** is its series of related events. Throughout the course of a story's plot, events unfold, build to a **climax** (or high point), and are then brought to a conclusion during the **resolution.**

Conflict The plot of a short story usually focuses on a **conflict,** or struggle. There are two main types of conflict in literature:

- An **external conflict** is a struggle between two characters, between an individual and a group, or between a character and a force of nature.
- An **internal conflict** is a struggle within the mind of one character.

Character The **characters** in a story are the personalities who participate in the action. Usually, characters are human beings, but they can also be animals or even objects. Writers use these methods of **characterization** to tell readers about characters:

- providing descriptions of what characters look like
- describing characters' words and actions
- showing characters interacting with one another
- sharing characters' thoughts and feelings

Setting The **setting** of a story is the time and place of the action.

- The time of a setting can be past, present, or future, and it may also include a specific year, season, or hour of day.
- Place can refer to the social, economic, or cultural environment as well as to a specific geographic location in a country, town, or community.

The setting provides a stage for the action of a story. It can also create a mood or an atmosphere or present a conflict for the characters to face.

Symbol A **symbol** is a person, place, or object that has a literal meaning and also stands for something larger, such as an idea or an emotion. Symbols may be particular to a specific literary work or universal.

Theme The **theme** of a short story is its central message or insight into life. This message may be stated or implied.

- A **stated theme** is expressed directly by the author.
- An **implied theme** is suggested indirectly through the experiences of the characters or through the events and the setting of the work.

Check Your Understanding

Choose the letter of the short story element that best matches each item.

1. A temple in India   **A** setting   **B** character
2. A man struggles against the ocean waves   **A** theme   **B** conflict
3. A poor woman is unhappy with her life   **A** character   **B** plot
4. A girl begins to appreciate her culture   **A** theme   **B** setting
5. Two enemies become friends   **A** setting   **B** plot

From the Author's Desk
Wayson Choy Introduces "The Jade Peony"

During World War II, while my immigrant parents worked all hours, I was cared for by Chinatown's village elders in Vancouver, Canada. These elders told me such vivid myths involving ghosts, magic amulets, hissing dragons, and talking foxes, that I dreamed one day that I would tell my own tales.

Finding Inspiration

As a student, when I was assigned to write a story based on the color "pink"—I was stuck. My aunt recalled that rare jades were pink in tone, and that afternoon, another aunt mentioned how the peonies were flowering in her garden.

Suddenly, something magical happened: the two ideas came together. My imagination glimpsed a wrinkled hand passing a carved pink jade into a boy's small palm. After imagining these **characters,** the first words of "The Jade Peony" came to me: "When grandmama died at the age of 83 . . ."

Themes: Meanings and Questions That Haunt You

After some research and a dozen revisions, I realized that I had been focusing on life and dying, and the realities of love between generations. Years later, I understood that there were **themes,** meanings and questions —*hauntings*—that had attached themselves to my story. For example, how many kinds of love were there? Were spirits real? And was dying the end of everything? One theme came to possess me: *Love has no rules.* Therefore, I now write believing that I, and my readers, will continue to discover similar meanings.

Symbol: What Does the Jade Peony Mean?

But I wondered why I came up with the jade peony—what, as a **symbol,** did the amulet stand for? I realized it has many layers of meaning, related to love and memory. I thought of the jade left to me by my mother and father, just as you might think about some important legacy left to you by a friend or a family member. I also thought of the apron my mother last wore before she was rushed to the hospital. Whenever I think of that apron, I see my dead mother alive again, a vivid ghost standing over her stove to feed us all. Finally, I as a writer created the symbol of the jade peony to make the people I love come alive again.

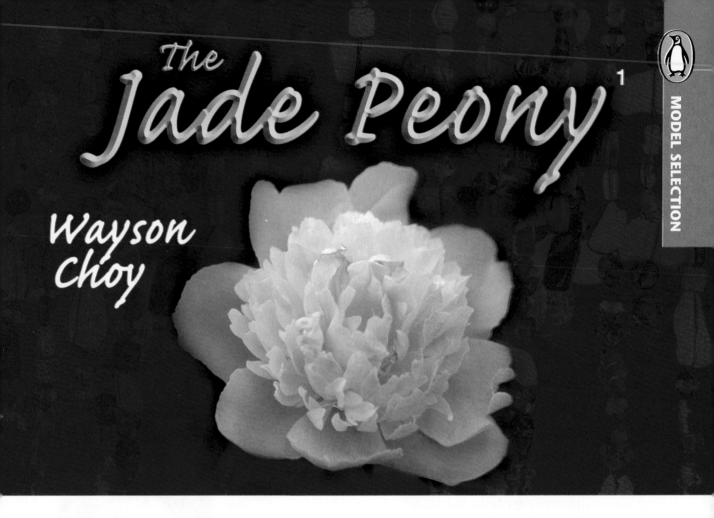

The Jade Peony

Wayson Choy

W hen Grandmama died at 83 our whole household held its breath. She had promised us a sign of her leaving, final proof that her present life had ended well. My parents knew that without any clear sign, our own family fortunes could be altered, threatened. My stepmother looked endlessly into the small cluttered room the ancient lady had occupied. Nothing was touched; nothing changed. My father, thinking that a sign should appear in Grandmama's garden, looked at the frost-killed shoots and cringed: *no, that could not be it.*

My two older teenage brothers and my sister, Liang, age 14, were embarrassed by my parents' behavior. What would all the white people in Vancouver[2] think of us? We were Canadians now, *Chinese-Canadians*, a hyphenated reality that my parents could never accept. So it seemed, for different reasons, we all held our breath waiting for *something.*

---

1. **Jade Peony** (pē′ ə nē) jade is a hard, dense gemstone; a peony is a common garden flower, the Chinese variety of which produces large, single blossoms in early summer.
2. **Vancouver** (van kōō′ vər) large city in the province of British Columbia, Canada.

Wayson Choy
Author's Insight
With references to signs and threatened fortunes, I wanted to create a ghostly mystery about the grandmother's dying.

Reading Check

What had Grandmama promised her family?

I was eight when she died. For days she had resisted going into the hospital . . . *a cold, just a cold* . . . and instead gave constant instruction to my stepmother and sister on the boiling of ginseng roots mixed with bitter extract.[3] At night, between wracking coughs and deadly silences, Grandmama had her back and chest rubbed with heated camphor[4] oil and sipped a bluish decoction[5] of an herb called Peacock's Tail. When all these failed to abate her fever, she began to arrange the details of her will. This she did with my father, confessing finally: "I am too stubborn. The only cure for old age is to die."

My father wept to hear this. I stood beside her bed; she turned to me. Her round face looked darker, and the gentleness of her eyes, the thin, arching eyebrows, seemed weary. I brushed the few strands of gray, brittle hair from her face; she managed to smile at me. Being the youngest, I had spent nearly all my time with her and could not imagine that we would ever be parted. Yet when she spoke, and her voice hesitated, cracked, the somber shadows of her room chilled me. Her wrinkled brow grew wet with fever, and her small body seemed even more diminutive.

"I—I am going to the hospital, Grandson." Her hand reached out for mine. "You know, Little Son, whatever happens I will never leave you." Her palm felt plush and warm, the slender, old fingers boney and firm, so magically strong was her grip that I could not imagine how she could ever part from me. Ever.

Her hands *were* magical. My most vivid memories are of her hands: long, elegant fingers, with impeccable nails, a skein[6] of fine, barely-seen veins, and wrinkled skin like light pine. Those hands were quick when she taught me, at six, simple tricks of juggling, learnt when she was a village girl in Southern Canton;[7] a troupe of actors had stayed on her father's farm. One of them, "tall and pale as the whiteness of petals," fell in love with her, promising to return. In her last years his image came back like a third being in our two lives. He had been magician, acrobat, juggler, and some of the things he taught her she had absorbed and passed on to me through her stories and games. But above all, without realizing it then, her hands conveyed to me the quality of their love.

Most marvelous for me was the quick-witted skill her hands revealed in making windchimes for our birthdays: windchimes in the likeness of her lost friend's only present to her, made of bits of

---

3. **ginseng** (jin′ sen′) **roots . . . bitter extract** ginseng is a Chinese herb known for its healing properties; bitter extract is a liquid made from bitter plants or herbs.
4. **camphor** (kam′ fər) *n.* thick substance made from the bark and wood of the camphor tree.
5. **decoction** (dē käk′ shən) *n.* substance extracted by boiling.
6. **skein** (skān) *n.* something that resembles coiled yarn or thread.
7. **Canton** (kan tän′) major port city in southeastern China.

Short Story
Plot Choy establishes a conflict around Grandmama's refusal to go to the hospital.

▼ **Critical Viewing**
In what ways does this sculpture convey a sense of "magical" hands similar to Grandmama's? **[Connect]**

string and scraps, in the center of which once hung a precious jade peony. This wondrous gift to her broke apart years ago, in China, but Grandmama kept the jade pendant[8] in a tiny red silk envelope, and kept it always in her pocket, until her death.

These were not ordinary, carelessly made chimes, such as those you now find in our Chinatown[9] stores, whose rattling noises drive you mad. But making her special ones caused <u>dissension</u> in our family, and some shame. Each one that she made was created from a treasure trove of glass fragments and castaway costume jewelry, in the same way that her first windchime had been made. The problem for the rest of the family was in the fact that Grandmama looked for these treasures wandering the back alleys of Keefer and Pender Streets,[10] peering into our neighbors' garbage cans, chasing away hungry, nervous cats and shouting curses at them.

"All our friends are laughing at us!" Older Brother Jung said at last to my father, when Grandmama was away having tea at Mrs. Lim's.

"We are not poor," Oldest Brother Kiam declared, "Yet she and Sek-Lung poke through those awful things as if—" he shoved me in frustration and I stumbled against my sister, "—they were beggars!"

"She will make Little Brother crazy!" Sister Liang said. Without warning, she punched me sharply in the back; I jumped. "You see, look how *nervous* he is!"

I lifted my foot slightly, enough to swing it back and kick Liang in the shin. She yelled and pulled back her fist to punch me again. Jung made a menacing move towards me.

"Stop this, all of you!" My father shook his head in exasperation. How could he dare tell the Grand Old One, his aging mother, that what was somehow appropriate in a poor village in China, was an <u>abomination</u> here. How could he prevent me, his youngest, from accompanying her? If she went walking into those alleyways alone she could well be attacked by hoodlums. "She is not a beggar looking for food. She is searching for—for. . . ."

My stepmother attempted to speak, then fell silent. She, too, seemed perplexed and somewhat ashamed. They all loved Grandmama, but she was *inconvenient*, unsettling.

As for our neighbors, most understood Grandmama to be harmlessly crazy, others that she did indeed make lovely toys but for what purpose? *Why?* they asked, and the stories she told me, of the juggler who smiled at her, flashed in my head.

---

8. **pendant** (pen´ dənt) *n.* hanging ornament, as on a necklace.
9. **Chinatown** (chī´ nə toun´) *n.* Chinese quarter of any city outside of China; in this case, of Vancouver.
10. **Keefer and Pender Streets** principal streets of Vancouver's Chinatown.

Vocabulary Builder
dissension (di sen´ shən) *n.* difference of opinion; disagreement

Wayson Choy
Author's Insight
Here I wanted to show how the wind chimes were symbolically important to some family members but provoked a lot of conflict and inner turmoil among the others.

Vocabulary Builder
abomination (ə bäm´ ə nā´ shən) *n.* anything hateful and disgusting

Reading Check

From whom did Grandmama learn juggling?

Finally, by their cutting remarks, the family did exert enough pressure so that Grandmama and I no longer openly announced our expeditions. Instead, she took me with her on "shopping trips," ostensibly for clothes or groceries, while in fact we spent most of our time exploring stranger and more distant neighborhoods, searching for splendid junk: jangling pieces of a vase, cranberry glass fragments embossed with leaves, discarded glass beads from Woolworth[11] necklaces. . . . We would sneak them all home in brown rice sacks, folded into small parcels, and put them under her bed. During the day when the family was away at school or work, we brought them out and washed every item in a large black pot of boiling lye[12] and water, dried them quickly, carefully, and returned them, sparkling, under her bed.

Our greatest excitement occurred when a fire gutted the large Chinese Presbyterian Church, three blocks from our house. Over the still-smoking ruins the next day, Grandmama and I rushed precariously over the blackened beams to pick out the stained glass that glittered in the sunlight. Small figure bent over, wrapped against the autumn cold in a dark blue quilted coat, happily gathering each piece like gold, she became my spiritual playmate: "There's a good one! *There!*"

Hours later, soot-covered and smelling of smoke, we came home with a carton full of delicate fragments, still early enough to steal them all into the house and put the small box under her bed. "These are special pieces," she said, giving the box a last push, "because they come from a sacred place." She slowly got up and I saw, for the first time, her hand begin to shake. But then, in her joy, she embraced me. Both of our hearts were racing, as if we were two dreamers. I buried my face in her blue quilt, and for a moment, the whole world seemed silent.

---

11. **Woolworth** a variety store belonging to the chain founded by Frank Woolworth in 1879.
12. **lye** (lī) *n.* substance derived from wood ashes, commonly used in making soap or for washing.

"My juggler," she said, "he never came back to me from Honan[13] . . . perhaps the famine. . . ." Her voice began to quake. "But I shall have my sacred windchime . . . I shall have it again."

One evening, when the family was gathered in their usual places in the parlor, Grandmama gave me her secret nod: a slight wink of her eye and a flaring of her nostrils. There was *trouble* in the air. Supper had gone badly, school examinations were due, father had failed to meet an editorial deadline at the *Vancouver Chinese Times*. A huge sigh came from Sister Liang.

"But it is useless this Chinese they teach you!" she lamented, turning to Stepmother for support. Silence. Liang frowned, dejected, and went back to her Chinese book, bending the covers back.

"Father," Oldest Brother Kiam began, waving his bamboo brush in the air, "you must realize that this Mandarin only confuses us. We are Cantonese[14] speakers. . . ."

"And you do not complain about Latin, French or German in your English school?" Father rattled his newspaper, a signal that his patience was ending.

"But, Father, those languages are *scientific*," Kiam jabbed his brush in the air. "We are now in a scientific, logical world."

Father was silent. We could all hear Grandmama's rocker.

"What about Sek-Lung?" Older Brother Jung pointed angrily at me. "He was sick last year, but this year he should have at least started Chinese school, instead of picking over garbage cans!"

"He starts next year," Father said, in a hard tone that immediately warned everyone to be silent. Liang slammed her book.

Grandmama went on rocking quietly in her chair. She complimented my mother on her knitting, made a remark about the "strong beauty" of Kiam's brushstrokes which, in spite of himself, immensely pleased him. All this babbling noise was her family torn and confused in a strange land: everything here was so very foreign and scientific.

The truth was, I was sorry not to have started school the year before. In my innocence I had imagined going to school meant certain privileges worthy of all my brothers' and sister's complaints. The fact that my lung infection in my fifth and sixth years, mistakenly diagnosed as TB,[15] earned me some <u>reprieve</u>, only made me long for school the more. Each member of the family took turns on Sunday,

Vocabulary Builder
reprieve (ri prēv´) *n.* temporary relief; postponement of a penalty

✓ **Reading Check**

What "treasures" do the old woman and her grandson find among the ruins of the church?

---

13. Honan (hō´ nän´) province in east central China.
14. Mandarin (man´ də rin) **. . . Cantonese** (kan´ tə nēz´) Mandarin is the most commonly spoken form of Chinese; Cantonese is a variety of Chinese spoken in some parts of China, including the cities of Canton and Hong Kong, and by most Chinese emigrants.
15. TB (tē´ bē´) *n.* abbreviation for tuberculosis, a contagious disease that begins in the lungs.

teaching me or annoying me. But it was the countless hours I spent with Grandmama that were my real education. Tapping me on my head she would say, "Come, Sek-Lung, we have *our* work," and we would walk up the stairs to her small crowded room. There, in the midst of her antique shawls, the old ancestral calligraphy and multi-colored embroidered hangings, beneath the mysterious shelves of sweet herbs and bitter potions, we would continue doing what we had started that morning: the elaborate windchime for her death.

"I can't last forever," she declared, when she let me in on the secret of this one. "It will sing and dance and glitter," her long fingers stretched into the air, pantomiming the waving motion of her ghost chimes; "My spirit will hear its sounds and see its light and return to this house and say goodbye to you."

Deftly she reached into the carton she had placed on the chair beside me. She picked out a fish-shape amber piece, and with a long needle-like tool and a steel ruler, she scored[16] it. Pressing the blade of a cleaver against the line, with the fingers of her other hand, she lifted up the glass until it cleanly *snapped* into the exact shape she required. Her hand began to tremble, the tips of her fingers to shiver, like rippling water.

"You see that, Little One?" She held her hand up. "That is my body fighting with Death. He is in this room now."

My eyes darted in panic, but Grandmama remained calm, undisturbed, and went on with her work. Then I remembered the glue and uncorked the jar for her. Soon the graceful ritual movements of her hand returned to her, and I became lost in the magic of her task: she dabbed a cabalistic[17] mixture of glue on one end and skillfully dropped the braided end of a silk thread into it. This part always amazed me: the braiding would slowly, *very* slowly, *unknot*, fanning out like a prized fishtail. In a few seconds the clear, homemade glue began to harden as I blew lightly over it, welding to itself each separate silk strand.

Each jam-sized pot of glue was precious; each large cork had been wrapped with a fragment of pink silk. I remember this part vividly, because each cork was treated to a special rite. First we went shopping in the best silk stores in Chinatown for the perfect square of silk she required. It had to be a deep pink, a shade of color blushing toward red. And the tone had to match — as closely as

▲ **Critical Viewing**
How does this image of a windchime compare to the ones Grandmama likes to make? [**Compare and Contrast**]

Wayson Choy
Author's Insight
I want to establish these realistic details—a pot of glue, a cork—so that what happens near the end with the appearance of an albino cat is rooted in the real.

---

16. scored (skôr'd) *v.* put a notch or groove in.
17. cabalistic (kab′ ə lis′ tik) *adj.* relating to a secret or mystical belief or practice.

possible — her precious jade carving, the small peony of white and light-red jade, her most lucky possession. In the center of this semi-translucent carving, no more than an inch wide, was a pool of pink light, its veins swirling out into the petals of the flower.

"This color is the color of my spirit," she said, holding it up to the window so I could see the delicate pastel against the broad strokes of sunlight. She dropped her voice, and I held my breath at the wonder of the color. "This was given to me by the young actor who taught me how to juggle. He had four of them, and each one had a center of this rare color, the color of Good Fortune." The pendant seemed to pulse as she turned it: "Oh, Sek-Lung! He had white hair and white skin *to his toes*! It's *true*, I saw him bathing." She laughed and blushed, her eyes softened at the memory. The silk had to match the pink heart of her pendant: the color was magical for her, to hold the unraveling strands of her memory. . . .

It was just six months before she died that we really began to work on her last windchime. Three thin bamboo sticks were steamed and bent into circlets; 30 exact lengths of silk thread, the strongest kind, were cut and braided at both ends and glued to stained glass. Her hands worked on their own command, each hand racing with a life of its own: cutting, snapping, braiding, knotting. . . . Sometimes she breathed heavily and her small body, growing thinner, sagged against me. *Death*, I thought, *He is in this room*, and I would work harder alongside her. For months Grandmama and I did this every other evening, a half dozen pieces each time. The shaking in her hand grew worse, but we said nothing. Finally, after discarding hundreds, she told me she had the necessary 30 pieces. But this time, because it was a sacred chime, I would not be permitted to help her tie it up or have the joy of raising it. "Once tied," she said, holding me against my disappointment, "not even I can raise it. Not a sound must it make until I have died."

"What will happen?"

"Your father will then take the center braided strand and raise it. He will hang it against my bedroom window so that my ghost may see it, and hear it, and return. I must say goodbye to this world properly or wander in this foreign land forever."

"You can take the streetcar!" I blurted, suddenly shocked that she actually meant to leave me. I thought I could hear the clear-chromatic chimes, see the shimmering colors on the wall: I fell against her and cried, and there in my crying I knew that she would die. I can still remember the touch of her hand on my head, and the smell of her thick woolen sweater pressed against my face. "I will always be with you, Little Sek-Lung, but in a different way . . . you'll see."

Short Story
Symbol In this passage, Choy connects the windchime with Grandmama's spirit, both in youth and old age.

Short Story
Plot With this discussion of the death, the author starts to bring the story full circle, back to the beginning discussion of "signs."

Reading Check

What does Grandmama say is the color of her spirit?

The Jade Peony ■ 193

Months went by, and nothing happened. Then one late September evening, when I had just come home from Chinese School, Grandmama was preparing supper when she looked out our kitchen window and saw a cat—a long, lean white cat—jump into our garbage pail and knock it over. She ran out to chase it away, shouting curses at it. She did not have her thick sweater on and when she came back into the house, a chill gripped her. She leaned against the door: "That was not a cat," she said, and the odd tone of her voice caused my father to look with alarm at her. "I can not take back my curses. It is too late." She took hold of my father's arm: "It was all white and had pink eyes like sacred fire."

My father started at this, and they both looked pale. My brothers and sister, clearing the table, froze in their gestures.

"The fog has confused you," Stepmother said. "It was just a cat."

But Grandmama shook her head, for she knew it was a sign. "I will not live forever," she said. "I am prepared."

The next morning she was confined to her bed with a severe cold. Sitting by her, playing with some of my toys, I asked her about the cat: "Why did father jump at the cat with the pink eyes? He didn't see it, you did."

"But he and your mother know what it means."

"What?"

"My friend, the juggler, the magician, was as pale as white jade, and he had pink eyes." I thought she would begin to tell me one of her stories, a tale of enchantment or of a wondrous adventure, but she only paused to swallow; her eyes glittered, lost in memory. She took my hand, gently opening and closing her fingers over it. "Sek-Lung," she sighed, "*he* has come back to me."

Then Grandmama sank back into her pillow and the embroidered flowers lifted to frame her wrinkled face. I saw her hand over my own, and my own began to tremble. I fell fitfully asleep by her side. When I woke up it was dark and her bed was empty. She had been taken to the hospital and I was not permitted to visit.

A few days after that she died of the complications of pneumonia. Immediately after her death my father came home and said nothing to us, but walked up the stairs to her room, pulled aside the drawn lace curtains of her window and lifted the windchimes to the sky.

I began to cry and quickly put my hand in my pocket for a handkerchief. Instead, caught between my fingers, was the small, round firmness of the jade peony. In my mind's eye I saw Grandmama smile and heard, softly, the pink center beat like a beautiful, cramped heart.

Q. Why did you tell this story in the first person?

A. I needed the reader to assume the world of the little boy—that is, to inhabit his world and to identify solely with his point of view. His "narrative voice" would tell his own truth as he experienced it with his beloved grandmother. The reader would then be locked into experiencing things that the more sensible family members could not understand. If the story works, you, the reader, might recall someone who loved or loves you as much.

Q. What is the meaning of the jade peony?

A. Chinese people believe that jade is very special, because the gemstone can inherit the good qualities, the spirit, of the person who owns it. Therefore, jade pieces, whether in the form of pendants, rings, or carved items, are often passed on from one beloved person to another.

Student Corner

Q. Why do you think the grandmother was able to develop such a close relationship with the narrator?
                                     —Jacquelyn Simone, Endicott, New York

A. The grandmother and grandson were left at home alone together for a long period. During this time, she shared with him her life stories and her love of the old ways, and the young boy was hungry to know everything from someone who paid him so much attention. They both had a need to belong to each other, since the rest of the family did not have much time for them, nor did the family entirely approve of the two searching in the alleyways for material to make the windchimes. In the end, they found something deeply meaningful between themselves, more than the others ever understood.

 ## Writing Workshop: *Work in Progress*

Problem/Solution Essay

Think of problems or issues that concern people in your school or community. Jot down five problems that you think can be solved. Then, choose one of those problems and write a statement that offers a possible solution. Put these notes in your writing folder.

Apply the Skills

Thinking About the Selection

1. **Respond:** What do you think of the relationship between Sek-Lung and his grandmother? Explain.

2. **(a) Recall:** Who gave the grandmother her first windchime? **(b) Infer:** Why do you think the making of windchimes became such a meaningful activity in the grandmother's later years?

3. **(a) Compare and Contrast:** How do Sek-Lung's reactions to his grandmother's activities differ from those of the other family members? **(b) Analyze:** How do you account for these differing attitudes within one family?

4. **(a) Infer:** What is different about the making of the grandmother's last windchime? **(b) Analyze:** What meaning will this windchime have for Sek-Lung and his family?

Short Story Review

5. Consider the setting, plot, and characters in "The Jade Peony." Which do you think is the most important element in this **short story**? Support your answer with details from the story.

6. **(a)** What is the underlying theme, or message, of this story? **(b)** Complete a chart like the one shown to examine details in the story. List events, actions, statements, or descriptions that you think are important to the story. Then, complete the rest of the chart. **(c)** Share your ideas with a partner. Finally, explain how your discussion did or did not change your interpretation of the story's theme.

What It Says	What It Means	Why It Is Important

QuickReview

Story at a Glance
A young boy forges a special bond with his grandmother.

Go Online
Assessment

For: Self-test
Visit: www.PHSchool.com
Web Code: epa-6201

Short Story: a brief work of fiction

Characters: the personalities who participate in the action of a story

Theme: the central message or insight of a literary work

Research the Author

Like Sek-Lung, Wayson Choy is both Chinese and Canadian. Using both Internet and print sources, create an **oral report** to discuss Choy's insights into his dual heritage. Follow these steps:

- Read biographical articles and interviews with Choy, and scan Choy's fictional works for comments that reflect his heritage.
- Select the most useful passages, and write a brief introduction. Then, write notes to connect and explain Choy's comments.
- Deliver your oral report to classmates. As you speak, include transitional words and phrases to clearly connect your ideas with passages from your research.

Skills You Will Learn

Literary Analysis: *Conflict and Resolution*

Reading Skill: *Identify Details to Make Inferences*

Reading Skill: *Evaluate Visual Aids*

Literary Analysis: *Irony and Surprise Ending*

Reading Skill: *Use Prior Knowledge to Make Inferences*

Literary Analysis: *Setting*

Literature You Will Read

Reading and Vocabulary Skills Preview

Reading: Make Inferences

> **Inferences** are logical assumptions about information or ideas that are not directly stated.

Standard Course of Study

- Analyze elements of informational environment in text when answering research questions. (IR.2.01.11)
- Make inferences and drawing conclusions when critiquing communication. (CT.4.03.6)

Skills and Strategies You Will Learn in Part 1

In Part 1 you will learn to

- **identify details** to **make inferences** (p. 292)
- **use prior knowledge** and experiences to **make inferences** (p. 320)
- **use visual aids** as a basis for **inferences** (p. 344)

Using the Skills and Strategies in Part 1

In Part 1, you will learn to pay attention to details and visual aids that act as thinking clues. You will also learn to add your own knowledge and experience to these details in order to infer ideas that are not directly stated.

Identifying details and applying your knowledge helps you to infer important concepts in a work.

This example shows you how you will apply the skills and strategies you will learn in Part 1.

> **Example:** Joe tensed when he heard the low growl and saw a dark shape coming toward the cabin. He held the lantern higher, then breathed a sigh of relief. "Skip!" he called out. "Where have you been?"

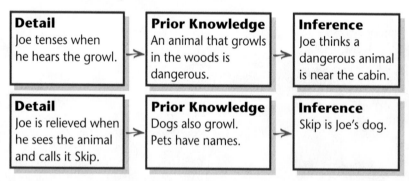

Detail	Prior Knowledge	Inference
Joe tenses when he hears the growl.	An animal that growls in the woods is dangerous.	Joe thinks a dangerous animal is near the cabin.
Joe is relieved when he sees the animal and calls it Skip.	Dogs also growl. Pets have names.	Skip is Joe's dog.

Academic Vocabulary: Words for Understanding Literature

The following words will help you talk and write about your understanding of literature.

Word	Definition	Example Sentence
aspect *n.*	an element or a part	One important *aspect* of Poe's writing is his use of details.
motive *n.*	the reason a person acts in a certain way.	The antagonist's *motive* was still not clear by the middle of the novel.
emotion *n.*	a feeling	The work evokes strong *emotions*.
circumstance *n.*	a fact or an event	We analyzed the *circumstances* that contributed to the conflict.
categorize *v.*	classify; place within a group	We *categorized* the symbols by color.

Vocabulary Skill: Roots

▶ A word **root** is the part of a word that contains its basic meaning.

In Part 1 you will learn:
- Latin root *–spec–* (p. 238)
- Latin root *–mot–* (p. 264)
- Latin root *–circum–* (p. 238)

Knowing the meaning of common Latin word roots helps you understand word meanings and see connections in word meanings. The chart shows two words that share the root *–spec–* meaning "see."

spectator	*spectacle*
one who sees or watches an event without taking part in it	something strange or remarkable to look at

Activity Use a dictionary to find a word that contains each root: *–spec–*, *–circum–*, and *–mot–*. Write a definition of each word, and explain how the word root relates to the definition.

Practice these skills with either "American History" (p. 202) or "The Most Dangerous Game" (p. 215).

Literary Analysis

Conflict is a struggle between opposing forces:

- With **external conflict,** a character struggles against an outside force, such as another character, society, or nature.

- With **internal conflict,** a character grapples with his or her own opposing feelings, beliefs, needs, or desires.

In narrative literature—works that tell stories—conflict and the search for a solution drive the plot. The solution usually occurs near the end of a story, during the **resolution.**

In some stories, however, the conflict is not truly solved. Instead, the character has an **epiphany,** or sudden flash of insight. The conflict remains, but the character's feelings about it change. As you read, notice conflicts characters face and decide whether they are truly resolved.

Reading Skill

Inferences are logical assumptions based on details in a story. Making inferences about a text helps you understand information that is not stated directly. To make inferences as you read, **ask questions** such as these about characters' feelings and behavior:

- *What does this detail show about the reasons for a character's actions or words?*

- *What does this passage say about the character's unspoken feelings?*

Use a chart like the one shown to make inferences as you read.

Standard Course of Study

- Apply a set of predetermined standards to critique communication. (CT.4.01.2)
- Uses varying sentence types purposefully, correctly, and for specific effect. (GU.6.01.1)
- Select verb tense to show an appropriate sense of time. (GU.6.01.2)

Detail
The door was painted green, the color of hope.

↓

Question
Why might a writer describe a door as having the color of an emotion?

↓

Inference
The door stands for opportunity.

Vocabulary Builder

American History

- **tenement** (ten´ ə mənt) *n.* apartment house, often run-down (p. 203) *Many families lived in the large <u>tenement</u>.*

- **profound** (prō found´) *adj.* deep; intense (p. 204) *Mia felt <u>profound</u> sorrow when her dog died.*

- **vigilant** (vij´ ə lənt) *adj.* watchful (p. 206) *The guard kept a <u>vigilant</u> eye on the candidate.*

- **dilapidated** (də lap´ ə dāt´ id) *adj.* decayed (p. 210) *The old furniture looked <u>dilapidated</u>.*

The Most Dangerous Game

- **palpable** (pal´ pə bəl) *adj.* able to be felt; easily perceived (p. 215) *The tension during the exam was <u>palpable</u>.*

- **indolently** (in´ də lənt lē) *adv.* lazily; idly (p. 217) *The sleepy cat yawned <u>indolently</u>.*

- **scruples** (scroo´ pəlz) *n.* misgivings about something one feels is wrong (p. 225) *Her <u>scruples</u> prevented her from lying.*

- **futile** (fyoot´ ´l) *adj.* useless; hopeless (p. 230) *My attempt to catch the mouse proved <u>futile</u>.*

Background

The Kennedy Assassination On November 22, 1963, President John F. Kennedy was shot and killed in Dallas, Texas, and the United States was plunged into mourning. Most people who lived through that time can still remember where they were when they heard the news. Kennedy's assassination and the nation's grief defined a generation. Key events in "American History" take place on that fateful day.

Connecting to the Literature

Reading/Writing Connection Just as the Kennedy assassination serves as the backdrop for "American History," events occurring in the world today become the backdrop for our own stories. Describe two major world events that have taken place in your lifetime. Use at least three of the following words: *transform, emerge, define, precipitate.*

READ MORE

by Judith Ortiz Cofer
The Latin Deli:
Prose and Poetry
An Island Like You

Meet the Author

Judith Ortiz **Cofer** (b. 1952)

Judith Ortiz Cofer spent her childhood in two different cultures. Born in Puerto Rico, she moved with her parents to Paterson, New Jersey, when she was four years old. She grew up mostly in Paterson, but she also spent time in Puerto Rico with her *abuela* (grandmother).

The Art of Storytelling It was from her grandmother that Ortiz Cofer learned the art of storytelling. "When my *abuela* sat us down to tell a story," she says, "we learned something from it, even though we always laughed. That was her way of teaching." In her own work, Ortiz Cofer teaches readers about the richness and difficulty of coming of age in two cultures at once.

Fast Facts

▶ Ortiz Cofer's first novel, *The Line of the Sun,* was nominated for a Pulitzer Prize.

▶ Ortiz Cofer teaches for Operation Homecoming, a writing program for U.S. military personnel.

Author Link

For: More about the author
Visit: www.PHSchool.com
Web Code: epe-9202

American History

Judith Ortiz Cofer

I once read in a *Ripley's Believe It or Not* column that Paterson, New Jersey, is the place where the Straight and Narrow (streets) intersect. The Puerto Rican <u>tenement</u> known as El Building was one block up from Straight. It was, in fact, the corner of Straight and Market; not "at" the corner, but *the* corner. At almost any hour of the day, El Building was like a monstrous jukebox, blasting out *salsas*[1] from open windows as the residents, mostly new immigrants just up from the island, tried to drown out whatever they were currently enduring with loud music. But the day President Kennedy was shot there was a <u>profound</u> silence in El Building; even the abusive tongues of viragoes,[2] the cursing of the unemployed, and the screeching of small children had been somehow muted. President Kennedy was a saint to these people. In fact, soon his photograph would be hung alongside the Sacred Heart and over the spiritist altars that many women kept in their apartments. He would become part of the hierarchy of martyrs they prayed to for favors that only one who had died for a cause would understand.

On the day that President Kennedy was shot, my ninth grade class had been out in the fenced playground of Public School Number 13. We had been given "free" exercise time and had been ordered by our P.E. teacher, Mr. DePalma, to "keep moving." That meant that the girls should jump rope and the boys toss basketballs through a hoop at the far end of the yard. He in the meantime would "keep an eye" on us from just inside the building.

It was a cold gray day in Paterson. The kind that warns of early snow. I was miserable, since I had forgotten my gloves, and my knuckles were turning red and raw from the jump rope. I was also taking a lot of abuse from the black girls for not turning the rope hard and fast enough for them.

"Hey, Skinny Bones, pump it, girl. Ain't you got no energy today?" Gail, the biggest of the black girls had the other end of the rope, yelled, "Didn't you eat your rice and beans and pork chops for breakfast today?"

The other girls picked up the "pork chops" and made it into a refrain: "pork chop, pork chop, did you eat your pork chop?" They entered the double ropes in pairs and exited without tripping or missing a beat. I felt a burning on my cheeks and then my glasses fogged up so that I could not manage to coordinate the jump rope with Gail.

---

1. *salsas* (säl´ səs) songs written in a particular Latin American musical style.
2. **viragoes** (vi rä´ gōz) fierce, irritable women who often shout.

◄ **Critical Viewing** Judging from this photograph of President Kennedy, why do you think people, like the adults in this story, felt so strongly about him? **[Interpret]**

Vocabulary Builder
tenement (ten´ ə mənt) *n.* apartment house, often run-down

profound (prō found´) *adj.* deep; intense

✓ **Reading Check**

On what memorable day in history does this story take place?

◀ Critical Viewing
How does the scene in this photograph compare to the view from the narrator's fire escape? [Compare and Contrast]

The chill was doing to me what it always did; entering my bones, making me cry, humiliating me. I hated the city, especially in winter. I hated Public School Number 13. I hated my skinny flat-chested body, and I envied the black girls who could jump rope so fast that their legs became a blur. They always seemed to be warm while I froze.

There was only one source of beauty and light for me that school year. The only thing I had anticipated at the start of the semester. That was seeing Eugene. In August, Eugene and his family had moved into the only house on the block that had a yard and trees. I could see his place from my window in El Building. In fact, if I sat on the fire escape I was literally suspended above Eugene's backyard. It was my favorite spot to read my library books in the summer. Until that August the house had been occupied by an old Jewish couple. Over the years I had become part of their family, without their knowing it, of course, I had a view of their kitchen and their backyard, and though I could not hear what they said, I knew when they were arguing, when one of them was sick, and many other things. I knew all this by watching them at mealtimes. I could see their kitchen table, the sink, and the stove. During good times, he sat at the table and read his newspapers while she fixed the meals. If they argued, he would leave and the old woman would sit and stare at nothing for a long time. When one of them was sick, the other would come and get things from the kitchen and carry them out on a tray. The old man had died in June. The last week of school I had not seen him at the table at all. Then one day I saw that there was a crowd in the kitchen. The old woman had finally emerged from the house on the arm of a stocky, middle-aged woman, whom I had seen there a few times before, maybe her daughter. Then a man had carried out suitcases. The house had stood empty for weeks. I had had to resist the temptation to climb down into the yard and water the flowers the old lady had taken such good care of.

Reading Skill
Making Inferences
Which details in this passage lead you to infer that the narrator is fond of Eugene?

By the time Eugene's family moved in, the yard was a tangled mass of weeds. The father had spent several days mowing, and when he finished, from where I sat, I didn't see the red, yellow, and purple clusters that meant flowers to me. I didn't see this family sit down at the kitchen table together. It was just the mother, a red-headed tall woman who wore a white uniform—a nurse's, I guessed it was; the father was gone before I got up in the morning and was never there at dinner time. I only saw him on weekends when they sometimes sat on lawn chairs under the oak tree, each hidden behind a section of the newspaper; and there was Eugene. He was tall and blond, and he wore glasses. I liked him right away because he sat at the kitchen table and read books for hours. That summer, before we had even spoken one word to each other, I kept him company on my fire escape.

Once school started I looked for him in all my classes, but P.S. 13 was a huge, overpopulated place and it took me days and many discreet questions to discover that Eugene was in honors classes for all his subjects; classes that were not open to me because English was not my first language, though I was a straight A student. After much maneuvering, I managed "to run into him" in the hallway where his locker was—on the other side of the building from mine—and in study hall at the library where he first seemed to notice me, but did not speak; and finally, on the way home after school one day when I decided to approach him directly, though my stomach was doing somersaults.

I was ready for rejection, snobbery, the worst. But when I came up to him, practically panting in my nervousness, and blurted out: "You're Eugene. Right?" He smiled, pushed his glasses up on his nose, and nodded. I saw then that he was blushing deeply. Eugene liked me, but he was shy. I did most of the talking that day. He nodded and smiled a lot. In the weeks that followed, we walked home together. He would linger at the corner of El Building for a few minutes then walk down to his two-story house. It was not until Eugene moved into that house that I noticed that El Building blocked most of the sun, and that the only spot that got a little sunlight during the day was the tiny square of earth the old woman had planted with flowers.

I did not tell Eugene that I could see inside his kitchen from my bedroom. I felt dishonest, but I liked my secret sharing of his evenings, especially now that I knew what he was reading since we chose our books together at the school library.

One day my mother came into my room as I was sitting on the window-sill staring out. In her abrupt way she said: "Elena, you are

Literary Analysis
Conflict What internal conflict does the narrator experience as she prepares to approach Eugene?

Reading Check

Who is Eugene and how does the narrator meet him?

"Listen," he repeated, "something awful has happened." A strange gurgling came from his throat, and he turned around and spat on the cement behind him.

"Gross," someone said, and there was a lot of laughter.

"The President is dead, you idiots. I should have known that wouldn't mean anything to a bunch of losers like you kids. Go home." He was shrieking now. No one moved for a minute or two, but then a big girl let out a "Yeah!" and ran to get her books piled up with the others against the brick wall of the school building. The others followed in a mad scramble to get to their things before somebody caught on. It was still an hour to the dismissal bell.

A little scared, I headed for El Building. There was an eerie feeling on the streets. I looked into Mario's drugstore, a favorite hangout for the high school crowd, but there were only a couple of old Jewish men at the soda-bar talking with the short order cook in tones that sounded almost angry, but they were keeping their voices low. Even the traffic on one of the busiest intersections in Paterson—Straight Street and Park Avenue—seemed to be moving slower. There were no horns blasting that day. At El Building, the usual little group of unemployed men were not hanging out on the front stoop making it difficult for women to enter the front door. No music spilled out from open doors in the hallway. When I walked into our apartment, I found my mother sitting in front of the grainy picture of the television set.

She looked up at me with a tear-streaked face and just said: "*Dios mio,*[5]" turning back to the set as if it were pulling at her eyes. I went into my room.

Though I wanted to feel the right thing about President Kennedy's death, I could not fight the feeling of elation that stirred in my chest. Today was the day I was to visit Eugene in his house. He had asked me to come over after school to study for an American history test with him. We had also planned to walk to the public library together. I looked down into his yard. The oak tree was bare of leaves and the ground looked gray with ice. The light through the large kitchen window of his house told me that El Building blocked the sun to such an extent that they had to turn lights on in the middle of the day. I felt ashamed about it. But the white kitchen table with the lamp hanging just above it looked cozy and inviting. I would soon sit there, across from Eugene, and I would tell him about my perch just above his house. Maybe I should.

In the next thirty minutes I changed clothes, put on a little pink lipstick, and got my books together. Then I went in to tell my mother

Reading Skill
Making Inferences
Which details in Elena's description of her walk home let you infer the anguish people feel over the assassination of the president?

Literary Analysis
Conflict Which details in this passage reveal Elena's internal conflict over her reaction to the president's death?

---

5. *Dios mio* (dē′ ōs mē′ ō) Spanish for "My God!"

that I was going to a friend's house to study. I did not expect her reaction.

"You are going out *today*?" The way she said "today" sounded as if a storm warning had been issued. It was said in utter disbelief. Before I could answer, she came toward me and held my elbows as I clutched my books.

"*Hija*,[6] the President has been killed. We must show respect. He was a great man. Come to church with me tonight."

She tried to embrace me, but my books were in the way. My first impulse was to comfort her, she seemed so distraught, but I had to meet Eugene in fifteen minutes.

"I have a test to study for, Mama. I will be home by eight."

"You are forgetting who you are, *Niña*.[7] I have seen you staring down at that boy's house. You are heading for humiliation and pain." My mother said this in Spanish and in a resigned tone that surprised me, as if she had no intention of stopping me from "heading for humiliation and pain." I started for the door. She sat in front of the TV holding a white handkerchief to her face.

I walked out to the street and around the chainlink fence that separated El Building from Eugene's house. The yard was neatly edged around the little walk that led to the door. It always amazed me how Paterson, the inner core of the city, had no apparent logic to

---

6. *Hija* (ē´ hä) Spanish for "daughter."
7. *Niña* (nē´ nyä) Spanish for "child."

Literary Analysis
Conflict On the evening of the assassination, how do Elena's plans conflict with her mother's?

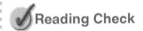Reading Check

What plans had Elena made with Eugene?

its architecture. Small, neat, single residences like this one could be found right next to huge, <u>dilapidated</u> apartment buildings like El Building. My guess was that the little houses had been there first, then the immigrants had come in droves, and the monstrosities had been raised for them—the Italians, the Irish, the Jews, and now us, the Puerto Ricans and the blacks. The door was painted a deep green: *verde*, the color of hope, I had heard my mother say it: *Verde-Esperanza.*[8]

I knocked softly. A few suspenseful moments later the door opened just a crack. The red, swollen face of a woman appeared. She had a halo of red hair floating over a delicate ivory face—the face of a doll—with freckles on the nose. Her smudged eye make-up made her look unreal to me, like a mannequin seen through a warped store window.

"What do you want?" Her voice was tiny and sweet-sounding, like a little girl's, but her tone was not friendly.

"I'm Eugene's friend. He asked me over. To study." I thrust out my books, a silly gesture that embarrassed me almost immediately.

"You live there?" She pointed up to El Building, which looked particularly ugly, like a gray prison with its many dirty windows and rusty fire escapes. The woman had stepped halfway out and I could see that she wore a white nurse's uniform with "St. Joseph's Hospital" on the name tag.

"Yes. I do."

She looked intently at me for a couple of heartbeats, then said as if to herself, "I don't know how you people do it." Then directly to me: "Listen. Honey. Eugene doesn't want to study with you. He is a smart boy. Doesn't need help. You understand me. I am truly sorry if he told you you could come over. He cannot study with you. It's nothing personal. You understand? We won't be in this place much longer, no need for him to get close to people—it'll just make it harder for him later. Run back home now."

I couldn't move. I just stood there in shock at hearing these things said to me in such a honey-drenched voice. I had never heard an accent like hers, except for Eugene's softer version. It was as if she were singing me a little song.

"What's wrong? Didn't you hear what I said?" She seemed very angry, and I finally snapped out of my trance. I turned away from the green door, and heard her close it gently.

Our apartment was empty when I got home. My mother was in someone else's kitchen, seeking the solace she needed. Father would come in from his late shift at midnight. I would hear them

---

8. *Verde-Esperanza* (ver´ dā es pā rän´ zä) Spanish for "green-hope."

Vocabulary Builder
dilapidated (də lap´ə dāt´ id) *adj.* falling to pieces or into disrepair

Reading Skill
Making Inferences
Based on the description of the woman's face, what do you think she was doing before Elena arrived?

talking softly in the kitchen for hours that night. They would not discuss their dreams for the future, or life in Puerto Rico, as they often did; that night they would talk sadly about the young widow and her two children, as if they were family. For the next few days, we would observe *luto* [9] in our apartment; that is, we would practice restraint and silence—no loud music or laughter. Some of the women of El Building would wear black for weeks.

That night, I lay in my bed trying to feel the right thing for our dead President. But the tears that came up from a deep source inside me were strictly for me. When my mother came to the door, I pretended to be sleeping. Sometime during the night, I saw from my bed the streetlight come on. It had a pink halo around it. I went to my window and pressed my face to the cool glass. Looking up at the light I could see the white snow falling like a lace veil over its face. I did not look down to see it turning gray as it touched the ground below.

---

9. *luto* (lōō´ tō) Spanish for "mourning."

▲ **Critical Viewing**
Do you think Elena would find this scene harsh or comforting? Explain. **[Speculate]**

Literary Analysis
Conflict and Epiphany What realization is the reason for Elena's tears?

Apply the Skills

American History

Thinking About the Selection

1. **Respond:** What would you like to say to Elena? Explain.
2. **(a) Recall:** In the first paragraph, what words does Elena use to describe her building? **(b) Recall:** How does she describe Eugene's house from her fire escape? **(c) Compare and Contrast:** Based on these descriptions, explain the contrast in Elena's feelings toward her own home and Eugene's house.
3. **(a) Recall:** What subject is Elena going to study with Eugene? **(b) Interpret:** What other reasons might Ortiz Cofer have for calling this story "American History"?
4. **(a) Analyze:** Where is Elena's mother and what is she doing when Elena returns from Eugene's house? **(b) Analyze:** In the last scene of the story, why does Elena say that her tears are just for herself?

Literary Analysis

5. **(a)** What is the main **conflict** in this story? Explain. **(b)** Is the main conflict primarily **internal** or **external**? Explain.
6. Use a chart like the one shown to provide specific details that reveal conflicts other than the main conflict.

Elena vs. another person	Elena vs. herself

7. Is there a **resolution** in this story or does Elena experience an **epiphany**, with no real end to the conflict? Support your answer with details from the story.

Reading Skill

8. **(a)** Identify three **inferences** you made while reading this story and the details you used to make them. **(b)** Did making inferences improve your understanding of the story? Explain.
9. **(a)** Write down two inferences you made about characters' responses to President Kennedy's assassination. Trade papers with a partner and compare the inferences you made. **(b)** Based on your inferences, discuss how the story would be different if Elena had tried to visit Eugene on a different day. **(c)** Pick one difference to share with the class.

Vocabulary Builder

Practice Use a word from the "American History" vocabulary list on page 200 to fill in the blank in each sentence. Then, explain the **context clues**, or key words and phrases, in each sentence that helped you.

1. During the blackout, the guard was more __?__ than usual.
2. The __?__ car had no wheels and was covered in rust.
3. She felt a __?__ sense of pride as she graduated with honors.
4. The serene garden contrasted with the bustling __?__.

Adding Words to Your Vocabulary Using a thesaurus, find an **antonym,** or word of opposite meaning, for each word in the vocabulary list for "American History" on page 200. Use each antonym in a sentence that makes the meaning of the word clear. (For more on using a thesaurus, see page R7.)

Writing

Write an **alternative ending** to "American History." Make sure your new ending meets these criteria:
- The ending flows logically out of earlier events.
- It is consistent with your understanding of the characters.
- It provides a satisfactory resolution to the conflict.

Use dialogue and details showing how characters feel and think.

For *Grammar, Vocabulary,* and *Assessment,*
see **Build Language Skills,** pages 238–239.

Extend Your Learning

Listening and Speaking Write and deliver a **speech** that eulogizes President Kennedy. As you write, imagine that your audience will be Elena and her classmates. Your language and tone should be appropriate for your audience and your purpose. While delivering your speech:
- Project your voice and maintain eye contact with your audience.
- Use vocal inflections and gestures that emphasize your message.

Research and Technology In a small group, create a **photo essay** about a day of national significance to the people of the United States. As a group, select a topic and conduct research to find photos. As you work, discuss the choice and arrangement of the photos and arrive at a consensus. Write suitable captions and display your photo essay.

Short Story

Background

Tests of Survival As civilizations advance, people no longer need to struggle for their basic survival. Nevertheless, some people still enjoy testing their bravery and physical skills in competitions. Today, computer games sometimes feature death-defying challenges. As this story shows, the sport of big-game hunting once served a similar purpose.

Connecting to the Literature

Reading/Writing Connection Think about a game you have played or observed that you would never want to face in reality. Imagine that the game has become real. Write a paragraph describing what might happen. Use at least three of these words: *contemplate, render, simulate, utilize.*

Review

For **Literary Analysis, Reading Skill,** and **Vocabulary Builder,** see page 200.

READ MORE

For another adventure story, read "To Build a Fire" by Jack London

Meet the Author

Richard **Connell** (1893–1949)

Richard Connell seemed destined to become a writer: He was a sports reporter at the age of ten! At sixteen, he was editing his father's newspaper, the *Poughkeepsie News-Press,* in upstate New York. Connell attended Harvard University, where he worked on the *Daily Crimson,* an early version of the humor magazine *National Lampoon.* During World War I, he edited his division's newspaper.

From Page to Screen In 1925, Connell published "The Most Dangerous Game." A year later, he settled in Beverly Hills, California, where he started working as a screenwriter. Twice nominated for Academy Awards, he became one of the most successful screenwriters of his day.

Fast Facts

▶ "The Most Dangerous Game" won the prestigious O. Henry Memorial Award for short fiction when it was first published.

▶ The 1932 film version of "The Most Dangerous Game" is called *The Hounds of Zaroff.*

 Go Online
Author Link

For: More about the author
Visit: www.PHSchool.com
Web Code: epe-9203

THE MOST DANGEROUS GAME

RICHARD CONNELL

"Off there to the right—somewhere—is a large island," said Whitney. "It's rather a mystery—"

"What island is it?" Rainsford asked.

"The old charts call it 'Ship-Trap Island,'" Whitney replied. "A suggestive name, isn't it? Sailors have a curious dread of the place. I don't know why. Some superstition—"

"Can't see it," remarked Rainsford, trying to peer through the dank tropical night that was <u>palpable</u> as it pressed its thick warm blackness in upon the yacht.

"You've good eyes," said Whitney, with a laugh, "and I've seen you pick off a moose moving in the brown fall bush at four hundred yards, but even you can't see four miles or so through a moonless Caribbean[1] night."

---

1. **Caribbean** (kar´ ə bē´ ən) the Caribbean Sea, a part of the Atlantic Ocean, bounded by the north coast of South America, Central America, and the West Indies.

▲ **Critical Viewing**
Based on the details in this image, what do you think this story will be about? **[Speculate]**

Vocabulary Builder
palpable (pal´ pə bēl) *adj.* able to be felt

"Not four yards," admitted Rainsford. "Ugh! It's like moist black velvet."

"It will be light in Rio," promised Whitney. "We should make it in a few days. I hope the jaguar guns have come from Purdey's. We should have some good hunting up the Amazon. Great sport, hunting."

"The best sport in the world," agreed Rainsford.

"For the hunter," amended Whitney. "Not for the jaguar."

"Don't talk rot, Whitney," said Rainsford. "You're a big-game hunter, not a philosopher. Who cares how a jaguar feels?"

"Perhaps the jaguar does," observed Whitney.

"Bah! They've no understanding."

"Even so, I rather think they understand one thing—fear. The fear of pain and the fear of death."

"Nonsense," laughed Rainsford. "This hot weather is making you soft, Whitney. Be a realist. The world is made up of two classes—the hunters and the huntees. Luckily, you and I are the hunters. Do you think we've passed that island yet?"

"I can't tell in the dark. I hope so."

"Why?" asked Rainsford.

"The place has a reputation—a bad one."

"Cannibals?" suggested Rainsford.

"Hardly. Even cannibals wouldn't live in such a God-forsaken place. But it's gotten into sailor lore, somehow. Didn't you notice that the crew's nerves seemed a bit jumpy today?"

"They were a bit strange, now you mention it. Even Captain Nielsen—"

"Yes, even that tough-minded old Swede, who'd go up to the devil himself and ask him for a light. Those fishy blue eyes held a look I never saw there before. All I could get out of him was: 'This place has an evil name among sea-faring men, sir.' Then he said to me, very gravely: 'Don't you feel anything?'—as if the air about us

Literary Analysis
Conflict How does Rainsford's attitude about hunting differ from Whitney's?

▼ **Critical Viewing**
In what ways does this image differ from the Caribbean Sea as it is described in the story? In what ways is it similar? **[Compare and Contrast]**

was actually poisonous. Now, you mustn't laugh when I tell you this—I did feel something like a sudden chill.

"There was no breeze. The sea was as flat as a plate-glass window. We were drawing near the island then. What I felt was a—a mental chill; a sort of sudden dread."

"Pure imagination," said Rainsford. "One superstitious sailor can taint the whole ship's company with his fear."

"Maybe. But sometimes I think sailors have an extra sense that tells them when they are in danger. Sometimes I think evil is a tangible thing—with wave lengths, just as sound and light have. An evil place can, so to speak, broadcast vibrations of evil. Anyhow, I'm glad we're getting out of this zone. Well, I think I'll turn in now, Rainsford."

"I'm not sleepy," said Rainsford. "I'm going to smoke another pipe on the afterdeck."

"Good night, then, Rainsford. See you at breakfast."

"Right. Good night, Whitney."

There was no sound in the night as Rainsford sat there, but the muffled throb of the engine that drove the yacht swiftly through the darkness, and the swish and ripple of the wash of the propeller.

Rainsford, reclining in a steamer chair, <u>indolently</u> puffed on his favorite brier. The sensuous drowsiness of the night was on him. "It's so dark," he thought, "that I could sleep without closing my eyes; the night would be my eyelids—"

An abrupt sound startled him. Off to the right he heard it, and his ears, expert in such matters, could not be mistaken. Again he heard the sound, and again. Somewhere, off in the blackness, someone had fired a gun three times.

Rainsford sprang up and moved quickly to the rail, mystified. He strained his eyes in the direction from which the reports had come, but it was like trying to see through a blanket. He leaped upon the rail and balanced himself there, to get greater elevation; his pipe,

Vocabulary Builder
indolently (in´ də lənt lē) *adv.* lazily; idly

✓**Reading Check**

What "two classes" does Rainsford believe make up the world?

striking a rope, was knocked from his mouth. He lunged for it; a short, hoarse cry came from his lips as he realized he had reached too far and had lost his balance. The cry was pinched off short as the blood-warm waters of the Caribbean Sea closed over his head.

He struggled up to the surface and tried to cry out, but the wash from the speeding yacht slapped him in the face and the salt water in his open mouth made him gag and strangle. Desperately he struck out with strong strokes after the receding lights of the yacht, but he stopped before he had swum fifty feet. A certain cool-headedness had come to him; it was not the first time he had been in a tight place. There was a chance that his cries could be heard by someone aboard the yacht, but that chance was slender, and grew more slender as the yacht raced on. He wrestled himself out of his clothes, and shouted with all his power. The lights of the yacht became faint and ever-vanishing fireflies; then they were blotted out entirely by the night.

Rainsford remembered the shots. They had come from the right, and doggedly he swam in that direction, swimming with slow, deliberate strokes, conserving his strength. For a seemingly endless time he fought the sea. He began to count his strokes; he could do possibly a hundred more and then—

Rainsford heard a sound. It came out of the darkness, a high screaming sound, the sound of an animal in an extremity of anguish and terror.

He did not recognize the animal that made the sound; he did not try to; with fresh vitality he swam toward the sound. He heard it again; then it was cut short by another noise, crisp, staccato.

"Pistol shot," muttered Rainsford, swimming on.

Ten minutes of determined effort brought another sound to his ears—the most welcome he had ever heard—the muttering and growling of the sea breaking on a rocky shore. He was almost on the rocks before he saw them; on a night less calm he would have been shattered against them. With his remaining strength he dragged himself from the swirling waters. Jagged crags appeared to jut into the opaqueness, he forced himself upward, hand over hand. Gasping, his hands raw, he reached a flat place at the top. Dense jungle came down to the very edge of the cliffs. What perils that tangle of trees and underbrush might hold for him did not concern Rainsford just then. All he knew was that he was safe from his enemy, the sea, and that utter weariness was on him. He flung himself down at the jungle edge and tumbled headlong into the deepest sleep of his life.

When he opened his eyes he knew from the position of the sun that it was late in the afternoon. Sleep had given him new vigor; a

Literary Analysis
Conflict With what external conflict is Rainsford suddenly confronted?

▶ **Critical Viewing** Why is Rainsford surprised to find a building, like the one shown here, on the remote island? **[Infer]**

sharp hunger was picking at him. He looked about him, almost cheerfully.

"Where there are pistol shots, there are men. Where there are men, there is food," he thought. But what kind of men, he wondered, in so forbidding a place? An unbroken front of snarled and ragged jungle fringed the shore.

He saw no sign of a trail through the closely knit web of weeds and trees; it was easier to go along the shore, and Rainsford floundered along by the water. Not far from where he had landed, he stopped.

Some wounded thing, by the evidence a large animal, had thrashed about in the underbrush; the jungle weeds were crushed down and the moss was lacerated; one patch of weeds was stained crimson. A small, glittering object not far away caught Rainsford's eye and he picked it up. It was an empty cartridge.

"A twenty-two," he remarked. "That's odd. It must have been a fairly large animal too. The hunter had his nerve with him to tackle it with a light gun. It's clear that the brute put up a fight. I suppose the first three shots I heard was when the hunter flushed his quarry and wounded it. The last shot was when he trailed it here and finished it."

He examined the ground closely and found what he had hoped to find—the print of hunting boots. They pointed along the cliff in the direction he had been going. Eagerly he hurried along, now slipping on a rotten log or a loose stone, but making headway; night was beginning to settle down on the island.

Bleak darkness was blacking out the sea and jungle when Rainsford sighted the lights. He came upon them as he turned a crook in the coast line, and his first thought was that he had come upon a village, for there were many lights. But as he forged along he saw to his great astonishment that all the lights were in one enormous building—a lofty structure with pointed towers plunging upward into the gloom. His eyes made out the shadowy outlines of a palatial château;[2] it was set on a high bluff, and on three sides of it cliffs dived down to where the sea licked greedy lips in the shadows.

"Mirage," thought Rainsford. But it was no mirage, he found, when he opened the tall spiked iron gate. The stone steps were real enough; the massive

---

2. palatial (pə lā´ shəl) **château** (sha tō´) a mansion as luxurious as a palace.

Reading Skill
Making Inferences
What inferences does Rainsford make based on the evidence of pistol shots?

Reading Check

As Rainsford swims for shore, what sounds does he hear coming out of the darkness?

door with a leering gargoyle[3] for a knocker was real enough; yet about it all hung an air of unreality.

He lifted the knocker, and it creaked up stiffly, as if it had never before been used. He let it fall, and it startled him with its booming loudness. He thought he heard steps within; the door remained closed. Again Rainsford lifted the heavy knocker, and let it fall. The door opened then, opened as suddenly as if it were on a spring, and Rainsford stood blinking in the river of glaring gold light that poured out. The first thing Rainsford's eyes discerned was the largest man Rainsford had ever seen—a gigantic creature, solidly made and black-bearded to the waist. In his hand the man held a long-barreled revolver, and he was pointing it straight at Rainsford's heart.

Out of the snarl of beard two small eyes regarded Rainsford.

"Don't be alarmed," said Rainsford, with a smile which he hoped was disarming. "I'm no robber. I fell off a yacht. My name is Sanger Rainsford of New York City."

The menacing look in the eyes did not change. The revolver pointed as rigidly as if the giant were a statue. He gave no sign that he understood Rainsford's words, or that he had even heard them. He was dressed in uniform, a black uniform trimmed with gray astrakhan.[4]

"I'm Sanger Rainsford of New York," Rainsford began again. "I fell off a yacht. I am hungry."

The man's only answer was to raise with his thumb the hammer of his revolver. Then Rainsford saw the man's free hand go to his forehead in a military salute, and he saw him click his heels together and stand at attention. Another man was coming down the broad marble steps, an erect, slender man in evening clothes. He advanced to Rainsford and held out his hand.

In a cultivated voice marked by a slight accent that gave it added precision and deliberateness, he said: "It is a very great pleasure and honor to welcome Mr. Sanger Rainsford, the celebrated hunter, to my home."

Automatically Rainsford shook the man's hand.

"I've read your book about hunting snow leopards in Tibet, you see," explained the man. "I am General Zaroff."

Rainsford's first impression was that the man was singularly handsome; his second was that there was an original, almost bizarre quality about the general's face. He was a tall man past middle age, for his hair was a vivid white; but his thick eyebrows and pointed military mustache were as black as the night from

Reading Skill
Making Inferences
Which details here lead you to infer that the two men Rainsford meets have a shared military past? Explain.

---

3. gargoyle (gär´ goil´) *n.* strange and distorted animal form projecting from a building.
4. astrakhan (as´ trə kən) *n.* loosely curled fur made from the skins of very young lambs.

which Rainsford had come. His eyes, too, were black and very bright. He had high cheek bones, a sharp-cut nose, a spare, dark face, the face of a man used to giving orders, the face of an aristocrat. Turning to the giant in uniform, the general made a sign. The giant put away his pistol, saluted, withdrew.

"Ivan is an incredibly strong fellow," remarked the general, "but he has the misfortune to be deaf and dumb. A simple fellow, but, I'm afraid, like all his race, a bit of a savage."

"Is he Russian?"

"He is a Cossack," said the general, and his smile showed red lips and pointed teeth. "So am I."

"Come," he said, "we shouldn't be chatting here. We can talk later. Now you want clothes, food, rest. You shall have them. This is a most restful spot."

Ivan had reappeared, and the general spoke to him with lips that moved but gave forth no sound.

"Follow Ivan, if you please, Mr. Rainsford," said the general. "I was about to have my dinner when you came. I'll wait for you. You'll find that my clothes will fit you, I think."

It was to a huge, beam-ceilinged bedroom with a canopied bed big enough for six men that Rainsford followed the silent giant. Ivan laid out an evening suit, and Rainsford, as he put it on, noticed that it came from a London tailor who ordinarily cut and sewed for none below the rank of duke.

The dining room to which Ivan conducted him was in many ways remarkable. There was a medieval magnificence about it; it suggested a baronial hall of feudal times with its oaken panels, its high ceiling, its vast refectory table where twoscore men could sit down to eat. About the hall were the mounted heads of many animals—lions, tigers, elephants, moose, bears; larger or more perfect specimens Rainsford had never seen. At the great table the general was sitting, alone.

"You'll have a cocktail, Mr. Rainsford," he suggested. The cocktail was surpassingly good; and, Rainsford noted, the table appointments were of the finest—the linen, the crystal, the silver, the china.

They were eating *borsch*, the rich, red soup with whipped cream so dear to Russian palates. Half apologetically General Zaroff said: "We do our best to preserve the amenities of civilization here. Please

Literature in Context

History Connection

Cossacks Ivan and Zaroff are Cossacks, members of a people from southern Russia who also made up a special Russian military unit. As a people, Cossacks were famous for their fierceness, and the soldiers enjoyed a privileged status. Because of their elite position, these soldiers were also fiercely independent. When the czar—the ruler of Russia—was overthrown in the Russian Revolution of 1917, Cossacks like Zaroff were executed or forced into exile. As a Cossack, Zaroff is unwilling to acknowledge that the rules of ordinary people apply to him.

Connect to the Literature

What traits does Zaroff exhibit that might be due, in part, to his having been a Cossack?

◄ **Czar Nicholas II,** overthrown in the Russian Revolution of 1917

✔ Reading Check

With what objects is Zaroff's dining room decorated?

The Most Dangerous Game ■ 221

forgive any lapses. We are well off the beaten track, you know. Do you think the champagne has suffered from its long ocean trip?"

"Not in the least," declared Rainsford. He was finding the general a most thoughtful and affable host, a true cosmopolite.[5] But there was one small trait of the general's that made Rainsford uncomfortable. Whenever he looked up from his plate he found the general studying him, appraising him narrowly.

"Perhaps," said General Zaroff, "you were surprised that I recognized your name. You see, I read all books on hunting published in English, French, and Russian. I have but one passion in my life, Mr. Rainsford, and it is the hunt."

"You have some wonderful heads here," said Rainsford as he ate a particularly well cooked filet mignon. "That Cape buffalo is the largest I ever saw."

"Oh, that fellow. Yes, he was a monster."

"Did he charge you?"

"Hurled me against a tree," said the general. "Fractured my skull. But I got the brute."

"I've always thought," said Rainsford, "that the Cape buffalo is the most dangerous of all big game."

For a moment the general did not reply; he was smiling his curious red-lipped smile. Then he said slowly: "No. You are wrong, sir. The Cape buffalo is not the most dangerous big game." He sipped his wine. "Here in my preserve on this island," he said in the same slow tone, "I hunt more dangerous game."

Rainsford expressed his surprise. "Is there big game on this island?"

The general nodded. "The biggest."

"Really?"

"Oh, it isn't here naturally, of course. I have to stock the island."

"What have you imported, general?" Rainsford asked. "Tigers?"

The general smiled. "No," he said. "Hunting tigers ceased to interest me some years ago. I exhausted their possibilities, you see. No thrill left in tigers, no real danger. I live for danger, Mr. Rainsford."

The general took from his pocket a gold cigarette case and offered his guest a long black cigarette with a silver tip; it was perfumed and gave off a smell like incense.

"We will have some capital hunting, you and I," said the general. "I shall be most glad to have your society."

"But what game—" began Rainsford.

___

5. **cosmopolite** (käz mäp´ ə lĭt´) *n.* person at home in all parts of the world.

Literary Analysis
Conflict Explain how Rainsford's discomfort in this passage is both an internal and an external conflict.

"I'll tell you," said the general. "You will be amused, I know. I think I may say, in all modesty, that I have done a rare thing. I have invented a new sensation. May I pour you another glass of port, Mr. Rainsford?"

"Thank you, general."

The general filled both glasses, and said: "God makes some men poets. Some He makes kings, some beggars. Me He made a hunter. My hand was made for the trigger, my father said. He was a very rich man with a quarter of a million acres in the Crimea,[6] and he was an ardent sportsman. When I was only five years old he gave me a little gun, specially made in Moscow for me, to shoot sparrows with. When I shot some of his prize turkeys with it, he did not punish me; he complimented me on my marksmanship. I killed my first bear in the Caucasus[7] when I was ten. My whole life has been one prolonged hunt. I went into the army—it was expected of noblemen's sons—and for a time commanded a division of Cossack cavalry, but my real interest was always the hunt. I have hunted every kind of game in every land. It would be impossible for me to tell you how many animals I have killed."

The general puffed at his cigarette.

"After the debacle[8] in Russia I left the country, for it was imprudent for an officer of the Czar to stay there. Many noble Russians lost everything. I, luckily, had invested heavily in American securities, so I shall never have to open a tea room in Monte Carlo or drive a taxi in Paris. Naturally, I continued to hunt—grizzlies in your Rockies, crocodiles in the Ganges, rhinoceroses in East Africa. It was in Africa that the Cape buffalo hit me and laid me up for six months. As soon as I recovered I started for the Amazon to hunt jaguars, for I had heard they were unusually cunning. They weren't." The Cossack sighed. "They were no match at all for a hunter with his wits about him, and a high-powered rifle. I was bitterly disappointed. I was lying in my tent with a splitting headache one night when a terrible thought pushed its way into my mind. Hunting was beginning to bore me! And hunting, remember, had been my life. I have heard that in America business men often go to pieces when they give up the business that has been their life."

"Yes, that's so," said Rainsford.

The general smiled. "I had no wish to go to pieces," he said. "I must do something. Now, mine is an analytical mind, Mr. Rainsford. Doubtless that is why I enjoy the problems of the chase."

"No doubt, General Zaroff."

Reading Skill
Making Inferences
How do the details about Zaroff's life support the inference that he feels neither guilt nor fear concerning hunting?

Reading Check

Why does Zaroff recognize Rainsford's name?

---

6. **Crimea** (krī mē′ ə) region in southwestern Ukraine extending into the Black Sea.
7. **Caucasus** (kô′ kə səs) mountain range between the Black and Caspian seas.
8. **debacle** (di bä′ kəl) *n.* bad defeat (Zaroff is referring to the Russian Revolution of 1917, a defeat for upper-class Russians like himself).

"So," continued the general, "I asked myself why the hunt no longer fascinated me. You are much younger than I am, Mr. Rainsford, and have not hunted as much, but you perhaps can guess the answer."

"What was it?"

"Simply this: hunting had ceased to be what you call 'a sporting proposition.' It had become too easy. I always got my quarry. Always. There is no greater bore than perfection."

The general lit a fresh cigarette.

"No animal had a chance with me any more. That is no boast; it is a mathematical certainty. The animal had nothing but his legs and his instinct. Instinct is no match for reason. When I thought of this it was a tragic moment for me, I can tell you."

Rainsford leaned across the table, absorbed in what his host was saying.

"It came to me as an inspiration what I must do," the general went on.

"And that was?"

The general smiled the quiet smile of one who has faced an obstacle and surmounted it with success. "I had to invent a new animal to hunt," he said.

"A new animal? You're joking."

"Not at all," said the general. "I never joke about hunting. I needed a new animal. I found one. So I bought this island, built this house, and here I do my hunting. The island is perfect for my purpose—there are jungles with a maze of trails in them, hills, swamps—"

"But the animal, General Zaroff?"

"Oh," said the general, "it supplies me with the most exciting hunting in the world. No other hunting compares with it for an instant. Every day I hunt, and I never grow bored now, for I have a quarry with which I can match my wits."

Rainsford's bewilderment showed in his face.

"I wanted the ideal animal to hunt," explained the general. "So I said: 'What are the attributes of an ideal quarry?' And the answer was, of course: 'It must have courage, cunning, and, above all, it must be able to reason.'"

"But no animal can reason," objected Rainsford.

"My dear fellow," said the general, "there is one that can."

"But you can't mean—" gasped Rainsford.

"And why not?"

"I can't believe you are serious, General Zaroff. This is a grisly joke."

"Why should I not be serious? I am speaking of hunting."

Literary Analysis
Conflict How was the "tragic moment" Zaroff refers to the sign of an internal conflict?

"Hunting? General Zaroff, what you speak of is murder."

The general laughed with entire good nature. He regarded Rainsford quizzically. "I refuse to believe that so modern and civilized a young man as you seem to be harbors romantic ideas about the value of human life. Surely your experiences in the war—"

"Did not make me condone cold-blooded murder," finished Rainsford stiffly.

Laughter shook the general. "How extraordinarily droll you are!" he said. "One does not expect nowadays to find a young man of the educated class, even in America, with such a naive, and, if I may say so, mid-Victorian point of view.[9] It's like finding a snuff-box in a limousine. Ah, well, doubtless you had Puritan ancestors. So many Americans appear to have had. I'll wager you'll forget your notions when you go hunting with me. You've a genuine new thrill in store for you, Mr. Rainsford."

"Thank you, I'm a hunter, not a murderer."

"Dear me," said the general, quite unruffled, "again that unpleasant word. But I think I can show you that your scruples are quite ill founded."

"Yes?"

"Life is for the strong, to be lived by the strong, and, if need be, taken by the strong. The weak of the world were put here to give the strong pleasure. I am strong. Why should I not use my gift? If I wish to hunt, why should I not? I hunt the scum of the earth—sailors from tramp ships—lascars,[10] blacks, Chinese, whites, mongrels—a thoroughbred horse or hound is worth more than a score of them."

"But they are men," said Rainsford hotly.

"Precisely," said the general. "That is why I use them. It gives me pleasure. They can reason, after a fashion. So they are dangerous."

"But where do you get them?"

The general's left eyelid fluttered down in a wink. "This island is called Ship-Trap," he answered. "Sometimes an angry god of the high seas sends them to me. Sometimes, when Providence is not so kind, I help Providence a bit. Come to the window with me."

Rainsford went to the window and looked out toward the sea.

"Watch! Out there!" exclaimed the general, pointing into the night. Rainsford's eyes saw only blackness, and then, as the general pressed a button, far out to sea Rainsford saw the flash of lights.

The general chuckled. "They indicate a channel," he said, "where there's none: giant rocks with razor edges crouch like a sea monster with wide-open jaws. They can crush a ship as easily as I crush this

---

9. **mid-Victorian point of view** a point of view emphasizing proper behavior and associated with the time of Queen Victoria of England (1819–1901).
10. **lascars** (las´ kərz) n. Indian or East Indian sailors, employed on European ships.

Literary Analysis
Conflict and Epiphany What does Rainsford suddenly understand about Zaroff?

Vocabulary Builder
scruples (skrōō´ pəlz) n. misgivings about something one thinks is wrong

Reading Check
What does Zaroff do to ease his boredom with hunting?

nut." He dropped a walnut on the hardwood floor and brought his heel grinding down on it. "Oh, yes," he said, casually, as if in answer to a question, "I have electricity. We try to be civilized here."

"Civilized? And you shoot down men?"

A trace of anger was in the general's black eyes, but it was there for but a second, and he said, in his most pleasant manner: "Dear me, what a righteous young man you are! I assure you I do not do the thing you suggest. That would be barbarous. I treat these visitors with every consideration. They get plenty of good food and exercise. They get into splendid physical condition. You shall see for yourself tomorrow."

"What do you mean?"

"We'll visit my training school," smiled the general. "It's in the cellar. I have about a dozen pupils down there now. They're from the Spanish bark San Lucar that had the bad luck to go on the rocks out there. A very inferior lot, I regret to say. Poor specimens and more accustomed to the deck than to the jungle."

He raised his hand, and Ivan, who served as waiter, brought thick Turkish coffee. Rainsford, with an effort, held his tongue in check.

"It's a game, you see," pursued the general blandly. "I suggest to one of them that we go hunting. I give him a supply of food and an excellent hunting knife. I give him three hours' start. I am to follow, armed only with a pistol of the smallest caliber and range. If my quarry eludes me for three whole days, he wins the game. If I find him"—the general smiled—"he loses."

"Suppose he refuses to be hunted?"

"Oh," said the general, "I give him his option, of course. He need not play the game if he doesn't wish to. If he does not wish to hunt, I turn him over to Ivan. Ivan once had the honor of serving as official knouter[11] to the Great White Czar, and he has his own ideas of sport. Invariably, Mr. Rainsford, invariably they choose the hunt."

"And if they win?"

The smile on the general's face widened. "To date I have not lost," he said.

Then he added, hastily: "I don't wish you to think me a braggart, Mr. Rainsford. Many of them afford only the most elementary sort of problem. Occasionally I strike a tartar.[12] One almost did win. I eventually had to use the dogs."

"The dogs?"

"This way, please. I'll show you."

Reading Skill
Making Inferences
Based on this description, what can you infer about the method Zaroff uses to lure his quarry to the island?

Literary Analysis
Conflict Is Zaroff's statement that his captives do not have to participate in the hunt true? Explain.

---

11. **knouter** (nout′ ər) *n.* someone who beats criminals with a leather whip, or knout.
12. **tartar** (tärt′ ər) *n.* stubborn, violent person.

The general steered Rainsford to a window. The lights from the windows sent a flickering illumination that made grotesque patterns on the courtyard below, and Rainsford could see moving about there a dozen or so huge black shapes; as they turned toward him, their eyes glittered greenly.

"A rather good lot, I think," observed the general. "They are let out at seven every night. If anyone should try to get into my house—or out of it—something extremely regrettable would occur to him." He hummed a snatch of song from the Folies Bergère.[13]

"And now," said the general, "I want to show you my new collection of heads. Will you come with me to the library?"

"I hope," said Rainsford, "that you will excuse me tonight, General Zaroff. I'm really not feeling at all well."

"Ah, indeed?" the general inquired solicitously. "Well, I suppose that's only natural, after your long swim. You need a good, restful night's sleep. Tomorrow you'll feel like a new man, I'll wager. Then we'll hunt, eh? I've one rather promising prospect—"

Rainsford was hurrying from the room.

"Sorry you can't go with me tonight," called the general. "I expect rather fair sport—a big, strong black. He looks resourceful—Well good night, Mr. Rainsford; I hope you have a good night's rest."

The bed was good, and the pajamas of the softest silk, and he was tired in every fiber of his being, but nevertheless Rainsford could not quiet his brain with the opiate of sleep. He lay, eyes wide open. Once he thought he heard stealthy steps in the corridor outside his room. He sought to throw open the door; it would not open. He went to the window and looked out. His room was high up in one of the towers. The lights of the château were out now, and it was dark and silent, but there was a fragment of sallow moon, and by its wan light he could see, dimly, the courtyard; there, weaving in and out in the pattern of shadow, were black, noiseless forms; the hounds heard him at the window and looked up, expectantly, with their green eyes. Rainsford went back to the bed and lay down. By

---

13. Folies (fô´ lē) **Bergère** (ber zher´) musical theater in Paris.

▲ **Critical Viewing**
Why might Zaroff have used dogs like these on his hunts? **[Connect]**

Reading Skill
Making Inferences
What kind of heads do you think Zaroff wants to show Rainsford? Explain.

✓ **Reading Check**
Who are the "pupils" in Zaroff's cellar?

many methods he tried to put himself to sleep. He had achieved a doze when, just as morning began to come, he heard, far off in the jungle, the faint report of a pistol.

General Zaroff did not appear until luncheon. He was dressed faultlessly in the tweeds of a country squire. He was solicitous about the state of Rainsford's health.

"As for me," sighed the general, "I do not feel so well. I am worried, Mr. Rainsford. Last night I detected traces of my old complaint."

To Rainsford's questioning glance the general said: "Ennui. Boredom."

Then, taking a second helping of crêpes suzette, the general explained: "The hunting was not good last night. The fellow lost his head. He made a straight trail that offered no problems at all. That's the trouble with these sailors; they have dull brains to begin with, and they do not know how to get about in the woods. They do excessively stupid and obvious things. It's most annoying. Will you have another glass of Chablis, Mr. Rainsford?"

"General," said Rainsford firmly, "I wish to leave this island at once."

The general raised his thickets of eyebrows; he seemed hurt. "But, my dear fellow," the general protested, "you've only just come. You've had no hunting—"

"I wish to go today," said Rainsford. He saw the dead black eyes of the general on him, studying him. General Zaroff's face suddenly brightened.

He filled Rainsford's glass with venerable Chablis from a dusty bottle.

"Tonight," said the general, "we will hunt—you and I."

Rainsford shook his head. "No, general," he said. "I will not hunt."

The general shrugged his shoulders and delicately ate a hothouse grape. "As you wish, my friend," he said. "The choice rests entirely with you. But may I not venture to suggest that you will find my idea of sport more diverting than Ivan's?"

He nodded toward the corner to where the giant stood, scowling, his thick arms crossed on his hogshead of chest.

"You don't mean—" cried Rainsford.

"My dear fellow," said the general, "have I not told you I always mean what I say about hunting? This is really an inspiration. I drink to a foeman worthy of my steel—at last."

The general raised his glass, but Rainsford sat staring at him.

"You'll find this game worth playing," the general said enthusiastically. "Your brain against mine. Your woodcraft against

Literary Analysis
Conflict How does Rainsford's statement about wishing to leave make his internal conflict an external one?

Reading Skill
Making Inferences What inference can you make about the hunting trip Zaroff is suggesting?

mine. Your strength and stamina against mine. Outdoor chess! And the stake is not without value, eh?"

"And if I win—" began Rainsford huskily.

"I'll cheerfully acknowledge myself defeated if I do not find you by midnight of the third day," said General Zaroff. "My sloop will place you on the mainland near a town."

The general read what Rainsford was thinking.

"Oh, you can trust me," said the Cossack. "I will give you my word as a gentleman and a sportsman. Of course you, in turn, must agree to say nothing of your visit here."

"I'll agree to nothing of the kind," said Rainsford.

"Oh," said the general, "in that case— But why discuss that now? Three days hence we can discuss it over a bottle of Veuve Cliquot, unless—"

The general sipped his wine.

Then a businesslike air animated him. "Ivan," he said to Rainsford, "will supply you with hunting clothes, food, a knife. I suggest you wear moccasins; they leave a poorer trail. I suggest too that you avoid the big swamp in the southeast corner of the island. We call it Death Swamp. There's quicksand there. One foolish fellow tried it. The deplorable part of it was that Lazarus followed him. You can imagine my feelings, Mr. Rainsford. I loved Lazarus; he was the finest hound in my pack. Well, I must beg you to excuse me now. I always take a siesta after lunch. You'll hardly have time for a nap, I fear. You'll want to start, no doubt. I shall not follow till dusk. Hunting at night is so much more exciting than by day, don't you think? Au revoir,[14] Mr. Rainsford, au revoir."

General Zaroff, with a deep, courtly bow, strolled from the room.

From another door came Ivan. Under one arm he carried khaki hunting clothes, a haversack of food, a leather sheath containing a long-bladed hunting knife; his right hand rested on a cocked revolver thrust in the crimson sash about his waist. . . .

Rainsford had fought his way through the bush for two hours. "I must keep my nerve. I must keep my nerve," he said through tight teeth.

He had not been entirely clear-headed when the château gates snapped shut behind him.

---

14. Au (ō′) **revoir** (rə vwär′) French for "until we meet again."

> **Reading Check**
>
> What two suggestions does Zaroff give Rainsford before they begin the hunt?

His whole idea at first was to put distance between himself and General Zaroff, and, to this end, he had plunged along, spurred on by the sharp rowels of something very like panic. Now he had got a grip on himself, had stopped, and was taking stock of himself and the situation.

He saw that straight flight was <u>futile</u>; inevitably it would bring him face to face with the sea. He was in a picture with a frame of water, and his operations, clearly, must take place within that frame.

"I'll give him a trail to follow," muttered Rainsford, and he struck off from the rude paths he had been following into the trackless wilderness. He executed a series of intricate loops; he doubled on his trail again and again, recalling all the lore of the fox hunt, and all the dodges of the fox. Night found him leg-weary, with his hands and face lashed by the branches, on a thickly wooded ridge. He knew it would be insane to blunder on through the dark, even if he had the strength. His need for rest was imperative and he thought: "I have played the fox, now I must play the cat of the fable." A big tree with a thick trunk and outspread branches was nearby, and, taking care to leave not the slightest mark, he climbed up into the crotch, and stretching out on one of the broad limbs, after a fashion, rested. Rest brought him new confidence and almost a feeling of security. Even so zealous a hunter as General Zaroff could not trace him there, he told himself; only the devil himself could follow that complicated trail through the jungle after dark. But, perhaps, the general was a devil—

An apprehensive night crawled slowly by like a wounded snake, and sleep did not visit Rainsford, although the silence of a dead world was on the jungle. Toward morning when a dingy gray was varnishing the sky, the cry of some startled bird focused Rainsford's attention in that direction. Something was coming through the bush, coming slowly, carefully, coming by the same winding way Rainsford had come. He flattened himself down on the limb, and through a screen of leaves almost

Vocabulary Builder
futile (fyo͞ot′ ′l) *adj.*
useless; hopeless

▼ **Critical Viewing**
How does this picture support Rainsford's thought that straight flight through the jungle is futile?
[Integrate Vocabulary]

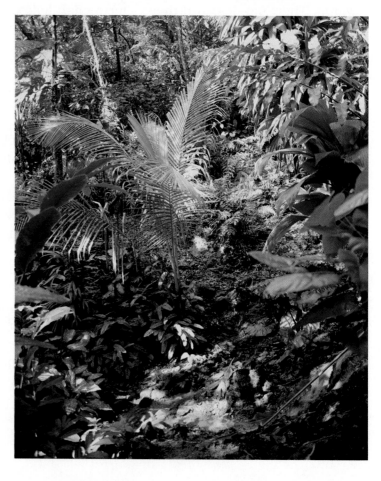

as thick as tapestry, he watched. The thing that was approaching was a man.

It was General Zaroff. He made his way along with his eyes fixed in utmost concentration on the ground before him. He paused, almost beneath the tree, dropped to his knees and studied the ground. Rainsford's impulse was to hurl himself down like a panther, but he saw the general's right hand held something metallic—a small automatic pistol.

The hunter shook his head several times, as if he were puzzled. Then he straightened up and took from his case one of his black cigarettes; its pungent incense-like smoke floated up to Rainsford's nostrils.

Rainsford held his breath. The general's eyes had left the ground and were traveling inch by inch up the tree. Rainsford froze there, every muscle tensed for a spring. But the sharp eyes of the hunter stopped before they reached the limb where Rainsford lay; a smile spread over his brown face. Very deliberately he blew a smoke ring into the air; then he turned his back on the tree and walked carelessly away, back along the trail he had come. The swish of the underbrush against his hunting boots grew fainter and fainter.

The pent-up air burst hotly from Rainsford's lungs. His first thought made him feel sick and numb. The general could follow a trail through the woods at night; he could follow an extremely difficult trail; he must have uncanny powers; only by the merest chance had the Cossack failed to see his quarry.

Rainsford's second thought was even more terrible. It sent a shudder of cold horror through his whole being. Why had the general smiled? Why had he turned back?

Rainsford did not want to believe what his reason told him was true, but the truth was as evident as the sun that had by now pushed through the morning mists. The general was playing with him! The general was saving him for another day's sport! The Cossack was the cat; he was the mouse. Then it was that Rainsford knew the full meaning of terror.

"I will not lose my nerve. I will not."

He slid down from the tree, and struck off again into the woods. His face was set and he forced the machinery of his mind to function. Three hundred yards from his hiding place he stopped where a huge dead tree leaned precariously on a smaller, living one. Throwing off his sack of food, Rainsford took his knife from its sheath and began to work with all his energy.

The job was finished at last, and he threw himself down behind a fallen log a hundred feet away. He did not have to wait long. The cat was coming again to play with the mouse.

Reading Skill
Making Inferences
Which details in the description of Zaroff's searching the tree suggest that he knows Rainsford is there?

Reading Check

On the first night of the hunt, where does Rainsford attempt to hide from Zaroff?

Following the trail with the sureness of a bloodhound, came General Zaroff. Nothing escaped those searching black eyes, no crushed blade of grass, no bent twig, no mark, no matter how faint, in the moss. So intent was the Cossack on his stalking that he was upon the thing Rainsford had made before he saw it. His foot touched the protruding bough that was the trigger. Even as he touched it, the general sensed his danger and leaped back with the agility of an ape. But he was not quite quick enough; the dead tree, delicately adjusted to rest on the cut living one, crashed down and struck the general a glancing blow on the shoulder as it fell; but for his alertness, he must have been smashed beneath it. He staggered, but he did not fall; nor did he drop his revolver. He stood there, rubbing his injured shoulder, and Rainsford, with fear again gripping his heart, heard the general's mocking laugh ring through the jungle.

"Rainsford," called the general, "if you are within the sound of my voice, as I suppose you are, let me congratulate you. Not many men know how to make a Malay mancatcher. Luckily, for me, I too have hunted in Malacca. You are proving interesting, Mr. Rainsford. I am going now to have my wound dressed; it's only a slight one. But I shall be back. I shall be back."

When the general, nursing his bruised shoulder, had gone, Rainsford took up his flight again. It was flight now, a desperate, hopeless flight, that carried him on for some hours. Dusk came, then darkness, and still he pressed on. The ground grew softer under his moccasins; the vegetation grew ranker, denser; insects bit him savagely. Then, as he stepped forward, his foot sank into the ooze. He tried to wrench it back, but the muck sucked viciously at his foot as if it were a giant leech. With a violent effort, he tore his foot loose. He knew where he was now. Death Swamp and its quicksand.

His hands were tight closed as if his nerve were something tangible that someone in the darkness was trying to tear from his grip. The softness of the earth had given him an idea. He stepped back from the quicksand a dozen feet or so, and, like some huge prehistoric beaver, he began to dig.

Rainsford had dug himself in in France when a second's delay meant death. That had been a placid pastime compared to his digging now. The pit grew deeper; when it was above his shoulders, he climbed out and from some hard saplings cut stakes and sharpened them to a fine point. These stakes he planted in the

Literary Analysis
Conflict Who seems to be winning the conflict at this point in the story? Explain.

Literature in Context — History Connection

World War I Trenches

When Rainsford digs himself in, he is drawing on his experiences as a soldier. During World War I (1914–1918), European armies on both sides dug hundreds of miles of deep, narrow ditches. The soldiers lived in these trenches, from where they would charge the enemy's trenches.

LIFE IN THE TRENCHES

- Throughout the war, approximately seven thousand British soldiers were killed, wounded, or disabled every day while serving in the trenches.
- Soldiers living in trenches were plagued by lice, rats, beetles, and frogs.
- The trenches smelled terrible due to dead bodies, overflowing latrines, and unwashed men.

▶ Soldiers' equipment included masks to protect them from mustard gas and other chemical weapons.

▶ A single pair of trench rats could produce as many as 880 offspring in one year.

Connect to the Literature Rainsford says his time in the trenches was "placid" compared to his experience on the island. How does this information about trenches clarify his fear?

---

bottom of the pit with the points sticking up. With flying fingers he wove a rough carpet of weeds and branches and with it he covered the mouth of the pit. Then, wet with sweat and aching with tiredness, he crouched behind the stump of a lightning-charred tree.

He knew his pursuer was coming; he heard the padding sound of feet on the soft earth, and the night breeze brought him the perfume of the general's cigarette. It seemed to Rainsford that the general was coming with unusual swiftness; he was not feeling his way along, foot by foot. Rainsford, crouching there, could not see the general, nor could he see the pit. He lived a year in a minute. Then he felt an impulse to cry aloud with joy, for he heard the sharp crackle of the breaking branches as the cover of the pit gave way; he heard the sharp scream of pain as the pointed stakes found their mark. He leaped up from his place of concealment. Then he cowered back. Three feet from the pit a man was standing, with an electric torch in his hand.

"You've done well, Rainsford," the voice of the general called. "Your Burmese tiger pit has claimed one of my best dogs. Again you score. I think, Mr. Rainsford, I'll see what you can do against my whole pack. I'm going home for a rest now. Thank you for a most amusing evening."

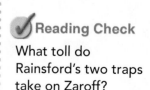

Reading Check

What toll do Rainsford's two traps take on Zaroff?

The Most Dangerous Game ■ 233

At daybreak Rainsford, lying near the swamp, was awakened by a sound that made him know that he had new things to learn about fear. It was a distant sound, faint and wavering, but he knew it. It was the baying of a pack of hounds.

Rainsford knew he could do one of two things. He could stay where he was and wait. That was suicide. He could flee. That was postponing the inevitable. For a moment he stood there, thinking. An idea that held a wild chance came to him, and, tightening his belt, he headed away from the swamp.

The baying of the hounds drew nearer, then still nearer, nearer, ever nearer. On a ridge Rainsford climbed a tree. Down a watercourse, not a quarter of a mile away, he could see the bush moving. Straining his eyes, he saw the lean figure of General Zaroff; just ahead of him Rainsford made out another figure whose wide shoulders surged through the tall jungle weeds; it was the giant Ivan, and he seemed pulled forward by some unseen force; Rainsford knew that Ivan must be holding the pack in leash.

They would be on him any minute now. His mind worked frantically. He thought of a native trick he had learned in Uganda. He slid down the tree. He caught hold of a springy young sapling and to it he fastened his hunting knife, with the blade pointing down the trail; with a bit of wild grapevine he tied back the sapling. Then he ran for his life. The hounds raised their voices as they hit the fresh scent. Rainsford knew now how an animal at bay feels.

He had to stop to get his breath. The baying of the hounds stopped abruptly, and Rainsford's heart stopped too. They must have reached the knife.

He shinnied excitedly up a tree and looked back. His pursuers had stopped. But the hope that was in Rainsford's brain when he

Literary Analysis
Conflict What new internal conflict does the sound of the baying dogs create for Rainsford?

▼ **Critical Viewing** How does this image clarify Rainsford's feeling that the island is a sort of prison, guarded by the surging sea? **[Connect]**

climbed died, for he saw in the shallow valley that General Zaroff was still on his feet. But Ivan was not. The knife, driven by the recoil of the springing tree, had not wholly failed.

"Nerve, nerve, nerve!" he panted, as he dashed along. A blue gap showed between the trees dead ahead. Ever nearer drew the hounds. Rainsford forced himself on toward that gap. He reached it. It was the shore of the sea. Across a cove he could see the gloomy gray stone of the château. Twenty feet below him the sea rumbled and hissed. Rainsford hesitated. He heard the hounds. Then he leaped far out into the sea. . . .

When the general and his pack reached the place by the sea, the Cossack stopped. For some minutes he stood regarding the blue-green expanse of water. He shrugged his shoulders. Then he sat down, took a drink of brandy from a silver flask, lit a perfumed cigarette, and hummed a bit from *Madame Butterfly*.[15]

General Zaroff had an exceedingly good dinner in his great paneled dining hall that evening. With it he had a bottle of Pol Roger and half a bottle of Chambertin. Two slight annoyances kept him from perfect enjoyment. One was the thought that it would be difficult to replace Ivan; the other was that his quarry had escaped him; of course the American hadn't played the game—so thought the general as he tasted his after-dinner liqueur. In his library he read, to soothe himself, from the works of Marcus Aurelius.[16] At ten he went up to his bedroom. He was deliciously tired, he said to himself, as he locked himself in. There was a little moonlight, so, before turning on his light, he went to the window and looked down at the courtyard. He could see the great hounds, and he called: "Better luck another time," to them. Then he switched on the light.

A man, who had been hiding in the curtain of the bed, was standing there.

"Rainsford!" screamed the general. "How in God's name did you get here?"

"Swam," said Rainsford. "I found it quicker than walking through the jungle."

The general sucked in his breath and smiled. "I congratulate you," he said. "You have won the game."

Rainsford did not smile. "I am still a beast at bay," he said, in a low, hoarse voice. "Get ready, General Zaroff."

The general made one of his deepest bows. "I see," he said. "Splendid! One of us is to furnish a repast for the hounds. The other will sleep in this very excellent bed. On guard, Rainsford. . . ."

He had never slept in a better bed, Rainsford decided.

---

15. Madame Butterfly an opera by Giacomo Puccini.
16. Marcus Aurelius (ô rē´ lē əs) Roman emperor and philosopher (A.D. 121–180).

Reading Skill
Making Inferences
When Rainsford leaps into the sea, what inference do you think the author wants you to make?

Apply the Skills

The Most Dangerous Game

Thinking About the Selection

1. **Respond:** What do you like or dislike about Rainsford? Explain.
2. **(a) Recall:** According to Zaroff, what is the most dangerous game? **(b) Make a Judgment:** Based on this attitude, would you call Zaroff "civilized"? Why or why not?
3. **(a) Recall:** Early in the story, what fears does Whitney believe jaguars feel? **(b) Contrast:** How does Rainsford's attitude toward these animals differ from Whitney's?
4. **(a) Recall:** Near the end, with what words does Zaroff congratulate Rainsford? **(b) Infer:** What action does Rainsford then take?
5. **Speculate:** How might Rainsford's experience on the island change him? Use evidence from the text to support your answer.

Literary Analysis

6. **(a)** What is the main **conflict** in this story? Explain. **(b)** Is the main conflict primarily **internal** or **external**? Explain.
7. Use a chart like the one shown to provide specific details that reveal conflicts other than the main conflict.

Rainsford vs. nature	Rainsford vs. himself

8. Is there a **resolution** in this story or does Rainsford experience an **epiphany** with no real end to the conflict? Support your answer with details from the story.

Reading Skill

9. **(a)** Identify three **inferences** you made while reading this story and the details you used to make them. **(b)** Did making inferences improve your understanding of the story? Explain.
10. **(a)** Write down two inferences you made about Whitney. Trade papers with a partner and compare the inferences you made. **(b)** Based on your inferences, discuss how the story would be different if it had been Whitney on the island with Zaroff. **(c)** Pick one difference to share with the class.

QuickReview

Story at a Glance
A big-game hunter finds himself being hunted.

—Assessment
For: Self-test
Visit: www.PHSchool.com
Web Code: epa-6203

Conflict: a struggle between opposing forces

Resolution: the stage of the plot in which the conflict is solved

Epiphany: a character's sudden flash of insight

Inference: a logical assumption a reader makes based on details in the text

Vocabulary Builder

Practice Use a word from the vocabulary list for "The Most Dangerous Game" on page 200 to fill in each blank. Then, explain the **context clues,** or key words and phrases, that helped you.

1. His cheating at the game demonstrated a lack of ___?___ .
2. At the wedding, the joy in the air seemed ___?___ .
3. She tried to climb, but her high heels made her efforts ___?___ .
4. The lazy sloth hung ___?___ from the tree branch.

Adding Words to Your Vocabulary Using a thesaurus, find an antonym for three words from the vocabulary list for "The Most Dangerous Game" on page 200. Use each antonym correctly in a sentence. (For more on using a thesaurus, see page R7.)

Writing

Write an **alternative ending** to "The Most Dangerous Game." Make sure your new ending meets these criteria:
- The ending flows logically out of earlier events.
- It is consistent with your understanding of the characters.
- It provides a satisfactory resolution to the conflict.

For *Grammar, Vocabulary,* and *Assessment,* see **Build Language Skills,** pp. 238–239.

Extend Your Learning

Listening and Speaking As Rainsford, write and deliver a **speech** to an audience of big-game hunters. In your speech, explain why your attitude toward big-game hunting has or has not changed as a result of story events. Your language and tone should be appropriate to your audience and purpose. As you deliver your speech in class:
- Project your voice and maintain eye contact with your audience.
- Use vocal inflections and gestures that emphasize your message.

Research and Technology In a small group, create a **photo essay** about two or three big-game species mentioned in the story. As you work, discuss the choice and arrangement of the photos as a group and arrive at a consensus. Write suitable captions and display your photo essay for the class.

Build Language Skills

Vocabulary Skill

Word Roots The **Latin root** -*spec*- means "look" or "see." This root appears in English words that have to do with "looking at," "looking upon," or "seeing" something. For example, when you discuss an *aspect* of a character, you look at a particular feature of the character.

The **Latin root** -*circum*- means "around" or "surrounding" and is used as part of several English words.

Practice List these words on your paper. Then, next to each word, write a brief explanation of how the root contributes to the word's meaning.

1. inspect   2. retrospect   3. circumvent   4. speculate   5. circumstance

Grammar Lesson

Regular Verbs A **verb** has four **principal parts:** the present, the present participle, the past, and the past participle. Most of the verbs in the English language, such as the verb *inspect,* are regular **verbs,** and you can form their principal parts following a predictable pattern. Notice that the final *e* may be dropped.

Present	Present Participle	Past	Past Participle
inspect	is inspecting	inspected	has inspected
race	is racing	raced	has raced

Practice Copy and complete the chart.

	Present	Present Participle	Past	Past Participle
look				
diverge				
expect				
observe				
walk				

𝒲G *Prentice Hall Writing and Grammar Connection: Chapter 23, Section 1*

MorePractice

For more practice with verbs, see the Grammar Handbook, p. R40.

Reading: Making Inferences

Directions: *Read the selection. Then, answer the questions.*

In sixth grade, I had one of the first in a lucky line of great English teachers who began to nurture in me a love of language, a love that had been there since my childhood of listening closely to words. Sister Maria Generosa did not make our class interminably diagram sentences from a workbook or learn a catechism of grammar rules. Instead, she asked us to write little stories imagining we were snowflakes, birds, pianos, a stone in the pavement, a star in the sky. What would it feel like to be a flower with roots in the ground? If the clouds could talk, what would they say? She had an expressive, dreamy look that was accentuated by the wimple that framed her face.

—from "My English," by Julia Alvarez

Standards Assessed

- IR.2.03.3
- IR.2.04.1
- IR.2.04.4

1. What can readers infer about the narrator?
   A She likes to write.
   B She doesn't like nature.
   C She has no imagination.
   D She thinks writers are dreamers.

2. What can readers infer about Sister Maria Generosa?
   A She doesn't understand grammar.
   B She also loves language.
   C She teaches religion.
   D She doesn't speak English.

3. What prior knowledge helps you make inferences about the narrator?
   A Sister Generosa also taught art.
   B Writing is part of the curriculum.
   C Teachers know grammar rules.
   D Writers generally love language.

4. Which detail is most helpful in making inferences about the narrator?
   A who began to nurture . . . of language,
   B did not make our class . . . of grammar rules.
   C write little stories . . . in the sky.
   D an expressive, dreamy look . . . her face.

Timed Writing: Interpretation [Critical Stance]

Review "The Most Dangerous Game" or "American History." Write a brief explanation of who the narrator is and how the narrator affects your impression of the story. Use examples from the story to illustrate your points. **(20 minutes)**

Writing Workshop: *Work in Progress*

Short Story

Using the work from your writing portfolio as an outline, fill in the steps between announcements. Add important moments in your character's life. Put this paper in your writing portfolio.

Reading Informational Materials

Signs and Instructions

In Part 1, you are learning how to make inferences while reading. Making inferences is also important in reading informational materials such as signs. Most signs depend on your ability to infer meaning from symbols and abbreviated statements. If you read "The Most Dangerous Game," you know that ocean waves and currents can be dangerous.

The signs and instructions here are posted to help swimmers and surfers avoid serious dangers.

About Signs and Instructions

Signs are a type of visual aid or symbol designed to communicate important messages quickly and effectively. Signs often include these elements:

- brief, clearly stated information
- large, easy-to-read lettering
- simple, bold pictures or symbols
- colors that help the words and pictures stand out

Instructions are not as concise as signs, but they provide direct statements and clear messages about how to handle particular situations.

Reading Skill

Like other visual aids, signs use pictures, color, and type to present information. An effective visual aid uses these elements to highlight different kinds of information on different parts of the message. When **evaluating visual aids,** look carefully at each element to see if it adds clarity and effectiveness to the message.

Standard Course of Study

- Create standards and apply them to critique presentation/product. (CT.4.01.3)
- Demonstrate comprehension of main idea and supporting details in critiquing communication. (CT.4.03.4)

How to Evaluate Signs and Instructions

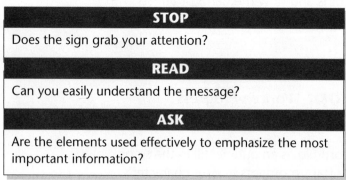

STOP
Does the sign grab your attention?
READ
Can you easily understand the message?
ASK
Are the elements used effectively to emphasize the most important information?

The word *warning* is the boldest element on the sign. The background for the word is orange—a color often used on warning signs and safety devices.

A simple picture illustrates the danger.

WARNING LEVEL: *DANGEROUS* . . . a potential for *loss of life or limb* exists.

CONDITION: Large powerful waves are generated by winds and storms at sea sometimes thousands of miles from the Hawaiian Islands. Seasonal high surf occurs on all shores of O'ahu. Typically, shorelines facing North, East and West receive high surf during Winter months. Shores facing Southeast and Southwest receive high surf during Summer months. Surf on the North shore may reach heights of *twenty-five* feet plus,—on the West shore, *fifteen* feet plus!

INSTRUCTIONS: If you're uncertain of your abilities, don't go into the ocean during high surf, heed all posted high surf warnings! Your life could depend on it!

The uppercase, red letters in each head let readers know that they are reading important information.

WARNING

STRONG CURRENT

YOU COULD BE SWEPT AWAY FROM SHORE AND COULD DROWN

IF IN DOUBT, DON'T GO OUT

> A specific warning message is stated briefly and clearly. The most important words are printed in the largest letters.

WARNING LEVEL: *DANGEROUS* . . . a potential for *loss of life or limb* exists.

> The information in the instructions is directly and simply stated.

CONDITION: These are swift moving channels of water against which it is difficult to swim. Strong currents frequently accompany high surf and rapid tide changes and can be recognized as a turbulent channel of water between areas where waves are breaking.

INSTRUCTIONS: When caught in a strong current — Try to keep a level head, i.e., don't panic! Wave one or both hands in the air, and scream or call for help. Swim diagonally to the current, not against it.

OCEAN SAFETY TIPS:

- Swim in Lifeguarded Areas
- Never Swim Alone.
- Don't Dive Into Unknown Water or Into Shallow Breaking Waves.
- Ask a Lifeguard About <u>Beach and Surf Conditions</u> Before Swimming.
- If You Are Unable to Swim Out of a Strong Current, Signal for Help.
- Rely on Your Swimming Ability Rather Than a Flotation Device.
- Look For, Read and Obey All <u>Beach Safety Signs and Symbols</u>.
- If In Doubt, Just Stay Out!

Reading: Evaluate Visual Aids

Directions: *Choose the letter of the best answer to each question.*

1. What specific danger does the first sign warn against?
   A deep water
   B sharp rocks
   C speedboats in the area
   D large, powerful waves

2. What is another way to describe "strong current"?
   A swift-moving channels of water
   B large waves along the shore
   C rocky area near a beach
   D deep water

3. If caught in a strong current, how should a person swim?
   A against the current
   B diagonally to the current
   C away from the current
   D sideways

Standards
Assessed

• IR.2.03.3
• IR.2.04.3
• CT.4.03.10

Reading: Comprehension and Interpretation

Directions: *Write your answers on a separate piece of paper.*

4. **(a)** Describe the picture on the sign that warns about a strong current.
   (b) In what ways does the picture illustrate the instructions? **(c)** Would you recommend any changes to make the sign more effective? Explain.
   [Evaluating]

5. **(a)** In what ways might signs like these benefit those who do not read English? **(b)** Using these signs as examples, explain why signs are useful to society. **[Applying]**

6. **(a)** What other words could you use to express the message "If in doubt, don't go out"? **(b)** How does the use of rhyme add to the effectiveness of the message? **(c)** Are these words the most effective words to include at the bottom of each sign? Explain. **[Evaluating]**

Timed Writing: Persuasion [Connections]

Propose a safety sign to be posted in your school or neighborhood. Describe the sign and identify its purpose. Give reasons why the sign is needed.
(20 minutes)

Practice these skills with either "The Gift of the Magi" (p. 246) or "The Interlopers" (p. 255).

NC **Standard Course of Study**

- State clearly a personal view is logical and coherent. (FA.3.02.1)
- Identify and use standards to critique and evaluate work. (CT.4.02.2)

Literary Analysis

Irony is a difference or a contradiction between appearance and reality or between what is expected and what actually happens.

- In **situational irony,** something happens in the story that contradicts the expectations of a character or a reader. For example, if a runner trains hard for a race, she should run well in it. However, if she trains so hard that she oversleeps and misses the race, that situation is ironic.

- A **surprise ending** often helps to create situational irony through a turn of events that takes a reader by surprise. To make a surprise ending believable, an author builds clues into the story that make the ending logical.

Irony and a surprise ending help convey the story's theme, or message.

Reading Skill

An **inference** is a logical assumption that you make based on details in a text. In addition to what the author tells you, you can also **use your own prior knowledge and experience** to make inferences.

- As you read, watch movies and plays, and observe the world every day, you gather knowledge and experiences.

- When you read something new, look for ways in which the characters and situations resemble ones you have seen before.

- Then, apply that knowledge and experience to make inferences.

Use a chart like the one shown to record your inferences.

Detail
The king yawns when he is told that his people are starving.

↓

My Experience
The best leaders are those who show concern for their people.

↓

Inference
The author wants me to believe that the king is a bad leader.

Vocabulary Builder

The Gift of the Magi

- **instigates** (in´ stə gāts´) *v.* urges on; stirs up (p. 247) *When he is not watched carefully, he instigates trouble.*

- **depreciate** (dē prē´ shē āt´) *v.* reduce in value (p. 248) *Items that do not depreciate are good investments.*

- **discreet** (di skrēt´) *adj.* careful about what one says or does (p. 250) *Being discreet is a good way to avoid hurting people's feelings.*

The Interlopers

- **precipitous** (prē sip´ ə təs) *adj.* steep; sheer (p. 256) *At the edge of the cliff, you will face a precipitous drop.*

- **condolences** (kən dō´ lən səz) *n.* expressions of sympathy with another in grief (p. 258) *The mourners shared their condolences.*

- **languor** (laŋ´ gər) *n.* lack of vigor; weakness (p. 260) *After two days without rest, languor overcame them.*

Build Understanding • *The Gift of the Magi*

Short Story

Background

The Value of Money In a story written years ago, prices may seem unrealistically low. The reason is inflation—the steady increase in the prices of most things over time. In this story, written around 1905, $32 is roughly one month's rent for Della and Jim. For most people today, $32 would not even cover one week's rent.

Connecting to the Literature

Reading/Writing Connection Even with unexpected dollar amounts in "The Gift of the Magi," most readers can easily understand the issue at the heart of the story: How can you express love through a gift when funds are tight? Write a few sentences to suggest an answer. Use at least three of these words: *adjust, embody, assist, emphasize.*

READ MORE

by O. Henry
"The Last Leaf"
"The Princess and the Puma"

Meet the Author

O. **Henry** (1862–1910)

Born in North Carolina, William Sydney Porter, better known as O. Henry, dropped out of school at sixteen to work in his uncle's drugstore. In 1882, he left to seek his fortune in Texas. He worked on a ranch, then at a bank, and eventually started writing sketches. He became a reporter, columnist, and cartoonist for the *Houston Post.*

Writing Stories in Prison In 1896, Porter was jailed for his involvement in a bank scandal. While in prison, he began writing stories. When he was released, Porter changed his name to O. Henry, moved to New York City, and developed into one of America's most celebrated writers of short fiction.

Fast Facts

▶ O. Henry's gift for storytelling was nurtured by his sister Evelina, who developed a game in which she would start a story and her brother would finish it.

▶ Since 1919, the O. Henry Awards have been given to the best short stories written each year.

Go **Online**
Author Link

For: More about the author
Visit: www.PHSchool.com
Web Code: epe-9204

The Gift of the Magi ■ 245

The Gift of the Magi

O. Henry

One dollar and eighty-seven cents. That was all. And sixty cents of it was in pennies. Pennies saved one and two at a time by bulldozing the grocer and the vegetable man and the butcher until one's cheeks burned with the silent imputation of parsimony[1] that such close dealing implied. Three times Della counted it. One dollar and eighty-seven cents. And the next day would be Christmas.

There was clearly nothing to do but flop down on the shabby little couch and howl. So Della did it. Which <u>instigates</u> the moral reflection that life is made up of sobs, sniffles, and smiles, with sniffles predominating.

While the mistress of the home is gradually subsiding from the first stage to the second, take a look at the home. A furnished flat at $8 per week. It did not exactly beggar description,[2] but it certainly had that word on the lookout for the mendicancy squad.[3]

In the vestibule below was a letter-box into which no letter would go, and an electric button from which no mortal finger could coax a ring. Also appertaining thereunto was a card bearing the name "Mr. James Dillingham Young."

The "Dillingham" had been flung to the breeze during a former period of prosperity when its possessor was being paid $30 per week. Now, when the income was shrunk to $20, the letters of "Dillingham" looked blurred, as though they were thinking seriously of contracting to a modest and unassuming D. But whenever Mr. James Dillingham Young came home and reached his flat above he was called "Jim" and greatly hugged by Mrs. James Dillingham Young, already introduced to you as Della. Which is all very good.

Della finished her cry and attended to her cheeks with the powder rag. She stood by the window and looked out dully at a gray cat walking a gray fence in a gray backyard. Tomorrow would be Christmas Day, and she had only $1.87 with which to buy Jim a present. She had been saving every penny she could for months, with this result. Twenty dollars a week doesn't go far. Expenses had been greater than she had calculated. They always are. Only $1.87 to buy a present for Jim. Her Jim. Many a happy hour she had spent planning for something nice for him. Something fine and rare and sterling—something just a little bit near to being worthy of the honor of being owned by Jim.

There was a pier glass between the windows of the room. Perhaps you have seen a pier glass in an $8 flat. A very thin and very agile person may, by observing his reflection in a rapid

1. **imputation** (im´ pyoo tā´ shən) **of parsimony** (pär´ sə mō´ nē) accusation of stinginess.
2. **beggar description** make description seem inadequate or useless.
3. **it certainly . . . mendicancy** (men´ di kən´ sē) **squad** it would have been noticed by the police who arrested beggars.

Vocabulary Builder
instigates (in´ stə gāts´) v. urges on; stirs up

Reading Skill
Inferences Based on this paragraph, what can you infer about Jim and the kind of person he would like to be?

Reading Check

How much money does Della have to buy a present for Jim?

sequence of longitudinal strips, obtain a fairly accurate conception of his looks. Della, being slender, had mastered the art.

Suddenly she whirled from the window and stood before the glass. Her eyes were shining brilliantly, but her face had lost its color within twenty seconds. Rapidly she pulled down her hair and let it fall to its full length.

Now, there were two possessions of the James Dillingham Youngs in which they both took a mighty pride. One was Jim's gold watch that had been his father's and his grandfather's. The other was Della's hair. Had the Queen of Sheba lived in the flat across the airshaft, Della would have let her hair hang out the window some day to dry just to <u>depreciate</u> Her Majesty's jewels and gifts. Had King Solomon been the janitor, with all his treasures piled up in the basement, Jim would have pulled out his watch every time he passed, just to see him pluck at his beard from envy.

So now Della's beautiful hair fell about her rippling and shining like a cascade of brown waters. It reached below her knee and made itself almost a garment for her. And then she did it up again nervously and quickly. Once she faltered for a minute and stood still while a tear or two splashed on the worn red carpet.

On went her old brown jacket; on went her old brown hat. With a whirl of skirts and with the brilliant sparkle still in her eyes, she fluttered out the door and down the stairs to the street.

Where she stopped the sign read: "Mme. Sofronie. Hair Goods of All Kinds." One flight up Della ran, and collected herself, panting. Madame, large, too white, chilly, hardly looked the "Sofronie."

"Will you buy my hair?" asked Della.

"I buy hair," said Madame. "Take yer hat off and let's have a sight at the looks of it."

Down rippled the brown cascade.

"Twenty dollars," said Madame, lifting the mass with a practiced hand.

"Give it to me quick," said Della.

Oh, and the next two hours tripped by on rosy wings. Forget the hashed metaphor. She was ransacking the stores for Jim's present.

She found it at last. It surely had been made for Jim and no one else. There was no other like it in any of the stores, and she had turned all of them inside out. It was a platinum fob chain simple and chaste in design, properly proclaiming its value by substance alone and not by meretricious ornamentation—as all good things should do. It was even worthy of The Watch. As soon as she saw it she knew that it must be Jim's. It was like him. Quietness and value—the description applied to both. Twenty-one dollars they took from her for it, and she hurried home with the 87 cents. With that

Vocabulary Builder
depreciate (dē prē´ shē āt´) v. to reduce in value

Reading Skill
Inferences Using your own prior knowledge and details from this passage, what can you infer about Della's thoughts and plans?

chain on his watch Jim might be properly anxious about the time in any company. Grand as the watch was he sometimes looked at it on the sly on account of the old leather strap that he used in place of a chain.

When Della reached home her intoxication gave way a little to prudence and reason. She got out her curling irons and lighted the gas and went to work repairing the ravages made by generosity added to love. Which is always a tremendous task, dear friends—a mammoth task.

Within forty minutes her head was covered with tiny, close-lying curls that made her look wonderfully like a truant schoolboy. She looked at her reflection in the mirror long, carefully, and critically.

"If Jim doesn't kill me," she said to herself, "before he takes a second look at me, he'll say I look like a Coney Island[4] chorus girl. But what could I do—oh! what could I do with a dollar and eighty-seven cents?"

At 7 o'clock the coffee was made and the frying-pan was on the back of the stove hot and ready to cook the chops.

Jim was never late. Della doubled the fob chain in her hand and sat on the corner of the table near the door that he always entered. Then she heard his step on the stair away down on the first flight, and she turned white for just a moment. She had a habit of saying little silent prayers about the simplest everyday things, and now she whispered: "Please God, make him think I am still pretty."

The door opened and Jim stepped in and closed it. He looked thin and very serious. Poor fellow, he was only twenty-two—and to be burdened with a family! He needed a new overcoat and he was without gloves.

Jim stopped inside the door, as immovable as a setter at the scent of quail. His eyes were fixed upon Della, and there was an

4. **Coney** (kō′ nē) **Island** beach and amusement park in Brooklyn, New York.

Cultural Connection

Watch Fob Chain A fob chain is central to the plot of "The Gift of the Magi." The word *fob* probably entered the English language from the German dialect word *fuppe,* meaning "pocket." During the nineteenth century, before the wristwatch became common, a man would carry a pocket watch that fit in a special vest pocket. To keep the watch from falling or becoming lost, it was fastened to the vest by means of a strap or chain (sometimes with an ornament, or a fob, at the end) that was attached to a pin with a locking clasp, making it secure. Sometimes, as pictured here, a chain's finely detailed metalwork elevated the piece to a work of art.

Connect to the Literature

A fob chain was often handed down from father to son, as was Jim Young's in O. Henry's story. Why might this fact alone make a fob chain very precious to its owner despite its modest cash value?

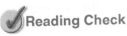

Reading Check

What does Della sell for twenty dollars?

Short Story

Background

Family Feuds A feud is a bitter, prolonged fight, typically between families or clans, that may continue for years or even generations. The brutality of a feud can make for gripping drama, as it does in "The Interlopers."

Connecting to the Literature

Reading/Writing Connection All people argue from time to time, but most disagreements do not last for a lifetime, as they do in "The Interlopers." Make a list of the possible ways in which a long-standing feud can be resolved. Use at least three of the following words: *analyze, focus, participate, verify.*

Review

For **Literary Analysis, Reading Skill,** and **Vocabulary Builder,** see page 244.

READ MORE

by Saki
"The Open Window"
"Sredni Vashtar"

Meet the Author

Saki (1870–1916)

Saki is the pen name of the British writer H. H. Munro. Munro was born in Burma and sent at age two to live in England. As a young adult, he returned to Burma to serve in the police force. However, poor health forced him to return to England, where he began work as a journalist.

Talent and Tragedy In 1904, Munro published a collection of short stories entitled *Reginald.* He went on to write several more collections of stories and two novels. The abrupt ending of Saki's own life was as shocking as one of his plot twists: When World War I broke out, he enlisted in the British army and was killed fighting in France.

Fast Facts

▶ Munro's pen name is thought to be taken from a character in Persian poet Omar Khayyam's *The Rubaiyat.*

▶ To honor Saki, the king of England issued a scroll that reads, "Let those who come after see to it that his name is not forgotten."

 Go Online
Author Link

For: More about the author
Visit: www.PHSchool.com
Web Code: epe-9205

THE INTERLOPERS

SAKI

In a forest of mixed growth somewhere on the eastern spurs of the Carpathians,[1] a man stood one winter night watching and listening, as though he waited for some beast of the woods to come within the range of his vision, and, later, of his rifle. But the game for whose presence he kept so keen an outlook was none that figured in the sportsman's calendar as lawful and proper for the chase: Ulrich von Gradwitz (ōōl´ rik fŏn gräd´ vitz) patrolled the dark forest in quest of a human enemy.

✓ **Reading Check**

Where does the story take place?

---

1. **Carpathians** (kär pā´ thē ənz) mountains in central Europe.

The forest lands of Gradwitz were of wide extent and well stocked with game; the narrow strip of <u>precipitous</u> woodland that lay on its outskirt was not remarkable for the game it harbored or the shooting it afforded, but it was the most jealously guarded of all its owner's territorial possessions. A famous lawsuit, in the days of his grandfather, had wrested it from the illegal possession of a neighboring family of petty landowners; the dispossessed party had never acquiesced in the judgment of the Courts, and a long series of poaching affrays[2] and similar scandals had embittered the relationships between the families for three generations. The neighbor feud had grown into a personal one since Ulrich had come to be head of his family; if there was a man in the world whom he detested and wished ill to it was Georg Znaeym (gā´ ôrg znä´ im), the inheritor of the quarrel and the tireless game-snatcher and raider of the disputed border-forest. The feud might, perhaps, have died down or been compromised if the personal ill will of the two men had not stood in the way; as boys they had thirsted for one another's blood, as men each prayed that misfortune might fall on the other, and this wind-scourged winter night Ulrich had banded together his foresters to watch the dark forest, not in quest of four-footed quarry, but to keep a lookout for the prowling thieves whom he suspected of being afoot from across the land boundary. The roebuck which usually kept in the sheltered hollows during a storm wind, were running like driven things tonight, and there was movement and unrest among the creatures that were wont to sleep through the dark hours. Assuredly there was a disturbing element in the forest, and Ulrich could guess the quarter from whence it came.

He strayed away by himself from the watchers whom he had placed in ambush on the crest of the hill, and wandered far down the steep slopes amid the wild tangle of undergrowth, peering through the tree trunks and listening through the whistling and skirling of the wind and the restless beating of the branches for sight or sound of the marauders. If only on this wild night, in this dark, lone spot, he might come across Georg Znaeym, man to man, with none to witness—that was the wish that was uppermost in his thoughts. And as he stepped round the trunk of a huge beech he came face to face with the man he sought.

The two enemies stood glaring at one another for a long silent moment. Each had a rifle in his hand, each had hate in his heart and murder uppermost in his mind. The chance had come to give full play to the passions of a lifetime. But a man who has been brought up under the code of a restraining civilization cannot easily

---

2. **poaching** (pōch´ iŋ) **affrays** (ə frāz´) disputes about hunting on someone else's property.

Reading Skill
Inferences What can you infer about the characters from their unwillingness to compromise?

Reading Skill
Inferences How does your knowledge of feuds help you infer the reason Ulrich hopes to meet Znaeym?

nerve himself to shoot down his neighbor in cold blood and without word spoken,
except for an offense against his hearth and
honor. And before the moment of hesitation had
given way to action a deed of Nature's own violence
overwhelmed them both. A fierce shriek of the storm
had been answered by a splitting crash over their heads,
and ere they could leap aside a mass of falling beech tree
had thundered down on them. Ulrich von Gradwitz found himself stretched on the ground, one arm numb beneath him and
the other held almost as helplessly in a tight tangle of forked
branches, while both legs were pinned beneath the fallen mass. His
heavy shooting-boots had saved his feet from being crushed to
pieces, but if his fractures were not as serious as they might have
been, at least it was evident that he could not move from his present
position till someone came to release him. The descending twigs had
slashed the skin of his face, and he had to wink away some drops of
blood from his eyelashes before he could take in a general view of
the disaster. At his side, so near that under ordinary circumstances
he could almost have touched him, lay Georg Znaeym, alive and
struggling, but obviously as helplessly pinioned down as himself. All
round them lay a thick-strewn wreckage of splintered branches and
broken twigs.

Relief at being alive and exasperation at his captive plight
brought a strange medley of pious thank-offerings and sharp curses
to Ulrich's lips. Georg, who was nearly blinded with the blood which
trickled across his eyes, stopped his struggling for a moment to listen, and then gave a short, snarling laugh.

"So you're not killed, as you ought to be, but you're caught, anyway," he cried; "caught fast. Ho, what a jest, Ulrich von Gradwitz
snared in his stolen forest. There's real justice for you!"

And he laughed again, mockingly and savagely.

"I'm caught in my own forest land," retorted Ulrich. "When my men
come to release us you will wish, perhaps, that you were in a better
plight than caught poaching on a neighbor's land, shame on you."

Georg was silent for a moment; then he answered quietly:

"Are you sure that your men will find much to release? I have
men, too, in the forest tonight, close behind me, and *they* will be
here first and do the releasing. When they drag me out from under

Literary Analysis
Irony Each character
wishes harm to the
other. What is the
irony in how the wish
is fulfilled?

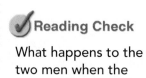
Reading Check

What happens to the
two men when the
tree falls?

these branches it won't need much clumsiness on their part to roll this mass of trunk right over on the top of you. Your men will find you dead under a fallen beech tree. For form's sake I shall send my <u>condolences</u> to your family."

"It is a useful hint," said Ulrich fiercely. "My men had orders to follow in ten minutes' time, seven of which must have gone by already, and when they get me out—I will remember the hint. Only as you will have met your death poaching on my lands I don't think I can decently send any message of condolence to your family."

"Good," snarled Georg, "good. We fight this quarrel out to the death, you and I and our foresters, with no cursed interlopers to come between us. Death and damnation to you, Ulrich von Gradwitz."

"The same to you, Georg Znaeym, forest-thief, game-snatcher."

Both men spoke with the bitterness of possible defeat before them, for each knew that it might be long before his men would

Vocabulary Builder
condolences (kən dō′ lən səz) *n.* expressions of sympathy with another in grief

Literary Analysis
Irony How do Georg's words give a twist to the meaning of *interlopers?*

seek him out or find him; it was a bare matter of chance which party would arrive first on the scene.

Both had now given up the useless struggle to free themselves from the mass of wood that held them down; Ulrich limited his endeavors to an effort to bring his one partially free arm near enough to his outer coat pocket to draw out his wine flask. Even when he had accomplished that operation it was long before he could manage the unscrewing of the stopper or get any of the liquid down his throat. But what a heaven-sent draft it seemed! It was an open winter, and little snow had fallen as yet, hence the captives suffered less from the cold than might have been the case at that season of the year; nevertheless, the wine was warming and reviving to the wounded man, and he looked across with something like a throb of pity to where his enemy lay, just keeping the groans of pain and weariness from crossing his lips.

✓ Reading Check

What is each man's hope for rescue?

▼ **Critical Viewing** What are some dangers the characters might face in a setting like this one? **[Analyze]**

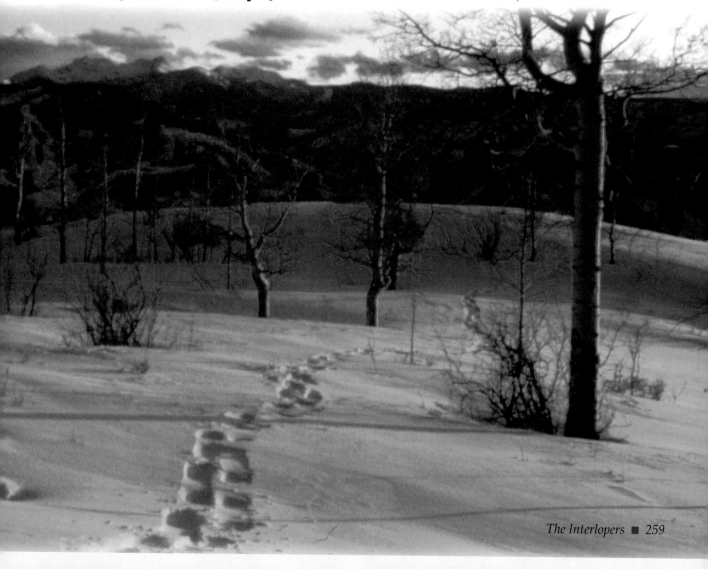

"Could you reach this flask if I threw it over to you?" asked Ulrich suddenly; "there is good wine in it, and one may as well be as comfortable as one can. Let us drink, even if tonight one of us dies."

"No, I can scarcely see anything; there is so much blood caked round my eyes," said Georg, "and in any case I don't drink wine with an enemy."

Ulrich was silent for a few minutes, and lay listening to the weary screeching of the wind. An idea was slowly forming and growing in his brain, an idea that gained strength every time that he looked across at the man who was fighting so grimly against pain and exhaustion. In the pain and <u>languor</u> that Ulrich himself was feeling the old fierce hatred seemed to be dying down.

Vocabulary Builder
languor (laŋ´ gər) *n.* a lack of vigor; weakness

"Neighbor," he said presently, "do as you please if your men come first. It was a fair compact. But as for me, I've changed my mind. If my men are the first to come you shall be the first to be helped, as though you were my guest. We have quarreled like devils all our lives over this stupid strip of forest, where the trees can't even stand upright in a breath of wind. Lying here tonight, thinking, I've come to think we've been rather fools; there are better things in life than getting the better of a boundary dispute. Neighbor, if you will help me to bury the old quarrel I—I will ask you to be my friend."

Georg Znaeym was silent for so long that Ulrich thought, perhaps, he had fainted with the pain of his injuries. Then he spoke slowly and in jerks.

Reading Skill
Inferences What can you infer that Georg is considering during this long silence?

"How the whole region would stare and gabble if we rode into the market square together. No one living can remember seeing a Znaeym and a von Gradwitz talking to one another in friendship. And what peace there would be among the forester folk if we ended our feud tonight. And if we choose to make peace among our people there is none other to interfere, no interlopers from outside . . . You would come and keep the Sylvester night beneath my roof, and I would come and feast on some high day at your castle . . . I would never fire a shot on your land, save when you invited me as a guest; and you should come and shoot with me down in the marshes where the wildfowl are. In all the countryside there are none that could hinder if we willed to make peace. I never thought to have wanted to do other than hate you all my life, but I think I have changed my mind about things too, this last half-hour. And you offered me your wine flask . . . Ulrich von Gradwitz, I will be your friend."

Literary Analysis
Irony What is surprising about this new meaning of *interlopers*?

For a space both men were silent, turning over in their minds the wonderful changes that this dramatic reconciliation would bring about. In the cold, gloomy forest, with the wind tearing in fitful gusts through the naked branches and whistling round the tree trunks, they lay and waited for the help that would now bring release and succor to both parties. And each prayed a private prayer that his men might be the first to arrive, so that he might be the first to show honorable attention to the enemy that had become a friend.

Presently, as the wind dropped for a moment, Ulrich broke silence.

"Let's shout for help," he said; "in this lull our voices may carry a little way."

"They won't carry far through the trees and undergrowth," said Georg, "but we can try. Together, then."

The two raised their voices in a prolonged hunting call.

"Together again," said Ulrich a few minutes later, after listening in vain for an answering halloo.

"I heard something that time, I think," said Ulrich.

"I heard nothing but the pestilential wind," said Georg hoarsely.

There was silence again for some minutes, and then Ulrich gave a joyful cry.

"I can see figures coming through the wood. They are following in the way I came down the hillside."

Both men raised their voices in as loud a shout as they could muster.

"They hear us! They've stopped. Now they see us. They're running down the hill toward us," cried Ulrich.

"How many of them are there?" asked Georg.

"I can't see distinctly," said Ulrich; "nine or ten."

"Then they are yours," said Georg; "I had only seven out with me."

"They are making all the speed they can, brave lads," said Ulrich gladly.

"Are they your men?" asked Georg. "Are they your men?" he repeated impatiently as Ulrich did not answer.

"No," said Ulrich with a laugh, the idiotic chattering laugh of a man unstrung with hideous fear.

"Who are they?" asked Georg quickly, straining his eyes to see what the other would gladly not have seen.

"*Wolves.*"

Literary Analysis
Irony In what way is the two men's cooperation an ironic situation?

Literary Analysis
Irony and Surprise Ending In what way does the story's surprise ending make the title ironic?

Apply the Skills

The Interlopers

Thinking About the Selection

1. **Respond:** With whom did you sympathize: Ulrich, Georg, neither, or both? Why?
2. **(a) Recall:** Whose family won possession of the disputed land in the lawsuit? **(b) Interpret:** Why does Georg not consider himself a poacher?
3. **(a) Recall:** How long has the dispute between Ulrich and Georg been going on? **(b) Infer:** Which factors about the feud seem to contribute the most to Ulrich's anger at Georg?
4. **(a) Recall:** In what condition does the fallen tree leave each man? **(b) Draw Conclusions:** Why do the men decide to end their feud?
5. **(a) Evaluate:** Considering the cause of their predicament, do you think the two men deserved their fate? Why or why not? **(b) Discuss:** Share your ideas with a partner and then explain how your answer has grown or changed.

Literary Analysis

6. **(a)** Identify **irony** in the story by using a chart like the one shown. In the first box, note the outcome that Ulrich and Georg expect when they first confront each other in the forest. In the second box, describe what actually happens.

What Characters Expect		What Actually Happens

   (b) What theme or message about life does this **situational irony** convey?
7. **(a)** Which details in "The Interlopers" make its **surprise ending** seem like a logical outcome of events? **(b)** Why are surprise endings such a popular device in literature and in movies?

Reading Skill

8. **(a)** What **inferences** do you think Saki intended readers to make about the characters of Ulrich and Georg? **(b)** Which details in the text support your inferences?
9. In what ways do your prior knowledge and experience of characters like Ulrich and Georg help you to make inferences about them? Explain.

Vocabulary Builder

Practice Explain why each statement below is true or false.

1. A drop of 2°F in a day is *precipitous*.
2. It is proper to express *condolences* to one who has suffered a loss.
3. A long drive can cause a feeling of *languor*.

Adding Words to Your Vocabulary The word *precipitous* is related to *precipitation,* which is often used as another term for *rain*. Use a dictionary to look up the meaning and origin of the word *precipitate.* Then, explain how the words *precipitous* and *precipitation* are related to each other. (For more on using a dictionary, see p. R6.)

Writing

Write a brief **news story** about Ulrich and Georg's experience. Your lead paragraph should make your reader want to read more.

- Focus on the questions *Who? What? When? Where? Why?* and *How?* Then, decide which of these facts to present in your lead.
- Read your lead paragraph to a classmate. Revise or eliminate any part that is not clear or that does not make your reader curious.
- Add a few more paragraphs to your report, including the details that tell the rest of the story.

For *Grammar, Vocabulary,* and *Assessment,* see **Build Language Skills,** pages 264–265.

Extend Your Learning

Listening and Speaking With a group of classmates, present a **debate** about the disputed land in "The Interlopers." Form groups to represent each man. Each group should then offer reasons to explain why its character is entitled to the land.

- Listen to your opponents' arguments and respond appropriately.
- After each team speaks for the same amount of time, ask the audience to decide which group was more persuasive.

Research and Technology The chilling ending of "The Interlopers" comes about because of the unexpected arrival of wolves. Prepare a **plan for an illustrated report** about wolves. Use library and Internet resources to find information, especially data about the interactions of wolves with people.

Build Language Skills

Vocabulary Skill

Word Roots The **Latin root** *-mot-* means "move." The root is contained in the word *motivate,* which means "causing something to move or act" and *motive,* which means "the reason that something acts." *Motivation* is the feeling of wanting to move or act.

Practice Use a dictionary to find two meanings for each of the following words. On a chart like the one shown, explain how each meaning is related to the idea of motion or taking action. Then, write a sentence for each meaning of each word.

motivation   motion   emotion   promote

	Meaning 1	Sentence 1	Meaning 2	Sentence 2
motor	Anything that produces motion	The car had a powerful motor.	To walk at a brisk pace	He motored around the corner.

Grammar Lesson

Irregular Verbs Unlike regular verbs, the past tense and past participle of **irregular verbs** are not formed by adding *-ed* to the present form. Instead, the past tense and past participle are formed in various ways. The past participle is always preceded by a helping verb. Look at the examples.

Present: run

Present Participle: running

Past: ran

Past Participle: (have) run

Practice Use a dictionary to help you identify present participle, past tense, and past participle for each verb. Write a sentence for each verb, using each principal part at least twice.

1. begin
2. hang
3. spring
4. fall
5. drive
6. sing
7. stand
8. swing
9. lead
10. won

MorePractice

For more practice with irregular verbs, see the Grammar Handbook, p. R40.

*W*G *Prentice Hall Writing and Grammar Connection: Chapter 23, Section 1*

Reading Skill: Make Inferences

Standards Assessed

• IR.2.01.10
• IR.2.04.2
• IR.2.04.4

Directions: *Read the selection, and then answer the questions.*

The thousand injuries of Fortunato I had borne as I best could, but when he ventured upon insult I vowed revenge. You, who so well know the nature of my soul, will not suppose, however, that I gave utterance to a threat. At *length* I would be avenged; this was a point definitely settled—but the very definitiveness with which it was resolved precluded the idea of risk. I must not only punish but punish with impunity. . . .

—from "The Cask of Amontillado," by Edgar Allan Poe

1. What can you infer about the narrator's relationship with Fortunato?
   A He has known Fortunato for a long time.
   B He has just met Fortunato.
   C He is related to Fortunato.
   D He admires Fortunato's skill as a wine-taster.

2. Based on details in the passage, which word would you use to describe the narrator?
   A forgiving
   B careless
   C patient
   D naive

3. What is a reasonable inference about Fortunato?
   A He always insults others.
   B He is aware of the narrator's dislike.
   C He knows the narrator.
   D He is afraid of the narrator and his friend.

4. What prior knowledge would be most helpful in making inferences about the speaker?
   A He lived in a time that allowed dueling.
   B His culture accepted revenge for dishonor.
   C The culture revered good will.
   D He and Fortunato were from different cultures.

Timed Writing: Explanation [Connections]

Review "The Gift of the Magi" or "The Interlopers." Explain the cause-effect chain of events in one of these works and how this sequence helps convey the theme. **(30 minutes)**

Writing Workshop: *Work in Progress*

Short Story

Using the work from your writing portfolio, write a letter from your character to a best friend explaining one event. In the letter, you should describe the event in detail and explain why it is important in the character's life.

Comparing Literary Works • Setting

Setting

The **setting** of a story is the time and place in which it occurs. The time may include not only the historical period but also a specific year, season, and hour of day. Place may involve not only geographical location, but also the social, economic, and cultural environment. Cultural aspects of a story's setting may be present in a variety of ways:

- the values and beliefs the characters hold
- the details of daily life, such as the work characters do, the foods they eat, and the clothing they wear
- the types of language, such a non-English words or slang, characters use. To build setting, a writer may include *idioms*—phrases, such as "raining cats and dogs," whose meanings differ from those of the individual words.

Standard Course of Study

- Compare effective strategies used in different presentations/products. (CT.4.01.4)
- Understand the importance of cultural and historical impact on texts. (LT.5.01.10)

Comparing Setting

The importance of setting varies from story to story.

- Sometimes, the setting simply provides a backdrop for the action. In such a story, the setting could change, but characters' actions and events would remain the same.
- Alternatively, the setting may shape the characters and plot of a story. For example, in a story set within a Native American culture, characters may make specific decisions and choices based on the expectations of their culture.

The stories presented here are set in very different places, but a particular culture and belief system play an important role in each one. As you read, use a chart like the one shown to identify setting details that suggest the place, time, and culture shown in each story.

Setting Details

The Man to Send Rain Clouds	Old Man of the Temple
Place:	Place:
Time:	Time:
Culture:	Culture:

Vocabulary Builder

The Man to Send Rain Clouds

- **penetrated** (pen´ i trāt´ ed) *v.* broke through (p. 272) *I pressed until the thumbtack* <u>penetrated</u> *the wall.*

- **perverse** (pər vurs´) *adj.* deviating from what is considered right (p. 272) *It would be* <u>perverse</u> *to go swimming on such a cold day.*

Old Man of the Temple

- **awry** (ə rī´) *adj.* not straight (p. 276) *Some bricks were* <u>awry</u>, *sticking out from the flat edge of wall.*

- **venture** (ven´ chər) *n.* an action involving risk (p. 280) *Stealing second base was a* <u>venture</u> *that paid off.*

Build Understanding

Connecting to the Literature

Reading/Writing Connection In both of these stories, the authors show the modern world combining with traditional ways. Write a few sentences in which you explain the benefits and drawbacks of maintaining traditions. Use at least three of the following words in your description: *challenge, display, emphasize, enrich.*

Meet the Authors

Leslie Marmon **Silko** (b. 1948)

Storytelling has always been an important part of Leslie Marmon Silko's life. Raised on the Laguna Pueblo reservation in New Mexico, she grew up listening to tribal stories told by her great-grandmother and great aunts. She has said that the oral tradition is "a collective memory and depends upon the whole community."

The Old and the New In her stories, novels, and poems, Silko explores what life is like for Native Americans in today's world. Many of her works capture the contrast between traditional values and beliefs and elements of modern life.

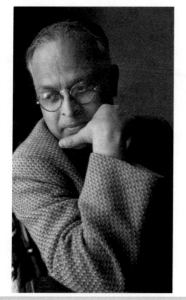

R. K. **Narayan** (1906–2001)

R. K. Narayan was born in the city of Madras in southern India. He was one of nine children in a middle-class family. After briefly working as a teacher, he became a writer. In 1960, his novel *The Guide* won India's highest literary honor.

Combining Themes Within a career that spanned nearly seventy years, Narayan wrote more than fifteen novels—as well as collections of short stories and essays. His works skillfully combine Western plots and themes with Indian subject matter.

For: More information about the authors
Visit: www.PHSchool.com
Web Code: epe-9207

The Man to Send Rain Clouds / Old Man of the Temple ■ 267

THE MAN TO SEND RAIN CLOUDS

Leslie Marmon Silko

They found him under a big cottonwood tree. His Levi jacket and pants were faded light blue so that he had been easy to find. The big cottonwood tree stood apart from a small grove of winterbare cottonwoods which grew in the wide, sandy arroyo.[1] He had been dead for a day or more, and the sheep had wandered and scattered up and down the arroyo. Leon and his brother-in-law, Ken, gathered the sheep and left them in the pen at the sheep camp before they returned to the cottonwood tree. Leon waited under the tree while Ken drove the truck through the deep sand to the edge of the arroyo. He squinted up at the sun and unzipped his jacket—it sure was hot for this time of year. But high and northwest the blue mountains were still in snow. Ken came sliding down the low, crumbling bank about fifty yards down, and he was bringing the red blanket.

Before they wrapped the old man, Leon took a piece of string out of his pocket and tied a small gray feather in the old man's long

Literary Analysis
Setting What do the details about the trees, mountains, and sheep reveal about the characters' way of life?

---

1. **arroyo** (ə rōī′ ō) *n.* a dry gully or hollow in the earth's surface.

white hair. Ken gave him the paint. Across the brown wrinkled forehead he drew a streak of white and along the high cheekbones he drew a strip of blue paint. He paused and watched Ken throw pinches of corn meal and pollen into the wind that fluttered the small gray feather. Then Leon painted with yellow under the old man's broad nose, and finally, when he had painted green across the chin, he smiled.

"Send us rain clouds, Grandfather." They laid the bundle in the back of the pickup and covered it with a heavy tarp before they started back to the pueblo.

They turned off the highway onto the sandy pueblo road. Not long after they passed the store and post office they saw Father Paul's car coming toward them. When he recognized their faces he slowed his car and waved for them to stop. The young priest rolled down the car window.

"Did you find old Teofilo?" he asked loudly.

Leon stopped the truck. "Good morning, Father. We were just out to the sheep camp. Everything is O.K. now."

▲ **Critical Viewing**
Which physical features of the New Mexico landscape does this photograph reveal? **[Analyze]**

Reading Check

How do Leon and Ken prepare the old man's body before they move it?

"Thank God for that. Teofilo is a very old man. You really shouldn't allow him to stay at the sheep camp alone."

"No, he won't do that any more now."

"Well, I'm glad you understand. I hope I'll be seeing you at Mass[2] this week—we missed you last Sunday. See if you can get old Teofilo to come with you." The priest smiled and waved at them as they drove away.

Louise and Teresa were waiting. The table was set for lunch, and the coffee was boiling on the black iron stove. Leon looked at Louise and then at Teresa.

"We found him under a cottonwood tree in the big arroyo near sheep camp. I guess he sat down to rest in the shade and never got up again." Leon walked toward the old man's bed. The red plaid shawl had been shaken and spread carefully over the bed, and a new brown flannel shirt and pair of stiff new Levi's were arranged neatly beside the pillow. Louise held the screen door open while Leon and Ken carried in the red blanket. He looked small and shriveled, and after they dressed him in the new shirt and pants he seemed more shrunken.

It was noontime now because the church bells rang the Angelus.[3] They ate the beans with hot bread, and nobody said anything until after Teresa poured the coffee.

Ken stood up and put on his jacket. "I'll see about the gravediggers. Only the top layer of soil is frozen. I think it can be ready before dark."

Leon nodded his head and finished his coffee. After Ken had been gone for a while, the neighbors and clanspeople came quietly to embrace Teofilo's family and to leave food on the table because the gravediggers would come to eat when they were finished.

The sky in the west was full of pale yellow light. Louise stood outside with her hands in the pockets of Leon's green army jacket that was too big for her. The funeral was over, and the old men had taken their candles and medicine bags[4] and were gone. She waited until the body was laid into the pickup before she said anything to Leon. She touched his arm, and he noticed that her hands were still dusty from the corn meal that she had sprinkled around the old man. When she spoke, Leon could not hear her.

"What did you say? I didn't hear you."

"I said that I had been thinking about something."

"About what?"

Literary Analysis
Setting Which detail here is a reminder of the Christian influence in the characters' lives?

---

2. **Mass** (mas) *n.* church service celebrated by Roman Catholics.
3. **Angelus** (an´ jə ləs) *n.* bell rung at morning, noon, and evening to announce a prayer.
4. **medicine bags** bags containing objects that were thought to have special powers.

"About the priest sprinkling holy water for Grandpa. So he won't be thirsty."

Leon stared at the new moccasins that Teofilo had made for the ceremonial dances in the summer. They were nearly hidden by the red blanket. It was getting colder, and the wind pushed gray dust down the narrow pueblo road. The sun was approaching the long mesa where it disappeared during the winter. Louise stood there shivering and watching his face. Then he zipped up his jacket and opened the truck door. "I'll see if he's there."

Ken stopped the pickup at the church, and Leon got out: and then Ken drove down the hill to the graveyard where people were waiting. Leon knocked at the old carved door with its symbols of the Lamb.[5] While he waited he looked up at the twin bells from the king of Spain with the last sunlight pouring around them in their tower.

The priest opened the door and smiled when he saw who it was. "Come in! What brings you here this evening?"

---

5. **the Lamb** Jesus Christ, as the sacrificial Lamb of God.

▲ **Critical Viewing**
How does the scene depicted in this painting compare to the images described in the story? **[Compare and Contrast]**

Reading Check

What do the old men take with them when the funeral is over?

The priest walked toward the kitchen, and Leon stood with his cap in his hand, playing with the earflaps and examining the living room—the brown sofa, the green armchair, and the brass lamp that hung down from the ceiling by links of chain. The priest dragged a chair out of the kitchen and offered it to Leon.

"No thank you, Father. I only came to ask you if you would bring your holy water to the graveyard."

The priest turned away from Leon and looked out the window at the patio full of shadows and the dining-room windows of the nuns' cloister[6] across the patio. The curtains were heavy, and the light from within faintly <u>penetrated</u>; it was impossible to see the nuns inside eating supper. "Why didn't you tell me he was dead? I could have brought the Last Rites[7] anyway."

Leon smiled. "It wasn't necessary, Father."

The priest stared down at his scuffed brown loafers and the worn hem of his cassock. "For a Christian burial it was necessary."

His voice was distant, and Leon thought that his blue eyes looked tired.

"It's O.K. Father, we just want him to have plenty of water."

The priest sank down into the green chair and picked up a glossy missionary magazine. He turned the colored pages full of lepers and pagans[8] without looking at them.

"You know I can't do that, Leon. There should have been the Last Rites and a funeral Mass at the very least."

Leon put on his green cap and pulled the flaps down over his ears. "It's getting late, Father. I've got to go."

When Leon opened the door Father Paul stood up and said, "Wait." He left the room and came back wearing a long brown over-coat. He followed Leon out the door and across the dim churchyard to the adobe steps in front of the church. They both stooped to fit through the low adobe entrance. And when they started down the hill to the graveyard only half of the sun was visible above the mesa.

The priest approached the grave slowly, wondering how they had managed to dig into the frozen ground; and then he remembered that this was New Mexico, and saw the pile of cold loose sand beside the hole. The people stood close to each other with little clouds of steam puffing from their faces. The priest looked at them and saw a pile of jackets, gloves, and scarves in the yellow, dry tumbleweeds that grew in the graveyard. He looked at the red blanket, not sure that Teofilo was so small, wondering if it wasn't some <u>perverse</u> Indian trick—something they did in March to ensure a good harvest—wondering if maybe old Teofilo was actually at sheep camp

---

6. **cloister** (klois´ tər) n. place devoted to religious seclusion.
7. **Last Rites** religious ceremony for a dying person or for someone who has just died.
8. **pagans** (pā´ gənz) n. people who are not Christians, Muslims, or Jews.

corraling the sheep for the night. But there he was, facing into a cold dry wind and squinting at the last sunlight, ready to bury a red wool blanket while the faces of his parishioners were in shadow with the last warmth of the sun on their backs.

His fingers were stiff, and it took him a long time to twist the lid off the holy water. Drops of water fell on the red blanket and soaked into dark icy spots. He sprinkled the grave and the water disappeared almost before it touched the dim, cold sand; it reminded him of something—he tried to remember what it was, because he thought if he could remember he might understand this. He sprinkled more water; he shook the container until it was empty, and the water fell through the light from sundown like August rain that fell while the sun was still shining, almost evaporating before it touched the wilted squash flowers.

The wind pulled at the priest's brown Franciscan robe[9] and swirled away the corn meal and pollen that had been sprinkled on the blanket. They lowered the bundle into the ground, and they didn't bother to untie the stiff pieces of new rope that were tied around the ends of the blanket. The sun was gone, and over on the highway the eastbound lane was full of headlights. The priest walked away slowly. Leon watched him climb the hill, and when he had disappeared within the tall, thick walls, Leon turned to look up at the high blue mountains in the deep snow that reflected a faint red light from the west. He felt good because it was finished, and he was happy about the sprinkling of the holy water; now the old man could send them big thunderclouds for sure.

9. Franciscan (fran sis´ kən) **robe** robe worn by a member of the Franciscan religious order, founded in 1209 by Saint Francis of Assisi.

Literary Analysis
Setting Which details in the last paragraph reflect Native American practices and beliefs? Explain.

Thinking About the Selection

1. **Respond:** What did you find most interesting about this story?
2. **(a) Recall:** What do Leon and Ken find at the beginning of the story? **(b) Infer:** Why does Leon avoid telling Father Paul about Teofilo's death at first?
3. **(a) Infer:** Why is Father Paul upset about the burial ceremony? **(b) Infer:** What insight into the Pueblo people does Father Paul gain during the ceremony?
4. **(a) Interpret:** What feelings does Leon experience when the burial ceremony is over? **(b) Draw Conclusions:** What do Leon's thoughts after Teofilo's burial reveal about his views of death? **(c) Compare and Contrast:** What does the ending reveal about the contrasts between Pueblo and Christian beliefs?

Old Man of the Temple

R. K. Narayan

The Talkative Man said:

It was some years ago that this happened. I don't know if you can make anything of it. If you do, I shall be glad to hear what you have to say; but personally I don't understand it at all. It has always mystified me. Perhaps the driver was drunk; perhaps he wasn't.

I had engaged a taxi for going to Kumbum, which, as you may already know, is fifty miles from Malgudi.[1] I went there one morning and it was past nine in the evening when I finished my business and started back for the town. Doss [däs], the driver, was a young fellow of about twenty-five. He had often brought his car for me and I liked him. He was a well-behaved, obedient fellow, with a capacity to sit and wait at the wheel, which is really a rare quality in a taxi driver. He drove the car smoothly, seldom swore at passers-by, and exhibited perfect judgment, good

▼ **Critical Viewing**
What mysterious events might occur in a temple like this?
[Speculate]

---

1. Malgudi (mäl gōō′ dē) fictional town about which Narayan often writes.

sense, and sobriety; and so I preferred him to any other driver whenever I had to go out on business.

It was about eleven when we passed the village Koopal [kōō päl'], which is on the way down. It was the dark half of the month and the surrounding country was swallowed up in the night. The village street was deserted. Everyone had gone to sleep; hardly any light was to be seen. The stars overhead sparkled brightly. Sitting in the back seat and listening to the continuous noise of the running wheels, I was half lulled into a drowse.

All of a sudden Doss swerved the car and shouted: "You old fool! Do you want to kill yourself ?"

I was shaken out of my drowse and asked: "What is the matter?"

Doss stopped the car and said, "You see that old fellow, sir. He is trying to kill himself. I can't understand what he is up to."

I looked in the direction he pointed and asked, "Which old man?"

"There, there. He is coming towards us again. As soon as I saw him open that temple door and come out I had a feeling, somehow, that I must keep an eye on him."

I took out my torch, got down, and walked about, but could see no one. There was an old temple on the roadside. It was utterly in ruins; most portions of it were mere mounds of old brick; the walls were <u>awry</u>; the doors were shut to the main doorway, and brambles and thickets grew over and covered them. It was difficult to guess with the aid of the torch alone what temple it was and to what period it belonged.

"The doors are shut and sealed and don't look as if they had been opened for centuries now," I cried.

"No, sir," Doss said coming nearer. "I saw the old man open the doors and come out. He is standing there; shall we ask him to open them again if you want to go in and see?"

I said to Doss, "Let us be going. We are wasting our time here."

We went back to the car. Doss sat in his seat, pressed the self-starter, and asked without turning his head, "Are you permitting this fellow to come with us, sir? He says he will get down at the next milestone."

"Which fellow?" I asked.

Doss indicated the space next to him.

"What is the matter with you, Doss? Have you had a drop of drink or something?"

"I have never tasted any drink in my life, sir," he said, and added, "Get down, old boy. Master says he can't take you."

"Are you talking to yourself?"

"After all, I think we needn't care for these unknown fellows on the road," he said.

"Doss," I pleaded. "Do you feel confident you can drive? If you feel dizzy don't drive."

"Thank you, sir," said Doss. "I would rather not start the car now. I am feeling a little out of sorts." I looked at him anxiously. He closed his eyes, his breathing became heavy and noisy, and gradually his head sank.

"Doss, Doss," I cried desperately. I got down, walked to the front seat, opened the door, and shook him vigorously. He opened his eyes, assumed a hunched-up position, and rubbed his eyes with his hands, which trembled like an old man's.

"Do you feel better?" I asked.

"Better! Better! Hi! Hi!" he said in a thin, piping voice.

"What has happened to your voice? You sound like someone else," I said.

"Nothing. My voice is as good as it was. When a man is eighty he is bound to feel a few changes coming on."

"You aren't eighty, surely," I said.

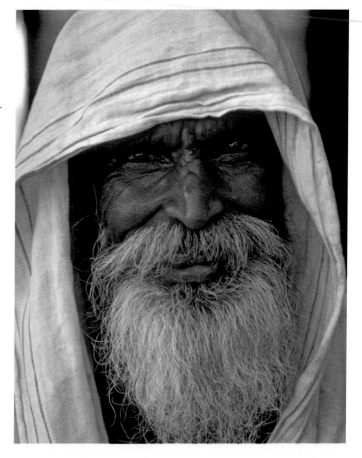

"Not a day less," he said. "Is nobody going to move this vehicle? If not, there is no sense in sitting here all day. I will get down and go back to my temple."

"I don't know how to drive," I said. "And unless you do it, I don't see how it can move."

"Me!" exclaimed Doss. "These new chariots! God knows what they are drawn by, I never understand, though I could handle a pair of bullocks[2] in my time. May I ask a question?"

"Go on," I said.

"Where is everybody?"

"Who?"

"Lots of people I knew are not to be seen at all. All sorts of new fellows everywhere, and nobody seems to care. Not a soul comes near the temple. All sorts of people go about but not one who cares to stop and talk. Why doesn't the king ever come this way? He used to go this way at least once a year before."

"Which king?" I asked.

▲ Critical Viewing
How does the man in this picture compare to your vision of the old man in the story? [Compare and Contrast]

 Reading Check
How old does Doss say he is when he wakes up?

---

2. **bullocks** (boŏl´ əks) young bulls.

"Let me go, you idiot," said Doss, edging towards the door on which I was leaning. "You don't seem to know anything." He pushed me aside, and got down from the car. He stooped as if he had a big hump on his back, and hobbled along towards the temple. I followed him, hardly knowing what to do. He turned and snarled at me: "Go away, leave me alone. I have had enough of you."

"What has come over you, Doss?" I asked.

"Who is Doss, anyway? Doss, Doss, Doss. What an absurd name! Call me by my name or leave me alone. Don't follow me calling 'Doss, Doss.'"

"What is your name?" I asked.

"Krishna Battar [krish′ nə bə tar′], and if you mention my name people will know for a hundred miles around. I built a temple where there was only a cactus field before. I dug the earth, burnt every brick, and put them one upon another, all single-handed. And on the day the temple held up its tower over the surrounding country, what a crowd gathered! The king sent his chief minister . . ."

"Who was the king?"

"Where do you come from?" he asked.

"I belong to these parts certainly, but as far as I know there has been only a collector at the head of the district. I have never heard of any king."

"Hi! Hi! Hi!" he cackled, and his voice rang through the gloomy silent village. "Fancy never knowing the king! He will behead you if he hears it."

"What is his name?" I asked.

This tickled him so much that he sat down on the ground, literally unable to stand the joke any more. He laughed an coughed uncontrollably.

"I am sorry to admit," I said, "that my parents have brought me up in such utter ignorance of worldly affairs that I don't know even my king. But won't you enlighten me? What is his name?"

"Vishnu Varma [vish′ noo vär′ mə], the emperor of emperors . . ."

I cast my mind up and down the range of my historical knowledge but there was no one by that name. Perhaps a local chief of pre-British days, I thought.

"What a king! He often visited my temple or sent his minister for the Annual Festival of the temple. But now nobody cares."

"People are becoming less godly nowadays," I said. There was silence for a moment. An idea occurred to me, I can't say why. "Listen to me," I said. "You ought not to be here any more."

"What do you mean?" he asked, drawing himself up, proudly.

"Don't feel hurt; I say you shouldn't be here any more because you are dead."

"Dead! Dead!" he said. "Don't talk nonsense. How can I be dead when you see me before you now? If I am dead how can I be saying this and that?"

"I don't know all that," I said. I argued and pointed out that according to his own story he was more than five hundred years old, and didn't he know that man's longevity was only a hundred? He constantly interrupted me, but considered deeply what I said.

He said: "It is like this . . . I was coming through the jungle one night after visiting my sister in the next village. I had on me some money and gold ornaments. A gang of robbers set upon me. I gave them as good a fight as any man could, but they were too many for me. They beat me down and knifed me; they took away all that I had on me and left thinking they had killed me. But soon I got up and tried to follow them. They were gone. And I returned to the temple and have been here since . . ."

I told him, "Krishna Battar, you are dead, absolutely dead. You must try and go away from here."

"What is to happen to the temple?" he asked.

"Others will look after it."

"Where am I to go? Where am I to go?"

"Have you no one who cares for you?" I asked.

"None except my wife. I loved her very much."

"You can go to her."

"Oh, no. She died four years ago . . ."

Four years! It was very puzzling. "Do you say four years back from now?" I asked.

"Yes, four years ago from now." He was clearly without any sense of time.

So I asked, "Was she alive when you were attacked by thieves?"

"Certainly not. If she had been alive she would never have allowed me to go through the jungle after nightfall. She took very good care of me."

"See here," I said. "It is imperative you should go away from here. If she comes and calls you, will you go?"

"How can she when I tell you that she is dead?"

I thought for a moment. Presently I found myself saying, "Think of her, and only of her, for a while and see what happens. What was her name?"

"Seetha [sē' thə], a wonderful girl . . ."

"Come on, think of her." He remained in deep thought for a while. He suddenly screamed, "Seetha is coming! Am I dreaming or what?

Literary Analysis
Setting What details of setting are revealed through the old man's story of the robbery?

Reading Check

Based on the old man's story, how old does the narrator think the old man is?

I will go with her . . ." He stood up, very erect; he appeared to have lost all the humps and twists he had on his body. He drew himself up, made a dash forward, and fell down in a heap.

Doss lay on the rough ground. The only sign of life in him was his faint breathing. I shook him and called him. He would not open his eyes. I walked across and knocked on the door of the first cottage. I banged on the door violently.

Someone moaned inside, "Ah, it is come!"

Someone else whispered, "You just cover your ears and sleep. It will knock for a while and go away." I banged on the door and shouted who I was and where I came from.

I walked back to the car and sounded the horn. Then the door opened, and a whole family crowded out with lamps. "We thought it was the usual knocking and we wouldn't have opened if you hadn't spoken."

"When was this knocking first heard?" I asked.

"We can't say," said one. "The first time I heard it was when my grandfather was living; he used to say he had even seen it once or twice. It doesn't harm anyone, as far as I know. The only thing it does is bother the bullock carts passing the temple and knock on the doors at night . . ."

I said as a <u>venture</u>, "It is unlikely you will be troubled any more."

It proved correct. When I passed that way again months later I was told that the bullocks passing the temple after dusk never shied now and no knocking on the doors was heard at nights. So I felt that the old fellow had really gone away with his good wife.

Thinking About the Selection

1. **Respond:** How would you have reacted if you were in the narrator's situation? Explain.

2. **(a) Recall:** Early in the story, what does Doss say he sees when the car swerves? **(b) Analyze:** Why does the narrator find Doss's words unbelievable?

3. **(a) Summarize:** Describe Doss's transformation. **(b) Analyze:** At first, how does the narrator react to the change? **(c) Extend:** In what ways does the narrator's reaction change?

4. **(a) Summarize:** How does the narrator finally get the ghost to go away? **(b) Connect:** What new information does the family at the end of the story provide? **(c) Support:** Do you think this information makes the story more or less effective? Explain.

5. **Evaluate:** How would you respond to the narrator's invitation to "hear what you have to say" about his story?

Apply the Skills

The Man to Send Rain Clouds • Old Man of the Temple

Comparing Setting

1. **(a)** Describe the place, time, and culture of each story. **(b)** For each story, note at least two details that describe each aspect of the setting—the geographical location, the time, and the cultural environment.

2. If the setting changed, could either story take place without being totally different? Explain.

Writing to Compare Literary Works

In an essay, compare and contrast the way the setting in each story influences the characters and story events. Use the following questions and chart to get started:

- How do the characters in each story live?
- What cultural values and beliefs are present in each story?
- Does the setting itself cause or somehow affect the events that take place in each story?
- Do any of the characters in each story change their thinking or behavior because of the setting? Explain.

The Man to Send Rain Clouds	Old Man of the Temple
Effect of Setting on Characters:	Effect of Setting on Characters:
↓	↓
Role of Setting:	Role of Setting:

Vocabulary Builder

Practice Answer each question. Explain your answer.

1. Would you fix a group of wall hangings that are *awry*?
2. Would it be *perverse* to wear sunglasses at night?
3. Would you be certain about the outcome of a new business *venture*?
4. Would you be glad if a nail *penetrated* your bicycle tire?

QuickReview

Setting: the time and place in which a story occurs

Go Online
Assessment

For: Self-test
Visit: www.PHSchool.com
Web Code: epa-6206

Reading

"That is the letter which I have just received Mr. Holmes, and my mind is made up that I will accept it. I thought, however, that before taking the final step I should like to submit the whole matter to your consideration."

"Well, Miss Hunter, if your mind is made up, that settles the question," said Holmes, smiling.

"But you would not advise me to refuse?"

"I confess that it is not the situation which I should like to see a sister of mine apply for."

—from *The Adventure of the Copper Beeches,* by Sir Arthur Conan Doyle

1. From Holmes's last reply, the reader can infer
   A that he is impolite and rude.
   B that he is politically conservative.
   C that he is polite and diplomatic.
   D that he does not approve of Miss Hunter.

2. From the conversation, the reader can infer
   A that Miss Hunter's mind is made up.
   B that Miss Hunter's mind is not really made up.
   C that Miss Hunter is asking Holmes's opinion out of habit.
   D that Miss Hunter doesn't care about Holmes's opinion.

3. The way the characters speak helps us infer that
   A the conversation is taking place in the future.
   B the conversation is taking place in the past.
   C the conversation is taking place in the present.
   D the conversation is taking place in the characters' minds.

4. Which would not be a reasonable inference given the passage?
   A Holmes and Miss Hunter know each other fairly well.
   B Holmes and Miss Hunter have talked before.
   C Miss Hunter respects Holmes's opinion.
   D Holmes and Miss Hunter have just met.

5. From the tone of this conversation, which of the following would be a reasonable inference?
   A Miss Hunter will follow Holmes's advice.
   B Miss Hunter will not follow Holmes's advice.
   C Miss Hunter will attempt to convince Holmes to change his mind.
   D Miss Hunter will ignore Holmes's advice.

Vocabulary

Directions: *Choose the word that best completes the sentence.*

6. Lisa wondered what Mary Ann's real _____ was in offering her a ride.
   A motive
   B attitude
   C opinion
   D topic

7. Examine each _____ of the story.
   A speculation
   B motivation
   C aspect
   D emotion

8. Although the candidate spoke with _____, no one believed he was sincere.
   A category
   B emotion
   C attitude
   D aspect

9. My biology homework is to study the _____ of Linnaeus's system of classification.
   A categories
   B emotions
   C attitudes
   D motives

10. The _____ that led to World War II are still debated by historians.
    A opinions
    B topics
    C circumstances
    D aspects

Directions: *Match each word with its definition.*

11. motionless
    A without direction
    B without looking ahead
    C without movement
    D without stopping

12. circulation
    A erratic motion
    B movement in a straight path
    C sporadic motion
    D movement around

13. motivity
    A the power of moving
    B the product of resting
    C the residual of stopping
    D the effect of being

14. spectacle
    A an interesting event
    B a moving object
    C a determined person
    D a remarkable sight

15. circumvent
    A to go around
    B to go through
    C to go back
    D to go inside

Narration: Short Story

Stories are one of the oldest and most familiar forms of literature. A traditional **short story** is a brief, fictional narrative composed of plot, setting, and characters. Follow the steps outlined in this workshop to write your own short story.

Assignment Write a short story that presents characters in a specific setting engaged in a conflict that is resolved.

What to Include Your short story should feature the following elements:
- a main character who takes part in the action
- details that establish a particular time, place, and mood
- a conflict, or problem, that is introduced, developed, and resolved
- a central theme, or message about life
- error-free grammar, including correct use of verbs

To preview the criteria on which your short story may be assessed, see the rubric on page 288.

Prewriting

Choosing Your Topic
Use sentence starters. Complete the following sentence starters to search for a topic. Note any memories or ideas they inspire.
- The strangest place I ever visited is . . .
- I was shocked to discover that . . .
- One person whom I will never forget is . . .

Focus on the sentence that sparks your imagination and jot down notes about a series of events that could form a plot.

Gathering Details
Develop characters. Use a chart like the one shown to note details that will help readers visualize your characters. Note how your characters speak, including any instances of dialect—regional speech—that will make them sound authentic.

Characters	Details
Giant	• Tall, shy • Follows, doesn't lead
Uno	• Nickname means "one" • Self-centered • Slick talker

Standard Course of Study
- Analyze connections among ideas, concepts, characters and experience in response. (WL.1.03.9)
- Recognize and analyze the characteristics of literary genres. (LT.5.01.2)
- Determine a character's traits. (LT.5.01.7)

Using the Form
You may use elements of this form in these types of writing:
- science fiction
- mysteries
- autobiographies

To get a feel for short stories, read "The Gift of the Magi" by O. Henry on page 245.

Work in Progress
Review the work you did on pages 195, 239, and 265.

Drafting

Shaping Your Writing

Plan the story line. Every paragraph in your story should help readers understand at least one of these elements:

- the **characters'** personalities, attitudes, and relationships
- the **setting** and its effect on events
- the **conflict** or struggles the characters face
- the **action** that occurs as a result of all of the above

Consider identifying one element, such as a place or an object, as a symbol that will help express the theme of your story.

Providing Elaboration

Show instead of tell. Use descriptions and dialogue to make events and characters vivid for your readers. Do not simply report that a street was noisy; give your readers details that let them hear the noise. Do not report that your characters had an argument; use dialogue to show it.

Revising

Revising Your Overall Structure

Maintain an effective sequence of events. Every detail in your story should deepen your portrayal of the characters or increase the tension of the conflict. Review your draft, noting any interruptions to the momentum of your plot. Consider modifying or deleting such interruptions.

For the complete student model, see page 287.

Student Model: Revising to Clarify Sequence

Then, we noticed something strange. ~~For a second I thought about what it was like back up on the grass.~~ There were other, different words painted on the wall and what they said scared us all: "Your friend is here. Don't try to find him."

> The writer omits a detail that slows the story down.

Revising Your Word Choice

Use active language. To create dynamic sentences, choose the active voice instead of the passive voice. Make sure that the subjects in your sentences perform the action.

> **Passive Voice:** The problem was solved by Curtis.
> **Active Voice:** Curtis solved the problem.

Integrating Grammar Skills

Revising Inconsistent Verb Tenses

Prentice Hall Writing and Grammar Connection: Chapter 23, Section 1

A tense is a form of a verb that expresses the time of an action. The six verb tenses are present, present perfect, past, past perfect, future, and future perfect. Inconsistent or unclear use of verb tenses can cause confusion in a story.

Identifying Inconsistent Verb Tenses Inconsistent verb tense occurs when a sentence begins in one tense and switches into another without explanation or logic.

> **Incorrect:** She *skied* every day we *go* to the mountains last winter.

> **Correct:** She *skied* every day we *went* to the mountains last winter.

Shifts in tense should always reflect a logical sequence.

> **Incorrect:** I *will be* on time today, but I *was* on time tomorrow.

> **Correct:** I *was* on time today, and I *will be* on time tomorrow.

Perfect tenses can clarify a sequence of actions.

> **Unclear:** By the time she *arrived,* we *started* the meeting.

> **Clear:** By the time she *arrived,* we *had started* the meeting.

Fixing Errors To maintain consistent use of verb tenses, scan your draft for shifts in tense.

1. **Identify the reason for each shift.** Correct any that are unnecessary.

2. **Determine which actions happened first.** When two actions occur at different times in the past, use the past perfect tense for the earlier action.

Uses of Past Perfect Tense	
Past action of condition completed before another	I had been to the museum before it was remodeled.
Continuing past action interrupted by another	I had been on the telephone when you rang the doorbell.

Apply It to Your Editing

Review a passage of your draft that includes both narrative and dialogue. Underline any shifts in tense that you find. Be sure that the shift represents a clear and logical time order. Fix any inconsistent tenses.

Student Model: **Randy Hays
Clackamas, OR**

The Oil Slick

The Oil Slick is a place where I play baseball with a bunch of friends. We call the field the "Oil Slick" because a boat carrying gallons of oil once sailed by. The boat sprang a leak, polluting the water around it. The Oil Slick also has a big hole in the outfield. . . .

My nickname is Giant. It suits me because I am the tallest player on the team. . . . I only know the nicknames of the others on my team. They're called Ant, Dash, Rip, X-Ray, Target, Eye, Animal, Uno, and Cover. . . .

This morning, I headed out to the Oil Slick, ready to play. However, before we started, Uno held a meeting. "As you know," he said, "there is a hole in the outfield."

"Who can tell me why the hole is there?" There was silence until Uno spoke again. "That's what I thought," he said. "Some people say there's treasure buried on this field. Somebody probably tried to dig for it, and they left that hole behind. I thought maybe we should dig, too, but then I figured that'd be stupid. It's probably just a rumor. We wouldn't find anything, diggin' holes."

Silence again until someone shouted. "Let's play already!" Everyone went to their positions and the game started. . . .

Rip hit the ball and it flew past the right-fielder, Eye. Concentrating on the ball, Eye ran toward the hole. He didn't know when to stop and he fell. . . .

We all ran and looked down the hole. Nobody had ever bothered to really look before, and it was deep, much deeper than we thought. Hoping to find Eye, we jumped in. . . .

When we saw what the hole truly was we forgot about Eye. We had expected dirt, rocks—the usual stuff you'd find in a hole. Instead, we saw smooth walls, stretching into the distance. All this time, without ever suspecting it, we had been playing above a maze of tunnels. . . .

We headed down the tunnel to our right. . . . These weren't ordinary tunnels. They had the names of famous baseball players carved right into the walls. Then, we noticed something strange. There were other, different words painted on the wall and what they said scared us all: "Your friend is here. Don't try to find him. Or else."

We continued through the tunnels until we emerged in a room which . . . had a sign that said, "You Found Him." Sure enough, there was Eye, leaning against a wall. He saw us and shouted, "Go! Now!"

But it was too late. A door slammed shut and we were trapped. Then, we heard a familiar voice. "You saw the warnings, but you didn't stop. Now you are trapped and the treasure is mine!". . .

Randy starts the story with a detailed description of an interesting setting.

The characters' quirky nicknames help the writer create a sense of what each one is like.

Randy uses dialogue to introduce the mystery of the hole in the field—the source of the story's conflict.

The conflict intensifies here.

Go Online
Read More

For: the complete student model
Visit: www.PHSchool.com
Web Code: epm-4201

Writing Workshop

Editing and Proofreading

Check your draft for errors in spelling, grammar, and punctuation.
Focus on Punctuating Dialogue: Make sure that your characters' spoken words are properly indented and demonstrate correct use of commas and quotation marks. Follow this example:

Prentice Hall Writing and Grammar Connection: Chapter 4

▶ **Example:** "Don't forget to call us," Natalie reminded us as we left.
　　　　　　Paul teased, "How *could* we forget?"

Publishing and Presenting

Consider one of the following ways to share your writing:
Deliver an oral presentation. Read your story aloud to your classmates. Get feedback from your classmates and make revisions based on their comments.
Create an anthology. Work with classmates to collect your stories in a single binder. Illustrate the stories with photographs or artwork and agree on a title for the collection. Contribute the anthology to the classroom or school library.

Reflecting on Your Writing

Writer's Journal Jot down your thoughts about writing a short story. Begin by answering these questions:
- Which prewriting and drafting strategies were most useful to you?
- How has the experience of writing a story affected the way you now read stories written by others?

Rubric for Self-Assessment

To assess your short story, use this rubric:

NC	Criteria	Rating Scale				
		not very				*very*
	Focus: How clear is the story's theme or message?	1	2	3	4	5
	Organization: How clearly do you introduce, develop, and resolve the conflict?	1	2	3	4	5
	Support/Elaboration: How well do you use details to establish time, place, and mood?	1	2	3	4	5
	Style: How well do you describe the characters and setting?	1	2	3	4	5
	Conventions: How correct is your grammar, especially your use of verb tenses?	1	2	3	4	5

Unit 2
Part 2
Cause and Effect

Skills You Will Learn

Literary Analysis: *Character and Characterization*
Reading Skill: *Ask Questions to Analyze Cause and Effect*

Literary Analysis: *Dialogue and Dialect*
Reading Skill: *Visualize the Action*

Reading Skill: *Evaluate Text Format*

Literary Analysis: *Symbolism and Allegory*

Literature You Will Read

Reading and Vocabulary Skills Preview

Reading: Cause and Effect

NC Standard Course of Study

> A **cause** is the reason for an action or event. An **effect** is the result of an action or event.

- Make inferences and draw conclusions based on text to answer research questions. (IR.2.01.6)
- Explain and interpret archetypal characters, themes, settings. (LT.5.01.5)

Skills and Strategies You Will Learn in Part 2

In Part 2 you will learn
- to **ask questions** to **analyze cause** and **effect** (p. 292).
- to **visualize** the action to **analyze cause** and **effect** (p. 320).
- to **evaluate text format** and **analyze the effects** of format presentation (p. 344).

Using the Skills and Strategies in Part 2

In Part 2 you will learn to ask questions that help you recognize the relationships between events. You will practice picturing the actions and breaking down a chain of events to analyze causes and effects. Asking questions will help you define the cause-and-effect relationships in the text. Visualizing the action can also clarify these relationships.

The example shows you how you can apply some of the skills you will learn in Part 2.

CAUSE	EFFECT	EFFECT	EFFECT
Character is worried about being late for an appointment	Character is thinking and drives beyond the gas station	Car runs out of gas	Character is late
	CAUSE	CAUSE	

Questions for analyzing causes and effects
- Why does the character miss the gas station?
- What is the result of missing the gas station?
- Why does the car run out of gas?
- What is the result of the car running out of gas?

Academic Vocabulary: Words for Understanding Literature

The following words will help you write and talk about the literature in this unit.

Word	Definition	Example Sentence
sequence *n.*	an arrangement in which one follows another	The *sequence* of events is the basis of the plot.
topic *n.*	the subject of a work or talk	The *topic* of that essay was interesting.
attitude *n.*	a way of acting that shows a disposition or opinion	The character's *attitude* was the cause of their disagreement.
verify *v.*	test whether something is true	*Verify* the cause-effect relationship.
imply *v.*	hint at or suggest	The author *implied* that the murderer was one of the principal characters.

Vocabulary Skills: Word Roots

▶ A word **root** can be used to infer the meaning of a word.

In Part 2 you will learn
- Latin root *-ver-* (p. 318)
- Latin root *-sequi-* (p. 342)

Knowing the meaning of word roots helps you understand and remember the meanings of words that contain them. Look at the following chart.

Activity Look up each example word in a dictionary. Then, write questions, using a different example word in each question. Trade questions with a partner and answer each other's questions.

Root	Meaning	Examples
-ver-	truth	verify, verdict
-sequi-	follow	sequence, sequel

Practice these skills with either "The Necklace" (p. 294) or "Rules of the Game" (p. 305).

NC **Standard Course of Study**

Literary Analysis

A **character** is a person, an animal, or even an object that participates in the action and experiences the events of a literary work. Writers communicate what characters are like through **characterization:**

- **Direct characterization:** The writer explains a character.
- **Indirect characterization:** The writer gives clues to a character by describing the character's behavior, words and thoughts, physical appearance, or how others react to the character.

Use a chart like this one to track characterization as you read.

- Demonstrate comprehension of main idea and supporting details. (FA.3.04.4)
- Analyze and evaluate the effects of author's craft and literary style. (LT.5.03.10)
- Analyze influences, contexts, or biases in literary text. (LT.5.03.8)

Story Details	What They Show About the Character
Narrator's comments	
Character's thoughts and words	
Character's actions	
Character's appearance	
What others say or think about character	

Reading Skill

A **cause** is an event, an action, or a feeling that produces a result. An **effect** is the result produced. As you read, **ask questions to analyze cause and effect.**

- What happened?
- Why did it happen?
- What happens as a result?

A single cause may produce several effects. For example, a character who was once a poor student starts to do well in school. This gives her greater self-esteem. Effects may, in turn, become causes. For example, that same character's new confidence leads her to audition for a play.

Vocabulary Builder

The Necklace

- **rueful** (rōō′ fəl) *adj.* feeling sorrow or regret (p. 294) *Her thoughtless comment soon made her <u>rueful</u>.*
- **resplendent** (ri splen′ dənt) *adj.* shining brightly (p. 297) *The winner's face was <u>resplendent</u> as he accepted the prize.*
- **disheveled** (di shev′ əld) *adj.* untidy (p. 300) *Val's <u>disheveled</u> hair showed he had overslept.*
- **profoundly** (prō found′ lē) *adv.* deeply (p. 301) *We were all <u>profoundly</u> moved by the long-lost brothers' reunion.*

Rules of the Game

- **pungent** (pun′ jənt) *adj.* producing a sharp smell (p. 306) *The use of <u>pungent</u> spices promised a savory meal.*
- **benevolently** (bə nev′ ə lənt lē) *adv.* in a well-meaning way (p. 310) *The officer smiled <u>benevolently</u> at the children.*
- **retort** (ri tôrt′) *n.* sharp or clever reply (p. 310) *Her <u>retort</u> silenced her critic.*
- **malodorous** (mal ō′ dər əs) *adj.* having a bad smell (p. 313) *The <u>malodorous</u> bag was filled with garbage.*

Build Understanding • *The Necklace*

Background

European Society During the nineteenth century, the old social order in Europe changed. Previously, society was divided into two main classes: nobles, who owned land, and peasants, who farmed it. However, as industry spread, a new middle class emerged and people could rise—or sink—in social position. Some sought to own material goods as a mark of higher social standing.

Connecting to the Literature

Reading/Writing Connection In "The Necklace," a character wishes she owned jewelry that is far more costly than she can afford. Write several reasons why a person might want to have expensive things. Use at least three of these words: *obtain, impress, exceed, identify.*

READ MORE

by Guy de Maupassant
A Day in the Country and Other Stories

Meet the Author

Guy de Maupassant (1850–1893)

Perhaps the best-known short-story writer in the world, Guy de Maupassant (gē də mō pä sän´) wrote tales that are realistic and pessimistic, and often offer surprise endings.

Friendship with Writers Following his army service, he settled in Paris, where he began to develop his skills as a writer, guided by the famous French author Gustave Flaubert. Maupassant also joined a circle of writers led by French novelist Emile Zola. With Zola's encouragement, Maupassant published his first short story, "Ball of Fat," in 1880. The story earned him immediate fame and freed him to write full time. "The Necklace" is perhaps his most widely read story.

Fast Facts

▶ Maupassant had a photographic memory.
▶ Maupassant wrote some 300 short stories, six novels, and other books.

Go Online
Author Link

For: More about the author
Visit: www.PHSchool.com
Web Code: epe-9208

The Necklace

Guy de Maupassant

She was one of those pretty, charming young women who are born, as if by an error of Fate, into a petty official's family. She had no dowry,[1] no hopes, not the slightest chance of being appreciated, understood, loved, and married by a rich and distinguished man; so she slipped into marriage with a minor civil servant at the Ministry of Education.

Unable to afford jewelry, she dressed simply: but she was as wretched as a déclassée, for women have neither caste nor breeding—in them beauty, grace, and charm replace pride of birth. Innate refinement, instinctive elegance, and suppleness of wit give them their place on the only scale that counts, and these qualities make humble girls the peers of the grandest ladies.

She suffered constantly, feeling that all the attributes of a gracious life, every luxury, should rightly have been hers. The poverty of her rooms—the shabby walls, the worn furniture, the ugly upholstery—caused her pain. All these things that another woman of her class would not even have noticed, tormented her and made her angry. The very sight of the little Breton girl who cleaned for her awoke <u>rueful</u> thoughts and the wildest dreams in her mind. She dreamt of thick-carpeted reception rooms with Oriental hangings, lighted by tall, bronze torches, and with two huge

---

1. dowry (dou′ rē) *n.* property that a woman brought to her husband at marriage.

Literary Analysis
Characterization
Using direct characterization, what does the author tell you about the young woman in the first two paragraphs?

Vocabulary Builder
rueful (rōō′ fəl) *adj.* feeling sorrow or regret

footmen in knee breeches, made drowsy by the heat from the stove, asleep in the wide armchairs. She dreamt of great drawing rooms upholstered in old silks, with fragile little tables holding priceless knick-knacks, and of enchanting little sitting rooms redolent of perfume, designed for tea-time chats with intimate friends—famous, sought-after men whose attentions all women longed for.

When she sat down to dinner at her round table with its three-day-old cloth, and watched her husband opposite her lift the lid of the soup tureen and exclaim, delighted: "Ah, a good homemade beef stew! There's nothing better . . ." she would visualize elegant dinners with gleaming silver amid tapestried walls peopled by knights and ladies and exotic birds in a fairy forest; she would think of exquisite dishes served on gorgeous china, and of gallantries whispered and received with sphinx-like smiles while eating the pink flesh of trout or wings of grouse.

She had no proper wardrobe, no jewels, nothing. And those were the only things that she loved—she felt she was made for them. She would have so loved to charm, to be envied, to be admired and sought after.

She had a rich friend, a schoolmate from the convent she had attended, but she didn't like to visit her because it always made her so miserable when she got home again. She would weep for whole days at a time from sorrow, regret, despair, and distress.

Then one evening her husband arrived home looking triumphant and waving a large envelope.

"There," he said, "there's something for you."

She tore it open eagerly and took out a printed card which said:

"The Minister of Education and Madame Georges Ramponneau [ma dam′ zhôrzh rə nō′] request the pleasure of the company of M. and Mme. Loisel [lwa zel′] at an evening reception at the Ministry on Monday, January 18th."

Instead of being delighted, as her husband had hoped, she tossed the invitation on the table and muttered, annoyed:

"What do you expect me to do with that?"

"Why, I thought you'd be pleased, dear. You never go out and this would be an occasion for you, a great one! I had a lot of trouble getting it. Everyone wants an invitation; they're in great demand and there are only a few reserved for the employees. All the officials will be there."

She looked at him, irritated, and said impatiently:

"I haven't a thing to wear. How could I go?"

It had never even occurred to him. He stammered:

"But what about the dress you wear to the theater? I think it's lovely. . . ."

Literary Analysis
Characterization
What does the husband's comment in this paragraph reveal indirectly about his character?

Reading Skill
Analyze Cause and Effect Why do visits to her rich friend always fill the young woman with despair?

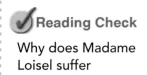Reading Check

Why does Madame Loisel suffer constantly?

He fell silent, amazed and bewildered to see that his wife was crying. Two big tears escaped from the corners of her eyes and rolled slowly toward the corners of her mouth. He mumbled:

"What is it? What is it?"

But, with great effort, she had overcome her misery; and now she answered him calmly, wiping her tear-damp cheeks:

"It's nothing. It's just that I have no evening dress and so I can't go to the party. Give the invitation to one of your colleagues whose wife will be better dressed than I would be."

He was overcome. He said:

"Listen, Mathilde [ma tēld'], how much would an evening dress cost—a suitable one that you could wear again on other occasions, something very simple?"

She thought for several seconds, making her calculations and at the same time estimating how much she could ask for without eliciting an immediate refusal and an exclamation of horror from this economical government clerk.

At last, not too sure of herself, she said:

"It's hard to say exactly but I think I could manage with four hundred francs."

He went a little pale, for that was exactly the amount he had put aside to buy a rifle so that he could go hunting the following summer near Nanterre, with a few friends who went shooting larks around there on Sundays.

However, he said:

"Well, all right, then. I'll give you four hundred francs. But try to get something really nice."

As the day of the ball drew closer, Madame Loisel seemed depressed, disturbed, worried—despite the fact that her dress was ready. One evening her husband said:

"What's the matter? You've really been very strange these last few days."

And she answered:

"I hate not having a single jewel, not one stone, to wear. I shall look so dowdy.[2] I'd almost rather not go to the party."

He suggested:

"You can wear some fresh flowers. It's considered very chic[3] at this time of year. For ten francs you can get two or three beautiful roses."

That didn't satisfy her at all.

"No . . . there's nothing more humiliating than to look poverty-stricken among a lot of rich women."

Reading Skill
Analyze Cause and Effect Why is the husband surprised by his wife's reaction to the party invitation?

---

2. dowdy (dou′dē) *adj.* shabby.
3. chic (shēk) *adj.* fashionable.

Then her husband exclaimed:

"Wait—you silly thing! Why don't you go and see Madame Forestier [fôr əs tyā´] and ask her to lend you some jewelry. You certainly know her well enough for that, don't you think?"

She let out a joyful cry.

"You're right. It never occurred to me."

The next day she went to see her friend and related her tale of woe.

Madame Forestier went to her mirrored wardrobe, took out a big jewel case, brought it to Madame Loisel, opened it, and said:

"Take your pick, my dear."

Her eyes wandered from some bracelets to a pearl necklace, then to a gold Venetian cross set with stones, of very fine workmanship. She tried on the jewelry before the mirror, hesitating, unable to bring herself to take them off, to give them back. And she kept asking:

"Do you have anything else, by chance?"

"Why yes. Here, look for yourself. I don't know which ones you'll like."

All at once, in a box lined with black satin, she came upon a superb diamond necklace, and her heart started beating with overwhelming desire. Her hands trembled as she picked it up. She fastened it around her neck over her high-necked dress and stood there gazing at herself ecstatically.

Hesitantly, filled with terrible anguish, she asked:

"Could you lend me this one—just this and nothing else?"

"Yes, of course."

She threw her arms around her friend's neck, kissed her ardently, and fled with her treasure.

The day of the party arrived. Madame Loisel was a great success. She was the prettiest woman there—<u>resplendent</u>, graceful, beaming, and deliriously happy. All the men looked at her, asked who she was, tried to get themselves introduced to her. All the minister's aides wanted to waltz with her. The minister himself noticed her.

She danced enraptured—carried away, intoxicated with pleasure, forgetting everything in this triumph of her beauty and the glory of her success, floating in a cloud of happiness formed by all this homage, all this admiration, all the desires she had stirred up—by this victory so complete and so sweet to the heart of a woman.

When she left the party, it was almost four in the morning. Her husband had been sleeping since midnight in a small, deserted sitting room, with three other gentlemen whose wives were having a wonderful time.

Literary Analysis
Characterization
What does Madame Loisel's comment reveal indirectly about her attitudes and values?

Vocabulary Builder
resplendent (ri splen´ dənt) *adj.* shining brightly

✔ Reading Check
Why does Madame Loisel visit Madame Forestier?

He brought her wraps so that they could leave and put them around her shoulders—the plain wraps from her everyday life whose shabbiness jarred with the elegance of her evening dress. She felt this and wanted to escape quickly so that the other women, who were enveloping themselves in their rich furs, wouldn't see her.

Loisel held her back.

"Wait a minute. You'll catch cold out there. I'm going to call a cab."

But she wouldn't listen to him and went hastily downstairs. Outside in the street, there was no cab to be found; they set out to look for one, calling to the drivers they saw passing in the distance.

They walked toward the Seine,[4] shivering and miserable. Finally, on the embankment, they found one of those ancient nocturnal broughams[5] which are only to be seen in Paris at night, as if they were ashamed to show their shabbiness in daylight.

It took them to their door in the Rue des Martyrs, and they went sadly upstairs to their apartment. For her, it was all over. And he was thinking that he had to be at the Ministry by ten.

She took off her wraps before the mirror so that she could see herself in all her glory once more. Then she cried out. The necklace was gone; there was nothing around her neck.

Her husband, already half undressed, asked:

"What's the matter?"

She turned toward him in a frenzy:

"The . . . the . . . necklace—it's gone."

He got up, thunderstruck.

"What did you say? . . . What! . . . Impossible!"

And they searched the folds of her dress, the folds of her wrap, the pockets, everywhere. They didn't find it.

He asked:

"Are you sure you still had it when we left the ball?"

"Yes. I remember touching it in the hallway of the Ministry."

"But if you had lost it in the street, we would have heard it fall. It must be in the cab."

"Yes, most likely. Do you remember the number?"

The New Necklace, 1910, William McGregor Paxton

▼ **Critical Viewing**
What important part of the story could this image illustrate?
[Connect]

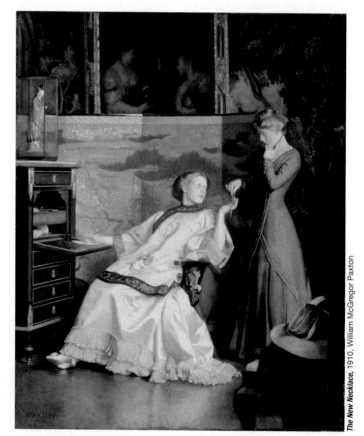

---

4. **Seine** (sān) river flowing through Paris.
5. **broughams** (brŌoms) *n.* horse-drawn carriages.

"No. What about you—did you notice it?"

"No."

They looked at each other in utter dejection. Finally Loisel got dressed again.

"I'm going to retrace the whole distance we covered on foot," he said, "and see if I can't find it."

And he left the house. She remained in her evening dress, too weak to go to bed, sitting crushed on a chair, lifeless and blank.

Her husband returned at about seven o'clock. He had found nothing.

He went to the police station, to the newspapers to offer a reward, to the offices of the cab companies—in a word, wherever there seemed to be the slightest hope of tracing it.

She spent the whole day waiting, in a state of utter hopelessness before such an appalling catastrophe.

Loisel returned in the evening, his face lined and pale; he had learned nothing.

"You must write to your friend," he said, "and tell her that you've broken the clasp of the necklace and that you're getting it mended. That'll give us time to decide what to do."

She wrote the letter at his dictation.

By the end of the week, they had lost all hope.

Loisel, who had aged five years, declared:

"We'll have to replace the necklace."

The next day they took the case in which it had been kept and went to the jeweler whose name appeared inside it. He looked through his ledgers:

"I didn't sell this necklace, madame. I only supplied the case."

Then they went from one jeweler to the next, trying to find a necklace like the other, racking their memories, both of them sick with worry and distress.

In a fashionable shop near the Palais Royal, they found a diamond necklace which they decided was exactly like the other. It was worth 40,000 francs. They could have it for 36,000 francs.

They asked the jeweler to hold it for them for three days, and they stipulated that he should take it back for 34,000 francs if the other necklace was found before the end of February.

Loisel possessed 18,000 francs left him by his father. He would borrow the rest.

He borrowed, asking a thousand francs from one man, five hundred from another, a hundred here, fifty there. He signed promissory notes,[6] borrowed at exorbitant rates, dealt with usurers and the entire race of moneylenders. He compromised his whole

---

6. **promissory** (präm′ i sôr′ē) **notes** written promises to pay back borrowed money.

Literary Analysis
Characterization
What do the Loisels' actions after the necklace is lost reveal about their individual characters?

Reading Check

What do the Loisels do to replace the necklace?

career, gave his signature even when he wasn't sure he would be able to honor it, and horrified by the anxieties with which his future would be filled, by the black misery about to descend upon him, by the prospect of physical privation and moral suffering, went to get the new necklace, placing on the jeweler's counter 36,000 francs.

When Madame Loisel went to return the necklace, Madame Forestier said in a faintly waspish tone:

"You could have brought it back a little sooner! I might have needed it."

She didn't open the case as her friend had feared she might. If she had noticed the substitution, what would she have thought? What would she have said? Mightn't she have taken Madame Loisel for a thief?

Reading Skill
Analyze Cause and Effect What fear prevents the Loisels from telling Madame Forestier the necklace was lost?

Madame Loisel came to know the awful life of the poverty-stricken. However, she resigned herself to it with unexpected fortitude. The crushing debt had to be paid. She would pay it. They dismissed the maid; they moved into an attic under the roof.

She came to know all the heavy household chores, the loathsome work of the kitchen. She washed the dishes, wearing down her pink nails on greasy casseroles and the bottoms of saucepans. She did the laundry, washing shirts and dishcloths which she hung on a line to dry; she took the garbage down to the street every morning, and carried water upstairs, stopping at every floor to get her breath. Dressed like a working-class woman, she went to the fruit store, the grocer, and the butcher with her basket on her arm, bargaining, outraged, contesting each sou[7] of her pitiful funds.

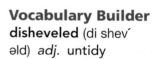

Every month some notes had to be honored and more time requested on others.

Her husband worked in the evenings, putting a shopkeeper's ledgers in order, and often at night as well, doing copying at twenty-five centimes a page.

And it went on like that for ten years.

After ten years, they had made good on everything, including the usurious rates and the compound interest.

Madame Loisel looked old now. She had become the sort of strong woman, hard and coarse, that one finds in poor families. Disheveled, her skirts askew, with reddened hands, she spoke in a loud voice, slopping water over the floors as she washed them. But sometimes, when her husband was at the office, she would sit down by the window and muse over that party long ago when she had been so beautiful, the belle of the ball.

Vocabulary Builder
disheveled (di shev´ əld) *adj.* untidy

---

7. sou (sōō) *n.* former French coin, worth very little; the centime (sän´ tēm´), mentioned later, was also of little value.

How would things have turned out if she hadn't lost that necklace? Who could tell? How strange and fickle life is! How little it takes to make or break you!

Then one Sunday when she was strolling along the Champs Elysées[8] to forget the week's chores for a while, she suddenly caught sight of a woman taking a child for a walk. It was Madame Forestier, still young, still beautiful, still charming.

Madame Loisel started to tremble. Should she speak to her? Yes, certainly she should. And now that she had paid everything back, why shouldn't she tell her the whole story?

She went up to her.

"Hello, Jeanne."

The other didn't recognize her and was surprised that this plainly dressed woman should speak to her so familiarly. She murmured:

"But . . . madame! . . . I'm sure . . . You must be mistaken."

"No, I'm not. I am Mathilde Loisel."

Her friend gave a little cry.

"Oh! Oh, my poor Mathilde, how you've changed!"

"Yes, I've been through some pretty hard times since I last saw you and I've had plenty of trouble—and all because of you!"

"Because of me? What do you mean?"

"You remember the diamond necklace you lent me to wear to the party at the Ministry?"

"Yes. What about it?"

"Well, I lost it."

"What are you talking about? You returned it to me."

"What I gave back to you was another one just like it. And it took us ten years to pay for it. You can imagine it wasn't easy for us, since we were quite poor. . . . Anyway, I'm glad it's over and done with."

Madame Forestier stopped short.

"You say you bought a diamond necklace to replace that other one?"

"Yes. You didn't even notice then? They really were exactly alike."

And she smiled, full of a proud, simple joy.

Madame Forestier, <u>profoundly</u> moved, took Mathilde's hands in her own.

"Oh, my poor, poor Mathilde! Mine was false. It was worth five hundred francs at the most!"

---

8. **Champs Elysées** (shän zā lē zā´) fashionable street in Paris.

Reading Skill
Analyze Cause and Effect What causes Madame Loisel to tremble at the sight of Madame Forestier?

Vocabulary Builder
profoundly (prō found´ lē) *adv.* deeply

Apply the Skills

The Necklace

Thinking About the Selection

1. **Respond:** Do you feel sorry for Madame Loisel at the end of the story? Why or why not?
2. **(a) Recall:** As the story begins, why is Madame Loisel unhappy with her life? **(b) Infer:** Do you think the author wants readers to sympathize with her unhappiness? Why or why not?
3. **(a) Recall:** How does her husband respond to Madame Loisel's disappointment over the invitation? **(b) Compare and Contrast:** How is M. Loisel different from his wife?
4. **(a) Interpret:** How does Madame Loisel change over the ten years as she works to pay off the cost of the necklace? **(b) Draw Conclusions:** What causes her to change?
5. **Analyze:** What message do you think the surprise ending about the necklace's actual value expresses? Explain.

Literary Analysis

6. Describe Madame Loisel's **character.** Support your answer with at least one example of each of the following methods of **indirect characterization** in the story: **(a)** Madame Loisel's actions and behavior; **(b)** her words and thoughts; and **(c)** the effect she has on other people.
7. **(a)** Is the conversation on the day of the ball in which the Loisels discuss Madame's attire an example of indirect or **direct characterization**? Explain. **(b)** What do you learn about both Monsieur and Madame Loisel's characters from this exchange?

Reading Skill

8. Use a chart like the one shown to **analyze cause and effect** in this story. **(a)** Note two causes for Madame Loisel's decision to borrow the necklace from Madame Forestier. **(b)** List three effects of this decision.

Causes		Effects
	She borrows the necklace	

9. Does Madame Loisel cause her own suffering? Explain your answer.

Vocabulary Builder

Practice Tell whether each sentence below makes sense. Use the meaning of the italicized vocabulary word to explain your answer.

1. After the party, the hostess was *rueful* about her graceful hospitality.
2. The tired campers were *resplendent* as they hiked in the rain.
3. Alan went to the interview *disheveled* and wearing a new suit.
4. The class was *profoundly* moved by the story of the heroic dog.

Adding Words to Your Vocabulary Using a thesaurus, find a **synonym,** or word with a similar meaning, for each word in the vocabulary list for "The Necklace" on page 292. Then, use each synonym correctly in a sentence. (For more on using a thesaurus, see page R7.)

Writing

Think about a lesson that you could teach the Loisels to help them move on with their lives. Create a **written presentation** that details your suggestions to them.

- Jot down some of the issues they might face. For each, consider what you might teach them and how best to convey your ideas.
- Based on your audience, purpose, and point of view as an outsider, choose an appropriate text structure for your presentation. For example, you might write an essay, or you might tell a story with a moral. Include an introduction to briefly explain your choice.

For *Grammar, Vocabulary,* and *Assessment,*
see **Build Language Skills,** pages 318–319.

Extend Your Learning

Listening and Speaking As Madame Loisel, write and deliver a **monologue** telling your husband the true value of the lost necklace.
- Consider the feelings and thoughts that Madame Loisel might want to share with her husband.
- Decide if Madame Loisel will defend herself or be apologetic.
- Use gestures and language appropriate to the character.

Research and Technology With classmates, use library and Internet resources to gather information about diamonds. Present your findings in an **informative brochure.** Take notes as you do your research, and decide which information would work best in a chart or drawing.

Short Story

Background

The Game of Chess A game of strategy, chess resembles a battle between two armies, each led by a figurehead king and a powerful queen. Chess may have started in India. After it spread to Persia (present-day Iran), Arab invaders introduced it to other lands. Today, it is played throughout the world.

Connecting to the Literature

Reading/Writing Connection In "Rules of the Game," chess becomes both a bridge between individuals and cultures and the source of an emotional tug of war within a family. Write a brief account of how games can both unite and divide people. Use at least three of these words: *induce, evoke, initiate, generate*.

Review

For **Literary Analysis, Reading Skills,** and **Vocabulary Builder,** see page 292.

READ MORE

by Amy Tan
The Kitchen God's Wife
The Hundred Secret Senses

Meet the Author

Amy **Tan** (b. 1952)

As a child, Amy Tan did not imagine that she would become a successful novelist. Her parents, who had emigrated from China to the San Francisco Bay area, wanted her to become a doctor. Doubting her abilities in science, Tan instead majored in English in college. She went on to become a successful business writer.

Finding Herself in Fiction In her mid-thirties, Tan began writing stories. While she was surprised by the pleasure writing fiction gave her, she was even more surprised by the content of her work. Tan had tried to play down her ethnicity, but in her fiction, she found herself exploring the experiences of Chinese American women. In 1985, Tan wrote "Rules of the Game," which she later included in her best-selling first novel, *The Joy Luck Club*.

Fast Facts

▶ When she was eight, Tan's essay "What the Library Means to Me" won first prize in a local contest.
▶ *The Joy Luck Club* was made into a popular film in 1993.

For: More about the author
Visit: www.PHSchool.com
Author Link Web Code: epe-9209

Rules of the Game

from The Joy Luck Club

Amy Tan

I was six when my mother taught me the art of invisible strength. It was a strategy for winning arguments, respect from others, and eventually, though neither of us knew it at the time, chess games.

"Bite back your tongue," scolded my mother when I cried loudly, yanking her hand toward the store that sold bags of salted plums. At home, she said, "Wise guy, he not go against wind. In Chinese we say, Come from South, blow with wind—poom!—North will follow. Strongest wind cannot be seen."

The next week I bit back my tongue as we entered the store with the forbidden candies. When my mother finished her shopping, she quietly plucked a small bag of plums from the rack and put it on the counter with the rest of the items.

My mother imparted her daily truths so she could help my older brothers and me rise above our circumstances. We lived in San Francisco's Chinatown. Like most of the other Chinese children who played in the back alleys of restaurants and curio shops, I didn't think we were poor. My bowl was always full, three five-course meals every day, beginning with a soup full of mysterious things I didn't want to know the names of.

We lived on Waverly Place, in a warm, clean, two-bedroom flat that sat above a small Chinese bakery specializing in steamed pastries and dim sum. In the early morning, when the alley was still

✅ Reading Check

What "art" did the narrator learn from her mother?

quiet, I could smell fragrant red beans as they were cooked down to a pasty sweetness. By daybreak, our flat was heavy with the odor of fried sesame balls and sweet curried chicken crescents. From my bed, I would listen as my father got ready for work, then locked the door behind him, one-two-three clicks.

At the end of our two-block alley was a small sandlot playground with swings and slides well-shined down the middle with use. The play area was bordered by wood-slat benches where old-country people sat cracking roasted watermelon seeds with their golden teeth and scattering the husks to an impatient gathering of gurgling pigeons. The best playground, however, was the dark alley itself. It was crammed with daily mysteries and adventures. My brothers and I would peer into the medicinal herb shop, watching old Li dole out onto a stiff sheet of white paper the right amount of insect shells, saffron-colored seeds and <u>pungent</u> leaves for his ailing customers. It was said that he once cured a woman dying of an ancestral curse that had eluded the best of American doctors. Next to the pharmacy was a printer who specialized in gold-embossed wedding invitations and festive red banners.

Farther down the street was Ping Yuen Fish Market. The front window displayed a tank crowded with doomed fish and turtles struggling to gain footing on the slimy green-tiled sides. A hand-written sign informed tourists, "Within this store, is all for food, not for pet." Inside, the butchers with their bloodstained white smocks deftly gutted the fish while customers cried out their orders and shouted, "Give me your freshest," to which the butchers always protested, "All are freshest." On less crowded market days, we would inspect the crates of live frogs and crabs which we were warned not to poke, boxes of dried cuttlefish, and row upon row of iced prawns, squid, and slippery fish. The sanddabs made me shiver each time; their eyes lay on one flattened side and reminded me of my mother's story of a careless girl who ran into a crowded street and was crushed by a cab. "Was smash flat," reported my mother.

At the corner of the alley was Hong Sing's, a four-table cafe with a recessed stairwell in front that led to a door marked "Tradesmen." My brothers and I believed the bad people emerged from this door at night. Tourists never went to Hong Sing's, since the menu was printed only in Chinese. A Caucasian man with a big camera once posed me and my playmates in front of the restaurant. He had us move to the side of the picture window so the photo would capture the roasted duck with its head dangling from a juice-covered rope. After he took the picture, I told him he should go into Hong Sing's and eat dinner. When he smiled and asked me what they served, I shouted, "Guts and duck's feet and octopus gizzards!" Then I ran off with my friends, shrieking with laughter as we scampered across the alley and hid in the entryway grotto of the China Gem Company, my heart pounding with hope that he would chase us.

My mother named me after the street that we lived on: Waverly Place Jong, my official name for important American documents. But my family called me Meimei [mā´ mā´], "Little Sister," I was the youngest, the only daughter. Each morning before school, my mother would twist and yank on my thick black hair until she had formed two tightly wound pigtails. One day, as she struggled to weave a hard-toothed comb through my disobedient hair, I had a sly thought.

I asked her, "Ma, what is Chinese torture?" My mother shook her head. A bobby pin was wedged between her lips. She wetted her palm and smoothed the hair above my ear, then pushed the pin in so that it nicked sharply against my scalp.

"Who say this word?" she asked without a trace of knowing how wicked I was being. I shrugged my shoulders and said, "Some boy in my class said Chinese people do Chinese torture."

"Chinese people do many things," she said simply. "Chinese people do business, do medicine, do painting. Not lazy like American people. We do torture. Best torture."

My older brother Vincent was the one who actually got the chess set. We had gone to the annual Christmas party held at the First Chinese Baptist Church at the end of the alley. The missionary ladies had put together a Santa bag of gifts donated by members of another church. None of the gifts had names on them. There were separate sacks for boys and girls of different ages.

One of the Chinese parishioners had donned a Santa Claus costume and a stiff paper beard with cotton balls glued to it. I think the only children who thought he was the real thing were too young to know that Santa Claus was not Chinese. When my turn came up, the Santa man asked me how old I was. I thought it was a trick question; I was seven according to the American formula and eight by the Chinese calendar. I said I was born on March 17, 1951. That seemed to satisfy him. He then solemnly asked if I had been a very, very good girl this year and did I believe in Jesus Christ and obey my parents. I knew the only answer to that. I nodded back with equal solemnity.

Literary Analysis
Characterization
What does Mrs. Jong's response to the accusation that Chinese people do torture reveal about her personality?

✓**Reading Check**

What gift does Vincent receive at the Christmas party?

Having watched the other children opening their gifts, I already knew that the big gifts were not necessarily the nicest ones. One girl my age got a large coloring book of biblical characters, while a less greedy girl who selected a small box received a glass vial of lavender toilet water. The sound of the box was also important. A ten-year-old boy had chosen a box that jangled when he shook it. It was a tin globe of the world with a slit for inserting money. He must have thought it was full of dimes and nickels, because when he saw that it had just ten pennies, his face fell with such undisguised disappointment that his mother slapped the side of his head and led him out of the church hall, apologizing to the crowd for her son who had such bad manners he couldn't appreciate such a fine gift.

As I peered into the sack, I quickly fingered the remaining presents, testing their weight, imagining what they contained. I chose a heavy, compact one that was wrapped in shiny silver foil and a red satin ribbon. It was a twelve-pack of Life Savers and I spent the rest of the party arranging and rearranging the candy tubes in the order of my favorites. My brother Winston chose wisely as well. His present turned out to be a box of intricate plastic parts; the instructions on the box proclaimed that when they were properly assembled he would have an authentic miniature replica of a World War II submarine.

Vincent got the chess set, which would have been a very decent present to get at a church Christmas party except it was obviously used and, as we discovered later, it was missing a black pawn and a white knight. My mother graciously thanked the unknown benefactor, saying, "Too good. Cost too much." At which point, an old lady with fine white, wispy hair nodded toward our family and said with a whistling whisper, "Merry, merry Christmas."

When we got home, my mother told Vincent to throw the chess set away. "She not want it. We not want it," she said, tossing her head stiffly to the side with a tight, proud smile. My brothers had deaf ears. They were already lining up the chess pieces and reading from the dog-eared instruction book.

I watched Vincent and Winston play during Christmas week. The chess board seemed to hold elaborate secrets waiting to be untangled. The chessmen were more powerful than Old Li's magic herbs that cured ancestral curses. And my brothers wore such serious faces that I was sure something was at stake that was greater than avoiding the tradesmen's door to Hong Sing's.

Literary Analysis
Characterization
What does Waverly's thought process in this paragraph reveal indirectly about her character?

Reading Skill
Cause and Effect
What effect does the gift of the chess board have on Waverly?

"Let me! Let me!" I begged between games when one brother or the other would sit back with a deep sigh of relief and victory, the other annoyed, unable to let go of the outcome. Vincent at first refused to let me play, but when I offered my Life Savers as replacements for the buttons that filled in for the missing pieces, he relented. He chose the flavors: wild cherry for the black pawn and peppermint for the white knight. Winner could eat both. As our mother sprinkled flour and rolled out small doughy circles for the steamed dumplings that would be our dinner that night, Vincent explained the rules, pointing to each piece. "You have sixteen pieces and so do I. One king and queen, two bishops, two knights, two castles, and eight pawns. The pawns can only move forward one step, except on the first move. Then they can move two. But they can only take men by moving crossways like this, except in the beginning, when you can move ahead and take another pawn."

"Why?" I asked as I moved my pawn. "Why can't they move more steps?"

"Because they're pawns," he said.

"But why do they go crossways to take other men. Why aren't there any women and children?"

"Why is the sky blue? Why must you always ask stupid questions?" asked Vincent. "This is a game. These are the rules. I didn't make them up. See. Here. In the book." He jabbed a page with a pawn in his hand. "Pawn. P-A-W-N. Pawn. Read it yourself."

My mother patted the flour off her hands. "Let me see book," she said quietly. She scanned the pages quickly, not reading the foreign English symbols, seeming to search deliberately for nothing in particular.

"This American rules," she concluded at last. "Every time people come out from foreign country, must know rules. You not know, judge say, Too bad, go back. They not telling you why so you can use their way go forward. They say, Don't know why, you find out yourself. But they knowing all the time. Better you take it, find out why yourself." She tossed her head back with a satisfied smile.

I found out about all the whys later. I read the rules and looked up all the big words in a dictionary. I borrowed books from the Chinatown library. I studied each chess piece, trying to absorb the power each contained.

I learned about opening moves and why it's important to control the center early on; the shortest distance between two points is straight down the middle. I learned about the middle game and why tactics between two adversaries are like clashing ideas; the one who plays better has the clearest plans for both attacking and getting

Literary Analysis
Characterization
What do you learn about Vincent based on this conversation?

Reading Check

How does Waverly convince Vincent to let her play chess?

out of traps. I learned why it is essential in the endgame to have foresight, a mathematical understanding of all possible moves, and patience; all weaknesses and advantages become evident to a strong adversary and are obscured to a tiring opponent. I discovered that for the whole game one must gather invisible strengths and see the endgame before the game begins.

I also found out why I should never reveal "why" to others. A little knowledge withheld is a great advantage one should store for future use. That is the power of chess. It is a game of secrets in which one must show and never tell.

I loved the secrets I found within the sixty-four black and white squares. I carefully drew a handmade chessboard and pinned it to the wall next to my bed, where at night I would stare for hours at imaginary battles. Soon I no longer lost any games or Life Savers, but I lost my adversaries. Winston and Vincent decided they were more interested in roaming the streets after school in their Hopalong Cassidy cowboy hats.

On a cold spring afternoon, while walking home from school, I detoured through the playground at the end of our alley. I saw a group of old men, two seated across a folding table playing a game of chess, others smoking pipes, eating peanuts, and watching. I ran home and grabbed Vincent's chess set, which was bound in a cardboard box with rubber bands. I also carefully selected two prized rolls of Life Savers. I came back to the park and approached a man who was observing the game.

"Want to play?" I asked him. His face widened with surprise and he grinned as he looked at the box under my arm.

"Little sister, been a long time since I play with dolls," he said, smiling <u>benevolently</u>. I quickly put the box down next to him on the bench and displayed my <u>retort</u>.

Lau Po, as he allowed me to call him, turned out to be a much better player than my brothers. I lost many games and many Life Savers. But over the weeks, with each diminishing roll of candies, I added new secrets. Lau Po gave me the names. The Double Attack from the East and West Shores. Throwing Stones on the Drowning Man. The Sudden Meeting of the Clan. The Surprise from the Sleeping Guard. The Humble Servant Who Kills the King. Sand in the Eyes of Advancing Forces. A Double Killing Without Blood.

There were also the fine points of chess etiquette. Keep captured men in neat rows, as well-tended prisoners. Never announce "Check" with vanity, lest someone with an unseen sword slit your throat. Never hurl pieces into the sandbox after you have lost a game, because then you must find them again, by yourself, after apologizing to all around you. By the end of the summer, Lau Po had taught me all he knew, and I had become a better chess player.

A small weekend crowd of Chinese people and tourists would gather as I played and defeated my opponents one by one. My mother would join the crowds during these outdoor exhibition games. She sat proudly on the bench, telling my admirers with proper Chinese humility, "Is luck."

A man who watched me play in the park suggested that my mother allow me to play in local chess tournaments. My mother smiled graciously, an answer that meant nothing. I desperately wanted to go, but I bit back my tongue. I knew she would not let me play among strangers. So as we walked home I said in a small voice that I didn't want to play in the local tournament. They would have American rules. If I lost, I would bring shame on my family.

"Is shame you fall down nobody push you," said my mother.

During my first tournament, my mother sat with me in the front row as I waited for my turn. I frequently bounced my legs to unstick them from the cold metal seat of the folding chair. When my name was called, I leapt up. My mother unwrapped something in her lap. It was her chang, a small tablet of red jade which held the sun's fire. "Is luck," she whispered, and tucked it into my dress pocket. I turned to my opponent, a fifteen-year-old boy from Oakland. He looked at me, wrinkling his nose.

As I began to play, the boy disappeared, the color ran out of the room, and I saw only my white pieces and his black ones waiting on the other side. A light wind began blowing past my ears. It whispered secrets only I could hear.

"Blow from the South," it murmured. "The wind leaves no trail." I saw a clear path, the traps to avoid. The crowd rustled. "Shhh! Shhh!" said the corners of the room. The wind blew stronger. "Throw sand from the East to distract him." The knight came forward ready for the sacrifice. The wind hissed, louder and louder. "Blow, blow, blow. He cannot see. He is blind now. Make him lean away from the wind so he is easier to knock down."

Reading Skill
Cause and Effect
What does Waverly anticipate would be the effect of her expressing her desire to play in local chess tournaments?

Reading Check

How does Waverly's mother respond to Waverly's admirers in the park?

"Check," I said, as the wind roared with laughter. The wind died down to little puffs, my own breath.

My mother placed my first trophy next to a new plastic chess set that the neighborhood Tao society had given to me. As she wiped each piece with a soft cloth, she said, "Next time win more, lose less."

"Ma, it's not how many pieces you lose," I said. "Sometimes you need to lose pieces to get ahead."

"Better to lose less, see if you really need."

At the next tournament, I won again, but it was my mother who wore the triumphant grin.

"Lost eight piece this time. Last time was eleven. What I tell you? Better off lose less!" I was annoyed, but I couldn't say anything.

I attended more tournaments, each one farther away from home. I won all games, in all divisions. The Chinese bakery downstairs from our flat displayed my growing collection of trophies in its window, amidst the dust-covered cakes that were never picked up. The day after I won an important regional tournament, the window encased a fresh sheet cake with whipped-cream frosting and red script saying, "Congratulations, Waverly Jong, Chinatown Chess Champion." Soon after that, a flower shop, headstone engraver, and funeral parlor offered to sponsor me in national tournaments. That's when my mother decided I no longer had to do the dishes. Winston and Vincent had to do my chores.

"Why does she get to play and we do all the work," complained Vincent.

"Is new American rules," said my mother. "Meimei play, squeeze all her brains out for win chess. You play, worth squeeze towel."

By my ninth birthday, I was a national chess champion. I was still some 429 points away from grand-master status, but I was touted as the Great American Hope, a child prodigy and a girl to boot. They ran a photo of me in *Life* magazine next to a quote in which Bobby Fischer[1] said, "There will never be a woman grand master." "Your move, Bobby," said the caption.

The day they took the magazine picture I wore neatly plaited braids clipped with plastic barrettes trimmed with rhinestones. I was playing in a large high school auditorium that echoed with phlegmy coughs and the squeaky rubber knobs of chair legs sliding across freshly waxed wooden floors. Seated across from me was an American man, about the same age as Lau Po, maybe fifty. I

Literary Analysis
Characterization
What do Waverly's mother's comments here reveal indirectly about her ambitions for Waverly?

Reading Skill
Cause and Effect
Why is Waverly's picture in *Life* magazine?

---

1. **Bobby Fischer** born in 1943, this American chess prodigy attained the high rank of grand master in 1958.

remember that his sweaty brow seemed to weep at my every move. He wore a dark, <u>malodorous</u> suit. One of his pockets was stuffed with a great white kerchief on which he wiped his palm before sweeping his hand over the chosen chess piece with great flourish.

In my crisp pink-and-white dress with scratchy lace at the neck, one of two my mother had sewn for these special occasions, I would clasp my hands under my chin, the delicate points of my elbows poised lightly on the table in the manner my mother had shown me for posing for the press. I would swing my patent leather shoes back and forth like an impatient child riding on a school bus. Then I would pause, suck in my lips, twirl my chosen piece in midair as if undecided, and then firmly plant it in its new threatening place, with a triumphant smile thrown back at my opponent for good measure.

I no longer played in the alley of Waverly Place. I never visited the playground where the pigeons and old men gathered. I went to school, then directly home to learn new chess secrets, cleverly concealed advantages, more escape routes.

But I found it difficult to concentrate at home. My mother had a habit of standing over me while I plotted out my games. I think she thought of herself as my protective ally. Her lips would be sealed tight, and after each move I made, a soft "Hmmmmph" would escape from her nose.

"Ma, I can't practice when you stand there like that," I said one day. She retreated to the kitchen and made loud noises with the pots and pans. When the crashing stopped, I could see out of the corner of my eye that she was standing in the doorway. "Hmmmmph!" Only this one came out of her tight throat.

▲ **Critical Viewing**
Based on details in the painting, who do you think is winning this chess game? Explain. **[Analyze]**

Vocabulary Builder
malodorous (mal ō´ dər əs) *adj.* having a bad smell

✓ **Reading Check**
What does Waverly achieve by her ninth birthday?

My parents made many concessions to allow me to practice. One time I complained that the bedroom I shared was so noisy that I couldn't think. Thereafter, my brothers slept in a bed in the living room facing the street. I said I couldn't finish my rice; my head didn't work right when my stomach was too full. I left the table with half-finished bowls and nobody complained. But there was one duty I couldn't avoid. I had to accompany my mother on Saturday market days when I had no tournament to play. My mother would proudly walk with me, visiting many shops, buying very little. "This my daughter Wave-ly Jong," she said to whoever looked her way.

One day, after we left a shop I said under my breath, "I wish you wouldn't do that, telling everybody I'm your daughter." My mother stopped walking. Crowds of people with heavy bags pushed past us on the sidewalk, bumping into first one shoulder, then another.

"Aiii-ya. So shame be with mother?" She grasped my hand even tighter as she glared at me.

I looked down. "It's not that, it's just so obvious. It's just so embarrassing."

"Embarrass you be my daughter?" Her voice was cracking with anger.

"That's not what I meant. That's not what I said."

"What you say?"

Reading Skill
Analyze Cause and Effect In what ways does Waverly's success at chess affect her family life? Explain.

I knew it was a mistake to say anything more, but I heard my voice speaking. "Why do you have to use me to show off? If you want to show off, then why don't you learn to play chess." My mother's eyes turned into dangerous black slits. She had no words for me, just sharp silence.

I felt the wind rushing around my hot ears. I jerked my hand out of my mother's tight grasp and spun around, knocking into an old woman. Her bag of groceries spilled to the ground.

"Aii-ya! Stupid girl!" my mother and the woman cried. Oranges and tin cans careened down the sidewalk. As my mother stooped to help the old woman pick up the escaping food, I took off.

I raced down the street, dashing between people, not looking back as my mother screamed shrilly, "Meimei! Meimei!" I fled down an alley, past dark curtained shops and merchants washing the grime off their windows. I sped into the sunlight, into a large street crowded with tourists examining trinkets and souvenirs. I ducked into another dark alley, down another street, up another alley. I ran until it hurt and I realized I had nowhere to go, that I was not running from anything. The alleys contained no escape routes.

My breath came out like angry smoke. It was cold. I sat down on an upturned plastic pail next to a stack of empty boxes, cupping my chin with my hands, thinking hard. I imagined my mother, first walking briskly down one street or another looking for me, then giving up and returning home to await my arrival. After two hours, I stood up on creaking legs and slowly walked home.

The alley was quiet and I could see the yellow lights shining from our flat like two tiger's eyes in the night. I climbed the sixteen steps to the door, advancing quietly up each so as not to make any warning sounds. I turned the knob; the door was locked. I heard a chair moving, quick steps, the locks turning—click! click! click!— and then the door opened.

"About time you got home," said Vincent. "Boy, are you in trouble."

He slid back to the dinner table. On a platter were the remains of a large fish, its fleshy head still connected to bones swimming upstream in vain escape. Standing there waiting for my punishment, I heard my mother speak in a dry voice.

"We not concerning this girl. This girl not have concerning for us."

Nobody looked at me. Bone chopsticks clinked against the insides of bowls being emptied into hungry mouths.

I walked into my room, closed the door, and lay down on my bed. The room was dark, the ceiling filled with shadows from the dinnertime lights of neighboring flats.

In my head, I saw a chessboard with sixty-four black and white squares. Opposite me was my opponent, two angry black slits. She wore a triumphant smile. "Strongest wind cannot be seen," she said.

Her black men advanced across the plane, slowly marching to each successive level as a single unit. My white pieces screamed as they scurried and fell off the board one by one. As her men drew closer to my edge, I felt myself growing light. I rose up into the air and flew out the window. Higher and higher, above the alley, over the tops of tiled roofs, where I was gathered up by the wind and pushed up toward the night sky until everything below me disappeared and I was alone.

I closed my eyes and pondered my next move.

Reading Skill
Analyze Cause and Effect Why do you think Waverly and her mother stop speaking to each other?

Apply the Skills

Rules of the Game

Thinking About the Selection

1. **Respond:** Which character did you find most realistic? Explain.
2. **(a) Recall:** Early in the story, what happens when Waverly asks for a bag of salted plums? **(b) Connect:** What happens when she stops asking? **(c) Apply:** How does Waverly later apply that strategy to her desire to play chess competitively?
3. **(a) Recall:** How does Mrs. Jong teach Waverly rules of behavior? **(b) Connect:** How does Waverly translate these rules into strategies for winning at chess? **(c) Extend:** How does she use these rules against her mother?
4. **(a) Describe:** What does Mrs. Jong do to show her pride in her daughter? **(b) Distinguish:** At the market, what does Mrs. Jong do that bothers Waverly? **(c) Assess:** Which aspects of the struggle between Waverly and Mrs. Jong are based on personal differences? Which are based on cultural differences? Explain.
5. **Speculate:** Who do you think will "win" the game between Waverly and her mother? Explain.

Literary Analysis

6. Describe the **character** of Waverly. Support your response with examples of her actions, behavior, words, and thoughts and with details about the effect she has on other people.
7. **(a)** Is the conversation in which Waverly and Mrs. Jong discuss Chinese torture an example of **direct characterization** or **indirect characterization?** Explain. **(b)** What do you learn about Mrs. Jong's character from this exchange?

Reading Skill

8. Use a chart like the one shown to **analyze cause and effect** in this story. **(a)** Note two causes for Waverly's success with chess. **(b)** List three effects of her success.

9. **(a)** Why does Mrs. Jong give Waverly special privileges? **(b)** How do these privileges affect Waverly and her relationship with her mother? Explain.

QuickReview

Story at a Glance
A young Chinese American girl tells how she learned to win at chess.

Go Online
—**Assessment**
For: Self-test
Visit: www.PHSchool.com
Web Code: epa-6208

Character: a person or an animal that participates in the action of a literary work

Characterization: methods writers use to reveal characters' traits; writers may use *direct* or *indirect* characterization

Cause: an event, an action, or a feeling that produces a result

Effect: the result produced by an event, action, or feeling

Vocabulary Builder

Practice Tell whether each sentence below makes sense. Use the meaning of the italicized vocabulary word to explain your answer.

1. The *pungent* scent of the baking pie drew the hungry crowd.
2. The girl was scared when the lady *benevolently* distributed cookies.
3. The audience was bored by the comedian's brilliant *retort*.
4. He gave his wife a bottle of expensive, *malodorous* perfume.

Adding Words to Your Vocabulary Using a thesaurus, find a **synonym,** or word with a similar meaning, for each word in the vocabulary list for "Rules of the Game" on page 292. Then, use each synonym correctly in a sentence. (For more on using a thesaurus, see page R7.)

Writing

Think about a lesson that you could teach Waverly and her mother to help them resolve their conflict. Create a **written presentation** that details your suggestions to them.

- Jot down some of the issues they face. For each, consider what you might teach them and how best to convey your ideas.
- Based on your audience, purpose, and point of view as an outsider, choose an appropriate text structure for your presentation. For example, you might write an essay, or you might tell a story with a moral. Include an introduction to briefly explain your choice.

For *Grammar, Vocabulary,* and *Assessment,*
see **Build Language Skills,** pages 318–319.

Extend Your Learning

Listening and Speaking As Waverly, write and deliver a **monologue** explaining to a friend what you love about chess.
- Consider the feelings and thoughts Waverly might want to share.
- Decide which aspects of Waverly's relationship with her mother she will want to discuss.
- Use gestures and language appropriate to the character.

Research and Technology With classmates, create an **informative brochure** on chess. Use library and Internet resources to research the rules and strategies of the game. Take notes as you do research, and decide which information would work best in a chart or drawing.

Build Language Skills

Vocabulary Skill

Word Roots The *Latin root -ver-* comes from the Latin word for truth: *verus.* English words that contain this root, such as *verify* and *verdict,* have meanings related to "truth."

Not all words with the letters *v-e-r* indicate the Latin root *-ver-.* English words with the letters *ver* may also be related to the root *-verd-,* meaning "green," or *-vert-,* meaning "turn."

Practice Copy the following words. Explain whether each word is related to the root that means *truth, green,* or *turn.* Use a dictionary to check your work. Then, use each word in a sentence.

1. verify
2. verdant
3. versatile
4. verity
5. verge

Grammar Lesson

Subjects and Predicates There are two essential components of a sentence—the subject and the predicate. The **subject** is the word or group of words in a sentence that tells whom or what the sentence is about. The **predicate** is the verb or verb phrase that tells what the subject of the sentence does or is.

▶ **Example:** Remington painted scenes of the wild West.
      (subject)   (predicate)
      Remington was a famous American artist.
      (subject)   (predicate)

Practice Write a sentence for each subject/predicate pair.

1. helped; work
2. museum; contains
3. are buying; we
4. Rowena; will decide
5. plane; landed

More Practice

For more practice with subjects and predicates, see the Grammar Handbook, p. R40.

W̶G Prentice Hall Writing and Grammar Connection: Chapter 20, Section 1

Reading Skill: Cause and Effect

Directions: *Read the selection. Then answer the questions.*

For decades each of the states imposed a comparatively lengthy residence requirement for voting—typically, at least a year in the State, and 60 or 90 days in the county.

In the Voting Rights Act Amendments of 1970, Congress prohibited any requirement longer than 30 days for presidential elections. In *Dunn v. Blumstein,* 1972, the Supreme Court found Tennessee's residence requirement unconstitutional. The Supreme Court said that "30 days appears to be an ample period of time."

Nearly half the states now require voters to live in the state for 30 days and in some states, like New Hampshire, the period is even shorter. Arizona is the only state requiring more than 30 days residency to vote.

Standards Assessed

• IR.2.02.3
• IR.2.03.4
• WL.1.02.2

1. Which of the following effects is correct?

   A 90 day requirements were changed.
   B Residency requirements changed in the 70's.
   C In 1972 Congress passed a new voting law
   D *Dunn* v. *Blumstein* changed Arizona law.

2. How many major reasons are given in the selection for the change in voting requirements?

   A Four
   B Three.
   C Two.
   D One.

3. Which is a direct cause of the current Tennessee residence requirement?

   A Voting Rights Act
   B *Dunn* v. *Blumstein,* 1972
   C the other states' regulations
   D the Amendments

4. According to the selection which cause/effect relationship is correct?

   A Supreme Court decision/change in voting requirements
   B change in voting requirements/Supreme Court decision
   C change in law/change in state requirements
   D change in state requirements/change in law

Timed Writing: Interpretation [Critical Stance]

Review "The Rules of the Game" or "The Necklace." Write a brief interpretation of the author's attitude toward one of the main characters. Use examples from the selection to support your interpretation. **(25 minutes)**

 ## Writing Workshop: *Work in Progress*

Cause and Effect Essay

It is often easier to see effects than to understand causes; much of science is the attempt to find causes for known effects. List ten effects for which you do not know the cause. Put this work in your writing portfolio.

Practice these skills with either "Blues Ain't No Mockin Bird" (p. 322) or "The Invalid's Story" (p. 333).

NC **Standard Course of Study**

- Narrate with a sense personal voice. (WL.1.01.4)
- Make inferences and draw conclusions based on text to answer research questions. (IR.2.01.6)

Literary Analysis

Dialogue is a conversation between or among characters in a literary work. In prose, dialogue is usually set off by quotation marks, and a new paragraph indicates a change in speaker. Writers use dialogue for these purposes:

- to reveal character traits and relationships
- to advance the action of the plot and develop the conflict
- to add variety, color, and realism to narratives

To make characters and settings more vivid, authors may write dialogue reflecting characters' dialect. **Dialect** is a way of speaking common to people of a region or group. A dialect's words, pronunciations, and grammar differ from those of the standard form of a language.

As you read, notice passages of dialogue and dialect and determine what they show about the characters and the setting.

Reading Skill

A **cause** is an event, an action, or a feeling that produces a result. An **effect** it the result produced. When reading a story, **visualize the action to analyze cause and effect.**

- Use text details to picture the setting, characters, and action.
- Use the details of your mental picture to help you identify the relationships between actions and events.

Organize your ideas in a chart like the one shown.

Cause
Steve turned on the sprinkler.

↓

Mental Picture
Matt on lawn Jaime on porch Sprinkler on lawn

↓

Effect
Matt got wet; Jaime just laughed.

Vocabulary Builder

Blues Ain't No Mockin Bird

- **formality** (fôr mal′ ə tē) *n.* attention to established rules or customs (p. 327) *His formality conveyed respect for his guests.*

- **reckless** (rek′ lis) *adj.* careless; rash (p. 328) *Reckless driving is a serious offense.*

The Invalid's Story

- **prodigious** (prō dij′ əs) *adj.* enormous (p. 334) *The Grand Canyon is a prodigious natural wonder.*

- **deleterious** (del′ ə tir′ ē əs) *adj.* harmful to health or well-being (p. 335) *Too much sun can be deleterious to one's skin.*

- **judicious** (jōō dish′ əs) *adj.* showing good judgment (p. 336) *Her decision to stay indoors during the storm was judicious.*

- **placidly** (plas′ id lē) *adv.* calmly; quietly (p. 337) *He smiled placidly, ignoring the noise.*

- **desultory** (des′ əl tôr′ ē) *adj.* random (p. 338) *They wandered through the park in a desultory way, with no clear destination.*

Background

Hawks Hawks are predators. They are fiercely territorial, and they often keep the same mate for life. Usually, hawks hunt rabbits, squirrels, and other birds. However, in rural areas they may kill and eat chickens. For a poor rural family like the one in this story, defending the family's flock of chickens from hawks is a matter of survival. Sometimes, when a farmer kills a hawk that has attacked his chickens, he displays it to frighten off other hawks.

Connecting to the Literature

Reading/Writing Connection In "Blues Ain't No Mockin Bird," a man protects his family and livestock. Write a few sentences about what kinds of things you feel are worth protecting or defending. Use at least three of these words: *intervene, oblige, promote, prohibit.*

READ MORE

by Toni Cade Bambara
The Sea Birds Are Still Alive: Collected Stories

Meet the Author

Toni Cade **Bambara** (1939–1995)

Toni Cade Bambara was a social activist and a writer of short stories, a novel, plays, television scripts, and documentaries. She started writing when she was in kindergarten and had her first story published when she was a senior in college.

"I write because I must," Bambara said. "If there were no more presses, no more publishing houses, I'd still be writing." She was equally devoted to social change and worked to improve the condition of African Americans. Her writing echoes that concern. Her stories are often praised for their vivid portrayals of the daily lives of African Americans in the twentieth century.

Fast Facts

▶ Toni Cade Bambara was born Miltona Cade. She added Bambara to her name after finding it on a sketchbook belonging to her great-grandmother.

▶ Bambara is the name of an African tribe known for its textiles.

For: More about the author
Visit: www.PHSchool.com
Web Code: epe-9210

Blues Ain't No Mockin Bird

Toni Cade Bambara

The puddle had frozen over, and me and Cathy went stompin in it. The twins from next door, Tyrone and Terry, were swingin so high out of sight we forgot we were waitin our turn on the tire. Cathy jumped up and came down hard on her heels and started tap-dancin. And the frozen patch splinterin every which way underneath kinda spooky. "Looks like a plastic spider web," she said. "A sort of weird spider, I guess, with many mental problems." But really it looked like the crystal paperweight Granny kept in the parlor. She was on the back porch, Granny was, making the cakes drunk. The old ladle dripping rum into the Christmas tins, like it used to drip maple syrup into the pails when we lived in the Judson's woods, like it poured cider into the vats when we were on the Cooper place, like it used to scoop buttermilk and soft cheese when we lived at the dairy.

"Go tell that man we ain't a bunch of trees."

"Ma'am?"

"I said to tell that man to get away from here with that camera." Me and Cathy look over toward the meadow where the men with the station wagon'd been roamin around all mornin. The tall man with a huge camera lassoed to his shoulder was buzzin our way.

"They're makin movie pictures," yelled Tyrone, stiffenin his legs and twistin so the tire'd come down slow so they could see.

"They're makin movie pictures," sang out Terry.

"That boy don't never have anything original to say," say Cathy grown-up.

By the time the man with the camera had cut across our neighbor's yard, the twins were out of the trees swingin low and Granny was onto the steps, the screen door bammin soft and scratchy against her palms. "We thought we'd get a shot or two of the house and everything and then—"

"Good mornin," Granny cut him off. And smiled that smile.

"Good mornin," he said, head all down the way Bingo does when you yell at him about the bones on the kitchen floor. "Nice place you got here, aunty. We thought we'd take a—"

"Did you?" said Granny with her eyebrows. Cathy pulled up her socks and giggled.

"Nice things here," said the man, buzzin his camera over the yard. The pecan barrels, the sled, me and Cathy, the flowers, the printed stones along the driveway, the trees, the twins, the toolshed.

"I don't know about the thing, the it, and the stuff," said Granny, still talkin with her eyebrows. "Just people here is what I tend to consider."

◀ **Critical Viewing** As you read, compare Granny with the woman in the illustration. **[Compare and Contrast]**

Literary Analysis
Dialogue and Dialect
Which features of the title and opening paragraph show that this story is written in dialect?

Reading Skill
Cause and Effect
Which details in the text help you to visualize the effect that the camera crew has on Granny?

✔**Reading Check**

What are the men doing on Granny's property?

Camera man stopped buzzin. Cathy giggled into her collar.

"Mornin, ladies," a new man said. He had come up behind us when we weren't lookin. "And gents," discoverin the twins givin him a nasty look. "We're filmin for the county," he said with a smile. "Mind if we shoot a bit around here?"

"I do indeed," said Granny with no smile. Smilin man was smiling up a storm. So was Cathy. But he didn't seem to have another word to say, so he and the camera man backed on out the yard, but you could hear the camera buzzin still. "Suppose you just shut that machine off," said Granny real low through her teeth, and took a step down off the porch and then another.

"Now, aunty," Camera said, pointin the thing straight at her.

"Your mama and I are not related."

Smilin man got his notebook out and a chewed-up pencil. "Listen," he said movin back into our yard, "we'd like to have a statement from you . . . for the film. We're filmin for the county, see. Part of the food stamp campaign. You know about the food stamps?"

Granny said nuthin.

"Maybe there's somethin you want to say for the film. I see you grow your own vegetables," he smiled real nice. "If more folks did that, see, there'd be no need—"

Granny wasn't sayin nuthin. So they backed on out, buzzin at our clothesline and the twins' bicycles, then back on down to the meadow. The twins were danglin in the tire, lookin at Granny. Me and Cathy were waitin, too, cause Granny always got somethin to say. She teaches steady with no let-up. "I was on this bridge one time," she started off. "Was a crowd cause this man was goin to jump, you understand. And a minister was there and the police and some other folks. His woman was there, too."

"What was they doin?" asked Tyrone.

"Tryin to talk him out of it was what they was doin. The minister talkin about how it was a mortal sin, suicide. His woman takin bites out of her own hand and not even knowin it, so nervous and cryin and talkin fast."

"So what happened?" asked Tyrone.

"So here comes . . . this person . . . with a camera, takin pictures of the man and the minister and the woman. Takin pictures of the man in his misery about to jump, cause life so bad and people been messin with him so bad. This person takin up the whole roll of film practically. But savin a few, of course."

"Of course," said Cathy, hatin the person. Me standin there wonderin how Cathy knew it was "of course" when I didn't and it was my grandmother.

Literary Analysis
Dialogue What does the dialogue between Granny and the film crew show about their attitudes toward each other?

▶ **Critical Viewing** Does this vegetable garden seem like one Granny would tend? Why or why not? **[Connect]**

After a while Tyrone say, "Did he jump?"

"Yeh, did he jump?" say Terry all eager. And Granny just stared at the twins till their faces swallow up the eager and they don't even care any more about the man jumpin. Then she goes back onto the porch and lets the screen door go for itself. I'm lookin to Cathy to finish the story cause she knows Granny's whole story before me even. Like she knew how come we move so much and Cathy ain't but a third cousin we picked up on the way last Thanksgivin visitin. But she knew it was on account of people drivin Granny crazy till she'd get up in the night and start packin. Mumblin and packin and wakin everybody up sayin, "Let's get on away from here before I kill me somebody." Like people wouldn't pay her for things like they said they would. Or Mr. Judson bringin us boxes of old clothes and raggedy magazines. Or Mrs. Cooper comin in our kitchen and touchin everything and sayin how clean it all was. Granny goin crazy, and Granddaddy Cain pullin her off the people, sayin, "Now,

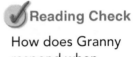

Reading Check

How does Granny respond when "Smilin" asks her to make a statement?

now, Cora." But next day loadin up the truck, with rocks all in his jaw, madder than Granny in the first place.

"I read a story once," said Cathy soundin like Granny teacher. "About this lady Goldilocks who barged into a house that wasn't even hers. And not invited, you understand. Messed over the people's groceries and broke up the people's furniture. Had the nerve to sleep in the folks' bed."

"Then what happened?" asked Tyrone. "What they do, the folks, when they come in to all this mess?"

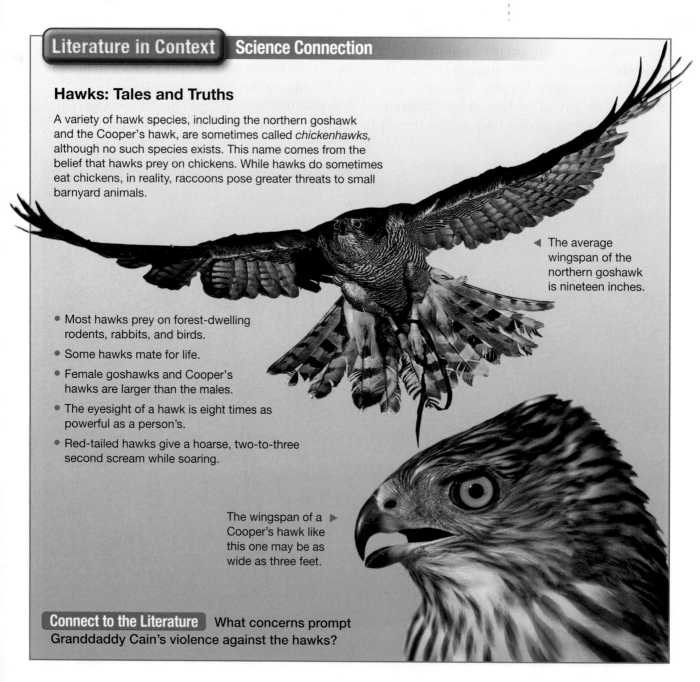

Literature in Context **Science Connection**

Hawks: Tales and Truths

A variety of hawk species, including the northern goshawk and the Cooper's hawk, are sometimes called *chickenhawks*, although no such species exists. This name comes from the belief that hawks prey on chickens. While hawks do sometimes eat chickens, in reality, raccoons pose greater threats to small barnyard animals.

◀ The average wingspan of the northern goshawk is nineteen inches.

- Most hawks prey on forest-dwelling rodents, rabbits, and birds.
- Some hawks mate for life.
- Female goshawks and Cooper's hawks are larger than the males.
- The eyesight of a hawk is eight times as powerful as a person's.
- Red-tailed hawks give a hoarse, two-to-three second scream while soaring.

The wingspan of a ▶ Cooper's hawk like this one may be as wide as three feet.

Connect to the Literature What concerns prompt Granddaddy Cain's violence against the hawks?

"Did they make her pay for it?" asked Terry, makin a fist. "I'd've made her pay me."

I didn't even ask. I could see Cathy actress was very likely to just walk away and leave us in mystery about this story which I heard was about some bears.

"Did they throw her out?" asked Tyrone, like his father sounds when he's bein extra nasty-plus to the washin-machine man.

"Woulda," said Terry. "I woulda gone upside her head with my fist and—"

"You woulda done whatcha always do—go cry to Mama, you big baby," said Tyrone. So naturally Terry starts hittin on Tyrone, and next thing you know they tumblin out the tire and rollin on the ground. But Granny didn't say a thing or send the twins home or step out on the steps to tell us about how we can't afford to be fightin amongst ourselves. She didn't say nuthin. So I get into the tire to take my turn. And I could see her leanin up against the pantry table, staring at the cakes she was puttin up for the Christmas sale, mumblin real low and grumpy and holdin her forehead like it wanted to fall off and mess up the rum cakes.

Behind me I hear before I can see Granddaddy Cain comin through the woods in his field boots. Then I twist around to see the shiny black oilskin cuttin through what little left there was of yellows, reds, and oranges. His great white head not quite round cause of this bloody thing high on his shoulder, like he was wearin a cap on sideways. He takes the shortcut through the pecan grove, and the sound of twigs snapping overhead and underfoot travels clear and cold all the way up to us. And here comes Smilin and Camera up behind him like they was goin to do somethin. Folks like to go for him sometimes. Cathy say it's because he's so tall and quiet and like a king. And people just can't stand it. But Smilin and Camera don't hit him in the head or nuthin. They just buzz on him as he stalks by with the chicken hawk slung over his shoulder, squawkin, drippin red down the back of the oilskin. He passes the porch and stops a second for Granny to see he's caught the hawk at last, but she's just starin and mumblin, and not at the hawk. So he nails the bird to the toolshed door, the hammerin crackin through the eardrums. And the bird flappin himself to death and droolin down the door to paint the gravel in the driveway red, then brown, then black. And the two men movin up on tiptoe like they was invisible or we were blind, one.

"Get them persons out of my flower bed, Mister Cain," say Granny moanin real low like at a funeral.

"How come your grandmother calls her husband 'Mister Cain' all the time?" Tyrone whispers all loud and noisy and from the city and

Literary Analysis
Dialogue and Dialect
What does the idiom "gone upside her head" probably mean?

Reading Check

What does Granddaddy do with the hawk?

don't know no better. Like his mama, Miss Myrtle, tell us never mind the <u>formality</u> as if we had no better breeding than to call her Myrtle, plain. And then this awful thing—a giant hawk—come wailin up over the meadow, flyin low and tilted and screamin, zigzaggin through the pecan grove, breakin branches and hollerin, snappin past the clothesline, flyin every which way, flyin into things <u>reckless</u> with crazy.

"He's come to claim his mate," say Cathy fast, and ducks down. We all fall quick and flat into the gravel driveway, stones scrapin my face. I squinch my eyes open again at the hawk on the door, tryin to fly up out of her death like it was just a sack flown into by mistake. Her body holdin her there on that nail, though. The mate beatin the air overhead and clutchin for hair, for heads, for landin space.

The camera man duckin and bendin and runnin and fallin, jigglin the camera and scared. And Smilin jumpin up and down swipin at the huge bird, tryin to bring the hawk down with just his raggedy ole cap. Granddaddy Cain straight up and silent, watchin the circles of the hawk, then aimin the hammer off his wrist. The giant bird fallin, silent and slow. Then here comes Camera and Smilin all big and bad now that the awful screechin thing is on its back and broken, here they come. And Granddaddy Cain looks up at them like it was the first time noticin, but not payin them too much mind cause he's listenin, we all listenin, to that low groanin music comin from the porch. And we figure any minute, somethin in my back tells me any minute now, Granny gonna bust through that screen with somethin in her hand and murder on her mind. So Granddaddy say above the buzzin, but quiet, "Good day, gentlemen." Just like that. Like he'd invited them in to play cards and they'd stayed too long and all the sandwiches were gone and Reverend Webb was droppin by and it was time to go.

They didn't know what to do. But like Cathy say, folks can't stand Granddaddy tall and silent and like a king. They can't neither. The smile the men smilin is pullin the mouth back and showin the teeth. Lookin like the wolf man, both of them. Then Granddaddy holds his hand out—this huge hand I used to sit in when I was a baby and he'd carry me through the house to my mother like I was a gift on a tray. Like he used to on the trains. They called the other men just waiters. But they spoke of Granddaddy separate and said, The Waiter. And said he had engines in his feet and motors in his hands and couldn't no train throw him off and couldn't nobody turn him round. They were big enough for motors, his hands were. He held that one hand out all still and it gettin to be not at all a hand but a person in itself.

"He wants you to hand him the camera," Smilin whispers to Camera, tiltin his head to talk secret like they was in the jungle or

Vocabulary Builder
formality (fôr mal´ ə tē) *n.* attention to established rules or customs
reckless (rek´ lis) *adj.* careless; rash

Reading Skill
Cause and Effect
How does the arrival of the screaming hawk affect the film crew? How does it affect Granddaddy Cain?

somethin and come upon a native that don't speak the language. The men start untyin the straps, and they put the camera into that great hand speckled with the hawk's blood all black and crackly now. And the hand don't even drop with the weight, just the fingers move, curl up around the machine. But Granddaddy lookin straight at the men. They lookin at each other and everywhere but at Granddaddy's face.

"We filmin for the county, see," say Smilin. "We puttin together a movie for the food stamp program . . . filmin all around these parts. Uhh, filmin for the county."

"Can I have my camera back?" say the tall man with no machine on his shoulder, but still keepin it high like the camera was still there or needed to be. "Please, sir."

Then Granddaddy's other hand flies up like a sudden and gentle bird, slaps down fast on top of the camera and lifts off half like it was a calabash[1] cut for sharing.

"Hey," Camera jumps forward. He gathers up the parts into his chest and everything unrollin and fallin all over. "Whatcha tryin to do? You'll ruin the film." He looks down into his chest of metal reels and things like he's protectin a kitten from the cold.

"You standin in the misses' flower bed," say Granddaddy. "This is our own place."

The two men look at him, then at each other, then back at the mess in the camera man's chest, and they just back off. One sayin over and over all the way down to the meadow, "Watch it, Bruno. Keep ya fingers off the film." Then Granddaddy picks up the hammer and jams it into the oilskin pocket, scrapes his boots, and goes into the house. And you can hear the squish of his boots headin through the house. And you can see the funny shadow he throws from the parlor window onto the ground by the string-bean patch. The hammer draggin the pocket of the oilskin out so Granddaddy looked even wider. Granny was hummin now—high not low and grumbly. And she was doin the cakes again, you could smell the molasses from the rum.

"There's this story I'm goin to write one day," say Cathy dreamer. "About the proper use of the hammer."

"Can I be in it?" Tyrone say with his hand up like it was a matter of first come, first served.

"Perhaps," say Cathy, climbin onto the tire to pump us up. "If you there and ready."

---

1. calabash (kal´ ə bash´) *n.* large gourd-like fruit.

Apply the Skills

Blues Ain't No Mockin Bird

Thinking About the Selection

1. **Respond:** Which character would you most like to meet? Why?
2. **(a) Recall:** Why are the photographers filming in the area?
   (b) Infer: What message does Granny give the men through her speech and actions?
3. Make a chart like the one shown. **(a) Compare:** In the first column, write the ways that the Camera and Smilin are like the hawks. **(b) Connect:** In the second column, write the ways that Granddaddy's actions are like the actions of the male hawk.
   (c) Discuss: Share your chart with a partner and discuss your responses. Then, in the third column, explain whether you think the hawks represent Granddaddy and Granny, Smilin and Camera, or both pairs.

Hawks and Camera and Smilin	Hawks and Granddaddy	What the Hawks Represent

4. **Make a Judgment:** Is Granddaddy's treatment of the photographers justified? Support your view with story details.

Literary Analysis

5. Identify one example of **dialogue** that indicates the tension is increasing between Granny and the filmmakers.
6. Identify one example of dialogue that shows Granny is tough.
7. **(a)** Explain how the spelling and grammar used in the following passage indicate that it is an example of **dialect.** "Granny always got somethin to say. She teaches steady with no let-up."
   (b) Rewrite the passage in Standard English. **(c)** Explain how the use of dialect makes the characters and setting more vivid.

Reading Skill

8. **(a)** What is the **cause** of Granddaddy's decision to disassemble the men's camera? **(b)** What is the **effect** of Granddaddy's action on the cameramen? **(c)** What is the effect on Granny?
9. Which visual details in the story help you to explain the causes and effects of Granddaddy's ruining the film?

Vocabulary Builder

Practice **Analogies** show the relationships between pairs of words. Use a word from the "Blues Ain't No Mockin Bird" vocabulary list on page 320 to complete each analogy. In each, your choice should create a word pair that matches the relationship between the first two words given. Explain the relationship that the pairs in each set share.

1. solution : intelligent :: accident : _____
2. sportsmanship : game :: _____ : ceremony

Adding Words to Your Vocabulary Using a thesaurus, find an **antonym,** or word of opposite meaning, for each word in the vocabulary list for "Blues Ain't No Mockin Bird" on page 320. Use each antonym in a sentence that makes the meaning of the word clear. (For more on using a thesaurus, see page R7.)

Writing

Write an **informal letter** from the point of view of a character in the story other than the narrator. Address the letter to a friend or relative and describe the events that the character observed.

- Before writing, list the personality traits of your character.
- Refer to your list as you write, making sure the details and language in your letter are consistent with the traits you listed.

For *Grammar, Vocabulary,* and *Assessment,* see **Build Language Skills,** pages 342–343.

Extend Your Learning

Listening and Speaking With a partner, role-play a **dialogue** between the cameraman and his boss. Follow these tips:
- Do not omit any important information, and do not exaggerate.
- Be polite, and use language appropriate to your situation.
- As the Boss, ask relevant questions and answers.
Read or perform the dialogue in class.

Research and Technology Work with a group of classmates to compile a **photo collection** of birds of prey like the hawks in "Blues Ain't No Mockin Bird." Consult library and Internet resources in your research of these birds, using keywords such as "hawks," "falcons," and "eagles." Print or copy the pictures and write an informative caption for each. Then, display your photo collection in class.

Short Story

Background

Nineteenth-Century Train Travel In the late nineteenth century, when this story takes place, trains were the fastest way to travel and transport cargo. Nonetheless, train cars in which people with cargo had to travel were uncomfortable. The cars were poorly ventilated boxes on wheels, and had only small windows.

Connecting to the Literature

Reading/Writing Connection In "The Invalid's Story," the author exaggerates the discomfort of two train travelers to create humor. Write a few sentences about why stories that create humor out of problems are funny. Use at least three of these words: *analyze, focus, participate, verify.*

Review

For **Literary Analysis, Reading Skill,** and **Vocabulary Builder,** see page 320.

READ MORE

by Mark Twain
Life on the Mississippi
The Adventures of Huckleberry Finn

Meet the Author

Mark **Twain** (1835–1910)

Born Samuel Clemens, Mark Twain grew up in the Mississippi River town of Hannibal, Missouri. He worked as a riverboat pilot, printer, prospector, reporter, and at many other jobs. Primarily, however, Clemens was a writer of comic stories, sketches, and novels. The most famous humorist of his day, he traveled the world entertaining people with his witty lectures.

"By the mark—twain" was a cry heard on the riverboats of Clemens's youth. It meant that the water was two fathoms deep—deep enough for a riverboat to pass unharmed. Harkening back to his youth working on those boats, Clemens took the name Mark Twain at age twenty-seven. Under that name, he wrote some of the most beloved fiction in American literature.

Fast Facts

▶ Mark Twain was the first writer to turn himself into a business. He even trademarked his name!
▶ Twain's first famous story was "The Celebrated Jumping Frog of Calaveras County."

Go Online
Author Link

For: More about the author
Visit: www.PHSchool.com
Web Code: epe-9211

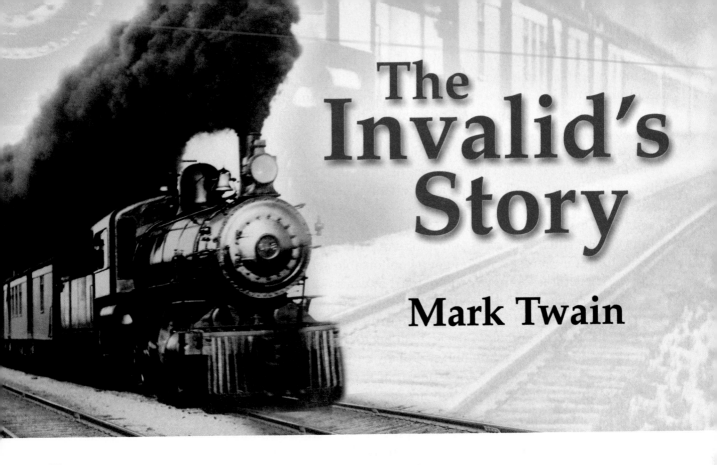

The Invalid's Story

Mark Twain

I seem sixty and married, but these effects are due to my condition and sufferings, for I am a bachelor, and only forty-one. It will be hard for you to believe that I, who am now but a shadow, was a hale, hearty man two short years ago—a man of iron, a very athlete!—yet such is the simple truth. But stranger still than this fact is the way in which I lost my health. I lost it through helping to take care of a box of guns on a two-hundred-mile railway journey one winter's night. It is the actual truth, and I will tell you about it.

I belong in Cleveland, Ohio. One winter's night, two years ago, I reached home just after dark, in a driving snowstorm, and the first thing I heard when I entered the house was that my dearest boyhood friend and schoolmate, John B. Hackett, had died the day before, and that his last utterance had been a desire that I would take his remains home to his poor old father and mother in Wisconsin. I was greatly shocked and grieved, but there was no time to waste in emotions; I must start at once. I took the card, marked "Deacon Levi Hackett, Bethlehem, Wisconsin," and hurried off through the whistling storm to the railway station. Arrived there I found the long white-pine box which had been described to me; I fastened the card to it with some tacks, saw it put safely aboard the express car, and then ran into the eating room to provide myself

Reading Check

What was John B. Hackett's dying wish?

with a sandwich and some cigars. When I returned, presently, there was my coffin-box back again, apparently, and a young fellow examining around it, with a card in his hands, and some tacks and a hammer! I was astonished and puzzled. He began to nail on his card, and I rushed out to the express car, in a good deal of a state of mind, to ask for an explanation. But no—there was my box, all right, in the express car; it hadn't been disturbed. [The fact is that without my suspecting it a <u>prodigious</u> mistake had been made. I was carrying off a box of guns which that young fellow had come to the station to ship to a rifle company in Peoria, Illinois, and he had got my corpse.] Just then the conductor sang out "All aboard," and I jumped into the express car and got a comfortable seat on a bale of buckets. The expressman was there, hard at work—a plain man of fifty, with a simple, honest, good-natured face, and a breezy, practical heartiness in his general style. As the train moved off a stranger skipped into the car and set a package of peculiarly mature and capable Limburger cheese[1] on one end of my coffin-box—I mean my box of guns. That is to say, I know now that it was Limburger cheese, but at that time I never had heard of the article in my life, and of course was wholly ignorant of its character. Well, we sped through the wild night, the bitter storm raged on, a cheerless misery stole over me, my heart went down, down, down! The old expressman made a brisk remark or two about the tempest and the arctic weather, slammed his sliding doors to, and bolted them, closed his window down tight, and then went bustling around, here and there and yonder, setting things to rights, and all the time contentedly humming "Sweet By and By" in a low tone, and flatting a

---

1. **Limburger cheese** cheese with a strong odor.

Vocabulary Builder
prodigious (prō dij′ əs)
adj. enormous

◀ **Critical Viewing**
Based on this 1874 painting of a railway station, what challenges did train travel pose at that time in history? **[Analyze]**

good deal. Presently I began to detect a most evil and searching odor stealing about on the frozen air. This depressed my spirits still more, because of course I attributed it to my poor departed friend. There was something infinitely saddening about his calling himself to my remembrance in this dumb, pathetic way, so it was hard to keep the tears back. Moreover, it distressed me on account of the old expressman, who, I was afraid, might notice it. However, he went humming tranquilly on, and gave no sign; and for this I was grateful. Grateful, yes, but still uneasy; and soon I began to feel more and more uneasy every minute, for every minute that went by that odor thickened up the more, and got to be more and more gamy and hard to stand. Presently, having got things arranged to his satisfaction, the expressman got some wood and made up a tremendous fire in his stove. This distressed me more than I can tell, for I could not but feel that it was a mistake. I was sure that the effect would be <u>deleterious</u> upon my poor departed friend. Thompson—the expressman's name was Thompson, as I found out in the course of the night—now went poking around his car, stopping up whatever stray cracks he could find, remarking that it didn't make any difference what kind of a night it was outside, he calculated to make us comfortable, anyway. I said nothing, but I believed he was not choosing the right way. Meantime he was humming to himself just as before; and meantime, too, the stove was getting hotter and hotter, and the place closer and closer. I felt myself growing pale and qualmish,[2] but grieved in silence and said nothing. Soon I noticed that the "Sweet By and By" was gradually fading out; next it ceased altogether, and there was an ominous stillness. After a few moments Thompson said—

"Pfew! I reckon it ain't no cinnamon't I've loaded up thish-year stove with!"

He gasped once or twice, then moved toward the cof—gun-box, stood over that Limburger cheese part of a moment, then came back and sat down near me, looking a good deal impressed. After a contemplative pause, he said, indicating the box with a gesture—

"Friend of yourn?"

"Yes," I said with a sigh.

"He's pretty ripe, ain't he!"

Nothing further was said for perhaps a couple of minutes, each being busy with his own thoughts; then Thompson said, in a low awed voice—

"Sometimes it's uncertain whether they're really gone or not—seem gone, you know—body warm, joints limber—and so, although

---

2. **qualmish** (kwäm´ ish) *adj.* suddenly sick.

Vocabulary Builder
deleterious (del´ ə tir´ ē əs) *adj.* harmful to health or well-being

Reading Skill
Cause and Effect
When you picture this scene, what details explain the cause of Thompson's gasp?

Reading Check
What does the narrator say depressed his spirits?

you think they're gone, you don't really know. I've had cases in my car. It's perfectly awful, becuz you don't know what minute they'll rise up and look at you!" Then, after a pause, and slightly lifting his elbow toward the box,—"But he ain't in no trance! No, sir, I go bail for him!"

We sat some time, in meditative silence, listening to the wind and the roar of the train; then Thompson said, with a good deal of feeling:

"Well-a-well, we've all got to go, they ain't no getting around it. Man that is born of woman is of few days and far between, as Scriptur'[3] says. Yes, you look at it any way you want to, it's awful solemn and cur'us: they ain't nobody can get around it; all's got to go—just everybody, as you may say. One day you're hearty and strong"— here he scrambled to his feet and broke a pane and stretched his nose out at it a moment or two, then sat down again while I struggled up and thrust my nose out at the same place, and this we kept on doing every now and then—"and next day he's cut down like the grass, and the places which knowed him then knows him no more forever, as Scriptur' says. Yes'ndeedy, it's awful solemn and cur'us; but we've all got to go, one time or another; they ain't no getting around it."

There was another long pause; then—

"What did he die of?"

I said I didn't know.

"How long has he ben dead?"

It seemed <u>judicious</u> to enlarge the facts to fit the probabilities; so I said:

"Two or three days."

But it did no good: for Thompson received it with an injured look which plainly said. "Two or three years, you mean." Then he went right along, <u>placidly</u> ignoring my statement, and gave his views at considerable length upon the unwisdom of putting off burials too long. Then he lounged off toward the box, stood a moment, then came back on a sharp trot and visited the broken pane, observing:

"'Twould 'a' ben a durn sight better, all around, if they'd started him along last summer."

Thompson sat down and buried his face in his red silk handkerchief, and began to slowly sway and rock his body like one who is doing his best to endure the almost unendurable. By this time the fragrance—if you may call it fragrance—was just about suffocating, as near as you can come at it. Thompson's face was turning gray: I

Vocabulary Builder
judicious (jōō dish´ əs)
adj. showing good judgment

placidly (plas´ id lē)
adv. calmly; quietly

---

3. **Scriptur'** scripture; the Bible.

knew mine hadn't any color left in it. By and by Thompson rested his forehead in his left hand, with his elbow on his knee, and sort of waved his red handkerchief toward the box with his other hand, and said:

"I've carried a many a one of 'em—some of 'em considerable overdue, too—but, lordy, he just lays over 'em all!—and does it easy. Cap, they was heliotrope[4] to him!"

This recognition of my poor friend gratified me, in spite of the sad circumstances, because it had so much the sound of a compliment.

Pretty soon it was plain that something had got to be done. I suggested cigars. Thompson thought it was a good idea. He said:

"Likely it'll modify him some."

We puffed gingerly along for a while, and tried hard to imagine that things were improved. But it wasn't any use. Before very long, and without any consultation, both cigars were quietly dropped from our nerveless fingers at the same moment. Thompson said, with a sigh:

"No, Cap, it don't modify him worth a cent. Fact is, it makes him worse, becuz it appears to stir up his ambition. What do you reckon we better do, now?"

I was not able to suggest anything: indeed, I had to be swallowing and swallowing all the time, and did not like to trust myself to speak. Thompson fell to maundering, in a <u>desultory</u> and low-spirited way, about the miserable experiences of this night: and he got to referring to my poor friend by various titles—sometimes military ones, sometimes civil ones; and I noticed that as fast as my poor friend's effectiveness grew, Thompson promoted him accordingly—gave him a bigger title. Finally he said:

"I've got an idea. Suppos'n' we buckle down to it and give the Colonel a bit of a shove toward t'other end of the car?—about ten foot, say. He wouldn't have so much influence, then, don't you reckon?"

I said it was a good scheme. So we took in a good fresh breath at the broken pane, calculating to hold it till we got through: then we went there and bent over that deadly cheese and took a grip on the box. Thompson nodded "All ready," and then we threw ourselves forward with all our might: but Thompson slipped, and slumped down with his nose on the cheese, and his breath got loose. He gagged and gasped, and floundered up and made a break for the door, pawing the air and saying hoarsely, "Don't hender me!—

---

4. **heliotrope** (hē´ lē ə trōp´) *n.* a sweet-smelling plant.

The Invalid's Story ■ 337

Literary Analysis
Dialogue and Dialect
Which features of Thompson's speech in this passage reflect a particular dialect?

Vocabulary Builder
desultory (des´ əl tôr´ ē) *adj.* random

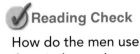Reading Check

How do the men use the window to lessen the effect of the odor?

gimme the road! I'm a-dying; gimme the road!" Out on the cold platform I sat down and held his head awhile, and he revived. Presently he said:

"Do you reckon we started the Gen'rul any?"

I said no: we hadn't budged him.

"Well, then, that idea's up the flume. We got to think up something else. He's suited wher' he is, I reckon; and if that's the way he feels about it, and has made up his mind that he don't wish to be disturbed, you bet he's a-going to have his own way in the business. Yes, better leave him right wher' he is, long as he wants it so; becuz he holds all the trumps, don't you know, and so it stands to reason that the man that lays out to alter his plans for him is going to get left."

But we couldn't stay out there in that mad storm; we should have frozen to death. So we went in again and shut the door, and began to suffer once more and take turns at the break in the window. By and by, as we were starting away from a station where we had stopped a moment Thompson pranced in cheerily, and exclaimed:

"We're all right, now! I reckon we've got the Commodore this time. I judge I've got the stuff here that'll take the tuck out of him."

It was carbolic acid. He had a carboy of it. He sprinkled it all around everywhere; in fact he drenched everything with it, rifle-box, cheese and all. Then we sat down, feeling pretty hopeful. But it wasn't for long. You see the two perfumes began to mix, and then—well, pretty soon we made a break for the door; and out there Thompson swabbed his face with his bandanna and said in a kind of disheartened way:

"It ain't no use. We can't buck agin him. He just utilizes everything we put up to modify him with, and gives it his own flavor and plays it back on us. Why, Cap, don't you know, it's as much as a hundred times worse in there now than it was when he first got a-going. I never did see one of 'em warm up to his work so, and take such a dumnation interest in it. No, sir, I never did, as long as I've ben on the road: and I've carried a many a one of 'em, as I was telling you."

We went in again after we were frozen pretty stiff; but my, we couldn't stay in, now. So we just waltzed back and forth, freezing, and thawing, and stifling, by turns. In about an hour we stopped at another station; and as we left it Thompson came in with a bag, and said—

"Cap, I'm a-going to chance him once more—just this once; and if we don't fetch him this time, the thing for us to do, is to just throw up the sponge and withdraw from the canvass. That's the way I put it up."

He had brought a lot of chicken feathers, and dried apples, and leaf tobacco, and rags, and old shoes, and sulphur, and asafetida, and one thing or another: and he piled them on a breadth of sheet iron in the middle of the floor, and set fire to them.

When they got well started. I couldn't see, myself, how even the corpse could stand it. All that went before was just simply poetry to that smell—but mind you, the original smell stood up out of it just as sublime as ever—fact is, these other smells just seemed to give it a better hold: and my, how rich it was! I didn't make these reflections there—there wasn't time—made them on the platform. And breaking for the platform, Thompson got suffocated and fell: and before I got him dragged out, which I did by the collar, I was mighty near gone myself. When we revived, Thompson said dejectedly:

"We got to stay out here, Cap. We got to do it. They ain't no other way. The Governor wants to travel alone, and he's fixed so he can outvote us."

And presently he added:

"And don't you know, we're pisoned. It's our last trip, you can make up your mind to it. Typhoid fever is what's going to come of this. I feel it a-coming right now. Yes, sir, we're elected, just as sure as you're born."

We were taken from the platform an hour later, frozen and insensible, at the next station, and I went straight off into a virulent fever, and never knew anything again for three weeks. I found out, then, that I had spent that awful night with a harmless box of rifles and a lot of innocent cheese; but the news was too late to save me; imagination had done its work, and my health was permanently shattered; neither Bermuda nor any other land can ever bring it back to me. This is my last trip; I am on my way home to die.

Reading Skill
Cause and Effect
What is the result of Thompson's final attempt to deal with the odor?

Reading Skill
Cause and Effect
What effect does the experience on the train have on the narrator's health?

Apply the Skills

The Invalid's Story

Thinking About the Selection

1. **Respond:** Did you find this story entertaining? Explain.
2. **(a) Recall:** What do the men believe is creating the awful smell? **(b) Connect:** What is actually creating the smell? **(c) Compare and Contrast:** In what ways does the contrast between what they think is true and what is really true contribute to the humor?
3. **(a) Interpret:** Why does Thompson say the corpse "wants to travel alone"? **(b) Analyze:** How does Thompson's description of the corpse as deliberately trying to smell bad add to the story's humor?
4. Make a chart like the one shown. **(a) Compare:** In the first column, write a list of sad details in the story. **(b) Connect:** In the second column, write the details that add humor to the story. **(c) Discuss and Evaluate:** Share your chart with a partner and discuss your responses. Then, in the third column, explain whether you think the story is sad, funny, or both.

Sad Details	Humorous Details	Evaluation

Literary Analysis

5. Identify one example of **dialogue** in the story that indicates the smell is increasing. Explain your choice.
6. Identify an example of dialogue that shows that Thompson and the narrator do not know each other well. Explain your choice.
7. **(a)** In what way do the spelling, grammar, and words used in the following passage indicate that it is an example of **dialect?**
    No, Cap, it don't modify him worth a cent. Fact is, it makes him worse, becuz it appears to stir up his ambition. What do you reckon we better do, now?
   (b) Rewrite the passage in Standard English. **(c)** Explain how the use of dialect makes the characters and setting more vivid.

Reading Skill

8. **(a)** What is the **cause** of the smell in the express car? **(b)** What **effect** does the smell have on Thompson and the narrator?
9. Which visual details in the story help you to explain why the characters are mistaken about the true cause of the smell?

QuickReview

Story at a Glance
Two travelers on a train endure an odor they mistakenly think comes from a corpse.

Go Online
Assessment
For: Self-test
Visit: www.PHSchool.com
Web Code: epa-6210

Dialogue: a conversation between or among characters in a literary work

Dialect: the unique form of a language spoken by people of a region or group

Cause: an event, an action, or a feeling that produces a result

Effect: the result produced by a cause

Vocabulary Builder

Practice **Analogies** show the relationships between pairs of words. Use a word from the vocabulary list for "The Invalid's Story" on page 320 to complete each analogy.

1. comedy : humorous :: measles : _____
2. graceful : clumsy :: _____ : foolish
3. tiny : small :: _____ : large
4. systematic : reliable :: _____ : unpredictable
5. violently : angry :: _____ : content

Adding Words to Your Vocabulary Using a thesaurus, find an **antonym,** or word of opposite meaning, for each word in the vocabulary list for "The Invalid's Story" on page 320. Use each antonym correctly in a sentence. (For more on using a thesaurus, see page R7.)

Writing

Write an **informal letter** from the point of view of Thompson. Address the letter to a friend or relative and describe what occurs in the story.
- Before you write, list Thompson's personality traits.
- Refer to your list as you write, making sure that the details and language in your letter fit the traits you listed.

For *Grammar, Vocabulary,* and *Assessment,* see **Build Language Skills,** pages 342–343.

Extend Your Learning

Listening and Speaking With a partner, assume the roles of the narrator and a doctor. Prepare and deliver a **dialogue** in which the narrator explains to the doctor why his health is "shattered."
- Do not omit any important information, and do not exaggerate.
- Be polite, and use language appropriate to your situation.
Read or perform the dialogue in class.

Research and Technology Mark Twain has one of America's most familiar faces. Work with a group to compile a **photo collection** that shows Twain at various ages. Consult library and Internet resources in your research. Print or copy the pictures and write an informative caption for each. Display your photo collection in class.

Build Language Skills

Vocabulary Skill

Word Roots The **Latin root** *-sequi-* means " follow." A *sequence* is "a following of one thing after another."

▶ **Example:** The witness described the sequence of events.

Words with the root *-sequi-* will have meanings related to the idea of following.

Practice From your knowledge of the root, predict the meaning of these words. Check the dictionary definition. Explain how your predicted meaning compares to the dictionary definition.

1. non sequitur
2. sequel
3. sequential
4. subsequent

Grammar Lesson

Active and Passive Voice A verb in the **active voice** expresses an action done **by** its subject. A verb in the **passive voice** expresses an action done **to** its subject.

Active voice:
Mark Twain *wrote* "The Invalid's Story." (The subject, *Mark Twain,* performs the action of the verb *wrote.*)

Passive voice:
"The Invalid's Story" *was written* by Mark Twain. (The subject, *"The Invalid's Story,"* receives the action of the verb *was written.*)

Use the active voice for lively, direct writing. Use the passive voice when you want to minimize the performer of the action or when the performer of the action is unknown.

Practice Copy the following sentences and underline the verb or verbs in each one. **(a)** Identify the underlined verbs as active or passive voice. **(b)** Explain whether the active or passive voice is a good choice for the sentence.

1. Matthew was ignored by the reporter.
2. The story was placed on the last page.
3. She wrote a story about a mysterious disappearance.
4. In the search for answers, the reporter was helped by two eyewitnesses.
5. A neighbor rescued the trapped child.

MorePractice

For more practice with active and passive voice, see the Grammar Handbook, p. R40.

*W*G *Prentice Hall Writing and Grammar Connection: Chapter 5, Section 4*

Reading: Cause and Effect

Directions: *Read the selection. Then answer the questions.*

Standards Assessed

• WL.1.01.4
• IR.2.04.1
• LT.5.01.8

   A fierce storm had been beating down on the isolated house since sunrise. Now, as the wind shrieked, Andrew glanced out the window just in time to see the huge oak tree quiver and begin to fall straight toward him. He ducked away and ran toward the kitchen. As he did so, he stumbled and fell roughly to the floor beneath his desk. He rolled over just in time to see the oak splinter the window and crash down on him. Andrew gasped for breath as the wind howled through the shattered window. The oak lay propped on the solid desk, inches from his eyes. Except for a slight scrape on his knee, he had escaped without injury.

1. Why did Andrew end up under the desk?
   A A storm had blown a tree through his window.
   B He knew he could not get to the kitchen in time.
   C He dove under the desk to avoid being injured.
   D He stumbled while trying to run to safety.

2. Why was Andrew able to avoid serious injury?
   A The tree was blocked by the window.
   B The desk prevented the tree from hitting him.
   C He leaped aside into the kitchen.
   D He ran quickly.

3. What was the effect of the storm?
   A injury
   B damage
   C impairment
   D affliction

4. What would you have to picture in order to visualize the action?
   A an oak tree
   B the exterior of the house
   C the interior of the house
   D a solid desk

Timed Writing: Description [Cognition]

Review "Blues Ain't No Mockin Bird" or "The Invalid's Story." Write a brief description of the setting of the story. **(30 minutes)**

 ## Writing Workshop: *Work in Progress*

Cause and Effect Essay

Highlight the one effect that you think is most interesting on your effect list. Write a list of questions that would help you define the cause for this effect. Put this paper in your writing portfolio.

Reading Informational Materials

Brochures

In Part 2, you are learning how to analyze causes and effects as you read literature. This skill is also useful when you read informational materials, such as brochures and advertisements. When writers and graphic designers create a brochure, they use specific design and organizational elements to produce the effects they want. If you read Mark Twain's "The Invalid's Story," you may have wanted to learn more about railways. The brochure that follows describes a museum that celebrates trains and railroads.

About Brochures

The **brochures** that organizations and businesses create can provide many types of information. They often include these features:

- Location map
- Contact information, including mailing address, e-mail address, and phone numbers
- Hours of operation and prices of admission
- Description of facilities, products, or services
- Photographs of products or services

Reading Skill

Brochures are designed so that words, colors, and images work together to present information in a logical and pleasing way. The **format** is the placement of text, including headings and captions, around design elements, such as pictures and maps. The format makes important information stand out. When you **evaluate text format,** you examine text and design features to determine the importance of the information presented. These features will help you distinguish between essential and nonessential information in printed materials.

Standard Course of Study

- Identify and use standards to critique and evaluate work. (CT.4.02.2)
- Analyze author's craft and argument style. (FA.3.04.9)
- Analyze and evaluate the effects of author's craft and style in response. (WL.1.03.8)

Evaluating Text Format	
Heads	What is the largest head on the page? What information do the heads emphasize?
Images	Are photographs included? Are maps or graphics included? Where? How do the images support information in the text?
Organization	What information appears on the first page? Why? What information appears inside? Why?

North Carolina Transportation Museum

The subhead grabs your attention by challenging you to discover something new. It also makes readers consider what "moved"—trains, people, or maybe even ideas.

Discover the People and Machines That Have Moved North Carolina

The locator map is placed so readers see it immediately. It shows major roads and landmarks.

North Carolina HISTORIC SITES

*Division of Archives and History
Department of Cultural Resources*

The museum's hours and cost of admission are located near the map. All the information needed to visit the museum is easy to find.

Hours:
Apr. 1–Oct. 31: Mon.–Sat. 9 A.M.–5 P.M.;
Sun. 1–5 P.M.
Nov. 1–Mar. 31: Tues.–Sat. 10 A.M.–4 P.M.
Sun. 1–4 P.M. Closed Mondays, New Year's
Day, Veterans Day, Thanksgiving Day, and
Christmas holidays.

Admission is free. Fee for train rides.
Group rates available. Groups are
requested to make advance reservations.

The Museum

Barber Junction — This is the gateway to fun and excitement at the North Carolina Transportation Museum. Get your tickets here for train rides around the site, and pick up information about tours and exhibits.

The Robert Julian Roundhouse — View more than twenty-five restored locomotives and rail cars along with extensive exhibits tracing the history of railroads in the state. Videos and interactive exhibits, along with shop areas at which locomotives are still worked on today, are highlights of this unique historic building.

Historic Spencer Shops — The North Carolina Transportation Museum is located on the site of Southern Railway's steam locomotive repair facility in Spencer. While the museum is young—founded in 1977—the story of the Spencer Shops reaches back more than one hundred years.

Spencer Shops' mission was to repair steam locomotives that hauled Southern's passenger trains and freight trains filled with North Carolina furniture, textiles, tobacco, and produce.

Southern Railway was one of the first U.S. rail systems to experiment with diesel-electric locomotives, and by 1953 Southern had retired its last steam engine. Spencer Shops started on the road to decline, and employment dropped steadily through the 1950s and 1960s until it finally came to a halt in the late 1970s.

LEARNING OPPORTUNITIES — Education is a primary
goal at the North Carolina Transportation Museum. A number of programs are offered to tour groups. In addition to 150,000 square feet of visual exhibits, hands-on activities are available, as are thirty-minute train rides around the site and rides on a restored turntable. Visitors who are here after the last train ride of the day can see the engine run onto the turntable and into the Roundhouse, where it remains for the night on cool evenings. A full-calendar of special events is offered, including temporary exhibits.

For more information, please contact:
North Carolina Transportation Museum
P.O. Box 165 Spencer, North Carolina 28159
(704) 636-2889
1-877-NCTMFUN
Fax (704) 639-1881
http://www.ah.dcr.state.nc.us/sections/hs/spencer/spencer.htm

---

Subheads call attention to activities and features of the museum.

The image of the man waving from the train shows the human connection to trains and presents them as much more than just equipment.

The brochure wraps up the presentation by inviting the reader to ask for more information. Contact information is clear and easy to find.

EOC Test Practice

Reading: Evaluating Text Format

Directions: *Choose the letter of the best answer to each question about the brochure for the North Carolina Transportation Museum.*

Standards Assessed

• IR.2.03.3
• IR.2.03.4
• WL.1.03.2

1. Why does the designer place the map on the first page?
   A The map is not related to the content of the second page.
   B The map is more attractive than a photograph.
   C This position makes the map more useful to the reader.
   D There was no space on the second page.

2. What is the main subject of the information on the second page?
   A where to get additional information
   B sites and activities at the museum
   C rates and fees at the museum
   D volunteer opportunities

3. Under which head would someone look to find information about programs offered to tour groups at the museum?
   A Hours
   B Historic Spencer Shops
   C Learning Opportunities
   D For more information

Reading: Comprehension and Interpretation

Directions: *Write your answers on a separate piece of paper.*

4. Why do you think the writer chose to place information about learning opportunities near the end of the second page rather than before the description of the museum sites? **[Generating]**

5. **(a)** On what specific historic site is the North Carolina Transportation Museum located? **(b)** Why do you think this location was chosen for the museum? **(c)** In what ways does this location affect the activities and services the museum provides? **[Generating]**

Timed Writing: Persuasion [Critical Stance]

Use the brochure information to write a letter to an elected official in which you request financial support for the museum. Explain how trains have impacted people's lives and why the museum deserves public funding. **(20 minutes)**

Symbolism and Allegory

A **symbol** is a person, a place, a thing, or an event that represents both itself and a larger idea or feeling. **Symbolism** is the use of symbols in literature. For example, a writer might use a dove as a symbol for peace or a voyage as a symbol for the journey of life.

An **allegory** is a poem or story that has parallel literal and symbolic meanings. On the literal level, the story appears simply as it is told. On the symbolic level, every element in the story, including the characters, events, descriptions, and features of the setting, has a symbolic meaning. For example, an allegory in which a sailor crosses the ocean in a small boat might have these symbolic equivalents:

- The sailor represents a human being.
- Storms at sea represent the struggles of life.
- Wind and sails represent the help of friends.

While an allegory can be understood on the literal level, its full meaning is only clear on the symbolic level. Often, allegories may seem less realistic than non-allegorical works. Their characters may seem simple or one-dimensional, because their symbolic value is more important than a realistic depiction. Often, writers use allegories to comment on current events.

Comparing Symbolism and Allegory

Symbols play an important role in both of the stories that follow. However, only one story is an allegory. As you read, use a chart like the one shown to interpret the symbols in each story. Then, determine which story uses symbols simply to enhance the meaning, and which is a full-blown, complete allegory.

NC	**Standard Course of Study**

- Understand the importance of cultural and historical impact on texts. (LT.5.01.10)
- Provide textual evidence to support understanding of response to literary text. (LT.5.03.3)

The Scarlet Ibis
Symbol: rotting brown petals
Meaning: the end of summer

The Golden Kite, the Silver Wind
Symbol: city wall shaped like a club
Meaning: a community's desire to protect itself

Vocabulary Builder

The Scarlet Ibis

- **imminent** (im´ ə nənt) *adj.* likely to happen soon (p. 354) *Clouds gathered and rain was imminent.*
- **infallibility** (in fal´ ə bil´ ə tē) *n.* condition of not being likely to fail (p. 356) *After several victories, the team had a sense of infallibility.*
- **precariously** (pri ker´ ē əs lē) *adv.* insecurely (p. 358) *She clung precariously to the ledge, high above the surging river.*

The Golden Kite, the Silver Wind

- **vile** (vīl) *adj.* evil; wicked (p. 363) *Such a vile crime is hard to forgive.*
- **ravenous** (rav´ ə nəs) *adj.* greedily or wildly hungry (p. 363) *After his workout, John was ravenous.*
- **spurn** (spurn) *v.* reject with contempt or disdain (p. 364) *She will spurn the gift because it came from an enemy.*

Build Understanding

Connecting to the Literature

Reading/Writing Connection Both of the following stories deal with conflicts, or struggles, between individuals or entire communities. Describe some situations that you think could cause feelings of competitiveness or jealousy between people. Use at least three of the following words in your response: *conform, confront, displace, rebel, react.*

Meet the Authors

James **Hurst** (b. 1922)

James Hurst grew up along the coast of North Carolina, a place of quiet landscapes and violent storms. After studying chemical engineering and opera and serving in the army during World War II, Hurst took a job at a New York bank. For thirty-four years, he worked as a banker and spent his evenings writing stories.

Creating Symbolism The "Scarlet Ibis," published in 1960, is Hurst's best-known story. Hurst has said that he "wanted [the ibis] to represent [the character of Doodle]—not Doodle's physical self, but his spirit."

Ray **Bradbury** (b. 1920)

Born in Waukegan, Illinois, Ray Bradbury grew up in Arizona and California. He has been writing for more than sixty years and has published more than 500 stories. His work has earned him many honors, including the World Fantasy Award for lifetime achievement and the Grand Master Award from the Science Fiction Writers of America.

Writing to Entertain Bradbury is best known for his works of fantasy and science fiction. "I write for fun," Bradbury has said. "I don't see myself as a philosopher. That's awfully boring. . . . My goal is to entertain myself and others."

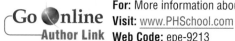

For: More information about the authors
Visit: www.PHSchool.com
Web Code: epe-9213

The Scarlet Ibis

James Hurst

It was in the clove of seasons, summer was dead but autumn had not yet been born, that the ibis lit in the bleeding tree. The flower garden was stained with rotting brown magnolia petals and iron-weeds grew rank amid the purple phlox. The five o'clocks by the chimney still marked time, but the oriole nest in the elm was unten-anted and rocked back and forth like an empty cradle. The last graveyard flowers were blooming, and their smell drifted across the cotton field and through every room of our house, speaking softly the names of our dead.

It's strange that all this is still so clear to me, now that the sum-mer has long since fled and time has had its way. A grindstone stands where the bleeding tree stood, just outside the kitchen door, and now if an oriole sings in the elm, its song seems to die up in the leaves, a silvery dust. The flower garden is prim, the house a gleam-ing white, and the pale fence across the yard stands straight and spruce. But sometimes (like right now), as I sit in the cool, green-draped parlor, the grindstone begins to turn, and time with all its changes is ground away—and I remember Doodle.

Doodle was just about the craziest brother a boy ever had. Of course, he wasn't a crazy crazy like old Miss Leedie, who was in love with President Wilson and wrote him a letter every day, but was a nice crazy, like someone you meet in your dreams. He was born when I was six and was, from the outset, a disappointment. He

Literary Analysis
Symbolism and Allegory What details about the flowers, weeds, and oriole nest symbolize death?

seemed all head, with a tiny body which was red and shriveled like an old man's. Everybody thought he was going to die—everybody except Aunt Nicey, who had delivered him. She said he would live because he was born in a caul[1] and cauls were made from Jesus' nightgown. Daddy had Mr. Heath, the carpenter, build a little mahogany coffin for him. But he didn't die, and when he was three months old Mama and Daddy decided they might as well name him. They named him William Armstrong, which was like tying a big tail on a small kite. Such a name sounds good only on a tombstone.

I thought myself pretty smart at many things, like holding my breath, running, jumping, or climbing the vines in Old Woman Swamp, and I wanted more than anything else someone to race to Horsehead Landing, someone to box with, and someone to perch with in the top fork of the great pine behind the barn, where across the fields and swamps you could see the sea. I wanted a brother. But Mama, crying, told me that even if William Armstrong lived, he would never do these things with me. He might not, she sobbed, even be "all there." He might, as long as he lived, lie on the rubber sheet in the center of the bed in the front bedroom where the white marquisette curtains billowed out in the afternoon sea breeze, rustling like palmetto fronds.[2]

It was bad enough having an invalid brother, but having one who possibly was not all there was unbearable, so I began to make plans to kill him by smothering him with a pillow. However, one afternoon as I watched him, my head poked between the iron posts of the foot of the bed, he looked straight at me and grinned. I skipped through the rooms, down the echoing halls, shouting, "Mama, he smiled. He's all there! He's all there!" and he was.

When he was two, if you laid him on his stomach, he began to try to move himself, straining terribly. The doctor said that with his weak heart this strain would probably kill him, but it didn't. Trembling, he'd push himself up, turning first red, then a soft purple, and finally collapse back onto the bed like an old worn-out doll. I can still see Mama watching him, her hand pressed tight across her mouth, her eyes wide and unblinking. But he learned to crawl (it was his third winter), and we brought him out of the front bedroom, putting him on the rug before the fireplace. For the first time he became one of us.

As long as he lay all the time in bed, we called him William Armstrong, even though it was formal and sounded as if we were referring to one of our ancestors, but with his creeping around on the

---

1. caul (kôl) *n.* membrane enclosing a baby at birth.
2. palmetto (pal met′ ō) **fronds** (frändz) *n.* palm leaves.

Reading Check

Who is Doodle?

deerskin rug and beginning to talk, something had to be done about his name. It was I who renamed him. When he crawled, he crawled backwards, as if he were in reverse and couldn't change gears. If you called him, he'd turn around as if he were going in the other direction, then he'd back right up to you to be picked up. Crawling backward made him look like a doodle-bug, so I began to call him Doodle, and in time even Mama and Daddy thought it was a better name than William Armstrong. Only Aunt Nicey disagreed. She said caul babies should be treated with special respect since they might turn out to be saints. Renaming my brother was perhaps the kindest thing I ever did for him, because nobody expects much from someone called Doodle.

Although Doodle learned to crawl, he showed no signs of walking, but he wasn't idle. He talked so much that we all quit listening to what he said. It was about this time that Daddy built him a go-cart and I had to pull him around. At first I just paraded him up and down the piazza, but then he started crying to be taken out into the yard and it ended up by my having to lug him wherever I went. If I so much as picked up my cap, he'd start crying to go with me and Mama would call from wherever she was, "Take Doodle with you."

He was a burden in many ways. The doctor had said that he mustn't get too excited, too hot, too cold, or too tired and that he must always be treated gently. A long list of don'ts went with him, all of which I ignored once we got out of the house. To discourage his coming with me, I'd run with him across the ends of the cotton rows and career him around corners on two wheels. Sometimes I accidentally turned him over, but he never told Mama. His skin was very sensitive, and he had to wear a big straw hat whenever he went out. When the going got rough and he had to cling to the sides of the go-cart, the hat slipped all the way down over his ears. He was a sight. Finally, I could see I was licked. Doodle was my brother and he was going to cling to me forever, no matter what I did, so I dragged him across the burning cotton field to share with him the only beauty I knew, Old Woman Swamp. I pulled the go-cart through the saw-tooth fern, down into the green dimness where the palmetto fronds whispered by the stream. I lifted him out and set him down in the soft rubber grass beside a tall pine. His eyes were round with wonder as he gazed

Literature in Context

Science Connection

Scarlet Ibis Found mostly in the South American tropics, the strikingly beautiful scarlet ibis is a wading bird with long legs, a long, slender neck, black-tipped wings, and a wingspan of more than three feet. It seldom appears in the United States north of Florida.

Connect to the Literature

Why would the discovery of a scarlet ibis in coastal North Carolina, the setting of this story, be unexpected and dramatic?

about him, and his little hands began to stroke the rubber grass. Then he began to cry.

"For heaven's sake, what's the matter?" I asked, annoyed.

"It's so pretty," he said. "So pretty, pretty, pretty."

After that day Doodle and I often went down into Old Woman Swamp. I would gather wildflowers, wild violets, honeysuckle, yellow jasmine, snakeflowers, and water lilies, and with wire grass we'd weave them into necklaces and crowns. We'd bedeck ourselves with our handiwork and loll about thus beautified, beyond the touch of the everyday world. Then when the slanted rays of the sun burned orange in the tops of the pines, we'd drop our jewels into the stream and watch them float away toward the sea.

There is within me (and with sadness I have watched it in others) a knot of cruelty borne by the stream of love, much as our blood sometimes bears the seed of our destruction, and at times I was mean to Doodle. One day I took him up to the barn loft and showed him his casket, telling him how we all had believed he would die. It was covered with a film of Paris green[3] sprinkled to kill the rats, and screech owls had built a nest inside it.

Doodle studied the mahogany box for a long time, then said, "It's not mine."

"It is," I said. "And before I'll help you down from the loft, you're going to have to touch it."

"I won't touch it," he said sullenly.

"Then I'll leave you here by yourself," I threatened, and made as if I were going down.

Doodle was frightened of being left. "Don't go leave me, Brother," he cried, and he leaned toward the coffin. His hand, trembling, reached out, and when he touched the casket he screamed. A screech owl flapped out of the box into our faces, scaring us and covering us with Paris green. Doodle was paralyzed, so I put him on my shoulder and carried him down the ladder, and even when we were outside in the bright sunshine, he clung to me, crying, "Don't leave me. Don't leave me."

When Doodle was five years old, I was embarrassed at having a brother of that age who couldn't walk, so I set out to teach him. We were down in Old Woman Swamp and it was spring and the sick-sweet smell of bay flowers hung everywhere like a mournful song. "I'm going to teach you to walk, Doodle," I said.

He was sitting comfortably on the soft grass, leaning back against the pine. "Why?" he asked.

---

3. **Paris green** poisonous green powder used chiefly as an insecticide.

Literary Analysis
Symbolism and Allegory Which details in this paragraph symbolize life and beauty?

Reading Check

What does the narrator force Doodle to touch?

The Scarlet Ibis ■ 353

I hadn't expected such an answer. "So I won't have to haul you around all the time."

"I can't walk, Brother," he said.

"Who says so?" I demanded.

"Mama, the doctor—everybody."

"Oh, you can walk," I said, and I took him by the arms and stood him up. He collapsed onto the grass like a half-empty flour sack. It was as if he had no bones in his little legs.

"Don't hurt me, Brother," he warned.

"Shut up. I'm not going to hurt you. I'm going to teach you to walk." I heaved him up again, and again he collapsed.

This time he did not lift his face up out of the rubber grass. "I just can't do it. Let's make honeysuckle wreaths."

"Oh yes you can, Doodle," I said. "All you got to do is try. Now come on," and I hauled him up once more.

It seemed so hopeless from the beginning that it's a miracle I didn't give up. But all of us must have something or someone to be proud of, and Doodle had become mine. I did not know then that pride is a wonderful, terrible thing, a seed that bears two vines, life and death. Every day that summer we went to the pine beside the stream of Old Woman Swamp, and I put him on his feet at least a hundred times each afternoon. Occasionally I too became discouraged because it didn't seem as if he was trying, and I would say, "Doodle, don't you want to learn to walk?"

He'd nod his head, and I'd say, "Well, if you don't keep trying, you'll never learn." Then I'd paint for him a picture of us as old men, white-haired, him with a long white beard and me still pulling him around in the go-cart. This never failed to make him try again.

Finally one day, after many weeks of practicing, he stood alone for a few seconds. When he fell, I grabbed him in my arms and hugged him, our laughter pealing through the swamp like a ringing bell. Now we knew it could be done. Hope no longer hid in the dark palmetto thicket but perched like a cardinal in the lacy toothbrush tree, brilliantly visible. "Yes, yes," I cried, and he cried it too, and the grass beneath us was soft and the smell of the swamp was sweet.

With success so <u>imminent</u>, we decided not to tell anyone until he could actually walk. Each day, barring rain, we sneaked into Old Woman Swamp, and by cotton-picking time Doodle was ready to show what he could do. He still wasn't able to walk far, but we could wait no longer. Keeping a nice secret is very hard to do, like holding your breath. We chose to reveal all on October eighth, Doodle's sixth birthday, and for weeks ahead we mooned around the house, promising everybody a most spectacular surprise. Aunt Nicey said that,

Literary Analysis
Symbolism and Allegory How is pride like "a seed that bears two vines"?

Vocabulary Builder
imminent (im´ ə nənt) *adj.* likely to happen soon

after so much talk, if we produced anything less tremendous than the Resurrection,[4] she was going to be disappointed.

At breakfast on our chosen day, when Mama, Daddy, and Aunt Nicey were in the dining room, I brought Doodle to the door in the go-cart just as usual and had them turn their backs, making them cross their hearts and hope to die if they peeked. I helped Doodle up, and when he was standing alone I let them look. There wasn't a sound as Doodle walked slowly across the room and sat down at his place at the table. Then Mama began to cry and ran over to him, hugging him and kissing him. Daddy hugged him too, so I went to Aunt Nicey, who was thanks praying in the doorway, and began to waltz her around. We danced together quite well until she came down on my big toe with her brogans, hurting me so badly I thought I was crippled for life.

Doodle told them it was I who had taught him to walk, so everyone wanted to hug me, and I began to cry.

"What are you crying for?" asked Daddy, but I couldn't answer. They did not know that I did it for myself; that pride, whose slave I was, spoke to me louder than all their voices, and that Doodle walked only because I was ashamed of having a crippled brother.

Within a few months Doodle had learned to walk well and his go-cart was put up in the barn loft (it's still there) beside his little mahogany coffin. Now, when we roamed off together, resting often, we never turned back until our destination had been reached, and to help pass the time, we took up lying. From the beginning Doodle was a terrible liar and he got me in the habit. Had anyone stopped to listen to us, we would have been sent off to Dix Hill.

▲ **Critical Viewing**
What can you tell about the brothers' relationship from the illustration and the details in the story?**[Interpret]**

✔ **Reading Check**

What surprise do the boys present?

---

4. the Resurrection (rez´ ə rek´ shən) the rising of Jesus Christ from the dead after his death and burial.

My lies were scary, involved, and usually pointless, but Doodle's were twice as crazy. People in his stories all had wings and flew wherever they wanted to go. His favorite lie was about a boy named Peter who had a pet peacock with a ten-foot tail. Peter wore a golden robe that glittered so brightly that when he walked through the sunflowers they turned away from the sun to face him. When Peter was ready to go to sleep, the peacock spread his magnificent tail, enfolding the boy gently like a closing go-to-sleep flower, burying him in the gloriously iridescent, rustling vortex.[5] Yes, I must admit it. Doodle could beat me lying.

Doodle and I spent lots of time thinking about our future. We decided that when we were grown we'd live in Old Woman Swamp and pick dog-tongue for a living. Beside the stream, he planned, we'd build us a house of whispering leaves and the swamp birds would be our chickens. All day long (when we weren't gathering dog-tongue) we'd swing through the cypresses on the rope vines, and if it rained we'd huddle beneath an umbrella tree and play stickfrog. Mama and Daddy could come and live with us if they wanted to. He even came up with the idea that he could marry Mama and I could marry Daddy. Of course, I was old enough to know this wouldn't work out, but the picture he painted was so beautiful and serene that all I could do was whisper Yes, yes.

Once I had succeeded in teaching Doodle to walk, I began to believe in my own <u>infallibility</u> and I prepared a terrific development program for him, unknown to Mama and Daddy, of course. I would teach him to run, to swim, to climb trees, and to fight. He, too, now believed in my infallibility, so we set the deadline for these accomplishments less than a year away, when, it had been decided, Doodle could start to school.

That winter we didn't make much progress, for I was in school and Doodle suffered from one bad cold after another. But when spring came, rich and warm, we raised our sights again. Success lay at the end of summer like a pot of gold, and our campaign got off to a good start. On hot days, Doodle and I went down to Horsehead Landing and I gave him swimming lessons or showed him how to row a boat. Sometimes we descended into the cool greenness of Old Woman Swamp and climbed the rope vines or boxed scientifically beneath the pine where he had learned to walk. Promise hung about us like the leaves, and wherever we looked, ferns unfurled and birds broke into song.

That summer, the summer of 1918, was blighted. In May and June there was no rain and the crops withered, curled up, then died under the thirsty sun. One morning in July a hurricane came out of

---

5. **vortex** (vôr′ teks′) *n.* rushing whirl, drawing in all that surrounds it.

Literary Analysis
Symbolism and Allegory How might the peacock and the boy symbolize death?

Vocabulary Builder
infallibility (in fal′ ə bil′ ə tē) *n.* condition of not being likely to fail

the east, tipping over the oaks in the yard and splitting the limbs of the elm trees. That afternoon it roared back out of the west, blew the fallen oaks around, snapping their roots and tearing them out of the earth like a hawk at the entrails of a chicken. Cotton bolls were wrenched from the stalks and lay like green walnuts in the valleys between the rows, while the cornfield leaned over uniformly so that the tassels touched the ground. Doodle and I followed Daddy out into the cotton field, where he stood, shoulders sagging, surveying the ruin. When his chin sank down onto his chest, we were frightened, and Doodle slipped his hand into mine. Suddenly Daddy straightened his shoulders, raised a giant knuckly fist, and with a voice that seemed to rumble out of the earth itself began cursing heaven, hell, the weather, and the Republican Party. Doodle and I, prodding each other and giggling, went back to the house, knowing that everything would be all right.

And during that summer, strange names were heard through the house: Chateau-Thierry, Amiens, Soissons, and in her blessing at the supper table, Mama once said, "And bless the Pearsons, whose boy Joe was lost at Belleau Wood."[6]

So we came to that clove of seasons. School was only a few weeks away, and Doodle was far behind schedule. He could barely clear the ground when climbing up the rope vines and his swimming was certainly not passable. We decided to double our efforts, to make that last drive and reach our pot of gold. I made him swim until he turned blue and row until he couldn't lift an oar. Wherever we went, I purposely walked fast, and although he kept up, his face turned red and his eyes became glazed. Once, he could go no further, so he collapsed on the ground and began to cry.

"Aw, come on, Doodle," I urged. "You can do it. Do you want to be different from everybody else when you start school?"

"Does it make any difference?"

"It certainly does," I said. "Now, come on," and I helped him up.

As we slipped through dog days, Doodle began to look feverish, and Mama felt his forehead, asking him if he felt ill. At night he didn't sleep well, and sometimes he had nightmares, crying out until I touched him and said, "Wake up, Doodle. Wake up."

It was Saturday noon, just a few days before school was to start. I should have already admitted defeat, but my pride wouldn't let me. The excitement of our program had now been gone for weeks, but still we kept on with a tired doggedness. It was too late to turn back, for we had both wandered too far into a net of expectations and had left no crumbs behind.

---

6. **Chateau-Thierry** (shä′ tō′ tē er′ ē), **Amiens** (ä myan′), **Soissons** (swä sôn′), . . . **Belleau** (be lō′) **Wood** places in France where battles were fought during World War I.

Literary Analysis
Symbolism and Allegory What might the "blighted" summer symbolize?

Reading Check

What plan does the narrator make for Doodle's future?

Daddy, Mama, Doodle, and I were seated at the dining-room table having lunch. It was a hot day, with all the windows and doors open in case a breeze should come. In the kitchen Aunt Nicey was humming softly. After a long silence, Daddy spoke. "It's so calm, I wouldn't be surprised if we had a storm this afternoon."

"I haven't heard a rain frog," said Mama, who believed in signs, as she served the bread around the table.

"I did," declared Doodle. "Down in the swamp."

"He didn't," I said contrarily.

"You did, eh?" said Daddy, ignoring my denial.

"I certainly did," Doodle reiterated, scowling at me over the top of his iced-tea glass, and we were quiet again.

Suddenly, from out in the yard, came a strange croaking noise. Doodle stopped eating, with a piece of bread poised ready for his mouth, his eyes popped round like two blue buttons. "What's that?" he whispered.

I jumped up, knocking over my chair, and had reached the door when Mama called, "Pick up the chair, sit down again, and say excuse me."

By the time I had done this, Doodle had excused himself and had slipped out into the yard. He was looking up into the bleeding tree. "It's a great big red bird!" he called.

The bird croaked loudly again, and Mama and Daddy came out into the yard. We shaded our eyes with our hands against the hazy glare of the sun and peered up through the still leaves. On the topmost branch a bird the size of a chicken, with scarlet feathers and long legs, was perched <u>precariously</u>. Its wings hung down loosely, and as we watched, a feather dropped away and floated slowly down through the green leaves.

"It's not even frightened of us," Mama said.

"It looks tired," Daddy added. "Or maybe sick."

Doodle's hands were clasped at his throat, and I had never seen him stand still so long. "What is it?" he asked.

Daddy shook his head. "I don't know, maybe it's—"

At that moment the bird began to flutter, but the wings were uncoordinated, and amid much flapping and a spray of flying feathers, it tumbled down, bumping through the limbs of the bleeding tree and landing at our feet with a thud. Its long, graceful neck jerked twice into an S, then straightened out, and the bird was still. A white veil came over the eyes and the long white beak unhinged. Its legs were crossed and its clawlike feet were delicately

▼ **Critical Viewing**
How would you react if this exotic bird—an ibis—showed up in your backyard? **[Relate]**

Vocabulary Builder
precariously (pri ker´ ē əs lē) *adv.* insecurely

curved at rest. Even death did not mar its grace, for it lay on the earth like a broken vase of red flowers, and we stood around it, awed by its exotic beauty.

"It's dead," Mama said.

"What is it?" Doodle repeated.

"Go bring me the bird book," said Daddy.

I ran into the house and brought back the bird book. As we watched, Daddy thumbed through its pages. "It's a scarlet ibis," he said, pointing to a picture. "It lives in the tropics—South America to Florida. A storm must have brought it here."

Sadly, we all looked back at the bird. A scarlet ibis! How many miles it had traveled to die like this, in our yard, beneath the bleeding tree.

"Let's finish lunch," Mama said, nudging us back toward the dining room.

"I'm not hungry," said Doodle, and he knelt down beside the ibis.

"We've got peach cobbler for dessert," Mama tempted from the doorway.

Doodle remained kneeling. "I'm going to bury him."

"Don't you dare touch him," Mama warned. "There's no telling what disease he might have had."

"All right," said Doodle. "I won't."

Daddy, Mama, and I went back to the dining-room table, but we watched Doodle through the open door. He took out a piece of string from his pocket and, without touching the ibis, looped one end around its neck. Slowly, while singing softly "Shall We Gather at the River," he carried the bird around to the front yard and dug a hole in the flower garden, next to the petunia bed. Now we were watching him through the front window, but he didn't know it. His awkwardness at digging the hole with a shovel whose handle was twice as long as he was made us laugh, and we covered our mouths with our hands so he wouldn't hear.

When Doodle came into the dining room, he found us seriously eating our cobbler. He was pale and lingered just inside the screen door. "Did you get the scarlet ibis buried?" asked Daddy.

Doodle didn't speak but nodded his head.

Literary Analysis
Symbolism and Allegory In what ways are the bird's uncoordinated movements similar to Doodle's? Explain.

Reading Check

What does Doodle find in the bleeding tree?

"Go wash your hands, and then you can have some peach cobbler," said Mama.

"I'm not hungry," he said.

"Dead birds is bad luck," said Aunt Nicey, poking her head from the kitchen door. "Specially red dead birds!"

As soon as I had finished eating, Doodle and I hurried off to Horsehead Landing. Time was short, and Doodle still had a long way to go if he was going to keep up with the other boys when he started school. The sun, gilded with the yellow cast of autumn, still burned fiercely, but the dark green woods through which we passed were shady and cool. When we reached the landing, Doodle said he was too tired to swim, so we got into a skiff and floated down the creek with the tide. Far off in the marsh a rail was scolding, and over on the beach locusts were singing in the myrtle trees. Doodle did not speak and kept his head turned away, letting one hand trail limply in the water.

After we had drifted a long way, I put the oars in place and made Doodle row back against the tide. Black clouds began to gather in the southwest, and he kept watching them, trying to pull the oars a little faster. When we reached Horsehead Landing, lightning was playing across half the sky and thunder roared out, hiding even the sound of the sea. The sun disappeared and darkness descended, almost like night. Flocks of marsh crows flew by, heading inland to their roosting trees, and two egrets, squawking, arose from the oyster-rock shallows and careened away.

Doodle was both tired and frightened, and when he stepped from the skiff he collapsed onto the mud, sending an armada of fiddler crabs rustling off into the marsh grass. I helped him up, and as he wiped the mud off his trousers, he smiled at me ashamedly. He had failed and we both knew it, so we started back home, racing the storm. We never spoke (What are the words that can solder cracked pride?), but I knew he was watching me, watching for a sign of mercy. The lightning was near now, and from fear he walked so close behind me he kept stepping on my heels. The faster I walked, the faster he walked, so I began to run. The rain was coming, roaring through the pines, and then, like a bursting Roman candle, a gum tree ahead of us was shattered by a bolt of lightning. When the deafening peal of thunder had died, and in the moment before the rain arrived, I heard Doodle, who had fallen behind, cry out, "Brother, Brother, don't leave me! Don't leave me!"

The knowledge that Doodle's and my plans had come to naught was bitter, and that streak of cruelty within me awakened. I ran as fast as I could, leaving him far behind with a wall of rain dividing us. The drops stung my face like nettles, and the wind flared the

Literary Analysis
Symbolism and Allegory What might "black clouds" symbolize? Explain.

wet glistening leaves of the bordering trees. Soon I could hear his voice no more.

I hadn't run too far before I became tired, and the flood of childish spite evanesced as well. I stopped and waited for Doodle. The sound of rain was everywhere, but the wind had died and it fell straight down in parallel paths like ropes hanging from the sky. As I waited, I peered through the downpour, but no one came. Finally I went back and found him huddled beneath a red nightshade bush beside the road. He was sitting on the ground, his face buried in his arms, which were resting on his drawn-up knees. "Let's go, Doodle," I said.

He didn't answer, so I placed my hand on his forehead and lifted his head. Limply, he fell backwards onto the earth. He had been bleeding from the mouth, and his neck and the front of his shirt were stained a brilliant red.

"Doodle! Doodle!" I cried, shaking him, but there was no answer but the ropy rain. He lay very awkwardly, with his head thrown far back, making his vermilion neck appear unusually long and slim. His little legs, bent sharply at the knees, had never before seemed so fragile, so thin.

I began to weep, and the tear-blurred vision in red before me looked very familiar. "Doodle!" I screamed above the pounding storm and threw my body to the earth above his. For a long long time, it seemed forever, I lay there crying, sheltering my fallen scarlet ibis from the heresy[7] of rain.

Literary Analysis
Symbolism and Allegory How are the details about the blood as well as Doodle's position beneath the bush similar to the scarlet ibis?

---

7. heresy (her′ ə sē) *n.* idea opposed to the beliefs of a religion or philosophy.

Thinking About the Selection

1. **Respond:** Do you blame the narrator for Doodle's death? Explain.

2. **(a) Recall:** Why does the narrator cry when everyone congratulates him for teaching Doodle to walk? **(b) Analyze:** What do the narrator's tears reveal about his conflicted, or mixed, feelings?

3. **(a) Recall:** What does Doodle do with the dead ibis?
   (b) Compare and Contrast: How does Doodle's reaction to the dead bird compare to those of his family members? **(c) Infer:** What do you think motivates Doodle to treat the ibis as he does?

4. **(a) Analyze:** Why do you think the narrator sets such demanding goals for Doodle? **(b) Draw Conclusions:** After Doodle's death, how do you think the narrator felt about his expectations of Doodle?

The Golden Kite, the Silver Wind

RAY BRADBURY

Background "The Golden Kite, the Silver Wind" was written during the Cold War, a period of intense rivalry between the United States and the former Soviet Union that shaped world politics in the second half of the twentieth century. During this time, each action by one country—the creation of a weapon, the launching of a satellite—was countered by a reaction from the other country. As you read, think about the parallels between the story events and the conflicts of the Cold War.

"In the shape of a pig?" cried the Mandarin.[1]

"In the shape of a pig," said the messenger, and departed.

"Oh, what an evil day in an evil year," cried the Mandarin. "The town of Kwan-Si, beyond the hill, was very small in my childhood. Now it has grown so large that at last they are building a wall."

"But why should a wall two miles away make my good father sad and angry all within the hour?" asked his daughter quietly.

"They build their wall," said the Mandarin, "in the shape of a pig! Do you see? Our own city wall is built in the shape of an orange. That pig will devour us, greedily!"

"Ah."

They both sat thinking.

Life was full of symbols and omens. Demons lurked everywhere, Death swam in the wetness of an eye, the turn of a gull's wing meant rain, a fan held so, the tilt of a roof, and, yes, even a city wall was of immense importance. Travelers and tourists, caravans, musicians, artists, coming upon these two towns, equally judging the

▼ **Critical Viewing**
How are the leader in this painting and the Mandarin in the story both similar and different? [**Compare and Contrast**]

---

1. **Mandarin** (man´ də rin) *n.* a high official of China; here, the ruling leader.

portents,[2] would say, "The city shaped like an orange? No! I will enter the city shaped like a pig and prosper, eating all, growing fat with good luck and prosperity!"

The Mandarin wept. "All is lost! These symbols and signs terrify. Our city will come on evil days."

"Then," said the daughter, "call in your stonemasons and temple builders. I will whisper from behind the silken screen and you will know the words."

The old man clapped his hands despairingly. "Ho, stonemasons!

"Ho, builders of towns and palaces!"

The men who knew marble and granite and onyx and quartz came quickly. The Mandarin faced them most uneasily, himself waiting for a whisper from the silken screen behind his throne. At last the whisper came.

"I have called you here," said the whisper.

"I have called you here," said the Mandarin aloud, "because our city is shaped like an orange, and the <u>vile</u> city of Kwan-Si has this day shaped theirs like a <u>ravenous</u> pig—"

Here the stonemasons groaned and wept. Death rattled his cane in the outer courtyard. Poverty made a sound like a wet cough in the shadows of the room.

"And so," said the whisper, said the Mandarin, "you raisers of walls must go bearing trowels and rocks and change the shape of our city!"

The architects and masons gasped. The Mandarin himself gasped at what he had said. The whisper whispered. The Mandarin went on: "And you will change our walls into a club which may beat the pig and drive it off!"

The stonemasons rose up, shouting. Even the Mandarin, delighted at the words from his mouth, applauded, stood down from his throne. "Quick!" he cried. "To work!"

When his men had gone, smiling and bustling, the Mandarin turned with great love to the silken screen. "Daughter," he whispered, "I will embrace you." There was no reply. He stepped around the screen, and she was gone.

Such modesty, he thought. She has slipped away and left me with a triumph, as if it were mine.

The news spread through the city; the Mandarin was acclaimed. Everyone carried stone to the walls. Fireworks were set off and the demons of death and poverty did not linger, as all worked together. At the end of the month the wall had been changed. It was now a mighty bludgeon with which to drive pigs, boars, even lions, far away. The Mandarin slept like a happy fox every night.

---

2. **portents** (pôr´ tents´) *n.* things that are thought to be signs of events to come; omens.

The Golden Kite, the Silver Wind ■ 363

Literary Analysis
Symbolism and Allegory What qualities do the people believe the image of a pig symbolizes?

Vocabulary Builder
vile (vīl) *adj.* evil; wicked

ravenous (rav´ ə nəs) *adj.* greedily or wildly hungry

Reading Check

Who whispers to the king from behind a silken screen?

"I would like to see the Mandarin of Kwan-Si when the news is learned. Such pandemonium and hysteria; he will likely throw himself from a mountain! A little more of that wine, oh Daughter-who-thinks-like-a-son."

But the pleasure was like a winter flower; it died swiftly. That very afternoon the messenger rushed into the courtroom. "Oh, Mandarin, disease, early sorrow, avalanches, grasshopper plagues, and poisoned well water!"

The Mandarin trembled.

"The town of Kwan-Si," said the messenger, "which was built like a pig and which animal we drove away by changing our walls to a mighty stick, has now turned triumph to winter ashes. They have built their city's walls like a great bonfire to burn our stick!"

The Mandarin's heart sickened within him, like an autumn fruit upon an ancient tree. "Oh, gods! Travelers will <u>spurn</u> us. Tradesmen, reading the symbols, will turn from the stick, so easily destroyed, to the fire, which conquers all!"

"No," said a whisper like a snowflake from behind the silken screen.

"No," said the startled Mandarin.

"Tell my stonemasons," said the whisper that was a falling drop of rain, "to build our walls in the shape of a shining lake."

The Mandarin said this aloud, his heart warmed.

"And with this lake of water," said the whisper and the old man, "we will quench the fire and put it out forever!"

The city turned out in joy to learn that once again they had been saved by the magnificent Emperor of ideas. They ran to the walls and built them nearer to this new vision, singing, not as loudly as before, of course, for they were tired, and not as quickly, for since it had taken a month to rebuild the wall the first time, they had had to neglect business and crops and therefore were somewhat weaker and poorer.

There then followed a succession of horrible and wonderful days, one in another like a nest of frightened boxes.

"Oh, Emperor," cried the messenger, "Kwan-Si has rebuilt their walls to resemble a mouth with which to drink all our lake!"

"Then," said the Emperor, standing very close to his silken screen, "build our walls like a needle to sew up that mouth!"

"Emperor!" screamed the messenger. "They make their walls like a sword to break your needle!"

The Emperor held, trembling, to the silken screen. "Then shift the stones to form a scabbard to sheathe that sword!"[3]

---

3. **scabbard** (skab´ ərd) **to sheathe** (shē*th*) **that sword!** case to hold the blade of the sword.

Literary Analysis
Symbolism and Allegory In what ways does the "winter flower" describe the fleeting pleasure the Mandarin feels?

Vocabulary Builder
spurn (spʉrn) *v.* reject with contempt or disdain

"Mercy," wept the messenger the following morn, "they have worked all night and shaped their walls like lightning which will explode and destroy that sheath!"

Sickness spread in the city like a pack of evil dogs. Shops closed. The population, working now steadily for endless months upon the changing of the walls, resembled Death himself, clattering his white bones like musical instruments in the wind. Funerals began to appear in the streets, though it was the middle of summer, a time when all should be tending and harvesting. The Mandarin fell so ill that he had his bed drawn up by the silken screen and there he lay, miserably giving his architectural orders. The voice behind the screen was weak now, too, and faint, like the wind in the eaves.

"Kwan-Si is an eagle. Then our walls must be a net for that eagle. They are a sun to burn our net. Then we build a moon to eclipse their sun!"

Like a rusted machine, the city ground to a halt.

At last the whisper behind the screen cried out:

"In the name of the gods, send for Kwan-Si!"

Upon the last day of summer the Mandarin Kwan-Si, very ill and withered away, was carried into our Mandarin's courtroom by four starving footmen. The two mandarins were propped up, facing each other. Their breaths fluttered like winter winds in their mouths. A voice said:

"Let us put an end to this."

The old men nodded.

"This cannot go on," said the faint voice. "Our people do nothing but rebuild our cities to a different shape every day, every hour. They have no time to hunt, to fish, to love, to be good to their ancestors and their ancestors' children."

"This I admit," said the mandarins of the towns of the Cage, the Moon, the Spear, the Fire, the Sword and this, that, and other things.

"Carry us into the sunlight," said the voice.

The old men were borne out under the sun and up a little hill. In the late summer breeze a few very thin children were flying dragon kites in all the colors of the sun, and frogs and grass, the color of the sea and the color of coins and wheat.

The first Mandarin's daughter stood by his bed.

"See," she said.

"Those are nothing but kites," said the two old men.

"But what is a kite on the ground?" she said. "It is nothing. What does it need to sustain it and make it beautiful and truly spiritual?"

"The wind, of course!" said the others.

"And what do the sky and the wind need to make them beautiful?"

Reading Check

What kind of wall does the daughter suggest should be built to defeat Kwan-si's sun?

"A kite, of course—many kites, to break the monotony, the sameness of the sky. Colored kites, flying!"

"So," said the Mandarin's daughter. "You, Kwan-Si, will make a last rebuilding of your town to resemble nothing more nor less than the wind. And we shall build like a golden kite. The wind will beautify the kite and carry it to wondrous heights. And the kite will break the sameness of the wind's existence and give it purpose and meaning. One without the other is nothing. Together, all will be beauty and cooperation and a long and enduring life."

Whereupon the two mandarins were so overjoyed that they took their first nourishment in days, momentarily were given strength, embraced, and lavished praise upon each other, called the Mandarin's daughter a boy, a man, a stone pillar, a warrior, and a true and unforgettable son. Almost immediately they parted and hurried to their towns, calling out and singing, weakly but happily.

And so, in time, the towns became the Town of Golden Kite and the Town of the Silver Wind. And harvestings were harvested and business tended again, and the flesh returned, and disease ran off like a frightened jackal. And on every night of the year the inhabitants in the Town of the Kite could hear the good clear wind sustaining them. And those in the Town of the Wind could hear the kite singing, whispering, rising, and beautifying them.

"So be it," said the Mandarin in front of his silken screen.

Literary Analysis
Symbolism and Allegory What kind of relationship do the kite and the wind symbolize?

Thinking About the Selection

1. **Respond:** Do you think the Mandarin's daughter gave her father good advice? Explain.

2. **(a) Interpret:** How do the townspeople react to the Mandarin's repeated instructions to rebuild the city?
   (b) Analyze Cause and Effect: How does the continued competition between the towns affect the people's health and well-being? Explain. **(c) Evaluate:** Should the people have continued to follow the Mandarin as a leader? Why or why not?

3. **(a) Evaluate:** Why are walls built as a kite and the wind more effective for a peaceful and harmonious relationship between the two towns? **(b) Draw Conclusions:** What lesson does this story teach for today's world?

Apply the Skills

The Scarlet Ibis • The Golden Kite, the Silver Wind

Comparing Symbolism

1. Use a chart like the one shown to analyze how the characters, events, and setting in "The Golden Kite, the Silver Wind" could be **symbols** for leaders and world events during the Cold War.

Symbol	Qualities	Meaning
Mandarin	Leader of his town; worried about losing business and reputation	Leader of a nation who wants to stay on top
Mandarin's daughter		
Walls		

2. **(a)** In "The Scarlet Ibis," what does the ibis symbolize? **(b)** Which story details support your conclusion? Explain.

3. Based on your analysis of the **symbolism** in both stories, which is an **allegory?** Explain.

Writing to Compare Literary Works

Write an essay in which you compare the use of symbolism in "The Scarlet Ibis" and "The Golden Kite, the Silver Wind." Use these questions to help you get started:

- What message or lesson does the author of each story express?
- How does the author of each selection use symbols to develop the message?
- If the symbols were omitted from either story, would its message remain the same? Explain.

Vocabulary Builder

Practice Use the situation described in each of the following items to write a sentence in which you use a word from the vocabulary list on page 348.

1. telling a terrible lie
2. hearing a train whistle getting louder
3. turning down an invitation
4. achieving perfect exam scores
5. having a meal after a long hike
6. climbing a sheer cliff

QuickReview

Symbol: an object, a person, or a place that stands for a larger idea or feeling

Symbolism: the use of symbols in a literary work

Allegory: a literary work that has parallel literal and symbolic meanings

Go Online
Assessment

For: Self-test
Visit: www.PHSchool.com
Web Code: epa-6211

Reading

Directions: *Questions 1–5 refer to the following selection.*

Increasing National Wealth: Mercantilists urged rulers to adopt policies to increase national wealth and government revenues. To boost production, governments exploited mineral and timber resources, built roads, and backed new industries. They imposed a single national currency and established standard weights and measures. Governments also sold monopolies to large producers in certain industries as well as to big overseas trading companies. Finally, governments imposed tariffs, or taxes on imported goods. Tariffs were designed to protect local industries from foreign competition by increasing the price of imported goods.

1. Standard weights and measures were an effect of which of the following?
   A a single national currency.
   B productivity.
   C mercantilism.
   D monopolies.

2. What was one effect of governments' attempt to boost production?
   A governments backed new industry.
   B governments backed foreign industry.
   C governments started the mineral industry.
   D governments took over certain industries.

3. Which of the following was not an effect of the effort to boost national wealth?
   A Tafiffs were imposed.
   B Monopolies were sold.
   C Roads were built.
   D Mercantilism was mandated.

4. Which of the following was a cause of imposing tariffs?
   A aid to foreign governments.
   B standardization of quality.
   C isolation of the government.
   D protection of local industries.

5. Which cause-and-effect pair is correct?
   A Mercantilism caused an increase in the national debt.
   B Mercantilism caused a decrease in national wealth.
   C Mercantilism had no effect on economic policy.
   D Mercantilism affected governments' policies.

Vocabulary

Standards Assessed

• FA.3.04.11
• CT.4.03.2
• LT.5.03.11

Directions: *Choose the word that best completes the sentence.*

6. We repeated the experiment to _____ the results.
   A stress
   B verify
   C sequence
   D imply

7. The actor's tone _____ that his character is discouraged.
   A stresses
   B verifies
   C explains
   D implies

8. The _____ of events in the plot gives the reader insight into the theme.
   A implication
   B veracity
   C explained
   D sequence

9. When you determine the author's _____, you understand the work more fully.
   A attitude
   B stress
   C veracity
   D implication

10. The _____ of the talk is "Evaluating Media."
    A attitude
    B stress
    C topic
    D explanation

Directions: *Use the definition of the root to choose the correct definition of the word.*

11. sequela
    A a movie version of a novel
    B a result that follows a cause
    C a fake appearance
    D a circular argument

12. verisimilitude
    A the state of motion
    B the appearance of being true or real
    C the setting or place of an event
    D the object that follows another

13. sequential
    A progressing randomly
    B progressing in a linear way
    C progressing in a circular way
    D progressing sporadically

14. verily
    A green
    B angled
    C truly
    D finally

15. veritable
    A not reasonable
    B not connected
    C not reliable
    D not false

Exposition: Cause-and-Effect Essay

Whether the subject is human nature, historical trends, or weather patterns, cause-and-effect reasoning explains why things happen. A **cause-and-effect essay** examines the relationship between or among two or more events, explaining how one causes another. In this workshop, you will write your own cause-and-effect essay.

Assignment: Write a cause-and-effect essay about an event or a condition in a subject area that interests you, such as business, the arts, technology, history, sports, or music.

What to Include: Your cause-and-effect essay should feature the following elements:
- a clear identification of a cause-and-effect relationship
- an analysis of specific aspects of the cause or causes that produce the effect
- facts, details, examples, and reasons that support your assertions and anticipate readers' questions
- a logical organization clarified by smooth transitions
- error-free grammar, including correct subject-verb agreement

To preview the criteria on which your cause-and-effect essay may be assessed, see the rubric on page 379.

Standard Course of Study
- Incorporate effective media and technology to inform about research. (IR.2.04.3)
- Analyze influences, contexts, or biases in argument. (FA.3.01

Using the Form
You may use elements of this form in these types of writing:
- science reports
- history papers
- health articles

Writing Workshop: Work in Progress

If you have completed the Work-in-Progress assignments, you have in your portfolio several ideas to pursue in your cause-and-effect essay. You may continue to develop these ideas, or you might explore a new idea as you complete this Writing Workshop.

Reading / Writing Connection

To get a feel for cause-and-effect essays, read the excerpt from *Silent Spring* by Rachel Carson on page 153.

Prewriting

Choosing Your Topic

To select a topic for your essay, use one of the following strategies:

- **Examine current events.** Scan newspapers or magazines for headlines that interest you. Use a three-column chart to examine possible causes and effects: In the middle column, write the event; in the left column, write possible causes; and in the right column, note possible effects. Review this chart for potential topics.

Causes	Event	Effect
• practice, focus • individual performance	Team Wins Championship	• increased fan interest • harder to buy tickets • revenue for city

- **List and freewrite.** Jot down any interesting events that come to mind from the worlds of business, science, technology, the arts, nature, politics, or sports. Then, circle the item that most intrigues you. Freewrite for three minutes about that topic. As you do, note any causes and effects that come to mind. Develop your topic from ideas you uncover in your freewriting.

Narrowing Your Topic

Categorize to narrow your topic. You may find that your topic is too big to manage in the scope of a single essay. Break your subject into smaller categories. For example, if your topic is about a record-breaking sports event, you might create categories such as "key player," "great coach," or "new equipment." Choose from your list of categories a more focused topic that interests you.

Gathering Details

Chart causes and effects. Using an index card or a self-sticking note, write the central event or circumstance that is your subject. Decide if you want to explore the causes that produced the event or the effects the event produced. In either case, write those factors on separate cards or notes. Write key details related to each cause or effect on the cards or notes. Then, arrange the cards or notes in a logical sequence.

Work in Progress
Review the work you did on pages 319 and 343.

Drafting

Shaping Your Writing

Choose a structure. In your opening paragraph, introduce your topic and show why it is important. Here are two possibilities for organizing the body paragraphs of your essay:

- **Chronological order** is particularly valuable when tracing a chain, or sequence, of cause and effect. However, a time-order relationship is not in itself proof of cause and effect.

- **Order of importance** begins with the least important point and works toward the most important point. This pattern is especially effective when you are presenting a series of effects produced by a single event.

Reading | Writing
Connection

For the complete student model, see page 378.

Providing Elaboration

Use logical evidence. As you draft your essay, avoid opinions, unsupported assertions, and trivial details. Rely on facts, statistics, and examples to build a convincing web of support.

> **Student Model: Building Ideas With Facts**
>
> The oceans have been around since the beginning of time, yet we know relatively little about them. They are constantly moving and changing, turning up water that has been down in the depths for hundreds of years. One of these currents is the North Atlantic, also known as the Great Ocean Conveyor Belt.

In his opening paragraph, the writer establishes his topic and its importance with statements of fact.

Use the TRI method to develop paragraphs. Follow these steps:

1. **Topic:** Write a sentence stating your topic or key idea; label it (T).

2. **Restatement:** Write a sentence restating your topic; label it (R).

3. **Illustration:** Illustrate your point through details, facts, examples, or personal experience; label this section (I).

Once you feel comfortable with the TRI pattern, you can shift the sequence to suit the information you present.

▶ **Example:** Originally, the color purple was associated with royalty. (**T**) Only kings, queens, and members of the nobility wore purple-colored clothing. (**R**) In England, Queen Elizabeth I actually made a law prohibiting anyone except herself and her relatives from wearing purple. (**I**)

From the Author's Desk

Wayson Choy
On Showing Cause and Effect

Wayson Choy

An origami butterfly sits on my computer to remind me that just as a butterfly must first go through various stages, my first draft will be "re-created" many times before it can take flight. During that process, I keep in mind that a sense of cause and effect is as important in fiction as in nonfiction. So, I hone the action and dialogue "to show not tell about" the causes and effects in my characters' lives. The following draft from my novel *All That Matters* demonstrates how I do that.

> *I aim for "showing not telling."*
> —————Wayson Choy

Professional Model:
from *All That Matters*

I had given up a late afternoon soccer practice to do some serious studying∧for Mr. Eades's first English test. There were plenty of others like us, books opened, eyes focused. Jenny pointed to the library seat∧across from hers, and her eyes said, *No fooling around!* ~~Truth was, she took her English studies more seriously than she took me. It was frustrating. I just wanted to be with her. She was always in charge.~~

∧As she pushed my books across the table, I thought that she and I should have, two months ago, declared ourselves an official couple, especially after our fifth double date together. But Jenny didn't want that.

∧ "Too showy," she had told me. "Maybe after we graduate. Next year."

∧She folded both our school sweaters together and neatly draped them over one of the empty chairs.

I needed to expand this account with more details to show causes and effects in the relationship between the narrator and his girlfriend, Jenny.

These two sentences tell that Jenny is an in-control girl who takes charge of the narrator. But I wanted to show it through dialogue and actions.

The act of folding the sweaters symbolizes Jenny's shaping of the relationship.

Writing Workshop

Revising

Revising Your Overall Structure

Clarify cause-and-effect relationships. Review your entire draft, focusing on the causes and effects you have presented. With two highlighters, use one color to mark phrases that present causes and the other to mark those that discuss effects. You may need to add details to strengthen connections, insert transitional words to make links clear, or eliminate causes or effects that do not support your main point.

Student Model: Revising to Clarify Cause and Effect

The mechanisms by which the current works are very simple. ~~The water~~ As the water moves north, it cools down and the salinity rises. ~~The~~ This occurs because the arctic climate cools the water as it moves north.

> This writer adds transitional words and phrases to clarify the cause-and-effect relationships.

Peer Review: Ask a partner to read your draft, and then conduct a conference about your work. Your reader should discuss the clarity of the cause-and-effect relationships you present throughout your essay. Consider modifying sentences, omitting or adding transitions, or reordering paragraphs to improve the logical flow of your ideas.

Revising Your Sentences

Combine short sentences. To evaluate the sentences in your writing, count the words in every sentence in your article, and record the numbers in the margin. If you find too many short sentences in your draft, look for places to combine them using the following strategies:

- Combine two sentences using subordinating clauses that start with conjunctions such as *after, although, despite, if,* and *whenever.*

- Use coordinating conjunctions such as *and, but, or, nor, for, so,* and *yet.*

▶ **Example: Short Sentences:**
> The team members lost hope. They found an unlikely inspiration to continue.
>
> **Combined:**
> The team members lost hope, but they found an unlikely inspiration to continue.

Integrating Grammar Skills

Revising to Correct Faulty Subject-Verb Agreement

For a subject and verb to agree, they must agree in number.

Identifying Errors in Subject-Verb Agreement Errors in agreement often occur with compound subjects, with subjects joined by *or* or *nor*, and with indefinite pronouns serving as subjects. In the following example, subjects are underlined and verbs are set in italic type.

Prentice Hall Writing and Grammar Connection: Chapter 25, Section 1

Compound Subject:
The <u>coach and the captain</u> *is going* *are going* to attend.

Subject Joined by *Or* or *Nor*:
<u>Either Jason or his brother</u> *are bringing* *is bringing* the snacks.

Indefinite Pronoun as Subject:
<u>Everybody</u> who supports our ideas *are helping* *is helping*.

If a plural subject is joined to a singular subject by *or* or *nor,* the verb should agree with the subject that is closer to it.

Correct: <u>Either the coach or the co-captains</u> *are going* to speak.

Correct: <u>Either the co-captains or the coach</u> *is going* to speak.

Fixing Errors To correct mismatched subjects and verbs, follow these steps:

1. **Identify whether the subject in a sentence is singular or plural.**

2. **Select the matching form of the verb:**
   - For compound subjects joined by *and,* use plural verb forms.
   - For singular subjects joined by *or* or *nor,* use singular verb forms.
   - When the subject is an indefinite pronoun, use the appropriate form of the verb. Use this chart for guidance.

Indefinite Pronouns	
Always Singular	anybody, anyone, anything, each, either, every, everybody, everyone, everything, neither, nobody, no one, nothing, somebody, someone, something
Always Plural	both, few, many, others, several
Singular or Plural	all, any, more, most, none, some

Apply It to Your Editing

Scan several paragraphs in your draft, underlining all compound subjects or indefinite pronouns. In each case, make sure that you have used the form of the verb that agrees with the subject.

Writing Workshop

Student Model: Glenn Milner
Charlotte, NC

Climate Effects of the North Atlantic Current

The oceans have been around since the beginning of time, yet we know relatively little about them. They are constantly moving and changing, turning up water that has been down in the depths for hundreds of years. One of these currents is the North Atlantic, also known as the Great Ocean Conveyor Belt.

The level of impact the current has on climate and the causes that change it are widely debated. The presumption held by most scientists is that we are currently experiencing global warming. Other theories state that global warming may influence the North Atlantic Current. This, consequently, may cause the exact opposite of warming— an ice age.

Models have shown that any change in speed or location of the current may well cause a rapid climate shift of great magnitude (Burroughs 17). This shift would be caused by two key changes: a decrease in salinity and an increase in the temperature of water in the North Atlantic Current. These factors would, in turn, cause the current to slow down or shut down, sending the Northern Hemisphere into an ice age.

The North Atlantic Current is a complicated system that runs for thousands of miles and combines water from all oceans. It moves heat from the tropics to the northern Atlantic. Robert Kunzig, the author of *The Restless Sea: Exploring the World Beneath the Waves . . .,* said that oceanographers call this the "global journey" of the Thermohaline Circulation, which is run by heat and salt (268). It is called a conveyor belt because warm water moves north on surface currents and then back south in deep cold-water currents, folding over itself like a conveyor belt. The heat has a drastic effect on the climate for the Northern Hemisphere. Without it, the average temperature would be much lower.

The mechanisms by which the current works are very simple. As the water moves north, it cools down. In addition, its salinity rises because winds that blow east to west across the equator transport moisture from the Atlantic to the Pacific, leaving the Atlantic more saline. The water that feeds the Atlantic from the Mediterranean is also salty because it is nearly landlocked and moisture evaporates from the Mediterranean, leaving it saltier (Mayewski 105). As the temperature decreases and salinity increases, the water becomes denser, causing it to sink. As it sinks, it spreads out deep in the ocean basin where it is pulled back toward the equator, thus creating the conveyor-like characteristics. . . .

Direct statements of fact form the basis of the essay.

The writer builds interest by acknowledging that there are differing opinions on the topic.

The coordinating conjunction *consequently* is particularly useful in a cause-and-effect essay.

The writer takes the knowledge level of his audience into account and provides explanations of scientific concepts. He supports his ideas with research.

The writer uses chronological order to explain the way the ocean currents work.

Go Online
Read More
For: the complete student model
Visit: www.PHSchool.com
Web Code: epm-4202

Editing and Proofreading

Check your draft for errors in spelling, grammar, and punctuation.
Focus on Sentence Clarity: Ensure that your sentences are clear by checking that the subjects agree with the verbs. In addition, be sure that every sentence expresses a complete thought.

Publishing and Presenting

Consider one of the following ways to share your work with others:
Present your essay. Use photographs, charts, and diagrams to help you explain the topic of your article. Include definitions of any challenging or specialized vocabulary your listeners will need to know in order to understand the information. Ask friends in the audience to provide feedback notes on your presentation.
Submit your essay for publication. If your essay focuses on a matter of local interest, send it to your school or community newspaper.

Prentice Hall Writing and Grammar Connection: Chapter 10

Reflecting on Your Writing

Writer's Journal Think about your experience of writing a cause-and-effect essay. Begin by answering these questions:

- What organizational strategy would you recommend to someone writing a cause-and-effect essay? Why?
- During the process of writing, what fresh information did you learn about the subject you chose?

Rubric for Self-Assessment

To assess your cause-and-effect essay, use the following rubric:

NC Criteria	Rating Scale *not very* ... *very*
Focus: How clearly do you identify and explore the cause-and-effect relationship?	1 2 3 4 5
Organization: How logical is your organization?	1 2 3 4 5
Support/Elaboration: How effective are your facts, details, and reasons?	1 2 3 4 5
Style: How well do you use transitional words and phrases?	1 2 3 4 5
Conventions: How correct is your grammar, especially your use of subject-verb agreement?	1 2 3 4 5

Communications Workshop

Evaluating a Speech

When you hear a formal speech or an informal talk, strive to be an active listener. Assess the credibility of the message and the effectiveness of the speaker's techniques. Learning how to evaluate a speech will give you a solid basis for improving your own oral presentations.

Evaluate Content

Create a context. Consider the following questions.

- What is the speaker's purpose?
- What knowledge, experience, or preparation equips the speaker to address the subject?
- What traditional, cultural, or historical influences shape the message?
- As a listener, what prior knowledge do you bring the speaker's topic?

Evaluate development of arguments. A good speaker presents arguments that are clearly stated, logically developed, and fully supported with evidence in the form of facts, statistics, anecdotes, and expert opinion. As an active listener, ask yourself whether the speaker's information is accurate, complete, and relevant. Assess whether the speaker's use of facts is fair and responsible or biased. Learn to anticipate weaknesses in certain types of argument.

Evaluate Delivery

Note the speaker's choice of language. Listen for the speaker's use of words and phrases with positive or negative connotations, or associations. Note repetition of key words or stress given to certain phrases. Be alert to the fact that some speakers, as a substitute for good evidence or logical argument, may rely on emotionally "loaded" language.

Note the speaker's technique. A speech is more than words. Use the following questions to analyze nonverbal elements.

- Is the speaker's tone of voice, word choice, and rate of speaking appropriate for the audience, subject, and occasion?
- What is the effect of the speaker's nonverbal signals such as eye contact, facial expressions, and gestures?
- When and why does the speaker pause, speak more loudly or softly, or speak more rapidly or slowly?

Activity ▶ *Analyze a Speech* ▶ With several classmates, view a political speech or a televised editorial. Using the evaluation tools from this workshop, assess the content and delivery of the speech and generate a list of positive and negative points.

 Standard Course of Study

- Provide textual evidence to support understanding of and response to text in answering questions. (IR.2.01.3)
- Analyze the effects of author's craft and style in informing audience. (IR.2.01.9)

Type of Argument	Potential Flaw
Analogy: Compares one situation to another	Are the two situations really alike?
Authority: Cites the opinion of an expert	Is the expert knowledgeable and unbiased?
Emotion: Appeals to the audience's feelings	Is the full argument balanced between logic and emotion?
Causation: Shows a cause-and-effect relationship	Does the speaker oversimplify his or her arguments?

The Sea-Wolf and Selected Stories

Jack London
Signet Classic, 1964

The *Sea-Wolf* is considered one of the greatest sea stories ever written, possibly because every reader finds his or her own connection with the character. The *Sea-Wolf* has been described as an adventure novel, a love story, a morality tale, and a novel of the sea. Set aboard a seal-hunting ship on the desolate Pacific Ocean, the plot centers around Wolf Larson's struggle for survival against the powerful forces of nature.

Literature of the Expanding Frontier

Prentice Hall Anthology
Prentice Hall, 1999

From the Leatherstocking Tales to John Steinbeck, this anthology conveys the wonder, excitement, and heartbreak of the western expansion in America. Pioneer stories, folk tales, stories of immigrants and the prairie all are pieces of this view of a different time and place.

The Sherlock Holmes Mysteries

Sir Arthur Conan Doyle
Signet Classic, 1985

Sherlock Holmes is the 1800's equivalent of James Bond. He lives in London, uses logic and resourceful ploys to solve mysteries, and takes on cases that seem impossible to solve. These mysteries are part of the classic stories that started the genre of detective novels.

To Kill a Mockingbird

Harper Lee
Warner Books, 1982

Set in the small Southern town of Maycomb, Alabama, during the Depression, *To Kill a Mockingbird* follows three years in the life of eight-year-old Scout Finch, her brother, Jem, and their father, Atticus— three years that encompass a mysterious neighbor, their father defending a young black man, and threats against Jem and Scout.

These titles are available in the Penguin/Prentice Hall Literature Library.
Consult your teacher before choosing one.

Think About It When you think of famous painters, you might imagine humorless people who work hard at producing serious "art." If that is the case, your imagination may be wrong! This poem by a contemporary American poet reveals the comic side of the great Spanish painter Francisco Goya (1746–1828). As you read this poem, think about why Goya would paint himself wearing this bizarre invention.

Candle Hat

Billy Collins

In most self-portraits it is the face that dominates:
Cézanne is a pair of eyes swimming in brushstrokes,
Van Gogh stares out of a halo of swirling darkness,
Rembrandt looks relieved, as if he were taking a breather
5 from painting *The Blinding of Samson.*

But in this one Goya stands well back from the mirror
and is seen posed in the clutter of his studio
addressing a canvas tilted back on a tall easel.

He appears to be smiling out at us as if he knew
10 we would be amused by the extraordinary hat on his head
which is fitted around the brim with candle holders,
a device that allowed him to work into the night.

You can only wonder what it would be like
to be wearing such a chandelier on your head
15 as if you were a walking dining room or concert hall.

But once you see this hat there is no need to read
any biography of Goya or to memorize his dates.

To understand Goya you only have to imagine him
lighting the candles one by one, then placing
20   the hat on his head, ready for a night of work.

Imagine him surprising his wife with his new invention,
then laughing like a birthday cake when she saw the glow.

Imagine him flickering through the rooms of his house
with all the shadows flying across the walls.

25   Imagine a lost traveler knocking on his door
one dark night in the hill country of Spain.
"Come in," he would say, "I was just painting myself,"
as he stood in the doorway holding up the wand of a brush,
illuminated in the blaze of his famous candle hat.

Meet the Author

Billy Collins (b. 1941) served as the Poet Laureate of the
United States from 2001 to 2003, and he has won many
other awards and honors for his poetry. Collins often uses
humor in his work, a quality that has helped endear him to
readers and changed many people's notions about poetry.

Readings in Contemporary Poetry
Talk About It

Use these questions to guide a discussion of "Candle Hat."

1. **(a)** In what main way is Goya's self-portrait different from other self-portraits? **(b)** What information about himself was Goya able to show because of this difference?

2. **(a)** Explain what the poet means by this statement: "Once you see this hat there is no need to read / any biography of Goya." **(b)** Do you agree? Why or why not?

3. In a group, discuss the role that art and artists can play in society.
   - In what ways was Goya's candle hat a fresh solution to a problem?
   - Why do you think the poet uses the word "Imagine" to begin the first line of the last three stanzas of the poem?
   - Is imagination important to society? Explain.
   - Imagine you are the "lost traveler." What would you say about the artist when you returned home? Explain.

   Choose a point-person to share your group's ideas with the class.

Unit 3

Types of Nonfiction:
Essays, Articles, and Speeches

Unit 3 Overview

PART 1: Identify Main Idea and Supporting Details
PART 2: Analyze and Evaluate Persuasive Texts

NC **Standard Course of Study**
In This Unit You Will

- Decide upon and use appropriate methods to answer research question. (IR.2.04.1)

- Incorporate effective media and technology to inform about research. (IR.2.04.3)

- Analyze influences, contexts, or biases in argument. (FA.3.01.4)

- Recognize and analyze the characteristics of literary genres. (LT.5.01.2)

- Make thematic connections. (LT.5.01.9)

- Uses varying sentence types purposefully, correctly, and for specific effect. (GU.6.01.1)

- Use vocabulary strategies to discern word meanings. (GU.6.01.6)

Introduction:
Types of Nonfiction

 From the Author's Desk

Rebecca Walker
Talks About the Forms

I have written both **articles,** brief nonfiction pieces often found in periodicals, and **essays,** nonfiction works of greater literary value in which authors express their emotions and thoughts. While I appreciate both forms, I am partial to the essay.

▲ **Rebecca Walker**
is a writer and an activist whose works have been widely anthologized.

Comparing Articles and Essays

The essay allows for the sharing of personal experience, the expression of emotion, and the subsequent creation of a subtle intimacy between author and reader. Some of the best essays are akin to life-changing conversations between parent and child, or teacher and student. Even after the author has died, her voice can reach through time to transform the reader.

While essays and articles both give accountings of real life, articles tend to be more objective in tone. They focus on the *what, when, where* and *why* of a particular situation, rather than on what the author feels about the answers to any of these questions. Although the author undoubtedly has a point of view, he or she strives for an objective rendering of fact.

An essay draws the reader into the author's world, pointing, suggesting, persuading. An article observes and presents, and leaves the reader to make up her own mind.

◄ **Critical Viewing**
Walker distinguishes between the objectivity of articles and the personal quality of essays. Which of these two forms does this image seem to represent? Why? **[Connect]**

Essays That Engage and Challenge the Reader

I have always loved essays in which the author uses his personal experience to challenge the reader to think about the world in a different way. By sharing intimate details of his private life, the author invites the reader to empathize with him and, as a result, to support his conclusions.

Because I believe that most human beings change their feelings long before they change their minds, it seems undeniable that the creation of this emotional link is vital to one's impact as an author.

For example, in 1881 Frederick Douglass forwarded the abolitionist cause by sensitizing readers to the plight of enslaved African-Americans in his deeply personal essay "My Escape from Slavery." And in 1929 Virginia Woolf convinced readers that women deserved autonomy by sharing her own longing for a modest space and small income in *A Room of One's Own*.

> *Intellectual freedom depends upon material things. Poetry depends upon intellectual freedom. And women have always been poor, not for two hundred years merely, but from the beginning of time. Women have had less intellectual freedom than the sons of Athenian slaves. . . . That is why I have laid so much stress on money and a room of one's own.*
>
> **from A Room of One's Own**
> —Virginia Woolf

These are just two of the authors and essays that affected the consciousness of entire generations, prompting not just individual enlightenment, but larger political reform. I admire the way these authors used their own lives as the basis for the theories they espouse. In essence they ask the reader: Shouldn't society be constructed to ensure my happiness, too?

More About Rebecca Walker

When she was 25, Rebecca Walker (b. 1969) was named by *Time* magazine as one of fifty influential American leaders under the age of forty. Her essays and articles have appeared in many magazines and publications, and her books are taught in high schools and colleges in the United States and Canada. She has received awards for both her writing and her work as an advocate for young women. As Walker's essay "Before Hip-Hop Was Hip-Hop" shows, she has a lively interest in youth culture.

Fast Facts

▶ In 1992, Walker co-founded the Third Wave Foundation, dedicated to empowering women aged 15–30 through scholarship grants and project funding.
▶ In 1997, Walker appeared in the film *Primary Colors*.

Exploring Types of Nonfiction

Essays, Articles, and Speeches

Essays and articles are short works of nonfiction. Their authors are usually identified and are always real people. Speeches are nonfiction literary works that are delivered by a speaker to an audience.

- An **essay** examines and discusses a focused topic, often including the writer's personal viewpoints.

- An **article** provides information about a topic, person, or event.

- A **speech**—written to be read aloud—presents a topic and may persuade, inform, explain, or entertain.

The writer contributes more than information to nonfiction.

- **Style** is the particular way in which a writer uses language. Style reflects an author's personality. Factors that contribute to an author's style include level of formality, use of figurative language, diction or word choice, sentence patterns, and methods of organization.

- **Tone** is the author's attitude toward both the subject and readers or listeners. In conversations, you can hear a speaker's tone in the way words and phrases are spoken. When reading, you can "hear" tone in an author's choice of words and details. The tone of a literary work can often be described with a single word such as: *pompous, playful, serious, personal, sarcastic,* or *friendly.*

- **Perspective** is the viewpoint or opinion an author expresses about the subject, either directly or indirectly. **Bias** occurs when a writer makes a one-sided presentation (for example, by ignoring relevant facts or by using emotional language that unfairly sways readers' or listeners' feelings).

- **Purpose** is the author's reason for writing. Common purposes are to inform, to persuade, to honor, to entertain, to explain, and to warn.

Types of Essays

Essays can be categorized by the author's purpose. These are common essay types:

- A **narrative essay** tells a story of actual events or an individual's life experiences.

- A **descriptive essay** creates an impression about a person, an object, or an experience by presenting physical details of sight, sound, smell, touch, or taste.

- An **expository essay** provides information, discusses ideas, or explains a process.

- A **persuasive essay** attempts to convince readers to take a specific course of action or adopt the writer's viewpoint.

- A **reflective essay** expresses the writer's thoughts and feelings in response to a personal experience or to an idea.

Check Your Understanding

Choose the letter of the answer that best matches each numbered item. Discuss your answers with a partner.

1. Formal, friendly, or casual   **a.** style   **b.** descriptive
2. Encouraging polite behavior   **a.** essay   **b.** bias
3. Retelling a historical event   **a.** persuasive   **b.** narrative
4. Explaining how Congress votes   **a.** expository   **b.** reflective
5. Comic, mysterious, or doubtful   **a.** tone   **b.** article

From the Author's Desk
Rebecca Walker Introduces "Before Hip-Hop Was Hip-Hop"

Writing is a lonely profession. A typical day for most writers does not include the lively banter enjoyed by those who work in brightly lit offices and interact in meeting rooms, elevators, and cafeterias.

A Portrait of the Writer at Work

We sit, usually completely alone, in our grand or modest workspaces, maybe with a cat or dog at our feet, a cup of tea or a bottle of water by the mousepad.

More often than not we work in silence, or maybe to the low hum of the television or the repetitive drone of a particularly evocative piece of music. We begin with a blank screen or piece of paper. If we are lucky, we have had some thought we find worthy, but more often we have not, and spend the next hours willing insight to dawn.

Purpose, Diction, Tone, and Level of Formality

Once we have a **purpose** and a direction, then the next bit of work begins: the arduous hunt for the **diction**, the words that can adequately express our still largely unborn revelation. Now we are looking for a feeling, a **tone** that will both track our thought and unlock its emotive power.

The choices we make in those moments—with what **level of formality** we will address the reader, what type of language we will employ, what **narrative structure** we will devise—all these and more create an experience. The result, like what you are reading right now, is a kind of literary transmission of the writer's soul, a revelation of the distinct imprint of her mind.

My Essay: A Different Perspective on Hip-Hop Culture

To face this hard and solitary work I must feel that I have something relevant to say. For instance, hip-hop culture is not often seen as a reflection of the deeply humanitarian impulses of urban youth. And yet I was there at its birth, I can testify to its noble roots. While writing the following essay I wondered, "If I don't tell this story, who will?"

Before Hip-Hop Was Hip-Hop

Rebecca Walker

If you ask most kids today about hip-hop, they'll spit out the names of recording artists they see on TV: Eminem, P. Diddy, J. Lo, Beyonce. They'll tell you about the songs they like and the clothes they want to buy. They'll tell you about the indisputable zones of hip-hop like "EO" (East Orange, New Jersey), the "ATL" (Atlanta, Georgia), and the "West Side" (Los Angeles, California), neighborhoods they feel they know because they've seen them in all the glossiest, "flossiest" music videos. Hip-hop is natural to these kids, like air or water, just there, a part of the digital landscape that streams through their lives.

I watch this cultural sea change with fascination. It astounds me that hip-hop has grown into a global industry, a force that dominates youth culture from Paris to Prague, Tokyo to Timbuktu. I can't

Rebecca Walker
Author's Insight
I chose to include slang to give the essay more flavor and authenticity. I wanted the reader to experience the language we created, not just read about it.

believe that in small, all-white towns like Lincoln, Nebraska, high school boys wear their clothes in the latest "steelo": pants sagging off their waists, sports jerseys hanging to their knees, baseball hats cocked to one side. Even in the pueblos of Mexico, where mariachi bands and old school crooners still rule, it is hip-hop that sells cars, sodas, and children's toys on TV. The vast empire of hip-hop amazes me because I knew hip-hop before it was hip-hop. I was there when it all began.

Way back then, in what today's ninth graders might call the ancient eighties, there was no MTV or VH-1. We found out about music by listening to the radio, flipping through the stacks at the record store, or buying "mix tapes" from local deejays at two dollars apiece. Back then, we carried combs in our back pockets and clipped long strands of feathers to the belt loops of our designer jeans. We wore our names in cursive gold letters around our necks or in big brass letters on our belt buckles. We picked up words and inverted them, calling something that we thought was really cool, "hot," and something that had a whole lot of life, "def."

We didn't know a whole new language was rolling off our tongues as we flipped English upside down and pulled some Spanish and even a few words from Africa into our parlance. We didn't know that young people for years to come would recycle our fashions and sample the bass lines from our favorite tracks. We thought we were just being kids and expressing ourselves, showing the grown-ups we were different from them in a way that was safe and fun. In fact we were at the epicenter[1] of one of America's most significant cultural revolutions, making it happen. Who knew?

Not me.

When I moved from Washington, D.C., to the Bronx the summer before seventh grade, I had one box of records, mostly albums I had ordered from the Columbia Record Club. In 1982, if you promised to buy a record a month for one whole year, the Club sent you eight records for a penny. I had Bruce Springsteen's "The River," REO Speedwagon's "The Letter,"

---

1. epicenter (ep´i sent´ ər) *n.* focal or central point.

"Belladonna" by Stevie Nicks. I had "Stairway to Heaven," by Led Zeppelin and the soundtrack from the movie *Saturday Night Fever*, which I played so many times I thought my mother would go crazy from listening to me belt out the lyrics with those lanky, swanky Bee Gees.

Along with my albums I had loads of 45s, what today we would call singles, little records with just two songs on them, that I bought at the record store near my school for just a dollar a piece. I had Chaka Khan's "I'm Every Woman," and Luther Vandross' "Never Too Much," and Chuck Brown and Soul Searcher's big hit, "Bustin' Loose." I had Michael Jackson's "Rock with You" and even Aretha Franklin's cover of "You Make me Feel Like a Natural Woman" which I sang along to in the mornings as I styled my hair.

If you had asked me then about rap music I would have shrugged my shoulders and looked at you like you were crazy. Rap music? What's that?

But then I started seventh grade and my whole world turned upside down. At Public School 141, I went to classes with kids from all over the Bronx. There were kids whose families came from Puerto Rico and the Dominican Republic, and kids whose families came from Russia and China. There were kids who were African-American and kids who were Irish-American, kids who were Italian-American and kids who were Greek-American. There were kids whose families were poor, kids whose families were well off, and kids whose families were somewhere in between. Some were Jewish, and others devout Catholics. Some were Muslim. Some of the Asian kids were even Buddhist.

The charge created by so many different elements coming together was <u>palpable</u>. The school crackled with energy, and as you can imagine, things weren't always smooth. There were some pretty <u>entrenched</u> cliques, and a few vicious fights on the schoolyard. But there was also so much "flavor." You could hear Spanish spoken with a thick "Nuyorican" accent to a kid wearing a "yamulke." A seemingly reserved Asian-American girl would get out of her parents' car, wait for them to drive off, and then unzip her coat to reveal a fire engine red Adidas sweatsuit. A guy in a preppy, button down shirt would "sport" gold chains with pendants of every denomination: the Jewish Star of David, the Arabic lettering for Allah, and a shiny gold cross. He was everything, that was his "steelo," and everyone gave him "props" for it.

When I got to 141, I felt like a blank canvas. Nothing had prepared me for the dynamism, the screaming self-expression of the place and its students. For the first few weeks I secretly studied the habits of the seventh, eighth and ninth graders with whom I walked

Nonfiction

Perspective Details of Walker's music preferences make it easier to understand how she sees her classmates and the world.

Vocabulary Builder
palpable (pal′ pə bəl) *adj.* able to be touched, felt, or handled; tangible
entrenched (en trenchd′) *adj.* securely established; unmoveable

Reading Check

What changed in Walker's life the summer before seventh grade?

the halls and shared the cafeteria. I was transfixed by the way they infused their words with attitude and drama, moving their hands and heads as they spoke. I was captivated by the way many of them walked and ran and joked with each other with confidence and <u>bravado</u>. I noted what they wore and how they wore it: the razor sharp creases of their Jordache jeans, the spotless sneakers with the laces left loose and untied.

Slowly, I began to add some of what I saw into my "look." I convinced my grandmother to buy me a name chain to wear around my neck, and my stepmother to buy me dark dyed designer jeans. I bought my first pair of Nike sneakers, red, white and blue Air Cortez's, with money I saved from my allowance.

One by one, I started to make friends—Diane, Loida, James, Jesus, Maya. When James and Jesus weren't making fun of me for being so "square," they took me to parties on the Grand Concourse, the big boulevard lined with old apartment buildings and department stores that ran through the Bronx. The parties were incredible, filled with young people who didn't drink, smoke or fight, but who just wanted to dance and laugh and ooh and ahhh over the "scratching" sounds and funky beats the DJ's coaxed out of their turntables.

A lot of the kids at the parties were "breakers" or "poppers and lockers," which meant they could breakdance, a style of movement that blends the Brazilian martial art of Capoeira with a dance called the Robot, and incorporates classical dance moves as well. The "breakers" moved in "crews" that competed against each other.

Vocabulary Builder
bravado (brə vä´ dō)
n. pretended courage or defiant confidence

Nonfiction Description By naming brands, Walker layers on details of the personal style she longed to achieve.

▼ **Critical Viewing** Which aspects of Walker's youthful experiences are captured in this scene? **[Connect]**

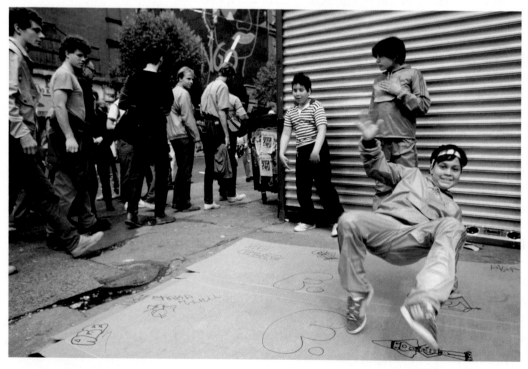

Standing in a circle we watched as members of the different groups "moonwalked" into the center, and then hurled themselves to the floor, spinning on their heads, kicking their legs into the air, and making elaborate hand gestures, each more intricate and acrobatic than the last. Everyone at the party who wasn't "breaking" was a judge by default, and we registered our scores by clapping and yelling.

When Loida and Diane weren't "capping on" or making fun of my clothes, they were "hipping" me to Kiss 98.7 and WBLS, the radio stations that had started to slip some of the songs we liked into their rotation. Songs like "Planet Rock" by Soul Sonic Force and "Take Me Home" by Lisa Lisa and the Cult Jam. After school and on the weekends, they took me to the street vendors that sold the accessories we all coveted: the big knockoff Porsche sunglasses everybody wanted but not everybody could afford, and the heavy gold chains people collected around their necks like so many pieces of string. Loida and Diane also took me around the city on the bus, familiarizing me with the routes of the M1 and M3 and M7, showing me all the different neighborhoods like Little Italy and Chinatown, Bed-Stuy and Harlem.

I remember looking out the big sliding glass windows of the bus at the lines drawn in concrete and glass and thinking that while the world outside seemed so divided, inside, in my circle, among my friends, those lines didn't seem to exist. Loida was Dominican and Diane was Puerto Rican. Our friend Mary was Irish-American, and Lisa was Italian-American. Maya's family was from Haiti. Julius was Russian-American. We were different ages, with different likes and dislikes, but we were united in our love of hip-hop. We loved the "dope"[2] beats, the ever changing and ever expanding <u>lexicon</u>, the outrageous dance moves, the cocky swagger, the feeling that we were part of something dynamic and "fresh"[3] that was bigger than any one of us. That world, that other realm that we created on the streets and in our minds, that streamed from the radio in the privacy of our bedrooms and coursed between us as we talked on the phone, that was where we lived.

That was where we felt free.

Looking back on it now, I can see that hip-hop was born of the diversity I found at 141. Unlike the hip-hop of today, it didn't come pre-packaged from a marketing department with millions of dollars to spend. Our hip-hop was the product of a bunch of kids from a bunch of different places trying to talk to each other, trying to create a common language that could cut through the many languages peo-

---

2. dope (dōp) *adj.* slang term meaning "great; irresistible."
3. fresh (fresh) *adj.* slang term meaning "new."

Nonfiction
Purpose Walker's extensive descriptions here and throughout are meant to explain and inform.

Vocabulary Builder
lexicon (lek´si kän´) *n.* the special vocabulary of a particular subject

Reading Check

In what "world" do Walker and her friends feel free?

ple spoke at home. Intuitively, kids were making a community where there was none; we were affirming our sameness in a world that seemed to only emphasize our difference. That desire to come together irrespective of superficial differences and sometimes in celebration of them, was what gave hip-hop authenticity, that was what kept it honest and as crucial to our well being as food. It's what kept it real.

I can't say much about hip-hop today, but I can say that old hip-hop, original hip-hop, changed my life forever. I only lived in the "Boogie Down Bronx" for a year, but those twelve months gave me so much. I learned that art could bring people together and make them forget their differences. I learned how good it could feel to move with a "posse," a group of friends who had my back no matter what. I learned that I could express myself and communicate with others through what I wore and how I walked and what music I liked. I learned that it doesn't take money or a special degree to transform the grit and drive and hardness of the city into something beautiful.

Loyalty. Community. Self-confidence. Creativity. Hip-hop taught me more about real life than anything I learned that year in class.

I hope when kids today look at shiny videos by their favorite hip-hop artists, they will see through the expensive cars and exotic locations, the women in skimpy outfits and the men trying to approximate a "gangsta" lean. I hope they will remember that hip-hop was born without a formula and without a lot of expensive props or violent undertones. I hope they will marvel at the fact that in the early days of hip-hop, young people were making it up as they went along, following their hearts, following what felt good. I hope they will think about what it takes to create culture that is unique and transcendent and honest, and I hope they begin to dream about creating a new world for themselves.

I hope hip-hop inspires them to make their own revolution.

Rebecca Walker
Author's Insight
I always liked this upbeat nickname for the Bronx, because it suggests dancing and having fun—not usually what this borough is known for.

▼ **Critical Viewing**
Which details in this image of a DJ suggest the energy of hip-hop? Explain. **[Interpret]**

Q. What kind of "revolution," if any, do you think young people are making now?

A. Young people today use technology to revolutionize the way people relate to each other across space, time, and culture. From instant text messaging to international Internet video gaming, young people are collapsing the distance between human beings, neutralizing physical and cultural divides through digital contact. This could become a powerful force for cross-cultural understanding and peace in the world.

Q. To what extent did you outline or plan your essay?

A. While I sometimes outline essays before I begin to write, I didn't outline this one. Instead, I allowed my memories to lead me through the piece, trusting they would reveal a story worth telling. Also, I knew I wanted the reader to come away from the essay feeling empowered, and with a fresh perspective on hip-hop. This intention was a powerful guide.

StudentCorner

Q. How did everyone at your school come up with a common language that you all understood?
                                    —Ryan Tuggle, Littleton, Colorado

A. We certainly weren't conscious of coming up with a common language! It wasn't an intellectual pursuit like a school paper or a science project. The process was intuitive, a natural outgrowth of the dynamic circumstances we found ourselves in. What we were was open to the possibility of finding a common language. I think this simple, human openness was responsible for all that came after.

 Writing Workshop: *Work in Progress*

Business Letter

For a business letter you may write, list several consumer items that have not lived up to your expectations. Note what has been disappointing about each one. Put this Product List in your writing portfolio.

Apply the Skills

Types of Nonfiction

Thinking About the Selection

1. **Respond:** What did you enjoy most about Walker's descriptions of hip-hop culture during her youth? Explain.

2. **(a) Recall:** According to Walker, why did PS 141 "crackle" with energy? **(b) Analyze Cause and Effect:** In what specific ways did hip-hop help Walker and her friends to bridge differences? **(c) Extend:** What other benefits did hip-hop provide to young people in that time and place? Explain.

3. **(a) Compare and Contrast:** What differences does Walker find between the music of her youth and today's hip-hop? **(b) Take a Position:** Do you think Walker's judgment is fair or biased? Explain your answer.

4. **(a) Interpret:** Why was it so important for Walker and her friends to define themselves through dress, special language, dance, and music? **(b) Generalize:** What strategies do teenagers use today to express themselves?

Types of Nonfiction Review

5. **(a)** Is the **tone** of Walker's **essay** personal or impersonal? **(b)** What other adjectives appropriately describe her tone? **(c)** Which details in the first three paragraphs support your answers?

6. **(a)** Use a chart like the one shown to analyze Walker's **style.** In each column, note passages that support your ideas. **(b)** In a small group, discuss the examples, and develop a one-sentence description of Walker's writing style.

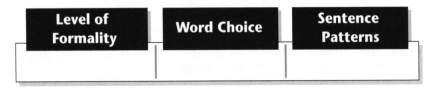

Level of Formality	Word Choice	Sentence Patterns

QuickReview

Essay at a Glance
This essay discusses the impact of hip-hop music and culture on the author's life

Assessment
For: Self-test
Visit: www.PHSchool.com
Web Code: epa-6301

Essay: a nonfiction work that explores a specific topic

Tone: the author's attitude toward both subject and audience, expressed in word choice and details

Style: the way in which an author uses language

Research the Author

Using library and Internet resources, create a popular culture **timeline** of Rebecca Walker's life. Follow these steps:

- Identify key events in her life. List them in order.
- Add details about music, fashion, and dance at the time of each event. Use photographs and illustrations when possible.
- Present your timeline to the class.

Unit 3
Part 1

Main Idea and Supporting Details

Skills You Will Learn

Literary Analysis: *Author's Style*
Reading Skill: *Generating Questions Prior to Reading*

Literary Analysis: *Expository Essay*
Reading Skill: *Rereading to Determine Main Idea*

Reading Skill: *Reading for Specific Information*

Literary Analysis: *Biographical Writing*

Literature You Will Read

Reading: Identifying Main Idea and Supporting Details

NC Standard Course of Study

- Demonstrate comprehension of main idea and supporting details in ansering research questions. (IR.2.01.4)
- Clearly stating the subject to be defined in research question. (IR.2.02.1)

> The **main idea** is the most important point in a literary work. **Supporting details** help identify the main idea.

Skills and Strategies You Will Learn in Part 1

In Part 1, you will learn

- to **generate questions** to **determine the main idea** and supporting details. (p. 402)
- to **reread** to **clarify the main idea.** (p. 424)
- to **apply** these skills when you **read technical documents** and other **forms of nonfiction.** (p. 446)

Using the Skills and Strategies in Part 1

In Part 1, you will learn to ask questions that help identify the stated and implied main idea. You will also learn to clarify and confirm main ideas by rereading. You will apply these skills as you read a variety of nonfiction texts.

The example shows how to use questions to find the main idea in nonfiction.

What is Mitosis?   When does Mitosis take place?

Mitosis is the process by which the cell nucleus is divided into two nuclei. Mitosis takes place in four phases: prophase, metaphase, anaphase, and telophase. The period between one mitosis and the next is called interphase. Chromosome replication occurs during interphase.

What is important about interphase?

Main Idea: The process of mitosis has four phases and an interphase.

Academic Vocabulary: Words for Interpreting Literature

The following words will help you write and talk about the literature in this unit.

Word	Definition	Sample Sentence
equivalent *adj.*	equal in meaning	The author's description of the mountain seems the *equivalent* of a prose poem.
contemplate *v.*	consider or think about	The poem requires the reader to *contemplate* the meaning of love.
abstract *n.*	summary	After reading the *abstract,* the students decided it was worth reading the article.
hence *adv.*	as a result; therefore	The conflict in the story was never resolved, and *hence* the reader was left confused.
illuminate *v.*	make clear	Their actions *illuminated* the characters' motives.

Vocabulary Skills You Will Learn in Part 1

> A **prefix** is a word part that is added to the beginning of a word or another word part.

In Part 1, you will learn
- Latin prefix *con-/com-* (p. 422)
- Latin prefix *equi-* (p. 444)

Knowing the meaning of common prefixes helps you understand an unfamiliar word.

(prefix)	+ (word root)	= word
com	+ prehendere	= comprehend
(meaning)	+ (meaning)	= new meaning
with	+ catch hold of	= catch hold of with thought; understand

Activity Use a dictionary to find one word that contains the prefix *con-* and one word that contains the spelling variation *com-*. Define each word by relating it to the idea of "with" or "together."

Practice these skills with either "A Celebration of Grandfathers" (p. 404) or "On Summer" (p. 415).

Literary Analysis

An author's **style** is his or her unique way of using language. Some elements that contribute to an author's style are:

- **Diction:** the words the author uses
- **Syntax:** the arrangement of words in sentences
- **Tone:** the author's attitude toward the audience or subject.

A writer's diction and syntax might be described as *formal* or *informal, technical* or *ordinary,* or *sophisticated* or *down-to-earth.* Tone might be described as *serious, playful, friendly,* or *harsh.*

Reading Skill

The **main idea** is the central message, insight, or opinion in a work of nonfiction. **Supporting details** are the pieces of evidence that a writer uses to prove the main idea. These details can include facts, statistics, quotations, or anecdotes. To **identify the main idea and supporting details** in a work, **generate questions prior to reading.** Before you read, ask yourself questions such as

- *Why did the author choose this title?*
- *How might events in the author's life influence his or her attitude?*

As you read, look for details that answer those questions and point to the main idea. Use a chart like the one shown to help you.

> **NC** **Standard Course of Study**
>
> - Summarize key events and/or points from text in critiquing communication. (CT.4.03.5)
> - Identify and analyze influences, contexts, or biases in communication. (CT.4.03.7)
> - Make thematic connections. (LT.5.01.9)

Question

Why is it significant that the author, a famous musician, grew up in poverty?

↓

Detail/Answer

He could not afford music lessons.

↓

Main Idea?

The author supports free music programs.

Vocabulary Builder

A Celebration of Grandfathers

- **perplexes** (pər pleks´ iz) *v.* confuses or puzzles (p. 405) *His odd behavior perplexes them.*
- **absurdity** (ab sʉr´ də tē) *n.* something ridiculous or nonsensical (p. 405) *Our reasonable request was treated as an absurdity.*
- **permeate** (pʉr´ mē āt´) *v.* spread or flow throughout (p. 406) *It didn't take long for the odor to permeate the entire apartment.*
- **anguish** (aŋ´ gwish) *n.* great pain or suffering (p. 410) *The troubled expression on her face revealed the anguish she felt inside.*

On Summer

- **aloofness** (ə lōōf´ nəs) *n.* quality of being distant or removed (p. 415) *His aloofness made him appear unfriendly.*
- **melancholy** (mel´ ən käl´ ē) *n.* sadness; gloom (p. 415) *The rain set a melancholy mood.*
- **pretentious** (prē ten´ shəs) *adj.* grand in a showy way (p. 419) *His pretentious manner only impressed those who had just met him.*
- **apex** (ā´ peks´) *n.* highest point; peak (p. 419) *Playing in the World Series was the apex of his baseball career.*

Background

New Mexican Culture Native Americans occupied present-day New Mexico thousands of years before the Spanish arrived in the late 1500s. The area remained under Spanish and then Mexican rule until 1848, when the United States gained control. Since then, people from all over the world have settled in New Mexico. As a result, the region has become a kind of cultural crossroads.

Connecting to the Literature

Reading/Writing Connection Growing up in New Mexico, Rudolfo Anaya learned respect for elders. Write five sentences explaining why our elders deserve respect. Use at least three of the following words: *appreciate, clarify, demonstrate, maximize.*

READ MORE

by
Rudolfo Anaya
"At a Crossroads"
A Chicano in China

Meet the Author

Rudolfo **Anaya** (b. 1937)

Born in New Mexico, Rudolfo Anaya is considered the founder of modern Chicano literature. His first novel, *Bless Me, Ultima,* was praised for its depiction of the culture and history of New Mexico. Today, it is considered a classic of American literature.

"I am an oral storyteller, but now I do it on the printed page." Anaya's storytelling reflects his interest in the folk tales of his native Hispanic culture, which combines Spanish, Mexican, and Central American influences. Anaya has won a number of awards, including the PEN Center West Award for his 1999 novel *Albuquerque.* He is currently a professor of English at the University of New Mexico.

Fast Facts

▶ The manuscript for *Bless Me, Ultima* was initially rejected by dozens of publishers, but the book has sold more than 360,000 copies.

▶ As a teenager, Anaya was paralyzed after he dove into an irrigation ditch and fractured two vertebrae in his neck. He recovered, but the ordeal forever changed his outlook on life.

Go **O**nline
Author Link

For: More about the author
Visit: www.PHSchool.com
Web Code: epe-9302

A Celebration of Grandfathers

Rudolfo A. Anaya

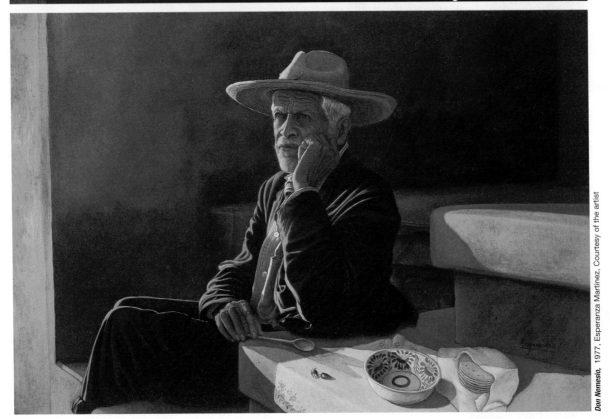

Don Nemesio, 1977, Esperanza Martinez, Courtesy of the artist

uenos días le de Dios, abuelo."[1] God give you a good day, grandfather. This is how I was taught as a child to greet my grandfather, or any grown person. It was a greeting of respect, a cultural value to be passed on from generation to generation, this respect for the old ones.

The old people I remember from my childhood were strong in their beliefs, and as we lived daily with them we learned a wise path of life to follow. They had something important to share with the young, and when they spoke the young listened. These old abuelos and abuelitas[2] had worked the earth all their lives, and so they

---

1. **Buenos días le de Dios, abuelo** (bwā′ nəs dē′ äs lā dā dē′ ōs ä bwä lō)
2. **abuelitas** (a bwā lē′ täs) grandmothers.

knew the value of nurturing, they knew the sensitivity of the earth. The daily struggle called for cooperation, and so every person contributed to the social fabric, and each person was respected for his contribution.

The old ones had looked deep into the web that connects all animate and inanimate forms of life, and they recognized the great design of the creation.

These *ancianos*[3] from the cultures of the Río Grande, living side by side, sharing, growing together, they knew the rhythms and cycles of time, from the preparation of the earth in the spring to the digging of the acequias[4] that brought the water to the dance of harvest in the fall. They shared good times and hard times. They helped each other through the epidemics and the personal tragedies, and they shared what little they had when the hot winds burned the land and no rain came. They learned that to survive one had to share in the process of life.

Hard workers all, they tilled the earth and farmed, ran the herds and spun wool, and carved their saints and their kachinas[5] from cottonwood late in the winter nights. All worked with a deep faith which <u>perplexes</u> the modern mind.

Their faith shone in their eyes; it was in the strength of their grip, in the creases time wove into their faces. When they spoke, they spoke plainly and with few words, and they meant what they said. When they prayed, they went straight to the source of life. When there were good times, they knew how to dance in celebration and how to prepare the foods of the fiestas.[6] All this they passed on to the young, so that a new generation would know what they had known, so the string of life would not be broken.

Today we would say that the old abuelitos lived authentic lives.

Newcomers to New Mexico often say that time seems to move slowly here. I think they mean they have come in contact with the inner strength of the people, a strength so solid it causes time itself to pause. Think of it. Think of the high, northern New Mexico villages, or the lonely ranches on the open llano.[7] Think of the Indian pueblo[8] which lies as solid as rock in the face of time. Remember the old people whose eyes seem like windows that peer into a distant past that makes <u>absurdity</u> of our contemporary world. That is what one feels when one encounters the old ones and their land, a pausing of time.

---

3. *ancianos* (än cē ä′ nōs) old people; ancestors.
4. **acequias** (ä sä kē′ əs) irrigation ditches.
5. **kachinas** (kə chē′ nəz) small wooden dolls, representing the spirit of an ancestor or a god.
6. **fiestas** (fē es′ təz) *n.* celebrations; feasts.
7. **llano** (yä′ nō) plain.
8. **pueblo** (pweb′ lō) *n.* village or town.

Literary Analysis
Style and Tone
Describe the author's tone as he discusses the "ancianos."

Vocabulary Builder
perplexes (pər pleks′ iz) *v.* confuses or puzzles
absurdity (ab sur′ də tē) *n.* something ridiculous or nonsensical

✓ **Reading Check**

What work did the ancianos do?

We have all felt time stand still. We have all been in the presence of power, the knowledge of the old ones, the majestic peace of a mountain stream or an aspen grove or red buttes rising into blue sky. We have all felt the light of dusk <u>permeate</u> the earth and cause time to pause in its flow.

I felt this when first touched by the spirit of Ultima, the old *curandera*[9] who appears in my first novel, *Bless Me, Ultima*. This is how the young Antonio describes what he feels:

> When she came the beauty of the llano unfolded before my eyes, and the gurgling waters of the river sang to the hum of the turning earth. The magical time of childhood stood still, and the pulse of the living earth pressed its mystery into my living blood. She took my hand, and the silent, magic powers she possessed made beauty from the raw, sun-baked llano, the green river valley, and the blue bowl which was the white sun's home. My bare feet felt the throbbing earth, and my body trembled with excitement. Time stood still . . .

At other times, in other places, when I have been privileged to be with the old ones, to learn, I have felt this inner reserve of strength upon which they draw. I have been held motionless and speechless by the power of curanderas. I have felt the same power when I hunted with Cruz, high on the Taos [tä´ ōs] mountain, where it was more than the incredible beauty of the mountain bathed in morning light, more than the shining of the quivering aspen, but a connection with life, as if a shining strand of light connected the particular and the cosmic. That feeling is an epiphany of time, a standing still of time.

But not all of our old ones are curanderos or hunters on the mountain. My grandfather was a plain man, a farmer from Puerto de Luna[10] on the Pecos River. He was probably a descendent of those people who spilled over the mountain from Taos, following the Pecos River in search of farmland. There in that river valley he settled and raised a large family.

Bearded and walrus-mustached, he stood five feet tall, but to me as a child he was a giant. I remember him most for his silence. In the summers my parents sent me to live with him on his farm, for I was to learn the ways of a farmer. My uncles also lived in that valley, the valley called Puerto de Luna, there where only the flow of the river and the whispering of the wind marked time. For me it was a magical place.

Vocabulary Builder
permeate (pu̇r´ mē āt´)
v. spread or flow throughout

Literary Analysis
Style How does Anaya's use of Spanish words add to his message of being connected to his culture?

---

9. *curandera* (ko͞o rän dä´ rä) medicine woman.
10. **Puerto de Luna** (pwer´ tō dä lo͞o´ ne) Port of the Moon, the name of a town.

I remember once, while out hoeing the fields, I came upon an anthill, and before I knew it I was badly bitten. After he had covered my welts with the cool mud from the irrigation ditch, my grandfather calmly said: "Know where you stand." That is the way he spoke, in short phrases, to the point.

One very dry summer, the river dried to a trickle, there was no water for the fields. The young plants withered and died. In my sadness and with the impulses of youth I said, "I wish it would rain!" My grandfather touched me, looked up into the sky and whispered, "Pray for rain." In his language there was a difference. He felt connected to the cycles that brought the rain or kept it from us. His prayer was a meaningful action, because he was a participant with the forces that filled our world, he was not a bystander.

El Leñador, 1934, Tom Lea, Collection of the Museum of New Mexico, Museum of Fine Arts

A young man died at the village one summer. A very tragic death. He was dragged by his horse. When he was found I cried, for the boy was my friend. I did not understand why death had come to one so young. My grandfather took me aside and said: "Think of the death of the trees and the fields in the fall. The leaves fall, and everything rests, as if dead. But they bloom again in the spring. Death is only this small transformation in life."

These are the things I remember, these fleeting images, few words.

I remember him driving his horse-drawn wagon into Santa Rosa in the fall when he brought his harvest produce to sell in the town. What a tower of strength seemed to come in that small man huddled on the seat of the giant wagon. One click of his tongue and the horses obeyed, stopped or turned as he wished. He never raised his whip. How unlike today when so much teaching is done with loud words and threatening hands.

I would run to greet the wagon, and the wagon would stop. "Buenos días le de Dios, abuelo," I would say. This was the

▲ Critical Viewing
How does the farmer in this painting compare with your image of the author's grandfather? **[Compare and Contrast]**

Reading Check
Why did Anaya's parents send him to stay with his grandfather during summers?

prescribed greeting of esteem and respect. Only after the greeting was given could we approach these venerable old people. "Buenos días te de Dios, mi hijo,"[11] he would answer and smile, and then I could jump up on the wagon and sit at his side. Then I, too, became a king as I rode next to the old man who smelled of earth and sweat and the other deep aromas from the orchards and fields of Puerto de Luna.

We were all sons and daughters to him. But today the sons and daughters are breaking with the past, putting aside los abuelitos. The old values are threatened, and threatened most where it comes to these relationships with the old people. If we don't take the time to watch and feel the years of their final transformation, a part of our humanity will be lessened.

I grew up speaking Spanish, and oh! how difficult it was to learn English. Sometimes I would give up and cry out that I couldn't learn. Then he would say, "Ten paciencia."[12] Have patience. *Paciencia*, a word with the strength of centuries, a word that said that someday we would overcome. *Paciencia*, how soothing a word

---

11. **mi hijo** (mē ē´ hō) my son.
12. **Ten paciencia** (ten pä sē en´ sē ä)

Reading Skill
Main Idea What main idea about the loss of values does Anaya state here?

▼ **Critical Viewing** Why do you think a writer like Anaya might find this New Mexican landscape inspiring? **[Speculate]**

coming from this old man who could still sling hundred-pound bags over his shoulder, chop wood for hours on end, and hitch up his own horses and ride to town and back in one day.

"You have to learn the language of the Americanos,"[13] he said. "Me, I will live my last days in my valley. You will live in a new time, the time of the gringos."[14]

A new time did come, a new time is here. How will we form it so it is fruitful? We need to know where we stand. We need to speak softly and respect others, and to share what we have. We need to pray not for material gain, but for rain for the fields, for the sun to nurture growth, for nights in which we can sleep in peace, and for a harvest in which everyone can share. Simple lessons from a simple man. These lessons he learned from his past which was as deep and strong as the currents of the river of life, a life which could be stronger than death.

He was a man; he died. Not in his valley, but nevertheless cared for by his sons and daughters and flocks of grandchildren. At the end, I would enter his room which carried the smell of medications and Vicks, the faint pungent odor of urine, and cigarette smoke. Gone were the aroma of the fields, the strength of his young

---

13. **Americanos** (ä mer′ ē kä′ nōs) Americans.
14. **gringos** (griŋ′ gōs) *n.* foreigners; North Americans.

Literary Analysis
Style How does the author's repetition of the phrase "We need" add urgency to his message?

Reading Check

Why does Anaya's grandfather tell him that he must learn English?

manhood. Gone also was his patience in the face of crippling old age. Small things bothered him; he shouted or turned sour when his expectations were not met. It was because he could not care for himself, because he was returning to that state of childhood, and all those wishes and desires were now wrapped in a crumbling old body.

"Ten paciencia," I once said to him, and he smiled. "I didn't know I would grow this old," he said. "Now, I can't even roll my own cigarettes." I rolled a cigarette for him, placed it in his mouth and lit it. I asked him why he smoked, the doctor had said it was bad for him. "I like to see the smoke rise," he said. He would smoke and doze, and his quilt was spotted with little burns where the cigarettes dropped. One of us had to sit and watch to make sure a fire didn't start.

I would sit and look at him and remember what was said of him when he was a young man. He could mount a wild horse and break it, and he could ride as far as any man. He could dance all night at a dance, then work the acequia the following day. He helped neighbors, they helped him. He married, raised children. Small legends, the kind that make up everyman's life.

He was 94 when he died. Family, neighbors, and friends gathered; they all agreed he had led a rich life. I remembered the last years, the years he spent in bed. And as I remember now, I am reminded that it is too easy to romanticize old age. Sometimes we forget the pain of the transformation into old age, we forget the natural breaking down of the body. Not all go gentle into the last years, some go crying and cursing, forgetting the names of those they loved the most, withdrawing into an internal <u>anguish</u> few of us can know. May we be granted the patience and care to deal with our ancianos.

For some time we haven't looked at these changes and needs of the old ones. The American image created by the mass media is an image of youth, not of old age. It is the beautiful and the young who are praised in this society. If analyzed carefully, we see that same damaging thought has crept into the way society views the old. In response to the old, the mass media have just created old people

Cultural Connection

Anaya's Best-Known Work In this essay, Anaya quotes from his novel *Bless Me, Ultima*. First published in 1972, the novel tells the story of a young boy, Antonio, who lives with his family in Guadalupe, New Mexico. Ultima, who is respected for her healing powers and her knowledge of the uses of plants, comes to live with Antonio's family. Ultima takes the boy under her wing and teaches him about the plants and trees of the area. She also teaches him some important lessons about life.

Connect to the Literature

Based on what you know about Anaya's writing, how would you expect him to describe the bond between people and the land? Explain your answer.

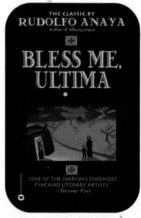

Vocabulary Builder
anguish (aŋ´ gwish) *n.* great pain or suffering

who act like the young. It is only the healthy, pink-cheeked, outgoing, older persons we are shown in the media. And they are always selling something, as if an entire generation of old people were salesmen in their lives. Commercials show very lively old men, who must always be in excellent health according to the new myth, selling insurance policies or real estate as they are out golfing; older women selling coffee or toilet paper to those just married. That image does not illustrate the real life of the old ones.

Real life takes into account the natural cycle of growth and change. My grandfather pointed to the leaves falling from the tree. So time brings with its transformation the often painful, wearing-down process. Vision blurs, health wanes; even the act of walking carries with it the painful reminder of the autumn of life. But this process is something to be faced, not something to be hidden away by false images. Yes, the old can be young at heart, but in their own way, with their own dignity. They do not have to copy the always-young image of the Hollywood star.

My grandfather wanted to return to his valley to die. But by then the families of the valley had left in search of a better future. It is only now that there seems to be a return to the valley, a revival. The new generation seeks its roots, that value of love for the land moves us to return to the place where our ancianos formed the culture.

I returned to Puerto de Luna last summer, to join the community in a celebration of the founding of the church. I drove by my grandfather's home, my uncles' ranches, the neglected adobe[15] washing down into the earth from whence it came. And I wondered, how might the values of my grandfather's generation live in our own? What can we retain to see us through these hard times? I was to become a farmer, and I became a writer. As I plow and plant my words, do I nurture as my grandfather did in his fields and orchards? The answers are not simple.

"They don't make men like that anymore," is a phrase we hear when one does honor to a man. I am glad I knew my grandfather. I am glad there are still times when I can see him in my dreams, hear him in my reverie. Sometimes I think I catch a whiff of that earthy aroma that was his smell, just as in lonely times sometimes I catch the fragrance of Ultima's herbs. Then I smile. How strong these people were to leave such a lasting impression.

So, as I would greet my abuelo long ago, it would help us all to greet the old ones we know with this kind and respectful greeting: "Buenos días le de Dios."

Reading Skill
Main Idea What main idea is supported by the detail of the neglected adobe homes?

---

15. **adobe** (ə dō´ bē) *n.* sun-dried clay brick.

Apply the Skills

A Celebration of Grandfathers

Thinking About the Selection

1. **Respond:** Which part of the essay is most powerful? Explain.
2. **(a) Recall:** What qualities of old people does Anaya remember from his childhood? **(b) Distinguish:** How are these qualities different from the images that Anaya says have been created by American mass media?
3. **(a) Recall:** What does Anaya's grandfather say is the "new time" in which Anaya will live? **(b) Infer:** What does the author imply about what this "new time" will bring for his people?
4. **(a) Draw Conclusions:** What opinion does Anaya offer on the way people should be treated as they grow old? **(b) Take a Position:** Do you agree with him? Explain. **(c) Discuss:** Discuss your answers with a partner. Then, explain how your answer has grown or changed as a result of the discussion.

Literary Analysis

5. At several points in his essay, Anaya strings together sentences that are structured in the same way, as in this example: "When they spoke, they spoke plainly and with few words, and they meant what they said. When they prayed, they went straight to the source of life. When there were good times, they knew how to dance in celebration. . . ." What effect does this aspect of the author's **syntax** create? Explain.
6. What one word might you use to describe the overall **tone** of "A Celebration of Grandfathers"? Explain.
7. Use a chart like the one shown to record examples of the **diction** and tone Anaya uses. Then, based on his diction and tone, write three adjectives in the center of the chart that describe Anaya's **style.**

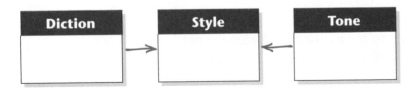

Diction	Style	Tone

Reading Skill

8. State the **main idea** of Anaya's essay in your own words.
9. **(a)** List three **supporting details** that serve as evidence for the point that Anaya makes in his essay. **(b)** Do you think the author adequately supports his main idea with details? Why or why not?

QuickReview

Essay at a Glance
The author celebrates his native culture in which older people are respected and honored.

Go Online
Assessment
For: Self-test
Visit: www.PHSchool.com
Web Code: epa-6302

Author's Style: an author's way of writing; elements of style include *diction, syntax,* and *tone.*

Main Idea: the central message, insight, or opinion in a work of nonfiction

Supporting Details: the pieces of evidence that a writer uses to prove a main idea

Vocabulary Builder

Practice Determine whether each sentence below is true or false. Use the meaning of the underlined word to explain your reasoning.

1. A poor instruction manual is one that _perplexes_ its reader.
2. It is a compliment to have a business idea labeled "an _absurdity_."
3. To prevent a stain, allow ink to _permeate_ the fabric.
4. Comforting someone in _anguish_ is a kind action.

Adding Words to Your Vocabulary Using a thesaurus, find a **synonym,** or word of similar meaning, for each word italicized above. Use each synonym in a sentence that makes the meaning of the word clear. (For more on using a thesaurus, see page R7.)

Writing

Anaya's essay reflects his admiration for his elders. Think of an older person whom you admire. Write a few paragraphs of **book jacket copy** for a biography of that person. Book jackets often provide a brief introduction to a subject to entice people to read more.
- Include some highlights of the person's life.
- Choose details that will make the reader want to know more.

For *Grammar, Vocabulary,* and *Assessment,* see **Build Language Skills,** pp. 422–423.

Extend Your Learning

Listening and Speaking Anaya claims that "the American image created by the mass media is an image of youth, not old age." In a small group, hold a **panel discussion** about the validity of this claim. Consider these questions as you prepare:
- What is the age of most people in television shows and films?
- What messages do these images convey?

Each panelist should prepare notes to use during the discussion and should elaborate upon or illustrate each other's comments.

Research and Technology Use the Internet and an atlas to gather information about the geography and history of Puerta de Luna, a town Anaya discusses in his essay. Then, make an **annotated map** of New Mexico that shows the location of this town. Include a side column listing facts about the town.

Build Understanding • *On Summer*

Background

The Great Migration Beginning in the early 1900s, hundreds of thousands of African Americans left the rural South for northern cities. They fled discrimination and the floods and pests that threatened their livelihood as farmers. Many left relatives behind and, like Hansberry's Chicago family, journeyed south in summertime to visit.

Connecting to the Literature

Reading/Writing Connection In "On Summer," the author's grandmother in Tennessee is a living link to her family's history. Write two or three sentences about a person, a place, or an object that reminds you of your connection with people of the past. Use at least three of these words: *embody, signify, dominate, react.*

Review

For **Literary Analysis, Reading Skill, and Vocabulary Builder,** see page 402

READ MORE

by Lorraine Hansberry

To Be Young, Gifted, and Black

The Sign in Sidney Brustein's Window

Meet the Author

Lorraine **Hansberry** (1930–1965)

Lorraine Hansberry grew up on the South Side of Chicago, where her father prospered as a real-estate broker. At the time, many white people closed their neighborhoods, refusing to sell or rent property to African Americans. Hansberry's father fought this practice, taking his case all the way to the Supreme Court, where he won.

A Pioneering Playwright As her father fought to integrate Chicago's neighborhoods, Hansberry laid claim to territories of the imagination. With the 1959 production of her play *A Raisin in the Sun,* she became the first African American woman to have a drama produced on Broadway.

Fast Facts

▶ *A Raisin in the Sun* won a New York Drama Critics' Circle Award in 1959.

▶ A 1961 movie version of the play won recognition at the Cannes Film Festival.

Go Online
—Author Link

For: More about the author
Visit: www.PHSchool.com
Web Code: epe-9303

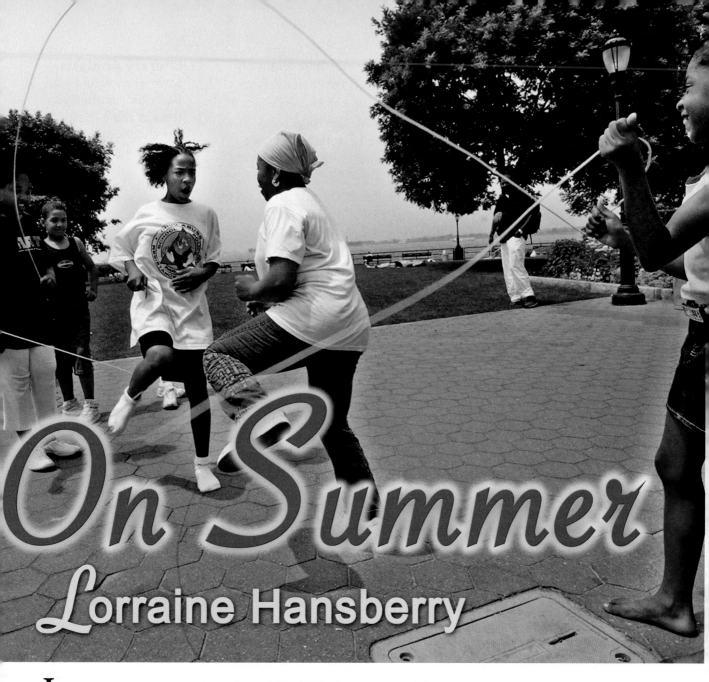

On Summer

Lorraine Hansberry

It has taken me a good number of years to come to any measure of respect for summer. I was, being May-born, literally an "infant of the spring" and, during the later childhood years, tended, for some reason or other, to rather worship the cold <u>aloofness</u> of winter. The adolescence, admittedly lingering still, brought the traditional passionate commitment to <u>melancholy</u> autumn—and all that. For the longest kind of time I simply thought that *summer* was a mistake.

In fact, my earliest memory of anything at all is of waking up in a darkened room where I had been put to bed for a nap on a summer's afternoon, and feeling very, very hot. I acutely disliked

Vocabulary Builder
aloofness (ə lōōf′ nəs) *n.* quality of being distant or removed
melancholy (mel′ ən käl′ ē) *n.* sadness; gloom

the feeling then and retained the bias for years. It had originally been a matter of the heat but, over the years, I came actively to associate displeasure with most of the usually celebrated natural features and social by-products of the season: the too-grainy texture of sand; the too-cold coldness of the various waters we constantly try to escape into, and the icky-perspiry feeling of bathing caps.

It also seemed to me, esthetically[1] speaking, that nature had got inexcusably carried away on the summer question and let the whole thing get to be rather much. By duration alone, for instance, a summer's day seemed maddeningly excessive; an utter overstatement. Except for those few hours at either end of it, objects always appeared in too sharp a relief against backgrounds; shadows too pronounced and light too blinding. It always gave me the feeling of walking around in a motion picture which had been too artsily-craftsily exposed. Sound also had a way of coming to the ear without that muting influence, marvelously common to winter, across patios or beaches or through the woods. I suppose I found it too stark and yet too intimate a season.

My childhood Southside summers were the ordinary city kind, full of the street games which other rememberers have turned into fine ballets these days and rhymes that anticipated what some people insist on calling modern poetry:

> Oh, Mary Mack, Mack, Mack
> All dressed in black, black, black
> With the silver buttons, buttons, buttons
> All down her back, back, back
> She asked her mother, mother, mother
> For fifteen cents, cents, cents
> To see the elephant, elephant, elephant
> Jump the fence, fence, fence
> Well, he jumped so high, high, high
> 'Til he touched the sky, sky, sky
> And he didn't come back, back, back
> 'Til the Fourth of Ju-ly, ly, ly!

Evenings were spent mainly on the back porches where screen doors slammed in the darkness with those really very special summertime sounds. And, sometimes, when Chicago nights got too steamy, the whole family got into the car and went to the park and slept out in the open on blankets. Those were, of course, the best times of all because the grownups were invariably reminded of

---

1. **esthetically** (es thet′ ik lē) *adv.* artistically.

Literary Analysis
Style How would you describe Hansberry's tone as she explains her childhood feelings about summer?

Literary Analysis
Style In what way does the made-up word *artsily-craftsily* add to the sense of Hansberry's disdain for summer?

having been children in rural parts of the country and told the best stories then. And it was also cool and sweet to be on the grass and there was usually the scent of freshly cut lemons or melons in the air. And Daddy would lie on his back, as fathers must, and explain about how men thought the stars above us came to be and how far away they were. I never did learn to believe that anything could be as far away as *that*. Especially the stars.

My mother first took us south to visit her Tennessee birthplace one summer when I was seven or eight, I think. I woke up on the back seat of the car while we were still driving through some place called Kentucky and my mother was pointing out to the beautiful hills on both sides of the highway and telling my brothers and my sister about how her father had run away and hidden from his master in those very hills when he was a little boy. She said that his mother had wandered among the wooded slopes in the moonlight and left food for him in secret places. They were very beautiful hills and I looked out at them for miles and miles after that wondering who and what a *master* might be.

I remember being startled when I first saw my grandmother rocking away on her porch. All my life I had heard that she was a great beauty and no one had ever remarked that they meant a half century before. The woman that I met was as wrinkled as a prune and could hardly hear and barely see and always seemed to be thinking of other times. But she could still rock and talk and even make wonderful cupcakes which were like cornbread, only sweet. She was captivated by automobiles and, even though it was well into the Thirties,[2] I don't think she had ever been in one before we came down and took her driving. She was a little afraid of them and could not seem to negotiate the windows, but she loved driving. She died the next summer and that is all that I remember about her, except that she was born in slavery and had memories of it and they didn't sound anything like *Gone With the Wind*.[3]

Like everyone else, I have spent whole or bits of summers in many different kinds of places since then: camps and resorts in the Middle West and New York State; on an island; in a tiny Mexican village; Cape Cod, perched atop the Truro bluffs at Longnook Beach that Millay wrote about; or simply strolling the streets of Provincetown[4] before the hours when the parties begin.

And, lastly, I do not think that I will forget days spent, a few summers ago, at a beautiful lodge built right into the rocky cliffs of a bay on the Maine coast. We met a woman there who had lived a

---

2. Thirties the 1930s.
3. Gone With the Wind novel set in the South during the Civil War period.
4. Provincetown resort town at the northern tip of Cape Cod, Massachusetts.

Literary Analysis
Style How does Hansberry's repetition of the word *And* to begin sentences emphasize the flow and abundance of her memories?

Reading Skill
Main Idea What information do these anecdotes about her trips to Tennessee add to your understanding of the author's childhood summers?

Reading Check

Whom does Hansberry visit in Tennessee?

purposeful and courageous life and who was then dying of cancer. She had, characteristically, just written a book and taken up painting. She had also been of radical viewpoint all her life; one of those people who energetically believe that the world *can* be changed for the better and spend their lives trying to do just that. And that was the way she thought of cancer; she absolutely refused to award it the stature of tragedy, a devastating instance of the brooding doom and inexplicability[5] of the absurdity of human destiny, etc., etc. The kind of characterization given, lately, as we all know, to far less formidable foes in life than cancer.

But for this remarkable woman it was a matter of nature in imperfection, implying, as always, work for man to do. It was an *enemy*, but a palpable one with shape and effect and source; and if it existed, it could be destroyed. She saluted it accordingly, without

---

5. inexplicability (in eks′ pli kə bil′ ə tē) *n.* condition of being unexplainable.

▼ **Critical Viewing**
How does this photograph of the Maine coast add to the description in the essay? **[Connect]**

despondency, but with a lively, beautiful and delightfully ribald anger. There was one thing, she felt, which would prove equal to its relentless ravages and that was the genius of man. Not his mysticism, but man with tubes and slides and the stubborn human notion that the stars are very much within our reach.

The last time I saw her she was sitting surrounded by her paintings with her manuscript laid out for me to read, because, she said, she wanted to know what a *young person* would think of her thinking; one must always keep up with what *young people* thought about things because, after all, they were *change.*

Every now and then her jaw set in anger as we spoke of things people should be angry about. And then, for relief, she would look out at the lovely bay at a mellow sunset settling on the water. Her face softened with love of all that beauty and, watching her, I wished with all my power what I knew that she was wishing: that she might live to see at least one more *summer.* Through her eyes I finally gained the sense of what it might mean; more than the coming autumn with its <u>pretentious</u> melancholy; more than an austere and silent winter which must shut dying people in for precious months; more even than the frivolous spring, too full of too many false promises, would be the gift of another summer with its stark and intimate assertion of neither birth nor death but life at the <u>apex</u>; with the gentlest nights and, above all, the longest days.

I heard later that she did live to see another summer. And I have retained my respect for the noblest of the seasons.

Literary Analysis
Style Which words convey Hansberry's feelings about the woman in Maine?

Vocabulary Builder
pretentious (prē ten´ shəs) *adj.* grand in a showy way
apex (ā´ peks´) *n.* highest point; peak

Apply the Skills

On Summer

Thinking About the Selection

1. **Respond:** How do Hansberry's ideas about summer compare with your own? Make a list of some of the reasons why you like and dis-like summer. Trade lists with a partner and discuss your answers. Then, explain how your answer has grown or changed as a result of the discussion.

2. **(a) Recall:** When does Hansberry first visit her grandmother? **(b) Infer:** Why do you think she includes the section about her grandmother in her essay?

3. **(a) Recall:** When does Hansberry's attitude toward summer change? **(b) Interpret:** At the end, she calls summer "the noblest of seasons." What do you think she means by this phrase?

4. **Evaluate:** How clearly do you think Hansberry explains the way her feelings about summer have changed? Explain your answer.

Literary Analysis

5. Hansberry begins many sentences in "On Summer" with the word *and*. What effect does this aspect of the author's **syntax** create? Explain.

6. What one word might you use to describe the overall **tone** of "On Summer"? Explain.

7. Review the last two paragraphs of "On Summer." Use a chart like the one shown to record examples of the **diction** and **tone** Hansberry uses in describing her associations with summer. Then, based on her diction and tone in these paragraphs, write three adjectives in the center of the chart to describe Hansberry's **style**.

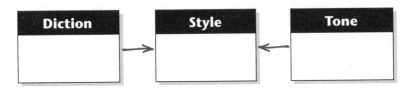

Reading Skill

8. State the **main idea** of "On Summer" in your own words.

9. **(a)** List three **supporting details** that serve as evidence for the point that Hansberry makes in the essay. **(b)** Do you think that the author adequately supports her main idea with details? Why or why not?

QuickReview

Essay at a Glance
The author describes how and why her feel-ings about summer have changed.

Assessment
For: Self-test
Visit: www.PHSchool.com
Web Code: epa-6303

Author's Style: an author's way of writing; elements of style include *diction*, *syntax*, and *tone*

Main Idea: the central message, insight, or opinion in a work of nonfiction

Supporting Details: the pieces of evidence that a writer uses to prove a main idea

Vocabulary Builder

Practice Determine whether each sentence below is true or false. Use the meaning of the underlined word to explain your reasoning.

1. Greeting someone with _aloofness_ shows respect for him or her.
2. Cheerful songs are meant to inspire _melancholy_ in a listener.
3. A _pretentious_ politician is likely to be unpopular with many voters.
4. One must climb a mountain to reach its _apex_.

Adding Words to Your Vocabulary Using a thesaurus, find a **synonym,** or word of similar meaning, for each italicized word above. Use each synonym in a sentence that makes the meaning of the word clear. (For more on using a thesaurus, see page R7.)

Writing

"On Summer" reflects Lorraine Hansberry's admiration for her elders. Think of an older person whom you admire. Write a few paragraphs of **book jacket copy** for a biography of that person. Book jackets often provide a brief introduction to a subject to entice people to read more.
- Include some highlights of the person's life.
- Choose details that will make the reader want to know more.

For _Grammar, Vocabulary,_ and _Assessment,_ see **Build Language Skills,** pp. 422–423.

Extend Your Learning

Listening and Speaking In a small group, hold a **panel discussion** on the pros and cons of each season of the year. Each panel member should speak in support of a favorite season. Consider these questions as you prepare:
- What in particular do you like about your favorite season?
- What are features of the season that others might dislike?

Each panelist should prepare notes to use during the discussion and should elaborate upon or illustrate each other's comments.

Research and Technology In her essay, Hansberry discusses the climate of Chicago, Illinois. Use the Internet and an atlas to gather data about Chicago's climate. Then, make an **annotated map** that shows Chicago in relation to the rest of the United States. Include a side column with facts about the city's climate.

Build Language Skills

Vocabulary Skill

Prefixes The prefix *con-* or *com-* means "with" or "together." This prefix appears in English words that relate to the ideas of joining or coming together. For example, the word *concurrent* means "happening *along with* something else."

▶ **Example:** The two classes I wanted to take were *concurrent,* so I could attend only one.

Com- at the beginning of a word is not always a prefix meaning *with* or *together.* Sometimes, *-com* adds emphasis to the base word as in *confirm.*

Practice Look up each word in a dictionary. Use the entry to help you locate the base word. Tell the part of speech for both words. Then, explain how the prefix contributes to their meanings.

▶ **Example:** Conjunction(n) a joining *together*; conjoin(v) join together.

1. compulsion
2. conjunction
3. commitment
4. confide
5. comparison

Grammar Lesson

Direct and Indirect Objects A **direct object** is a noun or pronoun that *receives* the action of an action verb. An **indirect object** appears with a direct object and names the person or thing that something is *given to* or *done for.*

You can determine whether a word is a direct object by asking *Whom?* or *What?* after an action verb. You can tell whether a word is an indirect object by asking *To or for whom?* or *To or for what?*

> The family bought *an old house.* (Direct object - answers the question, **what**)

> The rain pelted *the campers.* (Direct object - answers the question, **whom**)

> I wrote my brother (indirect object) letters. (direct object)

Practice For each item, write a sentence in which you use the word or phrase as directed in the parenthetical information.

1. fans (as a direct object)
2. muffins, toast, and bagels (as a direct object in a question)
3. dancers and singers (as a direct object in a statement)
4. Maria and Joe (as an indirect object in a question)
5. me (as an indirect object in a statement)

MorePractice

For more practice with direct and indirect objects, see the grammar Handbook p. R40.

W/*G* *Prentice Hall Writing and Grammar Connection: Chapter 20, Section 3*

EOC **Test Practice**

Reading: Main Idea and Supporting Details

Standards Assessed

• IR.2.02.3
• IR.2.03.3
• IR.2.03.4

Directions: *Read the selection. Then, answer the questions.*

Today, New Mexico is the home of over 50,000 Pueblo people, descendants of Indians who inhabited the area for nearly 2,000 years. The ancient Pueblo Indians are known for their villages of adobe "apartment buildings." These building were up to four stories tall. These apartments could have as many as 1,000 rooms. Ladders connected the lower floors to the upper floors. A family's section was arranged in a row of rooms from the center of the apartment complex, with rooms connected by doorways. The ground floor rooms were used for storage of grain and other goods.

1. A question to guide further reading to subsequent passages might be
   A What crops did the Pueblo people grow?
   B What architect designed these?
   C Would this be a good tourist attraction?
   D How did they build these dwellings?

2. The main idea of this paragraph is that
   A Pueblo people survived for nearly 2,000 years.
   B Ancient Pueblo Indians built adobe "apartment buildings."
   C Pueblos had as many as 1,000 rooms.
   D New Mexico is home to over 50,000 Pueblo people.

3. A key detail that would help define the main idea is
   A "Today, . . . Pueblo people. . . ."
   B "The ancient Pueblo Indians . . . buildings.'"
   C "Ladders connected . . . upper floors."
   D "The ground floor . . . other goods."

4. Which is not a supporting detail?
   A "Today, . . . Pueblo people. . ."
   B "Ladders connected . . . upper floors."
   C "A family's section was . . . connected by doorways. . . ."
   D "These buildings were . . . up to four stories tall."

Timed Writing: Evaluation [Critical Stance]

Review "On Summer" or "A Celebration of Grandfathers." Evaluate how well the author achieves his or her purpose. In your evaluation, cite details from the text to illustrate your points. **(20 minutes)**

Writing Workshop: *Work in Progress*

Business Letter

Choose one consumer item from your product list. Consider the types of information a company representative would need to know. Jot down three questions that would have to be answered for the reader to understand your complaint. Save these questions in your portfolio.

Practice these skills with either "The News" (p. 426) or "Single Room, Earth View" (p. 437).

Standard Course of Study

- Show appreciation for the significance of a personal account. (WL.1.01.3)
- Identify and analyze influences, contexts, or biases in communication. (CT.4.03.7)
- Analyze author's craft and style when critiquing communication. (CT.4.03.9)

Literary Analysis

An **expository essay** is a short piece of nonfiction that presents information, discusses ideas, or explains a process. The writer may use a variety of techniques to provide support, depth, and context:

- **Description:** including language that appeals to the senses
- **Comparison and contrast:** showing similarities and differences between two or among more than two items
- **Cause and effect:** explaining the relationship between events, actions, or situations by showing how one can result in another

Reading Skill

The **main idea** is the central message, insight, or opinion in a work of nonfiction. The **supporting details** are the pieces of evidence that a writer uses to prove his or her point. **Reread** to help you **identify the main idea and supporting details** in a work.

- Note key details to decide what the main idea might be.
- If a detail does not seem to support that main idea, reread the passage to be sure that you have not misinterpreted it.
- If necessary, revise your assumptions about the main idea.

Use a chart like the one shown to record the details of a work and the main idea they might support.

Vocabulary Builder

The News

- **compensation** (käm′ pən sā′ shən) *n.* anything that makes up for a loss, damage, or debt (p. 426) *When they ran out of prizes, they gave free tickets as* <u>compensation</u>.
- **temporal** (tem′ pə rəl) *adj.* having to do with time (p. 426) *His persistent lateness suggests that he has no* <u>temporal</u> *sense.*
- **revered** (ri vird′) *adj.* regarded with great respect and awe (p. 430) *Many students came to the retirement party for the* <u>revered</u> *teacher.*
- **daunting** (dônt′ iŋ) *adj.* intimidating (p. 431) *Climbing Mount Everest is a* <u>daunting</u> *task.*

Single Room, Earth View

- **articulate** (är tik′ yōō lit) *adj.* expressing oneself clearly and easily (p. 437) *The candidate is an* <u>articulate</u> *public speaker.*
- **novice** (näv′ is) *adj.* new to an activity; inexperienced (p. 438) *For a* <u>novice</u> *chess player, she shows great patience and maturity.*
- **diffused** (di fyōōzd′) *v.* spread out (p. 441) *The wind* <u>diffused</u> *the confetti over the field.*
- **extrapolating** (ek strap′ ə lāt′ iŋ) *v.* arriving at a conclusion by inferring from known facts (p. 441) *I decided I would like the whole CD by* <u>extrapolating</u> *from the first song.*

Build Understanding • *The News*

Background

Television News In 1948, only 400,000 American homes had a television. By 1960, more than 46 million American homes had a television, and TV began to take over as the news medium of choice. Today, television news is one of the most influential institutions in American culture.

Connecting to the Literature

Reading/Writing Connection In "The News," Neil Postman analyzes the pros and cons of television news. Write a short paragraph telling how you learn about newsworthy events and explaining which medium you prefer. Use at least three of these words: *analyze, rely, clarify, indicate.*

READ MORE
by
Neil Postman
Technopoly: The Surrender of Culture to Technology
The End of Education

Meet the Author

Neil **Postman** (1931–2003)

Neil Postman was a media critic and a revered professor of communications at New York University where he taught for over forty years. He called his field "media ecology," and his greatest concern was the effect that television was having on Americans.

Teachings on Television Born in New York, Postman received a doctorate in education from Columbia University. He also wrote twenty books and hundreds of articles. One of his most intense arguments is set forth in *The Disappearance of Childhood* (1982), in which he asserts that television exposes children to adult concerns far too early.

Fast Facts

▶ Postman once said, "You have to understand, what Americans do is watch television. I am not saying that's who they are. But that is what they *do*. Americans . . . watch . . . television."

▶ In 1987, Postman won the George Orwell Award from the National Council of Teachers of English.

For: More about the author
Visit: www.PHSchool.com
Web Code: epe-9304

The News

Neil Postman

The whole problem with news on television comes down to this: all the words uttered in an hour of news coverage could be printed on one page of a newspaper. And the world cannot be understood in one page. Of course, there is a <u>compensation</u>: television offers pictures, and the pictures move. It is often said that moving pictures are a kind of language in themselves, and there is a good deal of truth in this. But the language of pictures differs radically from oral and written language, and the differences are crucial for understanding television news.

To begin with, the grammar of pictures is weak in communicating past-ness and present-ness. When terrorists want to prove to the world that their kidnap victims are still alive, they photograph them holding a copy of a recent newspaper. The dateline on the newspaper provides the proof that the photograph was taken on or after that date. Without the help of the written word, film and videotape cannot portray <u>temporal</u> dimensions with any precision. Consider a film clip showing an aircraft carrier at sea. One might be able to identify the ship as Soviet[1] or American, but there would be no way of telling where in the world the carrier was, where it was headed, or when the pictures were taken. It is

Vocabulary Builder
compensation (käm´ pən sā´ shən) *n.* anything that makes up for a loss, damage, or debt

temporal (tem´ pə rəl) *adj.* having to do with time

---

1. **Soviet** (sō´ vē et´) belonging to the Soviet Union, the formerly socialist nation known today as Russia.

only through language—words spoken over the pictures or reproduced in them—that the image of the aircraft carrier takes on meaning as a portrayal of a specific event.

Still, it is possible to enjoy the image of the carrier for its own sake. One might find the hugeness of the vessel interesting; it signifies military power on the move. There is a certain drama in watching the planes come in at high speeds and skid to a stop on the deck. Suppose the ship were burning: that would be even more interesting. This leads to a second point about the language of pictures. The grammar of moving pictures favors images that change. That is why violence and destruction find their way onto television so often. When something is destroyed violently its constitution is altered in a highly visible way: hence the entrancing power of fire. Fire gives visual form to the ideas of consumption, disappearance, death—the thing which is burned is actually taken away by fire. It is at this very basic level that fires make a good subject for television news. Something was here, now it's gone, and the change is recorded on film.

Earthquakes and typhoons have the same power: before the viewer's eyes the world is taken apart. If a television viewer has relatives in Mexico City and an earthquake occurs there, then she may take an interest in the images of destruction as a report from a specific place and time. That is, she may look to television news for information about an important event. But film of an earthquake can still be interesting if the viewer cares nothing about the event itself. Which is only to say that there is another way of participating in the news—as a spectator who desires to be entertained. Actually to see buildings topple is exciting, no matter where the buildings are. The world turns to dust before our eyes.

Those who produce television news in America know that their medium favors images that move. That is why they despise "talking heads," people who simply appear in front of a camera and speak. When talking heads appear on television, there is nothing to record or document, no change in process. In the cinema the situation is somewhat different. On a movie screen, close-ups of a good actor speaking dramatically can sometimes be interesting to watch. When Clint Eastwood narrows his eyes and challenges his rival to shoot first, the spectator sees the cool rage of the Eastwood character take visual form, and the narrowing of the eyes is dramatic. But much of the effect of this small movement depends on the size of the movie screen and the darkness of the theater, which make Eastwood and his every action "larger than life."

The television screen is smaller than life. It occupies about 15 percent of the viewer's visual field (compared to about 70 percent for the movie screen). It is not set in a darkened theater closed off

◀ **Critical Viewing**
How does this backstage view of a news show compare with the news programs you may have seen on television? [Use Prior Knowledge]

Literary Analysis
Expository Essay
How do details about airplanes and fire support Postman's point that television favors change?

Reading Check

Why do television producers despise "talking heads"?

from the world but in the viewer's ordinary living space. This means that visual changes must be more extreme and more dramatic to be interesting on television. A narrowing of the eyes will not do. A car crash, an earthquake, a burning factory are much better.

With these principles in mind, let us examine more closely the structure of a typical newscast. In America, almost all news shows begin with music, the tone of which suggests important events about to unfold. (Beethoven's Fifth Symphony would be entirely appropriate.) The music is very important, for it equates the news with various forms of drama and ritual—the opera, for example, or a wedding procession—in which musical themes underscore the meaning of the event. Music takes us immediately into the realm of the symbolic, a world that is not to be taken literally. After all, when events unfold in the real world, they do so without musical accompaniment. More symbolism follows. The sound of teletype machines can be heard in the studio, not because it is impossible to screen this noise out, but because the sound is a kind of music in itself. It tells us that data are pouring in from all corners of the globe, a sensation reinforced by the world map in the background (or clocks noting the time on different continents).

Literary Analysis
Expository Essay
What topic will Postman analyze more closely in this essay?

▼ **Critical Viewing**
Which aspects of this picture would Postman say are typical of images in a television newscast? **[Connect]**

Types of Nonfiction

Already, then, before a single news item is introduced, a great deal has been communicated. We know that we are in the presence of a symbolic event, a form of theater in which the day's events are to be dramatized. This theater takes the entire globe as its subject, although it may look at the world from the perspective of a single nation. A certain tension is present, like the atmosphere in a theater just before the curtain goes up. The tension is represented by the music, the staccato beat of the teletype machines, and the sight of newsworkers scurrying around typing reports and answering phones. As a technical matter, it would be no problem to build a set in which the newsroom staff remained off camera, invisible to the viewer, but an important theatrical effect would be lost. By being busy on camera, the workers help communicate urgency about the events at hand, which it is suggested are changing so rapidly that constant revision of the news is necessary.

The staff in the background also helps signal the importance of the person in the center, the anchorman (or -woman) "in command" of both the staff and the news. The anchorman plays the role of host. He welcomes us to the newscast and welcomes us back from the different locations we visit during filmed reports. His voice, appearance, and manner establish the mood of the broadcast. It would be unthinkable for the anchor to be ugly, or a nervous sort who could not complete a sentence. Viewers must be able to believe in the anchor as a person of authority and skill, a person who would not panic in a crisis—someone to trust.

This belief is based not on knowledge of the anchorman's character or achievements as a journalist, but on his presentation of self while on the air. Does he look the part of a trusted man? Does he speak firmly and clearly? Does he have a warm smile? Does he project confidence without seeming arrogant? The value the anchor must communicate above all else is control. He must be in control of himself, his voice, his emotions. He must know what is coming next in the broadcast, and he must move smoothly and confidently from segment to segment. Again, it would be unthinkable for the anchor to break down and weep over a story, or laugh uncontrollably on camera, no matter how "human" these responses may be.

Reading Skill
Main Idea How do each of these details support Postman's idea that a newscast is a form of theater?

Reading Check

According to Postman, what value, above all else, must a news anchorperson convey?

Many other features of the newscast help the anchor to establish the impression of control. These are usually equated with professionalism in broadcasting. They include such things as graphics that tell the viewer what is being shown, or maps and charts that suddenly appear on the screen and disappear on cue, or the orderly progression from story to story, starting with the most important events first. They also include the absence of gaps or "deadtime" during the broadcast, even the simple fact that the news starts and ends at a certain hour. These common features are thought of as purely technical matters, which a professional crew handles as a matter of course. But they are also symbols of a dominant theme of television news: the imposition of an orderly world—called "the news"—upon the disorderly flow of events.

While the form of a news broadcast emphasizes tidiness and control, its content can best be described as chaotic. Because time is so precious on television, because the nature of the medium favors dynamic visual images, and because the pressures of a commercial structure require the news to hold its audience above all else, there is rarely any attempt to explain issues in depth or place events in their proper context. The news moves nervously from a warehouse fire to a court decision, from a guerrilla war to a World Cup match, the quality of the film often determining the length of the story. Certain stories show up only because they offer dramatic pictures. Bleachers collapse in South America: hundreds of people are crushed—a perfect television news story, for the cameras can record the face of disaster in all its anguish. Back in Washington, a new budget is approved by Congress. Here there is nothing to photograph because a budget is not a physical event; it is a document full of language and numbers. So the producers of the news will show a photo of the document itself, focusing on the cover where it says: "Budget of the United States of America." Or sometimes they will send a camera crew to the government printing plant where copies of the budget are produced. That evening, while the contents of the budget are summarized by a voice-over, the viewer sees stacks of documents being loaded into boxes at the government printing plant. Then a few of the budget's more important provisions will be flashed on the screen in written form, but this is such a time-consuming process—using television as a printed page—that the producers keep it to a minimum. In short, the budget is not televisable, and for that reason its time on the news must be brief. The bleacher collapse will get more minutes that evening.

With priorities of this sort, it is almost impossible for the news to offer an adequate account of important

▼ **Critical Viewing**
How does this image of ABC News anchorman Peter Jennings compare with Postman's description of a typical anchorperson? **[Compare and Contrast]**

events. Indeed, it is the trivial event that is often best suited for television coverage. This is such a commonplace that no one even bothers to challenge it. Walter Cronkite, a <u>revered</u> figure in television and anchorman of the CBS Evening News for many years, has acknowledged several times that television cannot be relied on to inform the citizens of a democratic nation. Unless they also read newspapers and magazines, television viewers are helpless to understand their world, Cronkite has said. No one at CBS has ever disagreed with his conclusion, other than to say, "We do the best we can."

Of course, it is a tendency of journalism in general to concentrate on the surface of events rather than underlying conditions; this is as true for the newspaper as it is for the newscast. But several features of television undermine whatever efforts journalists may make to give sense to the world. One is that a television broadcast is a series of events that occur in sequence, and the sequence is the same for all viewers. This is not true for a newspaper page, which displays many items simultaneously, allowing readers to choose the order in which they read them. If a newspaper reader wants only a summary of the latest tax bill, he can read the headline and the first paragraph of an article, and if he wants more, he can keep reading. In a sense, then, everyone reads a different newspaper, for no two readers will read (or ignore) the same items.

But all television viewers see the same broadcast. They have no choices. A report is either in the broadcast or out, which means that anything which is of narrow interest is unlikely to be included. As NBC News executive Reuven Frank once explained:

> A newspaper, for example, can easily afford to print an item of conceivable interest to only a fraction of its readers. A television news program must be put together with the assumption that each item will be of some interest to everyone that watches. Every time a newspaper includes a feature which will attract a specialized group it can assume it is adding at least a little bit to its circulation. To the degree a television news program includes an item of this sort . . . it must assume that its audience will diminish.

The need to "include everyone," an identifying feature of commercial television in all its forms, prevents journalists from offering lengthy or complex explanations, or from tracing the sequence of events leading up to today's headlines. One of the ironies of political life in modern democracies is that many problems which concern the "general welfare" are of interest only to

Vocabulary Builder
revered (ri vird′) *adj.* regarded with great respect and awe

Literary Analysis
Expository Essay
According to Postman, how are newspaper and television journalism both similar and different?

Reading Check

What does Walter Cronkite say about television news viewers who do not also read print media?

specialized groups. Arms control, for example, is an issue that literally concerns everyone in the world, and yet the language of arms control and the complexity of the subject are so <u>daunting</u> that only a minority of people can actually follow the issue from week to week and month to month. If it wants to act responsibly, a newspaper can at least make available more information about arms control than most people want. But commercial television cannot afford to do so.

▲ **Critical Viewing**
How might this man's experience of reading a newspaper differ from his experience of watching television news? **[Connect]**

Vocabulary Builder
daunting (dônt′ iŋ) *adj.*
intimidating

This illustrates an important point in the psychology of television's appeal. Many of the items in newspapers and magazines are not, in a strict sense, demanded by a majority of readers. They are there because some readers *might* be interested or because the editors think their readers *should* be interested. On commercial television, "might" and "should" are not the relevant words. The producers attempt to make sure that "each item will be of some interest to everyone that watches," as Reuven Frank put it. What this means is that a newspaper or magazine can challenge its audience in a way that television cannot. Print media have the luxury of suggesting or inviting interest, whereas television must always concern itself with conforming to existing interests. In a way, television is more strictly responsive to the demands of its huge audience. But there is one demand it cannot meet: the desire to be challenged, to be told "this is worth attending to," to be surprised by what one thought would not be of interest.

Another severe limitation on television is time. There is simply not enough of it. The evening news programs at CBS, NBC, and ABC all run for thirty minutes, eight of which are taken up by commercials. No one believes that twenty-two minutes for the day's news is adequate. For years news executives at ABC, NBC, and CBS have suggested that the news be expanded to one hour. But by tradition the half-hour after the national evening news is given over to the hundreds of local affiliate stations around the country to use as they see fit. They have found it a very profitable time to broadcast game shows or half-hour situation comedies, and they are reluctant to give up the income they derive from these programs.

The evening news produced by the three networks is profitable for both the networks and the local stations. The local stations are paid a fee by the network to broadcast the network news, and they profit from this fee since the news—produced by the network—costs them nothing. It is likely that they would also make money from a one-hour newscast, but not as much, they judge, as they do from the game shows and comedies they now schedule.

The result is that the evening news must try to do what cannot reasonably be done: give a decent account of the day's events in twenty-two minutes. What the viewer gets instead is a series of impressions, many of them purely visual, most of them unconnected to each other or to any sense of a history unfolding. Taken together, they suggest a world that is fundamentally ungovernable, where events do not arise out of historical conditions but rather explode from the heavens in a series of disasters that suggest a permanent state of crisis. It is this crisis—highly visual, ahistorical, and unsolvable—which the evening news presents as theater every evening.

Literary Analysis
Expository Essay
What sense of the world does television news cause?

The audience for this theater is offered a contradictory pair of responses. On the one hand, it is reassured by the smooth presentation of the news itself, especially the firm voice and steady gaze of the trusty anchorman. Newscasts frequently end with a "human-interest story," often with a sentimental or comic touch. Example: a little girl in Chicago writes Gorbachev a letter, and he answers her, saying that he and President Reagan are trying to work out their differences. This item reassures viewers that all is well, leaders are in command, we can still communicate with each other, and so on. But—and now we come to the other hand—the rest of the broadcast has told a different story. It has shown the audience a world that is out of control and incomprehensible, full of violence, disaster, and suffering. Whatever authority the anchorman may project through his steady manner is undermined by the terror inspired by the news itself.

Reading Skill
Main Idea What main idea does the anecdote about the little girl support?

This is where television news is at its most radical—not in giving publicity to radical causes, but in producing the impression of an ungovernable world. And it produces this impression not because the people who work in television are leftists or anarchists.[2] The anarchy in television news is a direct result of the commercial structure of broadcasting, which introduces into news judgments a single-mindedness more powerful than any ideology: the overwhelming need to keep people watching.

---

2. leftists . . . anarchists (an´ ər kists´) leftists desire to change the existing political order in the name of greater freedom for all; anarchists oppose any political authority.

Apply the Skills

The News

Thinking About the Selection

1. **Respond:** Do you agree with Postman about the limitations of television? Why or why not?
2. **(a) Recall:** According to Postman, what elements make a news broadcast like a form of theater? **(b) Interpret:** What problem does Postman see in the similarity between television news and theater?
3. **(a) Recall:** What value does Postman say the news anchor must project above all others? **(b) Connect:** How does the impression created by the anchor relate to the "radical" nature of television?
4. **(a) Recall:** How long does an evening news broadcast usually have to present all the news? **(b) Cause and Effect:** What effects do time limits have on television news?
5. **Take a Position:** Do you think that changes should be made in television news broadcasts to make them more intellectually challenging? Give reasons and examples to support your position.

Literary Analysis

6. What is the topic of Neil Postman's **expository essay?**
7. What quotations does Postman use to make information clear to readers?
8. **(a)** Using a chart like the one shown, identify passages in which Postman uses **description, comparison and contrast,** or **cause and effect.** Find one example of each technique. **(b)** Explain how each example adds depth and context to the information Postman presents in that passage.

	Example	Effect
Description		
Comparison/Contrast		
Cause and Effect		

Reading Skill

9. State the **main idea** of "The News" in your own words.
10. **(a)** List three **supporting details** that serve as evidence for the points that Neil Postman makes in his essay. **(b)** Do you think the author adequately supports his main idea with details? Why or why not?

QuickReview

Essay at a Glance
Neil Postman evaluates television as a news source.

Go Online
Assessment
For: Self-test
Visit: www.PHSchool.com
Web Code: epa-6304

Expository Essay: a short piece of nonfiction that presents information, discusses ideas, or explains a process. Writers may use *description, comparison and contrast,* and *cause and effect* to support ideas

Main Idea: the central message, insight, or opinion in a work of nonfiction

Supporting Details: the pieces of evidence that a writer uses to prove a main idea

---

Vocabulary Builder

Practice Review the vocabulary list for "The News" on page 424. Then, identify the word in each group that does not belong. Explain.

1. compensation, repayment, donation
2. temporal, necklace, clock
3. revered, scorn, ridicule
4. daunting, challenge, temptation

Adding Words to Your Vocabulary Using a thesaurus, find an **antonym**, or word of opposite meaning, for each vocabulary word. Use each antonym in a sentence that makes the meaning of the word clear. (For more on using a thesaurus, see page R7.)

Writing

Write the **script** for a public service announcement that encourages people to use a variety of news sources.
- Based on the Neil Postman essay, jot down details that might encourage people to use a variety of news sources.
- Describe visual elements that would create a persuasive message.
- In your script, include one direct quotation from Postman's essay, and describe the visual that would go with it.

For *Grammar, Vocabulary,* and *Assessment,* see **Build Language Skills,** pp. 444–445.

Extend Your Learning

Listening and Speaking In a group, videotape and watch several news broadcasts, paying special attention to the images presented. Then, give an **informal presentation** to discuss Postman's view that television news is dominated by the "need to keep people watching."
- Discuss the intellectual and emotional effects of the pictures.
- Point out what the pictures show about the broadcasters' intentions.
As you present, pause occasionally to summarize and evaluate your conclusions.

Research and Technology Use library and Internet resources to research the preparations that television journalists go through as they prepare a news story. Based on this information, write two **journal entries** that a reporter might write while preparing a story.

Essay

Background

First American Woman in Space On June 18, 1983, when she worked as a flight engineer and mission specialist aboard the shuttle *Challenger*, Sally Ride became the first American woman in space. Her historic mission allowed her to experience what she recounts in "Single Room, Earth View."

Connecting to the Literature

Reading/Writing Connection In this essay, Sally Ride describes what it is like to look at Earth from space. Write five sentences describing an experience you had of seeing something from a new perspective. Use at least three of the following words: *alter, contradict, emphasize, perceive.*

Review

For **Literary Analysis, Reading Skill,** and **Vocabulary Builder,** see page 424.

READ MORE

by
Sally Ride
To Space and Back
The Mystery of Mars
(with Tam O'Shaughnessy)

Meet the Author

Sally **Ride** (b. 1951)

Although best known as an astronaut, Sally Ride was also a talented athlete in her youth. She was a ranked player on the junior tennis circuit and considered turning professional before deciding to go to college instead.

The Right Stuff In 1978, Ride read a newspaper advertisement about NASA's search for astronauts. After extensive testing to be sure she had "the right stuff," NASA chose her as one of six women and twenty-five men accepted from among 8,000 applicants. Five years later, in 1983, she took her historic flight. Ride retired from NASA in 1987 and currently teaches physics at the University of California.

Fast Facts

▶ Sally Ride holds four degrees from Stanford University, including a Master's and a Doctorate.
▶ Ride played a key role in the investigations of both the *Challenger* and *Columbia* space shuttle disasters.

Go **O**nline
—Author Link

For: More about the author
Visit: www.PHSchool.com
Web Code: epe-9305

Single Room, Earth View

Sally Ride

Everyone I've met has a glittering, if vague, mental image of space travel. And naturally enough, people want to hear about it from an astronaut: "How did it feel . . . ?" "What did it look like . . . ?" "Were you scared?" Sometimes, the questions come from reporters, their pens poised and their tape recorders silently reeling in the words; sometimes, it's wide-eyed, ten-year-old girls who want answers. I find a way to answer all of them, but it's not easy.

Imagine trying to describe an airplane ride to someone who has never flown. An <u>articulate</u> traveler could describe the sights but would find it much harder to explain the difference in perspective provided by the new view from a greater distance, along with the feelings, impressions, and insights that go with that new perspective. And the difference is enormous: Spaceflight moves the traveler another giant step farther away. Eight and one-half thunderous minutes after launch, an astronaut is orbiting high above the Earth, suddenly able to watch typhoons form, volcanoes smolder, and meteors streak through the atmosphere below.

▲ Critical Viewing
Based on this photograph, why might travel in the space shuttle defy description? **[Connect]**

Vocabulary Builder
articulate (är tik´ yoo lit) *adj.* expressing oneself clearly and easily

While flying over the Hawaiian Islands, several astronauts have marveled that the islands look just like they do on a map. When people first hear that, they wonder what should be so surprising about Hawaii looking the way it does in the atlas. Yet, to the astronauts it is an absolutely startling sensation: The islands really *do* look as if that part of the world has been carpeted with a big page torn out of Rand-McNally, and all we can do is try to convey the surreal quality of that scene.

In orbit, racing along at five miles per second, the space shuttle circles the Earth once every 90 minutes. I found that at this speed, unless I kept my nose pressed to the window, it was almost impossible to keep track of where we were at any given moment—the world below simply changes too fast. If I turned my concentration away for too long, even just to change film in a camera, I could miss an entire land mass. It's embarrassing to float up to a window, glance outside, and then have to ask a crewmate, "What continent is this?"

We could see smoke rising from fires that dotted the entire east coast of Africa, and in the same orbit only moments later, ice floes jostling for position in the Antarctic. We could see the Ganges River dumping its murky, sediment-laden water into the Indian Ocean and watch ominous hurricane clouds expanding and rising like biscuits in the oven of the Caribbean.

Mountain ranges, volcanoes, and river deltas appeared in salt-and-flour relief, all leading me to assume the role of a <u>novice</u> geologist. In such moments, it was easy to imagine the dynamic upheavals that created jutting mountain ranges and the internal wrenchings that created rifts and seas. I also became an instant believer in plate tectonics; India really *is* crashing into Asia, and Saudi Arabia and Egypt really *are* pulling apart, making the Red Sea wider. Even though their respective motion is really no more than mere inches a year, the view from overhead makes theory come alive.

Spectacular as the view is from 200 miles up, the Earth is not the awe-inspiring "blue marble" made famous by the photos from the moon. From space shuttle height, we can't see the entire globe at a glance, but we can look down the entire boot of Italy, or up the East Coast of the United States from Cape Hatteras to Cape Cod. The panoramic view inspires an appreciation for the scale of some of nature's phenomena. One day, as I scanned the sandy expanse of Northern Africa, I couldn't find any of the familiar landmarks—colorful outcroppings of rock in Chad, irrigated patches of the Sahara. Then I realized they were obscured by a huge dust storm, a

Reading Skill
Main Idea Which details support Ride's point about the difficulties of describing space travel?

Vocabulary Builder
novice (näv´ is) *adj.* new to an activity; inexperienced

cloud of sand that enveloped the continent from Morocco to the Sudan.

Since the space shuttle flies fairly low (at least by orbital standards; it's more than 22,000 miles lower than a typical TV satellite), we can make out both natural and manmade features in surprising detail. Familiar geographical features like San Francisco Bay, Long Island, and Lake Michigan are easy to recognize, as are many cities, bridges, and airports. The Great Wall of China is not the only manmade object visible from space.

The signatures of civilization are usually seen in straight lines (bridges or runways) or sharp delineations (abrupt transitions from desert to irrigated land, as in California's Imperial Valley). A modern city like New York doesn't leap from the canvas of its surroundings, but its straight piers and concrete runways catch the eye—and around them, the city materializes. I found Salina, Kansas (and pleased my in-laws, who live there) by spotting its long runway amid the wheat fields near the city. Over Florida, I could see the launch pad where we had begun our trip, and the landing strip, where we would eventually land.

Some of civilization's more unfortunate effects on the environment are also evident from orbit. Oil slicks glisten on the surface of the Persian Gulf, patches of pollution-damaged trees dot the forests of central Europe. Some cities look out of focus, and their colors muted, when viewed through a pollutant haze. Not surprisingly, the effects are more noticeable now than they were a decade ago. An astronaut who has flown in both Skylab and the space shuttle reported that the horizon didn't seem quite as sharp, or the colors quite as bright, in 1983 as they had in 1973.

Of course, informal observations by individual astronauts are one thing, but more precise measurements are continually being made from space: The space shuttle has carried infrared film to document damage to citrus trees in Florida and in rain forests along the Amazon. It has carried even more sophisticated sensors in the payload bay. Here is one example: sensors used to measure atmospheric carbon monoxide levels, allowing scientists to study the environmental effects of city emissions and land-clearing fires.

Most of the Earth's surface is covered with water, and at first glance it all looks the same: blue. But with the right lighting conditions and a couple of orbits of practice, it's possible to make out the intricate patterns in the oceans—eddies and spirals become visible because of the subtle differences in water color or reflectivity.

Observations and photographs by astronauts have contributed significantly to the understanding of ocean dynamics, and some of

Literary Analysis
Expository Essay
What point about environmental change does Ride support with her descriptions in this paragraph?

Reading Check

What kinds of structures reveal the "signatures of civilization" from space?

the more intriguing discoveries prompted the National Aeronautics and Space Administration to fly an oceanographic observer for the express purpose of studying the ocean from orbit. Scientists' understanding of the energy balance in the oceans has increased significantly as a result of the discoveries of circular and spiral eddies tens of kilometers in diameter, of standing waves hundreds of kilometers long, and of spiral eddies that sometimes trail into one another for thousands of kilometers. If a scientist wants to study features on this scale, it's much easier from an orbiting vehicle than from the vantage point of a boat.

Believe it or not, an astronaut can also see the wakes of large ships and the contrails of airplanes. The sun angle has to be just right, but when the lighting conditions are perfect, you can follow otherwise invisible oil tankers on the Persian Gulf and trace major shipping lanes through the Mediterranean Sea. Similarly, when atmospheric conditions allow contrail formation, the thousand-mile-long condensation trails let astronauts trace the major air routes across the northern Pacific Ocean.

Part of every orbit takes us to the dark side of the planet. In space, night is very, very black—but that doesn't mean there's

Literary Analysis
Expository Essay
What relationship between space travel and ocean study does Ride identify here?

Literature in Context   Science Connection

The Changing Planet: Continental Drift

350 million years ago

54.8 to 33.7 million years ago

38 to 1.6 million years ago

- The continents were once part of a massive land mass.

- This land mass, named Pangea, started drifting apart 300 hundred million years ago.

- The continents are still moving a few inches farther apart each year.

The southern hemisphere "drifting" through time

Africa   India   Australia   Antarctica   South America

The Evidence:
Plants and animals in North America and Europe are very similar. Fossils from southern continents show that dinosaurs once roamed the entire area. In Africa and South America, 200-million-year-old matching lava has been found.

Connect to the Literature   The theories of plate tectonics and continental drift state that the Earth's crust is made of shifting "plates." What evidence for these theories might an astronaut see from space?

nothing to look at. The lights of cities sparkle; on nights when there was no moon, it was difficult for me to tell the Earth from the sky—the twinkling lights could be stars or they could be small cities. On one nighttime pass from Cuba to Nova Scotia, the entire East Coast of the United States appeared in twinkling outline.

When the moon is full, it casts an eerie light on the Earth. In its light, we see ghostly clouds and bright reflections on the water. One night, the Mississippi River flashed into view, and because of our viewing angle and orbital path, the reflected moonlight seemed to flow downstream—as if Huck Finn had tied a candle to his raft.

Of all the sights from orbit, the most spectacular may be the magnificent displays of lightning that ignite the clouds at night. On Earth, we see lightning from below the clouds; in orbit, we see it from above. Bolts of lightning are <u>diffused</u> by the clouds into bursting balls of light. Sometimes, when a storm extends hundreds of miles, it looks like a transcontinental brigade is tossing fireworks from cloud to cloud.

As the shuttle races the sun around the Earth, we pass from day to night and back again during a single orbit—hurtling into darkness, then bursting into daylight. The sun's appearance unleashes spectacular blue and orange bands along the horizon, a clockwork miracle that astronauts witness every 90 minutes. But I really can't describe a sunrise in orbit. The drama set against the black backdrop of space and the magic of the materializing colors can't be captured in an astronomer's equations or an astronaut's photographs.

I once heard someone (not an astronaut) suggest that it's possible to imagine what spaceflight is like by simply <u>extrapolating</u> from the sensations you experience on an airplane. All you have to do, he said, is mentally raise the airplane 200 miles, mentally eliminate the air noise and the turbulence, and you get an accurate mental picture of a trip in the space shuttle.

Not true. And while it's natural to try to liken spaceflight to familiar experiences, it can't be brought "down to Earth"—not in the final sense. The environment is different, the perspective is different. Part of the fascination with space travel is the element of the unknown—the conviction that it's different from earthbound experiences. And it is.

Vocabulary Builder
diffused (di fyo͞ozd´) *v.*
spread out

extrapolating
(ek strap´ ə lāt´ iŋ) *v.*
arriving at a conclusion
by inferring from known
facts

Apply the Skills

Single Room, Earth View

Thinking About the Selection

1. **Respond:** Based on Sally Ride's description of her experiences in space, would you like to be an astronaut? Why or why not?
2. **(a) Recall:** Which geological features did Ride observe from orbit? **(b) Interpret:** Why do you think Ride found it easier to imagine the workings of geological forces when she saw Earth from space?
3. **(a) Recall:** What "unfortunate effects" does Ride say she could see as she orbited the Earth? **(b) Analyze:** Why would these effects make colors seen in 1983 seem not as bright as those seen ten years earlier?
4. **Assess:** Have Ride's descriptions of Earth changed the way you think about our planet? Explain your answer.

Literary Analysis

5. What is the topic of Sally Ride's **expository essay?**
6. What scientific data does Ride use to make information clear to her readers?
7. **(a)** Using a chart like the one shown, identify passages in which Ride uses **description, comparison and contrast,** or **cause and effect.** Find one example of each technique. **(b)** Explain how each example adds depth and context to the information Ride presents in that passage.

	Example	Effect
Description		
Comparison/Contrast		
Cause and Effect		

Reading Skill

8. State the **main idea** of the essay "Single Room, Earth View" in your own words.
9. **(a)** List three **supporting details** that serve as evidence for the points that Sally Ride makes in her essay. **(b)** Do you think the author adequately supports her main idea with details? Why or why not?

QuickReview

Essay at a Glance
The first American woman in space explains what can be seen and understood about Earth from the perspective of space.

Go Online
—Assessment
For: Self-test
Visit: www.PHSchool.com
Web Code: epa-6305

Expository Essay: a short piece of nonfiction that presents information, discusses ideas, or explains a process. Writers can use *description, comparison and contrast,* and *cause and effect* to support ideas

Main Idea: the central message, insight, or opinion in a work of nonfiction

Supporting Details: the pieces of evidence that a writer uses to prove a main idea

Vocabulary Builder

Practice Review the vocabulary list for "Single Room, Earth View" on page 424. Then, identify the word in each group that does not belong with the others and explain your response.

1. articulate, eloquent, unclear
2. novice, seasoned, veteran
3. diffused, shared, withheld
4. extrapolating, rational, random

Adding Words to Your Vocabulary Using a thesaurus, find an **antonym,** or word of opposite meaning, for each vocabulary word. Use each antonym in a sentence that makes the meaning of the word clear. (For more on using a thesaurus, see page R7.)

Writing

Write the **script** for a commercial or public service announcement that NASA might use to attract candidates for astronaut training.
- Based on the Sally Ride essay, jot down details that might appeal to astronaut candidates.
- Describe visual elements that would attract candidates.
- In your script, include one direct quotation from Ride's essay, and describe the visual that would go with it.

For *Grammar, Vocabulary,* and *Assessment,* see **Build Language Skills,** pp. 444–445.

Extend Your Learning

Listening and Speaking In a group, study photographs of Earth taken from space and give an **informal presentation** to share the images with the rest of your class.
- Identify what natural features are shown in each photo.
- Point out "signatures of civilization" that the photos reveal.

As you present, pause occasionally to summarize and evaluate your conclusions.

Research and Technology Use library and Internet resources, including NASA's Web site, to research the training that astronauts undergo for space flight. Based on this information, write two **journal entries** that an astronaut might write while in training.

Build Language Skills

Single Room, Earth View • The News

Vocabulary Skill

Prefixes The **prefix** *equi-* means "equal." The prefix is contained in the word *equivalent,* which means "equal in meaning." In the field of mathematics, the prefix *-equi-* is used in the words *equilateral* and *equidistant* as a verbal reinforcement of a mathematical concept.

▶ **Example:** Her stony stare was the *equivalent* of a severe lecture on the importance of being punctual.

Practice All of the following words begin with the prefix *equi-*. Predict the meaning of each word. Check your definition in a dictionary. Then, use each word in an original sentence.

1. equidistant
2. equitable
3. equilateral
4. equivocal

Grammar Lesson

Predicate Nominatives and Predicate Adjectives A **predicate nominative** renames the subject of the sentence. The predicate nominative comes after a linking verb and renames, identifies, or explains the subject of the sentence. In a sentence with a predicate nominative, the linking verb acts as an equal sign between the subject and the predicate nominative.

▶ **Example:** The winner of the tournament is our **team**. *Team* renames *winner.*

A **predicate adjective** is an adjective that appears with a linking verb and *describes* the subject of the sentence.

▶ **Example:** The swimmer was *fast*. *Fast* describes *swimmer.*

Practice Circle and label the predicate nominative or predicate adjective in the following sentences. Then, use the predicate nominative or predicate adjective in a new sentence.

1. Swimming is good for strengthening muscles.
2. A sport is physical exertion for recreation or competition.
3. About 5,000 years ago, wrestling was essentially a survival skill.
4. The butterfly stroke appears graceful.
5. The winner of the tournament is our team.

MorePractice

For more practice with adjectives, see the Grammar Handbook, p. R40.

𝒲𝒢 Prentice Hall Writing and Grammar Connection: Chapter 20, Section 3

Reading Skill: Main Idea and Supporting Details

Directions: *Read the selection. Then, answer the questions.*

Standards Assessed

• IR.2.04.1
• IR.2.04.3
• WL.1.01.2

In the 1960s, however, the FCC began to impose regulations. Responding to complaints from over-the-air broadcasters that cable stations were refusing to carry local stations, the FCC ruled that every cable system had to carry the programs of all local stations as well as those of their own.

By the 1970s, the FCC began to impose more regulations. The agency mandated that cable systems provide at least twenty channels and obtain public approval of changes in their rates. In the 1980s, the FCC ruled that rates for cable services would be deregulated.

1. A detail that is **not** necessary to support the main idea of the passage is
   A "During the 1950s, the . . . FCC maintained a 'hands off' policy."
   B "The FCC ruled that every cable system. . . ."
   C "By the 1970s, the FCC began to impose more regulations."
   D "In the 1980s, the FCC ruled that rates for cable services would be deregulated."

2. Which detail's repetition signals that it should be part of the main idea?
   A the repetition of dates
   B the repetition of the word "channels"
   C the repetition of the word "ruled"
   D the repetition of the word "agency"

3. Which detail supports the main idea of the passage?
   A "The FCC began to impose . . . ."
   B "had to carry the programs. . . ."
   C "Cable systems provide. . . ."
   D "Complaints from . . ."

4. Which of the following is a main idea of the passage?
   A Cable systems need to be more accessible.
   B There has been a decrease in regulation of cable services.
   C The current cable industry seeks more control of the FCC.
   D The FCC has increasingly regulated the cable industry.

Timed Writing: Explanation

Review "Single Room, Earth View" or "The News." Explain how a different view can affect someone's attitude. State your thesis clearly, include examples, and explain how and why attitudes change. **(25 minutes)**

Writing Workshop: *Work in Progress*

Business Letter

From your writing portfolio, review the list of questions you generated. Answer each question using specific evidence: facts, dates, and examples. Formulate each answer to be clear and precise.

Reading Informational Materials

Technical Documents

In Part 1, you are learning how to identify the main idea and supporting details in literature. This skill is also useful when you read informational materials, such as journal articles or technical documents. Finding the main idea and supporting details helps you gather information more quickly and precisely. If you read Sally Ride's essay, "Single Room, Earth View," you may have wanted to know more about the space shuttle. The technical document that follows gives data and other information about this vehicle.

About Technical Documents

Technical documents provide detailed information on the use, construction, or design of items that are engineered or built. They often include these elements:

- descriptions of the item and its features
- explanations of what the item can do and how it performs under a range of conditions
- numeric data or specifications, such as size, weight, and measurements of performance
- descriptions of materials used to make the item
- diagrams and other graphics

Reading Skill

When you read technical documents, you are often **reading for specific information.** Diagrams, headings, labels, and a variety of visual features included in the document help lead you to the information you need. As you read, use a chart like the one shown to note the kinds of information you discover by using different features of the document.

Type of Information	Examples	Information Provided
Narrative text		
Diagrams	diagram of shuttle	parts of the shuttle launch configuration
Lists or Statistics		

Standard Course of Study

- Incorporate effective media and technology to inform about research. (IR.2.04.3)
- Select, monitor, and modify reading strategies appropriate to argumentative texts. (FA.3.04.1)

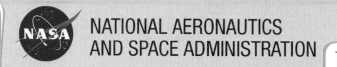

NATIONAL AERONAUTICS AND SPACE ADMINISTRATION

Shuttle Statistics

Length
Space Shuttle:
56.14 meters (184.2 feet)
Orbiter:
37.23 meters (122.17 feet)

Height
Orbiter on runway:
17.27 meters (56.67 feet)

Wingspan
23.79 meters (78.06 feet)

Weight*
At liftoff: 2,041,166 kilograms
(4.5 million pounds)

End of mission: 104,326 kilograms
(230,000 pounds)

Maximum cargo to orbit
28,803 kilograms (63,500 pounds)

SRB Separation
Two minutes after launch

External Tank Separation
8.5 minutes after launch

Altitude: 109.26 kilometers
59 nautical miles)

Velocity: 28,067 kph (17,440 mph)

Orbit
185 to 643 kilometers
(115 to 400 statute miles)

Velocity: 27,875 kph (17,321 mph)

*weight will vary depending on pay-
loads and on board consumables.

Space Shuttle Basics

The space shuttle is the world's first reusable spacecraft, and the first spacecraft in history that can carry large satellites both to and from orbit. The shuttle launches like a rocket, maneuvers in Earth orbit like a spacecraft and lands like an airplane. Each of the three space shuttle orbiters now in operation -- Discovery, Atlantis and Endeavour -- is designed to fly at least 100 missions. So far, altogether they have flown a combined total of less than one-fourth of that.

Columbia was the first space shuttle orbiter to be delivered to NASA's Kennedy Space Center, Fla., in March 1979. Columbia and the STS-107 crew were lost Feb. 1, 2003, during re-entry. The orbiter Challenger was delivered to KSC in July 1982 and was destroyed in an explosion during ascent in January 1986. Discovery was delivered in November 1983. Atlantis was delivered in April 1985. Endeavour was built as a replacement following the Challenger accident and was delivered to Florida in May 1991. An early space shuttle orbiter, the Enterprise, never flew in space but was used for approach and landing tests at the Dryden Flight Research Center and several launch pad studies in the late 1970s.

The space shuttle consists of three major components: the orbiter which houses the crew; a large external fuel tank that holds fuel for the main engines; and two solid rocket boosters which provide most of the shuttle's lift during the first two minutes of flight. All of the components are reused except for the external fuel tank, which burns up in the atmosphere after each launch.

Space Shuttle
(launch configuration)

External Tank

Solid Rocket Booster

Solid Rocket Booster

Orbiter

orbiter flight configuration
(w/satellite in payload bay)

The longest the shuttle has stayed in orbit on any single mission is 17.5 days on mission STS-80 in November 1996. Normally, missions may be planned for anywhere from five to 16 days in duration. The smallest crew ever to fly on the shuttle numbered two people on the first few missions. The largest crew numbered eight people. Normally, crews may range in size from five to seven people. The shuttle is designed to reach orbits ranging from about 185 kilometers to 643 kilometers (115 statute miles to 400 statute miles) high.

The shuttle has the most reliable launch record of any rocket now in operation. Since 1981, it has boosted more than 1.36 million kilograms (3 million pounds) of cargo into orbit. More than 600 crew members have flown on its missions. Although it has been in operation for almost 20 years, the shuttle has continually evolved and is significantly different today than when it first was launched. NASA has made literally thousands of major and minor modifications to the original design that have made it safer, more reliable and more capable today than ever before.

Since 1992 alone, NASA has made engine and system improvements that are estimated to have tripled the safety of flying the space shuttle, and the number of problems experienced while a space shuttle is in flight has decreased by 70 percent. During the same period, the cost of operating the shuttle has decreased by one and a quarter billion dollars annually — a reduction of more than 40 percent. At the same time, because of weight reductions and other improvements, the cargo the shuttle can carry has increased by 7.3 metric tons (8 tons.)

NASA is prepared to continue flying the shuttle for at least the next decade and plans to continue to improve the shuttle during the next five years, with goals of increasing its safety by improving the highest-risk components. NASA will also be working with the Columbia Accident Investigation Board to correct any problems the board may find as it works to determine the cause of the Columbia accident.

In managing and operating the space shuttle, NASA holds the safety of the crew as its highest priority.

Reading: Reading for Specific Information

Directions: *Choose the letter of the best answer to each question about "Space Shuttle Basics."*

Standards Assessed

- IR.2.02.5
- IR.2.03.2
- CT.4.03.1

1. Which space orbiters are now in use for space flights?
   A Discovery, Atlantis, and Endeavour
   B Columbia, Atlantis, and Enterprise
   C Challenger, Discovery, and Atlantis
   D Discovery, Atlantis, and Enterprise

2. What is the highest orbit the shuttle is designed to reach?
   A 185 kilometers
   B 185 statute miles
   C 400 kilometers
   D 400 statute miles

3. What is the shuttle's wingspan?
   A 56.24 meters
   B 37.23 meters
   C 17.27 meters
   D 23.79 meters

Reading: Comprehension and Interpretation

Directions: *Write your answers on a separate piece of paper.*

4. Why do you think the writer discusses the shuttle's launch record and design improvements? [**Generating**]

5. The writer of "Space Shuttle Basics" describes the external tank, the solid rocket boosters, and the orbiter. Why do you think the writer also provides a diagram of the shuttle showing these parts? [**Generating**]

Timed Writing: Exposition [Connections]

Review the "Shuttle Statistics" given in "Space Shuttle Basics." Then, explain the purpose and use of statistics or other numerical data in informational text. What is the benefit of providing this information numerically rather than as a running narrative? What is the benefit of providing numerical data in a list or chart form? Use details from "Space Shuttle Basics" in your answer. Make connections between the way the information is presented and the purposes for which it will probably be used. **(30 minutes)**

Comparing Literary Works • Biographical Writing

Biographical Writing

Biographical writing is a form of nonfiction in which a writer tells the life story of another person. Biographies are often written about historical figures, but they are also written about modern-day people. The best biographies do not just list the facts, events, or accomplishments in the subject's life. Although factual information is important, the author of a good biography presents an interpretation of those pieces of information. The biographer shows why an understanding of the subject's life is meaningful to readers.

Standard Course of Study

- Use reading strategies for preparation, engagement, reflection. (LT.5.01.1)
- Recognize and analyze the characteristics of literary genres. (LT.5.01.2)

Comparing Biographical Writing

In biographical writing, the details that an author chooses to describe help create our impression of the subject. Biographies often focus on one or all of the following aspects of a subject's life:

- personality
- relationships with family and others
- life events
- upbringing
- role in major social or historical events
- influence on others

Because biographies present the lives of real rather than fictional people, it is important that the biographer meet the highest standards of *ethics and truthfulness*. While he or she may interpret the facts and events of the subject's life, that interpretation must be reasonable and well supported. Using an organizer like the one shown, note details in these selections that describe specific aspects of each subject's life.

	Lincoln	Ashe
Personality		
Upbringing		
Relationships		
Life events		
Role in major events		
Influence on others		

Vocabulary Builder

from A Lincoln Preface

- **despotic** (des pät´ ik) *adj.* like an absolute ruler or tyrant (p. 453) *In a despotic move, the leader of the country abolished civil rights.*

- **censure** (sen´ shər) *n.* strong disapproval (p. 456) *The defeated candidate felt the censure of the voters.*

- **droll** (drōl) *adj.* funny in an odd way (p. 458) *While he did not laugh, he found the movie droll.*

Arthur Ashe Remembered

- **legacy** (leg´ ə sē) *n.* something handed down from an ancestor (p. 461) *The painter's legacy to her children was her love of art.*

- **enigma** (i nig´ mə) *n.* mystery (p. 461) *The cloaked and masked figure remains an enigma to us.*

- **lithe** (līth) *adj.* flexible (p. 462) *He has the lithe body of a swimmer.*

Build Understanding

Connecting to the Literature

Reading/Writing Connection The authors of these selections paint portraits of remarkable human beings. List some of the qualities that make a person special. Use at least three of the following words in your response: *commit, enrich, pursue, exceed, devote.*

Meet the Authors

Carl **Sandburg** (1878–1967)

Between the ages of thirteen and twenty, Carl Sandburg worked as a porter, scene changer, truck handler, dishwasher, and farm worker. Sandburg served briefly in Puerto Rico during the Spanish-American War, which brought on the strong anti-war feelings he would hold throughout his life.

Childhood Favorite Even as a child, Sandburg was fascinated by Abraham Lincoln. For thirty years, he collected material about Lincoln, and his single-mindedness paid off. Sandburg's six-volume work of Lincoln is considered the definitive biography of the former president.

John **McPhee** (b. 1931)

John McPhee's big break as a writer came in 1965, when *The New Yorker* magazine published his profile of Princeton basketball star Bill Bradley. That profile, which became the basis for McPhee's first book, combined two of the author's great loves: sports and his home town of Princeton, New Jersey, where he still lives today.

Broader Interests McPhee continues to write about sports, but he has broadened his subject matter to include the natural world, with books on Alaska, whales, and the birch-bark canoe. In recognition of his extraordinary prose, McPhee has won many important honors, including a Pulitzer Prize.

Go **Online**
Author Link

For: More about the authors
Visit: www.PHSchool.com
Web Code: epe-9307

from A Lincoln Preface
Carl Sandburg

▲ **Critical Viewing** Does this painting portray Lincoln as a man of great power? Explain. **[Make a Judgment]**

Lincoln Proclaiming Thanksgiving, Dean Cornwell, The Lincoln Museum, Fort Wayne, Indiana

Background

Ever since the birth of the United States in 1776, the issue of slavery had troubled the nation. Each time a new state entered the Union, congress debated fiercely over whether it would be a slaveholding or free state. In 1860, when Abraham Lincoln was elected president, he refused to support any Congressional proposal that would allow for new slave states. The southern slaveholding states resolved to fight to keep new states open to slavery. This conflict led to the outbreak of the Civil War in April 1861.

In the time of the April lilacs in the year 1865, a man in the City of Washington, D.C., trusted a guard to watch at a door, and the guard was careless, left the door, and the man was shot, lingered a night, passed away, was laid in a box, and carried north and west a thousand miles; bells sobbed; cities wore crepe;[1] people stood with hats off as the railroad burial car came past at midnight, dawn or noon.

During the four years of time before he gave up the ghost, this man was clothed with <u>despotic</u> power, commanding the most powerful armies till then assembled in modern warfare, enforcing drafts of soldiers, abolishing the right of habeas corpus,[2] directing politically and spiritually the wild, massive forces loosed in civil war.

Four billion dollars' worth of property was taken from those who had been legal owners of it, confiscated, wiped out as by fire, at his instigation and executive direction; a class of chattel[3] property recognized as lawful for two hundred years went to the scrap pile.

---

1. crepe (krāp) *n.* thin, black cloth worn to show mourning.
2. habeas corpus (hā´ bē əs kôr´ pəs) right of an imprisoned person to have a court hearing.
3. chattel (chat´´l) *n.* a movable item of personal property.

Vocabulary Builder
despotic (des pät´ ik) *adj.* like an absolute ruler or tyrant

Reading Check

What violent event happened in April 1865?

When the woman who wrote *Uncle Tom's Cabin*[4] came to see him in the White House, he greeted her, "So you're the little woman who wrote the book that made this great war," and as they seated themselves at a fireplace, "I do love an open fire: I always had one at home." As they were finishing their talk of the days of blood, he said, "I shan't last long after it's over."

An Illinois Congressman looked in on him as he had his face lathered for a shave in the White House and remarked, "If anybody had told me that in a great crisis like this the people were going out to a little one-horse town and pick out a one-horse lawyer for president, I wouldn't have believed it." The answer was, "Neither would I. But it was a time when a man with a policy would have been fatal to the country. I never had a policy. I have simply tried to do what seemed best each day, as each day came."

"I don't intend precisely to throw the Constitution overboard, but I will stick it in a hole if I can," he told a Cabinet officer. The enemy was violating the Constitution to destroy the Union, he argued, and therefore, "I will violate the Constitution, if necessary, to save the Union." He instructed a messenger to the Secretary of the Treasury, "Tell him not to bother himself about the Constitution. Say that I have that sacred instrument here at the White House, and I am guarding it with great care."

When he was renominated, it was by the device of seating delegates from Tennessee, which gave enough added votes to seat favorable delegates from Kentucky, Missouri, Louisiana, Arkansas, and from one county in Florida. Until late in that campaign of 1864, he expected to lose the November election; military victories brought the tide his way; the vote was 2,200,000 for him and 1,800,000 against him. Among those who bitterly fought him politically, and accused him of blunders or crimes, were Franklin Pierce, a former president of the United States; Horatio Seymour, the Governor of New York; Samuel F. B. Morse, inventor of the telegraph; Cyrus H. McCormick, inventor of the farm reaper; General George B. McClellan, a Democrat who had commanded the Army of the

▲ **Critical Viewing**
What impression of Lincoln does this painting convey? **[Describe]**

---

4. woman . . . Cabin Harriet Beecher Stowe (1811–1896), whose novel stirred up opinion against slavery.

Potomac; and the *Chicago Times,* a daily newspaper. In all its essential propositions the Southern Confederacy had the moral support of powerful, respectable elements throughout the North, probably more than a million votes believing in the justice of the cause of the South as compared with the North.

While propagandas raged, and the war winds howled, he sat in the White House, the Stubborn Man of History, writing that the Mississippi was one river and could not belong to two countries, that the plans for railroad connection from coast to coast must be pushed through and the Union Pacific[5] realized.

His life, mind and heart ran in contrasts. When his white kid gloves broke into tatters while shaking hands at a White House reception, he remarked, "This looks like a general bustification." When he talked with an Ohio friend one day during the 1864 campaign, he mentioned one public man, and murmured, "He's a thistle! I don't see why God lets him live." Of a devious Senator, he said, "He's too crooked to lie still!" And of a New York editor, "In early life in the West, we used to make our shoes last a great while with much mending, and sometimes, when far gone, we found the leather so rotten the stitches would not hold. Greeley is so rotten that nothing can be done with him. He is not truthful; the stitches all tear out." As he sat in the telegraph office of the War Department, reading cipher dispatches, and came to the words, Hosanna and Husband, he would chuckle, "Jeffy D.,"[6] and at the words, Hunter and Happy, "Bobby Lee."[7]

While the luck of war wavered and broke and came again, as generals failed and campaigns were lost, he held enough forces of the Union together to raise new armies and supply them, until generals were found who made war as victorious war has always been made, with terror, frightfulness, destruction, and valor and sacrifice past words of man to tell.

A slouching, gray-headed poet,[8] haunting the hospitals at Washington, characterized him as "the grandest figure on the crowded canvas of the drama of the nineteenth century—a Hoosier Michael Angelo."[9]

His own speeches, letters, telegrams and official messages during that war form the most significant and enduring document from any one man on why the war began, why it went on, and the dangers beyond its end. He mentioned "the politicians," over and again

Literary Analysis
Biographical Writing Which details present Lincoln as strong in the face of opposition? Explain.

Reading Check

Under what circumstances was Lincoln willing to violate the Constitution?

---

5. Union Pacific railroad chartered by Congress in 1862 to form part of a transcontinental system.
6. "Jeffy D." Jefferson Davis (1808–1889), president of the Confederacy.
7. "Bobby Lee" Robert E. Lee (1807–1870), commander in chief of the Confederate army.
8. slouching . . . poet Walt Whitman (1819–1892).
9. Michael Angelo Michelangelo (mī′ kəl an′ jə lō′) (1475–1564) famous Italian artist.

"the politicians," with scorn and blame. As the platoons filed before him at a review of an army corps, he asked, "What is to become of these boys when the war is over?"

He was a chosen spokesman: yet there were times he was silent; nothing but silence could at those times have fitted a chosen spokesman; in the mixed shame and blame of the immense wrongs of two crashing civilizations, with nothing to say, he said nothing, slept not at all, and wept at those times in a way that made weeping appropriate, decent, majestic.

His hat was shot off as he rode alone one night in Washington; a son he loved died as he watched at the bed; his wife was accused of betraying information to the enemy, until denials from him were necessary; his best companion was a fine-hearted and brilliant son with a deformed palate and an impediment of speech; when a Pennsylvania Congressman told him the enemy had declared they would break into the city and hang him to a lamp-post, he said he had considered "the violent preliminaries" to such a scene; on his left thumb was a scar where an ax had nearly chopped the thumb off when he was a boy; over one eye was a scar where he had been hit with a club in the hands of a man trying to steal the cargo off a Mississippi River flatboat; he threw a cashiered[10] officer out of his room in the White House, crying, "I can bear <u>censure</u>, but not insult. I never wish to see your face again."

As he shook hands with the correspondent of the London *Times*, he drawled, "Well, I guess the London *Times* is about the greatest power on earth—unless perhaps it is the Mississippi River." He rebuked with anger a woman who got on her knees to thank him for a pardon that saved her son from being shot at sunrise; and when an Iowa woman said she had journeyed out of her way to Washington just for a look at him, he grinned, "Well, in the matter of looking at one another, I have altogether the advantage."

He asked his Cabinet to vote on the high military command, and after the vote, told them the appointment had already been made; one Cabinet officer, who had been governor of Ohio, came away personally baffled and frustrated from an interview, to exclaim, to a private secretary, "That man is the most cunning person I ever saw in my life"; an Illinois lawyer who had been sent on errands carrying his political secrets, said, "He is a trimmer[11] and such a trimmer as the world has never seen."

He manipulated the admission of Nevada as a state in the Union, when her votes were needed for the Emancipation Proclamation, saying, "It is easier to admit Nevada than to raise another million of

---

10. **cashiered** (ka shird´) *adj.* dishonorably discharged.
11. **trimmer** (trim´ ər) *n.* person who changes his or her opinion to suit the circumstances.

soldiers." At the same time he went to the office of a former New York editor, who had become Assistant Secretary of War, and said the votes of three congressmen were wanted for the required three-quarters of votes in the House of Representatives, advising, "There are three that you can deal with better than anybody else. . . . Whatever promise you make to those men, I will perform it." And in the same week, he said to a Massachusetts politician that two votes were lacking, and, "Those two votes must be procured. I leave it to you to determine how it shall be done; but remember that I am President of the United States and clothed with immense power, and I expect you to procure those votes." And while he was thus employing every last resource and device of practical politics to constitutionally abolish slavery, the abolitionist[12] Henry Ward Beecher attacked him with javelins of scorn and detestation in a series of editorials that brought from him the single comment, "Is thy servant a dog?"

When the King of Siam sent him a costly sword of exquisite embellishment, and two elephant tusks, along with letters and a photograph of the King, he acknowledged the gifts in a manner as lavish as the Orientals. Addressing the King of Siam as "Great and Good Friend," he wrote thanks for each of the gifts, including "also two elephant's tusks of length and magnitude, such as indicate they could have belonged only to an animal which was a native of Siam." After further thanks for the tokens received, he closed the letter to the King of Siam with strange grace and humor, saying, "I appreciate most highly your Majesty's tender of good offices in forwarding to this Government a stock from which a supply of elephants might be raised on our soil. . . our political jurisdiction, however, does not reach a latitude so low as to favor the multiplication of the elephant, and steam on land as well as water has been our best agent of transportation . . . . Meantime, wishing for your Majesty a long and happy life, and, for the generous and emulous people of Siam, the highest possible prosperity, I commend both to the blessing of Almighty God."

He sent hundreds of telegrams, "Suspend death sentence" or "Suspend execution" of So-and-So, who was to be shot at sunrise.

Reading Check

Who was Lincoln's best companion?

---

12. abolitionist (ab´ ə lish´ ən ist) *n.* person in favor of doing away with slavery in the United States.

The telegrams varied oddly at times, as in one, "If Thomas Samplogh, of the First Delaware Regiment, has been sentenced to death, and is not yet executed, suspend and report the case to me." And another, "Is it Lieut. Samuel B. Davis whose death sentence is commuted? If not done, let it be done."

While the war drums beat, he liked best of all the stories told of him, one of two Quakeresses[13] heard talking in a railway car. "I think that Jefferson will succeed." "Why does thee think so?" "Because Jefferson is a praying man." "And so is Abraham a praying man." "Yes, but the Lord will think Abraham is joking."

An Indiana man at the White House heard him say, "Voorhees, don't it seem strange to you that I, who could never so much as cut off the head of a chicken, should be elected, or selected, into the midst of all this blood?"

A party of American citizens, standing in the ruins of the Forum in Rome, Italy, heard there the news of the first assassination of the first American dictator, and took it as a sign of the growing up and the aging of the civilization on the North American continent. Far out in Coles County, Illinois, a beautiful, gaunt old woman in a log cabin said, "I knowed he'd never come back."

Of men taking too fat profits out of the war, he said, "Where the carcass is there will the eagles be gathered together."

An enemy general, Longstreet, after the war, declared him to have been "the one matchless man in forty millions of people," while one of his private secretaries, Hay, declared his life to have been the most perfect in its relationships and adjustments since that of Christ.

Between the days in which he crawled as a baby on the dirt floor of a Kentucky cabin, and the time when he gave his final breath in Washington, he packed a rich life with work, thought, laughter, tears, hate, love.

With vast reservoirs of the comic and the <u>droll</u>, and notwithstanding a mastery of mirth and nonsense, he delivered a volume of addresses and letters of terrible and serious appeal, with import beyond his own day, shot through here and there with far, thin ironics, with paragraphs having raillery[14] of the quality of the Book of Job,[15] and echoes as subtle as the whispers of wind in prairie grass.

Perhaps no human clay pot has held more laughter and tears.

The facts and myths of his life are to be an American possession, shared widely over the world, for thousands of years, as the

---

13. **Quakeresses** (kwā′ kər es əz) *n.* female members of the religious group known as the Society of Friends, or Quakers.
14. **raillery** (rā′ lər ē) *n.* good-natured teasing.
15. **Book of Job** (jōb) *n.* book of the Old Testament in which Job is tested by God.

Literary Analysis
Biographical Writing What do you learn about Lincoln from the statement overheard by an Indiana man?

Vocabulary Builder
droll (drōl) *adj.* funny in an odd way

tradition of Knute or Alfred, Lao-tse or Diogenes, Pericles or Caesar,[16] are kept. This because he was not only a genius in the science of neighborly human relationships and an artist in the personal handling of life from day to day, but a strange friend and a friendly stranger to all forms of life that he met.

He lived fifty-six years of which fifty-two were lived in the West— the prairie years.

---

16. **Knute** (knō͞ot) **or Alfred, Lao-tse** (lou´ dzu´) **or Diogenes** (dī äj´ ə nēz´), **Pericles** (per´ ə klēz´) **or Caesar** (sē´ zər) well-known thinkers and leaders from different eras and places.

Literary Analysis
Biographical Writing According to Sandburg, what personal qualities make Lincoln a great historical figure?

Thinking About the Selection

1. **Respond:** Which story about Lincoln interested you the most? Why?

2. **(a) Recall:** To whom did Lincoln refer as "the little woman who wrote the book that made this great war"? **(b) Infer:** Why do you think Lincoln wanted to meet with this woman? **(c) Draw Conclusions:** What does Lincoln's interest in meeting this woman say about his character?

3. **(a) Recall:** How did Lincoln justify admitting Nevada to the Union? **(b) Connect:** What other examples of Lincoln's "practical" politics does the author note? **(c) Make a Judgment:** Does Sandburg seem to admire this aspect of Lincoln's character? Explain.

4. **(a) Recall:** According to Sandburg, what aspects of Lincoln's life will be "an American possession, shared widely over the world"? **(b) Interpret:** What does Sandburg mean by this comment?

5. **Evaluate:** Do you think Lincoln was justified in violating the Constitution to save the Union? Why or why not?

6. **Assess:** Sandburg says that Lincoln "packed a rich life with work, thought, laughter, tears, hate, and love." Do you think Sandburg provides examples of all of these qualities in this introduction to his biography of Lincoln?

Arthur Ashe Remembered

John McPhee

▲ **Critical Viewing** Based on this photograph, what emotions did Ashe express when he won the Wimbledon Championship in 1975? **[Assess]**

Background   Arthur Ashe was the first African American man to achieve greatness in tennis. When he was six years old, his mother died of heart disease. Ashe's father worked as a caretaker in a neighborhood park, where Ashe spent hours playing on the tennis courts. Ashe went on to win numerous honors in tennis, including the 1968 U.S. Open and the 1975 Wimbledon singles championship. Throughout his life, Ashe devoted himself to issues of human rights, education, and public health. After struggling with heart problems, he contracted AIDS from a transfusion during by-pass surgery. He founded the Arthur Ashe Foundation for the Defeat of AIDS before his death in 1993.

He once described his life as "a succession of fortunate circumstances." He was in his twenties then. More than half of his life was behind him. His memory of his mother was confined to a single image: in a blue corduroy bathrobe she stood in a doorway looking out on the courts and playing fields surrounding their house, which stood in the center of a Richmond playground. Weakened by illness, she was taken to a hospital that day, and died at the age of twenty-seven. He was six.

It was to be his tragedy, as the world knows, that he would leave his own child when she was six, that his life would be trapped in a medical irony as a result of early heart disease, and death would come to him prematurely, as it had to his mother.

His mother was tall, with long soft hair and a face that was gentle and thin. She read a lot. She read a lot to him. His father said of her, "She was just like Arthur Junior. She never argued. She was quiet, easygoing, kindhearted."

If by <u>legacy</u> her son never argued, he was also schooled, instructed, coached not to argue, and as he moved alone into alien country he fashioned not-arguing into an <u>enigma</u> and turned the enigma into a weapon. When things got tough (as I noted in these pages twenty-four years ago[1]), he had control. Even in very tight moments, other players thought he was toying with them. They rarely knew what he was thinking. They could not tell if he was angry. It was maddening, sometimes, to play against him. Never less than candid, he said that what he liked best about himself on a tennis court was his demeanor: "What it is is controlled cool, in a way. Always have the situation under control, even if losing. Never betray an inward sense of defeat."

---

1. twenty-four years ago McPhee refers to an article published in 1969.

Vocabulary Builder
legacy (leg´ ə sē) *n.* something handed down from an ancestor
enigma (i nig´ mə) *n.* mystery

Reading Check

What personality trait did Ashe share with his mother?

And of course he never did—not in the height of his athletic power, not in the statesmanship of the years that followed, and not in the endgame of his existence. If you wished to choose a single image, you would see him standing there in his twenties, his <u>lithe</u> body a braid of cables, his energy without apparent limit, in a court situation indescribably bad, and all he does is put his index finger on the bridge of his glasses and push them back up the bridge of his nose. In the shadow of disaster, he hits out. Faced with a choice between a conservative, percentage return or a one-in-ten flat-out blast, he chooses the blast. In a signature manner, he extends his left arm to point upward at lobs as they fall toward him. His over-heads, in fire bursts, put them away. His backhand is, if anything, stronger than his forehand, and his shots from either side for the most part are explosions. In motions graceful and decisive, though, and with reactions as fast as the imagination, he is a master of drop shots, of cat-and-mouse, of miscellaneous dinks and chips and (riskiest of all) the crosscourt half-volley. Other tennis players might be wondering who in his right mind would attempt something like that, but that is how Ashe plays the game: at the tensest moment, he goes for the all but impossible. He is predictably unpredictable. He is unreadable. His ballistic serves move in odd patterns and come off the court in unexpected ways. Behind his impassive face—behind the enigmatic glasses, the lifted chin, the first-mate-on-the-bridge look—there seems to be, even from this distance, a smile.

Literary Analysis
Biographical Writing How does this description of Ashe's tennis game portray his ability to remain calm and in control?

Thinking About the Selection

1. **Respond:** What did you find most interesting about Arthur Ashe? Explain.

2. **(a) Recall:** According to his father, how was Ashe like his mother?
   (b) Summarize: What does Ashe say he likes best about himself on the court? **(c) Draw Conclusions:** Based on this article, how would you describe Ashe's character?

3. **(a) Recall:** How did Ashe once describe his life?
   (b) Make a Judgment: Does this description seem accurate based on the information in this biography?

4. **(a) Summarize:** Summarize Ashe's approach to tennis. **(b) Apply:** In what ways might Ashe's approach to tennis be seen as an approach to life?

Apply the Skills

Comparing Biographical Writing

1. Identify at least three facts that each author includes about his subject. Then, explain what each fact shows about the subject.

2. **(a)** For each biography, note two statements the biographer makes that are interpretations of information about the subject. **(b)** What does each statement show about the biographer's feelings toward his subject? Explain.

Writing to Compare Literary Works

Write an essay in which you compare your reaction to the excerpt from *A Lincoln Preface* with *Arthur Ashe Remembered*. In your response, explain how the writer's attitude toward his subject affects your reaction. Use these questions to get started:

- Does each writer clearly convey why his subject is important?
- Did you respond more to the description of Abraham Lincoln or the description of Arthur Ashe? Why?
- What main impression do you think each writer wants to convey?

Using a chart like the one shown, find details to support your response. You can use these notes to build your essay.

Author	Main Impression	Details
Sandburg		
McPhee		

Vocabulary Builder

Practice Rewrite each of the following sentences using a word from the vocabulary list on page 450. Explain which sentence is stronger.

1. The dictator's abuse of power frightened the citizens.
2. The movie was peculiar, yet amusing.
3. The members of congress strongly disapprove of the president's decision.
4. The disappearance of various items caused everyone to wonder what could have happened.
5. The dancer could stretch and move in a flexible way.
6. The children felt fortunate to have several novels their mother had written when she was alive.

QuickReview

Biographical Writing: nonfiction writing in which a writer tells the story of another person's life

Go Online
Assessment
For: Self-test
Visit: www.PHSchool.com
Web Code: epa-6306

Reading

Directions: *Questions 1–5 are based on the following selection.*

For those without money, the road to that treasure house of the imagination begins at the public library. When I was a boy, the rooms were crowded with immigrants and their children. That is, with people who came from places where there were no libraries for the poor. With their children, they built the New York in which we now live.

Today, the libraries of this city are still doing that work. The libraries of Brooklyn and Queens are jammed with the new immigrants and their astonishing children, the people who will build the New York of tomorrow. The older people want information about this new world, and how to get better jobs and green cards and citizenship. Their American children want to vanish into books their parents cannot afford, thus filling themselves with the endless possibilities of the future.

—from "Libraries Face Sad Chapter," by Pete Hamill

1. **What is the subject of the passage?**
   A   immigrants
   B   libraries
   C   New York
   D   Brooklyn and Queens

2. **A detail that contributes to the main idea is that libraries are most important to**
   A   those with imagination.
   B   the poor.
   C   children.
   D   American citizens.

3. **The author states that "libraries of Brooklyn and Queens are jammed with the new immigrants." Which of the following does this detail support?**
   A   Brooklyn and Queens are important to immigrants.
   B   There are many new immigrants.
   C   Libraries are crowded places.
   D   Many immigrants make use of libraries.

4. **Which of the following best reflects the author's main idea in this passage?**
   A   Libraries are a vital resource for immigrants.
   B   Libraries contain vital information.
   C   Brooklyn and Queens have many libraries.
   D   Libraries are what built New York.

5. **Which detail best supports the main idea of the passage?**
   A   "Today, the libraries of this city are still doing that work."
   B   "The road to that treasure house of the imagination begins at the public library."
   C   "When I was a boy, the rooms were crowded with immigrants. . . ."
   D   "The older people want information about this new world. . . ."

Vocabulary

Directions: *Choose the word that best completes the sentence.*

Standards Assessed
• GU.6.01.6
• IR.2.01.4
• WL.1.03.8

6. Anna's explanation served to _____ the situation.
   A assume
   B illuminate
   C contemplate
   D appreciate

7. Jason wanted to _____ the meaning of her words.
   A display
   B contemplate
   C assume
   D contribute

8. I have read through forty _____ and still cannot find the right article.
   A contemplations
   B abstracts
   C illuminates
   D aspects

9. He lied to her, _____ her anger flared.
   A displayed
   B hence
   C contributed
   D involved

10. Adam's mumbled response was the _____ of a confession.
    A circumstance
    B illumination
    C appreciation
    D equivalent

11. During the _____, the day and the night are the same length.
    A concurrent
    B composition
    C equinox
    D equivalent

12. Sally reread her _____ several times before submitting it.
    A concurrent
    B composition
    C equinox
    D equilateral

13. The nation comprised a (n)_____ of states.
    A concurrent
    B equilateral
    C equivalent
    D confederation

14. The programs were shown _____, so each could only capture half of the limited audience.
    A confederately
    B concurrently
    C equilaterally
    D equitably

15. The judge was an honorable person, and no one doubted the _____ of the decision.
    A equivalence
    B concurrent
    C equity
    D composition

Workplace Writing: Business Letter

A **business letter** is a piece of correspondence that you write in the course of conducting business or professional matters. Effective business letters are clear, direct, courteous, and carefully formatted. Follow the steps outlined in this workshop to write your own business letter.

Assignment Write a business letter to a company in which you ask for information about a product or service you are interested in using.

What to Include Your letter should feature these elements:
- A heading, inside address, greeting, body, closing, and signature
- Formal, polite language, a clear purpose, and relevant background information
- Standard formatting with consistent spacing and indentation
- Error-free grammar, including correct use of compound subjects, objects, and complements

To preview the criteria on which your business letter may be assessed, see the rubric on page 470.

Prewriting

Choosing Your Topic

Brainstorm and Itemize Jot down a list of products or services that you currently use or are interested in using. For each, itemize by noting why this product or service interests you. Then, decide which details of performance, features, price, or reliability matter most to you. Review your work to choose a topic.

Products	Interest	Services	Interest
Bicycle repair kit	Which is the best?	Homework help	How much is too much?
Cell phone	Cheapest and best service?	Library research service	Help with the Internet?

Gathering Details

Conduct research. Use the Internet or your local phone book to locate the address of the company that provides the product or service you are investigating. Consider browsing stores that carry the products to learn more before you write.

Standard Course of Study
- Show appreciation for the significance of a personal account. (WL.1.01.3)
- Analyze text components and evaluate impact on text and on research. (IR.2.01.2)

Using the Form
You may use elements of this form in these types of writing:
- requests for information, appointments, or interviews
- formal complaints or commendations
- proposals

Work in Progress
Review the work you did on pages 397, 423, and 445.

Drafting

Shaping Your Writing

Select a format. Choose a standard business letter format, using a consistent font and spacing. You may use block format, in which each part of the letter begins at the left margin. Alternatively, you may use modified block format, in which the heading, closing, and signature are indented to the center of the page. Use the checklist shown here to verify that your draft includes all six elements of a business letter.

Providing Elaboration

Consider your audience. You are addressing a busy professional, so include only essential information. State information clearly and use formal vocabulary, style, and tone.

> ### Business Letter Elements
> - ☐ **Heading**—the writer's address and organization (if any) and the date
> - ☐ **Inside Address**—where the letter will be sent
> - ☐ **Greeting**—a salutation always punctuated by a colon
> - ☐ **Body**—a presentation of the writer's purpose
> - ☐ **Closing**—an appropriate farewell
> - ☐ **Signature**—a signed name

Revising

Revising Your Sentences

Highlight the active voice. A verb in the active voice expresses an action done *by* its subject. A verb in the passive voice expresses an action done *to* its subject.

Passive Voice: The vacuum cleaner *was broken* by the salesman.

Active Voice: The salesman *broke* the vacuum cleaner.

The active voice is preferable because it produces more direct and forceful sentences. Review your draft, highlighting verbs written in the passive voice; then, rewrite the sentences in the active voice where you can.

Revising Your Word Choice

Check your tone. To maintain a formal tone, avoid slang, contractions, and personal references. Review your draft, replacing casual language with more formal expressions.

Student Model: Revising to Create a Formal Tone

am in the market for a high-end,   I would like to obtain more
~~I want a good,~~ reliable server. ~~Can you get me some straight~~
information about your line of servers.
~~info on your products without a lot of runaround?~~

> The revision is more formal and polite.

Integrating Grammar Skills

Revising to Combine Choppy Sentences

Avoid choppy, disconnected sentences by combining two or more related ideas in a single sentence.

Methods of Sentence Combining Compound verbs—more than one verb linked to a single subject—can be used to combine two short sentences:

Prentice Hall Writing and Grammar Connection: Chapter 3, Section 1

> **Choppy:** I *disconnected* my phone. I *brought* it in for service.
> **Compound Verb:** I *disconnected* my phone and *brought* it in for service.

Compound objects—more than one object linked to a single verb—can help combine sentences.

> **Choppy:** I purchased *a scanner.* I purchased *a fax machine.*
> **Compound Object:** I purchased *a scanner and a fax machine.*

A third option is the use of **compound predicate nominatives** or **predicate adjectives**.

Predicate Nominative	Predicate Adjective
a noun or pronoun that appears with a linking verb and renames, identifies, or explains the subject Example: Juice is a <u>beverage</u>.	an adjective that appears with a linking verb and describes the subject Example: Juice is <u>expensive</u>.

> **Choppy:** My newest device *is a printer.* It is also *a scanner.* It is also *a fax machine.*
> **Compound Predicative Nominative:** My newest device *is a printer, scanner, and fax machine.*
> **Choppy:** The fax is *automated.* It is *fast.*
> **Compound Predicative Adjective:** The fax is *automated and fast.*

Fixing Choppy Sentences Scan your draft for sentence variety.

1. **Read your draft aloud.** Listen for overuse of short sentences.
2. **Identify sentences that can be combined.** Look for sentences that share a common subject or a common predicate element.
3. **Use a variety of sentence combining techniques.** Use compound verbs, compound direct objects, or compound predicate nominatives or predicate adjectives to create a wider variety of flowing sentences.

Apply It to Your Editing

Review the body paragraphs in your letter, looking for opportunities to express related ideas or information in a single sentence. Combine these elements using one of the methods presented here.

Student Model: Robin Weber
St. Petersburg, FL

Intelligent Productions
220 Any Street, Suite 112
Any Town, NY 10000
December 13, 2006

> The author uses modified block format.

G-2000 Computers
310 Infinite Loop
Any City, CA 94000

Dear Sir or Madam:

My business is currently in the market for several high-end, reliable server computers. I would like to obtain more information about your line of server products.

> The author states his purpose clearly and concisely.

The computers we use are operating twenty-four hours a day, seven days a week, as servers hosting a high-traffic Internet Web site. Therefore, it would be unacceptable for my company to purchase computers that require periods of inactivity in order to remain in working condition. We are also concerned about technical support issues and costs.

> In this paragraph, Robin provides important background information.

I would appreciate if you could send me the exact specifications on catalog items number 1444 and 2314. In addition, there is no information on warranties in your product descriptions. Any information you can provide in this regard would be very helpful in making my purchasing decision. Also, would it be possible to obtain a high volume discount? How would such an order affect delivery time?

> The letter includes specific questions that Robin would like answered.

Please send me any information you have on these matters. I look foward to hearing from you.

> In his conclusion, Robin summarizes the request using polite language.

Sincerely,

Robin Weber

Robin Weber

Editing and Proofreading

Check your draft for errors in format, grammar, and punctuation.

Focus on Accuracy: Make certain that the names of individuals and companies are spelled correctly and that the address is complete.

Publishing and Presenting

Consider one of the following ways to share your writing:

Send your letter. If your letter is written to an existing business, mail it. When you get a response, share it with classmates.

Conduct a discussion. Use your letter to begin a class discussion about the role of communication skills in everyday life. Improve the productivity of the discussion by being open to the variety of ideas your classmates suggest. Make notes on their comments, and add your letter and notes to your writing portfolio.

Reflecting on Your Writing

Writer's Journal Jot down your thoughts on the experience of writing a business letter. Begin by answering these questions.

- Which did you find easier, following the business letter format or maintaining a business-like tone? Explain.
- How will this experience change the way you write business letters in the future?

Prentice Hall Writing and Grammar Connection: Chapter 15

Rubric for Self-Assessment

To assess your business letter, use the following rubric:

NC Criteria	Rating Scale not very very
Focus: How clearly do you state your purpose?	1 2 3 4 5
Organization: How thoroughly do you incorporate all the elements of a business letter?	1 2 3 4 5
Support/Elaboration: How effectively do you provide background information?	1 2 3 4 5
Style: How formal and polite is your use of language?	1 2 3 4 5
Conventions: How correct is your grammar, especially your use of compound subjects, objects, and complements?	1 2 3 4 5

Persuasive Texts

Skills You Will Learn

Literary Analysis: *Persuasive Essay*
Reading Skill: *Rereading*

Literary Analysis: *Persuasive Speeches and Rhetorical Devices*
Reading Skill: *Reading Aloud*

Reading Skill: *Distinguishing Fact from Opinion*

Literary Analysis: *Humorous Essay*

Literature You Will Read

Reading and Vocabulary Skills Preview

Reading: Analyzing Persuasive Appeals

NC Standard Course of Study

▶ **Persuasive appeals** use logic or emotion to bring about a positive response to the writer's argument.

• Examine relevant reasons and evidence in argument. (FA.3.01.1)
• Note the progression of ideas that substantiate the argument proposal. (FA.3.01.2)

Skills and Strategies You Will Learn in Part 2

In Part 2, you will learn
- to **reread** the text to **analyze and evaluate persuasive appeals.** (p. 474)
- to **read the text aloud** to **analyze and evaluate persuasive appeals.** (p. 492)
- to **analyze persuasive nonfiction texts** using these skills. (p. 514)

Using the Skills and Strategies in Part 2

In Part 2, you will learn to recognize persuasive appeals. You will also learn to reread to recognize the kinds of appeals an author uses and to determine whether the appeal is valid and effective. Reading aloud will help you appreciate and analyze devices such as repetition that contribute to persuasive appeals. In Part 2, you will apply the skills and strategies you learn to a variety of nonfiction texts.

The model shows you how you can apply these skills and strategies.

reread, repetition reinforces the concept that this is one person's fault.

read aloud, negative connotation   *read aloud, negative connotation*

He *has refused* **his** Assent to Laws, the most wholesome and necessary for the public good. **He** *has forbidden* his Governors to pass Laws of immediate and pressing importance, unless suspended in their operation till **his** Assent should be obtained. . . .

Declaration of Independence 1776

reread text - use of pronoun rather than name is negative

Academic Vocabulary: Words for Analyzing Literature

The following words will help you write and talk about interpretations of the literature in this unit.

Word	Definition	Example Sentence
anticipate *v.*	expect something	Clues help the reader *anticipate* the story's climax.
internal *adj.*	on the inside	The plot centered on the main character's *internal* conflict.
derive *v.*	get from a source	I was able to *derive* some clues from the description of the characters.
texture *n.*	arrangement or structure of something	The author's description of the material's *texture* was a clue.
signify *v.*	be a sign of something	The author used dreams to *signify* the character's internal conflict.

Vocabulary Skills You Will Learn in Part 2

▶ A **prefix** is a word part that is added to the beginning of a word or another word part.

In Part 2, you will learn
- Latin prefix *ante-*   (p. 490)
- Latin prefix *inter-*   (p. 512)

Knowing the meaning of prefixes expands your vocabulary. Adding the definition of a prefix to a base word you are familiar with gives you a strategy for determining the meaning of new words.

▶ **Example:**

Unfamiliar Word: *antedate*
Prefix: *ante* = before
Word Root: *date* = specific time
Definition: *antedate*: before a specific time.

Practice these skills with either "Carry Your Own Skis" (p. 476) or "Libraries Face Sad Chapter" (p. 483).

Literary Analysis

A **persuasive essay** is a short nonfiction work that tries to convince a reader to think or act in a particular way. Persuasive essays usually include one or both of the following:

- **Appeals to reason:** logical arguments based on verifiable evidence, such as facts, statistics, or expert testimony

- **Appeals to emotion:** statements intended to affect listeners' feelings about a subject. These statements often include charged language—words with strong positive or negative associations.

An **author's motive** in a persuasive essay is his or her reason for, or interest in, persuading readers to accept his or her position.

Reading Skill

Persuasive appeals are the arguments the author makes. To **analyze and evaluate persuasive appeals,** identify passages in which the author makes an argument in support of his or her position. Then, **reread** those passages to test the author's logic and reasoning. Ask yourself the following questions.

- Is the author's argument supported by evidence, or is it based on faulty assumptions?
- Does the author link ideas clearly or make leaps in logic?
- Is the argument consistent or is it contradictory?

Use a chart like the one shown to record your analysis of the author's arguments. Then, decide whether the author has made a convincing persuasive appeal.

Claim	Logical?

Evaluation

Standard Course of Study

- Examine relevant reasons and evidence in argument. (FA.3.01.1)
- Make connections between argumentative works, self and related topics. (FA.3.04.8)
- Create standards and apply them to critique presentation/product. (CT.4.01.3)

Vocabulary Builder

Carry Your Own Skis

- **inevitability** (in ev´ i tə bil´ ə tē) *n.* quality of being certain to happen (p. 477) *The inevitability of losing did not keep the team from playing hard.*

- **potential** (pō ten´ shəl) *n.* possibility (p. 478) *She has the potential to be a great player, but she still needs a lot of practice.*

- **riddled** (rid´ld) *adj.* affected throughout (p. 479) *The old tree was riddled with wormholes.*

Libraries Face Sad Chapter

- **curtailed** (kər tāld´) *v.* cut short; reduced (p. 485) *The game was curtailed by darkness.*

- **medium** (mē´ dē əm) *n.* means of communication (p. 485) *Television is today's most popular medium.*

- **duration** (doo rā´ shən) *n.* length of time something lasts (p. 487) *Attendees remained standing for the duration of the ceremony.*

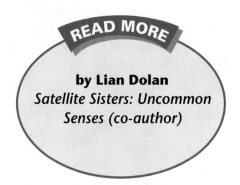

Background

Cold-Weather Clothing Before the development of synthetic, lightweight, waterproof fabrics that "breathe" and keep the wearer dry, keeping warm on the ski slopes meant wearing heavy wool and cotton clothing. Garments made from these fabrics would become wet and cold in the snow, and they would stay wet and cold until removed.

Connecting to the Literature

Reading/Writing Connection In "Carry Your Own Skis," Lian Dolan describes skiing in the mid-1960s: The absence of today's comfortable clothing and conveniences made skiing then seem like work. Yet Dolan's mother and aunt enjoyed the sport. Write five sentences explaining why some people enjoy activities that involve a degree of hardship. Use at least three of these words: *attain, challenge, concentrate, display, frustrate.*

READ MORE

by Lian Dolan
Satellite Sisters: Uncommon Senses (co-author)

Meet the Author

Lian **Dolan** (b. 1966)

Lian Dolan is one of the "Satellite Sisters," a group of five sisters who host a weekly radio show. Before helping launch the show, Dolan tried everything from working as a waitress to producing films. She also writes the column "The Chaos Chronicles" for *Working Mother* magazine.

"The Sassiest" Lian is known as the sassiest of the sisters, and she is not afraid to express her opinions on any topic. Even though Lian is the youngest of the five sisters, she directs all of their writing projects. She enjoys being the "Head Sister," giving orders to her older siblings.

Fast Facts

▶ Dolan's writing has appeared in national magazines such as *Good Housekeeping* and *O, The Oprah Magazine.*

▶ The Satellite Sisters live in four different cities on two continents. They link via satellite for their weekly radio show.

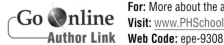

Go **O**nline
Author Link

For: More about the author
Visit: www.PHSchool.com
Web Code: epe-9308

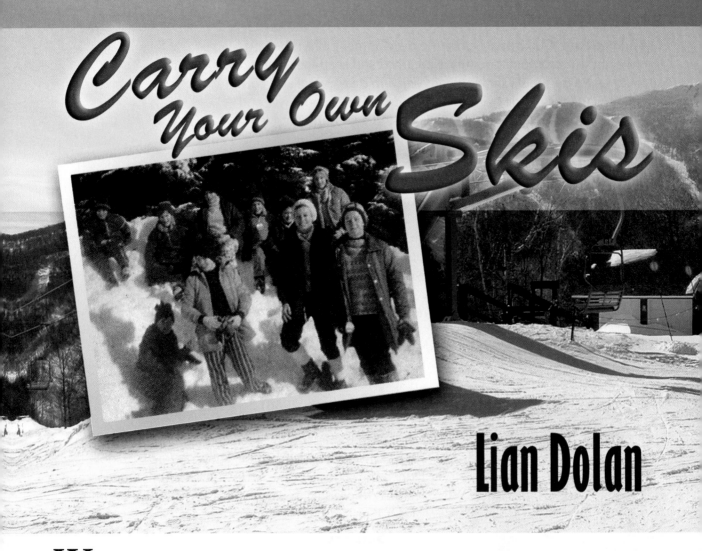

Carry Your Own Skis

Lian Dolan

W hen my mother was forty, she took up skiing. Or, more correctly, she and her twin sister took up skiing. They got on a bus, went to ski camp for a week, and learned to ski. After that, they'd get in the car and head up to Ladies Day at Powder Hill as often as they could to practice their stem christies.[1] Don't let the name fool you, Powder Hill (which later became the more Everest-like "Powder Ridge") was no pushover bunny slope.[2]

This was in the mid-sixties, when skiing was work—decades before valet parking, fondue lunches, and gear that actually keeps you dry, warm, and safe. My mother and my aunt took up the kind

Reading Skill
Persuasive Appeals
How do the details about ski lodges of the 1960s support the author's position that skiing used to be a less luxurious sport?

1. **stem christies** turns made by angling one ski and then bringing the other into alignment.
2. **bunny slope** gently sloping hill used for practice by beginning skiers.

of skiing that entailed wooden skis, tie boots, and rope tows[3] that could jerk your arm out of its socket. This was the kind of skiing where skiers, not the Sno-Cats, groomed the hill[4] in the morning. Ticket buyers were expected to sidestep up and down slopes and herringbone the lift lines.[5] The typical A-frame lodge had a big fireplace, a couple of bathrooms, rows of picnic tables, and maybe some hot chocolate for sale. At the end of the day, there were no hot toddies by a roaring fire in furry boots or drinks in the hot tub of a slopeside condo. Instead, my mother and her sister faced the inevitability of a station wagon with a dead battery and the long, dark drive back home in wet clothes.

Why did they learn to ski? It wasn't to spend some quality time outdoors together away from their responsibilities at home. They learned to ski so that they could take their collective children skiing, all seventeen of us. My mother's eight children and my aunt's nine. And learn to ski we did, eagerly. There was, however, one rule my mother had about skiing: Carry your own skis.

My mother didn't teach us to ski until we could carry our own skis from the car to the lodge in the morning and—this is key—from the lodge back to the car at the end of the day. Even cold, wet, and tired, we had to get our skis, poles, and boots back to that station wagon on our own. No falling behind. No dragging. And no whining. My mother had the responsibility for her gear, the giant lunch, the car, and the occasional trip to the ER for broken legs. We were in charge of our own gear and meeting at the end of the day. These were the conditions to be allowed to accompany siblings and cousins to the slopes. Carry your own skis or sit in the lodge all day.

No one wanted to get left in the lodge. A cold, wet day on the ice-blue slopes of New England, freezing in leather boots and the generation of ski clothes before microfibers was far preferable to being left out of all that fun. Miss the lunches of soggy tuna fish sandwiches and mini chocolate bars? No way! Sit in the lodge instead of side-slipping your way down a sheet of ice disguised as a trail or tramping through three feet of snow to get the pole you dropped under the chair lift? Not me! Forgo that last run of the day in near darkness, cold and alone and crying because your siblings have skied on ahead without you? Who'd want to miss all that fun? Sitting in the lodge all day just wasn't an option once we reached ski age. We were expected to participate. We learned to carry our own skis.

---

3. **rope tows** moving ropes that skiers hold to be pulled to the top of the hill.
4. **groomed the hill** packed and smoothed the snow.
5. **herringbone the lift lines** walk uphill to chair lift by stepping with skis pointed outward to avoid sliding back down the hill. The skis leave a "herringbone" pattern—a line of connected v-shapes—on the snow.

◀ **Critical Viewing**
What details in these photographs suggest they are from an earlier time? **[Infer]**

Vocabulary Builder
inevitability (in ev′ i tə bil′ ə tē) *n.* quality of being certain to happen

Literary Analysis
Persuasive Essay
Which details in this paragraph appeal to the emotions? Explain.

✔ **Reading Check**
Why did Dolan's mother and aunt learn to ski?

The lesson was simple, really. Be responsible for yourself and your stuff or you miss out. No one wanted to miss out. Getting across the icy parking lot and back seemed a small price to pay for the <u>potential</u> of great fun. And even if you dropped your poles or the bindings cut into your hands or you fell on your rear end, that was part of the experience. The "carry your own skis" mentality filtered into almost every area of our life as we were growing up. Doing homework, getting to practice, applying to college—be responsible for yourself and your stuff or you miss out.

I began to notice the people who hadn't learned to carry their own skis when I was as young as eleven. I didn't have a name for this concept yet, but I had the notion that maybe other kids operated by a different set of rules. They thought that somewhere, somebody was going to take care of things for them. I remember the girls at summer camp who never signed up to pack out or pack in for a camping trip, expecting that someone else would provide food or do all the cleanup for them. But me? I would sign up to make the PB&Js and to clean up the mess. I'd load the canoes onto the truck and take 'em off again. And the tent? I'd put it up and I'd take it down. I didn't know any different. As a result, I was invited to go on a lot of camping trips. The lodge and back, baby—that was my attitude.

In high school, the kids who didn't carry their own skis called their parents to bring in assignments they'd forgotten or to ask for a

Reading Skill
Persuasive Appeals
How does the author support her claim that some kids operate by different rules?

▼ **Critical Viewing**
Based on this photograph, does skiing look like work or recreation? **[Analyze]**

478

ride home instead of walking or taking the late bus. In college, the no-ski carriers all had pink T-shirts—a sure sign that they had never done laundry before—and they complained about how much work they had. Isn't that what college was about—doing your own laundry and finishing your work? Then you could get to the fun stuff.

The real world is <u>riddled</u> with people who have never learned to carry their own skis—the blame-shifters, the no-RSVPers, the coworkers who never participate in those painful group birthdays except if it's their own. I admit it: I don't really get these people.

I like the folks who clear the dishes, even when they're the guests. Or the committee members who show up on time, assignment completed and ready to pitch in on the next event. Or the neighbor who drives the carpool even though her kids are sick. I get these people. These people have learned to carry their own skis.

In early adulthood, carrying my own skis meant getting a job, paying off my student loans, and working hard for the company that was providing my paycheck. If I did those things, then I could enjoy the other areas of my life. Dull, yes, but freeing, too. When I wasn't responsible for myself or my stuff, I felt lousy. Sometimes I could get to the lodge, but I just couldn't get back to the station wagon at the end of the day. It was an unfamiliar feeling to let someone down by missing a deadline at work or not showing up for an early-morning run. . . . On days like that, the parking lot seemed bigger and icier than I had anticipated.

Now I have a life that includes a husband, two children, a dog, a house, friends, schools, and a radio show that involves lots of other people, including four sisters. The "stuff" of my life may seem much heavier than two skis, two boots, and two poles, but it isn't really—just a little bit trickier to carry. I have to do more balancing and let go of the commitments that I'd probably drop anyway. If I commit to more than I can handle, I miss out. That's when I think of Powder Hill.

The funny thing is, some of the worst moments of my childhood were spent on skis or in pursuit of skiing. The truth is, I didn't really like skiing as a kid. And I wasn't a very good skier. Most days, skiing for me was about freezing rain and constantly trying to catch up to my older, faster, more talented siblings. The hard falls on the hard ice. I can still feel the damp long underwear and the wet wool during the endless ride home. But whether I liked to ski or not didn't really matter. I was expected to learn to ski, and I did. And I also learned that in life you need to be responsible for yourself and your stuff or you miss out. The lodge and back, baby.

Vocabulary Builder
riddled (rid´'ld) *adj.*
affected throughout

Literary Analysis
Persuasive Essay
What does the paragraph beginning "I like . . . " suggest the author's motive for writing might be?

Reading Skill
Persuasive Appeals
Does the author clearly connect lessons learned from skiing with ideas about life? Explain.

Apply the Skills

Carry Your Own Skis

Thinking About the Selection

1. **Respond:** What more would you like to know about Dolan's childhood? Explain your answer.
2. **(a) Recall:** What is the one rule that Dolan's mother had about skiing? **(b) Make a Judgment:** Do you think Dolan's mother's expectations of her children are reasonable? Why or why not?
3. **(a) Recall:** What lesson does Dolan say she learned from carrying her own skis? **(b) Connect:** In what other aspects of life does the author say this lesson has guided her behavior?
4. **(a) Take a Position:** Do you agree or disagree with Dolan's claim that people who do not take responsibility miss out on things? Explain. **(b) Discuss:** Share your response with a partner, and then explain how the discussion has or has not changed your response to the question.

Literary Analysis

5. **(a)** In this **persuasive essay,** what is the author trying to persuade readers to think or do? **(b)** What evidence does she use to support her position?
6. **(a)** Using a chart like the one shown, identify three passages where Dolan argues for "the 'carry your own skis' mentality" in the left column. In the right column, indicate whether each passage is an appeal to reason or to emotion. Explain.

Passage	Reason or Emotion

   (b) Which kind of appeals does the author seem to favor—appeals to reason or appeals to emotion?
7. What do you think is the **author's motive** for trying to persuade readers to agree with her?

Reading Skill

8. When you **analyze and evaluate** the **persuasive appeal** in "Carry Your Own Skis," do you find the author's arguments to be well-reasoned and logical? Explain your answer.
9. **(a)** Did the author convince you to accept her position? Why or why not? **(b)** Which passages are especially convincing? Explain.

QuickReview

Essay at a Glance
The author describes how she learned personal responsibility by carrying her own skis as a child.

Go Online
Assessment
For: Self-test
Visit: www.PHSchool.com
Web Code: epa-6307

Persuasive Essay: a short nonfiction work that tries to convince a reader to think or act in a particular way

Author's Motive: the author's reason for persuading readers to accept his or her position

Analyze and Evaluate Persuasive Appeals: test the logic and reasoning of the arguments an author makes

Vocabulary Builder

Practice **Analogies** show the relationships between pairs of words. Use a word from the "Carry Your Own Skis" vocabulary list on page 474 to complete each analogy. In each, your choice should create a word pair that matches the relationship between the first two words given.

1. conflict : agreement :: uncertainty : _____
2. idea : reality :: _____ : actual
3. soaked : water :: _____ : dents

Adding Words to Your Vocabulary *Riddle,* the present-tense form of *riddled,* has a meaning different from the one used in the essay. Use a dictionary to discover this meaning. Then use *riddle* in three sentences reflecting this meaning. (For more on using a dictionary, see page R6.)

Writing

An **abstract** of a work is a type of summary. Readers check abstracts to see if an essay or article interests them or is relevant to their research. Write an abstract of "Carry Your Own Skis."

- Include the main point and briefly convey supporting details.
- Be sure your abstract will help those who have not read the essay.

For *Grammar, Vocabulary,* and *Assessment,* see **Build Language Skills,** pages 490–491.

Extend Your Learning

Listening and Speaking In "Carry Your Own Skis," Dolan describes the life lesson she learned while skiing. Choose a favorite activity, and give a **persuasive speech** that urges people to participate in it. Consider the following questions:
- What in particular do you enjoy about the activity?
- What life lessons could someone learn from it?

Practice in front of a mirror before giving your speech to the class.

Research and Technology With a group of classmates, research today's popular winter sports. Create and present a **comparative chart** that graphically shows which sports have the most active participants and the largest audience. Include a statement summarizing the information that the chart details.

Essay

Background

Public Libraries Although the first American library was established in 1638, it was not until the 1800s that public libraries became common in the United States. Since then, Americans have come to rely on public libraries as a free source of education, entertainment, and community.

Connecting to the Literature

Reading/Writing Connection In "Libraries Face Sad Chapter," Pete Hamill describes his visits to a public library as a young child. Think of one of the first times that you visited a library, and write to describe the experience. Use at least three of these words: *perceive, reveal, respond, dedicate, distribute.*

Review

For **Literary Analysis, Reading Skill,** and **Vocabulary Builder,** see page 474.

READ MORE

**by
Pete Hamill**
*Snow in August
Forever*

Meet the Author

Pete **Hamill** (b. 1935)

Pete Hamill has had two novels on *The New York Times* Bestseller List, but he is first and foremost a journalist. After quitting school at sixteen to work in the Brooklyn Navy Yard, Hamill joined the U.S. Navy. He completed his high school education while in the navy.

"The work was everything." In 1960, Hamill went to work as a reporter for the *New York Post* newspaper. Although he would write for several other newspapers in his career, Hamill loved his job at the *Post.* He wrote, "Nothing before (or since) could compare with walking into the *New York Post* at midnight, being sent into the dark scary city on assignment and coming back to write a story."

Fast Facts

▶ Hamill has served as editor-in-chief of both the *New York Post* and the *New York Daily News.*

▶ During Hamill's long career as a reporter, he covered wars in a number of countries.

Go Online
Author Link

For: More about the author
Visit: www.PHSchool.com
Web Code: epe-9309

LIBRARIES FACE SAD CHAPTER

PETE HAMILL

The library was four blocks from where we lived, on the corner of Ninth St. and Sixth Ave., and it was one of the treasure houses of our Brooklyn lives.

This was in the years before television, when we saw movies once a week at the Minerva or the Avon or the RKO Prospect, and fed our imaginations through radio and books. That is, it was in a time when *The Count of Monte Cristo* was as vivid in our minds, and talk, and dreams, as Jack Roosevelt Robinson. Dumas told the story of the count as vividly as Red Barber[1] recited the unfolding tale of No. 42.

We passed into that library between two mock-Corinthian columns that gave the building a majestic aura. For me, every visit was an astonishment. There was a children's room, first seen when I was 8, where I first read the wonderful Babar books, and then moved on to Howard Pyle's *Book of Pirates,* and all of Robert Louis Stevenson, with those rich, golden, mysterious illustrations by N.C. Wyeth.

There were bound volumes of a children's magazine called *St. Nicholas,* full of spidery drawings of animals that talked, and villains who didn't. There were picture books bursting with images of lost cities or the solar system. In that room, I learned that the world was larger than our neighborhood.

And then, at 10 or 11, I found my way into the adult stacks, to borrow books about the daily life of the Romans, the flight of Richard Hannay across Scotland, the conquests of Mexico and Peru, the cases of Sherlock Holmes. On a high shelf, presumed to be safe from the curious eyes of children, was a lavish (in memory) edition of *The Thousand and One Nights.*[2]

No teacher sent us to those leathery cliffs of books. Reading wasn't an assignment; it was a pleasure. We read for the combined thrills of villainy and heroism, along with knowledge of the vast world beyond the parish. Living in those other worlds, we could become other people: Jim Hawkins, or Edmund Dantes, or (most thrillingly) d'Artagnan, with his three musketeers.

1. *The Count of Monte Cristo . . .* **Red Barber** *The Count of Monte Cristo* is a nineteenth-century novel by Alexandre Dumas. Jackie Robinson was the first African American major league baseball player. He joined the Brooklyn Dodgers in 1947 and wore number 42. Dodgers games were broadcast on the radio, and the action was described by announcer Red Barber.
2. *The Thousand and One Nights* collection of ancient tales also known as the *Arabian Nights.* Although many of the tales, including "Aladdin," are now retold as children's stories, the original tellings are full of violence, bloodshed, poisonings, and betrayals.

Literary Analysis
Persuasive Essay
Which words here suggest that the author appeals to positive feelings about childhood and imagination?

▼ **Critical Viewing**
How might the young Pete Hamill have regarded these books? **[Speculate]**

We could live in the South Seas, or Paris, or the Rome of Caligula. It never occurred to us that we were inheriting our little share of civilization. But that's what was happening.

Built by Carnegie

The library of my childhood is still there, since 1975 known as the Park Slope Branch of the Brooklyn Public Library. It was built with grant money from my favorite capitalist, Andrew Carnegie, in 1906. But once again, as happened in 1992, the teeming imaginative life of libraries is in danger of being <u>curtailed</u>. Services might be cut. Hours trimmed. Staff reduced. The reason is the same: money, or the lack of it.

Such reductions are absolutely understandable. As we all know, Mayor Bloomberg has more than a $4 billion shortfall that must be made up. Unlike the spend-more tax-less leaders of the federal government, the government of New York City can't print money to keep things going. In this season of post-September 11 austerities,[3] something must give. I hope it isn't the libraries.

The reason is simple: In hard times, libraries are more important than ever. Human beings need what books give them better than any other <u>medium</u>. Since those ancient nights around prehistoric campfires, we have needed myth. And heroes. And moral tales. And information about the world beyond the nearest mountains or oceans.

Today, with books and movies more expensive than ever, and television entertainment in free fall to the lowest levels of stupidity, freely circulating books are an absolute necessity. They are quite simply another kind of food. We imagine, and then we live.

Hard times are also an opportunity. Parents and teachers all moan about the refusal of the young to read. Here is the chance to revive the power of the printed page. The Harry Potter books show

---

3. austerities (ô ster´ ə tēz) *n.* acts of self-discipline and self-denial.

Vocabulary Builder
curtailed (kər tāld´)
v. cut short; reduced
medium (mē´ dē əm)
n. means of
communication

✔️**Reading Check**

Why might library services be cut?

that the audience for young readers is potentially immense. A child who starts with Harry Potter can find his or her way to Dumas and Arthur Conan Doyle, to Mark Twain and Walt Whitman, and, yes, to Tolstoy and Joyce and Proust.

Immigrants' Appreciation

For those without money, the road to that treasure house of the imagination begins at the public library. When I was a boy, the rooms were crowded with immigrants and their children. That is, with people who came from places where there were no libraries for

▲ **Critical Viewing**
How does this photograph support Hamill's idea that a library is a "treasure house of the imagination"?
[Connect]

the poor. With their children, they built the New York in which we now live.

Today, the libraries of this city are still doing that work. The libraries of Brooklyn and Queens are jammed with the new immigrants and their astonishing children, the people who will build the New York of tomorrow. The older people want information about this new world, and how to get better jobs and green cards and citizenship. Their American children want to vanish into books their parents cannot afford, thus filling themselves with the endless possibilities of the future.

They are no different from the Irish, the Jews and the Italians of my childhood. My father only went to the eighth grade in Belfast. I remember my mother drilling him at our kitchen table for his citizenship test, and I know that he first read the Constitution in a book borrowed from the Prospect Branch of the Brooklyn Public Library. Lying in a darkened bed off that kitchen, I first heard the language of the Bill of Rights.

That process must go on in all the places where the poor now live. If it's impossible for the city to do it, then we must do it ourselves. Bloomberg can give us the hard numbers, explain the shortfall in the library budget and explain how much we need. Then we should try to make it up with the establishment of a private fund to maintain the libraries at full strength for the <u>duration</u> of the crisis.

All of us whose lives have been affected by the treasures of public libraries could contribute. The rich could emulate Carnegie, who used his wealth to create more than 1,600 public libraries, including 65 in New York. But the middle class could also send in small amounts from $10 to $50.

This would be a kind of voluntary tax. On one level, it would be a powerful pledge to maintain the life of the mind among all classes in this city. That is obviously in our own interest. But above all, it would be a means of honoring the labor of those men and women who got us here, and who paid taxes to buy books for all New Yorkers, and first took us by the hand and walked us into the treasure houses. We who dreamed of Ebbets Field and the Chateau d'If on the same American nights owe debts to New York that we can never pay. This is one that must be honored.

Vocabulary Builder
duration (d�ööͦ rā´ shən) *n.* length of time something lasts

Apply the Skills

Libraries Face Sad Chapter

Thinking About the Selection

1. **Respond:** Do you share Hamill's feelings about public libraries? Why or why not?
2. **(a) Recall:** What books and magazines does Hamill remember from early visits to the library? **(b) Infer:** What do these memories suggest about how Hamill felt about the library as a child?
3. **(a) Interpret:** What does Hamill mean by calling books "another kind of food"? **(b) Draw Conclusions:** What does this comparison suggest about the value he places on books?
4. **(a) Take a Position:** Do you agree or disagree with Hamill's claims about the importance of free public libraries? Explain.
   (b) Discuss: Share your response with a partner, and then explain how the discussion has or has not changed your response to the question.

Literary Analysis

5. **(a)** In this **persuasive essay,** what is the author trying to persuade readers to think or do? **(b)** What evidence does he use to support his position?
6. **(a)** Using a chart like the one shown, identify three passages where Hamill asserts his position on public libraries in the left column. In the right column, indicate whether each passage is an appeal to reason or to emotion. Explain.

Passage	Reason or Emotion

   (b) Which kind of appeals does the author seem to favor—appeals to reason or appeals to emotion?
7. What do you think is the **author's motive** for trying to persuade readers to agree with him?

Reading Skill

8. When you **analyze and evaluate** the **persuasive appeal** in "Libraries Face Sad Chapter," do you find the author's arguments to be well-reasoned and logical? Explain your answer.
9. **(a)** Did the author convince you to accept his position? Why or why not? **(b)** Which passages are especially convincing? Explain.

Vocabulary Builder

Practice **Analogies** show the relationships between pairs of words. Use a word from the "Libraries Face Sad Chapter" vocabulary list on page 474 to complete each analogy. In each, your choice should create a word pair that matches the relationship between the first two words.

1. sugar : sweetness :: time : _____
2. bucket : water :: _____ : information
3. arrived : departed :: continued : _____

Adding Words to Your Vocabulary *Media,* the term used to refer collectively to newspapers, television, and other sources of information, is the plural form of the word *medium.* Use a dictionary to look up the plural forms of *datum, curriculum,* and *millennium.* Then, use each singular and plural form correctly in a sentence that illustrates its meaning. (For more on using a dictionary, see page R6.)

Writing

An **abstract** of a work is a type of summary. Readers check abstracts to see if an essay or article interests them or is relevant to their research. Write an abstract of "Libraries Face Sad Chapter."
- Include the main point and briefly convey supporting details.
- Be sure your abstract will help those who have not read the essay.

For *Grammar, Vocabulary,* and *Assessment,* see **Build Language Skills,** pages 490–491.

Extend Your Learning

Listening and Speaking In his essay, Hamill argues to preserve libraries. Choose a favorite place and give a **persuasive speech** urging people to preserve it. Consider these questions:
- What in particular do you enjoy about the place?
- In what ways does it benefit the community?

Practice in front of a mirror before giving your speech to the class.

Research and Technology Hamill discusses his use of the library as a young person. Research the services offered today by libraries. Create and present a **comparative chart** that shows the variety of services and the average numbers of people using them. Include a statement summarizing the information in the chart.

Build Language Skills

Carry Your Own Skis • Libraries Face Sad Chapter

Vocabulary Skill

Prefixes

The **Latin prefix** *ante-* means "before" or "prior to." This prefix appears in words that relate to things that precede other things. The prefix of *anticipate* is **anti-** (a variant of the prefix *ante-*), which also means "before" or "prior to."

Practice Match the following words with the correct definition. Use a dictionary if necessary. Then, write a sentence using each word.

1. antecedent
2. antemeridian
3. anteroom
4. anterior
5. antebellum

a. to the front of something
b. a place through which one enters a room
c. before the war
d. a happening or thing that comes before
e. before noon

Grammar Lesson

Adjectives An **adjective** is a word used to give a noun or pronoun a more specific meaning. Adjectives modify nouns and pronouns by telling *what kind, which one, how many,* or *how much.*

Noun/ Pronoun	Question	Adjective and Noun/Pronoun
school	What kind?	martial arts school
student	Which one?	involved student
cars	How many?/How much?	three cars

Practice Identify each adjective. Then, write a new sentence replacing each adjective with a different adjective.

1. The crisp air was a clear sign that fall had arrived.
2. In the early morning, I heard the unmistakable sound of wild geese calling as they flew overhead.
3. It was the first day of autumn, and the air was filled with the pungent odor of fallen leaves.
4. Red and brown leaves crackled underfoot.
5. In a few months, the ground will be covered with a thick blanket of snow.

MorePractice

For more practice with adjectives, see the Grammar Hand-book, p. R40.

W̖G Prentice Hall Writing and Grammar Connection: Chapter 18, Section 1

Monitor Your Progress

Reading: Analyzing Persuasive Appeals

Directions: *Read the selection. Then, answer the questions.*

Perhaps the greatest environmental tragedy of our time is the destruction of the Amazon Rainforest. The rainforest has more species than any other area on Earth. Over 2,000 species of the plants are known to have value as medicines, but only about 10% of these have been studied. These species may disappear before scientists have a chance to study them and understand their value to human beings. Scientists agree that the disappearance of the rainforest will have a global impact. Some organizations recommend that nations buy and preserve rainforest land and educate local people about living in the rainforest without destroying it. These are small first steps in saving the rainforest, but they are worthy of our support.

Standards Assessed

- WL.1.03.3
- FA.3.03.1
- LT.5.03.6

1. The primary persuasive appeal that the author uses is
   A an appeal to emotion.
   B an appeal to ethics.
   C an appeal to belief.
   D an appeal to law.

2. A detail that does NOT persuade is
   A the destruction of the rainforest is a tragedy.
   B over 2,000 rainforest plants have value.
   C the rainforest has many species.
   D the disappearance of the rainforest may destroy the Earth.

3. The last sentence of the paragraph
   A summarizes the author's point of view.
   B provides a call to action.
   C provides a transition to the next idea.
   D explains the main idea.

4. Which of the following is an emotionally charged phrase?
   A "Greatest environmental tragedy . . ."
   B "Some organizations recommend . . ."
   C "10% of these have been studied . . ."
   D "It will have a global impact. . . ."

Timed Writing: Persuasion [Connection]

Choose an issue that is important to you and write a letter to the editor of your local newspaper persuading people to accept your viewpoint. Use persuasive appeals and support your points. **(20 minutes)**

 Writing Workshop: *Work in Progress*

Editorial

Identify and list at least three specific elements of music, fashion, books, or movies that currently influence you and your friends. Put this list in your writing portfolio.

Practice these skills with either "I Have a Dream" (p. 494) or "First Inaugural Address" (p. 503).

NC **Standard Course of Study**

- Apply a set of predetermined standards to critique communication. (CT.4.01.2)
- Identify and analyze influences, contexts, or biases. (FA.3.04.7)
- Use and place modifiers correctly. (GU.6.02.3)

Literary Analysis

A **persuasive speech** is a speech that tries to convince listeners to think or act in a certain way. Persuasive speeches may appeal to reason or emotion or both. In order to engage the audience, speakers often include **rhetorical devices,** patterns of words and ideas that create emphasis and stir emotion in the audience. Common rhetorical devices include the following:

- **Parallelism:** repeating a grammatical structure or an arrangement of words to create a sense of rhythm and momentum
- **Restatement:** expressing the same idea in different words to clarify and stress key points
- **Repetition:** expressing different ideas using the same words or images in order to reinforce concepts and unify the speech
- **Analogy:** drawing a comparison that shows a similarity between unlike things

Reading Skill

Persuasive techniques are devices used to influence the audience in favor of the author's argument. In addition to presenting evidence in a persuasive speech, a speaker may also use emotionally charged language and rhetorical devices, such as those listed above.

To analyze and evaluate persuasive techniques, **read aloud** to hear the effect. Notice the emotional impact of certain words and the rhythm and momentum created by specific word patterns. Consider both the purpose and effect of these persuasive techniques. Use a chart like the one shown to organize your analysis.

Technique:	
Purpose	**Effect**

Technique:	
Purpose	**Effect**

Vocabulary Builder

I Have a Dream

- **hallowed** (hal′ ōd) *adj.* sacred (p. 496) *The battlefield is considered by many to be <u>hallowed</u> ground.*
- **degenerate** (dē jen′ ər āt) *v.* grow worse (p. 497) *Don't let this discussion <u>degenerate</u> into a shouting match.*
- **creed** (krēd) *n.* statement of belief (p. 498) *The <u>creed</u> of brotherhood is preached by many who do not practice it.*

First Inaugural Address

- **abdicated** (ab′ di kāt id) *v.* gave up formally (p. 505) *The king <u>abdicated</u> his throne and left the country.*
- **evanescent** (ev′ ə nes′ ənt) *adj.* temporary; tending to disappear (p. 506) *The band's <u>evanescent</u> popularity was gone in a week.*
- **arduous** (är′ jōō əs) *adj.* difficult; laborious (p. 509) *Rebuilding the house by ourselves was an <u>arduous</u> task.*

Speech

Background

The Civil Rights Movement The U.S. Constitution guarantees certain rights to all Americans. The struggle of African Americans to have their rights recognized is known as the civil rights movement. Marked by demonstrations and legal challenges, this movement began in the 1950s and was led by figures like Martin Luther King, Jr.

Connecting to the Literature

Reading/Writing Connection In "I Have a Dream," Martin Luther King, Jr., challenges Americans to live up to national ideals of equality and justice. Write a short paragraph in which you describe some other ideals that you consider to be characteristically American. Use at least three of these words: *embody, comprise, define, invoke.*

READ MORE

by
Martin Luther King, Jr.
"Letter from a Birmingham Jail"

Meet the Author

Dr. Martin Luther King, Jr. (1929–1968)

Born in Atlanta, Georgia, Dr. Martin Luther King, Jr., was the most charismatic leader of the civil rights movement. During the 1950s and 1960s, King organized nonviolent protests to bring about equal rights for all Americans.

A Voice for the Oppressed King first came to national attention in 1956 in Montgomery, Alabama, when he organized a 382-day boycott of the city's segregated buses by African Americans. He went on to lead other protests and to speak out eloquently against poverty and social injustice. He was assassinated on April 4, 1968. His birthday, January 15, has since become a national holiday.

Fast Facts

▶ At thirty-five, King became the youngest man and only the third black man to be awarded a Nobel Peace Prize.
▶ The song "Pride (in the Name of Love)" by the famous rock band U2 is a tribute to Martin Luther King, Jr.

Go Online
Author Link

For: more about the author
Visit: www.PHSchool.com
Web Code: epe-9310

"I Have a Dream"

Martin Luther King, Jr.

Background Because speeches are written to be spoken aloud, they are a more fluid form of literature than most other nonfiction. A strong speaker will react to unspoken signals from his or her listeners and adjust a speech accordingly. He or she might change words or add whole phrases. This is the case with Dr. Martin Luther King, Jr., one of the greatest speakers of the modern age. The text that appears here represents the speech exactly as it was delivered by Dr. King on the steps of the Lincoln Memorial.

Five score years ago, a great American, in whose symbolic shadow we stand today, signed the Emancipation Proclamation. This momentous decree came as a great beacon light of hope to millions of Negro slaves who had been seared in the flames of withering injustice. It came as a joyous daybreak to end the long night of their captivity.

But one hundred years later, the Negro still is not free. One hundred years later, the life of the Negro is still sadly crippled by the manacles of segregation and the chains of discrimination. One hundred years later, the Negro lives on a lonely island of poverty in the midst of a vast ocean of material prosperity. One hundred years later, the Negro is still languished in the corners of American society and finds himself an exile in his own land. So we've come here today to dramatize a shameful condition.

In a sense we've come to our nation's Capital to cash a check. When the architects of our republic wrote the magnificent words of the Constitution and the Declaration of Independence, they were signing a promissory note[1] to which every American was to fall heir. This note was a promise that all men, yes, black men as well as white men, would be guaranteed the unalienable rights of life, liberty, and the pursuit of happiness.

It is obvious today that America has defaulted on this promissory note insofar as her citizens of color are concerned. Instead of honoring this sacred obligation, America has given the Negro people a bad check; a check which has come back marked "insufficient funds." But we refuse to believe that the bank of justice is bankrupt. We refuse to believe that there are insufficient funds in the great vaults of opportunity of this nation. And so we've come to cash this check—a check that will give us upon demand the riches of freedom

---

1. promissory (präm´ i sôr´ ē) **note** written promise to pay a specific amount.

Literary Analysis
Persuasive Speech
What idea does King's repetition of the phrase "One hundred years later" help to emphasize?

Literary Analysis
Persuasive Speech
Explain the analogy King makes between a financial transaction and the idea of justice.

Reading Check

What injustices are King and his listeners protesting?

◄ **Critical Viewing** Which details in this photograph demonstrate the importance of the event at which King gave his speech? **[Analyze]**

and the security of justice. We have also come to this <u>hallowed</u> spot to remind America of the fierce urgency of *now*. This is no time to engage in the luxury of cooling off or to take the tranquilizing drug of gradualism.

Now is the time to make real the promises of Democracy.

Now is the time to rise from the dark and desolate valley of segregation to the sunlit path of racial justice.

Now is the time to lift our nation from the quicksands of racial injustice to the solid rock of brotherhood.

Now is the time to make justice a reality for all of God's children.

It would be fatal for the nation to overlook the urgency of the moment. This sweltering summer of the Negro's legitimate discontent will not pass until there is an invigorating autumn of freedom and equality. Nineteen sixty-three is not an end, but a beginning. Those who hope that the Negro needed to blow off steam and will now be content will have a rude awakening if the nation returns to business as usual. There will be neither rest nor tranquillity in America until the Negro is granted his citizenship rights. The whirlwinds of revolt will continue to shake the foundations of our nation until the bright day of justice emerges.

Vocabulary Builder
hallowed (hal´ ōd) *adj.*
sacred

▼ Critical Viewing
How would you describe King's expression as he delivers his speech? **[Analyze]**

But there is something that I must say to my people who stand on the warm threshold which leads into the palace of justice. In the process of gaining our rightful place we must not be guilty of wrongful deeds. Let us not seek to satisfy our thirst for freedom by drinking from the cup of bitterness and hatred. We must forever conduct our struggle on the high plane of dignity and discipline. We must not allow our creative protest to <u>degenerate</u> into physical violence. Again and again we must rise to the majestic heights of meeting physical force with soul force. The marvelous new militancy which has engulfed the Negro community must not lead us to a distrust of all white people, for many of our white brothers, as evidenced by their presence here today, have come to realize that their destiny is tied up with our destiny. And they have come to realize that their freedom is inextricably bound to our freedom. We cannot walk alone.

And as we walk, we must make the pledge that we shall always march ahead. We cannot turn back. There are those who are asking the devotees of civil rights, "When will you be satisfied?" We can never be satisfied as long as the Negro is the victim of the unspeakable horrors of police brutality. We can never be satisfied as long as our bodies, heavy with the fatigue of travel, cannot gain lodging in the motels of the highways and the hotels of the cities. We cannot be satisfied as long as the Negro's basic mobility is from a smaller ghetto to a larger one. We cannot be satisfied as long as a Negro in Mississippi cannot vote and a Negro in New York believes he has nothing for which to vote. No, no, we are not satisfied, and we will not be satisfied until justice rolls down like waters and righteousness like a mighty stream.

I am not unmindful that some of you have come here out of great trials and tribulations. Some of you have come fresh from narrow jail cells. Some of you have come from areas where your quest for freedom left you battered by the storms of persecution and staggered by the winds of police brutality. You have been the veterans of creative suffering. Continue to work with the faith that unearned suffering is redemptive.

Go back to Mississippi, go back to Alabama, go back to South Carolina, go back to Georgia, go back to Louisiana, go back to the slums and ghettos of our northern cities, knowing that somehow this situation can and will be changed. Let us not wallow in the valley of despair.

I say to you today, my friends, so even though we face the difficulties of today and tomorrow, I still have a dream. It is a dream deeply rooted in the American dream.

Vocabulary Builder
degenerate (dē jen´ ər āt´) v. grow worse

Literary Analysis
Persuasive Speech
What key idea does King restate when he says, "We cannot walk alone"?

Reading Check

According to King, how should his people react to physical force?

I have a dream that one day this nation will rise up and live out the true meaning of its creed: "We hold these truths to be self-evident; that all men are created equal."

I have a dream that one day on the red hills of Georgia the sons of former slaves and the sons of former slaveowners will be able to sit down together at the table of brotherhood.

I have a dream that one day even the state of Mississippi, a state sweltering with the heat of injustice, sweltering with the heat of oppression, will be transformed into an oasis of freedom and justice.

I have a dream that my four little children will one day live in a nation where they will not be judged by the color of their skin but by the content of their character.

I have a dream today.

I have a dream that one day down in Alabama, with its vicious racists, with its governor still having his lips dripping with the words of interposition and nullification,[2] one day right down in Alabama little black boys and black girls will be able to join hands with little white boys and white girls as sisters and brothers.

I have a dream today.

I have a dream that one day every valley shall be exalted, every hill and mountain shall be made low, the rough places will be made plains, and the crooked places will be made straight, and the glory of the Lord shall be revealed, and all flesh shall see it together.[3]

This is our hope. This is the faith that I go back to the South with. With this faith we will be able to hew out of the mountain of despair a stone of hope. With this faith we will be able to transform the jangling discords of our nation into a beautiful symphony of brotherhood. With this faith we will be able to work together, to pray together, to struggle together, to go to jail together, to stand up for freedom together, knowing that we will be free one day.

This will be the day when all of God's children will be able to sing with new meaning

> My country, 'tis of thee,
> Sweet land of liberty,
>   Of thee I sing:
> Land where my fathers died,
> Land of the pilgrims' pride,
> From every mountainside
>   Let freedom ring.

---

2. interposition (in´ tər pə zish´ ən) **and nullification** (nul´ ə fi kā´ shən) disputed doctrine that a state can reject federal laws considered to be violations of its rights. Governor George C. Wallace used this doctrine to reject federal civil rights legislation.

3. every valley . . . all flesh shall see it together reference to a biblical passage (Isaiah 40:4–5). King is likening the struggle of African Americans to the struggle of the Israelites.

And if America is to be a great nation this must become true. So let freedom ring from the prodigious hilltops of New Hampshire. Let freedom ring from the mighty mountains of New York. Let freedom ring from the heightening Alleghenies of Pennsylvania!

Let freedom ring from the snowcapped Rockies of Colorado!

Let freedom ring from the curvacious slopes of California!

But not only that; let freedom ring from Stone Mountain of Georgia!

Let freedom ring from Lookout Mountain of Tennessee!

Let freedom ring from every hill and molehill of Mississippi. From every mountainside, let freedom ring.

And when this happens, when we allow freedom to ring, when we let it ring from every village and every hamlet, from every state and every city, we will be able to speed up that day when all of God's children, black men and white men, Jews and Gentiles, Protestants and Catholics, will be able to join hands and sing in the words of the old Negro spiritual, "Free at last! free at last! thank God almighty, we are free at last!"

▼ **Critical Viewing** Which part of the speech do you think King is delivering in this photograph? **[Connect]**

Apply the Skills

I Have a Dream

Thinking About the Selection

1. **Respond:** What feelings does Dr. King's "I Have a Dream" speech stir in you? Explain.
2. **(a) Recall:** Which words does King quote from "My Country 'Tis of Thee"? **(b) Interpret:** What message does he send to his audience by quoting these lines?
3. **(a) Recall:** Which different parts of the United States does King mention in his speech? **(b) Connect:** How does the mention of all of these places tie in with the overall message of his speech?
4. **(a) Hypothesize:** Why do you think "I Have a Dream" has lived on as one of the best-known speeches in modern history? **(b) Make a Judgment:** Do you think it deserves this standing? Explain.

Literary Analysis

5. In this **persuasive speech**, what is Martin Luther King, Jr., trying to persuade his audience to think or do?
6. **(a)** In what ways does King appeal to emotion in this speech? Explain. **(b)** In what ways does he appeal to reason? Explain.
7. **(a)** Using a chart like the one shown, identify examples in King's speech of the **rhetorical devices** listed. (You may not be able to find an example of every device.) **(b)** Describe the effect of each example you cite.

	Example	Effect
Restatement		
Repetition		
Parallelism		
Analogy		

Reading Skill

8. **(a)** Identify a passage in which King uses emotionally charged language as a **persuasive technique**. **(b)** What specific purpose do you think King had in using such language? Explain. **(c)** Describe the emotional effect of the words King uses in the passage.
9. Do you think that King uses emotionally charged language and rhetorical devices effectively and convincingly in this speech? Explain your answer.

QuickReview

Speech at a Glance
Martin Luther King, Jr., shares his dream of racial equality in America.

Go Online
Assessment
For: Self-test
Visit: www.PHSchool.com
Web Code: epa-6309

Persuasive Speech: a speech that tries to convince listeners to think or act in a certain way

Rhetorical Devices: patterns of words and ideas that speakers use to create emphasis and stir emotion. These devices include *parallelism, restatement, repetition,* and *analogy.*

Persuasive Techniques: devices used to influence the audience in favor of the author's argument

Vocabulary Builder

Practice Analogies show the relationships between pairs of words. Use a word from the "I Have a Dream" vocabulary list on page 492 to complete each analogy.

1. stumble : rise :: _____ : improve
2. oath : office :: _____ : religion
3. barren : desert :: _____ : church

Adding Words to Your Vocabulary Using a thesaurus, find a **synonym,** or word with a similar meaning, for each word in the "I Have a Dream" vocabulary list. Then, use each synonym correctly in a sentence. (For more on using a thesaurus, see page R7.)

Writing

Write a **proposal** to persuade your principal to invite a great speaker like Dr. King to address a school assembly.
- List some issues that concern students at your school.
- List possible speakers and the issues that each could discuss.
- Choose one speaker, and write a proposal supporting your choice.
End with an appeal to your principal to act on the proposal.

For *Grammar, Vocabulary,* and *Assessment,* see **Build Language Skills,** pages 512–513.

Extend Your Learning

Listening and Speaking Compose a **radio news report** that provides on-the-spot coverage of King's speech. Include the following:
- background information about the civil rights movement
- excerpts from King's speech
- a description of the speech's effect on the crowd

Broadcast your report to the class and record it for later evaluation.

Research and Technology In a group, create an **annotated source list** for a multimedia presentation about one aspect of the civil rights movement such as laws, marches, or leaders. Find sources of photographs and video and audio recordings of events. List each source following MLA format. (For more on MLA format, see page R33.) Briefly explain the information found in each source.

Build Understanding • *First Inaugural Address*

Speech

Background

The Great Depression On March 4, 1933, newly elected President Franklin Delano Roosevelt delivered his inaugural address to a nation close to despair. The Great Depression had weighed down American life for over three years. Americans sat by their radios to hear the new president's address, a speech he had written himself. In this speech, Roosevelt gave Americans hope.

Connecting to the Literature

Reading/Writing Connection The right words at the right time can inspire hope. Write a short paragraph describing a time when someone else's words inspired you. Use at least three of these words: *evoke, project, render, stimulate, transform.*

Review

For **Literary Analysis, Reading Skill,** and **Vocabulary Builder,** see page 492.

READ MORE

**by Franklin D. Roosevelt
Second Inaugural Address**

Meet the Author

Franklin Delano Roosevelt (1882–1945)

Franklin Delano Roosevelt had a relatively easy life until he was stricken with polio at age 39. Ironically, Roosevelt realized his potential as a leader only after falling victim to this illness. He was twice elected governor of New York and then in 1932 defeated President Herbert Hoover to become the nation's thirty-second president. Roosevelt won an unprecedented four terms as president.

A Leader in Dark Times Franklin Roosevelt led the nation through two great challenges: the Great Depression and World War II. The war was almost over when the president died of a cerebral hemorrhage in 1945.

Fast Facts

▶ Roosevelt helped found the March of Dimes, originally established to raise money to combat polio. His image was later put on the dime to honor his efforts.
▶ Roosevelt's wife, Eleanor, became one of the most active and widely admired first ladies in American history.

Go Online
Author Link

For: More about the author
Visit: www.PHSchool.com
Web Code: epe-9311

FIRST INAUGURAL ADDRESS
Franklin Delano Roosevelt

President Hoover, Mr Chief Justice, my friends:

This is a day of national consecration,[1] and I am certain that my fellow-Americans expect that on my induction into the Presidency I will address them with a candor and a decision which the present situation of our nation impels.

This is pre-eminently the time to speak the truth, the whole truth, frankly and boldly. Nor need we shrink from honestly facing conditions in our country today. This great nation will endure as it has endured, will revive and will prosper.

So first of all let me assert my firm belief that the only thing we have to fear is fear itself—nameless, unreasoning, unjustified terror which paralyzes needed efforts to convert retreat into advance.

✓ Reading Check

With what qualities does Roosevelt promise to address his audience?

---

1. **consecration** (kän′ si krā′ shən) *n.* dedication to something sacred.

In every dark hour of our national life a leadership of frankness and vigor has met with that understanding and support of the people themselves which is essential to victory. I am convinced that you will again give that support to leadership in these critical days.

In such a spirit on my part and on yours we face our common difficulties. They concern, thank God, only material things. Values have shrunken to fantastic levels; taxes have risen; our ability to pay has fallen, government of all kinds is faced by serious curtailment of income; the means of exchange are frozen in the currents of trade; the withered leaves of industrial enterprise lie on every side; farmers find no markets for their produce; the savings of many years in thousands of families are gone.

More important, a host of unemployed citizens face the grim problem of existence, and an equally great number toil with little return. Only a foolish optimist can deny the dark realities of the moment.

Yet our distress comes from no failure of substance. We are stricken by no plague of locusts.[2] Compared with the perils which our forefathers conquered because they believed and were not

2. **plague of locusts** according to Exodus 10:3–20, the plague of locusts was one of ten plagues inflicted by God on the Egyptians as punishment for enslaving the Israelites.

Reading Skill
Persuasive Techniques
How do you think Roosevelt wanted listeners to respond to the emotionally charged language here?

▼ **Critical Viewing**
This is a photograph of a bread line during the Great Depression. Why do you think conditions like this might make Americans fearful? **[Infer]**

afraid, we have still much to be thankful for. Nature still offers her bounty and human efforts have multiplied it. Plenty is at our doorstep, but a generous use of it languishes in the very sight of the supply.

Primarily, this is because the rulers of the exchange of mankind's goods have failed through their own stubbornness and their own incompetence, have admitted that failure and <u>abdicated</u>. Practices of the unscrupulous money changers stand indicted in the court of public opinion, rejected by the hearts and minds of men.

True, they have tried, but their efforts have been cast in the pattern of an outworn tradition. Faced by failure of credit, they have proposed only the lending of more money.

Stripped of the lure of profit by which to induce our people to follow their false leadership, they have resorted to exhortations, pleading tearfully for restored confidence. They know only the rules of a generation of self-seekers.

They have no vision, and when there is no vision the people perish.

The money changers have fled from their high seats in the temple[3] of our civilization. We may now restore that temple to the ancient truths.

The measure of the restoration lies in the extent to which we apply social values more noble than mere monetary profit.

---

3. **money changers . . . temple** allusion to Matthew 21:12–13, in which Jesus overturns the money changers' tables at the temple in Jerusalem. FDR is comparing those ancient money changers to modern bankers who took high risks with depositors' money and who charged excessive interest rates for loans.

Literary Analysis
Persuasive Speech
How might this description of national problems have changed people's minds about their troubles?

Vocabulary Builder
abdicated (ab′ di kāt′ id) v. gave up formally

 Reading Check

On whom does Roosevelt place the largest blame for the Great Depression?

Happiness lies not in the mere possession of money; it lies in the joy of achievement, in the thrill of creative effort.

The joy and moral stimulation of work no longer must be forgotten in the mad chase of <u>evanescent</u> profits. These dark days will be worth all they cost us if they teach us that our true destiny is not to be ministered unto but to minister to ourselves and to our fellowmen.

Recognition of the falsity of material wealth as the standard of success goes hand in hand with the abandonment of the false belief that public office and high political position are to be valued only by the standards of pride of place and personal profit; and there must be an end to a conduct in banking and in business which too often has given to a sacred trust the likeness of callous and selfish wrongdoing.

Small wonder that confidence languishes, for it thrives only on honesty, on honor, on the sacredness of obligations, on faithful protection, on unselfish performance. Without them it cannot live.

Restoration calls, however, not for changes in ethics alone. This nation asks for action, and action now.

Our greatest primary task is to put people to work. This is no unsolvable problem if we face it wisely and courageously. . . .

I favor as a practical policy the putting of first things first. I shall spare no effort to restore world trade by international economic readjustment, but the emergency at home cannot wait on that accomplishment.

The basic thought that guides these specific means of national recovery is not narrowly nationalistic.

It is the insistence, as a first consideration, upon the interdependence of the various elements in, and parts of, the United States—a recognition of the old and permanently important manifestation of the American spirit of the pioneer.

It is the way to recovery. It is the immediate way. It is the strongest assurance that the recovery will endure.

In the field of world policy I would dedicate this nation to the policy of the good neighbor—the neighbor who resolutely respects himself and, because he does so, respects the rights of others—the neighbor who respects his obligations and respects the sanctity of his agreements in and with a world of neighbors.

If I read the temper of our people correctly, we now realize as we have never before, our interdependence on each other; that we cannot merely take, but we must give as well; that if we are to go forward we must move as a trained and loyal army willing to sacrifice for the good of a common discipline, because, without such discipline, no progress is made, no leadership becomes effective.

Vocabulary Builder
evanescent (ev´ ə nes´ ənt) *adj.* temporary; tending to disappear

Literary Analysis
Persuasive Speech
Identify the parallelism in the paragraph beginning "It is the way . . ." and explain what it emphasizes.

We are, I know, ready and willing to submit our lives and property to such discipline because it makes possible a leadership which aims at a larger good.

This I propose to offer, pledging that the larger purposes will bind upon us all as a sacred obligation with a unity of duty hitherto evoked only in time of armed strife.

With this pledge taken, I assume unhesitatingly the leadership of this great army of our people, dedicated to a disciplined attack upon our common problems.

✓ **Reading Check**

What does Roosevelt say is the "greatest primary task" facing the nation?

Literature in Context   Social Studies Connection

Getting Back to Work: FDR and the WPA

In 1935, President Roosevelt established the Works Progress Administration (WPA) to aid struggling Americans. At the height of its activity, the WPA provided jobs to one third of the unemployed, ranging from artists to construction workers.

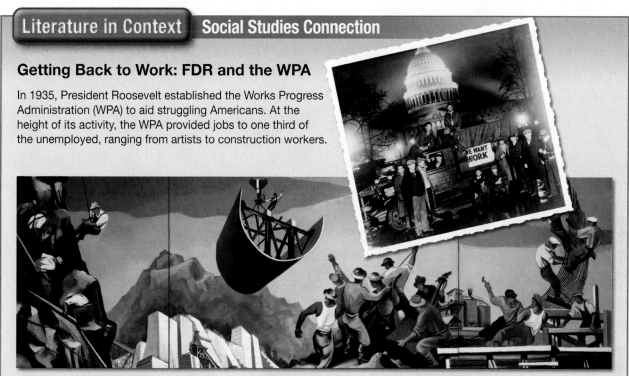

▲ Mural painted by WPA artist William Gropper shows the building of a WPA project dam.

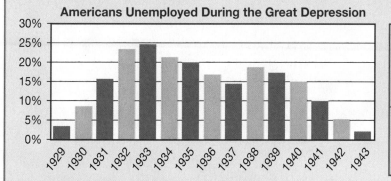

Americans Unemployed During the Great Depression

The WPA Projects		
WPA workers produced:	650,000	miles of roads
	125,000	public buildings
	75,000	bridges
	8,000	parks
	800	airports
WPA artists created:	2,566	murals
	100,000	paintings
	17,700	sculptures
	300,000	fine prints

Connect to the Literature President Roosevelt gave his First Inaugural Address in March of 1933. Basing your answer on the chart of unemployment, explain why this was a particularly hard time in American life.

Action in this image and to this end is feasible under the forms of government which we have inherited from our ancestors.

Our Constitution is so simple and practical that it is possible always to meet extraordinary needs by changes in emphasis and arrangement without loss of essential form.

That is why our constitutional system has proved itself the most superbly enduring political mechanism the modern world has produced. It has met every stress of vast expansion of territory, of foreign wars, of bitter internal strife, of world relations. . . .

I am prepared under my constitutional duty to recommend the measures that a stricken nation in the midst of a stricken world may require.

These measures, or such other measures as the Congress may build out of its experience and wisdom, I shall seek, within my constitutional authority, to bring to speedy adoption.

But in the event that the Congress shall fail to take one of these two courses, and in the event that the national emergency is still critical, I shall not evade the clear course of duty that will then confront me.

I shall ask the Congress for the one remaining instrument to meet the crisis—broad executive power to wage a war against the emergency as great as the power that would be given me if we were in fact invaded by a foreign foe.

For the trust reposed in me I will return the courage and the devotion that befit the time. I can do no less.

We face the <u>arduous</u> days that lie before us in the warm courage of national unity; with the clear consciousness of seeking old and precious moral values; with the clean satisfaction that comes from the stern performance of duty by old and young alike.

We aim at the assurance of a rounded and permanent national life.

We do not distrust the future of essential democracy. The people of the United States have not failed. In their need they have registered a mandate that they want direct, vigorous action.

They have asked for discipline and direction under leadership. They have made me the present instrument of their wishes. In the spirit of the gift I take it.

In this dedication of a nation we humbly ask the blessing of God. May He protect each and every one of us. May He guide me in the days to come.

◀ **Critical Viewing** This photograph of President Roosevelt was taken on the day of his first inauguration. Do you think he projects an image of confidence? Explain. **[Analyze]**

Literary Analysis
Persuasive Speech
What call to action does Roosevelt issue to Congress in this passage?

Vocabulary Builder
arduous (är′ joo əs)
adj. difficult; laborious

Apply the Skills

First Inaugural Address

Thinking About the Selection

1. **Respond:** What feelings does Roosevelt's speech stir in you? Why?
2. **(a) Recall:** What words does Roosevelt use to describe the financial leaders who had caused the country's financial problems? **(b) Interpret:** What message does he send to the American people by describing financial leaders in these terms?
3. **(a) Recall:** What does Roosevelt say about Americans from earlier periods in history? **(b) Speculate:** How do you think his listeners felt on hearing about earlier Americans?
4. **Make a Judgment:** Roosevelt's speech was made over seventy years ago to a country in economic ruin. Which parts of the speech do you think would be most appealing to Americans today? Which parts might be less appealing? Explain.

Literary Analysis

5. In this **persuasive speech**, what is President Roosevelt trying to persuade his audience to think or do?
6. **(a)** In what ways does Roosevelt appeal to emotion in his speech? Explain. **(b)** In what ways does he appeal to reason? Explain.
7. **(a)** Using a chart like the one shown, identify examples in Roosevelt's speech of the **rhetorical devices** listed. (You may not be able to find an example of every device.) **(b)** Describe the effect of each example you cite.

	Example	Effect
Restatement		
Repetition		
Parallelism		
Analogy		

Reading Skill

8. **(a)** Identify a passage in which Roosevelt uses emotionally charged language as a **persuasive technique**. **(b)** What specific purpose do you think he had in using such language in the passage? Explain. **(c)** Describe the emotional effect of the passage.
9. Does Roosevelt use emotionally charged language and rhetorical devices effectively in this speech? Explain your answer.

Vocabulary Builder

Practice Analogies show the relationships between pairs of words. Use a word from the "First Inaugural Address" vocabulary list on page 492 to complete each analogy.

1. coach : resigned :: ruler : _____
2. ongoing : rain :: _____ : lightning
3. vacation : relaxing :: labor : _____

Adding Words to Your Vocabulary Using a thesaurus, find a **synonym,** or word with a similar meaning, for each word in the "First Inaugural Address" vocabulary list. Then, use each synonym correctly in a sentence. (For more on using a thesaurus, see page R7.)

Writing

Write a **proposal** to persuade your principal to invite a great speaker like President Roosevelt to address a school assembly:
- List some issues that concern students at your school.
- List possible speakers and the issues that each could discuss.
- Choose a speaker, and write a proposal supporting your choice.

End with an appeal to your principal to act on the proposal.

For *Grammar, Vocabulary,* and *Assessment,*
see **Build Language Skills,** pages 512–513.

Extend Your Learning

Listening and Speaking Compose a **radio news report** that provides on-the-spot coverage of Roosevelt's speech. Include the following in your report:
- background information about the Great Depression
- excerpts from Roosevelt's speech
- a description of the speech's effect on the crowd

Broadcast your report to the class, and record it for later evaluation.

Research and Technology In a group, create an **annotated source list** for a multimedia presentation about one aspect of the Great Depression such as its causes, its effects, or the government's attempts to deal with it. Find sources of photographs and video and audio recordings from that time. Then, list those sources following MLA format. (For more on MLA format, see page R32.) Briefly explain the information found in each source.

Build Language Skills

Vocabulary Skill

Prefixes The **Latin prefix** *inter-* means "between, among, or within" and is contained in words that express a variety of ideas about "within" or "between." For example, *internal* expresses the idea of "within" something. Other words containing *inter-* relate to something between, such as the word *interfere,* which means "to come in between for some purpose."

▶ **Example:** Sally did not want to *interfere* in the argument between two of her good friends.

Practice All of the following words contain the prefix *inter-*. Write a definition of each word, explaining whether the word expresses the idea of *between, among,* or *within.* Then, use each word in a sentence.

1. interject
2. intermediate
3. interior
4. intermission
5. interval

Grammar Lesson

Adverbs *Adverbs* are words that modify verbs, adjectives, and other adverbs. They answer the questions *Where? When? In what way?* and *To what extent?* about the words they modify.

Modifying a verb: Dave drove the car <u>smoothly</u>. (The adverb *smoothly* modifies the verb *drove*.)

Modifying an adjective: He drove an <u>extremely</u> large car. (The adverb *extremely* modifies the adjective *large*.)

Modifying another adverb: He drove the car <u>very</u> smoothly. (The adverb *very* modifies the adverb *smoothly*.)

MorePractice

For more practice with adverbs, see the Grammar Handbook, p. R40.

Practice Circle each of the adverbs and underline the word or words it modifies. Indicate whether the modified word is a verb, an adjective, or an adverb. Rewrite each sentence, replacing the adverb with a new one.

1. He certainly felt that he was successful.
2. Grandmother took very good care of this house.
3. Lester sang so terribly.
4. Keri ran excitedly into the dining room.
5. The children hid away in the attic.

W̶G̶ Prentice Hall Writing and Grammar Connection: Chapter 18, Section 2

Reading Skill: Analyzing Persuasive Appeals

Directions: *Read the selection. Then, answer the questions.*

Standards Assessed

- IR.2.04.1
- IR.2.04.3
- IR.2.04.4

. . . as the first President of a united, democratic, nonracial, and nonsexist South Africa, to lead our country out of the valley of darkness. . . .

We know it well that none of us acting alone can achieve success. We must therefore act together as a united people. . . .

Let there be justice for all. . . .

<u>Never, never, and never again</u> shall it be that this beautiful land will again experience the oppression of one by another and suffer the indignity of being the skunk of the world.

The sun shall never set on so glorious a human achievement! Let freedom reign. God bless Africa!

—from *Glory and Hope,* by Nelson Mandela

1. The emotional terms "valley of darkness" and "skunk of the world" are meant to persuade Mandela's listeners that
  A South Africa did not deserve negative world opinion.
  B South Africa's recent history was a time of suffering and shame.
  C his government will solve most of people's problems.
  D South Africans are in danger of forgetting the lessons of their past.

2. What is the effect of the underlined phrase?
  A It comforts listeners with familiar words.
  B It surprises listeners with a new idea.
  C It rouses listeners with its repetition and rhythm.
  D It makes listeners ashamed.

3. The use of the statements beginning with "Let . . ." convey a tone of
  A happiness.
  B devotion.
  C confidence.
  D desperation.

Timed Writing: Evaluation [Critical Stance]

Review "I Have a Dream" by Dr. Martin Luther King, Jr., or President Franklin Roosevelt's First Inaugural Address. Write an evaluation of the persuasive techniques used in one of these selections. Include specific references from the text to support your ideas. **(30 minutes)**

Writing Workshop: *Work in Progress*

Editorial

Review the portfolio list of Cultural Influences. Identify one cultural factor that you feel has the greatest effect on you and your friends. In a two-column chart, jot down three positive and three negative aspects of this influence. Save this chart in your writing portfolio.

Reading Informational Materials

Historical Research Study

In Part 2, you learned how to analyze and evaluate persuasive texts. You will also find this skill useful when reading informational materials, such as advertisements, editorials, and historical studies. If you read President Roosevelt's "First Inaugural Address," you will see how the author of the following historical study analyzes his speech.

About Historical Research Studies

In a **historical research study,** the writer evaluates and interprets a speech, a document, or an event in history. When a writer studies a speech, he or she analyzes the words to understand both their meaning for people at the time and the meaning they may hold for people today. The writer also shows how the speech connects to other ideas and other historical events. A historical study typically includes these features:

- an introduction stating the author's thesis, or main idea
- a summary of all or part of the historical document
- facts and opinions
- quotations, examples, or statistics
- explanations and interpretations
- transitions to link ideas
- a conclusion restating the thesis and main points

Reading Skill

When reading a historical study, **distinguish fact from opinion.** A **fact** can be proved true. In contrast, an **opinion** is what someone thinks. It may be valid, but it cannot be proved. A valid opinion is supported by facts.

Statements using absolute words such as *always, everybody,* and *never* indicate **overgeneralizations.** Overgeneralizations are statements that may look factual, but they are usually too broad to be proven true and should be distinguished from facts. As you read, record the facts and opinions you find in a chart like the one shown.

NC Standard Course of Study

- Identify and analyze influences, contexts, or biases in response. (WL.1.03.6)
- Analyze influences, contexts, or biases in argument. (FA.3.01.4)
- Use various types of evidence to support an opinion. (FA.3.03.2)

Statement	Provable?	Fact or Opinion
In 1921, Roosevelt contracted polio.	Yes. Check a biography or an encyclopedia entry about Roosevelt.	Fact
Fear is a fog; it obscures the truth.	No	Opinion

from **Nothing To Fear:**
Lessons in Leadership from FDR

by Alan Axelrod

> The study begins with a quotation from FDR's speech. It reminds the reader of the speech and its famous line: "The only thing we have to fear is fear itself."

"This great nation will endure as it has endured, will revive and will prosper. So, first of all, let me assert my firm belief that the only thing we have to fear is fear itself—nameless, unreasoning, unjustified terror which paralyzes needed efforts to convert retreat into advance."

—First inaugural address, March 4, 1933

In *Defending Your Life,* a charmingly provocative 1991 movie written and directed by its star, Albert Brooks, we discover that the only truly unforgivable sin in life is fear. Killed in a head-on crash with a bus, yuppie Brooks finds himself transported to Judgment City, where he must "defend his life" before a pair of judges who will decide whether he is to be returned to Earth for another crack at life or be permitted to progress to the next plane of existence. His attorney (for the benevolent managers of the universe provide defense assistance) explains to him the nature of fear, which is, he says, a "fog" that obscures everything and that makes intelligent, productive action impossible.

> Axelrod uses this description of a popular movie as an engaging introduction.

It is a stimulating thought—that fear is not so much the sensation accompanying the realization of danger, but a fog, an obscurer of truth, an interference with how we may productively engage reality. Certainly this is the way FDR saw it. In 1921 polio threatened first to kill him and then paralyzed him, subjected him to a life of relentless pain, and nearly ended his career in public service. He could then and there have given in to the fog of fear, but he chose not to. He chose instead to understand polio, to see clearly the extent of his disability, and then to assess—also clearly—his options for overcoming that disability. He did not blink at the odds. He looked at them, contemplated them, assessed them, and then acted on them.

Franklin D. Roosevelt with a local child, 1941.

Now, more than a decade later, assuming the office of president of the United States, he began by asking the American people to sweep aside the fog of fear, "nameless, unreasoning, unjustified terror which paralyzes needed efforts to convert retreat into advance." He didn't ask them to stop being afraid, but to stop letting fear obscure their vision of reality. He asked the people to confront what they feared, so that they could see clearly what needed to be done and thereby overcome (and the word is significant) the terror that *paralyzes*.

In the second paragraph of his inaugural speech, FDR lifted the fog of fear. What did he reveal to his audience, the American people?

> Values have shrunken to fantastic levels; taxes have risen; our ability to pay has fallen; government of all kinds is faced by serious curtailment of income; the means of exchange are frozen in the currents of trade; the withered leaves of industrial enterprise lie on every side; farmers find no markets for their produce; the savings of many years in thousands of families are gone.

There is no sugarcoating of reality here! The fog has lifted, the scene is sharply etched and downright frightening: "a host of unemployed citizens face the grim problem of existence, and an equally great number toil with little return. Only a foolish optimist can deny the dark realities of the moment."

FDR did not blink at reality and he did not allow his audience to do so either. He embarked on this catalog of economic disasters by defining them as "our common difficulties," which "concern, thank God, only material things."

The fog was lifted and the president's listeners could see the reality they already knew, a reality of poverty and despair, to be sure; yet with the fog of fear lifted, they could see it in a new light: Our common difficulties "concern, thank God, only material things."

Not one to blink at disaster, FDR also saw a way out of it:

> Yet our distress comes from no failure of substance. We are stricken by no plague of locusts. Compared with the perils which our forefathers conquered because they believed and were not afraid, we have still much to be thankful for. Nature still offers her bounty and human efforts have multiplied it. Plenty is at our doorstep. . .

Lift the fog of fear and you could see that the Great Depression was not of natural, supernatural, or inevitable origin. It was not a plague of biblical proportion. Our kind has conquered worse in the past. Nature has not failed us.

Margin notes:

Axelrod provides information about the historical circumstances in which the speech was given.

Axelrod refers back to the "fog" described in the introduction. In later paragraphs, he continues to refer to the "fog of fear." This repetition helps tie the essay together.

Axelrod provides an opinion: "There is no sugarcoating of reality here!" Then, he presents lines from the speech to support the opinion.

What, then, was the problem?

> Plenty is at our doorstep, but a generous use of it languishes in the very sight of the supply. Primarily this is because rulers of the exchange of mankind's good have failed through their own stubbornness and their own incompetence, have admitted their failure, and have abdicated. Practices of unscrupulous money changers stand indicted in the court of public opinion, rejected by the hearts and minds of men.

> Axelrod provides a summary of the problems stated in the excerpt below.

The failure was a failure of particular human beings and the particular policies they pursued. "True," Roosevelt continued, these particular people "have tried, but their efforts have been cast in the pattern of an outworn tradition."

> Faced by failure of credit they have proposed only the lending of more money. Stripped of the lure of profit by which to induce our people to follow their false leadership, they have resorted to exhortation, pleading tearfully for restored confidence. They know only the rules of a generation of self-seekers. They have no vision, and when there is no vision the people perish.

> The word "always" is an absolute. It signals a statement that looks like a fact, but is probably not a fact.

As a leader FDR always navigated between the radically new and unprecedented, on the one hand, and the age-old and unchanging, on the other. Early in the speech he evoked the Old Testament image of a plague of locusts. He used another biblical image, this one from the New Testament, in referring to the "unscrupulous money changers." Then he went on to speak of the Depression as a problem created by old ways of thinking. It was, he said, a problem that could not be solved by "efforts . . . cast in the pattern of outworn tradition," the pattern of a "generation of self-seekers."

The implication was unmistakable: Conquering the Depression would require new thinking. And yet FDR once again linked this need for fresh imagination and bold, new action with the timeless wisdom of Judeo-Christian tradition. In Proverbs 29:18 we are told, "Where there is no vision, the people perish," and FDR tells us that the Depression was created and is perpetuated by leaders who "have no vision, and when there is no vision the people perish." He continued with his echo of the Gospels:

> Axelrod uses transitions such as "yet FDR once again linked" and "He continued" to tie ideas together and explain his arguments.

Franklin D. Roosevelt addressing Congress, 1941.

The money changers have fled from their high seats in the temple of our civilization. We may now restore that temple to the ancient truths. The measure of the restoration lies in the extent to which we apply social values more noble than mere monetary profit.

An inauguration is a beginning, as Roosevelt was well aware, and in his acceptance speech to the Democratic National Convention, he had already pledged to the American people a "New Deal." Americans would soon discover, during the dazzling first hundred days of the Roosevelt presidency, just how new a deal it would be, as program after innovative program was ushered into being. Yet all of this innovation was aimed at restoring the "temple of our civilization . . . to the ancient truths," the age-old redemption of the temple of the spirit from the grasp of the materialistic money changers.

Happiness lies not in the mere possession of money; it lies in the joy of achievement, in the thrill of creative effort. The joy and moral stimulation of work no longer must be forgotten in the mad chase of evanescent profits. These dark days will be worth all they cost us if they teach us that our true destiny is not to be ministered unto but to minister to ourselves and our fellow men.

Here then, in the space of the first few minutes of his first speech as leader of the American people, is what Franklin Roosevelt made visible in the absence of the fog of fear: that the economic disaster is serious, urgent, even life-threatening, *yet* it is an *economic* disaster, one concerning "thank God, only material things." Roosevelt's speech does not allow his listeners to turn away from the disaster. His words invite them to see beyond it, both to its cause in human errors, in the shortsighted pursuit of immediate material profit, and in the absence of greater vision, to its eventual resolution.

Franklin D. Roosevelt delivering a radio address, 1938.

That resolution is the subject of the rest of the speech, which broadly outlines innovative goals, policies, and programs aimed at ending the Great Depression. Yet the proposed means of resolution, radical as they may be, rest on restoring the "temple of our civilization . . . to the ancient truths." Paramount among these truths is a realization that "happiness lies not in the mere possession of money," that morals and ethics must not be sacrificed in "the mad chase of evanescent profits," and that our "true destiny is not to be ministered unto but to minister to ourselves and our fellow men."

In the final paragraphs, the author summarizes the main ideas discussed in the study.

Monitor Your Progress

Reading: Determining Fact and Opinion

Standards Assessed
• WL.1.03.6
• FA.3.03.2
• LT.5.01.2

Directions: *Choose the letter of the best answer to each question about the historical research study.*

1. Which statement from the text is an opinion?
   A "An inauguration is a beginning . . ."
   B "Our kind has conquered worse in the past."
   C "In 1921 polio threatened first to kill him."
   D "He evoked the . . . image of a plague of locusts."

2. Which statement from the text is a fact?
   A "He began by asking the American people to sweep aside the 'nameless, unreasoning, unjustified terror.'"
   B "Only a foolish optimist can deny the dark realities."
   C "Roosevelt was 'not one to blink at disaster.'"
   D "The only thing we have to fear is fear itself."

3. Which statement from the text is an overgeneralization?
   A "Taxes have risen; our ability to pay has fallen."
   B "They know only the rules of a generation of self-seekers."
   C "Happiness is not in the mere possession of money."
   D "This great nation will endure as it has endured."

Reading: Comprehension and Interpretation

Directions: *Write your answers on a separate piece of paper.*

4. What does Axelrod mean when he says that fear is a fog, "an obscurer of truth"? **[Generating]**

5. How does Axelrod support his belief that Roosevelt "navigated between the radically new . . . and the age-old and unchanging"? **[Analyzing]**

6. **(a)** Note two points at which Axelrod summarizes a section of the speech. **(b)** How effectively does each summary express the main idea of the original? Support your answer with details. **[Evaluating]**

Timed Writing: Analysis [Critical Stance]

Write an **analytical essay** discussing Axelrod's attitude toward President Roosevelt and his views of the Great Depression. In your analysis, address the following questions. Does Axelrod approve of Roosevelt's words and outlook? Does he seem convinced by Roosevelt's arguments? Use details from the essay to support your conclusions. **(30 minutes)**

Humorous Essay

A **humorous essay** is a form of nonfiction writing intended to make the reader laugh. In some forms of humorous writing, often described as harsh or biting, authors ridicule their subjects. In other forms of humorous writing, often described as gentle, authors treat their subjects with affection even as they make fun of them.

Humorous writing can include one or more of the following figures of speech:

- **hyperbole:** intentional (and sometimes outrageous) overstatement, or exaggeration—for example, describing a small patch of ice as a "vast, frozen wasteland."

- **understatement:** the presentation of an idea, person, or event in a way that makes it seen less than it is—for example, describing a huge loss as a "minor" setback.

In addition to these techniques, the comic writer's **diction**, or word choice, may include funny names, slang, or other examples of verbal humor.

Comparing Humorous Essays

Although humorous writing is meant to entertain, it can have other purposes as well. For example, humor can be used to convey a serious message.

Use an organizer like the one shown to identify the serious issues or ideas addressed in "The Talk" and "Go Deep to the Sewer." Then, think about the reasons the authors may have chosen to use humor to explore these issues.

> **Standard Course of Study**
>
> - Recognize and analyze the characteristics of literary genres. (LT.5.01.2)
> - Determine a character's traits. (LT.5.01.7)
> - Make thematic connections. (LT.5.01.9)

Go Deep to the Sewer

Detail
"I spent many happy years . . . hoping that a football would hit me before a Chevrolet did."

Issue
Cosby lacked open space in which to play.

Vocabulary Builder

The Talk

- **renegade** (ren´ ə gād´) *adj.* disloyal; traitorous (p. 523) *The renegade ballplayer signed up with the rival team.*

- **feisty** (fīs´ tē) *adj.* full of spirit; energetic (p. 523) *The feisty monkey took the banana from the visitor.*

Go Deep to the Sewer

- **lateral** (lat´ ər əl) *adj.* sideways (p. 526) *The rock climber moved up and then scaled in a lateral direction.*

- **interpretation** (in tʉr´ prə tā´ shən) *n.* a subjective, or personal, explanation (p. 526) *His interpretation helped me to understand the complicated play.*

Build Understanding

Connecting to the Literature

Reading/Writing Connection The authors of these essays recount youthful experiences that they found amusing later in life. Briefly describe a childhood incident that you might find funny as an adult. Use at least three of the following words: *derive, imply, react, anticipate, provoke.*

Meet the Authors

Gary **Soto** (b. 1952)

Gary Soto grew up in a Mexican American section of Fresno, California. As a child, he wanted to be either a priest or a scientist who studies fossils and bones. Then, in high school, he discovered great writers, including John Steinbeck and Robert Frost. In college, Soto started writing poetry.

Favorite Pastime Soto's favorite pastime is reading. He has said, "It appears these days I don't have much of a life because my nose is often stuck in a book. But I discovered that reading builds a life inside the mind." Soto has written several award-winning novels, short stories, and books of poetry.

Bill **Cosby** (b. 1937)

Bill Cosby grew up in the housing projects of Philadelphia, Pennsylvania. Although he left high school to join the navy, he earned a diploma through a correspondence course.

Finding Humor During the 1960s, Cosby began performing stand-up comedy. He based many of the characters in his early comedy routines, including Fat Albert and Junior Barnes, on school friends. Cosby has won numerous awards for his television shows and for his books. He has also earned a doctoral degree in education and several honorary degrees.

For: More information about the authors
Visit: www.PHSchool.com
Web Code: epe-9313

THE TALK

Gary Soto

▲ **Critical Viewing**
Based on this image and title, what topics do you think the author of this essay might discuss? Explain. **[Predict]**

My best friend and I knew that we were going to grow up to be ugly. On a backyard lawn—the summer light failing west of the mulberry tree where the house of the most beautiful girl on the street stood—we talked about what we could do: shake the second-base dirt from our hair, wash our hands of frog smells and canal water, and learn to smile without showing our crooked teeth. We had to stop spitting when girls were looking and learn not to pile food onto a fork and into a fat cheek already churning hot grub.

We were twelve, with lean bodies that were beginning to grow in weird ways. First, our heads got large, but our necks wavered, frail as crisp tulips. The eyes stayed small as well, receding into pencil dots on each side of an unshapely nose that cast remarkable shadows when we turned sideways. It seemed that Scott's legs sprouted muscle and <u>renegade</u> veins, but his arms, blue with ink markings, stayed short and hung just below his waist. My gangly arms nearly touched my kneecaps. In this way, I was built for picking up grounders and doing cartwheels, my arms swaying just inches from the summery grass.

We sat on the lawn, with the porch light off, waiting for the beautiful girl to turn on her bedroom light and read on her stomach with one leg stirring the air. This stirred us, and our dream was a clean dream of holding hands and airing out our loneliness by walking up and down the block.

When Scott asked whom I was going to marry, I said a brown girl from the valley. He said that he was going to marry a strawberry blonde who would enjoy Millerton Lake, dirty as it was. I said mine would like cats and the sea and would think nothing of getting up at night from a warm, restless bed and sitting in the yard under the icy stars. Scott said his wife would work for the first year or so, because he would go to trade school[1] in refrigeration. Since our town was made with what was left over after God made hell, there was money in air conditioning, he reasoned.

I said that while my wife would clean the house and stir pots of nice grub, I would drive a truck to my job as a carpenter, which would allow me to use my long arms. I would need only a stepladder to hand a fellow worker on the roof a pinch of nails. I could hammer, saw, lift beams into place, and see the work I got done at the end of the day. Of course, she might like to work, and that would be okay, because then we could buy two cars and wave at each other if we should see the other drive by. In the evenings, we would drink Kool-Aid and throw a slipper at our <u>feisty</u> dog at least a hundred times before we went inside for a Pop-Tart and hot chocolate.

Scott said he would work hard too, but now and then he would find money on the street and the two of them could buy extra things like a second TV for the bedroom and a Doughboy swimming pool for his three kids. He planned on having three kids and a ranch house on the river, where he could dip a hand in the water, drink, and say, "Ahh, tastes good."

But that would be years later. Now we had to do something about our looks. We plucked at the grass and flung it into each other's faces.

"Rotten luck," Scott said. "My arms are too short. Look at 'em."

"Maybe we can lift weights. This would make up for our looks," I said.

---

1. trade school school in which students specialize in learning one set of skills for a particular profession.

Vocabulary Builder
renegade (ren´ ə gād´) *adj.* disloyal; traitorous

Literary Analysis
Humorous Essay
Which details of the boys' youthful dreams might seem funny later in life?

Vocabulary Builder
feisty (fīs´ tē) *adj.* full of spirit; energetic

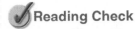Reading Check

What are the boys worried they will be like when they grow up?

"I don't think so," Scott said, depressed. "People like people with nice faces."

He was probably right. I turned onto my stomach, a stalk of grass in my mouth. "Even if I'm ugly, my wife's going to be good-looking," I said. "She'll have a lot of dresses and I'll have more shirts than I have now. Do you know how much carpenters make?"

Then I saw the bedroom light come on and the beautiful girl walk into the room drying her hair with a towel. I nudged Scott's short arm and he saw what I saw. We flicked the stalks of grass, stood up, and walked over to the fence to look at her scrub her hair dry. She plopped onto the bed and began to comb it, slowly at first because it was tangled. With a rubber band, she tied it back, and picked up a book that was thick as a good-sized sandwich.

Scott and I watched her read a book, now both legs in the air and twined together, her painted toenails like red petals. She turned the pages slowly, very carefully, and now and then lowered her face into the pillow. She looked sad but beautiful, and we didn't know what to do except nudge each other in the heart and creep away to the front yard.

"I can't stand it anymore. We have to talk about this," Scott said.

"If I try, I think I can make myself better looking," I said. "I read an article about a girl whitening her teeth with water and flour."

So we walked up the street, depressed. For every step I took, Scott took two, his short arms pumping to keep up. For every time Scott said, "I think we're ugly," I said two times, "Yeah, yeah, we're in big trouble."

Literary Analysis
Humorous Essay
What serious issue does Scott's statement raise? Explain.

Thinking About the Selection

1. **Respond:** What were your feelings for the boys as you read this essay? Explain.

2. **(a) Recall:** What jobs do the boys hope to have when they get older? **(b) Infer:** What do the boys' choice of future jobs suggest about their characters? Explain.

3. **(a) Infer:** Do you think this is the first time the boys have watched the beautiful girl? Why or why not? **(b) Draw Conclusions:** What does the girl in the window seem to represent for the two young boys?

4. **Speculate:** What advice do you think an adult might give the two boys to help them feel better about themselves?

Go Deep to the Sewer

Bill Cosby

The essence of childhood, of course, is play, which my friends and I did endlessly on streets that we reluctantly shared with traffic. As a daring receiver in touch football, I spent many happy years running up and down those asphalt fields, hoping that a football would hit me before a Chevrolet did.

▲ **Critical Viewing**
Based on this picture and the title, what do you anticipate about the topic of this essay? **[Predict]**

My mother was often a nervous fan who watched me from her window.

"Bill, don't get run over!" she would cry in a moving concern for me.

"Do you see me getting run over?" I would cleverly reply.

And if I ever had been run over, my mother had a seat for it that a scalper[1] would have prized.

Because the narrow fields of those football games allowed almost no <u>lateral</u> movement, an end run was possible only if a car pulled out and blocked for you. And so I worked on my pass-catching, for I knew I had little chance of ever living my dream: taking a handoff and sweeping to glory along the curb, dancing over the dog dung like Red Grange.

The quarterback held this position not because he was the best passer but because he knew how to drop to one knee in the huddle and diagram plays with trash.

"Okay, Shorty," Junior Barnes would say, "this is you: the orange peel."

"I don' wanna be the orange peel," Shorty replied. "The orange peel is Albert. I'm the gum."

---

1. scalper (skalp´ er) *n.* person who buys tickets and sells them later at higher than regular prices.

Vocabulary Builder
lateral (lat´ ər əl) *adj.*
sideways

▼ Critical Viewing
Why were manhole covers, like the one shown, useful for defining the field of play in the ballgames Cosby played as a child? **[Connect]**

"But let's make 'em think he's the orange peel," I said, "an' let 'em think Albert's the manhole."

"Okay, Shorty," said Junior, "you go out ten steps an' then cut left behind the black Oldsmobile."

"I'll sorta go in it first to shake my man," said Shorty, "an' then, when he don' know where I am, you can hit me at the fender."

"Cool. An' Arnie, you go down to the corner of Locust an' fake takin' the bus. An' Cos, you do a zig out to the bakery. See if you can shake your man before you hit the rolls."

"Suppose I start a fly pattern to the bakery an' then do a zig out to the trash can," I said.

"No, they'll be expecting that."

I spent most of my boyhood trying to catch passes with the easy grace of my heroes at Temple;[2] but easy grace was too hard for me. Because I was short and thin, my hands were too small to catch a football with arms extended on the run. Instead, I had to stagger backwards and smother the ball in my chest. How I yearned to grab the ball in my hands while striding smoothly ahead, rather than receiving it like someone who was catching a load of wet wash. Often, after a pass had bounced off my hands, I returned to the quarterback and glumly said, "Jeeze, Junior, I don' know what happened." He, of course, knew what had happened: he had thrown the ball to someone who should have been catching it with a butter-fly net.

Each of these street games began with a quick review of the rules: two-hand touch, either three or four downs, always goal-to-go, forward passing from anywhere, and no touchdowns called back because of traffic in motion. If a receiver caught a ball near an oncoming car while the defender was running for his life, the receiver had guts, and possibly a long excuse from school.

I will never forget one particular play from those days when I was trying so hard to prove my manhood between the manholes. In the huddle, as Junior, our permanent quarterback, dropped to one knee to arrange the garbage offensively, I said, "Hey, Junior, make me a decoy on this one."

Pretending to catch the ball was what I did best.

"What's a decoy?" he said.

"Well, it's—"

"I ain't got time to learn. Okay, Eddie, you're the Dr Pepper cap an' you go deep toward New Jersey."

"An' I'll fool around short," I said.

"No, Cos, you fake goin' deep an' then buttonhook at the DeSoto. An' Harold, you do a zig out between 'em. Somebody get free."

---

2. **Temple** Temple University in Philadelphia, Pennsylvania.

Literary Analysis
Humorous Essay
What is funny about these plays?

Literary Analysis
Humorous Essay
What serious issues about playing in the street do the rules reveal?

Reading Check

What do the boys use to "diagram" their plays?

Moments later, the ball was snapped to him and I started sprinting down the field with my defender, Jody, who was matching me stride for stride. Wondering if I would be able to get free for a pass sometime within the next hour, I stopped at the corner and began sprinting back to Junior, whose arm had been cocked for about fifteen seconds, as if he'd been posing for a trophy. Since Eddie and Harold also were covered, and since running from scrimmage was impossible on that narrow field, I felt that this might be touch football's first eternal play: Junior still standing there long after Eddie, Harold, and I had dropped to the ground, his arm still cocked as he tried to find some way to pass to himself.

But unlimited time was what we had and it was almost enough for us. Often we played in the street until the light began to fade and the ball became a blur in the dusk. If there is one memory of my childhood that will never disappear, it is a bunch of boys straining to find a flying football in the growing darkness of a summer night.

There were, of course, a couple of streetlamps on our field, but they were useful only if your pattern took you right up to one of them to make your catch. The rest of the field was lost in the night; and what an adventure it was to refuse to surrender to that night, to hear the quarterback cry "Ball!" and then stagger around in a kind of gridiron blindman's buff.

"Hey, you guys, dontcha think we should call the game?" said Harold one summer evening.

"Why do a stupid thing like that?" Junior replied.

"'Cause I can't see the ball."

"Harold, that don't make you special. Nobody can see the ball. But y' know it's up there."

And we continued to stagger around as night fell on Philadelphia and we kept looking for a football that could have been seen only on radar screens.

One day last year in a gym, I heard a boy say to his father, "Dad, what's a Spaldeen?"

This shocking question left me depressed, for it is one thing not to know the location of the White House or the country that gave its name to Swiss cheese, but when a boy doesn't know what a Spaldeen is, our educational system has failed. For those of you ignorant of basic American history, a Spaldeen was a pink rubber ball with more bounce than can be imagined today. Baseball fans talk about the lively ball, but a lively baseball is a sinking stone compared to a Spaldeen, which could be dropped from your eye level and bounce back there again, if you wanted to do something boring with it. And when you connected with a Spaldeen in stickball, you put a pink rocket in orbit, perhaps even over the

Literary Analysis
Humorous Essay
Which details about playing at night are exaggerated?

Literary Analysis
Humorous Essay
Which statements about Spaldeens are examples of hyperbole? Explain.

house at the corner and into another neighborhood, where it might gently bop somebody's mother sitting on a stoop.

I love to remember all the street games that we could play with a Spaldeen. First, of course, was stickball, an organized version of which is also popular and known as baseball. The playing field was the same rectangle that we used for football: it was the first rectangular diamond. And for this game, we had outfield walls in which people happened to live and we had bases that lacked a certain uniformity: home and second were manhole covers, and first and third were the fenders of parked cars.

One summer morning, this offbeat infield caused a memorable <u>interpretation</u> of the official stickball rules. Junior hit a two-sewer shot and was running toward what should have been third when third suddenly drove away in first. While the bewildered Junior tried to arrive safely in what had become a twilight zone, Eddie took my throw from center field and tagged him out.

"I'm not out!" cried Junior in outrage. "I'm right here on third!"

Vocabulary Builder
interpretation (in tʉr´ prə tā´ shən) *n.* a subjective, or personal, explanation

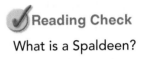 Reading Check

What is a Spaldeen?

◀ **Critical Viewing**
How do you think this stickball player compares to the boys in Cosby's essay? **[Compare]**

And he did have a point, but so did Eddie, who replied, not without a certain logic of his own, "But third ain't there anymore."

In those games, our first base was as mobile as our third; and it was a floating first that set off another lively division of opinion on the day that Fat Albert hit a drive over the spot from which first base had just driven away, leaving us without a good part of the right field foul line. The hit would have been at least a double for anyone with movable legs, but Albert's destination was first, where the play might have been close had the right fielder hit the cutoff man instead of a postman.

"Foul ball!" cried Junior, taking a guess that happened to be in his favor.

"You're out of your mind, Junior!" cried Albert, an observation that often was true, no matter what Junior was doing. "It went right over the fender!"

"What fender?"

"If that car comes back, you'll see it's got a fender," said Albert, our automotive authority.

However, no matter how many pieces of our field drove away, nothing could ever take away the sweetness of having your stick connect with a Spaldeen in a magnificent whoppp and drive it so high and far that it bounced off a window with a view of New Jersey and then caromed back to the street, where Eddie would have fielded it like Carl Furillo[3] had he not backed into a coal chute.

---

3. **Carl Furillo** baseball player for the Brooklyn Dodgers in the 1950s.

Thinking About the Selection

1. **Respond:** Would you enjoy playing stickball or football by the rules Bill Cosby describes? Explain.

2. **(a) Recall:** How does Cosby describe his physical size as a child? **(b) Analyze Cause and Effect:** How did Cosby's physical limitations affect his skill at football? **(c) Make a Judgment:** Do you think Cosby's physical size affected his enjoyment of the games? Explain.

3. **(a) Interpret:** What neighborhood features were part of the "diamond" on which Cosby and his friends played stickball? **(b) Analyze:** What does Cosby's description of the playing space show about the people who live in his neighborhood?

4. **(a) Speculate:** What does Cosby mean when he says, "The essence of childhood . . . is play"? **(b) Evaluate:** Do you agree with this idea? Explain.

Apply the Skills

The Talk • Go Deep to the Sewer

Comparing Humorous Essays

1. **(a)** Use a chart like the one shown to identify at least one example of **hyperbole**, one example of **understatement**, and one example of comic **diction** in each **humorous essay**.

Type	The Talk	Go Deep to the Sewer . . .
Hyperbole		
Understatement		
Comic Diction		

   (b) Explain how each example adds to the humor of the essay.

2. **(a)** In which story does the author use unusual or funny names as a humorous technique? **(b)** How do these names help to paint a comic portrait of the people they indicate?

3. Would you describe the humor of these essays as harsh or gentle? Explain your answer using details from the texts.

Writing to Compare Literary Works

In an essay, discuss and compare the serious ideas expressed in each of these essays. Consider why the authors chose to present these issues through humor. Use these questions to get started:
   - What challenges do the children in both essays face?
   - What challenges do they face in their futures?
   - What circumstances do you think may have added to those challenges? Note specific details from each essay that support your ideas.
   - How does the use of humor help to suggest that these challenges can be overcome?

Vocabulary Builder

Practice Review the vocabulary list on page 520. Then, answer each question. Explain your answer.

1. If you needed an employee who followed the rules, would you hire a *renegade* worker?

2. Would a tired animal be *feisty*?

3. Is someone's *interpretation* of an event the absolute truth?

4. Would someone climbing a ladder move in a *lateral* direction?

QuickReview

Humorous Essay: nonfiction writing intended to make the reader laugh

For: Self-test
Visit: www.PHSchool.com
Web Code: epa-6311

Reading

Directions: *Questions 1–5 are based on the following selection.*

Those who came before us made certain that this country rode the first waves of the industrial revolutions, the first waves of modern invention, and the first wave of nuclear power, and this generation does not intend to founder in the backwash of the coming age of space. We mean to be a part of it—we mean to lead it. For the eyes of the world now look into space, to the moon and to the planets beyond, and we have vowed that we shall not see it governed by a hostile flag of conquest, but by a banner of freedom and peace. We have vowed that we shall not see space filled with weapons of mass destruction, but with instruments of knowledge and understanding. . . .

We set sail on this new sea because there is new knowledge to be gained, and new rights to be won, and they must be won and used for the progress of all people. . . .

—from "Speech at Rice University, Houston, Texas, 1962,"
by President John F. Kennedy

1. **What is the subject of the passage?**
   A nuclear power
   B the space race
   C America's past achievements
   D important sea voyages

2. **What idea is the author trying to persuade his audience to accept?**
   A The industrial revolution was important.
   B Exploration is important.
   C Space travel is important.
   D America must be the most powerful nation.

3. **To what emotion in the audience does the first sentence appeal?**
   A to pride
   B to anger
   C to fear
   D to despair

4. **The second paragraph opens with which type of appeal?**
   A appeal to emotion
   B appeal to reason
   C appeal to authority
   D appeal to statistics

5. **How does the speaker use sound to add to the persuasive appeal in the phrase "new knowledge to be gained, and new rights to be won"?**
   A It has an internal rhyme.
   B It uses parallel structure.
   C It adds new ideas.
   D It is a musical phrase.

Vocabulary

Directions: *Choose the word that best completes the sentence.*

Standards Assessed

• IR.2.01.3
• FA.3.03.1
• GU.6.01.6

6. No one knew what he intended to _____ by his absence.
   A anticipate
   B derive
   C texture
   D signify

7. What information can you _____ from this?
   A participate
   B derive
   C display
   D contribute

8. I _____ the plot twist at the end of O'Henry's story.
   A anticipate
   B derive
   C participate
   D signify

9. We were glad to hear that she had no _____ injuries from the accident.
   A structural
   B textural
   C internal
   D trivial

10. The sweater had a very rough _____.
    A texture
    B illumination
    C anticipation
    D equivalence

11. Her _____ in other people's business was annoying.
    A antecede
    B antebellum
    C intersection
    D interference

12. This _____ mansion was built just before the Civil War began.
    A antecede
    B antebellum
    C intersection
    D interference

13. Many auto accidents have occurred at this _____.
    A antecede
    B antebellum
    C intersection
    D interference

14. The highest-ranking officer should _____ the others.
    A antecede
    B intercept
    C intersection
    D interference

15. They were able to _____ his message and learn of his plot.
    A antecede
    B intercept
    C antedate
    D interference

Spelling Workshop

Tools for Checking Spelling

Standard Course of Study

• Use and place modifiers correctly. (GU.6.02.3)

Sometimes it is hard to be sure that you have spelled certain words correctly. Fortunately, there are reference tools that can help you.

Computer Spell-checkers Most word-processing programs contain a feature that signals when you have typed a word incorrectly and suggests a replacement. Remember that computer programs can only check the words in their database. Here are some cautions about spell-checking programs:

- The program cannot tell you if you used the wrong homonym.
- It cannot tell if you have typed a title or proper name incorrectly.
- It cannot tell if you used the wrong word. The difference between "I bruised my knee" and "I braised my knee" is significant.
- The program may not always know the correct spelling for a word, especially if you are using a word that is not commonplace.

The e-mail was supposed to say "Take the boat around" not "aground".

Dictionaries Follow these steps to find spellings in a dictionary:

- **Check the first letters of a word.** Think of homophones for that sound.
- **Check the other letters.** Once you spell the first sound correctly, try sounding out the rest of the word. Look for likely spellings in the dictionary. If you don't find your word, look for more unusual spellings of the sound.

Practice Write one paragraph that contains errors a spell-checker would not find. Include at least four words from the list. Exchange paragraphs with a partner. Circle the errors and write the corrections.

Word List
waste
waist
eliminate
once
ounce
illuminate
colleagues
February
literally
metaphorically

Directions: There are errors in the following sentences. Some are misspellings. Others are problems with homonyms or other words used by mistake. Write the number of each sentence and the corrections it needs. If a sentence has no errors, write "none."

Standards Assessed

• GU.6.02.3

1. A small new mall has opened up in our busy city neighborhood.

2. Through not all the stores are filled yet, the ones I have seen so far look interesting.

3. The first store to open was a women's butique.

4. Its window is filled with stilish cloathes that girls my age would love to wear.

5. My friends and I can hardly wait to go inside.

6. There is also a small office supply store.

7. This should be useful for buying paper, ink cartriges, and other computer needs.

8. One really wired store looks like a haunted house from the outside.

9. In the window are groteskque masks and small carved gnomes.

10. Crazy black streamers hang for the ceiling.

11. The rumor is that a physic will be working part time there.

12. That place will be very useful the next time we play charades or have a costume party!

13. The director was literally beside himself with frustration.

14. Foreshadowing is when an author gives you clues to what is going to happen.

15. The sea goddess that loved Odysseus was Calypso.

16. James Thurber characterized Mitty as sort of absentminded.

17. We asked our parents to leave us go to the play.

18. I like football more then tennis.

19. He might of given us another chance; we didn't do anything horrible!

20. It is further to her house than we thought.

Persuasion: Editorial

One decisive and public way to take a stand on an issue is to write an **editorial**. An editorial is a brief persuasive essay that presents and defends an opinion. In this workshop, you will write an editorial on a subject of your choice.

Assignment Write an editorial about an issue that confronts your school or community.

What to Include Your editorial should feature the following elements:
- A clear thesis statement—a statement of your position on an issue
- Evidence that supports your position and anticipates your readers' counterarguments
- Effective organization
- Persuasive language that emphasizes your arguments
- Error-free grammar, including correct use of parallel structures

To preview the criteria on which your editorial may be assessed, see the rubric on page 543.

 ## Writing Workshop: *Work in Progress*

If you have completed the Work-In-Progress assignments, you have in your portfolio several ideas you might wish to pursue in your editorial. You may continue to develop these ideas, or you might choose to explore a new idea as you complete this Writing Workshop.

Standard Course of Study

- Narrate personal scenes located effectively in time and place. (WL.1.01.1)
- Narrate with a sense personal voice. (WL.1.01.4)
- Show understanding of personal reaction to the text through response. (WL.1.02.1)

Using the Form
You may use elements of this form in these types of writing:
- letters to the editor
- position papers
- speeches

To get a feel for editorials, read "Libraries Face Sad Chapter" by Pete Hamill on page 483.

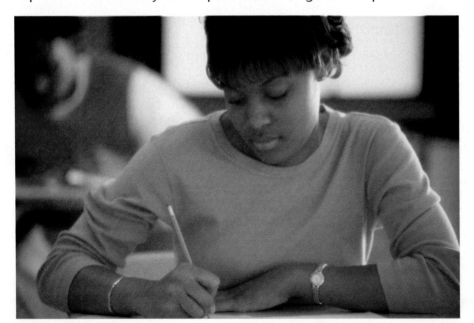

Prewriting

Choosing Your Topic

To select a topic for your editorial, use one of the following strategies:

- **Scan newspapers.** As you page through a newspaper, look for stories that matter to you on a personal level. Notice articles that describe situations that strike you as unfair, foolish, or harmful. Use one of these news stories as a topic for your editorial.

- **Work with a partner.** Pair up with a classmate and brainstorm for topics that are important to each of you, noting those that cause the most disagreement. Select an issue that has compelling arguments on both sides. Then, choose a position to support.

Narrowing Your Topic

Write a thesis statement. After reviewing the information you have in hand, decide which part of the issue to address. Write your opinion about the topic in one sentence. That sentence is your thesis statement, an expression of your position that you must now prepare to defend.

Gathering Details

Consider all sides of an issue. Gather evidence from a wide variety of sources. In a chart like the one shown, record evidence on both sides of an issue. Do not ignore information that contradicts or opposes your position. Your editorial will be more persuasive if you acknowledge and overcome opposing viewpoints. Plan to include summaries of opposing positions in order to refute them.

Support for school uniforms	Opposition to school uniforms
Reduce violence and discrimination	Take choice away from students
Create positive school image	Cause resentment among students

Appeal to logic and emotion. Effective persuasion speaks to both thought and feeling.
- *Logic:* Make a list of ideas, facts, and details that will make people think and analyze rather than feel.
- *Emotion:* Brainstorm for relevant anecdotes, or brief stories, descriptions, and personal examples that will affect readers' emotions. Quickly jot these down. As you work, experiment with language that carries strong emotional connotations:

Neutral connotation: Megan continues to work.
Strong connotation: Megan soldiers on.

Work in Progress
Review the work you did on pages 423 and 445.

Writing Workshop

Drafting

Shaping Your Writing

Create a structure for your draft. Plan a strategy for presenting your ideas.

- **Evaluate your arguments.** Review all the points that support your thesis and consider their impact on your intended audience. Then, rank them according to their persuasiveness.

- **Use an outline.** Use your ranking to write an outline showing order-of-importance organization. Start with your least important point and build toward your most persuasive point. In addition, be sure to indicate where you will address counterarguments. The chart shown demonstrates order-of-importance organization for an editorial.

Providing Elaboration

Distinguish between fact and opinion. Your thesis and arguments are statements of opinion that must be validated or supported with evidence. Facts—information that can be proved true—are the strongest evidence. Weak arguments pile opinions on top of opinions; strong arguments back opinions with relevant facts.

Provide evidence. For each point you make, produce convincing support. Types of effective evidence include the following:

- **Statistics:** numbers that show the impact of an issue or a proposal

- **Expert opinions:** the viewpoints or advice of those who have relevant training and experience

- **Personal observations:** your own experiences with the topic

- **Testimonials:** statements from observers that reinforce an argument

Organizing Your Arguments

↓

Present thesis statement.

↓

Present arguments to support thesis.

↓

Address counterarguments.

↓

Provide strongest argument in support of thesis.

↓

Conclude by restating thesis and presenting a memorable final thought or quotation.

Reading · Writing Connection

To read the complete student model, see page 542.

Student Model: Supporting Opinion With Fact

While it might make sense to have students' safety as a leading justification for requiring uniforms, safety hits the bottom of the list in a press release from the National Association of Elementary School Principals.

> The writer supports his opinion with a meaningful fact—one that references the expert opinions of school principals.

From the Author's Desk

Rebecca Walker

On Choosing the Right Details

Rebecca Walker

This excerpt is from the introductory essay to a book I edited about new perspectives on masculinity. I think about what I am going to write for a long time, maybe months, before committing my thoughts to the page. Long before I sat down to write, I knew I would prompt readers to think about masculinity in new ways by using this personal exchange between my son and me. What I didn't know was how I would finish the piece.

"Taking one's initial impulse to completion, that's the challenge . . ."
—————Rebecca Walker

Professional Model:

from *What Makes a Man:*

After a big bowl of his favorite pasta, he sat on a sofa in my study and read his science textbook as I wrote at my desk. . . . As we worked under the soft glow of paper lanterns, . . . I could feel a shift as he began to remember, deep in his body, that he was home, that he was safe, that he didn't have to brace to protect himself from the expectations of the outside world.

I wanted to convey a sense of peace and relaxation, so I added this detail to draw the reader into the tranquility of the "scene."

An hour or so passed like this before he announced that he had a question. . . . "I've been thinking that maybe I should play sports at school."

. . . I cocked my head to one side. "What brought this on?"

"I don't know," he said. "Maybe girls will like me if I play sports."

Excuse me?

I used italics here to suggest my surprise and outrage, and to reinforce a direct and intimate connection with the reader.

My boy is intuitive, smart, and creative . . . At the time he loved animals, Japanese anime, . . . and everything having to do with snowboarding. He liked to help both of his grandmothers in the garden. He read science fiction. . . . and was beginning what I thought would be a lifelong love affair with chess.

I included actual things my son enjoyed to add authenticity and texture, and to provide a strong counterpoint to sports.

Maybe girls would like him if he played sports?

Writing Workshop

Revising

Revising Your Overall Structure

Revise to address readers' concerns. Not all of your readers will agree with your position. Show them that you are aware of their questions and understand their concerns.

- Review your draft and highlight controversial claims that a critic of your position would oppose.
- To make sure you understand each opposing argument, write a summary that captures its main idea and line of reasoning.
- For each claim, develop strong counterarguments that you can back up with explanations and evidence.
- Find a point in your editorial where you can include this information smoothly.

To read the complete student model, see page 542.

Student Model: Revising to Address the Opposition

They keep students safe.
Dress codes make the difference where it counts. ∧ Students need to do nothing other than make sure their clothes meet acceptable standards.

Those who promote uniforms over dress codes are often concerned with safety, so the author revises to address that issue.

Revising Your Word Choice

Choose powerful words. To be persuasive, your essay should include words that convey meaning and emotion. Look at these examples:

Ordinary: Some adults *dislike* today's student fashions.
Powerful: Some adults *deplore* today's student fashions.

Ordinary: Joanna *did not want* to wear a uniform.
Powerful: Joanna *refused* to wear a uniform.

Review your earlier experiments with words that carry strong connotations. Determine whether to use those word choices.

Peer Review: Exchange drafts with a partner. Review each other's work, highlighting weak words that could be replaced by stronger ones. Then, revise your draft, replacing ordinary language with words that will make your readers feel and think. After you have made your revisions, exchange drafts with your partner again. Discuss whether the new word choices are effective.

Integrating Grammar Skills

Revising to Create Parallelism

Parallelism is the use of similar grammatical forms or patterns to express similar ideas. Effective use of parallelism adds rhythm and balance to your writing and strengthens connections among your ideas.

Sample Parallel Forms	
Nouns	sharp eyes, strong hands, deft fingers
Verbs	to ask, to learn, to share
Phrases	treating people fairly, being honest
Adverb clauses	when I am happy, when I am peaceful
Adjective clauses	those who read with care, those who act with concern

Identifying Nonparallel Constructions Parallel constructions place equal ideas in words, phrases, or clauses of similar types. Nonparallel constructions present equal ideas in an unnecessary mix of grammatical forms, producing awkward, distracting shifts for readers.

Nonparallel: Dress codes are <u>less restrictive, less costly,</u> and <u>are not a controversial system.</u>

Parallel: Dress codes are <u>less restrictive, less costly,</u> and <u>less controversial.</u>

Fixing Nonparallel Constructions To revise faulty parallelism, follow these steps:

1. **Identify similar or equal ideas within a sentence.**
2. **Determine whether the ideas are expressed in the same form—for example, all nouns or all prepositional phrases.**
3. **Rewrite the sentence so that all the elements match the stronger pattern.** Choose forms that produce the smoothest rhythm or require the fewest words.

Apply It to Your Editing

Review several paragraphs in your editorial, highlighting any sentences in which you present a series of ideas. In each case, make sure the constructions are parallel. If they are not, revise them.

Student Model: Braden Danbury
Cumming, Georgia

Dress Codes May Succeed
Where School Uniforms Have Failed

School uniforms are becoming increasingly popular as a way to combat school violence and discrimination. Uniforms, while they may help somewhat, cause problems of their own. Students argue that it is their right to wear what they choose and uniforms violate that right. A less strict code is the answer to both of these problems, keeping appropriate attire in the school while allowing individuals to choose what they wear.

> The author offers a clear thesis statement in the form of a proposal that addresses a key problem.

Uniforms require students to wear specific shirts and pants or skirts, thus eliminating the element of choice. School uniforms may cause friction between students and school officials, which can have negative consequences. Dress codes, on the other hand, are less restrictive than school uniforms and cause less resentment among students. Students enjoy choosing what to wear to school each day, coordinating what they wear with how they feel.

While students' safety is often cited as a leading justification for requiring uniforms, safety hits the bottom of the list in a press release from the National Association of Elementary School Principals. In fact, safety ranks below such trivial things as school image. This calls into question why uniforms are touted as the answer to school safety issues.

> Braden finds a way to deal with counterarguments based on safety concerns.

Dress codes make the difference where it counts. They keep students safe while forcing them to do nothing other than make sure their clothes meet acceptable standards. An added benefit of dress codes is that schools with uniform policies pay much more than schools with dress codes. Schools with uniforms have to design, order, sell, and distribute the uniforms they wish to have for their school. In addition, school officials spend time and resources making sure they receive payment for uniforms. These expenses may be hidden, but they are real. Dress codes are much less expensive to implement and follow.

> Braden offers evidence that supports his position.

With the rise in school violence, students and their dress often come under suspicion and scrutiny. In addition, the wide variety of clothing in our high schools may lead students to make prejudicial judgments about each other. Dress codes address the problems of violence without causing resentment among students. They are less strict, giving the students more freedom in how they dress, while allowing school officials to set general guidelines. The amount of money it would take to implement a dress code is a fraction of the cost of school uniforms. Dress codes are not the only answer, but they are a step toward combating violence and discrimination in the schools.

> The author restates his thesis and summarizes his evidence. He also offers an additional insight.

Editing and Proofreading

Check your draft for errors in format, grammar, and punctuation.

Focus on Spelling: An editorial that includes spelling errors loses its authority to convince. Check the spelling of each word. Look for words that you frequently misspell and make sure they are correct.

Publishing and Presenting

Consider one of the following ways to share your writing.

Deliver an oral presentation. Use your editorial as the basis for an oral presentation about your topic. As you speak, be sensitive to your audience. If they seem confused or doubtful, modify your word choice to clarify your ideas. After you finish, take a poll to determine whether or not you convinced your audience of your position.

Submit your editorial to a newspaper. Send your work to the school or community newspaper, or condense it into a letter to the editor.

Reflecting on Your Writing

Writer's Journal Think about the experience of writing an editorial. Begin by answering these questions:
- What new information have you learned about your topic?
- What did you learn about the process of writing persuasively? Do these insights apply to other types of writing?

Prentice Hall Writing and Grammar Connection: Chapter 7

Rubric for Self-Assessment

To assess your editorial, use the following rubric:

NC	Criteria	Rating Scale				
		not very				*very*
	Focus: How clearly does your thesis statement express an opinion?	1	2	3	4	5
	Organization: How effectively do you organize your arguments?	1	2	3	4	5
	Support/Elaboration: How well do you use evidence to support your position?	1	2	3	4	5
	Style: How powerful is your use of persuasive language?	1	2	3	4	5
	Conventions: How correct is your grammar, especially your use of parallel structures?	1	2	3	4	5

Communications Workshop

Delivering a Persuasive Speech

Persuasion is not merely a knack of public speaking; it is a valuable life skill that enables you to successfully present ideas and proposals. These speaking strategies can help you refine your persuasive speaking skills.

Organizing Content

Once you have determined your position on an issue, gather and arrange your evidence. You may want to use an order-of-importance organization, beginning with less-important points and leading up to your strongest argument. The Rating Evidence chart can help you assess the relative value of various types of evidence.

Know your audience. Understanding your audience offers a triple advantage. It allows you to:

- adjust word choice and evidence to the interests, cultural background, and knowledge levels of your listeners.

- anticipate questions and counterarguments. You can often disarm skeptical listeners by discussing and refuting their ideas.

- respond to the listeners' self-interests by showing how they are affected by the issue and might benefit from your proposals.

Rating Evidence

1. **Facts:** Provable statements about reality

2. **Statistics:** Numerical information about reality

3. **Expert opinions:** Informed viewpoints based on specialized training and observation

4. **General opinions:** Interesting but not necessarily reliable viewpoints

5. **Your opinion:** What needs to be proved by facts, statistics, and expert opinions

Giving the Speech

Effective persuasion begins in assurance. Demonstrate confidence in your ideas by your posture, bearing, and facial expression.

- Make eye contact with all your listeners, not just one or two people.

- Vary the volume and tone and pacing of your voice to emphasize key points and to keep your audience engaged.

- Edit your speech for Standard English grammar, syntax, and diction. Use slang only if it is appropriate for your audience and purpose.

- Include rhetorical devices, such as repetition or parallelism, to emphasize key ideas.

- Use hand gestures to support what you are saying.

Activity ⟩ *Prepare and Deliver a Persuasive Speech* ⟩ Choose a position on a current local or national issue about which you have strong feelings. Develop a persuasive speech in which you take a stand on this issue, and deliver it before your class. Then, poll your classmates to see if your speech has altered their perspective on the issue.

Biography and Autobiography

Prentice Hall, 2000

Anthology This collection of excerpts from twenty-two biographies and autobiographies presents glimpses into the compelling lives of fascinating and accomplished individuals.

Places Left Unfinished at the Creation of Time

John Philip Santos
Penguin Books, 1999

Memoir In this memoir, John Philip Santos weaves together dream fragments, family remembrances, and Chicano mythology, reaching back in time and place to blend the story of one Mexican family with the soul of an entire people. The story unfolds through unforgettable family figures: from Madrina, who was touched with epilepsy and prophecy ever since, as a girl, she saw a dying soul leave its body, to Teofilo, who was kidnapped as an infant and raised by the Kikapu Indians of Northern Mexico. At the heart of the book is Santos's search for the meaning of his grandfather's suicide in San Antonio, Texas, in 1939.

Narrative of Sojourner Truth

Sojourner Truth
Penguin Books, 1998

Autobiography Sojourner Truth was a woman transformed by the experience of slavery and the exhilaration of liberation. Born Isabella, she was emancipated when New York State outlawed slavery in 1827. Isabella cast aside her slave name and took the name Sojourner Truth, which more fully expressed her new mission in life. Truth embarked on a career as a prominent abolitionist and fiery orator, demanding the end of slavery in the United States. *Narrative of Sojourner Truth,* which describes her early life as a slave, was dictated by Truth to a neighbor and first published in 1850.

Touch the Top of the World

Erik Weihenmayer
Plume, 2002

Nonfiction Adventure When Erik Weihenmayer realized he had an eye disorder that would leave him sightless by the age of thirteen, he lost hope that he could ever live a full life. This book tells the story of his phenomenal road back from the brink of despair. Helped by his family and his own driving will to succeed, Weihenmayer disregards all of society's assumptions about the limitations of blindness, becoming a teacher and a world-class mountaineer.

These titles are available in the Penguin/Prentice Hall Literature Library.
Consult your teacher before choosing one.

Think About It In this newspaper story, a Connecticut woman gives a whole new meaning to the expression "thinking outside the box." Her experiment of sending pumpkins through the mail caught on with postal workers and friends far and wide. Come to think of it, what packaging would be better protection from shipping damage than a tough pumpkin shell?

from the Hartford Courant

Cheerful Gift Becomes a Tradition

Amy Ash Nixon

Armed with a hand-painted pumpkin, an index card with her grandfather's Florida address and a handful of push pins, Amy Hillebrecht walked into a Plainville post office 10 years ago to see if she could mail a pumpkin without packaging it.

"He didn't have the four seasons there, and my grandmother had died a few years earlier, and I thought it would cheer him up," said Hillebrecht, who has made the pumpkin mailing an autumn ritual.

On Friday, Hillebrecht, of Southington, waited in line to send off this year's batch of five decorated pumpkins to friends as near as Southington and as far away as Colorado.

"They're pumpkins, little sugar pumpkins, but when people receive them, they say it just makes their day, and how cool is that?" asked Hillebrecht.

A special education teacher at McGee Middle School in Berlin, Hillebrecht is not sure where the notion came from, but she recalled hearing someone wondering if they could mail a peanut butter and jelly sandwich in only a plastic bag with an address label.

Hillebrecht decided to conduct her own test and came up with pumpkins. She wondered whether a pumpkin would make it to Florida unscathed.

Not only did the pumpkin reach her grandfather, but it got there with tender loving care, she said.

"The man from the post office drove it to my grandfather's condo in the front seat of his car so it didn't get damaged, and it made both their days," she said.

The pumpkins are sent with nothing more than an address label taped to them and a priority mail sticker affixed to the stems.

Roy "Rocky" Roccapriore, a clerk at the Plainville Post Office, is an important part in Hillebrecht's annual mailing ritual. He's the person who helped Hillebrecht when she mailed her first pumpkin. She now goes to him each year.

On Friday morning, Roccapriore grinned a welcome and helped Hillebrecht tape the address labels on with stronger, waterproof tape.

"OK, this is the 2004 batch?" Roccapriore said. "OK. Four out of state, one in state."

Postage was about $5 to $6 apiece.

Customers waiting in line smiled at the oddity of the "packages" being weighed on the scale: fairly petite pumpkins with black hand-drawn eyes, noses and smiles with missing teeth.

Roccapriore said that Hillebrecht's pumpkin mailing is about his favorite experience as a mailman.

"You can't really put a price on doing something like this," he said. "They may only be pumpkins, but everyone smiles when they see them coming in, and I'm sure it's like that the whole way to where they're going."

One of the pumpkins mailed Friday was bound for Colorado, headed to Hillebrecht's friend, Hope Shenkman Kligerman.

Contacted shortly after her pumpkin began its journey, and unaware she was receiving one this year, Kligerman said, "Oh, oh, I'm getting one!"

"It's always so much fun to receive them," Kligerman said.

Meet the Author

Amy Ash Nixon is a general assignment reporter for *The Hartford Courant,* based in Hartford, the capital of Connecticut. The *Courant,* founded in 1764, is one of the oldest continuously published newspapers in the country.

Readings in Contemporary Culture
Talk About It

Use these questions to guide a discussion of the article.

1. **(a)** How did the postal workers react to Hillebrecht's first mailing?
   (b) Explain what postal worker Roccapriore meant when he said, "You can't really put a price on doing something like this."

2. In a group, consider why people give and receive gifts.
   - What factors make a gift especially valuable?
   - Who does a gift most benefit—the giver or the receiver? Explain.

   Choose a point-person to share your group's ideas with the class.

Unit 4 Overview

PART 1: Reading Fluently
PART 2: Paraphrasing

Standard Course of Study
In This Unit You Will

- Narrate personal scenes located effectively in time and place. (WL.1.01.1)
- Use visuals and media to make presentations effective in explaining procedures. (IR.2.03.3)
- Report the research for a specified audience. (IR.2.04.4)
- Analyze text components and evaluating impact on critiquing text. (CT.4.03.2)
- Recognize and analyze the characteristics of literary genres. (LT.5.01.2)
- Interpret literary devices. (LT.5.01.3)
- Explain how the writer creates literary elements. (LT.5.01.8)

Introduction:
Poetry

From the Author's Desk

Pat Mora
Talks About the Form

Pat Mora

I've lived near two rivers: the Rio Grande that separates my native state of Texas from Mexico and the Ohio River that separates Ohio from Kentucky. When I watch a river flowing by, I think about the journey it has made and where it's going. Rivers democratically gather branches and leaves as they move along. The sun and moon both travel on the ripples. Though water slips through our fingers, rivers carve canyons.

▲ **Pat Mora** has received numerous awards for works that depict the beauty and varied cultures of the American Southwest.

Poetry's River Includes You

As one of my favorite poets, Mary Oliver, says in the quotation on the next page, "Poetry is a river." You and I can be part of it. No one will compose the poem about popcorn or tennis shoes that you will. When you sit and bring all of yourself to the page, all you've seen, heard, read, and felt, and when you begin to play with words, you can eventually write a unique poem. You will choose your own **form; images,** words that appeal to the senses; and **speaker,** the person who says the words of the poem.

Paintings and music are unique in the same way. Many artists and musicians could see a teenager sitting alone at a party. Each artist would paint the scene differently; each musician would create different sounds to capture the scene, the mood.

▼ **Critical Viewing**
Pat Mora compares poetry to a river. What does this illustration suggest about the way the "river of poetry" affects its readers? **[Interpret]**

A Poem Is Like a River in a Room

I like the spareness of poetry. It demands that I remove the unnecessary. For example, I could have a grand time filling a room with objects I like—flowers, folk art, books, family photos. Suppose, though, that I decided to focus my attention. What if I allowed myself less space and chose each detail carefully because I wanted to create surprises for visitors, to have you not just see the room but experience it. Suppose that I put one small river flowing through the middle of the room.

Poetry is a river; many voices travel in it; poem after poem moves along in the exciting crests and falls of the river waves.

from A Poetry Handbook
—Mary Oliver

You walk in and stare and wonder, as readers sometimes wonder about poems, What's going on here? What's she trying to do? You listen to the river as I hope you listen to poems, and you hear something your neighbor or friend might miss. You connect with that river or that poem because you're you, and you're willing to risk releasing your imagination.

When I begin a poem, I sit with paper and pen. I try not to pressure myself to write a perfect first line. I write to get going, knowing I can discard whatever I write. The page is my landscape, and I'm like that river traveling along, exploring.

More About Pat Mora

In her works, Pat Mora (b. 1942) has explored the experience of being "American but hyphenated"; that is, a bilingual and bicultural Mexican American. She stresses the importance of family and cultural heritage, often using Spanish words and phrases in her writing. She has also published some works in bilingual editions.

Her poetry is spare, yet rich in imagery and feeling. Mora encourages her readers to write their own poems and to "enjoy the word-play."

Fast Facts

▶ Mora has hosted a radio show called *Voices: The Mexican American in Perspective.*
▶ In addition to being a writer and teacher, Mora has worked as a museum director and a college administrator.

Exploring Poetry

Elements of Poetry

Poetry is a literary form that combines the precise meanings of words with their emotional associations, sounds, and rhythms. Many poems are structured in **stanzas,** or groupings of lines. Specific stanza types include **couplets,** which have two lines, and **quatrains,** which have four lines.

Poets use **figurative language** such as metaphor, simile, personification, and onomatopoeia, to express ideas or feelings in a fresh way.

- Poets use **metaphors** to compare two apparently unlike things without using the words *like, as, than,* or *resembles,* as in "The sky is a patchwork quilt." Poets use **similes** to make such comparisons using connecting words, as in "The sky is like a patchwork quilt."

- **Personification** is language that attributes human qualities to non-human things.

- **Onomatopoeia** is the use of a word whose sound imitates its meaning. Examples of such words are *buzz, hiss, thud,* and *sizzle.*

- **Imagery** is descriptive language poets use to create word pictures, or **images.** Images are enhanced by **sensory language,** which provides details related to the senses.

Poets use a number of **sound devices** to achieve a musical quality.

- **Rhythm** is the pattern created by the stressed and unstressed syllables of words in sequence. A controlled pattern of rhythm is called **meter.**

- **Rhyme** is the repetition of identical or similar sounds in stressed syllables. A pattern of end rhymes is called a **rhyme scheme. Free verse** has no set meter or rhyme scheme.

- **Alliteration** is the repetition of the initial consonant sounds of words, as in the phrase *"dark days."* **Assonance** is the repetition of vowel sounds in nearby words, as in the phrase *"child of silence"* **Consonance** is the repetition of consonants within nearby words in which the separating vowels differ, as in the phrase *"live and love."*

- **Repetition** is the use of any language element more than once.

Types of Poetry

There are three main types of poetry.

- In a **narrative** poem, the writer tells a story in verse. Narratives can take many forms. For example, an **epic** is a long narrative poem about gods or heroes. In contrast, a **ballad** is a songlike narrative about an adventure or a romance.
- In a **dramatic** poem, the writer tells a story using a character's own thoughts or statements.
- A **lyric** is a brief poem in which the author expresses the feelings of a single speaker, creating a single effect on the reader. Lyrics are notable for their musical qualities, achieved through rhyme and rhythm.

Forms of Poetry

Other poems can be categorized by form—their particular patterns of rhyme, rhythm, line structure, stanza format, or other element.

- A **haiku** is a poem containing three unrhymed lines of five, seven, and five syllables. This Japanese poetic form uses imagery to convey a single vivid emotion.
- A **sonnet** is a fourteen-line lyric poem with formal patterns of rhyme, rhythm, and line structure.

▼ **Critical Viewing**
What simile could you write to describe this tornado? Explain.
[Synthesize]

Check Your Understanding

Choose the letter of the answer that best matches each numbered item.

1. descriptive sensory language   **A** rhythm   **B** imagery
2. tale of a legendary hero   **A** sonnet   **B** epic
3. words used in unusual ways   **A** figurative language   **B** couplet
4. organization of lines   **A** rhyme   **B** stanza
5. pattern of stressed sounds   **A** haiku   **B** meter

From the Author's Desk
Pat Mora Introduces "A Voice" and "Uncoiling"

I am a writer because I'm a reader, and because I love words in English and Spanish, their pleasure and power. I'm also a writer because of my mother. Mom, a reader who knew both Spanish and English, was my first editor and gave me good advice on my writing assignments and speeches.

"A Voice": Mom's Power Is a Key to the Theme

When I became interested in spending more time writing, I interviewed my family. Have you done that? Every family has good stories to tell. I listened and wrote about the way Mom and Mexicans or people of Mexican descent felt. I wrote about her in the children's book *The Rainbow Tulip;* in my family memoir, *House of Houses;* and in poems such as "A Voice."

When I was a teacher, my students and I would sometimes discuss the **theme** of a poem. What was the poem really about? What did it mean? Sometimes people avoid poetry because they think it's a puzzle. I don't write poetry to confuse you or to preach. I'm exploring with words. Writing poetry is taking a word journey.

I wanted to tell the story of Mom, a high school student, attending a speech contest. She felt frightened at feeling different. We all know that feeling. I also wanted to explore Mom's power in the life of our family.

"Uncoiling": Figurative Language Helps You See

If I use **figurative language** effectively, a phrase like "spunky as a peacock" or "lace lullabies" in the poem "Uncoiling" helps you see what I'm seeing or hearing. Poets spend time choosing words, sounds; poets play with possibilities. The desert is, like my mother, a powerful woman in my life. In "Uncoiling," I chose **personification** to create her on the page for you.

Poetry is a word journey. If I succeed, it's a word journey for you too. I discover and you discover as you read. Poetry asks us to use our imagination, to fill in the silences, to leap.

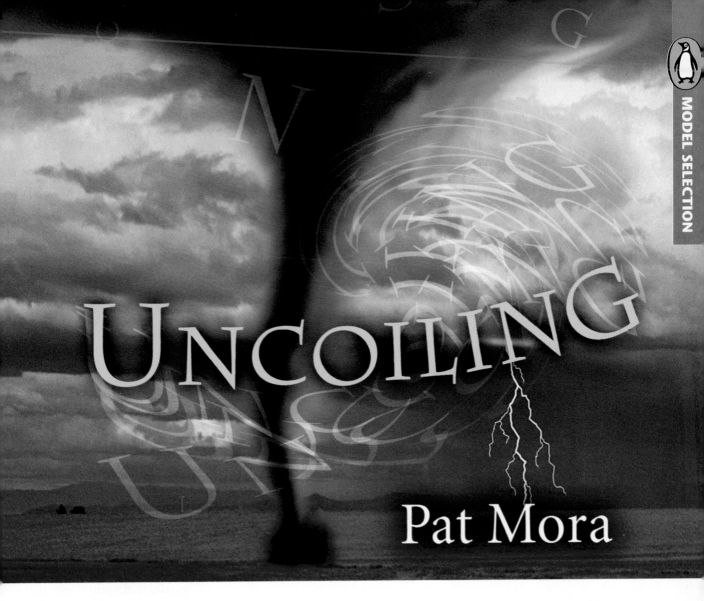

UNCOILING

Pat Mora

With thorns, she scratches
    on my window, tosses her hair dark with rain,
      snares lightning, cholla,[1] hawks, butterfly
        swarms in the tangles.

5 She sighs clouds,
     head thrown back, eyes closed, roars
                 and rivers leap,

boulders retreat like crabs
into themselves.

---

1. cholla (chōl′ yä) *n.* spiny cactus found in the southwestern United States and Mexico.

Pat Mora
Author's Insight
The desert, nature, is no wimp. It survives through strength. I chose verbs like "roars" to convey the desert's energy and power.

10 She spews gusts and thunder,
　　　spooks pale women who scurry to
　　　　lock doors, windows
　　　　　when her tumbleweed skirt starts its spin.

　　They sing lace lullabies
15　　so their children won't hear
　　　her uncoiling
　　　　through her lips, howling
　　　　　leaves off trees, flesh
　　　　　　off bones, until she becomes

20 sound, spins herself
　　　to sleep, sand stinging her ankles,
　　　　whirring into her raw skin like stars.

A Voice

Pat Mora

Even the lights on the stage unrelenting
as the desert sun couldn't hide the other
students, their eyes also unrelenting,
students who spoke English every night

5   as they ate their meat, potatoes, gravy.
Not you. In your house that smelled like
rose powder, you spoke Spanish formal
as your father, the judge without a courtroom

Pat Mora
Author's Insight
Food creates
connections in our
minds and gives us
cultural clues. What if
I'd said, "beans,
tortillas, chile"
instead?

in the country he floated to in the dark
10 on a flatbed truck. He walked slow
as a hot river down the narrow hall
of your house. You never dared to race past him

to say, "Please move," in the language
you learned effortlessly, as you learned to run,
15 the language forbidden at home, though your mother
said you learned it to fight with the neighbors.

You like winning with words. You liked
writing speeches about patriotism and democracy.
You liked all the faces looking at you, all those eyes.
20 "How did I do it?" you ask me now. "How did I do it

when my parents didn't understand?"
The family story says your voice is the voice
of an aunt in Mexico, <u>spunky</u> as a peacock.
Family stories sing of what lives in the blood.

25 You told me only once about the time you went
to the state capitol, your family proud as if
you'd been named governor. But when you looked
around, the only Mexican in the auditorium,

you wanted to hide from those strange faces.
30 Their eyes were pinpricks, and you faked
hoarseness. You, who are never at a loss
for words, felt your breath stick in your throat

like an ice cube. "I can't," you whispered.
"I can't." Yet you did. Not that day but years later.
35 You taught the four of us to speak up.
This is America, Mom. The undoable is done

in the next generation. Your breath moves
through the family like the wind
moves through the trees.

Q. Why did you use the title "A Voice" instead of the name of the person it is about?

A. Titles, like first and last lines, matter. The title is my first chance to snag your interest. I wanted to make you curious. Whose voice? Also, there's something powerful about a voice. Our voice, invisible as the wind, becomes part of the world. Mom's voice was hers (and how I loved it!), but it was—and is—also a force moving through us.

Q. How did you decide to give "Uncoiling" its shape on the page?

A. Most people don't like a wild desert storm. I do, probably because I always felt safe in my home. I liked watching and hearing the desert's power, but I never felt in danger. I wanted the poem's shape to convey a storm's disorder and lack of predictability. The lines aren't orderly. There's a bit of chaos right there on the page to help you experience the desert's mood.

Student Corner

Q. Do you add some of your own emotions when writing about a tornado?

—**Brandon Bishop, Grove City, Ohio**

A. I'd never heard a tornado warning until I moved to the Midwest as an adult. The storm in the poem isn't a tornado but a grand desert dust storm with tumble weeds flying. In El Paso, we could see the dust storm coming, and soon there was so much sand in the air that the mountain in the middle of town disappeared.

 Writing Workshop: *Work in Progress*

Response to Literature

For a response to literature you may write, make a list of literary characters that have made an impression on you. Underline the strong characters on your list and briefly note the qualities that give them their strength. Save this Character List in your writing portfolio.

Apply the Skills

Poetry

Thinking About the Selections

1. **Respond:** Which poem did you find more powerful? Why?

2. **(a) Infer:** In "Uncoiling," what kind of storm does the speaker describe? **(b) Interpret:** Identify three actions the storm takes in the first five stanzas. **(c) Analyze:** How do these actions show the storm's increasing violence?

3. **(a) Recall:** Who is the subject of "A Voice"? **(b) Interpret:** Which of this person's childhood accomplishments does the poet celebrate?

4. **(a) Summarize:** What happens to the person at the state capitol? **(b) Analyze:** According to the speaker, how is the failure of that day transformed later in the subject's life?

Poetry Review

5. In "Uncoiling," Mora uses **personification** to give human attributes to the storm. **(a)** What human qualities does the storm possess? **(b)** How does the storm's behavior compare with the actions of the women in the poem?

6. **(a)** In the first column of a chart like the one shown, list **images** of breathing, speaking, or vocalizing from each poem. In the second column, note the literal meaning of the image. In the third column, describe the effect of the image—the word picture it conveys or feeling it expresses. **(b)** In a small group, discuss your findings to make sure you have included all possible images. Agree on the single most effective image and share your conclusion with the class.

What it says	What it means	Effect

Research the Author

Prepare a **report** in which you describe Pat Mora's views about her dual-language heritage and literary career. Follow these steps:

- Using the Internet and your library, find biographical sources with comments about Mora's writing in both Spanish and English.
- Refer to at least five poems in which Mora mentions her dual-language heritage.
- Share your report with your class.

QuickReview

Poems at a Glance

Uncoiling portrays the violent power of a storm.

A Voice celebrates a mother's inspirational influence on her family.

Go Online
Assessment
For: Self-test
Visit: www.PHSchool.com
Web Code: epa-6401

Personification: a form of figurative language in which a nonhuman subject is given human traits

Imagery: descriptive language with which an author creates vivid word pictures

Skills You Will Learn

Literature You Will Read

Literary Analysis: *Figurative Language: Simile, Metaphor, Personification, and Paradox*
Reading Skill: *Reading in Sentences*

Reading Informational Materials

Reading Skill: *Making Generalizations*

Literary Analysis: *Sound Devices*
Reading Skill: *Using Your Senses*

Comparing Literary Works

Literary Analysis: *Imagery*

Reading and Vocabulary Skills Preview

Reading: Read Fluently

> **Reading fluently** means having the skills to read easily, smoothly, and expressively.

NC Standard Course of Study

- Select, monitor, and modify reading strategies appropriate to argumentative texts. (FA.3.04.1)
- Address clarity and style through grammar and usage. (GU.6.01.4)

Skills and Strategies You Will Learn in Part 1

In Part 1 you will learn

- to read **in sentences using punctuation** to help you **read fluently** (p. 564).
- to **use your senses** to help you **experience the images** described by a poet or an author (p. 590).
- to **make generalizations** about the meaning and imagery in poetry (p. 586).

Using the Skills and Strategies in Part 1

In Part 1, you will learn to read fluently—to read words smoothly in groups according to their meaning. You will practice using punctuation to group words. You will also practice relating words to your own knowledge through sensory details.

This example shows how you will apply the skills and strategies you will learn in Part 1.

Academic Vocabulary: Words for Analyzing Literature

The following words will help you as you read and analyze the literature in Part 1.

Word	Definition	Sample Sentence
considerable *adj.*	much or large; worth noting	His *considerable* talent was finally recognized.
deliberation *n.*	act of carefully thinking about an issue	Their *deliberations* about the validity of the theory lasted for two days.
transition *n.*	passing from one to another	There are *transitions* between ideas.
impact *n.*	force of a collision; shock	Imagery gave the poem great *impact*.
concept *n.*	idea	The poem was about the *concept* of life.

Vocabulary Skills: Suffixes

A **suffix** is a letter, syllable, or group of syllables added to a word to alter its meaning or function.

In Part 1 you will learn
- the Latin suffix *-able* (p. 584)
- the Latin suffix *-tion* (p. 610)

Knowing the meaning of common suffixes helps you to determine a word's meaning.

▶ **Example:**
deliberate (carefully thinking through an issue)

+

tion (the act of)

_____

deliberation
(the act of carefully thinking through an issue)

Activity Add either *-able* or *-tion* to the following words. Use a dictionary to check your spelling. Then, give an example for each word.

drink   like   attend   attract   transit

Build Skills

You can apply the instruction on this page to these poems.

Literary Analysis

Figurative language is language that is used imaginatively rather than literally. Figurative language includes one or more **figures of speech**, literary devices that make unexpected comparisons or change the usual meaning of words. The following are specific types of figures of speech:

- **Simile:** a comparison of two apparently unlike things using *like, as, than,* or *resembles:* "The sky is <u>like</u> a patchwork quilt."

- **Metaphor:** a comparison of one thing as if it were another: "The sky <u>is</u> a patchwork quilt."

- **Personification:** giving human characteristics to a nonhuman subject: "The <u>sea</u> was <u>angry</u> that day, my friends."

- **Paradox:** a statement, an idea, or a situation that seems contradictory but actually expresses a truth: "The more things change, the more they stay the same."

As you read, use a chart like the one shown to record examples of each type of figurative language you find.

Example

Her eyes are like diamonds.

↓

Type

Simile

↓

Meaning or Effect

The simile stresses the beauty and sparkle of the woman's eyes.

Reading Skill

Reading fluently is reading smoothly and continuously while also comprehending the text and appreciating the writer's artistry. To improve your fluency when reading poetry, **read in sentences.** Use punctuation rather than the ends of lines to determine where to pause or stop reading.

Vocabulary Builder

Poetry Collection 1

- **deferred** (dē furd′) *v.* put off until a future time (p. 566) *Jackie <u>deferred</u> her trip to Italy until she had more money.*

- **pensive** (pen′ siv) *adj.* deeply or seriously thoughtful (p. 569) *Everyone remembered the professor as a quiet and <u>pensive</u> man.*

Poetry Collection 2

- **discerning** (di surn′ iŋ) *adj.* having good judgment or understanding (p. 579) *The <u>discerning</u> viewer will realize what a bad movie this is.*

- **preliminaries** (prē lim′ ə ner′ ēz) *n.* steps or events before the main one (p. 581) *The <u>preliminaries</u> were more exciting than the game.*

Connecting to the Literature

Reading/Writing Connection In "Dreams," Langston Hughes advises readers to "hold fast" to dreams. Write a short paragraph explaining why you think dreams are so important to so many people. Use at least three of these words: *achieve, benefit, focus, maintain.*

Meet the Authors

Langston **Hughes** (1902–1967)

Dream Deferred (page 566), Dreams (page 567)

Born in Joplin, Missouri, Langston Hughes was the first African American to earn a living by writing literary works. As a young man, he held a variety of jobs—teacher, ranch hand, and farmer among others. He drew on all of these experiences, but primarily on his perspective as an African American, to create his great body of work.

William **Wordsworth** (1770–1850)

I Wandered Lonely as a Cloud (page 568)

William Wordsworth was born in England's rural Lake District. In 1798, he and fellow poet Samuel Taylor Coleridge published *Lyrical Ballads*—poems that use simple language to exalt everyday life. Emphasizing nature and the imagination, Wordsworth ushered in the age of Romanticism.

Gabriela **Mistral** (1889–1957)

Meciendo (page 570)

Born in Chile as Lucila Godoy y Alcayaga, this writer formed her pen name from the names of her two favorite poets, the Italian Gabriele D'Annunzio and the French Frederic Mistral. Gabriela Mistral wrote many moving poems about children and motherhood. She was awarded the Nobel Prize in Literature in 1945.

Jean **de Sponde** (1557–1595)

Sonnets on Love XIII (page 573)

The French poet Jean de Sponde was a true Renaissance man who served in the court of King Henry IV, dabbled in chemistry, and published scholarly editions of ancient Greek texts. "Sonnets on Love XIII" is part of his finest work, *Sonnets of Love and Death.*

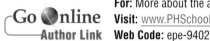

Go **Online**
Author Link

For: More about the authors
Visit: www.PHSchool.com
Web Code: epe-9402

Bernard's Daddy, Raymond Lark, Collection of Mary Moran, New Jersey, Photo courtesy of Edward Smith and Company

Dream Deferred
Langston Hughes

Harlem

What happens to a dream <u>deferred</u>?

    Does it dry up
    like a raisin in the sun?
5   Or fester like a sore—
    And then run?
    Does it stink like rotten meat?
    Or crust and sugar over—
    like a syrupy sweet?

10   Maybe it just sags

    like a heavy load.
    Or does it explode?

▲ **Critical Viewing**
Which line of "Dream Deferred" might you use as a caption for this image? Explain. **[Connect]**

Vocabulary Builder
deferred (dē fʉrd´) *adj.* put off until a future time

Dreams
Langston Hughes

Hold fast to dreams
For if dreams die
Life is a broken-winged bird
That cannot fly.

5   Hold fast to dreams
For when dreams go
Life is a barren field
Frozen with snow.

Reading Skill
Reading Fluently
How many sentences
are in the first stanza?

I WANDERED LONELY AS A CLOUD

WILLIAM WORDSWORTH

I wandered lonely as a cloud
That floats on high o'er vales[1] and hills,
When all at once I saw a crowd,
A host, of golden daffodils;
5   Beside the lake, beneath the trees,
Fluttering and dancing in the breeze.

Continuous as the stars that shine
And twinkle on the milky way,
They stretched in never-ending line
10   Along the margin of a bay:
Ten thousand saw I at a glance,
Tossing their heads in sprightly dance.

---

1. **o'er vales** over valleys.

Literary Analysis
Figurative Language
To what does the speaker compare the daffodils in the simile in lines 7–8?

The waves beside them danced; but they
Outdid the sparkling waves in glee;
15 A poet could not but be gay,
In such a jocund[2] company;
I gazed—and gazed—but little thought
What wealth the show to me had brought:

For oft, when on my couch I lie
20 In vacant or in <u>pensive</u> mood,
They flash upon that inward eye
Which is the bliss of solitude;
And then my heart with pleasure fills,
And dances with the daffodils.

---

2. jocund (jak´ ənd) *adj.* cheerful.

Vocabulary Builder
pensive (pen´ siv) *adj.*
deeply or seriously
thoughtful

Meciendo

Gabriela Mistral

El mar sus millares de olas
mece, divino.
Oyendo a los mares amantes,
mezo a mi niño.

5 El viento errabundo en la noche
mece a los trigos.
Oyendo a los vientos amantes,
mezo a mi niño.

Dios Padre sus miles de mundos
10 mece sin ruido.
Sintiendo su mano en la sombra,
mezo a mi niño.

▲ **Critical Viewing**
How well does this
photograph illustrate
the "loving sea"
described in the
poem? Explain.
[Evaluate]

Rocking (Meciendo)

Gabriela Mistral

translated by Doris Dana

The sea rocks her thousands of waves.
The sea is divine.
Hearing the loving sea,
I rock my son.

5 The wind wandering by night
rocks the wheat.
Hearing the loving wind,
I rock my son.

God, the Father, soundlessly rocks
10 His thousands of worlds.
Feeling His hand in the shadow,
I rock my son.

Literary Analysis
Figurative Language
What human traits
does the wind show in
the second stanza?

Apply the Skills

Poetry Collection 1

Thinking About the Selections

1. **Respond:** Which of these poems affected you the most? Why?
2. **(a) Recall:** To what two things does the speaker in "Dreams" compare life? **(b) Interpret:** Restate in your own words the advice that "Dreams" offers.
3. **(a) Recall:** How many questions does "Dream Deferred" ask? **(b) Contrast:** How is the last question different from the others?
4. **(a) Recall:** In "I Wandered Lonely as a Cloud," what natural sight does the speaker describe? **(b) Recall:** In "Meciendo/Rocking," what natural sights and sounds does the speaker describe? **(c) Compare and Contrast:** Explain how the natural sights and sounds affect both of the speakers.
5. **(a) Interpret:** In "Sonnets on Love XIII," to what does the speaker compare his love? **(b) Draw Conclusions:** What does this comparison suggest about the speaker's feelings? Explain.

Literary Analysis

6. **(a)** Identify one **simile** in "Dream Deferred" and one **metaphor** in "Dreams." **(b)** Explain what each **figure of speech** contributes to the overall meaning of the poem in which it appears.
7. **(a)** Identify one example of **personification** in Poetry Collection 1. **(b)** Explain how this use of **figurative language** contributes to the overall effect of the poem in which it appears.
8. **(a)** Identify the **paradox** in "Sonnets on Love XIII." **(b)** Explain how it seems contradictory but actually makes sense.

Reading Skill

9. **(a)** Using a graphic organizer like the one shown, rewrite one stanza in Poetry Collection 1 as a prose paragraph.

Stanza	Paragraph
God, the Father, soundlessly rocks His thousands of worlds. Feeling His hand in the shadow, I rock my son.	God, the Father, soundlessly rocks His thousands of worlds. Feeling His hand in the shadow, I rock my son.

(b) Read both the stanza and paragraph aloud. How does following the punctuation rather than the line breaks help you to **read fluently?**

QuickReview

Poems at a Glance
"Dream Deferred" explores the power of unfulfilled dreams.

"Dreams" advises readers to hold on to dreams.

"I Wandered Lonely as a Cloud" celebrates nature's beauty.

"Meciendo" finds comfort in nature's divine rhythms.

"Sonnets on Love XIII" addresses love's power and stability.

Go Online
Assessment
For: Self-test
Visit: www.PHSchool.com
Web Code: epa-6402

Figurative Language: language that is used imaginatively rather than literally, *including simile, metaphor, personification,* or *paradox*

Reading Fluently: reading smoothly and continuously with comprehension

Vocabulary Builder

Practice Analogies show the relationships between pairs of words. Use a word from the Collection 1 list on page 564 to complete each analogy. Your choice should create a word pair that matches the relationship between the first two words given. Explain the relationship.

1. rushed : hurried :: _____ : delayed
2. active : exercise :: _____ : ponder

Adding Words to Your Vocabulary Using a thesaurus, find a **synonym**, or word with a similar meaning, for *deferred* and *pensive*. Use each synonym in a sentence that makes the meaning of the word clear. (For more on using a thesaurus, see page R7.)

Writing

Using the scenes described by Wordsworth or Mistral as a model, write a **description of a scene** in nature. Create your own descriptive word picture in a few paragraphs or a poem.
- Choose a scene that you know firsthand or from photographs.
- List details in the scene that appeal to one or more of the senses.
- Refer to your list of details as you draft your description, and work to convey a unified impression.

For *Grammar, Vocabulary,* and *Assessment,* see **Build Language Skills,** pages 584–585.

Extend Your Learning

Listening and Speaking Use the poems in Poetry Collection 1 as the basis for an **impromptu speech** about dreams, nature, or love.
- Do not write a script or an outline; instead, consider the central point you want to convey.
- Work to use a variety of sentence structures.
- Use body language and eye contact to convey sincerity.
Invite your audience to give you feedback about your performance.

Research and Technology In a group, discuss and agree upon a **soundtrack** of appropriate music to accompany each poem in Poetry Collection 1. Research the music of the period in which each poem was written, and choose music that fits each poem's mood and ideas. Invite classmates to read the poems while the music is playing.

Build Understanding • *Poetry Collection 2*

Connecting to the Literature

Reading/Writing Connection In "All Watched Over by Machines of Loving Grace," Richard Brautigan imagines a world in which human beings and computers live in perfect harmony. Write two sentences about the positive role of computers in our lives, and write another two about the negative side of the computer age. Use at least three of these words: *maximize, minimize, accelerate, deny, interact.*

Review
For **Literary Analysis, Reading Skill,** and **Vocabulary Builder,** see page 564.

Meet the Authors

Richard **Brautigan** (1935–1984)
"All Watched Over by Machines of Loving Grace" (page 577)
With his 1967 novel *Trout Fishing in America,* Richard Brautigan became a spokesperson of the hippie generation. Ironically, he was at least fifteen years older than the hippies and a product of the Beat generation that preceded them. Nevertheless, his writing demonstrates his free spirit. His books present sketches of a counterculture that resists dependence on machines, industry, and business.

Emily **Dickinson** (1830–1886)
"Hope" is the thing with feathers (page 578);
Much Madness is divinest Sense— (page 579)
Despite her quiet exterior, Emily Dickinson's inner life overflowed with energy. She produced at least 1,775 poems. Dickinson looked deeply into simple subjects—a fly buzzing, a bird on a walk, the changing seasons. She also made profound explorations of love, death, and the relationship between the human and the divine. She remains unquestionably one of America's finest poets.

Stanley **Kunitz** (b. 1905)
The War Against the Trees (page 580)
Stanley Kunitz was born in Worcester, Massachusetts, and published his first book of poems in 1930. Kunitz has worked as an editor on many small magazines and has taught countless young poets. He was named the United States Poet Laureate in 2000.

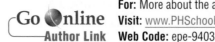

Go Online
Author Link

For: More about the authors
Visit: www.PHSchool.com
Web Code: epe-9403

All Watched Over by Machines of Loving Grace

Richard Brautigan

I like to think (and
the sooner the better!)
of a cybernetic meadow
where mammals and computers
5   live together in mutually
programming harmony
like pure water
touching clear sky.

I like to think
    (right now, please!)
10   of a cybernetic forest
filled with pines and electronics
where deer stroll peacefully
past computers
as if they were flowers
15   with spinning blossoms.

I like to think
    (it has to be!)
of a cybernetic ecology
where we are free of our labors
and joined back to nature,
20   returned to our mammal
brothers and sisters,
and all watched over
by machines of loving grace.

Literary Analysis
Figurative Language
What simile does the speaker use in lines 4–8 to describe the cybernetic meadow?

"Hope" is the thing with feathers—
EMILY DICKINSON

"Hope" is the thing with feathers—
That perches in the soul—
And sings the tune without the words—
And never stops—at all—

5   And sweetest—in the Gale[1]—is heard—
And sore must be the storm—
That could abash the little Bird
That kept so many warm—

I've heard it in the chillest land—
10   And on the strangest Sea—
Yet, never, in Extremity,
It asked a crumb—of Me.

---

1. Gale (gāl) *n.* strong wind.

Reading Skill
Reading Fluently
Where in the second stanza could you replace a dash with a period to signify the end of a sentence?

◀ **Critical Viewing**
Why might someone associate birds with hope? **[Speculate]**

Much Madness is divinest Sense—

EMILY DICKINSON

Much Madness is divinest Sense—
To a <u>discerning</u> Eye—
Much Sense—the starkest Madness—
'Tis the Majority
5 In this, as All, prevail—
Assent[1]—and you are sane—
Demur[2]—you're straightway dangerous—
And handled with a Chain—

---

1. Assent (ə sent´) *v.* agree.
2. Demur (dē mʉr´) *v.* hesitate because of doubts or objections.

Vocabulary Builder
discerning (di sʉrn´ iŋ)
adj. having good
judgment or
understanding

The WAR AGAINST the TREES

STANLEY KUNITZ

The man who sold his lawn to standard oil
Joked with his neighbors come to watch the show
While the bulldozers, drunk with gasoline,
Tested the virtue of the soil
5 Under the branchy sky
By overthrowing first the privet-row.

Forsythia-forays and hydrangea-raids
Were but <u>preliminaries</u> to a war
Against the great-grandfathers of the town,
10 So freshly lopped and maimed.
They struck and struck again,
And with each elm a century went down.

All day the hireling engines charged the trees,
Subverting them by hacking underground
15 In grub-dominions, where dark summer's mole
Rampages through his halls,
Till a northern seizure shook
Those crowns, forcing the giants to their knees.

I saw the ghosts of children at their games
20 Racing beyond their childhood in the shade,
And while the green world turned its death-foxed page
And a red wagon wheeled,
I watched them disappear
Into the suburbs of their grievous age.

25 Ripped from the craters much too big for hearts
The club-roots bared their amputated coils,
Raw gorgons matted blind, whose pocks and scars
Cried Moon! on a corner lot
One witness-moment, caught
30 In the rear-view mirrors of the passing cars.

◀ **Critical Viewing** What does a tree like the one shown represent to the speaker of the poem? **[Connect]**

Vocabulary Builder
preliminaries (prē lim´ ə ner´ ēz) *n.* steps or events before the main one

Literary Analysis
Figurative Language
What are the "giants" that are personified in line 18?

Apply the Skills

Poetry Collection 2

Thinking About the Selections

1. **Respond:** Which of these poems affected you the most? Why?
2. **(a) Recall:** To what does the speaker compare computers in the imaginary world of "All Watched Over by Machines of Loving Grace"? **(b) Interpret:** What does this comparison suggest about the speaker's feelings about computers in the real world?
3. **(a) Recall:** In "'Hope' is the thing with feathers—," when does hope sing the sweetest? **(b) Interpret:** Why does hope sing so well at these times?
4. **(a) Interpret:** In "The War Against the Trees," who or what is at war with the trees? **(b) Draw Conclusions:** What does the image of war suggest about the speaker's feelings toward the trees and what is happening to them? Explain.
5. **(a) Interpret:** In "Much Madness is divinest Sense—," what kind of behavior is considered insane? **(b) Evaluate:** Do you agree with the speaker's ideas? Why or why not?

Literary Analysis

6. **(a)** Identify a **simile** and a **metaphor** in Poetry Collection 2. **(b)** Explain what each **figure of speech** contributes to the overall meaning or effect of the poem in which it appears.
7. **(a)** Identify one example of **personification** in Collection 2. **(b)** Explain how this use of **figurative language** contributes to the overall meaning or effect of the poem in which it appears.
8. **(a)** Identify the **paradox** in "Much Madness is divinest Sense—." **(b)** Explain why it is a paradox.

Reading Skill

9. **(a)** Using a graphic organizer like the one shown, rewrite one stanza in Poetry Collection 2 as a prose paragraph.

Stanza	Paragraph
I've heard it in the chillest land— And on the strangest Sea— Yet, never, in Extremity, It asked a crumb—of Me.	I've heard it in the chillest land and on the strangest Sea, yet never, in Extremity, it asked a crumb of me.

(b) Read both the stanza and paragraph aloud. How does following the punctuation rather than the line breaks help you to **read fluently**?

QuickReview

Poems at a Glance
"All Watched Over by Machines of Loving Grace" presents a futuristic vision of a world run by computers.

"'Hope' is the thing with feathers—" discusses the power and constancy of hope.

"The War Against the Trees" explores the battle between "progress" and nature.

"Much Madness is divinest Sense—" explores the idea of sanity.

Assessment
For: Self-test
Visit: www.PHSchool.com
Web Code: epa-6403

Figurative Language: language that is used imaginatively rather than literally, including *simile, metaphor, personification,* or *paradox*

Reading Fluently: reading smoothly and continuously with comprehension

Vocabulary Builder

Practice **Analogies** show the relationships between pairs of words. Use a word from the Collection 2 list on page 564 to complete each analogy. Your choice should create a word pair that matches the relationship between the first two words given. Explain the relationship.

1. forgiving : fan :: _____ : expert
2. rehearsal : performance :: _____ : championship

Adding Words to Your Vocabulary Using a thesaurus, find a **synonym,** or word with a similar meaning, for *preliminaries* and *discerning.* Use each synonym in a sentence that makes the meaning of the word clear. (For more on using a thesaurus, see page R7.)

Writing

Using the scene described in "The War Against the Trees" as a model, write a **description of a scene** in nature. Create your own descriptive word picture in a few paragraphs or a poem.

- Choose a scene that you know firsthand or from photographs.
- List details in the scene that appeal to one or more of the senses.
- Refer to your list of details as you draft your description, and work to convey a unified impression.

For *Grammar, Vocabulary,* and *Assessment,* see **Build Language Skills,** pages 584–585.

Extend Your Learning

Listening and Speaking Use the poems in Poetry Collection 2 as the basis for an **impromptu speech** about dreams, nature, or love.

- Do not write a script or an outline; instead, consider the central point to convey.
- Work to use a variety of sentence structures.
- Use body language and eye contact to convey sincerity.

Invite your audience to give you feedback about your performance.

Research and Technology In a group, discuss and agree upon a **soundtrack** of appropriate music to accompany each poem in Poetry Collection 2. Research the music of the period in which each poem was written, and choose music that fits each poem's mood and ideas. Invite classmates to read the poems while the music is playing.

Build Language Skills

Vocabulary Skill

Suffixes The **Latin suffix** *-able* means "capable of being" or "having the quality of." Adding the suffix *-able* changes a base word to an adjective. For example, the word *considerable* means "worthy, or capable of, being considered." The addition of the suffix changes the verb "consider," to the adjective "considerable."

Practice Each of the following words contains the suffix *-able*. Write a definition of each word, and use it in a sentence.

1. usable
2. lovable
3. retractable
4. comfortable
5. washable

Grammar Lesson

Preposition and Object of the Preposition A **preposition** is a word that relates a noun or pronoun to another word in the sentence. Although most prepositions, such as *at, by, in,* and *with,* are single words, some prepositions, such as *because of* and *in addition to,* are **compound.** The **object of the preposition** is the noun or pronoun at the end of a prepositional phrase.

Common Prepositions: about, above, across, below, beyond, by, down, except, for, from, in, of, on, over, past, through, to, under, until, up, with

Common Compound Prepositions: according to, along with, in front of, instead of, next to

Object of a Preposition: Mr. Johnson ate <u>at a good restaurant.</u>
(*restaurant* is the object of the preposition *at*)

MorePractice

For more practice with prepositions and objects of the preposition, see the Grammar Handbook, R40.

Practice Rewrite the following sentences, substituting a different preposition for the italicized one. Then, write a brief explanation of how the new preposition changes the meaning of the sentence.

1. The cat ran *around* the tree.
2. Put the book *on* the desk.
3. The space probe traveled *to* Mars.
4. He ran *to* school.
5. Evelyn turned *on* the light.

W̶G Prentice Hall Writing and Grammar Connection: Chapter 19, Section 1.

Reading Skill: Read Fluently

Standards Assessed

• IR.2.02.4
• LT.5.01.2
• LT.5.01.9

Directions: *Read the poem. Then, answer the questions.*

I love to go out in late September
among the fat, overripe, icy, black blackberries
to eat blackberries for breakfast,
the stalks very prickly, a penalty
5 they earn for knowing the black art
of blackberry-making; and as I stand among them
lifting the stalks to my mouth, the ripest berries
fall almost unbidden to my tongue,
as words sometimes do, certain peculiar words
10 like *strengths* or *squinched,*
many-lettered, one-syllabled lumps,
which I squeeze, squinch open, and splurge well
in the silent, startled, icy, black language
of blackberry-eating in late September.

—Galway Kinnell

1. Which line tells what the speaker loves to do?
   A line 3
   B line 6
   C line 10
   D line 13

2. Which of the following lines ends with a subject separated from its verb in the next line?
   A line 1
   B line 4
   C line 7
   D line 12

3. What does the punctuation in line 9, signal?
   A the end of an extended metaphor
   B a new analogy.
   C the beginning of a series of similes
   D the start of the thematic explanation

4. How should lines 12-13 be read?
   A Pause briefly at the end of line 12.
   B Stop completely at the end of line 12.
   C Continue to the end of line 13.
   D Continue to the comma in line 13.

Timed Writing: Analysis [Critical Stance]

Review the poetry in *Poetry Collection 1* or *Poetry Collection 2*. Select a poem in which symbolism significantly contributes to the theme of the work. Explain how the symbols help convey the message of the poem.
(60 minutes)

Writing Workshop: *Work in Progress*

Descriptive Essay

For a descriptive essay you may write, make a list of three places. For each place write 10 words that describe the way the place looks. Put this Sight List in your writing portfolio.

Reading Informational Materials

Case Studies

In Part 1, you are learning how to read fluently while reading literature. Reading fluently helps you to group words into meaningful chunks. This skill will help you connect ideas when reading informational materials such as a case study. If you read about the field of computers in Richard Brautigan's "All Watched Over by Machines of Loving Grace," you might enjoy this case study about careers in robotics.

NG Standard Course of Study

- Select, monitor, and modify reading strategies appropriate to critiquing work. (CT.4.03.1)
- Selecting, monitoring, and modifying appropriate to literary purpose. (LT.5.03.1)

About Case Studies

A **case study** is a detailed analysis of a person, group, project, or situation. It provides a real-life example of what happens in specific situations and can serve as a model for similar initiatives. A case study usually has these elements:

- An introduction explaining what is being studied and why
- Facts, examples, and quotations
- Instances of *inductive reasoning*—reasoning from specific examples to a general concept
- Instances of *deductive reasoning*—applying a general principle to a specific case
- A conclusion and recommendation summarizing the information and providing ideas for how to apply it

Reading Skill

A case study presents specific details and examples to illustrate the subject. A reader uses these details to make generalizations. **Generalizations** are broad statements that are true when applied to a variety of circumstances. Making generalizations helps us make decisions, and it helps us apply our reading to our lives. As you read the case study "Careers in Robotics," use a chart like the one shown to make meaningful generalizations based on the details in the text.

Details	Generalization
• While in college, Matt and Gil had many different career goals. • After college, they both became successful engineers.	Even if you are unsure about your goals while in school, you can still find a good career.

Robotics Education Project

Careers in Robotics: A Case Study

Think you'll never use high school math? Think again . . .

In the introduction, the author tells who the subjects of the study are, explains what they do, and points out that there is "no single path" to becoming a robotics engineer.

Gil Jones and Matt Zucker may seem like regular guys just out of college—but they have one of the coolest jobs around! They are both software engineers for a company that makes underwater robots, otherwise known as autonomous underwater vehicles (AUVs). AUVs are small, unmanned submarines that use on-board artificial intelligence to complete survey tasks with little or no human supervision.

Although Matt and Gil do the same job now, the difference in how they got there shows there really is no single path to robotics.

Getting There

Quotations show that the information comes directly from the people being studied.

"I was a classic underachiever in high school," says Matt. "I got into college by the skin of my teeth. Once I got into college, though, I realized I wanted to focus on my interests. Studying something I liked really made it all worthwhile." In college at Vassar, Matt took his interests in biology and computers even further. He took classes in psychology, philosophy, anthropology, human brain and behavior, and artificial intelligence to work his way to a degree in cognitive science. His main interest? Helping robots and computers learn complex behaviors.

The writer analyzes some of the steps Gil took that prepared him for a career in robotics.

Gil, on the other hand, was a good student in high school, but didn't start out in robotics either—he was more interested in political science. At Swarthmore College, he was inspired by computer science. "I wanted to focus on artificial intelligence. I took an artificial intelligence class where we started playing with toy robots, using Handyboards and sensors." Gil really got interested in robotics through AAAI robotics competitions (imagine creating a robot that can serve hors d'oeuvres!), and when he graduated with a degree in computer science, a lot of his experience was with robots.

The bottom line, both Gil and Matt agree, is that you don't have to go to an engineering school. Liberal arts universities and colleges will also give you the skills you need to do robotics. If you're interested in a lot of things—physics, math, science, engineering, communications, and others—you'll do well.

Landing the Job

Both Gil and Matt did summer internships during college that provided them with work experience and an idea of how to get a job in robotics. During one summer, Gil worked for the Naval Research Laboratory doing software artificial intelligence research and then, after graduating, spent the summer preparing for another AAAI competition. When one of his friends got a job at a robotics company, Gil learned about the company and then applied to be a software engineer. Matt got an internship at the same company during the summer between his junior and senior years and was then offered a job following graduation. What's their best advice for getting internships and jobs? Perseverance! "Just find someone who works in robotics and ask them for advice," says Matt. Gil adds, "Sometimes it's difficult to get in, but keep trying. Think about doing an internship for free. Often internships are the first step through the door."

Research, Programming, and . . . Cruising(?)

One of the great things about this job is the variety. Sometimes they spend all day reading up on robotics research, sometimes they spend all day in front of a computer . . . and sometimes they spend all day hanging out on a boat testing the robot in the ocean! "You're making something that has a purpose, something that's part of a bigger project," says Gil. "You get to see if what you did worked. Of course, that means you're entirely responsible." Another perk, according to Matt, is that "you usually get to learn something big and new every few weeks." One warning: Pay attention in high school math classes. "You'll use trigonometry like crazy!"

Next Steps

Both Matt and Gil plan on going back to school sometime to do graduate work. Matt wants to study computer science, focusing on computer graphics and computer-human interfaces. Eventually, he wants to be a professor. Gil plans to go back to school specifically in robotics. He finds underwater robotics exciting because it requires autonomy, but there are a lot of other cool areas of robotics he'd like to explore.

The draw for both of them is that robotics is a quickly changing and very open field. As they point out, "You can do new stuff in any of the related areas and that's exciting!"

Reading: Making Generalizations

Standards Assessed
• CT.4.03.10
• LT.5.03.12
• WL.1.03.5

Directions: *Choose the letter of the best answer to each question.*

1. Which detail from the study supports the generalization that it is wise to explore different subjects before choosing a career?

   A "I got into college by the skin of my teeth."

   B "Matt took classes in psychology, philosophy, and anthropology."

   C "Gil and Matt did summer internships to get experience."

   D "You do not have to go to an engineering school."

2. An underachiever in high school, Matt pursued his interests in college and did well. What generalization can you make from Matt's experience?

   A Employers hire people who are interested in the field.

   B You have to like computer science to be good at robotics.

   C Hard work will result in good grades.

   D People learn better when they are interested in the subject.

3. Which detail from the study supports the generalization that one continues to study and learn after graduating from college?

   A "Sometimes they spend all day reading up on robotics."

   B "You get to see if what you did worked."

   C "Sometimes they spend all day on a boat testing robots."

   D "One of the great things about the job is variety."

Reading: Comprehension and Interpretation

Directions: *Write your answers on a separate piece of paper.*

4. What are the differences between Matt's path to a career in robotics and Gil's path? **[Organizing]**

5. Is this case study useful for students who are not interested in a career in robotics? Explain. **[Applying]**

Timed Writing: Exposition [Connections]

"Success is the sum of small efforts, repeated day in and day out."
—*Robert Collier*

Use inductive reasoning to support or refute the quotation. Cite details from the article in your response. **(25 minutes)**

You can apply the instruction on this page to these poems.

Poetry Collection 1
Summer, page 592
The Eagle, page 593
Analysis of Baseball, page 594

Poetry Collection 2
The Bells, page 599
Slam, Dunk, & Hook,
page 604
Jabberwocky, page 606

> **Standard Course of Study**
>
> • Analyze connections among ideas, concepts, characters and experience in response. (WL.1.03.9)
>
> • Make connections between argumentative works, self and related topics. (FA.3.04.8)

Literary Analysis

Poets use **sound devices** to emphasize the sound relation-ships among words. These devices include the following.

- **Alliteration:** the repetition of initial consonant sounds in stressed syllables: *"The fair breeze blew, the white foam flew . . ."*

- **Consonance:** the repetition of final consonant sounds in stressed syllables with different vowel sounds, as in *sit* and *cat*

- **Assonance:** the repetition of similar vowel sounds in stressed syllables that end with different consonants, as in *seal* and *meet*

- **Onomatopoeia:** the use of a word whose sound imitates its meaning, such as *pop* or *hiss*

All of these sound devices work to engage the reader's senses and create musical and emotional effects.

Senses	Words that appeal to senses
Sight	
Hearing	
Smell	
Taste	
Touch	

Reading Skill

Reading fluently is reading smoothly and continuously while also com-prehending the text and appreciating the writer's artistry. To avoid being tripped up by the meaning as you read, **use your senses.** To do so, notice language that appeals to the five senses. Record examples of sensory language in a chart like the one shown.

Vocabulary Builder

Poetry Collection 1

- **clasps** (klasps) *v.* grips (p. 593) *The driver clasps the wheel tightly to steer.*

- **azure** (azh´ ər) *adj.* blue (p. 593) *She painted the ceiling azure so it would look like the sky.*

Poetry Collection 2

- **voluminously** (və loo´ mə nəs lē) *adv.* fully; in great volume (p. 600) *Her coach praised her voluminously at the awards banquet.*

- **palpitating** (pal´ pə tāt´ iŋ) *adj.* beating rapidly; throbbing (p. 601) *The palpitating drums of the pep band excited the fans.*

- **metaphysical** (met´ ə fiz´ i kəl) *adj.* spiritual; beyond the physical (p. 605) *She says that songwriting is metaphysical; the songs come to her in dreams.*

- **jibed** (jībd) *v.* changed direction (p. 605) *As the wind shifted, the crew jibed to keep the sails full.*

Connecting to the Literature

Reading/Writing Connection The poem "Summer" is a celebration of the year's hottest season. Write a short paragraph describing your favorite season and what you love about it. Use at least three of these words: *anticipate, coincide, display, participate.*

Meet the Authors

Walter Dean **Myers** (b. 1937)
Summer (page 592)
Growing up poor in West Virginia, Walter Dean Myers never imagined himself becoming a writer. Although he was writing poems and stories by his early teens, he believed that his dream of a literary career would never be realized. Myers's dream was fulfilled, however, when he won a writing contest sponsored by the Council on Interracial Books for Children for his book *Where Does a Day Go?*

Alfred, **Lord Tennyson** (1809–1892)
The Eagle (page 593)
The most popular British poet during his lifetime, Alfred, Lord Tennyson rose from humble beginnings to the position of poet laureate of England. Although he was enthralled by the technological advances of the Victorian Era, Tennyson remained a poet of nature, bringing both imagination and feeling to descriptions of the landscape and its inhabitants.

May **Swenson** (1919–1989)
Analysis of Baseball (page 594)
May Swenson has been called "one of the surest poets, clear-eyed and absolute." She was born in Logan, Utah, and attended Utah State University. After working for a while as a newspaper reporter, she moved to New York City, where she worked as an editor and as a college lecturer. Her poems were published in such magazines as *The New Yorker, Harper's,* and *The Nation.* Swenson also served as a Chancellor of The Academy of American Poets from 1980 to 1989.

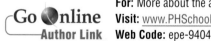

For: More about the authors
Visit: www.PHSchool.com
Web Code: epe-9404

SUMMER

Walter Dean Myers

I like hot days, hot days
Sweat is what you got days
Bugs buzzin from cousin to cousin
Juices dripping
5 Running and ripping
Catch the one you love days

Birds peeping
Old men sleeping
Lazy days, daisies lay
10 Beaming and dreaming
Of hot days, hot days,
Sweat is what you got days

▼ **Critical Viewing**
How well does this
photograph illustrate
the speaker's feelings
about summer?
Explain. **[Evaluate]**

The Eagle

Alfred, Lord Tennyson

He <u>clasps</u> the crag[1] with crooked hands;
Close to the sun in lonely lands,
Ring'd with the <u>azure</u> world, he stands.

The wrinkled sea beneath him crawls;
5 He watches from his mountain walls,
And like a thunderbolt he falls.

---

1. crag (krag) *n.* steep, rugged rock that rises above others or projects from a rock mass.

Vocabulary Builder
clasps (klasps) *v.* grips
azure (azh´ ər) *adj.* blue

Analysis Of Baseball

May Swenson

It's about
the ball,
the bat,
and the mitt.
5 Ball hits
bat, or it
hits mitt.
Bat doesn't
hit ball, bat
10 meets it.
Ball bounces
off bat, flies
air, or thuds
ground (dud)
15 or it
fits mitt.

Bat waits
for ball
to mate.
20 Ball hates
to take bat's
bait. Ball
flirts, bat's
late, don't
25 keep the date.
Ball goes in
(thwack) to mitt,
and goes out
(thwack) back
30 to mitt.

Ball fits
mitt, but
not all

**Literary Analysis
Sound Devices** What
final consonant sound
is repeated frequently
in the first ten lines of
the poem?

▶ **Critical Viewing**
Which words in the
poem might describe
the action in this
photograph?
[Connect]

the time.
35 Sometimes
ball gets hit
(pow) when bat
meets it,
and sails
40 to a place
where mitt
has to quit
in disgrace.
That's about
45 the bases
loaded,
about 40,000
fans exploded.

It's about
50 the ball,
the bat,
the mitt,
the bases
and the fans.
55 It's done
on a diamond,
and for fun.
It's about
home, and it's
60 about run.

Reading Skill
Reading Fluently To
what senses do the
words "40,000 fans
exploded" appeal?
Explain.

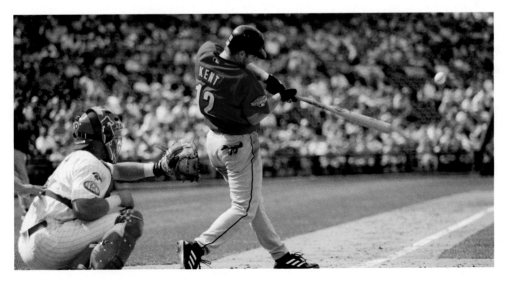

Analysis of Baseball ■ 595

Apply the Skills

Poetry Collection 1

Thinking About the Selections

1. **Respond:** How do each of these poems make you feel about their subjects? Explain.
2. **(a) Recall:** In lines 1–2 of "Summer," how does the speaker describe summer? **(b) Interpret:** What kind of juices might be dripping in line 4? **(c) Connect:** In what way is the image in line 4 a continuation of the one in line 2? Explain.
3. **(a) Infer:** What is the eagle watching for in line 5 of "The Eagle"? **(b) Interpret:** What is the eagle doing when he "falls" in line 6?
4. **Make a Judgment:** Do you think the poem "Analysis of Baseball" can be appreciated by someone who is unfamiliar with the rules of baseball? Why or why not?

Literary Analysis

5. **(a)** For each poem in Poetry Collection 1, use a chart like the one shown to identify one example of each **sound device** listed. **(b)** In what way does each example add to the musical feeling of each poem?

	Example	Effect
Alliteration		
Consonance		
Assonance		

6. **(a)** Identify an example of **onomatopoeia** in "Analysis of Baseball." **(b)** What sound does the word imitate? **(c)** How well does the word imitate the sound? Explain your answer.
7. **(a)** Which of these poems do you think makes the most effective use of sound devices? Explain your choice. **(b)** Discuss your idea with a small group and together decide on a single response to explain to the class.

Reading Skill

8. In what way does **reading fluently** help you to appreciate a poem's sound devices?
9. **(a)** Which of your senses, other than your sense of hearing, were most engaged by each of these poems? **(b)** Which specific words appealed to those senses?

QuickReview

Poems at a Glance
"**Summer**" celebrates the season.

"**The Eagle**" describes this awesome bird of prey.

"**Analysis of Baseball**" shares impressions of the game.

For: Self-test
Visit: www.PHSchool.com
Web Code: epa-6404

Sound Devices: language that emphasizes the sound relationships among words; sound devices include *alliteration, consonance, assonance,* and *onomatopoeia*

Reading Fluently: reading smoothly and continuously while comprehending the text and appreciating the writer's artistry

Vocabulary Builder

Practice Identify the word in each group that does not belong with the others. Explain your response.

1. clasps, hands, blanket   **2.** azure, bread, green

Adding Words to Your Vocabulary *Azure* describes a certain shade of blue: deep sky-blue. The words *scarlet, indigo,* and *emerald* also describe specific shades of colors. Use a dictionary to discover what these colors are. Then, write a sentence for each word that reflects the color's specific shade. (For more on using a dictionary, see page R6.)

Writing

Write an **editorial**—a brief piece of writing that presents one side of an issue—related to one of the poems in this collection. For example, using Tennyson's "The Eagle" as inspiration, you might write an editorial about the need to preserve the North American bald eagle.
- State the issue clearly and express your opinion reasonably.
- Anticipate questions from those who might disagree with you.

Have several people respond to your editorial, including someone who disagrees with you. If you hear a point that you should have addressed, consider adding it.

For *Grammar, Vocabulary,* and *Assessment,*
see **Build Language Skills,** pages 610–611.

Extend Your Learning

Listening and Speaking Prepare a **dramatic reading** that captures the musical qualities of one of the poems in the collection.
- Choose a poem and make notes about which words and sounds to emphasize and when to change your reading pace.
- Practice reading the poem aloud, recording yourself, if possible, so that you can hear and fix problem spots.

Present your dramatic reading in class.

Research and Technology In a group, create an **illustrated version** of one of the poems. Find photographs or original artwork. With the group, debate the merits of each choice and then reach an agreement about which images best capture the mood of the poem. Read the poem and share the art for classmates' enjoyment.

Build Understanding • *Poetry Collection 2*

Connecting to the Literature

Reading/Writing Connection The speaker in "The Bells" describes a range of ideas associated with the sounds of different bells. Write a short paragraph describing the ideas that an every-day sound sparks for you. Use at least three of these words: *signify, trigger, appreciate, contemplate, interpret.*

Review

For **Literary Analysis, Reading Skill,** and **Vocabulary Builder,** see page 590.

Meet the Authors

Edgar Allan **Poe** (1809–1849)
The Bells (page 599)
As poems like "The Bells" illustrate, Edgar Allan Poe was a master at using rhythm and sound devices to powerful effect. Many scholars believe that the idea for "The Bells" was suggested to Poe by Marie Louise Shew, a woman with medical training who treated Poe when his health began to fail.

Yusef **Komunyakaa** (b. 1947)
Slam, Dunk, & Hook (page 604)
Yusef Komunyakaa grew up in Bogalusa, Louisiana. During the mid-1960s, he served in Vietnam as a reporter and an editor for the military newspaper *The Southern Cross.* Komunyakaa later turned his attention to poetry, winning a Pulitzer Prize for his book *Neon Vernacular: New and Selected Poems* (1993). Komunyakaa has said that he likes "connecting the abstract to the concrete."

Lewis **Carroll** (1832–1898)
Jabberwocky (page 606)
Charles Lutwidge Dodgson was a professor of mathematics and a talented early photographer. Today, he is best remembered for two children's books he wrote under the pen name Lewis Carroll: *Alice's Adventures in Wonderland* (1865) and its sequel *Through the Looking Glass* (1871). Huge bestsellers almost from the moment they appeared, the "Alice" books have been the basis of numerous stage plays and films.

Go **Online**
Author Link
For: More about the authors
Visit: www.PHSchool.com
Web Code: epe-9405

The Bells

Edgar Allan Poe

I

Hear the sledges[1] with the bells—
Silver bells!
What a world of merriment their melody foretells!
How they tinkle, tinkle, tinkle,
5   In the icy air of night!
While the stars, that oversprinkle
All the heavens, seem to twinkle
     With a crystalline delight;
     Keeping time, time, time,
10   In a sort of Runic[2] rhyme,
To the tintinnabulation[3] that so musically wells
   From the bells, bells, bells, bells,
      Bells, bells, bells—
From the jingling and the tinkling of the bells.

---

1. sledges (slej´ iz) *n.* sleighs.
2. Runic (roo̅´ nik) *adj.* songlike; poetical.
3. tintinnabulation (tin´ ti nab´ yoo̅ la´ shlig;ən) *n.* ringing sound of bells.

> **✔ Reading Check**
>
> What type of bells does section one describe?

II

15   Hear the mellow wedding bells,

Golden bells!

What a world of happiness their harmony foretells!

Through the balmy air of night

How they ring out their delight!

20   From the molten golden-notes,

And all in tune,

What a liquid ditty[4] floats

To the turtle-dove[5] that listens, while she gloats

On the moon!

25   Oh, from out the sounding cells,

What a gush of euphony[6] <u>voluminously</u> wells!

How it swells!

How it dwells

On the future! how it tells

30   Of the rapture that impels

To the swinging and the ringing

Of the bells, bells, bells,

Of the bells, bells, bells, bells

Bells, bells, bells—

35   To the rhyming and the chiming of the bells!

III

Hear the loud alarum[7] bells!

Brazen[8] bells!

What a tale of terror now their turbulency tells!

In the startled ear of night

40   How they scream out their affright!

Too much horrified to speak,

They can only shriek, shriek,

Out of tune,

In a clamorous appealing to the mercy of the fire,

---

4. ditty (dit′ ē) *n.* short, simple song.

5. turtle-dove (turt′′l duv′) The turtle dove is traditionally associated with love.

6. euphony (yo͞o′ fə nē) *n.* pleasing sound.

7. alarum (ə ler′ əm) *adj.* sudden call to arms; alarm.

8. brazen (brā′ zən) *adj.* made of brass; having the ringing sound of brass.

45 In a mad expostulation[9] with the deaf and frantic fire
Leaping higher, higher, higher,
With a desperate desire,
And a resolute endeavor
Now—now to sit or never,
50 By the side of the pale-faced moon.
Oh, the bells, bells, bells!
What a tale their terror tells
Of Despair!
How they clang, and clash, and roar!
55 What a horror they outpour
On the bosom of the <u>palpitating</u> air!
Yet the ear it fully knows,
By the twanging
And the clanging,
60 How the danger ebbs and flows;
Yet the ear distinctly tells,
In the jangling,
And the wrangling,
How the danger sinks and swells,
65 By the sinking or the swelling in the anger of the bells—
Of the bells—
Of the bells, bells, bells, bells,
Bells, bells, bells—
In the clamor and the clangor of the bells!

Vocabulary Builder
palpitating (pal′ pə tāt′ iŋ) v. beating rapidly; throbbing

Literary Analysis
Sound Devices What is the effect of the repetition in lines 67–68?

IV

70 Hear the tolling of the bells—
Iron bells!
What a world of solemn thought their monody[10] compels!
In the silence of the night,
How we shiver with affright
75 At the melancholy menace of their tone!
For every sound that floats
From the rust within their throats
Is a groan.
And the people—ah, the people—

Reading Check

What kind of story do the wedding bells tell?

---

9. expostulation (ek späs′ chlig;ə lā′ shlig;ən) n. objection; complaint.
10. monody (pal′ pə tāt′ iŋ) n. poem of mourning; a steady sound; music in which one instrument or voice is dominant.

80	They that dwell up in the steeple,
	All alone,
	And who tolling, tolling, tolling,
	In that muffled monotone,
	Feel a glory in so rolling
85	On the human heart a stone—
	They are neither man nor woman—
	They are neither brute nor human—
	They are Ghouls:[11]
	And their king it is who tolls;
90	And he rolls, rolls, rolls,
	Rolls
	A pæan from the bells!
	And his merry bosom swells
	With the pæan of the bells!
95	And he dances and he yells;
	Keeping time, time, time,
	In a sort of Runic rhyme,
	To the pæan of the bells—
	Of the bells:
100	Keeping time, time, time,
	In a sort of Runic rhyme,
	To the throbbing of the bells—
	Of the bells, bells, bells—
	To the sobbing of the bells;
105	Keeping time, time, time,
	As he knells, knells, knells,
	In a happy Runic rhyme,
	To the rolling of the bells—
	Of the bells, bells, bells—
110	To the tolling of the bells,
	Of the bells, bells, bells, bells,
	Bells, bells, bells—
	To the moaning and the groaning of the bells.

Literary Analysis
Sound Devices What alliteration appears in lines 83–85?

Reading Skill
Reading Fluently Which repeated words in this stanza might sound like the repetitive tolling of bells?

---

11. Ghouls (go͞olz) *n.* evil spirits that rob graves.

◀ **Critical Viewing** Which kind of bells do you think this painting best illustrates? Why? **[Assess]**

Slam, Dunk, & Hook

Yusef Komunyakaa

Fast breaks. Lay ups. With Mercury's[1]
Insignia[2] on our sneakers,
We outmaneuvered the footwork
Of bad angels. Nothing but a hot

---

1. Mercury's Mercury was the Roman god of travel,
usually depicted with wings on his feet.
2. insignia (in sig′ nē ə) *n.* emblems or badges; logos.

Night Games, Ernie Barnes, Courtesy of The Company of Art, Los Angeles

5 Swish of strings like silk
  Ten feet out. In the roundhouse³
  Labyrinth⁴ our bodies
  Created, we could almost
  Last forever, poised in midair
10 Like storybook sea monsters.
  A high note hung there
  A long second. Off
  The rim. We'd corkscrew
  Up & dunk balls that exploded
15 The skullcap of hope & good
  Intention. Bug-eyed, lanky,
  All hands & feet . . . sprung rhythm.
  We were <u>metaphysical</u> when girls
  Cheered on the sidelines.
20 Tangled up in a falling,
  Muscles were a bright motor
  Double-flashing to the metal hoop
  Nailed to our oak.
  When Sonny Boy's mama died
25 He played nonstop all day, so hard
  Our backboard splintered.
  Glistening with sweat, we <u>jibed</u>
  & rolled the ball off our
  Fingertips. Trouble
30 Was there slapping a blackjack
  Against an open palm.
  Dribble, drive to the inside, feint,
  & glide like a sparrow hawk.
  Lay ups. Fast breaks.
35 We had moves we didn't know
  We had. Our bodies spun
  On swivels of bone & faith,
  Through a lyric slipknot
  Of joy, & we knew we were
40 Beautiful & dangerous.

◄ **Critical Viewing**
Which details in this painting relate to lines in "Slam, Dunk, & Hook"? **[Connect]**

Vocabulary Builder
metaphysical (met´ ə fiz´ i kəl) *adj.* spiritual; beyond the physical
jibed (jībd) *v.* changed direction

Literary Analysis
Sound Devices
What sound does the poet emphasize with the use of assonance in lines 30 and 31?

---

3. **roundhouse** (round´ hous´) *n.* area on the court beneath the basket.
4. **labyrinth** (lab´ ə rinth´) *n.* maze.

Jabberwocky
Lewis Carroll

'Twas brillig, and the slithy toves
   Did gyre and gimble in the wabe;
All mimsy were the borogoves,
   And the mome raths outgrabe.

5 "Beware the Jabberwock, my son!
   The jaws that bite, the claws that catch!
Beware the Jubjub bird, and shun
   The frumious Bandersnatch!"

He took his vorpal sword in hand:
10   Long time the manxome foe he sought—
So rested he by the Tumtum tree,
   And stood awhile in thought.

▼ **Critical Viewing**
Which aspects of this illustration convey the fantastical quality of "Jabberwocky"? **[Analyze]**

And as in uffish thought he stood,
  The Jabberwock, with eyes of flame,
15 Came whiffling through the tulgey wood,
  And burbled as it came!

One, two! One, two! And through and through
  The vorpal blade went snicker-snack!
He left it dead, and with its head
20 He went galumphing back.

"And hast thou slain the Jabberwock?
  Come to my arms, my beamish boy!
O frabjous day! Callooh! Callay!"
  He chortled in his joy.

25 'Twas brillig, and the slithy toves
  Did gyre and gimble in the wabe;
All mimsy were the borogoves,
  And the mome raths outgrabe.

Literary Analysis
Sound Devices What sound or noise does the onomatopoeia *burbled* reflect?

Literature in Context

Language Connection

Carroll's Invented Language In the first chapter of *Through the Looking-Glass,* Alice encounters a creature called a Jabberwock. She cannot understand it, so Humpty Dumpty explains some of the words it uses including these:

brillig: four o'clock in the afternoon, the time when you begin broiling things for dinner

toves: creatures that are something like badgers, something like lizards, and something like corkscrews

gyre: go round and round like a gyroscope

gimble: make holes like a gimlet (a hand tool that bores holes)

wabe: grass plot around a sundial

mome: having lost the way home

raths: something like green pigs

Connect to the Literature

What challenges do you think Carroll faced in writing a poem with invented language?

Apply the Skills

Poetry Collection 2

Thinking About the Selections

1. **Respond:** Which of these poems did you find most entertaining? Explain your choice.
2. **(a) Recall:** In lines 4–5 of "Slam, Dunk, & Hook," what sound does the speaker describe? **(b) Infer:** What action causes this sound?
3. **(a) Recall:** In "Jabberwocky," what does the hero do after being warned about the Jabberwock? **(b) Evaluate:** Do you think the poem pokes fun at heroism? Explain.
4. **Take a Position:** The poet T. S. Eliot once said that poetry can be enjoyed before it is understood. Could "The Bells" be used as evidence to support this idea? Explain.

Literary Analysis

5. **(a)** For each poem in Poetry Collection 2, use a chart like the one shown to identify one example of each **sound device** listed.
   (b) In what way does each example add to the musical feeling of each poem?

	Example	Effect
Alliteration		
Consonance		
Assonance		

6. **(a)** Identify an example of **onomatopoeia** in "The Bells."
   (b) What sound does the word imitate? **(c)** How well does the word imitate the sound? Explain your answer.
7. **(a)** Which of these poems do you think makes the most effective use of sound devices? Explain your choice. **(b)** Discuss your idea with a small group and together decide on a single response to explain to the class.

Reading Skill

8. In what way does **reading fluently** help you to appreciate a poem's sound devices?
9. **(a)** Which of your senses, other than your sense of hearing, were most engaged by each of these poems? **(b)** Which specific words appealed to those senses?

QuickReview

Poems at a Glance
"Slam, Dunk, & Hook" is a reminiscence of neighborhood basketball.

"Jabberwocky" is a poem about a fantastical creature.

"The Bells" describes the sounds of bells.

Go Online
Assessment
For: Self-test
Visit: www.PHSchool.com
Web Code: epa-6405

Sound Devices: language that emphasizes the sound relationships among words; sound devices include *alliteration, consonance, assonance,* and *onomatopoeia*

Reading Fluently: reading smoothly and continuously while comprehending the text and appreciating the writer's artistry

Vocabulary Builder

Practice Identify the word that does not belong and explain why.

1. metaphysical, concrete, bodily
2. jibed, turn, straight
3. voluminously, tiny, huge
4. palpitating, pulse, hum

Adding Words to Your Vocabulary *Jibe,* the present tense form of *jibed,* is a nautical term—a word related to sailing. *Tack, fathom,* and *headway* are other nautical terms used in conversation. Use a dictionary to learn the meanings of these words and how they relate to sailing. Then, write a sentence for each word that reflects its common usage. (For more on using a dictionary, see page R6.)

Writing

Write an **editorial**—a piece of writing that presents one side of an issue—related to one of the poems. Using "Slam, Dunk, & Hook" as inspiration, you could write about the need for more funding for neighborhood sports.

- State the issue clearly and express your opinion reasonably.
- Anticipate questions from those who might disagree with you.

Have several people respond to your editorial, including someone who disagrees with you. If you hear a point that you should have addressed, consider adding it.

For *Grammar, Vocabulary,* and *Assessment,* see **Build Language Skills,** pages 610–611.

Extend Your Learning

Listening and Speaking Prepare a **dramatic reading** that captures the musical qualities of one of the poems in the collection.

- Choose a poem and make notes about which words and sounds to emphasize and when to change your reading pace.
- Practice reading the poem aloud, recording yourself, if possible, so that you can hear and fix problem spots.

Present your dramatic reading in class.

Research and Technology In a group, create an **illustrated version** of one of the poems. Find photographs or original artwork. With the group, debate the merits of each choice and then reach an agreement about which images best capture the mood of the poem. Read the poem and share the art for classmates' enjoyment.

Build Language Skills

Vocabulary Skill

Suffixes The suffix *-tion* means "the act of" or "the state of being." When a word contains *-tion* as a suffix, it is a noun. For example, the verb *deliberate* means " carefully think through an issue." When the suffix *-tion* is added, the word *deliberation* means "the act of carefully thinking about an issue."

Practice: Add the suffix *-tion* to the following verbs and use each of the resulting nouns in a sentence.

1. standardize
2. instruct
3. transit
4. substitute
5. terminate

Grammar Lesson

Prepositional Phrases A **prepositional phrase** is a group of words beginning with a preposition and ending with a noun or pronoun. Prepositional phrases may function as adjectives or adverbs.

> **Adjective phrase:** The players *on their team* are more experienced.
> **Adverb phrase:** They played *with more skill.*

Practice Identify the prepositional phrase in each sentence. Tell whether it functions as an adjective or an adverb. Then, write a new sentence using the phrase.

1. We heard a noise in the yard.
2. Our teacher told us about the assignment.
3. Eddy made a picture *of a bird.*
4. We ran around the block.
5. He stood on the sidewalk.

WG *Prentice Hall Writing and Grammar Connection: Chapter 21, Section 1.*

MorePractice

For more practice with prepositional phrases, see the grammar Handbook p. R40.

Reading Skill: Read Fluently

Standards Assessed
• WL.1.02.1
• IR.2.04.1

Directions: *Read the selection. Then, answer the questions.*

1 In Xanadu did Kubla Khan
2 A stately pleasure dome decree:
3 Where Alph, the sacred river, ran
4 Through caverns measureless to man
5   Down to a sunless sea.
6 So twice five miles of fertile ground
7 With walls and towers were girdled round
8 And there were gardens bright with sinuous rills,
9 Where blossomed many an incense-bearing tree;
10 And here were forests ancient as the hills,
11 Enfolding sunny spots of greenery.

—from *Kubla Khan* by Samuel Taylor Coleridge

1. Why does each line begin with a capital letter?
   A It is a poetic convention.
   B It is the start of a sentence.
   C It signals that the reader should pause.
   D It shows that the words are proper nouns.

2. Line 9 relies on which two senses?
   A taste and touch
   B sight and sound
   C sight and smell
   D sound and touch

3. Which sense is most evoked in this poem?
   A touch
   B sight
   C taste
   D smell

4. How many sentences are in this poem?
   A four sentences
   B eleven sentences
   C two sentences
   D one sentence

Timed Writing: Analysis [Critical Stance]

Review *Poetry Collection 1* or *Poetry Collection 2*. Explain the meaning of the figurative language in one of the poems and evaluate the effectiveness of the comparison. **(35 minutes)**

Writing Workshop: *Work in Progress*

Descriptive Essay

Using your Sight List choose one place that is most interesting. Add a list of adjectives which describe other characteristics of the place, such as smells or sounds. Save this work in your writing portfolio.

Comparing Literary Works • Imagery

Imagery

Imagery is language that appeals to one or more of the senses—sight, hearing, touch, taste, and smell. The use of imagery allows writers to express their ideas with vividness and immediacy. Images create mental pictures for readers and allow them to make connections between their own experiences and the worlds presented in poems.

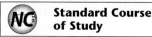

Standard Course of Study

- Judge different stylistic and literary devices in work. (CT.4.02.3)
- Interpret literary devices. (LT.5.01.3)

Comparing Imagery

Poets use imagery to give a sensuous basis to the experiences, thoughts, and feelings that they express in a poem. Through imagery, they convey to readers that the poem is a little world in itself, not just printed words on a page. These poetic worlds all relate to the one world we share, but each is unique. Two poets, for example, can use the same word to create different images, or they can describe similar images in different ways.

- In "Blackberry Eating," the word *black* stresses the rich color of blackberries. Combined with other details in the poem, this image appeals primarily to the senses of taste and sight.
- In "There Is No Word for Goodbye," the word *black* describes an elderly woman's eyes. The description appeals to the sense of sight and conveys an understanding of the woman's wisdom and depth.

Comparing imagery is an important step in analyzing the *aesthetic qualities* of a variety of poems. Poets, for example, often include patterns of images in their work. By making assertions about such image patterns, or *motifs*, you can better appreciate aesthetic differences and similarities among poems.

As you compare the imagery in these selections, start by noting that images appealing to the sense of touch play an important role. Then, you might note some differences among these image patterns.

As you read, compare the imagery in the poems. Use a chart like the one shown to identify images and note the senses they address.

Poem: "Blackberry Eating"	
Image: prickly stalks	
Sight	✔
Sound	
Taste	
Smell	
Touch	✔

Vocabulary Builder

Blackberry Eating

- **penalty** (pen´ əl tē) *n.* punishment (p. 615) *Mistakes are the <u>penalty</u> for working too quickly.*

- **unbidden** (un bid´ 'n) *adj.* without being asked; uninvited (p. 615) *The bee flew <u>unbidden</u> through the window.*

Daily

- **shriveled** (shriv´ əld) *adj.* shrunken and wrinkled (p. 616) *A raisin is a <u>shriveled</u> grape.*

- **scarred** (skärd) *adj.* marked or dented (p. 616) *The chair was <u>scarred</u> by the cat's scratching.*

Build Understanding

Connecting to the Literature

Reading/Writing Connection Each of the following poems uses language that appeals to the senses. Make a list of several common daily activities. Then, explain how each activity appeals to the senses of sight, sound, smell, taste, or touch. Use at least three of these words in your response: *emphasize, consume, appreciate, impact.*

Meet the Authors

Mary **Tall Mountain** (1918–1994)

An Athabaskan Indian, Mary Tall Mountain was born in Nulato, Alaska, a small town on the Yukon River. The Athabaskans are a group of tribes that speak a variety of related languages and live in the northwest United States, Alaska, and Canada. When Tall Mountain was six, her mother died and she was adopted by a family who removed her from her people and culture. In "There Is No Word for Goodbye," Tall Mountain reconnects with her Native American roots and language.

Galway **Kinnell** (b. 1927)

Galway Kinnell was born in Providence, Rhode Island. In his poetry, he addresses the themes of mortality, selfhood, and the power of nature. In explaining why he is drawn toward writing about nature, Kinnell has said, "Part of poetry's usefulness in the world is that it pays some of our huge, unpaid tribute to the things and creatures that share the earth with us."

Naomi Shihab **Nye** (b. 1952)

Naomi Shihab Nye was born in St. Louis to a Palestinian father and an American mother. She spent her teenage years in Jerusalem. A successful poet, she has worked as a visiting writer at several colleges and universities. Of poems, she has said, "I liked the space around them, and the way they took you to a deeper, quieter place, almost immediately."

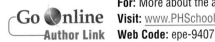

For: More about the authors
Visit: www.PHSchool.com
Web Code: epe-9407

THERE IS NO WORD FOR GOODBYE

MARY TALL MOUNTAIN

Sokoya, I said, looking through
    the net of wrinkles into
    wise black pools
    of her eyes.

5 What do you say in Athabaskan
    when you leave each other?
    What is the word
    for goodbye?

A shade of feeling rippled
10   the wind-tanned skin.
    Ah, nothing, she said,
    watching the river flash.

She looked at me close.
    We just say, Tlaa. That means,
15   See you.
    We never leave each other.
    When does your mouth
    say goodbye to your heart?

She touched me light
20   as a bluebell.
    You forget when you leave us,
    You're so small then.
    We don't use that word.

We always think you're coming back,
25   but if you don't,
    we'll see you some place else.
    You understand.
    There is no word for goodbye.

Sokoya: Aunt (mother's sister)

Literary Analysis
Imagery Which words suggest that Sokoya is an elder?

Literary Analysis
Imagery Which image in lines 19–23 appeals to the sense of touch?

BLACKBERRY EATING
GALWAY KINNELL

I love to go out in late September
among the fat, overripe, icy, black blackberries
to eat blackberries for breakfast,
the stalks very prickly, a <u>penalty</u>
5   they earn for knowing the black art
of blackberry-making; and as I stand among them
lifting the stalks to my mouth, the ripest berries
fall almost <u>unbidden</u> to my tongue,
as words sometimes do, certain peculiar words
10 like *strengths* or *squinched*,
many-lettered, one-syllabled lumps,
which I squeeze, squinch open, and splurge well
in the silent, startled, icy, black language
of blackberry-eating in late September.

Vocabulary Builder
penalty (pen´ əl tē)
n. punishment
unbidden (un bid´
'n) *adj.* without being
asked; uninvited

Thinking About the Selections

1. **Respond:** Which description did you like the most in each poem? Explain.

2. **(a) Recall:** In "There Is No Word for Goodbye," who is Sokoya?
   (b) Infer: Why do you think the speaker wants to know the word for goodbye?

3. **(a) Connect:** What does Sokoya want the speaker to understand in the final stanza? **(b) Draw Conclusions:** Do you think Sokoya's words are comforting to the speaker? Explain.

4. **(a) Recall:** In "Blackberry Eating," identify two words that the speaker compares to blackberries. **(b) Compare and Contrast:** According to the speaker, what do these words have in common with blackberries?

5. **(a) Draw Conclusions:** Which aspect of writing does this poem capture in lines 9–13? Explain. **(b) Speculate:** Do you think the speaker of this poem enjoys writing poetry? Why or why not?

DAILY

NAOMI SHIHAB NYE

These <u>shriveled</u> seeds we plant,
corn kernel, dried bean,
poke into loosened soil,
cover over with measured fingertips

5   These T-shirts we fold into
perfect white squares

These tortillas we slice and fry to crisp strips
This rich egg scrambled in a gray clay bowl

This bed whose covers I straighten
10   smoothing edges till blue quilt fits brown blanket
and nothing hangs out

This envelope I address
so the name balances like a cloud
in the center of the sky

15   This page I type and retype
This table I dust till the <u>scarred</u> wood shines
This bundle of clothes I wash and hang and wash again
like flags we share, a country so close
no one needs to name it

20   The days are nouns; touch them
The hands are churches that worship the world

Vocabulary Builder
shriveled (shriv´ əld)
adj. shrunken and
wrinkled

Literary Analysis
Imagery Which
senses does the
imagery of the bed
covers address?

Vocabulary Builder
scarred (skärd) *adj.*
marked or dented

Thinking About the Selection

1. **Respond:** Which words create the clearest picture? Explain.

2. **(a) Recall:** Identify at least five tasks the speaker describes. **(b) Infer:**
   Does she seem to take pleasure in doing these tasks? Explain.

3. **(a) Analyze:** How do the final two lines differ from those that come
   before? **(b) Draw Conclusions:** What is the speaker's outlook on life?

Apply the Skills

There Is No Word for Goodbye • Blackberry Eating • Daily

Comparing Imagery

1. **(a)** For each poem, provide one example of **imagery** that appeals to the sense of touch. **(b)** Provide one example of imagery that appeals to the sense of sight.

2. **(a)** Which poems include imagery that appeals to the sense of taste? **(b)** Which poem includes imagery that appeals to the sense of smell? **(c)** Do any of the poems include imagery that appeals to the sense of sound? Explain your answers with specific examples from the poems.

Writing to Compare Literary Works

In an essay, compare and contrast how the poet's use of imagery adds to the meaning of each poem. Use the following questions to get started:

- In "Blackberry Eating," how do the images of blackberries help you understand the poet's ideas about words?
- In "Daily," how do the images help you understand the speaker's affection for ordinary things?
- In "There Is No Word for Goodbye," how do the images of Sokoya help you understand the speaker's feelings for her aunt?

Use a chart like the one shown to help you in your response.

Poem	Imagery	Message Conveyed
"There Is No Word for Goodbye"		
"Blackberry Eating"		
"Daily"		

Vocabulary Builder

Practice Answer each question. Explain your answer.

1. Would you eat an apple that is *shriveled*?
2. If someone arrived *unbidden* to a party, would he or she be greeted warmly?
3. Would a football team be excited about receiving a *penalty*?
4. Would a *scarred* piece of furniture look new?

Go Online
Assessment
For: Self-test
Visit: www.PHSchool.com
Web Code: epa-6406

Reading

Directions: *Questions 1–5 refer to the following.*

> There will come soft rains and the smell of the ground,
> And swallows circling with their shimmering sound;
>
> And frogs in the pools singing at night,
> 4 And wild plum trees in tremulous white;
>
> Robins will wear their feathery fire
> Whistling their whims on a low fence-wire;
>
> And not one will know of the war, not one
> 8 Will care at last when it is done.
>
> Not one would mind, neither bird nor tree
> If mankind perished utterly;
>
> And Spring herself, when she woke at dawn,
> 12 Would scarcely know that we were gone.
>
> —"There Will Come Soft Rains" by Sara Teasdale

1. How many sentences are there in this poem?

  A four

  B three

  C two

  D one

2. Where is the first pause in lines 7–8?

  A at the end of line 7

  B at the end of line 8

  C after the word *war*

  D after the word *last*

3. What senses does the poet appeal to in the first four lines?

  A sight and smell

  B touch, smell, hearing

  C smell, sight, hearing

  D touch and smell

4. What is the image described in lines 5–6?

  A a redbird whistling in the wind

  B a robin that is on fire

  C a red-breasted robin sitting and singing on a fence

  D a bird with red feathers sitting on a fence wire

5. What point is the poet making in this poem?

  A If human beings disappeared, nothing in nature would notice.

  B Earth is most beautiful in the spring.

  C Soft rains come in the spring to awaken the earth.

  D Human beings are damaging the environment.

Vocabulary

Standards Assessed

- GU.6.01.3
- GU.6.01.6
- LT.5.01.3

Directions: *Choose the letter of the word that best completes the sentence.*

6. The _____ from the meteor left an enormous hole.
   - A deliberation
   - B transition
   - C impact
   - D concept

7. I am having difficulty writing _____ between the introduction and the first body paragraph in this essay.
   - A a deliberation
   - B a transition
   - C an impact
   - D a concept

8. He had difficulty understanding the _____ of infinity.
   - A transition
   - B concept
   - C impact
   - D consideration

9. He left his _____ fortune to charity.
   - A deliberate
   - B impact
   - C conceptual
   - D considerable

10. The judge reached his decision after careful and _____ thought.
    - A impact
    - B deliberate
    - C concept
    - D diminish

11. We need a snack that is _____.
    - A microwavate
    - B microwave
    - C microwaveable
    - D microed

12. An _____ of the problem helped us resolve it.
    - A articulacy
    - B articulated
    - C articulation
    - D articulative

13. He is very friendly and _____.
    - A amiable
    - B amenable
    - C animate
    - D amiably

14. I do not agree with his _____ of that work as "fantasy."
    - A categorized
    - B categorization
    - C categorizing
    - D categoric

15. I wonder whether or not this law is _____.
    - A enforceate
    - B enforce
    - C enforceably
    - D enforceable

Description: Descriptive Essay

Descriptive writing begins not in your imagination, but in your senses—in your ability to notice physical details. While valuable on its own, description also helps you share an experience or portray a person. Use the steps outlined in this workshop to write a descriptive essay.

Assignment Write a description of a place that you enjoy or that is meaningful to you.

What to Include Your descriptive essay should feature:
- sensory details that re-create sights, sounds, smells, tastes, and textures
- precise word choice that brings the subject into focus
- figurative language, such as metaphor and simile
- logical and consistent organization
- error-free grammar, especially your use of prepositional phrases

To preview the criteria on which your descriptive essay may be assessed, see the rubric on page 624.

Prewriting

Choosing Your Topic

Take notes. For a few days, be alert to the sights, sounds, smells, tastes, and textures you encounter in your daily routine. Jot down notes about the places you visit. Use the location that prompts the most entries as your topic.

Gathering Details

Plan to use figurative language. To create a vivid picture of your subject, use figurative language such as metaphors or similes. Compare an unfamiliar object or scene with something familiar to your readers.

Place	Basic Description	Figurative Language
school art room	Colorful paintbrushes sit in jars	Paintbrushes, <u>their heads heavy with color</u>, sit in jars. (metaphor)
	This is a place where lots of things can happen.	<u>Like a garden</u>, this is a place of possibilities. (simile)

 Standard Course of Study
- Use description, comparison, figurative language to elaborate ideas to inform audience (IR.2.02.4)
- Show appreciation for the significance of a personal account. (WL.1.01.3)

Using the Form

You may use elements of this form in these types of writing:
- autobiographical writing
- travel reports
- character sketches

To get a feel for descriptive essays, read the excerpt from *Silent Spring* on page 153.

Work in Progress

Review the work you did on pages 559, 585, and 611.

Drafting

Shaping Your Writing

Choose an effective organizational pattern. The following are two structures that work well with descriptive essays:

- **Spatial organization:** Describe your subject systematically from left to right, front to back, or top to bottom. Like a photographer, pan your "camera" over your subject, using transitional words and phrases like *above, below,* or *in the distance* that show spatial relationships.

- **Time-order organization:** Describe your subject as you first approach it and then as you move through or around it. In addition to words expressing spatial relationships, use words showing time-order relationships such as *initially, meanwhile,* or *finally.*

Providing Elaboration

Think about your audience. Consider your readers' knowledge of the place you are describing. If the place is unfamiliar, include more vivid details. If the place is familiar, draw your readers in by acknowledging shared experience.

Revising

Revising Your Overall Structure

Strengthen your main impression. A memorable descriptive essay conveys a single, strong impression of its subject. Review your work, adding details that support the main impression. Eliminate details that are irrelevant or distracting.

For the complete student model, see page 623.

Student Model: Revising to Strengthen the Main Impression

Inside I am met by a sound check of guitars vibrating through

speakers. I am surrounded by wood; wood floors, wood

ceiling, wood walls ∧ ; acoustic trampolines that make the music bounce around like mad.

> The writer adds detail to make the description more specific and vivid.

Revising Your Word Choice

Choose vivid words. Review your essay, circling vague or dull word choices. Consider replacements that paint a clear and colorful picture of your subject.

Dull: The air was *really* cold.

Vivid: The air was *piercingly* cold.

Integrating Grammar Skills

Revising to Vary Sentence Patterns

Overuse of the basic subject-verb pattern can make your writing stiff. To add interest, begin some sentences with prepositional phrases.

Identifying Prepositional Phrases A preposition is a word that relates a noun or pronoun to another word in the sentence. The combination of preposition and accompanying noun or pronoun—the object of the preposition—is called a prepositional phrase.

*Prentice Hall Writing and Grammar Connection:
Chapter 21, Section 1*

Preposition +	Noun/ Pronoun	=	Prepositional Phrase
over	moon		over the moon
under	porch		under the porch
behind	door		behind the red door

Many prepositions express spatial relationships. Appropriate use of such prepositions to begin sentences can clarify descriptive writing.

Varying Sentences With Prepositional Phrases In the following example, subjects are italicized, verbs are underlined, and prepositional phrases appear in parentheses.

> **Overuse of subject-verb pattern:** The *cave* <u>was hidden</u> (behind the trees). The *ground* <u>was</u> smooth (in front of it). *I* <u>pulled</u> away dead branches. *I* <u>saw</u> large paw prints (on the cave's dirt floor).

> **Revision:** The cave was hidden behind the trees. In front of it, the ground was smooth. I pulled away dead branches. On the cave's dirt floor, I saw large paw prints.

Follow these steps to vary your sentences in your writing.

1. **Read your draft aloud, listening for places where you overuse the subject-verb sentence pattern.**

2. **Rewrite some sentences to begin with a prepositional phrase.**

3. **If an introductory prepositional phrase contains four or more words, set it off with a comma.**

Apply It to Your Editing

Review the first and last paragraphs of your descriptive essay, looking for opportunities to vary a monotonous subject-verb sequence of sentences. Rewrite some sentences by beginning them with prepositional phrases.

Student Model: Zachary DeBoer
Raleigh, NC

Ziggy's Coffeehouse

As I enter the gates of the fenced-in courtyard of the humble coffeehouse, smooth stones crunch beneath my shoes and strings of Christmas lights twinkle like the stars overhead. A stranger takes my five-dollar bill and makes a mark on my hand. The freezing winter air is perfectly still while I walk up the ramp and step into the mildly dilapidated structure. Inside I am met by a sound check of guitars vibrating through speakers. I am surrounded by wood; wood floors, wood ceiling, wood walls; acoustic trampolines that make the music bounce around like mad. The guys and girls in the band tonight are good friends of mine. As they run through their set list, there is a strong sense of camaraderie between them. They dream of record deals and radio play and 25-city tours. Perhaps they imagine that their venue is not a small café, but a mammoth, sold-out arena. They put on their best performance, playing just for us and singing: "We should be dancing. We need be dancing."

The place smells like aged wood and fresh coffee, but my lack of even a few dollar bills means I'll be drinking water tonight. There are three platforms in the cafe; the lowest has a set of double doors on the stage right side that have been swung open. The heat lamps radiate warmth as the frigid air rushes in from the doors, like a cold front passing through on a hot September day. On the second tier, those who prefer to act like adults sip their skinny decaf lattes. They seem mildly interested in the music, but most are there for the lack of something better to do. Are they swaying because of the music or because they have put a bit too much sugar in their coffees? Outside in the parking lot, kids talk cars and sports and who knows what else? I'm so captivated by the band that my ears can't tell. They laugh intermittently, oblivious to the music playing inside.

On the lowest level, immediately in front of the stage, the real fans are found. We push the tables back and dance around like no one is watching us and we sing along with the songs we know at the top of our lungs. This is where we artists are, the free spirits, the *real* cool kids. I don't know most of them but I feel a connection with all of them. We are friends now, brothers and sisters, united by the music. We jump up and down, careful not to bump into each other or the tables; we are captivated by the music but respectful of those around us. We have been liberated from the bonds of everyday life. We are transported to a state of bliss. We are not escaping reality; instead, we are experiencing true reality. As the soft lights from the stage shine onto the mellow brown of the all-wood venue, I realize: On this night, at this moment, there is nowhere else I'd rather be than this place.

Zachary uses sensory details to make this introduction vivid and interesting.

The writer does not limit himself to describing the setting; he imagines the thoughts and feelings of the people, as well.

Zachary uses details related to all the senses, including smell and taste.

The writer pays attention to all elements of the scene.

Zachary uses description to make a meaningful point.

Writing Workshop

Editing and Proofreading

Check your draft for errors in spelling, grammar, and punctuation.

Focus on transitions: Make sure that you use transition words accurately and punctuate them correctly. If you begin a sentence with a transitional word or phrase, set it off wih a comma.

Publishing and Presenting

Consider one of the following ways to share your writing.

Prepare an oral presentation. Descriptive writing is well suited to being read aloud. Gather photographs or illustrations and select background music to enhance your reading.

Create a visitor's guide. With a group of classmates, assemble several essays that describe places of interest in your community and create a guidebook for visitors. Encourage everyone in the group to participate, either by sharing his or her essays, drawing illustrations, designing layouts, or producing the guidebook. If possible, provide copies of the guidebook to your local library, town hall, or chamber of commerce for distribution to the public.

Reflecting on Your Writing

Writer's Journal Jot down your thoughts on the experience of writing a descriptive essay. Begin by answering these questions.

- In what ways, if any, did your view of your subject change as you wrote about it?
- What do you enjoy most about descriptive writing? Explain.

> *Prentice Hall Writing and Grammar Connection: Chapter 6*

Rubric for Self-Assessment

To assess your descriptive essay, use the following rubric:

NC Criteria	Rating Scale				
	not very				*very*
Focus: How clearly do you describe your subject?	1	2	3	4	5
Organization: How logical and consistent is your organization?	1	2	3	4	5
Support/Elaboration: How well do you use sensory details?	1	2	3	4	5
Style: How effective is your use of figurative language?	1	2	3	4	5
Conventions: How correct is your grammar, especially your use of prepositional phrases?	1	2	3	4	5

Paraphrase

Skills You Will Learn

Literature You Will Read

Reading and Vocabulary Skills Preview

Reading: Paraphrase

> **Paraphrasing** is restating or explaining something in your own words.

Standard Course of Study

- Analyze connections among ideas, concepts, characters and experience in response. (WL.1.03.9)
- Interpret literary devices. (LT.5.01.3)
- Understand the importance of tone, mood, diction, and style. (LT.5.01.4)

Skills and Strategies You Will Learn in Part 2

In Part 2, you will learn

- **to picture the action** to help restate or **paraphrase** the action (p. 628).
- **to break down long sentences** so that they can be **paraphrased** (p. 657).
- **to evaluate Web sources** when researching articles on literature (p. 652).

Using the Skills and Strategies in Part 2

In Part 2, you will learn to paraphrase, or put something into your own words, to help you understand difficult or confusing text. You will learn to analyze the sentences in a poem, breaking them down into clauses and phrases. You will practice picturing action in order to restate the text in your own words.

The following example shows how you can apply these strategies.

1 If I could put the notion in his head:
2 "Why do they make good neighbors? Isn't it
3 Where there are cows? But here there are no cows.
4 Before I built a wall I'd ask to know
5 What I was walling in or walling out,
6 And to whom I was like to give offense.
7 Something there is that doesn't love a wall.
8 That wants it down."

　　　—from "Mending Wall" by Robert Frost

Break down the fourth sentence: Before I built a wall - I'd ask to know - what I was walling in or walling out - and to whom I was like to give offense.

Picture one person talking to another. The speaker is responding to something that the other has said.

Paraphrase: I would like him to think about why walls help neighbors get along. Walls are to keep cows in and we don't have cows.

Academic Vocabulary: Words for Analyzing Literature

The following words will help you as you read and analyze the literature in Part 2.

Word	Definition	Sample Sentence
usage *n.*	way of using something	The poet's *usage* of musical words adds to the beauty of the poem.
emphasize *v.*	to stress	Many poets *emphasize* rhythm.
mechanism *n.*	system or means of doing something; working parts of a machine	What *mechanism* does the author use to move the plot forward?
abstract *adj.*	not concrete; of thought	The author's use of *abstract* ideas made the work difficult to read.
distinct *adj.*	separate; well-defined	She has a *distinct* style.

Vocabulary Skill: Suffixes

> A **suffix** is a word ending that forms a new word and may change a word's part of speech.

In Part 2, you will learn
- the suffix *-age* (p. 650)
- the suffix *-ism* (p. 674)
- the suffix *-ize* (p. 674)

-age   Forms nouns related to conditions, results, costs, amounts, and places. (**marriage, postage, acreage, hermitage**)

-ism   Forms nouns related to conditions, systems, or practices, or examples. (**mechanism, skepticism, modernism, Americanism**)

-ize   Forms verbs related to making, becoming, combining, or doing what is indicated by the base word. (**Americanize, oxidize, theorize**)

Activity Add one of the suffixes to form the part of speech indicated. Check your spelling in a dictionary. Then, use the new word in a sentence.

1. active (noun)   **2.** patriot (noun)   **3.** computer (verb)
4. ton (noun)   **5.** general (verb)

You can apply the instruction on this page to these poems.

Poetry Collection 1
Casey at the Bat, page 631
Fifteen, page 633
Twister Hits Houston, page 635

Poetry Collection 2
The Raven, page 639
The Horses, page 644
The Writer, page 647

NC **Standard Course of Study**

- Make connections between literary works, self and related topics. (LT.5.03.9)
- Analyze the place and role of dialects and standard/nonstandard English. (GU.6.01.5)

Literary Analysis

Narrative poetry is verse that tells a story and includes the same literary elements as narrative prose: a plot, or sequence of events; specific settings; and characters who participate in the action.

Also like narrative prose, such as a short story, a narrative poem conveys a **mood,** or **atmosphere**—an overall feeling created by the setting, plot, words, and images. For example, a narrative poem's mood can be gloomy, joyous, or mysterious. Poetry's emphasis on precise words and images makes mood a powerful element in a narrative poem.

Reading Skill

Paraphrasing is restating in your own words what someone else has written or said. A paraphrase retains the meaning but is simpler. Paraphrasing helps you read poetry because poems often contain **figurative language,** words that are used imaginatively rather than literally. To paraphrase a narrative poem, **picture the action**.

- Based on details in the poem, form a mental image of the setting, the characters, and the characters' actions.

- To be sure that your mental picture is accurate, pay attention to the way that the poet describes the scene.

- Then, use your own words to describe your mental image of the scene and the action taking place in it.

As you read, use a chart like this one to record your paraphrases.

Lines of Poetry
Blue were her eyes as the fairy-flax, / Her cheeks like the dawn of day /

↓

Details in Lines of Poetry
Her eyes were blue. Her cheeks were red.

↓

Paraphrase
She had blue eyes and red cheeks.

Vocabulary Builder

Poetry Collection 1

- **pallor** (pal´ ər) *n.* unnatural paleness (p. 631) *His pallor made us realize how ill he was.*

- **writhing** (rī*th* iŋ) *v.* twisting; turning (p. 632) *He struggled to hold the writhing cat still.*

- **demure** (di myoor´) *adj.* modest (p. 633) *The movie star's demure behavior was refreshing in Hollywood.*

Poetry Collection 2

- **beguiling** (bē gīl´ iŋ) *v.* tricking; charming (p. 641) *The child's innocence was beguiling.*

- **respite** (res´ pit) *n.* rest; relief (p. 643) *The rain provided a respite from the long dry spell.*

- **archaic** (är kā´ ik) *adj.* from an earlier time; ancient (p. 645) *Some people say the old song is timeless; others say it is archaic.*

Connecting to the Literature

Reading/Writing Connection Each poem in this group has a unique mood or feeling. To get ready to appreciate the moods of these literary works, connect to details that influence your mood in everyday life—such as weather, events, or people's actions. Write several sentences about things that affect your mood. Use at least three of these words: *evoke, respond, reinforce, react, promote.*

Meet the Authors

Ernest Lawrence **Thayer** (1863–1940)
Casey at the Bat (p. 628)
It is not surprising that "Casey at the Bat" reads like a sports story in verse. The poet, Ernest Lawrence Thayer, worked for many years as a sports reporter on the staff of newspapers in New York and California. "Casey at the Bat" first appeared in the *San Francisco Examiner* in 1888. It became so popular that in 1953 it inspired an operetta called *The Mighty Casey.*

William **Stafford** (1914–1993)
Fifteen (p. 633)
Raised in Kansas, William Stafford did not publish his first book, *West of Your City,* until he was 46. However, he made up for lost time after that, publishing many collections, including *Traveling Through the Dark.* Fellow poet Robert Bly has said that Stafford's poems are "spoken like a friend over coffee."

Sandra **Cisneros** (b. 1954)
Twister Hits Houston (p. 635)
Sandra Cisneros was born in Chicago, but her family moved frequently between Chicago and Mexico City. She began her first novel, *The House on Mango Street,* while still a college student. Cisneros has worked with high school students, serving as poet-in-residence in several schools. She has received many awards for her writing.

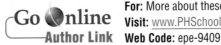

Go Online Author Link

For: More about these authors
Visit: www.PHSchool.com
Web Code: epe-9409

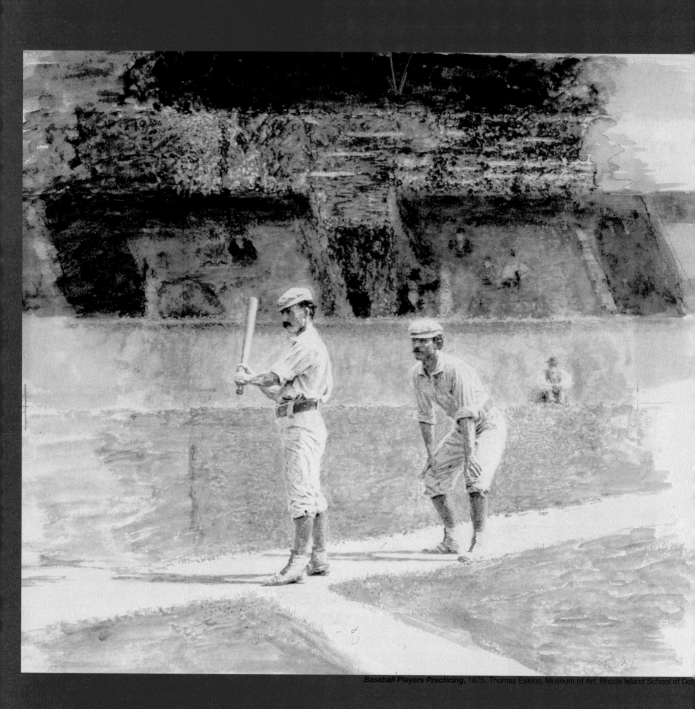

Baseball Players Practicing, 1875, Thomas Eakins, Museum of Art, Rhode Island School of Des

▲ **Critical Viewing** Compare and contrast the stance and attitude of the batter in this painting with Casey's stance and attitude. **[Compare and Contrast]**

CASEY AT THE BAT

ERNEST LAWRENCE THAYER

It looked extremely rocky for the Mudville nine that day;
The score stood two to four, with but an inning left to play.
So, when Cooney died at second, and Burrows did the same,
A <u>pallor</u> wreathed the features of the patrons of the game.

5 A straggling few got up to go, leaving there the rest,
With that hope which springs eternal within the human breast.
For they thought: "If only Casey would get a whack at that,"
They'd put even money now, with Casey at the bat.

But Flynn preceded Casey, and likewise so did Blake,
10 And the former was a pudd'n, and the latter was a fake.
So on that stricken multitude a deathlike silence sat;
For there seemed but little chance of Casey's getting to the bat.

But Flynn let drive a "single," to the wonderment of all.
And the much-despised Blakey "tore the cover off the ball."
15 And when the dust had lifted, and they saw what had occurred,
There was Blakey safe at second, and Flynn a-huggin' third.

Then from the gladdened multitude went up a joyous yell—
It rumbled in the mountaintops, it rattled in the dell;
It struck upon the hillside and rebounded on the flat;
20 For Casey, mighty Casey, was advancing to the bat.

There was ease in Casey's manner as he stepped into his place,
There was pride in Casey's bearing and a smile on Casey's face;
And when responding to the cheers he lightly doffed his hat,
No stranger in the crowd could doubt 'twas Casey at the bat.

Vocabulary Builder
pallor (pal´ ər) *n.*
unnatural paleness

Literary Analysis
Narrative Poetry
What is the setting of
this narrative poem?

Reading Check

Where are Blakey and
Flynn when Casey
comes to bat?

25 Ten thousand eyes were on him as he rubbed his hands with dirt,
Five thousand tongues applauded when he wiped them on his shirt;
Then when the <u>writhing</u> pitcher ground the ball into his hip,
Defiance glanced in Casey's eye, a sneer curled Casey's lip.

And now the leather-covered sphere came hurtling through the air,
30 And Casey stood a-watching it in haughty grandeur there.
Close by the sturdy batsman the ball unheeded sped;
"That ain't my style," said Casey. "Strike one," the umpire said.

From the benches, black with people, there went up a muffled roar,
Like the beating of the storm waves on the stern and distant shore.
35 "Kill him! kill the umpire!" shouted someone on the stand;
And it's likely they'd have killed him had not Casey raised his
hand.

With a smile of Christian charity great Casey's visage shone;
He stilled the rising tumult, he made the game go on;
He signaled to the pitcher, and once more the spheroid flew;
40 But Casey still ignored it, and the umpire said, "Strike two."

"Fraud!" cried the maddened thousands, and the echo
answered "Fraud!"
But one scornful look from Casey and the audience was awed;
They saw his face grow stern and cold, they saw his muscles
strain,
And they knew that Casey wouldn't let the ball go by again.

45 The sneer is gone from Casey's lips, his teeth are clenched in
hate.
He pounds with cruel vengeance his bat upon the plate:
And now the pitcher holds the ball, and now he lets it go,
And now the air is shattered by the force of Casey's blow.

Oh, somewhere in this favored land the sun is shining bright,
50 The band is playing somewhere, and somewhere hearts are
light:
And somewhere men are laughing, and somewhere children
shout,
But there is no joy in Mudville: Mighty Casey has struck out.

Vocabulary Builder
writhing (rīth̸ iŋ) *v.*
twisting; turning

Literary Analysis
**Narrative Poetry and
Mood** In what way
does the poem's
mood change in this
stanza?

Fifteen

William Stafford

South of the bridge on Seventeenth
I found back of the willows one summer
day a motorcycle with engine running
as it lay on its side, ticking over

5   slowly in the high grass. I was fifteen.

I admired all that pulsing gleam, the
shiny flanks, the <u>demure</u> headlights
fringed where it lay; I led it gently
to the road and stood with that

10   companion, ready and friendly. I was fifteen.

We could find the end of a road, meet
the sky on out Seventeenth. I thought about
hills, and patting the handle got back a
confident opinion. On the bridge we indulged

15   a forward feeling, a tremble. I was fifteen.

Thinking, back farther in the grass I found
the owner, just coming to, where he had flipped
over the rail. He had blood on his hand, was pale—
I helped him walk to his machine. He ran his hand

20   over it, called me a good man, roared away.

I stood there, fifteen.

Vocabulary Builder
demure (di myoor´) *adj.*
modest

Reading Skill
Paraphrase Picture
the action in lines 11
and 12, and then
restate the phrase
"meet the sky" in your
own words.

TWISTER *HITS* HOUSTON

Sandra Cisneros

Papa was on the front porch.
Mama was in the kitchen.
Mama was trying
to screw a lightbulb into a fixture.
5   Papa was watching the rain.
Mama, it's a cyclone for sure,
he shouted to his wife in the kitchen.
Papa who was sitting on his front porch
when the storm hit
10 said the twister ripped
the big black oak to splinter,
tossed a green sedan into his garden,
and banged the back door
like a mad cat wanting in.
15 Mama who was in the kitchen
said Papa saw everything,
the big oak ripped to kindling,
the green sedan land out back,
the back door slam and slam.
20 I missed it.
Mama was in the kitchen Papa explained.
Papa was sitting on the front porch.
The light bulb is still sitting
where I left it. Don't matter now.
25 Got no electricity anyway.

Reading Skill
Paraphrase Restate
the description in line
14 of the twister
banging the back
door.

◀ **Critical Viewing**   How does the power of
the tornado in this photograph add to your
understanding of the poem? **[Connect]**

Apply the Skills

Poetry Collection 1

Thinking About the Selections

1. **Recall:** Which of the poems in this collection do you think has the most exciting or interesting plot? Explain your answer.
2. **(a) Recall:** In "Casey at the Bat," what details does the speaker use to describe Casey? **(b) Infer:** What does the description suggest about Casey's personality? **(c) Draw Conclusions:** How might his personality have affected the game's outcome?
3. **(a) Recall:** In the third stanza of "Fifteen," what does the speaker imagine doing with the motorcycle? **(b) Interpret:** What does the motorcycle represent to him? Explain.
4. **(a) Recall:** What does the speaker's father do throughout the storm in "Twister Hits Houston"? **(b) Make a Judgment:** Is his behavior appropriate for the situation? Explain your answer.

Literary Analysis

5. **(a)** Using a chart like the one shown, identify and briefly describe the story elements in each **narrative poem** in Poetry Collection 1.

	Setting	Characters	Plot
"Casey at the Bat"			
"Fifteen"			
"Twister Hits Houston"			

   (b) Explain why you think each writer chose to bring these elements to life through poetry rather than prose.
6. Identify three lines or phrases in "Fifteen" that contribute to the poem's **mood,** or **atmosphere,** of longing. Explain each choice.
7. **(a)** Do you think a poem is an effective way in which to tell a story? Why or why not? **(b)** Share your response with a partner, and then explain how someone else's response did or did not change your own.

Reading Skill

8. **(a) Paraphrase** lines 29 through 32 of "Casey at the Bat."
   (b) Does the strategy of picturing the action make it easier to restate these lines in your own words? Explain.

QuickReview

Poems at a Glance
In **"Casey at the Bat,"** a baseball team's star player tries to win the game.

In **"Fifteen,"** a motorcycle at the side of a road sparks the speaker's imagination.

In **"Twister Hits Houston,"** the speaker witnesses a tornado's destructiveness.

For: Self-test
Visit: www.PHSchool.com
Web Code: epa-6407

Narrative Poetry: poetry that tells a story

Mood: *atmosphere* or feeling created in a literary work

Paraphrasing: restating in your own words what someone else has written or said

Vocabulary Builder

Practice **Analogies** show the relationships between pairs of words. Use a word from the Poetry Collection 1 vocabulary list on page 628 to complete each analogy. In each, your choice should create a word pair that matches the relationship between the first two words given.

1. flapping : bird :: _____ : snake
2. blush : red :: _____ : white
3. boastful : proud :: _____ : humble

Adding Words to Your Vocabulary Using a thesaurus, find a **synonym** for each word in the Poetry Collection 1 vocabulary list on page 628. Use each synonym in a sentence that makes the meaning of the word clear. (For more on using a thesaurus, see page R7.)

Writing

Imagine that you are making a film based on "Casey at the Bat." Write a **description of the scene** that could be used to develop a script.
- Jot down details about the characters, setting, and action.
- Explain the mood you want to set and note how details about characters, setting, and action can evoke this mood.
- Suggest camerawork, lighting, and other elements.

Ask a classmate to decide if your writing conveys the poem's mood.

For *Grammar, Vocabulary,* and *Assessment,* see **Build Language Skills,** pages 650–651.

Extend Your Learning

Listening and Speaking With a partner, role-play a **dialogue** between the speaker of "Fifteen" and the motorcyclist.
- Review the poem to find relevant details.
- Decide on each person's main concerns.
- Use conversational styles, including humor, expressions, slang, or more formal words, appropriate to each character.

Listen carefully, and respond as your own character.

Research and Technology Use library and Internet resources to gather statistics for a **fact sheet** about tornadoes in the United States. Find out where, when, how often, and how severely tornadoes strike. Be sure to include statistics for tornadoes in Houston, Texas.

Poetry

Connecting to the Literature

Reading/Writing Connection Each poem in this group has a unique mood or feeling. To get ready to appreciate the moods of these literary works, connect to details that influence your mood in everyday life—such as weather, events, or people's actions. Write several sentences about things that affect your mood. Use at least three of these words: *evoke, respond, reinforce, react, promote.*

Review

For **Literary Analysis, Reading Skill,** and **Vocabulary Builder,** see page 628.

Meet the Authors

Edgar Allan **Poe** (1809–1849)
The Raven (p. 639)
One of the first great American storytellers, Edgar Allan Poe often explored dark and bizarre events in his stories and poems. His inspiration may have come from his own life, which was often filled with sadness. He found some happiness in his marriage to Virginia Clemm, but after her death, Poe became depressed and antisocial. Many of his poems and stories focus on an ideal love that is lost.

Edwin **Muir** (1887–1959)
The Horses (p. 644)
An author of numerous books of poetry as well as several novels, Edwin Muir had visions of the future that were rooted in his past. He spent his early years on a farm in the Orkney Islands, north of Scotland. Much of the imagery in his poetry comes from these islands.

Richard **Wilbur** (b. 1921)
The Writer (p. 647)
As a young man, Richard Wilbur planned to be a cartoonist. Instead, he became an award-winning poet. By the time he was thirty, Wilbur had published two collections of poetry and established himself as an important young writer. In 1987, Wilbur was appointed Poet Laureate of the United States.

Go Online
—Author Link

For: More about these authors
Visit: www.PHSchool.com
Web Code: epe-9410

The Raven

Edgar Allan Poe

Once upon a midnight dreary, while I pondered, weak and weary,
 Over many a quaint and curious volume of forgotten lore,
While I nodded, nearly napping, suddenly there came a tapping,
As of someone gently rapping, rapping at my chamber door.
5 "Tis some visitor," I muttered, "tapping at my chamber door—
  Only this, and nothing more."

Ah, distinctly I remember it was in the bleak December,
And each separate dying ember wrought its ghost upon the floor.
Eagerly I wished the morrow—vainly I had tried to borrow
10 From my books surcease[1] of sorrow—sorrow for the lost Lenore—
For the rare and radiant maiden whom the angels name Lenore—
  Nameless here for evermore.

---

1. surcease (sʉr sēs´) *n.* end.

Literary Analysis
Narrative Poetry
Which details provide information about the setting and main character?

Reading Check

What sorrow is the speaker hoping to ease by reading?

And the silken, sad, uncertain rustling of each purple curtain
Thrilled me—filled me with fantastic terrors never felt before;
15 So that now, to still the beating of my heart, I stood repeating
"'Tis some visitor entreating entrance at my chamber door—
Some late visitor entreating entrance at my chamber door—
This it is and nothing more."

Presently my soul grew stronger; hesitating then no longer,
20 "Sir," said I, "or Madam, truly your forgiveness I implore;
But the fact is I was napping, and so gently you came rapping,
And so faintly you came tapping, tapping at my chamber door,
That I scarce was sure I heard you"—here I opened wide the door—
Darkness there, and nothing more.

25 Deep into that darkness peering, long I stood there wondering, fearing,
Doubting, dreaming dreams no mortal ever dared to dream before;
But the silence was unbroken, and the darkness gave no token,
And the only word there spoken was the whispered word, "Lenore!"
This *I* whispered, and an echo murmured back the word, "Lenore!"
30 Merely this, and nothing more.

Then into the chamber turning, all my soul within me burning,
Soon I heard again a tapping somewhat louder than before.
"Surely," said I, "surely that is something at my window lattice;
Let me see, then, what thereat[2] is, and this mystery explore—
35 Let my heart be still a moment and this mystery explore—
'Tis the wind, and nothing more!"

---

2. **thereat** (ther at´) *adv.* there.

Reading Skill
Paraphrase Picture the action the speaker describes and paraphrase this stanza.

Literary Analysis
Narrative Poetry
How has the speaker's emotional state changed since the first stanza?

Literature in Context

Culture Connection

Pallas When the speaker says "a bust of Pallas" in line 41, he refers to a sculpture of the head and shoulders of the ancient Greek goddess Pallas Athena. Athena was the goddess of wisdom, skills, and warfare. She was also the patron goddess of Athens, the cultural center of ancient Greece. She was considered the guardian of the city.

Connect to the Literature

Do you think the speaker keeps a bust of Pallas because he values her as a symbol of warfare, as a symbol of wisdom, or neither? Explain.

Open here I flung the shutter, when, with many a flirt[3] and flutter,
In there stepped a stately raven of the saintly days of yore;
Not the least obeisance[4] made he; not an instant stopped or
   stayed he;
40   But, with mien[5] of lord or lady, perched above my chamber door—
Perched upon a bust of Pallas just above my chamber door—
      Perched, and sat, and nothing more.

Then this ebony bird <u>beguiling</u> my sad fancy[6] into smiling,
By the grave and stern decorum of the countenance[7] it wore,
45   "Though thy crest be shorn and shaven, thou," I said, "art sure
   no craven,[8]
Ghastly grim and ancient raven wandering from the Nightly
   shore—
Tell me what thy lordly name is on the Night's Plutonian[9] shore!"
      Quoth[10] the raven, "Nevermore."

Much I marveled this ungainly fowl to hear discourse so plainly,
50   Though its answer little meaning—little relevancy bore;
For we cannot help agreeing that no sublunary[11] being
Ever yet was blessed with seeing bird above his chamber door—
Bird or beast upon the sculptured bust above his chamber door,
      With such name as "Nevermore."

55   But the raven, sitting lonely on the placid bust, spoke only
That one word, as if his soul in that one word he did outpour.
Nothing farther then he uttered—not a feather then he fluttered—
Till I scarcely more than muttered, "Other friends have flown
   before—
On the morrow *he* will leave me, as my hopes have flown before."
60   Quoth the raven, "Nevermore."

Wondering at the stillness broken by reply so aptly spoken,
"Doubtless," said I, "what it utters is its only stock and store,
Caught from some unhappy master whom unmerciful Disaster
Followed fast and followed faster—so, when Hope he would
   adjure,[12]

---

3. flirt (flʉrt) *n.* quick, uneven movement.
4. obeisance (ō bā´ səns) *n.* bow or another sign of respect.
5. mien (mēn) *n.* manner.
6. fancy (fan´ sē) *n.* imagination.
7. countenance (koʊunt´'n əns) *n.* facial appearance.
8. craven (krā´ vən) *n.* coward (usually an adjective).
9. Plutonian (plōō tō´ nē ən) *adj.* like the underworld, ruled over by the ancient Roman god Pluto.
10. quoth (kwōth) *v.* said.
11. sublunary (sub lōōn´ ər ē) *adj.* earthly.
12. adjure (ə jʊor´) *v.* appeal to; ask earnestly.

Reading Skill
Paraphrase In your own words, describe how the raven behaved as it entered the chamber.

Vocabulary Builder
beguiling (bē gīl´ iŋ) *v.* tricking; charming

✓**Reading Check**

What one word does the raven repeat?

65 Stern Despair returned, instead of the sweet Hope he dared
   adjure—
         That sad answer, 'Nevermore.'"

But the raven still beguiling all my sad soul into smiling,
Straight I wheeled a cushioned seat in front of bird, and bust, and
   door;
Then upon the velvet sinking, I betook myself to linking
70 Fancy unto fancy, thinking what this ominous bird of yore—
What this grim, ungainly, ghastly, gaunt, and ominous bird of yore
         Meant in croaking "Nevermore."

This I sat engaged in guessing, but no syllable expressing
To the fowl whose fiery eyes now burned into my bosom's core;
75 This and more I sat divining,[13] with my head at ease reclining
On the cushion's velvet lining that the lamplight gloated o'er,
But whose velvet violet lining with the lamplight gloating o'er,
         She shall press, ah, nevermore!

---

13. divining (də vīn´ iŋ) *v.* guessing.

Literary Analysis
Narrative Poetry
What two conflicts or
problems does the
narrator face in this
stanza?

◄ **Critical Viewing**
Which features of a
raven make it appear
more mysterious than
other birds? **[Analyze]**

Then, methought, the air grew denser, perfumed from an unseen censer[14]

80   Swung by angels whose faint footfalls tinkled on the tufted floor.
"Wretch," I cried, "thy God hath lent thee—by these angels he hath sent thee
Respite—respite and Nepenthe[15] from thy memories of Lenore!
Let me quaff this kind Nepenthe and forget this lost Lenore!"
        Quoth the raven, "Nevermore."

85   "Prophet!" said I, "thing of evil!—prophet still, if bird or devil!—
Whether Tempter sent, or whether tempest tossed thee here ashore,
Desolate, yet all undaunted, on this desert land enchanted—
On this home by Horror haunted—tell me truly, I implore—
Is there—is there balm in Gilead?[16]—tell me—tell me, I implore!"
90   Quoth the raven, "Nevermore."

"Prophet!" said I, "thing of evil!—prophet still, if bird or devil!
By that Heaven that bends above us—by that God we both adore—
Tell this soul with sorrow laden if, within the distant Aidenn,[17]
It shall clasp a sainted maiden whom the angels name Lenore—
95   Clasp a rare and radiant maiden whom the angels name Lenore."
        Quoth the raven, "Nevermore."

"Be that word our sign of parting, bird or fiend!" I shrieked, upstarting—
"Get thee back into the tempest and the Night's Plutonian shore!
Leave no black plume as a token of that lie thy soul hath spoken!
100 Leave my loneliness unbroken!—quit the bust above my door!
Take thy beak from out my heart, and take thy form from off my door!"
        Quoth the raven, "Nevermore."

And the raven, never flitting, still is sitting, still is sitting
On the pallid bust of Pallas just above my chamber door;
105 And his eyes have all the seeming of a demon that is dreaming,
And the lamplight o'er him streaming throws his shadow on the floor;
And my soul from out that shadow that lies floating on the floor
        Shall be lifted—nevermore!

---

14. **censer** (sen´ sər) *n.* container for burning incense.
15. **Nepenthe** (nē pen´ thē) *n.* drug believed by the ancient Greeks to cause forgetfulness of sorrow.
16. **balm** (bäm) **in Gilead** (gil´ ē əd) cure for suffering; the Bible refers to a medicinal ointment, or balm, made in a region called Gilead.
17. **Aidenn** name meant to suggest Eden or paradise.

Vocabulary Builder
respite (res´ pit) *n.* rest; relief

Literary Analysis
Narrative Poetry and Mood How does the mood here compare with the mood at the beginning of the poem? Explain.

THE HORSES

EDWIN MUIR

Barely a twelvemonth after
The seven days war that put the world to sleep,
Late in the evening the strange horses came.
By then we had made our covenant with silence,
5   But in the first few days it was so still
We listened to our breathing and were afraid.
On the second day
The radios failed; we turned the knobs; no answer.
On the third day a warship passed us, heading north,
10   Dead bodies piled on the deck. On the sixth day
A plane plunged over us into the sea. Thereafter
Nothing. The radios dumb;
And still they stand in corners of our kitchens,
And stand, perhaps, turned on, in a million rooms
15   All over the world. But now if they should speak,
If on a sudden they should speak again,
If on the stroke of noon a voice should speak,
We would not listen, we would not let it bring
That old bad world that swallowed its children quick
20   At one great gulp. We would not have it again.
Sometimes we think of the nations lying asleep,
Curled blindly in impenetrable sorrow,
And then the thought confounds us with its strangeness.

The tractors lie about our fields; at evening
25   They look like dank sea-monsters couched and waiting.
We leave them where they are and let them rust:

**Literary Analysis
Narrative Poetry**
Which details in the
first stanza reveal that
the poem takes place
in the future?

► Critical Viewing
Do these horses
appear "stubborn and
shy" like the ones
described in the
poem? **[Compare and
Contrast]**

'They'll moulder away and be like other loam'.[1]
We make our oxen drag our rusty ploughs,
Long laid aside. We have gone back
30 Far past our fathers' land.
                                    And then, that evening
Late in the summer the strange horses came.
We heard a distant tapping on the road,
A deepening drumming; it stopped, went on again
35 And at the corner changed to hollow thunder.
We saw the heads
Like a wild wave charging and were afraid.
We had sold our horses in our fathers' time
To buy new tractors. Now they were strange to us
40 As fabulous steeds set on an ancient shield
Or illustrations in a book of knights.
We did not dare go near them. Yet they waited,
Stubborn and shy, as if they had been sent
By an old command to find our whereabouts
45 And that long-lost <u>archaic</u> companionship.
In the first moment we had never a thought
That they were creatures to be owned and used.
Among them were some half-a-dozen colts
Dropped in some wilderness of the broken world,
50 Yet new as if they had come from their own Eden.[2]
Since then they have pulled our ploughs and borne our loads,
But that free servitude still can pierce our hearts.
Our life is changed; their coming our beginning.

---

1. loam (lōm) *n.* dark, rich soil.
2. Eden in the Bible, the garden where life began with Adam and Eve; paradise.

Reading Skill
Paraphrase Picture
the scene here
and paraphrase
lines 31–32.

Vocabulary Builder
archaic (är kā´ ik) *adj.*
from an earlier time;
ancient

The Writer

RICHARD WILBUR

In her room at the prow[1] of the house
Where light breaks, and the windows are tossed with linden,[2]
My daughter is writing a story.

    I pause in the stairwell, hearing
5 From her shut door a commotion of typewriter-keys
Like a chain hauled over a gunwale.[3]

Young as she is, the stuff
Of her life is a great cargo, and some of it heavy:
I wish her a lucky passage.

10 But now it is she who pauses,
As if to reject my thought and its easy figure.
A stillness greatens, in which

The whole house seems to be thinking,
And then she is at it again with a bunched clamor
15 Of strokes, and again is silent.

Literary Analysis
Narrative Poetry
What details about the characters and setting are introduced in the first stanza?

---

1. prow (prou) *n.* front part of a ship or boat.
2. linden (lin´ dən) *n.* type of tree.
3. gunwale (gun´ əl) *n.* upper edge of the side of a ship or boat.

I remember the dazed starling[4]
Which was trapped in that very room, two years ago;
How we stole in, lifted a sash

And retreated, not to affright it;
20 And how for a helpless hour, through the crack of the door,
We watched the sleek, wild, dark

And iridescent creature
Batter against the brilliance, drop like a glove
To the hard floor, or the desk-top,

25 And wait then, humped and bloody,
For the wits to try it again; and how our spirits
Rose when, suddenly sure,

It lifted off from a chair-back,
Beating a smooth course for the right window
30 And clearing the sill of the world.

It is always a matter, my darling,
Of life or death, as I had forgotten. I wish
What I wished you before, but harder.

---

4. starling (stär′ lin) *n.* bird with black feathers that shine in a greenish or purplish way.

Reading Skill
Paraphrase Picture the action here and paraphrase lines 16–23.

▼ **Critical Viewing**
Do you think a typewriter like this would allow a writer more or less creativity than a computer? **[Speculate]**

Apply the Skills

Poetry Collection 2

Thinking About the Selections

1. **Recall:** Which of the poems in this collection do you think has the most exciting or interesting plot? Explain your answer.
2. **(a) Recall:** In the first line of "The Raven," which two adjectives does the speaker use to describe his state of mind?
   (b) Draw Conclusions: What words would you use to describe the speaker's state of mind at the end of the poem? **(c) Analyze Cause and Effect:** What has caused the speaker to change?
3. **(a) Recall:** What has happened to the tractors in "The Horses"?
   (b) Interpret: Why does the poet place the tractors and the horses side by side?
4. **Analyze:** Why does the speaker of "The Writer" recall the incident of the trapped starling? Explain your answer.

Literary Analysis

5. **(a)** Using a chart like the one shown, identify and briefly describe the story elements in each **narrative poem** in Poetry Collection 2.

	Setting	Characters	Plot
"The Raven"			
"The Horses"			
"The Writer"			

   (b) Explain why you think each writer chose to bring these elements to life through poetry rather than prose.
6. Identify three lines or phrases in "The Horses" that contribute to the poem's mysterious and dreamlike **mood,** or **atmosphere.** Explain your choices.
7. **(a)** Do you think a poem is an effective way in which to tell a story? Why or why not? **(b)** Share your response with a partner, and then explain how someone else's response did or did not change your own.

Reading Skill

8. **(a) Paraphrase** lines 37 through 39 of "The Raven." **(b)** Does the strategy of picturing the action make it easier to restate these lines in your own words? Explain.

QuickReview

Poems at a Glance
In **"The Raven,"** the speaker is haunted by a mysterious bird.

In **"The Horses,"** the speaker describes a strange vision of the future.

In **"The Writer,"** the speaker is moved by the sound of his daughter typing a story.

Go Online
Assessment
For: Self-test
Visit: www.PHSchool.com
Web Code: epa-6408

Narrative Poetry: poetry that tells a story

Mood: *atmosphere* or feeling created in a literary work

Paraphrasing: restating in your own words what someone else has written or said

Vocabulary Builder

Practice **Analogies** show the relationships between pairs of words. Use a word from the Poetry Collection 2 vocabulary list on page 628 to complete each analogy. In each, your choice should create a word pair that matches the relationship between the first two words given.

1. stale : fresh :: _____ : modern
2. exercise : tiredness :: _____ : rest
3. teaching : professor :: _____ : trickster

Adding Words to Your Vocabulary Using a thesaurus, find a **synonym** for each word in the Poetry Collection 2 vocabulary list on page 628. Use each synonym in a sentence that makes the meaning of the word clear. (For more on using a thesaurus, see page R7.)

Writing

Imagine that you have been hired by a movie studio to make a short film based on "The Raven." Write a **description of the scene** that could be used to develop a script.
- Jot down details about the characters, setting, and action.
- Explain the mood you want to set and note how details about characters, setting, and action can evoke this mood.
- Suggest camerawork, lighting, and other elements.

Ask a classmate to decide if your writing conveys the poem's mood.

For *Grammar*, *Vocabulary*, and *Assessment*, see **Build Language Skills**, pages 650–651.

Extend Your Learning

Listening and Speaking With a partner, role-play a **dialogue** between the father and daughter in "The Writer."
- Review the poem to find relevant details.
- Decide on each person's main concerns.
- Use conversational styles, including humor, expressions, slang, or more formal words, appropriate to each character.

Listen carefully, and respond as your own character.

Research and Technology Use library and Internet resources to gather information for a **fact sheet** about ravens: what these birds look like, where they are found, and other key facts. Compare the details in your fact sheet with those in the poem.

Build Language Skills

Vocabulary Skill

Suffixes The **Latin suffix** *-age* means "that which relates to the act of or the condition of." This suffix creates nouns—often from other nouns.

▶ **Example:** "He is descended from a *line* of kings. His *lineage* means he will inherit the throne."

Practice As in the example that has been given, write sentence pairs for each of the following. Use the base word in the first sentence and the base + *-age*-word in the second sentence.

1. short   **2.** drain   **3.** post   **4.** marry   **5.** acre

Grammar Skill

Appositive Phrase An **appositive phrase** is a noun or pronoun with modifiers that adds information to the noun or pronoun it is placed next to. Appositive phrases that contain modifiers are set off with commas. Using appositives is a good way to make your writing more concise.

> **Less concise:**
> The *Iliad* relates the events of the Trojan war. The Trojan war was a legendary struggle between Greece and Troy.

Look at the more concise revision, in which the sentences are combined with an appositive phrase (underlined):

> **Appositive:**
> The *Iliad* relates the events of the Trojan war, <u>a legendary struggle between Greece and Troy.</u>

MorePractice

For more practice with appositve phrases, see the grammar Handbook, p. R40.

Practice Combine the sentences using appositive phrases.

1. The *Iliad* begins when Paris runs off with Queen Helen. Paris was a Prince of Troy.

2. Achilles eventually kills Hector. Achilles is a powerful Greek warrior.

3. Hector is the greatest fighter in Troy. Hector is Paris' brother.

4. The Trojan war is the backdrop of the *Iliad.* The Trojan war was between the Greeks and Trojans.

5. Queen Helen was known for her beauty. Queen Helen was the wife of King Menelaus.

𝒲𝒢 *Prentice Hall Writing and Grammar Connection: Chapter 10, Section 4.*

Reading Skill: Paraphrase

Directions: *Read the poem. Then, answer the questions.*

I wandered lonely as a cloud
That floats on high o'er vales and hills
When all at once I saw a crowd,
A host of golden daffodils;
5 Beside the lake, beneath the trees,
Fluttering and dancing in the breeze.

Continuous as the stars that shine
And twinkle on the milky way,
They stretched in never ending line
10 Along the margin of a bay:
Ten thousand saw I at a glance,
Tossing their heads in sprightly dance.

    —from "I Wandered Lonely as a Cloud" by William Wordsworth

Standards Assessed

- IR.2.02.4
- FA.3.03.2
- LT.5.01.11

1. Which is the best paraphrase of line 6?
   A moving in the water
   B moving in the wind
   C dancing by the lake
   D dancing in the crowd

2. Which is a reasonable paraphrase of lines 4–7?
   A the stars keep on going
   B you see numerous stars
   C there were many daffodils
   D the line of trees seemed endless

3. Which of the following statements represents the best paraphrase of the first stanza?
   A Clouds and daffodils are part of nature, unlike human beings.
   B Walking by myself, I was amazed to see a huge field of daffodils.
   C I was by myself, but there were many daffodils, and I felt lonely.
   D It was a windy day, but I did not mind because of the beauty of the daffodils.

Timed Writing: Analysis [Connections]

Review the poems in **Poetry Collection 1** and **Poetry Collection 2**. Choose one poem in which the poet describe a universal human trait. Write an explanation of how the poet transmits a sense of this characteristic. Use specifics from the work as support. **(40 minutes)**

Writing Workshop: *Work in Progress*

Response to Literature

Review your notes about strong characters in "Uncoiling" and "A Voice." Identify the character that makes the strongest impression on you. Jot down details from the poem that help create that impression. Put your annotations in your writing portfolio.

Reading Informational Materials

Web Sites

In Part 2, you are learning how to paraphrase while reading literature. Paraphrasing is also useful when reading informational materials, such as newspaper articles and Web sites. Paraphrasing allows you to state the information in your own words to better understand the material. If you read Sandra Cisneros's "Twister Hits Houston," you could use this Web site to find facts about twisters.

About Web Sites

A **Web site** is a collection of information at a specific address on the World Wide Web. Software known as a **browser** enables you to access Web sites with your computer and the Internet. To connect to a site, type a Web address, or URL (Uniform Resource Locator), or click on a word or picture that links to it. Usually, you will be connected to a **home page**, which is like a table of contents. Web sites often have these features:

- A **keyword** or pull-down search function. In a keyword search, you type in a word, and the browser searches the site. A pull-down search provides choices of topics.
- A **bulletin board,** which lists relevant news or questions
- An **e-mail address** of someone at the site

Reading Skill

All Web sites do not present equally reliable information, so **evaluating Web sources** is essential. First, identify the sponsor of the site and assess the sponsor's credentials and expertise. Then, determine whether the sponsor is biased or favors a particular point of view. Bias can be revealed through opinions or through information that is either stressed or omitted. Finally, consider whether the information on the Web site is current. The URL ending indicates the general type of sponsor:

URL Ending	Description	Usual Intent
.edu or .gov	Site is maintained by an educational institution or government agency.	to provide reliable information
.org	Site is probably maintained by a nonprofit organization.	to provide information about an issue or a cause
.com	Site is maintained commercially or personally.	to sell or promote something
.net	Site is maintained by a network.	varies

Standard Course of Study

- Analyze elements of informational environment in text when answering research questions. (IR.2.01.11)
- Report the research for a specified audience. (IR.2.04.4)

The emblem and URL indicate that this is a U.S. government site.

The "Search" button leads to a page where you can search by keyword.

National Oceanic and Atmosphere Administration

READING INFORMATIONAL MATERIALS

Home Page Menu ⬥

| Home | Contacts | Media | Disclaimer | Search | People Locator |

Weather Page

Fujita Tornado Damage Scale

Category F0: Light Damage (<73 mph); Some damage to chimneys and sign boards, branches broken off trees, shallow-rooted trees pushed over.

Category F1: Moderate Damage (73-112 mph); Peels surface off roofs; mobile homes pushed off foundations or overturned; moving autos blown off road.

Category F2: Considerable Damage (113-157 mph); Roofs torn off frame houses; mobile homes demolished; boxcars overturned; large trees snapped or uprooted; light-object missiles generated; cars lifted off ground.

Category F3: Severe Damage (158-206 mph); Roofs and some walls torn off well-constructed houses, trains overturned; most trees in forest uprooted; heavy cars lifted off ground and thrown.

Category F4: Devastating Damage (207-260 mph); Well-constructed houses leveled; structures with weak foundations blown off some distance; cars thrown and large missiles generated.

Category F5: Incredible Damage (261-318 mph); Strong frame houses lifted off foundations and swept away; automobile sized missiles fly through the air in excess of 100 meters (109 yards); trees debarked.

Tornadoes

Tornadoes are one of nature's most violent storms. In an average year, about 1,000 tornadoes are reported across the United States, resulting in 80 deaths and over 1,500 injuries. A tornado is a violently rotating column of air extending from a thunderstorm to the ground. The most violent tornadoes are capable of tremendous destruction with wind speeds of 250 mph or more. Damage paths can be in excess of one mile wide and 50 miles long.

Tornadoes come in all shapes and sizes and can occur anywhere in the U.S. at any time of the year. In the southern states, peak tornado season is March through May, while peak months in the northern states are during the summer.

Preparedness Guides

• Are you prepared for Nature's Most Violent Storms?. A preparedness guide including safety information for schools prepared by the National Weather Service, FEMA and the American Red Cross.

• Thunderstorms and Camping Safety

• Weather Safety for Kids - Owlie Skywarn's Weather Book about Tornadoes

More Info . . .

• Weather Glossary for Storm Spotters

These links connect to pages with more information. For example, clicking on "Weather Safety for Kids" takes you to the web page shown on the page 654.

• Storm Reports - includes monthly tornado statistics, deadly tornadoes, current severe weather reports and more from the National Weather Service's Storm Prediction Center.

• Tornadoes of the 20th Century - a list of the more notable tornado outbreaks that occurred in the U.S. during the 20th century.

http://www.crh.noaa.gov/mkx/owlie/tornadoe1.htm

Click on these links to find additional information about the topics listed.

National Weather Service
Owlie Skywarn's Weather Book
Watch Out...Storms Ahead!

Owlie's Front Page

View My Safety Tips About...
Tornadoes
  Watches
  Warnings
Lightning
Flash Floods
Hurricanes
Winter Weather
Carbon Monoxide

TORNADO!

If you ever see a big black cloud with a funnel-like extension beneath it, watch out. It could be a tornado.

A tornado looks like a funnel with the fat part at the top. Inside it winds may be swirling around at 300 miles an hour. If it goes through a town, the tornado could flatten houses and buildings, lift up cars and trucks, shatter mobile homes into splinters. Sometimes the path is narrow but everything in the path gets wrecked. But you don't always see the funnel. It may be raining too hard. Or the tornado may come at night. Listen for the tornado's roar. Some people say it sounds like a thousand trains.

What to do if...

You are in your house	**You are downtown or in a shopping mall**	**You are outside**
You are in school	**You are in a mobile home**	**In Conclusion...**

This line identifies the date when the web page was updated.

Last updated June 22, 20__
URL: http://www.crh.noaa.gov/mkx/owlie/tornado1.htm

This page provides an e-mail address so users can contact someone at the web site with comments or questions.

Educators and students should send their questions to the NOAA outreach team at noaa-outreach@noaa.gov.

Reading: Evaluating Web Sources

Directions: *Choose the letter of the best answer to each question about the NOAA Web site on "Tornadoes."*

Standards
Assessed

• IR.2.03.3
• IR.2.04.1
• IR.2.04.3

1. For which of the following topics would this site provide valid information?
   A climate changes due to global warming
   B tide tables for the coming season
   C average temperatures and rainfall in your state
   D tornadoes during the 1980s and 1990s

2. Which link would you use to find reliable data on current storms in your area?
   A Storm Reports
   B Nature's Most Violent Storms?
   C Safety Tips about "Tornadoes"
   D Weather Glossary for Storm Spotters

3. How do you know the information on this site is reliable?
   A This is a government-sponsored weather Web site.
   B The site has pages for kids.
   C The site looks scientific.
   D Only experts would have access to this information.

Reading: Comprehension and Interpretation

Directions: *Write your answers on a separate piece of paper.*

4. Which link or links on the home page lead to information about measures schools can take to ensure the safety of students and teachers? **[Knowledge]**

5. Paraphrase the descriptions of Category F0 and Category F5 on the Fujita Tornado Damage Scale. **[Organizing]**

Timed Writing: Evaluation [Connections]

Write an evaluation of the Web site that answers these questions: What are its most helpful features? Who would find it the most useful? Is there anything that should be added to the site to make it better? Would you recommend this site to someone researching severe weather? **(35 minutes)**

Build Skills
Poetry Collection 1 • Poetry Collection 2

You can apply the instruction on this page to these poems.

Poetry Collection 1
We never know how high we are, page 659
The Road Not Taken, page 661
Macavity: The Mystery Cat, page 662

Poetry Collection 2
Fire and Ice, page 667
maggie and milly and molly and may, page 668
The Seven Ages of Man, page 671

NC **Standard Course of Study**

• Avoid fragments, run-ons, and comma splices. (GU.6.02.1)
• Analyze elements of informational environment in text when answering research questions. (IR.2.01.11)

Literary Analysis

Rhyme is the repetition of sounds at the ends of words. There are several types of rhyme:

- **Exact rhyme:** the repetition of words that end with the same vowel and consonant sounds, as in *love* and *dove*

- **Slant rhyme:** the repetition of words that end with similar sounds but do not rhyme perfectly, as in *prove* and *glove*

- **End rhyme:** the rhyming of words at the ends of lines

- **Internal rhyme:** the rhyming of words within a line

A **rhyme scheme** is a regular pattern of end rhymes in a poem or stanza. A rhyme scheme is described by assigning one letter of the alphabet to each rhyming sound. For example, in "Ring Out, Wild Bells," Alfred, Lord Tennyson uses the rhyme scheme *abba*:

Ring out, wild bells, to the wild <u>sky</u>,	*a*
The flying cloud, the frosty <u>light</u>:	*b*
The year is dying in the <u>night</u>;	*b*
Ring out, wild bells, and let him <u>die</u>.	*a*

Meter is the rhythmical pattern in a line of poetry. It results from the arrangement of stressed (´) and unstressed (˘) syllables. When you read aloud a line with a regular meter, you can hear the steady rhythmic pulse of the stressed syllables:

The flying cloud, the frosty light

Half a league, half a league, / Half a league onward

Not all poems include rhyme, a rhyme scheme, or a regular meter. However, poets often use one or more of these techniques to create musical effects and achieve a sense of unity in their poems.

As you read the poetry in this collection, notice rhyme and meter.

- Look for examples of different types of rhyme.
- Determine if the lines follow a rhyme scheme.
- Notice whether or not the lines follow a regular meter.

Build Skills (Continued)

Reading Skill

Paraphrasing is restating in your own words what someone else has written or said. A paraphrase should retain the essential meaning and ideas of the original but should be simpler to read. One way to simplify the text that you are paraphrasing is to **break down long sentences.** Divide long sentences into parts and paraphrase those parts.

- If a sentence contains multiple subjects or verbs, see if it can be separated into smaller sentences that each contain one subject and one verb.

- If a sentence contains colons, semicolons, or dashes, create separate sentences by treating those punctuation marks as periods.

- If a sentence contains long phrases or long passages in parentheses, turn each phrase or parenthetical passage into a separate sentence.

Poets often write sentences that span several lines to give their poems fluidity. By breaking down long sentences and paraphrasing them, you can enjoy a poem's fluid quality without missing its meaning.

As you read poetry and break down long sentences to paraphrase lines, use a chart like the one shown to record your work.

Original Lines	Lines in Smaller Sentences	Paraphrase
I celebrate myself and sing myself, / And what I assume you shall assume, / For every atom belonging to me as good belongs to you.	I celebrate myself. I sing myself. What I assume you shall assume. Every atom belonging to me as good belongs to you.	I celebrate myself and share my joy with you. What is mine is also yours.

Vocabulary Builder

Poetry Collection 1

- **warp** (wôrp) *v.* twist; distort (p. 659) *Skilled artists can warp wood into different shapes.*

- **diverged** (dī vʉrjd´) *v.* branched out in different directions (p. 661) *When the highway diverged, we were not sure which way to go.*

- **bafflement** (baf´ əl mənt) *n.* puzzlement; bewilderment (p. 662) *To the bafflement of many, the jet pilot was afraid of heights.*

- **depravity** (dē prav´ ə tē) *n.* crookedness; corruption (p. 663) *The criminal's depravity was well-known, and his arrest was cheered.*

Poetry Collection 2

- **suffice** (sə fīs´) *v.* be enough (p. 667) *Five tables will suffice for a party of this size.*

- **languid** (laŋ´ gwid) *adj.* drooping; weak (p. 668) *The heat of the summer afternoon made us all feel languid.*

- **woeful** (wō´ fəl) *adj.* full of sorrow (p. 671) *His woeful story brought us to tears.*

- **treble** (treb´ əl) *n.* high-pitched voice or sound (p. 671) *The harsh treble of her alarm clock woke everyone in the house.*

Poetry

Connecting to the Literature

Reading/Writing Connection In "The Road Not Taken," Robert Frost writes about making a difficult choice—a choice that is different from what most people would choose. Think about why people sometimes choose to do things that are difficult, challenging, or even unpopular. Use at least three of these words: *challenge, compel, conform, distinguish.*

Meet the Authors

Emily **Dickinson** (1830–1886)
We never know how high we are (p. 659)
Emily Dickinson's life in Amherst, Massachusetts, seemed to be quiet and uneventful. Yet the emotional power of her poems shows the wide range of her energy and imagination. She found profound meanings in simple subjects, and her poems still delight readers.

Robert **Frost** (1874–1963)
The Road Not Taken (p. 661)
In January 1961, when John F. Kennedy became president of the United States, he called on fellow New Englander Robert Frost to recite two poems at the inauguration. At the time, Frost was America's most famous living poet. He became famous when *A Boy's Will* (1913) and *North of Boston* (1914) won praise in both England and America.

T. S. **Eliot** (1888–1965)
Macavity: The Mystery Cat (p. 662)
A whimsical poem like "Macavity: The Mystery Cat" was a rarity in the writing of Thomas Sterns Eliot. He was better known for serious, philosophical poems. Born in the United States, Eliot settled in England. He became a highly influential poet and won the Nobel Prize in 1948.

For: More about these authors
Visit: www.PHSchool.com
Web Code: epe-9411

We never know how high we are

Emily Dickinson

We never know how high we are
Till we are asked to rise
And then if we are true to plan
Our statures touch the skies—
The Heroism we recite
Would be a normal thing
Did not ourselves the Cubits[1] <u>warp</u>
For fear to be a King—

Vocabulary Builder
warp (wôrp) *v.* twist;
distort

---

1. Cubits (kyōō´ bits) *n.* ancient measure using the length of the arm from the end of the middle finger to the elbow (about 18–22 inches).

The Road Not Taken
Robert Frost

Two roads <u>diverged</u> in a yellow wood,
And sorry I could not travel both
And be one traveler, long I stood
And looked down one as far as I could
5 To where it bent in the undergrowth;

Then took the other, as just as fair,
And having perhaps the better claim,
Because it was grassy and wanted wear;
Though as for that, the passing there
10 Had worn them really about the same,

And both that morning equally lay
In leaves no step had trodden black.
Oh, I kept the first for another day!
Yet knowing how way leads on to way,
15 I doubted if I should ever come back.

I shall be telling this with a sigh
Somewhere ages and ages hence:
Two roads diverged in a wood, and I—
I took the one less traveled by,
20 And that has made all the difference.

Vocabulary Builder
diverged (dī vʉrjd´) v.
branched out in
different directions

Reading Skill
Paraphrase In your
own words, restate
the decision the
speaker makes in
lines 6–8.

Literary Analysis
**Rhyme and Rhyme
Scheme** What is the
rhyme scheme of
stanza four?

◀ **Critical Viewing** Based on this image, explain why the
idea of a fork in a road is an effective symbol for a life choice.
[Support]

Macavity: The Mystery Cat

T.S. Eliot

Macavity's a Mystery Cat: he's called the Hidden Paw—
For he's the master criminal who can defy the Law.
He's the <u>bafflement</u> of Scotland Yard,[1] the Flying Squad's[2]
    despair:
5   For when they reach the scene of crime—*Macavity's not*
      there!

Macavity, Macavity, there's no one like Macavity,
He's broken every human law, he breaks the law of gravity.
His powers of levitation would make a fakir[3] stare,
10   And when you reach the scene of crime—*Macavity's not there!*
You may seek him in the basement, you may look up in the
      air—
But I tell you once and once again, *Macavity's not there!*

Macavity's a ginger cat, he's very tall and thin;
15   You would know him if you saw him, for his eyes are sunken in.

---

1. Scotland Yard London police.
2. Flying Squad criminal-investigation department.
3. fakir (fə kir´) *n.* Muslim or Hindu beggar who claims to perform miracles.

Vocabulary Builder
bafflement (baf´ əl mənt) *n.* puzzlement; bewilderment

Literary Analysis
Rhyme What type of rhyme does this stanza contain?

His brow is deeply lined with thought, his head is highly
        domed;
His coat is dusty from neglect, his whiskers are uncombed.
He sways his head from side to side, with movements like a
20   snake;
And when you think he's half asleep, he's always wide awake.

Macavity, Macavity, there's no one like Macavity,
For he's a fiend in feline shape, a monster of <u>depravity</u>.
You may meet him in a by-street, you may see him in the
25   square—
But when a crime's discovered, then *Macavity's not there!*

He's outwardly respectable. (They say he cheats at cards.)
And his footprints are not found in any file of Scotland Yard's.
And when the larder's looted, or the jewel-case is rifled,
30   Or when the milk is missing, or another Peke's[4] been stifled,
Or the greenhouse glass is broken, and the trellis past repair—
Ay, there's the wonder of the thing! *Macavity's not there!*

And when the Foreign Office find a Treaty's gone astray,
Or the Admiralty lose some plans and drawings by the way,
35   There may be a scrap of paper in the hall or on the stair—
But it's useless to investigate—*Macavity's not there!*
And when the loss has been disclosed, the Secret Service say:
'It *must* have been Macavity!'—but he's a mile away.
You'll be sure to find him resting, or a-licking of his thumbs,
40   Or engaged in doing complicated long division sums.

Macavity, Macavity, there's no one like Macavity,
There never was a Cat of such deceitfulness and suavity.
He always has an alibi, and one or two to spare:
At whatever time the deed took place—MACAVITY WASN'T
45   THERE!
And they say that all the Cats whose wicked deeds are widely
        known
(I might mention Mungojerrie, I might mention Griddlebone)
Are nothing more than agents for the Cat who all the time
50   Just controls their operations: the Napoleon of Crime![5]

---

4. Peke short for Pekingese, a small dog with long, silky hair and a pug nose.
5. the Napoleon of Crime criminal mastermind; emperor of crime—just as Napoleon Bonaparte
(1769–1821) was a masterful military strategist who had himself crowned emperor.

Vocabulary Builder
depravity (dē prav´ ə tē) *n.* crookedness; corruption

Reading Skill
Paraphrase Break down the sentence in lines 43–44 into three smaller sentences. Restate each sentence in your own words.

Apply the Skills

Poetry Collection 1

Thinking About the Selections

1. **Respond:** Which poem sounds best when read aloud? Why?
2. Fill out a three-column chart like the one shown. **(a) Recall:** In the first column, identify the decision faced by the speaker of "The Road Not Taken." **(b) Interpret:** In the second column, tell what other kinds of decisions this choice might represent.
   (c) Discuss: Share your chart with a partner. In the third column, explain how the message of the poem applies to people your age.

What Does It Say?	What Does It Mean?	Why Is It Important?

3. **(a) Recall:** According to "We never know how high we are," what happens when people are asked to rise to an occasion?
   (b) Interpret: According to the speaker of the poem, why is heroism not "a normal thing"?
4. **Speculate:** Which qualities of cats might have caused T. S. Eliot to associate them with criminal activities in "Macavity: The Mystery Cat"? Explain.

Literary Analysis

5. Identify two lines in "The Road Not Taken" that illustrate both **exact rhyme** and **end rhyme.** Explain your choices.
6. Which two words in line 31 of "Macavity: The Mystery Cat" illustrate both **slant rhyme** and **internal rhyme?**
7. **(a)** Use letters to identify the **rhyme scheme** in "We never know how high we are." **(b)** In what way does the shift in rhyme scheme midway through the poem help to signal a turning point in the poem's message?
8. **(a)** Which poem has lines with a more regular **meter,** "The Road Not Taken" or "We never know how high we are"? Explain.
   (b) Which do you find more enjoyable to read, lines with a regular meter or lines with an irregular meter? Explain.

Reading Skill

9. **(a) Paraphrase** the first stanza of "The Road Not Taken" by re-writing it as a series of sentences. **(b)** In what way does **breaking down long sentences** make this poem's meaning more clear?

QuickReview

Poems at a Glance
"The Road Not Taken" explains a crucial decision.
"We never know how high we are" explores the nature of heroism.
"Macavity: The Mystery Cat" describes a feline criminal mastermind.

Go Online
Assessment

For: Self-test
Visit: www.PHSchool.com
Web Code: epa-6409

Rhyme: repetition of sounds at the ends of words; types include *exact rhyme, slant rhyme, end rhyme,* and *internal rhyme.*
Rhyme Scheme: a regular pattern of end rhymes
Meter: the rhythmical pattern in a line of poetry
Paraphrasing: restating in your own words what someone else has written or said

Vocabulary Builder

Practice Decide if each statement is true or false. Then, explain.

1. Two people whose opinions *diverged* would be in disagreement.
2. Reporters are taught to *warp* the facts of events they cover.
3. *Bafflement* is a likely reaction to a bizarre event.
4. Laws are written to encourage *depravity* in society.

Adding Words to Your Vocabulary Using a thesaurus, find a synonym for the italicized words in the Practice. Use each synonym correctly in a sentence. (For more on using a thesaurus, see page R7.)

Writing

Write a **poem** using the same rhyme scheme as a poem in Collection 1.

- Choose a poem and identify its rhyme scheme.
- Decide on a topic, an event, an experience, or an emotion that you would like to be the subject of your poem.
- Brainstorm for a list of images, details, phrases, or words.
- Draft your lines, making them rhyme only after you have expressed your ideas and feelings.

Ask a classmate to identify your poem's rhyme scheme.

For *Grammar, Vocabulary,* and *Assessment,*
see **Build Language Skills,** pages 674–675.

Extend Your Learning

Listening and Speaking With classmates, hold a **panel discussion** about possible interpretations of a poem in Poetry Collection 1.

- Before you begin, state the purpose of the discussion.
- During the discussion, demonstrate effective listening by paraphrasing the others' comments. Then, express your own ideas clearly.
- Analyze and reflect on ideas while also paying close attention.

Reach a consensus—one acceptable to most people panelists. Present a position statement of this interpretation.

Research and Technology Assemble an **annotated electronic database** of texts by and about Robert Frost. Conduct research to make a list of biographies and criticism about Frost. Identify books Frost wrote and listen to recordings of his work. For each source, write a statement noting the kind and quality of information it offers.

Build Understanding • *Poetry Collection 2*

Connecting to the Literature

Reading/Writing Connection In "The Seven Ages of Man," one of Shakespeare's characters says that people play many different roles during their lives—taking on different identities, attitudes, relationships, and responsibilities at different ages. Make a list of what you think are the seven most important periods or ages in a person's life and give a reason for each. Use at least three of these words: *acquire, alter, cease, coincide, embody.*

Review
For **Literary Analysis, Reading Skill,** and **Vocabulary Builder,** see pages 656–657.

Meet the Authors

Robert **Frost** (1874–1963)
Fire and Ice (p. 667)
Like the title of his poem "Fire and Ice," Robert Frost seemed warm to some people, cold to other people. All agreed, however, that poetry came first in his life. Frost produced a large body of work and became the most popular American poet of his time, winning four Pulitzer Prizes.

E. E. **Cummings** (1894–1962)
maggie and milly and molly and may (p. 668)
Born in Cambridge, Massachusetts, Edward Estlin Cummings graduated from Harvard University. Both as poet and playwright, Cummings became notorious for his unconventional style, which reflected his individualistic outlook. Much of his work is playful and lyrical, and he often disregarded rules of grammar, spelling, and punctuation.

William **Shakespeare** (1564–1616)
The Seven Ages of Man (p. 671)
Shakespeare forged a perfect blend of high drama and exalted language. He wrote more than three dozen plays, and because of the timelessness of his themes and the beauty of his language, lines from his plays are quoted more often than those of any other writer. "The Seven Ages of Man" is considered one of his best speeches. (For more on William Shakespeare, see page 726.)

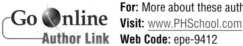

Go **O**nline
Author Link
For: More about these authors
Visit: www.PHSchool.com
Web Code: epe-9412

FIRE AND ICE

Robert Frost

Some say the world will end in fire,
Some say in ice.
From what I've tasted of desire
I hold with those who favor fire.
5   But if it had to perish twice,
I think I know enough of hate
To say that for destruction ice
Is also great
And would <u>suffice</u>.

Vocabulary Builder
suffice (sə fīs´) v. be
enough

maggie and milly and molly and may
E. E. Cummings

maggie and milly and molly and may
went down to the beach (to play one day)

and maggie discovered a shell that sang
so sweetly she couldn't remember her troubles, and

5   milly befriended a stranded star
whose rays five <u>languid</u> fingers were;

and molly was chased by a horrible thing
which raced sideways while blowing bubbles: and

may came home with a smooth round stone
10 as small as a world and as large as alone.

For whatever we lose (like a you or a me)
it's always ourselves we find in the sea

Vocabulary Builder
languid (laŋ´ gwid)
adj. drooping; weak

Literary Analysis
Rhyme What type of rhyme does Cummings use in the first and last stanzas?

▶ **Critical Viewing** How well does this photograph illustrate the "stranded star" in the poem? **[Evaluate]**

The Seven Ages of Man, Folger Shakespeare Library, Washington, D.C.

The Seven Ages of Man
William Shakespeare

All the world's a stage,
And all the men and women merely players:[1]
They have their exits and their entrances;
And one man in his time plays many parts,
5 His acts being seven ages. At first the infant,
Mewling[2] and puking in the nurse's arms.
And then the whining schoolboy, with his satchel,
And shining morning face, creeping like snail
Unwillingly to school. And then the lover,
10 Sighing like furnace, with a <u>woeful</u> ballad
Made to his mistress' eyebrow. Then a soldier,
Full of strange oaths, and bearded like the pard,[3]
Jealous in honor,[4] sudden and quick in quarrel,
Seeking the bubble reputation
15 Even in the cannon's mouth. And then the justice,[5]
In fair round belly with good capon[6] lined,
With eyes severe and beard of formal cut,
Full of wise saws and modern instances;[7]
And so he plays his part. The sixth age shifts
20 Into the lean and slippered pantaloon,[8]
With spectacles on nose and pouch on side,
His youthful hose[9] well saved, a world too wide
For his shrunk shank;[10] and his big manly voice,
Turning again toward childish <u>treble</u>, pipes
25 And whistles in his sound. Last scene of all,
That ends this strange eventful history,
Is second childishness, and mere oblivion,
Sans[11] teeth, sans eyes, sans taste, sans everything.

---

1. **players** actors.
2. **mewling** (myo͞ol′ iŋ) v. whimpering; crying weakly.
3. **pard** (pärd) n. leopard or panther.
4. **Jealous in honor** very concerned about his honor.
5. **justice** judge.
6. **capon** (kā′ pän′) n. roasted chicken.
7. **wise saws and modern instances** sayings and examples that show the truth of the sayings.
8. **pantaloon** (pan′ tə lo͞on′) n. thin, foolish old man who was a character in old comedies.
9. **hose** (hōz) n. stockings.
10. **shank** (shaŋk) n. leg.
11. **sans** (sanz) prep. without; lacking.

The Seven Ages of Man ■ 671

Literary Analysis
Meter What is the pattern of stressed and unstressed syllables in lines 2–4?

Vocabulary Builder
woeful (wō′ fəl) adj. full of sorrow
treble (treb′ əl) n. high-pitched voice

◀ **Critical Viewing**
How do the images in this stained-glass window add to your understanding of the poem? **[Relate]**

Apply the Skills

Poetry Collection 2

Thinking About the Selections

1. **Respond:** Which poem sounds best when read aloud? Why?
2. Fill out a three-column chart like the one shown. **(a) Recall:** In the first column, identify which emotions the speaker in "Fire and Ice" associates with fire and ice. **(b) Interpret:** In the second column, explain why fire and ice are fitting metaphors for these emotions. **(c) Discuss:** Share your chart with a partner. Then, in the third column, explain how the poem's message applies to teenagers.

What Does It Say?	What Does It Mean?	Why Is It Important?

3. **(a) Recall:** In "maggie and milly and molly and may," what experience does each character have? **(b) Connect:** How does each character's experience support the conclusion in the poem's final line?
4. **Assess:** Does "The Seven Ages of Man" in any way change your perspective about the stages of life? Why or why not?

Literary Analysis

5. Identify two lines in "maggie and milly and molly and may" that illustrate both **exact rhyme** and **end rhyme.** Explain your choices.
6. Which two words in line 17 of "The Seven Ages of Man" illustrate both **slant rhyme** and **internal rhyme?**
7. **(a)** Use letters to identify the **rhyme scheme** in "Fire and Ice." **(b)** In what way does the shift in rhyme scheme midway through the poem help to signal a turning point in the poem's message?
8. **(a)** Which poem has lines with a more regular **meter,** "Fire and Ice" or "The Seven Ages of Man"? Explain. **(b)** Which do you find more enjoyable to read, lines with a regular meter or lines with an irregular meter? Explain.

Reading Skill

9. **(a) Paraphrase** the first ten lines of "maggie and milly and molly and may" by rewriting them as a series of sentences. **(b)** In what way does **breaking down long sentences** make this poem's meaning more clear?

QuickReview

Poems at a Glance
"Fire and Ice" examines the destructive power of desire and hate.
"maggie and milly and molly and may" explores the significance of a trip to the sea.
"The Seven Ages of Man" presents a human life as having seven stages.

For: Self-test
Visit: www.PHSchool.com
Web Code: epa-6410

Rhyme: repetition of sounds at the ends of words; types include *exact rhyme, slant rhyme, end rhyme,* and *internal rhyme*

Rhyme Scheme: a regular pattern of end rhymes
Meter: the rhythmical pattern in a line of poetry
Paraphrasing: restating in your own words what someone else has written or said

Vocabulary Builder

Practice Decide if each statement is true or false. Then, explain.

1. If something will *suffice*, it will be satisfactory.
2. Coaches hope their players will be *languid* during a game.
3. A *woeful* sight is likely to inspire pity.
4. A *treble* is a deep sound like a foghorn.

Adding Words to Your Vocabulary Using a thesaurus, find a synonym for the italicized words in the Practice. Use each synonym correctly in a sentence. (For more on using a thesaurus, see page R7.)

Writing

Write a **poem** using the same rhyme scheme as a poem in Poetry Collection 2.
- Choose a poem and identify its rhyme scheme.
- Decide on a topic, an event, an experience, or an emotion that you would like to be the subject of your poem.
- Brainstorm for a list of images, details, phrases, or words.
- Draft your lines, making them rhyme only after you have expressed your ideas and feelings.

Ask a classmate to identify your poem's rhyme scheme.

For *Grammar, Vocabulary,* and *Assessment,*
see **Build Language Skills,** pages 674–675.

Extend Your Learning

Listening and Speaking With classmates, hold a **panel discussion** about possible interpretations of a poem in Poetry Collection 2.
- Before you begin, state the purpose of the discussion.
- During the discussion, demonstrate effective listening by paraphrasing the others' comments. Then express your own ideas clearly.
- Analyze and reflect on ideas while following the discussion.

Reach a consensus, one acceptable to most panelists. Present a position statement of this interpretation.

Research and Technology Assemble an **annotated electronic database** of texts by and about Robert Frost. Conduct research to make a list of biographies and criticism about Frost. Identify books Frost wrote and listen to recordings of his work. For each source, write a statement noting the kind and quality of information it offers.

Build Language Skills

Vocabulary Skill

Suffixes The word *witticism* contains the **suffix** *-ism,* which means "a condition of being" or "the result of" and forms nouns. *Witticism* is a noun that means "a clever or witty remark" and is based on *wit* or *witty.*

The suffix *-ize,* meaning "to engage in" or "to cause to be," forms verbs. For example, the word *stabilize* is the verb form of the noun *stable* and means "make stable."

Practice: In the following sentences, decide what part of speech is needed to complete the sentence. Supply a word ending in *-ism,* or *-ize.* You may choose a word from the list or supply one of your own. Explain your choices.

heroism   evolutionaize   symbolize   symbolism

1. Many people believed his _____ cost him the election.
2. This idea will _____ the system.
3. What do you think we can use to _____ this idea?
4. Her _____ in the face of such great danger made everyone admire her.
5. He liked the _____ in the story.

Grammar Lesson

An **infinitive** is a verb form preceded by the word *to* that acts as a noun, an adjective, or an adverb. An infinitive phrase is an infinitive with its modifiers or complements. Like infinitives, infinitive phrases can function as nouns, adjectives, or adverbs.

> **Infinitive:**
> To play requires patience and practice. (infinitive acting as a noun)
>
> **Infinitive Phrase:**
> Jeanne was not afraid <u>to speak her mind.</u> (infinitive acting as an adverb by modifying *afraid*)

Practice Identify the infinitive or infinitive phrase. Then, rewrite the sentence using a different infinitive or infinitive phrase.

1. The police wanted to get a statement from the owner.
2. Soon there were no more rabbits to chase.
3. They wanted to throw the debris overboard.
4. The airplane was designed to soar over the mountains.
5. Asking for help was her last hope to pass the test.

W͟G *Prentice Hall Writing and Grammar Connection: Chapter 21, Section 1.*

MorePractice

For more practice with infinitives and infinitive phrases, see the Grammar Handbook, p. R40.

Reading Skill: Paraphrase

Standards Assessed

• WL.1.02.2
• IR.2.04.3
• LT.5.01.2

(1) No wonder that Alexander carried the *Iliad* with him on his expeditions in a precious casket. (2) A written word is the choicest of relics. (3) It is something at once more intimate with us and more universal than any other work of art. (4) It is the work of art nearest to life itself. (5) It may be translated into every language, and not only be read but actually breathed from all human lips;—not be represented on canvas or in marble only, but be carved out of the breath of life itself. (6) The symbol of an ancient man's thought becomes a modern man's speech. (7) Two thousand summers have imparted to the monuments of Grecian literature, as to her marbles, only a maturer golden and autumnal tint, for they have carried their own serene and celestial atmosphere into all lands to protect them against the corrosion of time. (8) Books are the treasured wealth of the world and the fit inheritance of generations and nations.

—from *Walden* by Henry David Thoreau

1. The words "maturer golden and autumnal tint" can be paraphrased as
   A ancient and yellowed.
   B better and aged.
   C old and irrelevant.
   D important and overlooked.

2. The word "it" in sentence 4 refers to
   A Alexander.
   B a precious casket.
   C the written word.
   D a relic.

3. Sentence 7 can be briefly paraphrased as
   A time makes books better.
   B Grecian literature is important.
   C the corrosion of time applies to literature.
   D Grecian marble and Grecian literature are comparable.

4. Which of the following best states the main idea of the passage?
   A Sentence 1
   B Sentence 4
   C Sentence 7
   D Sentence 8

Timed Writing: Interpretation [Critical Stance]

Interpret Robert Frost's "The Road Not Taken" or "Fire and Ice." Identify the theme and support your interpretation with evidence from the text. **(40 minutes)**

Writing Workshop: *Work in Progress*

Response to Literature

Review your notes and write a one-sentence conclusion about that character. Or, describe in one sentence a connection between the character and an influential person in your own life experience. Use that sentence as the thesis for your response to literature.

Lyric Poetry

Lyric poetry is poetry with a musical quality in which the author expresses the thoughts and feelings of a single speaker. Unlike the author of a narrative poem, the author of a lyric does not try to tell a complete story. Instead, the poet describes an emotion or a mood, often by using vivid imagery, or language that appeals to the senses. A lyric poem is relatively short and in it, the poet usually achieves a single, unified effect.

Comparing Forms of Lyric Poetry: Sonnet, Haiku, and Free Verse

There are a variety of lyric forms that can create different effects:

- A **sonnet** is a fourteen-line poem that is usually written in iambic pentameter and usually rhymes. Two common sonnet types are the Italian, or Petrarchan, and the English, or Shakespearean. The chart shown describes an English, or Shakespearean, sonnet.
- A **haiku** is an unrhymed Japanese verse form arranged into three lines of five, seven, and five syllables. The author of a haiku often uses a striking image from nature to convey a strong emotion.
- A **free verse** poem does not follow a regular pattern of rhythm or rhyme. The author of free verse employs sound and rhythmic devices, such as alliteration and repetition, and may even use rhyme—but not in a regular pattern.

As you read, think about ways in which the form of the poem helps to shape or emphasize the poet's meaning.

Standard Course of Study

- Recognize and analyze the characteristics of literary genres. (LT.5.01.2)
- Explain and interpret archetypal characters, themes, settings. (LT.5.01.5)
- Summarize key events and/or points from literary text. (LT.5.03.6)

Shakespearean Sonnet
formatting: usually presented with no spaces between the stanzas, which are unified by their distinct ideas and rhyme schemes
three quatrains (four-line stanzas): each explores a different aspect of the poem's theme
final couplet: the two lines at the end of a sonnet present a concluding comment
rhyme scheme: the lines in each quatrain follow a regular pattern of *abab cdcd efef gg*

Vocabulary Builder

Women

- **stout** (stout) *adj.* sturdy (p. 678) *The wrestler was strong and had a <u>stout</u> build.*

I Hear America Singing

- **intermission** (in'tər mish'ən) *n.* any kind of break; more specifically, a break during a performance (p. 681) *Although I was thirsty, I waited until <u>intermission</u> to get a drink.*

Sonnet 30

- **woes** (wōz) *n.* great sorrows (p. 682) *Her troubles and <u>woes</u> are a real burden.*
- **wail** (wāl) *n.* lament; cry of deep sorrow (p. 682) *When the child saw her broken doll, she let out a prolonged <u>wail</u>.*

Build Understanding

Connecting to the Literature

Reading/Writing Connection These poems address a wide range of topics. List subjects that you think are suited to poetry. For each, write one sentence explaining why. Use three of these words: *signify, elaborate, emerge, stress, embrace.*

Meet the Authors

Alice **Walker** (b. 1944)

Alice Walker was born in Eatonton, Georgia. From the age of eight, she kept a journal and wrote poems. Today, Walker is an acclaimed novelist, short story writer, essayist, and poet. Her many works include the novel *The Color Purple,* which was made into a popular film.

Bashō (1644–1694) and **Chiyojo** (1703–1775)

One of the greatest Japanese poets, Bashō raised the haiku from a comic form to a high art. When he was young, he lived in luxury as the companion to the son of a lord. Later, he lived alone and devoted himself to haiku. Chiyojo was the wife of a samurai's servant. When her husband died, she became a nun and began studying poetry.

Walt **Whitman** (1819–1892)

American poet Walt Whitman celebrated the freedom of the individual and sang the praises of democracy. He published his first book of poetry, *Leaves of Grass,* at his own expense. Although it was a commercial failure, today *Leaves of Grass* is considered one of the most influential volumes in the history of American literature.

William **Shakespeare** (1564–1616)

English poet and playwright William Shakespeare is one of the most famous and beloved writers of all time. Experts believe Shakespeare possessed the largest vocabulary of any writer in history. His nearly forty plays, including *Romeo and Juliet, Hamlet,* and *Othello,* are still performed around the world, almost 400 years after his death.

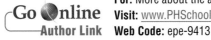

Go **Online**
Author Link

For: More about the authors
Visit: www.PHSchool.com
Web Code: epe-9413

Women

ALICE WALKER

Background In "Women," the speaker praises African American women who fought for public school desegregation in the American South. Until the 1950s, African American and white students attended different schools in the South. In 1954, the U.S. Supreme Court ruled that segregated public schooling was unconstitutional.

▲ **Critical Viewing**
Is the artist's attitude toward these women similar to the one expressed by the poet? **[Compare]**

They were women then
My mama's generation
Husky of voice—<u>Stout</u> of
Step
5 With fists as well as
Hands
How they battered down
Doors
And ironed
10 Starched white
Shirts
How they led
Armies
Headragged Generals
15 Across mined
Fields
Booby-trapped
Ditches
To discover books
20 Desks
A place for us
How they knew what we
Must know
Without knowing a page
25 Of it
Themselves.

Vocabulary Builder
stout (stout) *adj.* sturdy

Literary Analysis
Lyric Poetry Which words and images convey the women's determination to help their children? Explain.

THREE HAIKU

Daniel C. Buchanan, translator

Temple bells die out.
The fragrant blossoms remain.
A perfect evening!
                    —Bashō

Dragonfly catcher,
How far have you gone today
In your wandering?
                    —Chiyojo

Bearing no flowers,
I am free to toss madly
Like the willow tree.
                    —Chiyojo

Thinking About the Selections

1. **Respond:** Which of these poems do you like best? Why?

2. **(a) Recall:** In "Women," what do the women want to "discover" and for whom? **(b) Interpret:** In lines 22–26, why is the women's knowledge so remarkable?

3. **(a) Recall:** In Bashō's haiku, what dies out and what remains? **(b) Interpret:** To which senses does Bashō's haiku appeal? **(c) Analyze:** Why are these senses most appropriate in a poem about evening?

4. **Assess:** Would the first Chiyojo haiku be as effective if it were written as a statement rather than as a question? Explain.

5. **Explain:** In the second Chiyojo haiku, what impression does the speaker convey by comparing herself to a willow tree?

Reading:

Directions: *Read the selection. Then, answer the questions.*

> The poetry of earth is never dead:
> When all the birds are faint with the hot sun,
> And hide in cooling trees, a voice will run
> 4 From hedge to hedge about the new-mown mead;
> That is the Grasshopper's—he takes the lead
> In summer luxury,—he has never done
> With his delights; for when tired out with fun
> 8 He rests at ease beneath some pleasant weed.

> —from *On the Grasshopper and the Cricket*, by John Keats

1. What is taking place in lines 2–5?
  A While birds sit in cool trees, the Grasshopper sings.
  B Birds are fainting in the sun and you can hear someone mowing the field.
  C Birds are fainting, and the Grasshopper takes the lead.
  D A Grasshopper is hiding from the heat.

2. Line 8 can be paraphrased as
  A the Grasshopper hides from the birds.
  B the birds rest in the weeds.
  C the Grasshopper rests in the weeds.
  D the weeds are a good hiding place.

Directions: *Read the passage and answer the questions.*

(1) John Keats was born in London, England, on October 31, 1795. (2) His parents died when he was young, and Keats was brought up by relatives. (3) Leigh Hunt, an editor of the *Examiner,* published the first sonnets by Keats and introduced him to an influential circle of poets.

3. Sentence 2 could be rephrased as
  A Keats was brought up by his aunt after his parents died.
  B Keats's parents died young and then he was raised by his aunt.
  C Keats died young after being raised by relatives.
  D Keats's relatives took care of his parents after his death.

4. The words "influential circle" mean
  A a group of friends who wrote poetry.
  B the same religious group.
  C important people with a common bond.
  D people with connections.

5. When paraphrasing sentence 3,
  A the sentence should be broken down into three parts.
  B the appositive is necessary.
  C the appositive is not necessary.
  D the sentence should be combined with sentence 2.

Vocabulary

Standards Assessed

• IR.2.04.1
• LT.5.01.5
• GU.6.01.6

Directions: *Choose the word that best completes the sentence.*

6. **He used imagery to _____ the point of the poem.**
   A trivialize
   B derive
   C emphasize
   D mechanize

7. **The poem was so _____ that no one could understand it.**
   A distinct
   B emphasized
   C abstract
   D mechanized

8. **The poet's unusual _____ of familiar words was striking.**
   A abstraction
   B distinction
   C usage
   D mechanism

9. **The character's boasting was his defense _____.**
   A distinction
   B emphasis
   C mechanism
   D usage

10. **The poem contains two _____ images.**
   A trivia
   B derived
   C distinct
   D mechanized

Directions: *Use the definition of the suffix to choose the correct definition for the numbered word.*

11. **sterilize**
   A to make something sterile
   B the result of being sterile
   C the result of being destroyed
   D the condition of being sterile

12. **criticism**
   A to offer suggestions
   B related to literary writers
   C the act of making judgments
   D to disapprove

13. **acreage**
   A related to the size of a piece of land
   B to divide a piece of land
   C related to farming
   D farmland

14. **mechanize**
   A a part of a machine
   B to cause something to be done by machine
   C to make machines
   D a machine

15. **coverage**
   A to cause to be covered
   B to allow to be covered
   C the result of being covered
   D the condition of being covered

Spelling Workshop

 Standard Course of Study

• Edit for spelling and mechanics. (GU.6.02.4)

Words with Affixes

Affixes Prefixes and suffixes, called affixes, are part of many English words. The base word does not change when you add a prefix. Suffixes may cause a spelling change to the end of the base word as well as within the base word.

Suffixes and Spelling Changes Suffixes can be added to base words in a number of different ways. Often, they cause no spelling change to the base word. Sometimes, though, final *e*'s are dropped or final *y*'s change to *i*. The final consonant in a word may change as well, as in *suspend-suspension*. The trickiest changes occur when the internal spelling of the base word changes. Many of the words in this list fall into this final category, so make particular note of the spelling of those words.

Internal changes are always difficult operations.

Practice On your paper, write the word from the Word List that is related to each word below. Underline any places where a spelling change occurs when a suffix is added. Explain the changes.

1. generous
2. ecstasy
3. proclaim
4. maintain
5. accompany
6. pretend
7. pronounce
8. spontaneous
9. repeat
10. consume

Word List
accompaniment
proclamation
pronounceable
consumption
repetition
maintenance
generosity
ecstatic
spontaneity
pretentious

Monitor Your Progress

EOC Test Practice

Standards Assessed

• GU.6.02.4

A. Directions: *Write the letter of the sentence in which the underlined word is spelled correctly.*

1. **A** To achieve <u>spontaniety</u> in your piano playing, you must first practice.
   B <u>Repitition</u> of scales and simple pieces can help you improve.
   C <u>Accompaniement</u> from other instruments should not distract you.
   D One day, you will be <u>ecstatic</u> at your improvement.

2. **A** The mayor issued a new <u>proclaimation.</u>
   B It honored the <u>generosity</u> of volunteer helpers.
   C It praised the improvements made by <u>maintenence</u> workers.
   D It urged the <u>consumeption</u> of locally grown produce.

3. **A** Ida May often seems very <u>pretendsious.</u>
   B Her <u>pronounciation</u> of words like "to-mah-to" is laughable.
   C Her constant <u>repeatition</u> of "Really?" gets everyone irritated.
   D There is very little <u>spontaneity</u> in her speech or her ideas.

4. **A** My dad is on a <u>maintenance</u> diet to keep his weight down.
   B When he lost 40 pounds, he was <u>ecstastic.</u>
   C He still needs to watch his <u>consumpsion</u> of salty snacks.
   D Potato chips are his constant <u>accompanyment</u> when watching sports.

B. Directions: *Write the letter of the word that would be the correct spelling to fill in the blank.*

1. The governor's _____ established a new holiday.
   A proclaimation
   B proclamasion
   C proclaimasion
   D proclamation

2. The head of student council made a very _____ speech.
   A pretentious
   B pretendious
   C pretendsious
   D pretentous

3. My pet bird's _____ of food is amazing.
   A consumtion
   B consumeption
   C consumption
   D consumetion

4. The scientific term was not _____.
   A prononcable
   B pronounceable
   C pronunceable
   D pronownceable

5. A new language can be learned by constant _____.
   A repetition
   B repeatition
   C repitition
   D repetision

6. She often sings with no _____.
   A accompaniement
   B accompanyment
   C accompanement
   D accompaniment

Writing Workshop

Response to Literature

Standard Course of Study

- Use description, comparison, figurative language to elaborate ideas to inform audience (IR.2.02.4)
- Show appreciation for the significance of a personal account. (WL.1.01.3)

Often, our first reactions to creative works—poems, stories, songs, or films—are superficial: *I loved it! I hated it! I didn't get it!* By contrast, a formal **response to literature** gives you an opportunity to explore and explain the effects of a specific work. In doing so, you deepen your understanding of the work and also gain a greater appreciation of literary technique in general. Follow the steps in this workshop to write an essay in response to a literary selection of your choice.

Assignment Write a response to a work of literature that engages you as a reader.

What to Include Your response to literature should feature the following elements:

- an analysis of the work's content, its related ideas, and its effect on you
- a thesis statement that characterizes your response
- a focus on a single aspect or an overall view of the work
- evidence from the literary work or other texts to support the opinions you present
- error-free grammar, including correct usage when making comparisions

To preview the criteria on which your response to literature may be assessed, see the rubric on page 695.

Using the Form

You may use elements of this form in these types of writing:

- journals
- critical reviews
- literary analyses
- annotated bibliographies

Writing Workshop: *Work in Progress*

If you have completed the Work-in-Progress assignments, you have several ideas in your portfolio that you might pursue in your response to literature. You may continue to develop these ideas, or you might explore a new idea as you complete this Writing Workshop.

Reading ▸ *Writing* ◂ *Connection*

To get a feel for responses to literature, read the excerpt from *Nothing to Fear: Lessons in Leadership from FDR* by Alan Axelrod on page 515.

Prewriting

Choosing Your Topic

Make a top-ten list. Think of stories, poems, or other works of literature that you found memorable. Create a top-ten list of these titles and authors. Next to each entry, briefly note your initial reactions to the work and any ideas you might want to share about it. Review your list and choose one work as your topic.

Narrowing Your Topic

Clarify your purpose. Determine the specific purpose, or goal, of your essay. For example, you may want to share your enthusiasm for a new writer, find fresh insights into a well-known poem, or analyze the meaning of a short story. Write a statement of purpose for your essay. Use both the title and the author's name in your statement:

> **Example statement of purpose:** *In this essay, I will analyze the character of General Zaroff in Richard Connell's short story "The Most Dangerous Game."*

Identify types of details you will need. The purpose or goal of your essay determines the kinds of details you need to include. Consider these tips:
- **To praise,** include concrete details about what you liked.
- **To analyze,** back up your ideas with evidence from the selection.
- **To explain a personal response,** show how the work connects to your own experiences and ideas.

Gathering Details

Find supporting evidence. Return to the work of literature you have selected to find examples, excerpts, and direct quotations that relate to your topic. Prepare a series of index cards, with one card for every idea that you want to prove. Write your main point or idea across the top of the card. Underneath, write your notes on the details you gathered from the text to support that point or idea.

By breaking down the details and referring them back to your purpose, you will be able to present complex ideas in a sustained and compelling manner.

Work in Progress
Review the work you did on pages 651 and 675.

Identifying Supporting Evidence
What I want to prove:
General Zaroff's civilized exterior conceals a ruthless, heartless murderer.
How I can prove it:
His elegant castle is also a prison.

Writing Workshop

Drafting

Shaping Your Writing

Identify your thesis. Your draft should have a clear thesis statement that you will develop and support throughout your essay. Review your notes to draft a single sentence that combines the statement of purpose you wrote earlier with the ideas and evidence you have accumulated. Use this thesis statement to direct the writing of your essay.

> **Example thesis statement:** *In Richard Connell's short story "The Most Dangerous Game," the character of General Zaroff reveals the murderous mind lurking behind an illusion of refinement.*

Organize your ideas. Create an organizational chart like the one shown to present your ideas in a logical way. Be sure that your introduction includes your thesis and that every paragraph supports it.

Providing Elaboration

Consider your audience. The nature of your audience—who they are and what they know—influences the amount and kind of information you include in your response to literature. For example, if your audience already knows the work, limit the background information and proceed to your core ideas. If your audience is unfamiliar with the work, give more context and explanation.

Provide supporting details. Include evidence from the literary work for every claim you make in your essay. Consider these suggestions:

- **Quotations** can illustrate a character's attitude, a writer's word choice, or an essayist's opinion. Be sure that quotations are exact and enclosed in quotation marks.

- **Examples** of a character's actions or of a specific literary element can enhance your analysis.

- **Paraphrases,** or restatements in your own words, can help you explain a writer's theme, discuss the conflict, analyze a character, or clarify key ideas. Paraphrases must accurately reflect the original text.

Avoid padding your draft with irrelevant passages or unnecessary summaries of the plot.

Organize Your Ideas

Introduction
- Grab attention
- Identify author and title
- Offer brief summary
- State thesis

Body
- Present supporting ideas
- Introduce each new idea in a new paragraph
- Use details to support each idea

Conclusion
- Restate thesis
- Make a final point or present a final question or insight

From the Author's Desk

Pat Mora

Pat Mora

On Responding to Literature

Many of my best teachers are authors I will never meet. In the essay "Unseen Teachers," I explore how authors help me experience the world more intensely. Literature and all forms of art can make us more human.

This passage from the essay was inspired by a quotation from Southwest artist Georgia O'Keeffe saying that she was trying to prompt the viewer to notice. As I tried to show, writers who see their work as part of a group's struggle for justice do the same.

"I love words and their interweavings."
—Pat Mora

Professional Model:

from "Unseen Teachers," from *Nepantla*

I still smile at her [Georgia O'Keeffe's] laughing confession that by painting huge flowers, she forced us to notice. . . .

I love art and often get ideas in museums. Many readers know O'Keeffe's paintings of flowers. Here, they make my thesis colorful and concrete.

We too seek to force a society to notice the bitter and the sweet. Often we both participate in our communities and are solitary writers, a tension. The mere cover of Denise Levertov's *The Poet in the World* reminds me of her firm conviction: "Both life and poetry fade, wilt, shrink when they are divorced." Lorna Dee Cervantes, Sandra Cisneros, Alice Walker, Lucille Clifton, Amy Tan, Joy Harjo, and Linda Hogan are thick in the struggle of their people, and their writing is part of that struggle. Though the daily realities—high dropout rates, low per capita income, high unemployment— continue, these women teach me that the arrangement and rearrangement of work on the page is neither elitist nor irrelevant. It is the appropriate task of the person who weaves words for people's use.

I debated what names to include and what realities to list. These authors support the diversity that's a theme for the book.

Braids or weaves I wondered? Both, like writing, are hand activities. I chose weaves because weavers create both basic items of clothing and beautiful art pieces.

Writing Workshop

Revising

Revising Your Overall Structure

Revise to eliminate unnecessary information. Review your draft to identify instances in which the information you provide may distract from your main idea.

- Underline your thesis and the main ideas of each paragraph.
- Highlight sentences that do not support your thesis.
- Consider revising details to make a tighter connection to your main idea.
- Eliminate any paragraphs or details that do not clearly contribute to your analysis.

To read the complete student model, see page 694.

> **Student Model: Cutting Unnecessary Details**
>
> When we first encounter General Zaroff, our initial reaction is one of delight and admiration for his wealth and charm. Zaroff lives in a massive castle, feasts on the finest delicacies, and wears expensive clothes. ~~He had previously been in the army and his strong personality has a frightening quality.~~

The writer eliminates this sentence because it does not support his main point.

Revising Your Word Choice

Check words of praise or criticism. Review your response to literature, making sure your word choices are precise and that they accurately reflect both your purpose and your attitude to the literary work.

Vague: This *factual* account of the author's life is *interesting* to read.

Precise: This *honest* account of the author's life *captures* the reader's attention.

In addition, pay close attention to the degree, or form, of the adjectives you use, especially when making comparisons. Use the degree that accurately reflects your meaning.

Comparative degree: Zaroff is a *more disagreeable* character than Rainsford. *(Compares two items)*

Superlative degree: Zaroff is the *most disagreeable* character in the story. *(Compares more than two items)*

Peer Review: Exchange drafts with a partner. Review each other's work, circling words that convey approval or criticism or express degrees of comparison. Determine whether you have used these words correctly and whether they are precise or vague. Then, revise your draft, replacing vague, dull, or incorrect language with choices that pinpoint your meaning.

Integrating Grammar Skills

Revising Common Usage Problems

Many students frequently misuse certain words and expressions.

Usage Problems With *Among* **and** *Between*. *Among* and *between* are not interchangeable. *Among* always implies three or more elements. *Between* is generally used only with two elements. *Between* should be followed either by a plural (between trips; between friends) or by two expressions joined by *and*—not by *or* or *to*.

Prentice Hall Writing and Grammar Connection: Chapter 27, Section 2

> **Among:** Panic swept *among* the crew of Rainsford's yacht.
> **Between:** Rainsford had to choose *between* fleeing and dying.

Usage Problems With *Like, As,* **and** *As If Like* is a preposition meaning "similar to" or "such as." It should not be used in place of *as, as if,* or *as though,* which are conjunctions that introduce clauses.

> **As:** Rainsford fled, just *as* Zaroff had planned.
> **As if:** It looks *as if* it might rain.

Like is properly used as a preposition in phrases of comparison.

> **Like:** In his basic nature, Zaroff is *like* a predator. *Like* Rainsford, I too came to despise Zaroff.

Fixing Errors To fix usage problems, follow these steps:

1. **Revising usage problems with** *among* **and** *between:*
    - Identify the number of elements involved.
    - Use *between* with phrases involving two elements.
    - Use *among* with phrases involving three or more elements.

2. **Revising usage problems with** *like, as, as if,* **or** *as though:*
    - Determine how you are using the word.
    - If *like* is used to make a comparison, the usage is correct.
    - If you have used *like* to introduce a clause, replace it with the conjunction *as, as if,* or *as though.*

Apply It to Your Editing

Review the first page of your essay and highlight any uses of *between, among, like, as,* and *as if.* Use the methods described to revise any incorrect usage.

Writing Workshop

Student Model: Jeff Rutherford
Broken Arrow, OK

Characterization of General Zaroff

The title indicates that the essay will focus on a single character.

What lies at the heart of a refined man? In Richard Connell's short story "The Most Dangerous Game," the deranged, yet cunning and elegant, General Zaroff shares his taste for hunting with an unsuspecting visitor. Although he is civilized in his dress and habits, Zaroff's beliefs reveal a murderous mind behind the illusion of a charming, charismatic man.

Jeff uses strong language to state his thesis clearly.

When we first encounter General Zaroff, our initial reaction is one of delight and admiration for his wealth and charm. Zaroff lives in a massive castle, feasts on the finest delicacies, and wears expensive clothes. His luxurious surroundings and lifestyle reflect a highly civilized, eloquent, and proper gentleman. As readers soon learn, however, there is more to Zaroff than food and elegance.

Beneath Zaroff's fine qualities lies an overwhelming attitude of arrogance. This attitude comes from his firm belief that his way of thinking is superior to that of the average person. Zaroff also fancies himself a phenomenal hunter: "My hand was made for the trigger," he claims. It is this deadly mixture of arrogance, superior hunting skills, and belief that it is natural for the strong to prevail over the weak that makes him disregard the value of human life.

Direct quotations provide evidence for this understanding of Zaroff.

Zaroff's extreme beliefs lead him to conclude that only the intelligent mind of a human being can provide him with the dangerous game he desires. Rationalizing that "the weak were created to please the strong," he chooses to hunt humans instead of animals. Unfortunately, Rainsford steps into this situation. The major conflicts in "The Most Dangerous Game" demonstrate what happens during such an inhumane hunt.

However, the general's arrogance and disregard for human life blind him to the fear and desperation of his prey. His attitude leads to his own demise at the hands of Rainsford, his prey. The characterization of Zaroff as a murderer hiding behind a mask of civility shows that beneath even the most beautiful rose can lie a sharp and deadly thorn.

Jeff concludes his response with an analogy that neatly summarizes his analysis.

Editing and Proofreading

Check your draft for errors in format, grammar, and punctuation.
Focus on Direct Quotations: Make sure that the direct quotations that you have taken from the work of literature are accurate and enclosed by quotation marks. Use an indented block style—without quotation marks—when quoting a passage of more than ten lines.

Publishing and Presenting

Consider one of the following ways to share your writing.
Deliver an oral presentation. Read your response to literature aloud. Have a copy of the literary work on hand in the event that your classmates wish to read or review it.
Publish a collection of responses to literature. Gather the essays of several of your classmates. Organize them in a binder and make the collection available in the school library.

Reflecting on Your Writing

Writer's Journal Think about the experience of writing a response to literature. Begin by answering these questions:

- What fresh insights about the work did you discover as you prepared your response? Explain.
- If you could begin this writing process again, what might you do differently? Why?
- After writing your response, what questions about the literary work do you still have? How might you answer these questions?

Prentice Hall Writing and Grammar Connection: Chapter 13

Rubric for Self-Assessment

To assess your response to literature, use the following rubric:

NC Criteria	Rating Scale
	not very very
Focus: How clear is your thesis statement?	1 2 3 4 5
Organization: How thoroughly do you analyze the work's content, ideas, or effect on the reader?	1 2 3 4 5
Support/Elaboration: How effectively do you include evidence from the literary work?	1 2 3 4 5
Style: How clearly do you use words of praise or criticism?	1 2 3 4 5
Conventions: How correct is your grammar, especially your use of *among* and *between,* and *like* and *as?*	1 2 3 4 5

Oral Interpretation of Literature

As you prepare your interpretation, you will deepen your understanding of a literary work. In presenting the interpretation, you will share your appreciation with others. The following strategies can help you prepare and deliver your oral interpretation.

 Standard Course of Study

- Consider the audience's degree of knowledge in explaining procedures. (IR.2.03.1)
- Interpret literary devices. (LT.5.01.3)
- Explain and interpret archetypal characters, themes, settings. (LT.5.01.5)

Preparing the Interpretation

Understand the literature. Your interpretation should be based on an accurate understanding of the literary work's content and meaning. Make sure you are thoroughly familiar with your selection.

Rehearse the interpretation. Make a copy of the literary work on which to write performance notes. Plan and practice appropriate gestures, facial expressions, intonations, and timing until they feel natural. If certain words or phrases become stumbling points, memorize them to assure confidence and poise. Always practice aloud. Use the checklist shown here to help you prepare.

Consider your audience. Provide context to help you audience better understand the literary work you are presenting. Write an introduction to help your readers visualize the situation and characters you may also include information about the author and the circumstances in which he or she wrote the selection.

Giving the Interpretation

Your familiarity with the selection should give you the freedom to maintain eye contact with your audience as you read.

Reading poetry. Use the poem's punctuation, not the ends of lines, as cues to pause when reading. Avoid lapsing into sing-song rhythms; instead, maintain a flow that sounds like natural speech. Vary your volume and pace to create emphasis.

Reading stories and plays. When expressing a character's quoted words, use a change in intonation to distinguish speech from narration. Modulate your vocal inflections, facial expressions, and posture to indicate whether a speaker is male or female, adult or child.

Oral Interpretation Tips

- Read the text multiple times.
- Mark performance notes and cues on your reading copy.
- Choose appropriate gestures, costumes, and props to suggest characters or situations.
- Vary your pace and tone of voice to create emphasis.

Activity ▶ **Prepare and Deliver an Oral Interpretation** ▶ Choose a favorite poem, story, or play and prepare an oral interpretation using the strategies outlined above. After presenting the interpretation to your class, ask your classmates to evaluate how well the presentation reflected the content and meaning of the work of literature.

The Canterbury Tales

Geoffrey Chaucer

Globe Ferron, 1995

Book of Tales The classic collection of tales told by fictional pilgrims from all walks of life is translated here into modern English. The stories range from the funny to the bitter, giving an expansive view of life in Chaucer's day.

Poems by Robert Frost: A Boy's Will and North of Boston

Robert Frost

Signet, 2001

Collection These first two collections of poetry by one of America's most beloved poets bring the people and the landscape of rural New England to life. Frost introduces characteristic themes—the value of manual labor, the beauty of nature, the individual versus the community—and experiments with narrative poetry and blank verse.

Alice in Wonderland

Lewis Carroll

Novel Alice falls into a strange world that has some odd parallels to our own. The rabbit, who is always late, the queen, who is always yelling, and Alice's own confusion will strike a familiar chord in many students.

The Complete Poetry of Edgar Allan Poe

Edgar Allan Poe

Collection The poems that have delighted and frightened generations of readers are collected in this anthology. Included are the poems famous for their psychological impact such as "The Raven" and "The Bells."

These titles are available in the Penguin/Prentice Hall Literature Library.
Consult your teacher before choosing one.

Think About It Looked at one way, music has nothing to do with fame or fortune. We sing at holidays and we dance at weddings. We celebrate in songs, and we lament our losses. Music is a personal expression and a reflection of life. However, music is also big business. A hit song can earn its composer millions of dollars. In this story, these two views of music come into conflict for one sad man.

The Serenade in Nine Innings

Judith Ortiz Cofer

It seems that my father had a dream as a young man—of having a song he wrote recorded. It was not a love song or a song about love betrayed, which is the prime topic of Puerto Rican popular music; it was instead a lyrical piece about the only activity that gave him pure joy: baseball. He had been, at eighteen, a star pitcher for his high-school team, but then he broke his ankle in a collision with another player. The song was a dirge, a mournful hymn to his moment of glory, too soon gone; a melody sent into space like a time capsule to preserve a moment. My father played a few chords on an old guitar and sang it to his compañeros at Chavo's cafeteria one afternoon while he rested his swollen foot on a shoeshine stool. It was fiesta week in the pueblo, so there were also many strangers present—itinerant musicians, who made the circuit of festivals around the island. Some of these men congratulated my father on his fine composition; in fact, it was their compliments that planted the seed of hope in his heart. For weeks, as he recuperated and courted my mother, he perfected the lyrics and set them to a simpler melody, one that reflected the feelings of yearning he had after meeting her. And she traded her heart for his song.

It was the week when they announced their engagement that he heard it—his song—played on the radio. Of course it had a different title—not "Serenade in Nine Innings," later to be referred to by him simply as "La Serenata," a title he had finally settled on after much thought. The rhythm had been speeded up so now it sounded more like a mambo rather than the bolero he had intended it to be. He had his friends listen to it, and they all agreed it was "Serenade" and it had been stolen! My father took a bus to the radio station in Ponce, pushed and harangued his way to the manager, who laughed in his face when he heard the story, dismissing him with "Go home and write another hit tune, son, and I'll believe you."

No one outside the pueblo ever believed him, of course. And he never tried writing another song, as far as I know. But for years, he noted how many times he heard the song played, computing in a series of ledgers how much money it had made for the thieves. In due time the story of his near brush with fame and fortune, the lost dream, became his cuento for life.

Meet the Author
Judith Ortiz Cofer (b. 1952) spent her childhood shuttling back and forth between her birthplace of Puerto Rico and her home in Paterson, New Jersey. The two cultures of her childhood would later have a profound impact on Ortiz Cofer's writing, which includes poetry, essays, novels, short stories, and creative nonfiction.

Readings in Contemporary Literature
Talk About It

Use these questions to guide a discussion of this story.

1. **(a)** What did the father do after he broke his ankle and was unable to play baseball? **(b)** What "seed of hope" did the musicians' compliments plant in his heart?

2. **(a)** How did the radio station manager respond to the father's protest? **(b)** What did the father never do again? **(c)** In addition to the song, what else was taken from him?

3. In a group, discuss the role that hope and striving can play in one's life.
   - What became the father's *cuento* for life?
   - How else might the father have reacted to this setback?
   - Have you ever done something for which you did not receive credit? Were you able to feel proud anyway? Explain.

   Choose a point-person to share your group's ideas with the class.

Drama

Unit 5 Overview

PART 1: Summarizing
PART 2: Drawing Conclusions

NC **Standard Course of Study**
In This Unit You Will

- Identify, evaluate, and analyze the impact of text components. (WL.1.03.2)
- Analyze the effects of author's craft and style in informing audience. (IR.2.01.9)
- Use layout and design elements to enhance presentation of procedure. (IR.2.03.4)
- Report the research for a specified audience. (IR.2.04.4)
- Use reading strategies for preparation, engagement,reflection. (LT.5.01.1)
- Explain and interpret archetypal characters, themes, settings. (LT.5.01.5)
- Use vocabulary strategies to discern word meanings. (GU.6.01.6)

Introduction
Drama

Gary L.
Blackwood

Gary L. Blackwood

Talks About the Form

I consider myself, in all modesty, fairly successful as a playwright. Yet, even in a good year, only about ten percent of the money I make comes from productions of my plays; the other ninety percent is from my novels and nonfiction books.

So why, you may ask—as my wife often does—do I bother writing **drama** at all? Why not just devote all my time and effort to books?

▲ **Gary L. Black-wood** has written more than twenty novels and nonfiction books for young readers, in addition to several plays.

When the House Lights Go Down

The short answer is, "Because I love the theater." During high school and college, and for several years afterward, I was mainly interested in **acting.** But when my first play was produced I discovered that performing in someone else's play wasn't nearly as much fun as watching other people perform my play. (Actually, I ended up acting in my own play when the lead got sick, but that's another story.)

It's a great feeling, of course, to see a new book in print for the first time, or to get a glowing review or an enthusiastic fan letter. But it doesn't compare to the feeling you get when the house lights go down and the stage lights come up and **actors** start saying **dialogue** that you created and the **audience** responds with laughter or, better yet, with rapt silence.

▲ **Critical Viewing** Blackwood describes the excitement of hearing his words spoken by actors. How does this illustration suggest the way actors bring a text to life? **[Connect]**

Drama: Actual People Doing Actual Things

I experience that same sort of excitement even when the drama or comedy I'm watching isn't mine. As indispensable as books and movies are, the theater offers something they don't: No matter how skimpy the **set** is, no matter how much the dialogue differs from everyday speech, you still get the sensation that what's taking place onstage is real. And it is. It's not just images projected on a screen, or letters printed on a page. It's actual people doing actual things and actually speaking, with no quotation marks, no description, no exposition, no soundtrack.

Never the Same

Because it's live, not printed or recorded, you can never see the same play twice. Each **performance** is different. And a large part of what makes it different is the audience. Our reaction to the play actually contributes to it, influences it.

After you experience any work of art, you have that moment of asking yourself, "From this I've learned . . . what?" . . . That's the bottom line question, and I believe that artists have a responsibility to address that—of course, not giving an answer, but at least giving an audience comfort with the realization that we're all wrestling with the same questions.

from an interview in The Dramatist

—Israel Horovitz

Another reason I love the theater is that it tends to challenge its audience more than books and movies do. I think most playwrights—including Israel Horovitz, who is quoted here—are less interested in offering an escape from real life than they are in reflecting real life and commenting on it.

More About Gary L. Blackwood

Before Gary L. Blackwood (b. 1945) adapted his popular novel *The Shakespeare Stealer* for the stage, he had written some notable plays: *Dark Horse*, a prizewinning courtroom drama, and *The Count of One*, a drama about the use of hypnotism. One of his books of historical fiction, *The Year of the Hangman*, is set in Colonial America. *Beyond the Door*

Fast Facts

▶ Blackwood attended a one-room schoolhouse where the library consisted of a single small bookcase He sold his first story when he was nineteen.

Exploring Drama

Elements of Drama

A drama, or play, is a story written to be performed by actors. It features **characters** facing a **conflict,** or struggle, that propels the sequence of events called the **plot.** The conflict reaches a **climax,** the point of greatest tension, and is then resolved. The **dialogue,** or speeches of the characters, tells the story, and not, as in fiction, the voice of a narrator.

These elements are specific to drama:

- **Acts** and **scenes** are the basic units of drama. A drama may consist of one or more acts, each of which may contain any number of scenes.

Drama coach.

- The author of a play, called the **playwright,** provides the **script,** or text, of a play. The script contains both dialogue and stage directions.

- **Stage directions** tell how the work is to be performed, or staged. Providing details about sets, lighting, sound effects, props, costumes, and acting, directions are often printed in italics and set off in brackets. Some playwrights use abbreviations to provide additional direction about where on or offstage a speech may be delivered. These include O.S. for offstage; D.S.; for downstage, or close to the audience; and U.S. for upstage, or far from the audience.

- **Sets** are the constructions indicating where the drama takes place. A set may include painted backdrops, wooden frames, and other elements.
- **Props** are movable objects, like swords or pens, that actors use onstage.

All the elements of drama combine in performance to produce the vivid illusion of reality known as **dramatic effect.** Through this effect, the dramatist explores a **theme,** or insight into life.

Types of Drama and Dramatic Speech

The ancient Greeks, who developed drama, created two types of plays:

- A **tragedy** shows the downfall or death of the **tragic hero,** or main character. In ancient Greek drama, the hero was an outstanding person brought low by a **tragic flaw,** a mistaken action or defect in character. In modern tragedy, the hero can be an ordinary person destroyed by an evil in society. Greek tragedy included a **chorus,** a group of performers who commented on the action. William Shakespeare sometimes used a single actor to perform the role of the chorus.

- A **comedy** has a happy ending, usually after an amusing series of predicaments. While tragedy emphasizes human greatness, comedy stresses the weaknesses of ordinary people or of society itself.

For both kinds of drama, you sometimes need to understand the **historical context,** the background of the era in which the play is set or written. In addition to dialogue involving conversations between two or more characters, dramatists use these types of **dramatic speech:**

- A **monologue** is a long, uninterrupted speech delivered by a character to other characters who are onstage but remain silent.
- A **soliloquy** is a speech in which a character alone on stage reveals private thoughts and feelings that the audience is allowed to overhear.
- An **aside** is a brief remark in which a character expresses private thoughts to the audience rather than to other characters.

▲ **Critical Viewing**
What type of dramatic speech do you think the actors shown here might be delivering? Explain. **[Analyze]**

Check Your Understanding

Choose the letter of the answer that best completes each numbered item.

1. The sequence of events in a play is the   **a.** tragedy   **b.** plot
2. A flawed, noble character is vital to a   **a.** theme   **b.** tragedy
3. Unlike tragedy, comedy has a   **a.** happy ending   **b.** dialogue
4. Costume details are found in   **a.** monologues   **b.** stage directions
5. A brief remark made to the audience is   **a.** an aside   **b.** a soliloquy

From the Author's Desk
Gary Blackwood Introduces *The Shakespeare Stealer*

Adapting my young adult novel *The Shakespeare Stealer* for the stage was a whole new experience for me. I'd written plenty of original plays, and even turned novels by other authors into plays, but I'd never tried to dramatize one of my own books.

From the Page to the Stage

It's not an easy thing to do. When you're the author of the book, your tendency is to try to put as much of it as possible into the play. My first draft was over two hours long and had roughly twenty **characters**. The problem was, the theater that initially produced it wanted a one-hour play that could be performed by nine actors.

So I set to work cutting cherished **scenes** (including the sword battle with the thieves, which appears in the first **act** of the play), giving the boot to beloved characters, and doubling—having each actor play several roles. I kept on cutting right up until opening night.

No Horses or Rivers on the Set!

The second theater to produce it wanted a full-length play. Back went most of the deleted scenes, plus some new ones. Naturally, even in a longer version, I couldn't keep everything from the novel. I couldn't very well have the actors on horseback, for example, or practically drowning in the Thames River, as they do in the book.

To simplify matters and make the play move quickly, I kept the number of scene changes to a minimum, and let a single **set**—called a unit set—represent several different locations.

Historical Context: Re-creating Another Time Period

Despite all this, the play is very demanding technically. The **historical context** is just as important as it is in the book. In the book, however, I could get away with an occasional brief description of the clothing, the Globe Theatre, the sword fighting moves, etc. On the stage all that has to actually be re-created from brief **stage directions** included in the **script**. So the actors have to cope with early seventeenth-century costumes and **props**, learn Elizabethan sword fighting techniques, and approximate London and Yorkshire accents.

from The Shakespeare Stealer

Gary Blackwood

Characters

* SANDER COOKE
* DR. TIMOTHY BRIGHT, 50s or 60s
* WIDGE, 14
* FALCONER/SIMON BASS (must be played by the same actor), 30s or 40s
* THIEF #1, 30s
* THIEF #2, 30s
* THIEF #3, late teens
* LIBBY, 40s–60s

Prologue

SANDER: I bid you welcome. For an hour or so
I ask you to imagine, if you will,
That this poor stage is not a stage at all
But England, some four hundred years ago.
That the actors who—I hope—will soon appear
Are something more than they appear to be,
That they are not mere shadows on a stage
But men and women of another age.

▲ **Critical Viewing**
What does the actor's expression suggest about Widge's feelings at this moment? **[Interpret]**

Act I

At the rear of the playing area is a shallow, two-story set with a narrow flight of steps leading to the upper story. In the center of the upper story is a single wide doorway draped with a curtain. The lower story has two smaller openings, one at Left and one at Right, also covered by curtains. At various times, this set will represent DR. TIMOTHY BRIGHT'S *apothecary, with* WIDGE'S *living quarters upstairs;* SIMON BASS'S *house; and the backstage area at the Globe Theatre.*

At Lights Up, it is DR. BRIGHT'S *apothecary in Berwick-in-Elmet, Yorkshire, c. 1601. A table at Center contains glass and earthenware jars and beakers. One of the containers bubbles over a pot filled with burning pitch.* WIDGE *sits on a stool at the table, copying something from a small bound notebook onto loose sheets of paper, using a plumbago pencil—a stick of graphite wrapped in paper, similar to a grease pencil or charcoal pencil.* WIDGE *is a slight boy of fourteen with a "pudding basin" or bowl haircut. He wears a working-class tunic.*

All is quiet and peaceful for a long moment. Then the audience is startled by the entrance of DR. TIMOTHY BRIGHT, *a florid, overweight man in his forties or fifties, who is slightly deaf. He strides on brandishing a walking stick, and roaring—but he is nearly as comical as he is menacing.*

BRIGHT: You! . . . clod-pated drivel! (WIDGE *reacts, knocking a beaker to the floor, where it shatters, enraging* BRIGHT *even more*) You . . . halfwitted hoddypeak! Do you know what you've done?!

WIDGE: (*Puts the table between himself and* BRIGHT) I—I didn't mean to! I'll clean it up at once!

BRIGHT: Not *that*, you simpleton! This! (*He waves a paper about*) It's from the bishop's secretary. I've been accused of stealing sermons from my fellow rectors! How in heaven's name did the bishop get wind of this? Have you let a hint drop to anyone of what you were up to? Anyone at all?

WIDGE: Nay, I never! So help me God and halidom!

BRIGHT: Has anyone shown any signs of suspecting you?

WIDGE: Nay, no one.

BRIGHT: You're lying. No, don't bother to deny it. I've the proof here. The rector at Leeds caught you red-handed. Isn't that so? Isn't that so?

(*murmurs*) Aye.

BRIGHT: What's that? Speak up, boy!

Drama
Stage Directions
Blackwood's detailed descriptions of set and props reinforce the time setting of the play.

WIDGE: Aye! It was a fortnight ago. 'A spotted me scribbling away, and afore I could make me escape, 'a collared me and snatched away me table-book!

BRIGHT: Why did you not tell me this sooner?

WIDGE: I was afeared. I kenned you'd be angry.

BRIGHT: You were right. But . . . if he took away your transcription of his sermon, then . . . then whose sermon was it that I . . . (*he doesn't want to say "stole"*) . . . used as my model last Sunday?

WIDGE: Well . . . I—I wrote it all out as best I could remember . . .

BRIGHT: You? I delivered a sermon composed by my idle-headed apprentice? You deceitful little whelp! When will you learn not to lie to me? Well, by St. Pintle, I'll teach you right from wrong! Come here! (WIDGE *dodges the man's grasp, circling the table, but then he slips on the contents of the broken beaker, and is caught.* BRIGHT *raises the stick as if to strike;* WIDGE *cowers and flinches. But then* BRIGHT *tosses him aside and, puffing with the exertion, plops down on the stool*) Ahh, what's the use of it? If I haven't beaten some sense into you by now, I never will. (*shakes his head*) When I think of all I've done for you, all the years I've invested in you. When I took you in five years ago—

WIDGE: Seven.

BRIGHT: Eh? What's that?

WIDGE: It's been seven years, sir.

BRIGHT: That's beside the point. When I took you in, you were a <u>feckless</u>, illiterate orphan with no prospects whatever in the world. I taught you to read and cipher, taught you about medicine, even taught you my system of swift writing, and this is what I get in return? (*waves the paper*) If someone were to offer it, I'd sell your services for a farthing; it's far more than you're worth. Yes, and I expect you'd jump at the chance to change masters, wouldn't you? Eh? (*The way* WIDGE *hangs his head makes it clear that he would*) Well, all I can say is, be careful what you wish for, boy. There are far worse places than this, believe me, and far worse masters than me.

WIDGE: (*aside*) Aye, the Devil, for one.

BRIGHT: What's that?

Gary Blackwood
Author's Insight
Unless you use a narrator, everything in a play has to be conveyed through dialogue. In the book, the information in this scene is revealed through exposition, an explanation of background material.

Vocabulary Builder
feckless (fek´ lis) *adj.*
careless; irresponsible

Reading Check

What has Bright been accused of stealing?

◄ **Critical Viewing** How does Widge's posture and attitude reflect his feelings about Dr. Bright? [**Connect**]

WIDGE: Nothing. (*He sets about cleaning up the broken beaker, while* BRIGHT *checks his boiling potion. The silence is broken by the sound of an iron door knocker pounding O.S. Right*)

BRIGHT: Yes, yes, coming. Bloody patients. Why can't they be sick in the daytime? (*He crosses to Left, reaches O.S to open a door, then backs up as* FALCONER *enters, a tall figure in a hooded cloak, looking as grim as Death. Beneath the cloak he carries a rapier. We seldom see his face, but when he does reveal a glimpse of it, we see that he has a bushy, dark beard and a hooked nose. A nasty scar disfigures one side of his face*) G-good evening, sir. How may I serve you?

FALCONER: (*seems to reach for his rapier, but instead takes a leather bound book from beneath his cloak. In a deep, almost spectral voice*) This is yours, is it not?

BRIGHT: (*moves hesitantly closer to the man*) Why, yes. Yes, it is. It's a copy of my book on charactery.

FALCONER: Does it work?

BRIGHT: I beg your pardon?

FALCONER: Your system of charactery. Does it work?

BRIGHT: Of course it works. Using my system of swift writing, one may without effort transcribe the written or the spoken word—

FALCONER: How long does it take?

BRIGHT: As I was about to say, one may set down speech as rapidly as it is spoken—

FALCONER: (*impatient*) Yes, yes, but how long to learn it?

BRIGHT: Well, that depends upon the aptitude of the—

FALCONER: How long?

BRIGHT: (*nervously, stretching the truth*) Oh, two months, perhaps three. Well, let's say four. Five, at the outside.

FALCONER: (*tosses the book rather contemptuously onto the table*) To how many have you taught this system of yours?

BRIGHT: Let me see . . . There's my apprentice, here, and then.

FALCONER: How many?

BRIGHT: Well . . . one, actually.

FALCONER: And how proficient is he?

Drama
Staging Detailed description of Falconer provides valuable information for both costumers and actors when staging the play.

Vocabulary Builder
spectral (spek´ trəl) *adj.* like a phantom or ghost

Gary Blackwood
Author's Insight
Since dialogue comes more easily to me than narrative and description, there are long passages of it in my novels. Scenes like this one are taken almost directly from the book.

Literature in Context | Culture Connection

Shorthand and Speedwriting

Dr. Timothie Bright was a real person who developed a "swift-writing" system in 1588. Efforts to create a fast way of recording speech go back more than 2,000 years.

- In 63 B.C., Marcus Tiro invented a system of abbreviations to transcribe speeches. His ampersand (&) is still used today.
- Nineteenth century writer Charles Dickens used Gurney's system, developed in 1707.
- Both the Pitman and Gregg systems, invented during the 1800s are still in use.

accept
almost
although
burn
busy

▲ Bright's system used 500 signs instead of words.

▲ Court reporters today use stenograph machines to record testimony at the speed of speech.

▲ Text-messaging is a new form of swift-writing. (This message means "See you later, okay?")

Connect to the Literature In an age when books were scarce, why might Widge's swift-writing skills be highly valued?

BRIGHT: Oh, quite proficient. Extremely. (WIDGE *is surprised to hear this*)

FALCONER: Show me.

BRIGHT: (*to* WIDGE) Are you deaf, boy? The gentleman wishes a demonstration of your skill.

WIDGE: (*picks up notebook and pencil*) What must I write?

FALCONER: Write this: "I hereby convey to the bearer of this paper the services of my former apprentice—"

WIDGE: Go on. I've kept up wi' you.

FALCONER: Your name.

WIDGE: Pardon?

FALCONER: What is your name?

BRIGHT: Widge. It's Widge. (*laughs as if to show that he realizes how odd it sounds*)

Drama
Dramatic Effect The author's instruction to actors about how to react to specific events or dialogue adds to the play's illusion of reality.

Reading Check

What kind of system has Dr. Bright invented?

from *The Shakespeare Stealer* ■ 711

FALCONER: "—my former apprentice Widge, in consideration of which I have accepted the amount of ten pounds sterling."

BRIGHT: (*staggered*) Ten p—?!

WIDGE: Is that all, then?

FALCONER: Let me see it. (WIDGE *hands him the notebook. Skeptical*) You've copied down every word?

WIDGE: Aye.

FALCONER: Read it back.

WIDGE: (*takes notebook*) "I hereby convey to the bearer of this paper the services of my former apprentice, Widge, in consideration— (*the meaning of the words finally sinks in*) Do you— does this mean—?

FALCONER: Copy it out, now, in a normal hand.

BRIGHT: (*when* WIDGE *hesitates*) Go on. Do as he says! (*While* WIDGE *copies it out,* FALCONER *takes out a purse and counts out ten sovereigns onto the table, with* BRIGHT *watching greedily*)

FALCONER: If there's anything you want to take along, you'd best fetch it now, boy. I'll be outside. (*to* BRIGHT) Where can I water my horse?

BRIGHT: On the north side of the house, there's a trough. (*to* WIDGE) Go on, lad. (*through the following* WIDGE *goes upstairs, collects his meager belongings, including a leather wallet on a strap. To* FALCONER) I hope you'll keep a close eye on the boy. (*The concern this implies is belied by* BRIGHT'S *next line*) He can be sluggish if you don't stir him from time to time with a stick. (FALCONER *exits*) Move your bones, boy, before he changes his mind. (WIDGE *descends the stairs reluctantly*)

WIDGE: Must I go with him, then?

BRIGHT: (*busy fondling the sovereigns*) Eh? Of course you must. He's paid for you, and far more handsomely than I would have dreamed.

WIDGE: Will you not bid me farewell, at least, sir?

BRIGHT: (*perfunctorily*) Of course, of course. Fair 'chieve you, boy, fair 'chieve you.

Transition

Drama
Stage Directions
By simply indicating "Transition," Blackwood lets the director devise the best way to show a change of scene.

(FALCONER *enters at Down Right, looking about warily, trailed by* WIDGE, *who is rubbing his backside*)

WIDGE: Gog's blood, I'm glad to be off that horse.

FALCONER: It won't be for long. Here. (*Hands* WIDGE *a journey cake, nibbles at one himself, still looking about alertly. They pass a flask of something back and forth*)

WIDGE: When will we be at our destination?

FALCONER: When we get there.

WIDGE: These woods are much more . . . wild than around Berwick, and more dense. It feels almost as though they're closing in on us. (*shivers*)

FALCONER: Stop your wagging tongue. You'll have every cutpurse within a league down upon us.

WIDGE: Cutpurse? (*looks about even more fearfully*) You mean . . . there are thieves in these woods? (*realizes he's still talking*) Sorry.

(*Horse whinnies O.S. Right.* FALCONER *reacts, abruptly puts away the flask and loosens his rapier in its sheath, looking about and listening intently.* THREE THIEVES *enter at Left, one armed with a pistol, two with swords*)

THIEF #1: Don't move, if you value your life.

FALCONER: (*unexpectedly amiable*) God rest you, gentlemen.

THIEF #1: God, is it? Don't tell me you're a parson.

FALCONER: No, no. Far from it.

THIEF #1: Good. I don't like doing business with parsons. They're too parsimonious. (*Laughs*) All right, let's have it, then.

FALCONER: Have what?

THIEF #1: (*Laughs again*) Have what, 'a says! Have what? Why, have a pot of ale wi' us, of course. (*More soberly*) Come now, enough pleasantries. Let's have your purse, man.

FALCONER: (*Pulls out his hefty purse. Still amiable*) Ah. Forgive me for not taking your meaning.

THIEF #1: Oh, aye, an you forgive me for taking your purse.

(FALCONER *steps to the man, who holds out a hand for the purse. Instead of handing it over,* FALCONER *swings it swiftly upward, catching Thief #1 alongside the head. The man cries out, crumples to*

Gary Blackwood
Author's Insight
Shakespeare was very fond of *puns*—humorous plays on words that sound alike—so I made liberal use of them, too. Since they depend on words sounding alike, they work even better in a play than in a book.

Vocabulary Builder
parsimonious (pär′ sə mō′ nē əs) *adj.* miserly; stingy

Reading Check

Why does Widge leave Bright to go with Falconer?

the ground; his pistol goes off wildly. The other thieves spring forward. FALCONER *draws his rapier, parries an ineffectual blow, kicks the man in the groin.* WIDGE *picks up a rock, but has no chance to use it.* FALCONER *grasps the third man's blade in his cloak-wrapped hand, yanks it away, and slices the man's ribs with his own sword. With the thieves lying about groaning,* FALCONER *lifts his purse with the point of his sword, flips it in the air, catches it, then shakes a single coin from it and throws it at the men's feet)*

FALCONER: If this is a toll road, you might simply have tolled me.

THIEF #1: *(laughs, then groans in pain)* Would that you had been a parson after all.

FALCONER: *(to WIDGE)* Come. *(starts Off Right)*

WIDGE: What you did back there—I've never seen the like of it.

FALCONER: Yes, well, you haven't seen much, have you?

Transition

(A bed has been brought on upstairs, and a writing desk and two chairs downstairs. FALCONER *and* WIDGE *enter at Right.* WIDGE *is walking stiffly, wincing)*

WIDGE: Are we in London, then?

FALCONER: *(scoffing)* Hardly. This is Leicester.

*(*LIBBY, *a sympathetic, plain woman in a maid's garb, emerges from one of the downstairs doorways)*

LIBBY: Welcome back, sir.

FALCONER: The boy will be staying the night. Show him to the garret. *(Exits upstage)*

LIBBY: Yes, sir. *(looking Widge over)* Where you from, then?

WIDGE: Berwick-in-Elmet.

LIBBY: Where's that?

WIDGE: Up Yorkshire way. Near Leeds.

LIBBY: I see. Well, come. We'd best get you to your room. *(Leads him up the steps)* I'll bring you some food up in a bit. Here you are. It's not much.

WIDGE: More than I'm used to. Mind you, it could be a pit of snakes for all I care, I'm that exhausted. *(sinks down on the bed)* You didn't seem surprised at all, that 'a came back wi' me in tow.

LIBBY: Nothing the master does surprises me. Have a good rest.

Drama

Dialogue Falconer's awful pun on the word *told* restores a humorous tone to the scene after a violent struggle.

▶ **Critical Viewing** Based on this photograph of Widge with Libby, do you think his new life will be better than his old one? **[Predict]**

Transition

(WIDGE *wakes up, rubs eyes, looks around at the unfamiliar sur-roundings then hobbles downstairs.* LIBBY *is at the bottom of the steps*)

LIBBY: I was just coming to wake you. The master said to bring you to him as soon as you were up. I don't think he expected you to sleep so late. (*They cross to where* SIMON BASS *sits at the writing desk. He is played by the same actor who plays* FALCONER, *minus the hooded cloak, the curly black wig, the hooked nose, the swarthy skin, the beard, the scar, and the high boots that make him several inches taller.* BASS *is much more approachable and genial, but a prickliness lurks beneath the surface*)

WIDGE: Will 'a be cross wi' me, do you wis?

LIBBY: I can't say. He's a queer one, the master is. (*sotto voce*) Not to tell him I said so, now. (*Leaning into desk area*) I've brought the boy, sir.

BASS: (*without turning; we still assume it's* FALCONER *sitting there*) Come in, Widge. (WIDGE *enters the "room", clearly awed by the fur-nishings*) Sit down.

WIDGE: Eh? Oh. (*sits*) Sorry. It's just that I've never seen such a grand room, with so many books, not even at Squire Cheyney's.

MODEL SELECTION

Gary Blackwood

Author's Insight
It's hard to change costume and makeup this quickly. To give the actor enough time, I created a conversation between Widge and Libby.

 Reading Check

Where does Falconer bring Widge?

BASS: Wait until you see the houses in London. (*He turns, rises. We and* WIDGE *get our first good look at him. Widge is obviously bewildered*)

WIDGE: Who—who are you?

BASS: My name is Simon Bass. I'm your new master.

WIDGE: But—but I thought—

BASS: You thought the one who brought you here was to be your master.

WIDGE: Aye.

BASS: (*shrugs*) Falconer is not the most communicative of men, I warrant, nor the most genial. But he is reliable and effective. I could not go to Yorkshire myself . . . for various reasons. He got you here safe and sound, it appears.

WIDGE: (*squirming on his sore rear end*) Well, safe, at any rate.

BASS: Let's get down to business. You'll want to know what's expected of you.

WIDGE: Aye.

BASS: Very well. The first thing I expect is for you to say "yes," rather than *"aye."* I'd just as soon you did not sound like a complete rustic. Understood?

WIDGE: Aye—I mean, yes.

BASS: Excellent. Now, when you go to London—

WIDGE: London?

BASS: Yes. It's a large city to the south.

WIDGE: I ken that, but—

BASS: Let me finish, then ask questions. You will be attending a play called *The Tragedy of Hamlet, Prince of Denmark.* You will copy down the play, every word of it, in Dr. Bright's charactery, and then you will deliver it to me. (WIDGE *looks uncomfortable*) Do you have some objection to that?

WIDGE: Nay, not especially. It's only words, after all. It's just that— Well, when a wight back home caught me copying his sermons, 'a got very upset wi' me.

Drama

Dialogue Here and throughout the play, Blackwood uses words like *aye* and *rustic* to reinforce the setting in time and place.

Vocabulary Builder
rustic (rus´tik) *adj.*
simple, plain, or artless; rural

Reading Check

What does Bass want Widge to do in London?

◀ **Critical Viewing**   Which details in this photograph show that Bass, at left, is more sophisticated than Widge? **[Compare and Contrast]**

BASS: Then you'll have to make certain you don't get caught, won't you? You will use a small tablebook, easily concealed . . . (*rummages through his desk*) You see how easily it's concealed? Even I can't find it. Ah, here it is. (*hands it to* WIDGE) Keep it in your wallet. You have a plumbago pencil?

WIDGE: Ay—Yes. An I might ask—for what purpose am I to do this?

BASS: Does it matter?

WIDGE: Nay; I was only curious. The only plays I've ever seen are the ones the church does at Easter and Yuletide, and those certainly didn't seem worth stealing.

BASS: (*being prickly now*) I would prefer it if you did not use that term. I am not a thief. I am a man of business, and one of my more profitable ventures is a company of players. They are not so successful as the Lord Chamberlain's Men or the Admiral's Men, of course, but they draw a sizable audience here in the Midlands. If we could stage a current work, by a well-known poet, we could double our profits. Now, sooner or later someone will pry this *Tragedy of Hamlet* from the grasp of its author, Mr. Shakespeare, just as they have his earlier plays. I would like that someone to be me. If I wait for others to do it, they will do a botched job, cobbled together from various sources, none of them very reliable. Mr. Shakespeare deserves better. He is a poet of quality, perhaps of genius, and if his work is to be borrowed, it should be done properly. That is your mission. If you fulfill it satisfactorily, the reward will be considerable.

WIDGE: And . . . what an I do not?

BASS: Falconer will make certain that you do.

WIDGE: Oh. I didn't ken that 'a would go wi' me.

BASS: Did you suppose I would send you off to London on your own? I might as well send you to Guiana. Go and rest now, or soak your haunches, or whatever you will. You'll be leaving for London early in the morning. (*He exits.* WIDGE *shuffles downstage as* LIBBY *enters at Left*)

Drama

Conflict With this speech, Blackwood lays out the central elements of his plot. Readers can link the title of the play with Bass's information to predict how the play will develop.

Q. Where did you get the idea for *The Shakespeare Stealer*?

A. I'd studied Elizabethan theater in college, and learned about how acting companies stole plays from one another. But it wasn't until I stumbled across a brief mention of Dr. Timothy Bright and his system of swift-writing that I came up with the notion of having someone steal *Hamlet* by copying it down in shorthand. In my first version of the story, that someone was Dr. Bright, not Widge.

Q. What was it like to play the lead role in your own play?

A. As an actor, I approached it much the same as I would any other play. I didn't know the lines by heart, so I still had to learn them, and I still had to listen to the director. As a playwright, I would have preferred to see what someone else would bring to the role.

Q. When the director and actors are rehearsing your play, do they ask your advice?

A. The director serves as liaison between the actors and the playwright, so I seldom gave advice directly to the actors. Generally, directors just do things the way they think best and assume that, if I have a problem with it, I'll let them know.

StudentCorner

Q. How much of *The Shakespeare Stealer* is fact and how much is fiction?

—Jessica Meyer, Crawfordsville, Indiana

A. As far as I know, everything relating to Elizabethan theater and plays is accurate. I couldn't hope to re-create 16th century speech, but I did include lots of authentic words and phrases ("clod-pated drivel," "wight"). With the exception of Widge, Simon Bass, and Julian, all the major characters are based on real people.

 Writing Workshop: *Work in Progress*

How-to Essay

For a how-to essay you may write, record five tasks that you do well. Choose one of those tasks and make a list of steps necessary to accomplish it. Put this Task List in your writing portfolio.

Apply the Skills

Drama

Thinking About the Selection

1. **Respond:** Do you think Bass's assignment to Widge is unethical or wrong? Why or why not?

2. **(a) Recall:** What special skill has Widge been taught by Dr. Bright? **(b) Summarize:** What happened when the rector at Leeds caught Widge transcribing a sermon? **(c) Infer:** What does this episode show about Widge's talent as a writer?

3. **(a) Infer:** How did Falconer learn about Dr. Bright's swift-writing system? Explain. **(b) Speculate:** Why does Falconer test Widge?

4. **(a) Recall:** How does Bass plan to profit from Widge's skill? **(b) Take a Position:** Do you see any similarities between Bass's plan and modern-day practices involving music or movies? Explain.

Drama Review

5. **(a)** Note three details in the **stage directions** that establish the setting of the **drama** in Shakespearean England. **(b)** Note three examples of **dialogue** that reinforce that setting.

6. **(a)** Use a chart like the one shown to explore how characters use **props** to reveal their personalities. **(a)** In the first column, list props that are used by Dr. Bright, Widge, and Falconer. In the second column, record how the characters use each prop. In the third column, describe what their actions show about their personalities. **(b)** In a small group, discuss your findings and share them with the class.

Prop	How It Is Used	What It Shows

Research the Author

Gary Blackwood has written several books that continue Widge's adventures. Write the **foreword,** or introductory material, to a collection of these works. Include summaries and statements by critics. Write to interest your peers in reading these works.

- Use the Internet and your library to locate Blackwood works that feature Widge and Shakespeare.
- Gather enough information to summarize the plots.
- Read the reviews, and identify key passages to use in your writing.
- Write your foreword and share it with the class.

Summarize

Skills You Will Learn

Literary Analysis: *Dialogue and Stage Directions*
Reading Skill: *Using Text Aids*

Literary Analysis: *Blank Verse*
Reading Skill: *Reading in Sentences*

Literary Analysis: *Soliloquy, Aside, and Monologue; Allusion*
Reading Skill: *Paraphrasing*

Literary Analysis: *Dramatic Irony; Comic Relief and Puns*
Reading Skill: *Breaking Down Long Sentences*

Literary Analysis: *Tragedy; Character's Motive*
Reading Skill: *Cause and Effect*

Reading Skill: *Skimming and Scanning*

Literary Analysis: *Archetypal Theme*

Literature You Will Read

Reading: Summarize

**Standard Course
of Study**

- Summarize key events
  and/or points from
  argumentative text.
  (FA.3.04.5)
- Selecting, monitoring,
  and modifying
  appropriate to literary
  purpose. (LT.5.03.1)
- Summarize key events
  and/or points. (LT.5.03.6)

▶ To **summarize** is to briefly state the most important points
of a text in your own words.

When you summarize, you retell the events and ideas in the original work
in your own words. Because a summary includes only the most
important points, it is significantly shorter than the original work.

Skills and Strategies You Will Learn in Part 1

In Part 1, you will learn
- to use **text aids** to determine important points to **summarize.**
  (p. 728)
- to **read according to punctuation** to **group ideas.** (p. 756)
- to **paraphrase,** or restate something in your own words. (p. 780)
- to **break down long sentences** and **paraphrase** them. (p. 814)
- to **identify cause-and-effect** relationships that you would
  include in a **summary.** (p. 832)
- to **skim and scan** to identify the most important points in a piece
  of writing. (p. 852)

Using the Skills and Strategies in Part 1

In Part 1, you will learn strategies that help you break down a text to
identify the most important ideas and the relationships among them.
You will also practice restating ideas in your own words and organizing
them in a summary.

The Tragedy of Romeo and Juliet is one of the most famous love stories
of all time. However, this play is much more than a simple love story.
Written by William Shakespeare in the fifteenth century, [a] the play
continues to be enjoyed by audiences more than 500 years later. [b]
The reason *Romeo and Juliet,* like the rest of Shakespeare's work,
enjoys an enduring popularity is that it touches on a timeless theme. [c]

[a] The comma helps you group the words in this long sentence into
two ideas about the play.

[b] If you break down the sentence, you can paraphrase the main part.

[c] The cause of the play's popularity is one of the main points in the
text and would be included in a summary.

Academic Vocabulary: Words for Connecting Themes in Literature

The following words will help you to write and talk about themes in the literature in this unit.

Word	Definition	Example Sentence
condense v.	shorten or make concise	The summary *condenses* the action.
relevant adj.	related to	The theme is as *relevant* today as it was in Shakespeare's time.
ambiguous adj.	numerous possible meanings	We discussed the *ambiguous* ending.
elaborate v., adj.	work out in detail; extremely detailed	The author *elaborates* on her ideas. There were *elaborate* descriptions of the island.
illuminate v.	make clear; provide insight	The speech will *illuminate* his motives.

Vocabulary Skill: Word Roots

▶ A **word root** is the basic meaning of a word.

In Part 1 you will learn
- the word root *-labor-* (p. 812)
- the word root *-lum-* (p. 850)

The word root *-labor-,* meaning "work", is also a word root for words, such as *elaborate.* The word root *-lum-* is found in words with meanings related to "light."

Activity Write what you think each word means, using the word's root as a clue. Paraphrase, or restate in your own words, the dictionary definition. Then explain why your predicted definition is, or is not, accurate.

	luminous	belabor	laboratory	luminary
Predicted Definition				
Actual Definition				
Explanation				

Romeo and Juliet

Of all the love stories ever written, that of Romeo and Juliet is the most famous. To many people, Shakespeare's tragic lovers represent the essence of romantic love. When Shakespeare wrote *The Tragedy of Romeo and Juliet*, he was a young man, and the play is a young man's play about young love.

The Theater in Shakespeare's Day

Romeo and Juliet, like most of Shakespeare's plays, was produced in a public theater. Public theaters were built around roofless courtyards without artificial light. Performances, therefore, were given only during daylight hours. Surrounding the courtyard were three levels of galleries with benches on which wealthier playgoers sat. Less wealthy spectators, called groundlings, stood and watched a play from the courtyard, which was called the pit.

Most of Shakespeare's plays were performed in the Globe theater. No one is certain exactly what the Globe looked like, though Shakespeare tells us it was round or octagonal. We know that it was open to the sky and held between 2,500 and 3,000 people. Scholars disagree about its actual dimensions and size. The discovery of its foundation in 1989 was exciting because the excavation has revealed clues about the plays, the actors, and the audience. The tiny part of the foundation initially uncovered yielded a great number of hazelnut shells. Hazelnuts were Elizabethan popcorn; people munched on them all during the performance.

The stage was a platform that extended into the pit. Actors entered and left the stage from doors located behind the platform. The portion of the galleries behind and above the stage was used primarily as dressing and

▼ **Critical Viewing**
Which attribute of the Globe is emphasized in this painting?
[Analyze]

The Globe Theatre, London

storage rooms. The second-level gallery right above the stage, however, was used as an upper stage. It would have been here that the famous balcony scene in *Romeo and Juliet* was enacted.

There was no scenery in the theaters of Shakespeare's day. Settings were indicated by references in the dialogue. As a result, one scene could follow another in rapid succession. The actors wore elaborate clothing. It was, in fact, typical Elizabethan clothing, not costuming. Thus, the plays produced in Shakespeare's day were fast-paced, colorful productions. Usually, a play lasted two hours.

▲ **Critical Viewing** Which part of the replica of the Globe theater do you think is being built in this picture? **[Analyze]**

One other difference between Shakespeare's theater and today's is that acting companies in the sixteenth century were made up only of men and boys. Women did not perform on the stage. This was not considered proper for a woman. As a general rule, boys of eleven, twelve, or thirteen—before their voices changed—performed the female roles.

The Globe Today

Building a replica of Shakespeare's Globe was the dream of American actor Sam Wanamaker. After long years of fund-raising and construction, the theater opened in London to its first full season on June 8, 1997, with a production of *Henry V*. Like the earlier Globe, this one is made of wood, with a thatched roof and lime plaster covering the walls. The stage and the galleries are covered, but the "bear pit," where the modern-day groundlings stand, is open to the skies, exposing the spectators to the weather.

Drama

Meet the Author

William **Shakespeare** (1564–1616)

Go **Online**
Author Link

For: More information about the author
Visit: www.PHSchool.com
Web Code: eqe-9504

Almost 400 years after William Shakespeare's death, his thirty seven plays continue to be read widely and produced frequently throughout the world. They have as powerful an impact on audiences today as when they were first staged.

Starting in Stratford Not much is known about Shakespeare's early life. One reason for this lack of information is that playwrights during Shakespeare's time were not considered very important people socially. Therefore, no biographies were written about him until many years after his death. Church and town records in his hometown of Stratford-on-Avon—a busy market town about seventy-five miles northwest of London—provide some clues about Shakespeare's beginnings, however. His mother, whose maiden name was Mary Arden, was the daughter of his father's landlord. His father, John, was a prosperous merchant in Stratford and even served a term as the town's mayor. John Shakespeare's social standing made it possible for William to attend Stratford Grammar School free of charge until the age of fourteen. There, he studied Latin and Greek, as well as British and world history. Shakespeare would later put all of these lessons to use in his plays about historical figures such as Julius Caesar, Pericles, Macbeth, Richard III, and Henry IV.

Building a Love of Theater Because Stratford was a commercial center, traveling companies of professional actors visited several times a year. Young William probably attended many of these performances, inspiring his interest in the stage. In 1582, at the age of eighteen, Shakespeare married and was soon the father of three children. It is uncertain how Shakespeare spent the next few years, but he did not settle down in Stratford. His heart was set on London and the theater, so he followed his heart there sometime before 1592, leaving his patient family behind. Stratford nevertheless remained an important part of Shakespeare's life, and he visited often. Once he had achieved success in London, Shakespeare purchased one of Stratford's nicest homes for his family, and he retired there after his playwriting career ended.

Stage Celebrity By 1594, William Shakespeare, now a Londoner, had developed a reputation as an actor, had written several plays, and had become the principal playwright of the Lord Chamberlain's

Men, a successful London theater company. He was also a part owner of the company, which meant that he earned money in three ways—from fees for his plays, from his acting salary, and from his share of the profits of the company. In 1599, the company built the famous Globe theater, where most of Shakespeare's plays were performed. When James I became king in 1603, Shakespeare and his partners renamed the company The King's Men. Shakespeare stayed with the company until 1610, when he retired to Stratford-on-Avon.

When Were They Written? Because Shakespeare wrote his plays to be performed, not published, no one knows exactly when each play was written. However, scholars have charted several distinct periods in Shakespeare's development as a playwright. During his early years, he wrote a number of comedies, several histories, and two tragedies. *Romeo and Juliet*—inspiration for the musical *West Side Story* as well as ballets, songs, stories, and movies—was written around 1595. Between that date and the turn of the seventeenth century, Shakespeare wrote several of his finest romantic comedies (*As You Like It, Twelfth Night,* and *Much Ado About Nothing*). During the first decade of the seventeenth century, Shakespeare created his greatest tragedies (*Hamlet, Othello, King Lear, Macbeth, Antony and Cleopatra,* and *Coriolanus*). Finally, toward the end of his career, Shakespeare wrote several plays referred to as romances or tragicomedies. Shakespeare's plays were finally published in a one-volume edition in 1623, seven years after his death. More than 1,000 copies of the first printing were sold for the considerable sum of one pound each—equivalent to more than $50 in today's currency.

Shakespeare's Impact on English

In addition to introducing many new words into the language, Shakespeare penned hundreds of memorable lines that are familiar to millions of people throughout the world—even to people who have never read one of his plays. The following are just a few of his most famous lines.

From *Hamlet*:

To be, or not to be: that is the question: / Whether 'tis nobler in the mind to suffer / The slings and arrows of outrageous fortune, / Or take arms against a sea of troubles. . . .

Romeo and Juliet

Parting is such sweet sorrow. . . .

Julius Caesar

Friends, Romans, countrymen, lend me your ears; / I come to bury Caesar, not to praise him.

Literary Analysis

Dialogue is conversation between characters. In prose, dialogue is usually set off with quotation marks. In drama, it generally follows the name of the speaker, as in this example:

> **BENVOLIO.** My noble uncle, do you know the cause?
>
> **MONTAGUE.** I neither know it nor can learn of him.

Dialogue reveals the personalities and relationships of the characters and advances the action of the play.

Stage directions are notes in the text of a play that describe how the work should be performed, or staged. These instructions are usually printed in italics and are sometimes set in brackets or parentheses. They describe scenes, lighting, and sound effects, as well as the appearance and physical actions of characters, as in this example:

> *Scene iii.* FRIAR LAWRENCE's *cell.*
>
> [*Enter* FRIAR LAWRENCE *alone, with a basket.*]

As you read, notice how the dialogue and stage directions work together to help you "see" and "hear" the play in your mind.

Reading Skill

Summarizing is briefly stating the main points in a piece of writing. Pausing to summarize what you have read helps you to check your comprehension before you read further. To be sure that you understand Shakespeare's language before you summarize **use text aids**—the numbered explanations that appear with the text.

- If you are confused by a passage, check to see if there is a footnote or side note and read the corresponding explanation.
- Reread the passage, using the information from the note to be sure you grasp the meaning of the passage.

As you read Act I, use a chart like the one shown to record a summary of each scene.

NC **Standard Course of Study**

- Summarize key events and/or points from text in critiquing communication. (CT.4.03.5)
- Provide textual evidence to support understanding of response to argumentative text. (FA.3.04.3)
- Classify terms and identify characteristics to inform audience. (IR.2.02.2)

ACT I	
Scene	Summary of Action

Vocabulary Builder

- **pernicious** (pər nish′ əs) *adj.* causing great injury or ruin (p. 734) *The spy's activities had a pernicious effect on the top-secret project.*

- **augmenting** (ôg ment′ iŋ) *v.* increasing; enlarging (p. 736) *With small deposits each week, our family is augmenting its savings.*

- **grievance** (grēv′ əns) *n.* complaint (p. 736) *The board investigated the worker's grievance against his supervisor.*

- **transgression** (trans gresh′ ən) *n.* wrong doing; sin (p. 737) *Stealing from the poor is a transgression against humanity.*

Background

Shakespeare's Source Shakespeare based his play about star-crossed lovers from feuding Italian families on a poem published in 1562 by Arthur Brooke. Brooke's 3,000-line poem has a highly moral tone: Disobedience, as well as fate, leads to the deaths of the two lovers. Shakespeare portrayed the young lovers more sympathetically. He also elevated these everyday characters by presenting their tale in a tragedy—a serious type of drama that traditionally involved kings, emperors, or other characters of great importance.

Connecting to the Literature

Reading/Writing Connection *The Tragedy of Romeo and Juliet* was inspired by tales of ill-fated love that came before it. In turn, the play has inspired countless other interpretations. In a few sentences, explain why a romantic tragedy is an inspiring subject for writers, painters, and composers alike. Use at least three of these words: *illustrate, contrast, emphasize, reinforce, adapt.*

Elizabethan Language

As you read *Romeo and Juliet,* most of the unfamiliar words from Elizabethan English will be explained in footnotes. However, the following words appear so frequently that learning them now will make your reading of the play easier.

against for; in preparation for

alack alas (an exclamation of sorrow)

anon soon

aye yes

but only; except

e'en even

e'er ever

haply perhaps

happy fortunate

hence away; from here

hie hurry

hither here

marry indeed

whence where

wherefore why

wilt will

withal in addition; notwithstanding

would wish

The Tragedy of
ROMEO
and JULIET

William Shakespeare

CHARACTERS

CHORUS	**SAMPSON**, servant to Capulet
ESCALUS, Prince of Verona	**GREGORY**, servant to Capulet
PARIS, a young count, kinsman to the Prince	**PETER**, servant to Juliet's nurse
MONTAGUE	**ABRAM**, servant to Montague
CAPULET	**AN APOTHECARY**
AN OLD MAN, of the Capulet family	**THREE MUSICIANS**
ROMEO, son to Montague	**AN OFFICER**
MERCUTIO, kinsman to the Prince and friend to Romeo	**LADY MONTAGUE**, wife to Montague
BENVOLIO, nephew to Montague and friend to Romeo	**LADY CAPULET**, wife to Capulet
TYBALT, nephew to Lady Capulet	**JULIET**, daughter to Capulet
FRIAR LAWRENCE, Franciscan	**NURSE TO JULIET**
FRIAR JOHN, Franciscan	**CITIZENS OF VERONA**, Gentlemen and Gentlewomen of both houses, Maskers, Torchbearers, Pages, Guards, Watchmen, Servants, and Attendants
BALTHASAR, servant to Romeo	

Scene: Verona; Mantua

[*Enter* CHORUS.]

PROLOGUE

    CHORUS. Two households, both alike in dignity.[1]
      In fair Verona, where we lay our scene,
    From ancient grudge break to new mutiny.[2]
      Where civil blood makes civil hands unclean.[3]
5 From forth the fatal loins of these two foes
      A pair of star-crossed[4] lovers take their life;
    Whose misadventured piteous overthrows[5]
      Doth with their death bury their parents' strife.
    The fearful passage of their death-marked love,
10   And the continuance of their parents' rage,
    Which, but[6] their children's end, naught could remove,
      Is now the two hours' traffic[7] of our stage;
    The which if you with patient ears attend,
    What here shall miss, our toil shall strive to mend.[8]

[*Exit.*]

1. dignity high social rank.
2. mutiny violence.
3. Where . . . unclean in which the blood of citizens stains citizens' hands.
4. star-crossed ill-fated by the unfavorable positions of the stars.
5. Whose . . . overthrows whose unfortunate, sorrowful destruction.

6. but except.
7. two hours' traffic two hours' business.

8. What . . . mend What is not clear in this prologue we actors shall try to clarify in the course of the play.

Scene i. Verona. A public place.

[*Enter* SAMPSON *and* GREGORY, *with swords and bucklers,*[1] *of the house of Capulet.*]

    SAMPSON. Gregory, on my word, we'll not carry coals.[2]

    GREGORY. No, for then we should be colliers.[3]

    SAMPSON. I mean, an we be in choler, we'll draw.[4]

    GREGORY. Ay, while you live, draw your neck out of collar.[5]

5   **SAMPSON.** I strike quickly, being moved.

    GREGORY. But thou art not quickly moved to strike.

    SAMPSON. A dog of the house of Montague moves me.

    GREGORY. To move is to stir, and to be valiant is to stand.
    Therefore, if thou art moved, thou run'st away.

10   **SAMPSON.** A dog of that house shall move me to stand. I
    will take the wall[6] of any man or maid of Montague's.

    GREGORY. That shows thee a weak slave; for the weakest
    goes to the wall.

    SAMPSON. 'Tis true; and therefore women, being the weaker
15   vessels, are ever thrust to the wall. Therefore I will push
    Montague's men from the wall and thrust his maids to the
    wall.

    GREGORY. The quarrel is between our masters and us their
    men.

    SAMPSON. 'Tis all one. I will show myself a tyrant. When I have
    fought with the men, I will be civil with the maids—I will cut
20   off their heads.

    GREGORY. The heads of the maids?

    SAMPSON. Ay, the heads of the maids or their maidenheads.
    Take it in what sense thou wilt.

    GREGORY. They must take it in sense that feel it.

25   **SAMPSON.** Me they shall feel while I am able to stand;
    and 'tis known I am a pretty piece of flesh.

    GREGORY. 'Tis well thou art not fish; if thou hadst, thou hadst
    been Poor John. Draw thy tool![7] Here comes two of the
    house of Montagues.

[*Enter two other Servingmen,* ABRAM *and* BALTHASAR.]

30   **SAMPSON.** My naked weapon is out. Quarrel! I will back thee.

1. **bucklers** small shields.
2. **carry coals** endure insults.
3. **colliers** sellers of coal.
4. **an . . . draw** If we are angered, we'll draw our swords.
5. **collar** hangman's noose.

6. **take the wall** assert superiority by walking nearer the houses and therefore farther from the gutter.

Literary Analysis
Dialogue What does this conversation among servants reveal about the Montagues?

7. **tool** weapon.

GREGORY. How? Turn thy back and run?

SAMPSON. Fear me not.

GREGORY. No, marry. I fear thee!

SAMPSON. Let us take the law of our sides;[8] let them begin.

35 **GREGORY.** I will frown as I pass by, and let them take it as they list.[9]

SAMPSON. Nay, as they dare. I will bite my thumb[10] at them, which is disgrace to them if they bear it.

ABRAM. Do you bite your thumb at us, sir?

SAMPSON. I do bite my thumb, sir.

40 **ABRAM.** Do you bite your thumb at us, sir?

SAMPSON. [*Aside to* GREGORY] Is the law of our side if I say ay?

GREGORY. [*Aside to* SAMPSON] No.

SAMPSON. No, sir, I do not bite my thumb at you, sir; but I bite my thumb, sir.

45 **GREGORY.** Do you quarrel, sir?

ABRAM. Quarrel, sir? No, sir.

SAMPSON. But if you do, sir, I am for you. I serve as good a man as you.

ABRAM. No better.

SAMPSON. Well, sir.

[*Enter* BENVOLIO.]

50 **GREGORY.** [*Aside to* SAMPSON.] Say "better." Here comes one of my master's kinsmen.

SAMPSON. Yes, better, sir.

ABRAM. You lie.

SAMPSON. Draw, if you be men. Gregory, remember thy swashing[11] blow.   [*They fight.*]

55 **BENVOLIO.** Part, fools!
Put up your swords. You know not what you do.

[*Enter* TYBALT.]

TYBALT. What art thou drawn among these heartless hinds?[12] Turn thee, Benvolio; look upon thy death.

BENVOLIO. I do but keep the peace. Put up thy sword,
60   Or manage it to part these men with me.

Reading Skill
Summarizing How does footnote 8 help you understand Sampson's logic in line 36?

8. **take . . . sides** make sure the law is on our side.
9. **list** please.
10. **bite . . . thumb** make an insulting gesture.

Literary Analysis
Stage Directions Which words in the stage directions in line 41 clarify that Sampson is not speaking to Abram?

11. **swashing** hard downward swordstroke.

12. **heartless hinds** cowardly servants. *Hind* also means "a female deer."

Reading Check

With which family are the quarreling servants affiliated?

TYBALT. What, drawn, and talk of peace? I hate the word
As I hate hell, all Montagues, and thee.
Have at thee, coward!   [*They fight.*]

[*Enter an* OFFICER, *and three or four* CITIZENS *with clubs or partisans.*[13]]

      OFFICER. Clubs, bills,[14] and partisans! Strike! Beat them down!
65   Down with the Capulets! Down with the Montagues!

[*Enter old* CAPULET *in his gown, and his* WIFE.]

      CAPULET. What noise is this? Give me my long sword, ho!

      LADY CAPULET. A crutch, a crutch! Why call you for a sword?

      CAPULET. My sword, I say! Old Montague is come
And flourishes his blade in spite[15] of me.

[*Enter old* MONTAGUE *and his* WIFE.]

70 **MONTAGUE.** Thou villain Capulet!—Hold me not; let me go.

      LADY MONTAGUE. Thou shalt not stir one foot to seek a foe.

[*Enter* PRINCE ESCALUS, *with his Train.*[16]]

      PRINCE. Rebellious subjects, enemies to peace,
Profaners[17] of this neighbor-stainèd steel—
Will they not hear? What, ho! You men, you beasts,

13. **partisans** spearlike weapons with broad blades.

14. **bills** weapons consisting of hook-shaped blades with long handles.

15. **spite** defiance.

16. **Train** attendants.

17. **Profaners** those who show disrespect or contempt.

Literature in Context

History Connection

Prince of Verona When Prince Escalus intervenes in the fight between the Capulets and the Montagues, he does so under his authority as the podesta, or "chief magistrate," of Verona. The powers and duties of the podesta combined those of a modern mayor, chief of police, and head of the local militia. Scholars believe that Shakespeare based the character of Prince Escalus on Bartolomeo della Scala, who ruled the northern Italian city of Verona during the late-thirteenth and early-fourteenth centuries.

Connect to the Literature

Which part of his authority is Prince Escalus exercising in this scene—mayor, police chief, or head of the army? Explain.

75 That quench the fire of your <u>pernicious</u> rage
With purple fountains issuing from your veins!
On pain of torture, from those bloody hands
Throw your mistempered[18] weapons to the ground
And hear the sentence of your moved prince.
80 Three civil brawls, bred of an airy word
By thee, old Capulet, and Montague,
Have thrice disturbed the quiet of our streets
And made Verona's ancient citizens
Cast by their grave beseeming ornaments[19]
85 To wield old partisans, in hands as old,
Cank'red with peace, to part your cank'red hate.[20]
If ever you disturb our streets again,
Your lives shall pay the forfeit of the peace.
For this time all the rest depart away.
90 You, Capulet, shall go along with me;
And, Montague, come you this afternoon,
To know our farther pleasure in this case,
To old Freetown, our common judgment place.
Once more, on pain of death, all men depart.

[*Exit all but* MONTAGUE, *his* WIFE, *and* BENVOLIO.]

95 **MONTAGUE.** Who set this ancient quarrel new abroach?[21]
Speak, nephew, were you by when it began?

BENVOLIO. Here were the servants of your adversary
And yours, close fighting ere I did approach.
I drew to part them. In the instant came
100 The fiery Tybalt, with his sword prepared;
Which, as he breathed defiance to my ears,
He swung about his head and cut the winds,
Who, nothing hurt withal, hissed him in scorn.
While we were interchanging thrusts and blows,
105 Came more and more, and fought on part and part,[22]
Till the Prince came, who parted either part.

LADY MONTAGUE. O, where is Romeo? Saw you him today?
Right glad I am he was not at this fray.

BENVOLIO. Madam, an hour before the worshiped sun
110 Peered forth the golden window of the East,
A troubled mind drave me to walk abroad:
Where, underneath the grove of sycamore
That westward rooteth from this city side,
So early walking did I see your son.

115	Towards him I made, but he was ware[23] of me
	And stole into the covert[24] of the wood.
	I, measuring his affections[25] by my own,
	Which then most sought where most might not be found,[26]
	Being one too many by my weary self,
120	Pursued my humor not pursuing his,[27]
	And gladly shunned who gladly fled from me.

23. **ware** aware; wary.

24. **covert** hidden place.

25. **measuring . . . affections** judging his feelings.

26. **Which . . . found** which wanted to be where there was no one else.

27. **Pursued . . . his** followed my own mind by not following after Romeo.

MONTAGUE. Many a morning hath he there been seen,
 With tears <u>augmenting</u> the fresh morning's dew,
 Adding to clouds more clouds with his deep sighs;
125 But all so soon as the all-cheering sun
 Should in the farthest East begin to draw
 The shady curtains from Aurora's bed,
 Away from light steals home my heavy[28] son
 And private in his chamber pens himself,
130 Shuts up his windows, locks fair daylight out,
 And makes himself an artificial night.
 Black and portentous[29] must this humor prove
 Unless good counsel may the cause remove.

Vocabulary Builder
augmenting (ôg ment´ iŋ) v. increasing; enlarging

28. **heavy** sad, moody.

29. **portentous** promising bad fortune.

BENVOLIO. My noble uncle, do you know the cause?

135 **MONTAGUE.** I neither know it nor can learn of him.

BENVOLIO. Have you importuned[30] him by any means?

30. **importuned** questioned deeply.

MONTAGUE. Both by myself and many other friends;
 But he, his own affections' counselor,
 Is to himself—I will not say how true—
140 But to himself so secret and so close,
 So far from sounding[31] and discovery,
 As is the bud bit with an envious worm
 Ere he can spread his sweet leaves to the air
 Or dedicate his beauty to the sun.
145 Could we but learn from whence his sorrows grow,
 We would as willingly give cure as know.

31. **sounding** understanding.

[*Enter* ROMEO.]

BENVOLIO. See, where he comes. So please you step aside;
 I'll know his <u>grievance</u>, or be much denied.

Vocabulary Builder
grievance (grēv´ əns) n. injustice; complaint

MONTAGUE. I would thou wert so happy by thy stay
150 To hear true shrift.[32] Come, madam, let's away.

[*Exit* MONTAGUE *and* WIFE.]

32. **I . . . shrift** I hope you are lucky enough to hear him confess the truth.

BENVOLIO. Good morrow, cousin.

ROMEO.   Is the day so young?

BENVOLIO. But new struck nine.

ROMEO.   Ay me! Sad hours seem long.
  Was that my father that went hence so fast?

BENVOLIO. It was. What sadness lengthens Romeo's hours?

155 **ROMEO.** Not having that which having makes them short.

BENVOLIO. In love?

ROMEO. Out—

BENVOLIO. Of love?

ROMEO. Out of her favor where I am in love.

160 **BENVOLIO.** Alas that love, so gentle in his view,[33]
  Should be so tyrannous and rough in proof![34]

ROMEO. Alas that love, whose view is muffled still,[35]
  Should without eyes see pathways to his will!
  Where shall we dine? O me! What fray was here?
165 Yet tell me not, for I have heard it all.
  Here's much to do with hate, but more with love.[36]
  Why then, O brawling love, O loving hate,
  O anything, of nothing first created!
  O heavy lightness, serious vanity,
170 Misshapen chaos of well-seeming forms,
  Feather of lead, bright smoke, cold fire, sick health,
  Still-waking sleep, that is not what it is!
  This love feel I, that feel no love in this.
  Dost thou not laugh?

BENVOLIO.   No, coz,[37] I rather weep.

ROMEO. Good heart, at what?

175 **BENVOLIO.**   At thy good heart's oppression.

ROMEO. Why, such is love's <u>transgression</u>.
  Griefs of mine own lie heavy in my breast,
  Which thou wilt propagate, to have it prest
  With more of thine.[38] This love that thou hast shown
180 Doth add more grief to too much of mine own.
  Love is a smoke made with the fume of sighs;
  Being purged, a fire sparkling in lovers' eyes;
  Being vexed, a sea nourished with loving tears.
  What is it else? A madness most discreet,[39]

185   A choking gall,[40] and a preserving sweet.
      Farewell, my coz.

BENVOLIO.   Soft![41] I will go along.
      And if you leave me so, you do me wrong.

ROMEO. Tut! I have lost myself; I am not here;
      This is not Romeo, he's some other where.

190   **BENVOLIO.** Tell me in sadness,[42] who is that you love?

ROMEO. What, shall I groan and tell thee?

BENVOLIO.   Groan? Why, no;
      But sadly tell me who.

ROMEO. Bid a sick man in sadness make his will.
      Ah, word ill urged to one that is so ill!
195   In sadness, cousin, I do love a woman.

BENVOLIO. I aimed so near when I supposed you loved.

ROMEO. A right good markman. And she's fair I love.

BENVOLIO. A right fair mark, fair coz, is soonest hit.

ROMEO. Well, in that hit you miss. She'll not be hit
200   With Cupid's arrow. She hath Dian's wit,[43]
      And, in strong proof[44] of chastity well armed,
      From Love's weak childish bow she lives uncharmed.
      She will not stay[45] the siege of loving terms,
      Nor bide th' encounter of assailing eyes,
205   Nor ope her lap to saint-seducing gold.
      O, she is rich in beauty; only poor
      That, when she dies, with beauty dies her store.[46]

BENVOLIO. Then she hath sworn that she will still live chaste?

40. gall a bitter liquid.

41. Soft! Hold on a minute.

42. in sadness seriously.

43. Dian's wit the mind of Diana, goddess of chastity.
44. proof armor.
45. stay endure; put up with.

46. That . . . store in that her beauty will die with her if she does not marry and have children.

ROMEO. She hath, and in that sparing make huge waste;

210 For beauty, starved with her severity,
Cuts beauty off from all posterity.[47]
She is too fair, too wise, wisely too fair
To merit bliss by making me despair.[48]
She hath forsworn to[49] love, and in that vow

215 Do I live dead that live to tell it now.

BENVOLIO. Be ruled by me; forget to think of her.

ROMEO. O, teach me how I should forget to think!

BENVOLIO. By giving liberty unto thine eyes.
Examine other beauties.

ROMEO.   'Tis the way

220 To call hers, exquisite, in question more.[50]
These happy masks that kiss fair ladies' brows,
Being black puts us in mind they hide the fair.
He that is strucken blind cannot forget
The precious treasure of his eyesight lost.

225 Show me a mistress that is passing fair:
What doth her beauty serve but as a note
Where I may read who passed that passing fair?[51]
Farewell. Thou canst not teach me to forget.

BENVOLIO. I'll pay that doctrine, or else die in debt.[52]   [*Exit all.*]

Scene ii. A street.

[*Enter* CAPULET, COUNTY PARIS, *and the* CLOWN, *his servant.*]

CAPULET. But Montague is bound as well as I,
In penalty alike; and 'tis not hard, I think,
For men so old as we to keep the peace.

PARIS. Of honorable reckoning[1] are you both,

5 And pity 'tis you lived at odds so long.
But now, my lord, what say you to my suit?

CAPULET. But saying o'er what I have said before:
My child is yet a stranger in the world,
She hath not seen the change of fourteen years;

10 Let two more summers wither in their pride
Ere we may think her ripe to be a bride.

PARIS. Younger than she are happy mothers made.

CAPULET. And too soon marred are those so early made.

47. in . . . posterity By denying herself love and marriage, she wastes her beauty, which will not live on in future generations.

48. She . . . despair She is being too good—she will earn happiness in heaven by dooming me to live without her love.

49. forsworn to sworn not to.

50. 'Tis . . . more That way will only make her beauty more strongly present in my mind.

51. who . . . fair who surpassed in beauty that very beautiful woman.

52. I'll . . . debt I will teach you to forget, or else die trying.

1. reckoning reputation.

◀ **Critical Viewing**
What does this photograph reveal about the feelings of Romeo and Benvolio? **[Analyze]**

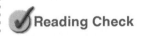 **Reading Check**

What advice does Benvolio give to Romeo about the woman he loves?

Earth hath swallowed all my hopes[2] but she;
15 She is the hopeful lady of my earth.[3]
But woo her, gentle Paris, get her heart;
My will to her consent is but a part.
An she agree, within her scope of choice
Lies my consent and fair according voice,[4]
20 This night I hold an old accustomed feast,
Whereto I have invited many a guest,
Such as I love; and you among the store,
One more, most welcome, makes my number more.
At my poor house look to behold this night
25 Earth-treading stars[5] that make dark heaven light.
Such comfort as do lusty young men feel
When well-appareled April on the heel
Of limping Winter treads, even such delight
Among fresh fennel buds shall you this night
30 Inherit at my house. Hear all, all see,
And like her most whose merit most shall be;
Which, on more view of many, mine, being one,
May stand in number, though in reck'ning none.[6]
Come, go with me. [*To* SERVANT, *giving him a paper*]
        Go, sirrah, trudge about
35 Through fair Verona; find those persons out
Whose names are written there, and to them say
My house and welcome on their pleasure stay.[7]

[*Exit with* PARIS.]

SERVANT. Find them out whose names are written here? It is
written that the shoemaker should meddle with his yard and
the tailor with his last, the fisher with his pencil and the
40 painter with his nets;[8] but I am sent to find those persons
whose names are here writ, and can never find what names
the writing person hath here writ. I must to the learned.
In good time![9]

[*Enter* BENVOLIO *and* ROMEO.]

BENVOLIO. Tut, man, one fire burns out another's burning;
45 One pain is less'ned by another's anguish;
Turn giddy, and be holp by backward turning;[10]
One desperate grief cures with another's languish.
Take thou some new infection to thy eye,
And the rank poison of the old will die.

2. hopes children.

3. She . . . earth My hopes for
the future rest in her; she will
inherit all that is mine.

4. and . . . voice If she
agrees, I will consent to and
agree with her choice.

5. Earth-treading stars
young ladies.

6. Which . . . none If you look
at all the young girls, you may
see her as merely one among
many, and not worth special
admiration.

7. stay await.

**Reading Skill
Summarizing** Use
footnote 8 to help you
summarize the
servant's remarks
here.

8. shoemaker . . . nets The
servant is confusing workers
and their tools. He intends to
say that people should stick
with what they know.

9. In good time! Just in time!
The servant has seen Benvolio
and Romeo, who can read.

10. Turn . . . turning If you are
dizzy from turning one way,
turn the other way.

50 **ROMEO.** Your plantain leaf[11] is excellent for that.

BENVOLIO. For what, I pray thee?

ROMEO.   For your broken shin.

BENVOLIO. Why, Romeo, art thou mad?

ROMEO. Not mad, but bound more than a madman is;
    Shut up in prison, kept without my food,
55 Whipped and tormented and—God-den,[12] good fellow.

SERVANT. God gi' go-den. I pray, sir, can you read?

ROMEO. Ay, mine own fortune in my misery.

SERVANT. Perhaps you have learned it without book.
    But, I pray, can you read anything you see?

60 **ROMEO.** Ay, if I know the letters and the language.

SERVANT. Ye say honestly. Rest you merry.[13]

ROMEO. Stay, fellow; I can read. [*He reads the letter.*]
    "Signior Martino and his wife and daughters;
    County Anselm and his beauteous sisters;
65 The lady widow of Vitruvio;
    Signior Placentio and his lovely nieces;
    Mercutio and his brother Valentine;
    Mine uncle Capulet, his wife and daughters;
    My fair niece Rosaline; Livia;
70 Signior Valentio and his cousin Tybalt;
    Lucio and the lively Helena."
    A fair assembly. Whither should they come?

SERVANT. Up.

ROMEO. Whither? To supper?

75 **SERVANT.** To our house.

ROMEO. Whose house?

SERVANT. My master's.

ROMEO. Indeed I should have asked you that before.

SERVANT. Now I'll tell you without asking. My master is the
    great rich Capulet; and if you be not of the house of
80 Montagues, I pray come and crush a cup of wine. Rest you
    merry.   [*Exit.*]

BENVOLIO. At this same ancient[14] feast of Capulet's
    Sups the fair Rosaline whom thou so loves;
    With all the admirèd beauties of Verona.
85 Go thither, and with unattainted[15] eye

---

11. **plantain leaf** leaf used to stop bleeding.

12. **God-den** good afternoon; good evening.

13. **Rest you merry** May God keep you happy—a way of saying farewell.

Literary Analysis
Stage Directions
What important information in the stage directions clarifies Romeo's speech here?

14. **ancient** long-established; traditional.
15. **unattainted** unprejudiced.

Reading Check

Why does Capulet's servant talk to Romeo and Benvolio?

Compare her face with some that I shall show,
And I will make thee think thy swan a crow.

ROMEO. When the devout religion of mine eye
Maintains such falsehood, then turn tears to fires:
90 And these, who, often drowned, could never die,
Transparent heretics, be burnt for liars!¹⁶
One fairer than my love? The all-seeing sun
Ne'er saw her match since first the world begun.

BENVOLIO. Tut! you saw her fair, none else being by,
95 Herself poised with herself in either eye;¹⁷
But in that crystal scales¹⁸ let there be weighed
Your lady's love against some other maid
That I will show you shining at this feast,
And she shall scant show well that now seems best.

100 **ROMEO.** I'll go along, no such sight to be shown,
But to rejoice in splendor of mine own.¹⁹   [*Exit all.*]

Scene iii. A room in Capulet's house.

[*Enter* CAPULET'S WIFE, *and* NURSE.]

LADY CAPULET. Nurse, where's my daughter? Call her forth to
me.

NURSE. Now, by my maidenhead at twelve year old,
I bade her come. What, lamb! What, ladybird!
God forbid, where's this girl? What, Juliet!
[*Enter* JULIET.]

16. **When . . . liars!** When I
see Rosaline as just a plain-
looking girl, may my tears turn
to fire and burn my eyes out!

17. **Herself . . . eye** Rosaline
compared with no one else.
18. **crystal scales** your eyes.

19. **mine own** my own love,
Rosaline.

▼ **Critical Viewing** What do this picture and the conversation
among Juliet, Lady Capulet, and the Nurse tell you about their
relationship? **[Infer]**

5 **JULIET.** How now? Who calls?

NURSE.   Your mother.

JULIET.   Madam, I am here
What is your will?

LADY CAPULET. This is the matter—Nurse, give leave[1] awhile;
We must talk in secret. Nurse, come back again.
I have rememb'red me; thou's hear our counsel.[2]
10 Thou knowest my daughter's of a pretty age.

NURSE. Faith, I can tell her age unto an hour.

LADY CAPULET. She's not fourteen.

NURSE.   I'll lay fourteen of my teeth—
And yet, to my teen[3] be it spoken, I have but four—
She's not fourteen. How long is it now
To Lammastide?[4]

15 **LADY CAPULET.**   A fortnight and odd days.[5]

NURSE. Even or odd, of all days in the year,
Come Lammas Eve at night shall she be fourteen.
Susan and she (God rest all Christian souls!)
Were of an age.[6] Well, Susan is with God;
20 She was too good for me. But, as I said,
On Lammas Eve at night shall she be fourteen;
That shall she, marry; I remember it well.
'Tis since the earthquake now eleven years.
And she was weaned (I never shall forget it),
25 Of all the days of the year, upon that day;
For I had then laid wormwood to my dug,
Sitting in the sun under the dove house wall.
My lord and you were then at Mantua.
Nay, I do bear a brain. But, as I said,
30 When it did taste the wormwood on the nipple
Of my dug and felt it bitter, pretty fool,
To see it tetchy and fall out with the dug!
Shake, quoth the dovehouse! 'Twas no need, I trow,
To bid me trudge.
35 And since that time it is eleven years,
For then she could stand high-lone; nay, by th' rood,
She could have run and waddled all about;
For even the day before, she broke her brow;
And then my husband (God be with his soul!
40 'A was a merry man) took up the child.
"Yea," quoth he, "dost thou fall upon thy face?

1. **give leave** Leave us alone.
2. **thou's . . . counsel** You shall hear our conference.

3. **teen** sorrow.
4. **Lammastide** August 1, a holiday celebrating the summer harvest.
5. **A fortnight and odd days** two weeks plus a few days.
6. **Susan . . . age** Susan, the Nurse's child, and Juliet were the same age.

Literary Analysis
Dialogue What do the Nurse's words here reveal about her devotion to Juliet?

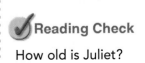
Reading Check

How old is Juliet?

Thou wilt fall backward when thou hast more wit;
Wilt thou not, Jule?" and, by my holidam,
The pretty wretch left crying and said, "Ay."

45 To see now how a jest shall come about!
I warrant, and I should live a thousand years,
I never should forget it. "Wilt thou not, Jule?" quoth he,
And, pretty fool, it stinted and said, "Ay."

LADY CAPULET. Enough of this. I pray thee hold thy peace.

50 **NURSE.** Yes, madam. Yet I cannot choose but laugh
To think it should leave crying and say, "Ay."
And yet, I warrant, it had upon it brow
A bump as big as a young cock'rel's stone;
A perilous knock; and it cried bitterly.

55 "Yea," quoth my husband, "fall'st upon thy face?
Thou wilt fall backward when thou comest to age,
Wilt thou not, Jule?" It stinted and said, "Ay."

JULIET. And stint thou too, I pray thee, nurse, say I.

NURSE. Peace, I have done. God mark thee to His grace!

60 Thou wast the prettiest babe that e'er I nursed.
And I might live to see thee married once,
I have my wish.

LADY CAPULET. Marry, that "marry" is the very theme
I came to talk of. Tell me, daughter Juliet,

65 How stands your dispositions to be married?

JULIET. It is an honor that I dream not of.

NURSE. An honor? Were not I thine only nurse,
I would say thou hadst sucked wisdom from thy teat.

LADY CAPULET. Well, think of marriage now. Younger than you,

70 Here in Verona, ladies of esteem,
Are made already mothers. By my count,
I was your mother much upon these years
That you are now a maid.[7] Thus then in brief;
The valiant Paris seeks you for his love.

75 **NURSE.** A man, young lady! Lady, such a man
As all the world—Why, he's a man of wax.[8]

LADY CAPULET. Verona's summer hath not such a flower.

NURSE. Nay, he's a flower, in faith—a very flower.

LADY CAPULET. What say you? Can you love the gentleman?

80 This night you shall behold him at our feast.

Literary Analysis
Dialogue What does
the conversation
here reveal about the
Nurse's personality?

7. I . . . maid I was your mother when I was as old as you are
now.
8. he's . . . wax He's a model
of a man.

Reading Skill
Summarizing Use the
information in
footnote 8 and the
dialogue to help you
summarize the Nurse's
opinion of Paris.

Read o'er the volume of young Paris' face,
And find delight writ there with beauty's pen;
Examine every married lineament,
And see how one another lends content;⁹
85 And what obscured in this fair volume lies
Find written in the margent¹⁰ of his eyes.
This precious book of love, this unbound lover,
To beautify him only lacks a cover.¹¹
The fish lives in the sea, and 'tis much pride
90 For fair without the fair within to hide.
That book in many's eyes doth share the glory,
That in gold clasps locks in the golden story;
So shall you share all that he doth possess,
By having him making yourself no less.

95 **NURSE.** No less? Nay, bigger! Women grow by men.

LADY CAPULET. Speak briefly, can you like of Paris' love?

JULIET. I'll look to like, if looking liking move;¹²
But no more deep will I endart mine eye
Than your consent gives strength to make it fly.¹³

[*Enter* SERVINGMAN.]

100 **SERVINGMAN.** Madam, the guests are come, supper served up,
you called, my young lady asked for, the nurse cursed in the
pantry, and everything in extremity. I must hence to wait. I
beseech you follow straight.   [*Exit.*]

LADY CAPULET. We follow thee. Juliet, the County stays.¹⁴

105 **NURSE.** Go, girl, seek happy nights to happy days.   [*Exit all.*]

Scene iv. A street.

[*Enter* ROMEO, MERCUTIO, BENVOLIO, *with five or six other*
MASKERS; TORCHBEARERS.]

ROMEO. What, shall this speech¹ be spoke for our excuse?
Or shall we on without apology?

BENVOLIO. The date is out of such prolixity.²
We'll have no Cupid hoodwinked with a scarf,
5 Bearing a Tartar's painted bow of lath,
Scaring the ladies like a crowkeeper,
Nor no without-book prologue, faintly spoke
After the prompter, for our entrance;
But, let them measure us by what they will,
10 We'll measure them a measure and be gone.

9. Examine . . . content
Examine every harmonious feature of his face, and see how each one enhances every other. Throughout this speech, Lady Capulet compares Paris to a book.
10. margent margin. Paris's eyes are compared to the margin of a book, where whatever is not clear in the text (the rest of his face) can be explained by notes.
11. cover metaphor for wife.

Literary Analysis
Dialogue What does the dialogue here reveal about Juliet's attitude toward marriage and Paris?

12. I'll . . . move If looking favorably at someone leads to liking him, I will look at Paris in a way that will lead to liking him.
13. But . . . fly But I will not look harder than you want me to.
14. the County stays The Count, Paris, is waiting.

1. this speech Romeo asks whether he and his companions, being uninvited guests, should follow custom by announcing their arrival in a speech.
2. The . . . prolixity Such wordiness is outdated. In the following lines, Benvolio says, in sum, "Let us forget about announcing our entrance with a show. The other guests can look over as they see fit. We will dance a while, then leave."

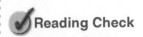

Reading Check

Why has Lady Capulet come to talk to Juliet?

ROMEO. Give me a torch. I am not for this ambling.
Being but heavy,[3] I will bear the light.

MERCUTIO. Nay, gentle Romeo, we must have you dance.

ROMEO. Not I, believe me. You have dancing shoes
15   With nimble soles; I have a soul of lead
So stakes me to the ground I cannot move.

MERCUTIO. You are a lover. Borrow Cupid's wings
And soar with them above a common bound

ROMEO. I am too sore enpiercèd with his shaft
20   To soar with his light feathers; and so bound
I cannot bound a pitch above dull woe.
Under love's heavy burden do I sink.

MERCUTIO. And, to sink in it, should you burden love—
Too great oppression for a tender thing.

25 **ROMEO.** Is love a tender thing? It is too rough,
Too rude, too boist'rous, and it pricks like thorn.

MERCUTIO. If love be rough with you, be rough with love.
Prick love for pricking, and you beat love down.
Give me a case to put my visage[4] in.
30   A visor for a visor![5] What care I

3. heavy weighed down with sadness.

▼ **Critical Viewing**
Which details in this photograph show how Romeo and his friends prepare to attend the feast? **[Analyze]**

4. visage mask.
5. A visor . . . visor! A mask for a mask—which is what my real face is like!

What curious eye doth quote deformities?[6]
Here are the beetle brows shall blush for me.

BENVOLIO. Come, knock and enter; and no sooner in
But every man betake him to his legs.[7]

35 **ROMEO.** A torch for me! Let wantons light of heart
Tickle the senseless rushes[8] with their heels;
For I am proverbed with a grandsire phrase,[9]
I'll be a candleholder and look on;
The game was ne'er so fair, and I am done.[10]

40 **MERCUTIO.** Tut! Dun's the mouse, the constable's own word![11]
If thou art Dun,[12] we'll draw thee from the mire
Of this sir-reverence love, wherein thou stickest
Up to the ears. Come, we burn daylight, ho!

ROMEO. Nay, that's not so.

MERCUTIO.   I mean, sir, in delay
45 We waste our lights in vain, like lights by day.
Take our good meaning, for our judgment sits
Five times in that ere once in our five wits.[13]

ROMEO. And we mean well in going to this masque,
But 'tis no wit to go.

MERCUTIO.   Why, may one ask?

ROMEO. I dreamt a dream tonight.

50 **MERCUTIO.**   And so did I.

ROMEO. Well, what was yours?

MERCUTIO.   That dreamers often lie.

ROMEO. In bed asleep, while they do dream things true.

MERCUTIO. O, then I see Queen Mab[14] hath been with you.
She is the fairies' midwife, and she comes
55 In shape no bigger than an agate stone
On the forefinger of an alderman,
Drawn with a team of little atomies[15]
Over men's noses as they lie asleep;
Her wagon spokes made of long spinners'[16] legs,
60 The cover, of the wings of grasshoppers;
Her traces, of the smallest spider web;
Her collars, of the moonshine's wat'ry beams;
Her whip, of cricket's bone; the lash, of film;[17]
Her wagoner, a small gray-coated gnat,

6. quote deformities notice my ugly features.
7. betake . . . legs start dancing.
8. Let . . . rushes Let fun-loving people dance on the floor coverings.
9. proverbed . . . phrase directed by an old saying.
10. The game . . . done No matter how much enjoyment may be had, I will not have any.
11. Dun's . . . word! Lie low like a mouse—that is what a constable waiting to make an arrest might say.
12. Dun proverbial name for a horse.

Literary Analysis
Dialogue What contrast between Mercutio and Romeo does the dialogue reveal?

13. Take . . . wits Understand my intended meaning. That shows more intelligence than merely following what your senses perceive.
14. Queen Mab the queen of fairyland.

15. atomies creatures.
16. spinners spiders.
17. film spider's thread.

Reading Check

How does Romeo feel about going to the Capulets' feast?

65   Not half so big as a round little worm
       Pricked from the lazy finger of a maid;
       Her chariot is an empty hazelnut,
       Made by the joiner squirrel or old grub,[18]
       Time out o' mind the fairies' coachmakers.

70   And in this state she gallops night by night
       Through lovers' brains, and then they dream of love;
       On courtiers' knees, that dream on curtsies straight;
       O'er lawyers' fingers, who straight dream on fees;
       O'er ladies' lips, who straight on kisses dream,

75   Which oft the angry Mab with blisters plagues,
       Because their breath with sweetmeats[19] tainted are.
       Sometimes she gallops o'er a courtier's nose,
       And then dreams he of smelling out a suit;[20]
       And sometime comes she with a tithe pig's[21] tail

80   Tickling a parson's nose as 'a lies asleep,
       Then he dreams of another benefice.[22]
       Sometime she driveth o'er a soldier's neck,
       And then dream he of cutting foreign throats,
       Of breaches, ambuscadoes,[23] Spanish blades,

85   Of healths[24] five fathom deep; and then anon
       Drums in his ear, at which he starts and wakes,
       And being thus frighted, swears a prayer or two
       And sleeps again. This is that very Mab
       That plats[25] the manes of horses in the night

90   And bakes the elflocks[26] in foul sluttish hairs,
       Which once untangled much misfortune bodes.
       This is the hag, when maids lie on their backs,
       That presses them and learns them first to bear,
       Making them women of good carriage.[27]
       This is she—

95 **ROMEO.**   Peace, peace, Mercutio, peace!
       Thou talk'st of nothing.

     MERCUTIO.   True, I talk of dreams;
       Which are the children of an idle brain,
       Begot of nothing but vain fantasy;
       Which is as thin of substance as the air,

100   And more inconstant than the wind, who woos
       Even now the frozen bosom of the North
       And, being angered, puffs away from thence,
       Turning his side to the dew-dropping South.

     BENVOLIO. This wind you talk of blows us from ourselves.
105   Supper is done, and we shall come too late.

---

18. old grub insect that bores holes in nuts.

19. sweetmeats candy.

20. smelling . . . suit finding someone who has a petition (suit) for the king and who will pay the courtier to gain the king's favor for the petition.
21. tithe pig pig donated to a parson.
22. benefice church appointment that included a guaranteed income.
23. ambuscadoes ambushes.
24. healths toasts ("To your health!").
25. plats tangles.
26. elflocks tangled hair.

27. carriage posture.

Reading Skill
Summarizing Review Mercutio's speech and summarize his ideas about Queen Mab.

Literary Analysis
Dialogue What do Mercutio's comments about dreams reveal about his character?

ROMEO. I fear, too early; for my mind misgives
    Some consequence yet hanging in the stars
    Shall bitterly begin his fearful date
    With this night's revels and expire the term
110   Of a despisèd life, closed in my breast,
    By some vile forfeit of untimely death.[28]
    But he that hath the steerage of my course
    Direct my sail! On, lusty gentlemen!

BENVOLIO. Strike, drum.

        [*They march about the stage, and retire to one side.*]

Scene v. A hall in Capulet's house.

[SERVINGMEN *come forth with napkins.*]

FIRST SERVINGMAN. Where's Potpan, that he helps not to
    take away? He shift a trencher![1] He scrape a trencher!

SECOND SERVINGMAN. When good manners shall lie all in one
    or two men's hands, and they unwashed too, 'tis a foul thing.

5 **FIRST SERVINGMAN.** Away with the join-stools, remove the
    court cupboard, look to the plate. Good thou, save me a
    piece of marchpane,[2] and, as thou loves me, let the porter
    let in Susan Grindstone and Nell. Anthony, and Potpan!

SECOND SERVINGMAN. Ay, boy, ready.

10 **FIRST SERVINGMAN.** You are looked for and called for,
    asked for and sought for, in the great chamber.

THIRD SERVINGMAN. We cannot be here and there too.
    Cheerly, boys! Be brisk awhile, and the longer liver
    take all.   [*Exit.*]

[*Enter* CAPULET, *his* WIFE, JULIET, TYBALT, NURSE, *and all the* GUESTS
and GENTLEWOMEN *to the* MASKERS.]

15 **CAPULET.** Welcome, gentlemen! Ladies that have their toes
    Unplagued with corns will walk a bout[3] with you.
    Ah, my mistresses, which of you all
    Will now deny to dance? She that makes dainty,[4]
    She I'll swear hath corns. Am I come near ye now?
20   Welcome, gentlemen! I have seen the day
    That I have worn a visor and could tell
    A whispering tale in a fair lady's ear,
    Such as would please. 'Tis gone, 'tis gone, 'tis gone.

Reading Skill
Summarizing Use
footnote 28 to help
you summarize
Romeo's response to
Benvolio.

28. my mind . . . death My
mind is fearful that some future
event, fated by the stars, shall
start to run its course tonight
and cut my life short.

1. trencher wooden platter.

2. marchpane marzipan, a
confection made of sugar and
almonds.

3. walk a bout dance a turn.
4. makes dainty hesitates,
acts shy.

Reading Check

What does Romeo
fear might happen in
the near future?

You are welcome, gentlemen! Come, musicians,
    play.

[*Music plays, and they dance.*]

25 A hall,[5] a hall! Give room! And foot it, girls.
    More light, you knaves, and turn the tables up,
    And quench the fire; the room is grown too hot.
    Ah, sirrah, this unlooked-for sport comes well.
    Nay, sit; nay, sit, good cousin Capulet;
30 For you and I are past our dancing days.
    How long is't now since last yourself and I
    Were in a mask?

SECOND CAPULET. By'r Lady, thirty years.

CAPULET. What, man? 'Tis not so much, 'tis not so
    much;
35 'Tis since the nuptial of Lucentio,
    Come Pentecost as quickly as it will,
    Some five-and-twenty years, and then we masked.

SECOND CAPULET. 'Tis more, 'tis more. His son is
    elder, sir;
    His son is thirty.

CAPULET.   Will you tell me that?
40 His son was but a ward[6] two years ago.

ROMEO. [*To a* SERVINGMAN] What lady's that which doth
    enrich the hand
    Of yonder knight?

SERVINGMAN. I know not, sir.

ROMEO. O, she doth teach the torches to burn bright!
    It seems she hangs upon the cheek of night
45 As a rich jewel in an Ethiop's ear—
    Beauty too rich for use, for earth too dear!
    So shows a snowy dove trooping with crows
    As yonder lady o'er her fellows shows.
    The measure done, I'll watch her place of stand
50 And, touching hers, make blessèd my rude hand.
    Did my heart love till now? Forswear[7] it, sight!
    For I ne'er saw true beauty till this night.

TYBALT. This, by his voice, should be a Montague.
    Fetch me my rapier, boy. What! Dares the slave
55 Come hither, covered with an antic face,[8]
    To fleer[9] and scorn at our solemnity?

5. **A hall** clear the floor, make
room for dancing.
6. **ward** minor.

Literary Analysis
Stage Directions
What do the stage
direction in line 41
and the dialogue that
follows reveal about
Romeo?

7. **Forswear** deny.
8. **antic face** strange, fantastic mask.
9. **fleer** mock.

Now, by the stock and honor of my kin,
To strike him dead I hold it not a sin.

CAPULET. Why, how now, kinsman? Wherefore storm you so?

60 **TYBALT.** Uncle, this is a Montague, our foe,
A villain, that is hither come in spite
To scorn at our solemnity this night.

CAPULET. Young Romeo is it?

TYBALT.   'Tis he, that villain Romeo.

CAPULET. Content thee, gentle coz,[10] let him alone.
65 'A bears him like a portly gentleman,[11]
And, to say truth, Verona brags of him
To be a virtuous and well-governed youth.
I would not for the wealth of all this town
Here in my house do him disparagement.[12]
70 Therefore be patient; take no note of him.
It is my will, the which if thou respect,
Show a fair presence and put off these frowns,
An ill-beseeming semblance[13] for a feast.

TYBALT. It fits when such a villain is a guest.
I'll not endure him.

75 **CAPULET.**   He shall be endured.
What, goodman[14] boy! I say he shall. Go to![15]
Am I the master here, or you? Go to!
You'll not endure him, God shall mend my soul![16]
You'll make a mutiny among my guests!
80 You will set cock-a-hoop.[17] You'll be the man!

TYBALT. Why, uncle, 'tis a shame.

CAPULET.   Go to, go to!
You are a saucy boy. Is't so, indeed?
This trick may chance to scathe you.[18] I know what.
You must contrary me! Marry, 'tis time—
85 Well said, my hearts!—You are a princox[19]—go!
Be quiet, or—more light, more light!—For shame!
I'll make you quiet. What!—Cheerly, my hearts!

TYBALT. Patience perforce with willful choler meeting[20]
Makes my flesh tremble in their different greeting.
90 I will withdraw; but this intrusion shall,
Now seeming sweet, convert to bitt'rest gall.   [*Exit.*]

ROMEO. If I profane with my unworthiest hand

10. **coz** Here, "coz" is used as a term of address for a relative.
11. **'A . . . gentleman** He behaves like a dignified gentleman.
12. **disparagement** insult.
13. **ill-beseeming semblance** inappropriate appearance.
14. **goodman** term of address for someone below the rank of gentleman.
15. **Go to!** expression of angry impatience.
16. **God . . . soul!** expression of impatience, equivalent to "God save me!"
17. **You will set cock-a-hoop** You want to swagger like a barnyard rooster.

Literary Analysis
Dialogue What does the dialogue between Capulet and Tybalt show about their relationship?

18. **This . . . you** This trait of yours may turn out to hurt you.
19. **princox** rude youngster; wise guy.
20. **Patience . . . meeting** enforced self-control mixing with strong anger.

Reading Check

How does Capulet respond when Tybalt says he will not tolerate Romeo's presence at the party?

This holy shrine,[21] the gentle sin is this:
My lips, two blushing pilgrims, ready stand

95   To smooth that rough touch with a tender kiss.

JULIET. Good pilgrim, you do wrong your hand too much,
Which mannerly devotion shows in this;
For saints have hands that pilgrims' hands do touch
And palm to palm is holy palmers'[22] kiss.

100 **ROMEO.** Have not saints lips, and holy palmers too?

JULIET. Ay, pilgrim, lips that they must use in prayer.

ROMEO. O, then, dear saint, let lips do what hands do!
They pray; grant thou, lest faith turn to despair.

JULIET. Saints do not move,[23] though grant for prayers' sake.

105 **ROMEO.** Then move not while my prayer's effect I take.
Thus from my lips, by thine my sin is purged.   [*Kisses her.*]

JULIET. Then have my lips the sin that they have took.

ROMEO. Sin from my lips? O trespass sweetly urged![24]
Give me my sin again.   [*Kisses her.*]

JULIET.   You kiss by th' book.[25]

110 **NURSE.** Madam, your mother craves a word with you.

ROMEO. What is her mother?

NURSE.   Marry, bachelor,
Her mother is the lady of the house,
And a good lady, and a wise and virtuous.

21. **shrine** Juliet's hand.

22. **palmers** pilgrims who at one time carried palm branches from the Holy Land.
23. **move** initiate involvement in earthly affairs.

Literary Analysis
Dialogue and Stage Directions What do the dialogue and stage directions in this passage reveal about Romeo's and Juliet's feelings?

24. **O . . . urged!** Romeo is saying, in substance, that he is happy. Juliet calls his kiss a sin, for now he can take it back—by another kiss.
25. **by th' book** as if you were following a manual of courtly love.

◀ **Critical Viewing** Which details in this photograph show Romeo's and Juliet's affection for each other? [**Draw Conclusions**]

I nursed her daughter that you talked withal.
115 I tell you, he that can lay hold of her
Shall have the chinks.²⁶

ROMEO.   Is she a Capulet?
O dear account! My life is my foe's debt.²⁷

BENVOLIO. Away, be gone; the sport is at the best.

ROMEO. Ay, so I fear; the more is my unrest.

120 **CAPULET.** Nay, gentlemen, prepare not to be gone;
We have a trifling foolish banquet towards.²⁸
Is it e'en so?²⁹ Why then, I thank you all.
I thank you, honest gentlemen. Good night.
More torches here! Come on then; let's to bed.
125 Ah, sirrah, by my fay,³⁰ it waxes late;
I'll to my rest.   [*Exit all but* JULIET *and* NURSE.]

JULIET. Come hither, nurse. What is yond gentleman?

NURSE. The son and heir of old Tiberio.

JULIET. What's he that now is going out of door?

130 **NURSE.** Marry, that, I think, be young Petruchio.

JULIET. What's he that follows here, that would not dance?

NURSE. I know not.

JULIET. Go ask his name—If he is married,
My grave is like to be my wedding bed.

135 **NURSE.** His name is Romeo, and a Montague,
The only son of your great enemy.

JULIET. My only love, sprung from my only hate!
Too early seen unknown, and known too late!
Prodigious³¹ birth of love it is to me
140 That I must love a loathèd enemy.

NURSE. What's this? What's this?

JULIET.   A rhyme I learnt even now.
Of one I danced withal.   [*One calls within,* "Juliet."]

NURSE.   Anon, anon!
Come, let's away; the strangers all are gone.   [*Exit all.*]

26. **chinks** cash.
27. **My life . . . debt** Since Juliet is a Capulet, Romeo's life is at the mercy of the enemies of his family.

28. **towards** being prepared.
29. **Is . . . so?** Is it the case that you really must leave?
30. **fay** faith.

Literary Analysis
Dialogue and Stage Directions How can you tell that the dialogue that follows line 126 is a private conversation?

31. **Prodigious** monstrous; foretelling misfortune.

Apply the Skills

The Tragedy of Romeo and Juliet, Act I

Thinking About the Selection

1. **Respond:** If you were Romeo or Juliet, would you pursue a relationship with the other? Explain.
2. **(a) Recall:** Based on Act I, what do you know about Romeo's and Juliet's lives? **(b) Compare and Contrast:** How are their personalities similar and different?
3. **(a) Recall:** What information about the two households is presented in the Prologue? **(b) Connect:** In what way does Juliet's comment in Act I, Scene v, lines 137–138 echo the Prologue?
4. **Analyze:** How do the comments of Mercutio and Benvolio add to your understading of Romeo's character?
5. **(a) Analyze:** What threats to Romeo and Juliet's love already exist in Act I? **(b) Speculate:** How do you think Romeo and Juliet will react to these threats?
6. **Evaluate:** Based on Romeo's behavior in Act I, do you think Shakespeare accurately portrays a teenager in love? Explain.

Literary Analysis

7. Using a chart like the one shown, explain what the **dialogue** involving the Nurse, Juliet, and Lady Capulet in Act I, Scene iii reveals about each character.

Character	Dialogue		Reveals

8. Most of the **stage directions** in Act I mark the characters' entrances and exits. **(a)** Identify three examples of stage directions that do more than simply dictate characters' movements on and off stage. **(b)** Explain what each of these directions tells us about the characters and the action.

Reading Skill

9. **Use text aids** to restate Capulet's scolding of Tybalt in Act I, Scene v, lines 77–87 in your own words.
10. **(a)** Using text aids to clarify her meaning, explain the play on words in Juliet's speech in Act I, Scene v, lines 96–99.
    (b) Summarize her speech in a few sentences.

QuickReview

Act I at a Glance
Romeo and Juliet meet at a ball given by Juliet's family. They fall immediately in love, only to discover that their families are enemies.

Assessment

For: Self-test
Visit: www.PHSchool.com
Web Code: epa-6502

Dialogue: conversation between characters

Stage Directions: notes in the text of a play that describe how the work should be performed or staged

Summarizing: briefly stating the main points in a piece of writing

Vocabulary Builder

Practice An **oxymoron** is a phrase combining contradictory or opposing ideas, often used as a figure of speech for poetic effect. Review the vocabulary list on page 728. Then, explain the meaning of each phrase and tell why each one is an oxymoron.

1. pernicious blessing
2. augmenting scarcity
3. flattering grievance
4. honorable transgression

Adding Words to Your Vocabulary *Diminishing* and *abridging* are both antonyms for the word *augmenting*. Use a dictionary to find the precise meaning of each word. For each word, write a sentence using it correctly. Then, share your sentences with classmates and discuss their differences and similarities. (For more on using a dictionary, see page R6.)

Writing

As either Romeo or Juliet, write a **letter to an advice columnist** requesting help with the problem of falling in love with someone whom you are not supposed to love.
  • First, list the reasons your love may be doomed.
  • Next, write a letter that explains your list and asks for advice.
After you have written your letter as Romeo or Juliet, write a response as the advice columnist. Suggest to Romeo or Juliet how he or she might handle this difficult situation. Share your letters with the class and discuss the power of writing using more than one voice.

For *Grammar, Vocabulary,* and *Assessment,*
see **Build Language Skills,** pages 812–813.

Extend Your Learning

Listening and Speaking Select a scene from Act I and plan a **staged performance** with classmates. Choose a scene with at least three characters. Then, plan and rehearse the scene.
  • Decide who will play each role.
  • As you rehearse take turns critiquing the group's work.
Take care to express your thoughts clearly with attention to others, and convey criticism in a respectful way. Perform the scene for the class, and invite comments from the audience.

Literary Analysis

Blank verse is unrhymed poetry written in a meter called iambic pentameter. A line written in iambic pentameter includes five stressed syllables, each preceded by an unstressed syllable, as in the following example:

But soft! What light through yonder window breaks?

It is the east, and Juliet is the sun!

Much of *The Tragedy of Romeo and Juliet* is written in blank verse. Shakespeare uses its formal meter to reinforce character rank. Important or aristocratic characters typically speak in blank verse. Minor or comic characters often do not speak in verse.

Based on your understanding of blank verse, use a chart like the one shown to identify characters' rank in this play.

Reading Skill

Summarizing is briefly stating the main points in a piece of writing. Stopping periodically to summarize what you have read helps you to check your comprehension before you read further.

Summarizing is especially useful when reading a play that has long passages of blank verse. When you encounter one of these passages, **read in sentences**—just as if you were reading a poem. Pause according to punctuation instead of at the end of each line. As you become more accustomed to the form, you will be able to increase your speed.

Once you have grasped the meanings of individual sentences in blank verse, you can more easily and more accurately summarize long passages.

Vocabulary Builder

- **procure** (prō kyoor´) *v.* get; obtain (p. 765) *The hungry man tried to procure food.*

- **predominant** (prē däm´ ə nənt) *adj.* having dominating influence over others (p. 767) *Despite some disagreement, the predominant tone of the meeting was one of unity.*

- **intercession** (in´ tər sesh´ ən) *n.* act of pleading on another's behalf (p. 767) *Thanks to the intercession by Andy and Paula, Jim was allowed into the concert without a ticket.*

- **sallow** (sal´ ō) *adj.* of a sickly, pale-yellowish color (p. 768) *When her sickness passed, her face no longer looked sallow.*

- **lamentable** (lam´ ən tə bəl) *adj.* distressing; sad (p. 769) *His lack of concern about his health is lamentable.*

- **unwieldy** (un wēl´ dē) *adj.* awkward; clumsy (p. 776) *Joe's sprained ankle made him unwieldy on the dance floor.*

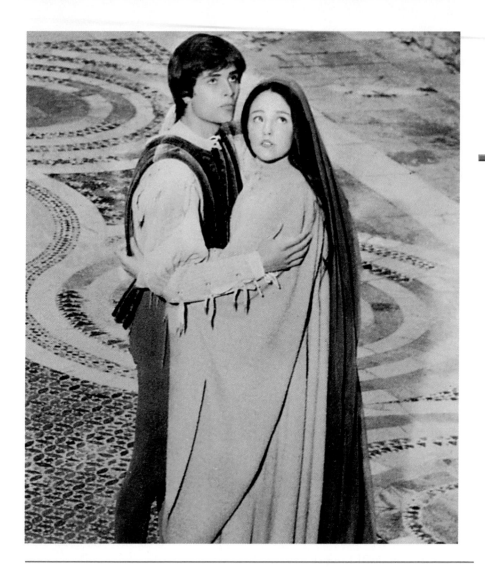

Review and Anticipate

Act I reveals a bitter, long-standing feud between the Montagues and the Capulets. It also introduces the play's title characters, who meet at a feast and immediately fall in love, only to discover that they come from opposing sides of the feud.

Based on what you have learned about the personalities of Romeo and Juliet, how do you expect them to respond to their love for each other and to the problems it poses? How do you think their families will react?

[*Enter* CHORUS.]

CHORUS. Now old desire[1] doth in his deathbed lie,
    And young affection gapes to be his heir;[2]
    That fair[3] for which love groaned for and would die,

ACT II

PROLOGUE

1. **old desire** Romeo's love for Rosaline.

2. **young . . . heir** Romeo's new love for Juliet is eager to replace his love for Rosaline.

3. **fair** beautiful woman (Rosaline).

With tender Juliet matched, is now not fair.
5 Now Romeo is beloved and loves again,
   Alike bewitchèd[4] by the charm of looks;
But to his foe supposed he must complain,[5]
   And she steal love's sweet bait from fearful hooks.
Being held a foe, he may not have access
10 To breathe such vows as lovers use to swear,
And she as much in love, her means much less
   To meet her new belovèd anywhere;
But passion lends them power, time means to meet,
Temp'ring extremities with extreme sweet.[6]
[*Exit.*]

Scene i. Near CAPULET'S orchard.

[*Enter* ROMEO *alone.*]

ROMEO. Can I go forward when my heart is here?
   Turn back, dull earth,[1] and find thy center[2] out.

[*Enter* BENVOLIO *with* MERCUTIO. ROMEO *retires.*]

BENVOLIO. Romeo! My cousin Romeo! Romeo!

MERCUTIO.   He is wise.
   And, on my life, hath stol'n him home to bed.

5 **BENVOLIO.** He ran this way and leapt this orchard wall.
   Call, good Mercutio.

MERCUTIO.   Nay, I'll conjure[3] too.
   Romeo! Humors! Madman! Passion! Lover!
   Appear thou in the likeness of a sigh;
   Speak but one rhyme, and I am satisfied!
10 Cry but "Ay me!" pronounce but "love" and "dove";
   Speak to my gossip[4] Venus one fair word,
   One nickname for her purblind son and heir,
   Young Abraham Cupid, he that shot so true
   When King Cophetua loved the beggar maid!
15 He heareth not, he stirreth not, he moveth not;
   The ape is dead,[5] and I must conjure him.
   I conjure thee by Rosaline's bright eyes,
   By her high forehead and her scarlet lip,
   By her fine foot, straight leg, and quivering thigh,
20 And the demesnes that there adjacent lie,
   That in thy likeness thou appear to us!

BENVOLIO. And if he hear thee, thou wilt anger him.

---

4. Alike bewitched Both Romeo and Juliet are enchanted.

5. complain address his words of love.

6. Temp'ring . . . sweet easing their difficulties with great delights.

1. dull earth lifeless body.

2. center heart, or possibly soul (Juliet).

3. conjure recite a spell to make Romeo appear.

4. gossip merry old lady.

5. The ape is dead Romeo, like a trained monkey, seems to be playing.

Literary Analysis
Blank Verse Based on the overall meter of his speech, how can you tell that Mercutio is an aristocrat?

MERCUTIO. This cannot anger him. 'Twould anger him
    To raise a spirit in his mistress' circle
25   Of some strange nature, letting it there stand
    Till she had laid it and conjured it down.
    That were some spite; my invocation
    Is fair and honest; in his mistress' name,
    I conjure only but to raise up him.

30 **BENVOLIO.** Come, he hath hid himself among these trees
    To be consorted[6] with the humorous[7] night.
    Blind is his love and best befits the dark.

MERCUTIO. If love be blind, love cannot hit the mark.
    Now will he sit under a medlar tree
35   And wish his mistress were that kind of fruit
    As maids call medlars[8] when they laugh alone.
    O, Romeo, that she were, O that she were
    An open et cetera, thou a pop'rin pear!
    Romeo, good night. I'll to my truckle bed;[9]
40   This field bed is too cold for me to sleep.
    Come, shall we go?

BENVOLIO.   Go then, for 'tis in vain
    To seek him here that means not to be found.

                          [Exit with others.]

6. **consorted** associated.

7. **humorous** humid; moody, like a lover.

8. **medlars** applelike fruits.

9. **truckle bed** trundlebed, placed under a larger bed when not in use.

Scene ii. CAPULET'S orchard.

ROMEO. *[Coming forward]* He jests at scars that never felt a wound.

[Enter JULIET at a window.]

    But soft! What light through yonder window breaks?
    It is the East, and Juliet is the sun!
    Arise, fair sun, and kill the envious moon,
5   Who is already sick and pale with grief
    That thou her maid art far more fair than she.
    Be not her maid, since she is envious.
    Her vestal livery[1] is but sick and green,
    And none but fools do wear it. Cast it off.
10   It is my lady! O, it is my love!
    O, that she knew she were!
    She speaks, yet she says nothing. What of that?
    Her eye discourses; I will answer it.
    I am too bold; 'tis not to me she speaks.
15   Two of the fairest stars in all the heaven,
    Having some business, do entreat her eyes

Literary Analysis
Blank Verse Which line in Romeo's speech breaks the pattern of five stressed syllables per line?

1. **livery** clothing or costume worn by a servant.

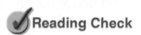

Reading Check

Whom does Romeo see at the window?

To twinkle in their spheres² till they return.
What if her eyes were there, they in her head?
The brightness of her cheek would shame those stars
20 As daylight doth a lamp; her eyes in heaven
Would through the airy region stream so bright
That birds would sing and think it were not night.
See how she leans her cheek upon that hand,
O, that I were a glove upon that hand,
That I might touch that cheek!

JULIET.   Ay me!

25 **ROMEO.**   She speaks.
O, speak again, bright angel, for thou art
As glorious to this night, being o'er my head,
As is a wingèd messenger of heaven
Unto the white-upturnèd wond'ring eyes
30 Of mortals that fall back to gaze on him
When he bestrides the lazy puffing clouds
And sails upon the bosom of the air.

JULIET. O Romeo, Romeo! Wherefore art thou Romeo?³
Deny thy father and refuse thy name;
35 Or, if thou wilt not, be but sworn my love,
And I'll no longer be a Capulet.

ROMEO. [*Aside*] Shall I hear more, or shall I speak at this?

JULIET. 'Tis but thy name that is my enemy.
Thou art thyself, though not⁴ a Montague.
40 What's Montague? It is nor hand, nor foot,
Nor arm, nor face, nor any other part
Belonging to a man. O, be some other name!
What's in a name? That which we call a rose
By any other name would smell as sweet.
45 So Romeo would, were he not Romeo called,
Retain that dear perfection which he owes⁵
Without that title. Romeo, doff⁶ thy name;
And for thy name, which is no part of thee,
Take all myself.

ROMEO.   I take thee at thy word.
50 Call me but love, and I'll be new baptized;
Henceforth I never will be Romeo.

JULIET. What man art thou, thus bescreened in night,
So stumblest on my counsel?⁷

ROMEO.   By a name
I know not how to tell thee who I am.

2. **spheres** orbits.

3. **Wherefore . . .
Romeo?** Why are you
Romeo—a Montague?

4. **though not** even if you
were not.

**Reading Skill
Summarizing** Briefly
summarize Juliet's
speech about Romeo's
name.

5. **owes** owns; possesses.

6. **doff** remove.

7. **counsel** secret thoughts.

55 My name, dear saint, is hateful to myself
    Because it is an enemy to thee.
    Had I it written, I would tear the word.

    JULIET. My ears have yet not drunk a hundred words
    Of thy tongue's uttering, yet I know the sound.
60 Art thou not Romeo, and a Montague?

    ROMEO. Neither, fair maid, if either thee dislike.

    JULIET. How camest thou hither, tell me, and wherefore?
    The orchard walls are high and hard to climb,
    And the place death, considering who thou art,
65 If any of my kinsmen find thee here.

    ROMEO. With love's light wings did I o'erperch[8] these walls;
    For stony limits cannot hold love out,
    And what love can do, that dares love attempt.
    Therefore thy kinsmen are no stop to me.

70 **JULIET.** If they do see thee, they will murder thee.

    ROMEO. Alack, there lies more peril in thine eye
    Than twenty of their swords! Look thou but sweet,
    And I am proof[9] against their enmity.

    JULIET. I would not for the world they saw thee here.

75 **ROMEO.** I have night's cloak to hide me from their eyes;
    And but[10] thou love me, let them find me here.
    My life were better ended by their hate
    Than death proroguèd,[11] wanting of thy love.

    JULIET. By whose direction found'st thou out this place?

80 **ROMEO.** By love, that first did prompt me to inquire.
    He lent me counsel, and I lent him eyes.
    I am no pilot; yet, wert thou as far
    As that vast shore washed with the farthest sea,
    I should adventure[12] for such merchandise.

85 **JULIET.** Thou knowest the mask of night is on my face;
    Else would a maiden blush bepaint my cheek
    For that which thou hast heard me speak tonight.
    Fain would I dwell on form[13]—fain, fain deny
    What I have spoke; but farewell compliment![14]
90 Dost thou love me? I know thou wilt say "Ay";
    And I will take thy word. Yet, if thou swear'st,
    Thou mayst prove false. At lovers' perjuries,
    They say Jove laughs. O gentle Romeo,
    If thou dost love, pronounce it faithfully.
95 Or if thou thinkest I am too quickly won,

> **Literary Analysis**
> **Blank Verse** In line 57, how do the stressed syllables reinforce Romeo's meaning?

8. o'erperch fly over.

9. proof protected, as by armor.

10. And but unless.

11. proroguèd postponed.

12. adventure risk a long journey, like a sea adventurer.

13. Fain . . . form eagerly would I follow convention (by acting reserved).

14. compliment conventional behavior.

Reading Check

Why does Romeo say his name is hateful to him?

I'll frown and be perverse[15] and say thee nay,
So thou wilt woo; but else, not for the world.
In truth, fair Montague, I am too fond,[16]
And therefore thou mayst think my havior light;[17]
100 But trust me, gentleman, I'll prove more true
Than those that have more cunning to be strange.[18]
I should have been more strange, I must confess,
But that thou overheard'st, ere I was ware,
My truelove passion. Therefore pardon me,
105   And not impute this yielding to light love,
Which the dark night hath so discoverèd.[19]

ROMEO. Lady, by yonder blessèd moon I vow,
That tips with silver all these fruit-tree tops—

JULIET. O, swear not by the moon, th' inconstant moon,
110 That monthly changes in her circle orb,
Lest that thy love prove likewise variable.

ROMEO. What shall I swear by?

15. **be perverse** act contrary to my true feelings.

16. **fond** affectionate.

17. **my havior light** my behavior immodest or unserious.

18. **strange** distant and cold.

19. **discoverèd** revealed.

◀ **Critical Viewing**
How does Juliet's expression in this picture compare with the feelings she has conveyed in the play so far? **[Connect]**

JULIET.   Do not swear at all;
Or if thou wilt, swear by thy gracious self,
Which is the god of my idolatry,
And I'll believe thee.

115 **ROMEO.** heart's dear love—

JULIET. Well, do not swear. Although I joy in thee,
I have no joy of this contract[20] tonight.
It is too rash, too unadvised, too sudden;
Too like the lightning, which doth cease to be
120   Ere one can say it lightens. Sweet, good night!
This bud of love, by summer's ripening breath,
May prove a beauteous flow'r when next we meet.
Good night, good night! As sweet repose and rest
Come to thy heart as that within my breast!

125 **ROMEO.** O, wilt thou leave me so unsatisfied?

JULIET. What satisfaction canst thou have tonight?

ROMEO. Th' exchange of thy love's faithful vow for mine.

JULIET. I gave thee mine before thou didst request it;
And yet I would it were to give again.

130 **ROMEO.** Wouldst thou withdraw it? For what purpose, love?

JULIET. But to be frank[21] and give it thee again.
And yet I wish but for the thing I have.
My bounty[22] is as boundless as the sea,
My love as deep; the more I give to thee,
135   The more I have, for both are infinite,
I hear some noise within. Dear love, adieu!

[NURSE *calls within.*]

Anon, good nurse! Sweet Montague, be true.
Stay but a little, I will come again.   [*Exit.*]

ROMEO. O blessèd, blessèd night! I am afeard,
140   Being in night, all this is but a dream,
Too flattering-sweet to be substantial.[23]

[*Enter* JULIET *again.*]

JULIET. Three words, dear Romeo, and good night indeed.
If that thy bent[24] of love be honorable,
Thy purpose marriage, send me word tomorrow,
145   By one that I'll <u>procure</u> to come to thee,
Where and what time thou wilt perform the rite;
And all my fortunes at thy foot I'll lay
And follow thee my lord throughout the world.

Literary Analysis
Blank Verse The five stressed syllables of lines 112 and 115 are split between the two speakers. What does this weaving together of dialogue suggest about the speakers' relationship?

20. **contract** betrothal.

21. **frank** generous.

22. **bounty** what I have to give.

23. **substantial** real.
24. **bent** purpose; intention.

Vocabulary Builder
procure (prō kyoor´)
v. get; obtain

Reading Check

Why does Juliet tell Romeo not to swear his love by the moon?

NURSE. [*Within*] Madam!

150 **JULIET.** I come anon.—But if thou meanest not well,
I do beseech thee—

NURSE. [*Within*] Madam!

JULIET. By and by[25] I come.—
To cease thy strife[26] and leave me to my grief.
Tomorrow will I send.

ROMEO. So thrive my soul—

JULIET. A thousand times good night! [*Exit.*]

Literary Analysis
Blank Verse Three speakers share the rhythm of line 151. Does the Nurse's interruption complete or break the blank verse?

25. By and by at once.

26. strife efforts.

Literature in Context — Culture Connection

Falconry

When Juliet longs for "a falc'ners voice," she is referring to someone who practices falconry, the sport of hunting with falcons. Falcon are swift, hawk-like birds of prey. The falconer trains the bird to respond to a combination of physical and vocal commands.

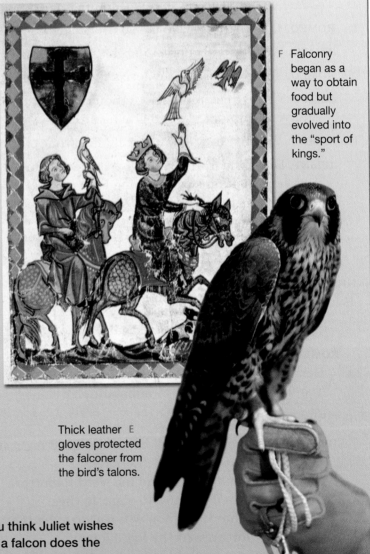

F Falconry began as a way to obtain food but gradually evolved into the "sport of kings."

During Shakespeare's time one's rank in society determined the kind of bird one could own:

Rank	Type of Bird
King	Gyr falcon
Prince	Peregrine falcon (male)
Knight	Saker falcon
Squire	Lanner falcon
Lady	Merlin (female)
Yeoman	(a landowner) Goshawk
Servants, children	Kestrel

Thick leather E gloves protected the falconer from the bird's talons.

Connect to the Literature Why do you think Juliet wishes Romeo would respond to her voice as a falcon does the falconer's commands?

155 **ROMEO.** A thousand times the worse, to want thy light!
　　Love goes toward love as schoolboys from their books;
　　But love from love, toward school with heavy looks.

[*Enter* JULIET *again.*]

　　JULIET. Hist! Romeo, hist! O for a falc'ner's voice
　　　To lure this tassel gentle²⁷ back again!
160　Bondage is hoarse²⁸ and may not speak aloud,
　　　Else would I tear the cave where Echo²⁹ lies
　　　And make her airy tongue more hoarse than mine
　　　With repetition of "My Romeo!"

　　ROMEO. It is my soul that calls upon my name.
165　How silver-sweet sound lovers' tongues by night,
　　　Like softest music to attending ears!

　　JULIET. Romeo!

　　ROMEO.　　My sweet?

　　JULIET.　　　　　　　　What o'clock tomorrow
　　　Shall I send to thee?

　　ROMEO.　　　　　　By the hour of nine.

　　JULIET. I will not fail. 'Tis twenty year till then.
170　　I have forgot why I did call thee back.

　　ROMEO. Let me stand here till thou remember it.

　　JULIET. I shall forget, to have thee still stand there,
　　　Rememb'ring how I love thy company.

　　ROMEO. And I'll stay, to have thee still forget,
175　Forgetting any other home but this.

　　JULIET. 'Tis almost morning. I would have thee gone—
　　　And yet no farther than a wanton's³⁰ bird,
　　　That lets it hop a little from his hand,
　　　Like a poor prisoner in his twisted gyves,³¹
180　And with a silken thread plucks it back again,
　　　So loving-jealous of his liberty.

　　ROMEO. I would I were thy bird.

　　JULIET.　　　　　　　　　Sweet, so would I.
　　　Yet I should kill thee with much cherishing.
　　　Good night, good night! Parting is such sweet sorrow
185　That I shall say good night till it be morrow.　　[*Exit.*]

　　ROMEO. Sleep dwell upon thine eyes, peace in thy breast!
　　　Would I were sleep and peace, so sweet to rest!

Literary Analysis
Blank Verse Based on the fact that Romeo and Juliet speak in blank verse, what can you conclude about their character rank?

27. tassel gentle male falcon.

28. Bondage is hoarse Being bound in by my family restricts my speech.

29. Echo In classical mythology, the nymph Echo, unable to win the love of Narcissus, wasted away in a cave until nothing was left of her but her voice.

30. wanton's spoiled, playful child's.

31. gyves (jīvz) chains.

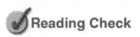

Reading Check

What plan do Romeo and Juliet make for the following day?

Hence will I to my ghostly friar's[32] close cell,[33]
His help to crave and my dear hap[34] to tell.   [*Exit.*]

Scene iii. *Friar Lawrence cell.*

[*Enter* FRIAR LAWRENCE *alone, with a basket.*]

FRIAR. The gray-eyed morn smiles on the frowning night,
Check'ring the eastern clouds with streaks of light;
And fleckèd[1] darkness like a drunkard reels
From forth day's path and Titan's burning wheels.[2]
5 Now, ere the sun advance his burning eye
The day to cheer and night's dank dew to dry,
I must upfill this osier cage[3] of ours
With baleful[4] weeds and precious-juicèd flowers.
The earth that's nature's mother is her tomb.
10 What is her burying grave, that is her womb;
And from her womb children of divers kind[5]
We sucking on her natural bosom find,
Many for many virtues excellent,
None but for some, and yet all different.
15 O, mickle[6] is the powerful grace[7] that lies
In plants, herbs, stones, and their true qualities;
For naught so vile that on the earth doth live
But to the earth some special good doth give;
Nor aught so good but, strained[8] from that fair use,
20 Revolts from true birth,[9] stumbling on abuse.
Virtue itself turns vice, being misapplied,
And vice sometime by action dignified.

[*Enter* ROMEO.]

Within the infant rind[10] of this weak flower
Poison hath residence and medicine power;[11]
25 For this, being smelt, with that part cheers each part;[12]
Being tasted, stays all senses with the heart.[13]
Two such opposèd kings encamp them still[14]
In man as well as herbs—grace and rude will;
And where the worser is <u>predominant</u>,
30 Full soon the canker[15] death eats up that plant.

ROMEO. Good morrow, father.

FRIAR.   Benedicite![16]
What early tongue so sweet saluteth me?
Young son, it argues a distemperèd head[17]
So soon to bid good morrow to thy bed.

32. ghostly friar's spiritual father's.

33. close cell small room.

34. dear hap good fortune.

Reading Skill
Summarizing Briefly state the main points of the Friar's speech in lines 1–30.

1. **fleckèd** spotted.

2. **Titan's burning wheels** wheels of the sun god's chariot.

3. **osier cage** willow basket.

4. **baleful** poisonous.

5. **divers kind** different kinds.

6. **mickle** great.

7. **grace** divine power.

8. **strained** turned away.

9. **Revolts . . . birth** conflicts with its real purpose.

10. **infant rind** tender skin.

11. **and medicine power** and medicinal quality has power.

12. **with . . . part** with that quality—odor—revives each part of the body.

13. **stays . . . heart** kills (stops the working of the five senses along with the heart).

14. **still** always.

15. **canker** destructive caterpillar.

Vocabulary Builder
predominant (prē dăm′ ə nənt) *adj.* having dominating influence over others

16. **Benedicite!** God bless you!

17. **distemperèd head** troubled mind.

35 Care keeps his watch in every old man's eye,
    And where care lodges, sleep will never lie;
    But where unbruisèd youth with unstuffed[18] brain
    Doth couch his limbs, there golden sleep doth reign,
    Therefore thy earliness doth me assure
40 Thou art uproused with some distemp'rature;[19]
    Or if not so, then here I hit it right—
    Our Romeo hath not been in bed tonight.

ROMEO. That last is true. The sweeter rest was mine.

FRIAR. God pardon sin! Wast thou with Rosaline?

45 **ROMEO.** With Rosaline, my ghostly father? No.
    I have forgot that name and that name's woe.

FRIAR. That's my good son! But where hast thou been then?

ROMEO. I'll tell thee ere thou ask it me again.
    I have been feasting with mine enemy,
50 Where on a sudden one hath wounded me
    That's by me wounded. Both our remedies
    Within thy help and holy physic[20] lies.
    I bear no hatred, blessèd man, for, lo,
    My intercession likewise steads my foe.[21]

55 **FRIAR.** Be plain, good son, and homely in thy drift.[22]
    Riddling confession finds but riddling shrift.[23]

ROMEO. Then plainly know my heart's dear love is set
    On the fair daughter of rich Capulet;
    As mine on hers, so hers is set on mine,
60 And all combined, save[24] what thou must combine
    By holy marriage. When and where and how
    We met, we wooed, and made exchange of vow,
    I'll tell thee as we pass; but this I pray,
    That thou consent to marry us today.

65 **FRIAR.** Holy Saint Francis! What a change is here!
    Is Rosaline, that thou didst love so dear,
    So soon forsaken? Young men's love then lies
    Not truly in their hearts, but in their eyes.
    Jesu Maria! What a deal of brine[25]
70 Hath washed thy sallow cheeks for Rosaline!
    How much salt water thrown away in waste
    To season love, that of it doth not taste!
    The sun not yet thy sighs from heaven clears,
    Thy old groans ring yet in mine ancient ears.
75 Lo, here upon thy cheek the stain doth sit
    Of an old tear that is not washed off yet.

If e'er thou wast thyself, and these woes thine,
Thou and these woes were all for Rosaline.
And art thou changed? Pronounce this sentence then:

80 Women may fall[26] when there's no strength[27] in men.

ROMEO. Thou chidst me oft for loving Rosaline.

FRIAR. For doting,[28] not for loving, pupil mine.

ROMEO. And badst[29] me bury love.

FRIAR.   Not in a grave
To lay one in, another out to have.

85 **ROMEO.** I pray thee chide me not. Her I love now
Doth grace[30] for grace and love for love allow.[31]
The other did not so.

FRIAR.   O, she knew well
Thy love did read by rote, that could not spell.[32]
But come, young waverer, come go with me.

90 In one respect I'll thy assistant be;
For this alliance may so happy prove
To turn your households' rancor[33] to pure love.

ROMEO. O, let us hence! I stand on[34] sudden haste.

FRIAR. Wisely and slow. They stumble that run fast.   [*Exit all.*]

26. fall be weak or inconstant.

27. strength constancy; stability.

28. doting being infatuated.

29. badst urged.

30. grace favor.

31. allow give.

32. Thy . . . spell your love recited words from memory with no understanding of them.

33. rancor hatred.

34. stand on insist on.

Scene iv. A street.

[*Enter* BENVOLIO *and* MERCUTIO.]

MERCUTIO. Where the devil should this Romeo be? Came he not home tonight?

BENVOLIO. Not to his father's. I spoke with his man.

MERCUTIO. Why, that same pale hardhearted wench, that
5 Rosaline, torments him so that he will sure run mad.

BENVOLIO. Tybalt, the kinsman to old Capulet, hath sent a letter to his father's house.

MERCUTIO. A challenge, on my life.

BENVOLIO. Romeo will answer it.

10 **MERCUTIO.** Any man that can write may answer a letter.

BENVOLIO. Nay, he will answer the letter's master, how he dares, being dared.

Literary Analysis
Blank Verse In what way is Mercutio's and Benvolio's speech different in this scene than it was earlier in Act II?

MERCUTIO. Alas, poor Romeo, he is already dead: stabbed
with a white wench's black eye; run through the ear
with a love song; the very pin of his heart cleft with the
blind bow-boy's butt-shaft;[1] and is he a man to encounter
Tybalt?

BENVOLIO. Why, what is Tybalt?

MERCUTIO. More than Prince of Cats.[2] O, he's the courageous
captain of compliments.[3] He fights as you sing
pricksong[4]—keeps time, distance, and proportion; he
rests his minim rests,[5] one, two, and the third in your
bosom! The very butcher of a silk button,[6] a duelist, a
duelist! A gentleman of the very first house,[7] of the first
and second cause.[8] Ah, the immortal passado! The
punto reverso! The hay![9]

BENVOLIO. The what?

MERCUTIO. The pox of such antic, lisping, affecting fantasti-
coes—these new tuners of accent![10] "By Jesu, a very good
blade! A very tall man! A very good whore!" Why,
is not this a <u>lamentable</u> thing, grandsir, that we
should be thus afflicted with these strange flies, these
fashionmongers, these pardon-me's,[11] who stand so
much on the new form that they cannot sit at ease on
the old bench? O, their bones, their bones!

[*Enter* ROMEO.]

BENVOLIO. Here comes Romeo! Here comes Romeo!

MERCUTIO. Without his roe, like a dried herring.[12] O flesh,
flesh, how art thou fishified! Now is he for the numbers[13]
that Petrarch flowed in. Laura, to his lady, was
a kitchen wench (marry, she had a better love to berhyme
her), Dido a dowdy, Cleopatra a gypsy, Helen
and Hero hildings and harlots, Thisbe a gray eye or so,
but not to the purpose. Signior Romeo, bon jour!
There's a French salutation to your French slop. You
gave us the counterfeit fairly last night.

ROMEO. Good morrow to you both. What counterfeit did I
give you?

MERCUTIO. The slip,[14] sir, the slip. Can you not conceive?

ROMEO. Pardon, good Mercutio. My business was great,
and in such a case as mine a man may strain courtesy.

Line numbers: 15, 20, 25, 30, 35, 40, 45

1. blind bow-boy's butt-shaft Cupid's blunt arrow.

2. Prince of Cats Tybalt, or a variation of it, is the name of the cat in medieval stories of Reynard the Fox.

3. captain of compliments master of formal behavior.

4. as you sing pricksong with attention to precision.

5. rests . . . rests observes all formalities.

6. button exact spot on his opponent's shirt.

7. first house finest school of fencing.

8. the first and second cause reasons that would cause a gentleman to challenge another to a duel.

9. passado! . . . punto reverso! . . . hay! lunge . . . backhanded stroke . . . home thrust.

10. The pox . . . accent May the plague strike these absurd characters with their phony manners.

Vocabulary Builder
lamentable (lam´ ən tə bəl) *adj.* distressing; sad

11. these pardon-me's these men who are always saying "Pardon me".

12. Without . . . herring worn out.

13. numbers verses of love poems.

14. slip escape. *Slip* is also a term for a counterfeit coin.

Reading Check

What does the Friar think Romeo and Juliet's love will do for the Capulets and Montagues?

50 **MERCUTIO.** That's as much as to say, such a case as yours
constrains a man to bow in the hams.[15]

ROMEO. Meaning, to curtsy.

MERCUTIO. Thou hast most kindly hit it.

ROMEO. A most courteous exposition.

55 **MERCUTIO.** Nay, I am the very pink of courtesy.

ROMEO. Pink for flower.

MERCUTIO. Right.

ROMEO. Why, then is my pump[16] well-flowered.

MERCUTIO. Sure wit, follow me this jest now till thou hast
60 worn out thy pump, that, when the single sole of it is
worn, the jest may remain, after the wearing, solely
singular.[17]

ROMEO. O single-soled jest, solely singular for the singleness![18]

MERCUTIO. Come between us, good Benvolio! My wits faints.

65 **ROMEO.** Swits and spurs, swits and spurs; or I'll cry a
match.[19]

15. hams hips.

16. pump shoe.

17. when . . . singular the jest will outwear the shoe and will then be all alone.

18. O . . . singleness! O thin joke, unique for only one thing—weakness!

19. Swits . . . match Drive your wit harder to beat me or else I will claim victory in this match of word play.

Literature in Context

History Connection

Mercutio's Allusions The women Mercutio names as he taunts Romeo are famous figures in European literature and history. Laura was the name of a woman to whom the Italian poet Petrarch addressed much of his love poetry. Dido, according to Roman mythology, was the queen of Carthage and love interest of Aeneas, the founder of Rome. Cleopatra was the famed Egyptian queen with whom Julius Caesar and later Mark Antony fell in love. Helen, Hero, and Thisbe are all legendary beauties in Greek mythology. Mercutio mocks Romeo by saying that Romeo thinks none of them compare with Rosaline.

Connect to the Literature

Why is Mercutio's use of grand references and exaggerated language a fitting way to tease Romeo?

MERCUTIO. Nay, if our wits run the wild-goose chase, I
  am done; for thou hast more of the wild goose in one of
70 thy wits than, I am sure, I have in my whole five. Was I
  with you there for the goose?

ROMEO. Thou wast never with me for anything when thou
  wast not there for the goose.

MERCUTIO. I will bite thee by the ear for that jest.

75 **ROMEO.** Nay, good goose, bite not!

MERCUTIO. Thy wit is a very bitter sweeting;[20] it is a most sharp
  sauce.

ROMEO. And is it not, then, well served in to a sweet goose?

MERCUTIO. O, here's a wit of cheveril,[21] that stretches from an
80 inch narrow to an ell broad!

ROMEO. I stretch it out for that word "broad," which added
  to the goose, proves thee far and wide a broad goose.

MERCUTIO. Why, is not this better now than groaning for
  love? Now art thou sociable, now art thou Romeo; now
85 art thou what thou art, by art as well as by nature. For
  this driveling love is like a great natural[22] that runs
  lolling[23] up and down to hide his bauble[24] in a hole.

BENVOLIO. Stop there, stop there!

MERCUTIO. Thou desirest me to stop in my tale against the
  hair.[25]

90 **BENVOLIO.** Thou wouldst else have made thy tale large.

MERCUTIO. O, thou art deceived! I would have made it
  short; for I was come to the whole depth of my tale,
  and meant indeed to occupy the argument[26] no longer.

ROMEO. Here's goodly gear![27]

[*Enter* NURSE *and her Man,* PETER.]

95   A sail, a sail!

MERCUTIO. Two, two! A shirt and a smock.[28]

NURSE. Peter!

PETER. Anon.

NURSE. My fan, Peter.

100 **MERCUTIO.** Good Peter, to hide her face; for her fan's the
  fairer face.

NURSE. God ye good morrow, gentlemen.

MERCUTIO. God ye good-den, fair gentlewoman.

Literary Analysis
Blank Verse Why do
you think Romeo does
not speak in blank
verse in this
conversation with his
friends?

20. **sweeting** kind of apple.

21. **cheveril** easily stretched
kid leather.

22. **natural** idiot.

23. **lolling** with tongue hanging out.

24. **bauble** toy.

25. **the hair** natural
inclination.

26. **occupy the argument**
talk about the matter.

27. **goodly gear** good stuff
for joking (Romeo sees Nurse
approaching).

28. **A shirt and a smock** a
man and a woman.

Reading Check

How does Romeo
respond when
Mercutio says that
Romeo gave his
friends "the slip" the
night before?

NURSE. Is it good-den?

105 **MERCUTIO.** 'Tis no less, I tell ye; for the bawdy hand of the dial is now upon the prick of noon.

NURSE. Out upon you! What a man are you!

ROMEO. One, gentlewoman, that God hath made, himself to mar.

NURSE. By my troth, it is well said. "For himself to mar,"
110 quoth 'a? Gentlemen, can any of you tell me where I may find the young Romeo?

ROMEO. I can tell you; but young Romeo will be older when you have found him than he was when you sought him. I am the youngest of that name, for fault²⁹ of a
115 worse.

NURSE. You say well.

MERCUTIO. Yea, is the worst well? Very well took,³⁰ i' faith! Wisely, wisely.

NURSE. If you be he, sir, I desire some confidence³¹ with you.

120 **BENVOLIO.** She will endite him to some supper.

MERCUTIO. A bawd, a bawd, a bawd! So ho!

ROMEO. What hast thou found?

MERCUTIO. No hare, sir; unless a hare, sir, in a lenten pie, that is something stale and hoar ere it be spent.

[*He walks by them and sings.*]

125

An old hare hoar,
And an old hare hoar,
Is very good meat in Lent;
But a hare that is hoar
Is too much for a score

130
When it hoars ere it be spent.

Romeo, will you come to your father's? We'll to dinner thither.

ROMEO. I will follow you.

MERCUTIO. Farewell, ancient lady. Farewell, [*singing*] "Lady, lady, lady."³²
[*Exit* MERCUTIO, BENVOLIO.]

135 **NURSE.** I pray you, sir, what saucy merchant was this that was so full of his ropery?³³

Literary Analysis
Blank Verse How does Shakespeare reveal Romeo and Mercutio's intelligence even when they are not speaking in blank verse?

29. **fault** lack.

30. **took** understood.

31. **confidence** Nurse means "conference."

32. **"Lady . . . lady"** line from an old ballad, "Chaste Susanna."

33. **ropery** Nurse means "roguery," the talk and conduct of a rascal.

▶ **Critical Viewing**
How does Romeo's behavior with the other young Montagues contrast with his behavior with Juliet? [**Compare and Contrast**]

ROMEO. A gentleman, nurse, that loves to hear himself talk and will speak more in a minute than he will stand to in a month.

140 **NURSE.** And 'a[34] speak anything against me, I'll take him down, and 'a were lustier than he is, and twenty such Jacks; and if I cannot, I'll find those that shall. Scurvy knave! I am none of his flirt-gills;[35] I am none of his skainsmates.[36] And thou must stand by too, and suffer
145 every knave to use me at his pleasure!

PETER. I saw no man use you at his pleasure. If I had, my weapon should quickly have been out, I warrant you. I dare draw as soon as another man, if I see occasion in a good quarrel, and the law on my side.

150 **NURSE.** Now, afore God, I am so vexed that every part about me quivers. Scurvy knave! Pray you, sir, a word; and, as I told you, my young lady bid me inquire you out. What she bid me say, I will keep to myself; but first let me tell ye, if ye should lead her in a fool's paradise, as
155 they say, it were a very gross kind of behavior, as they say; for the gentlewoman is young; and therefore, if you should deal double with her, truly it were an ill thing to be off'red to any gentlewoman, and very weak[37] dealing.

34. 'a he.

35. flirt-gills common girls.
36. skainsmates criminals; cutthroats.

37. weak unmanly.

Reading Check

Who interrupts Romeo and his friends to ask about Romeo?

ROMEO. Nurse, commend[38] me to thy lady and mistress.
I protest unto thee—

160

NURSE. Good heart, and i' faith I will tell her as much.
Lord, Lord, she will be a joyful woman.

ROMEO. What wilt thou tell her, nurse? Thou dost not
mark me.

165

NURSE. I will tell her, sir, that you do protest, which, as I
take it, is a gentlemanlike offer.

ROMEO. Bid her devise
Some means to come to shrift[39] this afternoon;
And there she shall at Friar Lawrence' cell
Be shrived and married. Here is for thy pains.

170

NURSE. No, truly, sir; not a penny.

ROMEO. Go to! I say you shall.

NURSE. This afternoon, sir? Well, she shall be there.

ROMEO. And stay, good nurse, behind the abbey wall.
Within this hour my man shall be with thee
And bring thee cords made like a tackled stair.[40]
Which to the high topgallant[41] of my joy
Must be my convoy[42] in the secret night.
Farewell. Be trusty, and I'll quit[43] thy pains.
Farewell. Commend me to thy mistress.

175

180

NURSE. Now God in heaven bless thee! Hark you, sir.

ROMEO. What say'st thou, my dear nurse?

NURSE. Is your man secret? Did you ne'er hear say,
Two may keep counsel, putting one away?[44]

185

ROMEO. Warrant thee my man's as true as steel.

NURSE. Well, sir, my mistress is the sweetest lady. Lord,
Lord! When 'twas a little prating[45] thing—O, there is a
nobleman in town, one Paris, that would fain lay knife
aboard;[46] but she, good soul, had as lieve[47] see a toad,
a very toad, as see him. I anger her sometimes, and tell
her that Paris is the properer man; but I'll warrant
you, when I say so, she looks as pale as any clout[48]
in the versal world.[49] Doth not rosemary and Romeo
begin both with a letter?

190

195

ROMEO. Ay, nurse; what of that? Both with an R.

NURSE. Ah, mocker! That's the dog's name.[50] R is for the—
No; I know it begins with some other letter; and she
hath the prettiest sententious[51] of it, of you and rosemary,
that it would do you good to hear it.

200

38. commend convey my respect and best wishes.

39. shrift confession.

Reading Skill
Summarizing Read in sentences to summarize the Nurse's warning to Romeo.

40. tackled stair rope ladder.

41. topgallant summit.

42. convoy conveyance.

43. quit reward; pay you back for.

44. Two . . . away Two can keep a secret if one is ignorant, or out of the way.

45. prating babbling.

46. fain . . . aboard eagerly seize Juliet for himself.

47. had as lieve would as willingly.

48. clout cloth.

49. versal world universe.

50. dog's name *R* sounds like a growl.

51. sententious Nurse means "sentences"—clever, wise sayings.

ROMEO. Commend me to thy lady.

NURSE. Ay, a thousand times. [*Exit* ROMEO.] Peter!

PETER. Anon.

NURSE. Before, and apace.⁵² [*Exit, after* PETER.]

Scene v. CAPULET'S orchard.

[*Enter* JULIET.]

    JULIET. The clock struck nine when I did send the nurse;
      In half an hour she promised to return.
      Perchance she cannot meet him. That's not so.
      O, she is lame! Love's heralds should be thoughts,
5   Which ten times faster glides than the sun's beams
      Driving back shadows over low'ring¹ hills.
      Therefore do nimble-pinioned doves draw Love,²
      And therefore hath the wind-swift Cupid wings.
      Now is the sun upon the highmost hill
10   Of this day's journey, and from nine till twelve
      Is three long hours; yet she is not come.
      Had she affections and warm youthful blood,
      She would be as swift in motion as a ball;
      My words would bandy her³ to my sweet love,
15   And his to me.
      But old folks, many feign⁴ as they were dead—
      Unwieldy, slow, heavy and pale as lead.

[*Enter* NURSE *and* PETER.]

      O God, she comes! O honey nurse, what news?
      Hast thou met with him? Send thy man away.

20 **NURSE.** Peter, stay at the gate. [*Exit* PETER.]

    JULIET. Now, good sweet nurse—O Lord, why lookest thou sad?
      Though news be sad, yet tell them merrily;
      If good, thou shamest the music of sweet news
      By playing it to me with so sour a face.

25 **NURSE.** I am aweary, give me leave⁵ awhile.
      Fie, how my bones ache! What a jaunce⁶ have I!

    JULIET. I would thou hadst my bones, and I thy news.
      Nay, come, I pray thee speak. Good, good nurse, speak.

    NURSE. Jesu, what haste? Can you not stay a while?
30   Do you not see that I am out of breath?

    JULIET. How art thou out of breath when thou hast breath
      To say to me that thou art out of breath?

Literary Analysis
Blank Verse What is the effect of hearing Romeo's blank verse after long passages of prose?

52. Before, and apace Go ahead of me, and quickly.

1. low'ring darkening.

2. Therefore . . . Love therefore, doves with quick wings pull the chariot of Venus, goddess of love.

3. bandy her send her rapidly.

4. feign act.

Vocabulary Builder
unwieldy (un wēl′ dē) *adj.* awkward; clumsy

5. give me leave excuse me; give me a moment's rest.

6. jaunce rough trip.

Reading Check

What does Romeo ask the Nurse to tell Juliet?

The excuse that thou dost make in this delay
Is longer than the tale thou dost excuse.

35 Is thy news good or bad? Answer to that.
Say either, and I'll stay the circumstance.[7]
Let me be satisfied, is't good or bad?

NURSE. Well, you have made a simple[8] choice; you know
not how to choose a man. Romeo? No, not he. Though

40 his face be better than any man's, yet his leg excels all
men's; and for a hand and a foot, and a body, though
they be not to be talked on, yet they are past compare.
He is not the flower of courtesy, but, I'll warrant him,
as gentle as a lamb. Go thy ways, wench; serve God.

45 What, have you dined at home?

JULIET. No, no. But all this I did know before.
What says he of our marriage? What of that?

NURSE. Lord, how my head aches! What a head have I!
It beats as it would fall in twenty pieces.

50 My back a[9] t'other side—ah, my back, my back!
Beshrew[10] your heart for sending me about
To catch my death with jauncing up and down!

JULIET. I' faith, I am sorry that thou art not well.
Sweet, sweet, sweet nurse, tell me, what says my love?

55 **NURSE.** Your love says, like an honest gentleman, and a
courteous, and a kind, and a handsome, and, I warrant,
a virtuous—Where is your mother?

JULIET. Where is my mother? Why, she is within.
Where should she be? How oddly thou repliest!

60 "Your love says, like an honest gentleman,
'Where is your mother?'"

NURSE.   O God's Lady dear!
Are you so hot?[11] Marry come up, I trow.[12]
Is this the poultice[13] for my aching bones?
Henceforward do your messages yourself.

65 **JULIET.** Here's such a coil![14] Come, what says Romeo?

NURSE. Have you got leave to go to shrift today?

JULIET. I have.

NURSE. Then hie you hence to Friar Lawrence' cell;
There stays a husband to make you a wife.

70 Now comes the wanton[15] blood up in your cheeks:
They'll be in scarlet straight at any news.
Hie you to church: I must another way,

▶ **Critical Viewing**
Which details in this
picture reflect the
feelings Romeo and
Juliet have for each
other? **[Interpret]**

7. stay the circumstance
wait for the details.

8. simple foolish; simple-
minded.

9. a on.

10. Beshrew shame on.

Literary Analysis
Blank Verse What
might Shakespeare
be indicating about
the Nurse's character
by having her switch
between prose and
blank verse?

11. hot impatient; hot-
tempered.

12. Marry . . . trow Indeed,
cool down, I say.

13. poultice remedy.

14. coil disturbance.

15. wanton excited.

Reading Check

How does the Nurse
describe Romeo?

To fetch a ladder, by the which your love
Must climb a bird's nest soon when it is dark.
75   I am the drudge, and toil in your delight:
But you shall bear the burden soon at night.
Go; I'll to dinner; hie you to the cell.

JULIET. Hie to high fortune! Honest nurse, farewell.

                                                  [Exit all.]

Scene vi. Friar Lawrence cell.

[Enter FRIAR LAWRENCE *and* ROMEO.]

  FRIAR. So smile the heavens upon this holy act
That afterhours with sorrow chide us not![1]

  ROMEO. Amen, amen! But come what sorrow can,
It cannot countervail[2] the exchange of joy
5   That one short minute gives me in her sight.
Do thou but close our hands with holy words,
Then love-devouring death do what he dare—
It is enough I may but call her mine.

  FRIAR. These violent delights have violent ends
10   And in their triumph die, like fire and powder,[3]
Which, as they kiss, consume. The sweetest honey
Is loathsome in his own deliciousness
And in the taste confounds[4] the appetite.
Therefore love moderately: long love doth so;
15   Too swift arrives as tardy as too slow.

[Enter JULIET.]

  Here comes the lady. O, so light a foot
Will ne'er wear out the everlasting flint.[5]
A lover may bestride the gossamers[6]
That idles in the wanton summer air,
20   And yet not fall; so light is vanity.[7]

  JULIET. Good even to my ghostly confessor.

  FRIAR. Romeo shall thank thee, daughter, for us both.

  JULIET. As much to him,[8] else is his thanks too much.

  ROMEO. Ah, Juliet, if the measure of thy joy
25   Be heaped like mine, and that thy skill be more
To blazon it,[9] then sweeten with thy breath
This neighbor air, and let rich music's tongue
Unfold the imagined happiness that both
Receive in either by this dear encounter.

Literary Analysis
Blank Verse What effect is created by making Juliet's last line rhyme with the Nurse's last line?

1. **That . . . not!** that the future does not punish us with sorrow.

2. **countervail** equal.

3. **powder** gunpowder.

4. **confounds** destroys.

5. **flint** stone.

6. **gossamers** spider webs.

7. **vanity** foolish things that cannot last.

8. **As . . . him** the same greeting to him.

9. **and . . . it** and if you are better able to proclaim it.

30 **JULIET.** Conceit, more rich in matter than in words,
   Brags of his substance, not of ornament.[10]
   They are but beggars that can count their worth;
   But my true love is grown to such excess
   I cannot sum up sum of half my wealth.

35 **FRIAR.** Come, come with me, and we will make short work;
   For, by your leaves, you shall not stay alone
   Till Holy Church incorporate two in one.   [*Exit all.*]

10. Conceit . . . ornament
Understanding does not need
to be dressed up in words.

▲ **Critical Viewing** How does this image of fifteenth-century Verona
reflect scenery and intrigues in Romeo and Juliet's lives? **[Synthesize]**

Apply the Skills

The Tragedy of Romeo and Juliet, Act II

Thinking About the Selection

1. **(a) Respond:** Is Friar Lawrence wise to agree to marry Romeo and Juliet? Explain. **(b) Discuss:** In a small group, share your responses. As a group, choose one idea to share with the class.
2. **(a) Recall:** Where do Romeo and Juliet first mutually declare their love? **(b) Interpret:** What role does darkness play in the scene?
3. **(a) Recall:** What weakness in Romeo does the Friar point out before agreeing to help? **(b) Compare and Contrast:** How do the Friar's motives differ from the couple's own motives?
4. **(a) Recall:** For whom does Juliet wait in Act II, Scene v? **(b) Analyze:** What are her feelings as she waits?
5. **Evaluate:** Why do you think the love scene in Capulet's garden is one of the most famous dramatic scenes in all literature?

Literary Analysis

6. Copy the following passages of **blank verse.** Then, indicate the pattern of accented (´) and unaccented (˘) syllables in each line.
   (a) Act II, Scene ii, lines 43–51
   (b) Act II, Scene vi, lines 3–8
7. Using a chart like the one shown, rewrite the following two lines, marking stressed and unstressed syllables. Then, identify the key words stressed in each line, and explain what meaning is conveyed by the emphasis on those words.
   (a) ROMEO. Can I go forward when my heart is here?
   (b) JULIET. But my true love is grown to such excess.

Blank Verse Pattern	Key Words	Significance

8. **(a)** Identify the aristocratic and common people in Acts I and II based on whether or not they speak in blank verse. **(b)** Why do you think Shakespeare chose to have aristocratic characters speak in blank verse instead of ordinary prose?

Reading Skill

9. **(a)** How many sentences are in lines 1–8 of Act II, Scene v? **(b)** Write a **summary** of these lines.

QuickReview

Act II at a Glance
Romeo and Juliet pledge their love to each other. With the aid of Juliet's Nurse and Friar Lawrence, they arrange to be married in secret by the Friar.

For: Self-test
Visit: www.PHSchool.com
Web Code: epa-6503

Blank Verse: unrhymed poetry written in iambic pentameter, a meter consisting of five stressed syllables, each preceded by an unstressed syllable

Summarizing: briefly stating the main points in a piece of writing

Vocabulary Builder

Practice Answer each question. Then, explain your answer.

1. Where would you go to _procure_ groceries?
2. What is the _predominant_ feeling at a celebration?
3. How many people are needed for an _intercession_ to occur?
4. Is a _sallow_ complexion a sign of good health?
5. If a situation is _lamentable,_ are people likely to be happy about it?
6. Is an _unwieldy_ package something you would want to carry far?

Adding Words to Your Vocabulary The word _intercession_ might easily be confused with _interception_. Use a dictionary to find out the meaning of the word _interception,_ and then write a few sentences explaining how an intercession is different from an interception. (For more on using a dictionary, see page R6.)

Writing

A **parody** is a humorous piece of writing that mocks the characteristics of another work. A parody may be gentle or scathing, and it may distort the plot, characters, themes, or language of its target. Write a parody of the famous balcony scene in _Romeo and Juliet_. In your writing, make light of Romeo and Juliet's exaggerated professions of love.

- Reread the scene and take notes about elements of that could be funny.
- Choose a focus. For example, you might decide that no one would speak the way Shakespeare's lovers do.
- Write your parody as a script for an original play, including dialogue and stage directions.

For _Grammar, Vocabulary,_ and _Assessment,_ see **Build Language Skills,** pages 812–813.

Extend Your Learning

Research and Technology Conduct research to create an **annotated flowchart** that displays and explains the structure of the nobility in sixteenth-century Verona. Your flowchart should show the relative positions of the Prince, Count Paris, the Montagues, and the Capulets. Organize text and images logically, and use correct grammar. Remember to document sources for both ideas and images. (For more on citing sources, see page R32.) Include the flowchart in your multimedia portfolio.

Literary Analysis

Plays often include these types of **dramatic speeches:**

- **Soliloquy:** a lengthy speech in which a character—usually alone on stage—expresses his or her true thoughts or feelings. Soliloquies are unheard by other characters.

- **Aside:** a character revealing his or her true thoughts or feelings in a remark that is unheard by other characters

- **Monologue:** a lengthy speech by one person. Unlike a soliloquy, a monologue is addressed to other characters.

Dramatic speeches often include **allusions**—references to well-known people, places, or events from mythology or literature. For example, in Act II, Mercutio insultingly calls Tybalt "Prince of Cats," alluding to a cat named Tybalt in French fables.

As you read, consider what each type of speech reveals about the speaker and his or her relationships with other characters. Use a chart like the one shown to note the effect of any allusions you find.

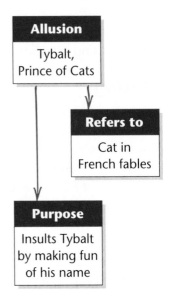

Allusion

Tybalt, Prince of Cats

Refers to

Cat in French fables

Purpose

Insults Tybalt by making fun of his name

Reading Skill

Summarizing is briefly stating the main points in a piece of writing. Before you summarize a long passage of a play by Shakespeare, you should **paraphrase** it or restate the lines in your own words. For example, compare these two versions of a speech by Romeo:

> **Shakespeare's version:** "This gentleman, the prince's near ally / My very friend hath got his mortal hurt / In my behalf. . . ."
> **Paraphrase:** My good friend, a close relative of the prince, has been fatally wounded in defending me.

Once you have paraphrased small portions of text, you can more easily and accurately summarize an entire passage.

Vocabulary Builder

- **gallant** (gal´ ənt) *adj.* brave and noble (p. 787) *We called the firefighters <u>gallant</u>, but they said they were just doing their job.*

- **fray** (frā) *n.* noisy fight (p. 788) *The crew argued, but the captain stayed above the <u>fray</u>.*

- **martial** (mär´ shəl) *adj.* military (p. 789) *The band played <u>martial</u> music to honor the soldiers.*

- **exile** (ek´ sīl´) *v.* banish (p. 790) *Years ago, rulers would <u>exile</u> criminals to faraway places.*

- **eloquence** (el´ ə kwəns) *n.* speech or writing that is graceful and persuasive (p. 791) *The <u>eloquence</u> of her speech moved the audience.*

- **fickle** (fik´ əl) *adj.* changeable (p. 802) *His <u>fickle</u> sense of style made buying clothes hard.*

ACT III

Review and Anticipate

In Act II, Romeo and Juliet express their mutual love and enlist the aid of Juliet's nurse and Friar Lawrence to arrange a secret marriage ceremony. As the act closes, the young couple is about to be married. Before performing the ceremony, the Friar warns, "These violent delights have violent ends. . . ." How might this statement hint at events that will occur in Act III or later in the play?

Scene i. A public place.

[*Enter* MERCUTIO, BENVOLIO, *and* MEN.]

    BENVOLIO. I pray thee, good Mercutio, let's retire.
      The day is hot, the Capulets abroad,
      And, if we meet, we shall not 'scape a brawl,
      For now, these hot days, is the mad blood stirring.

5 **MERCUTIO.** Thou art like one of these fellows that, when he
      enters the confines of a tavern, claps me his sword upon the
      table and says, "God send me no need of thee!" and by the
      operation of the second cup draws him on the drawer,[1] when
      indeed there is no need.

10 **BENVOLIO.** Am I like such a fellow?

    MERCUTIO. Come, come, thou art as hot a Jack in thy mood as
      any in Italy; and as soon moved to be moody, and as soon
      moody to be moved.[2]

1. and . . . drawer and by the effect of the second drink, draws his sword against the waiter.

2. and . . . moved and as quickly stirred to anger as you are eager to be so stirred.

Reading Check

Why does Benvolio want to get off the street?

BENVOLIO. And what to?

15 **MERCUTIO.** Nay, and there were two such, we should have none shortly, for one would kill the other. Thou! Why, thou wilt quarrel with a man that hath a hair more or a hair less in his beard than thou hast. Thou wilt quarrel with a man for cracking nuts, having no other reason but because thou
20 hast hazel eyes. What eye but such an eye would spy out such a quarrel? Thy head is as full of quarrels as an egg is full of meat; and yet thy head hath been beaten as addle³ as an egg for quarreling. Thou hast quarreled with a man for coughing in the street, because he hath wakened thy dog that hath lain asleep in the sun. Didst thou not fall out with
25 a tailor for wearing his new doublet⁴ before Easter? With another for tying his new shoes with old riband?⁵ And yet thou wilt tutor me from quarreling!⁶

BENVOLIO. And I were so apt to quarrel as thou art, any man should buy the fee simple⁷ of my life for an hour and a quarter.⁸

30 **MERCUTIO.** The fee simple? O simple!⁹

[*Enter* TYBALT, PETRUCHIO, *and* OTHERS.]

BENVOLIO. By my head, here comes the Capulets.

MERCUTIO. By my heel, I care not.

TYBALT. Follow me close, for I will speak to them.
35 Gentlemen, good-den. A word with one of you.

MERCUTIO. And but one word with one of us? Couple it with something; make it a word and a blow.

TYBALT. You shall find me apt enough to that, sir, and you will give me occasion.¹⁰

40 **MERCUTIO.** Could you not take some occasion without giving?

TYBALT. Mercutio, thou consortest¹¹ with Romeo.

MERCUTIO. Consort?¹² What, dost thou make us minstrels? And thou make minstrels of us, look to hear nothing but discords.¹³ Here's my fiddlestick; here's that shall make you
45 dance. Zounds,¹⁴ consort!

BENVOLIO. We talk here in the public haunt of men.
Either withdraw unto some private place,
Or reason coldly of your grievances,
Or else depart. Here all eyes gaze on us.

Literary Analysis
Dramatic Speeches
Which details of Mercutio's speech indicate that it is a monologue and not a soliloquy?

3. addle scrambled; crazy.

4. doublet jacket.

5. riband ribbon.

6. tutor . . . quarreling instruct me not to quarrel.

7. fee simple complete possession.

8. an hour and a quarter length of time that a man with Mercutio's fondness for quarreling may be expected to live.

9. O simple! O stupid!

Reading Skill
Summarizing How would you paraphrase the exchange between Tybalt and Mercutio?

10. occasion cause; reason.

11. consortest associate with.

12. Consort associate with; "consort" also meant a group of musicians.

13. discords harsh sounds.

14. Zounds exclamation of surprise or anger ("By God's wounds").

50 **MERCUTIO.** Men's eyes were made to look, and let them gaze.
    I will not budge for no man's pleasure, I.

[*Enter* ROMEO.]

    TYBALT. Well, peace be with you, sir. Here comes my man.[15]

    MERCUTIO. But I'll be hanged, sir, if he wear your livery.[16]
    Marry, go before to field,[17] he'll be your follower!
55   Your worship in that sense may call him man.

    TYBALT. Romeo, the love I bear thee can afford
    No better term than this: thou art a villain.[18]

    ROMEO. Tybalt, the reason that I have to love thee
    Doth much excuse the appertaining[19] rage
60   To such a greeting. Villain am I none.
    Therefore farewell. I see thou knowest me not.

    TYBALT. Boy, this shall not excuse the injuries
    That thou hast done me; therefore turn and draw.

    ROMEO. I do protest I never injured thee,
65   But love thee better than thou canst devise[20]
    Till thou shalt know the reason of my love;
    And so, good Capulet, which name I tender[21]
    As dearly as mine own, be satisfied.

    MERCUTIO. O calm, dishonorable, vile submission!
70   Alla stoccata[22] carries it away.   [*Draws.*]
    Tybalt, you ratcatcher, will you walk?

    TYBALT. What wouldst thou have with me?

    MERCUTIO. Good King of Cats, nothing but one of your
    nine lives. That I mean to make bold withal,[23] and, as
75   you shall use me here-after, dry-beat[24] the rest of the
    eight. Will you pluck your sword out of his pilcher[25]
    by the ears? Make haste, lest mine be about your
    ears ere it be out.

    TYBALT. I am for you.   [*Draws.*]

    ROMEO. Gentle Mercutio, put thy rapier up.

80 **MERCUTIO.** Come, sir, your passado!   [*They fight.*]

    ROMEO. Draw, Benvolio; beat down their weapons.
    Gentlemen, for shame! Forbear this outrage!
    Tybalt, Mercutio, the Prince expressly hath
    Forbid this bandying in Verona streets.

15. man man I am looking for; "man" also meant "manservant."

16. livery servant's uniform.

17. field dueling place.

18. villain low, vulgar person.

19. appertaining appropriate.

20. devise understand; imagine.

21. tender value.

22. Alla stoccata at the thrust—an Italian fencing term that Mercutio uses as a nickname for Tybalt.

23. make bold withal make bold with; take.

24. dry-beat thrash.

25. pilcher scabbard.

Reading Check

From whom is Mercutio protecting Romeo when he draws his sword?

85   Hold, Tybalt! Good Mercutio!

[TYBALT *under* ROMEO'S *arm thrusts* MERCUTIO *in, and flies.*]

MERCUTIO.   I am hurt.
A plague a²⁶ both houses! I am sped.²⁷
Is he gone and hath nothing?

BENVOLIO.   What, art thou hurt?

MERCUTIO. Ay, ay, a scratch, a scratch. Marry, 'tis enough.
Where is my page? Go, villain, fetch a surgeon. [*Exit* PAGE.]

90 **ROMEO.** Courage, man. The hurt cannot be much.

MERCUTIO. No, 'tis not so deep as a well, nor so wide as
a church door; but 'tis enough, 'twill serve. Ask for
me tomorrow, and you shall find me a grave man. I
am peppered,²⁸ I warrant, for this world. A plague a

▲ **Critical Viewing**
Which details in this
photograph suggest
that the duel between
Mercutio and Tybalt
could have been
stopped? **[Analyze]**

26. a on.

27. sped wounded; done
for.

28. peppered finished off.

95 both your houses! Zounds, a dog, a rat, a mouse, a
cat, to scratch a man to death! A braggart, a rogue,
a villain, that fights by the book of arithmetic!²⁹ Why
the devil came you between us? I was hurt under
your arm.

ROMEO. I thought all for the best.

MERCUTIO. Help me into some house, Benvolio,
100   Or I shall faint. A plague a both your houses!
They have made worms' meat of me. I have it,³⁰
And soundly too. Your houses! [*Exit* MERCUTIO *and* BENVOLIO.]

ROMEO. This gentleman, the Prince's near ally,³¹
My very friend, hath got his mortal hurt
105   In my behalf—my reputation stained
With Tybalt's slander—Tybalt, that an hour
Hath been my cousin. O sweet Juliet,
Thy beauty hath made me effeminate
And in my temper soft'ned valor's steel!

[*Enter* BENVOLIO.]

110 **BENVOLIO.** O Romeo, Romeo, brave Mercutio is dead!
That <u>gallant</u> spirit hath aspired³² the clouds.
Which too untimely here did scorn the earth.

ROMEO. This day's black fate on moe³³ days doth depend;³⁴
This but begins the woe others must end.

[*Enter* TYBALT.]

115 **BENVOLIO.** Here comes the furious Tybalt back again.

ROMEO. Alive in triumph, and Mercutio slain?
Away to heaven respective lenity,³⁵
And fire-eyed fury be my conduct³⁶ now!
Now, Tybalt, take the "villain" back again
120   That late thou gavest me; for Mercutio's soul
Is but a little way above our heads,
Staying for thine to keep him company.
Either thou or I, or both, must go with him.

TYBALT. Thou, wretched boy, that didst consort him here,
125   Shalt with him hence.

ROMEO.   This shall determine that.
                         [*They fight.* TYBALT *falls.*]

BENVOLIO. Romeo, away, be gone!

29. **by . . . arithmetic** by for-mal rules.

Reading Skill
Summarizing Para-phrase Mercutio's line "A plague a both your houses!" and summarize his reasons for uttering this curse.

30. **I have it** I have got my deathblow.

31. **ally** relative.

32. **aspired** climbed to.

Vocabulary Builder
gallant (gal´ ənt) *adj.*
brave and noble

33. **moe** more.

34. **depend** hang over.

35. **respective lenity** thoughtful mercy.

36. **conduct** guide.

Reading Check

What is the outcome of the duel between Tybalt and Mercutio?

The citizens are up, and Tybalt slain.
Stand not amazed. The Prince will doom thee death
If thou art taken. Hence, be gone, away!

130 **ROMEO.** O, I am fortune's fool!³⁷

BENVOLIO.   Why dost thou stay?

                                           [*Exit* ROMEO.]

[*Enter* CITIZENS.]

CITIZEN. Which way ran he that killed Mercutio?
Tybalt, that murderer, which way ran he?

BENVOLIO. There lies that Tybalt.

CITIZEN.   Up, sir, go with me.
I charge thee in the Prince's name obey.

[*Enter* PRINCE, OLD MONTAGUE, CAPULET, *their* WIVES, *and all.*]

135 **PRINCE.** Where are the vile beginners of this <u>fray</u>?

BENVOLIO. O noble Prince, I can discover³⁸ all
The unlucky manage³⁹ of this fatal brawl.

37. fool plaything.

Vocabulary Builder
fray (frā) *n.* noisy fight

38. discover reveal.

39. manage course.

▼ **Critical Viewing**
Based on this photograph, how would you describe bystanders' reactions to Romeo's slaying of Tybalt? **[Infer]**

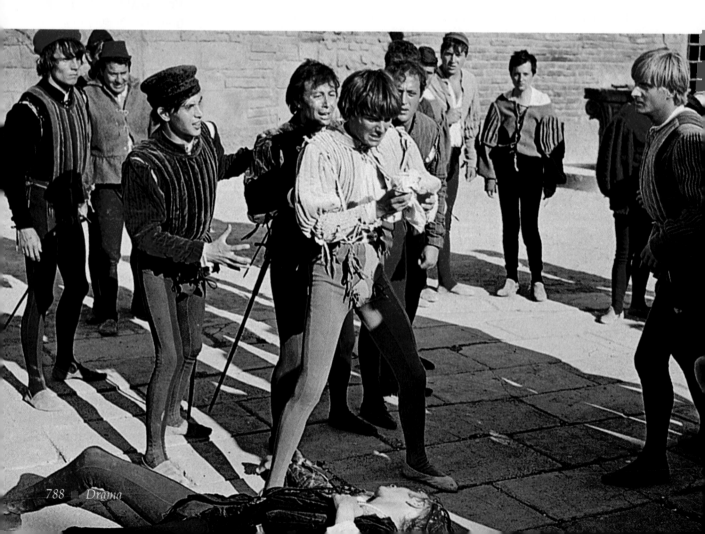

There lies the man, slain by young Romeo,
That slew thy kinsman, brave Mercutio.

140 **LADY CAPULET.** Tybalt, my cousin! O my brother's child!
O Prince! O cousin! Husband! O, the blood is spilled
Of my dear kinsman! Prince, as thou art true,
For blood of ours shed blood of Montague.
O cousin, cousin!

145 **PRINCE.** Benvolio, who began this bloody fray?

BENVOLIO. Tybalt, here slain, whom Romeo's hand did slay.
Romeo, that spoke him fair, bid him bethink
How nice⁴⁰ the quarrel was, and urged withal
Your high displeasure. All this—utterèd
150 With gentle breath, calm look, knees humbly bowed—
Could not take truce with the unruly spleen⁴¹
Of Tybalt deaf to peace, but that he tilts⁴²
With piercing steel at bold Mercutio's breast;
Who, all as hot, turns deadly point to point,
155 And, with a <u>martial</u> scorn, with one hand beats
Cold death aside and with the other sends
It back to Tybalt, whose dexterity
Retorts it. Romeo he cries aloud,
"Hold, friends! Friends, part!" and swifter than his tongue,
160 His agile arm beats down their fatal points,
And 'twixt them rushes; underneath whose arm
An envious⁴³ thrust from Tybalt hit the life
Of stout Mercutio, and then Tybalt fled;
But by and by comes back to Romeo,
165 Who had but newly entertained⁴⁴ revenge,
And to't they go like lightning; for, ere I
Could draw to part them, was stout Tybalt slain;
And, as he fell, did Romeo turn and fly.
This is the truth, or let Benvolio die.

170 **LADY CAPULET.** He is a kinsman to the Montague;
Affection makes him false, he speaks not true.
Some twenty of them fought in this black strife,
And all those twenty could but kill one life.
I beg for justice, which thou, Prince, must give.
175 Romeo slew Tybalt; Romeo must not live.

PRINCE. Romeo slew him; he slew Mercutio.
Who now the price of his dear blood doth owe?

MONTAGUE. Not Romeo, Prince; he was Mercutio's friend;

40. **nice** trivial.

41. **spleen** angry nature.
42. **tilts** thrusts.

Vocabulary Builder
martial (mär′ shəl) *adj.*
military

Literary Analysis
Dramatic Speeches
Which details of
Benvolio's speech
suggest that he is
trying to portray
Romeo favorably?

43. **envious** full of hatred.

44. **entertained** considered.

Reading Check

What makes Lady
Capulet distrust
Benvolio's account of
the brawl?

His fault concludes but what the law should end,
The life of Tybalt.⁴⁵

180 **PRINCE.** And for that offense
Immediately we do <u>exile</u> him hence.
I have an interest in your hate's proceeding.
My blood⁴⁶ for your rude brawls doth lie a-bleeding;
But I'll amerce⁴⁷ you with so strong a fine
185 That you shall all repent the loss of mine.
I will be deaf to pleading and excuses;
Nor tears nor prayers shall purchase out abuses.
Therefore use none. Let Romeo hence in haste,
Else, when he is found, that hour is his last.
190 Bear hence this body and attend our will.⁴⁸
Mercy but murders, pardoning those that kill.

[*Exit with others.*]

Vocabulary Builder
exile (ek′ sīl′) *v.* banish

46. My blood Mercutio was related to the Prince.
47. amerce punish.

48. attend our will await my decision.

Scene ii. CAPULET'S *orchard.*

[*Enter* JULIET *alone.*]

JULIET. Gallop apace, you fiery-footed steeds,¹
Towards Phoebus' lodging!² Such a wagoner
As Phaëton³ would whip you to the west
And bring in cloudy night immediately.
5 Spread thy close curtain, love-performing night,
That runaways' eyes may wink,⁴ and Romeo
Leap to these arms untalked of and unseen.
Lovers can see to do their amorous rites,
And by their own beauties; or, if love be blind,
10 It best agrees with night. Come, civil night,
Thou sober-suited matron all in black,
And learn me how to lose a winning match,
Played for a pair of stainless maidenhoods.
Hood my unmanned blood, bating in my cheeks,⁵
15 With thy black mantle till strange⁶ love grow bold,
Think true love acted simple modesty,
Come, night; come, Romeo; come, thou day in night;
For thou wilt lie upon the wings of night
Whiter than new snow upon a raven's back.
20 Come, gentle night; come, loving, black-browed night;
Give me my Romeo; and when I shall die,
Take him and cut him out in little stars,
And he will make the face of heaven so fine
That all the world will be in love with night
25 And pay no worship to the garish sun.

1. fiery-footed steeds horses of the sun god, Phoebus.

2. Phoebus' lodging below the horizon.

Literary Analysis
Dramatic Speeches
How can you tell that Juliet's speech is a soliloquy?

3. Phaëton Phoebus' son, who tried to drive his father's horses but was unable to control them.

4. That runaways' eyes may wink so that the eyes of busybodies may not see.

5. Hood . . . cheeks hide the untamed blood that makes me blush.

6. strange unfamiliar.

Mythology Connection

Cockatrice In a play on words, Juliet links "Ay" with the dangerous "eye" of a cockatrice (Act III, scene ii, line 47). The cockatrice is a serpent that, according to myth, could kill with a look or transform people into stone. The creature resembles a snake with the head and yellow feathers of a rooster. It feared the song of the rooster and its own reflection in a mirror.

Connect to the Literature

How does Juliet's allusion to a cockatrice reinforce the nature of her conversation with the Nurse?

O, I have bought the mansion of a love,
But not possessed it; and though I am sold,
Not yet enjoyed. So tedious is this day
As is the night before some festival
30   To an impatient child that hath new robes
And may not wear them. O, here comes my nurse,

[*Enter* NURSE, *with cords.*]

And she brings news; and every tongue that speaks
But Romeo's name speaks heavenly <u>eloquence</u>.
Now, nurse, what news? What hast thou there, the cords
That Romeo bid thee fetch?

35 **NURSE.**   Ay, ay, the cords.

JULIET. Ay me! What news? Why dost thou wring thy hands?

NURSE. Ah, weraday![7] He's dead, he's dead, he's dead!
We are undone, lady, we are undone!
Alack the day! He's gone, he's killed, he's dead!

JULIET. Can heaven be so envious?

40 **NURSE.**   Romeo can,
Though heaven cannot. O Romeo, Romeo!
Who ever would have thought it? Romeo!

JULIET. What devil art thou that dost torment me thus?
This torture should be roared in dismal hell.
45   Hath Romeo slain himself? Say thou but "Ay,"
And that bare vowel "I" shall poison more
Than the death-darting eye of cockatrice.

Vocabulary Builder
eloquence (el´ ə kwəns) *n.* speech that is graceful and persuasive

7. **Ah, weraday!** alas!

Reading Check

What punishment does the Prince order for Romeo?

I am not I, if there be such an "Ay,"[8]
Or those eyes' shot[9] that makes thee answer "Ay."
50　　If he be slain, say "Ay"; or if not, "No."
Brief sounds determine of my weal or woe.

NURSE. I saw the wound, I saw it with mine eyes,
(God save the mark![10]) here on his manly breast.
A piteous corse,[11] a bloody piteous corse;
55　　Pale, pale as ashes, all bedaubed in blood,
All in gore-blood. I sounded[12] at the sight.

JULIET. O, break, my heart! Poor bankrout,[13] break at once!
To prison, eyes; ne'er look on liberty!
Vile earth, to earth resign;[14] end motion here,
60　　And thou and Romeo press one heavy bier![15]

NURSE. O Tybalt, Tybalt, the best friend I had!
O courteous Tybalt! Honest gentleman!
That ever I should live to see thee dead!

JULIET. What storm is this that blows so contrary?[16]
65　　Is Romeo slaught'red, and is Tybalt dead?
My dearest cousin, and my dearer lord?
Then, dreadful trumpet, sound the general doom![17]
For who is living, if those two are gone?

NURSE. Tybalt is gone, and Romeo banishèd;
70　　Romeo that killed him, he is banishèd.

JULIET. O God! Did Romeo's hand shed Tybalt's blood?

NURSE. It did, it did! Alas the day, it did!

JULIET. O serpent heart, hid with a flow'ring face!
Did ever dragon keep so fair a cave?
75　　Beautiful tyrant! Fiend angelical!
Dove-feathered raven! Wolvish-ravening lamb!
Despisèd substance of divinest show!
Just opposite to what thou justly seem'st—
A damnèd saint, an honorable villain!
80　　O nature, what hadst thou to do in hell
When thou didst bower the spirit of a fiend
In mortal paradise of such sweet flesh?
Was ever book containing such vile matter
So fairly bound? O, that deceit should dwell
In such a gorgeous palace!

85　**NURSE.**　　　　　　　There's no trust,
No faith, no honesty in men; all perjured,

8. "Ay" yes.

9. eyes' shot the Nurse's glance.

10. God save the mark! May God save us from evil!

11. corse corpse.

12. sounded swooned; fainted.

13. bankrout bankrupt.

14. Vile . . . resign let my body return to the earth.

15. bier platform on which a corpse is displayed before burial.

16. contrary in opposite directions.

17. dreadful . . . doom let the trumpet that announces doomsday be sounded.

**Reading Skill
Summarizing** Briefly summarize Juliet's remarks about Romeo in lines 73–85.

All forsworn,[18] all naught, all dissemblers.[19]
Ah, where's my man? Give me some aqua vitae.[20]
These griefs, these woes, these sorrows make me old.
Shame come to Romeo!

90 **JULIET.**   Blistered be thy tongue
For such a wish! He was not born to shame.
Upon his brow shame is ashamed to sit;
For 'tis a throne where honor may be crowned
Sole monarch of the universal earth.
95 O, what a beast was I to chide at him!

NURSE. Will you speak well of him that killed your cousin?

JULIET. Shall I speak ill of him that is my husband?
Ah, poor my lord, what tongue shall smooth thy name
When I, thy three-hours wife, have mangled it?
100 But wherefore, villain, didst thou kill my cousin?
That villain cousin would have killed my husband.
Back, foolish tears, back to your native spring!
Your tributary[21] drops belong to woe,
Which you, mistaking, offer up to joy.
105 My husband lives, that Tybalt would have slain;
And Tybalt's dead, that would have slain my husband.
All this is comfort; wherefore weep I then?
Some word there was, worser than Tybalt's death,
That murd'red me. I would forget it fain;
110 But O, it presses to my memory
Like damnèd guilty deeds to sinners' minds!
"Tybalt is dead, and Romeo—banishèd."
That "banishèd," that one word "banishèd,"
Hath slain ten thousand Tybalts. Tybalt's death
115 Was woe enough, if it had ended there;
Or, if sour woe delights in fellowship
And needly will be ranked with[22] other griefs,
Why followed not, when she said "Tybalt's dead,"
Thy father, or thy mother, nay, or both,
120 Which modern[23] lamentation might have moved?
But with a rearward[24] following Tybalt's death,
"Romeo is banishèd"—to speak that word
Is father, mother, Tybalt, Romeo, Juliet,
All slain, all dead. "Romeo is banishèd"—
125 There is no end, no limit, measure, bound,
In that word's death; no words can that woe sound.
Where is my father and my mother, nurse?

18. **forsworn** are liars.
19. **dissemblers** hypocrites.
20. **aqua vitae** brandy.

21. **tributary** in tribute.

Literary Analysis
Dramatic Speeches
What makes this speech a monologue but not a soliloquy?

22. **needly . . . with** must be accompanied by.

23. **modern** ordinary.
24. **rearward** follow up; literally, a rear guard.

Reading Check

What is Juliet's initial reaction to Romeo's involvement in Tybalt's death?

NURSE. Weeping and wailing over Tybalt's corse.
Will you go to them? I will bring you thither.

130 **JULIET.** Wash they his wounds with tears? Mine shall be spent,
When theirs are dry, for Romeo's banishment.
Take up those cords. Poor ropes, you are beguiled,
Both you and I, for Romeo is exiled.
He made you for a highway to my bed;
135 But I, a maid, die maiden-widowèd.
Come, cords; come, nurse. I'll to my wedding bed;
And death, not Romeo, take my maidenhead!

NURSE. Hie to your chamber. I'll find Romeo
To comfort you. I wot²⁵ well where he is.
140 Hark ye, your Romeo will be here at night.
I'll to him; he is hid at Lawrence' cell.

JULIET. O, find him! Give this ring to my true knight
And bid him come to take his last farewell. [*Exit* with NURSE]

Scene iii. *Friar Lawrence's cell.*

[*Enter* FRIAR LAWRENCE.]

FRIAR. Romeo, come forth; come forth, thou fearful man.
Affliction is enamored of thy parts,¹
And thou art wedded to calamity.

▲ **Critical Viewing**
How does Romeo's expression in this picture compare to your impression of him as you read? **[Compare and Contrast]**

25. wot know.

1. Affliction . . . parts misery is in love with your attractive qualities.

[*Enter* ROMEO.]

ROMEO. Father, what news? What is the Prince's doom?[2]
5   What sorrow craves acquaintance at my hand
     That I yet know not?

FRIAR.   Too familiar
     Is my dear son with such sour company.
     I bring thee tidings of the Prince's doom.

ROMEO. What less than doomsday[3] is the Prince's doom?

10 **FRIAR.** A gentler judgment vanished[4] from his lips—
     Not body's death, but body's banishment.

ROMEO. Ha, banishment? Be merciful, say "death";
     For exile hath more terror in his look,
     Much more than death. Do not say "banishment."

15 **FRIAR.** Here from Verona art thou banishèd.
     Be patient, for the world is broad and wide.

ROMEO. There is no world without[5] Verona walls,
     But purgatory, torture, hell itself.
     Hence banishèd is banished from the world,
20   And world's exile is death. Then "banishèd"
     Is death mistermed. Calling death "banishèd,"
     Thou cut'st my head off with a golden ax
     And smilest upon the stroke that murders me.

FRIAR. O deadly sin! O rude unthankfulness!
25   Thy fault our law calls death;[6] but the kind Prince,
     Taking thy part, hath rushed[7] aside the law,
     And turned that black word "death" to "banishment."
     This is dear mercy, and thou seest it not.

ROMEO. 'Tis torture, and not mercy. Heaven is here,
30   Where Juliet lives; and every cat and dog
     And little mouse, every unworthy thing,
     Live here in heaven and may look on her;
     But Romeo may not. More validity,[8]
     More honorable state, more courtship lives
35   In carrion flies than Romeo. They may seize
     On the white wonder of dear Juliet's hand
     And steal immortal blessing from her lips,
     Who, even in pure and vestal modesty,
     Still blush, as thinking their own kisses sin;
40   But Romeo may not, he is banishèd.
     Flies may do this but I from this must fly;
     They are freemen, but I am banishèd.

2. doom final decision.

3. doomsday my death.

4. vanished escaped; came forth.

5. without outside.

6. Thy fault . . . death for what you did our law demands the death penalty.

7. rushed pushed.

Reading Skill
Summarizing
Paraphrase Romeo's complaint in lines 29–33, and then summarize his reaction to his banishment.

8. validity value.

Reading Check

What punishment does the Friar say Romeo could have received for his crime?

Romeo and Juliet, Act III ■ 795

And sayest thou yet that exile is not death?
Hadst thou no poison mixed, no sharp-ground knife,
45   No sudden mean⁹ of death, though ne'er so mean,¹⁰
But "banishèd" to kill me—"banishèd"?
O friar, the damnèd use that word in hell;
Howling attends it! How hast thou the heart,
Being a divine, a ghostly confessor,
50   A sin-absolver, and my friend professed,
To mangle me with that word "banishèd"?

FRIAR. Thou fond mad man, hear me a little speak.

ROMEO. O, thou wilt speak again of banishment.

FRIAR. I'll give thee armor to keep off that word;
55   Adversity's sweet milk, philosophy,
To comfort thee, though thou art banishèd.

ROMEO. Yet "banishèd"? Hang up philosophy!
Unless philosophy can make a Juliet,
Displant a town, reverse a prince's doom,
60   It helps not, it prevails not. Talk no more.

FRIAR. O, then I see that madmen have no ears.

ROMEO. How should they, when that wise men have no eyes?

FRIAR. Let me dispute¹¹ with thee of thy estate.¹²

ROMEO. Thou canst not speak of that thou dost not feel.
65   Wert thou as young as I, Juliet thy love,
An hour but married, Tybalt murderèd,
Doting like me, and like me banishèd,
Then mightst thou speak, then mightst thou tear thy hair,
And fall upon the ground, as I do now,
70   Taking the measure of an unmade grave.

[*Enter* NURSE *and knock.*]

FRIAR. Arise, one knocks. Good Romeo, hide thyself.

ROMEO. Not I; unless the breath of heartsick groans
Mistlike infold me from the search of eyes. [*Knock.*]

FRIAR. Hark, how they knock! Who's there? Romeo, arise;
75   Thou wilt be taken.—Stay awhile!—Stand up; [*Knock.*]
Run to my study.—By and by!¹³—God's will,
What simpleness¹⁴ is this.—I come, I come! [*Knock.*]
Who knocks so hard? Whence come you? What's your will?

[*Enter* NURSE.]

9. mean method.

10. mean humiliating.

Reading Skill
Summarizing
Summarize Romeo's
ideas in lines 57–60.
What do they suggest
about his state of
mind?

11. dispute discuss.

12. estate condition; situation.

13. By and by! In a minute!
(said to the person knocking).

14. simpleness silly behavior
(Romeo does not move).

NURSE. Let me come in, and you shall know my errand.
　　I come from Lady Juliet.

80 **FRIAR.** 　　　　　　　　　　Welcome then.

NURSE. O holy friar, O, tell me, holy friar,
　　Where is my lady's lord, where's Romeo?

FRIAR. There on the ground, with his own tears made drunk.

NURSE. O, he is even in my mistress' case,
85 　　Just in her case! O woeful sympathy!
　　Piteous predicament! Even so lies she,
　　Blubb'ring and weeping, weeping and blubb'ring.
　　Stand up, stand up! Stand, and you be a man.
　　For Juliet's sake, for her sake, rise and stand!
90 　　Why should you fall into so deep an O?[15]

ROMEO. [*Rises.*] Nurse—

NURSE. Ah sir, ah sir! Death's the end of all.

ROMEO. Spakest thou of Juliet? How is it with her?
　　Doth not she think me an old murderer,
95 　　Now I have stained the childhood of our joy
　　With blood removed but little from her own?
　　Where is she? And how doth she? And what says
　　My concealed lady[16] to our canceled love?

NURSE. O, she says nothing, sir, but weeps and weeps;
100 　　And now falls on her bed, and then starts up,
　　And Tybalt calls; and then on Romeo cries,
　　And then down falls again.

ROMEO. 　　　　　　　As if that name,
　　Shot from the deadly level[17] of a gun,
　　Did murder her; as that name's cursèd hand
105 　　Murdered her kinsman. O, tell me, friar, tell me, In
　　what vile part of this anatomy Doth my name lodge?
　　Tell me, that I may sack[18] The hateful mansion.

[*He offers to stab himself, and* NURSE *snatches the dagger away.*]

FRIAR. 　　　　　　　Hold thy desperate hand.
　　Art thou a man? Thy form cries out thou art;
110 　　Thy tears are womanish, thy wild acts denote
　　The unreasonable fury of a beast.
　　Unseemly[19] woman in a seeming man!
　　And ill-beseeming beast in seeming both![20]
　　Thou hast amazed me. By my holy order,
115 　　I thought thy disposition better tempered.

Literary Analysis
Dramatic Speeches
What does this brief speech by the Nurse reveal about her relationship with Romeo?

15. **O** cry of grief.

16. **concealed lady** secret bride.

17. **level** aim.

18. **sack** plunder.

19. **Unseemly** inappropriate (because unnatural).

20. **And . . . both!** Romeo has inappropriately lost his human nature because he seems like a man and woman combined.

Reading Check

What does Romeo nearly do before the Nurse stops him?

Hast thou slain Tybalt? Wilt thou slay thyself?
And slay thy lady that in thy life lives,
By doing damnèd hate upon thyself?
Why railest thou on thy birth, the heaven, and earth?
120 Since birth and heaven and earth, all three do meet
In thee at once; which thou at once wouldst lose.
Fie, fie, thou shamest thy shape, thy love, thy wit,[21]
Which, like a usurer,[22] abound'st in all,
And usest none in that true use indeed
125 Which should bedeck[23] thy shape, thy love, thy wit.
Thy noble shape is but a form of wax,
Digressing from the valor of a man;
Thy dear love sworn but hollow perjury,
Killing that love which thou hast vowed to cherish;
130 Thy wit, that ornament to shape and love,
Misshapen in the conduct[24] of them both,
Like powder in a skilless soldier's flask,[25]
Is set afire by thine own ignorance,
And thou dismemb'red with thine own defense.[26]
135 What, rouse thee, man! Thy Juliet is alive,
For whose dear sake thou wast but lately dead.[27]
There art thou happy.[28] Tybalt would kill thee,
But thou slewest Tybalt. There art thou happy.
The law, that threat'ned death, becomes thy friend
140 And turns it to exile. There art thou happy.
A pack of blessings light upon thy back;
Happiness courts thee in her best array;
But, like a misbehaved and sullen wench,[29]
Thou puts up[30] thy fortune and thy love.
145 Take heed, take heed, for such die miserable.
Go get thee to thy love, as was decreed,
Ascend her chamber, hence and comfort her.
But look thou stay not till the watch be set,[31]
For then thou canst not pass to Mantua,
150 Where thou shalt live till we can find a time
To blaze[32] your marriage, reconcile your friends,
Beg pardon of the Prince, and call thee back
With twenty hundred thousand times more joy
Than thou went'st forth in lamentation.
155 Go before, nurse. Commend me to thy lady,
And bid her hasten all the house to bed,
Which heavy sorrow makes them apt unto.[33]
Romeo is coming.

21. **wit** mind; intellect.

22. **Which, like a usurer** who, like a rich money-lender.

23. **bedeck** do honor to.

24. **conduct** management.

25. **flask** powder flask.

26. **And thou . . . defense** the friar is saying that Romeo's mind, which is now irrational, is destroying rather than aiding him.

27. **but lately dead** only recently declaring yourself dead.

28. **happy** fortunate.

29. **wench** low, common girl.

30. **puts up** pouts over.

31. **watch be set** watchmen go on duty.

32. **blaze** announce publicly.

33. **apt unto** likely to do.

Reading Skill
Summarizing Briefly state the main points of the Friar's speech to Romeo.

NURSE. O Lord, I could have stayed here all the night
160　To hear good counsel. O, what learning is!
　　My lord, I'll tell my lady you will come.

ROMEO. Do so, and bid my sweet prepare to chide.[34]

[NURSE *offers to go in and turns again.*]

NURSE. Here, sir, a ring she bid me give you, sir.
　　Hie you, make haste, for it grows very late.　　[*Exit.*]

165　**ROMEO.** How well my comfort is revived by this!

FRIAR. Go hence; good night; and here stands all your state:[35]
　　Either be gone before the watch be set,
　　Or by the break of day disguised from hence.
　　Sojourn[36] in Mantua. I'll find out your man,
170　And he shall signify[37] from time to time
　　Every good hap to you that chances here.
　　Give me thy hand. 'Tis late. Farewell; good night.

ROMEO. But that a joy past joy calls out on me,
　　It were a grief so brief to part with thee.
175　Farewell.　　　　　　　　　　　　[*Exit all.*]

Scene iv. A room in CAPULET'S *house.*

[*Enter old* CAPULET, *his* WIFE, *and* PARIS.]

CAPULET. Things have fall'n out, sir, so unluckily
　　That we have had no time to move[1] our daughter.
　　Look you, she loved her kinsman Tybalt dearly,
　　And so did I. Well, we were born to die.
5　'Tis very late; she'll not come down tonight.
　　I promise you, but for your company,
　　I would have been abed an hour ago.

PARIS. These times of woe afford no times to woo.
　　Madam, good night. Commend me to your daughter.

10　**LADY.** I will, and know her mind early tomorrow;
　　Tonight she's mewed up to her heaviness.[2]

CAPULET. Sir, Paris, I will make a desperate tender[3]
　　Of my child's love. I think she will be ruled
　　In all respects by me; nay more, I doubt it not.
15　Wife, go you to her ere you go to bed;
　　Acquaint her here of my son[4] Paris' love
　　And bid her (mark you me?) on Wednesday next—
　　But soft! What day is this?

---

34. **chide** rebuke me (for slaying Tybalt).

35. **here . . . state** this is your situation.

36. **Sojourn** remain.

37. **signify** let you know.

1. **move** discuss your proposal with.

Literary Analysis
Dramatic Speeches
Is Paris's brief remark in line 8 an aside? Explain.

2. **mewed . . . heaviness** locked up with her sorrow.

3. **desperate tender** risky offer.

4. **son** son-in-law.

✓**Reading Check**

What reason do the Capulets give Paris to explain why Juliet cannot see him?

PARIS.   Monday, my lord.

    CAPULET. Monday! Ha, ha! Well, Wednesday is too soon.
20   A⁵ Thursday let it be—a Thursday, tell her,
    She shall be married to this noble earl.
    Will you be ready? Do you like this haste?
    We'll keep no great ado⁶—a friend or two;
    For hark you, Tybalt being slain so late,
25   It may be thought we held him carelessly,⁷
    Being our kinsman, if we revel much.
    Therefore we'll have some half a dozen friends,
    And there an end. But what say you to Thursday?

    PARIS. My lord, I would that Thursday were tomorrow.

30 **CAPULET.** Well, get you gone. A Thursday be it then.
    Go you to Juliet ere you go to bed;
    Prepare her, wife, against⁸ this wedding day.
    Farewell, my lord.—Light to my chamber, ho!
    Afore me,⁹ it is so very late
35   That we may call it early by and by.
    Good night.   *[Exit all.]*

Scene v. *CAPULET'S orchard.*

[Enter ROMEO *and* JULIET *aloft.]*

    JULIET. Wilt thou be gone? It is not yet near day.
    It was the nightingale, and not the lark,
    That pierced the fearful hollow of thine ear.
    Nightly she sings on yond pomegranate tree.
5   Believe me, love, it was the nightingale.

    ROMEO. It was the lark, the herald of the morn;
    No nightingale. Look, love, what envious streaks
    Do lace the severing¹ clouds in yonder East.
    Night's candles² are burnt out, and jocund day
10   Stands tiptoe on the misty mountaintops.
    I must be gone and live, or stay and die.

    JULIET. Yond light is not daylight; I know it, I.
    It is some meteor that the sun exhales³
    To be to thee this night a torchbearer
15   And light thee on thy way to Mantua.
    Therefore stay yet; thou need'st not to be gone.

    ROMEO. Let me be ta'en, let me be put to death.
    I am content, so thou wilt have it so.

---

5. A on.

6. We'll . . . ado We will not make a great fuss.

7. held him carelessly did not respect him enough.

Reading Skill
Summarizing
Summarize Lord Capulet's remarks about the timing of Juliet's marriage to Paris.

8. against for.

9. Afore me indeed (a mild oath).

1. severing parting.

2. Night's candles stars.

3. exhales sends out.

Literature Connection

The Nightingale and the Lark The nightingale and the lark are two birds that appear frequently in literature, particularly in poetry. Both birds are admired and adored for their beautiful singing, and they also have symbolic associations. The nightingale and its song are traditionally associated with night; the lark and its song with dawn. Shakespeare draws on these associations in this exchange between Romeo and Juliet.

Connect to the Literature

Why do Romeo and Juliet have negative associations with the lark at this point in the play?

   I'll say yon gray is not the morning's eye,
20 'Tis but the pale reflex of Cynthia's brow;[4]
   Nor that is not the lark whose notes do beat
   The vaulty heaven so high above our heads.
   I have more care to stay than will to go.
   Come, death, and welcome! Juliet wills it so.
25 How is't, my soul? Let's talk; it is not day.

  JULIET. It is, it is! Hie hence, be gone, away!
   It is the lark that sings so out of tune,
   Straining harsh discords and unpleasing sharps.[5]
   Some say the lark makes sweet division;[6]
30 This doth not so, for she divideth us.
   Some say the lark and loathèd toad change eyes;[7]
   O, now I would they had changed voices too,
   Since arm from arm that voice doth us affray,[8]
   Hunting thee hence with hunt's-up[9] to the day.
35 O, now be gone! More light and light it grows.

  ROMEO. More light and light—more dark and dark our woes.

[*Enter* NURSE.]

  NURSE. Madam!

  JULIET. Nurse?

4. reflex . . . brow reflection of the moon (Cynthia was a name for the moon goddess).

Literary Analysis
Dramatic Speeches
What meaning does the allusion in line 20 add to Romeo's speech?

5. sharps shrill high notes.

6. division melody.

7. change eyes exchange eyes (because the lark has a beautiful body with ugly eyes and the toad has an ugly body with beautiful eyes).

8. affray frighten.

9. hunt's-up morning song for hunters.

✓ Reading Check

What do the Capulets plan for Juliet on Thursday?

NURSE. Your lady mother is coming to your chamber.
40   The day is broke; be wary, look about.   [*Exit.*]

JULIET. Then, window, let day in, and let life out.

ROMEO. Farewell, farewell! One kiss, and I'll descend.
                                [*He goeth down.*]

JULIET. Art thou gone so, love-lord, ay husband-friend?
    I must hear from thee every day in the hour,
45   For in a minute there are many days.
    O, by this count I shall be much in years[10]
    Ere I again behold my Romeo!

ROMEO. Farewell!
    I will omit no opportunity
50   That may convey my greetings, love, to thee.

JULIET. O, think'st thou we shall ever meet again?

ROMEO. I doubt it not; and all these woes shall serve
    For sweet discourses[11] in our times to come.

JULIET. O God, I have an ill-divining[12] soul!
55   Methinks I see thee, now thou art so low,
    As one dead in the bottom of a tomb.
    Either my eyesight fails, or thou lookest pale.

ROMEO. And trust me, love, in my eye so do you.
    Dry sorrow drinks our blood.[13] Adieu, adieu!   [*Exit.*]

60 **JULIET.** O Fortune, Fortune! All men call thee <u>fickle</u>.
    If thou art fickle, what dost thou[14] with him
    That is renowned for faith? Be fickle, Fortune,
    For then I hope thou wilt not keep him long
    But send him back.

[*Enter* MOTHER.]

65 **LADY CAPULET.** Ho, daughter! Are you up?

JULIET. Who is't that calls? It is my lady mother.
    Is she not down so late,[15] or up so early?
    What unaccustomed cause procures her hither?[16]

LADY CAPULET. Why, how now, Juliet?

JULIET.   Madam, I am not well.

70 **LADY CAPULET.** Evermore weeping for your cousin's death?
    What, wilt thou wash him from his grave with tears?
    And if thou couldst, thou couldst not make him live.
    Therefore have done. Some grief shows much of love;
    But much of grief shows still some want of wit.

Reading Skill
Summarizing Identify the key points of the farewell conversation between Romeo and Juliet.

10. **much in years** much older.

11. **discourses** conversations.

12. **ill-divining** predicting evil.

13. **Dry sorrow . . . blood** It was once believed that sorrow drained away the blood.

14. **dost thou** do you have to do.

Vocabulary Builder
fickle (fik´ əl) *adj.* changeable

15. **Is she . . . late** Has she stayed up so late?

16. **What . . . hither?** What unusual reason brings her here?

75 **JULIET.** Yet let me weep for such a feeling[17] loss.

LADY CAPULET. So shall you feel the loss, but not the friend
    Which you weep for.

JULIET.   Feeling so the loss,
    I cannot choose but ever weep the friend.

LADY CAPULET. Well, girl, thou weep'st not so much for his death
80   As that the villain lives which slaughtered him.

JULIET. What villain, madam?

LADY CAPULET.   That same villain Romeo.

JULIET. [*Aside*] Villain and he be many miles asunder.[18]—
    God pardon him! I do, with all my heart;
    And yet no man like he doth grieve my heart.

85 **LADY CAPULET.** That is because the traitor murderer lives.

JULIET. Ay, madam, from the reach of these my hands.
    Would none but I might venge my cousin's death!

LADY CAPULET. We will have vengeance for it, fear thou not.
    Then weep no more. I'll send to one in Mantua,
90   Where that same banished runagate[19] doth live,
    Shall give him such an unaccustomed dram[20]
    That he shall soon keep Tybalt company;
    And then I hope thou wilt be satisfied.

JULIET. Indeed I never shall be satisfied
95   With Romeo till I behold him—dead[21]—
    Is my poor heart so for a kinsman vexed.
    Madam, if you could find out but a man
    To bear a poison, I would temper[22] it;
    That Romeo should, upon receipt thereof,
100   Soon sleep in quiet. O, how my heart abhors
    To hear him named and cannot come to him,
    To wreak[23] the love I bore my cousin
    Upon his body that hath slaughtered him!

LADY CAPULET. Find thou the means, and I'll find such a man.
105   But now I'll tell thee joyful tidings, girl.

JULIET. And joy comes well in such a needy time.
    What are they, beseech your ladyship?

LADY CAPULET. Well, well, thou hast a careful[24] father, child;
    One who, to put thee from thy heaviness,
110   Hath sorted out[25] a sudden day of joy
    That thou expects not nor I looked not for.

---

17. feeling deeply felt.

Literary Analysis
Dramatic Speeches
What qualities of an aside do you find in lines 82–84?

18. asunder apart.

19. runagate renegade; runaway.

20. unaccustomed dram unexpected dose of poison.

21. dead Juliet is deliberately ambiguous here. Her mother thinks *dead* refers to Romeo. But Juliet is using the word with the following line, in reference to her heart.

22. temper mix; weaken.

23. wreak (rēk) avenge; express.

24. careful considerate.

25. sorted out selected.

Reading Check

What are Lady Capulet's plans for Romeo?

▲ **Critical Viewing** Do you think these actors accurately convey Juliet's response to her parents' plan for her marriage? **[Evaluate]**

JULIET. Madam, in happy time!²⁶ What day is that?

LADY CAPULET. Marry, my child, early next Thursday morn
  The gallant, young, and noble gentleman,
115   The County Paris, at Saint Peter's Church,
  Shall happily make thee there a joyful bride.

JULIET. Now by Saint Peter's Church, and Peter too,
  He shall not make me there a joyful bride!
  I wonder at this haste, that I must wed
120   Ere he that should be husband comes to woo.
  I pray you tell my lord and father, madam,
  I will not marry yet; and when I do, I swear
  It shall be Romeo, whom you know I hate,
  Rather than Paris. These are news indeed!

125 **LADY CAPULET.** Here comes your father. Tell him so yourself,
  And see how he will take it at your hands.

[*Enter* CAPULET *and* NURSE.]

CAPULET. When the sun sets the earth doth drizzle dew,
  But for the sunset of my brother's son
  It rains downright.
130   How now? A conduit,²⁷ girl? What, still in tears?
  Evermore show'ring? In one little body
  Thou counterfeits a bark,²⁸ a sea, a wind:
  For still thy eyes, which I may call the sea,
  Do ebb and flow with tears; the bark thy body is,
135   Sailing in this salt flood; the winds, thy sighs,
  Who, raging with thy tears and they with them,
  Without a sudden calm will overset
  Thy tempest-tossèd body. How now, wife?
  Have you delivered to her our decree?

140 **LADY CAPULET.** Ay, sir; but she will none, she gives you
    thanks.²⁹
  I would the fool were married to her grave!

CAPULET. Soft! Take me with you,³⁰ take me with you, wife.
  How? Will she none? Doth she not give us thanks?
  Is she not proud?³¹ Doth she not count her blest,
145   Unworthy as she is, that we have wrought³²
  So worthy a gentleman to be her bride?

JULIET. Not proud you have, but thankful that you have.
  Proud can I never be of what I hate,
  But thankful even for hate that is meant love.

150 **CAPULET.** How, how, how, how, chopped-logic?³³ What is this?

26. in happy time just in time.

27. conduit water pipe.

28. bark boat.

Reading Skill
Summarizing
Summarize the comparison Lord Capulet makes in lines 130–138.

29. she will none . . . thanks she will have nothing to do with it, thank you.

30. Soft! Take . . . you Wait a minute. Let me understand you.

31. proud pleased.

32. wrought arranged.

33. chopped-logic contradictory, unsound thought and speech.

Reading Check

Rather than Paris, whom does Juliet threaten to marry?

"Proud"—and "I thank you"—and "I thank you not"—
And yet "not proud"? Mistress minion[34] you,
Thank me no thankings, nor proud me no prouds,
But fettle[35] your fine joints 'gainst Thursday next
155 To go with Paris to Saint Peter's Church,
Or I will drag thee on a hurdle[36] thither.
Out, you greensickness carrion![37] Out, you baggage![38]
You tallow-face![39]

LADY CAPULET.   Fie, fie! What, are you mad?

JULIET. Good father, I beseech you on my knees,
160 Hear me with patience but to speak a word.

CAPULET. Hang thee, young baggage! Disobedient wretch!
I tell thee what—get thee to church a Thursday
Or never after look me in the face.
Speak not, reply not, do not answer me!
165 My fingers itch. Wife, we scarce thought us blest
That God had lent us but this only child;
But now I see this one is one too much,
And that we have a curse in having her.
Out on her, hilding![40]

NURSE.   God in heaven bless her!
170 You are to blame, my lord, to rate[41] her so.

CAPULET. And why, my Lady Wisdom? Hold your tongue,
Good Prudence. Smatter with your gossips, go![42]

NURSE. I speak no treason.

CAPULET.   O, God-i-god-en!

NURSE. May not one speak?

CAPULET.   Peace, you mumbling fool!
175 Utter your gravity[43] o'er a gossip's bowl,
For here we need it not.

LADY CAPULET.   You are too hot.

CAPULET. God's bread![44] It makes me mad.
Day, night; hour, tide, time; work, play;
Alone, in company; still my care hath been
180 To have her matched; and having now provided
A gentleman of noble parentage,
Of fair demesnes,[45] youthful, and nobly trained,
Stuffed, as they say, with honorable parts,[46]
Proportioned as one's thought would wish a man—
185 And then to have a wretched puling[47] fool,

34. **Mistress minion** Miss
Uppity.

35. **fettle** prepare.

36. **hurdle** sled on which prisoners were taken to their execution.

37. **greensickness
carrion** anemic lump of flesh.

38. **baggage** naughty girl.

39. **tallow-face** wax-pale
face.

Literary Analysis
Dramatic Speeches
What feelings and
personality traits does
Lord Capulet reveal in
this brief speech?

40. **hilding** worthless person.

41. **rate** scold; berate.

42. **Smatter . . . go!** Go chatter with the other old women.

43. **gravity** wisdom.

44. **God's bread!** By the holy
Eucharist!

45. **demesnes** property.

46. **parts** qualities.

47. **puling** whining.

A whining mammet,[48] in her fortune's tender,[49]
To answer "I'll not wed, I cannot love;
I am too young, I pray you pardon me"!
But, and you will not wed, I'll pardon you!
190 Graze where you will, you shall not house with me.
Look to't, think on't; I do not use to jest.
Thursday is near; lay hand on heart, advise:[50]
And you be mine, I'll give you to my friend;
And you be not, hang, beg, starve, die in the streets,
195 For, by my soul, I'll ne'er acknowledge thee,
Nor what is mine shall never do thee good.
Trust to't. Bethink you. I'll not be forsworn.[51]   [*Exit.*]

JULIET. Is there no pity sitting in the clouds
That sees into the bottom of my grief?
200 O sweet my mother, cast me not away!
Delay this marriage for a month, a week;
Or if you do not, make the bridal bed
In that dim monument where Tybalt lies.

LADY CAPULET. Talk not to me, for I'll not speak a word.
205 Do as thou wilt, for I have done with thee.   [*Exit.*]

48. **mammet** doll.

49. **in . . . tender** when good fortune is offered her.

50. **advise** consider.

Reading Skill
Summarizing Summarize the threat that Lord Capulet makes to Juliet in this monologue.

51. **forsworn** made to violate my promise.

✔**Reading Check**

How do the Capulets respond to the Nurse's attempts to defend Juliet?

◀ **Critical Viewing** In what ways does this picture suggest both Juliet's strength and her vulnerability? Explain. **[Interpret]**

JULIET. O God!—O nurse, how shall this be prevented?
My husband is on earth, my faith in heaven.[52]
How shall that faith return again to earth
Unless that husband send it me from heaven
210 By leaving earth?[53] Comfort me, counsel me.
Alack, alack, that heaven should practice stratagems[54]
Upon so soft a subject as myself!
What say'st thou? Hast thou not a word of joy?
Some comfort, nurse.

NURSE.   Faith, here it is.
Romeo is banished; and all the world to nothing[55]
That he dares ne'er come back to challenge[56] you;
Or if he do, it needs must be by stealth.
Then, since the case so stands as now it doth,
I think it best you married with the County.
220 O, he's a lovely gentleman!
Romeo's a dishclout to him.[57] An eagle, madam,
Hath not so green, so quick, so fair an eye
As Paris hath. Beshrew my very heart,
I think you are happy in this second match,
225 For it excels your first; or if it did not,
Your first is dead—or 'twere as good he were
As living here and you no use of him.

JULIET. Speak'st thou from thy heart?

NURSE. And from my soul too; else beshrew them both.

230 **JULIET.** Amen!

NURSE. What?

JULIET. Well, thou hast comforted me marvelous much.
Go in; and tell my lady I am gone,
Having displeased my father, to Lawrence' cell,
235 To make confession and to be absolved.[58]

NURSE. Marry, I will; and this is wisely done.   [*Exit.*]

JULIET. Ancient damnation![59] O most wicked fiend!
Is it more sin to wish me thus forsworn,
Or to dispraise my lord with that same tongue
240 Which she hath praised him with above compare
So many thousand times? Go, counselor!
Thou and my bosom henceforth shall be twain.[60]
I'll to the friar to know his remedy.
If all else fail, myself have power to die.   [*Exit.*]

---

52. my faith in heaven my marriage vow is recorded in heaven.

53. leaving earth dying.

54. stratagems tricks; plots.

55. all . . . nothing the odds are overwhelming.

56. challenge claim.

57. a dishclout to him a dishcloth compared with him.

58. absolved receive forgiveness for my sins.

59. Ancient damnation! Old devil!

60. Thou . . . twain You will from now on be separated from my trust.

Literary Analysis
Dramatic Speeches
What feelings toward her Nurse does Juliet reveal in this soliloquy?

▶ **Critical Viewing**
Why is a balcony well suited for a soliloquy? **[Assess]**

Apply the Skills

The Tragedy of Romeo and Juliet, Act III

Thinking About the Selection

1. **Respond:** What would you do if you were in Romeo or Juliet's situation? Explain.
2. **(a) Recall:** Make a three-column chart. In the first column, write the remark regarding the Montagues and Capulets that Mercutio makes three times as he is dying. **(b) Infer:** In the second column, explain what Mercutio means by this exclamation. **(c) Interpret:** In the third column, explain how his remark reinforces ideas set forth in the play's Prologue.

Mercutio's Dying Remark

What Does It Say?	What Does It Mean?	Why Is It Important?

3. **(a) Recall:** How and why does Romeo kill Tybalt? **(b) Interpret:** What does Romeo mean when he says, after killing Tybalt, "I am fortune's fool"?
4. **(a) Analyze:** Describe the clashing emotions Juliet feels when the Nurse reports Tybalt's death and Romeo's punishment. **(b) Compare and Contrast:** In what ways are Romeo's and Juliet's reactions to Romeo's banishment similar and different? Explain.
5. **Resolve:** How might Tybalt's death have been avoided?

Literary Analysis

6. **(a)** What thoughts and feelings does Juliet express in the **soliloquy** that opens Scene ii of Act III? **(b)** When Juliet makes an **allusion** to Phoebus and Phaëton, what is she hoping will happen soon?
7. What criticisms of Romeo does the Friar address in his Scene iii **monologue** beginning, "Hold thy desperate hand"?
8. **(a)** In Act III, Scene v, when her mother refers to Romeo as a villain, Juliet utters the **aside,** "Villain and he be many miles asunder." What does Juliet mean? **(b)** Why is it important that the audience, but not Lady Capulet, hears Juliet's remark?

Reading Skill

9. **(a) Paraphrase** lines 29–51 in Act III, Scene iii. **(b)** Based on your paraphrase, write a few sentences that **summarize** what Romeo says to the Friar in these lines.

QuickReview

Act III at a Glance
After Juliet's cousin, Tybalt, kills Mercutio, Romeo kills Tybalt and is banished from Verona. The newly-weds have one night together before Romeo flees. Juliet's parents plan to marry her to Count Paris.

For: Self-test
Visit: www.PHSchool.com
Web Code: epa-6504

Dramatic Speeches: words spoken by a single character to comment on the action. Common types include *soliloquy, monologue,* and *aside.*

Summarizing: briefly stating the main points in a piece of writing

Vocabulary Builder

Practice Identify which words in each group are synonyms and which is an antonym. Explain your response.

1. gallant, courageous, cowardly
2. fray, truce, brawl
3. exile, banishment, welcome
4. martial, peaceful, war-like
5. eloquence, expressive, inarticulate
6. fickle, unpredictable, constant

Adding Words to Your Vocabulary The word *martial* literally means "of Mars." Mars is the ancient Roman god of war, and so *martial* describes anything related to war. The words *jovial* and *mercurial* also owe their meanings to associations with certain Roman gods. Use a dictionary to find out the meaning of each word and how it relates to a particular Roman god. Then, write a few sentences explaining how the origin of each word is reflected in its everyday usage. (For more on using a dictionary, see page R6.)

Writing

Imagine that you are the editor of a newspaper in Verona at the time of the play. Write an **editorial** addressing the Prince's response to the deaths of Tybalt and Mercutio.

- Reread the Prince's dialogue in the scene.
- Decide whether Romeo's sentence was appropriate, and explain.
- Write the editorial, supporting your ideas with details from Acts I–III.

Share your editorial with classmates, and encourage them to write letters to the editor in support of or in opposition to your editorial.

For *Grammar, Vocabulary,* and *Assessment,* see **Build Language Skills,** pages 812–813.

Extend Your Learning

Research and Technology In a small group view a film of the ballet *Romeo and Juliet* by Russian composer Sergei Prokofiev. Take notes on how the dance, the music, and the camerawork communicate the play's ideas. Locate a review of the film and compare it to your own opinion. Then, use your notes to present a **film review** for the rest of the class.

Build Language Skills

Vocabulary Skill

Word Roots The **Latin word root** *-labor-* means "work." Words that contain this word root have meanings related to work. For example, *elaborate* means "work out in great detail." You can help yourself remember the "detail" part of the definition by remembering that to add details, or to elaborate, is more work than skipping the details.

Practice Use each form of *elaborate* and *labor* in a sentence. Look at the meaning of each word and the examples of its use in a dictionary. Revise your sentences as needed.

1. (a) elaboration   (b) elaborately   (c) elaborated
2. (a) labor   (b) laboriously   (c) laboring

Grammar Skill

Participle and Participle Phrases A **participle** is a verb form that is used as an adjective. **Present participles** end in *-ing*. The **past participles** of regular verbs end in *-ed*.

A **participle phrase** is a group of words that functions as an adjective in the sentence and contains a participle.

Present Participle	*growing* child
Past Participle	*troubled* child
Participle Phrase	*Focusing* intently, the driver managed to avoid an accident.

Practice Change the sentence pattern in each of the following so the participle is in a different place in the sentence. Explain how this changes the emphasis on the subject.

1. Discovered in the northwest, petroleum reserves helped to boost the economy of New Mexico.
2. Twenty years later, the federal government, looking for a sparsely populated area, went to New Mexico.
3. There have been several treaties, initiated by the United States, that try to limit nuclear weapons.
4. Depending on mutual self-interest, these treaties hold countries accountable for their weapons.

MorePractice

For more practice with participles and participle phrases, see the grammar handbook, p. R40.

W͞G Prentice Hall Writing and Grammar Connection: Chapter 21, Section 11.

Reading Skill: Summarize

Standards Assessed
- WL.1.01.1
- IR.2.01.1
- IR.2.01.8

Directions: *Read the selection. Then, answer the questions.*

> Full of vexation come I, with complaint
> Against my child, my daughter Hermia.—
> Stand forth, Demetrium.—My noble lord,
> 25 This man hath my consent to marry her.—
> Stand forth, Lysander. And, my gracious duke,
> This man hath bewitched the bosom of my child. . . .
> I beg the ancient privilege of Athens:
> As she is mine, I may dispose of her,
> 35 Which shall be either to this gentleman
> Or to her death, according to our law. . . .
>
> from *A Midsummer Night's Dream* by William Shakespeare

1. What happens in line 24?
  A Demetrium steps forward.
  B Demetrium marries Hermia.
  C Demetrius consents to marry Hermia.
  D Demetrius leaves.

2. Which of the following statements accurately paraphrases the ideas in lines 22–23?
  A I come here very angry, to compliment my daughter, Hermia.
  B I am full of complaints, and my daughter, Hermia, is against me.
  C I am angry, and my daughter, Hermia, knows it.
  D I am here to complain about my daughter, who has made me very angry.

3. The most important point in lines 33–36 is that
  A Hermia lives in Athens.
  B Hermia is the daughter of the speaker.
  C Hermia will either marry or be killed.
  D Hermia's father knows the law.

Timed Writing: Interpretation [Connections]

> "What's in a name?
> That which we call a rose
> by any other name would smell as sweet"
>
> from *Romeo and Juliet* by William Shakespeare

Interpret this quotation from the play. Paraphrase the idea expressed in the lines, and explain its significance. **(30 minutes)**

 ## Writing Workshop: *Work in Progress*

How-to Essay

Review the Step List from your writing portfolio. Visualize performing each step and mark if you have forgotten a step. After you are finished visualizing the task, go back and fill in the missing steps. Put this work in your writing portfolio.

Literary Analysis

Dramatic irony is a contradiction between what a character thinks and says and what the audience or reader knows is true. For example, in Act III, Capulet plans Juliet's wedding to Paris. He does not know what you know: that Juliet is already married to Romeo. Dramatic irony involves the audience emotionally in the story.

Shakespeare knew his audience could become *too* involved in the intense emotion of *Romeo and Juliet*. Therefore, he made sure to include the following elements to lighten the play's mood:

- **Comic relief:** a technique used to interrupt a serious scene by introducing a humorous character or situation
- **Puns:** plays on words involving a word with multiple meanings or two words that sound alike but have different meanings. For example, the dying Mercutio makes a pun involving two meanings of the word *grave:* "Ask for me tomorrow, and you shall find me a grave man."

As you read, notice how Shakespeare uses dramatic irony, comic relief, and puns to balance emotional suspense with laughter and wit.

Reading Skill

Summarizing is briefly stating the main points in a piece of writing. Stopping periodically to summarize what you have read helps you to check your comprehension before you read further.

Before you summarize a long passage of Shakespearean dialogue, you should **break down long sentences.**

- If a sentence contains multiple subjects or verbs, separate it into smaller sentences with one subject and one verb.
- If a sentence contains colons, semicolons, or dashes, treat them as periods in order to make smaller sentences.

Use a chart like this to help you break down long sentences.

Line of Dialogue

Immoderately she weeps for Tybalt's death,/ And therefore have I little talked of love;/ For Venus smiles not in a house of tears.

Line in Smaller Sentences

1. Immoderately she weeps for Tybalt's death.
2. Therefor have I little talked of love.
3. Venus smiles not in a house of tears.

Summary of Line

Paris has not talked of love with Juliet because she is crying over Tybalt's death.

Vocabulary Builder

- **pensive** (pen´ siv) *adj.* thinking deeply (p. 816) *She listened intently, looking pensive.*
- **enjoined** (en joind´) *v.* ordered (p. 820) *The jurors were enjoined not to discuss the case.*
- **wayward** (wā´ wərd) *adj.* headstrong (p. 821) *The wayward boy did not listen to anyone and insisted on working alone.*

- **dismal** (diz´ məl) *adj.* causing gloom or misery (p. 821) *The dismal sight of his abandoned house made the old man sad.*
- **loathsome** (lōth´ səm) *adj.* disgusting; detestable (p. 823) *The loathsome smell of rotten eggs filled the laboratory.*

ACT IV

Review and Anticipate

Romeo and Juliet are married for only a few hours when disaster strikes. In Act III, Juliet's cousin Tybalt kills Mercutio, and then Romeo kills Tybalt. This leads to Romeo's banishment from Verona. To make matters worse, Juliet's parents are determined to marry her to Paris. Will Romeo and Juliet ever be able to live together as husband and wife? What, if anything, can the lovers now do to preserve their relationship?

Scene i. FRIAR LAWRENCE'S cell.

[*Enter* FRIAR LAWRENCE *and* COUNTY PARIS.]

    FRIAR. On Thursday, sir? The time is very short.

    PARIS. My father¹ Capulet will have it so,
        And I am nothing slow to slack his haste.²

    FRIAR. You say you do not know the lady's mind.
5   Uneven is the course;³ I like it not.

    PARIS. Immoderately she weeps for Tybalt's death,
        And therefore have I little talked of love;
        For Venus smiles not in a house of tears.

1. father future father-in-law.

2. I . . . haste I will not slow him down by being slow myself.

3. Uneven . . . course irregular is the plan.

✓ Reading Check

What is the Friar's complaint to Paris about the impending wedding?

Now, sir, her father counts it dangerous
10   That she do give her sorrow so much sway,
And in his wisdom hastes our marriage
To stop the inundation⁴ of her tears,
Which, too much minded⁵ by herself alone,
May be put from her by society.
15   Now do you know the reason of this haste.

FRIAR. [*Aside*] I would I knew not why it should be slowed.—
Look, sir, here comes the lady toward my cell.

[*Enter* JULIET.]

PARIS. Happily met, my lady and my wife!

JULIET. That may be, sir, when I may be a wife.

20   **PARIS.** That "may be" must be, love, on Thursday next.

JULIET. What must be shall be.

FRIAR.   That's a certain text.⁶

PARIS. Come you to make confession to this father?

JULIET. To answer that, I should confess to you.

PARIS. Do not deny to him that you love me.

25   **JULIET.** I will confess to you that I love him.

PARIS. So will ye, I am sure, that you love me.

JULIET. If I do so, it will be of more price,⁷
Being spoke behind your back, than to your face.

PARIS. Poor soul, thy face is much abused with tears.

30   **JULIET.** The tears have got small victory by that,
For it was bad enough before their spite.⁸

PARIS. Thou wrong'st it more than tears with that report.

JULIET. That is no slander, sir, which is a truth;
And what I spake, I spake it to my face.

35   **PARIS.** Thy face is mine, and thou hast sland'red it.

JULIET. It may be so, for it is not mine own.
Are you at leisure, holy father, now,
Or shall I come to you at evening mass?

FRIAR. My leisure serves me, <u>pensive</u> daughter, now.
40   My lord, we must entreat the time alone.⁹

PARIS. God shield¹⁰ I should disturb devotion!

---

4. **inundation** flood.

5. **minded** thought about.

Literary Analysis
Dramatic Irony In what way does Paris's comment show that he does not understand the real reason that Juliet is crying?

6. **That's . . . text** That is a certain truth.

7. **price** value.

8. **before their spite** before the harm that the tears did.

Vocabulary Builder
pensive (pen′ siv)
adj. thinking deeply

9. **entreat . . . alone** ask to have this time to ourselves.

10. **shield** forbid.

Juliet, on Thursday early will I rouse ye.
Till then, adieu, and keep this holy kiss.   [*Exit.*]

JULIET. O, shut the door, and when thou hast done so,
45   Come weep with me—past hope, past care, past help!

FRIAR. O Juliet, I already know thy grief;
It strains me past the compass of my wits.[11]
I hear thou must, and nothing may prorogue[12] it,
On Thursday next be married to this County.

50 **JULIET.** Tell me not, friar, that thou hearest of this,
Unless thou tell me how I may prevent it.
If in thy wisdom thou canst give no help,
Do thou but call my resolution wise
And with this knife I'll help it presently.[13]
55   God joined my heart and Romeo's, thou our hands;
And ere this hand, by thee to Romeo's sealed,
Shall be the label to another deed,[14]
Or my true heart with treacherous revolt
Turn to another, this shall slay them both.
60   Therefore, out of thy long-experienced time,
Give me some present counsel; or, behold,
'Twixt my extremes and me[15] this bloody knife
Shall play the umpire, arbitrating[16] that
Which the commission of thy years and art
65   Could to no issue of true honor bring.[17]
Be not so long to speak. I long to die
If what thou speak'st speak not of remedy.

FRIAR. Hold, daughter. I do spy a kind of hope,
Which craves[18] as desperate an execution
70   As that is desperate which we would prevent.
If, rather than to marry County Paris,
Thou hast the strength of will to slay thyself,
Then is it likely thou wilt undertake
A thing like death to chide away this shame,
75   That cop'st with death himself to scape from it;[19]
And, if thou darest, I'll give thee remedy.

JULIET. O, bid me leap, rather than marry Paris,
From off the battlements of any tower,
Or walk in thievish ways,[20] or bid me lurk
80   Where serpents are; chain me with roaring bears,
Or hide me nightly in a charnel house,[21]
O'ercovered quite with dead men's rattling bones,

---

11. **past . . . wits** beyond the ability of my mind to find a remedy.

12. **prorogue** delay.

13. **presently** at once.

14. **Shall . . . deed** shall give the seal of approval to another marriage contract.

15. **'Twixt . . me** between my misfortunes and me.

16. **arbitrating** deciding.

17. **Which . . . bring** which the authority that derives from your age and ability could not solve honorably.

Literary Analysis
Puns Which two meanings of the word "long" does Juliet use to make a pun in line 66?

18. **craves** requires.

19. **That cop'st . . . it** that bargains with death itself to escape from it.

20. **thievish ways** roads where criminals lurk.

21. **charnel house** vault for bones removed from graves to be reused.

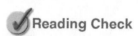Reading Check

What does Juliet threaten to do to avoid marrying Paris?

With reeky[22] shanks and yellow chapless[23] skulls;
Or bid me go into a new-made grave
85 And hide me with a dead man in his shroud—
Things that, to hear them told, have made me tremble—
And I will do it without fear or doubt,
To live an unstained wife to my sweet love.

FRIAR. Hold, then. Go home, be merry, give consent
90 To marry Paris. Wednesday is tomorrow.
Tomorrow night look that thou lie alone;
Let not the nurse lie with thee in thy chamber.
Take thou this vial, being then in bed,
And this distilling liquor drink thou off;
95 When presently through all thy veins shall run
A cold and drowsy humor;[24] for no pulse
Shall keep his native[25] progress, but surcease;[26]
No warmth, no breath, shall testify thou livest;
The roses in thy lips and cheeks shall fade
100 To wanny ashes,[27] thy eyes' windows[28] fall
Like death when he shuts up the day of life;
Each part, deprived of supple government,[29]

22. **reeky** foul-smelling.

23. **chapless** jawless.

24. **humor** fluid; liquid.

25. **native** natural.

26. **surcease** stop.

27. **wanny ashes** to the color of pale ashes.

28. **eyes' windows** eyelids.

29. **supple government** ability for maintaining motion.

▼ **Critical Viewing**
According to the play, what power does the vial hold? **[Connect]**

Shall, stiff and stark and cold, appear like death;
And in this borrowed likeness of shrunk death
105 Thou shalt continue two-and-forty hours,
And then awake as from a pleasant sleep.
Now, when the bridegroom in the morning comes
To rouse thee from thy bed, there art thou dead.
Then, as the manner of our country is,
110 In thy best robes uncovered on the bier[30]
Thou shalt be borne to that same ancient vault
Where all the kindred of the Capulets lie.
In the meantime, against[31] thou shalt awake,
Shall Romeo by my letters know our drift;[32]
115 And hither shall he come; and he and I
Will watch thy waking, and that very night
Shall Romeo bear thee hence to Mantua.
And this shall free thee from this present shame,
If no inconstant toy[33] nor womanish fear
120 Abate thy valor[34] in the acting it.

JULIET. Give me, give me! O, tell not me of fear!

FRIAR. Hold! Get you gone, be strong and prosperous
In this resolve. I'll send a friar with speed
To Mantua, with my letters to thy lord.

125 **JULIET.** Love give me strength, and strength shall help afford.
Farewell, dear father.   [*Exit with* FRIAR.]

Scene ii. Hall in CAPULET'S house.

[*Enter* FATHER CAPULET, MOTHER, NURSE, *and* SERVINGMEN, *two or three.*]

CAPULET. So many guests invite as here are writ.
                              [*Exit a* SERVINGMAN.]
Sirrah, go hire me twenty cunning[1] cooks.

SERVINGMAN. You shall have none ill, sir; for I'll try[2] if they can
lick their fingers.

5 **CAPULET.** How canst thou try them so?

SERVINGMAN. Marry, sir, 'tis an ill cook that cannot lick his own
fingers.[3] Therefore he that cannot lick his fingers goes not
with me.

CAPULET. Go, begone.

                              [*Exit* SERVINGMAN.]

30. uncovered on the bier displayed on the funeral platform.

31. against before.

32. drift purpose; plan.

33. inconstant toy passing whim.

34. Abate thy valor Lessen your courage.

Literary Analysis
Dramatic Irony What information does Juliet now have that Romeo does not?

1. cunning skillful.

2. try test.

3. 'tis . . . fingers It is a bad cook who will not taste his own cooking.

Reading Check

According to the Friar, how will Romeo learn of Juliet's plan to meet him?

We shall be much unfurnished[4] for this time.

10 What, is my daughter gone to Friar Lawrence?

NURSE. Ay, forsooth.[5]

CAPULET. Well, he may chance to do some good on her.
A peevish self-willed harlotry it is.[6]

[*Enter* JULIET.]

NURSE. See where she comes from shrift with merry look.

15 **CAPULET.** How now, my headstrong? Where have you been
gadding?

JULIET. Where I have learnt me to repent the sin
Of disobedient opposition
To you and your behests,[7] and am <u>enjoined</u>
By holy Lawrence to fall prostrate[8] here
20 To beg your pardon. Pardon, I beseech you!
Henceforward I am ever ruled by you.

CAPULET. Send for the County. Go tell him of this.
I'll have this knot knit up tomorrow morning.

JULIET. I met the youthful lord at Lawrence' cell
25 And gave him what becomèd[9] love I might,
Not stepping o'er the bounds of modesty.

CAPULET. Why, I am glad on't. This is well. Stand up.
This is as't should be. Let me see the County.
Ay, marry, go, I say, and fetch him hither.
30 Now, afore God, this reverend holy friar,
All our whole city is much bound[10] to him.

JULIET. Nurse, will you go with me into my closet[11]
To help me sort such needful ornaments[12]
As you think fit to furnish me tomorrow?

35 **LADY CAPULET.** No, not till Thursday. There is time enough.

CAPULET. Go, nurse, go with her. We'll to church tomorrow.

[*Exit* JULIET *and* NURSE.]

LADY CAPULET. We shall be short in our provision.[13]
'Tis now near night.

CAPULET.   Tush, I will stir about,
And all things shall be well, I warrant thee, wife.
40 Go thou to Juliet, help to deck up her.[14]
I'll not to bed tonight; let me alone.
I'll play the housewife for this once. What, ho![15]

---

4. unfurnished unprepared.

5. forsooth in truth.

6. A peevish . . . it is It is the ill-tempered, selfish behavior of a woman without good breeding.

Vocabulary Builder
enjoined (en join′) *v.* ordered

7. behests requests.

8. fall prostrate lie face down in humble submission.

9. becomèd suitable; proper.

Literary Analysis
Dramatic Irony What is ironic about Lord Capulet's relief in this scene?

10. bound indebted.

11. closet private room.

12. ornaments clothes.

13. short . . . provision lacking time for preparation.

14. deck up her dress her; get her ready.

15. What, ho! Capulet is calling for his servants.

They are all forth; well, I will walk myself
To County Paris, to prepare up him
45   Against tomorrow. My heart is wondrous light,
Since this same <u>wayward</u> girl is so reclaimed.

                          [*Exit with* MOTHER.]

Scene iii. JULIET'S chamber.

[*Enter* JULIET *and* NURSE.]

    JULIET. Ay, those attires are best; but, gentle nurse,
    I pray thee leave me to myself tonight;
    For I have need of many orisons[1]
    To move the heavens to smile upon my state,[2]
5   Which, well thou knowest, is cross[3] and full of sin.

[*Enter* MOTHER.]

    LADY CAPULET. What, are you busy, ho? Need you my help?

    JULIET. No, madam; we have culled[4] such necessaries
    As are behoveful[5] for our state tomorrow.
    So please you, let me now be left alone,
10   And let the nurse this night sit up with you:
    For I am sure you have your hands full all
    In this so sudden business.

    LADY CAPULET.   Good night.
    Get thee to bed, and rest: for thou hast need.

                  [*Exit* MOTHER *and* NURSE.]

    JULIET. Farewell! God knows when we shall meet again.
15   I have a faint cold fear thrills through my veins
    That almost freezes up the heat of life.
    I'll call them back again to comfort me.
    Nurse!—What should she do here?
    My <u>dismal</u> scene I needs must act alone.
20   Come, vial.
    What if this mixture do not work at all?
    Shall I be married then tomorrow morning?
    No, no! This shall forbid it. Lie thou there.

                  [*Lays down a dagger.*]

    What if it be a poison which the friar
25   Subtly hath minist'red[6] to have me dead,
    Lest in this marriage he should be dishonored
    Because he married me before to Romeo?

Vocabulary Builder
wayward (wā′ wərd)
adj. headstrong

1. **orisons** prayers.
2. **state** condition.
3. **cross** selfish; disobedient.

Reading Skill
Summarizing Briefly state the reasons Juliet gives her Nurse and Lady Capulet for why she should be alone.

4. **culled** chosen.
5. **behoveful** desirable; appropriate.

Vocabulary Builder
dismal (diz′ məl)
adj. causing gloom or misery

6. **minist'red** given me.

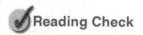Reading Check

How does Juliet regain her parents' favor?

I fear it is; and yet methinks it should not,
For he hath still been tried[7] a holy man.
30 How if, when I am laid into the tomb,
I wake before the time that Romeo
Come to redeem me? There's a fearful point!
Shall I not then be stifled in the vault,
To whose foul mouth no healthsome air breathes in,
35 And there die strangled ere my Romeo comes?
Or, if I live, is it not very like
The horrible conceit[8] of death and night,
Together with the terror of the place—
As in a vault, an ancient receptacle
40 Where for this many hundred years the bones
Of all my buried ancestors are packed;
Where bloody Tybalt, yet but green in earth,[9]
Lies fest'ring in his shroud; where, as they say,
At some hours in the night spirits resort—
45 Alack, alack, is it not like[10] that I,
So early waking—what with loathsome smells,
And shrieks like mandrakes[11] torn out of the earth,
That living mortals, hearing them, run mad—
O, if I wake, shall I not be distraught,[12]
50 Environèd[13] with all these hideous fears,
And madly play with my forefathers' joints,
And pluck the mangled Tybalt from his shroud,
And, in this rage, with some great kinsman's bone
As with a club dash out my desp'rate brains?
55 O, look! Methinks I see my cousin's ghost
Seeking out Romeo, that did spit his body
Upon a rapier's point. Stay, Tybalt, stay!
Romeo, Romeo, Romeo, I drink to thee.
                    [*She falls upon her bed within the curtains.*]

Scene ii. Hall in CAPULET'S house.

[*Enter* LADY OF THE HOUSE *and* NURSE.]

LADY CAPULET. Hold, take these keys and fetch more spices,
    nurse.

◄ **Critical Viewing** Do you think Juliet's decision to take the potion is
courageous? Why or why not? **[Evaluate]**

7. tried proved.

8. conceit idea; thought.

9. green in earth newly entombed.

10. like likely.

Vocabulary Builder
loathsome (lōth´ səm)
adj. disgusting;
detestable

11. mandrakes plants with forked roots that resemble human legs. The mandrake was believed to shriek when uprooted and cause the hearer to go mad.

12. distraught insane.

13. Environèd surrounded.

Reading Skill
Summarizing Summarize the fears that Juliet expresses in this soliloquy.

Reading Check

What does Juliet do after her mother and the Nurse leave her chambers?

NURSE. They call for dates and quinces[1] in the pastry.[2]

[*Enter old* CAPULET.]

    CAPULET. Come, stir, stir, stir! The second cock hath crowed,
       The curfew bell hath rung, 'tis three o'clock.
5   Look to the baked meats, good Angelica;[3]
       Spare not for cost.

    NURSE.   Go, you cotquean,[4] go,
       Get you to bed! Faith, you'll be sick tomorrow
       For this night's watching.[5]

    CAPULET. No, not a whit. What, I have watched ere now
10   All night for lesser cause, and ne'er been sick.

    LADY CAPULET. Ay, you have been a mouse hunt[6] in your time;
       But I will watch you from such watching now.
                    [*Exit* LADY *and* NURSE.]

    CAPULET. A jealous hood,[7] a jealous hood!
[*Enter three or four* FELLOWS *with spits and logs and baskets.*]
                  Now, fellow,
     What is there?

15 **FIRST FELLOW.** Things for the cook, sir; but I know not what.

    CAPULET. Make haste, make haste. [*Exit* FIRST FELLOW.] Sirrah,
       fetch drier logs.
       Call Peter; he will show thee where they are.

    SECOND FELLOW. I have a head, sir, that will find out logs
       And never trouble Peter for the matter.

20 **CAPULET.** Mass,[8] and well said; a merry whoreson, ha!
       Thou shalt be loggerhead.[9]
             [*Exit* SECOND FELLOW, *with the others.*]
     Good faith, 'tis day.
     The County will be here with music straight,
     For so he said he would.   [*Play music.*]
            I hear him near.
     Nurse! Wife! What, ho! What, nurse, I say!

[*Enter* NURSE.]
25   Go waken Juliet; go and trim her up.
     I'll go and chat with Paris. Hie, make haste,
     Make haste! The bridegroom he is come already:
     Make haste, I say.   [*Exit.*]

---

1. quinces golden, apple-shaped fruits.

2. pastry baking room.

3. Angelica This is probably the Nurse's name.

4. cotquean (kat′ kwēn′) man who does housework.

5. watching staying awake.

6. mouse hunt woman chaser.

7. jealous hood jealousy.

8. Mass by the Mass (an oath).

9. loggerhead blockhead.

Literary Analysis
Puns In what way does Capulet's pun in line 21 contribute to the mood of Scene iv?

Scene iii. JULIET'S chamber.

> **NURSE.** Mistress! What, mistress! Juliet! Fast,[1] I warrant her,
>   she.
>   Why, lamb! Why, lady! Fie, you slugabed.[2]
>   Why, love, I say! Madam; Sweetheart! Why, bride!
>   What, not a word? You take your pennyworths now;
> 5 Sleep for a week; for the next night, I warrant,
>   The County Paris hath set up his rest
>   That you shall rest but little. God forgive me!
>   Marry, and amen. How sound is she asleep!
>   I needs must wake her. Madam, madam, madam!
> 10 Ay, let the County take you in your bed;
>   He'll fright you up, i' faith. Will it not be?
>
>   *[Draws aside the curtains.]*
>   What, dressed, and in your clothes, and down again?[3]
>   I must needs wake you. Lady! Lady! Lady!
>   Alas, alas! Help, help! My lady's dead!
> 15 O weraday that ever I was born!
>   Some *aqua vitae*, ho! My lord! My lady!

[Enter MOTHER.]

> **LADY CAPULET.** What noise is here?
>
> **NURSE.**   O lamentable day!
>
> **LADY CAPULET.** What is the matter?
>
> **NURSE.**   Look, look! O heavy day!
>
> **LADY CAPULET.** O me, O me! My child, my only life!
> 20 Revive, look up, or I will die with thee!
>   Help, help! Call help.

[Enter FATHER.]

> **CAPULET.** For shame, bring Juliet forth; her lord is come.
>
> **NURSE.** She's dead, deceased; she's dead, alack the day!
>
> **LADY CAPULET.** Alack the day, she's dead, she's dead, she's
>   dead!
>
> 25 **CAPULET.** Ha! Let me see her. Out alas! She's cold,
>   Her blood is settled, and her joints are stiff;
>   Life and these lips have long been separated.
>   Death lies on her like an untimely frost
>   Upon the sweetest flower of all the field.

1. **Fast** fast asleep.

2. **slugabed** sleepyhead.

Literary Analysis
Dramatic Irony In what way does the Nurse's carefree chatter add to the irony of the scene?

3. **down again** back in bed.

Reading Check

What does the Nurse find when she draws aside the curtains in Juliet's chamber?

NURSE. O lamentable day!

30 **LADY CAPULET.** O woeful time!

CAPULET. Death, that hath ta'en her hence to make me wail,
Ties up my tongue and will not let me speak.

[*Enter* FRIAR LAWRENCE *and the* COUNTY PARIS, *with* MUSICIANS.]

FRIAR. Come, is the bride ready to go to church?

CAPULET. Ready to go, but never to return.
35 O son, the night before thy wedding day
Hath Death lain with thy wife. There she lies,
Flower as she was, deflowerèd by him.
Death is my son-in-law, Death is my heir;
My daughter he hath wedded. I will die
40 And leave him all. Life, living, all is Death's.

PARIS. Have I thought, love, to see this morning's face,
And doth it give me such a sight as this?

LADY CAPULET. Accursed, unhappy, wretched, hateful day!
Most miserable hour that e'er time saw
45 In lasting labor of his pilgrimage!
But one, poor one, one poor and loving child,
But one thing to rejoice and solace[4] in,
And cruel Death hath catched it from my sight.

NURSE. O woe! O woeful, woeful, woeful day!
50 Most lamentable day, most woeful day
That ever ever I did yet behold!
O day, O day, O day! O hateful day!
Never was seen so black a day as this.
O woeful day! O woeful day!

55 **PARIS.** Beguiled,[5] divorcèd, wrongèd, spited, slain!
Most detestable Death, by thee beguiled,
By cruel, cruel thee quite overthrown.
O love! O life!—not life, but love in death!

CAPULET. Despised, distressèd, hated, martyred, killed!
60 Uncomfortable[6] time, why cam'st thou now
To murder, murder our solemnity?[7]
O child, O child! My soul, and not my child!
Dead art thou—alack, my child is dead,
And with my child my joys are burièd!

**Literary Analysis
Dramatic Irony** In
what way does the
Friar's question add
to the dramatic irony
of the scene?

**Literary Analysis
Dramatic
Irony** How is effect
of the pun in
lines 46–47 different
from the effect of
the comic puns
earlier in Act IV?

4. solace find comfort.

5. Beguiled cheated.

6. Uncomfortable painful,
upsetting.

7. solemnity solemn rites.

Culture Connection

Rosemary When the Capulets discover Juliet apparently dead, the Friar advises, "Dry up your tears and stick your rosemary / On this fair corse." Rosemary is an evergreen herb that traditionally signifies remembrance, loyalty, and love. Shakespeare often included references to herbs in his plays for symbolic purposes, and rosemary is one herb that turned up often in his works. *Hamlet, King Lear, The Winter's Tale,* and *Pericles* all include references to rosemary as a symbol of remembrance.

Connect to the Literature

Why do you think the Friar tells the Capulets to lay a sprig of rosemary on Juliet's body?

65 **FRIAR.** Peace, ho, for shame! Confusion's cure lives not
   In these confusions.[8] Heaven and yourself
   Had part in this fair maid—now heaven hath all,
   And all the better is it for the maid.
   Your part in her you could not keep from death,
70 But heaven keeps his part in eternal life.
   The most you sought was her promotion,
   For 'twas your heaven she should be advanced;
   And weep ye now, seeing she is advanced
   Above the clouds, as high as heaven itself?
75 O, in this love, you love your child so ill
   That you run mad, seeing that she is well.[9]
   She's not well married that lives married long,
   But she's best married that dies married young.
   Dry up your tears and stick your rosemary[10]
80 On this fair corse, and, as the custom is,
   And in her best array bear her to church:
   For though fond nature[11] bids us all lament,
   Yet nature's tears are reason's merriment.[12]

   CAPULET. All things that we ordainèd festival[13]
85 Turn from their office to black funeral—
   Our instruments to melancholy bells,
   Our wedding cheer to a sad burial feast;
   Our solemn hymns to sullen dirges[14] change;
   Our bridal flowers serve for a buried corse;
90 And all things change them to the contrary.

8. Confusion's . . . confusions The remedy for this calamity is not to be found in these outcries.

9. well blessed in heaven.

10. rosemary evergreen herb signifying love and remembrance.

11. fond nature mistake-prone human nature.

12. Yet . . . merriment While human nature causes us to weep for Juliet, reason should cause us to be happy (since she is in heaven).

13. ordainèd festival planned to be part of a celebration.

14. dirges funeral hymns.

Reading Check

What does the Friar recommend that the Capulets do when they discover Juliet and believe she is dead?

FRIAR. Sir, go you in; and, madam, go with him;
And go, Sir Paris. Everyone prepare
To follow this fair corse unto her grave.
The heavens do low'r[15] upon you for some ill;
95　　Move them no more by crossing their high will.

> [*Exit, casting rosemary on her and shutting the curtains.*
> *The* NURSE *and* MUSICIANS *remain.*]

FIRST MUSICIAN. Faith, we may put up our pipes and be gone.

NURSE. Honest good fellows, ah, put up, put up!
For well you know this is a pitiful case.[16]　　　　　[*Exit.*]

FIRST MUSICIAN. Ay, by my troth, the case may be amended.

[*Enter* PETER.]

100　**PETER.** Musicians, O, musicians, "Heart's ease," "Heart's ease"!
O, and you will have me live, play "Heart's ease."

FIRST MUSICIAN. Why "Heart's ease"?

PETER. O, musicians, because my heart itself plays "My heart is full."
O, play me some merry dump[17] to comfort me.

105　**FIRST MUSICIAN.** Not a dump we! 'Tis no time to play now.

PETER. You will not then?

FIRST MUSICIAN. No.

PETER. I will then give it you soundly.

FIRST MUSICIAN. What will you give us?

110　**PETER.** No money, on my faith, but the gleek.[18] I will give you[19] the minstrel.[20]

FIRST MUSICIAN. Then will I give you the serving-creature.

PETER. Then will I lay the serving-creature's dagger on your pate.
I will carry no crotchets.[21] I'll re you, I'll fa you. Do you note me?

115　**FIRST MUSICIAN.** And you re us and fa us, you note us.

SECOND MUSICIAN. Pray you put up your dagger, and put out your wit.
Then have at you with my wit!

Literary Analysis
Dramatic Irony In what way does the dramatic irony of the Friar's words heighten the play's suspense?

15. low'r frown.

16. case situation; instrument case.

17. dump sad tune.

18. gleek scornful speech.

19. give you call you.

20. minstrel a contemptuous term (as opposed to "musician").

21. crotchets whims; quarter notes.

PETER. I will dry-beat you with an iron wit, and put up my iron dagger. Answer me like men.

120 "When griping grief the heart doth wound,
And doleful dumps the mind oppress,
Then music with her silver sound"—
Why "silver sound"? Why "music with her silver sound"?
What say you, Simon Catling?

125 **FIRST MUSICIAN.** Marry, sir, because silver hath a sweet sound.

PETER. Pretty! What say you, Hugh Rebeck?

SECOND MUSICIAN. I say "silver sound" because musicians sound for silver.

PETER. Pretty too! What say you, James Soundpost?

130 **THIRD MUSICIAN.** Faith, I know not what to say.

PETER. O, I cry you mercy,²² you are the singer. I will say for you. It is "music with her silver sound" because musicians have no gold for sounding.
"Then music with her silver sound
135 With speedy help doth lend redress." [*Exit.*]

FIRST MUSICIAN. What a pestilent knave is this same!

SECOND MUSICIAN. Hang him, Jack! Come, we'll in here, tarry for the mourners, and stay dinner. [*Exit with others.*]

Literary Analysis
Puns What kind of mood does the pun in line 127 help to create in this scene?

22. cry you mercy beg your pardon.

Apply the Skills

The Tragedy of Romeo and Juliet, Act IV

Thinking About the Selection

1. **(a) Respond:** Should Romeo and Juliet have followed Friar Lawrence's advice? Why or why not? **(b) Discuss:** Share your response with a partner, and then discuss how hearing someone else's response did or did not change your own.
2. **(a) Recall:** What is Friar Lawrence's plan for Juliet? **(b) Analyze:** Why do you think Juliet trusts the Friar?
3. **(a) Recall:** What three fears does Juliet reveal in her Act IV, Scene iii, soliloquy? **(b) Interpret:** What does the soliloquy reveal about her personality?
4. **(a) Evaluate:** Do you think drinking the potion is a brave act or a foolish act? Explain. **(b) Draw Conclusions:** How has Juliet changed in the course of the play?

Literary Analysis

5. In what way is Juliet's encounter with Paris in Friar Lawrence's cell an instance of **dramatic irony?**
6. Complete a chart like the one shown to demonstrate why Capulet's statement in Act IV, Scene iv, line 25 is an example of dramatic irony.

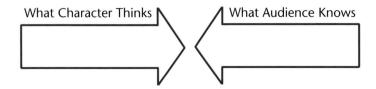

What Character Thinks | What Audience Knows

7. Explain how Capulet's encounter with the fellows in Act IV, Scene ii, represents an example of **comic relief.**
8. **(a)** Explain the **pun** in the Nurse's exchange with the First Musician in Act IV, Scene v, lines 97–98. **(b)** In what way is the conversation that follows among the musicians and Peter an example of comic relief?

Reading Skill

9. **(a) Summarize** lines 50–59 of Juliet's monologue to Friar Lawrence in Act IV, Scene i. **(b)** In what way does breaking down this long sentence into smaller ones make the meaning of Juliet's speech clearer?

QuickReview

Act IV at a Glance
Juliet promises to marry Paris and then avoids the wedding by drinking a potion that puts her in a deathlike sleep. Her family grieves to find Juliet apparently lifeless on her wedding day.

Assessment
For: Self-test
Visit: www.PHSchool.com
Web Code: epa-6505

Dramatic Irony: a contradiction between what a character thinks and says and what the audience or reader knows is true

Comic Relief: a humorous character or situation that lightens the mood of a serious scene

Pun: a play on words

Summarizing: briefly stating the main points in a piece of writing

Vocabulary Builder

Practice Indicate whether each of the following statements is *True* or *False*. Revise the sentences that are false to make them true.

1. Clowns make children laugh by appearing *pensive*.
2. If you have been *enjoined* to attend an event, you should not go.
3. A *wayward* person would probably dislike orders.
4. If you were in a *dismal* mood, you would be good company.
5. A *loathsome* meal is not likely to be eaten quickly.

Adding Words to Your Vocabulary Using a thesaurus, find a **synonym,** or word with a similar meaning, for each italicized word in the Practice items. Then, use each synonym correctly in a sentence. (For more on using a thesaurus, see page R7.)

Writing

Write an **abstract,** or summary, of what has happened so far in *Romeo and Juliet.* Imagine that you are writing for an audience member who has missed everything up to the beginning of Act V.
- Review Acts I–IV and list of the major events in the play so far.
- Describe the main characters, noting relationships among them.
- Note the most memorable scenes in Acts I–IV and the overall mood.
- Use the information you compile to write a one-paragraph summary of the play's action.

Read your abstract to someone who has not read *Romeo and Juliet.* Clarify any information that your reader finds confusing.

For *Grammar, Vocabulary,* and *Assessment,* see **Build Language Skills,** pages 850–851.

Extend Your Learning

Research and Technology With a partner, create a **multimedia presentation** on Renaissance music. Use library or Internet resources to collect examples of music that would have been played by musicians in Act IV, Scene v. Find pictures of instruments from the period as well. Present your findings in class and lead a discussion about the cultural values the music expresses.

Literary Analysis

A **tragedy** is a drama in which the central character, who is of noble stature, meets with disaster or great misfortune. The tragic hero's downfall is usually the result of one of the following:

- *fate*, or the idea of a pre-planned destiny
- a serious character flaw
- some combination of both

Motive is an important element of a tragic hero's character. A character's motive is the reason for his or her thoughts or actions. In many of Shakespeare's tragedies, the hero's motives are basically good, but misguided. As a result, the hero suffers a tragic fate that may seem undeserved.

Although tragedies are sad, they can also be uplifting. They show the greatness and nobility of the human spirit when faced with grave challenges. As you read the conclusion of *Romeo and Juliet,* consider what positive message might be conveyed by the play's tragic events.

Reading Skill

Summarizing is briefly stating the main points in a piece of writing. In summarizing the action, it is useful to first **identify causes and effects.**

- A *cause* is an event, action, or emotion that produces a result.
- An *effect* is the result produced by the cause.

Tragedies often involve a chain of events that advance the plot and lead to the final tragic outcome. Understanding the sequence of causes and effects will help you to summarize complicated plots like the one in *Romeo and Juliet.* As you read Act V, use a chart like this to record causes and effects.

Cause
Juliet takes the potion.

↓

Effect/Cause
Everyone thinks she is dead.

↓

Effect

Vocabulary Builder

- **remnants** (rem´ nənts) *n.* what is left over; remainders (p. 834) *The remnants of the house still stood after the fire.*

- **penury** (pen´ yoo rē) *n.* extreme poverty (p. 835) *His choice was either to find work or to live in penury.*

- **haughty** (hôt´ ē) *adj.* arrogant (p. 838) *He acts haughty onstage, but humble offstage.*

- **ambiguities** (am´ bə gyoo´ ə tēz) *n.* statements or events whose meanings are unclear (p. 845) *Voters were confused by the ambiguities in the candidate's speech.*

- **scourge** (skʉrj) *n.* instrument for inflicting punishment (p. 847) *Longer practices were the scourge that the coach used to punish the players for their laziness.*

ACT V

Review and Anticipate

To prevent her marriage to Paris, Juliet has taken the Friar's potion and, as Act V begins, is in a temporary deathlike sleep. Her unsuspecting family plans her funeral. Meanwhile, the Friar has sent a messenger to Mantua to tell Romeo of the ruse, so that he may return and rescue Juliet from her family tomb. What do you think might go wrong with the Friar's plan?

Scene i. MANTUA. A STREET.

[*Enter* ROMEO.]

> **ROMEO.** If I may trust the flattering truth of sleep,[1]
> My dreams presage[2] some joyful news at hand.
> My bosom's lord[3] sits lightly in his throne,
> And all this day an unaccustomed spirit
> 5   Lifts me above the ground with cheerful thoughts.
> I dreamt my lady came and found me dead
> (Strange dream that gives a dead man leave to think!)
> And breathed such life with kisses in my lips
> That I revived and was an emperor.
> 10   Ah me! How sweet is love itself possessed,
> When but love's shadows[4] are so rich in joy!

[*Enter* ROMEO'S MAN, BALTHASAR, *booted.*]

> News from Verona! How now, Balthasar?

1. flattering . . . sleep pleasing illusions of dreams.

2. presage foretell.

3. bosom's lord heart.

4. shadows dreams; unreal images.

✔ Reading Check

Why is Romeo in a good mood?

Dost thou not bring me letters from the friar?
How doth my lady? Is my father well?
15 How fares my Juliet? That I ask again,
For nothing can be ill if she be well.

MAN. Then she is well, and nothing can be ill.
Her body sleeps in Capels' monument,[5]
And her immortal part with angels lives.
20 I saw her laid low in her kindred's vault
And presently took post[6] to tell it you.
O, pardon me for bringing these ill news,
Since you did leave it for my office,[7] sir.

ROMEO. Is it e'en so? Then I defy you, stars!
25 Thou knowest my lodging. Get me ink and paper
And hire post horses. I will hence tonight.

MAN. I do beseech you, sir, have patience.
Your looks are pale and wild and do import
Some misadventure.[8]

ROMEO.   Tush, thou art deceived.
30 Leave me and do the thing I bid thee do.
Hast thou no letters to me from the friar?

MAN. No, my good lord.

ROMEO.   No matter. Get thee gone.
And hire those horses. I'll be with thee straight.

[*Exit* BALTHASAR.]

Well, Juliet, I will lie with thee tonight.
35 Let's see for means. O mischief, thou art swift
To enter in the thoughts of desperate men!
I do remember an apothecary,[9]
And hereabouts 'a dwells, which late I noted
In tatt'red weeds, with overwhelming brows,
40 Culling of simples.[10] Meager were his looks,
Sharp misery had worn him to the bones;
And in his needy shop a tortoise hung,
An alligator stuffed, and other skins
Of ill-shaped fishes; and about his shelves
45 A beggarly account[11] of empty boxes,
Green earthen pots, bladders, and musty seeds,
Remnants of packthread, and old cakes of roses[12]
Were thinly scatterèd, to make up a show.
Noting this penury, to myself I said,
50 "And if a man did need a poison now
Whose sale is present death in Mantua,

Literary Analysis
Motive What motivates Romeo's questions?

5. **Capels' monument** the Capulets' burial vault.

6. **presently took post** immediately set out on horseback.

7. **office** duty.

Literary Analysis
Tragedy In what way does Romeo's remark in line 24 reinforce fate's role in the tragedy?

8. **import / Some misadventure** suggest some misfortune.

9. **apothecary** one who prepares and sells drugs and medicines.

10. **In tatt'red . . . simples** in torn clothing, with overhanging eyebrows, sorting out herbs.

11. **beggarly account** small number.

12. **cakes of roses** pressed rose petals (used for perfume).

Vocabulary Builder
remnants (rem′ nənts) *n.* what is left over; remainders

penury (pen′ yo͞o rē) *n.* extreme poverty

Here lives a caitiff[13] wretch would sell it him."
O, this same thought did but forerun my need,
And this same needy man must sell it me.
55　As I remember, this should be the house.
Being holiday, the beggar's shop is shut.
What, ho! Apothecary!

[*Enter* APOTHECARY.]

APOTHECARY.　　　Who calls so loud?

ROMEO. Come hither, man. I see that thou art poor.
Hold, there is forty ducats.[14] Let me have
60　A dram of poison, such soon-speeding gear[15]
As will disperse itself through all the veins
That the life-weary taker may fall dead,
And that the trunk[16] may be discharged of breath
As violently as hasty powder fired
65　Doth hurry from the fatal cannon's womb.

APOTHECARY. Such mortal drugs I have; but Mantua's law
Is death to any he that utters[17] them.

ROMEO. Art thou so bare and full of wretchedness
And fearest to die? Famine is in thy cheeks,
70　Need and oppression starveth in thy eyes,
Contempt and beggary hangs upon thy back:
The world is not thy friend, nor the world's law;
The world affords no law to make thee rich;
Then be not poor, but break it and take this.

75　**APOTHECARY.** My poverty but not my will consents.

ROMEO. I pay thy poverty and not thy will.

APOTHECARY. Put this in any liquid thing you will
And drink it off, and if you had the strength
Of twenty men, it would dispatch you straight.

80　**ROMEO.** There is thy gold—worse poison to men's souls,
Doing more murder in this loathsome world,
Than these poor compounds[18] that thou mayst not sell.
I sell thee poison; thou hast sold me none.
Farewell. Buy food and get thyself in flesh.
85　Come, cordial[19] and not poison, go with me
To Juliet's grave; for there must I use thee.　　　　[*Exit all.*]

13. caitiff miserable.

14. ducats (duk´ əts) gold coins.

15. soon-speeding gear fast-working stuff.

16. trunk body.

17. utters sells.

Literary Analysis
Motive What is the apothecary's motive for selling Romeo the poison?

18. compounds mixtures.

19. cordial health-giving drink.

Reading Check

What does Romeo learn from Balthasar?

Scene ii. FRIAR LAWRENCE'S cell.

[*Enter* FRIAR JOHN *to* FRIAR LAWRENCE.]

    JOHN. Holy Franciscan friar, brother, ho!

[*Enter* FRIAR LAWRENCE.]

    LAWRENCE. This same should be the voice of Friar John.
       Welcome from Mantua. What says Romeo?
       Or, if his mind be writ, give me his letter.

5 **JOHN.** Going to find a barefoot brother out,
       One of our order, to associate[1] me
       Here in this city visiting the sick,
       And finding him, the searchers of the town,
       Suspecting that we both were in a house
10   Where the infectious pestilence did reign,
       Sealed up the doors, and would not let us forth,
       So that my speed to Mantua there was stayed.

    LAWRENCE. Who bare my letter, then, to Romeo?

    JOHN. I could not send it—here it is again—
15   Nor get a messenger to bring it thee,
       So fearful were they of infection.

1. associate accompany.

Reading Skill
Summarizing Briefly state the causes and effects of Friar John's failure to deliver Friar Lawrence's letter.

Literature in Context

History Connection

Plague Searchers The Black Plague, or Black Death, was a disease that swept through Europe, Asia, and the Middle East during the 1300s, with outbreaks continuing until 1400. It is thought that as much as a third of Europe's population died of the disease between 1347 and 1351. During an outbreak of plague, officials would appoint plague searchers to quarantine people infected with the disease and dispose of victims' remains. In *Romeo and Juliet,* Friar John is quarantined by plague searchers who fear he has been infected. As a result, he is unable to deliver Friar Lawrence's letter to Romeo.

Connect to the Literature
What does the Black Death add to the tragedy in *Romeo and Juliet*?

LAWRENCE. Unhappy fortune! By my brotherhood,
　The letter was not nice,[2] but full of charge,
　Of dear import;[3] and the neglecting it
20　May do much danger. Friar John, go hence,
　Get me an iron crow and bring it straight
　Unto my cell.

JOHN. 　　　Brother, I'll go and bring it thee. 　　　[*Exit.*]

LAWRENCE. Now must I to the monument alone.
　Within this three hours will fair Juliet wake.
25　She will beshrew[4] me much that Romeo
　Hath had no notice of these accidents;[5]
　But I will write again to Mantua,
　And keep her at my cell till Romeo come—
　Poor living corse, closed in a dead man's tomb! 　[*Exit.*]

Scene iii. A churchyard; in it a monument belonging to the CAPULETS.

[*Enter* PARIS *and his* PAGE *with flowers and sweet water.*]

PARIS. Give me thy torch, boy. Hence, and stand aloof.[1]
　Yet put it out, for I would not be seen.
　Under yond yew trees lay thee all along,[2]
　Holding thy ear close to the hollow ground.
5　So shall no foot upon the churchyard tread
　(Being loose, unfirm, with digging up of graves)
　But thou shalt hear it. Whistle then to me,
　As signal that thou hearest something approach.
　Give me those flowers. Do as I bid thee, go.

10 **PAGE.** [*Aside*] I am almost afraid to stand alone
　Here in the churchyard; yet I will adventure.[3] 　[*Retires.*]

PARIS. Sweet flower, with flowers thy bridal bed I strew
　　(O woe! thy canopy is dust and stones)
　Which with sweet[4] water nightly I will dew;
15　　Or, wanting that, with tears distilled by moans.
　The obsequies[5] that I for thee will keep
　Nightly shall be to strew thy grave and weep.[*Whistle* BOY.]
　The boy gives warning something doth approach.
　What cursèd foot wanders this way tonight
20　To cross[6] my obsequies and true love's rite?
　What, with a torch? Muffle me, night, awhile. 　[*Retires.*]

[*Enter* ROMEO, *and* BALTHASAR *with a torch, a mattock, and a crow of iron.*]

---

2. nice trivial.

3. full of charge, / Of dear import urgent and important.

4. beshrew blame.

5. accidents happenings.

Literary Analysis
Motive What motivates Friar Lawrence's decision to go to the monument?

1. aloof apart.

2. lay . . . along lie down flat.

3. adventure chance it.

4. sweet perfumed.

5. obsequies memorial ceremonies.

6. cross interrupt.

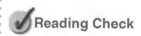Reading Check

Why was Friar John unable to deliver the letter to Romeo?

ROMEO. Give me that mattock and the wrenching iron.
  Hold, take this letter. Early in the morning
  See thou deliver it to my lord and father.
25 Give me the light. Upon thy life I charge thee,
  Whate'er thou hearest or seest, stand all aloof
  And do not interrupt me in my course.
  Why I descend into this bed of death
  Is partly to behold my lady's face,
30 But chiefly to take thence from her dead finger
  A precious ring—a ring that I must use
  In dear employment.[7] Therefore hence, be gone.
  But if thou, jealous,[8] dost return to pry
  In what I farther shall intend to do,
35 By heaven, I will tear thee joint by joint
  And strew this hungry churchyard with thy limbs.
  The time and my intents are savage-wild,
  More fierce and more inexorable[9] far
  Than empty[10] tigers or the roaring sea.

40 **BALTHASAR.** I will be gone, sir, and not trouble ye.

ROMEO. So shalt thou show me friendship. Take thou that.
  Live, and be prosperous; and farewell, good fellow.

BALTHASAR. [*Aside*] For all this same, I'll hide me hereabout.
  His looks I fear, and his intents I doubt.   [*Retires.*]

45 **ROMEO.** Thou detestable maw,[11] thou womb of death,
  Gorged with the dearest morsel of the earth,
  Thus I enforce thy rotten jaws to open,
  And in despite[12] I'll cram thee with more food.

                    [ROMEO *opens the tomb.*]

PARIS. This is that banished <u>haughty</u> Montague
50 That murd'red my love's cousin—with which grief
  It is supposed the fair creature died—
  And here is come to do some villainous shame
  To the dead bodies. I will apprehend[13] him.
  Stop thy unhallowèd toil, vile Montague!
55 Can vengeance be pursued further than death?
  Condemnèd villain, I do apprehend thee.
  Obey, and go with me; for thou must die.

ROMEO. I must indeed; and therefore came I hither.
  Good gentle youth, tempt not a desp'rate man.
60 Fly hence and leave me. Think upon these gone;
  Let them affright thee. I beseech thee, youth,

Put not another sin upon my head
By urging me to fury. O, be gone!
By heaven, I love thee better than myself,
65   For I come hither armed against myself.
Stay not, be gone. Live, and hereafter say
A madman's mercy bid thee run away.

PARIS. I do defy thy conjurations.[14]
And apprehend thee for a felon[15] here.

70 **ROMEO.** Wilt thou provoke me? Then have at thee, boy!
[*They fight.*]

PAGE. O Lord, they fight! I will go call the watch.
                               [*Exit.* PARIS *falls.*]

PARIS. O, I am slain! If thou be merciful,
Open the tomb, lay me with Juliet.   [*Dies.*]

ROMEO. In faith, I will. Let me peruse[16] this face.
75   Mercutio's kinsman, noble County Paris!
What said my man when my betossèd[17] soul
Did not attend[18] him as we rode? I think

◀ **Critical Viewing**
Do you think this image of Romeo accurately conveys his feelings as he enters the Capulets' tomb? Why or why not? **[Evaluate]**

Romeo and Juliet, Act V ■ *839*

He told me Paris should have married Juliet.
Said he not so, or did I dream it so?
80 Or am I mad, hearing him talk of Juliet,
To think it was so? O, give me thy hand,
One writ with me in sour misfortune's book!
I'll bury thee in a triumphant grave.
A grave? O, no, a lanthorn,[19] slaught'red youth,
85 For here lies Juliet, and her beauty makes
This vault a feasting presence[20] full of light.
Death, lie thou there, by a dead man interred.

                      [*Lays him in the tomb.*]

How oft when men are at the point of death
Have they been merry! Which their keepers[21] call
90 A lightning before death. O, how may I
Call this a lightning? O my love, my wife!
Death, that hath sucked the honey of thy breath,
Hath had no power yet upon thy beauty.
Thou art not conquered. Beauty's ensign[22] yet
95 Is crimson in thy lips and in thy cheeks,
And death's pale flag is not advancèd there.

19. lanthorn windowed structure on top of a room to admit light; also, a lantern.

20. feasting presence chamber fit for a celebration.

21. keepers jailers.

22. ensign banner.

Literary Analysis
Tragedy What tragic mistake does Romeo make regarding Juliet's appearance?

◄ **Critical Viewing**
What clues about Juliet's appearance, as it is shown here, should have led Romeo to realize she was still alive?
[Support]

Tybalt, liest thou there in thy bloody sheet?
O, what more favor can I do to thee
Than with that hand that cut thy youth in twain
100 To sunder²³ his that was thine enemy?
Forgive me, cousin! Ah, dear Juliet,
Why art thou yet so fair? Shall I believe
That unsubstantial Death is amorous,²⁴
And that the lean abhorrèd monster keeps
105 Thee here in dark to be his paramour?
For fear of that I still will stay with thee
And never from this pallet²⁵ of dim night
Depart again. Here, here will I remain
With worms that are thy chambermaids. O, here
110 Will I set up my everlasting rest
And shake the yoke of inauspicious²⁶ stars
From this world-wearied flesh. Eyes, look your last!
Arms, take your last embrace! And, lips, O you
The doors of breath, seal with a righteous kiss
115 A dateless²⁷ bargain to engrossing²⁸ death!
Come, bitter conduct;²⁹ come, unsavory guide!
Thou desperate pilot,³⁰ now at once run on
The dashing rocks thy seasick weary bark!
Here's to my love! [*Drinks.*] O true apothecary!
120 Thy drugs are quick. Thus with a kiss I die.   [*Falls.*]

[*Enter* FRIAR LAWRENCE, *with lanthorn, crow, and spade.*]

FRIAR. Saint Francis be my speed!³¹ How oft tonight
Have my old feet stumbled³² at graves! Who's there?

BALTHASAR. Here's one, a friend, and one that knows you well.

FRIAR. Bliss be upon you! Tell me, good my friend,
125 What torch is yond that vainly lends his light
To grubs³³ and eyeless skulls? As I discern,
It burneth in the Capels' monument.

BALTHASAR. It doth so, holy sir; and there's my master,
One that you love.

FRIAR.   Who is it?

BALTHASAR.   Romeo.

130 **FRIAR.** How long hath he been there?

BALTHASAR.   Full half an hour.

FRIAR. Go with me to the vault.

BALTHASAR.   I dare not, sir.

23. **sunder** cut off.

24. **amorous** full of love.

25. **pallet** bed.

26. **inauspicious** promising misfortune.

27. **dateless** eternal.

28. **engrossing** all-encompassing.

29. **conduct** guide (poison).

30. **pilot** captain (Romeo himself).

31. **speed** help.

32. **stumbled** stumbling was thought to be a bad omen.

Literary Analysis
Tragedy In what way is Friar Lawrence's late arrival another example of chance contributing to this tragedy?

33. **grubs** worms.

✓**Reading Check**
Does Friar Lawrence arrive in time to save Romeo?

My master knows not but I am gone hence,
And fearfully did menace me with death
If I did stay to look on his intents.

135 **FRIAR.** Stay then; I'll go alone. Fear comes upon me.
O, much I fear some ill unthrifty³⁴ thing.

BALTHASAR. As I did sleep under this yew tree here,
I dreamt my master and another fought,
And that my master slew him.

FRIAR.   Romeo!
140   Alack, alack, what blood is this which stains
The stony entrance of this sepulcher?
What mean these masterless³⁵ and gory swords
To lie discolored by this place of peace?   [*Enters the tomb.*]
Romeo! O, pale! Who else? What, Paris too?
145 And steeped in blood? Ah, what an unkind³⁶ hour
Is guilty of this lamentable chance!
The lady stirs.   [JULIET *rises.*]

JULIET. O comfortable³⁷ friar! Where is my lord?
I do remember well where I should be,
150 And there I am. Where is my Romeo?

FRIAR. I hear some noise. Lady, come from that nest
Of death, contagion, and unnatural sleep.
A greater power than we can contradict
Hath thwarted our intents. Come, come away.
155 Thy husband in thy bosom there lies dead;
And Paris too. Come, I'll dispose of thee
Among a sisterhood of holy nuns.
Stay not to question, for the watch is coming.
Come, go, good Juliet. I dare no longer stay.

160 **JULIET.** Go, get thee hence, for I will not away.   [*Exit* FRIAR.]
What's here? A cup, closed in my truelove's hand?
Poison, I see, hath been his timeless³⁸ end.
O churl!³⁹ Drunk all, and left no friendly drop
To help me after? I will kiss thy lips.
165 Haply some poison yet doth hang on them
To make me die with a restorative.⁴⁰   [*Kisses him.*]
Thy lips are warm!

CHIEF WATCHMAN. [*Within*] Lead, boy. Which way?

JULIET. Yea, noise? Then I'll be brief. O happy⁴¹ dagger!
                              [*Snatches* ROMEO'S *dagger.*]
170   This is thy sheath; there rust, and let me die.
                              [*She stabs herself and falls.*]

▶ **Critical Viewing**
Does Juliet appear
more sorrowful or
fearful in this picture?
[Analyze]

34. **unthrifty** unlucky.

35. **masterless** discarded
(without masters).

36. **unkind** unnatural.

37. **comfortable** comforting.

Literary Analysis
Motive Why do you
think Friar Lawrence
wants to "dispose of
Juliet" in a sisterhood
of nuns?

38. **timeless** untimely; too
soon.

39. **churl** rude fellow.

40. **restorative** medicine.

41. **happy** convenient; oppor-
tune.

Reading Check

What does Juliet do
when she finds Romeo
dead?

[*Enter* PARIS' BOY *and* WATCH.]

  BOY. This is the place. There, where the torch doth burn.

  CHIEF WATCHMAN. The ground is bloody. Search about the
   churchyard.
   Go, some of you; whoe'er you find attach.[42]

              [*Exit some of the* WATCH.]
   Pitiful sight! Here lies the County slain;
175   And Juliet bleeding, warm, and newly dead,
   Who here hath lain this two days burièd.
   Go, tell the Prince; run to the Capulets;
   Raise up the Montagues; some others search.
              [*Exit others of the* WATCH.]
   We see the ground whereon these woes do lie,
180   But the true ground[43] of all these piteous woes
   We cannot without circumstance descry.[44]

[*Enter some of the* WATCH, *with* ROMEO'S MAN, BALTHASAR.]

  SECOND WATCHMAN. Here's Romeo's man. We found him in the
   churchyard.

  CHIEF WATCHMAN. Hold him in safety till the Prince come
   hither.

[*Enter* FRIAR LAWRENCE *and another* WATCHMAN.]

  THIRD WATCHMAN. Here is a friar that trembles, sighs and weeps.
185   We took this mattock and this spade from him
   As he was coming from this churchyard's side.

  CHIEF WATCHMAN. A great suspicion! Stay the friar too.

[*Enter the* PRINCE *and* ATTENDANTS.]

  PRINCE. What misadventure is so early up,
   That calls our person from our morning rest?

[*Enter* CAPULET *and his* WIFE *with others.*]

190 **CAPULET.** What should it be, that is so shrieked abroad?

  LADY CAPULET. O, the people in the street cry "Romeo,"
   Some "Juliet," and some "Paris"; and all run
   With open outcry toward our monument.

  PRINCE. What fear is this which startles in your ears?

195 **CHIEF WATCHMAN.** Sovereign, here lies the County Paris slain;
   And Romeo dead; and Juliet, dead before,
   Warm and new killed.

  PRINCE. Search, seek, and know how this foul murder comes.

  CHIEF WATCHMAN. Here is a friar, and slaughtered Romeo's man,

42. **attach** arrest.

43. **ground** cause.

44. **without circumstance
descry** see clearly without
details.

**Literary Analysis
Tragedy** How might
the tragic ending have
been averted if the
characters had come
to the churchyard in a
different order?

200   With instruments upon them fit to open
    These dead men's tombs.

    CAPULET. O heavens! O wife, look how our daughter bleeds!
    This dagger hath mista'en, for, lo, his house[45]
    Is empty on the back of Montague,
205   And it missheathèd in my daughter's bosom!

    LADY CAPULET. O me, this sight of death is as a bell
    That warns my old age to a sepulcher.

[*Enter* MONTAGUE *and others.*]

    PRINCE. Come, Montague; for thou art early up
    To see thy son and heir more early down.

210 **MONTAGUE.** Alas, my liege,[46] my wife is dead tonight! Grief of
    my son's exile hath stopped her breath. What further woe
    conspires against mine age?

    PRINCE. Look, and thou shalt see.

    MONTAGUE. O thou untaught! What manners is in this,
215   To press before thy father to a grave?

    PRINCE. Seal up the mouth of outrage[47] for a while,
    Till we can clear these <u>ambiguities</u>
    And know their spring, their head, their true descent;
    And then will I be general of your woes[48]
220   And lead you even to death. Meantime forbear,
    And let mischance be slave to patience.[49]
    Bring forth the parties of suspicion.

    FRIAR. I am the greatest, able to do least,
    Yet most suspected, as the time and place
225   Doth make against me, of this direful[50] murder;
    And here I stand, both to impeach and purge[51]
    Myself condemnèd and myself excused.

    PRINCE. Then say at once what thou dost know in this.

    FRIAR. I will be brief, for my short date of breath[52]
230   Is not so long as is a tedious tale.
    Romeo, there dead, was husband to that Juliet;
    And she, there dead, that's Romeo's faithful wife.
    I married them; and their stol'n marriage day
    Was Tybalt's doomsday, whose untimely death
235   Banished the new-made bridegroom from this city;
    For whom, and not for Tybalt, Juliet pined.
    You, to remove that siege of grief from her,
    Betrothed and would have married her perforce

---

45. house sheath.

46. liege (lēj) lord.

Reading Skill
Summarizing Summarize the losses that the families have experienced as a result of Romeo and Juliet's relationship.

Vocabulary Builde
ambiguities (am´ bə gyōō´ ə tēz) *n.* statements or events whose meanings are unclear

47. mouth of outrage violent cries.
48. general . . . woes leader in your sorrow.
49. let . . . patience Be patient in the face of misfortune.

50. direful terrible.

51. impeach and purge accuse and declare blameless.

52. date of breath term of life.

Reading Check

What effect did Romeo's exile have on his mother?

To County Paris. Then comes she to me

240 And with wild looks bid me devise some mean
To rid her from this second marriage,
Or in my cell there would she kill herself.
Then gave I her (so tutored by my art)
A sleeping potion; which so took effect

245 As I intended, for it wrought on her
The form of death. Meantime I writ to Romeo
That he should hither come as[53] this dire night
To help to take her from her borrowed grave,
Being the time the potion's force should cease,

250 But he which bore my letter, Friar John,
Was stayed by accident, and yesternight
Returned my letter back. Then all alone
At the prefixèd hour of her waking
Came I to take her from her kindred's vault;

255 Meaning to keep her closely[54] at my cell
Till I conveniently could send to Romeo.
But when I came, some minute ere the time
Of her awakening, here untimely lay
The noble Paris and true Romeo dead.

260 She wakes; and I entreated her come forth
And bear this work of heaven with patience;
But then a noise did scare me from the tomb,
And she, too desperate, would not go with me,
But, as it seems, did violence on herself.

265 All this I know, and to the marriage
Her nurse is privy;[55] and if aught in this
Miscarried by my fault, let my old life
Be sacrificed some hour before his time
Unto the rigor[56] of severest law.

270 **PRINCE.** We still have known thee for a holy man.
Where's Romeo's man? What can he say to this?

 BALTHASAR. I brought my master news of Juliet's death;
And then in post he came from Mantua
To this same place, to this same monument.

275 This letter he early bid me give his father,
And threat'ned me with death, going in the vault,
If I departed not and left him there.

 PRINCE. Give me the letter. I will look on it.
Where is the County's page that raised the watch?

280 Sirrah, what made your master[57] in this place?

Literary Analysis
Tragedy What examples of fate or character flaws do you find in the tragic events that the Friar recounts?

53. **as** on.

54. **closely** hidden; secretly.

55. **privy** secretly informed about.

56. **rigor** strictness.

57. **made your master** was your master doing.

BOY. He came with flowers to strew his lady's grave;
And bid me stand aloof, and so I did.
Anon comes one with light to ope the tomb;
And by and by my master drew on him;
285   And then I ran away to call the watch.

PRINCE. This letter doth make good the friar's words,
Their course of love, the tidings of her death;
And here he writes that he did buy a poison
Of a poor pothecary and therewithal
290   Came to this vault to die and lie with Juliet.
Where be these enemies? Capulet, Montague,
See what a <u>scourge</u> is laid upon your hate,
That heaven finds means to kill your joys with love.
And I, for winking at[58] your discords too,
295   Have lost a brace[59] of kinsmen. All are punished.

CAPULET. O brother Montague, give me thy hand.
This is my daughter's jointure,[60] for no more
Can I demand.

MONTAGUE.   But I can give thee more;
For I will raise her statue in pure gold,
300   That whiles Verona by that name is known,
There shall no figure at such rate[61] be set
As that of true and faithful Juliet.

CAPULET. As rich shall Romeo's by his lady's lie—
Poor sacrifices of our enmity![62]

305 **PRINCE.** A glooming[63] peace this morning with it brings.
     The sun for sorrow will not show his head.
Go hence, to have more talk of these sad things;
     Some shall be pardoned, and some punishèd;
For never was a story of more woe
310   Than this of Juliet and her Romeo.   *[Exit all.]*

Vocabulary Builder
scourge (skurj) *n.*
instrument for
inflicting punishment

58. winking at closing my
eyes to.

59. brace pair (Mercutio and
Paris).

60. jointure wedding gift;
marriage settlement.

61. rate value.

62. enmity hostility.

63. glooming cloudy;
gloomy.

Literary Analysis
Motive What might
be Lord Montague's
motive for the
promise he makes to
Lord Capulet?

Apply the Skills

The Tragedy of Romeo and Juliet, Act V

Thinking About the Selection

1. **Respond:** Were you surprised by the way in which this play ends? Why or why not?
2. **(a) Recall:** In Act V, Scene i, what causes Romeo to exclaim, "Then I defy you, stars"? **(b) Connect:** In what way are Romeo's words consistent with what you know of his character?
3. **(a) Recall:** Identify at least three events that cause the Friar's scheme to fail. **(b) Analyze:** Why is it not surprising that the scheme fails?
4. **(a) Recall:** How does the relationship between the feuding families change at the end of the play? **(b) Draw Conclusions:** Were Romeo and Juliet's deaths necessary for this change to occur? Explain. **(c) Make a Judgment:** Is the end of long-term violence between their families a fair exchange for the deaths of Romeo and Juliet? Explain.

Literary Analysis

5. **(a)** Use a chart like the one shown to identify details of the elements that contribute to the **tragedy** in the play.

Romeo's and Juliet's Personalities	Fate or Chance	Other Causes

   (b) Which element is most responsible for the tragic events? Explain.
6. **(a)** What is the Friar's **motive** for helping Romeo and Juliet? **(b)** To what extent is he responsible for their tragedy? Explain.
7. What theme or message does Shakespeare attempt to convey through the tragic events in the play?
8. What positive message about the human spirit, if any, does this tragic play offer? Explain.

Reading Skill

9. **(a)** What events cause Romeo and Paris to arrive at Juliet's tomb at the same time? **(b)** What is the effect of their arriving at the same time?
10. **(a)** Analyze the chain of causes and effects that leads to the tragic ending of the play. **(b) Summarize** the events that occur at the tomb.

Vocabulary Builder

Practice Identify the word in each group that does not belong with the others. Explain your response.

1. remnants, future, past
2. penury, poor, wealthy
3. haughty, proud, insecure
4. ambiguities, absolute, uncertain
5. scourge, pleasure, happiness

Adding Words to Your Vocabulary The word *haughty* has many **synonyms,** or words with a similar meaning. One of those words is *supercilious,* a word with an interesting origin that has to do with eyebrows. Use a dictionary to find out the origin of the word *supercilious.* Then, write a few sentences explaining how the origin of this word relates to its everyday usage. (For more on using a dictionary, see page R6.)

Writing

As Friar Lawrence, write a **persuasive letter** to both Lord Capulet and Lord Montague. The letter should urge them to end their feud.

- Make a list of factual evidence and emotional pleas that might convince the families to end their feud.
- Begin your draft by explaining the marriage.

Ask a classmate to read your draft from the point of view of both families. Revise your letter if it appears to favor one side.

For *Grammar, Vocabulary,* and *Assessment,*
see **Build Language Skills,** pages 850–856.

Extend Your Learning

Listening and Speaking As a class, conduct a **mock trial** to investigate the causes of the tragedy in *Romeo and Juliet.*

- Assign roles: the main characters of the play, the lawyers, and the judge. The rest of the class should serve as the jury.
- Take depositions, or statements in which each character tells the story from his or her perspective.
- Use language—formal, informal, slang, or jargon—that fits the social, cultural, regional, and professional status of each character.

Jury member hearing from both witnesses and lawyers should work to distinguish between valid claims and *propaganda*—arguments that twist or ignore facts to present a biased and distorted picture of events.

Build Language Skills

Vocabulary Skill

Word Roots The **word root** *-lum-* means "light." Words that contain the word root *-lum-* have meanings related to light. For example, *illuminate* means, literally, "brings light to." It is often used in the figurative sense: When a fact or an idea is brought to light, it is *illuminated,* or clarified.

▶ **Example:** Juliet's conversation with the nurse is *illuminating.*

Practice Write a sentence using each of the words that contains the root *-lum-*. Then, check the meaning and examples of usage of each word in a dictionary revise your sentences.

1. (a) illumination (b) illuminating **3.** (a) luminescent (b) luminescence

2. (a) luminous (b) luminously **4.** (a) luminary (b) luminaries

Grammar Skill

Gerund and Gerund Phrase A **gerund** is a form of a verb that acts as a noun. It can function as a subject, an object, a predicate noun, or the object of a preposition. A **gerund phrase** is a gerund and its modifiers. A gerund phrase also acts as a noun.

Subject	*Remodeling* the building's style was a good idea.
Direct Object	Michael enjoys *painting.*
Predicate Noun	His favorite sport is *fishing.*
Object of the Preposition	Lucille never gets tired of *singing.*
Gerund Phrase	The *loud, shrill howling* continued all morning.

MorePractice

For more practice with gerunds, see the Grammar Handbook, p. R40.

Practice Change one of the verbs to gerund and use of gerund, or gerund phrase, to combine the two sentences.

1. He suggests that we walk to school. It would be good exercise.

2. There are sounds that mean danger. A scream is one of those sounds.

3. The cat made a strange sound. It was a screech.

4. The soccer player ran. The defense chased him.

5. Science is fun for me. I like to study the environment.

𝒲𝒢 *Prentice Hall Writing and Grammar Connection: Chapter 21, Section 1.*

Reading Skill: Summarize

Standards Assessed

- WL.1.01.1
- IR.2.01.1
- IR.2.01.8

Directions: *Read the selection. Answer the questions.*

Last Friday was opening night for the Drama Club's production of *Cats*. The performances and the music was terrific. The cast has been rehearsing for months and it showed. There were a few blunders, but most of the audience did not notice. Jim missed his entrance on the opening dance number, but he was only a second late. It is surprising that there were not more mistakes. The stomach virus that caused so many class absences last week also led to about half the cast missing the last dress rehearsals. The audience gave the cast and crew a well-deserved standing ovation.

1. Which of the following is the most important idea to include in a summary?
   A Jim was a few seconds late.
   B Adance number had a mistake.
   C The Drama Club performed *Cats*.
   D There was a standing ovation.

2. What is the best paraphrase of the first three sentences of the selection?
   A The Drama Club had its first performance of *Cats* last Friday.
   B After months of rehearsal, the Drama Club gave an amazing opening night show of *Cats*.

   C On Friday, the performances were fantastic and the music was good.
   D Last Friday, the Drama Club produced a wonderful *Cats*. They had rehearsed for months.

3. What is the most important result of the stomach virus to include in a summary of this selection?
   A Students missed class.
   B Jim missed the performance.
   C Actors missed rehearsals.
   D Jim missed his entrance.

Timed Writing: Interpretation [Critical Stance]

In a tragedy the tragic hero meets with disaster because of a character flaw or fate. Who is the tragic hero in Romeo and Juliet? Defend your choice, and argue whether fate or a character flaw contributed most to the disaster. Use specific details from the text to support your interpretation. **(40 minutes)**

 Writing Workshop: *Work in Progress*

How-to Essay

Review the Steps List from your writing portfolio. Use stick figures to make a "cartoon frame" for each step on your list. Then, in each dialogue bubble, write a sentence in which you explain the step. Save this work in your writing portfolio.

Reading Informational Materials

Atlases

In Part 1, you are learning how to summarize as you read. This skill is also useful when reading encyclopedia or atlas entries. When you read an atlas entry, summarizing helps you identify the main point and it helps you better understand what you have read. If you read "Romeo and Juliet," you might be interested in the atlas entry about Italy, the setting of the play.

About Atlases

An **atlas** is a book of maps showing physical features of the world, such as cities, mountains, rivers, and roads. Some atlases include facts and statistics about the places presented. Many modern atlases provide brief articles on topics such as population, climate, government, transportation, and tourism.

A map in an atlas is usually accompanied by a legend, a key that explains the symbols and colors used in the map. For example, symbols might represent features such as national or state capitals. Color codes might be used to indicate land height or population densities. The legend may also indicate to what mileage the map is scaled.

Reading Skill

Atlases provide a broad range of information. To find the material you need, adjust your reading rate by **skimming and scanning.**

- By skimming, you get an idea of the organization and scope of the work before reading it closely. To skim, read quickly, taking in words in groups. Stop for headings and other text that is set off, such as bold text.

- By scanning, you can quickly locate specific information. Move your eyes rapidly over the page. Look for words related to the information you are seeking. Stop and read the paragraphs that contain these words.

Use the questions shown in the box to guide you as you skim and scan the atlas that follows.

Questions to Ask When Skimming and Scanning

- What information is provided in the legend of the map?
- In the atlas article, which text is set in large or bold print?
- What are the main subheads on the page?
- For each subhead, what is one key fact you can find quickly?

Standard Course of Study

- Report the research for a specified audience. (IR.2.04.4)

- Recognize and analyze the characteristics of literary genres. (LT.5.01.2)

ITALY

Adapted from Dorling Kindersley World Reference Atlas

ITALY

Total Land Area : 294 060 sq. km
(301 270 sq. miles)

POPULATION

over 1 000 000
over 500 000
over 100 000
over 50 000
over 10 000

The legend explains the meaning of the symbols found on the map.

LAND HEIGHT

3000m/9843ft
2000m/6562ft
1000m/3281ft
500m/1640ft
200m/656ft
Sea Level

The map shows the cities and towns of Italy.

Reading Informational Materials

The atlas article begins with a list of basic information about the country depicted in the map.

ITALY

Official Name: *Italian Republic*
Capital: *Rome*
Population: *57.2 million*
Currency: *Italian lira*
Official Language: *Italian*

Lying in southern Europe, Italy comprises the famous boot-shaped peninsula stretching 500 miles into the Mediterranean and a number of islands—Sicily and Sardinia being the largest. The Alps form a natural boundary to the north, while the Apennine Mountains run the length of the peninsula. The south is an area of seismic activity, epitomized by the volcanoes of Mounts Etna and Vesuvius. United under ancient Roman rule, Italy subsequently developed into a series of competing kingdoms and states, not fully reunited until 1870. Italian politics was dominated by the Christian Democrats (CD) from 1945 to 1992 under a system of political patronage and a succession of short-lived governments. Investigations into corruption from 1992 on led to the demise of this system in the elections of 1994.

Subheads break the information into the same specific categories for each country.

CLIMATE

Southern Italy has a Mediterranean climate; the north is more temperate. Summers are hot and dry, especially in the south. Temperatures range from 75°F to over 81°F in Sardinia and Sicily. Southern winters are mild; northern ones are cooler and wetter. The mountains usually experience heavy snow. The Adriatic coast suffers from cold winds such as the bora.

Symbols highlight key information in each category.

TRANSPORTATION

 Leonardo da Vinci (Fiumicino), Rome 15.55m passengers   791 ships (10.13m dwt)

Many of Italy's key routes are congested. The trans-Apennine *autostrada* (expressway) from Bologna to Florence is being doubled in size. A high-speed train program (*treno ad alta velocità—TAV*) is planned to link Turin, Milan, Venice, Bologna, Florence and Naples to Rome. Most of Italy's exports travel by road, via Switzerland and Austria. Only 16% goes by sea.

TOURISM

 27.5m visitors   Up 4% in 1994

Italy has been a tourist destination since the 16th century and probably invented the concept. Roman Popes consciously aimed to make their city the most beautiful in the world to attract travelers. In the 18th century, Italy was the focus of any Grand Tour. Today, its many unspoilt centers of Renaissance culture continue to make Italy one of the world's major tourism destinations. The industry accounts for 3% of Italy's GDP, and hotels and restaurants employ one million out of a working population of 21 million.

Most visitors travel to the northern half of the country, to cities such as Rome, Florence, Venice and Padova. Many are increasingly traveling to the northern lakes. Beach resorts such as Rimini attract a large, youthful crowd in summer. Italy is also growing in popularity as a skiing destination.

PEOPLE

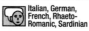 Italian, German, French, Rhaeto-Romanic, Sardinian   505 people per sq. mile

Italy is a remarkably homogenous society. Most Italians are Roman Catholics, and Italy has far fewer ethnic minorities than its EU neighbors. Most are fairly recent immigrants from Ethiopia, the Philippines and Egypt. A sharp rise in illegal immigration in the 1980's and 1990's, from North and West Africa, Turkey and Albania, generated a right-wing backlash and tighter controls. It became a major election issue in 1993 and a factor in the rise of the federalist Northern League.

Reading: Skimming and Scanning

Directions: *Choose the letter of the best answer to each question about the atlas entry.*

Standards Assessed

• IR.2.03.4
• FA.3.04.1
• LT.5.01.1

1. What is the approximate population of Assisi?

   A over 1,000,000

   B over 100,000

   C over 50,000

   D over 10,000

2. If you were scanning the atlas article for information about the weather of southern Italy in the winter, under which subhead would you stop and read?

   A Climate

   B Transportation

   C Tourism

   D People

3. Under which subhead would you skim to find the religion of the majority of people in Italy?

   A Climate

   B Transportation

   C Tourism

   D People

Reading: Comprehension and Interpretation

Directions: *Write your answers on a separate piece of paper.*

4. Which four seas border Italy? **[Knowledge]**
5. Why is Rome printed in bold, capital letters on the map? **[Generating]**
6. What percentage of Italy's exports travel by sea? **[Integrating]**

Timed Writing: Exposition [Interpreting]

Summarize the information presented in this atlas entry about Italy. Using information from both the graphics and text, briefly describe the country's size and location, its land and climate, and its people. Then, note key facts that would help tourists make the most of a trip there. **(40 minutes)**

Archetypal Theme: Ill-fated Love

An **archetype** is a plot, character, image, or setting that appears in literature from around the world and throughout history. Archetypes represent truths about life and are said to mirror the working of the human mind. Common archetypes include the following:

- Characters: the hero; the outcast
- Plot types: the quest, or search; the task
- Symbol: water as a symbol of life; fire as a symbol of power

A **theme** is the central idea, message, or insight of a literary work. **Archetypal themes** are those that develop or explore fundamental, or archetypal, ideas. One example of an archetypal theme is ill-fated love, which appears in literature from all over the world.

Comparing Presentations of an Archetypal Theme

Works of literature may differ in their presentations of the same archetypal theme for many reasons, including these:

- the values of the era in which the work was written
- the author's purpose for writing
- the author's culture and language, including any literary styles and expectations

As you read Ovid's "Pyramus and Thisbe," make comparisons to Shakespeare's treatment of a similar tale in *Romeo and Juliet*. Refer to the Prologue in Act I (lines 1–13), the balcony scene (Act II, Scene ii, lines 49–189), and the death scene (Act V, Scene iii, lines 22–170) in *Romeo and Juliet*. Then, consider Shakespeare's treatment of the same story in *A Midsummer Night's Dream*. Use a chart like the one shown to organize your observations.

NC Standard Course of Study

- Understand the importance of cultural and historical impact on texts. (LT.5.01.10)
- Explain and interpret archetypal characters, themes, settings. (LT.5.01.5)

Characters	
Similarities	Differences

Events	
Similarities	Differences

Vocabulary Builder

"Pyramus and Thisbe"

- **lament** (lə ment´) *v.* express deep sorrow; mourn (p. 859) *Many friends showed up at the funeral to lament their loss.*

- **inevitable** (in ev´ i tə bəl) *adj.* unavoidable, certain (p. 860) *After he missed his nap, the toddler's tantrum was inevitable.*

from *A Midsummer Night's Dream*

- **enamored** (en am´ ərd) *v.* filled with love and desire; charmed (p. 867) *She was enamored of his personality, not his looks.*

- **enthralled** (en thrôld) *v.* held as in a spell; captivated (p. 867) *The audience sat enthralled by the movie's special effects.*

Build Understanding

Connecting to the Literature

Reading/Writing Connection *Romeo and Juliet*, "Pyramus and Thisbe," and *A Midsummer Night's Dream* all tell of young people in love who face serious obstacles. Write a paragraph in which you explain why people enjoy love stories, whether they end happily or sadly. Use at least three of the following words in your response: *enrich, sustain, console, transform, unify.*

Meet the Author

Ovid (43 B.C.–A.D. 17)

Educated in Rome, Ovid began his career writing poems about love and pleasure. However, the emperor Augustus wanted citizens to focus on morality and work toward an ideal Roman state. In response, Ovid decided to write about myths and traditional stories, such as "Pyramus and Thisbe."

Achievement and Exile After completing his master-piece, *Metamorphoses,* in A.D. 8, Ovid was banished to a remote village on the Black Sea. The reasons for his banish-ment are not entirely clear, but the emperor might have felt that Ovid's work endangered public morals. Exile to a half-civilized place on the edge of the empire was a severe pun-ishment for this worldly poet. Although he continued to write, he was never allowed to return to Rome.

William **Shakespeare** (1564–1616)

The greatest of all playwrights, William Shakespeare was born in the town of Stratford-on-Avon and gained his successes in the flourishing theatrical world of London. He worked as an actor, playwright, and part owner of a theatre company, earning enough to retire to Strat-ford in 1610.

Kings and Clowns, Lovers and Villains Shakespeare's 37 plays are populated with a wide range of characters which embody the depth and variety of human experience. No writer has played a more significant role in shaping the English language and English literature.

Go Online
Author Link

For: More information about the authors
Visit: www.PHSchool.com
Web Code: epe-9503

from **A Midsummer Night's Dream**

William Shakespeare

Background In *A Midsummer Night's Dream*, Shakespeare creates comedy out of misunderstandings, magic transformations, and the interactions of characters from three different worlds: the noble class, the working class, and the realm of the fairy spirits. In this scene, several local craftsmen (the "Clowns") prepare to put on a play for the duke's wedding. Robin, the fairy king's jester, discovers the actors and decides to play a trick on one of them. All of this happens as Titania, the queen of the fairies, sleeps nearby. The actors do not know that Titania is under a spell that will cause her to fall in love with the first person she sees upon waking.

Act III, Scene i

With TITANIA *still asleep onstage, enter the* CLOWNS, BOTTOM, QUINCE, SNOUT, STARVELING, SNUG, *and* FLUTE.

BOTTOM. Are we all met?

QUINCE. Pat,[1] pat. And here's a marvels convenient place for our rehearsal. This green plot shall be our stage, this hawthorn brake[2] our tiring-house,[3] and we will do it in action as we will
5 do it before the Duke.

BOTTOM. Peter Quince?

QUINCE. What sayest thou, bully[4] Bottom?

BOTTOM. There are things in this comedy of Pyramus and Thisbe that will never please. First, Pyramus must draw a sword to kill
10 himself, which the ladies cannot abide. How answer you that?

SNOUT. By 'r lakin,[5] a parlous fear.

STARVELING. I believe we must leave the killing out, when all is done.[6]

◀ **Critical Viewing** How would you describe Titania in the image shown here?

---

1. **pat** exactly; right on time.

2. **brake** thicket.

3. **tiring house** room used for dressing, or attiring.

4. **bully** jolly fellow.

5. **By 'r lakin** shortened version of "By your ladykin (little lady)."

6. **when all is done** after all.

✔ **Reading Check**

Who is asleep onstage when the Clowns enter?

BOTTOM. Not a whit! I have a device to make all well. Write me a
15 prologue, and let the prologue seem to say we will do no harm
with our swords, and that Pyramus is not killed indeed. And, for
the more better assurance, tell them that I, Pyramus, am not
Pyramus, but Bottom the weaver. This will put them out of fear.

QUINCE. Well, we will have such a prologue, and it shall be written
20 in eight and six.[7]

BOTTOM. No, make it two more. Let it be written in eight and
eight.

SNOUT. Will not the ladies be afeard of the lion?

STARVELING. I fear it, I promise you.

25 **BOTTOM.** Masters, you ought to consider with yourself, to bring
in God shield us! a lion among ladies is a most dreadful thing.
For there is not a more fearful wildfowl than your lion living,
and we ought to look to it.

SNOUT. Therefore another prologue must tell he is not a lion.

30 **BOTTOM.** Nay, you must name his name, and half his face must
be seen through the lion's neck, and he himself must speak
through, saying thus, or to the same defect: "Ladies," or "Fair
ladies, I would wish you," or "I would request you," or "I would
entreat you not to fear, not to tremble! My life for yours. If you
35 think I come hither as a lion, it were pity of my life.[8] No, I am no
such thing. I am a man as other men are." And there indeed let
him name his name and tell them plainly he is Snug the joiner.

7. eight and six ballad meter containing alternating eight- and six-syllable lines.

Literary Analysis
Archetypal Theme
How do the Clowns plan to soften their presentation of the lion?

8. it were . . . my life risky for me.

Literature in Context

Humanities Connection

Almanacs

When Bottom calls for an almanac, he is referring to a type of book
that was very popular in Elizabethan times. The almanac was essentially
a calendar, but it also provided lists of upcoming natural events, such
as tides, full moons, and eclipses. The book was especially useful to
farmers because it included gardening tips and weather predictions.
Almanacs of various kinds are still published and consulted today.

Connect to the Literature

Do you think the "Clowns" are wise to rely on the accuracy of the
almanac with regard to moonlight? Why or why not?

QUINCE. Well, it shall be so. But there is two hard things: that is, to bring the moonlight into a chamber, for you know Pyramus
40 and Thisbe meet by moonlight.

SNOUT. Doth the moon shine that night we play our play?

BOTTOM. A calendar, a calendar! Look in the almanac. Find out moonshine, find out moonshine.

QUINCE *takes out a book.*

45 **QUINCE.** Yes, it doth shine that night.

BOTTOM. Why, then, may you leave a casement of the great chamber window, where we play, open, and the moon may shine in at the casement.

QUINCE. Ay, or else one must come in with a bush of thorns[9] and
50 a lantern and say he comes to disfigure[10] or to present the person of Moonshine. Then there is another thing: we must have a wall in the great chamber, for Pyramus and Thisbe, says the story, did talk through the chink of a wall.

SNOUT. You can never bring in a wall. What say you, Bottom?

55 **BOTTOM.** Some man or other must present Wall. And let him have some plaster, or some loam, or some roughcast[11] about him to signify wall, or let him hold his fingers thus, and through that cranny shall Pyramus and Thisbe whisper.

QUINCE. If that may be, then all is well. Come, sit down, every
60 mother's son, and rehearse your parts. Pyramus, you begin. When you have spoken your speech, enter into that brake, and so everyone according to his cue.

Enter ROBIN invisible to those onstage.

ROBIN. *(aside)*
What hempen homespuns[12] have we swaggring
65   here
So near the cradle[13] of the Fairy Queen?
What, a play toward?[14] I'll be an auditor—
An actor too perhaps, if I see cause.

QUINCE. Speak, Pyramus.—Thisbe, stand forth.

BOTTOM. *(as Pyramus)*
70 Thisbe, the flowers of odious savors sweet—

QUINCE. Odors, odors!

BOTTOM. *(as Pyramus)*
    . . . odors savors sweet.
So hath thy breath, my dearest Thisbe dear—

---

9. a bush of thorns according to legend, the man in the moon collected firewood on Sundays and was thus banished to the sky.

10. disfigure Quince means *figure,* as in "symbolize" or "stand for."

11. plaster . . . roughcast three different blended materials, each used for plastering walls.

12. hempen homespuns characters wearing clothing homemade from hemp, probably from the country.

13. cradle bower where Titania sleeps.

14. toward being rehearsed.

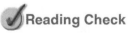 **Reading Check**

How do the Clowns plan to present the wall that separates Pyramus and Thisbe?

But hark, a voice! Stay thou but here awhile.

75 And by and by I will to thee appear. *(He exits.)*

ROBIN. *(aside)*
A stranger Pyramus than e'er played here.

(He exits.)

FLUTE. Must I speak now?

QUINCE. Ay, marry, must you, for you must understand he goes but to see a noise that

80 he heard and is to come again.

FLUTE. *(as Thisbe)*
Most radiant Pyramus, most lily-white of hue,
Of color like the red rose on triumphant[15] brier,
Most brisky juvenal[16] and eke[17] most lovely Jew,[18]
As true as truest horse, that yet would never tire.

85 I'll meet thee, Pyramus, at Ninny's tomb.[19]

QUINCE. "Ninus tomb," man! Why, you must not speak that yet. That you answer to Pyramus. You speak all your part[20] at once, cues and all.— Pyramus, enter. Your cue is past. It is "never tire."

FLUTE. O!

90 *(As Thisbe)* As true as truest horse, that yet would
    never tire.

Enter ROBIN, *and* BOTTOM *as Pyramus with the ass-head.*[21]

BOTTOM. *(as Pyramus)*
If I were fair, fair Thisbe, I were[22] only thine.

95 **QUINCE.** O monstrous! O strange! We are haunted. Pray, masters, fly, masters! Help!

        QUINCE, FLUTE, SNOUT, SNUG,
        and STARVELING *exit.*

ROBIN. I'll follow you. I'll lead you about a round,[23]
Through bog, through bush, through brake,
        through brier.

100 Sometime a horse I'll be, sometime a hound,
A hog, a headless bear, sometime a fire.[24]

15. **triumphant** splendid; magnificent.

16. **juvenal** juvenile; a young person.

17. **eke** also.

18. **Jew** shortening of "jewel" to complete the rhyme.

19. **Ninny's tomb** refers to Ninus, legendary founder of biblical city of Nineveh.

20. **part** script containing stage cues, which Flute is accused of missing or mis-reading.

21. **with the ass-head** wearing an ass-head.

22. **were** would be.

23. **about a round** in a round-about, like a circle dance.

24. **fire** will-o'-the-wisp.

And neigh, and bark, and grunt, and roar, and
      burn,
Like horse, hound, hog, bear, fire, at every turn.

      He exits.

105 **BOTTOM.** Why do they run away? This is a knavery of them to
make me afeard.

      Enter SNOUT.

SNOUT. O Bottom, thou art changed! What do I see on thee?

BOTTOM. What do you see? You see an ass-head of your own,
do you? *(SNOUT exits.)*

      Enter QUINCE.

110 **QUINCE.** Bless thee, Bottom, bless thee! Thou art translated![25]
(He exits.)

BOTTOM. I see their knavery. This is to make an ass of me, to
fright me, if they could. But I will not stir from this place, do
what they can. I will walk up and down here, and I will sing,
that they shall hear I am not afraid. *(He sings.)* The ouzel
115 cock,[26] so black of hue,
      With orange-tawny bill,
      The throstle[27] with his note so true,
      The wren with little quill—[28]

TITANIA. *(waking up)*
What angel wakes me from my flow'ry bed?

BOTTOM. *(sings)*
120   *The finch, the sparrow, and the lark,*
      The plainsong cuckoo[29] gray,
    Whose note full many a man doth mark
      And dares not answer "nay"—[30]
for, indeed, who would set his wit to so foolish a bird? Who
125 would give a bird the lie[31] though he cry "cuckoo" never so?[32]

TITANIA.
I pray thee, gentle mortal, sing again. Mine ear is much <u>enam-
ored</u> of thy note,
So is mine eye <u>enthralled</u> to thy shape,
And thy fair virtue's force perforce doth move me[33]
130 On the first view to say, to swear, I love thee.

BOTTOM. Methinks, mistress, you should have little reason for
that. And yet, to say the truth, reason and love keep little
company together nowadays. The more the pity that some

Literary Analysis
Archetypal Theme
How does Bottom's
transformation make
fun of the character of
Pyramus?

25. translated changed;
transformed.

26. ouzel cock male black-
bird.

27. throstle thrush; a bird.

28. quill literally, a small reed
pipe, but here meaning a tiny
piping song.

29. plainsong cuckoo bird
whose song is likened to
church music called plainsong.

30. Whose . . . "nay" whose
song married men listen to as
a sign that their wives may be
unfaithful, and who cannot
deny that this may be so.

**31. Who would . . . the
lie** who would use his intelligence to answer a foolish bird,
yet who would dare to contradict the cuckoo's taunt?

32. never so over and over;
ever so much.

33. thy . . . move me your
beauty is so powerful it moves
me whether I want it to or not.

Vocabulary Builder
enamored (en am´ ərd)
v. filled with love and
desire; charmed

enthralled (en *thr*ôld)
v. held as in a spell;
captivated

✓ **Reading Check**

What physical change
happens to Bottom?

honest neighbors will not make them friends. Nay, I can gleek[34]
135 upon occasion.

TITANIA.
Thou art as wise as thou art beautiful.

BOTTOM. Not so neither; but if I had wit enough to get out of this wood, I have enough to serve mine own turn.

TITANIA.
Out of this wood do not desire to go.
140 Thou shalt remain here whether thou wilt or no.
I am a spirit of no common rate.[35]
The summer still doth tend[36] upon my state,
And I do love thee. Therefore go with me.
I'll give thee fairies to attend on thee,
145 And they shall fetch thee jewels from the deep
And sing while thou on pressèd flowers dost sleep.

▲ **Critical Viewing**
How do Titania and Bottom seem to feel about each other in this image?
[Describe]

34. gleek jest; joke.

35. rate value; rank.

36. still doth tend still serves.

And I will purge thy mortal grossness[37] so
That thou shalt like an airy spirit go.—
Peaseblossom, Cobweb, Mote,[38] and Mustardseed!

Enter four Fairies: PEASEBLOSSOM, COBWEB,
MOTE, *and* MUSTARDSEED.

150 **PEASEBLOSSOM.** Ready.

COBWEB. And I.

MOTE. And I.

MUSTARDSEED. And I.

ALL. Where shall we go?

TITANIA.
Be kind and courteous to this gentleman.
Hop in his walks and gambol in his eyes;
Feed him with apricocks and dewberries.[39]
With purple grapes, green figs, and mulberries;
The honey-bags steal from the humble-bees,
160 And for night-tapers crop their waxen thighs
And light them at the fiery glowworms' eyes
To have my love to bed and to arise;
And pluck the wings from painted butterflies
To fan the moonbeams from his sleeping eyes.
165 Nod to him, elves, and do him courtesies.

PEASEBLOSSOM. Hail, mortall

COBWEB. Hail!

MOTE. Hail!

MUSTARDSEED. Hail!

170 **BOTTOM.** I cry your Worships mercy,[40] heartily.—
I beseech your Worship's name.

COBWEB. Cobweb.

BOTTOM. I shall desire you of more acquaintance, good Master
Cobweb. If I cut my finger, I shall make bold with you.[41]—Your
175 name, honest gentleman?

PEASEBLOSSOM. Peaseblossom.

BOTTOM. I pray you, commend me to Mistress Squash,[42] your
mother, and to Master Peascod,[43] your father. Good Master
Peaseblossom, I shall desire you of more acquaintance, too.—Your
180 name, I beseech you, sir?

MUSTARDSEED. Mustardseed.

---

37. mortal grossness the physical, mortal state of human beings.

38. Mote a speck, but also moth, as this word was pronounced similarly.

39. apricocks and dewberries apricots and blackberries.

Literary Analysis
Archetypal Theme
How do Titania's commands emphasize the absurdity of her feelings toward Bottom?

40. cry . . . mercy beg your pardon.

41. Master . . . you cobwebs were used to stop bleeding.

42. squash an unripe pea pod.

43. peascod a ripe pea pod.

Reading Check

How does Titania want the fairies to treat Bottom?

BOTTOM. Good Master Mustardseed, I know your patience[44] well. That same cowardly, giantlike ox-beef hath devoured many a gentleman of your house. I promise you, your kindred
185 hath made my eyes water ere now. I desire you of more acquaintance, good Master Mustardseed.

TITANIA. Come, wait upon him. Lead him to my bower.
The moon, methinks, looks with a watery eye,
And when she weeps, weeps every little flower,
190 Lamenting some enforcèd chastity.[45]
Tie up my lover's tongue. Bring him silently.

They exit.

44. your patience your story; your experience.

45. enforcèd chastity violated; required.

Thinking About the Selection

1. **Respond:** Which aspect of this excerpt did you find funniest? Explain.

2. **(a) Recall:** What are the Clowns trying to accomplish in this scene? **(b) Analyze Cause and Effect:** What events prevent their success? Explain.

3. **(a) Recall:** How is Bottom transformed? **(b) Infer:** Is Bottom aware of his transformation? Explain. **(c) Analyze:** Does the transformation alter Bottom's personality as well as his appearance? Why or why not?

4. **(a) Recall:** Who is Titania? **(b) Analyze:** In what ways does the match between Titania and Bottom mock typical portrayals of romantic love?

5. **Analyze:** Does Bottom's transformation actually reveal a truth about his character? Explain.

6. **(a) Summarize:** What alterations to script and costumes do the Clowns plan in order to minimize the frightening aspects of their play? **(b) Speculate:** Do you think the Clowns' eventual audience will enjoy their production of "Pyramus and Thisbe"? Why or why not?

Apply the Skills

Romeo and Juliet • **Pyramus and Thisbe** •

from A Midsummer Night's Dream

Comparing Archetypal Themes

1. Use a chart like the one shown to identify the characters, obstacles, and main events in Shakespeare's *Romeo and Juliet* and Ovid's "Pyramus and Thisbe."

Selection	Characters	Obstacles	Main Events
Romeo and Juliet			
Pyramus and Thisbe			

2. **(a)** Using your chart, explain similarities in the way both *Romeo and Juliet* and "Pyramus and Thisbe" present the **archetypal theme of ill-fated love. (b)** What are the differences in the way the two selections present this theme?

3. **(a)** Why is Titania's and Bottom's love ill-fated? **(b)** How do these reasons compare to the obstacles faced by Romeo and Juliet or Pyramus and Thisbe?

Writing to Compare Literary Works

In an essay, compare and contrast the way Shakespeare uses the characters and events from "Pyramus and Thisbe" in *Romeo and Juliet,* and the way he uses them in *A Midsummer Night's Dream.* Discuss why you think Shakespeare would explore the same story in both a tragedy and a comedy. Use the following questions to help you write your essay.

- How do the different settings and characters in each of Shakespeare's plays affect the two presentations of the archetypal theme?
- How do you think Shakespeare wanted audiences to feel while watching the ill-fated love in *Romeo and Juliet?*
- How do you think he wanted audiences to feel while watching Titania's and Bottom's ill-fated love?

Vocabulary Builder

Practice For each item, write a sentence correctly using the word pairs.

1. enamored; wonderful
2. inevitable; surprise
3. enthralled; view
4. lament; tragedy

QuickReview

Theme: the central idea of a literary work

Archetype: a plot, character, setting, symbol, or image that recurs in the literature of many different cultures

Archetypal theme: the central message of a literary work that is based on an archetypal idea

Go Online
Assessment
For: Self-test
Visit: www.PHSchool.com
Web Code: epa-6507

Reading: Summarize

Directions: *Questions 1–4 are based on the following selection.*

Many of Shakespeare's plays were performed in the Globe Theater. It was a wooden structure with a thatched roof over the stage. The audience surrounded the stage on three sides. Those who wished to sit down in a covered gallery could do so for a price.

Because the audience surrounded the stage on three sides, Shakespeare often wrote a word for an actor to repeat three times. For example, in one play, a character says, "Tomorrow, and tomorrow, and tomorrow. . . ." This repetition allowed an actor to address all sides of the audience.

In 1613, a spark from a cannon fired during a performance of *Henry VIII* set fire to the thatched roof, and the Globe burned down. It was rebuilt, this time with a tile roof, and it stood until 1644, when it was destroyed again, this time by the Puritans.

1. **What is the best way to group ideas in a paraphrase of the sentence that begins, "It was rebuilt . . ."?**
   A The theater was rebuilt with a tile roof and lasted until the Puritans tore it down in 1644.
   B The theater that was torn down by the Puritans had a tile roof and it lasted until 1644.
   C In 1644, the Puritans tore down the theater that had been rebuilt with a tile roof.
   D The tile roof on the rebuilt theater lasted until 1644, when the Puritans tore the theater down.

2. **What is the most important idea in the second paragraph?**
   A The lines that were repeated were repeated three times.
   B In one play, a character says, "Tomorrow, and tomorrow, and tomorrow. . . ."

   C The audience surrounded the stage on three sides.
   D Shakespeare wrote some lines to be repeated so that an actor could turn to each section of the audience.

3. **Which pair of details are necessary to summarize the cause of the fire that destroyed the first Globe?**
   A *Henry VIII*; 1613
   B theater destroyed; tile roof
   C spark; thatched roof
   D no one hurt; theater rebuilt

4. **What is the most important effect of the cannon being shot during *Henry VIII*?**
   A The new theater was built with a tile roof.
   B The original Globe was destroyed.
   C No one was badly hurt.
   D The rebuilt theater stood until 1644.

Vocabulary

Standards Assessed

- FA.3.04.4
- GU.6.01.6
- WL.1.03.4

Directions: *Choose the letter of the word that is the best definition of the italicized word in the context of the sentence.*

5. Even though the play is set in ancient times it is *relevant* to today's readers.
   - A conforming
   - B proper
   - C pertinent
   - D harmonious

6. Ramon was hoping that a discussion would *illuminate* his understanding of the play.
   - A irradiate
   - B clarify
   - C interpret
   - D lighten

7. The writer needs to *condense* this story; we don't have that much space in the magazine.
   - A summarize
   - B shorten
   - C constrict
   - D consolidate

8. You must *elaborate* on the details of the incident to make it more interesting.
   - A garnish
   - B expand
   - C embellish
   - D complicate

9. Harry felt that the character's motives were *ambiguous* and not clearly developed.
   - A faint
   - B inconspicuous
   - C vague
   - D intricate

Directions: *Choose the word that means the same as the italicized word.*

10. a *laborious* task
    - A hard work
    - B made or done with ease
    - C mental exertion
    - D pains

11. an *elaborate* plan
    - A complicated and detailed
    - B foolproof
    - C risky and dangerous
    - D difficult to perform

12. the *illumination* of the room
    - A filling with light
    - B understanding
    - C entrance or doorway
    - D explanation

13. an *elaborately* decorated room
    - A done without effort
    - B professionally designed
    - C worked out in great detail
    - D carefully put together

14. how he *elaborates*
    - A complicated and detailed
    - B adds details
    - C subtracts details
    - D without details

Exposition: How-to Essay

A **how-to essay** provides step-by-step instructions that tell readers how to accomplish a specific task. The best how-to essays are enriched by a writer's practical experience, so that readers can avoid mistakes and follow the best path to a desired outcome. Use the steps outlined in this workshop to write a how-to essay.

Assignment Write a how-to essay about an activity or a process that you know well.

What to Include Your how-to essay should feature the following elements:
- specific factual information presented logically and accurately
- step-by-step directions for each stage in the process
- examples and definitions that demonstrate key concepts
- instructions that anticipate readers' questions
- error-free grammar, including your use of modifying phrases

To preview the criteria on which your how-to essay may be assessed, see the rubric on page 878.

Prewriting

Choosing Your Topic

Make a calendar. For each day of the week, write down your activities. Then, identify an activity from your calendar to describe in a how-to essay. Or, describe another activity with which you are familiar.

Gathering Details

List the materials. Write down all the materials, tools, and information your readers will need to accomplish the activity you plan to describe. First, make a list of items needed. Then, note all the steps involved—in the order in which they occur. Take time to identify basic rules of behavior: for example, about safety, care of equipment, or working with others

Materials for Making Pizza Dough

1. Oven set, at 450°
2. Pizza Stone
3. 314 cup warm water
4. 2 cups flour
5.

Standard Course of Study

- Report the research for a specified audience. (IR.2.04.4)
- Note the progression of ideas that substantiate the argument proposal. (FA.3.01.2)

Using the Form
You may use how-to elements in these types of writing:
- repair instructions
- travel directions
- recipes
- training manuals
- problem solving

Work in Progress
Review the work you did on pages 719, 813, and 851.

Drafting

Shaping Your Writing

Organize information. After gathering all the information you want to include in your draft, select an organization that will make sense to your readers. Chronological, or step-by-step, order is usually best suited to this kind of writing. Use the chart shown to help you organize your information effectively.

Providing Elaboration

Use graphic devices and formatting. Locate or create graphics to reinforce your instructions, and place them at appropriate points in your essay. If you have access to a computer, use graphics features to create helpful diagrams and drawings. Use the automatic numbering or bulleting feature to indicate each step in the process you are describing.

Organizing Information

1. State the purpose of your how-to-essay.
2. List the materials and conditions necessary to complete the activity.
3. Provide examples to demonstrate the activity.
4. List steps to complete in consecutive order.
5. Suggest solutions to common problems when performing the activity.

Revising

Revising Your Paragraphs

Revise for clarity. Look over your draft to identify instructions, steps, or information that may be unclear to your reader. Mark these sections and go back to them, rewriting or adding language that better explains your points. If the order in which you have explained steps is confusing, rearrange paragraphs to create a better flow of information.

Student Model: Revising for Clarity

Once you feel confident enough, begin to "run"ʌ--read aloud--your lines . . . with another person. . . .ʌThis prepares you for being onstage with other actors.

Carmen defined a term that may be unfamiliar to readers and added information to explain the value of a strategy.

Revising Your Word Choice

Revise for transitions. Look for sections in your draft that need transitional language to connect the steps in your activity. In this example, the words *first* and *then* make the instruction easier to understand.

> **Example:** Wash the bowl and add the eggs.
> *First,* wash the bowl, and *then* add the eggs.

Reading Writing Connection

To read the complete student model, see page 877.

Writing Workshop

Integrating Grammar Skills

Revising to Combine Sentences With Phrases

To avoid a series of too many simple sentences, combine some sentences by converting the idea in one sentence into a modifying phrase in another sentence.

Identifying Modifying Phrases An **appositive phrase** is a group of words that clarifies the meaning of a noun or pronoun. The following sentences can be combined using an appositive phrase.

Prentice Hall Writing and Grammar Connection: Chapter 22, Section 4

Original: Sophia is a talented actress. She has appeared in over twenty productions.

Combined: Sophia, *a talented actress,* has appeared in over twenty productions. (appositive phrase)

Verbal phrases, which use verbs as nouns, adjectives, or adverbs, can also be used to combine sentences. Verbal phrases may be classified as participial, gerund, and infinitive, depending on their function.

When adding a modifying phrase to a sentence, place the phrase close to the word it modifies. A misplaced modifier can confuse readers.

Participial	*Finding himself alone onstage,* Aaron paced nervously.	Adjective modifies *Aaron*
Gerund	*Meeting with new people* is difficult for some people.	Noun acts as subject of sentence
Infinitive	The director's advice was *to focus first on learning the lines.*	Noun acts as complement of verb *was*

Misplaced: *Hanging from a silken thread,* Jeremy noticed a spider. (Participial phrase seems to modify *Jeremy.*)

Correct: Jeremy noticed a spider *hanging from a silken thread.*

Combining With Phrases Follow these steps to revise a series of short sentences by using phrases to combine them.

1. **Express the information from one sentence as an appositive or a verbal phrase.**

2. **Insert the phrase in a new sentence, locating it near the word or words being modified.**

3. **Make sure that the revised sentence is punctuated correctly.**

Apply It to Your Editing

Review the last four paragraphs of your draft, looking for short sentences that might be combined using appositive, participial, gerund, or infinitive phrases. Consider combining these sentences.

Student Model: Carmen Rose Viviano-Crafts
Syracuse, NY

Preparing for a Dramatic Role

One of the first challenges of a new dramatic role is the task of memorizing lines. Use the following guidelines to memorize lines more efficiently:

1. Read the entire play at least twice to familiarize yourself with the setting and situations. When performing, it is essential to know what is going on around you in order to provide the appropriate reactions.

2. Highlight or underline all your lines to identify when your character speaks.

3. Begin to concentrate solely on your parts. Look at the script scene by scene, memorizing one or two scenes a day, depending on how much time you have. Reading the lines out loud speeds up the process by making the lines more memorable.

4. Once you feel confident enough, begin to "run" your lines. Read them aloud, with another person reading the other characters' lines. This prepares you for being onstage with other actors.

5. When you begin rehearsing with fellow cast members, you will be able to try out different ways of saying things, and you'll start to develop your character. Here are the steps to use when developing a character:

   • If your role is based on a real person, research that person or observe someone in a similar situation. Try to find out as much information as you can so that you can play the part realistically.
   • If you are playing a fictional character, study the script closely. The character's words can tell you about his or her feelings, likes, and dislikes.
   • Once you have learned some aspects of your character, begin to delve into the mind and soul of the person. Make up an entire life story for your character. The more you know about the person, the easier it is to put yourself in his or her place. Think of a past experience to relate to something your character is going through. Bring the emotions you felt in that situation to your character's situation.
   • Finally, conduct general conversations with other cast members, with each of you speaking from your own character's point of view. Ask things like "How do you feel about me?" and "How do you think I feel about you?" This lets you know how you are perceived by the other actors/characters in the play and allows you to react more realistically.

6. After each rehearsal, consider what worked well and what felt wrong to you. Use your after-rehearsal notes as feedback to improve your next performance.

The numbering system allows Carmen to present information logically.

By offering time suggestions, the essay anticipates readers' questions and concerns.

Advice about conducting research elaborates on the writer's earlier suggestions.

These ideas explain the valueof each strategy.

Writing Workshop

Editing and Proofreading

Check your draft for errors in spelling, grammar, and punctuation.

Focus on Lists: If you include bullets or numbered lists in your essay, be sure that you use these elements consistently in your final draft. Check that numbers are consecutive and that bullets are the same size and shape. In addition, check that spacing is consistent and appropriate.

Publishing and Presenting

Consider one of the following ways to share your writing:
Deliver an oral presentation. Share your essay with classmates and give an instructional presentation. If the process you describe can be done in a classroom, have a classmate demonstrate the steps as you describe them. Ask for feedback about the clarity of your presentation.
Prepare a how-to manual. With a group of classmates, collect several how-to essays into a booklet. Add step-by-step photographs or illustrations to your instructions. Make the collection available to the class.

Reflecting on Your Writing

Writer's Journal Jot down your thoughts about writing a how-to essay. Begin by answering these questions.
- What new insights have you acquired about the process that you have explained?
- In what ways is a how-to essay similar to and different from other types of writing?

Rubric for Self-Assessment

To evaluate your how-to essay, use the following rubric:

Criteria	Rating Scale not very very
Focus: How specific is your focus?	1 2 3 4 5
Organization: How logical is your organization of the process into steps?	1 2 3 4 5
Support/Elaboration: How effective are your examples in demonstrating key concepts?	1 2 3 4 5
Style: How well do your instructions anticipate readers' questions?	1 2 3 4 5
Conventions: How correct is your grammar, especially your use of modifying phrases?	1 2 3 4 5

Draw Conclusions

Skills You Will Learn

Literary Analysis: *Comedy and Dramatic Irony*
Reading Skill: *Drawing Conclusions From Dialogue and Stage Directions*

Reading Skill: *Evaluating the Author's Credibility*

Literary Analysis: *Satire*

Literature You Will Read

Reading and Vocabulary Skills Preview

Reading: Draw Conclusions

> A **conclusion** is a decision or an opinion reached by logically combining details.

NC Standard Course of Study

- Summarize key events and/or points from argumentative text. (FA.3.04.5)
- Analyze and evaluate the effects of author's craft and literary style. (LT.5.03.10)

Skills and Strategies You Will Learn in Part 2

In Part 2, you will learn
- to **draw conclusions** based on **dialogue** and **stage directions.** (p. 882)
- to **evaluate an author's credibility** before you **draw conclusions.** (p. 892)

Using the Skills and Strategies in Part 2

In Part 2, you will learn to pull details together to draw conclusions. You will practice identifying these details in dialogue and stage directions and learn strategies for using them to draw conclusions. In addition, you will learn how to evaluate an author's credibility.

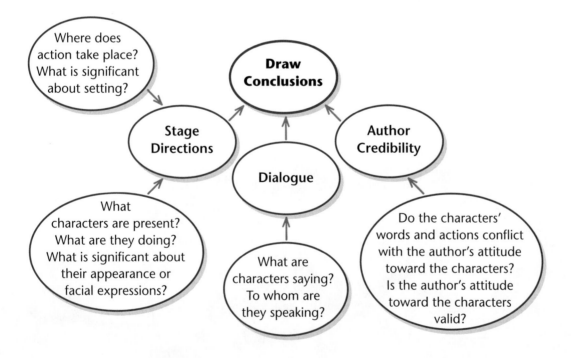

Academic Vocabulary: Words for Connecting Themes in Literature

The following words will help you write and talk about themes in the literature of this unit.

Word	Definition	Example Sentence
revise *v.*	read carefully to correct	The new events led us to *revise* our interpretation of the theme.
convince *v.*	overcome doubts; persuade	The disastrous outcome *convinced* the character he had made poor choices.
implement *v.*	put into action; fulfill or accomplish	Writers *implement* a variety of techniques to develop characters.
strategy *n.*	science of managing or planning; plan	Fortunately, the villain's *strategy* failed.
compile *v.*	put together; compose by gathering materials	I will *compile* a list of characters in the play.

Vocabulary Skill: Word Roots

▶ A **word root** is the basic unit of meaning in a word.

In Part 2 you will learn
- Latin word root *-vis-* or *-vid-* (p. 890)
- Latin word root *-vinc-* (p. 890)

As word roots pass through different languages over time, they sometimes develop more than one form. For example, words that have meanings related to *seeing* may either contain the word root *-vis-*, as in *visible*, or *-vid-*, as in *video*.

Activity Look up each example word on the chart. For each word, tell what meanings the word root or related words had and how the word root contributes to the current meaning of the word.

Related Roots	-vis-, -vid-	-vince-, -vict-
Meaning	see	conquer
Example Words	revise, vision, video	convince, victory, evict

Literary Analysis

Comedy is a form of drama that is lighter in mood than tragedy, ends happily, and aims primarily to amuse. The humor in comic plays may arise from one or more of the following elements:

- funny names
- witty dialogue
- comic situations, such as deception by a character, misunderstandings, or mistaken identities

The humor of comic situations often relies on **dramatic irony**, which is a contradiction between what a character thinks and says and what the audience knows to be true. In comedies, the audience often knows the truth about a situation in the play while the characters remain unaware. As a result, the characters' statements and behavior may seem funny to the audience.

Standard Course of Study

- State clearly a personal view is logical and coherent. (FA.3.02.1)
- Analyze connections between ideas, concepts, characters and experiences in argumentative text. (FA.3.04.10)
- Identify and analyze influences, contexts, or biases. (FA.3.04.7)

Reading Skill

A **conclusion** is a decision or an opinion that you reach based on details in a text. In drawing conclusions, you consider both stated and implied information. To draw conclusions about characters in a play, **use both dialogue and stage directions** to find meaningful information.

- Consider what characters' words suggest about their personalities and circumstances.
- Read stage directions closely for details about the scene, characters' appearances, and characters' behavior. Take note of other information that could prove essential to the plot or ideas expressed in the play.

As you read, use a chart like the one shown to record conclusions you draw about characters.

Information Provided

Traveler wants to talk about himself.

↓

Conclusion

He thinks he is an important man.

Vocabulary Builder

- **anonymous** (ə nän′ ə məs) *adj.* without a known or acknowledged name (p. 884) *These poems were composed a long time ago by anonymous writers.*

- **trundle** (trun′ dəl) *v.* to roll along (p. 884) *While we were chatting, the shopping cart began trundle down the aisle.*

- **discreetly** (di skrēt′ lē) *adv.* without drawing attention (p. 886) *The candidate avoided embarrassment by discreetly straightening his crooked tie during the debate.*

- **cunning** (kun′ iŋ) *adj.* skilled in deception (p. 886) *The small but cunning animal is usually able to outwit and escape its predators.*

Background

Inspectors General "The Inspector-General" is set in imperial Russia, before the 1917 communist revolution, when the country was ruled by an emperor, or czar. To oversee the many officials in Russia's vast expanse, the czars employed inspectors general. They observed how local schools, courts, and hospitals were functioning. Many resented the czar's authority, however, and inspectors general were often unwelcome.

Connecting to the Literature

Reading/Writing Connection In "The Inspector-General," an official in disguise finds out more than he wants to know. Imagine a scene in which someone—a public official, an athlete, a celebrity—secretly overhears people talking about him or her. Write a few sentences describing the person's reactions to such a conversation. Use at least three of these words: *distort, ignore, interpret, respond, injure.*

READ MORE

by Anton Chekhov
The Marriage Proposal
The Cherry Orchard

Meet the Author

Anton **Chekhov** (1860–1904)

Anton Chekhov grew up in a small Russian coastal town. He later attended medical school in Moscow, where he began writing humorous stories. Writing soon became his major focus.

Passion and Compassion Chekhov wrote many short stories as well as several acclaimed plays, including *The Seagull* (1896), *Uncle Vanya* (1897), and *The Three Sisters* (1901). His characters range from old peasants to young society women, from those whom life has treated kindly, to those who are disappointed. Chekhov treats them all with respect and sympathy. His humor and ability to portray characters of great depth and authenticity have helped make Chekhov a beloved aothor.

Fast Facts

▶ In 1890, Chekhov journeyed across Siberia to write a report on conditions at the convict settlement of Sakhalin.

▶ Chekhov married a famous actress, Olga Knipper.

Go Online
Author Link
For: More about the author
Visit: www.PHSchool.com
Web Code: epe-9504

The Inspector-General

Anton Chekhov

Adapted by Michael Frayn

The curtain goes up to reveal falling snow and a cart facing away from us. Enter the storyteller, who begins to read the story. Meanwhile, the traveler enters. He is a middle-aged man of urban appearance, wearing dark glasses and a long overcoat with its collar turned up. He is carrying a small traveling bag. He climbs into the cart and sits facing us.

STORYTELLER. The Inspector General. In deepest incognito[1], first by express train, then along back roads, Pyotr Pavlovich Posudin[2] was hastening toward the little town of N, to which he had been summoned by an <u>anonymous</u> letter. "I'll take them by surprise," he thought to himself. "I'll come down on them like a thunderbolt out of the blue. I can just imagine their faces when they hear who I am . . ." [*Enter the DRIVER, a peasant, who climbs onto the cart, so that he is sitting with his back to us, and the cart begins to <u>trundle</u> slowly away from us.*] And when he'd thought to himself for long enough, he fell into conversation with the driver of the cart. What did he talk about? About himself, of course. [*Exit the STORYTELLER*]

Vocabulary Builder
anonymous (ə nän′ ə məs) *adj.* without a known or acknowledged name

trundle (trun′ dəl) *v.* to roll along

---

1. **incognito** (in′ käg nē′ tō) *n.* a disguised condition.
2. **Pyotr Pavlovich Posudin** (pyō′ tər päv lō′ vich pō syōō′ dən)

TRAVELER. I gather you've got a new Inspector-General in these parts.

DRIVER. True enough.

TRAVELER. Know anything about him? [*The driver turns and looks at the* TRAVELER, *who turns his coat collar up a little higher.*]

DRIVER. Know anything about him? Of course we do! We know everything about all of them up there! Every last little clerk—we know the color of his hair and the size of his boots! [*He turns back to the front, and the* TRAVELER *permits himself a slight smile.*]

TRAVELER. So, what do you reckon? Any good, is he? [*The* DRIVER *turns around.*]

DRIVER. Oh, yes, he's a good one, this one.

TRAVELER. Really?

DRIVER. Did one good thing straight off.

TRAVELER. What was that?

DRIVER. He got rid of the last one. Holy terror he was! Hear him coming five miles off! Say he's going to this little town. Some-where like we're going, say. He'd let all the world know about it a month before. So now he's on his way, say, and it's like thunder and lightning coming down the road. And when he gets where he's going he has a good sleep, he has a good eat and drink—and then he starts. Stamps his feet, shouts his head off. Then he has another good sleep, and off he goes.

TRAVELER. But the new one's not like that?

DRIVER. Oh, no, the new one goes everywhere on the quiet, like. Creeps around like a cat. Don't want no one to see him, don't want no one to know who he is. Say he's going to this town down the road here. Someone there sent him a letter on the sly, let's say. "Things going on here you should know about." Something of that kind. Well, now, he creeps out of his office, so none of them up there see him go. He hops on a train just like anyone else, just like you or me. Then when he gets off he don't go jumping into a cab or nothing fancy. Oh, no. He wraps himself up from head to toe so you can't see his face, and he wheezes away like an old dog so no one can recognize his voice.

TRAVELER. Wheezes? That's not wheezing! That's the way he talks! So I gather.

▲ **Critical Viewing**
How might the people of a small town like this react to the arrival of an inspector? **[Speculate]**

Reading Skill
Drawing Conclusions
What conclusion about the inspector general can you draw from the stage direction that he "permits himself a slight smile"?

Reading Check

Why is the inspector general traveling to the town?

DRIVER. Oh, is it? But the tales they tell about him. You'd laugh till you burst your tripes![3]

TRAVELER. [*sourly*]. I'm sure I would.

DRIVER. He drinks, mind!

TRAVELER. [*startled*]. Drinks?

DRIVER. Oh, like a hole in the ground. Famous for it.

TRAVELER. He's never touched a drop! I mean, from what I've heard.

DRIVER. Oh, not in public, no. Goes to some great ball—"No thank you, not for me." Oh, no, he puts it away at home! Wakes up in the morning, rubs his eyes, and the first thing he does, he shouts, "Vodka!" So in runs his valet with a glass. Fixed himself up a tube behind his desk, he has. Leans down, takes a pull on it, no one the wiser.

TRAVELER. [offended]. How do you know all this, may I ask?

DRIVER. Can't hide it from the servants, can you? The valet and the coachman have got tongues in their heads. Then again, he's on the road, say, going about his business, and he keeps the bottle in his little bag. [*The* TRAVELER <u>discreetly</u> *pushes the traveling bag out of the* DRIVER'S *sight.*] And his housekeeper . . .

TRAVELER. What about her?

DRIVER. Runs circles around him, she does, like a fox round his tail. She's the one who wears the trousers.[4] The people aren't half so frightened of him as they are of her.

TRAVELER. But at least he's good at his job, you say?

DRIVER. Oh, he's a blessing from heaven, I'll grant him that.

TRAVELER. Very <u>cunning</u>—you were saying.

DRIVER. Oh, he creeps around all right.

TRAVELER. And then he pounces, yes? I should think some people must get the surprise of their life, mustn't they?

DRIVER. No, no—let's be fair, now. Give him his due. He don't make no trouble.

TRAVELER. No, I mean, if no one knows he's coming . . .

DRIVER. Oh, that's what he thinks, but we all know.

TRAVELER. You know?

---

3. **tripes** (trips) *n.* parts of the stomach, usually of an ox or a sheep, when used as food.
4. **wears the trousers** has the greatest authority; is really in charge.

Literary Analysis
Comedy How does your knowledge of the traveler's true identity make this dialogue humorous?

Vocabulary Builder
discreetly (di skrēt′ lē) *adv.* without drawing attention

Vocabulary Builder
cunning (kun′ iŋ) *adj.* skilled in deception

DRIVER. Oh, some gentleman gets off the train at the station back there with his greatcoat up to his eyebrows and says, "No, I don't want a cab, thank you, just an ordinary horse and cart for me." Well, we'd put two and two together, wouldn't we! Say it was you, now, creeping along down the road here. The lads would be down there in a cab by now! By the time you got there the whole town would be as regular as clockwork! And you'd think to yourself, "Oh, look at that! As clean as a whistle! And they didn't know I was coming!" No, that's why he's such a blessing after the other one. This one believes it!

TRAVELER. Oh, I see.

DRIVER. What, you thought we wouldn't know him? Why, we've got the electric telegraph these days! Take today, now. I'm going past the station back there this morning, and the fellow who runs the buffet comes out like a bolt of lightning. Arms full of baskets and bottles. "Where are you off to?" I say. "Doing drinks and refreshments for the Inspector-General!" he says, and he jumps into a carriage and goes flying off down the road here. So there's the old Inspector-General, all muffled up like a roll of carpet, go ing secretly along in a cart somewhere—and when he gets there, nothing to be seen but vodka and cold salmon!

TRAVELER. [*shouts*]. Right—turn around, then . . . !

DRIVER. [*to the horse*]. Whoa, boy! Whoa! [*To the* TRAVELER.] Oh, so what's this, then? Don't want to go running into the Inspector-General, is that it? [*The* TRAVELER *gestures impatiently for the* DRIVER *to turn the cart around.*]
[DRIVER *to the horse.*] Back we go, then, boy. Home we go. [*He turns the cart around, and the* TRAVELER *takes a swig from his traveling bag.*] Though if I know the old devil, he's like as not turned around and gone home again himself. [*Blackout.*]

◀ **Critical Viewing**
How does the countryside depicted in this painting compare to the setting of the play? **[Compare and Contrast]**

Reading Skill
Drawing Conclusions
What conclusion can you draw based on the Traveler's sudden order to turn around?

Apply the Skills

The Inspector-General

Thinking About the Selection

QuickReview

Play at a Glance
A smug inspector-general is outsmarted by a peasant.

1. **(a) Respond:** What questions do you still have after reading "The Inspector-General"? Write your questions in the first column of a three-column chart like the one shown. **(b) Discuss:** Trade lists with a partner. In the second column of the chart, try to answer your partner's questions. Then, discuss the questions and answers. **(c) Assess:** In the third column, explain how your understanding of the work has or has not changed based on the discussion.

Questions	Partner's Answers	Understanding of the Play

2. **(a) Recall:** What does the traveler do when the driver mentions that the inspector-general keeps a flask of vodka? **(b) Infer:** What does this action tell you about the traveler?
3. **(a) Recall:** According to the driver, what preparations does the town make for the inspector-general's arrival? **(b) Interpret:** Why does the driver's account provoke the traveler's demand to turn around?
4. **Evaluate:** Who do you think is the wiser and cleverer man, the driver or the traveler? Explain.

Literary Analysis

5. Note specific ways in which "The Inspector-General" does or does not meet these criteria for **comedy**: it ends happily; it uses witty dialogue; it presents a comic situation; it seeks to amuse.
6. **(a)** What information, conveyed by the Storyteller, sets up the **dramatic irony** in "The Inspector General"? **(b)** Identify an exchange between the Driver and the Traveler that highlights the dramatic irony of the situation.

Reading Skill

7. What **conclusions** can you draw about the character of the Traveler based on the stage directions *sourly, startled,* and *offended* that precede three of his lines?
8. What conclusions can you draw about the character of the Driver based on his dialogue with the Traveler? Explain your answer.

Comedy: a form of drama that ends happily and aims primarily to amuse

Dramatic Irony: a contradiction between what a character thinks and says and what the audience knows to be true

Conclusion: decision or opinion based on details in a text

Go Online
—Assessment
For: Self-test
Visit: www.PHSchool.com
Web Code: epe-6508

Vocabulary Builder

Practice Indicate whether each statement is *True* or *False*. Explain your answers. Then, revise false sentences to make them true.

1. Someone making an *anonymous* donation wants recognition.
2. A tricycle is something that might *trundle*.
3. The best way to send a message *discreetly* is to shout.
4. If a man is *cunning*, he may not always tell the truth.

Adding Words to Your Vocabulary Using a thesaurus, find one synonym, and one antonym for each italicized word in the Practice section. Then, use each new word correctly in a sentence. (For more on using a thesaurus, see page R7.)

Writing

Write a brief **play** in which students outwit a bully. Use a realistic school setting and be sure that dialogue sounds true-to-life.

Create *dramatic irony* by including scenes in which the audience knows something the bully does not know. Write to entertain and teach without being cruel, even to the character of the bully.

For *Grammar, Vocabulary,* and *Assessment,* see **Build Language Skills,** pages 890–891.

Extend Your Learning

Listening and Speaking With two other students, prepare a **Readers Theatre presentation** of "The Inspector-General." Do not provide props or staging; instead, focus on a well-prepared reading of the play. Remember that your purpose is to entertain your audience.
- Choose roles—the Traveler, the Driver, and a narrator.
- Experiment to find a suitable tone of voice and style of delivery. Perform the play in front of a small group or the entire class.

Research and Technology Use library and Internet resources to research what life was like in Russia during the rule of the czars, including the role of inspectors general at this time. As you research, take careful notes and observe which research terms and processes help you locate the best information. Organize your findings in an **informational chart** and present it to your class.

Build Language Skills

Vocabulary Skill

Word Roots The **Latin word roots** *-vis-* and its variant *-vid-* mean "see." Words that contain these word roots, such as *visible* and *video,* have meanings related to "seeing." The **word root** *-vinc-*, along with its variant *-vict-*, means "conquer." Words that contain these word roots have meanings that can be traced back to ideas about winning or being stronger. For example, to *convince* someone, you must have a stronger argument than the other person has.

Practice Check the meaning of each italicized word in a dictionary. Then, answer each question in a complete sentence that incorporates the italicized word and the underlined word.

▶ **Example: Q:** Does a person who cannot <u>see</u> the road signs have good enough *vision* to drive? Explain.

A: A person who cannot see road signs does not have good enough vision to drive and might have accidents.

1. What do you <u>look</u> for when you *revise* something you have written?
2. If <u>invisible</u> means "not able to be seen," what do you think *invincible* means?
3. What is one *victory* that makes you proud to have been the <u>winner</u>?

Grammar Lesson

Main and Subordinate Clauses A **clause**, a group of words that contains a subject and a verb, can be a **main** (independent) **clause** or a **subordinate** (dependent) **clause.** If the group of words needs additional information to make sense, it is a subordinate clause. Subordinate clauses can function as noun, adjective, or adverbial clauses.

▶ **Example:** Main clause   The reporter shouted.
            Subordinate clause   but the reporter shouted

Practice Define each of the following as a main or subordinate clause. Then, add to each subordinate clause to make it a main clause.

1. when the phone rang
2. the phone rang
3. decisions are difficult at times
4. but decisions are difficult
5. the Dead Sea in Israel has a lower elevation

MorePractice

For more practice with main and subordinate clauses, see the Grammar Handbook, p. R40.

WG Prentice Hall Writing and Grammar Connection: Chapter 20, Section 3.

Reading Skill: Draw Conclusions

Standards Assessed

- IR.2.02.3
- IR.2.03.2
- IR.2.03.4

Directions: *Read the selection. Then, answer the questions.*

The social significance of Chekhov's dramatic art is a vast theme. . . . What did he intend in presenting these characters and these situations? Why did he believe it was necessary "to depict life as it is and people as they are . . ."?

Perhaps in his aversion from everything stilted, affected, and pretentious he just created out of the sincerity and directness of his— very Russian—character. Perhaps his natural tolerance, his saving sense of humour, and deep sympathy with human beings moved him to show that people—however misguided, silly, ineffectual—are still lovable.

from Introduction: *Anton Chekhov: Plays,* Elisaveta Fen

1. The phrase "natural tolerance" could best be replaced by
   A recognition and respect for people.
   B inate ability to depict situations.
   C response to the humorous.
   D development of background.

2. The language in the selection leads the reader to conclude that
   A the author is a critic of Chekhov's writing.
   B the author admires Chekhov's writing.
   C the author is a sociologist evaluating Chekhov's writing.
   D the author makes excuses for Chekhov's work.

3. From descriptive details in the selection, the reader can conclude that
   A Chekhov wrote mainly fantasy.
   B Chekhov wrote mainly documentaries.
   C Chekhov wrote about high society.
   D Chekhov wrote about normal people.

Timed Writing: Interpretation [Critical Stance]

Symbolism plays a significant role in both *Romeo and Juliet* and *The Inspector General.* Choose one of the plays and explain how one set of symbols contributes to a major theme in the work. Support your views with specifics from the play. **(60 minutes)**

 ## Writing Workshop: *Work in Progress*

Research Report

For a research report you may be asked to write, discuss the details in Blackwood's scene that seem drawn from historical research: for example, details about language, dress, writing, materials, or theater. Keep these notes in your writing portfolio.

Reading Informational Materials

Book Review

In Part 2, you learned how to draw conclusions when you read literature. Drawing conclusions is also important when reading informational material such as editorials and reviews because it helps you weigh the facts and details in a text and form your own opinions. If you read Anton Chekhov's "The Inspector General," you may be interested in this review of a translation of Chekhov's plays.

About Reviews

Reviews are essays that express the writer's opinion about a created work, such as a book, a film, a recording, or a performance. Reviews appear in newspapers, magazines, and on Web sites, and are sometimes collected in books. In addition to expressing the reviewer's opinion, many reviews provide background and history about both the work and its creator. Based on information in a review, readers may decide if they want to read the book, see the play, or watch the movie. Reviews often include these features:

- An introduction that states the main idea or thesis
- Opinions about the strengths and weaknesses of the subject
- Examples, quotations, facts, or other support for the opinion
- A conclusion that restates the opinion and gives a recommendation

Reading Skill

Before you accept the opinions of a reviewer, evaluate the author's credibility. When you **evaluate the author's credibility,** you judge whether he or she is knowledgeable and fair. An unfair reviewer may express **bias,** an opinion he or she formed prior to experiencing a work. Credible authors avoid bias and present a balanced view. Use a chart like the one shown to evaluate the credibility of the author of the review, "Chekhov in American."

Evaluating the Credibility of an Author	
Writer's expertise or level of knowledge	Familiar with Chekhov's plays. Knows facts and other details about Chekhov. Cites Tolstoy, Chekhov, and Schmidt.
Intent or reasons for writing	
Bias toward the subject	
Thorough support for opinions	

Standard Course of Study

- Analyze the effects of author's craft and style in informing audience. (IR.2.01.9)
- Recognize and analyze the characteristics of literary genres. (LT.5.01.2)

THE PLAYS OF

Anton
CHEKHOV

A New Translation
by Paul Schmidt

"The Gold Standard in
Russian-English Translation"

Chekhov in American

Adam Kirsch

A Review of a Translation of Chekhov's Plays

In the introduction, the reviewer states his general subject—Chekhov's plays. He also gives background on the plays and identifies a controversy.

In the English-speaking world Anton Chekhov is far better known for his plays than for his short stories. But during his lifetime Chekhov's stories made his reputation; his plays were given a more ambivalent reception, even by his fellow writers. Shortly after Chekhov's death, in 1904, Tolstoy voiced a common feeling that plays like *Uncle Vanya* and *Three Sisters* weren't quite dramas. "To evoke a mood," he said in an interview, "you want a lyrical poem. Dramatic forms serve, and ought to serve, quite different aims. In a dramatic work the author ought to deal with some problem that has yet to be solved and every character in the play ought to solve it according to the idiosyncrasies of his own character. . . . But you won't find anything of the kind in Chekhov."

In this criticism Tolstoy hit on exactly those features that have made Chekhov's plays the fundamental works of modern drama. Like lyric poems, they favor mood over plot; there is no overriding "problem," and when problems do appear, the playwright never

seems to endorse any solutions. Chekhov's dramatic form allowed him to present things on the stage "just as complicated and just as simple as . . . in real life," as he famously wrote. "People are sitting at a table having dinner, that's all, but at the same time their happiness is being created, or their lives are being torn apart."

But Chekhov's emphasis on tone and mood, and his faithful re-creation of ordinary conversation with all its hesitations, references, and silences, make him an unusually difficult playwright to translate. Just as difficult to convey is the class dynamic that Chekhov treated again and again: there is no precise English, much less American, equivalent of his gentry, trying to live a city life on income from vast, ungovernable, debt-ridden estates. To an audience that doesn't share Chekhov's basic cultural knowledge, his plays can seem far more meandering, depressing, and vague than they were intended to be.

Here, the reviewer introduces a specific focus— the challenges of translating Chekhov.

In his new translation of Chekhov's complete plays Paul Schmidt has these problems very much in mind. Both an actor and a Russian scholar, Schmidt sets out to give us a Chekhov who makes sense. He writes in his introduction, "Above all, I hope these translations will provide actors and directors with a clear sense of how the plays are meant to work and how they should sound." His guiding stars are clarity and relevance — particularly relevance to an American audience. "I want to emphasize," he writes, "that this is an American translation, not simply another 'English' translation."

The result is a surprisingly lively Chekhov, colloquial and clear, which will come as a revelation to those who know the playwright through the widely read but rather stiff British translations of Constance Garnett and Elisaveta Fen. Everything about Schmidt's book, from the organization and footnotes to the language itself, is meant to clear away the obscurity and sentimentality with which Chekhov is often burdened. The plays that emerge are funnier and more muscular than one might have expected.

The most striking element in Schmidt's "American" translation is his attempt to put Chekhov's Russian into modern American idiom. There's no doubt that we sorely need such a translation; even the most casual dialogue can sound faintly absurd in the starchy British English of many popular editions of Chekhov. Take, for instance, this exchange from Act I of *Ivanov* in Elisaveta Fen's Penguin translation.

> **ANNA PETROVNA:** Who was it talking here just now? Was it you, Misha? Why are you stamping about like that?
>
> **BORKIN:** Anyone who had to

deal with your cher Nicolàs would stamp about!

> **ANNA PETROVNA:** I say, Misha, will you have some hay brought to the croquet lawn?
>
> **BORKIN:** Leave me alone, please.
>
> **ANNA PETROVNA:** Tut-tut, what a tone of voice!

Schmidt turns this passage into something American actors can plausibly say onstage.

> **ANNA:** What's going on out there? Is that you, Misha? What are you marching around like that for?
>
> **BORKIN:** Trying to talk sense into your friend Nicholas here. Voilà. Enough to make anybody start marching.
>
> **ANNA:** Misha, I want some hay brought up to the croquet lawn; don't forget to tell them.
>
> **BORKIN:** Oh, leave me alone, will you?
>
> **ANNA:** How rude! Will you please not take that tone with me?

For a playwright as frequently misunderstood as Chekhov, this is perhaps the greatest service that any translator could have performed. A generation from now Schmidt's American English may sound as antiquated as Elisaveta Fen's British English, but until then Schmidt's Chekhov should be the first choice for any American reader.

The writer uses a quotation to further explain and support his opinion.

This clearly stated evaluation is the main point of the review.

Examples of two different translations vividly illustrate the reviewer's opinion.

In the final paragraph, the writer restates his opinion about Schmidt's work.

EOC Test Practice

Reading: Evaluating Credibility of an Author

Directions: *Choose the letter of the best answer to each question.*

Standards Assessed
- WL.1.03.8
- CT.4.03.8
- LT.5.01.8

1. In this review, Adam Kirsch clearly expresses this opinion:

    A Chekhov's plays are stronger in English than in Russian.

    B Chekhov's plays are important dramatic works.

    C Chekhov should have written poetry instead of drama.

    D Chekhov's plays are not interesting.

2. Kirsch thinks Schmidt's translations

    A can only be understood by American audiences.

    B should have been done by someone else.

    C do not accurately reproduce the mood of the original plays.

    D will become the standard translations for many generations.

3. Kirsch's main purpose in writing this review is to

    A express an opinion about Schmidt's translation.

    B describe what he likes about Chekhov's plays.

    C explain why Tolstoy's criticism of Chekhov's plays is incorrect.

    D explain the themes and plots in Chekhov's plays.

4. Which of the following details contributes to Kirch's credibility?

    A He has read many works by and about Chekhov.

    B He likes Chekhov's work.

    C He does not like most English translations of Chekhov's work.

    D He is published in a newspaper.

Reading: Comprehension and Interpretation

Directions: *Write your answers on a separate piece of paper.*

5. Explain the main problem Kirsch has with most English translations of Chekhov. **[Knowledge]**

6. Describe the differences between the two versions of dialogue spoken by Anna and Borkin that Kirsch quotes. **[Organizing]**

Timed Writing: Exposition [Critical Stance]

Chekhov once said that dramas present things "just as complicated and just as simple as . . . in real life." Think about one play, television show, or movie that presents a realistic, or ordinary, depiction of life. Explain how the drama you choose illustrates Chekhov's words. **(40 minutes)**

Comparing Literary Works • *Satire*

Satire

Satire is writing that exposes and makes fun of the foolishness and faults of an individual, institution, society, or situation. Although a satire often makes readers laugh, it may also aim to correct the flaws that it criticizes. Some satires address serious social problems, while others address less important issues and subjects.

Standard Course of Study

- Explain how point of view is developed and its effect on texts. (LT.5.01.6)
- Demonstrate comprehension of main idea and supporting details in literary texts. (LT.5.03.5)

Comparing Satires

Satirical writings vary in style and **tone**, the writer's attitude toward the subject, the audience, or both.

- A satire may be gentle and sympathetic or angry and bitter in tone.
- A satire may use sarcasm or irony—language that means the opposite of what it says. For example, a satirist may mention the "overwhelming generosity" of someone who is a noted miser.
- A satire may exaggerate faults in order to make them both funny and obvious.

In addition, the **perspective**, or viewpoint, of the satirist plays key role. Some satirists write as outside onlookers, while others include themselves as objects of the satire.

As you read the excerpts from *The Importance of Being Earnest* and *Big Kiss,* answer questions like those in the chart to better understand the satire. Then, compare and contrast the satirie elements of each selection.

Questions About Satire	
subject	• What or whom is ridiculed? • Is the topic serious or trivial? • Does the writer include him- or herself as an object of the satire?
tone	• Is the tone gentle or harsh? • Does the writer use sarcasm or irony?
purpose	• Is the satire funny? • Does the satirist want to correct the flaws he/she exposes?

Vocabulary Builder

from The Importance of Being Earnest

- **demonstrative** (di män´ strə tiv) *adj.* showing feelings openly (p. 899) *She was demonstrative in her affection for the child, hugging her often.*

- **ignorance** (ig´ nə rəns) *n.* lack of knowledge or education (p. 902) *The driver exhibited ignorance, so the police officer explained the law.*

from Big Kiss

- **allotment** (ə lät´ mənt) *n.* share; portion (p. 906) *When they divided the supplies, my allotment was small.*

- **assiduous** (ə sij´ oo əs) *adj.* done with constant and careful attention; diligent (p. 909) *She is assiduous about studying.*

Build Understanding

Connecting to the Literature

Reading/Writing Connection Both of these selections poke fun at an aspect of society or of people's behavior. List a few television shows, movies, or comedians that poke fun at politics, the entertainment industry, or another area of life. Then, briefly explain why you think satire can help people see subjects differently. Use at least three of the following words in your response: *assess, confront, contradict, minimize, construct.*

Meet the Authors

Oscar **Wilde** (1854–1900)

Oscar Wilde was educated in Dublin and at Oxford University, where he became notorious for his wit. While he wrote poems and celebrated works of fiction, it was in his plays, that Wilde's genius found its voice.

The Importance of Being Funny In a series of brilliant comedies, including *A Woman of No Importance* and *An Ideal Husband,* Wilde targeted the straight-laced manners and hypocrisy of English society in the 1890s. His masterpiece is *The Importance of Being Earnest* (1895), a drama about Victorian values that still entertains audiences today.

Henry **Alford** (b. 1962)

Henry Alford calls himself an "investigative humorist," a comic journalist who unearths humor wherever it hides. Armed with dry wit and charm, he uncovers what makes popular culture funny, amazing, or outrageous.

Comic Escapades *Big Kiss: One Actor's Desperate Attempt to Claw His Way to the Middle* chronicles Alford's adventures as he tries to become an actor. He faces humiliation at the hands of acting teachers and directors, but he relishes his minor victory as an extra in *Godzilla.*

Go **Online**
Author Link

For: More information about the authors
Visit: www.PHSchool.com
Web Code: epe-9505

from The Importance of Being Earnest

Oscar Wilde

The following excerpt is from Act I of The Importance of Being Earnest. *The play takes place in England in the 1890s, during the reign of Queen Victoria, a time when elegance, manners, and social status were of great importance. In this scene, John Worthing, nicknamed Jack, visits the London apartment of his friend Algernon. Jack loves Algernon's cousin, Gwendolen. In order to maintain his spotless reputation at his home in the country, Jack takes on a different identity when he is in the city. When he is out in the country, he pretends to have a brother named Ernest, and when he visits London, Jack pretends to be Ernest. Gwendolen knows nothing about Jack's real name or his double identity.*

CHARACTERS

John Worthing, JP

Lady Bracknell

Hon. Gwendolen Fairfax

Lady Bracknell and Algernon go into the music room, Gwendolen remains behind

JACK. Charming day it has been, Miss Fairfax.

GWENDOLEN. Pray don't talk to me about the weather, Mr Worthing. Whenever people talk to me about the weather, I always feel quite certain that they mean something else. And that makes me so nervous.

JACK. I do mean something else.

GWENDOLEN. I thought so. In fact, I am never wrong.

JACK. And I would like to be allowed to take advantage of Lady Bracknell's temporary absence. . . .

GWENDOLEN. I would certainly advise you to do so. Mamma has a way of coming back suddenly into a room that I have often had to speak to her about.

JACK. *(nervously)* Miss Fairfax, ever since I met you I have admired you more than any girl . . . I have ever met since . . . I met you.

GWENDOLEN. Yes, I am quite aware of the fact. And I often wish that in public, at any rate, you had been more <u>demonstrative</u>. For me you have always had an irresistible fascination. Even before I met you I was far from indifferent to you. *(Jack looks at her in amazement)* We live, as I hope you know, Mr Worthing, in an age of ideals. The fact is constantly mentioned in the more expensive monthly magazines, and has reached the provincial pulpits I am told; and my ideal has always been to love someone of the name of Ernest. There is something in that name that inspires absolute confidence. The moment Algernon first mentioned to me that he had a friend called Ernest, I knew I was destined to love you.

JACK. You really love me, Gwendolen?

GWENDOLEN. Passionately!

JACK. Darling! You don't know how happy you've made me.

◀ **Critical Viewing** Judging from the actor playing Jack in this photograph, what do you think Jack will be like? **[Predict]**

Literary Analysis
Satire Which words here make fun of Gwendolen's haughtiness?

Vocabulary Builder
demonstrative
(di män´ strə tiv) *adj.* showing feelings openly

Reading Check
What is Gwendolen's "ideal"?

GWENDOLEN. My own Ernest!

JACK. But you don't really mean to say that you couldn't love me if my name wasn't Ernest?

GWENDOLEN. But your name is Ernest.

JACK. Yes, I know it is. But supposing it was something else? Do you mean to say you couldn't love me then?

GWENDOLEN. *(glibly)* Ah! that is clearly a metaphysical speculation, and like most metaphysical speculations has very little reference at all to the actual facts of real life, as we know them.

JACK. Personally, darling, to speak quite candidly, I don't much care about the name Ernest. . . . I don't think the name suits me at all.

GWENDOLEN. It suits you perfectly. It is a divine name. It has music of its own. It produces vibrations.

JACK. Well, really, Gwendolen, I must say that I think there are lots of other much nicer names. I think Jack, for instance, a charming name.

GWENDOLEN. Jack? . . . No, there is very little music in the name Jack, if any at all, indeed. It does not thrill. It produces absolutely no vibrations. . . . I have known several Jacks, and they all, without exception, were more than usually plain. Besides, Jack is a notorious domesticity for John! And I pity any woman who is married to a man called John. She would probably never be allowed to know the entrancing pleasure of a single moment's solitude. The only really safe name is Ernest.

JACK. Gwendolen, I must get christened at once—I mean we must get married at once. There is no time to be lost.

GWENDOLEN. Married, Mr Worthing?

JACK. *(astounded)* Well . . . surely. You know that I love you, and you led me to believe, Miss Fairfax, that you were not absolutely indifferent to me.

GWENDOLEN. I adore you. But you haven't proposed to me yet. Nothing has been said at all about marriage. The subject has not even been touched on.

JACK. Well . . . may I propose to you now?

GWENDOLEN. I think it would be an admirable opportunity. And to spare you any possible disappointment, Mr Worthing, I think it only fair to tell you quite frankly beforehand that I am fully determined to accept you.

JACK. Gwendolen!

GWENDOLEN. Yes, Mr Worthing, what have you got to say to me?

JACK. You know what I have got to say to you.

GWENDOLEN. Yes, but you don't say it.

JACK. Gwendolen, will you marry me? *(Goes on his knees)*

GWENDOLEN. Of course I will, darling. How long you have been about it! I am afraid you have had very little experience in how to propose.

JACK. My own one, I have never loved anyone in the world but you.

GWENDOLEN. Yes, but men often propose for practice. I know my brother Gerald does. All my girlfriends tell me so. What wonderfully blue eyes you have, Ernest! They are quite, quite blue. I hope you will always look at me just like that, especially when there are other people present.

(Enter Lady Bracknell)

LADY BRACKNELL. Mr Worthing! Rise, sir, from this semi-recumbent posture. It is most indecorous.

GWENDOLEN. Mamma! *(He tries to rise; she restrains him)* I must beg you to retire. This is no place for you. Besides, Mr Worthing has not quite finished yet.

LADY BRACKNELL. Finished what, may I ask?

GWENDOLEN. I am engaged to Mr Worthing, mamma.

(They rise together)

LADY BRACKNELL. Pardon me, you are not engaged to anyone. When you do become engaged to someone, I, or your father, should his health permit him, will inform you of the fact. An engagement should come on a young girl as a surprise, pleasant or unpleasant, as the case may be. It is hardly a matter that she could be allowed to arrange for herself. . . . And now I have a few questions to put to you, Mr Worthing. While I am making these inquiries, you, Gwendolen, will wait for me below in the carriage.

GWENDOLEN. *(reproachfully)* Mamma!

Literary Analysis
Satire What does Lady Bracknell's use of elaborate expressions suggest about her character?

Reading Check

What is Gwendolen's response to Jack's proposal?

LADY BRACKNELL. In the carriage, Gwendolen!

Gwendolen goes to the door. She and Jack blow kisses to each other behind Lady Bracknell's back. Lady Bracknell looks vaguely about as if she could not understand what the noise was. Finally turns round

Gwendolen, the carriage!

GWENDOLEN. Yes, mamma.

Goes out, looking back at Jack

LADY BRACKNELL. *(sitting down)* You can take a seat, Mr Worthing. *(Looks in her pocket for note-book and pencil)*

JACK. Thank you, Lady Bracknell, I prefer standing.

LADY BRACKNELL. *(pencil and note-book in hand)* I feel bound to tell you that you are not down on my list of eligible young men, although I have the same list as the dear Duchess of Bolton has. We work together, in fact. However, I am quite ready to enter your name, should your answers be what a really affectionate mother requires. How old are you?

JACK. Twenty-nine.

LADY BRACKNELL. A very good age to be married at. I have always been of opinion that a man who desires to get married should know either everything or nothing. Which do you know?

JACK. *(after some hesitation)* I know nothing, Lady Bracknell.

LADY BRACKNELL. I am pleased to hear it. I do not approve of anything that tampers with natural <u>ignorance</u>. Ignorance is like a delicate exotic fruit; touch it and the bloom is gone. The whole theory of modern education is radically unsound. Fortunately in England, at any rate, education produces no effect whatsoever. If it did, it would prove a serious danger to the upper classes, and probably lead to acts of violence in Grosvenor Square. What is your income?

JACK. Between seven and eight thousand a year.

Literary Analysis
Satire Is Lady Bracknell truly "a really affectionate mother?" Explain.

Vocabulary Builder
ignorance (ig′ nə rəns) *n.* lack of knowledge or education

LADY BRACKNELL. *(makes a note in her book)* In land, or in investments?

JACK. In investments, chiefly.

LADY BRACKNELL. That is satisfactory. What between the duties expected of one during one's lifetime, and the duties exacted from one after one's death, land has ceased to be either a profit or a pleasure. It gives one position, and prevents one from keeping it up. That's all that can be said about land.

JACK. I have a country house with some land, of course, attached to it, about fifteen hundred acres, I believe; but I don't depend on that for my real income. In fact, as far as I can make out, the poachers are the only people who make anything out of it.

LADY BRACKNELL. A country house! How many bedrooms? Well, that point can be cleared up afterwards. You have a town house, I hope? A girl with a simple, unspoiled nature, like Gwendolen, could hardly be expected to reside in the country.

JACK. Well, I own a house in Belgrave Square, but it is let by the year to Lady Bloxham. Of course, I can get it back whenever I like, at six months' notice.

LADY BRACKNELL. Lady Bloxham? I don't know her.

JACK. Oh, she goes about very little. She is a lady considerably advanced in years.

LADY BRACKNELL. Ah, nowadays that is no guarantee of respectability of character. What number in Belgrave Square?

JACK. 149.

LADY BRACKNELL. *(shaking her head)* The unfashionable side. I thought there was something. However, that could easily be altered.

JACK. Do you mean the fashion, or the side?

LADY BRACKNELL. *(sternly)* Both, if necessary, I presume. What are your politics?

JACK. Well, I am afraid I really have none. I am a Liberal Unionist.

LADY BRACKNELL. Oh, they count as Tories. They dine with us. Or come in the evening, at any rate. Now to minor matters. Are your parents living?

JACK. I have lost both my parents.

▲ Critical Viewing
How do these actresses' portrayals of Lady Bracknell and Gwendolen compare to your mental image of the characters? **[Compare and Contrast]**

Literary Analysis
Satire Does Gwendolen really have a "simple, unspoiled, nature"? Explain.

Reading Check
On what list of Lady Bracknell's does Jack's name not appear?

LADY BRACKNELL. Both? . . . That seems like carelessness. Who was your father? He was evidently a man of some wealth. Was he born in what the Radical papers call the purple of commerce, or did he rise from the ranks of the aristocracy?

JACK. I am afraid I really don't know. The fact is, Lady Bracknell, I said I had lost my parents. It would be nearer the truth to say that my parents seem to have lost me. . . . I don't actually know who I am by birth. I was . . . well, I was found.

LADY BRACKNELL. Found!

JACK. The late Mr Thomas Cardew, an old gentleman of a very charitable and kindly disposition, found me, and gave me the name of Worthing, because he happened to have a first-class ticket for Worthing in his pocket at the time. Worthing is a place in Sussex. It is a seaside resort.

LADY BRACKNELL. Where did the charitable gentleman who had a first-class ticket for this seaside resort find you?

JACK. *(gravely)* In a hand-bag.

LADY BRACKNELL. A hand-bag?

JACK. *(very seriously)* Yes, Lady Bracknell. I was in a hand-bag—a somewhat large, black leather handbag, with handles to it—an ordinary hand-bag in fact.

LADY BRACKNELL. In what locality did this Mr James, or Thomas, Cardew come across this ordinary hand-bag?

JACK. In the cloak-room at Victoria Station. It was given to him in mistake for his own.

LADY BRACKNELL. The cloak-room at Victoria Station?

JACK. Yes. The Brighton line.

LADY BRACKNELL. The line is immaterial. Mr Worthing, I confess I feel somewhat bewildered by what you have just told me. To be born, or at any rate bred, in a hand-bag, whether it had handles or not, seems to me to display a contempt for the ordinary decencies of family life that reminds one of the worst excesses of the French Revolution. And I presume you know what that unfortunate movement led to? As for the particular locality in which the hand-bag was found, a cloak-room at a railway station might serve to conceal a social indiscretion—has probably, indeed, been used for that purpose before now—but it could hardly be regarded as an assured basis for a recognized position in good society.

JACK. May I ask you then what you would advise me to do? I need

Literary Analysis
Satire How does Jack's explanation of being "found" make fun of the Victorian value of proper lineage and family ties?

Literary Analysis
Satire Explain how Lady Bracknell's use of exaggeration adds to the satire.

hardly say I would do anything in the world to ensure Gwendolen's happiness.

LADY BRACKNELL. I would strongly advise you, Mr Worthing, to try and acquire some relations as soon as possible, and to make a definite effort to produce at any rate one parent, of either sex, before the season is quite over.

JACK. Well, I don't see how I could possibly manage to do that. I can produce the hand-bag at any moment. It is in my dressing-room at home. I really think that should satisfy you, Lady Bracknell.

LADY BRACKNELL. Me, sir! What has it to do with me? You can hardly imagine that I and Lord Bracknell would dream of allowing our only daughter—a girl brought up with the utmost care—to marry into a cloak-room, and form an alliance with a parcel? Good morning, Mr Worthing!

Lady Bracknell sweeps out in majestic indignation

JACK. Good morning! (*Algernon, from the other room, strikes up the Wedding March. Jack looks perfectly furious, and goes to the door*) For goodness' sake don't play that ghastly tune, Algy! How idiotic you are!

Literary Analysis
Satire How does Lady Bracknell's final demand add to the satire?

Thinking About the Selection

1. **Respond:** Would you like to spend time with the characters in this play? Why or why not?

2. **(a) Recall:** How does Gwendolen respond to Jack's proposal? **(b) Infer:** How would you describe Gwendolen's feelings toward Jack?

3. **(a) Recall:** According to Lady Bracknell, how should a young girl learn she is engaged? **(b) Infer:** What do Lady Bracknell's remarks suggest about Victorian attitudes toward marriage and family?

4. **(a) Summarize:** Write a summary of the personal information that Lady Bracknell needs from Jack. **(b) Interpret:** In what ways does Lady Bracknell find Jack both acceptable and unacceptable as a possible husband? **(c) Assess:** Based on her judgment of Jack, describe Lady Bracknell's character.

5. **(a) Draw Conclusions:** What values does Lady Bracknell hold dear? Explain. **(b) Compare and Contrast:** How do you think Lady Bracknell's values compare to the values of most people today? Explain.

from **BIG KISS**

ONE ACTOR'S DESPERATE ATTEMPT TO
CLAW HIS WAY TO THE MIDDLE

Henry Alford

I n the acting profession, as in life, you must make the most of your tiny <u>allotment</u>. He who waits until he has been cast as Othello to pull out all the stops is setting himself up for disappointment—it will be Othello, not Desdemona,[1] who is strangled in this production. So when a classmate told me she was helping to cast extras for the remake of Godzilla, I quickly recommended myself for duty. I clearly had not slayed them at improv camp in Wisconsin; here was an opportunity to channel my feelings of disappointment into bravura acting. And perhaps, in so doing, to achieve every extra's dream: to be awarded a line of dialogue.

My classmate called me two days later and said that the filming, to be done that Sunday, would involve prodigious amounts of stage rain. I assured her that I was no stranger to adverse meteorological conditions, natural and man-made, and, as such, could "play wet."

1. **Othello. . . Desdemona** In Shakespeare's play, *Othello,* kills his wife, Desdemona, because he believes she had an affair. He later discovers she had been faithful and his grief causes him to kill himself.

Vocabulary Builder
allotment (ə lät′ mənt)
n. share; portion

Literary Analysis
Satire Which details make Alford's role as an extra sound important?

The pay for non-Screen Actors Guild[2] talent was seventy-five dollars; I needed to be available all day and night. I was to wear a raincoat and carry a black umbrella.

The harbinger[3] of location shooting in a metropolitan area is a table on the sidewalk, heaped high with haggard bagels. When I arrived at the appointed location in the Financial District that Sunday morning at six-thirty, although the chaos I found there—Teamsters[4] bickering over sports scores, thick black cables veining the streets as if to depict the late stages of arteriosclerosis—had all the earmarks of filmmaking, I did not see the telltale breadstuffs and so was moved to ask the first walkie-talkie-wielding individual I saw, "Where are the bagels?"

"Are you SAG or non-SAG?" she asked.

"Non."

"You're in the tent."

She pointed to a huge, dun-colored tent around which loitered hundreds of men and women, many of whom were also wearing raincoats and carrying umbrellas. "My people," I exclaimed. I walked over to the tent and, seeing a line formed at one of the twenty or so tables thereunder, queued up. Four minutes later the casting people had checked my name off on a list and I had been given a voucher, the form by which I would be paid.

All was actor-clogged; I could barely find an empty seat at a table. I was glad I finally did—we proceeded to wait for two hours. During this time, small groups of us were presented to a young, unshaven man from Wardrobe who was, by turns, exhausted and sniffy. He looked at the camouflage cap that the fortysomething gentleman ahead of me in line was wearing and said, "I don't know anyone who would wear that cap." Then he scanned me—that is to say, my tan raincoat, my black umbrella, and my wingtips encased in black rubbers—and yawned, "You're fine."

Shortly thereafter we were herded down to the set in groups of thirty or forty. The set was Federal Hall, the majestic site of George Washington's inauguration, rich in Corinthian columns and impressive stairways, which dead-ends Broad Street in the manner of a lion's gaping jaws. Halfway up its main stairs was a podium, festooned with red, white, and blue bunting and a sign reading RE-ELECT MAYOR EBERT. I wondered aloud, "Where's the reptile?"

The self-appointed expert in my group explained, "They're gonna blue-screen[5] him in later."

We lined up on the sidewalk and then, one by one, walked through a small, cordoned-off area where a sweet, pale, bespecta-

Literary Analysis
Satire What does the word "herded" convey about the experience of extras?

Reading Check

What does Alford say is every extra's dream?

---

2. **Screen Actors Guild (SAG)** labor union for performers.
3. **harbinger** (här´ bin jər) something that comes before to give an indication of what follows.
4. **Teamsters** (tēm´ stərz) members of a large labor union for truck drivers and other occupations.

cled man was handing out props. It looked like about a third of the extras were being given still cameras and two thirds were being given placards reading RE-ELECT EBERT.

"I hope I get a camera," the woman standing behind me in line said.

Eager to be filmed shooting at Godzilla, I responded, "I hope I get a Taser."

Moments later I was handed three props—a fake 35 millimeter camera, a fanny pack, and a press badge. I looked at the badge. The first thing I noticed was that the photo on it was of the man who had just handed it to me. Hovering over the photo was the name Sean Haworth and the call letters WAQR. These call letters sounded more like radio than TV to me; but then why was I carrying a still camera?

Rather than let this seeming contradiction bother me, I decided to base my character interpretation on it. What if Sean Haworth labored under the impression that if he took a good enough photograph it would be aired on the radio? Wouldn't this, character-wise, raise the stakes, and imbue him with the driven quality that makes for an interesting dramatic character? Poor Sean, you can almost hear the editorial staff at WAQR whispering over the water cooler. If only he understood that ours is an aural medium.

But five minutes later an assistant director who had assembled about a hundred of us in front of Federal Hall took away my camera.

"I based my character interpretation on that!" I exclaimed, hoping that this would translate to him as "Serious actor. Could handle a line of dialogue."

"I need it for up front," he reported tersely, then walked to the front of the crowd.

One of my fellow colleagues—a vivacious English as a Second Language tutor and sometime actress in her early thirties with whom I had fallen into conversation back in the tent—witnessed my loss of camera and counseled, "You were probably overpropped anyway."

"Yes," I responded, "my work was getting proppy."

We proceeded to work for almost eleven hours, lunch break included, on variations of a single shot. In it, about four hundred of us New Yorkers are standing in the rain, listening to Mayor Ebert

▼ Critical Viewing
How do the "extras" in this image from the movie *Godzilla* help increase the impact of the scene? **[Analyze]**

Literary Analysis
Satire Explain the satire in Alford's reaction when the assistant director takes his camera.

---

5. **blue-screen** filming against a blue background, in order to apply special effects later.

Recipe for a Monster

He's big, he's green, he's mean, and his breath is radioactive. Godzilla—named "Gojira" in his native Japan—has been stomping on Tokyo since 1954 when he made his movie debut. A dinosaur transformed into a giant monster as the result of atomic testing, Godzilla's appearance was created by scientists and sculptors using the ingredients below.

Take 1 Tyrannosaurus skeleton

Add 1 Chinese dragon

Mix in a pinch of crocodile

Raise the heat. Serve with a heaping portion of special effects.

Connect to the Literature How do you think Alford's performance might have changed if Godzilla had been played by an actor instead of being a special effect?

(Michael Lerner) give a speech. All of a sudden, we hear a thump. Some of the crowd—those born between January and April, to be precise—look behind them, down Broad Street, whence the sound originates. The mayor continues to netter on when thump! May through August now look down the street, too, expressing restlessness, a sense of discomfort, the vague possibility that this little piece of earth they call their own will soon be rent asunder. Then seconds later a third THUMP!: Godzilla appears, causing the crowd, regardless of natal season, to shriek with abandon, perhaps to drop umbrellas or placards, and to run off in a prescribed direction.

Since I was born in February, my prescribed direction was straight ahead, up the thirty or so stairs of Federal Hall. So, hearing my thump, I would look behind me down Broad Street in highly nuanced, ever-burgeoning panic; erupt into a despair-tinged, Edvard Munch-calibre scream[6] on hearing the third thump; run northward, negotiating my way through what was, by now, a very festival of bad acting; ascend the stairs two at a time; look behind me again while closing my umbrella (note the elegant adherence to decorum, even in the face of apocalypse); and then hurl my body against Federal Hall's massive stone doors in an attempt to gain entry.

> **Reading Check**
>
> How do the filmmakers divide the crowd of extras into two groups?

---

6. **Edvard Munch-calibre scream** an outcry with the intensity of *The Scream,* a famous painting by Norwegian artist Edvard Munch [munk] (1863–1944), which shows a person screaming.

I loved this work. I would be hard-pressed to recount any event from my personal or professional life that more accurately typified the phrase crazy fun. Yes, my colleagues and I encountered much wetness; the rain machines were <u>assiduous</u> in their ministrations. Moreover, no lines of dialogue were being doled out by the director or assistant directors. But the acting task at hand wedded blitz-krieg-strength drama with stuntman-strength athleticism and, as such, was wholly engaging. Screaming at full force in the canyons of Wall Street on a Sunday morning was particularly liberating. On the first few takes (by the end of the day we would do more than twenty) I would yell, "There he is!" By the eighth take I was screaming, "Here comes trouble!" By the late afternoon, punchy, I was shrieking, in an accent vaguely Caribbean, vaguely Cockney, "'Zilla monster ate me baby!" causing the self-appointed expert to glare at me and say, "Let's keep it real, huh?"

This statement might have chastened were it not for the other extras. Seldom have I seen such a preponderance of scenery-chewing; my colleagues' every utterance and movement seemed to offer ready proof that vaudeville[7] is not dead. Several of the extras, in an attempt to make themselves noticed, would run directly at the camera. Another one, a tall, fiftysomething woman who appeared to be a recent graduate of the Lucille Ball School of Clown Makeup, made such a spectacle of repeatedly dropping and then retrieving her umbrella that an assistant director was forced to take the umbrella away from her; the woman, divested of her gimmick, then devoted her energies to shrieking.

"That woman just screamed right in my eardrum," the ESL tutor told me between takes, motioning with her head toward the offender.

"Yes," I acknowledged, "her work is particularly broad."

---

7. **vaudeville** (vôd′ vil) old-fashioned stage shows of mixed specialty acts, including songs, dances, and comic skits.

Vocabulary Builder
assiduous (ə sij′ o͞o əs) *adj.* done with constant and careful attention; diligent

Literary Analysis
Satire How do the extras' hopes to be noticed compare to their actual experiences? Explain.

Thinking About the Selection

1. **(a) Recall:** According to Alford's opening paragraph, what is every extra's dream? **(b) Analyze:** Even though his dream does not come true, does he still feel his experience was worthwhile? Explain.

2. **(a) Recall:** What are Alford and the other extras required to do during the scene? **(b) Generalize:** What do they actually do? **(c) Analyze:** Why do they do so much more than required?

3. **Evaluate:** Based on Alford's account, what do you think are the pros and cons of being an extra in a movie? Explain.

Apply the Skills

from *The Importance of Being Earnest* • from *Big Kiss*

Comparing Satires

1. **(a)** Use a chart like the one shown to identify elements of **satire** in both *The Importance of Being Earnest* and *Big Kiss.*

Selection	Subject of the Satire	Foolishness or Faults Exposed	Author's Tone of Attitude
The Importance of Being Earnest			
Big Kiss			

   (b) Explain specific ways in which both selections use humor to expose people's foolishness or flaws.
2. **(a)** Which selection satirizes serious social issues and which satirizes trivial or light-hearted issues? **(b)** Which selection is harsher towards the people it satirizes? Explain.

Writing to Compare Literary Works

The **perspective**, or vantage point, of the writer helps to shape the satire. In *The Importance of Being Earnest,* Wilde is not part of the events he satirizes. In the excerpt from *Big Kiss,* Alford is a participant in the action, satirizing himself along with the other actors. In an essay, discuss how these different perspectives affect the satire. Use these questions to help organize your thoughts:

- What purpose do you think Wilde had in writing this play about Victorian society?
- Do you think Wilde likes his characters, or finds them funny?
- Does Alford's point of view make him more, or less, sympathetic to the other actors he satirizes?
- How do Alford's inner thoughts and feelings add to the humor of the satire?
- Which satire do you think is more successful? Why?

Vocabulary Builder

Practice Use each word pair below correctly in a sentence.

1. assiduous/energy
2. prodigious/tiny
3. allotment/unfair
4. ignorance/school
5. demonstrative/speaker

QuickReview

Satire: writing that exposes and makes fun of the foolishness and faults of an individual, institution, society, or situation

Go **Online**
Assessment
For: Self-test
Visit: www.PHSchool.com
Web Code: epa-6509

Reading

Directions: *Questions 1–5 are based on the following selection.*

[*Scene: The lights are brought up on the [small-town] drugstore.* WAITRESS *is there.* INEZ STANLEY *comes into the drugstore. She stands for a moment thinking. The* WAITRESS *goes over to her.*]

WAITRESS.	Can I help you?
INEZ.	Yes, you can if I can think of what I came in here for. Just gone completely out of my mind. I've been running around all day. You see, I'm expecting some company tonight. My brother Horace. He's coming on a visit.

[ELIZABETH CREWS *and her daughter* EMILY *come into the drugstore.* EMILY *is about seventeen and very pretty. This afternoon, however, it is evident that she is unhappy.*]

ELIZABETH.	We've just been by your house.
INEZ.	You have? Hello, Emily.
EMILY.	Hello.
ELIZABETH.	We made some [candy] and took it over for Horace.
INEZ.	Well, that's so sweet of you.
ELIZABETH.	What time is he coming in?
INEZ.	Six thirty.

1. **What is taking place in this scene?**
   A A woman and her daughter meet the woman's friend in a drugstore.
   B A woman is shopping for a dress for her daughter.
   C Two teenagers are discussing a dance.
   D Three women are meeting for lunch.

2. **What can you conclude about Inez?**
   A She is in an angry mood.
   B She is worried about her brother.
   C She is in a hurry.
   D She is distracted.

3. **What can you conclude about Emily?**
   A She does not like Inez.
   B She is anxious to see Horace.
   C She is not her usual self this day.
   D She is angry with her mother.

4. **Based on the dialogue, what might you conclude about Inez's husband, Herman?**
   A He is a very generous and loving husband.
   B He insists on having his meals on time.
   C He does not like Inez to go visiting.
   D He likes to help out around the house.

5. **What can you conclude about Elizabeth and Emily?**
   A Elizabeth and Emily are devoted to each other.
   B Elizabeth seems to be domineering.
   C Emily is a sullen and difficult daughter.
   D Emily treats her mother with disrespect.

Vocabulary

Standards
Assessed

• GU.6.01.6
• LT.5.03.10
• LT.5.03.7

Directions: *Choose the word that best completes the sentence.*

6. Margaret was able to _____ her friend to go to the movies.
   A compile
   B revise
   C convince
   D implement

7. The committee decided to _____ the plan for a new school building.
   A convince
   B implement
   C compile
   D strategize

8. Virginia developed a _____ for studying for the exam.
   A compilation
   B strategy
   C mechanism
   D trial

9. She did not have time to _____ the draft of her essay.
   A compile
   B revise
   C convince
   D implement

10. The reporter had to _____ his list of sources for the article.
    A compile
    B convince
    C revise
    D implement

Directions: *Choose the correct word for each definition or explanation.*

11. the state of having overcome a challenge
    A conviction
    B vision
    C victorious
    D convict

12. one who goes to see an exhibit
    A supervisor
    B convict
    C visionary
    D visitor

13. one who oversees and directs another's work
    A supervisor
    B visionary
    C revisionist
    D convict

14. one who has been found guilty and imprisoned
    A victim
    B visionary
    C supervisor
    D convict

15. an image of something beyond one's self
    A revision
    B vision
    C convict
    D visionary

Reading and Vocabulary Skills Review ■ *913*

Spelling Workshop

Using Silent *e*

In English, silent *e* performs a number of jobs. Knowing these jobs will help you determine when you should and should not add silent *e* to the end of a word.

In addition, there are rules for when to keep or drop the *e* at the end of a word when adding suffixes. Knowing these rules will help you spell different forms of a word correctly.

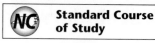

Standard Course of Study

• Edit for spelling and mechanics. (GU.6.02.4)

" Well, get rid of that guy! "

Reasons to end a word with silent *e*
- It makes the vowel in the preceding syllable say its name.
- English words usually do not end with a *v* or a *u.*
- It softens the final *c* or *g.*
- It avoids a syllable with no vowel. This usually applies to words that end with the *l* sound, like *bottle.*
- It helps avoid confusion. Words that end in a consonant followed by an *s* look like plurals. The *e* following the consonant *s* combination eliminates confusion.

Drop the *e*
- When the ending you are adding begins with a vowel: amaze, amazing

Keep the *e*
- When the ending you are adding begins with a consonant: amaze, amazement

Practice A Write each word from the word list. Identify the reason that helps you remember to use an *e* at the end of the word. Then, identify another word that illustrates the reason.

Practice B Use the rules for keeping or dropping the *e* to add the word endings indicated.

1. revise + ing
2. alternative + ly
3. involve + ing
4. involve + ment

Word List
alternative
circumstance
revise
involve
resource
college
credible
rectangle
dense
engage

Directions: *Choose the sentence in which all the words are spelled correctly.*

Standards Assessed

• GU.6.02.4

1. **A** We looked for an alternative solution to the problem.
   B The circumstances made it difficult to bring the task to completeion.
   C The expert we had hired was an excellent resours.
   D In the end, we had to revis the plan.

2. **A** Their involvment was very helpful.
   B The shrubs around the house grew densly.
   C I am almost finished completeing my college application.
   D We drew a rectangle around the word we needed to study.

3. **A** The author gave credibl reasons for accepting his ideas.
   B We hoped to find an alternativ way to get to the store.
   C His story is engaging because the characters are so interesting.
   D Alternatively, you could involv several other students.

4. **A** We consulted several credibel resources.
   B The dense foliage blocked the sun.
   C We wanted to go to the party, but we had another engagment.
   D My sister started collage this year.

5. **A** The painting was abstract, with several rectangals of different colors.
   B We spent a long time revising the paper.
   C The circumstanses were favorable for us to succeed.
   D This book is a good resourc for the information.

6. **A** We hoped more students would become involvd.
   B The dens fog made driving difficult.
   C Colege is a good place to meet new people.
   D He gave a credible reason for being late.

7. **A** Did you involve all the students by asking their opinons?
   B Consult several resoursis before making a decision.
   C We tried to engage the children in a conversation, but they were shy.
   D An alternativ game plan was needed.

8. **A** The zookeeper tried engageing the monkeys with new toys.
   B We need to revize the plan before we present it.
   C We identified the circumstance that was causing the problem.
   D This book is an alternativ to the one that you are reading.

9. **A** He told an incredibel story.
   B We needed to revise only a few words.
   C She announced her engagment on Saturday.
   D We will involve everyone in coming up with an alternateve plan.

10. **A** We wanted to announce the news yesterday, but the announcment did not come out until today.
    B Who will help you when you are revising your paper?
    C The roads were clogged with dens traffic.
    D That is an incredable idea.

Research Writing: Research Report

A **research report** presents and interprets information gathered through the extensive study of a subject. Use the steps outlined in this workshop to write a research report.

Assignment Write a research report on a subject that is both interesting and worth exploring in depth.

What to Include Your research report should feature the following characteristics of research writing:

- a thesis statement that is clearly expressed
- factual support from a variety of reliable, credited sources
- a clear organization that includes an introduction, a body, and a conclusion
- a bibliography or works-cited list that provides a complete listing of research sources formatted in an approved style
- error-free grammar, including the correct use of adverb clauses

To preview the criteria on which your research report may be assessed, see the rubric on page 927.

Standard Course of Study

- Clearly stating the subject to be defined in research question. (IR.2.02.1)
- Report the research for a specified audience. (IR.2.04.4)

Using the Form
You may use elements of research in these types of writing:

- lab reports
- documentaries
- annotated bibliographies
- histories
- persuasive essays

Writing Workshop: *Work in Progress*

If you have completed the Work-in-Progress assignment, you have several ideas in your portfolio that you might wish to pursue in your report. You may continue to develop these ideas, or you might explore a new idea as you complete this Writing Workshop.

To get a feel for research writing, read the selection from *Nothing To Fear* by Alan Axelrod on page 515.

Prewriting

Choosing Your Topic

- **Brainstorm for Categories** Identify an area of general interest, and rapidly list more specific categories that come to mind. For example, from the general area of art, you might list the following: sculpture, drawing, painting, and ceramics. Repeat the process: from painting, you might list Impressionism, Cubism, and Pop Art. Continue listing categories until you find a topic that you would like to research.

- **Notebook Review** Flip through the notebooks you keep for each class in school to find subjects or ideas that spark your interest. Choose one of these as the topic of your research paper.

Narrowing Your Topic

Identify an open-ended research question. Before you begin, consider a question that you would like to answer about your topic. Review your notes and jot down a question that expresses this interest clearly. The question will help you identify specific information and avoid gathering details and data that are too broad for your purpose. In fact, the answer to your question may become your thesis statement.

    Question: How did the school of painting called Impressionism begin?

Gathering Details Through Research

Use a variety of primary and secondary sources. As you study your topic, use both *primary sources* (firsthand or original accounts, such as interview transcripts and newspaper articles) and *secondary sources* (accounts that are not original, such as encyclopedia entries).

Find appropriate sources. Depending on your topic, you may find the information you need in specialized resources such as almanacs (for social, cultural, and natural statistics), government publications (for law, government programs, and information on subjects such as agriculture), information services, and microfiche (for back issues of periodicals). Consult your librarian to determine the best sources to use.

    You can find sources of specific information through a card catalog, an online search, or these more complex resources:

Databases: Access databases of information to find appropriate sources: For example, the Modern Language Association (MLA) database indexes articles on topics within the humanities.

Work in Progress
Review the work you did on page 891.

Gathering Details Through Research, (continued)

Indexes: Locate magazine or newspaper articles by consulting the *Readers' Guide to Periodical Literature.*

SAMPLE *READERS' GUIDE* ENTRY

Question your sources. As you locate information, choose sources representing a variety of viewpoints. If you find information you do not trust, consult a second source to verity its validity.

Record and organize information. Take notes as you locate pertinent information, and keep a reference list of every source you use.

- **Source Cards:** Create a separate source card that identifies the author, title, publisher, city, date of publication, and page number of each source you consult. For Internet sources, record the name and Web address of the site, as well as the date you accessed the information.

- **Notecards:** For each item of information, create a separate notecard that includes both the fact or idea and its source.

Quote accurately. Responsible research begins with the first note you take. Be sure to quote and paraphrase your sources accurately so you can identify these sources later. In your notes, circle all quotes and paraphrases to distinguish them from your own comments. When photocopying from a source, include the copyright information. Be sure to include the Web addresses of printouts from online sources.

Source Card

> [A]
>
> Marsh, Peter, M.D. *Eye to Eye: How People Interact.* Topsfield, MA: Salem House Publishers, 1988. (p. 54)

Note Card

> Gestures vary from culture to culture. The American "OK" symbol (thumb and forefinger) is considered insulting in Greece and Turkey.
>
> Source Card: A

Drafting

Shaping Your Writing

Propose a thesis statement. Review your notes and take a position that can be supported by most of the information that you have gathered. Include this position in your draft in the form of a thesis statement.

> **Sample Thesis Statement:** Claude Monet's handling of light in his water lily paintings is typical of Impressionist techniques.

Choose a text structure. Use your thesis statement and your knowledge of your audience to choose an organizational structure. Consider these options:

- **Chronological order:** present events in the order in which they occur; ideal for reporting a subject's history

- **Order of importance:** present details in order of increasing or decreasing significance; ideal for building an argument

- **Comparison and contrast:** present similarities and differences; ideal for addressing two or more subjects

Write an outline. To make an outline, use headings to identify the main idea you will cover in each section of your report. Order these ideas so they flow logically. Use this outline to develop your draft.

Providing Elaboration

Make direct references to sources. Use one of these methods to incorporate the facts, examples, and quotations you have found:

- **Direct Quotation** Enclose a writer's exact words in quotation marks. Be sure any omission does not alter the intent of the passage. Indicate omitted words with **ellipses,** or three dots.

- **Paraphrase** Restate a writer's specific ideas in your own words, accurately reflecting the writer's meaning.

- **Summary** Condense an extended idea into a brief statement in your own words. Use a summary to introduce background information or to review the key ideas of your own report.

Credit your sources. To avoid **plagiarism**—presenting another's work as your own—you must include documentation every time you use another writer's ideas. Circle all ideas and words in your draft that are not your own. Note the author's last name and the page numbers of material used. Later, you can use these notes to create formal citations.

Gary L. Blackwood

On Showing, Not Telling

Gary L.
Blackwood

To me, research is as much fun as beachcombing: You never know what fascinating items you're going to find. Since books are generally more reliable than the Internet, I do most of my beachcombing in libraries. I know that some people consider nonfiction dull, but I find good nonfiction more compelling than a novel, because I know the events really happened. Who could invent a story as singular and mysterious as that of Kaspar Hauser, which I came upon while researching my four-volume work *Unsolved History*?

"It helps to read sentences aloud."
—**Gary L. Blackwood**

Professional Model:

from *Perplexing People*, a volume in the *Unsolved History* series published by Benchmark Books (Marshall Cavendish) Sept. 2005

~~Sometime in the afternoon of~~ ₍On₎ May 26, 1828, a peculiar boy of about sixteen appeared, seemingly from nowhere, on a street in the German city of Nuremberg. His clothing was shabby and ill-fitting and he walked with a ~~peculiar~~ ₍strange₎ waddling gait, as though intoxicated. His face wore a vacant expression; he spoke and understood only a few words. Within a year he would become one of the ~~best known and most discussed~~ ₍most celebrated and controversial₎ people in Europe. . . .

Writing can be factual without also being sleep-inducing. I try to liven things up by using vivid adjectives.

The police questioned the boy, but his replies consisted of two phrases in ungrammatical German: "Don't know" and "I want to be a horseman as my father is." When they gave him paper and a pen ~~and asked to write his name and address,~~ he produced a series of scribbles, of which only two were intelligible: "cavalryman" and "Kaspar Hauser."

To add interest and a feeling of authenticity, I use a lot of quotes from primary sources—people who actually witnessed or participated in the events or chroniclers of the time.

Good prose—whether it's fiction or nonfiction—is clear and concise. I do a lot of cutting of superfluous words and phrases, and I may reword a sentence half a dozen times before I'm satisfied with it.

Revising

Revising Your Overall Structure

Evaluate your sources. Underline any fact in your draft that may not have a trustworthy source. For example, you may have found information from a newspaper or a Web site known for sensationalizing or exaggerating events. Try to confirm this information through a more reliable source, such as an established encyclopedia, a scholarly Web site, or a reputable newspaper. If you cannot verify essential information, consider removing it from your draft.

Student Model: Evaluating Sources

A good way for people to convey a positive message is to avoid certain movements. ~~When people cross their arms it is always a sign of defensiveness.~~

> The writer found that this was a controversial claim that was supported by only one source. Since it was inessential to her basic argument, she chose to eliminate it.

Revising Your Word Choice

Revise to vary word choice. Except for specific terminology required by your topic, avoid overuse of words and expressions. Review your draft to identify words that you may have overused. For each, generate a list of possible synonyms, and substitute them as appropriate.

Example Synonym Banks
   invention: innovation, development, contrivance, device
   theory: belief, policy, system, position, idea, supposition

Peer Review: Exchange drafts with a partner. As you read each other's reports, circle or highlight words that recur over and over. Working together, identify replacements to improve word variety in the writing.

Revising Your Format

Revise to follow a consistent format. As you finalize your report, be sure that it meets your teacher's criteria for length, format, and documentation of sources. The Modern Language Association (MLA) requires parenthetical citations of sources and a works-cited list that includes only the sources used in the report.

   To credit sources within a research paper, include direct documentation in the form of footnotes, endnotes, or parenthetical citations. At the end of your paper, provide a reference list giving complete bibliographic information. If possible, use the footnoting function in a word processing program to aid your efforts.

Preparing a Reference List

Bibliographic Form Present your sources in a standardized format. Include authors' names, source titles, place of publication, publishers, and the dates of publication. For online references, indicate the date on which you accessed the site. The following examples are in MLA format:

For a book with one author:

Wolfe, Tom. *The Right Stuff.* New York: Bantam Books, 1979.

For an article:

Quittner, Joshua. "Digital Video Daze." *Time.* 2 Nov. 1998: 112.

For an online source:

"Half Past Autumn: Newshour Transcript" *Online Newshour.* 19 Oct. 1998. http://www.pbs.org/newshour/bb/entertainment/jan–june98/gordon_1/

Footnotes and endnotes When using footnotes or endnotes to provide citation, include full details about the source and cite the page number. Indicate a citation by placing a number at the end of a passage. Place footnote documentation at the bottom of the page on which the number appears; place endnote documentation on a page preceding the reference list.

First footnote or endnote for a book:

1. Wolfe, Tom, *The Right Stuff* (New York: Bantam books, 1979), 61.

Subsequent footnotes or endnotes citing same source:

2. Wolfe 92.

Parenthetical citations To cite parenthetically, include source information in parentheses after the quoted material. This information, along with your reference list, directs readers to your source.

In her analysis of heroic behavior, Lewis suggests, "If you look inside yourself, you might find a hero waiting" (Lewis 90).

For more information on citing sources, see page R33–34.

Integrating Grammar Skills

Revising to Combine Sentences Using Adverb Clauses

Adverb clauses can be used to combine information from two sentences into one sentence. Often, the revised sentence will make an intended meaning more obvious.

Prentice Hall Writing and Grammar Connection: Chapter 21, Section 2

Two sentences: I joined the panel. Jay is the leader.
Combined: I joined the panel because Jay is the leader.

Identifying Adverb Clauses A clause is any group of words with a subject and a verb. An *independent clause* can stand by itself as a complete sentence; a *subordinate clause* is not complete because it does not express a full idea. An *adverb clause* is a subordinate clause that modifies a noun in a sentence. It begins with a subordinating conjunction that tells *where, when, in what way, to what extent, under what condition,* or *why.*

When: *After I read the report,* I agreed with the mayor.
Condition: Don will ask for a refund *if you will go with him.*
In what way: The bulldog yawned *as if he were utterly bored.*
Why: I drew a map *so that they would not get lost.*

Combining Sentences When combining two short sentences using adverb clauses, follow these steps.

1. **Look for a relationship between the ideas of the two clauses.**

2. **Select the appropriate subordinate conjunction to show that relationship.** Place the adverb clause at the beginning or end of the combined sentence—wherever it conveys your intent more clearly.

3. **Use a comma to separate a subordinate clause only when it begins a sentence.**

Common Subordinate Conjunctions			
after	because	since	when
although	before	so that	whenever
as	even though	unless	whether
as soon as	if	until	while

Apply It to Your Editing

Review several paragraphs of your report and highlight any consecutive short sentences that you find. Look for a possible adverbial relationship (*where, when, in what way,* and so on) in two of the sentences. Following the steps outlined here, combine the sentences using an appropriate subordinating conjunction.

Writing Workshop

Student Model: Lyndsey Regan
Canyon Country, CA

Body Language

When we speak to other people, they are not only listening to our actual words, but sensing our facial expression, tone of voice, gestures, level of eye contact, posture, and movements as well. Nonverbal communication, or body language, makes up approximately 65 percent of human communication (Aylesworth 3). Body language has a major impact on how others perceive what we say. It can also be a tool for miscommunication when the speaker and listener are from different cultures or are communicating through technology that deprives them of visual cues. In fact, we often realize the importance of body language only when we cannot interpret someone else's body language correctly.

In *Eye to Eye: How People Interact,* Dr. Peter Marsh explains that before we speak, our gestures, posture, and facial expressions are already broadcasting messages to those around us. While we are speaking, these gestures continue to communicate messages—usually clarifying what we are saying, but sometimes contradicting us in telltale ways (Marsh 116–119).

Often, body language is an unconscious act that triggers the most developed senses in other people—hearing and sight (Aylesworth 18). That is why body language is such a great way to emphasize words and ideas. Many people take advantage of this. Advertisers, for example, cast actors in their commercials who use body language that appeals to viewers.

Studies have shown that people's body language changes when they are not telling the truth (Vrij, Edward, Roberts, and Bull 239–263). If someone's body language is inconsistent with what he or she is saying, people tend to believe what the body is telling them. A good way for people to convey a positive message is to avoid certain movements, like fidgeting or letting your eyes wander. Instead, good communicators maintain steady eye contact, nod in agreement, and smile. You may notice that people on television, like hosts of infomercials and talk-shows, generally display this positive body language when speaking.

The opening line captures the reader's attention by presenting a surprising perspective.

The author expresses her thesis statement clearly and concisely.

Lyndsey smoothly introduces a research source and explains the ideas it provided.

Body language is usually learned, but it can also be inherited. It is affected by age, gender, background, and situation. The meaning of body language can change depending on cultural context. According to Dr. Marsh, each culture has developed its own repertoire of symbolic gestures, many with original associations that have now long been forgotten (Marsh 53–54). This causes people to be alarmed by foreign visitors or nervous around people when they visit new countries.

In the United States, people have a wide variety of regional influences because the country is a melting pot of diverse cultures. A gesture that means the same thing throughout the Unite States is the "OK" sign made with the thumb and forefinger. This gesture is interpreted similarly in some European countries, but if you were to perform this sign in Greece or Turkey, it would be considered very insulting (Marsh 54).

> Whenever Lyndsey presents a specific piece of evidence that is not her own idea or common knowledge, she cites it using the appropriate format.

There are other cultural differences in body language within Europe. In Germany, body language often reflects social status, and Germans often use body language for emphasis. Italian gestures are often passionate, emotional expressions communicated with the face, arms, and shoulders. Italians often use body language to clarify themselves or to express urgency. In France, people tend to use more formal gestures. They are generally not as expressive or insistent as Italians. The body language of the French is not nearly as casual as we are used to in America (Ruesch and Kees 23–25). As you can see by exploring a few examples from different cultures, there are many differences in body language. Therefore, when you communicate with people from other countries, take special care in your use of body language.

Technological advancements in our society affect the way we communicate. For example, when we speak on the telephone, we are unable to see the person on the other end of the line. The message that a person may be trying to convey may be misinterpreted without the additional visual information provided by his or her body language. With electronic mail, there is no visual or verbal communication whatsoever. As a result, people cannot completely understand the meaning of what is being communicated. Therefore, people using e-mail should be careful about what they write. To avoid miscommunication, communicating the old-fashioned way—in person—may be the best approach.

> The author's organizational structure is logical and clear. First, she discusses how body language is used in a variety of cultures. Next, she gives examples of what happens when we do not have body language to guide us.

Writing Workshop

In conclusion, body language is a significant component of communication, even though we are often not aware of it. Body language, like facial expression and gestures, frequently enables people to clearly understand one another, but we must remember that people cannot always be read like a book. With cultural differences, body language can take on different meanings, and this allows for potential miscommunication. Changes in technology present a different kind of problem but with a similar result. When body language cannot be seen, people may misinterpret the meaning of the communicator, making them angry or confused. As you can see, the additional information we provide with our body language plays a major role in how we communicate our thoughts and ideas.

Works-Cited List

Aylesworth, Thomas G. *Understanding Body Talk.* New York: F. Watts, 1979.

Marsh, Peter, M.D. *Eye to Eye: How People Interact.* Topsfield, MA: Salem House Publishers, 1988.

Ruesch, Jurgen, and Weldon Kees. *Nonverbal Communication: Notes on the Visual Perception of Human Relations.* Berkeley, CA: University of California Press, 1969.

Vrij, Aldert, Katherine Edward, Kim P. Roberts, and Ray Bull. "Detecting Deceit via Analysis of Verbal and Nonverbal Behavior." *Journal of Nonverbal Behavior,* Winter 2000: 239–263.

After her conclusion, Lyndsey presents the complete information for the works cited in her report using MLA, a common style for citation.

Editing and Proofreading

Check your draft to correct errors in format, grammar, and punctuation.

Focus on Format: Make sure that you have accurately followed the preferred system for crediting sources within your paper and for listing bibliographical information at the end. Double-check the punctuation and capitalization of these elements. (For more on formatting citations, see page R32–R34.)

Publishing and Presenting

Consider one of the following ways to share your writing:
Deliver an oral presentation. Read your research report aloud to your classmates. You may also consider recreating the report as a multimedia presentation using presentation software. Add appropriate visual aids as needed. You may want to provide a copy of your bibliography or works-cited page to any students who wish to learn more.
Organize a panel discussion. If several of your classmates have written on a similar topic, plan a discussion to compare and contrast your findings. Speakers can summarize their research before opening the panel to questions from the class.

Reflecting on Your Writing

Writer's Journal Jot down your thoughts on the experience of writing a research report. Begin by answering these questions:
- How did writing a research report affect your appreciation, understanding, or opinion of your topic?
- What were the best and worst parts of this experience?

> *Prentice Hall Writing and Grammar Connection: Chapter 12*

Rubric for Self-Assessment

To assess your research report, use the following rubric:

NC	Criteria	Rating Scale				
		not very				*very*
	Focus: How clear is your thesis statement?	1	2	3	4	5
	Organization: How logical and consistent is your organization?	1	2	3	4	5
	Support/Elaboration: How effective and varied is your support?	1	2	3	4	5
	Style: How well do you summarize background information?	1	2	3	4	5
	Conventions: According to an accepted format, how complete and accurate are your citations?	1	2	3	4	5

Communications Workshop

Multimedia Presentation of a Research Report

 Standard Course of Study

• Identify, evaluate, and analyze the impact of text components. (WL.1.03.2)

• Prioritize and organize the information for investigation. (IR.2.04.2)

• Analyze text components and evaluating impact on literary text. (LT.5.03.2)

Modern classrooms offer students several ways to add sound and visuals to a verbal report. Students may choose from an array of equipment to make multimedia presentations. The following strategies will help you develop and deliver a multimedia presentation of a research report.

Organizing Content

Your choice of media depends on the equipment available to you, your topic, and your target audience. Use the following tips:

- Use a two-column format for your outline. Arrange the content of your report in the left column; plan media elements in the right column. Use this same pattern in your final script: Run your speaking text in the left column and your media cues in the right.
- Choose media appropriate to your content. Dry recitation of statistics can be replaced with colorful graphs and charts. If your report is historical, incorporate music from the time period. Photographs or video images may clarify complex procedures.
- Distribute media use evenly throughout your report. This will make it easier for you to manage the equipment and to maintain audience interest.

Preparing the Presentation

An effective multimedia presentation is the result of planning and practice. These tips may help you prepare:

- If possible, rehearse your presentation in the room where it will take place. Check sightlines to make sure that your visual materials will be seen by all of your audience. Do a sound check as well.
- Make sure that words on your slides are readable; do not put too much content on any one slide.
- Practice shifting from spoken content to media elements. Plan what you will do and say if any piece of equipment fails.

Feedback Form for Multimedia Presentations

Rating System

+ = Excellent   ✓ = Average   – = Weak

Content and Organization

Media appropriate to topic _____

Media well distributed _____

Media enhances key points _____

Delivery:

Equipment functioning _____

Media visible and audible _____

Smooth transitions _____

Activity ▶ *Presentation and Feedback* ▶ Use a research report from your portfolio as the basis of a multimedia presentation. Plan and practice your presentation using the guidelines above. After your presentation, use the Feedback Form to collect comments from your classmates.

Julius Caesar

William Shakespeare
Globe Fearon, 1996

Drama Shakespeare's tale of power and betrayal is retold in modern English. The classic story invites the audience into a world of power and corruption where the lines of loyalty blur and it is sometimes difficult to decide who is a friend and who is a foe.

Four Plays by Tennessee Williams

Tennessee Williams
Signet Classic, 1976

Each of the four plays represents a masterpiece of American theater. The Williams plays deal poignantly with the drama of daily life. These are works in which there are ordinary people making decisions that dramatically change their lives and the lives of those closest to them.

Twentieth Century American Drama

A Prentice Hall Anthology
Prentice Hall, 2000

Drama Collection This collection contains four of the most important plays of twentieth-century America. *The Crucible,* Miller's famous refutation of oppression and censorship, is set during the Salem witch trials. *The Glass Menagerie,* by Tennessee Williams, is set in the Midwest during the Great Depression. *Our Town* and *Death of a Salesman* add to this look at America and American values.

Six Characters in Search of an Author

Luigi Pirandello
Signet Classic, 1998

Drama Pirandello's best-known play challenges audiences to decide which is more real: an actor or a character. During a rehearsal, the cast and crew of a play are visited by six characters who need to have their story told. This innovative drama breaks down theatrical barriers while questioning the reality of life itself.

These titles are available in the Penguin/Prentice Hall Literature Library.

Think About It Hurricanes are dangerous storms—sometimes hundreds of miles long. These enormous storms have two main parts: the eye and the wall of clouds that surround it. The eye of the storm is calm with very few clouds. However, the wall of clouds outside of the eye produces powerful winds and heavy rainfall. As you read, try to imagine these dangerous winds carrying the objects the speaker describes.

Problems With Hurricanes

Victor Hernández Cruz

A campesino[1] looked at the air
And told me:
With hurricanes it's not the wind
or the noise or the water.
5   I'll tell you he said:
it's the mangoes, avocados
Green plantains[2] and bananas
flying into town like projectiles.

How would your family
10   feel if they had to tell
The generations that you
got killed by a flying
Banana.

---

1. campesino (käm′ pe sē′ nō) *n.* Spanish term for a simple farmer or another person who lives in a rural area.
2. plantains (plan′ tinz) *n.* starchy tropical fruits that resemble bananas.

Death by drowning has honor
15 If the wind picked you up
and slammed you
Against a mountain boulder
This would not carry shame
But
20 to suffer a mango smashing
Your skull
or a plantain hitting your
Temple at 70 miles per hour
is the ultimate disgrace.

25 The campesino takes off his hat—
As a sign of respect
toward the fury of the wind
And says:
Don't worry about the noise
30 Don't worry about the water
Don't worry about the wind—
If you are going out
beware of mangoes
And all such beautiful
35 sweet things.

Meet the Author

Victor Hernández Cruz (b. 1949) is one of the pioneering poets who created the Nuyorican style of poetry, a new form that combines the English of New York City, the Spanish of Puerto Rico, and street slang. Cruz has twice been crowned the World Heavyweight Poetry champion in Taos, New Mexico.

Readings in Contemporary Poetry
Talk About It

Use these questions to guide a discussion of this poem.

1. **(a)** According to the campesino, what is the biggest safety concern in a hurricane? **(b)** Is this statement funny, true, or both?

2. Cruz uses playful words to describe a serious subject. In a group, consider how his word choices affect the poem.
   - Which words would not belong in a more serious poem?
   - How are the final two lines of the poem different from the rest? Are "beautiful sweet things" only fruit? Do these final lines change the poem's meaning in any way?

   Choose a point-person to share your group's ideas with the class.

Problems with Hurricanes ■ 931

Themes in Literature
Heroism

Unit 6 Overview

PART 1: Analyzing the Influence of Cultural and Historical Context

PART 2: Compare and Contrast

Standard Course of Study
In This Unit You Will

- Select, monitor and modify reading strategies appropriate to answering research questions. (IR.2.01.1)
- Analyze connections among ideas, concepts, characters and experiences to inform audience. (IR.2.01.10)
- Apply a set of predetermined standards to critique communication. (CT.4.01.2)
- Compare effective strategies used in different presentations/products. (CT.4.01.4)
- Use preparation, engagement, and reflection appropriate to critique text. (CT.4.02.1)
- Use reading strategies for preparation, engagement, reflection. (LT.5.01.1)
- Edit for spelling and mechanics. (GU.6.02.4)

Introduction
Themes in Literature: Heroism

Dean
Smith

Coach Dean Smith and John Kilgo
Talk About Leadership and Heroism

▲ **Dean Smith,** the legendary basketball coach, has collaborated with John Kilgo on a book about coaching and leadership.

Before I agreed to write a book on the **theme of leadership,** I had to be convinced that a college basketball coach qualified as a true leader. I wondered whether all leaders have something in common, from heroic political figures like Nelson Mandela to mythic heroes like Odysseus down to coaches of winning teams.

Does Coaching Qualify as Leadership?

Each season, as North Carolina's basketball coach, I led thirteen to fifteen dedicated, talented young men who loved playing the sport. I knew as I began my career in coaching that I had to motivate, teach, and discipline fairly, and to care deeply about those I led, just as all effective leaders do. Experts in leadership later proved to me that coaching is leadership.

If a coach is a leader and teacher, the game of basketball itself could teach our society some important lessons. The game reflects the ideals of our **culture.** In college basketball, we begin the game 0–0. There's no advantage for being rich, no disadvantage for being poor. Basketball teaches us that people of all races and nationalities, holding various political and religious beliefs, can excel when given a fair and equal chance.

◄ **Critical Viewing**
How does the figure in this picture demonstrate qualities of leadership? **[Interpret]**

True Heroes Help Others

For me, the true heroes of basketball are not the players out for themselves, but those who help their team and their community. Before each practice at North Carolina, a Thought for the Day, which had nothing to do with basketball, was given to each player. He was expected to memorize it and be able to recite it if called upon.

One day's thought was: "Do something every day for someone who can't pay you back." We wanted our players to be involved with their community, take part in campus politics, make friends on campus with non-athletes, and experience the fulfillment one receives from helping someone in need, with no desire to be recognized publicly for the good works. I required this not for the sport, but to teach players about our culture and its values.

Grandpere, while you're over in that neighborhood, I noticed that Jim Abbot's ten year old boy is dragging his leg in a brace that didn't look right to me. . . . Why don't you hop into your car tomorrow and have Stephen drive you through the district? You'll be amazed what it does to you to make connections with people who need you. . . .
from *Magnificent Obsession*
—Lloyd C. Douglas

The inspiration for my belief in helping others came not only from the example set by my parents but also from literature, the novel *Magnificent Obsession,* which I quote from here.

This novel is the story of a wealthy doctor who gives away his fortune to people in need who cannot pay him back. This passage, in which a character encourages his wealthy grandfather to help the poor, shows that true leaders, true heroes, are givers, not takers.

More About Dean Smith and John Kilgo

Dean Smith (b. 1931), who spent thirty-six years coaching the University of North Carolina's Tar Heels, has been called the greatest college basketball coach who ever lived. He has the most wins for coaching in college basketball history: 879. John Kilgo (b. 1935), who has spent forty years writing about North Carolina sports, publishes a magazine called *Carolina Blue.* For fifteen years, he was a co-host of Smith's TV show.

Fast Facts

▶ Smith was inducted into the Naismith Basketball Hall of Fame in 1983.
▶ He was named Sportsman of the Year by *Sports Illustrated* in 1997.

Exploring Themes in Literature

Universal Themes in the Oral Tradition

Written literature grew out of the **oral tradition,** the passing of stories, poems, and sayings by word of mouth. Around campfires and at other gatherings, people told tales about love, ambition, and friendship. Expressing their human concerns in stories, they explored **universal themes,** insights into life that are true for many different times and cultures. The following are examples of common universal themes:

- the importance of heroism
- the strength of loyalty
- the power of love
- the dangers of greed

Storytellers explored such themes by means of **archetypes,** the situations, characters, images, and symbols that appear in the tales of various cultures. Here are some important archetypes:

Cornered by Mike Baldwin

10-16 © 2004 Mike Baldwin / Dist. by Universal Press Syndicate www.cornered.com
cornered@comic.com

- the **hero's quest,** in which a brave or clever person undergoes tests or trials while searching for something of great value

- the struggle between the **protagonist,** the main character, and the **antagonist,** a person or force that opposes the protagonist

- the **monster,** a nonhuman or semi-human creature that menaces human society and must be destroyed by the hero

- the **trickster,** a clever character who can fool others but often gets into trouble through curiosity

- the **circle** as a symbol of loyalty, completion, or protection

The **historical context** is the social and cultural background of a particular tale. This context influences the presentation of archetypes. Yet, even with cultural variations, one can recognize archetypes across time and culture.

Forms That Express Universal Themes

Anonymous storytellers developed various forms to express universal themes and archetypes. At first, these forms lived only in the memory, and a tale might vary with every telling. Later in history, stories were written down and individual authors emerged.

- **Myths** explain the actions of gods and the humans who interact with them. Myths also explain the causes of natural phenomena.
- **Folk tales** focus on human or animal heroes and, unlike myths, are not primarily concerned with gods or creation.
- **Legends** are folk tales that recount the adventures of a human hero and are based on a historical truth. A legend told in an exaggerated way is a **tall tale.**
- **Epics** are long narrative poems that describe the exploits of larger-than-life heros. The hero usually engages in a dangerous journey or quest that is important to the history of a group or culture.

All of these narrative forms express the **values,** ideals, and behaviors cherished by a society. **Shared values** are held in common by people across cultures. In contrast, **culturally distinct values** are specific to a group. In a literary work, **cultural details** are the beliefs, traditions, and customs that reflect a particular society. Modern literature, though written by individuals rather than fashioned by a group, can also express universal themes.

Check Your Understanding

Decide which lettered term or phrase best matches the numbered phrase.

1. example of a universal theme   **a.** the monster   **b.** the power of love
2. brave person on a quest   **a.** epic hero   **b.** antagonist
3. important archetype   **a.** trickster   **b.** culture
4. passing on of tales by word of mouth   **a.** narrative form   **b.** oral tradition
5. legend told in an exaggerated way   **a.** tall tale   **b.** myth

From the Author's Desk
Dean Smith and John Kilgo Introduce *The Carolina Way*

Both of my parents were schoolteachers in my hometown of Emporia, Kansas. I developed a passion for athletics at an early age, but my parents insisted that sports not interfere with my studies, and if they did, sports took a backseat.

My parents received much joy and fulfillment from helping students learn and develop into good citizens, and were the major influences that led me to a career of teaching and coaching.

Creating a Culture of Unselfishness

At the University of North Carolina, I wanted to build a program in which all the players on the team, regardless of their backgrounds, respected each other, and highly talented players saw the wisdom of putting team goals in front of individual awards.

The Brightest Statistic

While a winning basketball program is very important at UNC, we established from the start that academics came first. Thanks to our players, we won 879 games and many championships in my thirty-six years as UNC's coach, but the statistic that stands brightest is that 96.6 percent of our players graduated, and more than a third of those went on to professional and graduate school.

Success Means Building Character

The university administration supported our efforts to build a program that emphasized education first, and the fact that we won almost eighty percent of our games says much about the players we had in our program. Thanks to them, some now refer to our method as "The Carolina Way."

That is also the title of the book I wrote about my coaching experience and philosophy. My **purpose** in writing this book was to demonstrate the methods we used to promote unselfish play and dedication to scholarship. And I was writing for an **audience** that I hoped would include not only athletes and sports fans but anyone who plays or works with others. As you read this excerpt from the book, you may be surprised to learn that I rarely talked to my players about winning!

Play Hard;
Play Together;
Play Smart

from The Carolina Way

Dean Smith with John Kilgo

I never went into a season as North Carolina's head coach thinking we'd just plug things into the previous year's plan and duplicate ourselves. As I said, we never had the same team return, and there were any number of other variables from one year to the next. We couldn't have had the long run of success that we enjoyed if we'd been too stubborn to change and come up with new ideas and different ways to play the game.

▲ Critical Viewing
What does this photograph tell you about the way Coach Dean Smith (in the blue suit) works with his players? **[Analyze]**

I will repeat this several times in this book: Don't fear change. Sometimes change can refresh a stale team; sometimes it's mandated by changing personnel; sometimes the rules of the game change. We adapted each year to hide our weaknesses and accentuate our strengths.

Although we didn't have a system at North Carolina, we certainly had a philosophy. We believed in it strongly and didn't stray very far from it. It pretty much stayed the same from my first year as head coach. It was our mission statement; our strategic plan, our entire approach in a nutshell: Play hard; play smart; play together.

Hard meant with effort, determination, and courage; *together* meant unselfishly, trusting your teammates, and doing everything possible not to let them down; *smart* meant with good execution and poise, treating each possession as if it were the only one in the game.

That was our philosophy; we believed that if we kept our focus on those <u>tenets</u>, success would follow. Our North Carolina players seldom heard me or my assistants talk about winning. Winning would be the by-product of the process. There could be no shortcuts.

Making winning the ultimate goal usually isn't good teaching. Tom Osborne, the great former football coach of the University of Nebraska, said that making winning the goal can actually get in the way of winning. I agree. So many things happened in games that were beyond our control: the talent and experience of the teams; bad calls by officials; injuries; bad luck.

By sticking to our philosophy, we asked realistic things from our players. A player could play hard. He could play unselfishly and do things to help his teammates succeed. He could play intelligently if we did the job in practice as coaches. We measured our success by how we did in those areas.

When we put these elements together, the players had fun, one of my goals as their coach. I wanted our players to enjoy the experience of playing basketball for North Carolina. Each player on our team knew he was important. Each did a terrific job of sharing the ball, which also made the game enjoyable for more players. All won and lost as a team.

Of course it is easier to talk about playing hard, playing smart, and playing together than it is to do all three. It begins by the recruiting of unselfish players, who subscribe to the philosophy of team over individual. In a summer physical education class I once taught at the Air Force Academy there was one young man who shot every time he touched the ball. Exasperated from watching him, I pulled his four teammates off the court. He asked who would throw the ball inbounds to him. "You understand that it takes at least one more player," I said to him.

Dean Smith
Author's Insight
A system signifies being rigid and unwilling to accept change. Our philosophy welcomed new and better ways of doing things.

Vocabulary Builder
tenets (ten´ itz) *n.* principles or beliefs

Dean Smith
Author's Insight
We asked our players to concentrate only on those things within their control. This philosophy also eliminates excuse-making.

Themes in Literature
Leadership Smith describes his ideas about successful coaching.

Playing Hard

Maybe a player wasn't the fastest, the tallest, or the most athletic person on the court. In the course of any given game that was out of his control. But each of them could control the effort with which he played. "Never let anyone play harder than you," I told them. "That is part of the game you can control." If another team played harder than we did, we had no excuse for it. None. We worked on it in every practice. If a player didn't give maximum effort, we dealt with it right then. We stopped practice and had the entire team run sprints for the offending player. We played a style of basketball that was physically exhausting and made it impossible for a player to go full throttle for forty minutes. When he got tired, he flashed the tired signal, a raised fist, and we substituted for him. He could put himself back in the game once he had rested. We didn't want tired players on the court because they usually tried to rest on defense. That wouldn't work in our plan. Therefore we watched closely in practice and in games to make sure players played hard. If they slacked off, it was important to catch them and get them out of the game, or if it occurred in practice, to have the entire team run.

▼ **Critical Viewing**
How does this photograph show that Coach Smith's players (in white) "play hard"?
[Connect]

Playing Together

One of the first things I did at the beginning of preseason practice was to spell out for our players the importance of team play. Basketball is a game that counts on togetherness. I pointed out that seldom, if ever, did the nation's leading scorer play on a ranked team. He certainly didn't play on a championship team. I made them understand that our plan would fall apart if they didn't take care of one another: set screens; play team defense; box out; pass to the open man. One man who failed to do his job unselfishly could undermine the efforts of the four other players on the court.

Dean Smith
Author's Insight
Basketball is fun for the players when everyone on the team is treated equally and with respect. Players savor team accomplishments long after individual ones are forgotten.

Reading Check

According to Coach Smith, what can a player always control?

Playing Smart

We taught and drilled until we made the things we wanted to see become habits. The only way to have a smart team is to have one that is fundamentally sound. We didn't skimp on fundamentals. We worked on them hard in practice and repeated them until they were down cold. We didn't introduce something and then move away from it before we had nailed it. Our entire program was built around practice, which we will talk more about in a later chapter. Practice, competitive games, late-game situations, and my relationship with our players are what I've missed most since I retired from coaching. We expected our team to execute well and with precision. If we practiced well and learned, we could play smart. It was another thing we could control.

I stay in touch with many members of my extended family, former Carolina basketball players. These men have brought great happiness to my life. Ninety-six percent of them earned their college degrees, and one-third of those continued their studies at graduate and professional schools. It's the way a teacher's career should be judged. Our former players are doing great things for people in all walks of life.

The Carolina Way isn't the only way, that's for certain. But playing hard, playing smart, playing together certainly worked well for us.

Our trophy case is full, but far more important, our Museum of Good Memories runneth over.

Themes in Literature
Cultural Context
Details here show the values and behaviors that lead to success.

▼ Critical Viewing
How does this photograph show that Coach Smith emphasizes the whole team, not just the "star" player? **[Analyze]**

Q. Did you develop your coaching "philosophy" over the years, or did you formulate it at the start of your career?

A. I learned basketball from my father, who was my high school coach, from my college coaches at the University of Kansas, Dr. Forrest (Phog) Allen and Dick Harp, and from Bob Spear and Frank McGuire, whom I assisted at the Air Force Academy and North Carolina, respectively. I had my own ideas, of course, which I updated annually to best suit our personnel and to adapt to rules changes. I also received valuable ideas from all of my assistant coaches at North Carolina.

Q. Do you remain in touch with your players after they have graduated?

A. Yes. I'm constantly in touch with our former players. Seldom does a week go by that I don't talk to at least a few of them. One of the best compliments given to me came from Phil Ford, who was National Player of the Year for us in 1978, when he said: "When I signed with Coach Smith and North Carolina, I knew I'd be getting a great coach for four years. I ended up with a great coach for four years and a friend for a lifetime."

StudentCorner

Q. How would kids who don't play a sport apply your methods?
—Lisa Avilez, Zion, Illinois

A. By concentrating on things within your control. Our players were taught to play hard, play smart, play together. Non-athletes can study and work hard, make intelligent life decisions, and be unselfish in their relationships with family and friends. You can also treat each individual honestly and with respect.

 Writing Workshop: *Work in Progress*

Writing for Assessment

To prepare for general assessments, make a list of literary works or historical events you might use to discuss the theme of courage. Jot down your ideas about how each item illustrates courage. Save this Courage List in your portfolio.

Apply the Skills

Themes in Literature: Heroism

Thinking About the Selection

1. **Respond:** Do you agree that playing a sport the right way is more important than winning? Explain.

2. **(a) Recall:** According to Smith, which factors in sports are beyond a team's control? **(b) Draw Conclusions:** How does Smith's philosophy provide a response to the unexpected in sports?

3. **(a) Recall:** According to Smith, how should a teacher's career be judged? **(b) Evaluate:** By his standards, is Smith's lifework meaningful because he was a teacher or because he was a coach? Explain.

Reviewing Themes in Literature

4. Using a three-column chart like the one shown, analyze the values that Smith emphasized as basketball coach for North Carolina. **(a)** In the first column, list the three **values** or goals that Smith taught. In the second column, give a specific example of how Smith promoted each value among his players. In the third column, suggest ways in which Smith's values can be applied to people in any walk of life. **(b)** Discuss your ideas in a small group, and add any new insights to your chart. **(c)** Share your ideas with the class.

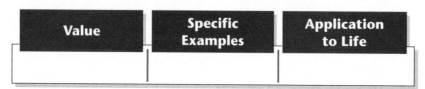

Value	Specific Examples	Application to Life

5. Do you think that sports are an essential part of the **cultural context** of the United States? Use details from Smith's essay to support your answer.

Research the Author

Many of Dean Smith's players have achieved great success in life. Use comments from Smith's former players to create a **testimonial poster** that shows the positive results of Smith's coaching beliefs.

- Using both Internet and library sources, identify famous athletes, coaches, or leaders who have played for Dean Smith.
- Collect comments about Smith made by these former players. Focus on statements relating to values that have aided their success.
- Present these comments on a poster. Include photographs of Smith and the people whom you quote.

Skills You Will Learn

Literature You Will Read

Reading: Analyzing Cultural and Historical Context

> The **cultural and historical context** is the social and cultural information, including the attitudes and customs, of the time and place in which a work is set.

 Standard Course of Study

- Analyze connections among ideas, concepts, characters and experiences to inform audience. (IR.2.01.10)
- Analyze influences, contexts, or biases in anwering research questions. (IR.2.01.7)

Skills and Strategies you will learn in Part 1

- **to use background and prior knowledge** to **identify the influences** of **cultural and historical context** in your own reading (p. 948)
- **to relate to your own experiences** to help you understand the **influence of the cultural and historical context** (p. 992)
- **to follow directions** in order to help you **analyze cultural and historical contexts** (p. 1022)

Using the Skills and Strategies in Part 1

In Part 1, you will learn to recognize how the culture and time period in which a work of literature is set affects the work. You will also learn how your own experiences help you relate to a different culture and to use directions in text to add to your cultural understanding.

The following chart shows the key questions you can ask to analyze cultural and historical context.

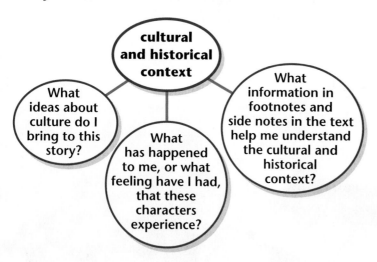

Academic Vocabulary: Words for Developing Concepts in Literature

These words will help you write and talk about concepts in literature.

Word	Definition	Example Sentence
controversy *n.*	a discussion over opposing viewpoints; a dispute	The **controversy** over who authored the poem continues.
technique *n.*	methods used to create an artistic work	Repetition of words and phrases is one **technique** used in epic poetry.
appraise *v.*	judge the quality or worth of something; set a value on something	Her article attempts to **appraise** the work of ancient Greek poets.
confirm *v.*	prove the truth or authenticity	Scholars can **confirm** that the manuscript was authentic.
complex *adj.*	complicated or intricate	The poem was filled with **complex** detail.

Vocabulary Skill: Word Roots

▶ A **word root** is the part of the word that contain its basic meaning.

In Part 1, you will learn

- Latin prefix *contra-* (p. 990)
- Greek word root *-techni-* (p. 1020)

Word parts help you determine the meaning of an unfamiliar word. Knowing that "contra" means "against" helps you define words such as "contradict," which means "speak against."

Activity Write the definition of each of the following word roots. Then, write the definition of the word with *contra-* added.

1. diction/contradiction

2. alto/contralto

3. distinguish/contradistinguish

4. position/contraposition

Practice these skills with the excerpt from the *Odyssey,* Part 1

Literary Analysis

An **epic hero** is the larger-than-life central character in an **epic**—a long narrative poem about important events in the history or folklore of a nation or culture. Through adventurous deeds, the epic hero demonstrates traits that are valued by the society in which the epic originates. Here, Odysseus shows his courage and leadership:

> Now, by the gods, I drove my big hand spike
> deep in the embers, charring it again,
> and cheered my men along with battle talk
> to keep their courage up; no quitting now.

Many epics begin *in medias res* ("in the middle of things"), meaning that much of the important action in the story occurred before the point at which the poem begins. Therefore, the epic hero's adventures are often recounted in a **flashback,** a scene that interrupts the sequence of events in a narrative to relate earlier events.

Reading Skill

The **historical and cultural context** of a work is the backdrop of details of the time and place in which the work is set or in which it was written. These details include specific events, beliefs, and customs. When you read a work from another time and culture, **use background and prior knowledge** to analyze the influence of the historical and cultural context.

- Read the author biography, footnotes, and other text aids.
- Note how characters' behavior and attitudes reflect the context.

As you read, use a chart like the one shown to note the influence of ancient Greek culture in Homer's *Odyssey.*

 Standard Course of Study

- Examine the use of strategies in a presentation to critique communication. (CT.4.01.1)
- Compare effective strategies used in different presentations/products. (CT.4.01.4)
- Demonstrate comprehension of main idea and supporting details. (CT.4.03.4)

Historical / Cultural Detail

"Now Zeus the lord of cloud roused in the north a storm against the ships. . . ."

Background

Zeus is king of the gods in Greek mythology.

Analysis

The *Odyssey* reflects a belief that the gods participate actively in the lives of mortals.

Vocabulary Builder

- **plundered** (plun´ dərd) *v.* took goods by force; looted (p. 951) *The fierce pirates captured the merchant ship and* plundered *it.*

- **dispatched** (di spacht´) *v.* finished quickly (p. 960) *Remarkably, she* dispatched *this assignment a full hour before anyone else did.*

- **mammoth** (mam´ əth) *adj.* enormous (p. 963) *The* mammoth *ship made all others in the harbor look tiny.*

- **assuage** (ə swāj´) *v.* to calm; pacify (p. 971) *Gentle words may* assuage *their anger.*

- **bereft** (bē reft´) *adj.* deprived (p. 973) *Bereft of sleep, she struggled to stay awake in class.*

- **ardor** (är´ dər) *n.* passion; enthusiasm (p. 978) *The audience cheered with* ardor.

- **insidious** (in sid´ ē əs) *adj.* characterized by craftiness and betrayal (p. 981) *The traitor's* insidious *actions led to the city's downfall.*

Build Understanding • from the *Odyssey*

Background

The Trojan War The *Odyssey* describes the experiences of the Greek hero Odysseus as he made his way home after the Trojan War. According to legend, the Trojan War was sparked when Paris ran off with Helen. A Greek force attacked Troy (in modern-day Turkey) to recapture her and was finally victorious after ten years of fighting.

READ MORE

by Homer
The *Iliad*

Connecting to the Literature

Reading/Writing Connection In the *Odyssey*, Homer describes a journey filled with amazing adventures. Write a paragraph that tells of a journey you have taken or imagined. Describe something challenging or amazing that occurred. Use at least three of these words: *coincide, eliminate, encounter, highlight, interact.*

Meet the Author

Homer (ca. 800 B.C.)

Homer is the legendary poet credited with writing the *Iliad* and the *Odyssey*. Their length and scope, gripping stories, imagery, and style have captured readers' imaginations for almost 3,000 years.

Did Homer Exist? Scholars disagree about whether the *Iliad* and the *Odyssey* were really written by Homer. According to tradition, Homer was born in western Asia Minor and was blind. However, many scholars feel confident that the *Iliad* and the *Odyssey* are the result of generations of oral poetic composition, masterpieces to which numerous ancient singers contributed. If Homer existed, he may have been the greatest in a long line of Greek epic storytellers.

Fast Facts

▶ The adjective *Homeric* means "large-scale; massive; epic in scope."
▶ Homer's stories have been the basis for many Hollywood movies, including *Troy* in 2004.

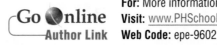

Go Online
Author Link

For: More information about the author
Visit: www.PHSchool.com
Web Code: epe-9602

from the

ODYSSEY

Homer Translated by Robert Fitzgerald

Ulysses Deriding Polyphemus, 1819, J.M.W. Turner, The National Gallery, London

▲ **Critical Viewing** Do the images in this painting evoke feelings of hope or doom? Explain? **[Analyze]**

PART 1
The Adventures of Odysseus

In the opening verses, Homer addresses the muse of epic poetry. He asks her help in telling the tale of Odysseus.

Sing in me, Muse,[1] and through me tell the story
of that man skilled in all ways of contending,
the wanderer, harried for years on end,
after he <u>plundered</u> the stronghold
5 on the proud height of Troy.[2]

               He saw the townlands
and learned the minds of many distant men,
and weathered many bitter nights and days
in his deep heart at sea, while he fought only
to save his life, to bring his shipmates home.
10 But not by will nor valor could he save them,
for their own recklessness destroyed them all—
children and fools, they killed and feasted on
the cattle of Lord Helios,[3] the Sun,
and he who moves all day through heaven
15 took from their eyes the dawn of their return.
Of these adventures, Muse, daughter of Zeus,[4]
tell us in our time, lift the great song again.

Note: In translating the *Odyssey*, Fitzgerald spelled Greek names to suggest the sound of the original Greek. In these excerpts, more familiar spellings have been used. For example, Fitzgerald's "Kirkê," "Kyklops," and "Seirênês" are spelled here as "Circe," "Cyclops," and "Sirens."

1. Muse (myo͞oz) any one of the nine goddesses of the arts, literature, and sciences; the spirit that is thought to inspire a poet or other artist.
2. Troy (troi) city in northwest Asia Minor; site of the Trojan War.

Vocabulary Builder
plundered (plun´ dərd)
v. took goods by force; looted

3. Helios (hē´ lē äs´) sun god.

4. Zeus (zo͞os) king of the gods.

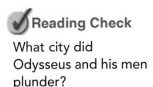

Reading Check

What city did Odysseus and his men plunder?

CHARACTERS

Alcinous (al sin´ ō əs)—king of the Phaeacians, to whom Odysseus tells his story

Odysseus (ō dis´ ē əs)—king of Ithaca

Calypso (kə lip´ sō)—sea goddess who loved Odysseus

Circe (sʉr´ sē)—enchantress who helped Odysseus

Zeus (zo͞os)—king of the gods

Apollo (ə päl´ ō)—god of music, poetry, prophecy, and medicine

Agamemnon (ag´ ə mem´ nän´)—king and leader of Greek forces

Poseidon (pō sī´ dən)—god of sea, earthquakes, horses, and storms at sea

Athena (ə thē´ nə)—goddess of wisdom, skills, and warfare

Polyphemus (päl´ i fē´ məs)—the Cyclops who imprisoned Odysseus

Laertes (lā ʉr´ tēz´)—Odysseus' father

Cronus (krō´ nəs)—Titan ruler of the universe; father of Zeus

Perimedes (per´ ə mē´ dēz)—member of Odysseus' crew

Eurylochus (yo͞o ril´ ə kəs)—another member of the crew

Tiresias (tī rē´ sē əs)—blind prophet who advised Odysseus

Persephone (pər sef´ ə nē)—wife of Hades

Telemachus (tə lem´ ə kəs)—Odysseus and Penelope's son

Sirens (sī´ rənz)—creatures whose songs lure sailors to their deaths

Scylla (sil´ ə)—sea monster of gray rock

Charybdis (kə rib´ dis)—enormous and dangerous whirlpool

Lampetia (lam pē´ shə)—nymph

Hermes (hʉr´ mēz´)—herald and messenger of the gods

Eumaeus (yo͞o mē´ əs)—old swineherd and friend of Odysseus

Antinous (an tin´ ō əs)—leader among the suitors

Eurynome (yo͞o rin´ ə mē)—housekeeper for Penelope

Penelope (pə nel´ ə pē)—Odysseus' wife

Eurymachus (yo͞o ri´ mə kəs)—suitor

Amphinomus (am fin´ ə məs)—suitor

Sailing from Troy

Ten years after the Trojan War, Odysseus departs from the goddess Calypso's island. He arrives in Phaeacia, ruled by Alcinous. Alcinous offers a ship to Odysseus and asks him to tell of his adventures.

"I am Laertes'[5] son, Odysseus.

       Men hold me

formidable for guile[6] in peace and war:

20 this fame has gone abroad to the sky's rim.

My home is on the peaked sea-mark of Ithaca[7]
under Mount Neion's wind-blown robe of leaves,
in sight of other islands—Dulichium,
Same, wooded Zacynthus—Ithaca

25 being most lofty in that coastal sea,
and northwest, while the rest lie east and south.
A rocky isle, but good for a boy's training;
I shall not see on earth a place more dear,
though I have been detained long by Calypso,[8]

30 loveliest among goddesses, who held me
in her smooth caves, to be her heart's delight,
as Circe of Aeaea,[9] the enchantress,
desired me, and detained me in her hall.
But in my heart I never gave consent.

35 Where shall a man find sweetness to surpass
his own home and his parents? In far lands
he shall not, though he find a house of gold.

What of my sailing, then, from Troy?

       What of those years
of rough adventure, weathered under Zeus?

40 The wind that carried west from Ilium[10]
brought me to Ismarus, on the far shore,
a strongpoint on the coast of Cicones.[11]
I stormed that place and killed the men who fought.
Plunder we took, and we enslaved the women,

45 to make division, equal shares to all—
but on the spot I told them: 'Back, and quickly!
Out to sea again!' My men were mutinous,[12]

5. Laertes (lā ʉr´ tēz´)

6. guile (gīl) *n.* craftiness; cunning.

7. Ithaca (i*th*´ ə kə) island off the west coast of Greece.

Literary Analysis
Epic Hero For what quality does Odysseus say he is famous?

8. Calypso (kə lip´ sō) sea goddess who loved Odysseus.

9. Circe (sʉr´ sē) **of Aeaea** (ē´ ē ə)

10. Ilium (il ē əm) Troy.

11. Cicones (si kō´ nēz)

12. mutinous (myo͞ot´'n əs) *adj.* rebellious.

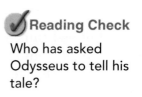

Reading Check

Who has asked Odysseus to tell his tale?

fools, on stores of wine. Sheep after sheep
they butchered by the surf, and shambling cattle,
50 feasting,—while fugitives went inland, running
to call to arms the main force of Cicones.
This was an army, trained to fight on horseback
or, where the ground required, on foot. They came
with dawn over that terrain like the leaves
55 and blades of spring. So doom appeared to us,
dark word of Zeus for us, our evil days.
My men stood up and made a fight of it—
backed on the ships, with lances kept in play,
from bright morning through the blaze of noon
60 holding our beach, although so far outnumbered;
but when the sun passed toward unyoking time,
then the Achaeans,[13] one by one, gave way.
Six benches were left empty in every ship
that evening when we pulled away from death.
65 And this new grief we bore with us to sea:
our precious lives we had, but not our friends.
No ship made sail next day until some shipmate
had raised a cry, three times, for each poor ghost
unfleshed by the Cicones on that field.

The Lotus-Eaters

70   Now Zeus the lord of cloud roused in the north
a storm against the ships, and driving veils
of squall moved down like night on land and sea.
The bows went plunging at the gust; sails
cracked and lashed out strips in the big wind.
75   We saw death in that fury, dropped the yards,
unshipped the oars, and pulled for the nearest lee:[14]
then two long days and nights we lay offshore
worn out and sick at heart, tasting our grief,
until a third Dawn came with ringlets shining.
80   Then we put up our masts, hauled sail, and rested,
letting the steersmen and the breeze take over.

I might have made it safely home, that time,
but as I came round Malea the current
took me out to sea, and from the north
85   a fresh gale drove me on, past Cythera.

13. Achaeans (ə kē´ ənz)
n. Greeks; here, Odysseus'
men.

Reading Skill
Historical and
Cultural Context
What beliefs and
values are reflected in
lines 65–69?

14. lee (lē) *n.* area sheltered
from the wind.

Literary Analysis
Epic Hero and
Flashback What
words in line 82
remind you that this
part is a flashback?

Nine days I drifted on the teeming sea
before dangerous high winds. Upon the tenth
we came to the coastline of the Lotus-Eaters,
who live upon that flower. We landed there
90 to take on water. All ships' companies
mustered alongside for the mid-day meal.
Then I sent out two picked men and a runner
to learn what race of men that land sustained.
They fell in, soon enough, with Lotus-Eaters,
95 who showed no will to do us harm, only
offering the sweet Lotus to our friends—
but those who ate this honeyed plant, the Lotus,
never cared to report, nor to return:
they longed to stay forever, browsing on
100 that native bloom, forgetful of their homeland.
I drove them, all three wailing, to the ships,
tied them down under their rowing benches,
and called the rest: 'All hands aboard;
come, clear the beach and no one taste
105 the Lotus, or you lose your hope of home.'
Filing in to their places by the rowlocks
my oarsmen dipped their long oars in the surf,
and we moved out again on our sea faring.

Literary Analysis
Epic Hero Which characteristics of an epic hero does Odysseus show in this episode?

Thinking About the Selection

1. **Respond:** What is your first impression of Odysseus? Which of his qualities do you admire? Explain.

2. **(a) Recall:** While on Ismarus, in what ways do Odysseus' men disobey orders? **(b) Analyze Cause and Effect:** What is the result of this disobedience? **(c) Speculate:** What lesson might Odysseus take away from this experience?

3. **(a) Recall:** What happens to the men who eat the Lotus? **(b) Infer:** What does this episode suggest about the main problem that Odysseus has with his men? **(c) Evaluate:** Do you think Odysseus responds appropriately to the three men who long to stay with the Lotus-Eaters? Why or why not?

4. **(a) Recall:** Note two points at which Odysseus mentions a desire to return home. **(b) Infer:** What significant role might his longing for home play in Odysseus' epic journey?

from the *Odyssey, Part I* ■ 955

The Cyclops

In the next land we found were Cyclopes,[15]
110   giants, louts, without a law to bless them.
In ignorance leaving the fruitage of the earth in mystery
to the immortal gods, they neither plow
nor sow by hand, nor till the ground, though grain—
wild wheat and barley—grows untended, and
115   wine-grapes, in clusters, ripen in heaven's rains.
Cyclopes have no muster and no meeting,
no consultation or old tribal ways,
but each one dwells in his own mountain cave
dealing out rough justice to wife and child,
120   indifferent to what the others do. . . .

As we rowed on, and nearer to the mainland,
at one end of the bay, we saw a cavern
yawning above the water, screened with laurel,
and many rams and goats about the place
125   inside a sheepfold—made from slabs of stone
earthfast between tall trunks of pine and rugged
towering oak trees.
                A prodigious[16] man
slept in this cave alone, and took his flocks
to graze afield—remote from all companions,
130   knowing none but savage ways, a brute
so huge, he seemed no man at all of those
who eat good wheaten bread; but he seemed rather
a shaggy mountain reared in solitude.
We beached there, and I told the crew
135   to stand by and keep watch over the ship:
as for myself I took my twelve best fighters
and went ahead. I had a goatskin full
of that sweet liquor that Euanthes' son,
Maron, had given me. He kept Apollo's[17]
140   holy grove at Ismarus; for kindness
we showed him there, and showed his wife and child,
he gave me seven shining golden talents[18]
perfectly formed, a solid silver winebowl,
and then this liquor—twelve two-handled jars
145   of brandy, pure and fiery. Not a slave
in Maron's household knew this drink; only
he, his wife and the storeroom mistress knew;

15. Cyclopes (sī klō′ pēz′) *n.* plural form of **Cyclops** (sī′ kläps′), race of giants with one eye in the middle of the forehead.

Reading Skill
Historical and Cultural Context Based on Odysseus' criticism of the Cyclopes, what kind of society do you think the Greeks valued?

16. prodigious (prō dij′ əs) *adj.* enormous.

Reading Skill
Historical and Cultural Context What does this passage reveal about ancient Greek attitudes toward the importance of community?

17. Apollo (ə päl′ ō) god of music, poetry, prophecy, and medicine.

18. talents units of money in ancient Greece.

and they would put one cupful—ruby-colored,
honey-smooth—in twenty more of water,
150 but still the sweet scent hovered like a fume
over the winebowl. No man turned away
when cups of this came round.

                                    A wineskin full
I brought along, and victuals[19] in a bag,
for in my bones I knew some towering brute
155 would be upon us soon—all outward power,
a wild man, ignorant of civility.

We climbed, then, briskly to the cave. But Cyclops
had gone afield, to pasture his fat sheep,
so we looked round at everything inside:
160 a drying rack that sagged with cheeses, pens
crowded with lambs and kids,[20] each in its class:
firstlings apart from middlings, and the 'dewdrops,'
or newborn lambkins, penned apart from both.
And vessels full of whey[21] were brimming there—
165 bowls of earthenware and pails for milking.
My men came pressing round me, pleading:

19. victuals (vit′ ə'lz) *n.* food or other provisions.

20. kids young goats.

21. whey (hwā) *n.* thin, watery part of milk separated from the thicker curds.

☑ **Reading Check**

Where is Cyclops when Odysseus and his men enter the cave?

◄ **Critical Viewing**
How does this image of Apollo compare with your impressions of the ancient Greek gods? **[Compare and Contrast]**

'Why not
take these cheeses, get them stowed, come back,
throw open all the pens, and make a run for it?
We'll drive the kids and lambs aboard. We say
170   put out again on good salt water!'

                      Ah,
how sound that was! Yet I refused. I wished
to see the cave man, what he had to offer—
no pretty sight, it turned out, for my friends.
We lit a fire, burnt an offering,
175   and took some cheese to eat; then sat in silence
around the embers, waiting. When he came
he had a load of dry boughs[22] on his shoulder
to stoke his fire at suppertime. He dumped it
with a great crash into that hollow cave,
180   and we all scattered fast to the far wall.
Then over the broad cavern floor he ushered
the ewes he meant to milk. He left his rams
and he-goats in the yard outside, and swung
high overhead a slab of solid rock
185   to close the cave. Two dozen four-wheeled wagons,
with heaving wagon teams, could not have stirred
the tonnage of that rock from where he wedged it
over the doorsill. Next he took his seat
and milked his bleating ewes. A practiced job
190   he made of it, giving each ewe her suckling;
thickened his milk, then, into curds and whey,
sieved out the curds to drip in withy[23] baskets,
and poured the whey to stand in bowls
cooling until he drank it for his supper.
195   When all these chores were done, he poked the fire,
heaping on brushwood. In the glare he saw us.

'Strangers,' he said, 'who are you? And where from?
What brings you here by seaways—a fair traffic?
Or are you wandering rogues, who cast your lives
200   like dice, and ravage other folk by sea?'

We felt a pressure on our hearts, in dread
of that deep rumble and that mighty man.
But all the same I spoke up in reply:

Literary Analysis
Epic Hero What character flaw does the hero Odysseus reveal by refusing to leave the cave?

22. boughs (bouz) *n.* tree branches.

23. withy (with′ ē) *adj.* made from tough, flexible twigs.

'We are from Troy, Achaeans, blown off course
205 by shifting gales on the Great South Sea;
homeward bound, but taking routes and ways
uncommon; so the will of Zeus would have it.
We served under Agamemnon,[24] son of Atreus—
the whole world knows what city
210 he laid waste, what armies he destroyed.
It was our luck to come here; here we stand,
beholden for your help, or any gifts
you give—as custom is to honor strangers.
We would entreat you, great Sir, have a care
215 for the gods' courtesy; Zeus will avenge
the unoffending guest.'

                        He answered this

from his brute chest, unmoved:

                               'You are a ninny,
or else you come from the other end of nowhere,
telling me, mind the gods! We Cyclopes
220 care not a whistle for your thundering Zeus
or all the gods in bliss; we have more force by far.
I would not let you go for fear of Zeus—
you or your friends—unless I had a whim[25] to.
Tell me, where was it, now, you left your ship—
225 around the point, or down the shore, I wonder?'

He thought he'd find out, but I saw through this,
and answered with a ready lie:

                               'My ship?
Poseidon[26] Lord, who sets the earth a-tremble,
broke it up on the rocks at your land's end.
230 A wind from seaward served him, drove us there.
We are survivors, these good men and I.'

Neither reply nor pity came from him,
but in one stride he clutched at my companions
and caught two in his hands like squirming puppies
235 to beat their brains out, spattering the floor.
Then he dismembered them and made his meal,
gaping and crunching like a mountain lion—
everything: innards, flesh, and marrow bones.
We cried aloud, lifting our hands to Zeus,
240 powerless, looking on at this, appalled;

24. Agamemnon (ag´ ə mem´ nän´) king who led the Greek army during the Trojan War.

Reading Skill
Historical and Cultural Context What ancient Greek beliefs regarding the gods, military might, and respect for strangers does Odysseus express in his words to the Cyclops?

25. whim (hwim) n. sudden thought or wish to do something.

26. Poseidon (pō sī dən) god of the sea, earthquakes, horses, and storms at sea.

Literary Analysis
Epic Hero In what way does Odysseus' response show that he is "formidable for guile"?

✓**Reading Check**

What does Odysseus tell the Cyclops happened to his ship?

but Cyclops went on filling up his belly
with manflesh and great gulps of whey,
then lay down like a mast among his sheep.
My heart beat high now at the chance of action,
245   and drawing the sharp sword from my hip I went
along his flank to stab him where the midriff
holds the liver. I had touched the spot
when sudden fear stayed me: if I killed him
we perished there as well, for we could never
250   move his ponderous doorway slab aside.
So we were left to groan and wait for morning.

When the young Dawn with fingertips of rose
lit up the world, the Cyclops built a fire
and milked his handsome ewes, all in due order,
255   putting the sucklings to the mothers. Then,
his chores being all <u>dispatched</u>, he caught
another brace²⁷ of men to make his breakfast,
and whisked away his great door slab
to let his sheep go through—but he, behind,
260   reset the stone as one would cap a quiver.²⁸
There was a din²⁹ of whistling as the Cyclops
rounded his flock to higher ground, then stillness.
And now I pondered how to hurt him worst,
if but Athena³⁰ granted what I prayed for.
265   Here are the means I thought would serve my turn:

a club, or staff, lay there along the fold—
an olive tree, felled green and left to season³¹
for Cyclops' hand. And it was like a mast
a lugger³² of twenty oars, broad in the beam—
270   a deep-sea-going craft—might carry:
so long, so big around, it seemed. Now I
chopped out a six foot section of this pole
and set it down before my men, who scraped it;
and when they had it smooth, I hewed again
275   to make a stake with pointed end. I held this
in the fire's heart and turned it, toughening it,
then hid it, well back in the cavern, under
one of the dung piles in profusion there.
Now came the time to toss for it: who ventured
280   along with me? whose hand could bear to thrust
and grind that spike in Cyclops' eye, when mild

Literary Analysis
Epic Hero How do
lines 244–250 show
Odysseus' ability to
think ahead?

Vocabulary Builder
dispatched (di spacht´)
v. finished quickly

27. brace (brās) *n.* pair.

28. cap a quiver (kwiv´
ər) close a case holding
arrows.

29. din (din) *n.* loud, continuous noise; uproar.

30. Athena (ə thē´ nə)
goddess of wisdom, skills,
and warfare.

**31. felled green and left to
season** chopped down and
exposed to the weather to age
the wood.

32. lugger (lug´ ər) *n.* small
sailing vessel.

▼ **Critical Viewing**
What traits does
this statue of
Athena illustrate?
[Interpret]

sleep had mastered him? As luck would have it,
the men I would have chosen won the toss—
four strong men, and I made five as captain.

285   At evening came the shepherd with his flock,
his woolly flock. The rams as well, this time,
entered the cave: by some sheepherding whim—
or a god's bidding—none were left outside.
He hefted his great boulder into place
290   and sat him down to milk the bleating ewes
in proper order, put the lambs to suck,
and swiftly ran through all his evening chores.
Then he caught two more men and feasted on them.
My moment was at hand, and I went forward
295   holding an ivy bowl of my dark drink,
looking up, saying:

                              'Cyclops, try some wine.
Here's liquor to wash down your scraps of men.
Taste it, and see the kind of drink we carried
under our planks. I meant it for an offering
300   if you would help us home. But you are mad,
unbearable, a bloody monster! After this,
will any other traveler come to see you?'

He seized and drained the bowl, and it went down
so fiery and smooth he called for more:

305   'Give me another, thank you kindly. Tell me,
how are you called? I'll make a gift will please you.
Even Cyclopes know the wine grapes grow
out of grassland and loam in heaven's rain,
but here's a bit of nectar and ambrosia!'[33]

310   Three bowls I brought him, and he poured them down.
I saw the fuddle and flush come over him,
then I sang out in cordial tones:

                              'Cyclops,
you ask my honorable name? Remember
the gift you promised me, and I shall tell you.
315   My name is Nohbdy: mother, father, and friends,
everyone calls me Nohbdy.'

Literary Analysis
Epic Hero What heroic qualities does Odysseus reveal as he plots against the Cyclops?

Literary Analysis
Epic Hero What plan do you think Odysseus has in mind by offering the Cyclops the wine?

33. nectar (nek′ tər) **and ambrosia** (am brō′ zhə) drink and food of the gods.

Reading Check

What does Odysseus plan to do with the stake that he and his men make?

And he said:

'Nohbdy's my meat, then, after I eat his friends.
Others come first. There's a noble gift, now.'

Even as he spoke, he reeled and tumbled backward,
320 his great head lolling to one side; and sleep
took him like any creature. Drunk, hiccuping,
he dribbled streams of liquor and bits of men.

Now, by the gods, I drove my big hand spike
deep in the embers, charring it again,
325 and cheered my men along with battle talk
to keep their courage up: no quitting now.
The pike of olive, green though it had been,
reddened and glowed as if about to catch.
I drew it from the coals and my four fellows
330 gave me a hand, lugging it near the Cyclops
as more than natural force nerved them; straight
forward they sprinted, lifted it, and rammed it
deep in his crater eye, and leaned on it
turning it as a shipwright turns a drill
335 in planking, having men below to swing
the two-handled strap that spins it in the groove.
So with our brand we bored[34] that great eye socket
while blood ran out around the red-hot bar.
Eyelid and lash were seared; the pierced ball
340 hissed broiling, and the roots popped.

In a smithy
one sees a white-hot axehead or an adze
plunged and wrung in a cold tub, screeching steam—
the way they make soft iron hale and hard—:
just so that eyeball hissed around the spike.
345 The Cyclops bellowed and the rock roared round him,
and we fell back in fear. Clawing his face
he tugged the bloody spike out of his eye,
threw it away, and his wild hands went groping;
then he set up a howl for Cyclopes
350 who lived in caves on windy peaks nearby.
Some heard him; and they came by divers[35] ways
to clump around outside and call:

'What ails you,

Polyphemus?[36] Why do you cry so sore
in the starry night? You will not let us sleep.

Reading Skill
Historical and Cultural Context What cultural values are represented in Odysseus' reference to "the gods" in line 323?

34. bored (bôrd) *v.* made a hole in.

35. divers (dī′ vərz) *adj.* several; various.

36. Polyphemus (päl′ i fē′ məs)

355　Sure no man's driving off your flock? No man
　　has tricked you, ruined you?'

　　　　　　　　　　　　　　　　　Out of the cave

　　the <u>mammoth</u> Polyphemus roared in answer:

　　'Nohbdy, Nohbdy's tricked me, Nohbdy's ruined me!'

　　To this rough shout they made a sage[37] reply:

360　'Ah well, if nobody has played you foul
　　there in your lonely bed, we are no use in pain
　　given by great Zeus. Let it be your father,
　　Poseidon Lord, to whom you pray.'

　　　　　　　　　　　　　　　　　So saying

　　they trailed away. And I was filled with laughter
365　to see how like a charm the name deceived them.
　　Now Cyclops, wheezing as the pain came on him,
　　fumbled to wrench away the great doorstone
　　and squatted in the breach with arms thrown wide
　　for any silly beast or man who bolted—
370　hoping somehow I might be such a fool.
　　But I kept thinking how to win the game:
　　death sat there huge; how could we slip away?
　　I drew on all my wits, and ran through tactics,
　　reasoning as a man will for dear life,
375　until a trick came—and it pleased me well.
　　The Cyclops' rams were handsome, fat, with heavy
　　fleeces, a dark violet.

　　　　　　　　　　　　　　　Three abreast

　　I tied them silently together, twining
　　cords of willow from the ogre's bed;
380　then slung a man under each middle one
　　to ride there safely, shielded left and right.
　　So three sheep could convey each man. I took
　　the woolliest ram, the choicest of the flock,
　　and hung myself under his kinky belly,
385　pulled up tight, with fingers twisted deep
　　in sheepskin ringlets for an iron grip.
　　So, breathing hard, we waited until morning.

　　When Dawn spread out her fingertips of rose
　　the rams began to stir, moving for pasture,

Vocabulary Builder
mammoth (mam´ əth) *adj.* enormous

37. **sage** (sāj) *adj.* wise.

Literary Analysis
Epic Hero What does Odysseus' gleeful response to his successful trick reveal about his character?

 Reading Check

What do the other Cyclopes think Polyphemus is saying when he says, "Nohbdy's tricked me"?

390　and peals of bleating echoed round the pens
　　　where dams with udders full called for a milking.
　　　Blinded, and sick with pain from his head wound,
　　　the master stroked each ram, then let it pass,
　　　but my men riding on the pectoral[38] fleece
395　the giant's blind hands blundering never found.
　　　Last of them all my ram, the leader, came,
　　　weighted by wool and me with my meditations.
　　　The Cyclops patted him, and then he said:

　　　'Sweet cousin ram, why lag behind the rest
400　in the night cave? You never linger so,
　　　but graze before them all, and go afar
　　　to crop sweet grass, and take your stately way
　　　leading along the streams, until at evening
　　　you run to be the first one in the fold.
405　Why, now, so far behind? Can you be grieving
　　　over your Master's eye? That carrion rogue[39]
　　　and his accurst companions burnt it out
　　　when he had conquered all my wits with wine.
　　　Nohbdy will not get out alive, I swear.
410　Oh, had you brain and voice to tell
　　　where he may be now, dodging all my fury!
　　　Bashed by this hand and bashed on this rock wall
　　　his brains would strew the floor, and I should have
　　　rest from the outrage Nohbdy worked upon me.'

415　He sent us into the open, then. Close by,
　　　I dropped and rolled clear of the ram's belly,
　　　going this way and that to untie the men.
　　　With many glances back, we rounded up
　　　his fat, stiff-legged sheep to take aboard,
420　and drove them down to where the good ship lay.
　　　We saw, as we came near, our fellows' faces
　　　shining; then we saw them turn to grief
　　　tallying those who had not fled from death.
　　　I hushed them, jerking head and eyebrows up,
425　and in a low voice told them: 'Load this herd;
　　　move fast, and put the ship's head toward the breakers.'
　　　They all pitched in at loading, then embarked
　　　and struck their oars into the sea. Far out,
　　　as far off shore as shouted words would carry,
430　I sent a few back to the adversary:

38. pectoral (pek′ tə rəl)
adj. located in or on the chest.

39. carrion (kar′ ē ən) **rogue**
(rōg) repulsive scoundrel.

**Literary Analysis
Epic Hero** What
details of this speech
show that Polyphemus
is far less clever than
Odysseus?

'O Cyclops! Would you feast on my companions?
Puny, am I, in a cave man's hands?
How do you like the beating that we gave you,
you damned cannibal? Eater of guests
435 under your roof! Zeus and the gods have paid you!'

The blind thing in his doubled fury broke
a hilltop in his hands and heaved it after us.
Ahead of our black prow it struck and sank
whelmed in a spuming geyser, a giant wave
440 that washed the ship stern foremost back to shore.
I got the longest boathook out and stood
fending us off, with furious nods to all
to put their backs into a racing stroke—
row, row, or perish. So the long oars bent
445 kicking the foam sternward, making head
until we drew away, and twice as far.
Now when I cupped my hands I heard the crew
in low voices protesting:

                                    'Godsake, Captain!
Why bait the beast again? Let him alone!'

450 'That tidal wave he made on the first throw
all but beached us.'

                              'All but stove us in!'
'Give him our bearing with your trumpeting,
he'll get the range and lob a boulder.'

                                             'Aye
He'll smash our timbers and our heads together!'
455 I would not heed them in my glorying spirit,
but let my anger flare and yelled:

                                          'Cyclops,
if ever mortal man inquire
how you were put to shame and blinded, tell him
Odysseus, raider of cities, took your eye:
460 Laertes' son, whose home's on Ithaca!'

At this he gave a mighty sob and rumbled:
'Now comes the weird[40] upon me, spoken of old.
A wizard, grand and wondrous, lived here—Telemus,[41]
a son of Eurymus;[42] great length of days

Literary Analysis
Epic Hero Despite
his heroism, what
human weaknesses
does Odysseus
reveal as he sails
away?

40. weird (wird) *n.* fate or
destiny.

41. Telemus (tel e´ məs)

42. Eurymus (yo͞o rim´ əs)

Reading Check

How do the men
escape from Cyclops'
cave?

465　he had in wizardry among the Cyclopes,
　　and these things he foretold for time to come:
　　my great eye lost, and at Odysseus' hands.
　　Always I had in mind some giant, armed
　　in giant force, would come against me here.
470　But this, but you—small, pitiful and twiggy—
　　you put me down with wine, you blinded me.
　　Come back, Odysseus, and I'll treat you well,
　　praying the god of earthquake[43] to befriend you—
　　his son I am, for he by his avowal
475　fathered me, and, if he will, he may
　　heal me of this black wound—he and no other
　　of all the happy gods or mortal men.'

　　Few words I shouted in reply to him:

　　'If I could take your life I would and take
480　your time away, and hurl you down to hell!
　　The god of earthquake could not heal you there!'

　　At this he stretched his hands out in his darkness
　　toward the sky of stars, and prayed Poseidon:

　　'O hear me, lord, blue girdler of the islands,
485　if I am thine indeed, and thou art father:
　　grant that Odysseus, raider of cities, never
　　see his home: Laertes' son, I mean,
　　who kept his hall on Ithaca. Should destiny
　　intend that he shall see his roof again
490　among his family in his father land,
　　far be that day, and dark the years between.
　　Let him lose all companions, and return
　　under strange sail to bitter days at home.'

43. god of earthquake
Poseidon.

Reading Skill
Historical and Cultural Context What do lines 472–493 suggest about ancient Greek beliefs about the gods' involvement in the mortal world?

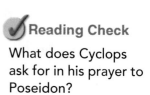**Reading Check**

What does Cyclops ask for in his prayer to Poseidon?

Polyphemus, The Cyclops N. C. Wyeth, Delaware Art Museum

▲ **Critical Viewing** Odysseus and his surviving men escape in their ship as the blinded Cyclops hurls boulders and curses. How does this illustration compare to your mental image of the scene? **[Analyze]**

In these words he prayed, and the god heard him.
495 Now he laid hands upon a bigger stone
and wheeled around, titanic for the cast,
to let it fly in the black-prowed vessel's track.
But it fell short, just aft the steering oar,
and whelming seas rose giant above the stone
500 to bear us onward toward the island.
                                    There
as we ran in we saw the squadron waiting,
the trim ships drawn up side by side, and all
our troubled friends who waited, looking seaward.
We beached her, grinding keel in the soft sand,
505 and waded in, ourselves, on the sandy beach.
Then we unloaded all the Cyclops' flock
to make division, share and share alike,
only my fighters voted that my ram,
the prize of all, should go to me. I slew him
510 by the seaside and burnt his long thighbones
to Zeus beyond the stormcloud, Cronus'[44] son,
who rules the world. But Zeus disdained my offering:
destruction for my ships he had in store
and death for those who sailed them, my companions.
515 Now all day long until the sun went down
we made our feast on mutton and sweet wine,
till after sunset in the gathering dark
we went to sleep above the wash of ripples.

When the young Dawn with fingertips of rose
520 touched the world, I roused the men, gave orders
to man the ships, cast off the mooring lines;
and filing in to sit beside the rowlocks
oarsmen in line dipped oars in the gray sea.
So we moved out, sad in the vast offing,[45]
525 having our precious lives, but not our friends.

44. Cronus (krō′ nəs) Titan who was ruler of the universe until he was overthrown by his son Zeus.

Literary Analysis
Epic Hero What admirable quality does Odysseus show by dividing the sheep among his men?

45. offing (ôf′ iŋ) *n.* distant part of the sea visible from the shore.

The Land of the Dead

Odysseus and his men sail to Aeolia, where Aeolus,[46] king of the winds, sends Odysseus on his way with a gift: a sack containing all the winds except the favorable west wind. When they are near home, Odysseus' men open the sack, letting loose a storm that drives them back to Aeolia. Aeolus casts them out, having decided that they are detested by the gods. They sail for seven days and arrive in the land of the Laestrygonians,[47] a race of cannibals. These creatures destroy all of Odysseus' ships except the one he is sailing in. Odysseus and his reduced crew escape and reach Aeaea, the island ruled by the sorceress-goddess Circe. She transforms half of the men into swine. Protected by a magic herb, Odysseus demands that Circe change his men back into human form. Before Odysseus departs from the island a year later, Circe informs him that in order to reach home he must journey to the land of the dead, Hades, and consult the blind prophet Tiresias.

46. Aeolia (ē ō´ lē ə) . . .
Aeolus (ē´ ə ləs)

47. Laestrygonians (les tri gō´ nē ənz)

We bore down on the ship at the sea's edge
and launched her on the salt immortal sea,
stepping our mast and spar in the black ship;
embarked the ram and ewe and went aboard
530   in tears, with bitter and sore dread upon us.
But now a breeze came up for us astern—
a canvas-bellying landbreeze, hale shipmate
sent by the singing nymph with sunbright hair;[48]
so we made fast the braces, took our thwarts,
535   and let the wind and steersman work the ship
with full sail spread all day above our coursing,
till the sun dipped, and all the ways grew dark
upon the fathomless unresting sea.

        By night
our ship ran onward toward the Ocean's bourne,
540   the realm and region of the Men of Winter,
hidden in mist and cloud. Never the flaming
eye of Helios lights on those men
at morning, when he climbs the sky of stars,
nor in descending earthward out of heaven;
545   ruinous night being rove over those wretches.
We made the land, put ram and ewe ashore,
and took our way along the Ocean stream
to find the place foretold for us by Circe.

48. singing nymph . . . hair Circe.

Reading Skill
Historical and Cultural Context
What details here suggest that the source of wind was mysterious to ancient Greeks?

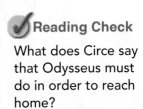
Reading Check

What does Circe say that Odysseus must do in order to reach home?

Odysseus in the Land of the Dead, N. C. Wyeth, Delaware Art Museum

▲ **Critical Viewing** What can you infer about ancient Greek beliefs concerning death and the afterlife from lines 555–577 and from this illustration? **[Infer]**

There Perimedes and Eulylochus[49]
550 pinioned[50] the sacred beasts. With my drawn blade
I spaded up the votive[51] pit, and poured
libations[52] round it to the unnumbered dead:
sweet milk and honey, then sweet wine, and last
clear water; and I scattered barley down.
555 Then I addressed the blurred and breathless dead,
vowing to slaughter my best heifer for them
before she calved, at home in Ithaca,
and burn the choice bits on the altar fire;
as for Tiresias, I swore to sacrifice
560 a black lamb, handsomest of all our flock.
Thus to <u>assuage</u> the nations of the dead
I pledged these rites, then slashed the lamb and ewe,
letting their black blood stream into the wellpit.
Now the souls gathered, stirring out of Erebus,[53]
565 brides and young men, and men grown old in pain,
and tender girls whose hearts were new to grief;
many were there, too, torn by brazen lanceheads,
battle-slain, bearing still their bloody gear.
From every side they came and sought the pit
570 with rustling cries; and I grew sick with fear.
But presently I gave command to my officers
to flay those sheep the bronze cut down, and make
burnt offerings of flesh to the gods below—
to sovereign Death, to pale Persephone.[54]
575 Meanwhile I crouched with my drawn sword to keep
the surging phantoms from the bloody pit
till I should know the presence of Tiresias.[55]

One shade came first—Elpenor, of our company,
who lay unburied still on the wide earth
580 as we had left him—dead in Circe's hall,
untouched, unmourned, when other cares compelled us.
Now when I saw him there I wept for pity
and called out to him:

49. Perimedes (per´ ə mē´ dēz)
and Eurylochus (yoo ril´ ə kəs)

50. pinioned (pin´ yənd) v.
confined or shackled.

51. votive (vōt´ iv) adj. done to
fulfill a vow or express thanks.

52. libations (lī bā´ shənz) n.
wine or other liquids poured
upon the ground as a sacrifice
or offering.

Vocabulary Builder
assuage (ə swāj´) v.
calm; pacify

53. Erebus (er´ ə bəs) dark
region under the earth through
which the dead pass before
entering the realm of Hades.

54. Persephone (pər sef´ ə
nē) wife of Hades.

55. Tiresias (tī rē´ sē əs)

✓ Reading Check

Whom is Odysseus
trying to summon by
making sacrifices?

'How is this, Elpenor,
how could you journey to the western gloom
585 swifter afoot than I in the black lugger?'
He sighed, and answered:

'Son of great Laertes,
Odysseus, master mariner and soldier,
bad luck shadowed me, and no kindly power;
ignoble death I drank with so much wine.
590 I slept on Circe's roof, then could not see
the long steep backward ladder, coming down,
and fell that height. My neckbone, buckled under,
snapped, and my spirit found this well of dark.
Now hear the grace I pray for, in the name
595 of those back in the world, not here—your wife
and father, he who gave you bread in childhood,
and your own child, your only son, Telemachus,[56]
long ago left at home.

When you make sail
and put these lodgings of dim Death behind,
600 you will moor ship, I know, upon Aeaea Island;
there, O my lord, remember me, I pray,
do not abandon me unwept, unburied,
to tempt the gods' wrath, while you sail for home;
but fire my corpse, and all the gear I had,
605 and build a cairn[57] for me above the breakers—
an unknown sailor's mark for men to come.
Heap up the mound there, and implant upon it
the oar I pulled in life with my companions.'

He ceased, and I replied:

'Unhappy spirit,
610 I promise you the barrow and the burial.'

So we conversed, and grimly, at a distance,
with my long sword between, guarding the blood,
while the faint image of the lad spoke on.
Now came the soul of Anticlea, dead,
615 my mother, daughter of Autolycus,[58]
dead now, though living still when I took ship
for holy Troy. Seeing this ghost I grieved,
but held her off, through pang on pang of tears,
till I should know the presence of Tiresias.

▲ **Critical Viewing**
How do the characters
on this vase compare
with your image of the
characters in the
Odyssey? **[Compare
and Contrast]**

56. **Telemachus** (tə lem´ ə kəs)

57. **cairn** (kern) *n.* conical
heap of stones built as a monument.

58. **Autolycus** (ô täl´ i kəs)

Reading Skill
**Historical and
Cultural Context**
What ancient Greek
values and beliefs are
suggested by
Elpenor's requests?

620 Soon from the dark that prince of Thebes[59] came forward
bearing a golden staff; and he addressed me:

'Son of Laertes and the gods of old,
Odysseus, master of landways and seaways,
why leave the blazing sun, O man of woe,
625 to see the cold dead and the joyless region?
Stand clear, put up your sword;
let me but taste of blood, I shall speak true.'

At this I stepped aside, and in the scabbard
let my long sword ring home to the pommel silver,
630 as he bent down to the somber blood. Then spoke
the prince of those with gift of speech:

               'Great captain,
a fair wind and the honey lights of home
are all you seek. But anguish lies ahead;
the god who thunders on the land prepares it,
635 not to be shaken from your track, implacable,
in rancor for the son whose eye you blinded.
One narrow strait may take you through his blows:
denial of yourself, restraint of shipmates.
When you make landfall on Thrinacia first
640 and quit the violet sea, dark on the land
you'll find the grazing herds of Helios
by whom all things are seen, all speech is known.
Avoid those kine,[60] hold fast to your intent,
and hard seafaring brings you all to Ithaca.
645 But if you raid the beeves, I see destruction
for ship and crew. Though you survive alone,
<u>bereft</u> of all companions, lost for years,
under strange sail shall you come home, to find
your own house filled with trouble: insolent men
650 eating your livestock as they court your lady.
Aye, you shall make those men atone in blood!
But after you have dealt out death—in open
combat or by stealth—to all the suitors,
go overland on foot, and take an oar,
655 until one day you come where men have lived
with meat unsalted, never known the sea,
nor seen seagoing ships, with crimson bows
and oars that fledge light hulls for dipping flight.
The spot will soon be plain to you, and I

Reading Skill
Historical and
Cultural Context
What ancient Greek value is reflected in the "narrow strait" that Tiresias describes (lines 637–638)?

60. kine (kīn) *n.* cattle.

Vocabulary Builder
bereft (bē reft´) *adj.*
deprived

Reading Check

According to Tiresias, what will Odysseus find when he returns home?

660 can tell you how: some passerby will say,
   "What winnowing fan is that upon your shoulder?"
   Halt, and implant your smooth oar in the turf
   and make fair sacrifice to Lord Poseidon:
   a ram, a bull, a great buck boar; turn back,
665 and carry out pure hecatombs[61] at home
   to all wide heaven's lords, the undying gods,
   to each in order. Then a seaborne death
   soft as this hand of mist will come upon you
   when you are wearied out with rich old age,
670 your country folk in blessed peace around you.
   And all this shall be just as I foretell.'

61. hecatombs (hek′ ə tōmz′) *n.* large-scale sacrifices to the gods in ancient Greece; often, the slaughter of 100 cattle at one time.

Thinking About the Selection

1. **Respond:** What do you think of Odysseus' plan for escaping from Polyphemus? Explain.

2. **(a) Recall:** Before the meeting with the Cyclops, what had Odysseus received from Maron at Ismarus? **(b) Generalize:** What does the encounter with Maron reveal about ancient Greek attitudes regarding hospitality?

3. **(a) Recall:** How do Odysseus and his companions expect to be treated by the Cyclops? **(b) Infer:** What "laws" of behavior and attitude does Polyphemus violate?

4. **(a) Summarize:** How do Odysseus and his crew escape from the Cyclops? **(b) Evaluate:** What positive and negative character traits does Odysseus demonstrate in his adventure with the Cyclops?

5. **(a) Compare and Contrast:** Compare and Contrast Odysseus' reactions to the three ghosts he meets in the Land of the Dead— Elpenor, Anticlea, and Tiresias. **(b) Analyze:** What character trait does Odysseus display in the Land of the Dead that he did not reveal earlier?

6. **(a) Summarize:** What difficulty does Tiresias predict for the journey to come? **(b) Speculate:** Why would Odysseus continue, despite the grim prophecies?

7. **(a) Assess:** Judging from Tiresias' prediction, which heroic qualities will Odysseus need to rely upon as he continues his journey? Explain.

The Sirens

Odysseus returns to Circe's island. The goddess reveals his course to him and gives advice on how to avoid the dangers he will face: the Sirens, who lure sailors to their destruction; the Wandering Rocks, sea rocks that destroy even birds in flight; the perils of the sea monster Scylla and, nearby, the whirlpool Charybdis;[62] and the cattle of the sun god, which Tiresias has warned Odysseus not to harm.

62. Charybdis (kə rib´ dis)

As Circe spoke, Dawn mounted her golden throne,
and on the first rays Circe left me, taking
her way like a great goddess up the island.

675   I made straight for the ship, roused up the men
to get aboard and cast off at the stern.
They scrambled to their places by the rowlocks
and all in line dipped oars in the gray sea.
But soon an offshore breeze blew to our liking—

680   a canvas-bellying breeze, a lusty shipmate
sent by the singing nymph with sunbright hair.
So we made fast the braces, and we rested,
letting the wind and steersman work the ship.
The crew being now silent before me, I

685   addressed them, sore at heart:

                          'Dear friends,
more than one man, or two, should know those things
Circe foresaw for us and shared with me,
so let me tell her forecast: then we die
with our eyes open, if we are going to die,

690   or know what death we baffle if we can. Sirens
weaving a haunting song over the sea
we are to shun, she said, and their green shore
all sweet with clover; yet she urged that I
alone should listen to their song. Therefore

695   you are to tie me up, tight as a splint,
erect along the mast, lashed to the mast,
and if I shout and beg to be untied,
take more turns of the rope to muffle me.'

I rather dwelt on this part of the forecast,
700   while our good ship made time, bound outward down
the wind for the strange island of Sirens.

Literary Analysis
Epic Hero What does Odysseus reveal about his character by sharing information with his men?

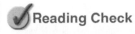

Reading Check

What instructions does Odysseus give his shipmates as they prepare to deal with the Sirens?

▲ Critical Viewing The sorceress Circe both helps and hinders Odysseus on his journey home. What can you tell about Circe from this illustration? [Deduce]

Then all at once the wind fell, and a calm
came over all the sea, as though some power
lulled the swell.

                  The crew were on their feet
705   briskly, to furl the sail, and stow it; then,
each in place, they poised the smooth oar blades
and sent the white foam scudding by. I carved
a massive cake of beeswax into bits
and rolled them in my hands until they softened—
710   no long task, for a burning heat came down
from Helios, lord of high noon. Going forward
I carried wax along the line, and laid it
thick on their ears. They tied me up, then, plumb
amidships, back to the mast, lashed to the mast,
715   and took themselves again to rowing. Soon,
as we came smartly within hailing distance,
the two Sirens, noting our fast ship
off their point, made ready, and they sang:

>   *This way, oh turn your bows,*
> 720   *Achaea's glory,*
>   *As all the world allows—*
>   *Moor and be merry.*
>
>   *Sweet coupled airs we sing.*
>   *No lonely seafarer*
> 725   *Holds clear of entering*
>   *Our green mirror.*
>
>   *Pleased by each purling note*
>   *Like honey twining*

Reading Skill
Historical and Cultural Context
What does Odysseus' mention of Helios reveal about ancient Greek beliefs regarding astronomical events?

☑ **Reading Check**

How does Odysseus keep his shipmates from hearing the Sirens sing?

From her throat and my throat,
Who lies a-pining?

Sea rovers here take joy
Voyaging onward,
As from our song of Troy
Graybeard and rower-boy
Goeth more learnèd.

All feats on that great field
In the long warfare,
Dark days the bright gods willed,
Wounds you bore there,

Argos' old soldiery [63]
On Troy beach teeming,
Charmed out of time we see.
No life on earth can be
Hid from our dreaming.

The lovely voices in <u>ardor</u> appealing over the water
made me crave to listen, and I tried to say
'Untie me!' to the crew, jerking my brows;
but they bent steady to the oars. Then Perimedes
got to his feet, he and Eurylochus,
and passed more line about, to hold me still.
So all rowed on, until the Sirens
dropped under the sea rim, and their singing
dwindled away.

                                    My faithful company
rested on their oars now, peeling off
the wax that I had laid thick on their ears;
then set me free.

Scylla and Charybdis

                         But scarcely had that island
faded in blue air than I saw smoke
and white water, with sound of waves in tumult—
a sound the men heard, and it terrified them.
Oars flew from their hands; the blades went knocking
wild alongside till the ship lost way,
with no oar blades to drive her through the water.

Literary Analysis
Epic Hero Which details in the Sirens' song are designed to flatter the epic hero?

63. Argos' old soldiery soldiers from Argos, a city in ancient Greece.

Vocabulary Builder
ardor (är´ dər) *n.* passion; enthusiasm

Well, I walked up and down from bow to stern,
trying to put heart into them, standing over
765 every oarsman, saying gently,

'Friends,
have we never been in danger before this?
More fearsome, is it now, than when the Cyclops
penned us in his cave? What power he had!
Did I not keep my nerve, and use my wits
770 to find a way out for us?

Now I say
by hook or crook this peril too shall be
something that we remember.

Heads up, lads!
We must obey the orders as I give them.
Get the oar shafts in your hands, and lay back
775 hard on your benches; hit these breaking seas.
Zeus help us pull away before we founder.
You at the tiller, listen, and take in
all that I say—the rudders are your duty;
keep her out of the combers and the smoke;[64]
780 steer for that headland; watch the drift, or we
fetch up in the smother, and you drown us.'

That was all, and it brought them round to action.
But as I sent them on toward Scylla,[65] I
told them nothing, as they could do nothing.
785 They would have dropped their oars again, in panic,
to roll for cover under the decking. Circe's
bidding against arms had slipped my mind,
so I tied on my cuirass[66] and took up
two heavy spears, then made my way along
790 to the foredeck—thinking to see her first from there,
the monster of the gray rock, harboring
torment for my friends. I strained my eyes
upon the cliffside veiled in cloud, but nowhere
could I catch sight of her.
And all this time,
795 in travail,[67] sobbing, gaining on the current,
we rowed into the strait—Scylla to port
and on our starboard beam Charybdis, dire

Literary Analysis
Epic Hero What parts of Odysseus' speech demonstrate his strength as a leader?

64. the combers (kōm′ ərs) **and the smoke** the large waves that break on the beach and the ocean spray.

65. Scylla (sil′ ə)

66. cuirass (kwi ras′) *n.* armor for the upper body.

67. travail (trə vāl′) *n.* very hard work.

Reading Check

What demand does Odysseus make of his men as they approach the rough waters?

gorge[68] of the salt seatide. By heaven! when she
vomited, all the sea was like a cauldron
800 seething over intense fire, when the mixture
suddenly heaves and rises.

                                 The shot spume
soared to the landside heights, and fell like rain.
But when she swallowed the sea water down
we saw the funnel of the maelstrom,[69] heard
805 the rock bellowing all around, and dark
sand raged on the bottom far below.
My men all blanched against the gloom, our eyes
were fixed upon that yawning mouth in fear
of being devoured.

                         Then Scylla made her strike,
810 whisking six of my best men from the ship.
I happened to glance aft at ship and oarsmen
and caught sight of their arms and legs, dangling
high overhead. Voices came down to me
in anguish, calling my name for the last time.

815 A man surfcasting on a point of rock
for bass or mackerel, whipping his long rod
to drop the sinker and the bait far out,
will hook a fish and rip it from the surface
to dangle wriggling through the air:

                               so these
820 were borne aloft in spasms toward the cliff.

She ate them as they shrieked there, in her den,
in the dire grapple, reaching still for me—
and deathly pity ran me through
at that sight—far the worst I ever suffered,
825 questing the passes of the strange sea.

                            We rowed on.
The Rocks were now behind; Charybdis, too,
and Scylla dropped astern.

The Cattle of the Sun God

In the small hours of the third watch, when stars
that shone out in the first dusk of evening
830 had gone down to their setting, a giant wind

---

68. gorge (gôrj) *n.* throat or gullet.

69. maelstrom (māl´ strəm) *n.* large, violent whirlpool.

Literary Analysis
Epic Hero What quality of heroic leadership does Odysseus show in lines 823–825?

blew from heaven, and clouds driven by Zeus
shrouded land and sea in a night of storm;
so, just as Dawn with fingertips of rose
touched the windy world, we dragged our ship
835 to cover in a grotto, a sea cave
where nymphs had chairs of rock and sanded floors.
I mustered all the crew and said:

                'Old shipmates,
our stores are in the ship's hold, food and drink;
the cattle here are not for our provision,
840 or we pay dearly for it.

                Fierce the god is
who cherishes these heifers and these sheep:
Helios; and no man avoids his eye.'

To this my fighters nodded. Yes. But now
we had a month of onshore gales, blowing
845 day in, day out—south winds, or south by east.
As long as bread and good red wine remained
to keep the men up, and appease their craving,
they would not touch the cattle. But in the end,
when all the barley in the ship was gone,
850 hunger drove them to scour the wild shore
with angling hooks, for fishes and seafowl,
whatever fell into their hands; and lean days
wore their bellies thin.

                The storms continued.
So one day I withdrew to the interior
855 to pray the gods in solitude, for hope
that one might show me some way of salvation.
Slipping away, I struck across the island
to a sheltered spot, out of the driving gale.
I washed my hands there, and made supplication
860 to the gods who own Olympus,[70] all the gods—
but they, for answer, only closed my eyes
under slow drops of sleep.

             Now on the shore Eurylochus
made his <u>insidious</u> plea:

                'Comrades,' he said,
'You've gone through everything; listen to what I say.
865 All deaths are hateful to us, mortal wretches,
but famine is the most pitiful, the worst
end that a man can come to.

Reading Skill
Historical and Cultural Context
Which details here suggest that ancient Greeks believed the gods controlled the weather?

Reading Skill
Historical and Cultural Context
How does this passage show that ancient Greeks believed their gods had human-like emotions?

70. Olympus (ō lim′ pəs) Mount Olympus, home of the gods.

Vocabulary Builder
insidious (in sid′ ē əs) *adj.* characterized by craftiness and betrayal

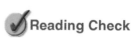Reading Check

Who owns the heifers and sheep on the island?

Will you fight it?

Come, we'll cut out the noblest of these cattle
for sacrifice to the gods who own the sky;
870 and once at home, in the old country of Ithaca,
if ever that day comes—
we'll build a costly temple and adorn it
with every beauty for the Lord of Noon.[71]
But if he flares up over his heifers lost,
875 wishing our ship destroyed, and if the gods
make cause with him, why, then I say: Better
open your lungs to a big sea once for all
than waste to skin and bones on a lonely island!'

Thus Eurylochus; and they murmured 'Aye!'
880 trooping away at once to round up heifers.
Now, that day tranquil cattle with broad brows
were gazing near, and soon the men drew up
around their chosen beasts in ceremony.
They plucked the leaves that shone on a tall oak—
885 having no barley meal—to strew the victims,
performed the prayers and ritual, knifed the kine
and flayed each carcass, cutting thighbones free
to wrap in double folds of fat. These offerings,
with strips of meat, were laid upon the fire.
890 Then, as they had no wine, they made libation
with clear spring water, broiling the entrails first;
and when the bones were burnt and tripes shared,
they spitted the carved meat.

Just then my slumber
left me in a rush, my eyes opened,
895 and I went down the seaward path. No sooner
had I caught sight of our black hull, than savory
odors of burnt fat eddied around me;
grief took hold of me, and I cried aloud:

'O Father Zeus and gods in bliss forever,
900 you made me sleep away this day of mischief!
O cruel drowsing, in the evil hour!
Here they sat, and a great work they contrived.'[72]

Lampetia[73] in her long gown meanwhile
had borne swift word to the Overlord of Noon:

71. Lord of Noon Helios.

Literary Analysis
Epic Hero How are
the values of
Eurylochus different
from those of
Odysseus?

72. contrived (kən trīvd')
v. thought up; devised.

73. Lampetia (lam pē′ shə) a
nymph.

Real Places and Imaginary Events in the *Odyssey*

Odysseus' journey carries him to real places, including Troy, Sparta, and the Strait of Gibraltar. However, in the story, many of these real places are populated by imaginary creatures, such as the Cyclops and the Sirens. The combination of real places and fantastic events is part of the story's appeal.

Connect to the Literature Why does the inclusion of real places make the story's imaginary events more believable?

905   'They have killed your kine.'

               And the Lord Helios
   burst into angry speech amid the immortals:

   'O Father Zeus and gods in bliss forever,
   punish Odysseus' men! So overweening,
   now they have killed my peaceful kine, my joy
910   at morning when I climbed the sky of stars,
   and evening, when I bore westward from heaven.
   Restitution or penalty they shall pay—
   and pay in full—or I go down forever
   to light the dead men in the underworld.'

915   Then Zeus who drives the stormcloud made reply:

Reading Check

What do Odysseus' shipmates do while he is sleeping?

from the *Odyssey, Part I* ■ 983

'Peace, Helios: shine on among the gods,
shine over mortals in the fields of grain.
Let me throw down one white-hot bolt, and make
splinters of their ship in the winedark sea.'

920   —Calypso later told me of this exchange,
as she declared that Hermes[74] had told her.
Well, when I reached the sea cave and the ship,
I faced each man, and had it out; but where
could any remedy be found? There was none.
925   The silken beeves[75] of Helios were dead.
The gods, moreover, made queer signs appear:
cowhides began to crawl, and beef, both raw
and roasted, lowed like kine upon the spits.

Now six full days my gallant crew could feast
930   upon the prime beef they had marked for slaughter
from Helios' herd; and Zeus, the son of Cronus,
added one fine morning.

                              All the gales
had ceased, blown out, and with an offshore breeze
we launched again, stepping the mast and sail,
935   to make for the open sea. Astern of us
the island coastline faded, and no land
showed anywhere, but only sea and heaven,
when Zeus Cronion piled a thunderhead
above the ship, while gloom spread on the ocean.
940   We held our course, but briefly. Then the squall
struck whining from the west, with gale force, breaking
both forestays, and the mast came toppling aft
along the ship's length, so the running rigging
showered into the bilge.

                              On the afterdeck
945   the mast had hit the steersman a slant blow
bashing the skull in, knocking him overside,
as the brave soul fled the body, like a diver.
With crack on crack of thunder, Zeus let fly
a bolt against the ship, a direct hit,
950   so that she bucked, in reeking fumes of sulphur,
and all the men were flung into the sea.
They came up 'round the wreck, bobbing awhile
like petrels[76] on the waves.

74. Hermes (hur´ mēz´) *n.*
god who serves as herald and
messenger of the other gods.

75. beeves (bēvz) *n.*
alternate plural form of "beef."

Literary Analysis
Epic Hero and
Flashback
What details in
lines 920–921 clarify
the flashback
presented here?

76. petrels (pe´ trəlz) *n.*
small, dark sea birds.

No more seafaring
homeward for these, no sweet day of return;
955 the god had turned his face from them.

                                    I clambered

fore and aft my hulk until a comber
split her, keel from ribs, and the big timber
floated free; the mast, too, broke away.
A backstay floated dangling from it, stout
960 rawhide rope, and I used this for lashing
mast and keel together. These I straddled,
riding the frightful storm.

                                    Nor had I yet

seen the worst of it: for now the west wind
dropped, and a southeast gale came on—one more
965 twist of the knife—taking me north again,
straight for Charybdis. All that night I drifted,
and in the sunrise, sure enough, I lay
off Scylla mountain and Charybdis deep.
There, as the whirlpool drank the tide, a billow
970 tossed me, and I sprang for the great fig tree,
catching on like a bat under a bough.
Nowhere had I to stand, no way of climbing,
the root and bole[77] being far below, and far
above my head the branches and their leaves,
975 massed, overshadowing Charybdis pool.
But I clung grimly, thinking my mast and keel
would come back to the surface when she spouted.
And ah! how long, with what desire, I waited!
till, at the twilight hour, when one who hears
980 and judges pleas in the marketplace all day
between contentious men, goes home to supper,
the long poles at last reared from the sea.

Now I let go with hands and feet, plunging
straight into the foam beside the timbers,
985 pulled astride, and rowed hard with my hands
to pass by Scylla. Never could I have passed her
had not the Father of gods and men,[78] this time,
kept me from her eyes. Once through the strait,
nine days I drifted in the open sea
990 before I made shore, buoyed up by the gods,

Literary Analysis
Epic Hero Which of
Odysseus' heroic
qualities does he
demonstrate in this
passage?

77. **bole** (bōl) *n.* tree trunk.

78. **Father . . . men** Zeus.

Reading Check

How is Odysseus' ship
destroyed?

La Nef de Telemachus (The Ship of Telemachus), New York Public Library Picture Collection

▲ **Critical Viewing** In the *Odyssey*, Odysseus' son Telemachus searches for his father in a ship like this one. From what you observe in the painting, how does this ship compare with modern ships? **[Compare and Contrast]**

upon Ogygia[79] Isle. The dangerous nymph
Calypso lives and sings there, in her beauty,
and she received me, loved me.

But why tell
the same tale that I told last night in hall
995　to you and to your lady? Those adventures
made a long evening, and I do not hold
with tiresome repetition of a story."

79. **Ogygia** (o jij′ ī ə)

**Literary Analysis
Epic Hero and
Flashback** In what
way do lines 994–997
remind you that
Odysseus is telling his
story to an audience?

Thinking About the Selection

1. **Respond:** In which adventure in this section do you think Odysseus acts most heroically? Explain.

2. **(a) Recall:** How do the Sirens lure travelers to their destruction? **(b) Compare and Contrast:** How does the danger posed by the Sirens compare to that posed by the Lotus-Eaters?

3. **(a) Make a Judgment:** Was Odysseus right not to tell his men about his decision to sail toward Scylla? **(b) Hypothesize:** What might have happened if Odysseus had told them everything?

4. **(a) Recall:** What does Eurylochus say to persuade the crew to kill the cattle of the sun god? **(b) Analyze:** After all the men have experienced, why do you think they still disobey Odysseus' command? **(c) Relate:** If you had been in their position, do you think you would have eaten the cattle? Why or why not?

5. **(a) Make a Judgment:** Do the members of the crew deserve the punishment they receive for killing the cattle? Explain.

Apply the Skills

from the *Odyssey*, Part 1

Thinking About the Selection

1. **Respond:** If you were one of Odysseus' crew, how would you feel about having him as your leader? Explain your response.
2. **(a) Recall:** In the episode of the Lotus-Eaters, how does Odysseus handle the men who ate the lotus? **(b) Interpret:** What does Odysseus understand that his men do not?
3. **(a) Recall:** In the episode of the Cattle of the Sun God, why does the crew kill the cattle? **(b) Interpret:** How does Odysseus react to this action? **(c) Analyze:** What does Odysseus' reaction show about the importance of the gods to him?
4. **(a) Evaluate:** The *Odyssey* has entertained people for thousands of years. Why do you think it has remained such an enduring work of literature? **(b) Discuss:** In a small group, share your ideas. As a group, choose one response to share with the class.

Literary Analysis

5. **(a)** Using a chart like the one shown as a model, identify three other actions that the **epic hero** Odysseus performs. **(b)** For each action, identify the character trait that it reveals. **(c)** Based on your responses, explain which character traits the ancient Greeks admired most.

Action		**Trait**
Resists temptations of Calypso and Circe.	**Odysseus**	Self-control

6. Odysseus recounts most of the action in Part 1 in the form of a **flashback.** List the events of Part 1 in chronological sequence, beginning with the end of the Trojan War.
7. The epic hero recounts his own adventures. In what way does this affect your reaction to the events he describes? Explain.

Reading Skill

8. Consider the **cultural and historical context** of Homer's *Odyssey.* What role do ancient Greek religious beliefs play in the epic? Explain your answer.
9. What abilities or features of modern technology could have helped Odysseus on his journey had they been available in ancient times? Explain your answer.

QuickReview

Part 1 at a Glance
The hero Odysseus enjoys amazing adventures and endures great hardships on his quest to return home.

Go nline
—Assessment
For: Self-test
Visit: www.PHSchool.com
Web Code: epa-6602

Epic Hero: the larger-than-life central character in an epic

Flashback: a scene that interrupts the sequence of events in a narrative to relate earlier events

Historical and Cultural Context: the events, beliefs, and customs that define the time and place in which a work is set or in which it was written

Vocabulary Builder

Practice Identify the word in each group that does not belong with the others. Explain your response.

1. *plundered,* robbed, donated
2. *dispatched,* hesitated, completed
3. *mammoth,* small, tiny
4. *assuage,* soothe, increase
5. *bereft,* after, without
6. *ardor,* spirited, careless
7. *insidious,* traitorous, friendly

Adding Words to Your Vocabulary The word *dispatched* is the past-tense form of the verb *dispatch,* which means "finish quickly." Use a dictionary to find the definition of the noun *dispatcher,* which has a very different meaning. Then, explain how the words are related. (For more on using a dictionary, see page R6.)

Writing

Write an **everyday epic.** Choose an everyday event and write an account that makes it seem larger than life. Recite your work for the class.

- Outline the plot of your story, adding points for epic traits such as adventure, bravery, and extreme challenges. Plan appearances by gods and monsters.
- Use multiple points of view. Begin with the voice of a speaker outside the story, and then have one of the characters tell the tale.

For *Grammar, Vocabulary,* and *Assessment,* see **Build Language Skills,** pages 990–991.

Extend Your Learning

Listening and Speaking With two classmates, improvise an **everyday conversation** among ordinary Greeks discussing *Odysseus'* exploits. Each character's statements should reflect the ancient Greek values shown in the *Odyssey.*

Research and Technology Use library and Internet resources to research the complete story of the *Odyssey.* Then, create an **illustrated travelogue** that shows the sequence of Odysseus' wanderings. Include pictures of the places that Odysseus visited, and describe the events that took place in each location.

Build Language Skills

from the *Odyssey*, Part 1

Vocabulary Skill

Word Roots Knowing that the *prefix contra-* means "against" provides a clue to the meaning of the word *controversy*, which is "parties having opinions against each other."

▶ **Example:** There is a *controversy* over who actually wrote the Shakespearean plays.

Practice Use each of the following words in an original sentence. Then, explain how knowing the meaning of the prefix *contra-* provides a context clue for understanding the sentence.

1. contraband   2. contradict   3. contraindicate   4. contraposition

Grammar Lesson

Simple and Compound Sentences A **simple sentence** consists of a single independent clause. Although a simple sentence is just one independent clause with one subject and one verb, the subject, verb, or both may be compound.

A **compound sentence** consists of two or more independent clauses. The clauses can be joined by a comma and a coordinating conjunction or by a semicolon.

MorePractice

For more practice with simple and compound sentences, see the Grammar Handbook, p. R40.

Simple sentence	He remembered an old story.
Simple sentence with compound subject	He and she remembered an old story.
Compound sentence	The stars shone, and they remembered an old story.

Practice Identify each of the following sentences as simple or compound. For compound sentences, identify the coordinating conjunction.

1. Marvin went outside.
2. He looked down the street, but he saw no one.
3. The weather was perfect after the rain.
4. He wanted to start a game, so he looked for his friends.
5. They played all afternoon and into the evening.

W︠G Prentice Hall Writing and Grammar Connection: Chapter 21, Section 2

Monitor Your Progress

Reading Skill: Analyzing Cultural and Historical Context

Standards Assessed
• WL.1.01.1
• IR.2.04.1
• LT.5.01.2

Directions: *Read the selection. Then, answer the questions.*

King Acrisius of Argos had one child, a daughter, Danae. She was extremely beautiful, but this was no comfort to the King, who wished for a son. He journeyed to Delphi to ask the god if there was any hope that some day he would be the father of a boy. The priestess told him no, and added that his daughter would have a son who would kill him.

—"Perseus"

1. From the cultural and historical context of this passage, what can a reader infer that the ancient Greeks valued?
   A beautiful children above all
   B boy and girl children equally
   C girls more highly than boys
   D boys more highly than girls

2. From the cultural and historical context of this passage, what can a reader infer that the ancient Greeks believed?
   A All kings must journey to Delphi.
   B Oracles can foretell the future.
   C Greek princesses were more beautiful than any others.
   D Every generation fears destruction by its own offspring.

3. What common human trait does the king demonstrate?
   A a desire to know the future
   B the wish to have a daughter
   C a lack of respect
   D the desire to travel

4. From the context of this passage, what can the reader infer?
   A The culture is similar to modern American culture.
   B The culture has several points in common with modern American culture.
   C The culture has little in common with modern American culture.
   D The culture is not indicated.

Timed Writing: Explanation [Critical Stance]

The *Odyssey* has always been considered an important work. Write an explanation of why Western culture has valued this epic. Use details from the text to support your assumptions. **(30 minutes)**

 Writing Workshop: *Work in Progress*

Assessment Writing

Using your Background List, add major characters and stages of the plot of the literary works. Then, add the major cause-effect sequence to each historical event. Save this work in your writing portfolio.

Literary Analysis

An **epic simile** is an elaborate comparison that may extend for several lines. Epic similes may use the words *like, as, just as,* or *so* to make the comparison. Unlike a normal simile, which draws a comparison to a single, distinct image, an epic simile is longer and more involved. It might recall an entire place or story. In Part 1, lines 268–271, Odysseus uses an epic simile to stress the size of the fallen tree from which he creates a weapon.

> And it was like a mast / a lugger of twenty oars,
> broad in the beam— / a deep-sea-going craft—might carry: /
> so long, so big around, it seemed.

As you read, notice how Homer uses epic similes—sometimes called Homeric similes—to bring descriptions to life.

NC **Standard Course of Study**

- Apply a set of predetermined standards to critique communication. (CT.4.01.2)
- Provide textual evidence to support understanding of critical text. (CT.4.03.3)
- Use and place modifiers correctly. (GU.6.02.3)

Reading Skill

The **historical and cultural context** of a work is the backdrop of details of the time and place in which the work is set or in which it was written. These details include the events, beliefs, and customs of a specific culture and time. When you **identify influences on your own reading and responses,** the historical and cultural context reflected in a work becomes more apparent.

- As you read a work from another time and culture, keep your own beliefs and customs in mind.
- Notice the ways in which your reactions to ideas and situations in the work differ from the reactions of the characters.
- Consider whether your reactions reflect your cultural values.

Use a chart like the one shown to note the differences between your own influences and those reflected in the *Odyssey*.

Detail in Text

Odysseus says he and his crew plundered Ismarus.

Meaning for Characters

Winners can take valuables from the defeated.

Meaning in My Culture

Looting is shameful.

Vocabulary Builder

- **dissemble** (di sem´ bəl) *v.* conceal under a false appearance; disguise (p. 994) *The spy was able to dissemble and seem like a patriot.*

- **incredulity** (in´ krə dōō´ lə tē) *n.* unwillingness or inability to believe (p. 996) *During the eclipse, they were silent with incredulity.*

- **bemusing** (bē myōōz´ iŋ) *v.* stupefying or muddling (p. 999) *After bemusing the audience, the speaker received little applause.*

- **equity** (ek´ wit ē) *n.* fairness; justice (p. 1004) *Laws are meant to treat everyone with equity.*

- **maudlin** (môd´ lin) *adj.* tearfully and foolishly sentimental (p. 1004) *The soap opera evoked maudlin responses in the audience.*

- **contempt** (kən tempt´) *n.* disdain or scorn (p. 1011) *A good athlete shows respect, not contempt, for an opponent.*

from the

Odyssey

Homer Translated by Robert Fitzgerald

PART 2

The Return of Odysseus

Review and Anticipate

In Part 1 of the Odyssey, *Odysseus and his companions face many perils on their voyage from Troy to Ithaca. At some moments, they are tempted to forsake their voyage; at others, their lives are endangered by powerful enemies. Ultimately, Odysseus' men bring about their own destruction at the hand of Zeus when they kill the cattle belonging to Helios.*

As Part 2 begins, Odysseus is alone when he reaches Ithaca after a twenty-year absence. What do you predict will happen when Odysseus arrives home?

"Twenty years gone, and I am back again . . ."

Odysseus has finished telling his story to the Phaeacians. The next day, young Phaeacian noblemen conduct him home by ship. He arrives in Ithaca after an absence of twenty years. The goddess Athena appears and informs him of the situation at home. Numerous suitors, believing Odysseus to be dead, have been continually seeking the hand of his wife, Penelope, in marriage, while overrunning Odysseus' palace and enjoying themselves at Penelope's expense. Moreover, they are plotting to murder Odysseus' son, Telemachus, before he can inherit his father's lands. Telemachus, who, like Penelope, still hopes for his father's return, has journeyed to Pylos and Sparta to learn what he can about his father's fate. Athena disguises Odysseus as a beggar and directs him to the hut of Eumaeus,[1] his old and faithful swineherd. While Odysseus and Eumaeus are eating breakfast, Telemachus arrives. Athena then appears to Odysseus.

1. Eumaeus (yo͞o mē´ əs)

         . . . From the air
she walked, taking the form of a tall woman,
handsome and clever at her craft, and stood
1000 beyond the gate in plain sight of Odysseus,
unseen, though, by Telemachus, unguessed,
for not to everyone will gods appear.
Odysseus noticed her; so did the dogs,
who cowered whimpering away from her. She only
1005 nodded, signing to him with her brows,
a sign he recognized. Crossing the yard,
he passed out through the gate in the stockade
to face the goddess. There she said to him:

"Son of Laertes and the gods of old,
1010 Odysseus, master of landways and seaways,
<u>dissemble</u> to your son no longer now.
The time has come: tell him how you together
will bring doom on the suitors in the town.
I shall not be far distant then, for I
1015 myself desire battle."

                  Saying no more,
she tipped her golden wand upon the man,
making his cloak pure white, and the knit tunic
fresh around him. Lithe and young she made him,

▲ **Critical Viewing** What can you tell about Eumaeus from this illustration? **[Infer]**

ruddy with sun, his jawline clean, the beard
1020 no longer gray upon his chin. And she
withdrew when she had done.

                                 Then Lord Odysseus
reappeared—and his son was thunderstruck.
Fear in his eyes, he looked down and away
as though it were a god, and whispered:

                                       "Stranger,
1025 you are no longer what you were just now!
Your cloak is new; even your skin! You are
one of the gods who rule the sweep of heaven!
Be kind to us, we'll make you fair oblation[2]
and gifts of hammered gold. Have mercy on us!"

1030 The noble and enduring man replied:

"No god. Why take me for a god? No, no.
I am that father whom your boyhood lacked
and suffered pain for lack of. I am he."

Held back too long, the tears ran down his cheeks
1035 as he embraced his son.

                                 Only Telemachus,
uncomprehending, wild
with incredulity, cried out:

                                    "You cannot
be my father Odysseus! Meddling spirits
conceived this trick to twist the knife in me!
1040 No man of woman born could work these wonders
by his own craft, unless a god came into it
with ease to turn him young or old at will.
I swear you were in rags and old,
and here you stand like one of the immortals!"

1045 Odysseus brought his ranging mind to bear
and said:

                         "This is not princely, to be swept
away by wonder at your father's presence.
No other Odysseus will ever come,
for he and I are one, the same; his bitter
1050 fortune and his wanderings are mine.
Twenty years gone, and I am back again
on my own island.

**Reading Skill
Historical and
Cultural Context**
What do lines 1021–
1029 suggest about
the way ancient
Greeks responded
to the presence of
a god?

2. oblation (äb lā´ shən)
n. offering to a god.

**Vocabulary Builder
incredulity** (in´ krə doo͞´
lə tē) *n.* unwillingness
or inability to believe

As for my change of skin,
that is a charm Athena, Hope of Soldiers,
uses as she will; she has the knack
1055 to make me seem a beggar man sometimes
and sometimes young, with finer clothes about me.
It is no hard thing for the gods of heaven
to glorify a man or bring him low."

When he had spoken, down he sat.
                                 Then, throwing
1060 his arms around this marvel of a father
Telemachus began to weep. Salt tears
rose from the wells of longing in both men,
and cries burst from both as keen and fluttering
as those of the great taloned hawk,
1065 whose nestlings farmers take before they fly.
So helplessly they cried, pouring out tears,
and might have gone on weeping so till sundown,
had not Telemachus said:

                                 "Dear father! Tell me
what kind of vessel put you here ashore
1070 on Ithaca? Your sailors, who were they?
I doubt you made it, walking on the sea!"

Then said Odysseus, who had borne the barren sea:

"Only plain truth shall I tell you, child.
Great seafarers, the Phaeacians, gave me passage
1075 as they give other wanderers. By night
over the open ocean, while I slept,
they brought me in their cutter,[3] set me down
on Ithaca, with gifts of bronze and gold
and stores of woven things. By the gods' will
1080 these lie all hidden in a cave. I came
to this wild place, directed by Athena,
so that we might lay plans to kill our enemies.
Count up the suitors for me, let me know
what men at arms are there, how many men.
1085 I must put all my mind to it, to see
if we two by ourselves can take them on
or if we should look round for help."
                                 Telemachus
replied:

Literary Analysis
Epic Simile To what are Odysseus' and Telemachus' cries compared in the epic simile in lines 1063-1065?

3. cutter (kut´ər) *n.* small, swift ship or boat carried aboard a large ship to transport personnel or supplies.

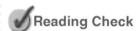

Reading Check

Why is Telemachus initially doubtful that the man before him is Odysseus, his father?

              "O Father, all my life your fame
as a fighting man has echoed in my ears—
1090   your skill with weapons and the tricks of war—
but what you speak of is a staggering thing,
beyond imagining, for me. How can two men
do battle with a houseful in their prime?[4]
For I must tell you this is no affair
1095   of ten or even twice ten men, but scores,
throngs of them. You shall see, here and now.
The number from Dulichium alone
is fifty-two picked men, with armorers,
a half dozen; twenty-four came from Same,
1100   twenty from Zacynthus; our own island
accounts for twelve, high-ranked, and their retainers,
Medon the crier, and the Master Harper,
besides a pair of handymen at feasts.
If we go in against all these
1105   I fear we pay in salt blood for your vengeance.
You must think hard if you would conjure up
the fighting strength to take us through."

                             Odysseus

who had endured the long war and the sea
answered:

                        "I'll tell you now.

1110   Suppose Athena's arm is over us, and Zeus
her father's, must I rack my brains for more?"

Clearheaded Telemachus looked hard and said:

"Those two are great defenders, no one doubts it,
but throned in the serene clouds overhead;
1115   other affairs of men and gods they have
to rule over."

                   And the hero answered:
"Before long they will stand to right and left of us
in combat, in the shouting, when the test comes—
our nerve against the suitors' in my hall.
1120   Here is your part: at break of day tomorrow
home with you, go mingle with our princes.
The swineherd later on will take me down
the port-side trail—a beggar, by my looks,
hangdog and old. If they make fun of me
1125   in my own courtyard, let your ribs cage up

4. in their prime in the best or most vigorous stage of their lives.

Reading Skill
Historical and Cultural Context
What does Odysseus' statement in lines 1109–1111 suggest about ancient Greek beliefs about the gods' interest in human affairs?

your springing heart, no matter what I suffer,
no matter if they pull me by the heels
or practice shots at me, to drive me out.
Look on, hold down your anger. You may even
1130 plead with them, by heaven! in gentle terms
to quit their horseplay—not that they will heed you,
rash as they are, facing their day of wrath.
Now fix the next step in your mind.

                                              Athena,
     counseling me, will give me word, and I
1135 shall signal to you, nodding: at that point
     round up all armor, lances, gear of war
     left in our hall, and stow the lot away
     back in the vaulted storeroom. When the suitors
     miss those arms and question you, be soft
1140 in what you say: answer:

                         'I thought I'd move them
     out of the smoke. They seemed no longer those
     bright arms Odysseus left us years ago
     when he went off to Troy. Here where the fire's
     hot breath came, they had grown black and drear.
1145 One better reason, too, I had from Zeus:
     suppose a brawl starts up when you are drunk,
     you might be crazed and bloody one another,
     and that would stain your feast, your courtship. Tempered
     iron can magnetize a man.'
                                      Say that.

1150 But put aside two broadswords and two spears
     for our own use, two oxhide shields nearby
     when we go into action. Pallas Athena
     and Zeus All-Provident will see you through,
     <u>bemusing</u> our young friends.
                              Now one thing more.
1155 If son of mine you are and blood of mine,
     let no one hear Odysseus is about.
     Neither Laertes, nor the swineherd here,
     nor any slave, nor even Penelope.
     But you and I alone must learn how far
1160 the women are corrupted; we should know
     how to locate good men among our hands,
     the loyal and respectful, and the shirkers[5]
     who take you lightly, as alone and young."

Literature in Context

Cultural Connection

Athena Athena was the goddess of wisdom, skills, and warfare. When she helps Odysseus in this epic, it is not the first time that she offers assistance to a Greek hero. In Homer's *Iliad,* Athena helps the Greek hero Achilles defeat the Trojan warrior Hector. Athena favored Achilles for his unmatched skill in battle, but Odysseus was her favorite among the Greeks. He displayed not only skill in warfare, but also ingenuity and cunning.

Connect to the Literature

Which of Odysseus' deeds in the *Odyssey* might have helped him to earn Athena's favor? Explain.

Vocabulary Builder
bemusing (bē myo͞oz´ iŋ) *v.* stupefying or muddling

5. shirkers (shʉrk´ ərz) *n.* people who get out of doing what needs to be done.

 Reading Check

How does Odysseus tell his son to respond if the suitors "practice shots" on Odysseus?

Argus

*Odysseus heads for town with Eumaeus. Outside the palace,
Odysseus' old dog, Argus, is lying at rest as his long-absent
master approaches.*

While he spoke

an old hound, lying near, pricked up his ears
1165 and lifted up his muzzle. This was Argus,
trained as a puppy by Odysseus,
but never taken on a hunt before
his master sailed for Troy. The young men, afterward,
hunted wild goats with him, and hare, and deer,
1170 but he had grown old in his master's absence.
Treated as rubbish now, he lay at last
upon a mass of dung before the gates—
manure of mules and cows, piled there until
fieldhands could spread it on the king's estate.
1175 Abandoned there, and half destroyed with flies,
old Argus lay.

But when he knew he heard

Odysseus' voice nearby, he did his best
to wag his tail, nose down, with flattened ears,
having no strength to move nearer his master.
1180 And the man looked away,
wiping a salt tear from his cheek; but he
hid this from Eumaeus. Then he said:

"I marvel that they leave this hound to lie
here on the dung pile;
1185 he would have been a fine dog, from the look of him,
though I can't say as to his power and speed
when he was young. You find the same good build
in house dogs, table dogs landowners keep
all for style."

And you replied, Eumaeus:

1190 "A hunter owned him—but the man is dead
in some far place. If this old hound could show
the form he had when Lord Odysseus left him,
going to Troy, you'd see him swift and strong.
He never shrank from any savage thing
1195 he'd brought to bay in the deep woods; on the scent

▼ Critical Viewing
What can you infer
about the ancient
Greeks based on the
fact that they depicted
their gods on everyday
objects like this urn?
[Infer]

no other dog kept up with him. Now misery
has him in leash. His owner died abroad,
and here the women slaves will take no care of him.
You know how servants are: without a master
1200 they have no will to labor, or excel.
For Zeus who views the wide world takes away
half the manhood of a man, that day
he goes into captivity and slavery."

Eumaeus crossed the court and went straight forward
1205 into the megaron[6] among the suitors:
but death and darkness in that instant closed
the eyes of Argus, who had seen his master,
Odysseus, after twenty years.

The Suitors

*Still disguised as a beggar, Odysseus enters his home. He is
confronted by the haughty[7] suitor Antinous.[8]*

But here Antinous broke in, shouting:

                                             "God!
1210 What evil wind blew in this pest?

                                             Get over,
stand in the passage! Nudge my table, will you?
Egyptian whips are sweet
to what you'll come to here, you nosing rat,
making your pitch to everyone!
1215 These men have bread to throw away on you
because it is not theirs. Who cares? Who spares
another's food, when he has more than plenty?"

With guile Odysseus drew away, then said:

"A pity that you have more looks than heart.
1220 You'd grudge a pinch of salt from your own larder
to your own handyman. You sit here, fat
on others' meat, and cannot bring yourself
to rummage out a crust of bread for me!"

Then anger made Antinous' heart beat hard,
1225 and, glowering under his brows, he answered:

Reading Skill
**Historical and
Cultural Context**
How do Eumaeus'
beliefs about
servitude and slavery
compare with those of
your own culture?

6. **megaron** (meg´ ə rön)
n. great, central hall of the
house, usually containing a
center hearth.

7. **haughty** (hôt´ ē) *adj.*
arrogant.

8. **Antinous** (an tin´ ō əs)

Reading Check

How does Antinous
react to Odysseus,
who is disguised as a
beggar?

"Now!
You think you'll shuffle off and get away
after that impudence?[9] Oh, no you don't!"

The stool he let fly hit the man's right shoulder
on the packed muscle under the shoulder blade—
1230   like solid rock, for all the effect one saw.
Odysseus only shook his head, containing
thoughts of bloody work, as he walked on,
then sat, and dropped his loaded bag again
upon the door sill. Facing the whole crowd
1235   he said, and eyed them all:

"One word only,
my lords, and suitors of the famous queen.
One thing I have to say.
There is no pain, no burden for the heart
when blows come to a man, and he defending
1240   his own cattle—his own cows and lambs.
Here it was otherwise. Antinous
hit me for being driven on by hunger—
how many bitter seas men cross for hunger!
If beggars interest the gods, if there are Furies[10]
1245   pent in the dark to avenge a poor man's wrong, then may
Antinous meet his death before his wedding day!"

Then said Eupeithes' son, Antinous:

"Enough.
Eat and be quiet where you are, or shamble elsewhere,
unless you want these lads to stop your mouth
1250   pulling you by the heels, or hands and feet,
over the whole floor, till your back is peeled!"

But now the rest were mortified, and someone
spoke from the crowd of young bucks to rebuke him:

"A poor show, that—hitting this famished tramp—
1255   bad business, if he happened to be a god.
You know they go in foreign guise, the gods do,
looking like strangers, turning up
in towns and settlements to keep an eye
on manners, good or bad."

But at this notion

1002 ■ *Themes in Literature: Heroism*

Reading Skill
Historical and
Cultural Context
What conflicting
values does this
exchange between
Antinous and
Odysseus reveal?

9. impudence (im´ pyōō
dəns) *n.* quality of being
shamelessly bold; disrespectful.

Reading Skill
Historical and
Cultural Context
What values regarding
the use of physical
force are evident in
this speech?

10. Furies (fyoor´ ēz) *n.* three
terrible female spirits who
punish the doers of
unavenged crimes.

Reading Skill
Historical and
Cultural Context
What ancient Greek
belief is conveyed
in this suitor's speech?

1260   Antinous only shrugged.

                                         Telemachus,
        after the blow his father bore, sat still
        without a tear, though his heart felt the blow.
        Slowly he shook his head from side to side,
        containing murderous thoughts.

                                         Penelope
1265   on the higher level of her room had heard
        the blow, and knew who gave it. Now she murmured:

        "Would god you could be hit yourself, Antinous—
        hit by Apollo's bowshot!"

                                   And Eurynome[11]

        her housekeeper, put in:

                                   "He and no other?
1270   If all we pray for came to pass, not one
        would live till dawn!"

                          Her gentle mistress said:

        "Oh, Nan, they are a bad lot; they intend
        ruin for all of us; but Antinous
        appears a blacker-hearted hound than any.
1275   Here is a poor man come, a wanderer,
        driven by want to beg his bread, and everyone
        in hall gave bits, to cram his bag—only
        Antinous threw a stool, and banged his shoulder!"

        So she described it, sitting in her chamber
1280   among her maids—while her true lord was eating.
        Then she called in the forester and said:

        "Go to that man on my behalf, Eumaeus,
        and send him here, so I can greet and question him.
        Abroad in the great world, he may have heard
1285   rumors about Odysseus—may have known him!"

Penelope

In the evening, Penelope interrogates the old beggar.

"Friend, let me ask you first of all:
who are you, where do you come from, of what nation

11. **Eurynome** (yo͞o rin′ əm ē)

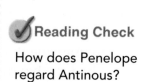

Reading Check

How does Penelope regard Antinous?

and parents were you born?"

And he replied:

"My lady, never a man in the wide world
1290 should have a fault to find with you. Your name
has gone out under heaven like the sweet
honor of some god-fearing king, who rules
in <u>equity</u> over the strong: his black lands bear
both wheat and barley, fruit trees laden bright,
1295 new lambs at lambing time—and the deep sea
gives great hauls of fish by his good strategy,
so that his folk fare well.

O my dear lady,
this being so, let it suffice to ask me
of other matters—not my blood, my homeland.
1300 Do not enforce me to recall my pain.
My heart is sore; but I must not be found
sitting in tears here, in another's house:
it is not well forever to be grieving.
One of the maids might say—or you might think—
1305 I had got <u>maudlin</u> over cups of wine."

And Penelope replied:

"Stranger, my looks,
my face, my carriage,[12] were soon lost or faded
when the Achaeans crossed the sea to Troy,
Odysseus my lord among the rest.
1310 If he returned, if he were here to care for me,
I might be happily renowned!
But grief instead heaven sent me—years of pain.
Sons of the noblest families on the islands,
Dulichium, Same, wooded Zacynthus,[13]
1315 with native Ithacans, are here to court me,
against my wish; and they consume this house.
Can I give proper heed to guest or suppliant
or herald on the realm's affairs?

How could I?
wasted with longing for Odysseus, while here
1320 they press for marriage.

Ruses[14] served my turn
to draw the time out—first a close-grained web
I had the happy thought to set up weaving
on my big loom in hall. I said, that day:

Vocabulary Builder
equity (ek´ wit ē)
n. fairness; justice

Vocabulary Builder
maudlin (môd´ lin)
adj. tearfully and
foolishly sentimental

12. **carriage** (kar´ ij)
n. posture.

13. **Zacynthus** (za sin´ *th*us)

14. **ruses** (ro͞oz´ iz) *n.* tricks.

'Young men—my suitors, now my lord is dead,
1325   let me finish my weaving before I marry,
or else my thread will have been spun in vain.
It is a shroud I weave for Lord Laertes
when cold Death comes to lay him on his bier.
The country wives would hold me in dishonor
1330   if he, with all his fortune, lay unshrouded.'
I reached their hearts that way, and they agreed.
So every day I wove on the great loom,
but every night by torchlight I unwove it;
and so for three years I deceived the Achaeans.
1335   But when the seasons brought a fourth year on,
as long months waned, and the long days were spent,
through impudent folly in the slinking maids
they caught me—clamored up to me at night;
I had no choice then but to finish it.
1340   And now, as matters stand at last,
I have no strength left to evade a marriage,
cannot find any further way; my parents
urge it upon me, and my son
will not stand by while they eat up his property.
1345   He comprehends it, being a man full-grown,
able to oversee the kind of house
Zeus would endow with honor.

                             But you too

confide in me, tell me your ancestry.
You were not born of mythic oak or stone."

---

*Penelope again asks the beggar to tell about himself. He
makes up a tale in which Odysseus is mentioned and
declares that Penelope's husband will soon be home.*

1350   "You see, then, he is alive and well, and headed
homeward now, no more to be abroad
far from his island, his dear wife and son.
Here is my sworn word for it. Witness this,
god of the zenith, noblest of the gods,[15]
1355   and Lord Odysseus' hearthfire, now before me:
I swear these things shall turn out as I say.
Between this present dark and one day's ebb,
after the wane, before the crescent moon,
Odysseus will come."

**Reading Skill
Historical and
Cultural Context**
How do the ancient
Greek ideas in
Penelope's speech
about honoring the
dead compare to
modern ideas?

**15. god of the zenith, noblest
of the gods** Zeus.

Reading Check

How was Penelope
able to delay marriage
for three years?

▲ **Critical Viewing** The winner of the archery contest will win Penelope's hand in marriage. What details or artistic techniques capture the tension in this scene? **[Interpret]**

The Challenge

Pressed by the suitors to choose a husband from among them,
Penelope says she will marry the man who can string
Odysseus' bow and shoot an arrow through twelve axhandle
sockets. The suitors try and fail. Still in disguise, Odysseus
asks for a turn and gets it.

                        And Odysseus took his time,
1360 turning the bow, tapping it, every inch,
for borings that termites might have made
while the master of the weapon was abroad.
The suitors were now watching him, and some
jested among themselves:

                                    "A bow lover!"

1365 "Dealer in old bows!"

                        "Maybe he has one like it
at home!"

                "Or has an itch to make one for himself."

"See how he handles it, the sly old buzzard!"

And one disdainful suitor added this:
"May his fortune grow an inch for every inch he bends it!"

1370 But the man skilled in all ways of contending,
satisfied by the great bow's look and heft,
like a musician, like a harper, when
with quiet hand upon his instrument
he draws between his thumb and forefinger
1375 a sweet new string upon a peg: so effortlessly
Odysseus in one motion strung the bow.
Then slid his right hand down the cord and plucked it,
so the taut gut vibrating hummed and sang
a swallow's note.

                In the hushed hall it smote the suitors
1380 and all their faces changed. Then Zeus thundered
overhead, one loud crack for a sign.
And Odysseus laughed within him that the son

Literary Analysis
Epic Simile Which
of Odysseus' qualities
is highlighted in the
epic simile in lines
1372–1379?

 Reading Check

What means does
Penelope decide she
will use to choose a
husband?

of crooked-minded Cronus had flung that omen down.
He picked one ready arrow from his table
1385　where it lay bare: the rest were waiting still
in the quiver for the young men's turn to come.
He nocked[16] it, let it rest across the handgrip,
and drew the string and grooved butt of the arrow,
aiming from where he sat upon the stool.

　　　　　　　　　　　　　　　Now flashed
1390　arrow from twanging bow clean as a whistle
through every socket ring, and grazed not one,
to thud with heavy brazen head beyond.

　　　　　　　　　　　　　　Then quietly
Odysseus said:

　　　　　　　　　　"Telemachus, the stranger
you welcomed in your hall has not disgraced you.
1395　I did not miss, neither did I take all day
stringing the bow. My hand and eye are sound,
not so contemptible as the young men say.
The hour has come to cook their lordships' mutton—
supper by daylight. Other amusements later,
1400　with song and harping that adorn a feast."

He dropped his eyes and nodded, and the prince
Telemachus, true son of King Odysseus,
belted his sword on, clapped hand to his spear,
and with a clink and glitter of keen bronze
1405　stood by his chair, in the forefront near his father.

16. nocked (näk′d) set an arrow into the bowstring.

▲ **Critical Viewing**
Does the hunter pictured here show the same race as does Odysseus in lines 1370–1392? Explain. **[Compare and Contrast]**

Thinking About the Selection

1. **Respond:** If you were Telemachus or Penelope, how would you react to the stranger's arrival? Why?

2. **(a) Recall:** Who does Telemachus think Odysseus is when they first reunite? **(b) Compare and Contrast:** Compare Odysseus' emotions with those of Telemachus at their reunion.

3. **(a) Recall:** Describe Antinous' treatment of Odysseus. **(b) Analyze Cause and Effect:** Why do you think Antinous treats Odysseus as he does?

4. **(a) Recall:** What does Odysseus tell Penelope about himself? **(b) Infer:** Why do you think Odysseus chooses not to reveal his identity to his wife? **(c) Take a Position:** Is it wrong for Odysseus to deceive Penelope? Explain.

Odysseus' Revenge

Now shrugging off his rags the wiliest[17] fighter of the islands
leapt and stood on the broad doorsill, his own bow in his
  hand.
He poured out at his feet a rain of arrows from the quiver
and spoke to the crowd:

        "So much for that. Your clean-cut game is over.
1410 Now watch me hit a target that no man has hit before,
if I can make this shot. Help me, Apollo."

He drew to his fist the cruel head of an arrow for Antinous
just as the young man leaned to lift his beautiful drinking
  cup,
embossed, two-handled, golden: the cup was in his fingers:
1415 the wine was even at his lips: and did he dream of death?
How could he? In that revelry[18] amid his throng of friends
who would imagine a single foe—though a strong foe
  indeed—
could dare to bring death's pain on him and darkness on his
  eyes?
Odysseus' arrow hit him under the chin
1420 and punched up to the feathers through his throat.

Backward and down he went, letting the winecup fall
from his shocked hand. Like pipes his nostrils jetted
crimson runnels, a river of mortal red,
and one last kick upset his table
1425 knocking the bread and meat to soak in dusty blood.
Now as they craned to see their champion where he lay
the suitors jostled in uproar down the hall,
everyone on his feet. Wildly they turned and scanned
the walls in the long room for arms; but not a shield,
1430 not a good ashen spear was there for a man to take and
  throw.
All they could do was yell in outrage at Odysseus:

"Foul! to shoot at a man! That was your last shot!"
"Your own throat will be slit for this!"
              "Our finest lad is down!
You killed the best on Ithaca."
          "Buzzards will tear your eyes out!"
1435 For they imagined as they wished—that it was a wild shot,
an unintended killing—fools, not to comprehend

---

17. wiliest (wīl´ ē əst) *adj.* craftiest; slyest.

18. revelry (rev´ əl rē) *n.* noisy festivity.

Reading Skill
Historical and Cultural Context
Does the manner in which Odysseus kills Antinous agree with your idea of a "fair fight"? Explain.

Reading Check

Whom does Odysseus kill first?

The Slaughter of the Suitors, N. C. Wyeth, Delaware Art Museum

▲ Critical Viewing Do you think this illustration presents the slaughter of the suitors accurately? Explain. [Evaluate]

they were already in the grip of death.
But glaring under his brows Odysseus answered:

"You yellow dogs, you thought I'd never make it
1440 home from the land of Troy. You took my house to
　　　plunder. . .
You dared bid for my wife while I was still alive.
Contempt was all you had for the gods who rule wide
　　　heaven,
contempt for what men say of you hereafter.
Your last hour has come. You die in blood."

1445 As they all took this in, sickly green fear
pulled at their entrails, and their eyes flickered
looking for some hatch or hideaway from death.
Eurymachus[19] alone could speak. He said:

"If you are Odysseus of Ithaca come back,
1450 all that you say these men have done is true.
Rash actions, many here, more in the countryside.
But here he lies, the man who caused them all.
Antinous was the ringleader, he whipped us on
to do these things. He cared less for a marriage
1455 than for the power Cronion has denied him
as king of Ithaca. For that
he tried to trap your son and would have killed him.
He is dead now and has his portion. Spare
your own people. As for ourselves, we'll make
1460 restitution of wine and meat consumed,
and add, each one, a tithe of twenty oxen
with gifts of bronze and gold to warm your heart.
Meanwhile we cannot blame you for your anger."

Odysseus glowered under his black brows
1465 and said:
　　　　　"Not for the whole treasure of your fathers,
all you enjoy, lands, flocks, or any gold
put up by others, would I hold my hand.
There will be killing till the score is paid.
You forced yourselves upon this house. Fight your way out,
1470 or run for it, if you think you'll escape death.
I doubt one man of you skins by."

They felt their knees fail, and their hearts—but heard
Eurymachus for the last time rallying them.

Vocabulary Builder
contempt (kən tempt′)
n. disdain or scorn

Reading Skill
Historical and
Cultural Context
What cultural values
are revealed by
Odysseus' explanation
for his anger in
lines 1441–1444?

19. **Eurymachus** (yoo ri′ mə
kəs)

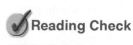
Reading Check

What does
Eurymachus offer
Odysseus to try to
calm his anger?

"Friends," he said, "the man is implacable.
1475 Now that he's got his hands on bow and quiver
he'll shoot from the big doorstone there
until he kills us to the last man.

                               Fight, I say,
let's remember the joy of it. Swords out!
Hold up your tables to deflect his arrows.
1480 After me, everyone: rush him where he stands.
If we can budge him from the door, if we can pass
into the town, we'll call out men to chase him.
This fellow with his bow will shoot no more."

He drew his own sword as he spoke, a broadsword of fine
     bronze,
1485 honed like a razor on either edge. Then crying hoarse and
     loud
he hurled himself at Odysseus. But the kingly man let fly
an arrow at that instant, and the quivering feathered butt
sprang to the nipple of his breast as the barb stuck in his
     liver.
The bright broadsword clanged down. He lurched and fell
     aside,
1490 pitching across his table. His cup, his bread and meat,
were spilt and scattered far and wide, and his head slammed
     on the ground.
Revulsion, anguish in his heart, with both feet kicking out,
he downed his chair, while the shrouding wave of mist closed
     on his eyes.

Amphinomus now came running at Odysseus,
1495 broadsword naked in his hand. He thought to make
the great soldier give way at the door.
But with a spear throw from behind Telemachus hit him
between the shoulders, and the lancehead drove
clear through his chest. He left his feet and fell
1500 forward, thudding, forehead against the ground.
Telemachus swerved around him, leaving the long dark
     spear
planted in Amphinomus. If he paused to yank it out
someone might jump him from behind or cut him down with
     a sword
at the moment he bent over. So he ran—ran from the tables
1505 to his father's side and halted, panting, saying:

"Father let me bring you a shield and spear,

Literary Analysis
Epic Simile Why is the comparison of Eurymachus' sharp sword to a razor only a simile and not an epic simile?

1012 ■ *Themes in Literature: Heroism*

a pair of spears, a helmet.
I can arm on the run myself; I'll give
outfits to Eumaeus and this cowherd.
1510 Better to have equipment."

                                    Said Odysseus:
"Run then, while I hold them off with arrows
as long as the arrows last. When all are gone
if I'm alone they can dislodge me."

                              Quick
upon his father's word Telemachus
1515 ran to the room where spears and armor lay.
He caught up four light shields, four pairs of spears,
four helms of war high-plumed with flowing manes,
and ran back, loaded down, to his father's side.
He was the first to pull a helmet on
1520 and slide his bare arm in a buckler strap.
The servants armed themselves, and all three took their
        stand
beside the master of battle.

                              While he had arrows
he aimed and shot, and every shot brought down
one of his huddling enemies.
1525 But when all barbs had flown from the bowman's fist,
he leaned his bow in the bright entryway
beside the door, and armed: a four-ply shield
hard on his shoulder, and a crested helm,
horsetailed, nodding stormy upon his head,
1530 then took his tough and bronze-shod spears. . . .

───────────────────────────────────────

*Aided by Athena, Odysseus, Telemachus, Eumaeus, and
other faithful herdsmen kill all the suitors.*

───────────────────────────────────────

And Odysseus looked around him, narrow-eyed,
for any others who had lain hidden
while death's black fury passed.

                              In blood and dust
he saw that crowd all fallen, many and many slain.

1535 Think of a catch that fishermen haul in to a half-moon bay
in a fine-meshed net from the whitecaps of the sea:
how all are poured out on the sand, in throes for the salt sea,
twitching their cold lives away in Helios' fiery air:
so lay the suitors heaped on one another.

Reading Skill
**Historical and
Cultural Context**
What cultural values
are reflected in
Telemachus' behavior
toward his father?

Literary Analysis
Epic Simile Which
aspects of the slain
suitors' appearance
does the epic simile in
lines 1535–1539
emphasize?

Reading Check

Who helps Odysseus
defeat the suitors?

Build Language Skills

Vocabulary Skill

Word Roots *Word roots* can provide *context clues* to help you understand unfamiliar words. The **Greek word root** *-techni- (-techn-)* is used in words related to art, skill, or craft, such as the word *technique.*

▶ **Example:** Our society depends on *technology* to function.

Practice Use each of the following in a sentence that would help someone understand what the word means.

1. technician   2. technical   3. technicality
4. technocracy   5. technography

Grammar Lesson

Complex and Compound-Complex Sentences   A **complex sentence** consists of one independent clause, which can stand by itself as a sentence, and at least one subordinate clause, which cannot stand by itself as a sentence. A **compound-complex sentence** consists of two or more independent clauses and one or more subordinate clauses.

> **Complex sentence:** When the lights came on, he saw the audience.
> **Compound-complex sentence:** When the lights came on, he saw the audience, and he waved to his parents.

Practice Identify each sentence as complex or compound-complex. Identify the independent clauses and the subordinate clauses.

1. The shield that the warrior carried in the first battle was made of oxhide.
2. We read the play when our teacher assigned it, but we did not see the movie.
3. She solved the mystery, and she left for Uruguay, which is a country in South America.
4. Arthur bought the magnificent painting that he admired in the gallery.
5. He was late for his appointment with the guidance counselor because his alarm clock did not ring.

More**Practice**

For more practice with complex and compound-complex sentences, see the Grammar Handbook, p. R40.

W͟G͟ Prentice Hall Writing and Grammar Connection: Chapter 21, Section 2

Reading Skill: Analyzing Cultural and Historical Context

Standards Assessed

• WL.1.02.2
• WL.1.03.2
• IR.2.01.1

Directions: *Read the selection. Then, answer the questions.*

The King was convinced that the only way to save himself was to kill his daughter, Danae, before she could have a child. The oracle had foretold his death at the hands of her son. Yet, he was afraid of the gods who prohibited shedding the blood of kin. Acrisius was fearful of killing Danae so instead he had a house built of bronze. He had the house sunk underground with only part of the roof open so light and air could come through. He had Danae put in the house and guarded carefully. One day she was visited by Zeus disguised in a shower of gold. The myth tells us that Danae had a son whose father was Zeus.

1. From the context of this passage, what can a reader infer?
   A The ancient Greeks believed in fate but sometimes tried to alter it.
   B The ancient Greeks felt that a person's fate could never be changed.
   C The ancient Greeks believed that the gods would always make them happy.
   D The ancient Greeks had no way of knowing what the gods meant for them.

2. From the cultural and historical context of this passage, what can a reader infer about the ancient Greeks?
   A They lived in bronze houses sunk underground.
   B They believed that the clouds were really gold mines.

   C They felt that daughters had the right to disobey their fathers.
   D They believed that the gods could appear in any shape or form.

3. What assumption can the reader make about Greek culture?
   A They believed the gods were not important.
   B They believed the gods could be swayed.
   C They believed the gods were myths.
   D They believed the gods were real.

4. Which concept does our society share with this myth?
   A Murder is not allowed.
   B Oracles are believed.
   C Kings are all powerful.
   D Power is not to be used harshly.

Timed Writing: Interpretation (Critical Stance)

Write an essay in which you interpret the character of Penelope based on the decisions she makes and the actions she performs. Cite specific events in the *Odyssey,* identify Penelope's decisions and actions, and interpret why she does what she does. **(45 minutes)**

 ## Writing Workshop: *Work in Progress*

Assessment Writing

Use your background list to generate possible writing questions. What general question might you ask about one of the historical events or literary works on your list?

Reading Informational Materials

Applications

In Part 1, you learned how to analyze the influence of cultural and historical context by reading the *Odyssey* by Homer. The application that follows relates to an opportunity to understand history and other cultures even more deeply through archaeological exploration.

About Applications

Applications are documents that companies, schools, and other organizations use to gather information and determine whether someone is qualified to serve in a job or to participate in a program. People also complete applications when they want to rent an apartment, take out a loan, get a driver's license, or achieve other such goals. A person may be asked for the following types of information on an application:

- personal information, such as name, address, and date of birth
- educational background
- specific experience that applies to the position
- references from people who know the applicant

Reading Skill

Following directions is a critical skill when completing any application. Often, the information on an application is the only data decision-makers have about an applicant. Therefore, the application must be complete and accurate. In addition, the ability to follow directions shows that you can read and think clearly. The following checklist will help guide you in completing an application.

Standard Course of Study

- Select, monitor and modify reading strategies appropriate to answering research questions. (IR.2.01.1)
- Address clarity and style through grammar and usage. (GU.6.01.4)

Following Directions on an Application: A Checklist
Gather details about your education, work experience, and references before starting.
Read the application thoroughly before you begin.
Write neatly, using blue or black ink.
Respond specifically and accurately.
If you have questions, ask for help.
Before listing anyone as a personal reference, make sure he or she is willing to write a letter or speak for you.

THE AMERICAN SCHOOL OF CLASSICAL STUDIES AT ATHENS

BULLETIN

EXCAVATIONS IN THE ATHENIAN AGORA VOLUNTEER PROGRAM SUMMER 20_ _

> This section gives general information about the available opportunities.

The American School of Classical Studies at Athens announces a program for volunteer excavators wishing to participate in the archaeological excavations of the Athenian Agora during the summer of 2005. Approximately thirty-five volunteers are chosen on the basis of academic qualifications and interest in the archaeological field. All participants are expected to work the entire six-week season.

Work of the Volunteer Staff

> This section provides more specific information about the work and the responsibilities of volunteers.

The Volunteer Staff will participate in all aspects of the archaeological field-work under the supervision of a staff of field archaeologists and technical experts, all of whom have extensive field experience and advanced academic training in classical archaeology. Volunteers will be trained in the basic techniques of excavation: working with pick, trowel, shovel, and wheelbarrow; cleaning and investigating stratigraphy; delicate cleaning of artifacts in the ground; sifting of excavated earth and techniques of flotation; washing and basic conservation of pottery and other objects; clerical work involved in the keeping of excavation records. All tasks will be assigned in rotation, and volunteers are expected to participate in them all. Room and a modest allowance for board are provided for the time volunteers are working at the excavations. Travel arrangements to and from Greece are the responsibility of each volunteer.

The 20_ _ Season

The excavations of 20_ _ are planned for six weeks beginning early June and continuing until late July. Fieldwork is in progress five days a week, Monday through Friday, from 7 a.m. to 3 p.m. with a 30-minute break at midmorning. Volunteers are expected to be on the site during these hours and to work at the excavations for the full six weeks.

To request applications or additional information, please see the contact information on page 3.

> The due date for the application is indicated in bold, underlined type so it stands out.

POSTMARK DEADLINE: DECEMBER 15, 20 _ _.
Applicants can expect to receive notification after February 15, 20_ _.

EXCAVATIONS IN THE ATHENIAN AGORA
APPLICATION FOR VOLUNTEER PROGRAM 2006

Full Name: _____

Address: _____

_____

Telephone: _____ Date of Birth: _____

EDUCATION

High School _____

Dates Attended: _____ Date (or Expected Date of graduation): _____

List courses (if any) taken in Archaeology, Classics, and related fields (continue on back if necessary): _____

_____

_____

_____

> The first part of this section asks for archeology-related experience. The second asks for any similar experience, such as membership in a history or science club.

List any ARCHAEOLOGICAL EXPERIENCE:

Give name of site, name of Director, dates: _____

_____

_____

Special qualifications and other relevant information: _____

_____

Dates Available: Full Season (6 weeks) _____

PERSONAL STATEMENT:

Please attach a personal statement explaining your interest in the Agora Excavations. Please discuss more fully your qualifications, career goals and interests, and any other relevant information. This essay should not exceed more than one side of one 8 1/2 x 11 page.

> In addition to this brief form, the organization requires each applicant to write a short essay in which he or she explain's his or her interest.

INTERVIEW:

I will telephone to arrange date for interview _____

I cannot be interviewed because of distance _____

REFEREES:

Give names and addresses of <u>two</u> persons whom <u>you have asked</u> to write in support of your application. They should be familiar with your academic studies and/or archaeological interest. _____

_____

> Referees are people with good credentials who can recommend the applicant for the position.

Signature: _____ Date: _____

Completed applications and letters of recommendation should be sent to the appropriate address listed on page 3. All application materials should be post-marked no later than December 15, 20_ _.

Monitor Your Progress

Reading: Following Directions

Directions: *Choose the letter of the best answer to each question about the application.*

1. What is a responsibility of each volunteer?

   A to pay all expenses during the course of the fieldwork

   B to notify the program director of all travel arrangements

   C to receive training in archaeology before the program starts

   D to participate in all excavation tasks

2. What additional information should an applicant provide on the write-on-lines under "Education"?

   A high school grade point average

   B literature classes taken

   C archaeology and classics courses taken

   D hours completed for graduation

3. What specific directions are given regarding the personal essay that accompanies the application?

   A The essay should be no longer than five pages.

   B The essay should be stapled to the application.

   C The essay should be no longer than a single 8 1/2 × 11 page.

   D The essay should have a cover sheet.

Reading: Comprehension and Interpretation

Directions: *Write your answers on a separate sheet of paper.*

4. Explain the purpose of the personal essay. **[Applying]**

5. What kind of information might an organization learn from referees that is different from information the applicant provides? **[Organizing]**

Timed Writing: Persuasion [Connections]

Imagine you are applying for the program represented on this application. Write the requested essay that would accompany the form. Describe your goals and ambitions clearly. Avoid clichés or jargon and use formal, polite language that shows respect toward your audience. **(45 minutes)**

Comparing Literary **Works** *Contemporary Interpretations*

Contemporary Interpretations

A **contemporary interpretation** of a literary work is a new piece of writing, such as a poem, story, or play, that a modern-day author bases on an ancient work. An **allusion** is a reference to a well-known person, place, event, literary work, or work of art. The characters and events of Homer's *Odyssey* are timeless and universal in their appeal and meaning and have inspired many contemporary interpretations. By reinventing Homer's tales, or by making allusions to them, modern-day writers shed new light on Homer's ancient words. The new literary work thus makes a powerful connection between the people of different countries, eras, and cultures. Contemporary interpretations may allude to any aspects of the original work, including plot, characters, settings, imagery, language, or theme.

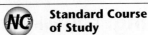

Standard Course of Study

- Understand the importance of cultural and historical impact on texts. (LT.5.01.10)
- Understand the importance of tone, mood, diction, and style. (LT.5.01.4)

Comparing Contemporary Interpretations

Even when they are based on the same work, contemporary interpretations can differ widely in purpose and theme. The writers' cultural and historical backgrounds, attitudes, and beliefs profoundly affect their perceptions of the ancient work. These factors also influence their creation of the new literary work. As you read, use a chart like the one shown to note the allusion each poet makes to the *Odyssey*. Then, think about the ways in which the allusion helps the poet to express a new meaning.

Poem:
Allusion to the *Odyssey:*
Meaning:

Vocabulary Builder

An Ancient Gesture

- **authentic** (ô then′ tik) *adj.* genuine; true (p. 1029) *Lab tests prove that the document is* <u>authentic</u> *and not a forgery.*

Siren Song

- **picturesque** (pik′ chər esk′) *adj.* like or suggesting a picture (p. 1031) *The grand and* <u>picturesque</u> *desert landscape stretched out before us.*

Prologue and Epilogue from the *Odyssey*

- **siege** (sēj) *n.* encirclement of a fortified place by an opposing armed force intending to take it (p. 1032) *The castle withstood the* <u>siege</u> *for two months.*

Ithaca

- **lofty** (lôf′ tē) *adj.* very high; noble (p. 1035) *With* <u>lofty</u> *goals you can achieve great things.*

- **defrauded** (dē frôd′ id) *v.* cheated (p. 1036) *By charging too much, they* <u>defrauded</u> *the public.*

Build Understanding

Connecting to the Literature

Reading/Writing Connection Each poem in this section draws inspiration from Homer's *Odyssey*. This ancient poem features Odysseus as its central heroic figure. List Odysseus' heroic qualities, and then write a paragraph in which you explain the qualities that define a hero today. Use at least three of the following words in your response: *integrate, manifest, confront, enlighten, integrate.*

Meet the Author

Edna St. Vincent **Millay** (1892–1950)

Edna St. Vincent Millay is remembered for her artistic experimentation and her rebelliousness. Her poetry collection *The Harp Weaver and Other Poems* (1923) earned her a Pulitzer Prize.

Margaret **Atwood** (b. 1939)

Much of Margaret Atwood's writing is about what it means to be a woman in a period of social change. In "Siren Song," Atwood presents another of her themes—the role of mythology in people's lives.

Derek **Walcott** (b. 1930)

Born in St. Lucia, an island in the Carribbean Sea, Walcott writes poems that reflect his background. In 1992, he won the Nobel Prize in Literature. "Prologue" and "Epilogue" are from his stage version of the *Odyssey*.

Constantine **Cavafy** (1863–1933)

Constantine Cavafy was born to Greek parents in Alexandria, Egypt. "Ithaca" showcases his creative method: using Greek mythology to speak to the modern reader.

Go Online
Author Link

For: More about the authors
Visit: www.PHSchool.com
Web Code: epe-9603

AN ANCIENT GESTURE

Edna St. Vincent Millay

▲ **Critical Viewing** What is Penelope's attitude toward the suitors?
How can you tell? **[Infer; Support]**

I thought, as I wiped my eyes on the corner of my apron:
Penelope did this too.
And more than once: you can't keep weaving all day
And undoing it all through the night;
5   Your arms get tired, and the back of your neck gets tight;
And along towards morning, when you think it will never
    be light,
And your husband has been gone, and you don't know
    where, for years,
Suddenly you burst into tears;
There is simply nothing else to do.

10   And I thought, as I wiped my eyes on the corner of my apron:
This is an ancient gesture, <u>authentic</u>, antique,
In the very best tradition, classic, Greek;
Ulysses[1] did this too.
But only as a gesture,—a gesture which implied
15   To the assembled throng that he was much too moved
    to speak.
He learned it from Penelope . . .
Penelope, who really cried.

Literary Analysis
Contemporary Interpretations What connection does the speaker make between herself and Penelope?

Vocabulary Builder
authentic (ô then´ tik) *adj.* genuine; true

---

1. **Ulysses** Latin name for Odysseus.

Thinking About the Selection

1. **Respond:** Does this poem make you feel more or less sympathetic to Penelope than the *Odyssey* did? Explain.

2. **(a) Recall:** What is the "ancient gesture"? **(b) Summarize:** According to the speaker, what caused Penelope to employ this gesture? **(c) Infer:** What might have caused the speaker to make a similar gesture?

3. **(a) Recall:** According to the speaker, who else made this ancient gesture? **(b) Compare and Contrast:** How did this gesture differ from Penelope's? **(c) Analyze:** What do the different qualities of their gestures show about these characters?

4. **(a) Assess:** What questions about the speaker are left unanswered? **(b) Analyze Cause and Effect:** What effect do these unanswered questions create?

5. **Speculate:** What advice do you think Penelope would give to the speaker of this poem? Explain.

Prologue and Epilogue from the Odyssey

Derek Walcott

PROLOGUE

Sound of surf.

BILLY BLUE *(Sings)*

Gone sing 'bout that man because his stories please us,
Who saw trials and tempests for ten years after Troy.

I'm Blind Billy Blue, my main man's sea-smart Odysseus,
Who the God of the Sea drove crazy and tried to destroy.

5   Andra moi ennepe mousa polutropon hos mala polla . . .
The shuttle of the sea moves back and forth on this line,

All night, like the surf, she shuttles and doesn't fall
Asleep, then her rosy fingers at dawn unstitch the design.

When you hear this chord
(Chord)

                  Look for a swallow's wings,
10 A swallow arrowing seaward like a messenger

Passing smoke-blue islands, happy that the kings
Of Troy are going home and its ten years' <u>siege</u> is over.

So my blues drifts like smoke from the fire of that war,
Cause once Achilles was ashes, things sure fell apart.

15 Slow-striding Achilles, who put the hex on Hector
A swallow twitters in Troy. That's where we start.
(Exit.)

Literary Analysis
Contemporary Interpretations What actions in lines 6–8 reflect the *Odyssey*? Explain.

Vocabulary Builder
siege (sēj) *n.* encirclement of a fortified place by an opposing armed force intending to take it

EPILOGUE

BILLY BLUE *(Sings)*

    I sang of that man against whom the sea still rages,
    Who escaped its terrors, that despair could not destroy,

    Since that first blind singer, others will sing down the ages
20   Of the heart in its harbour, then long years after Troy,
    after Troy.

    And a house, happy for good, from a swallow's omen,
    Let the trees clap their hands, and the surf whisper amen.

    For a rock, a rock, a rock, a rock-steady woman
    Let the waves clap their hands and the surf whisper amen.

25   For that peace which, in their mercy, the gods allow men.
    (Fade. Sound of surf.)

> **Literary Analysis**
> **Contemporary Interpretations** Which words suggest that the story of the *Odyssey* will always be meaningful?

Thinking About the Selection

1. **Respond:** Do you think the speaker is someone whom you would like to know? Explain.
2. **(a) Recall:** In the Prologue, who is the speaker's "main man"?
    (b) Interpret: What is the speaker's attitude toward this "main man"?
3. **(a) Recall:** What is the speaker's name? **(b) Infer:** What type of music does the speaker sing? **(c) Analyze:** Considering the loneliness, death, and defeat that occur in the *Odyssey,* why is the speaker's musical style appropriate?
4. **(a) Recall:** How is Penelope described in the Epilogue?
    (b) Infer: What seems to be the speaker's attitude toward Penelope?
5. **(a) Generalize:** Overall, which elements from the *Odyssey* seem most interesting to Walcott? **(b) Evaluate:** Do you think the poet treats the original text with respect? Why or why not?

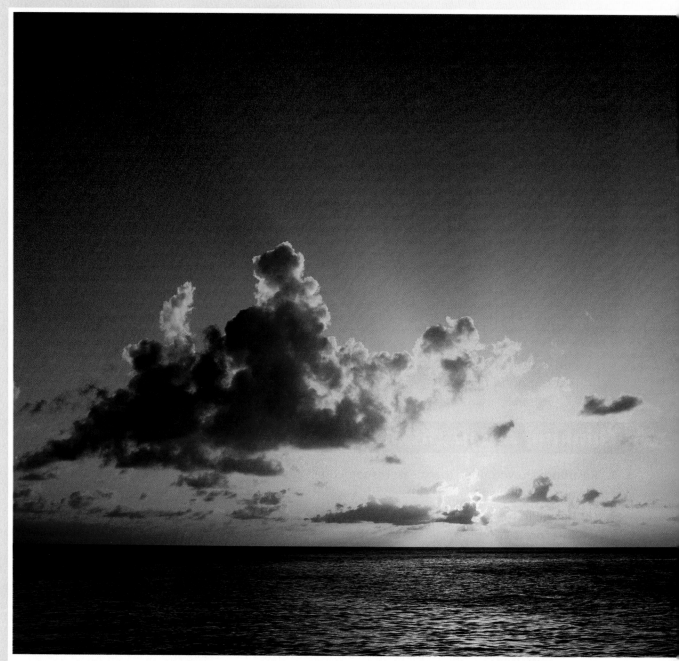

▲ Critical Viewing Which aspects of this image relate to Odysseus' journey? [Connect]

ITHACA

Constantine Cavafy

When you start on your journey to Ithaca,
then pray that the road is long,
full of adventure, full of knowledge.
Do not fear the Lestrygonians[1]
5   and the Cyclopes and the angry Poseidon.
You will never meet such as these on your path,
if your thoughts remain <u>lofty</u>, if a fine
emotion touches your body and your spirit.
You will never meet the Lestrygonians,
10   the Cyclopes and the fierce Poseidon,
if you do not carry them within your soul,
if your soul does not raise them up before you.

Then pray that the road is long.
That the summer mornings are many,
15   that you will enter ports seen for the first time
with such pleasure, with such joy!
Stop at Phoenician markets,
and purchase fine merchandise,
mother-of-pearl and corals, amber and ebony,

Vocabulary Builder
lofty (lôf´ tē) *adj.* very high; noble

Reading Check

What advice does the speaker give about meeting the Lestrygonians?

---

1. Lestrygonians (les tri gō´ nē ənz) cannibals who destroy all of Odysseus' ships except his own and kill the crews.

20 and pleasurable perfumes of all kinds,
   buy as many pleasurable perfumes as you can;
   visit hosts of Egyptian cities,
   to learn and learn from those who have knowledge.

   Always keep Ithaca fixed in your mind.
25 To arrive there is your ultimate goal.
   But do not hurry the voyage at all.
   It is better to let it last for long years;
   and even to anchor at the isle when you are old,
   rich with all that you have gained on the way,
30 not expecting that Ithaca will offer you riches.

   Ithaca has given you the beautiful voyage.
   Without her you would never have taken the road.
   But she has nothing more to give you.

   And if you find her poor, Ithaca has not <u>defrauded</u> you.
35 With the great wisdom you have gained, with so much
      experience,
   You must surely have understood by then what Ithaca
      means.

Literary Analysis
Contemporary Interpretations How does Odysseus' desire for an end to his journey differ from the contemporary poet's attitude toward the journey?

Vocabulary Builder
defrauded (dē frôd′ id)
v. cheated

Thinking About the Selection

1. **Respond:** Does the journey described in this poem appeal to you? Explain.

2. **(a) Recall:** According to the speaker, how can you avoid meeting the Lestrygonians, the Cyclopes, and Poseidon? **(b) Infer:** Why might a person carry such terrors as these in his or her own soul?

3. **(a) Recall:** What three things does the speaker say you should pray for on the journey to Ithaca? **(b) Connect:** What activities and pleasures are linked to these prayers?

4. **(a) Recall:** According to the speaker, why is Ithaca important?
   (b) Interpret: What might Ithaca symbolize for the poet?

5. **(a) Interpret:** What message is conveyed in the last three lines of the poem? **(b) Assess:** Do you agree with this message? Explain.

6. **(a) Speculate:** What advice might the speaker have given to Odysseus during his long journey? **(b) Take a Position:** Do you agree with this advice? Explain.

Apply the Skills

An Ancient Gesture • *Siren Song* • *Prologue* and *Epilogue* from the *Odyssey* • *Ithaca*

Comparing Contemporary Interpretations

1. The author of each **contemporary interpretation** in this section uses Homer's ideas as inspiration for new ideas. Use a chart like the one shown to explain how each poem is like and unlike Homer's *Odyssey*.

Poem:

Similar to Homer: Different from Homer:

2. Select one poem in this section and identify the comment the poet is making about modern life. Support your explanation with details from your completed chart.

3. **(a)** Identify an **allusion** in two of the poems. **(b)** Explain what the reference adds to the meaning of the poem. **(c)** Tell which allusion you think is more effective, and why.

Writing to Compare Literary Works

Each poet in this section finds something valuable in the *Odyssey* to use in his or her literary work. In an essay, discuss specific ways in which Odysseus' journey provides worthwhile material for modern-day writers. Use the following questions to get started:

- What is each contemporary author's reason for writing?
- What conflicts or situations in the *Odyssey* might be viewed very differently by modern-day writers?
- What modern-day conflict or situation does Homer help each poet address?
- Which poem did you enjoy most? Why?

Vocabulary Builder

Practice For each item, write a sentence in which you correctly use the given word pair.

1. authentic; genuine
2. picturesque; pleasing
3. siege; danger
4. lofty; challenge
5. defrauded; honest

QuickReview

Contemporary Interpretation: a present-day literary work that refers to an ancient work to convey contemporary ideas

Allusion: reference to a well-known person, place, event, literary work, or work of art

Go Online
—Assessment

For: Self-test
Visit: www.PHSchool.com
Web Code: epa-6604

Reading: Analyzing Cultural and Historical Context

Directions: *Questions 1–5 are based on the following selection.*

> [Telemachus speaks.] "You cannot
> be my father Odysseus! Meddling spirits
> conceived this trick to twist the knife in me!
> 1040   No man of woman born could work these wonders
> by his own craft, unless a god came into it
> with ease to turn him young or old at will.
> I swear you were in rags and old,
> and here you stand like one of the immortals!"
>
> 1045   Odysseus brought his ranging mind to bear and said:
>   "This is not princely, to be swept
> away by wonder at your father's presence.
> No other Odysseus will ever come,
> for he and I are one, the same; his bitter
> 1050   fortune and his wanderings are mine.
> Twenty years gone, and I am back again
> on my own island.
>   As for my change of skin,
> that is a charm [the goddess] Athena, Hope of Soldiers,
> uses as she will; . . .
>
> —from the *Odyssey*

1. **Telemachus realizes his father has returned. What common human emotions does he express in the first three lines?**
   A   anger and hatred
   B   surprise and shock
   C   fear
   D   love

2. **What does Telemachus believe caused his father to appear to be an old man?**
   A   his father's tricks
   B   meddling spirits
   C   trickery
   D   time

3. **How is what Odysseus tells his son in lines 1048–1050 similar to what any father might tell a son?**
   A   He scolds him for being easily tricked.
   B   He tells him to behave appropriately.
   C   He tells him to believe the gods.
   D   He scolds him for not recognizing his own father.

4. **According to the passage, what did the Greeks believe about the gods?**
   A   They were cruel and vengeful.
   B   They did not care about human beings.
   C   They could affect the lives of humans.
   D   They were all-powerful.

Vocabulary

Standards
Assessed

• GU.6.01.6
• WL.1.02.3
• WL.1.03.6

Directions: *Choose the letter of the word that best completes the sentence.*

5. Jerry's playing _____ was remarkable.
   A   controversy
   B   complex
   C   technique
   D   impact

6. The plot was so _____ that few could follow it.
   A   complex
   B   confirmed
   C   controversial
   D   deliberate

7. He found it difficult to _____ the value of the art.
   A   contemplate
   B   complicate
   C   diminish
   D   appraise

8. The story caused a great deal of _____.
   A   complexity
   B   controversy
   C   technique
   D   appraisal

9. The board met to _____ the appointment of the new president.
   A   impact
   B   diminish
   C   confirm
   D   complicate

Directions: *Using the definition of the word roots, choose the word that best fits the context of the sentence.*

10. Andy needed _____ assistance to fix the problem.
    A   technical
    B   contrary
    C   contradictory
    D   technocratic

11. The new _____ allowed them to communicate more easily.
    A   technography
    B   contravention
    C   technology
    D   technocrat

12. In _____ to the inexperience of his opponent, Julio had years of experience in the sport.
    A   contravention
    B   contradistinction
    C   technography
    D   technology

13. He attempted to _____ the law by using a false identification card.
    A   contradict
    B   technographic
    C   contravene
    D   technologically

14. The evidence was so _____ that the jury could not agree on a verdict.
    A   contradictory
    B   technographic
    C   technological
    D   contrapuntal

Writing Workshop

Writing for Assessment: Timed Essay

Teachers often use **timed essays**, written responses to prompts or questions, to measure your mastery of essential skills. Usually, the essay must be completed within a specific—and brief—time period. Use the steps in this workshop to sharpen your skills in writing a timed essay.

Assignment Write a timed essay in response to this prompt, or ask your teacher to provide you with one.

- In an *essay*, identify and discuss a character from a literary work or a film who was brave in the face of danger.

What to Include: Your timed essay should feature these elements:
- a direct response to the test question or prompt
- a clear, well-supported thesis statement or main idea
- specific information about the topic drawn from your knowledge
- a clear organization
- on-time completion
- error-free grammar, including correct sentence formation

To preview the criteria on which your timed essay may be assessed, see the rubric on page 1044.

Prewriting

Spend about a quarter of your time prewriting.

Choosing Your Topic

Review the prompts. When you are given a choice among questions, choose the one that relates to the topic you know the best. Or, choose the question that engages your strongest skills.

Gathering Details

Clarify the question. Circle the verbs in the assignment that define what is expected. Use these key words to direct your response.

- **Analyze:** examine how various elements contribute to the whole.
- **Describe:** give main features and examples of each.
- **Compare and contrast:** stress how two works or other items are alike and different.
- **Discuss:** support a generalization with facts and examples.
- **Explain:** clarify by probing reasons, causes, results, and effects.
- **Defend:** support your position with examples from the text.

After reviewing the question, write a sentence to express the idea you will develop. Then, gather a few details to support this idea.

NC **Standard Course of Study**

- Narrate personal scenes located effectively in time and place. (WL.1.01.1)
- Analyze use of language for a particular effect in argument. (FA.3.01.3)

Using the Form
You will use writing for assessment strategies in the following situations:
- end-of-year tests
- standardized tests
- college entrance exams, such as SAT and ACT

Work in Progress
Review the work you did on pages 943, 991, and 1021.

Drafting

Spend about half your time drafting.

Make a quick outline. Start with a sketch, or brief outline, of your essay. State your thesis in the *introduction*. In the *body* of the essay, present at least two main points that support your thesis. In the *conclusion*, restate the answer to the essay question and sum up your main points.

Fill in the details. Using your outline, draft your response, incorporating facts, examples and quotations that support your ideas. Do not include a detail unless you can connect it to your thesis.

Revising

Spend about a quarter of your time revising and editing.

Revising Your Overall Structure

Revise for Unity. You will not be able to do a complete revision of your draft. When you have finished writing, compare the first paragraph of your essay with the last:

- The first paragraph should contain a focus or thesis that clearly responds to the essay question.

- The final paragraph should restate your thesis and summarize your supporting evidence.

- If the main points of the first and final paragraphs do not connect, revise either paragraph to make the writing more coherent. Add transitions or more information in the body paragraphs.

Reading Writing Connection

To read the complete student model, see page 1043.

Revising Word Choice

Revise for formal language. Neatly replace informal or vague words with more appropriate and formal language.

Informal: The railroad was the *thing* that most contributed to the success of new businesses.

Formal: The railroad was the *factor* that most contributed to the success of new businesses.

Student Model: Revising a Conclusion

I think that Jackie Joyner-Kersee and Stevie Wonder are admirable for overcoming their disabilities.ʌ*Stevie Wonder overcame blindness to bring music to the world. Joyner-Kersee stunned us with her athleticism, despite her asthma.* They teach me to never give up.

> The writer summarizes his supporting arguments to give greater weight and clarity to his thesis.

Integrating Grammar Skills

Revising to Correct Fragments and Run-ons

Sentence errors are common in writing that is done for assessment. A **fragment** is a group of words that does not express a complete thought but is punctuated as if it were a sentence. A **run-on** is two or more complete sentences that are not properly joined or separated.

Identifying and Correcting Fragments Fragments incomplete thoughts express. Often, they offer information that belongs to a nearby sentence. Correct fragments by attaching them to these sentences.

> **Fragment:** They waited at the bus stop. *Huddled under an umbrella.*
> **Revised:** They waited at the bus stop, huddled under an umbrella.

Other fragments can be corrected through expansion—adding the words needed to make complete sentence.

> **Fragment:** *As long as you agree to help.*
> **Expanded:** I will wash the car as long as you agree to help.

Identifying and Correcting Run-ons Run-ons include sentences that are fused without any punctuation at all or that are linked by only a comma.

> **Fused:** She speaks Spanish fluently she does not speak Italian at all.
> **Comma splice:** She speaks Spanish fluently, she does not speak Italian at all.

Three Ways to Correct a Run-on Sentence

Use an appropriate end mark to separate a run-on into two sentences. Begin the second sentence with a capital letter.	She speaks Spanish fluently. She does not speak Italian at all.
Use a comma and a coordinating conjunction, such as *and, but, or, for, and nor,* to combine two related independent clauses.	She speaks Spanish fluently, but she does not speak Italian at all.
Use a semicolon to connect two closely related ideas.	She speaks Spanish fluently; she does not speak Italian at all.

Apply It to Your Editing

Scan the body paragraphs of your timed essay for fragments and run-ons by looking for sentences that seem too short or too long. Neatly correct any sentence problems you find using the strategies that have been presented.

Prentice Hall Writing and Grammar Connection: Chapter 22, Section 4

Student Model: Eddie Harris
Chicago, IL

Question: *In an essay, discuss how someone you admire overcame an obstacle in order to succeed.*

The best way to overcome a disability is to face it head-on and not let it prevent you from achieving great things. This is the lesson I draw from the lives of two people whom I admire—the musician Stevie Wonder and the track-and-field star Jackie Joyner-Kersee. I respect them for their courage and strength in overcoming obstacles. Both are African Americans with disabilities who defied obstacles in order to be successful in their fields.

Stevie Wonder became blind after he was born prematurely and received too much oxygen. But that did not stop him from becoming one of the best musicians ever. He started out singing rock and roll songs outside a church in Detroit. Eventually, he found his way to Motown Studios at a time when Motown was one of the top recording studios in America. There his career skyrocketed. He became one of the best Motown singers even though he was only ten years old.

He has since been nominated for more Grammy awards than any other musician. His blindness is no disability for him. On the music charts, Stevie Wonder opened the gates for a new sound . . . not just for African Americans but for everyone else as well.

Another person that I admire for the way she overcame obstacles is Jackie Joyner-Kersee, a famous track-and-field star. She was born in East St. Louis, Illinois, and her family was very poor. Her parents thought that track and field was inappropriate for a girl. When she was nine, she entered her first track-and-field competition. Even though she lost, she didn't give up. Jackie entered another race. Her parents were shocked when she won.

In the late 1980s, she was diagnosed with asthma. This has not interfered with her performance as an athlete. Jackie is a world champion in both the long jump and heptathlon and has many Olympic medals to prove it.

Jackie Joyner-Kersee continues to be a role model for young people with disabilities like me. I think that Jackie Joyner-Kersee and Stevie Wonder are admirable for overcoming their disabilities. Stevie Wonder overcame blindness to bring music to the world. Joyner-Kersee stunned us with her athleticism, despite her asthma. They teach me to never give up, no matter how intimidating the obstacles I face in life.

Eddie uses a general statement to introduce his response to the essay question.

The writer presents a thesis statement that focuses his answer to the essay question.

In the body of the essay, Eddie supports his general statement with specific factual information.

He concludes by restating his thesis and reinforcing it with personal insight.

Writing Workshop

Editing and Proofreading

Check your draft to correct errors in spelling, grammar, and punctuation.

Focus on Legibility: Because you will not have time to make a clean copy of your final draft, make sure your revisions and corrections are clear and readable. Draw a single line through words you wish to delete, and use a caret [^] or an arrow to show where you are adding words.

Publishing and Presenting

Consider one of the following ways to share your writing:
Organize a study group. Compare your timed essay with those of your classmates. Discuss with the group the ways you could improve your essay writing.
Prepare for future exams. Use your essay as a study tool. Review the grade you received and the scorer's comments to help you improve future performance.

Reflecting on Your Writing

Writer's Journal Jot down your thoughts about writing a timed essay. Begin by answering these questions.
- What strategy in this workshop might best help you complete your next essay test?
- What do you find most challenging about taking an essay test?

Prentice Hall Writing and Grammar Connection: Chapter 14

Rubric for Self-Assessment

To assess your timed essay, use the following rubric:

NC	Criteria	Rating Scale				
		not very				very
	Focus: How clear is your thesis statement or main idea?	1	2	3	4	5
	Organization: How logical is your organization?	1	2	3	4	5
	Support/Elaboration: How effectively do you include specific information drawn from your experience, your reading, or class discussion?	1	2	3	4	5
	Style: How direct is your response to the question or prompt?	1	2	3	4	5
	Conventions: How correct is your grammar, especially your avoidance of fragments and run-ons?	1	2	3	4	5

Unit 6
Part 2

Compare and Contrast

Skills You Will Learn

Literary Analysis: *Protagonist and Antagonist*
Reading Skill: *Generating Questions After Reading*

Reading Skill: *Setting a Purpose for Reading*

Literary Analysis: *Author's Purpose and Philosophical Assumptions*
Reading Skill: *Using Self-Monitoring*

Literary Analysis: *Heroes in Tall Tale and Myth*

Literature You Will Read

Reading and Vocabulary Skills Preview

Reading: Compare and Contrast

Standard Course of Study

> A **comparison** tells how two or more things are alike. A **contrast** tells how two or more things are different. When you compare and contrast, you identify similarities and differences between two or among more than two things.

- Use description, comparison, figurative language to elaborate ideas to inform audience (IR.2.02.4)
- Compare effective strategies used in different presentations/products. (CT.4.01.4)

Skills and Strategies you will learn in Part 2

- **to compare and contrast characters** to help **determine the protagonist and antagonist** in a piece of literature (p. 1048)
- **to generate questions after reading** to clarify comparisons and contrasts (p. 1048)
- **to compare and contrast ideas** to **self-monitor your reading** (p. 1098)
- **to set a purpose for reading** to focus on **comparing and contrasting** (p. 1094)

Using the Skills and Strategies in Part 2

In Part 2, you will learn that comparing and contrasting is a basic reasoning skill that will help you analyze similarities and differences of elements within a text. For example, comparing and contrasting characters in a piece of literature will help you identify their strengths and weaknesses. After you set a purpose for reading, comparing and contrasting ideas will help you monitor your reading.

The following chart shows how you can apply these strategies.

Purpose: To identify differences in characters and in ideas

John: wealthy, private school, loves mountain climbing

well educated, concerned about environment

George: from farmland, public school, loves mountain biking

Academic Vocabulary: Words for Evaluating Literature

These words will also help you as you write and talk about your evaluation of the literary techniques and themes.

Word	Definition	Example Sentence
cogent *adj.*	convincing; powerfully appealing	He expressed a **cogent** argument in his defense.
significant *adj.*	important; full of meaning	The character's loss of the gold ring was a **significant** event in the story.
defect *n.*	an imperfection	His pride was a fatal **defect**.
compelling *v.*	forcing or pressuring	The importance of the quest was **compelling** him to continue despite the danger.
coherent *adj.*	orderly or logical; sticking together	His paper was **coherent**.

Vocabulary Skill: Context Clues

▶ A **word root** is the part of the word that contains its basic meaning.

In Part 2, you will learn

- the Latin word root *-sign-* (p. 1092)   • the Latin word root *-her-* (p. 1110)

WORD ROOTS	
-her-: "cling or stick"	-sign-: "signal; meaning"
We will adhere to the rules.	*Distant thunder signifies a storm.*
"We will stick to the rules."	"Distant thunder means a storm is coming"

Activity Write a sentence for each word. Explain how knowing the meaning of a root helps you understand the meaning of the sentence.

1. signature   **2.** signify   **3.** inherent

Practice these skills with either "Three Skeleton Key" (p. 1050) or "The Red-headed League" (p. 1067).

Literary Analysis

The **protagonist** is the chief character in a literary work. Some literary works also have an **antagonist**—a character or force that opposes the protagonist. The antagonist is often another character, but may also be an external force, such as nature.

Although the protagonist is not always an admirable or even a likeable character, readers are interested in what happens to him or her.

- The protagonist's motives may be universally understood feelings and goals, such as curiosity, or the search for love.
- The protagonist's conflict with the antagonist may represent a universal struggle, such as the conflict between good and evil.

As you read, fill in a chart like the one shown.

Reading Skill

Comparing and contrasting characters is recognizing and thinking about their similarities and differences. You can compare different characters within a work, characters from different works, or a single character at different points. As you read, ask questions about each character whom you are comparing. Then, **generate questions after reading** that are specific to the story.

- What are the character's actions?
- What are the character's reasons for his or her actions?
- What qualities does the character demonstrate?

Use your questions and answers to think about the significance of the similarities and differences you discover.

Standard Course of Study

- Apply a set of predetermined standards to critique communication. (CT.4.01.2)
- Provide textual evidence to support understanding of critical text. (CT.4.03.3)
- Use and place modifiers correctly. (GU.6.02.3)

Vocabulary Builder

Three Skeleton Key

- **lurched** (lʉrcht) *v.* moved awkwardly and suddenly (p. 1053) *The newborn calf lurched forward as he tried to stand.*
- **diminution** (dim′ ə nōō′ shən) *n.* lessening (p. 1058) *The players' diminution of enthusiasm caused them to play poorly.*
- **derisive** (di rī′ siv) *adj.* mocking (p. 1061) *The critic's derisive laugh offended the artist.*

The Red-headed League

- **introspective** (in′ trə spek′ tiv) *adj.* having to do with looking into one's own thoughts and feelings (p. 1080) *The touching movie put me in an introspective mood.*
- **vex** (veks) *v.* annoy (p. 1081) *My allergies continued to vex me throughout the spring.*
- **formidable** (fôr′ mə də bəl) *adj.* awe-inspiring (p. 1081) *Mt. Everest is a formidable sight.*

Build Understanding • *Three Skeleton Key*

Background

Lighthouses A lighthouse, or "light," is a tower built on an island or other prominent point to warn ships away from treacherous areas near a coast. The tower is usually several stories high, with a large, bright, movable light at the top. Most lighthouses are now automated, but they used to be occupied by people who maintained and operated the light, moving the beam across the water when a ship approached. A lighthouse is often located on a key, which is a small island or a reef near a larger land mass.

Connecting to the Literature

Reading/Writing Connection Lighthouse operators, like those in this story, often had little contact with the outside world during their shifts. Write a short paragraph describing the positive and negative aspects of such isolation. Use at least three of these words: *isolate, access, forgo, induce.*

READ MORE

George Toudouze
Histoire de la Marine

Meet the Author

George G. **Toudouze** (1877–1971)

The award-winning writer, editor, and scholar George Gustave Toudouze was born in Paris, France.

Writer of the Sea A maritime expert, Toudouze wrote nineteen books about the ocean and served as chief editor of *The French Maritime and Colonial League*. He also earned a doctorate of letters at the Sorbonne, one of the oldest and most distinguished universities in the world, and he went on to become a professor of history and dramatic literature at the Paris Conservatory. His claim to fame, however, rests entirely upon one story, "Three Skeleton Key," which was published in 1937 in *Esquire* magazine.

Fast Facts

▶ "Three Skeleton Key" is the only story of Toudouze's to appear in English.

▶ The story became the basis for a successful radio play, broadcast in 1949.

Go Online
Author Link

For: More information about the author
Visit: www.PHSchool.com
Web Code: epe-9607

Three Skeleton Key

George G. Toudouze

My most terrifying experience? Well, one does have a few in thirty-five years of service in the Lights, although it's mostly monotonous routine work—keeping the light in order, making out the reports.

When I was a young man, not very long in the service, there was an opening in a lighthouse newly built off the coast of Guiana,[1] on a small rock twenty miles or so from the mainland. The pay was high, so in order to reach the sum I had set out to save before I married, I volunteered for service in the new light.

Three Skeleton Key, the small rock on which the light stood, bore a bad reputation. It earned its name from the story of the three convicts who, escaping from Cayenne[2] in a stolen dugout canoe, were wrecked on the rock during the night, managed to escape the sea but eventually died of hunger and thirst. When they were discovered, nothing remained but three heaps of bones, picked clean by the birds. The story was that the three skeletons, gleaming with phosphorescent light,[3] danced over the small rock, screaming. . . .

But there are many such stories, and I did not give the warnings of the old-timers at the Isle de Sein[4] a second thought. I signed up, boarded ship, and in a month I was installed at the light.

Picture a gray, tapering cylinder, welded to the solid black rock by iron rods and concrete, rising from a small island twenty odd miles from land. It lay in the midst of the sea, this island, a small, bare piece of stone, about one hundred fifty feet long, perhaps forty wide. Small, barely large enough for a man to walk about and stretch his legs at low tide.

This is an advantage one doesn't find in all lights, however, for some of them rise sheer from the waves, with no room for one to move save within the light itself. Still, on our island, one must be careful, for the rocks were treacherously smooth. One misstep and down you would fall into the sea—not that the risk of drowning was so great, but the waters about our island swarmed with huge sharks who kept an eternal patrol around the base of the light.

Still, it was a nice life there. We had enough provisions to last for months, in the event that the sea should become too rough for the supply ship to reach us on schedule. During the day we would work about the light, cleaning the rooms, polishing the metalwork and the lens and reflector of the light itself, and at night we would sit on

Literary Analysis
Protagonist and Antagonist Which details in the first four paragraphs suggest that the narrator is the central character in this story?

✔️**Reading Check**

What is especially dangerous about the waters surrounding Three Skeleton Key?

1. Guiana (gē an´ə) region on the northern coast of South America.
2. Cayenne (kī en´) capital city of French Guiana.
3. phosphorescent (fäs´fə res´ənt) **light** a glowing light produced by certain natural chemical reactions.
4. Isle de Sein (ēl´ də sen´) island off the northwestern coast of France.

the gallery and watch our light, a twenty thousand candle-power lantern, swinging its strong, white bar of light over the sea from the top of its hundred-twenty-foot tower. Some days, when the air would be very clear, we could see the land, a thread-like line to the west. To the east, north and south stretched the ocean. Landsmen, perhaps, would soon have tired of that kind of life, perched on a small island off the coast of South America for eighteen weeks, until one's turn for leave ashore came around. But we liked it there, my two fellow-tenders and myself—so much so that, for twenty-two months on end with the exception of shore leaves, I was greatly satisfied with the life on Three Skeleton Key.

I had just returned from my leave at the end of June, that is to say mid-winter in that latitude, and had settled down to the routine with my two fellow-keepers, a Breton[5] by the name of Le Gleo and the head-keeper, Itchoua, a Basque[6] some dozen years or so older than either of us.

Eight days went by as usual, then on the ninth night after my return, Itchoua, who was on night duty, called Le Gleo and me, sleeping in our rooms in the middle of the tower, at two in the morning. We rose immediately and, climbing the thirty or so steps that led to the gallery, stood beside our chief.

Itchoua pointed, and following his finger, we saw a big three-master, with all sail set, heading straight for the light. A queer course, for the vessel must have seen us, our light lit her with the glare of day each time it passed over her.

Now, ships were a rare sight in our waters, for our light was a warning of treacherous reefs, barely hidden under the surface and running far out to sea. Consequently we were always given a wide berth, especially by sailing vessels, which cannot maneuver as readily as steamers.

No wonder that we were surprised at seeing this three-master heading dead for us in the gloom of early morning. I had immediately recognized her lines, for she stood out plainly, even at the distance of a mile, when our light shone on her.

She was a beautiful ship of some four thousand tons, a fast sailor that had carried cargoes to every part of the world, plowing the seas unceasingly. By her lines she was identified as Dutch-built, which was understandable as Paramaribo and Dutch Guiana are very close to Cayenne.

Watching her sailing dead for us, a white wave boiling under her bows, Le Gleo cried out:

---

5. Breton (bret′n) person born or living in Brittany, a region on the northwestern coast of France.
6. Basque (bask) member of a people who inhabit a region between Spain and France on the Bay of Biscay.

▶ **Critical Viewing**
How does this photograph of a Dutch sailing ship help establish the time period of the story? **[Connect]**

Reading Skill
Contrasting Characters What difference in the characters' ages does the narrator point out?

"What's wrong with her crew? Are they all drunk or insane? Can't they see us?"

Itchoua nodded soberly, looked at us sharply as he remarked: "See us? No doubt—if there is a crew aboard!"

"What do you mean, chief?" Le Gleo had started, turned to the Basque, "Are you saying that she's the Flying Dutchman?"[7]

His sudden fright had been so evident that the older man laughed:

"No, old man, that's not what I meant. If I say that no one's aboard, I mean she's a derelict."

Then we understood his queer behavior. Itchoua was right. For some reason, believing her doomed, her crew had abandoned her. Then she had righted herself and sailed on, wandering with the wind.

The three of us grew tense as the ship seemed about to crash on one of our numerous reefs, but she suddenly <u>lurched</u> with some change of the wind, the yards swung around, and the derelict came clumsily about and sailed dead away from us.

In the light of our lantern she seemed so sound, so strong, that Itchoua exclaimed impatiently:

"But why the devil was she abandoned? Nothing is smashed, no sign of fire—and she doesn't sail as if she were taking water."

Le Gleo waved to the departing ship:

"Bon voyage!"[8] he smiled at Itchoua and went on. "She's leaving us, chief, and now we'll never know what—"

"No she's not!" cried the Basque. "Look! She's turning!"

As if obeying his words, the derelict three-master stopped, came about and headed for us once more. And for the next four hours the vessel played around us—zigzagging, coming about,[9] stopping, then suddenly lurching forward. No doubt some freak of current and wind, of which our island was the center, kept her near us.

Then suddenly, the tropic dawn broke, the sun rose and it was day, and the ship was plainly visible as she sailed past us. Our light

Vocabulary Builder
lurched (lʉrcht) *v.*
moved awkwardly and suddenly

Reading Check

In the middle of the night, what surprising sight does Itchoua show his companions?

---

7. **Flying Dutchman** fabled ghost ship doomed to sail forever
8. **Bon voyage** (bän′ voi äzh′) French for "pleasant journey;" a farewell to a traveler.
9. **coming about** changing direction according to the direction of the wind.

extinguished, we returned to the gallery with our glasses and inspected her.

The three of us focused our glasses on her poop,[10] saw standing out sharply, black letters on the white background of a life-ring, the stenciled name:

"*Cornelius-de-Witt*, Rotterdam."

We had read her lines correctly, she was Dutch. Just then the wind rose and the *Cornelius-de-Witt* changed course, leaned to port and headed straight for us once more. But this time she was so close that we knew she would not turn in time.

"Thunder!" cried Le Gleo, his Breton soul aching to see a fine ship doomed to smash upon a reef, "She's going to pile up! She's gone!"

I shook my head:

"Yes, and a shame to see that beautiful ship wreck herself. And we're helpless."

There was nothing we could do but watch. A ship sailing with all sail spread, creaming the sea with her forefoot as she runs before the wind, is one of the most beautiful sights in the world—but this time I could feel the tears stinging my eyes as I saw this fine ship headed for her doom.

All this time our glasses were riveted on her, and we suddenly cried out together:

"The rats!"

Now we knew why this ship, in perfect condition, was sailing without her crew aboard. They had been driven out by the rats. Not those poor specimens of rats you see ashore, barely reaching the

---

10. poop (p$\overline{oo}$p) *n.* raised deck at the rear of a sailing ship.

Reading Skill
Contrasting Characters In what ways are Le Gleo's and the narrator's reactions to the doomed ship similar and different?

▼ **Critical Viewing** Based on this photograph, which of a rat's traits make it well-suited for life on a ship? [**Analyze**]

length of one foot from their trembling noses to the tip of their skinny tails, wretched creatures that dodge and hide at the mere sound of a footfall.

No, these were ships' rats, huge, wise creatures, born on the sea, sailing all over the world on ships, transferring to other, larger ships as they multiply. There is as much difference between the rats of the land and these maritime rats as between a fishing smack and an armored cruiser.

The rats of the sea are fierce, bold animals. Large, strong and intelligent, clannish and seawise, able to put the best of mariners to shame with their knowledge of the sea, their uncanny ability to foretell the weather.

And they are brave, these rats, and vengeful. If you so much as harm one, his sharp cry will bring hordes of his fellows to swarm over you, tear you and not cease until your flesh has been stripped from the bones.

The ones on this ship, the rats of Holland, are the worst, superior to other rats of the sea as their brethren are to the land rats. There is a well-known tale about these animals.

A Dutch captain, thinking to protect his cargo, brought aboard his ship—not cats—but two terriers, dogs trained in the hunting, fighting and killing of vicious rats. By the time the ship, sailing from Rotterdam, had passed the Ostend light, the dogs were gone and never seen again. In twenty-four hours they had been overwhelmed, killed and eaten by the rats.

At times, when the cargo does not suffice, the rats attack the crew, either driving them from the ship or eating them alive. And

Reading Skill
Contrasting Characters In what way are the rats on the *Cornelius-de-Witt* different from other rats in the world?

✔**Reading Check**

What detail do the men notice that shows that the crew of the *Cornelius-de-Witt* did not abandon ship?

Three Skeleton Key ■ 1055

studying the *Cornelius-de-Witt*, I turned sick, for her small boats were all in place. She had not been abandoned.

Over her bridge, on her deck, in the rigging, on every visible spot, the ship was a writhing mass—a starving army coming towards us aboard a vessel gone mad!

Our island was a small spot in that immense stretch of sea. The ship could have grazed us, passed to port or starboard with its ravening cargo—but no, she came for us at full speed, as if she were leading the regatta at a race, and impaled herself on a sharp point of rock.

There was a dull shock as her bottom stove in, then a horrible crackling as the three masts went overboard at once, as if cut down with one blow of some gigantic sickle. A sighing groan came as the water rushed into the ship, then she split in two and sank like a stone.

But the rats did not drown. Not these fellows! As much at home in the sea as any fish, they formed ranks in the water, heads lifted, tails stretched out, paws paddling. And half of them, those from the forepart of the ship, sprang along the masts and onto the rocks in the instant before she sank. Before we had time even to move, nothing remained of the three-master save some pieces of wreckage floating on the surface and an army of rats covering the rocks left bare by the receding tide.

Thousands of heads rose, felt the wind and we were scented, seen! To them we were fresh meat, after possible weeks of starving. There came a scream, composed of innumerable screams, sharper than the howl of a saw attacking a bar of iron, and in the one motion, every rat leaped to attack the tower!

We barely had time to leap back, close the door leading onto the gallery, descend the stairs and shut every window tightly. Luckily the door at the base of the light, which we never could have reached in time, was of bronze set in granite and was tightly closed.

The horrible band, in no measurable time, had swarmed up and over the tower as if it had been a tree, piled on the embrasures of

Literary Analysis
Protagonist and Antagonist What details here might make readers sympathetic toward the narrator? Why?

▼ **Critical Viewing** Which details in the photograph make this rat appear fearsome, like the ones in "Three Skeleton Key"? **[Analyze]**

the windows, scraped at the glass with thousands of claws, covered the lighthouse with a furry mantle and reached the top of the tower, filling the gallery and piling atop the lantern.

Their teeth grated as they pressed against the glass of the lantern-room, where they could plainly see us, though they could not reach us. A few millimeters of glass, luckily very strong, separated our faces from their gleaming, beady eyes, their sharp claws and teeth. Their odor filled the tower, poisoned our lungs and rasped our nostrils with a pestilential, nauseating smell. And there we were, sealed alive in our own light, prisoners of a horde of starving rats.

That first night, the tension was so great that we could not sleep. Every moment, we felt that some opening had been made, some window given away, and that our horrible besiegers were pouring through the breach. The rising tide, chasing those of the rats which had stayed on the bare rocks, increased the numbers clinging to the walls, piled on the balcony—so much so that clusters of rats clinging to one another hung from the lantern and the gallery.

With the coming of darkness we lit the light, and the turning beam completely maddened the beasts. As the light turned, it successively blinded thousands of rats crowded against the glass, while the dark side of the lantern-room gleamed with thousands of points of light, burning like the eyes of jungle beasts in the night.

All the while we could hear the enraged scraping of claws against the stone and glass, while the chorus of cries was so loud that we had to shout to hear one another. From time to time, some of the rats fought among themselves and a dark cluster would detach itself, falling into the sea like a ripe fruit from a tree. Then we would see phosphorescent streaks as triangular fins slashed the water—sharks, permanent guardians of our rock, feasting on our jailors.

The next day we were calmer, and amused ourselves by teasing the rats, placing our faces against the glass which separated us. They could not fathom the invisible barrier which separated them from us, and we laughed as we watched them leaping against the heavy glass.

But the day after that, we realized how serious our position was. The air was foul; even the heavy smell of oil within our stronghold could not dominate the fetid odor of the beasts massed around us, and there was no way of admitting fresh air without also admitting the rats.

The morning of the fourth day, at early dawn, I saw the wooden framework of my window, eaten away from the outside, sagging inwards. I called my comrades and the three of us fastened a sheet of tin in the opening, sealing it tightly. When we had completed the task, Itchoua turned to us and said dully:

**Literary Analysis
Protagonist and
Antagonist** With what external force are the narrator, Le Gleo, and Itchoua now in conflict?

**Reading Skill
Comparing
Characters** In what way do the sharks and the rats behave similarly?

 Reading Check

What do the rats do almost immediately after landing on the island?

"Well—the supply boat came thirteen days ago, and she won't be back for twenty-nine." He pointed at the white metal plate sealing the opening through the granite—"If that gives way—" he shrugged—"they can change the name of this place to Six Skeletons Key."

The next six days and seven nights, our only distraction was watching the rats whose holds were insecure fall a hundred and twenty feet into the maws of the sharks—but they were so many that we could not see any <u>diminution</u> in their numbers.

Thinking to calm ourselves and pass the time, we attempted to count them, but we soon gave up. They moved incessantly, never still. Then we tried identifying them, naming them.

One of them, larger than the others, who seemed to lead them in their rushes against the glass separating us, we named "Nero";[11] and there were several others whom we had learned to distinguish through various peculiarities.

But the thought of our bones joining those of the convicts was always in the back of our minds. And the gloom of our prison fed these thoughts, for the interior of the light was almost completely dark, as we had to seal every

---

11. Nero (nir´ ō) (A.D. 37–68) Roman emperor who was notoriously cruel.

▼ **Critical Viewing**
Why are even the fierce ship rats no match for a school of sharks like these? **[Assess]**

window in the same fashion as mine, and the only space that still admitted daylight was the glassed-in lantern-room at the very top of the tower.

Then Le Gleo became morose and had nightmares in which he would see the three skeletons dancing around him, gleaming coldly, seeking to grasp him. His maniacal, raving descriptions were so vivid that Itchoua and I began seeing them also.

It was a living nightmare, the raging cries of the rats as they swarmed over the light, mad with hunger; the sickening, strangling odor of their bodies—

True, there is a way of signaling from lighthouses. But to reach the mast on which to hang the signal we would have to go out on the gallery where the rats were.

**Literary Analysis
Protagonist and
Antagonist** In addition to the rats, what other problems do the men face?

Reading Check

What happens in Le Gleo's nightmares?

There was only one thing left to do. After debating all of the ninth day, we decided not to light the lantern that night. This is the greatest breach of our service, never committed as long as the tenders of the light are alive; for the light is something sacred, warning ships of danger in the night. Either the light gleams, a quarter hour after sundown, or no one is left alive to light it.

Well, that night, Three Skeleton Light was dark, and all the men were alive. At the risk of causing ships to crash on our reefs, we left it unlit, for we were worn out—going mad!

At two in the morning, while Itchoua was dozing in his room, the sheet of metal sealing his window gave way. The chief had just time enough to leap to his feet and cry for help, the rats swarming over him.

But Le Gleo and I, who had been watching from the lantern-room, got to him immediately, and the three of us battled with the horde of maddened rats which flowed through the gaping window. They bit, we struck them down with our knives—and retreated.

We locked the door of the room on them, but before we had time to bind our wounds, the door was eaten through and gave way, and we retreated up the stairs, fighting off the rats that leaped on us from the knee-deep swarm.

I do not remember, to this day, how we ever managed to escape. All I can remember is wading through them up the stairs, striking them off as they swarmed over us; and then we found ourselves, bleeding from innumerable bites, our clothes shredded, sprawled across the trapdoor in the floor of the lantern-room—without food or drink. Luckily, the trapdoor was metal set into the granite with iron bolts.

The rats occupied the entire light beneath us, and on the floor of our retreat lay some twenty of their fellows, who had gotten in with us before the trapdoor closed, and whom we had killed with our knives. Below us, in the tower, we could hear the screams of the rats as they devoured everything edible that they found. Those on the outside squealed in reply, and writhed in a horrible curtain as they stared at us through the glass of the lantern-room.

Itchoua sat up, stared silently at his blood trickling from the wounds on his limbs and body, and running in thin streams on the floor around him. Le Gleo, who was in as bad a state (and so was I, for that matter) stared at the chief and me vacantly, started as his gaze swung to the multitude of rats against the glass, then suddenly began laughing horribly:

"Hee! Hee! The Three Skeletons! Hee! Hee! The Three Skeletons are now *six* skeletons! *Six* skeletons!"

He threw his head back and howled, his eyes glazed, a trickle of saliva running from the corners of his mouth and thinning the

Literary Analysis
Protagonist and Antagonist What do you think motivates the narrator and Le Gleo to risk their own lives to help Itchoua?

blood flowing over his chest. I shouted to him to shut up, but he did not hear me, so I did the only thing I could to quiet him—I swung the back of my hand across his face.

The howling stopped suddenly, his eyes swung around the room, then he bowed his head and began weeping softly, like a child.

Our darkened light had been noticed from the mainland, and as dawn was breaking, the patrol was there to investigate the failure of our light. Looking through my binoculars, I could see the horrified expression on the faces of the officers and crew when, the daylight strengthening, they saw the light completely covered by a seething mass of rats. They thought, as I afterwards found out, that we had been eaten alive.

But the rats had also seen the ship, or had scented the crew. As the ship drew nearer, a solid phalanx[12] left the light, plunged into the water and, swimming out, attempted to board her. They would have succeeded, as the ship was hove to, but the engineer connected his steam to a hose on the deck and scalded the head of the attacking column, which slowed them up long enough for the ship to get under way and leave the rats behind.

Then the sharks took part. Belly up, mouths gaping, they arrived in swarms and scooped up the rats, sweeping through them like a sickle through wheat. That was one day that sharks really served a useful purpose.

The remaining rats turned tail, swam to the shore, and emerged dripping. As they neared the light, their comrades greeted them with shrill cries, with what sounded like a <u>derisive</u> note predominating. They answered angrily and mingled with their fellows. From the several tussles that broke out, they resented being ridiculed for their failure to capture the ship.

But all this did nothing to get us out of our jail. The small ship could not approach, but steamed around the light at a safe distance, and the tower must have seemed fantastic, some weird, many-mouthed beast hurling defiance at them.

Finally, seeing the rats running in and out of the tower through the door and the windows, those on the ship decided that we had perished and were about to leave when Itchoua, regaining his senses, thought of using the light as a signal. He lit it and, using a plank placed and withdrawn before the beam to form the dots and dashes, quickly sent out our story to those on the vessel.

Our reply came quickly. When they understood our position—how we could not get rid of the rats, Le Gleo's mind going fast,

---

12. **phalanx** (fā′laŋks′) *n.* group of individuals advancing in a close, compact formation.

Reading Skill
Contrasting Characters What differences between the narrator and Le Gleo do their reactions make clear?

Vocabulary Builder
derisive (di rī′ siv) *adj.* mocking

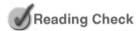
Reading Check

What do the men do that results in the arrival of a patrol ship?

Itchoua and myself covered with bites, cornered in the lantern-room without food or water—they had a signalman send us their reply.

His arms swinging like those of a windmill, he quickly spelled out: "Don't give up. Hang on a little longer! We'll get you out of this!"

Then she turned and steamed at top speed for the coast, leaving us little reassured.

She was back at noon, accompanied by the supply ship, two small coast guard boats, and the fire boat—a small squadron. At twelve-thirty the battle was on.

After a short reconnaissance,[13] the fire boat picked her way slowly through the reefs until she was close to us, then turned her powerful jet of water on the rats. The heavy stream tore the rats from their places, hurled them screaming into the water where the sharks gulped them down. But for every ten that were dislodged, seven swam ashore, and the stream could do nothing to the rats within the tower. Furthermore, some of them, instead of returning to the rocks, boarded the fire boat, and the men were forced to battle them hand to hand. They were true rats of Holland, fearing no man, fighting for the right to live!

---

13. **reconnaissance** (ri kän´ə səns) *n.* exploratory survey or examination.

▲ Critical Viewing
Based on this photograph, how easily do you think the sharks could sweep through the rats? Explain. **[Evaluate]**

Reading Skill
Comparing Characters What similarity between the rats and the men does the narrator's remark about the rats reveal?

Nightfall came, and it was as if nothing had been done, the rats were still in possession. One of the patrol boats stayed by the island; the rest of the flotilla[14] departed for the coast. We had to spend another night in our prison. Le Gleo was sitting on the floor, babbling about skeletons, and as I turned to Itchoua, he fell unconscious from his wounds. I was in no better shape and could feel my blood flaming with fever.

Somehow the night dragged by, and the next afternoon I saw a tug, accompanied by the fire boat, coming from the mainland with a huge barge in tow. Through my glasses, I saw that the barge was filled with meat.

Literary Analysis
Protagonist and Antagonist In what way does human intelligence ultimately overcome the rats' brutality?

Risking the treacherous reefs, the tug dragged the barge as close to the island as possible. To the last rat, our besiegers deserted the rock, swam out and boarded the barge reeking with the scent of freshly cut meat. The tug dragged the barge about a mile from shore, where the fire boat drenched the barge with gasoline. A well placed incendiary shell from the patrol boat set her on fire.

The barge was covered with flames immediately, and the rats took to the water in swarms, but the patrol boat bombarded them with shrapnel from a safe distance, and the sharks finished off the survivors.

A whaleboat from the patrol boat took us off the island and left three men to replace us. By nightfall we were in the hospital in Cayenne.

What became of my friends? Well, Le Gleo's mind had cracked and he was raving mad. They sent him back to France and locked him up in an asylum,[15] the poor devil; Itchoua died within a week; a rat's bite is dangerous in that hot, humid climate, and infection sets in rapidly.

Reading Skill
Contrasting Characters How is Le Gleo changed by the attack?

As for me—when they fumigated[16] the light and repaired the damage done by the rats, I resumed my service there. Why not? No reason why such an incident should keep me from finishing out my service there, is there?

Besides—I told you I liked the place—to be truthful, I've never had a post as pleasant as that one, and when my time came to leave it forever, I tell you that I almost wept as Three Skeleton Key disappeared below the horizon.

---

14. flotilla (flō til′ ə) *n.* small fleet.
15. asylum (ə sī′ ləm) *n.* institution for the care of the mentally ill.
16. fumigated (fyoo′ mə gāt′ id) *v.* disinfected with fumes.

Apply the Skills

Three Skeleton Key

Thinking About the Selection

1. **Respond:** What feelings does this story stir in you and why?
2. **(a) Recall:** How do the rats come to the lighthouse? **(b) Infer:** What impression of the rats does this method of arrival create? **(c) Summarize:** Explain how the rescuers defeat the rats.
3. **(a) Recall:** What does Itchouca say about the name of the island and what will happen if the window seal gives way? **(b) Infer:** What does he mean by this remark? **(c) Interpret:** How does this remark create suspense and add meaning to the story's title?
4. **(a) Categorize:** Which details portray the rats as intelligent and organized and which portray them as mindlessly vicious? **(b) Evaluate:** Does Toudouze make you believe that actual rats would be capable of the actions he describes? Explain.

Literary Analysis

5. **(a)** Identify the **protagonist** in the narrative. **(b)** What is the protagonist's goal? **(c)** Why are readers interested in whether the protagonist achieves his goal?
6. **(a)** Identify the **antagonist**. **(b)** What is the antagonist's goal?
7. **(a)** Why is the story's conflict interesting? **(b)** What universal struggle does this conflict represent?

Reading Strategy

8. What are two specific questions you can ask to help you **compare and contrast** the narrator's actions, reasoning, and outlook at the beginning of the attack and at the end?
9. **(a)** Complete a Venn diagram like the one shown to compare and contrast the narrator's outlook at the beginning of the story with his outlook at the end of the story. **(b)** Explain whether the narrator has or has not changed as a result of his experience.

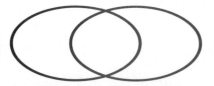

Beginning Only   **End Only**

Beginning and End

10. **(a)** In what ways do the narrator, Le Gleo, and Itchoua act differently from one another during the attack? **(b)** What is one reason the author may have for showing these three different reactions?

QuickReview

Story at a Glance
Three men are trapped in an island lighthouse besieged by bloodthirsty rats.

Go **O**nline
—**Assessment**
For: Self-test
Visit: www.PHSchool.com
Web Code: epa-6605

Protagonist: the character in a literary work whose fortunes are of greatest interest to readers

Antagonist: a character or force in conflict with the protagonist

Comparing and Contrasting: recognizing similarities and differences

Vocabulary Builder

Practice **Analogies** show the relationships between pairs of words. Use a word from the "Three Skeleton Key" vocabulary list on page 1048 to complete each analogy.

1. enlargement : increase :: _____ : decrease
2. glided : graceful :: _____ : clumsy
3. complimentary : praise :: _____ : ridicule

Adding Words to Your Vocabulary Using a dictionary and a thesaurus, find an antonym, for each vocabulary word in the story. Explain your choices. Then, use each correctly in a sentence. (For more on using a dictionary and a thesaurus, see pp. R6–7.)

Writing

Imagine that you are one of the characters in "Three Skeleton Key" other than the narrator. Write three **journal entries** describing the events in the story as they unfold.

- Review the story and create a timeline for the major events.
- Decide which days you will record in your journal.
- Write your thoughts about what happens each day.

As you write, stay in character, making sure that your journal reflects any changes that the character experiences in the story.

For *Grammar, Vocabulary,* and *Assessment,* see **Build Language Skills,** pages 1092–1093.

Extend Your Learning

Listening and Speaking With another student, role-play an **interview** between a television talk show host and the narrator of "Three Skeleton Key." Listen carefully to what your partner says in the interview, and respond with appropriate questions or answers. After the role play, give each other feedback on your work.

Research and Technology Research the topic of ship rats and prepare an **oral report** for the class. Find answers to these questions:

- How do these rats differ physically from other rats?
- Where do such rats live, and how long can they survive?

Refer to multiple sources, such as the Internet, encyclopedias, and science books. Compare what you learn to Toudouze's descriptions.

Short Story

Background
Sherlock Holmes This story is one of many tales about the exploits of the world's most famous fictional detective, Sherlock Holmes. Often depicted wearing a plaid cape and a deerstalker cap, Sherlock Holmes is recognized by people everywhere.

Connecting to the Literature
Reading/Writing Connection Sherlock Holmes has remarkable powers of observation. Test your skill by describing a familiar object. Use at least three of these words: *perceive, observe, differentiate, reveal.*

Review
For **Literary Analysis, Reading Skill,** and **Vocabulary Builder,** see page 1048.

READ MORE

by Sir Arthur Conan Doyle
The Complete Sherlock Holmes
The Lost World

Meet the Author

Sir Arthur **Conan Doyle** (1859–1930)

Sir Arthur Conan Doyle began his career as a doctor. He also pursued a career in writing. In a few years, he sold his first novel, *A Study in Scarlet*, which introduced Sherlock Holmes to the world.

The World's Favorite Detective It is likely that Conan Doyle modeled Sherlock Holmes on Dr. Joseph Bell, a professor of his who could diagnose illnesses from clues that other physicians had missed. Conan Doyle made the narrator of the Holmes mysteries Dr. John Watson. Watson greatly admires Holmes but can never match his friend's powers of observation and reasoning.

Readers grew to love Sherlock Holmes. When Conan Doyle killed him off in a story in 1893, readers protested so strongly that the author was forced to bring back the beloved detective.

Fast Facts
▶ Although Holmes is often depicted in a plaid cape and deerstalker hat, the stories never mention such clothing.
▶ The famous catchphrase "Elementary, my dear Watson" was only used in films—never in Conan Doyle's stories.

Go **Online**
Author Link

For: More information about the author
Visit: www.PHSchool.com
Web Code: epe-9608

THE RED-HEADED LEAGUE

SIR ARTHUR CONAN DOYLE

I had called upon my friend, Mr. Sherlock Holmes, one day in the autumn of last year and found him in deep conversation with a very stout, florid-faced, elderly gentleman with fiery red hair. With an apology for my intrusion, I was about to withdraw when Holmes pulled me abruptly into the room and closed the door behind me.

"You could not possibly have come at a better time, my dear Watson," he said cordially.

"I was afraid that you were engaged."

"So I am. Very much so."

"Then I can wait in the next room."

"Not at all. This gentleman, Mr. Wilson, has been my partner and helper in many of my most successful cases, and I have no doubt that he will be of the utmost use to me in yours also."

The stout gentleman half rose from his chair and gave a bob of greeting, with a quick little questioning glance from his small, fat-encircled eyes.

"Try the settee,"[1] said Holmes, relapsing into his armchair and putting his finger tips together, as was his custom when in judicial moods. "I know, my dear Watson, that you share my love of all that is bizarre and outside the conventions and humdrum routine of everyday life. You have shown your relish for it by the enthusiasm which has prompted you to chronicle, and, if you will excuse my saying so, somewhat to embellish so many of my own little adventures.

"Your cases have indeed been of the greatest interest to me," I observed.

"You will remember that I remarked the other day, just before we went into the very simple problem presented by Miss Mary Sutherland, that for strange effects and extraordinary combinations we must go to life itself, which is always far more daring than any effort of the imagination."

"A proposition which I took the liberty of doubting."

"You did, Doctor, but none the less you must come round to my view, for otherwise I shall keep on piling fact upon fact on you until your reason breaks down under them and acknowledges me to be right. Now, Mr. Jabez Wilson here has been good enough to call upon me this morning, and to begin a narrative which promises to be one of the most singular which I have listened to for some time. You have heard me remark that the strangest and most unique things are very often connected not with the larger but with the smaller crimes, and occasionally, indeed, where there is room for doubt whether any positive crime has been committed. As far as I have heard it is impossible for me to say whether the present case is an instance of crime or not, but the course of events is certainly among the most singular that I have ever listened to. Perhaps, Mr. Wilson, you would have the great kindness to recommence your narrative. I ask you not merely because my friend Dr. Watson has not heard the opening part but also because the peculiar nature of the story makes me anxious to have every possible detail from your lips. As a rule, when I have heard some slight indication of the course of events, I am able to guide myself by the thousands of

---

1. **settee** (se tē′) *n.* small sofa.

Reading Skill
Comparing Characters According to Holmes, what do he and Watson have in common?

Literary Analysis
Protagonist and Antagonist What details in Holmes's speech here help present him as a protagonist?

other similar cases which occur to my memory. In the present instance I am forced to admit that the facts are, to the best of my belief, unique."

The portly client puffed out his chest with an appearance of some little pride and pulled a dirty and wrinkled newspaper from the inside pocket of his great coat. As he glanced down the advertisement column, with his head thrust forward and the paper flattened out upon his knee, I took a good look at the man and endeavored, after the fashion of my companion, to read the indications which might be presented by his dress or appearance.

I did not gain very much, however, by my inspection. Our visitor bore every mark of being an average commonplace British tradesman, obese, pompous, and slow. He wore rather baggy gray shepherd's check trousers, a not over-clean black frock coat, unbuttoned in the front, and a drab waistcoat with a heavy brassy Albert chain, and a square pierced bit of metal dangling down as an ornament. A frayed top hat and a faded brown overcoat with a wrinkled velvet collar lay upon a chair beside him. Altogether, look as I would, there was nothing remarkable about the man save his blazing red head, and the expression of extreme chagrin and discontent upon his features.

Sherlock Holmes's quick eye took in my occupation, and he shook his head with a smile as he noticed my questioning glances. "Beyond the obvious facts that he has at some time done manual labor, that he takes snuff,[2] that he is a Freemason,[3] that he has been in China, and that he has done a considerable amount of writing lately, I can deduce nothing else."

Mr. Jabez Wilson started up in his chair, with his forefinger upon the paper, but his eyes upon my companion.

"How, in the name of good fortune, did you know all that, Mr. Holmes?" he asked. "How did you know, for example, that I did manual labor? It's as true as gospel, for I began as a ship's carpenter."

"Your hands, my dear sir. Your right hand is quite a size larger than your left. You have worked with it, and the muscles are more developed."

"Well, the snuff, then, and the Freemasonry?"

"I won't insult your intelligence by telling you how I read that, especially as, rather against the strict rules of your order, you use an arc-and-compass breastpin."

"Ah, of course, I forgot that. But the writing?"

Reading Skill
Contrasting Characters How are Watson and Holmes different in terms of their powers of observation?

Reading Check

What facts about Mr. Wilson does Holmes deduce based on Wilson's appearance?

---

2. snuff (snuf) *n.* powdered tobacco.
3. Freemason member of a secret society.

"What else can be indicated by that right cuff so very shiny for five inches, and the left one with the smooth patch near the elbow where you rest it upon the desk?"

"Well, but China?"

"The fish that you have tattooed immediately above your right wrist could only have been done in China. I have made a small study of tattoo marks and have even contributed to the literature of the subject. That trick of staining the fishes' scales of a delicate pink is quite peculiar to China. When, in addition, I see a Chinese coin hanging from your watch-chain, the matter becomes even more simple."

Mr. Jabez Wilson laughed heavily. "Well, I never!" said he. "I thought at first that you had done something clever, but I see that there was nothing in it, after all."

"I begin to think, Watson," said Holmes, "that I make a mistake in explaining. '*Omne ignotum pro magnifico*,'[4] you know, and my poor little reputation, such as it is, will suffer shipwreck if I am so candid. Can you not find the advertisement, Mr. Wilson?"

"Yes, I have got it now," he answered with his thick red finger planted halfway down the column. "Here it is. This is what began it all. You just read it for yourself, sir."

I took the paper from him and read as follows:

To THE RED-HEADED LEAGUE:

On account of the bequest of the late Ezekiah Hopkins, of Lebanon, Pennsylvania, U. S. A., there is now another vacancy open which entitles a member of the League to a salary of £4 a week for purely nominal services. All red-headed men who are sound in body and mind, and above the age of twenty-one years, are eligible. Apply in person on Monday, at eleven o'clock, to Duncan Ross, at the offices of the League, 7 Pope's Court, Fleet Street.

"What on earth does this mean?" I ejaculated after I had twice read over the extraordinary announcement.

Holmes chuckled and wriggled in his chair, as was his habit when in high spirits. "It is a little off the beaten track, isn't it?" said

4. *Omne ignotum pro magnifico* (äm′ nā ig nō′ təm prō mag nē′ fē kō) Latin for "Whatever is unknown is magnified."

Literature in Context

Math Connection

Pound Conversions The advertisement that concerns Mr. Wilson announces a salary of four pounds a week. The pound is the monetary unit of Great Britain. Its equivalency in American dollars fluctuates depending on current economic conditions. At the time Doyle wrote the story, one British pound equaled about $4.85, so four pounds would have equaled about $19.40. This was considered a large amount at the time in which the story is set, particularly for easy work.

Connect to the Literature

Why might an offer of a large sum of money "for purely nominal services" be cause for suspicion?

he. "And now, Mr. Wilson, off you go at scratch and tell us all about yourself, your household, and the effect which this advertisement had upon your fortunes. You will first make a note, Doctor, of the paper and the date."

"It is *The Morning Chronicle* of April 27, 1890. Just two months ago."

"Very good. Now, Mr. Wilson?"

"Well, it is just as I have been telling you, Mr. Sherlock Holmes," said Jabez Wilson, mopping his forehead; "I have a small pawnbroker's business at Coburg Square, near the City. It's not a very large affair, and of late years it has not done more than just give me a living. I used to be able to keep two assistants, but now I only keep one; and I would have a job to pay him but that he is willing to come for half wages so as to learn the business."

"What is the name of this obliging youth?" asked Sherlock Holmes.

"His name is Vincent Spaulding, and he's not such a youth, either. It's hard to say his age. I should not wish a smarter assistant, Mr. Holmes; and I know very well that he could better himself and earn twice what I am able to give him. But, after all, if he is satisfied, why should I put ideas in his head?"

"Why, indeed? You seem most fortunate in having an employee who comes under the full market price. It is not a common experience among employers in this age. I don't know that your assistant is not as remarkable as your advertisement."

"Oh, he has his faults, too," said Mr. Wilson. "Never was such a fellow for photography. Snapping away with a camera when he ought to be improving his mind, and then diving down into the cellar like a rabbit into its hole to develop his pictures. That is his main fault, but on the whole he's a good worker. There's no vice in him."

"He is still with you, I presume?"

"Yes, sir. He and a girl of fourteen, who does a bit of simple cooking and keeps the place clean—that's all I have in the house, for I am a widower and never had any family. We live very quietly, sir, the three of us; and we keep a roof over our heads and pay our debts, if we do nothing more.

"The first thing that put us out was that advertisement. Spaulding, he came down into the office just this day eight weeks, with this very paper in his hand, and he says:

"'I wish to the Lord, Mr. Wilson, that I was a red-headed man.'

"'Why that?' I asks.

"'Why,' says he, 'here's another vacancy on the League of the Red-headed Men. It's worth quite a little fortune to any man who

Literary Analysis
Protagonist and Antagonist Which details in the description of Vincent Spaulding attract Holmes's notice?

Reading Check

Who is eligible for the position posted in the advertisement?

gets it, and I understand that there are more vacancies than there are men, so that the trustees are at their wits' end what to do with the money. If my hair would only change color, here's a nice little crib all ready for me to step into.'

"'Why, what is it, then?' I asked. You see, Mr. Holmes, I am a very stay-at-home man, and as my business came to me instead of my having to go to it, I was often weeks on end without putting my foot over the doormat. In that way I didn't know much of what was going on outside, and I was always glad of a bit of news.

"'Have you never heard of the League of the Red-headed Men?' he asked with his eyes open.

"'Never.'

"'Why, I wonder at that, for you are eligible yourself for one of the vacancies.'

"'And what are they worth?' I asked.

"'Oh, merely a couple of hundred a year, but the work is slight, and it need not interfere very much with one's other occupations.'

"Well, you can easily think that that made me prick up my ears, for the business has not been over-good for some years, and an extra couple of hundred would have been very handy.

"'Tell me all about it,' said I.

"'Well,' said he, showing me the advertisement, 'you can see for yourself that the League has a vacancy, and there is the address where you should apply for particulars. As far as I can make out, the League was founded by an American millionaire, Ezekiah Hopkins, who was very peculiar in his ways. He was himself red-headed, and he had a great sympathy for all red-headed men; so when he died it was found that he had left his enormous fortune in the hands of trustees, with instructions to apply the

Reading Skill
Contrasting Characters In what ways does Wilson's lack of awareness of the outside world present a contrast to Holmes and Watson?

interest to the providing of easy berths to men whose hair is of that color. From all I hear it is splendid pay and very little to do.

"'But,' said I, 'there would be millions of red-headed men who would apply.'

"'Not so many as you might think,' he answered. 'You see it is really confined to Londoners, and to grown men. This American had started from London when he was young, and he wanted to do the old town a good turn. Then, again, I have heard it is no use your applying if your hair is light red, or dark red, or anything but real bright, blazing, fiery red. Now, if you cared to apply, Mr. Wilson, you would just walk in; but perhaps it would hardly be worth your while to put yourself out of the way for the sake of a few hundred pounds.'

"Now, it is a fact, gentlemen, as you may see for yourselves, that my hair is of a very full and rich tint, so that it seemed to me that if there was to be any competition in the matter I stood as good a chance as any man that I had ever met. Vincent Spaulding seemed to know so much about it that I thought he might prove useful so I just ordered him to put up the shutters for the day and to come right away with me. He was very willing to have a holiday,[5] so we shut the business up and started off for the address that was given us in the advertisement.

"I never hope to see such a sight as that again, Mr. Holmes. From north, south, east, and west every man who had a shade of red in his hair had tramped into the city to answer the advertisement. Fleet Street was choked with red-headed folk, and Pope's Court looked like a coster's orange barrow.[6] I should not have thought there were so many in the whole country as were brought together by that single advertisement. Every shade of color they were—straw, lemon, orange, brick, Irish-setter, liver, clay; but, as Spaulding said, there were not many who had the real vivid flame-colored tint. When I saw how many were waiting, I would have given it up in despair; but Spaulding would not hear of it. How he did it I could not imagine, but he pushed and pulled and butted until he got me through the crowd, and right up to the steps which led to the office. There was a double stream upon the stair, some going up in hope, and some coming back dejected; but we wedged in as well as we could and soon found ourselves in the office."

"Your experience has been a most entertaining one," remarked Holmes as his client paused and refreshed his memory with a huge pinch of snuff. "Pray continue your very interesting statement."

"There was nothing in the office but a couple of wooden chairs and a deal table, behind which sat a small man with a head that

Reading Skill
Contrasting Characters Who seems more invested in Wilson's joining the Red-headed League—Wilson or Spaulding? Explain.

Reading Check

Who helps Wilson push through the crowd of men applying for the Red-headed League?

---

5. **holiday** day off from work; vacation.
6. **coster's orange barrow** pushcart of a seller of oranges.

was even redder than mine. He said a few words to each candidate as he came up, and then he always managed to find some fault in them which would disqualify them. Getting a vacancy did not seem to be such a very easy matter, after all. However, when our turn came the little man was much more favorable to me than to any of the others, and he closed the door as we entered, so that he might have a private word with us.

"'This is Mr. Jabez Wilson,' said my assistant, 'and he is willing to fill a vacancy in the League.'

"'And he is admirably suited for it,' the other answered. 'He has every requirement. I cannot recall when I have seen anything so fine.' He took a step backward, cocked his head on one side, and gazed at my hair until I felt quite bashful. Then suddenly he plunged forward, wrung my hand, and congratulated me warmly on my success.

"'It would be injustice to hesitate, said he. 'You will, however, I am sure, excuse me for taking an obvious precaution.' With that he seized my hair in both his hands, and tugged until I yelled with the pain. 'There is water in your eyes,' said he as he released me. 'I perceive that all is as it should be. But we have to be careful, for we have twice been deceived by wigs and once by paint. I could tell you tales of cobbler's wax which would disgust you with human nature.' He stepped over to the window and shouted through it at the top of his voice that the vacancy was filled. A groan of disappointment came up from below, and the folk all trooped away in different directions until there was not a red head to be seen except my own and that of the manager.

"'My name,' said he, 'is Mr. Duncan Ross, and I am myself one of the pensioners upon the fund left by our noble benefactor. Are you a married man, Mr. Wilson? Have you a family?'

"I answered that I had not.

"His face fell immediately.

"'Dear me!' he said gravely, 'that is very serious indeed! I am sorry to hear you say that. The fund was, of course, for the propagation and spread of the red-heads as well as for their maintenance. It is exceedingly unfortunate that you should be a bachelor.'

"My face lengthened at this, Mr. Holmes, for I thought that I was not to have the vacancy after all; but after thinking it over for a few minutes he said that it would be all right.

"'In the case of another,' said he, 'the objection might be fatal, but we must stretch a point in favor of a man with such a head of hair as yours. When shall you be able to enter upon your new duties?'

"'Well, it is a little awkward, for I have a business already,' said I.

**Reading Skill
Contrasting
Characters** In what way is the man's behavior toward Mr. Wilson different from his behavior toward the other candidates?

"'Oh, never mind about that, Mr. Wilson!' said Vincent Spaulding. 'I should be able to look after that for you.'

"'What would be the hours?' I asked.

"'Ten to two.'

"Now a pawnbroker's business is mostly done of an evening, Mr. Holmes, especially Thursday and Friday evening, which is just before pay-day; so it would suit me very well to earn a little in the mornings. Besides, I knew that my assistant was a good man, and that he would see to anything that turned up.

"'That would suit me very well,' said I. 'And the pay?'

"'Is £4 a week.'

"'And the work?'

"'Is purely nominal.'

"'What do you call purely nominal?'

"'Well, you have to be in the office, or at least in the building, the whole time. If you leave, you forfeit your whole position forever. The will is very clear upon that point. You don't comply with the conditions if you budge from the office during that time.'

"'It's only four hours a day, and I should not think of leaving,' said I.

"'No excuse will avail,' said Mr. Duncan Ross; 'neither sickness nor business nor anything else. There you must stay, or you lose your billet.'[7]

"'And the work?'

"'Is to copy out the Encyclopedia Britannica. There is the first volume of it in that press. You must find your own ink, pens, and blotting-paper, but we provide this table and chair. Will you be ready tomorrow?'

"'Certainly,' I answered.

"'Then, good-bye, Mr. Jabez Wilson, and let me congratulate you once more on the important position which you have been fortunate enough to gain.' He bowed me out of the room, and I went home with my assistant, hardly knowing what to say or do, I was so pleased at my own good fortune.

"Well, I thought over the matter all day, and by evening I was in low spirits again; for I had quite persuaded myself that the whole affair must be some great hoax or fraud, though what its object might be I could not imagine. It seemed altogether past belief that anyone could make such a will, or that they would pay such a sum for doing anything so simple as copying out the Encyclopedia Britannica. Vincent Spaulding did what he could to cheer me up, but by bedtime I had reasoned myself out of the whole thing. However,

---

7. billet (bil′ it) *n.* position; job.

Literary Analysis
Protagonist and Antagonist Which details in the description of Wilson's responsibilities make Ross seem like a suspicious character?

Reading Check

Who offers to look after Wilson's pawnbroker business while he is at his other job?

in the morning I determined to have a look at it anyhow, so I bought a penny bottle of ink, and with a quill-pen, and seven sheets of foolscap paper, I started off for Pope's Court.

"Well, to my surprise and delight, everything was as right as possible. The table was set out ready for me, and Mr. Duncan Ross was there to see that I got fairly to work. He started me off upon the letter A, and then he left me; but he would drop in from time to time to see that all was right with me. At two o'clock he bade me good-day, complimented me upon the amount that I had written, and locked the door of the office after me.

"This went on day after day, Mr. Holmes, and on Saturday the manager came in and planked down four golden sovereigns for my week's work. It was the same next week, and the same the week after. Every morning I was there at ten, and every afternoon I left at two. By degrees Mr. Duncan Ross took to coming in only once of a morning, and then, after a time, he did not come in at all. Still, of course, I never dared to leave the room for an instant, for I was not sure when he might come, and the billet was such a good one, and suited me so well, that I would not risk the loss of it.

"Eight weeks passed away like this, and I had written about Abbots and Archery and Armor and Architecture and Attica, and hoped with diligence that I might get on to the B's before very long. It cost me something in foolscap, and I had pretty nearly filled a shelf with my writings. And then suddenly the whole business came to an end."

"To an end?"

"Yes, sir. And no later than this morning. I went to my work as usual at ten o'clock, but the door was shut and locked, with a little square of cardboard hammered on to the middle of the panel with a tack. Here it is, and you can read for yourself."

He held up a piece of white cardboard about the size of a sheet of notepaper. It read in this fashion:

THE RED-HEADED LEAGUE IS DISSOLVED.
October 9, 1890.

Sherlock Holmes and I surveyed this curt announcement and the rueful face behind it, until the comical side of the affair so completely overtopped every other consideration that we both burst out into a roar of laughter.

"I cannot see that there is anything very funny," cried our client, flushing up to the roots of his flaming head. "If you can do nothing better than laugh at me, I can go elsewhere."

"No, no," cried Holmes, shoving him back into the chair from which he had half risen. "I really wouldn't miss your case for the world. It is most refreshingly unusual. But there is, if you will excuse my saying so, something just a little funny about it. Pray what steps did you take when you found the card upon the door?"

"I was staggered, sir. I did not know what to do. Then I called at the offices round, but none of them seemed to know anything about it. Finally, I went to the landlord, who is an accountant living on the ground floor, and I asked him if he could tell me what had become of the Red-headed League. He said that he had never heard of any such body. Then I asked him who Mr. Duncan Ross was. He answered that the name was new to him.

"'Well,' said I, 'the gentleman at No. 4.'

"'What, the red-headed man?'

"'Yes.'

"'Oh,' said he, 'his name was William Morris. He was a solicitor[8] and was using my room as a temporary convenience until his new premises were ready. He moved out yesterday.'

"'Where could I find him?'

"'Oh, at his new offices. He did tell me the address. Yes, 17 King Edward Street, near St. Paul's.'

"I started off, Mr. Holmes, but when I got to that address it was a manufactory of artificial kneecaps, and no one in it had ever heard of either Mr. William Morris or Mr. Duncan Ross."

"And what did you do then?" asked Holmes.

Reading Skill
Contrasting Characters How do the reactions of Watson and Holmes to the announcement compare with Mr. Wilson's? Explain.

Literary Analysis
Protagonist and Antagonist What does William Morris's dishonesty about his identity suggest about his character?

Reading Check

After eight weeks at his new job, what does Wilson find posted on the door?

"I went home to Saxe-Coburg Square, and I took the advice of my assistant. But he could not help me in any way. He could only say that if I waited I should hear by post. But that was not quite good enough, Mr. Holmes. I did not wish to lose such a place without a struggle, so, as I had heard that you were good enough to give advice to poor folk who were in need of it, I came right away to you."

"And you did very wisely," said Holmes. "Your case is an exceedingly remarkable one, and I shall be happy to look into it. From what you have told me I think that it is possible that graver issues hang from it than might at first sight appear."

"Grave enough!" said Mr. Jabez Wilson. "Why, I have lost four pound a week."

"As far as you are personally concerned," remarked Holmes, "I do not see that you have any grievance against this extraordinary league. On the contrary, you are, as I understand, richer by some £30, to say nothing of the minute knowledge which you have gained on every subject which comes under the letter A. You have lost nothing by them."

"No, sir. But I want to find out about them, and who they are, and what their object was in playing this prank—if it was a prank—upon me. It was a pretty expensive joke for them, for it cost them two and thirty pounds."

"We shall endeavor to clear up these points for you. And, first, one or two questions, Mr. Wilson. This assistant of yours who first called your attention to the advertisement— how long had he been with you?"

"About a month then."

"How did he come?"

"In answer to an advertisement."

"Was he the only applicant?"

"No, I had a dozen."

**Literary Analysis
Protagonist and
Antagonist** What
reason might Holmes
have for being
suspicious of Vincent
Spaulding?

"Why did you pick him?"

"Because he was handy and would come cheap."

"At half-wages, in fact."

"Yes."

"What is he like, this Vincent Spaulding?"

"Small, stout-built, very quick in his ways. No hair on his face, though he's not short of thirty. Has a white splash of acid upon his forehead."

Holmes sat up in his chair in considerable excitement. "I thought as much," said he. "Have you ever observed that his ears are pierced for earrings?"

"Yes, sir. He told me that a gypsy had done it for him when he was a lad."

"Hum!" said Holmes, sinking back in deep thought. "He is still with you?"

"Oh, yes, sir; I have only just left him."

"And has your business been attended to in your absence?"

"Nothing to complain of, sir. There's never very much to do of a morning."

"That will do, Mr. Wilson. I shall be happy to give you an opinion upon the subject in the course of a day or two. Today is Saturday, and I hope that by Monday we may come to a conclusion."

"Well, Watson," said Holmes when our visitor had left us, "what do you make of it all?"

"I make nothing of it," I answered frankly. "It is a most mysterious business."

"As a rule," said Holmes, "the more bizarre a thing is the less mysterious it proves to be. It is your commonplace, featureless crimes which are really puzzling, just as a commonplace face is the most difficult to identify. But I must be prompt over this matter."

"What are you going to do, then?" I asked.

"To smoke," he answered. "It is quite a three pipe problem, and I beg that you won't speak to me for fifty minutes." He curled himself up in his chair, with his thin knees drawn up to his hawk-like nose, and there he sat with his eyes closed and his black clay pipe thrusting out like the bill of some strange bird. I had come to the conclusion that he had dropped asleep, and indeed was nodding myself, when he suddenly sprang out of his chair with the gesture of a man who has made up his mind and put his pipe down upon the mantelpiece.

"Sarasate[9] plays at the St. James's Hall this afternoon," he remarked. "What do you think, Watson? Could your patients spare you for a few hours?"

---

9. **Sarasate** (sä rä sä′ tä) Spanish violinist and composer.

Literary Analysis
Protagonist and Antagonist What does Holmes's expectation of reaching a conclusion in two days reveal about his character?

Reading Check

What reasons does Mr. Wilson give for hiring Vincent Spaulding?

"I have nothing to do today. My practice is never very absorbing."

"Then put on your hat and come. I am going through the City first, and we can have some lunch on the way. I observe that there is a good deal of German music on the program, which is rather more to my taste than Italian or French. It is <u>introspective</u>, and I want to introspect. Come along!"

We traveled by the Underground as far as Aldersgate; and a short walk took us to Saxe-Coburg Square, the scene of the singular story which we had listened to in the morning. It was a poky, little, shabby-genteel place, where four lines of dingy two-storied brick houses looked out into a small railed-in enclosure, where a lawn of weedy grass and a few clumps of faded laurel bushes made a hard fight against a smoke-laden and uncongenial atmosphere. Three gilt balls and a brown board with "JABEZ WILSON" in white letters, upon a corner house, announced the place where our red-headed client carried on his business. Sherlock Holmes stopped in front of it with his head on one side and looked it all over, with his eyes shining brightly between puckered lids. Then he walked slowly up the street, and then down again to the corner, still looking keenly at the houses. Finally he returned to the pawnbroker's, and, having thumped vigorously upon the pavement with his stick two or three times, he went up to the door and knocked. It was instantly opened by a bright-looking, clean-shaven young fellow, who asked him to step in.

"Thank you," said Holmes, "I only wished to ask you how you would go from here to the Strand."

"Third right, fourth left," answered the assistant promptly, closing the door.

"Smart fellow, that," observed Holmes as we walked away. "He is, in my judgment, the fourth smartest man in London, and for daring I am not sure that he has not a claim to be third. I have known something of him before."

"Evidently," said I, "Mr. Wilson's assistant counts for a good deal in this mystery of the Red-headed League. I am sure that you inquired your way merely in order that you might see him."

"Not him."

"What then?"

"The knees of his trousers."

"And what did you see?"

"What I expected to see."

"Why did you beat the pavement?"

"My dear doctor, this is a time for observation, not for talk. We are spies in an enemy's country. We know something of Saxe-Coburg Square. Let us now explore the parts which lie behind it."

Vocabulary Builder
introspective (in′ trə spek′ tiv) *adj.* having to do with one's own thoughts and feelings

Reading Skill
Comparing Characters Based on Holmes's remark about Spaulding, what trait do the two men share? Explain.

The road in which we found ourselves as we turned round the corner from the retired Saxe-Coburg Square presented as great a contrast to it as the front of a picture does to the back. It was one of the main arteries which conveyed the traffic of the City to the north and west. The roadway was blocked with the immense stream of commerce flowing in a double tide inward and outward, while the footpaths were black with the hurrying swarm of pedestrians. It was difficult to realize as we looked at the line of fine shops and stately business premises that they really abutted on the other side upon the faded and stagnant square which we had just quitted.

"Let me see," said Holmes, standing at the corner and glancing along the line, "I should like just to remember the order of the houses here. It is a hobby of mine to have an exact knowledge of London. There is Mortimer's, the tobacconist, the little newspaper shop, the Coburg branch of the City and Suburban Bank, the Vegetarian Restaurant, and McFarlane's carriage-building depot. That carries us right on to the other block. And now, Doctor, we've done our work, so it's time we had some play. A sandwich and a cup of coffee, and then off to violin land, where all is sweetness and delicacy and harmony, and there are no red-headed clients to <u>vex</u> us with their conundrums."

My friend was an enthusiastic musician, being himself not only a very capable performer but a composer of no ordinary merit. All the afternoon he sat in the stalls wrapped in the most perfect happiness, gently waving his long, thin fingers in time to the music, while his gently smiling face and his languid, dreamy eyes were as unlike those of Holmes, the sleuthhound, Holmes the relentless, keen-witted, ready-handed criminal agent, as it was possible to conceive. In his singular character the dual nature alternately asserted itself, and his extreme exactness and astuteness represented, as I have often thought, the reaction against the poetic and contemplative mood which occasionally predominated in him. The swing of his nature took him from extreme languor to devouring energy; and, as I knew well, he was never so truly <u>formidable</u> as when, for days on end, he had been lounging in his armchair amid his improvisations and his black-letter editions. Then it was that the lust of the chase would suddenly come upon him, and that his brilliant reasoning power would rise to the level of intuition, until those who were unacquainted with his methods would look askance at him as on a man whose knowledge was not that of other mortals. When I saw him that afternoon so enwrapped in the music at St. James's Hall I felt that an evil time might be coming upon those whom he had set himself to hunt down.

"You want to go home, no doubt, Doctor," he remarked as we emerged.

Vocabulary Builder
vex (veks) *v.* annoy

formidable (fôr´ mə də bəl) *adj.* awe-inspiring

Reading Check

Which aspect of Spaulding's appearance does Holmes want to observe?

"Yes, it would be as well."

"And I have some business to do which will take some hours. This business at Coburg Square is serious."

"Why serious?"

"A considerable crime is in contemplation. I have every reason to believe that we shall be in time to stop it. But today being Saturday rather complicates matters. I shall want your help tonight."

"At what time?"

"Ten will be early enough."

"I shall be at Baker Street at ten."

"Very well. And, I say, Doctor, there may be some little danger, so kindly put your army revolver in your pocket." He waved his hand, turned on his heel, and disappeared in an instant among the crowd.

I trust that I am not more dense than my neighbors, but I was always oppressed with a sense of my own stupidity in my dealings with Sherlock Holmes. Here I had heard what he had heard, I had seen what he had seen, and yet from his words it was evident that he saw clearly not only what had happened but what was about to happen, while to me the whole business was still confused and grotesque. As I drove home to my house in Kensington I thought over it all, from the extraordinary story of the red-headed copier of the Encyclopedia down to the visit to Saxe-Coburg Square, and the ominous words with which he had parted from me. What was this nocturnal expedition, and why should I go armed? Where were we going, and what were we to do? I had the hint from Holmes that this smooth-faced pawnbroker's assistant was a formidable man—a man who might play a deep game. I tried to puzzle it out, but gave it up in despair and set the matter aside until night should bring an explanation.

It was a quarter past nine when I started from home and made my way across the Park, and so through Oxford Street to Baker Street. Two hansoms were standing at the door, and as I entered the passage I heard the sound of voices from above. On entering his room I found Holmes in animated conversation with two men, one of whom I recognized as Peter Jones, the official police agent, while the other was a long, thin, sadfaced man, with a very shiny hat and oppressively respectable frock coat.

Literature in Context

Culture Connection

Hansoms The hansom, also known as the hansom cab, is a two-wheeled covered carriage for two passengers that is pulled by one horse. The cab was named for its inventor, Joseph Hansom (1803–1882), a London architect. By the late 1850s, the hansom was popular in New York and Boston as well as in London. Customers could enjoy a scenic and romantic ride in private with an unobstructed view because the driver sat above and behind the passengers' cab. Today, updated hansom cabs are a popular tourist attraction in New York's Central Park. However, in this story, they are a common form of transportation.

Connect to the Literature

What problems would traveling by hansom pose for someone rushing to stop a crime?

"Ha! our party is complete," said Holmes, buttoning up his pea-jacket and taking his heavy hunting crop from the rack. "Watson, I think you know Mr. Jones, of Scotland Yard? Let me introduce you to Mr. Merryweather, who is to be our companion in tonight's adventure."

"We're hunting in couples again, Doctor, you see," said Jones in his consequential way. "Our friend here is a wonderful man for starting a chase. All he wants is an old dog to help him to do the running down."

"I hope a wild goose may not prove to be the end of our chase," observed Mr. Merryweather gloomily.

"You may place considerable confidence in Mr. Holmes, sir," said the police agent loftily. "He has his own little methods, which are, if he won't mind my saying so, just a little too theoretical and fantastic, but he has the makings of a detective in him. It is not too much to say that once or twice, as in that business of the Sholto murder and the Agra treasure, he has been more nearly correct than the official force."

"Oh, if you say so, Mr. Jones, it is all right," said the stranger with deference. "Still, I confess that I miss my rubber.[10] It is the first Saturday night for seven-and-twenty years that I have not had my rubber."

"I think you will find," said Sherlock Holmes, "that you will play for a higher stake tonight than you have ever done yet, and that the play will be more exciting. For you, Mr. Merryweather, the stake will be some £30,000; and for you, Jones, it will be the man upon whom you wish to lay your hands."

"John Clay, the murderer, thief, smasher, and forger. He's a young man, Mr. Merryweather, but he is at the head of his profession, and I would rather have my bracelets on him than on any criminal in London. He's a remarkable man, is young John Clay. His grandfather was a royal duke, and he himself has been to Eton[11] and Oxford.[12] His brain is as cunning as his fingers, and though we meet signs of him at every turn, we never know where to find the man himself. He'll crack a crib[13] in Scotland one week, and be raising money to build an orphanage in Cornwall the next. I've been on his track for years and have never set eyes on him yet."

"I hope that I may have the pleasure of introducing you tonight. I've had one or two little turns also with Mr. John Clay, and I agree with you that he is at the head of his profession. It is past ten,

---

10. **rubber** a term for a type of card game.
11. **Eton** famous British secondary school for boys.
12. **Oxford** oldest university in Great Britain.
13. **crack a crib** commit burglary.

**Reading Skill
Comparing
Characters** Despite their differences, in what ways are Sherlock Holmes and John Clay similar?

Reading Check

With whom is Holmes speaking when Watson arrives?

however, and quite time that we started. If you two will take the first hansom, Watson and I will follow in the second."

Sherlock Holmes was not very communicative during the long drive and lay back in the cab humming the tunes which he had heard in the afternoon. We rattled through an endless labyrinth of gas-lit streets until we emerged into Farrington Street.

"We are close there now," my friend remarked. "This fellow Merryweather is a bank director, and personally interested in the matter. I thought it as well to have Jones with us also. He is not a bad fellow, though an absolute imbecile in his profession. He has one positive virtue. He is as brave as a bulldog and as tenacious as a lobster if he gets his claws upon anyone. Here we are, and they are waiting for us."

We had reached the same crowded thoroughfare in which we had found ourselves in the morning. Our cabs were dismissed, and, following the guidance of Mr. Merryweather, we passed down a narrow passage and through a side door, which he opened for us. Within there was a small corridor, which ended in a very massive iron gate. This also was opened, and led down a flight of winding stone steps, which terminated at another formidable gate. Mr. Merryweather stopped to light a lantern, and then conducted us down a dark, earth-smelling passage, and so, after opening a third door, into a huge vault or cellar, which was piled all round with crates and massive boxes.

"You are not very vulnerable from above," Holmes remarked as he held up the lantern and gazed about him.

"Nor from below," said Mr. Merryweather, striking his stick upon the flags which lined the floor. "Why, dear me, it sounds quite hollow!" he remarked, looking up in surprise.

"I must really ask you to be a little more quiet!" said Holmes severely. "You have already imperiled the whole success of our expedition. Might I beg that you would have the goodness to sit down upon one of those boxes, and not to interfere?"

The solemn Mr. Merryweather perched himself upon a crate, with a very injured expression upon his face, while Holmes fell upon his knees upon the floor and, with the lantern and a magnifying lens, began to examine minutely the cracks between the stones. A few seconds sufficed to satisfy him, for he sprang to his feet again and put his glass in his pocket.

"We have at least an hour before us," he remarked, "for they can hardly take any steps until the good pawnbroker is safely in bed. Then they will not lose a minute, for the sooner they do their work the longer time they will have for their escape. We are at present, Doctor—as no doubt you have divined—in the cellar of the City branch of one of the principal London banks. Mr. Merryweather is the chairman of directors, and he will explain to you that there are reasons why the more daring criminals of London should take a considerable interest in this cellar at present."

"It is our French gold," whispered the director. "We have had several warnings that an attempt might be made upon it."

"Your French gold?"

"Yes. We had occasion some months ago to strengthen our resources and borrowed for that purpose 30,000 napoleons from the Bank of France. It has become known that we have never had occasion to unpack the money, and that it is still lying in our cellar. The crate upon which I sit contains 2,000 napoleons packed between layers of lead foil. Our reserve of bullion is much larger at present than is usually kept in a single branch office, and the directors have had misgivings upon the subject."

"Which were very well justified," observed Holmes.

"And now it is time that we arranged our little plans. I expect that within an hour matters will come to a head. In the meantime, Mr. Merryweather, we must put the screen over that dark lantern."

"And sit in the dark?"

"I am afraid so. I had brought a pack of cards in my pocket, and I thought that, as we were a *partie carrée*,[14] you might have your rubber after all. But I see that the enemy's preparations have gone so far that we cannot risk the presence of a light. And, first of all, we

Literary Analysis
Protagonist and Antagonist What kind of enemy does Holmes anticipate he and his companions will face?

Reading Check

Where does Mr. Merryweather lead Holmes and his companions?

---

14. *partie carrée* (pär tē´ cä rā´) French for "group of four."

must choose our positions. These are daring men, and though we shall take them at a disadvantage, they may do us some harm unless we are careful. I shall stand behind this crate, and do you conceal yourselves behind those. Then, when I flash a light upon them, close in swiftly. If they fire, Watson, have no compunction about shooting them down."

I placed my revolver, cocked, upon the top of the wooden case behind which I crouched. Holmes shot the slide across the front of his lantern and left us in pitch darkness—such an absolute darkness as I have never before experienced. The smell of hot metal remained to assure us that the light was still there, ready to flash out at a moment's notice. To me, with my nerves worked up to a pitch of expectancy, there was something depressing and subduing in the sudden gloom, and in the cold dank air of the vault.

"They have but one retreat," whispered Holmes. "That is back through the house into Saxe-Coburg Square. I hope that you have done what I asked you, Jones?"

"I have an inspector and two officers waiting at the front door."

"Then we have stopped all the holes. And now we must be silent and wait."

What a time it seemed! From comparing notes afterwards it was but an hour and a quarter, yet it appeared to me that the night must have almost gone, and the dawn be breaking above us. My limbs were weary and stiff, for I feared to change my position; yet my nerves were worked up to the highest pitch of tension, and my hearing was so acute that I could not only hear the gentle breathing of my companions, but I could distinguish the deeper, heavier in-breath of the bulky Jones from the thin, sighing note of the bank director. From my position I could look over the case in the direction of the floor. Suddenly my eyes caught the glint of a light.

At first it was but a lurid spark upon the stone pavement. Then it lengthened out until it became a yellow line, and then, without any warning or sound, a gash seemed to open and a hand appeared; a white, almost womanly hand, which felt about in the center of the little area of light. For a minute or more the hand, with its writhing fingers, protruded out of the floor. Then it was withdrawn as suddenly as it appeared, and all was dark again save the single lurid spark which marked a chink between the stones.

Its disappearance, however, was but momentary. With a rending, tearing sound, one of the broad, white stones turned over upon its side and left a square, gaping hole, through which streamed the light of a lantern. Over the edge there peeped a clean-cut, boyish face, which looked keenly about it, and then, with a hand on either side of the aperture, drew itself shoulder-high and

Literary Analysis
Protagonist and Antagonist What details of Watson's account help build the suspense of the conflict?

Reading Skill
Comparing Characters In what ways is the first burglar's appearance similar to that of Vincent Spaulding?

waist-high, until one knee rested upon the edge. In another instant he stood at the side of the hole and was hauling after him a companion, lithe and small like himself, with a pale face and a shock of very red hair.

"It's all clear," he whispered. "Have you the chisel and the bags? Great Scott! Jump, Archie, jump, and I'll swing for it."

Sherlock Holmes had sprung out and seized the intruder by the collar. The other dived down the hole, and I heard the sound of rending cloth as Jones clutched at his skirts. The light flashed upon the barrel of a revolver, but Holmes's hunting crop came down on the man's wrist, and the pistol clinked upon the stone floor.

"It's no use, John Clay," said Holmes blandly. "You have no chance at all."

"So I see," the other answered with the utmost coolness. "I fancy that my pal is all right, though I see you have got his coattails."

"There are three men waiting for him at the door," said Holmes.

"Oh, indeed! You seem to have done the thing very completely. I must compliment you."

"And I you," Holmes answered. "Your red-headed idea was very new and effective."

"You'll see your pal again presently," said Jones. "He's quicker at climbing down holes than I am. Just hold out while I fix the derbies."[15]

"I beg that you will not touch me with your filthy hands," remarked our prisoner as the handcuffs clattered upon his wrists. "You may not be aware that I have royal blood in my veins. Have the

---

15. **derbies** handcuffs.

✓ **Reading Check**

What color is Clay's accomplice's hair?

goodness, also, when you address me always to say 'sir' and 'please.'"

"All right," said Jones with a stare and a snigger. "Well, would you please, sir, march upstairs, where we can get a cab to carry your Highness to the police station?"

"That is better," said John Clay serenely. He made a sweeping bow to the three of us and walked quietly off in the custody of the detective.

"Really, Mr. Holmes," said Mr. Merryweather as we followed them from the cellar, "I do not know how the bank can thank you or repay you. There is no doubt that you have detected and defeated in the most complete manner one of the most determined attempts at bank robbery that have ever come within my experience."

"I have had one or two little scores of my own to settle with Mr. John Clay," said Holmes. "I have been at some small expense over this matter, which I shall expect the bank to refund, but beyond that I am amply repaid by having had an experience which is in many ways unique, and by hearing the very remarkable narrative of the Red-headed League."

"You see, Watson," he explained in the early hours of the morning as we sat over a glass of whisky and soda in Baker Street, "it was perfectly obvious from the first that the only possible object of this rather fantastic business of the advertisement of the League, and the copying of the Encyclopedia, must be to get this not over-bright pawnbroker out of the way for a number of hours every day. It was a curious way of managing it, but, really, it would be difficult to suggest a better. The method was no doubt suggested to Clay's ingenious mind by the color of his accomplice's hair. The £4 a week was a lure which must draw him, and what was it to them, who were playing for thousands? They put in the advertisement, one rogue has the temporary office, the other rogue incites the man to apply for it, and together they manage to secure his absence every morning in the week. From the time that I heard of the assistant having come for half wages, it was obvious to me that he had some strong motive for securing the situation."

"But how could you guess what the motive was?"

"Had there been women in the house, I should have suspected a mere vulgar intrigue. That, however, was out of the question. The man's business was a small one, and there was nothing in his house which could account for such elaborate preparations, and such an expenditure as they were at. It must, then, be something out of the house. What could it be? I thought of the assistant's fondness for photography, and his trick of vanishing into the cellar. The cellar! There was the end of this tangled clue. Then I made

Reading Skill
Contrasting Characters What difference between Holmes and Clay is revealed by Holmes's refusal to accept a reward?

inquiries as to this mysterious assistant and found that I had to deal with one of the coolest and most daring criminals in London. He was doing something in the cellar—something which took many hours a day for months on end. What could it be, once more? I could think of nothing save that he was running a tunnel to some other building.

"So far I had got when we went to visit the scene of action. I surprised you by beating upon the pavement with my stick. I was ascertaining whether the cellar stretched out in front or behind. It was not in front. Then I rang the bell, and, as I hoped, the assistant answered it. We have had some skirmishes, but we had never set eyes upon each other before. I hardly looked at his face. His knees were what I wished to see. You must yourself have remarked how worn, wrinkled, and stained they were. They spoke of those hours of burrowing. The only remaining point was what they were burrowing for. I walked round the corner, saw that the City and Suburban Bank abutted on our friend's premises, and felt that I had solved my problem. When you drove home after the concert I called upon Scotland Yard and upon the chairman of the bank directors, with the result that you have seen."

"And how could you tell that they would make their attempt tonight?" I asked.

"Well, when they closed their League offices that was a sign that they cared no longer about Mr. Jabez Wilson's presence—in other words, that they had completed their tunnel. But it was essential that they should use it soon, as it might be discovered, or the bullion might be removed. Saturday would suit them better than any other day, as it would give them two days for their escape. For all these reasons I expected them to come tonight."

"You reasoned it out beautifully," I exclaimed in unfeigned admiration. "It is so long a chain, and yet every link rings true."

"It saved me from ennui,"[16] he answered, yawning. "Alas! I already feel it closing in upon me. My life is spent in one long effort to escape from the commonplaces of existence. These little problems help me to do so."

"And you are a benefactor of the race," said I.

He shrugged his shoulders. "Well, perhaps, after all, it is of some little use," he remarked. "'L'homme c'est rien—l'oeuvre c'est tout,'[17] as Gustave Flaubert wrote to George Sand."[18]

---

16. ennui (än′ wē′) *n.* boredom.
17. L'homme c'est rien—l'oeuvre c'est tout (lum se rē en′ luvr se too) French for "Man is nothing—the work is everything."
18. Gustave Flaubert (goos täv′ flō ber′) . . . **George Sand** notable French novelists of the nineteenth century.

Literary Analysis
Protagonist and Antagonist What was Clay's (Spaulding's) motivation in arranging for Wilson to be out of the house?

Literary Analysis
Protagonist and Antagonist What does Holmes claim is his reason for solving crimes?

Apply the Skills

The Red-headed League

Thinking About the Selection

1. **(a) Respond:** What did you think of Holmes's solution to the mystery? **(b)** Did you find it a satisfying ending? Explain.
2. **(a) Recall:** Why does Jabez Wilson visit Sherlock Holmes? **(b) Infer:** Why does Holmes find Wilson's story interesting?
3. **(a) Recall:** What happens the night of the attempted burglary? **(b) Analyze Cause and Effect:** Which clues found at Saxe-Coburg Square lead to Holmes's solution of the mystery? **(c) Speculate:** What details could have been misinterpreted, leading to an incorrect conclusion?
4. **(a) Recall:** What remark does Holmes make about commonplace crimes? **(b) Infer:** What does Holmes mean? **(c) Interpret:** What does his remark suggest about the qualities that make a great detective?

Literary Analysis

5. **(a)** Identify the **protagonist** in the narrative. **(b)** What is the protagonist's goal? **(c)** Why are readers interested in whether the protagonist achieves his goal?
6. **(a)** Identify the **antagonist**. **(b)** What is the antagonist's goal?
7. **(a)** Why is the story's conflict interesting? **(b)** What universal struggle does this conflict represent?

Reading Strategy

8. What are two specific questions you can ask after reading to help you **compare and contrast** Holmes's actions, reasoning, and outlook at the beginning of the case and after it is solved?
9. **(a)** Use a Venn diagram to compare and contrast Holmes's character at the beginning and end of the story.

Beginning Only

End Only

Beginning and End

   (b) Explain whether Holmes changes during the story.
10. **(a)** In what ways do Watson, Holmes, and Wilson act differently from one another during the case? **(b)** What is one reason the author may have for showing these three different reactions?

Vocabulary Builder

Practice Analogies show the relationships between pairs of words. Use a word from the vocabulary list for "The Red-headed League" on page 1048 to complete each analogy.

1. kind : gentle :: _____ : fearsome
2. burn : candle :: _____ : problem
3. descending : downward :: _____ : inward

Adding Words to Your Vocabulary Using a dictionary and a thesaurus, find an antonym for each vocabulary word. Explain your choices. Then, use each correctly in a sentence. (For more on using a dictionary and a thesaurus, see pp. R6–7.)

Writing

Imagine that you are one of the characters in "The Red-headed League" other than Dr. Watson. Write three **journal entries** describing the events in the story as they unfold.

- Review the story and create a timeline for the major events.
- Decide which days you will record in your journal.
- Write your thoughts about what happens each day.

As you write, stay in character, making sure that your journal reflects any changes that the character experiences in the story.

For *Grammar, Vocabulary,* and *Assessment,*
see **Build Language Skills,** pages 1092–1093.

Extend Your Learning

Listening and Speaking With another student, role-play an **interview** in which Officer Jones interrogates John Clay about his plan. Listen carefully to what your partner says in the interview, and respond with appropriate questions or answers. After the role play, give each other feedback on your work.

Research and Technology Research the science of detective work and prepare an **oral report** for the class. Find information on fingerprinting, lie detectors, and police sketches. Refer to multiple sources, such as the Internet, encyclopedias, and criminology books. Compare what you learn to Holmes's methods.

Build Language Skills

Vocabulary Skill

Word Roots The Latin word **root -sign-** means "sign or meaning." It can stand on its own, as in the word *sign,* or it can be the word root of another word, such as *signify,* meaning "to mean something or to stand for something." This word root can be a context clue to help you figure out the meaning of a sentence.

Practice Use each of the following *-sign-* words in a sentence. Then, exchange papers with another student and write a sentence explaining how knowing the meaning of *-sign-* helps you understand the sentence.

1. signal
2. ensign
3. assign
4. resign

Grammar Lesson

Using Commas Correctly Use commas when you need to indicate a short pause in your writing. Two basic principles guide all comma usage.

MorePractice

For more practice with commas, see the Grammar Handbook, p. R40.

USE COMMAS TO SEPARATE . . .	USE COMMAS TO SET OFF . . .
— **two independent clauses in a compound sentence** I turned the ignition key, but the car did not start.	— **an introductory word, phrase, or clause** Coincidentally, we all ended up at the same beach.
— **three or more words, phrases, or clauses in a series** He spoke with passion, with gravity, and with sorrow.	— **parenthetical or nonessential expressions** The magazine, which I unfortunately misplaced, had some great articles.
— **parts of dates, places, or certain titles** We went to Sonoma, California, for the weekend.	— **direct quotations** President Roosevelt declared, "The only thing we have to fear is fear itself."

Practice Copy each sentence, and add commas where they are necessary, indicating which rule(s) you are following. (Note: Every sentence may not require a comma.)

1. "Please leave the building" said the fire marshal.
2. Actually my sister is older than my brother.
3. His voice is powerful deep and resonant and these qualities which I envy make him a fine speaker.

W *Prentice Hall Writing and Grammar Connection: Chapter 29, Section 2*

Reading Skill: Compare and Contrast

Standards
Assessed

• IR.2.04.1
• IR.2.04.4
• LT.5.01.6

Directions: *Read the selection. Then, answer the questions.*

He felt silent, amazed and bewildered to see that his wife was crying. . . .

He mumbled: "What is it? What is it?"

But, with great effort, she had overcome her misery; and now she answered him calmly, wiping her tear-damp cheeks:

"It's nothing. It's just that I have no evening dress and so I can't go to the party. Give the invitation to one of your colleagues whose wife will be better dressed than I would be."

He was overcome. He said:

"Listen, Mathilde, how much would an evening dress cost. . .

She thought for several seconds, making her calculations and at the same time estimating how much she could ask for without eliciting an immediate refusal . . . from the economical government clerk.

—from "The Necklace" by Guy de Maupassant

1. Which of the following is not a fact that defines the wife's character?
   A She wants to go to the dance.
   B She wishes her husband paid more attention to her.
   C She calculates how much she can ask for.
   D She cries to gain sympathy.

2. Which question would be most helpful in *contrasting* the husband and wife?
   A Does she really want to go to the ball?
   B Why is he confused by her reaction?
   C How do their feelings about money differ?
   D Why does the wife cry?

Timed Writing: Explanation (Connnections)

Review "Three Skeleton Key" or "The Red-headed League." For either story, explain the key details that provide clues to the mystery's solution and how the author presents these clues. **(40 minutes)**

Writing Workshop: *Work in Progress*

Comparison and Contrast

For a comparison-and-contrast essay you may write, choose two places that you know well. For each, note the purpose, sound, and look of the place. Save this Comparison Lst in your writing portfolio.

Reading Informational Materials

Encyclopedia Entries

In Part 2, you learned how to compare and contrast when you read literature. This skill is also useful when reading informational materials such as biographies, magazine articles, and encyclopedia entries. Comparing and contrasting helps you understand ideas, data, and other information by exploring their similarities and differences. If you read "The Red-Headed League" by Sir Arthur Conan Doyle, you will appreciate this encyclopedia entry about detective stories.

Standard Course of Study

• Summarizing key events and/or points from text. for research. (IR.2.01.5)

• Analyze elements of literary environment found in text. (LT.5.03.12)

About Encyclopedia Entries

Encyclopedias are reference works containing factual articles. There are many types of encyclopedias. General encyclopedias provide information in all subject areas. Specialized encyclopedias provide information on particular subjects, such as twentieth-century inventors or African American writers. Encyclopedias are published in both electronic format, such as CD-ROM, and in print, or book, form. Most print encyclopedias consist of many volumes, which are arranged alphabetically. Articles within each volume are usually arranged alphabetically by topic. Encyclopedia entries often have the following characteristics:

- an introduction in which the author identifies the topic and gives an overview
- subheads with which the author organizes information and helps readers locate specific facts
- sources for additional information

Reading Skill

Setting a purpose for reading can help you focus, save time, and get the most out of a work. For example, your purpose for reading might be to gain general knowledge about a topic, to find a specific piece of information, or to analyze an author's ideas. To set a purpose for reading, first decide what you want to learn about a topic. Preview the material to get a sense of its scope and organization. Then, use a K-W-L chart like the one shown to set a specific purpose for your reading.

What I Know	What I Want to Know	What I Learned
Arthur Conan Doyle wrote detective stories.	When were the first detective stories written?	Edgar Allen Poe wrote the first detective story in 1841.

Detective Story

Detective story is a work of fiction about a puzzling crime, a number of clues, and a detective who solves the mystery. In most detective stories, the crime is murder and the clues lead to or away from the solution.

> The first paragraph defines the detective story and gives an overview of the characters and plots used.

The pattern of most detective stories is the same, whether the tale is a novel, a novelette, or a short story. The author presents the crime, the detective, and several clues and suspects. The detective follows the clues and may even discover additional crimes. The climax of the story comes when the detective reveals the criminal and tells how the mystery was solved.

> Bold subheads call attention to main ideas.

Certain conventions have developed from the detective story pattern. The author is expected to "play fair" with the reader. That is, the reader should be given exactly the same information that the detective uses to find the criminal. Readers can treat the story as a battle of wits between themselves and the detective.

The detective in most of these stories is not a professional police officer but a private consultant. For example, G. K. Chesterton's Father Brown is a priest, Rex Stout's Nero Wolfe is a gourmet and intellectual, and S. S. Van Dine's Philo Vance is a sophisticated socialite. Fictional professional detectives include Wilkie Collins's Sgt. Cuff, John Creasey's Inspector Gideon (written under the name of J. J. Marric), and Georges Simenon's Inspector Maigret. Romance or financial gain may be a factor in a detective story, but the main theme is the mystery and its solution.

History of the detective story began with Edgar Allan Poe's "The Murders in the Rue Morgue" (1841). With this story and "The Mystery of Marie Rogêt" and "The Purloined Letter," Poe created the literary tradition of detective fiction. His detective was C. Auguste Dupin, a brilliant amateur who uses logic to solve mysteries.

Charles Dickens tried the new form in *Bleak House* (1852–1853) and in his unfinished novel, *The Mystery of Edwin Drood*. Wilkie Collins's *The Moonstone* (1868) was one of the most important early detective novels. Sherlock Holmes and his comrade, Dr. John Watson, appeared in 1887 in Sir Arthur Conan Doyle's *A Study in Scarlet*. Holmes is the most famous character in detective fiction—and perhaps in all fiction.

> The discussion of the history of the detective story is given in chronological, or time, order. The main writers in the development of the detective story are cited.

Detective Story

The early 1900's were a period of excitement and originality in detective fiction. In *The Singing Bone* (1912), the English author R. Austin Freeman introduced the *inverted* detective story, in which the criminal is known from the beginning. The mystery is whether—and how—the criminal will be uncovered. The American writer Jacques Futrelle created a character called the Thinking Machine, and the Hungarian-born Baroness Orczy introduced the Old Man in the Corner. The period from 1925 to 1935 brought the publication of the first or major works by such masters as Margery Allingham, Nicholas Blake, John Dickson Carr, Dame Agatha Christie, Erle Stanley Gardner, Dashiell Hammett, Michael Innes, Msgr. Ronald Knox, Ngaio Marsh, Ellery Queen, Dorothy Sayers, Georges Simenon, Rex Stout, and S. S. Van Dine.

In the 1920's, *Black Mask* magazine introduced a distinctly American style of mystery, often called "private eye" or "hard-boiled" mysteries. These stories focused on a tough detective hero and featured action and violence and a colorful narrative style. Dashiell Hammett was the leader of this style in the 1920's, followed a decade later by Raymond Chandler. The style continues to enjoy great popularity today.

During the mid- and late 1900's, a new generation of detective-story writers gained popularity. They included the American writers Sue Grafton, Tony Hillerman, Emma Lathen, Elmore Leonard, Ross Macdonald, John D. MacDonald, Ed McBain, Walter Mosley, Sara Paretsky, and Robert B. Parker; the English writers Dick Francis, P. D. James, James McClure, and Ruth Rendell; Jan-willem Van de Wetering of the Netherlands; and the Swedish team of Maj Sjöwall and Per Wahlöö.

David Geherin

Related articles in *World Book* include:

Chandler, Raymond	Hillerman, Tony
Chesterton, G. K.	Holmes, Sherlock
Christie, Dame	James, P. D.
Agatha	MacDonald, John D.
Collins, Wilkie	Marsh, Dame Ngaio
Cornwell, Patricia	McBain, Ed
Creasey, John	Orczy, Baroness
Doyle, Sir Arthur	Parker, Robert B.
Conan	Poe, Edgar Allan
Francis, Dick	Queen, Ellery
Gardner, Erle Stanley	Rinehart, Mary R.
Grafton, Sue	Sayers, Dorothy L.
Grimes, Martha	Simenon, Georges
Hammett, Dashiell	Stout, Rex
Heyer, Georgette	Van Dine, S. S.

Additional resources

Henderson, Lesley, ed. *Twentieth-Century Crime and Mystery Writers,* 3rd ed. St. James Pr., 1991.
Symons, Julian. *Bloody Murder: From the Detective Story to the Crime Novel.* 3rd ed. Mysterious Pr., 1992.

The entry gives specific details, including dates and principal writers, but it doesn't go into great depth about these writers.

The encyclopedia credits the author of the entry.

"Related articles" refers the reader to other entries in the encyclopedia that give more information on detective stories. "Additional resources" directs a reader to sources of more in-depth information.

Reading: Setting a Purpose for Reading

Directions: *Choose the letter of the best answer to each question about reading the encyclopedia entry.*

Standards Assessed

• WL.1.03.1
• CT.4.02.1
• LT.5.01.1

1. Which is the most likely purpose for reading this entry?
   A to learn about movies based on detective stories
   B to learn about short stories
   C to learn which writers are famous for detective stories
   D to learn detailed information about one writer

2. Where in the entry would you find information about ways in which the character of the detective has changed over time?
   A in the introduction
   B in the section with the subhead "The pattern"
   C in the section with the subhead "History"
   D in the final paragraph

3. Which of the following details would you learn by reading the "Detective Story" entry?
   A in-depth critical reactions to detective stories
   B how Edgar Allan Poe came up with ideas for detective stories
   C why detective story writers during the 1920s were so popular
   D the names of popular detective story writers of the 1990s

Reading: Comprehension and Interpretation

Directions: *Write your answers on a separate piece of paper.*

4. What is the typical pattern of most detective stories? **[Organizing]**
5. What does it mean for an author of a detective story to "play fair" with the reader? **[Applying]**
6. Explain the "distinctly American style of mystery" that was introduced in the 1920s. **[Organizing]**

Timed Writing: Exposition [Connections]

Explain why detective stories belong in the larger category of narrative fiction by identifying the elements they share with short stories and novels. Then, explain what makes detective stories different from other forms of narrative fiction. In your answer, use details from the encyclopedia entry and from literature as support. **(45 minutes)**

Build Skills   *There Is a Longing • Glory and Hope*

Practice these skills with either "There Is a Longing" (p. 1100) or "Glory and Hope" (p. 1105).

Literary Analysis

An author's **purpose,** or goal, is shaped by his or her **philosophical assumptions,** or basic beliefs. These philosophical assumptions may be a political ideology, moral or ethical beliefs, or assumptions about human nature. In some cases, the author may use these basic beliefs as support for his or her argument. The response of the **audience,** or readers, to the author's work will depend on whether the audience shares the basic beliefs underlying the author's purpose.

To read critically, identify the basic beliefs and assumptions in the author's work. Determine whether you accept them and whether others in the intended audience would be likely to accept them. Then, evaluate whether these assumptions help the author achieve his or her purpose. Use a chart like the one shown to record your ideas as you read.

Reading Skill

Comparing and contrasting is recognizing similarities and differences. In persuasive writing, authors often use a compare and contrast organization to show the similarities and differences between one point of view and another. As you read, use self-monitoring techniques like the ones shown to make sure you understand the comparisons.

- Identify the things or ideas being compared.
- Restate the similarities and differences in your own words.
- Explain the significance of the similarities and differences.

If you cannot identify, restate, or explain the author's points, reread to clarify or to find words or phrases that were unclear.

 Standard Course of Study

- Analyze connections between ideas, concepts, characters and experiences in argumentative text. (FA.3.04.10)
- Examine the use of strategies in a presentation to critique communication. (CT.4.01.1)

Philosophical Assumptions

The basic beliefs included in the author's work

Evaluation

How basic beliefs do or do not support author's purpose

Vocabulary Builder

There Is a Longing

- **determination** (dē tʉr′ mi nā′ shən) *n.* firm intention (p. 1100) *The runner's determination enabled him to win the race.*
- **endurance** (en dʊr′ əns) *n.* ability to withstand hardship (p. 1100) *Surviving the hurricane required courage and endurance.*

Glory and Hope

- **confer** (kən fʉr′) *v.* give (p. 1105) *The school will confer an honorary degree on the singer.*
- **pernicious** (pər nish′ əs) *adj.* destructive (p. 1106) *A pernicious insect destroyed the tree.*
- **covenant** (kuv′ ə nənt) *n.* agreement or contract, especially a sacred one (p. 1107) *They made a covenant to be friends forever.*

Speech

Background

The Struggle of Native Americans When Europeans settled in the Americas, they encountered tribal peoples who had lived on the land for thousands of years. The initial fear and prejudice led to violence and many native tribes were destroyed. Nevertheless, Native American culture survived. Today, Native Americans continue to discover ways to succeed in the twenty-first century while maintaining their own cultural identity.

READ MORE

by the Author
My Heart Soars (1974)
My Spirit Soars (1982)

Connecting to the Literature

Reading/Writing Connection Chief Dan George recognizes the importance of cultural identity. Write a paragraph to explain why it is or is not important to connect to your heritage and history. Use at least three of these words: *reinforce, contemporary, domestic, spectrum.*

Meet the Author

Chief Dan **George** (1899–1981)

Chief Dan George had many careers, including actor and writer. Chief of a Salish Band of Native Americans in British Columbia, Canada, he was deeply concerned about improving the relationships between Native Americans and other North Americans.

Celebrity Activist Chief Dan George used the prominence he gained from his film and television roles to raise public awareness about the plight of Canada's native peoples. By the 1960s, he had become an unofficial spokesman for Native Americans and the environment. Throughout all of his endeavors against injustice, he always advocated peace over violence.

Fast Facts

▶ His Native American name is "Tes-wah-no."
▶ He was nominated for an Academy Award as Best Supporting Actor for his role in the movie *Little Big Man.*

Go Online
Author Link

For: More information about the author
Visit: www.PHSchool.com
Web Code: epe-9609

THERE IS A

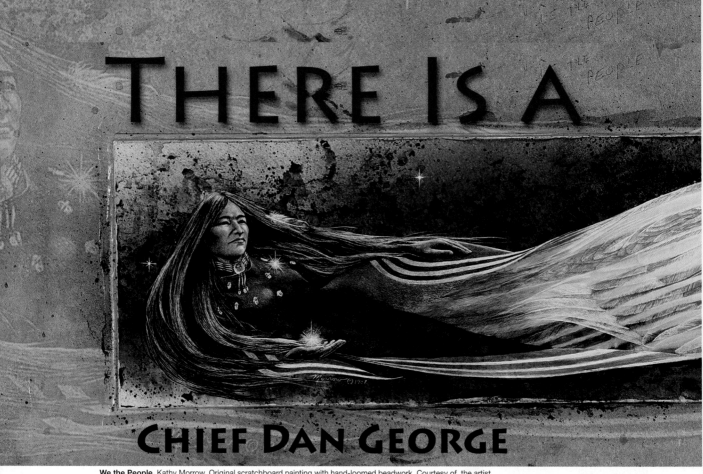

CHIEF DAN GEORGE

We the People, Kathy Morrow, Original scratchboard painting with hand-loomed beadwork. Courtesy of the artist.

There is a longing in the heart of my people
to reach out and grasp that which is needed
for our survival. There is a longing among
the young of my nation to secure for themselves
5   and their people the skills that will
provide them with a sense of worth and
purpose. They will be our new warriors.
Their training will be much longer and
more demanding than it was in olden days.
10 The long years of study will demand more
<u>determination</u>; separation from home and
family will demand <u>endurance</u>. But they
will emerge with their hand held forward,
not to receive welfare, but to grasp the
15 place in society that is rightly ours.

I am a chief, but my power to make war
is gone, and the only weapon left to me
is speech. It is only with tongue and speech
that I can fight my people's war.

Vocabulary Builder
determination (dē tur´
mi nā´ shən) *n.* firm
intention
endurance (en door´
əns) *n.* ability to
withstand hardship

LONGING

20 Oh, Great Spirit![1] Give me back the courage
of the olden Chiefs. Let me wrestle with
my surroundings. Let me once again,
live in harmony with my environment.
Let me humbly accept this new culture
25 and through it rise up and go on. Like
the thunderbird[2] of old, I shall rise again
out of the sea; I shall grab the instruments
of the white man's success—his
education, his skills. With these new tools
30 I shall build my race into the proudest
segment of your society. I shall see our
young braves and our chiefs sitting in
the houses of law and government, ruling
and being ruled by the knowledge and
35 freedoms of our great land.

▲ **Critical Viewing**
Which images in this
painting reflect ideas
found in the speech?
[Analyze]

Literary Analysis
Philosophical
Assumptions What
belief about the keys
to success in the "new
culture" does this
passage reflect?

---

1. **Great Spirit** for many Native Americans, the greatest power or god.
2. **thunderbird** powerful supernatural creature that was thought to produce thunder by flapping its
wings and to produce lightning by opening and closing its eyes. In the folklore of some Native
American nations, the thunderbird is in constant warfare with the powers beneath the waters.

Apply the Skills

There Is a Longing

Thinking About the Selection

1. **(a) Respond:** Which statements in "There Is a Longing" affected you the most? Explain. **(b) Discuss:** Share your response with a partner. Explain how hearing someone else's response did or did not change your own.
2. **(a) Recall:** What does Chief Dan George say is his community's longing? **(b) Infer:** What is his greatest fear?
3. **(a) Recall:** What training will the new warriors have to endure? **(b) Analyze:** Why does Chief Dan George believe that this training is necessary?
4. **(a) Infer:** In what way is Chief Dan George different from the "olden" chiefs? **(b) Interpret:** What does the chief mean when he refers to fighting a war "with tongue and speech"?
5. **Assess:** Do you think the chief's goal of achieving success through education and skills is the best means for improving his people's lives? Explain.

Literary Analysis

6. **(a)** What is Chief Dan George's **purpose** in writing? **(b)** What are the **philosophical assumptions**, or basic beliefs, that help to shape his purpose?
7. **(a)** For what **audience** did Chief Dan George originally write? **(b)** What details in the text indicate his intended audience? **(c)** Do you think his intended audience shared his basic beliefs? Support your answer with details from the text.
8. Using Chief Dan George's speech as an example, explain how the audience for a speech can change over time.

Reading Skill

9. **(a)** Use a chart like the one shown to record the ideas Chief Dan George presents about the past, present, and future.

Past	Present	Future

   (b) Explain the point Chief Dan George makes by **comparing and contrasting** the past, present, and future.

QuickReview

Speech at a Glance
A Native American chief calls for changes to improve the lives of his people.

Go Online
Assessment
For: Self-test
Visit: www.PHSchool.com
Web Code: epa-6607

Purpose: what the author hopes to accomplish by communicating his or her message

Philosophical Assumptions: basic beliefs

Audience: the people who will read or hear the author's message

Comparing and Contrasting: recognizing similarities and differences

Vocabulary Builder

Practice Indicate whether each statement is *True* or *False*. Explain your answers. Then, revise any sentences that are false to make them true.

1. Difficult tasks require <u>determination</u> to be completed.
2. Rock climbing requires less <u>endurance</u> than television watching.

Adding Words to Your Vocabulary Using a thesaurus, find a **synonym**, or word with a similar meaning, for each italicized word. Then, use each synonym correctly in a sentence. (For more on using a thesaurus, see page R7.)

Writing

In "There Is a Longing," Chief Dan George presents a vision for the future of his people. Write a **letter** to Chief Dan George expressing your feelings about the speech and identifying passages that you found most inspiring.

- List words that describe how the speech makes you feel. Next to each word, write the line or lines from the speech that evoke that emotion.
- Tell the author why you are writing and why you think "There Is a Longing" has a message for *all* readers.
- As you draft, use a friendly yet respectful tone.

For *Grammar, Vocabulary,* and *Assessment,* see **Build Language Skills,** pages 1110–1111.

Extend Your Learning

Listening and Speaking In a group, hold a **panel discussion** on the kind of world you hope future generations will enjoy. Keep in mind the issues that Chief Dan George addresses. Consider these tips:

- Make note cards to use for extemporaneous, or unrehearsed, delivery of your ideas.
- Show respect for everyone's opinions and speak in turn.

Analyze the process to decide how to improve future discussions.

Research and Technology Use library and Internet resources to prepare an **outline** for a biographical report about Chief Dan George or another famous Native American. Include basic facts, major accomplishments, and beliefs and values.

Background

Apartheid In Afrikaans, one of the languages of South Africa, *apartheid* means "apartness." Apartheid is the policy of segregation and discrimination that was once practiced against nonwhites by the South African government. When apartheid became law in 1948, it affected housing, education, and transportation. In order to help end apartheid, many nations reduced trade with South Africa. Apartheid was finally abolished in 1991.

Connecting to the Literature

Reading/Writing Connection In "Glory and Hope," Nelson Mandela gives some of the reasons he feels love for his country and pride in its triumph. Write several sentences about reasons people might feel pride, love, or hope for their country. Use at least three of the following words: *derive, signify, devote, evoke.*

Review

For **Literary Analysis, Reading Skill,** and **Vocabulary Builder,** see page 1098.

READ MORE

by the Author *Long Walk to Freedom: The Autobiography of Nelson Mandela*

Meet the Author

Nelson **Mandela** (b. 1918)

Nelson Rolihlahla Mandela was born in South Africa, a nation whose white government maintained a strict policy of apartheid, or legal discrimination against blacks. In 1944, Mandela began protesting apartheid. Twenty years later, after several arrests, he was sentenced to life in prison for acts of protest.

Freedom for a Man and a Nation In 1990, after long years of imprisonment, Mandela was released. He continued to fight for equal rights for all South Africans. In 1991, apartheid was finally abolished and, in 1993, Mandela and South African president F. W. de Klerk shared the Nobel Prize for Peace. The next year, Mandela became the first black man to be elected president of South Africa. He retired from public life in 1999, and he currently lives in his birthplace, Qunu, Transkei.

Fast Facts

▶ Nelson Mandela once said, "The struggle is my life."
▶ Mandela's prison for so many years, Robben Island, has now been turned into a learning center.

Go Online
Author Link
For: More information about the author
Visit: www.PHSchool.com
Web Code: epe-9610

GLORY AND HOPE

Nelson Mandela

Your majesties, your royal highnesses, distinguished guests, comrades and friends: Today, all of us do, by our presence here, and by our celebrations in other parts of our country and the world, <u>confer</u> glory and hope to newborn liberty.

Out of the experience of an extraordinary human disaster that lasted too long must be born a society of which all humanity will be proud.

Our daily deeds as ordinary South Africans must produce an actual South African reality that will reinforce humanity's belief in justice, strengthen its confidence in the nobility of the human soul and sustain all our hopes for a glorious life for all.

All this we owe both to ourselves and to the peoples of the world who are so well represented here today.

To my compatriots, I have no hesitation in saying that each one of us is as intimately attached to the soil of this beautiful country as are the famous jacaranda trees of Pretoria and the mimosa trees of the bushveld.[1]

Each time one of us touches the soil of this land, we feel a sense of personal renewal. The national mood changes as the seasons change.

We are moved by a sense of joy and exhilaration when the grass turns green and the flowers bloom.

That spiritual and physical oneness we all share with this common homeland explains the depth of the pain we all carried in our

▲ **Critical Viewing**
What does this photograph of outgoing South African president F. W. de Klerk and Nelson Mandela suggest about the two men's vision for their country? **[Analyze]**

Vocabulary Builder
confer (kən fur´) v. give

✔ **Reading Check**
What does Mandela say must be born "out of the experience of an extraordinary human disaster"?

---

1. bushveld (bŏŏsh´ velt) n. South African grassland with abundant shrubs and thorny vegetation.

hearts as we saw our country tear itself apart in terrible conflict, and as we saw it spurned, outlawed and isolated by the peoples of the world, precisely because it has become the universal base of the <u>pernicious</u> ideology and practice of racism and racial oppression.

We, the people of South Africa, feel fulfilled that humanity has taken us back into its bosom, that we, who were outlaws not so long ago, have today been given the rare privilege to be host to the nations of the world on our own soil.

We thank all our distinguished international guests for having come to take possession with the people of our country of what is, after all, a common victory for justice, for peace, for human dignity.

We trust that you will continue to stand by us as we tackle the challenges of building peace, prosperity, nonsexism, nonracialism and democracy.

We deeply appreciate the role that the masses of our people and their democratic, religious, women, youth, business, traditional and other leaders have played to bring about this conclusion. Not least among them is my Second Deputy President, the Honorable F. W. de Klerk.

We would also like to pay tribute to our security forces, in all their ranks, for the distinguished role they have played in securing

Vocabulary Builder
pernicious (pər nish´ əs) *adj.* destructive

Literature in Context | Humanities Connection

Voices for Change

By raising worldwide awareness of the injustices suffered under South Africa's racially divided system, artists of all kinds played a vital role in helping the country become a more just society.

▲ South African novelist **Nadine Gordimer** writes about the pain of racial divisions in her homeland.

▲ Playwright **Athol Fugard** was one of the first white South African dramatists to collaborate with black actors.

▲ On Broadway from 1988 to 1989, **Sarafina!** was a popular musical about protests that took place in South Africa in 1976.

▲ The album "Sun City" raised more than $1 million dollars for South Africa's freedom fight. "Little Steven" Van Zandt (left) organized the project and Bono (right) participated.

Connect to the Literature How might the efforts of artists around the world have given Nelson Mandela and other South Africans hope for the future?

our first democratic elections and the transition to democracy, from bloodthirsty forces which still refuse to see the light.

The time for the healing of the wounds has come.

The moment to bridge the chasms that divide us has come.

The time to build is upon us.

We have, at last, achieved our political emancipation. We pledge ourselves to liberate all our people from the continuing bondage of poverty, deprivation, suffering, gender and other discrimination.

We succeeded to take our last steps to freedom in conditions of relative peace. We commit ourselves to the construction of a complete, just and lasting peace.

We have triumphed in the effort to implant hope in the breasts of the millions of our people. We enter into a <u>covenant</u> that we shall build the society in which all South Africans, both black and white, will be able to walk tall, without any fear in their hearts, assured of their inalienable right to human dignity—a rainbow nation at peace with itself and the world.

Vocabulary Builder
covenant (kuv´ə nənt) *n.* agreement or contract, especially a sacred one

As a token of its commitment to the renewal of our country, the new Interim Government of National Unity will, as a matter of urgency, address the issue of amnesty for various categories of our people who are currently serving terms of imprisonment.

We dedicate this day to all the heroes and heroines in this country and the rest of the world who sacrificed in many ways and surrendered their lives so that we could be free.

Their dreams have become reality. Freedom is their reward.

We are both humbled and elevated by the honor and privilege that you, the people of South Africa, have bestowed on us, as the first President of a united, democratic, nonracial and nonsexist South Africa, to lead our country out of the valley of darkness.

We understand it still that there is no easy road to freedom.

We know it well that none of us acting alone can achieve success.

We must therefore act together as a united people, for national reconciliation, for nation building, for the birth of a new world.

Let there be justice for all.

Let there be peace for all.

Let there be work, bread, water and salt for all.

Let each know that for each the body, the mind and the soul have been freed to fulfill themselves.

Never, never and never again shall it be that this beautiful land will again experience the oppression of one by another and suffer the indignity of being the skunk of the world.

The sun shall never set on so glorious a human achievement!

Let freedom reign. God bless Africa!

Reading Skill
Comparing and Contrasting What important difference does Mandela point out about South Africa's future as compared to its past?

Glory and Hope ■ 1107

Apply the Skills

Glory and Hope

Thinking About the Selection

1. **(a) Respond:** What do you admire most about the message in "Glory and Hope"? Explain. **(b) Discuss:** Share your response with a partner. Explain how hearing someone else's response did or did not change your own.
2. **(a) Recall:** What does Nelson Mandela say is "newborn" in his country? **(b) Interpret:** What emotion does the word "newborn" add to his remarks?
3. **(a) Recall:** Into what "covenant" does Mandela say the South African people are now entering? **(b) Generalize:** Which ideas in the speech are especially important for safeguarding the human rights of all people throughout today's world?
4. **(a) Interpret:** What do the words "glory" and "hope" mean? **(b) Connect:** How does the title of the speech connect with the ideas that Mandela conveys?
5. **Take a Position:** Basing your answer on Mandela's speech, what do you think was the new leader's greatest challenge? Explain.

Literary Analysis

6. **(a)** What is Nelson Mandela's **purpose** in his speech? **(b)** What are the **philosophical assumptions,** or basic beliefs, that help to shape his purpose?
7. **(a)** For what **audience** did Nelson Mandela originally speak? **(b)** What details in the text indicate his intended audience? **(c)** Do you think his intended audience shared his basic beliefs? Support your answer with details from the text.
8. **(a)** Using Nelson Mandela's speech as an example, explain how the audience for a speech can change over time.

Reading Skill

9. **(a)** Use a chart like the one shown to record the ideas Nelson Mandela presents about the past, present, and future.

Past	Present	Future

(b) Explain the point that Nelson Mandela makes by **comparing and contrasting** the past, present, and future.

QuickReview

Speech at a Glance
At his presidential inauguration, Nelson Mandela celebrates South Africa's triumph over apartheid and envisions a future of freedom and peace.

Go Online
Assessment
For: Self-test
Visit: www.PHSchool.com
Web Code: epa-6608

Purpose: what the author hopes to accomplish by communicating his or her message

Philosophical Assumptions: basic beliefs

Audience: the people who will read or hear the author's message

Comparing and Contrasting: recognizing similarities and differences

Vocabulary Builder

Practice Indicate whether each statement is *True* or *False.* Explain your answers. Then, revise any sentences that are false to make them true.

1. A signature serves to *confer* authenticity to a document.
2. A *pernicious* idea is always welcome at a team meeting.
3. Each party in a *covenant* hopes that the other party will break it.

Adding Words to Your Vocabulary Using a thesaurus, find a **synonym,** or word with a similar meaning, for each italicized word in the Practice section. Then, use each synonym correctly in a sentence. (For more on using a thesaurus, see page R7.)

Writing

In "Glory and Hope," Nelson Mandela presents a vision for the future of his people. Write a **letter** to Nelson Mandela expressing your feelings about the speech and identifying inspiring passages.

- Make a list of words that describe how the speech makes you feel. Next to each word, write the sentence or sentences from the speech that evoke that emotion.
- Tell the author why you are writing and why you think "Glory and Hope" has a message for *all* readers.
- As you draft, use a friendly yet respectful tone.

For *Grammar, Vocabulary,* and *Assessment,*
see **Build Language Skills,** pages 1110–1111.

Extend Your Learning

Listening and Speaking In a group, hold a **panel discussion** on the kind of world you hope future generations will enjoy. Keep in mind the issues that Mandela addresses. Consider these tips:
- Make note cards to use for extemporaneous, or unrehearsed, delivery of your ideas.
- Show respect for everyone's opinions and speak in turn.

Analyze the process to decide how to improve future discussions.

Research and Technology Use library and Internet resources to prepare an **outline** for a biographical report about Nelson Mandela. Be sure that your outline includes the basic facts of his life, his major accomplishments, and his beliefs.

Build Language Skills

Vocabulary Skill

Word Roots The **Latin word root** *-her-* means "to cling or stick to" and is the word root for the word *inherent,* which means "something that is an inseparable quality of something else."

Practice: The underlined words in the following sentences contain the word root *-her-*. Explain how the meaning of the word root is a clue to the meaning of the sentence.

1. The paper lacked <u>coherence</u>.
2. Dan's <u>adherence</u> to the policy is admirable.
3. The accident left him <u>incoherent</u>.

Grammar Lesson

Using Colons, Semicolons, and Ellipsis Points Correctly

Punctuation helps a writer clarify the meaning of a sentence. A **colon** is used mainly to list items following an independent clause. A **semi-colon** is used to join independent clauses that are closely related. A semicolon is also used to separate independent clauses or items in a series that already contains several commas.

Ellipsis points (. . .) are punctuation marks that show that something has not been expressed. Ellipsis points usually indicate

- words that have been left out of a quotation.
- a series that continues beyond the items mentioned.
- time passing or action occurring in a narrative.

Colon The flowers seemed human: nodding, bending, dancing.
Semicolon The teacher lifted the desk herself; the sight greatly impressed the students.
Ellipsis Points He struck out . . . but the end of the game would surprise them all.

Practice Write these sentences on your paper, adding colons, semicolons, or ellipsis points wherever necessary.

1. The astronauts looked out beyond the planets, beyond the stars, beyond.
2. The sweatshirt fit perfectly it completed the disguise.
3. She knew the best things to eat whole grains, fruits, vegetables.
4. They came they saw they conquered.
5. I left the woods and I would never be the same again.

MorePractice

For more practice with punctuation, see the Grammar Handbook, p. R40.

Reading Skill: Comparing and Contrasting

Standards Assessed

• WL.1.02.1
• FA.3.03.1
• LT.5.03.3

Directions: *Read the passage, and then answer the questions that follow. Mark the letters of your answers on a bubble sheet if your teacher provides one; otherwise, write the letters of the correct answers on a separate piece of paper.*

I have a dream that one day this nation will rise up and live out the true meaning of its creed: "We hold these truths to be self-evident; that all men are created equal."

I have a dream that one day on the red hills of Georgia the sons of former slaves and the sons of former slaveowners will be able to sit down together at a table of brotherhood.

I have a dream that one day even the state of Mississippi, a desert state sweltering with the heat of injustice and oppression, will be transformed into an oasis of freedom and justice.

I have a dream that my four little children will one day live in a nation where they will not be judged by the color of their skin but by the content of their character.

—from "I Have a Dream," Martin Luther King, Jr.

1. In this speech, the speaker compares
   A brothers to sisters.
   B slaves to slaveowners.
   C injustice and oppression to the heat of a desert.
   D truths that are self-evident to truths that are not self-evident.

2. In this speech, the speaker contrasts
   A freedom and justice.
   B his four little children.
   C Georgia and Mississippi.
   D the present and the future.

Timed Writing: Analysis

Review "There Is a Longing" or "Glory and Hope." Using quotations from the text, write an analysis of what the speaker wants for his people. **(60 minutes)**

 ## Writing Workshop: *Work in Progress*

Comparison and Contrast

Add to the Comparison List in your writing portfolio. For each place add your emotional response to that place. Then, use a Venn diagram to compare and contrast the two places. Save your work in your portfolio.

Comparing Literary Works • *Tall Tale and Myth*

Tall Tale and Myth

A **tall tale** is a type of folk tale that contains some or all of the following features:

- a larger-than-life central hero
- far-fetched situations and amazing feats
- humor
- *hyperbole,* or exaggeration

The exaggerated situations and descriptions in a tall tale, offered in vivid and often increasingly ridiculous detail, highlight how unbelievable the story really is.

Tall tales are a particularly American form of story. Many tall tales originated during the American frontier period and reflect the challenges and values of that place and time.

A **myth** is an anonymous story that explains the actions of gods or human heroes, the reasons for certain traditions, or the causes of natural features. Many cultures have their own *mythology,* or collection of myths, that expresses the central values of the people who madeup these stories and passed them on by word of mouth.

Mythic heroes often share three characteristics:

- they have at least one divine parent,
- they gain special knowledge or weapons, and
- they face seemingly impossible tasks.

Comparing Tall Tales and Myths

In general, tell tales describe how humans make things happen on their own, while myths tell how gods shape human life. Tall tales are often a type of *legend*, a traditional story about the past that is usually based on historical fact. Myths, in contrast, are religious in origin. However, both these forms developed in the *oral tradition*—they were passed on by word of mouth, and both express the values of the people who created them.

Use a chart like one shown to compare and contrast these two selections.

Vocabulary Builder

Pecos Bill: The Cyclone

- **usurped** (yōō surpt´) *v.* took power or position without right (p. 1117) *The young knight imprisoned the king and usurped the throne.*

- **skeptics** (skep´ tiks) *n.* people who doubt and question generally accepted ideas (p. 1120) *He was one of the skeptics who did not believe the world was flat.*

Perseus

- **mortified** (môrt´ ə fīd´) *adj.* extremely embarrassed (p. 1123) *She blushed, mortified at her mistake.*

- **revelry** (rev´ əl rē) *n.* noisy merrymaking (p. 1125) *Parades filled the city with the spirit of revelry.*

Build Understanding

Connecting to the Literature

Reading/Writing Connection Both Pecos Bill and Perseus are larger-than-life heroes who triumph over terrifying opponents. Write a paragraph about what you think it means to be larger than life. Use at least three of the following words in your response: *impact, negate, illuminate, exceed, undertake.*

Meet the Author

Harold W. **Felton** (1902–1991)

Harold William Felton practiced law and worked for the Internal Revenue Service, but over the years, he became increasingly interested in the legends and folklore of the United States.

Collector and Reteller Felton published collections of stories about folk heroes and the cowboys of the West. His book *Legends of Paul Bunyan* contains more than one hundred folk tales about the great logger.

Edith **Hamilton** (1867–1963)

Edith Hamilton was a groundbreaking educator who helped found the Bryn Mawr School in Baltimore, the first college pre-paratory school for women. She taught a generation of young women not to limit their goals simply because they were not men.

Modern Woman, Ancient Tales After leaving Bryn Mawr, Hamilton began writing articles about ancient Greece, which she later turned into a book entitled *The Greek Way* (1930). Her other books include *The Roman Way* (1932) and *Mythology* (1942), which are both beautifully crafted retellings of the Greek myths.

Go **Online**
Author Link

For: More about the authors
Visit: www.PHSchool.com
Web Code: epe-9611

PECOS BILL
THE CYCLONE

HAROLD W. FELTON

One of Bill's greatest feats, if not the greatest feat of all time, occurred unexpectedly one Fourth of July. He had invented the Fourth of July some years before. It was a great day for the cowpunchers.[1] They had taken to it right off like the real Americans they were. But the celebration had always ended on a dismal note. Somehow it seemed to be spoiled by a cyclone.

Bill had never minded the cyclone much. The truth is he rather liked it. But the other celebrants ran into caves for safety. He invented cyclone cellars for them. He even named the cellars. He called them "'fraid holes." Pecos wouldn't even say the word "afraid." The cyclone was something like he was. It was big and strong too. He always stood by musing pleasantly as he watched it.

The cyclone caused Bill some trouble, though. Usually it would destroy a few hundred miles of fence by blowing the postholes away. But it wasn't much trouble for him to fix it. All he had to do was to go and get the postholes and then take them back and put the fence posts in them. The holes were rarely ever blown more than twenty or thirty miles.

In one respect Bill even welcomed the cyclone, for it blew so hard it blew the earth away from his wells. The first time this happened, he thought the wells would be a total loss. There they were, sticking up several hundred feet out of the ground. As wells they were useless. But he found he could cut them up into lengths and sell them for postholes to farmers in Iowa and Nebraska. It was very profitable, especially after he invented a special posthole saw to cut them with. He didn't use that type of posthole himself. He got the prairie dogs to dig his for him. He simply caught a few gross[2] of prairie dogs and set them down at proper intervals. The prairie dog would dig a hole. Then Bill would put a post in it. The prairie dog would get disgusted and go down the row ahead of the others and dig another hole. Bill fenced all of Texas and parts of New Mexico and Arizona in this manner. He took a few contracts and fenced most of the Southern Pacific right of way too. That's the reason it is so crooked. He had trouble getting the prairie dogs to run a straight fence.

As for his wells, the badgers dug them. The system was the same as with the prairie dogs. The labor was cheap so it didn't make much difference if the cyclone did spoil some of the wells. The

---

1. **cowpunchers** (kou′ pun′ chərz) *n.* cowboys.
2. **gross** (grōs) *n.* twelve dozen.

◀ **Critical Viewing** Does this cyclone seem capable of destroying a "few hundred miles of fence"? Explain. **[Assess]**

Literary Analysis
Tall Tale and Myth
Which description in the first paragraph contains hyperbole?

Reading Check

Where does Pecos Bill get the postholes he sells to farmers in Iowa and Nebraska?

badgers were digging all of the time anyway. They didn't seem to care whether they dug wells or just badger holes.

One year he tried shipping the prairie dog holes up north, too, for postholes. It was not successful. They didn't keep in storage and they couldn't stand the handling in shipping. After they were installed they seemed to wear out quickly. Bill always thought the difference in climate had something to do with it.

Literary Analysis
Tall Tale and Myth
Which realistic details in this paragraph add humor?

It should be said that in those days there was only one cyclone. It was the first and original cyclone, bigger and more terrible by far than the small cyclones of today. It usually stayed by itself up north around Kansas and Oklahoma and didn't bother anyone much. But it was attracted by the noise of the Fourth of July celebration and without fail managed to put in an appearance before the close of the day.

On this particular Fourth of July, the celebration had gone off fine. The speeches were loud and long. The contests and games were hard fought. The high point of the day was Bill's exhibition with Widow Maker, which came right after he showed off Scat and Rat.[3] People seemed never to tire of seeing them in action. The mountain lion was almost useless as a work animal after his accident, and the snake had grown old and somewhat infirm, and was troubled with rheumatism in his rattles. But they too enjoyed the Fourth of July and liked to make a public appearance. They relived the old days.

Literary Analysis
Tall Tale and Myth
Which details give this tall tale a particularly American flavor?

Widow Maker had put on a good show, bucking as no ordinary horse could ever buck. Then Bill undertook to show the gaits[4] he had taught the palomino.[5] Other mustangs at that time had only two gaits. Walking and running. Only Widow Maker could pace. But now Bill had developed and taught him other gaits. Twenty-seven in all. Twenty-three forward and three reverse. He was very proud of the achievement. He showed off the slow gaits and the crowd was eager for more.

He showed the walk, trot, canter, lope, jog, slow rack, fast rack, single foot, pace, stepping pace, fox trot, running walk and the others now known. Both men and horses confuse the various gaits nowadays. Some of the gaits are now thought to be the same, such as the rack and the single foot. But with Widow Maker and Pecos Bill, each one was different. Each was precise and to be distinguished from the others. No one had ever imagined such a thing.

---

3. Widow Maker . . . Scat and Rat. Widow Maker is a mustang, a type of wild horse. Scat is Bill's mountain lion, and Rat is Bill's pet rattlesnake.
4. gaits (gāts) *n.* foot movements of a horse.
5. palomino (pal' ə mē' nō) *n.* golden-tan or cream-colored horse that has a white, silver, or ivory tail and, often, white spots on the face and legs.

Then the cyclone came! All of the people except Bill ran into the 'fraid holes. Bill was annoyed. He stopped the performance. The remaining gaits were not shown. From that day to this horses have used no more than the gaits Widow Maker exhibited that day. It is unfortunate that the really fast gaits were not shown. If they were, horses might be much faster today than they are.

Bill glanced up at the cyclone and the quiet smile on his face faded into a frown. He saw the cyclone was angry. Very, very angry indeed.

The cyclone had always been the center of attention. Everywhere it went people would look up in wonder, fear and amazement. It had been the undisputed master of the country. It had observed Bill's rapid climb to fame and had seen the Fourth of July celebration grow. It had been keeping an eye on things all right.

In the beginning, the Fourth of July crowd had aroused its curiosity. It liked nothing more than to show its superiority and power by breaking the crowd up sometime during the day. But every year the crowd was larger. This preyed on the cyclone's mind. This year it did not come to watch. It deliberately came to spoil the celebration. Jealous of Bill and of his success, it resolved to do away with the whole institution of the Fourth of July once and for all. So much havoc and destruction would be wrought that there would never be another Independence Day Celebration. On that day, in future years, it would circle around the horizon leering and gloating. At least, so it thought.

The cyclone was resolved, also, to do away with this bold fellow who did not hold it in awe and run for the 'fraid hole at its approach. For untold years it had been the most powerful thing in the land. And now, here was a mere man who threatened its position. More! Who had <u>usurped</u> its position!

When Bill looked at the horizon and saw the cyclone coming, he recognized the anger and rage. While a cyclone does not often smile, Bill had felt from the beginning that it was just a grouchy fellow who never had a pleasant word for anyone. But now, instead of merely an unpleasant character, Bill saw all the viciousness of which an angry cyclone is capable. He had no way of knowing that the cyclone saw its kingship tottering and was determined to stop this man who threatened its supremacy.

But Bill understood the violence of the onslaught even as the monster came into view. He knew he must meet it. The center of the cyclone was larger than ever before. The fact is, the cyclone had been training for this fight all winter and spring. It was in best form and at top weight. It headed straight for Bill intent on his destruction. In an instant it was upon him. Bill had sat quietly and silently on the great pacing mustang. But his mind was working

Vocabulary Builder
usurped (yōō sʉrpt´)
v. took power or position without right

Reading Check

Why is the cyclone angry with Bill?

rapidly. In the split second between his first sight of the monster and the time for action he had made his plans. Pecos Bill was ready! Ready and waiting!

Green clouds were dripping from the cyclone's jaws. Lightning flashed from its eyes as it swept down upon him. Its plan was to envelop Bill in one mighty grasp. Just as it was upon him, Bill turned Widow Maker to its left. This was a clever move for the cyclone was right-handed, and while it had been training hard to get its left in shape, that was not its best side. Bill gave rein to his mount. Widow Maker wheeled and turned on a dime which Pecos had, with great foresight and accuracy, thrown to the ground to mark the exact spot for this maneuver. It was the first time that anyone had thought of turning on a dime. Then he urged the great horse forward. The cyclone, filled with surprise, lost its balance and rushed forward at an increased speed. It went so fast that it met itself coming back. This confused the cyclone, but it did not confuse Pecos Bill. He had expected that to happen. Widow Maker went into his twenty-first gait and edged up close to the whirlwind. Soon they were running neck and neck.

At the proper instant Bill grabbed the cyclone's ears, kicked himself free of the stirrups and pulled himself lightly on its back. Bill never used spurs on Widow Maker. Sometimes he wore them for show and because he liked the jingling sound they made. They made a nice accompaniment for his cowboy songs. But he had not been singing, so he had no spurs. He did not have his rattlesnake for a quirt.[6] Of course there was no bridle. It was man against monster! There he was! Pecos Bill astride a raging cyclone, slick heeled and without a saddle!

The cyclone was taken by surprise at this sudden turn of events. But it was undaunted. It was sure of itself. Months of training had given it a conviction that it was invincible. With a mighty heave, it twisted to its full height. Then it fell back suddenly, twisting and turning violently, so that before it came back to earth, it had turned around a thousand times. Surely no rider could ever withstand such an attack. No rider ever had. Little wonder. No one had ever ridden a cyclone before. But Pecos Bill did! He fanned the tornado's ears with his hat and dug his heels into the demon's flanks and yelled, "Yipee-ee!"

Literature in Context

Science Connection

Cyclones A cyclone is an area of rapidly spinning winds that is associated with severe thunderstorms. The rotating winds can reach speeds of 250 miles per hour and are capable of lifting even very heavy objects into the column of circulating air. Cyclones develop when warm and cold masses of air collide, causing abrupt changes in wind speed and direction. Cyclones that were over a mile wide and that have spread damage along a fifty-mile path have been recorded. Unlike Pecos Bill, most people are smart enough to take shelter underground when they see a cyclone coming.

Connect to the Literature

Why might a literary character like Bill be especially beloved by people who live in areas affected by cyclones?

---

6. quirt (kwɜrt) *n.* riding whip with a braided lash and a short handle.

The people who had run for shelter began to come out. The audience further enraged the cyclone. It was bad enough to be disgraced by having a man astride it. It was unbearable not to have thrown him. To have all the people see the failure was too much! It got down flat on the ground and rolled over and over. Bill retained his seat throughout this ruse. Evidence of this desperate but futile stratagem[7] remains today. The great Staked Plains, or as the Mexicans call it, Llano Estacado is the result. Its small, rugged mountains were covered with trees at the time. The rolling of the cyclone destroyed the mountains, the trees, and almost everything else in the area. The destruction was so complete, that part of the country is flat and treeless to this day. When the settlers came, there were no landmarks to guide them across the vast unmarked space, so they drove stakes in the ground to mark the trails. That is the reason it is called "Staked Plains." Here is an example of the proof of the events of history by careful and painstaking research. It is also an example of how seemingly inexplicable geographical facts can be explained.

It was far more dangerous for the rider when the cyclone shot straight up to the sky. Once there, the twister tried the same thing it had tried on the ground. It rolled on the sky. It was no use. Bill could not be unseated. He kept his place, and he didn't have a sky hook with him either.

As for Bill, he was having the time of his life, shouting at the top of his voice, kicking his opponent in the ribs and jabbing his thumb in its flanks. It responded and went on a wild bucking rampage over the entire West. It used all the bucking tricks known to the wildest broncos as well as those known only to cyclones. The wind howled furiously and beat against the fearless rider. The rain poured. The lightning flashed around his ears. The fight went on and on. Bill enjoyed himself immensely. In spite of the elements he easily kept his place. . . .

The raging cyclone saw this out of the corner of its eye. It knew then who the victor was. It was twisting far above the Rocky Mountains when the awful truth came to it. In a horrible heave it disintegrated! Small pieces of cyclone flew in all directions. Bill still kept his seat on the main central portion until that rained out from under him. Then he jumped to a nearby streak of lightning and slid down it toward earth. But it was raining so hard that the rain put out the lightning. When it fizzled out from under him, Bill dropped the rest of the way. He lit in what is now called Death Valley. He hit quite hard, as is apparent from the fact that he so compressed the

---

7. futile (fyōōt′ ′l) **stratagem** (strat′ ə jəm) useless or hopeless plan.

Literary Analysis
Tall Tale and Myth
In his encounter with the cyclone, which details show Bill's physical strength and lack of fear?

Reading Check

What does Bill do with the cyclone that had never been done before?

place that it is still two hundred and seventy-six feet below sea level. The Grand Canyon was washed out by the rain, though it must be understood that this happened after Paul Bunyan had given it a good start by carelessly dragging his ax behind him when he went west a short time before.

The cyclones and the hurricanes and the tornadoes nowadays are the small pieces that broke off of the big cyclone Pecos Bill rode. In fact, the rainstorms of the present day came into being in the same way. There are always <u>skeptics</u>, but even they will recognize the logic of the proof of this event. They will recall that even now it almost always rains on the Fourth of July. That is because the rainstorms of today still retain some of the characteristics of the giant cyclone that met its comeuppance at the hands of Pecos Bill.

Bill lay where he landed and looked up at the sky, but he could see no sign of the cyclone. Then he laughed softly as he felt the warm sand of Death Valley on his back. . . .

It was a rough ride though, and Bill had resisted unusual tensions and pressures. When he got on the cyclone he had a twenty-dollar gold piece and a bowie knife in his pocket. The tremendous force of the cyclone was such that when he finished the ride he found that his pocket contained a plugged nickel[8] and a little pearl-handled penknife. His two giant six-shooters were compressed and transformed into a small water pistol and a popgun.

It is a strange circumstance that lesser men have monuments raised in their honor. Death Valley is Bill's monument. Sort of a monument in reverse. Sunk in his honor, you might say. Perhaps that is as it should be. After all, Bill was different. He made his own monument. He made it with his hips, as is evident from the great depth of the valley. That is the hard way.

---

8. **plugged nickel** fake nickel.

Thinking About the Selection

1. **Respond:** Which parts of the tale did you find funniest? Explain.

2. **(a) Recall:** What term does Bill use to refer to the cyclone cellars?
   (b) Interpret: What do you learn about the character of Pecos Bill from his reaction to the cellars?

3. **(a) Recall:** What word is Bill unwilling to say aloud?
   (b) Draw Conclusions: How does his resolve never to say this word explain, in part, why he is a folk hero?

4. **(a) Interpret:** What are three human characteristics of the cyclone?
   (b) Compare: How does the cyclone resemble Pecos Bill himself?

Literary Analysis
Tall Tale and Myth
According to the tale, how does Bill create a natural phenomenon?

Vocabulary Builder
skeptics (skep´ tiks) *n.* people who doubt and question generally accepted ideas

Literary Analysis
Tall Tale and Myth
Which details in this paragraph are examples of humorous exaggeration?

Perseus

Edith Hamilton

▲ **Critical Viewing** The man with the sword is Perseus as an adult. Judging from this painting, how do you think others perceive him? **[Interpret]**

King Acrisius [a kris′ ē əs] of Argos had only one child, a daughter, Danaë [dan′ ā ē]. She was beautiful above all the other women of the land, but this was small comfort to the King for not having a son. He journeyed to Delphi to ask the god if there was any hope that some day he would be the father of a boy. The priestess told him no, and added what was far worse: that his daughter would have a son who would kill him.

The only sure way to escape that fate was for the King to have Danaë instantly put to death—taking no chances, but seeing to it himself. This Acrisius would not do. His fatherly affection was not strong, as events proved, but his fear of the gods was. They visited with terrible punishment those who shed the blood of kindred.

Reading Check

What does the priestess say Danae's son will do?

Acrisius did not dare slay his daughter. Instead, he had a house built all of bronze and sunk underground, but with part of the roof open to the sky so that light and air could come through. Here he shut her up and guarded her.

> So Danaë endured, the beautiful,
> To change the glad daylight for brass-bound walls,
> And in that chamber secret as the grave
> She lived a prisoner. Yet to her came
> Zeus in the golden rain.

As she sat there through the long days and hours with nothing to do, nothing to see except the clouds moving by overhead, a mysterious thing happened, a shower of gold fell from the sky and filled her chamber. How it was revealed to her that it was Zeus who had visited her in this shape we are not told, but she knew that the child she bore was his son.

For a time she kept his birth secret from her father, but it became increasingly difficult to do so in the narrow limits of that bronze house and finally one day the little boy—his name was Perseus— was discovered by his grandfather. "Your child!" Acrisius cried in great anger. "Who is his father?" But when Danaë answered proudly, "Zeus," he would not believe her. One thing only he was sure of, that the boy's life was a terrible danger to his own. He was afraid to kill him for the same reason that had kept him from killing her, fear of Zeus and the Furies who pursue such murderers. But if he could not kill them outright, he could put them in the way of tolerably certain death. He had a great chest made, and the two placed in it. Then it was taken out to sea and cast into the water.

In that strange boat Danaë sat with her little son. The daylight faded and she was alone on the sea.

> When in the carven chest the winds and waves
> Struck fear into her heart she put her arms,
> Not without tears, round Perseus tenderly
> She said, "O son, what grief is mine.
> But you sleep softly, little child,
> Sunk deep in rest within your cheerless home,
> Only a box, brass-bound. The night, this darkness visible,
> The scudding waves so near to your soft curls,
> The shrill voice of the wind, you do not heed,
> Nestled in your red cloak, fair little face."

Through the night in the tossing chest she listened to the waters that seemed always about to wash over them. The dawn came, but with no comfort to her for she could not see it. Neither could she see that around them there were islands rising high above the sea, many islands. All she knew was that presently a wave seemed to lift them and carry them swiftly on and then, retreating, leave them on something solid and motionless. They had made land; they were safe from the sea, but they were still in the chest with no way to get out.

Fate willed it—or perhaps Zeus, who up to now had done little for his love and his child—that they should be discovered by a good man, a fisherman named Dictys. He came upon the great box and broke it open and took the pitiful cargo home to his wife who was as kind as he. They had no children and they cared for Danaë and Perseus as if they were their own. The two lived there many years, Danaë content to let her son follow the fisherman's humble trade, out of harm's way. But in the end more trouble came. Polydectes [pol i dek′ tèz], the ruler of the little island, was the brother of Dictys, but he was a cruel and ruthless man. He seems to have taken no notice of the mother and son for a long time, but at last Danaë attracted his attention. She was still radiantly beautiful even though Perseus by now was full grown, and Polydectes fell in love with her. He wanted her, but he did not want her son, and he set himself to think out a way of getting rid of him.

There were some fearsome monsters called Gorgons who lived on an island and were known far and wide because of their deadly power. Polydectes evidently talked to Perseus about them; he probably told him that he would rather have the head of one of them than anything else in the world. This seems practically certain from the plan he devised for killing Perseus. He announced that he was about to be married and he called his friends together for a celebration, including Perseus in the invitation. Each guest, as was customary, brought a gift for the bride-to-be, except Perseus alone. He had nothing he could give. He was young and proud and keenly <u>mortified</u>. He stood up before them all and did exactly what the King had hoped he would do, declared that he would give him a present better than any there. He would go off and kill Medusa and bring back her head as his gift. Nothing could have suited the King better. No one in his senses would have made such a proposal. Medusa was one of the Gorgons,

> And they are three, the Gorgons, each with wings
> And snaky hair, most horrible to mortals.
> Whom no man shall behold and draw again
> The breath of life,

for the reason that whoever looked at them were turned instantly into stone. It seemed that Perseus had been led by his angry pride into making an empty boast. No man unaided could kill Medusa.

▲ **Critical Viewing**
Which scene in the story does this art illustrate? **[Connect]**

Vocabulary Builder
mortified (môrt′ ə fīd′) *adj.* extremely embarrassed

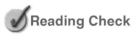 **Reading Check**

What does Perseus promise to give the king as a gift?

Perseus ■ *1123*

But Perseus was saved from his folly. Two great gods were watching over him. He took ship as soon as he left the King's hall, not daring to see his mother first and tell her what he intended, and he sailed to Greece to learn where the three monsters were to be found. He went to Delphi, but all the priestess would say was to bid him seek the land where men eat not Demeter's golden grain, but only acorns. So he went to Dodona, in the land of oak trees, where the talking oaks were which declared Zeus's will and where the Selli lived who made their bread from acorns. They could tell him, however, no more than this, that he was under the protection of the gods. They did not know where the Gorgons lived.

When and how Hermes and Athena came to his help is not told in any story, but he must have known despair before they did so. At last, however, as he wandered on, he met a strange and beautiful person. We know what he looked like from many a poem, a young man with the first down upon his cheek when youth is loveliest, carrying, as no other young man ever did, a wand of gold with wings at one end, wearing a winged hat, too, and winged sandals. At sight of him hope must have entered Perseus' heart, for he would know that this could be none other than Hermes, the guide and the giver of good.

This radiant personage told him that before he attacked Medusa he must first be properly equipped, and that what he needed was in the possession of the nymphs of the North. To find the nymphs' abode, they must go to the Gray Women who alone could tell them the way. These women dwelt in a land where all was dim and shrouded in twilight. No ray of sun looked ever on that country, nor the moon by night. In that gray place the three women lived, all gray themselves and withered as in extreme old age. They were strange creatures, indeed, most of all because they had but one eye for the three, which it was their custom to take turns with, each removing it from her forehead when she had had it for a time and handing it to another.

All this Hermes told Perseus and then he unfolded his plan. He would himself guide Perseus to them. Once there Perseus must keep hidden until he saw one of them take the eye out of her forehead to pass it on. At that moment, when none of the three could see, he must rush forward and seize the eye and refuse to give it back until they told him how to reach the nymphs of the North.

He himself, Hermes said, would give him a sword to attack Medusa with—which could not be bent or broken by the Gorgon's scales, no matter how hard they were. This was a wonderful gift, no doubt, and yet of what use was a sword when the creature to be struck by it could turn the swordsman into stone before he was

▲ **Critical Viewing**
Who is portrayed in this art? Explain how you know. **[Connect]**

within striking distance? But another great deity was at hand to help. Pallas Athena stood beside Perseus. She took off the shield of polished bronze which covered her breast and held it out to him. "Look into this when you attack the Gorgon," she said. "You will be able to see her in it as in a mirror, and so avoid her deadly power."

Now, indeed, Perseus had good reason to hope. The journey to the twilight land was long, over the stream of Ocean and on to the very border of the black country where the Cimmerians dwell, but Hermes was his guide and he could not go astray. They found the Gray Women at last, looking in the wavering light like gray birds, for they had the shape of swans. But their heads were human and beneath their wings they had arms and hands. Perseus did just as Hermes had said, he held back until he saw one of them take the eye out of her forehead. Then before she could give it to her sister, he snatched it out of her hand. It was a moment or two before the three realized they had lost it. Each thought one of the others had it. But Perseus spoke out and told them he had taken it and that it would be theirs again only when they showed him how to find the nymphs of the North. They gave him full directions at once; they would have done anything to get their eye back. He returned it to them and went on the way they had pointed out to him. He was bound, although he did not know it, to the blessed country of the Hyperboreans [hī per bō′ rē anz], at the back of the North Wind, of which it is said: "Neither by ship nor yet by land shall one find the wondrous road to the gathering place of the Hyperboreans." But Perseus had Hermes with him, so that the road lay open to him, and he reached that host of happy people who are always banqueting and holding joyful <u>revelry</u>. They showed him great kindness: they welcomed him to their feast, and the maidens dancing to the sound of flute and lyre paused to get for him the gifts he sought. These were three: winged sandals, a magic wallet which would always become the right size for whatever was to be carried in it, and, most important of all, a cap which made the wearer invisible. With these and Athena's shield and Hermes' sword Perseus was ready for the Gorgons. Hermes knew where they lived, and leaving the happy land the two flew back across Ocean and over the sea to the Terrible Sisters' island.

By great good fortune they were all asleep when Perseus found them. In the mirror of the bright shield he could see them clearly, creatures with great wings and bodies covered with golden scales and hair a mass of twisting snakes. Athena was beside him now as well as Hermes. They told him which one was Medusa and that was important, for she alone of the three could be killed; the other two were immortal. Perseus on his winged sandals hovered above them, looking, however, only at the shield. Then he aimed a stroke down

Literary Analysis
Tall Tale and Myth
What heroic qualities does Perseus reveal in his encounter with the Gray Women?

Vocabulary Builder
revelry (rev′ əl rē) *n.* noisy merrymaking

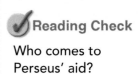

Reading Check

Who comes to Perseus' aid?

Perseus ■ 1125

at Medusa's throat and Athena guided his hand. With a single sweep of his sword he cut through her neck and, his eyes still fixed on the shield with never a glance at her, he swooped low enough to seize the head. He dropped it into the wallet which closed around it. He had nothing to fear from it now. But the two other Gorgons had awakened and, horrified at the sight of their sister slain, tried to pursue the slayer. Perseus was safe; he had on the cap of darkness and they could not find him.

> So over the sea rich-haired Danaë's son,
> Perseus, on his winged sandals sped,
> Flying swift as thought.
> In a wallet of silver,
> A wonder to behold,
> He bore the head of the monster,
> While Hermes, the son of Maia,
> The messenger of Zeus,
> Kept ever at his side.

On his way back he came to Ethiopia and alighted there. By this time Hermes had left him. Perseus found, as Hercules was later to find, that a lovely maiden had been given up to be devoured by a horrible sea serpent. Her name was Andromeda and she was the daughter of a silly vain woman,

> That starred Ethiop queen who strove
> To set her beauty's praise above
> The sea-nymphs, and their power offended.

She had boasted that she was more beautiful than the daughters of Nereus, the Sea-god. An absolutely certain way in those days to draw down on one a wretched fate was to claim superiority in anything over any deity[1]; nevertheless people were perpetually doing so. In this case the punishment for the arrogance the gods detested fell not on Queen Cassiopeia [kas′ ē ō pē′ ə], Andromeda's mother, but on her daughter. The Ethiopians were being devoured in numbers by the serpent; and, learning from the oracle that they could be freed from the pest only if Andromeda were offered up to it, they forced Cepheus [sē′ fəs], her father, to consent. When Perseus arrived the maiden was on a rocky ledge by the sea, chained there to wait for the coming of the monster. Perseus saw her and on the instant loved her. He waited beside her until the great snake came for its prey; then he cut its head off just as he had the Gorgon's. The headless body dropped back into the water; Perseus took Andromeda to her parents and asked for her hand, which they gladly gave him.

Literary Analysis
Tall Tale and Myth
What special knowledge helps Perseus kill Medusa?

---

1. deity (dē′ ə tē) *n.* a god.

◀ Critical Viewing
In what ways does this painting emphasize Perseus' physical strength and bravery? [Interpret]

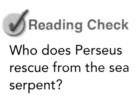

Reading Check

Who does Perseus rescue from the sea serpent?

With her he sailed back to the island and his mother, but in the house where he had lived so long he found no one. The fisherman Dictys' wife was long since dead, and the two others, Danaë and the man who had been like a father to Perseus, had had to fly and hide themselves from Polydectes, who was furious at Danaë's refusal to marry him. They had taken refuge in a temple, Perseus was told. He learned also that the King was holding a banquet in the palace and all the men who favored him were gathered there. Perseus instantly saw his opportunity. He went straight to the palace and entered the hall. As he stood at the entrance, Athena's shining buckler on his breast, the silver wallet at his side, he drew the eyes of every man there. Then before any could look away he held up the Gorgon's head; and at the sight one and all, the cruel King and his servile courtiers, were turned into stone. There they sat, a row of statues, each, as it were, frozen stiff in the attitude he had struck when he first saw Perseus.

When the islanders knew themselves freed from the tyrant it was easy for Perseus to find Danaë and Dictys. He made Dictys king of the island, but he and his mother decided that they would go back with Andromeda to Greece and try to be reconciled to Acrisius, to see if the many years that had passed since he had put them in the chest had not softened him so that he would be glad to receive his daughter and grandson. When they reached Argos, however, they found that Acrisius had been driven away from the city, and where he was no one could say. It happened that soon after their arrival Perseus heard that the King of Larissa, in the North, was holding a great athletic contest, and he journeyed there to take part. In the discus-throwing when his turn came and he hurled the heavy missile, it swerved and fell among the spectators. Acrisius was there on a visit to the King, and the discus struck him. The blow was fatal and he died at once.

So Apollo's oracle was again proved true. If Perseus felt any grief, at least he knew that his grandfather had done his best to kill him and his mother. With his death their troubles came to an end. Perseus and Andromeda lived happily ever after. Their son, Electryon, was the grandfather of Hercules.

Medusa's head was given to Athena, who bore it always upon the aegis, Zeus's shield, which she carried for him.

Literary Analysis
Tall Tale and Myth
How do the events at the end of the story relate to situations described at the beginning?

Thinking About the Selection

1. **Respond:** Which of Perseus' adventures would make the best action-adventure movie? Why?

2. **(a) Recall:** Why does Perseus set out to kill Medusa? **(b) Infer:** What detail of Perseus' background might have led Athena and Hermes to help Perseus in his quest?

3. **(a) Summarize:** Explain the weapons Perseus uses and the actions he takes to kill Medusa. **(b) Hypothesize:** What might have happened to Perseus if he had not received help from the gods?

4. **(a) Interpret:** What lesson do you think this ancient myth taught its first audiences? **(b) Extend:** In what ways is this myth still relevant today? Explain.

Apply the Skills

Pecos Bill: The Cyclone • Perseus

Comparing Tall Tales and Myths

1. Use a chart like the one shown to identify the ways in which "Pecos Bill: The Cyclone" contains the elements of a **tall tale**.

Larger-than-life hero	Far-fetched situations	Amazing feats	Humor	Hyperbole

2. **(a)** What divine actions does the **myth** of Perseus describe? **(b)** In what ways is Perseus a typical **mythic hero?**

3. **(a)** What weapons, skills, and knowledge does Perseus use to defeat the Medusa? **(b)** What weapons, skills, and knowledge does Pecos Bill use to defeat the cyclone? **(c)** In what ways are Pecos Bill's and Perseus' achievements both similar and different?

4. **(a)** What makes Pecos Bill a hero? **(b)** What makes Perseus a hero?

Writing to Compare Literary Works

The heroes of tall tales and myths usually represent some aspects of the cultures that create them. At the same time, every hero embodies some universal qualities—traits that are valued in all cultures. In an essay, compare and contrast the values that Pecos Bill and Perseus represent. Use these questions to help organize your thoughts:

- Whom does each hero respect? What does each fear?
- What does each hero desire? What does each accomplish?
- Does the hero act primarily on his own behalf or on behalf of others?

Vocabulary Builder

Practice For each item, use a word from the vocabulary list on page 1112 in a sentence describing the situation.

1. trying to convince those with different ideas
2. celebrating a championship season
3. embarrassment at forgetting a gift
4. taking over a coach's job

QuickReview

Tall Tale: a folk tale that features humor, exaggeration, and a hero who performs amazing deeds

Myth: an anonymous tale that explains the actions of gods and heroes or the causes of natural phenomena

Go Online
Assessment
For: Self-test
Visit: www.PHSchool.com
Web Code: epa-6609

Reading: Compare and Contrast

Directions: *Questions 1–5 are based on the following selection.*

ANTIGONE. I thought so. And that is why I wanted you
To come out here with me. There is something we must do.

ISMENE. Why do you speak so strangely?

ANTIGONE. Listen, Ismene:
Creon buried our brother Eteocles
With military honors, gave him a soldier's funeral,
And it was right that he should; but Polyneices [Antigone's other brother],
Who fought as bravely and died as miserably,—
They say that Creon has sworn
No one shall bury him, no one mourn for him,
But his body must lie in the fields, a sweet treasure
For carrion birds to find as they search for food.
That is what they say, and our good Creon is coming here
To announce it publicly; and the penalty—
Stoning to death in the public square!
                              There it is,
And now you can prove what you are:
A true sister, or a traitor to your family.

ISMENE. Antigone, you are mad! What could I possibly do?

ANTIGONE. Ismene, I am going to bury him. Will you come?

ISMENE. Bury him! You have just said the new law forbids it.

—from *Antigone,* by Sophocles

1. **What issue is the source of conflict in this passage?**
   A   the war of the Argives
   B   the relationship between the sisters
   C   the burial of Polyneices
   D   the death of Eteocles

2. **How are Antigone and Ismene similar?**
   A   Both have suffered the same loss.
   B   Both are angry at Creon.
   C   Both are determined to avenge the death of their brother.
   D   Both believe Creon is a just king.

3. **How are Antigone and Ismene different?**
   A   Antigone loves her brothers; Ismene does not.
   B   Antigone is defiant; Ismene is obedient.
   C   Antigone believes in upholding the law; Ismene believes in following one's heart.
   D   Antigone mourns the loss of her brothers; Ismene is indifferent to their loss.

Vocabulary

Directions: *Choose the best definition for each italicized word.*

Standards Assessed

• CT.4.02.1
• CT.4.03.2
• LT.5.03.11

4. **Both opponents in the debate present** *cogent* **evidence to support their position.**
   A sticky
   B forceful and to the point
   C confusing and meaningless
   D self-righteous

5. **The main character found his conscience was** *compelling* **him to tell the truth.**
   A driving
   B clarifying
   C not allowing
   D signaling

6. **The rules are clear and** *coherent.*
   A strict
   B serious
   C transparent
   D consistent

7. **This work is a** *significant* **addition to the literary criticism of Greek poetry.**
   A trivial
   B meaningful
   C exceptional
   D useless

8. **The lack of strong characters is a major** *defect* **of the play.**
   A perfection
   B importance
   C shortcoming
   D addition

Directions: *Choose the correct definition of each word.*

9. **insignificant**
   A trivial
   B the lack of a plan
   C full of meaning
   D being an obvious clue

10. **coherently**
    A confusedly
    B in a loud manner
    C full of importance
    D clearly

11. **design**
    A to give a signal
    B to mark out or make a plan
    C to confuse
    D to create an image

12. **reassign**
    A to make meaningless
    B to mark out for a purpose once again
    C to make clear
    D to hand over or give authority to

13. **inherently**
    A inseparably within
    B in a clear way
    C unconditionally
    D in a confused manner

Spelling Workshop

Spelling on College Entrance Exams

Spelling items come up on most college entrance exams. Doing well with them involves paying attention to small things, recalling a few basic rules, and knowing your own spelling weaknesses.

Spell It Right Spelling is not the most important part of college entrance exams. However, spelling items do occur in English usage sections of most tests. Use these recommendations to help you prepare.

- Look for homophone errors, easily confused words, or simple words that are spelled incorrectly. Remember, for instance, that *a lot* is two words and that *you're,* not *your,* is the contraction for "you are."
- Review word formation rules that people sometimes forget.
  — When adding endings to multisyllable words whose final letters are a consonant + y, double the final consonant if the accent is on the final syllable.
  — When adding prefixes to words, do not drop any letters.
  — When adding suffixes to words, remember that final consonant + *y* usually changes to *i*. Final *e*'s are usually dropped when the suffix begins with a vowel—but not when the base word ends in *ce* or *ge*.
- Know the words that give you trouble and work out memory tricks to help with them.

Practice For each word on the word list write a memory aid. Share the memory aid with a partner or the class.

Example: to **adapt** is **A** necessary survival skill.

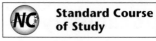

Standard Course of Study

- Edit for spelling and mechanics. (GU.6.02.4)

Word List
adapt
adopt
preferred
misshapen
courageous
loneliness
acclaim
sophomore
parentheses
preceding

I could have adapted if they adopted a "no test" policy!

Monitor Your Progress

A. Directions: *Write the letter of the item that contains a spelling, punctuation, capitalization, or usage error. Choose E if there are no errors in the sentence.*

Standards Assessed

• GU.6.02.4

1. <u>My sister</u> is a <u>sophomore</u> at the
       (A)   (B)
     <u>University of Dayton</u> in Ohio, <u>so</u> last year,
          (C)   (D)
     she attended a community college. No error
                              (E)

2. The <u>preceeding</u> day, the third
         (A)
     <u>Friday of the month</u>, Travis
        (B)
     <u>had gone</u> for his regular <u>doctor's</u>
      (C)   (D)
     appointment. No error
           (E)

3. Some <u>people, such as</u> the volunteers
           (A)
     at <u>Price Hospital</u>, are content to stay out
       (B)
     of the <u>limelight, others</u>, though, must
          (C)
     have constant <u>acclaim</u>. No error
            (D)   (E)

4. <u>Writers who</u> overuse <u>parenthesees</u> in
        (A)   (B)
     <u>their essays</u> tend not only to confuse
       (C)
     readers <u>but also to</u> annoy them. No error
         (D)   (E)

B. Directions: *Write the letter of the version of the underlined section that makes the item correct and appropriate. If you think the original version is best, choose "NO CHANGE."*

When my grandmother first planted the little <u>tree, it was a sad, mishapen</u>
                                        1

stick. As summer passed, though, it <u>adopted to its</u>
                            2

environment. It clearly <u>preferred well-irrigated soil, so</u> we watered
                           3

it constantly.

1. **A** NO CHANGE
    B tree it was a sad, mishapen
    C tree, it was a sad, misshapen
    D tree, it would be a sad, mishapen

2. **A** NO CHANGE
    B adapted to its
    C adopted to his
    D adapted to it's

3. **A** NO CHANGE
    B prefered well-irrigated soil, so
    C prefered well-irrigated soil so
    D preferred well-irrigated soil, but

Exposition: Comparison-and-Contrast Essay

You make comparisons every day. Whether you are considering foods, ideas, actions, or careers, comparative thinking is an underlying factor of almost every choice you make. A **comparison-and-contrast essay** is a written exploration of the similarities and differences between two things or among more than two things. Use the steps outlined in this workshop to write a comparison-and-contrast essay.

Assignment Write a comparison-and-contrast essay about two events, ideas, or historical leaders.

What to Include Your comparison-and-contrast essay should have the following characteristics:
an analysis and discussion of similarities and differences between two or among more than two things, people, places, or ideas

- accurate, factual details about each subject
- a purpose for comparising and contrasting
- a balanced presentation of each subject using either subject-by-subject or point-by-point organization
- error-free grammar, including varied sentence structure and length

To preview the criteria on which your comparison-and-contrast essay may be assessed, see the rubric on page 1141.

Writing Workshop: *Work in Progress*

If you have completed the Work-in-Progress assignments, you have several ideas in your portfolio that you might wish to pursue in your essay. You may continue to develop these ideas, or you might choose to explore a new idea as you complete this Writing Workshop.

Standard Course of Study

- Use description, comparison, figurative language to elaborate ideas to inform audience (IR.2.02.4)
- Compare effective strategies used in different presentations/products. (CT.4.01.4)

Using the Form

You will use elements of comparison and contrast in these types of writing:

- essays on historical figures and events
- consumer reports
- essays on works of art, literature, or music

Reading **Writing** Connection

To get a feel for comparison-and-contrast writing, read "The News" by Neil Postman, on page 426

Prewriting

Choosing Your Topic

In your essay, compare things that are both closely related and significantly different. Use these strategies for choosing a topic.

- **Finding Related Pairs** Explore topics in terms of clear opposites, clear similarities, or close relationships. Start with names of people, places, objects, or ideas. Note related subjects that come to mind. Notice relationships that interest you, and choose one to develop.

- **Exploring Categories** Working with a group, make a list of categories, such as famous athletes, famous artists, vacation spots, or favorite foods. Then, choose one category, and discuss it in greater depth. Identify specific topics within the category that present clear similarities and differences.

Work in Progress
Review the work you did on pages 1111 and 1093.

> **Brainstorming for Topic Pairs**
>
> Hockey vs. soccer
> Middle school vs. high school
> Love for my town vs. boredom with it
> Music vs. literature
> Video vs. DVD

Narrowing Your Topic

Specify your purpose. To identify a purpose for your essay, consider the following possibilities:

- **To persuade**—You want readers to accept your opinion that one subject is preferable to another.

- **To explain**—You want readers to understand something special about the subjects.

- **To describe**—You want readers to understand the basic similarities and differences between your subjects.

Gathering Details

Use a Venn diagram. Gather and organize details for your essay using a Venn diagram. Record similarities in the space where the circles overlap, and note differences in the outer sections of the circles.

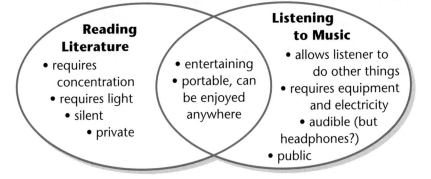

Reading Literature
- requires concentration
- requires light
- silent
- private

(overlap)
- entertaining
- portable, can be enjoyed anywhere

Listening to Music
- allows listener to do other things
- requires equipment and electricity
- audible (but headphones?)
- public

Writing Workshop

Drafting

Shaping Your Writing

Choose an organization. Select an organization that suits your topic. Point-by-point and subject-by-subject plans are the most common types of organization used in comparison-and-contrast writing.

- **Point-by-Point Organization** Move between your subjects as you discuss points of comparison. First, compare one element of both subjects, and then address another element of both subjects. Continue this process until you have covered all the features. This method allows you to sharpen your points of similarity and difference.

Point-by-Point Plan

Point 1
- Subject A
- Subject B
Point 2
- Subject A
- Subject B

Subject-by-Subject Plan

Subject A
- Point 1
- Point 2
Subject B
- Point 1
- Point 2

- **Subject-by-Subject Organization** Compare your subjects as complete units. First, discuss all the features of one subject; then, discuss all the features of the other. While this format allows you to focus on one subject at a time, take care that you address the same features and devote equal time to each subject.

To read the complete student model, see page 1140.

Providing Elaboration

Support generalizations with specifics. Whether your purpose in comparing and contrasting two subjects is to describe, to persuade, or to explain, provide enough detail to fully develop your points. Support your statements about similarities and differences with facts, examples, and other forms of evidence.

Student Model: Providing Specific Details

I am fond of the size of Bernice and I detest it, too. I'm glad that only fifteen cars is a major traffic jam. But I hate that I have to drive sixteen miles to the nearest major store. I love and hate that my town is so small that I know everybody's first, middle, and last names. I like it because I have a "tab" at the grocery store . . . .

Lauren gives specific, balanced support for each "love" and "hate" statement.

From the Author's Desk

Coach Dean Smith and John Kilgo

On Word Choice

Dean Smith

"Good writing is hard work."
—Coach Dean Smith and John Kilgo

John Kilgo, my co-author, took notes of our conversations related to this book and put my ideas into written form. I have strong feelings about what I want my words to convey, which means we did extensive rewriting and revising. When we finally signed off on a chapter, it was always shorter, sharper in focus, and less repetitive than the original.

Professional Model:

from *The Carolina Way*

A steady focus on taking care of the little things, attending diligently to the many details involved with building a team, helped us produce a mind-set that enhanced our ability to handle the big things. . . . Here are some of the so-called little things that we integrated into our program:

Punctuality: Players knew I arrived early for meetings and practices, and I expected everyone to be there and ready to go. . . . Tardiness is the ~~definition~~ ∧height of arrogance. In effect, you're saying, "My time is more important than yours." Being on time is being considerate of others. . . .

Swearing: We discouraged it in our program. When a player cursed in practice, the entire team ran for him. . . . This is not an easy subject to talk about because it can sound ~~sanctimonious~~ ∧pious. . . . However, I believe that anger can be expressed without using profanity.

Top priority: We checked on the class attendance of our players, as well as their grades and academic progress.

We used the phrase "produce a mind-set," because it's important for readers to know that our program had a strong philosophy concerning team-building techniques that we instilled in our players beginning with the first day they stepped on campus.

We first wrote that tardiness is the "definition" of arrogance, but changed it to "height of arrogance" on the rewrite. Using "height of arrogance" seemed to more strongly emphasize how unacceptable tardiness was in our program.

We first used "sanctimonious" in describing the difficulty in even discussing the subject of swearing, but changed it to "pious," which sounds less "preachy," or at least we thought so at the time. Also, words have a rhythm, and "pious" just seemed to fit better here.

Writing Workshop

Revising

Revising Your Paragraphs

Revise to make comparisons and contrasts clear. Using two different colors, mark your draft to distinguish between the two subjects you discuss. Whether you have used point-by-point or subject-by-subject organization, this color coding will clearly reveal whether or not you have made a balanced presentation of both subjects. If necessary, expand or reduce coverage of one of your subjects to achieve balance. Next, evaluate the places where the two colors—and subjects—meet. Add transitional words to make the shifts clear.

To read the complete student model, see page 1140.

Student Model: Revising for Clarity

~~I love and hate the security in my town for a number of reasons.~~ ^I love it because I know that it is my dogs scratching at my door at 5:30 in the morning and not some dangerous stranger. In my town, a fifteen-car traffic jam is front-page news. On the other hand, ^I hate that it gets a little boring sometimes. I don't want criminals at my door, but a little excitement would be nice.

> A topic sentence helps call out the point of comparison. The transition *on the other hand* shows readers the shift between subjects.

Revising Your Word Choice

Revise to add specifics. To help your readers understand the comparisons you make, add enough detail to explain the differences and similarities you see. Look for places where you can add information that strengthens your description or analysis.

Peer Review: Exchange drafts with a partner. As you read each other's essay, circle any vague language that you find. Consider choices that convey your meaning more precisely. Then, discuss with your reader specific details that would make your comparisions more vivid. Consider adding these details.

Vague: In contrast to literature, popular music forms a soundtrack for our lives.

Specific: In contrast to literature that we must read to enjoy, popular music, like the Top 40 tunes we hear on the radio, forms a soundtrack for our lives. We can enjoy it as we drive, shop, or even fall asleep at night.

Integrating Grammar Skills

Revising to Vary Sentence Structure and Length

A sequence of sentences of the same length and the same structural pattern can have a tedious effect on readers. By varying sentence length, introducing new sentence beginnings, and inverting subject-verb order, you can make your paragraphs more interesting and readable.

Vary sentence length. Once you have identified an unbroken series of long sentences, look for an opportunity to include a short sentence. Since the short sentence will draw the reader's attention, use it to emphasize an important detail or idea. Be sure that the short sentence is a complete thought and not a fragment.

> **Original:** Memories of long hours of practice, the brutal weather, the aches and bruises of an endless season were erased by the single shining fact that we had won the championship.
>
> **Revised:** Memories of long hours of practice, the brutal weather, the aches and bruises of an endless season were erased by a single shining fact. We had won the championship.

Vary sentence beginnings. If you have written a series of sentences beginning with a noun or pronoun, look for opportunities to start sentences with different parts of speech.

> **Adverb clause:** *Anywhere you go,* you will still find most people care about others.
>
> **Prepositional phrase:** *After a long Saturday of work,* Sarah did not feel like going out.
>
> **Complement:** *Most interesting to me* was an electronic display of the battlefield. (complement of the verb *was*)
>
> **Direct object:** *Our report* I gave to the editor; my opinion I kept to myself. (objects of the verb *gave*)

Vary subject-verb order. You can vary sentence beginnings by reversing the usual subject-verb order.

> **Original:** The mystery guest is here at last.
> **Inverted:** Here at last is the mystery guest.

Apply It to Your Editing

As you review the three longest paragraphs in your draft, place brackets around each sentence. Examine the length and pattern of each sentence to look for ways to improve their variety. Change sentence lengths, alter sentence beginnings, and invert subject-verb order.

Prentice Hall Writing and Grammar Connection: Chapter 22, Section 3

Writing Workshop

Student Model: Lauren De Loach
Bernice LA

Ambivalence

When I consider my conflicting feelings about my hometown, I see that there are things that I love and hate about living in Bernice, Louisiana, a nineties version of Mayberry. I love the security of a small town, and I hate it. I love the way that my town is not clouded by the smog of a city, and I hate it too. I love it and I hate that I love it.

I love and hate the security in my town for a number of reasons. I love it because I know that it is my dogs scratching at my door at 5:30 in the morning and not some dangerous stranger. In my town, a fifteen-car traffic jam is front-page news. On the other hand, I hate that it gets a little boring sometimes. I don't want criminals at my door, but a little excitement would be nice.

I am fond of the size of Bernice and I detest it, too. I'm glad that only fifteen cars is a major traffic jam. But I hate that I have to drive sixteen miles to the nearest major store. I love and hate that my town is so small that I know everybody's first, middle, and last names. I like it because I have a "tab" at the grocery store and the drug store, so that eliminates the necessity of money. I hate that everybody knows me because that means that everybody finds out about whom I'm dating, whom I once dated, my height, weight, and age. I also hate that we all know each other so well that the most entertaining news we can come up with to put in the *Bernice Banner* is that Peggy Jane and her brother JC visited their Aunt Goosey Lou in the nursing home. But by knowing everyone so well, I've made friends who are trustworthy because we know all of one another's deepest secrets.

Even though I say that I detest some things, home wouldn't be home without these silly quirks. I love that my parents and their friends are known as the "elite group" because they have traveled beyond Texas, Arkansas, and Mississippi. I love saying that I have read the *Iliad* to people who think I would not read such a book. I know that it sounds like I love the provincialism that small towns can impose, but the smells of fresh-cut grass and the gardenia bush outside my door are what make my home my home.

This is what I love and what I hate, but I don't really. The overall feeling I get from living in Bernice is ambivalence. I love it and I hate that I love such goofy things. But the parts of home that seem so trivial are the ones that make you who you are. That makes a place your home.

Lauren's essay will compare two feelings: what she loves and what she hates about her hometown.

Using a point-by-point organization, Lauren addresses the first contrast in her attitudes about her town: She feels ambivalence about its security.

These facts support the writer's ideas and opinions.

Lauren's comparison allows her to be funny, but it also helps her reflect on her ideas.

Editing and Proofreading

Check your draft to correct errors in spelling, grammar, and punctuation.

Focus on Compound Sentences: Comparison-and-contrast essays often contain compound sentences—those with two independent clauses joined by a semicolon or a coordinating conjunction, such as *or, and,* or *but.* Check that you have correctly punctuated these sentences.

> **Conjunction:** I liked the chili, but it was spicy.
>
> **Semicolon:** I rushed out; I was late for the bus.

Publishing and Presenting

Consider one of the following ways to share your writing:
Deliver an oral presentation. Read your comparison-and-contrast essay aloud to an audience of your classmates. If possible, include props or visuals to enhance the reading.
Make a poster. Present your comparison-and-contrast findings visually in a poster. Using a graphic organizer such as a Venn diagram, show the differences and similarities of your subjects. If possible, add photographs and illustrations to show the distinctive elements of your subjects.

Reflecting on Your Writing

Writer's Journal Jot down your thoughts on writing a comparison-and-contrast essay. Begin by answering these questions.
- Did your ideas change as you compared your subjects?
- Which strategy for prewriting, drafting, revising, or editing helped you the most with this assignment?

> *Prentice Hall Writing and Grammar Connection: Chapter 9*

Rubric for Self-Assessment

To assess your comparison-and-contrast essay, use the following rubric:

NC Criteria	Rating Scale
	not very .... very
Focus: How clear is your purpose for comparing and contrasting?	1 2 3 4 5
Organization: How balanced is your organization?	1 2 3 4 5
Support/Elaboration: How accurate and factual are the details you use to support your ideas?	1 2 3 4 5
Style: How effectively do you use transitions to clarify ideas?	1 2 3 4 5
Conventions: How correct is your grammar, especially related to your use of varied sentence structure and length?	1 2 3 4 5

Communications Workshop

Comparing Media Coverage

Modern news media have developed a broad array of techniques and technologies for conveying their messages. Use the following comparison strategies to assess the accuracy and objectivity of media coverage, and evaluate media impact on your life.

NC Standard Course of Study

- Analyze use of language for a particular effect in argument. (FA.3.01.3)
- Interpret literary devices. (LT.5.01.3)

Comparing Coverage

With a team of classmates, record news reports from two different news programs. Try to select items that are reported on the same event or issue, that aired on the same day, and that are about the same length. As you view each news report several times, make inferences and ask questions. Consider the following:

- **Clarity** Does the on-air reporter clearly present the *who, what, how, when,* and *why* elements of the story? Is the "headline"—the main point—prominent in the newscast?
- **Tone** What is the reporter's tone? Does the reporter use language that is factual or emotional, objective or involved?
- **Credibility** What facts are used to build the story? Are informational sources reliable and objective? Are potential biases acknowledged?
- **Images** Are photographs and video clips used? Are these images relevant to the content of the story?
- **Quotations** Who is interviewed or quoted? What is the role of each speaker? Does the speaker have an inherent bias? Do the interviews contribute facts, insights, emotions, entertainment, or propaganda to the story?
- **Balance** Does the story include multiple perspectives or viewpoints about the event or issue? Does the story tilt toward a particular argument or viewpoint?

Presenting Your Findings

Consider one of the following patterns of organization.

- **Whole-to-whole** Present a complete analysis of one of the broadcasts; then, do the same for the other. Be sure to cover the same factors in each analysis. Summarize your conclusions about both newscasts.
- **Part-to-part** Organize your discussion according to specific categories. For example, discuss both stories in terms of credibility, use of images, tone, and so on.

Activity *Analysis and Presentation* Using the above guidelines, analyze two different news broadcasts of the same story. Present your findings to the class. If possible, illustrate your findings with clips from the broadcasts.

The War of the Worlds

H.G. Wells

Globe Fearon, 1993

Novel In this realistically told science fiction tale, invaders from outer space attack the Earth. A radio adaptation of the story once convinced listeners that the invasion was real—they fled their homes.

Strange Case of Dr. Jekyll and Mr. Hyde

Robert Louis Stevenson

Prentice Hall, 2000

Novel This is the story of a mild-mannered doctor who explores his dark side—with terrifying results. Fascinated with the idea of evil, the story's main character, Dr. Jekyll, develops a potion that changes him into the violent Mr. Hyde. Before long, however, Jekyll finds himself transforming into Hyde without the aid of the potion, leaving him, along with terrified readers, to wonder which personality will finally win out.

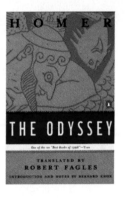

The Left Hand of Darkness

Ursula Le Guin

Ace Books, 1969

Novel This is the journal of a Terran, sent as an envoy from the Council of Ekumen to form an alliance with the planet Getham. Getham is a unique planet—it is ruled by a king who distrusts technology, yet harbors a group of people whose psychological understanding is unparalleled in the universe.

The Odyssey

Homer translated by Robert Fagles

Penguin Books, 1996

Epic This is the story of Odysseus, a Greek hero of the Trojan War who offended Poseidon. The *Odyssey* chronicles Odysseus' ten year adventurous journey home as he and his crew wandered through uncharted oceans filled with mythical and human enemies. At home the situation is dismal. Presuming that Odysseus is dead, suitors for his wife's hand are draining the country's resources and plotting to kill his son. This epic has survived for 3000 years because it explores the passion and problems of powerful people.

These titles are available in the Penguin/Prentice Hall Literature Library.

Think About It A restaurant called Windows on the World was once one of New York City's landmarks. From its great windows on the 107th floor of the World Trade Center, diners could gaze upon the city and its vast suburbs. Many people worked in this restaurant, arriving early each morning to prepare food or to set the elegant tables. When the towers fell on September 11, 2001, those workers lost their lives.

Alabanza:
In Praise of Local 100
Martín Espada

for the 43 members of Hotel Employees and Restaurant Employees Local 100, working at the Windows on the World restaurant who lost their lives in the attack on the World Trade Center

Alabanza[1] Praise the cook with the shaven head
and a tattoo on his shoulder that said *Oye*,
a blue-eyed Puerto Rican with people from Fajardo,
the harbor of pirates centuries ago.
5   Praise the lighthouse in Fajardo, candle
glimmering white to worship the dark saint of the sea.
Alabanza. Praise the cook's yellow Pirates cap
worn in the name of Roberto Clemente, his plane
that flamed into the ocean loaded with cans for Nicaragua,
10   for all the mouths chewing the ash of earthquakes.
Alabanza. Praise the kitchen radio, dial clicked
even before the dial on the oven, so that music and Spanish
rose before bread. Praise the bread. *Alabanza*.

---

1. Alabanza (äl´ə ban´ za) Spanish for "praise."

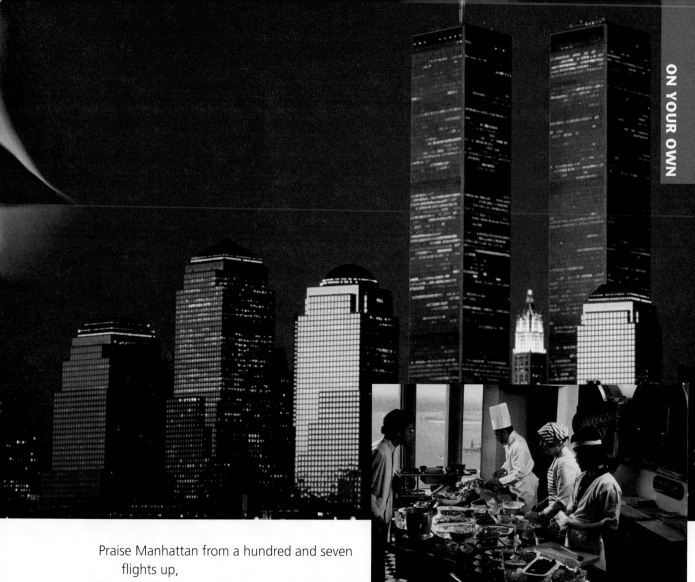

Praise Manhattan from a hundred and seven
flights up,

15 like Atlantis glimpsed through the windows of
an ancient aquarium.
Praise the great windows where immigrants from the kitchen
could squint and almost see their world, hear the chant of nations:
Ecuador, México, Republica Dominicana,

20 *Haiti, Yemen, Ghana, Bangladesh.*
Alabanza. Praise the kitchen in the morning,
where the gas burned blue on every stove
and exhaust fans fired their diminutive propellers,
hands cracked eggs with quick thumbs

25 or sliced open cartons to build an altar of cans.
Alabanza. Praise the busboy's music, the chime-chime
of his dishes and silverware in the tub.
Alabanza. Praise the dish-dog, the dishwasher
who worked that morning because another dishwasher

30 could not stop coughing, or because he needed overtime
to pile the sacks of rice and beans for a family

floating away on some Caribbean island plagued by frogs.
Alabanza. Praise the waitress who heard the radio in the kitchen
and sang to herself about a man gone. *Alabanza.*

35   After the thunder wilder than thunder,
after the booming ice storm of glass from the great windows,
after the radio stopped singing like a tree full of terrified frogs,
after night burst the dam of day and flooded the kitchen,
for a time the stoves glowed in darkness like the lighthouse in Fajardo,

40   like a cook's soul. Soul I say, even if the dead cannot tell us
about the bristles of God's beard because God has no face,
soul I say, to name the smoke-beings flung in constellations
across the night sky of this city and cities to come.
Alabanza I say, even if God has no face.

45   *Alabanza.* When the war began, from Manhattan to Kabul
two constellations of smoke rose and drifted to each other,
mingling in icy air, and one said with an Afghan tongue:
Teach me to dance. We have no music here.
And the other said with a Spanish tongue:

50   *I will teach you. Music is all we have.*

Meet the Author
Martín Espada (b. 1957) was born in Brooklyn, New York. His poems draw upon his Puerto Rican heritage as well as his early work experiences, which ranged from gas station attendant to lawyer. Espada is currently a professor of English at the University of Massachusetts in Amherst.

Readings in Contemporary Literature
Talk About It
Use these questions to guide a discussion of the poem.

1. **(a)** Why are the workers able to "hear the chant of nations"?
   (b) How does this "chant of nations" change in the last five lines?

2. In a group, discuss why the author may have chosen to write about this group of people rather than others who perished on that day.
   - Why do you think that the poet repeats the Spanish word for praise? What is he praising?
   - The poet imagines a meeting of the souls of those who died in the attacks and in the war that followed. What is he suggesting about the connections between these two groups?

Choose a point-person to share your group's ideas with the class.

RESOURCES

GLOSSARY

High utility and academic vocabulary words appear in green.

A

abdicated (ab´ di kāt´ id) *v.* gave up formally

abomination (ə bäm´ ə nā´ shən) *n.* anything hateful and disgusting

abstract (ab´ strakt´) *adj.* not concrete; of thought

abstract (ab strakt´) *n., v.* a summary, summarize

absurdity (ab sʉr´ də tē) *n.* something ridiculous or nonsensical

allotment (ə lät´ mənt) *n.* share; portion

aloofness (ə lōōf´ nəs) *n.* quality of being distant or removed

ambiguities (am´ bə gyōō´ ə tēz) *n.* statements or events whose meanings are unclear

ambiguous (am big´yōō əs) *adj.* having more than one possible meaning

amicably (am´ i kə blē) *adv.* in a friendly way

anguish (aŋ´ gwish) *n.* great pain or suffering

anonymous (ə nän´ ə məs) *adj.* without a known or acknowledged name

anticipate (an tis´ə pāt´) *v.* expect something.

apex (ā´ peks´) *n.* highest point; peak

appreciate (ə prē´shē āt´) *v.* to recognize; to understand and be grateful for

archaic (är kā´ ik) *adj.* seldom used; old-fashioned

ardor (är´ dər) *n.* passion; enthusiasm

arduous (är´ jōō əs) *adj.* difficult; laborious

articulate (är tik´ yōō lit) *adj.* expressing oneself clearly and easily

aspect (as´pekt´) *n.* an element or part

assiduous (ə sij´ ōō əs) *adj.* done with constant and careful attention; diligent

assuage (ə swāj´) *v.* calm; pacify

atonement (ə tōn´ mənt) *n.* act of making up for a wrongdoing or injury

augmenting (ôg ment´ iŋ) *v.* increasing; enlarging

authentic (ô then´ tik) *adj.* genuine; true

awry (ə rī´) *adj.* not straight

azure (azh´ ər) *adj.* sky blue

B

bafflement (baf´ əl mənt) *n.* puzzlement; bewilderment

bemusing (bē myōōz´ iŋ) *v.* stupefying or muddling

benevolently (bə nev´ ə lənt lē) *adv.* in a well-meaning way

bereft (bē reft´) *adj.* deprived

bilingual (bī liŋ´ gwəl) *adj.* capable of using two languages

blight (blīt) *n.* something that destroys or prevents growth

bravado (brə vä´ dō) *n.* pretended courage or defiant confidence when one is really afraid

C

categorize (kat´ə gə rīz´) *v.* to classify, place within a group

censure (sen´ shər) *n.* strong disapproval

circumstance (sʉr´ cəm stans´) *n.* a fact or event

clasps (klasps) *v.* grips

cogent (kō´jənt) *adj.* convincing; powerfully appealing

coherent (cō her´ənt) *adj.* orderly or logical; sticking together

compelling (cəm pel´iŋ) *v.* forcing or pressuring

compensation (käm´ pən sā´ shən) *n.* anything that makes up for a loss, damage, or debt

compile (kəm pīl´) *v.* put together; compose by gathering materials

complex (cäm pleks´) *adj.* complicated or intricate

comprehension (käm´ prē hen´ shen) *n.* understanding

concept (kän´sept´) *n.* an idea; a general notion of a class of objects

condense (kən dens´) *v.* shorten or make more concise; concentrate

condolences (kən dō´ lən sez) *n.* expressions of sympathy with another in grief

confer (kən fʉr´) *v.* give

confirm (cən fʉrm´) *v.* prove the truth or authenticity

considerable (cən sid´er ə bəl) *adj.* much or large; worth noting

contemplate (kän´təm plat´) *v.* consider or think about

contemporary (kən tem´pə rer´ē) *adj.* recent or current; living or happening at the same time

contempt (kən tempt´) *n.* disdain or scorn

contribute (cən trib´yōōt) *v.* give, add, provide

controversy (cän´ trə v r´sē) *n.* a discussion over opposing viewpoints; a dispute

convince (kən vins´) *v.* overcome the doubts of; persuade

GLOSSARY

countenance (kount´ʼn əns) *n.* face

covenant (kuv´ə nənt) *n.* agreement or contract, especially a sacred one

creed (krēd) *n.* statement of belief

cunning (kun´ iŋ) *adj.* skilled in deception

curtailed (kər tāld. ´) *v.* cut short; reduced

D

daunting (dônt´ iŋ) *adj.* intimidating

defect (dē´ fekt´) *n.* a lack of something important; an imperfection

deferred (dē fʉrd´) *adj.* put off until a future time

defrauded (dē frôd´ id) *v.* cheated

degenerate (dē jen´ ər āt´) *v.* grow worse

deleterious (del´ ə tir´ ē əs) *adj.* harmful to health or well-being

deliberation (di lib´ər ā´shən) *n.* the act of carefully thinking about an issue

demonstrative (di män´ strə tiv) *adj.* showing feelings openly

demure (di myour´) *adj.* modest

depravity (dē prav´ ə tē) *n.* crookedness; corruption

depreciate (dē prē´ shē āt´) *v.* to reduce in value

derisive (di rī´ siv) *adj.* mocking

derive (di rīv´) *v.* get from a source

despotic (des pät´ ik) *adj.* like an absolute ruler or tyrant

desultory (des´ əl tôr´ ē) *adj.* random

detect (dē tekt´) *v.* to discover

determination (dē tʉr´ mi nā´ shən) *n.* firm intention

diffused (di fyo͞ozd´) *v.* spread out

dilapidated (də lap´ə dāt´ id) *adj.* falling to pieces or into disrepair

diminution (dim´ ə no͞o´ shən) *n.* lessening

discerning (di sʉrn´ iŋ) *adj.* having or showing good judgment or understanding

disconsolately (dis kän´ sə lit lē) *adv.* so unhappily that nothing will comfort

discreet (di skrēt´) *adj.* careful about what one says or does; unnoticeable

discreetly (di skrēt´ lē) *adv.* without drawing attention

disheveled (di shev´ əld) *adj.* untidy

dishevelment (di shev´ əl ment) *n.* state of being untidy

dismal (diz´ məl) *adj.* causing gloom or misery

dispatched (di spacht´) *v.* finished quickly

display (di splā´) *v.* to exhibit; to show

dissemble (di sem´ bəl) *v.* conceal under a false appearance; disguise

dissension (di sen´ shən) *n.* difference of opinion; disagreement

distinct (di stiŋkt´) *adj.* different from; separate and well-defined

distraught (di strôt´) *adj.* extremely troubled or confused

diverged (dī vʉrjd´) *v.* branched out in different directions

droll (drōl) *adj.* funny in an odd way

duration (doo rā´ shən) *n.* length of time something lasts

E

elaborate (ē lab´ə rāt´) *v., adj.* work out in detail; extremely detailed

eloquence (el´ ə kwəns) *n.* speech that is graceful and persuasive

elusive (ē lo͞o´ siv) *adj.* hard to grasp or retain mentally

emotion (ē´ mō´shən) *n.* a feeling

emphasize (em´fə sīz´) *v.* to stress; to give special importance to

emulate (em´ yo͞o lāt´) *v.* imitate

enamored (en am´ ərd) *v.* filled with love and desire; charmed

endurance (en door´ əns) *n.* ability to withstand hardship

enigma (i nig´ mə) *n.* mystery

enjoined (en joind´) *v.* ordered

enthralled (en thrōld´) *v.* held as in a spell; captivated

entrenched (en trench´d´) *adj.* securely established

equity (ek´ wit ē) *n.* fairness; justice

equivalent (ē kwiv´ə lənt) *adj.* equal in meaning

evanescent (ev´ ə nes´ ənt) *adj.* temporary; tending to disappear

exile (ek´ sīl´) *v.* banish

explicit (eks plis´ it) *adj.* clearly stated

extrapolating (ek strap´ ə lāt´ iŋ) *v.* arriving at a conclusion by inferring from known facts

F

feckless (fek´ lis) *adj.* careless; irresponsible

feisty (fīs´ tē) *adj.* full of spirit; energetic

fertile (fʉrt´ʼl) *adj.* able to make plants grow

fickle (fik´ əl) *adj.* changeable

forebears (fôr´ berz´) *n.* ancestors

formality (fôr mal´ ə tē) *n.* attention to established rules or customs

formidable (fôr´ mə də bəl) *adj.* awe-inspiring

fray (frā) *n.* noisy fight

furtive (fʉr´ tiv) *adj.* sneaky

futile (fyo͞ot´ ʼl) *adj.* useless; hopeless

G

gallant (gal´ ənt) adj. brave and noble

grievance (grēv´ əns) n. injustice; complaint

H

hallowed (hal´ ōd) adj. sacred

haughty (hôt´ ē) adj. arrogant

hence (hens) adv. as a result; therefore

humble (hum´ bəl) adj. modest; having humility

I

ignorance (ig´ nə rəns) n. lack of knowledge or education

illuminate (I lo͞o´mə nāt´) v. make clear; provide insight

imminent (im´ ə nənt) adj. likely to happen soon

impact (im pakt´) n. the force of a shock; a violent collision

implement (im´plə ment) v. put into action; fulfill or accomplish

implications (im´ pli kā´ shənz) n. indirect results

incognito (in´ käg nē´ tō´) n. a disguised condition

incredulity (in´ krə do͞o´ lə tē) n. inability to believe

indolently (in´ də lənt lē) adv. lazily; idly

inevitability (in ev´ i tə bil´ ə tē) n. quality of being certain to happen

inevitable (in ev´ i tə bəl) adj. unavoidable, certain

infallibility (in fal´ ə bil´ ə tē) n. condition of not being likely to fail

inscrutable (in skro͞ot´ ə bəl) adj. baffling; mysterious

insidious (in sid´ ē əs) adj. characterized by craftiness and betrayal

insolent (in´ sə lənt) adj. boldly disrespectful

J

jibed (jībd) v. changed direction

judicious (jo͞o dish´ əs) adj. showing good judgment

L

lament (lə ment´) v. express deep sorrow; mourn

lamentable (lam´ ən tə bəl) adj. distressing; sad

languid (laŋ´ gwid) adj. drooping; weak

languor (laŋ´ gər) n. a lack of vigor; weakness

lateral (lat´ ər əl) adj. sideways

legacy (leg´ ə sē) n. something handed down from an ancestor

lexicon (lek´si kän´) n. the special vocabulary of a particular author, field of study, and so on

lithe (līth) adj. flexible

loathsome (lōth´ səm) adj. disgusting; detestable

lofty (lôf´ tē) adj. very high; noble

lurched (lēcht) v. moved awkwardly and suddenly

M

maladies (mal´ ə dēz) n. diseases

malodorous (mal ō´ dər əs) adj. having a bad smell

mammoth (mam´ əth) adj. enormous

martial (mär´ shəl) adj. military

maudlin (môd´ lin) adj. tearfully and foolishly sentimental

mechanism (mek´ə niz´əm) n. a system or means of doing something; the working parts of a machine

medium (mē´ dē əm) n. means of communication

melancholy (mel´ ən käl´ ē) n. sadness; gloom

metaphysical (met´ ə fiz´ i kəl) adj. spiritual; beyond the physical

meticulously (mə tik´ yo͞o ləs lē) adv. very carefully and precisely

moribund (môr´ i bund´) adj. dying

mortified (môrt´ ə fīd´) adj. extremely embarrassed

motive (mōt´ iv) n. the reason a person acts in a certain way.

N

naive (nä ēv´) adj. unsophisticated

novice (näv´ is) adj. new to an activity; inexperienced

O

obstinacy (äb´ stə nə sē) n. stubbornness

ominous (äm´ ə nəs) adj. threatening

P

pallid (pal´ id) adj. pale

pallor (pal´ ər) n. unnatural paleness

palpable (pal´ pə bəl) adj. able to be felt

palpitating (pal´ pə tāt´ iŋ) v. beating rapidly; throbbing

Glossary ■ R-3

GLOSSARY

parsimonious (pär′ sə mō′ nē əs) *adj.* miserly; stingy

participate (pär tis′ə pāt′) *v.* to take part in, to join

penalty (pen′ əl tē) *n.* punishment

penetrated (pen′ i trāt′ ed) *v.* broke through

pensive (pen′ siv) *adj.* thinking deeply or seriously

penury (pen′ yoo rē) *n.* extreme poverty

perennial (pə ren′ ē əl) *adj.* happening over and over; perpetual

permeate (pur′ mē āt′) *v.* spread or flow throughout

pernicious (pər nish′ əs) *adj.* causing great injury or ruin

perplexes (pər pleks′ iz) *v.* confuses or puzzles

pertinent (purt′ 'n ənt) *adj.* relevant; having a connection to the matter at hand

perverse (pər vurs′) *adj.* deviating from what is considered right or reasonable

picturesque (pik′ chər esk′) *adj.* like or suggesting a picture

placidly (plas′ id lē) *adv.* calmly; quietly

plundered (plun′ dərd) *v.* took goods by force; looted

poignant (poin′ yənt) *adj.* emotionally touching

potential (pō ten′ shl) *n.* possibility

precariously (pri ker′ ē əs lē) *adv.* insecurely

precipitous (prē sip′ ə təs) *adj.* steep; sheer

precluded (prē klood′ id) *v.* prevented

predominant (prē däm′ ə nənt) *adj.* having dominating influence over others

preliminaries (prē lim′ ə ner′ ēz) *n.* steps or events before the main one

pretentious (prē ten′ shəs) *adj.* grand in a showy way

procure (prō kyoor′) *v.* get; obtain

prodigious (prō dij′ əs) *adj.* enormous

profound (prō found′) *adj.* deep; intense

profoundly (prō found′ lē) *adv.* deeply

pungent (pun′ jənt) *adj.* producing a sharp smell

purged (purjd) *v.* cleansed

R

rancor (raŋ′ kər) *n.* ill will

ravenous (rav′ ə nəs) *adj.* greedily or wildly hungry

reciprocate (ri sip′ rə kāt′) *v.* return

reckless (rek′ lis) *adj.* careless; rash

relevant (rel′ə vənt) *adj.* related to in a significant way

remnants (rem′ nənts) *n.* what is left over; remainders

renegade (ren′ ə gād′) *adj.* disloyal; traitorous

reprieve (ri prēv′) *n.* temporary relief; postponement of a penalty

resplendent (ri splen′ dənt) *adj.* shining brightly

retort (ri tôrt′) *n.* sharp or clever reply

retribution (re′ trə byoo′ shən) *n.* payback; punishment for a misdeed

revelry (rev′ əl rē) *n.* noisy merry-making

revered (ri vird′) *adj.* regarded with great respect and awe

reverie (rev′ ə rē) *n.* dreamy thought of pleasant things

revise (ri vīz′) *v.* read carefully to correct; change or amend

riddled (rid′ 'ld) *adj.* affected throughout or in every part

rueful (roo′ fəl) *adj.* feeling sorrow or regret

rustic (rus′tik) *adj.* simple, plain, or artless; rural

S

sallow (sal′ ō) *adj.* of a sickly, pale-yellowish hue

scarred (skärd) *adj.* marked or dented

scourge (skurj) *n.* instrument for inflicting punishment

scruples (skroo′ pəlz) *n.* misgivings about something one thinks is wrong

shriveled (shriv′ əld) *adj.* shrunken and wrinkled

siege (sēj) *n.* encirclement of a forti-fied place by an opposing armed force intending to take it

significant (sig nif′ə cənt) *adj.* important; full of meaning

signify (sig′nə fī′) *v.* to be a sign of something

skeptics (skep′ tiks) *n.* people who doubt and question generally accepted ideas

specific (spə sif′ik) *adj.* precise, or definite

spectral (spek′ trəl) *adj.* like a phan-tom or ghost

spunky (spuŋ′ kē) *adj.* courageous; spirited

spurn (sp rn) *v.* reject with con-tempt or disdain

stout (stout) *adj.* sturdy

strategy (strat′ ə jē) *n.* the science of managing or planning; a plan of action

suffice (sə fīs′) *v.* be enough

T

tantalizingly (tan′ tə līz′ iŋ lē) *adv.* in a teasing way

technique (tek′nēk′) *n.* methods used to create an artistic work

temporal (tem′ pə rəl) *adj.* having to do with time

tenement (ten´ ə mənt) *n.* apartment house, often run-down

tenets (ten´ itz) *n.* principles or beliefs

texture (teks´chər) *n.* the arrangement or structure of something

transgression (trans gresh´ ən) *n.* wrongdoing; sin

transition (tran zish´ən) *n.* passing from one place, idea or condition to another

treble (treb´ əl) *n.* high-pitched voice

trivial (triv´ ē əl) *adj.* of little or no importance

trundle (trun´ dəl) *v.* roll along

tumultuous (tōō mul´ chōō əs) *adj.* greatly disturbed; in an uproar

U

unbidden (un bid´ 'n) *adj.* without being asked; uninvited

unpalatable (un pal´ it ə bəl) *adj.* distasteful; unpleasant

unrequited (un ri kwīt´ id) *adj.* not returned or repaid

unwieldy (un wēl´ dē) *adj.* awkward; clumsy

usage (yōō´sij) *n.* the way of using something

usurped (yōō sʉrpt´) *v.* took power or position without right

V

venture (ven´ chər) *n.* an action involving risk

vex (veks) *v.* annoy

vigilant (vij´ ə lənt) *adj.* watchful

vile (vīl) *adj.* evil; wicked

vindictive (vin dik´tiv) *adj.* revengeful; inclined to seek vengeance

vital (vīt´'l) *adj.* necessary or essential

voluminously (və lōō´ mə nəs lē) *adv.* fully; of great volume

W

wail (wāl) *v.* grieve; lament

warp (wôrp) *v.* twist; distort

wayward (wā´ wərd) *adj.* headstrong

woeful (wō´ fəl) *adj.* full of sorrow

woes (wōz) *n.* great sorrows

writhing (rīth´ iŋ) *v.* twisting; turning

WHAT'S IN A WORD?

Using a Dictionary

A **dictionary** is a reference book containing an alphabetical list of words along with their pronunciations, definitions, and other information about them. Dictionaries are helpful when you need to find the meaning, the pronunciation, or the part of speech of a word. You may also consult a dictionary to trace a word's *etymology*, or its origins. Etymology explains how words change, how they are borrowed from other languages, and how new words are invented, or "coined."

A Sample Dictionary Entry

Here is an entry from a dictionary. Notice what it tells about the word *anthology*.

> **anthology** (an thäl´ə jē) *n., pl.* **–gies** [Gr. *anthologia*, a garland, collection of short poems < *anthologos*, gathering flowers < *anthos*, flower + *legein*, to gather] a collection of poems, stories, songs, excerpts, etc., chosen by the compiler

Dictionaries provide the *denotation* of each word, or its objective meaning. The symbol < means "comes from" or "is derived from." In this case, the Greek words for "flower" and "gather" combined to form a Greek word that meant a garland, and then that word became an English word that means a collection of literary flowers—a collection of literature like the one you are reading now.

Idiomatic Expressions

Dictionaries also provide information about idiomatic expressions. An idiomatic expression is a phrase that means something different from the combined meanings of its individual words. For example, "lay eyes on" is an idiomatic expression meaning "to see." Another common idiomatic expression is "raining cats and dogs," which means, "it is raining very hard." In a dictionary, idiomatic expressions are usually included in the entry for the keyword in the phrase.

Activities

1. Look up the word *obscure* in a dictionary. (a) What is its etymology? (b) Explain what its etymology reveals about the development of English.

2. Look up the word *boot* in a dictionary. (a) Identify at least two idiomatic expressions associated with the word.
   (b) Explain what each idiomatic expression means.

Using a Thesaurus

A **thesaurus** is a book of synonyms, or words that have similar meanings. Words in a thesaurus are often arranged by concept, such as "wisdom," or "wealth." Use a thesaurus to increase your vocabulary or to find alternative words to express your meaning.

- Do not choose a word just because it sounds interesting or smart. Choose the word that expresses exactly the meaning you intend.
- When choosing a word, note both its *denotative* and *connotative* meanings. A word's connotations are the emotional associations that it calls to mind. The connotation may not reflect your intentions even if the denotation does so.
- To avoid errors, look up the word in a dictionary to check its precise meaning and to make sure you are using it properly.

A Sample Thesaurus Entry

Here is an entry from a thesaurus. Notice what it tells about the word *book*.

> **book** *noun*
>
> A printed and bound work: tome, volume. *See* WORDS.
>
> **book** *verb* 1. To register in or as if in a book: catalog, enroll, inscribe, list, set down, write down. *See* REMEMBER. 2. To cause to be set aside, as for one's use, in advance: bespeak, engage, reserve. *See* GET.

If the word can be used as different parts of speech, as *book* can, the thesaurus entry provides synonyms for the word as each part of speech. A thesaurus entry also gives specific synonyms for each connotation of the word.

Activity:

Look up the word *pacify* in a thesaurus. (a) What are three synonyms for this word? (b) Explain how the connotations of the synonyms differ.

THE HISTORY OF ENGLISH

A Merging of Cultures

Old English English began about the year 500 when Germanic tribes from the middle of Europe traveled west and settled in Britain. These peoples—the Angles, Saxons, and Jutes—spoke a Germanic language that combined with Danish and Norse when Vikings attacked Britain and added some Latin elements when Christian missionaries arrived. The result was Old English, which looked like this:

> Hwaet! We Gar-Dena   in gear-dagum,
>
> peod-cyninga,   prym gefrunon,
>
> hu da aepelingas   ellen fremedon!

These words are the opening lines of the Old English epic poem *Beowulf*, probably composed in the eighth century. In modern English, they mean: "Listen! We know the ancient glory of the Spear-Danes, and the heroic deeds of those noble kings!"

Middle English The biggest change in English took place after the Norman Conquest of Britain in 1066. The Normans spoke a dialect of Old French, and Old English changed dramatically when the Normans became the new aristocracy. From about 1100 to 1500, the people of Britain spoke what we now call Middle English.

> A Knyght ther was, and that a worthy man,
>
> That fro the tyme that he first bigan
>
> To riden out, he loved chivalrie,
>
> Trouthe and honour, fredom and curtesie.

These lines from the opening section of Geoffrey Chaucer's *Canterbury Tales* (c. 1400) are much easier for us to understand than the lines from *Beowulf*. They mean: "There was a knight, a worthy man who, from the time he began to ride, loved chivalry, truth, honor, freedom, and courtesy."

Modern English During the Renaissance, with its emphasis on reviving classical culture, Greek and Latin languages exerted a strong influence on the English language. In addition, Shakespeare added about two thousand words to the language. Grammar, spelling, and pronunciation continued to change. Modern English was born.

> But soft! What light through yonder window breaks?
>
> It is the East, and Juliet is the sun!

These lines from Shakespeare's *Romeo and Juliet* (c. 1600) need no translation, although it is helpful to know that "soft" means "speak softly." Since Shakespeare's day, conventions of usage and grammar have continued to change. For example, the *th* at the ends of many verbs has become *s*. In Shakespeare's time, it was correct to say "Romeo *hath* fallen in love." In our time, it is right to say "he *has* fallen in love." However, the changes of the past five hundred years are not nearly as drastic as the changes from Old English to Middle English, or from Middle English to Modern English. We still speak Modern English.

Old Words, New Words

Modern English has a larger vocabulary than any other language in the world. The *Oxford English Dictionary* contains about a half million words, and it is estimated that another half million scientific and technical terms do not appear in the dictionary. Here are the main ways that new words enter the language:

- **War**—Conquerors introduce new terms and ideas—and new vocabulary, such as *anger*, from Old Norse.
- **Immigration**—When large groups of people move from one country to another, they bring their languages with them, such as *boycott*, from Ireland.
- **Travel and Trade**—Those who travel to foreign lands and those who do business in faraway places bring new words back with them, such as *shampoo,* from Hindi.
- **Science and Technology**—In our time, the amazing growth of science and technology adds multitudes of new words to English, such as *Internet.*

English is also filled with **borrowings**, words taken directly from other languages. Sometimes, borrowed words maintain the same meanings they have in their original languages: *pajamas* (Hindi), *sauna* (Finnish), *camouflage* (French), *plaza* (Spanish). Sometimes borrowed words take on new meanings. *Sleuth*, for example, an Old Norse word for *trail*, now means the person who follows a trail—a detective.

Mythology contributed to our language too. Some of the days of the week are named after Norse gods—Wednesday was Woden's Day, Thursday was Thor's Day. Greek and Roman myths have given us many words, such as *jovial* (from Jove), *martial* (from Mars), *mercurial* (from Mercury), and *herculean* (from Hercules).

Americanisms are words, phrases, or usages that originated in American English or that are unique to the way Americans speak. They are expressions of our national character in all its variety: *easy as pie, prairie dog, bamboozle, panhandle, halftime, fringe benefit, bookmobile, jackhammer, southpaw, lickety split.*

Activity:
Look up the following words in a dictionary. Describe the most probable ways in which these words entered American English.

   bloom   bandana   souvenir   volcano   pixel

The Influence of English
There are about three hundred million native English speakers, and about the same number who speak English as a second language. Although more people speak Mandarin Chinese, English is the dominant language of trade, tourism, international diplomacy, science, and technology.

Language is a vehicle of both communication and culture, and the cultural influence of English in the twenty-first century is unprecedented in the history of the world's languages. Beyond business and science, English spreads through sports, pop music, Hollywood movies, television, and journalism. A book that is translated into English reaches many more people than it would in its native language alone. Perhaps most significantly, English dominates the Internet. The next time you log on, notice how many Web sites from around the world also have an English version. The global use of English is the closest the world has ever come to speaking an international language.

Activity:
Choose one area of culture—such as sports, fashion, the arts, or technology—and identify three new words that English has recently added to the *world's* vocabulary. (a) In what ways does a shared language benefit the world? (b) In what ways might a global language be a detriment to the world?

LITERARY TERMS HANDBOOK

ACT *See* Drama.

ALLEGORY An *allegory* is a story or tale with two or more levels of meaning—a literal level and one or more symbolic levels. The events, setting, and characters in an allegory are symbols for ideas and qualities.

ALLITERATION *Alliteration* is the repetition of initial consonant sounds. Writers use alliteration to give emphasis to words, to imitate sounds, and to create musical effects. In the following line from Edgar Allan Poe's "The Raven" (p. 639), there is alliteration of the *w* sound:

> Once upon a midnight dreary, *w*hile I pondered *w*eak and *w*eary, . . .

ALLUSION An *allusion* is a reference to a well-known person, place, event, literary work, or work of art. In O. Henry's "The Gift of the Magi" (p. 246), the title and details of the story refer to the biblical account of the Magi, wise men who brought gifts to the baby Jesus.

ANALOGY An *analogy* makes a comparison between two or more things that are similar in some ways but otherwise unalike.

ANECDOTE An *anecdote* is a brief story about an interesting, amusing, or strange event told to entertain or to make a point. In "A Lincoln Preface" (p. 452), Carl Sandburg tells anecdotes about Abraham Lincoln.

See also Narrative.

ANTAGONIST An *antagonist* is a character or force in conflict with a main character, or protagonist.

ANTICLIMAX Like a climax, an *anticlimax* is the turning point in a story. However, an anticlimax is always a letdown. It's the point at which you learn that the story will not turn out the way you had expected. In Thayer's "Casey at the Bat" (p. 630), the anticlimax occurs when Casey strikes out instead of hitting a game-winning run as everyone had expected.

ARCHETYPE An *archetype* is a type of character, detail, image, or situation that appears in literature from around the world and throughout history. Some critics believe that archetypes reveal deep truths about human experience.

ASIDE An *aside* is a short speech delivered by a character in a play in order to express his or her true thoughts and feelings. Traditionally, the aside is directed to the audience and is presumed to be inaudible to the other actors.

ASSONANCE *Assonance* is the repetition of vowel sounds followed by different consonants in two or more stressed syllables. Assonance is found in the phrase "weak and weary" in Edgar Allan Poe's "The Raven" (p. 639).

ATMOSPHERE *See* Mood.

AUTOBIOGRAPHY An *autobiography* is a form of nonfiction in which a writer tells his or her own life story. An autobiography may tell about the person's whole life or only a part of it. An example of an autobiography is the excerpt from *A White House Diary* (p. 98).

See also Biography *and* Nonfiction.

BALLAD A *ballad* is a songlike poem that tells a story, often one dealing with adventure and romance. Most ballads are written in four- to six-line stanzas and have regular rhythms and rhyme schemes. A ballad often features a refrain—a regularly repeated line or group of lines.

See also Oral Tradition.

BIOGRAPHY A *biography* is a form of nonfiction in which a writer tells the life story of another person. Biographies have been written about many famous people, historical and contemporary, but they can also be written about "ordinary" people. An example of a biography is the excerpt from *Arthur Ashe Remembered* (p. 460).

See also Autobiography *and* Nonfiction.

BLANK VERSE *Blank verse* is poetry written in unrhymed iambic pentameter lines. This verse form was widely used by William Shakespeare.

See also Meter.

CHARACTER A *character* is a person or an animal who takes part in the action of a literary work. The main character, or protagonist, is the most important character in a story. This character often changes in some important way as a result of the story's events. In Richard Connell's "The Most Dangerous Game" (p. 215), Rainsford is the main character and General Zaroff is the antagonist, or character who opposes the main character.

Characters are sometimes classified as round or flat, dynamic or static. A *round character* shows many different traits—faults as well as virtues. A *flat character* shows only one trait. A *dynamic character* develops and grows during the course of the story; a *static character* does not change.

See also Characterization and Motivation.

CHARACTERIZATION *Characterization* is the act of creating and developing a character. In *direct characterization*, the author directly states a character's traits. For example, at the beginning of "The Necklace" (p. 294), Maupassant directly characterizes Madame Loisel: "She was one of those pretty, charming young women . . ."

In *indirect characterization*, an author provides clues about a character by describing what a character looks like, does, and says, as well as how other characters react to him or her. It is up to the reader to draw conclusions about the character based on this indirect information.

The most effective indirect characterizations usually result from showing characters acting or speaking.

See also Character.

CLIMAX The *climax* of a story, novel, or play is the high point of interest or suspense. The events that make up the rising action lead up to the climax. The events that make up the falling action follow the climax.

See also Conflict, Plot, *and* Anticlimax.

COMEDY A *comedy* is a literary work, especially a play, that has a happy ending. Comedies often show ordinary characters in conflict with society. These conflicts are resolved through misunderstandings, deceptions, and concealed identities, which result in the correction of moral faults or social wrongs. Types of comedy include *romantic comedy*, which involves problems among lovers, and the *comedy of manners*, which satirically challenges the social customs of a sophisticated society. Comedy is often contrasted with tragedy, in which the protagonist meets an unfortunate end.

COMIC RELIEF *Comic relief* is a technique that is used to interrupt a serious part of a literary work by introducing a humorous character or situation.

CONFLICT A *conflict* is a struggle between opposing forces. Characters in conflict form the basis of stories, novels, and plays.

There are two kinds of conflict: external and internal. In an *external conflict*, the main character struggles against an outside force. This force may be another character, as in Richard Connell's "The Most Dangerous Game" (p. 215), in which Rainsford struggles with General Zaroff. The outside force could also be the standards or expectations of a group, such as the family prejudices that Romeo and Juliet struggle against. Their story (p. 730) shows them in conflict with society. The outside force may be nature itself, a person-against-nature conflict. The two men who are trapped by a fallen tree in Saki's "The Interlopers" (p. 255) face such a conflict.

An *internal conflict* involves a character in conflict with himself or herself. In "Checkouts" (p. 74), two young people who meet by chance in a supermarket agonize over whether they should speak to each other.

See also Plot.

CONNOTATION The *connotation* of a word is the set of ideas associated with it in addition to its explicit meaning.

See also Denotation.

CONSONANCE *Consonance* is the repetition of final consonant sounds in stressed syllables with different vowel sounds, as in *hat* and *sit.*

CONTEMPORARY INTERPRETATION A *contemporary interpretation* is a literary work of today that responds to and sheds new light on a well-known, earlier work of literature. Such an interpretation may refer to any aspect of the older work, including plot, characters, settings, imagery, language, and theme. Edna St. Vincent Millay's poem "An Ancient Gesture" (p. 1028), for example, provides a modern perspective on the characters Penelope and Odysseus in the *Odyssey.*

COUPLET A *couplet* is a pair of rhyming lines, usually of the same length and meter. In the following couplet from a poem by William Shakespeare, the speaker comforts himself with the thought of his love:

> For thy sweet love remember'd such wealth brings
>
> That then I scorn to change my state with kings.

See also Stanza.

DENOTATION The *denotation* of a word is its dictionary meaning, independent of other associations that the word may have. The denotation of the word *lake*, for example, is an inland body of water. "Vacation spot" and "place where the fishing is good" are connotations of the word *lake.*

See also Connotation.

DENOUEMENT *See* Plot.

DESCRIPTION A *description* is a portrait in words of a person, place, or object. Descriptive writing uses sensory details, those that appeal to the senses: sight, hearing, taste, smell, and touch. Description can be found in all types of writing. Rudolfo Anaya's essay "A Celebration of Grandfathers" (p. 404) contains descriptive passages.

DEVELOPMENT *See* Plot.

DIALECT *Dialect*, the form of language spoken by people in a particular region or group, may involve changes to the pronunciation, vocabulary, and sentence structure of standard English. An example from Mark Twain's "The Invalid's Story" (p. 333) is a character's use of the term *yourn* for *yours*.

DIALOGUE A *dialogue* is a conversation between characters that may reveal their traits and advance the action of a narrative. In fiction or nonfiction, quotation marks indicate a speaker's exact words, and a new paragraph usually indicates a change of speaker. Following is an exchange between the narrator and his frail younger brother, Doodle, in "The Scarlet Ibis" (p. 350):

> "Aw, come on Doodle," I urged. "You can do it. Do you want to be different from everybody else when you start school?"
>
> "Does it make any difference?"

Quotation marks are not used in a *script*, the printed copy of a play. Instead, the dialogue follows the name of the speaker, as in this example from Chekhov's *The Inspector General* (p. 884):

> **DRIVER.** Oh, yes, he's a good one, this one.

DICTION *Diction* refers to an author's choice of words, especially with regard to range of vocabulary, use of slang and colloquial language, and level of formality. These lines from Ernest Lawrence Thayer's poem "Casey at the Bat" are an example of colloquial, informal diction: "It looked extremely rocky for the Mudville nine that day; / The score stood two to four; with but an inning left to play."

See also Connotation *and* Denotation.

DIRECT CHARACTERIZATION *See* Characterization.

DRAMA A *drama* is a story written to be performed by actors. The script of a drama is made up of *dialogue*—the words the actors say—and *stage directions*, which are comments on how and where action happens.

The drama's *setting* is the time and place in which the action occurs. It is indicated by one or more sets, including furniture and backdrops, that suggest interior or exterior scenes. *Props* are objects, such as a sword or a cup of tea, that are used onstage.

At the beginning of most plays, a brief *exposition* gives the audience some background information about the characters and the situation. Just as in a story or novel, the plot of a drama is built around characters in conflict.

Dramas are divided into large units called *acts,* which are divided into smaller units called *scenes*. A long play may include many sets that change with the scenes, or it may indicate a change of scene with lighting.

See also Dialogue, Genre, Stage Directions, *and* Tragedy. Romeo and Juliet (p. 730) is a long play in five acts.

DRAMATIC IRONY *See* Irony.

DRAMATIC MONOLOGUE A *dramatic monologue* is a poem in which a character reveals himself or herself by speaking to a silent listener.

DRAMATIC POETRY *Dramatic poetry* is poetry that utilizes the techniques of drama. The dialogue used in Edgar Allan Poe's "The Raven" (p. 639) makes it dramatic dialogue. A *dramatic monologue* is a poem spoken by one person, addressing a silent listener.

END RHYME *See* Rhyme.

EPIC An *epic* is a long narrative poem about the deeds of gods or heroes. Homer's *Odyssey* (p. 950) is an example of epic poetry. It tells the story of the Greek hero Odysseus, the king of Ithaca.

An epic is elevated in style and usually follows certain patterns. The poet begins by announcing the subject and asking a Muse—one of the nine goddesses of the arts, literature, and sciences—to help. An *epic hero* is the larger-than-life central character in an epic. Through behavior and deeds, the epic hero displays qualities that are valued by the society in which the epic originated.

See also Epic Simile *and* Narrative Poem.

EPIC SIMILE An *epic simile*, also called *Homeric simile*, is an elaborate comparison of unlike subjects. In this example from the *Odyssey* (p. 950), Homer compares the bodies of men killed by Odysseus to a fisherman's catch heaped up on the shore:

> Think of a catch that fishermen haul in to a
>   half-moon bay
>
> in a fine-meshed net from the whitecaps of the sea:
> how all are poured out on the sand, in throes
>   for the salt sea,
>
> twitching their cold lives away in Helios' fiery air:
>   so lay the suitors heaped on one another.

See also Figurative Language *and* Simile.

EPIPHANY An *epiphany* is a character's sudden flash of insight into a conflict or situation. At the end of Judith Ortiz Cofer's story "American History" (p. 202) for example, the central character experiences an epiphany.

ESSAY An *essay* is a short nonfiction work about a particular subject. While classification is difficult, five types of essays are sometimes identified.

A *descriptive essay* seeks to convey an impression about a person, place, or object. In "A Celebration of Grandfathers" (p. 404), Rudolfo Anaya describes the cultural values that his grandfather and other "old ones" from his childhood passed down.

A *narrative essay* tells a true story. In "The Washwoman" (p. 26), Isaac Bashevis Singer tells of his childhood in Poland.

An *expository essay* gives information, discusses ideas, or explains a process. In "Single Room, Earth View" (p. 437), Sally Ride describes what it is like to be in outer space.

A *persuasive essay* tries to convince readers to do something or to accept the writer's point of view. Pete Hamill's "Libraries Face Sad Chapter" (p. 483) is a persuasive essay.

A *visual essay* is an exploration of a topic that conveys its ideas through visual elements as well as language. Like a standard essay, a visual essay presents an author's views of a single topic. Unlike other essays, however, much of the meaning in a visual essay is conveyed through illustrations or photographs.

See also Description, Exposition, Genre, Narration, Nonfiction, *and* Persuasion.

EXPOSITION *Exposition* is writing or speech that explains a process or presents information. In the plot of a story or drama, the exposition is the part of the work that introduces the characters, the setting, and the basic situation.

EXTENDED METAPHOR In an *extended metaphor*, as in regular metaphor, a writer speaks or writes of a subject as though it were something else. An extended metaphor sustains the comparison for several lines or for an entire poem.

See also Figurative Language *and* Metaphor.

FALLING ACTION *See* Plot.

FANTASY A *fantasy* is highly imaginative writing that contains elements not found in real life. Examples of fantasy include stories that involve supernatural elements, stories that resemble fairy tales, and stories that deal with imaginary places and creatures.

See also Science Fiction.

FICTION *Fiction* is prose writing that tells about imaginary characters and events. The term is usually used for novels and short stories, but it also applies to dramas and narrative poetry. Some writers rely on their imaginations alone to create their works of fiction. Others base their fiction on actual events and people, to which they add invented characters, dialogue, and plot situations.

See also Genre, Narrative, *and* Nonfiction.

FIGURATIVE LANGUAGE *Figurative language* is writing or speech not meant to be interpreted literally. It is often used to create vivid impressions by setting up comparisons between dissimilar things.

Some frequently used figures of speech are *metaphors, similes*, and *personifications*.

See also Literal Language.

FLASHBACK A *flashback* is a means by which authors present material that occurred earlier than the present tense of the narrative. Authors may include this material in a characters' memories, dreams, or accounts of past events.

FOIL A *foil* is a character who provides a contrast to another character. In *Romeo and Juliet* (p. 730), the fiery temper of Tybalt serves as a foil to the good nature of Benvolio.

FOOT *See* Meter.

FORESHADOWING *Foreshadowing* is the use in a literary work of clues that suggest events that have yet to occur. This technique helps to create suspense, keeping readers wondering about what will happen next.

See also Suspense.

FREE VERSE *Free verse* is poetry not written in a regular pattern of meter or rhyme. Like Whitman's "I Hear America Singing" (p. 680), however, it may use parallelism and various sound devices.

GENRE A *genre* is a category or type of literature. Literature is commonly divided into three major genres: poetry, prose, and drama. Each major genre is in turn divided into smaller genres, as follows:

1. Poetry: Lyric Poetry, Concrete Poetry, Dramatic Poetry, Narrative Poetry, and Epic Poetry

2. Prose: Fiction (Novels and Short Stories) and Nonfiction (Biography, Autobiography, Letters, Essays, and Reports)

3. Drama: Serious Drama and Tragedy, Comic Drama, Melodrama, and Farce

See also Drama, Poetry, *and* Prose.

HAIKU The *haiku* is a three-line verse form. The first and third lines of a haiku each have five syllables. The second line has seven syllables. A haiku seeks to convey a single vivid emotion by means of images from nature.

HOMERIC SIMILE *See* Epic Simile.

HYPERBOLE A *hyperbole* is a deliberate exaggeration or overstatement. In Mark Twain's "The Notorious Jumping Frog of Calaveras County," the claim that Jim Smiley would follow a bug as far as Mexico to win a bet is a hyperbole. As this example shows, hyperboles are often used for comic effect.

IAMB *See* Meter.

IDIOM An *idiom* is an expression that is characteristic of a language, region, community or class of people. *Idiomatic expressions* often arise from figures of speech and therefore cannot be understood literally. In "The Invalid's Story" (p. 333), for example, a character uses the idiom *throw up the sponge*, meaning "surrender."

See *also* Dialect.

IMAGE An *image* is a word or phrase that appeals to one or more of the five senses—sight, hearing, touch, taste, or smell. Writers use images to re-create sensory experiences in words.

See also Description.

IMAGERY *Imagery* is the descriptive or figurative language used in literature to create word pictures for the reader. These pictures, or images, are created by details of sight, sound, taste, touch, smell, or movement.

INDIRECT CHARACTERIZATION *See* Characterization.

INTERNAL RHYME *See* Rhyme.

IRONY *Irony* is the general term for literary techniques that portray differences between appearance and reality, or expectation and result. In *verbal irony*, words are used to suggest the opposite of what is meant. In *dramatic irony*, there is a contradiction between what a character thinks and what the reader or audience knows to be true. In *irony of situation*, an event occurs that directly contradicts the expectations of the characters, the reader, or the audience.

LITERAL LANGUAGE *Literal language* uses words in their ordinary senses. It is the opposite of *figurative language*. If you tell someone standing on a diving board to jump in, you speak literally. If you tell someone on the street to jump in a lake, you are speaking figuratively.

See also Figurative Language.

LYRIC POEM A *lyric poem* is a highly musical verse that expresses the thoughts, observations, and feelings of a single speaker.

MAIN CHARACTER *See* Character.

METAPHOR A *metaphor* is a figure of speech in which one thing is spoken of as though it were something else. Unlike a simile, which compares two things using *like* or *as*, a metaphor implies a comparison between them. In

"Dreams" (p. 567), Langston Hughes uses a metaphor to show what happens to a life without dreams:

> . . . if dreams die
>
> Life is a broken-winged bird
>
> That cannot fly.

See also Extended Metaphor *and* Figurative Language.

METER The *meter* of a poem is its rhythmical pattern. This pattern is determined by the number and types of stresses, or beats, in each line. To describe the meter of a poem, you must scan its lines. Scanning involves marking the stressed and unstressed syllables, as shown with the following two lines from "I Wandered Lonely as a Cloud" by William Wordsworth (p. 568):

> Ĭ wán|dĕřed lŏne|lў ás| ă clóud
>
> Thăt floáts | ŏn hígh| o' ĕr váles| ănd hílls.

As you can see, each strong stress is marked with a slanted line (´) and each unstressed syllable with a horseshoe symbol (˘). The stressed and unstressed syllables are then divided by vertical lines (|) into groups called *feet*. The following types of feet are common in English poetry:

1. *Iamb:* a foot with one unstressed syllable followed by a stressed syllable, as in the word "again"

2. *Trochee:* a foot with one stressed syllable followed by an unstressed syllable, as in the word "wonder"

3. *Anapest:* a foot with two unstressed syllables followed by one strong stress, as in the phrase "on the beach"

4. *Dactyl:* a foot with one strong stress followed by two unstressed syllables, as in the word "wonderful"

5. *Spondee:* a foot with two strong stresses, as in the word "spacewalk"

Depending on the type of foot that is most common in them, lines of poetry are described as *iambic, trochaic, anapestic,* and so forth.

Lines are also described in terms of the number of feet that occur in them, as follows:

1. *Monometer:* verse written in one-foot lines
   All things
   Must pass
   Away.

2. *Dimeter:* verse written in two-foot lines
   Thomas | Jefferson
   What do | you say
   Under the | gravestone
   Hidden | away?
   —Rosemary and Stephen Vincent Benét, "Thomas Jefferson, 1743–1826"

3. *Trimeter:* verse written in three-foot lines
   I know | not whom | I meet
   I know | not where | I go.

4. *Tetrameter:* verse written in four-foot lines

5. *Pentameter:* verse written in five-foot lines

6. *Hexameter:* verse written in six-foot lines

7. *Heptameter:* verse written in seven-foot lines

Blank verse, used by Shakespeare in *Romeo and Juliet* (p. 730), is poetry written in unrhymed iambic pentameter.

Free verse, used by Walt Whitman in "I Hear America Singing" (p. 680), is poetry that does not follow a regular pattern of meter and rhyme.

MONOLOGUE A *monologue* in a play is a speech by one character that, unlike a *soliloquy*, is addressed to another character or characters. An example from Shakespeare's *Romeo and Juliet* (p. 730) is the speech by the Prince of Verona in Act 1, Scene i, lines 72–94).

See also Soliloquy.

MONOMETER *See* Meter.

MOOD *Mood*, or *atmosphere*, is the feeling created in the reader by a literary work or passage. The mood is often suggested by descriptive details. Often the mood can be described in a single word, such as lighthearted, frightening, or despairing. Notice how this passage from Edgar Allan Poe's "The Cask of Amontillado" (p. 61) contributes to an eerie, fearful mood:

> "The niter!" I said; "see, it increases. It hangs like moss upon the vaults. We are below the river's bed. The drops of moisture trickle among the bones. Come, we will go back ere it is too late."

See also Tone.

MORAL A *moral* is a lesson taught by a literary work, especially a fable—many fables, for example, have a stated moral at the end. It is customary, however, to discuss contemporary works in terms of the themes they explore, rather than a moral that they teach.

MOTIVATION *Motivation* is a reason that explains or partially explains why a character thinks, feels, acts, or behaves in a certain way. Motivation results from a combination of the character's personality and the situation he or she must deal with. In "Checkouts" (p. 74), the main character is motivated by conflicting feelings.

See also Character *and* Characterization.

MYTH A myth is a *fictional* tale that describes the actions of gods and heroes or explains the causes of natural phenomena. Unlike legends, myths emphasize

supernatural rather than historical elements. Many cultures have collections of myths, and the most familiar in the Western world are those of the ancient Greeks and Romans. "Perseus" (p. 1121) is a retelling of a famous ancient Greek myth.

See also Oral Tradition.

NARRATION *Narration* is writing that tells a story. The act of telling a story in speech is also called narration. Novels and short stories are fictional narratives. Nonfiction works—such as news stories, biographies, and autobiographies—are also narratives. A narrative poem tells a story in verse.

See also Anecdote, Essay, Narrative Poem, Nonfiction, Novel, *and* Short Story.

NARRATIVE A *narrative* is a story told in fiction, nonfiction, poetry, or drama.

See also Narration.

NARRATIVE POEM A *narrative poem* is one that tells a story. "Casey at the Bat" (p. 630) is a humorous narrative poem about the last inning of a baseball game. Edgar Allan Poe's "The Raven" (p. 639) is a serious narrative poem about a man's grief over the loss of a loved one.

See also Dramatic Poetry, Epic, *and* Narration.

NARRATOR A *narrator* is a speaker or character who tells a story. The writer's choice of narrator determines the story's *point of view*, which directs the type and amount of information the writer reveals.

When a character in the story tells the story, that character is a *first-person narrator*. This narrator may be a major character, a minor character, or just a witness. Readers see only what this character sees, hear only what he or she hears, and so on. The first-person narrator may or may not be reliable. We have reason, for example, to be suspicious of the first-person narrator of Edgar Allan Poe's "The Cask of Amontillado" (p. 61).

When a voice outside the story narrates, the story has a *third-person narrator*. An omniscient, or all-knowing, third-person narrator can tell readers what any character thinks and feels. For example, in Guy de Maupassant's "The Necklace" (p. 294), we know the feelings of both Monsieur and Madame Loisel. A limited third-person narrator sees the world through one character's eyes and reveals only that character's thoughts. In James Thurber's "The Secret Life of Walter Mitty" (p. 124), the narrator reveals only Mitty's experiences and feelings.

See also Speaker.

NONFICTION *Nonfiction* is prose writing that presents and explains ideas or that tells about real people, places, ideas, or events. To be classified as nonfiction, a work must be true. "Single Room, Earth View" (p. 437) is a nonfictional account of the view of Earth from space.

See also Autobiography, Biography, *and* Essay.

NOVEL A *novel* is a long work of fiction. It has a plot that explores characters in conflict. A novel may also have one or more subplots, or minor stories, and several themes.

OCTAVE *See* Stanza.

ONOMATOPOEIA *Onomatopoeia* is the use of words that imitate sounds. *Whirr, thud, sizzle*, and *hiss* are typical examples. Writers can deliberately choose words that contribute to a desired sound effect.

ORAL TRADITION The *oral tradition* is the passing of songs, stories, and poems from generation to generation by word of mouth. Many folk songs, ballads, fairy tales, legends, and myths originated in the oral tradition.

See also Myth.

OXYMORON An *oxymoron* is a combination of words, or parts of words, that contradict each other. Examples are "deafening silence," "honest thief," "wise fool," and "bittersweet." This device is effective when the apparent contradiction reveals a deeper truth, as in Act 2, Scene ii, line 184 of *Romeo and Juliet* (p. 730) when Juliet bids goodbye to Romeo: "Parting is such *sweet sorrow.*"

PARADOX A *paradox* is a statement that seems contradictory but that actually may be true. Because a paradox is surprising, it catches the reader's attention.

PARALLELISM *See* Rhetorical Devices.

PENTAMETER *See* Meter.

PERSONIFICATION *Personification* is a type of figurative language in which a nonhuman subject is given human characteristics. William Wordsworth personifies daffodils when he describes them as "Tossing their heads in sprightly dance" (p. 568).

See also Figurative Language.

PERSUASION *Persuasion* is writing or speech that attempts to convince the reader to adopt a particular opinion or course of action.

PLOT *Plot* is the sequence of events in a literary work. In most novels, dramas, short stories, and narrative poems, the plot involves both characters and a central conflict. The plot usually begins with an *exposition* that introduces the setting, the characters, and the basic situation. This is followed by the *inciting incident*, which introduces the central conflict. The conflict then increases during the *development* until it reaches a high point of interest or suspense, the *climax*. All the events leading up to the climax make up the *rising action*. The climax is followed by the *falling action*, which leads to the *denouement*, or *resolution*, in which a general insight or change is conveyed.

POETRY *Poetry* is one of the three major types of literature, the others being prose and drama. Most poems make use of highly concise, musical, and emotionally charged language. Many also make use of imagery, figurative language, and special devices of sound such as rhyme. Poems are often divided into lines and stanzas and often employ regular rhythmical patterns, or meters. However, some poems are written out just like prose, while others are written in free verse.

See also Genre.

POINT OF VIEW *See* Narrator.

PROSE *Prose* is the ordinary form of written language. Most writing that is not poetry, drama, or song is considered prose. Prose is one of the major genres of literature and occurs in two forms: fiction and nonfiction.

See also Fiction, Genre, *and* Nonfiction.

PROTAGONIST The *protagonist* is the main character in a literary work.

See also Antagonist *and* Character.

PUN A *pun* is a play on words involving a word with two or more different meanings or two words that sound alike but have different meanings. In *Romeo and Juliet* (p. 730), the dying Mercutio makes a pun involving two meanings of the word *grave*, "serious" and "burial site": "Ask for me tomorrow, and you shall find me a grave man" (Act 3, Scene i, lines 92–93).

QUATRAIN A *quatrain* is a stanza or poem made up of four lines, usually with a definite rhythm and rhyme scheme.

REPETITION *Repetition* is the use of any element of language—a sound, a word, a phrase, a clause, or a sentence—more than once.

Poets use many kinds of repetition. Alliteration, assonance, rhyme, and rhythm are repetitions of certain sounds and sound patterns. A refrain is a repeated line or group of lines. In both prose and poetry, repetition is used for musical effects and for emphasis.

See also Alliteration, Assonance, Rhyme, *and* Rhythm.

RESOLUTION *See* Plot.

RHETORICAL DEVICES *Rhetorical devices* are special patterns of words and ideas that create emphasis and stir emotion, especially in speeches or other oral presentations. *Parallelism*, for example, is the repetition of a grammatical structure in order to create a rhythm and make words more memorable. In his "I Have a Dream" speech (p. 494), Martin Luther King, Jr., uses parallel statements beginning, "I have a dream that . . ."

Other common rhetorical devices include *restatement*, expressing the same idea in different words, and *rhetorical questions*, questions with obvious answers.

RHYME *Rhyme* is the repetition of sounds at the ends of words. *End rhyme* occurs when the rhyming words come at the ends of lines, as in "The Desired Swan Song" by Samuel Taylor Coleridge:

> Swans sing before they die—'twere no bad *thing*
> Should certain persons die before they *sing*.

Internal rhyme occurs when the rhyming words appear in the same line, as in the first line of Edgar Allan Poe's "The Raven" (p. 639):

> Once upon a midnight *dreary*, while I pondered, weak and *weary*,

Exact rhyme involves the repetition of words with the same vowel and consonant sounds like *ball* and *hall*. *Slant rhyme* involves the repetition of words that sound alike but do not rhyme exactly, like *grove* and *love*.

See also Repetition *and* Rhyme Scheme.

RHYME SCHEME A *rhyme scheme* is a regular pattern of rhyming words in a poem. The rhyme scheme of a poem is indicated by using different letters of the alphabet for each new rhyme. In an *aabb* stanza, for example, line 1 rhymes with line 2 and line 3 rhymes with line 4. William Wordsworth's poem "I Wandered Lonely as a Cloud" (p. 568) uses an *ababcc* rhyme pattern:

I wandered lonely as a cloud	a
That floats on high o'er vales and hills,	b
When all at once I saw a crowd,	a
A host, of golden daffodils;	b
Beside the lake, beneath the trees,	c
Fluttering and dancing in the breeze.	c

Many poems use the same pattern of rhymes, though not the same rhymes, in each stanza.

See also Rhyme.

RHYTHM *Rhythm* is the pattern of *beats*, or *stresses*, in spoken or written language. Some poems have a very specific pattern, or meter, whereas prose and free verse use the natural rhythms of everyday speech.

See also Meter.

RISING ACTION *See* Plot.

ROUND CHARACTER *See* Character.

SATIRE A *satire* is a literary work that ridicules the foolishness and faults of individuals, an institution, society, or even humanity in general.

SCENE *See* Drama.

SCIENCE FICTION *Science fiction* is writing that tells about imaginary events involving science or technology. Many science-fiction stories are set in the future. Arthur C. Clarke's "If I Forget Thee, Oh Earth . . ." (p. 148) is set on the moon after a nuclear disaster on Earth.

See also Fantasy.

SENSORY LANGUAGE *Sensory language* is writing or speech that appeals to one or more of the senses.

See also Image.

SESTET *See* Stanza.

SETTING The *setting* of a literary work is the time and place of the action. Time can include not only the historical period—past, present, or future—but also a specific year, season, or time of day. Place may involve not only the geographical place—a region, country, state, or town—but also the social, economic, or cultural environment.

In some stories, setting serves merely as a backdrop for action, a context in which the characters move and speak. In others, however, setting is a crucial element.

See also Mood.

SHORT STORY A *short story* is a brief work of fiction. In most short stories, one main character faces a conflict that is resolved in the plot of the story. Great craftsmanship must go into the writing of a good story, for it has to accomplish its purpose in relatively few words.

See also Fiction *and* Genre.

SIMILE A *simile* is a figure of speech in which the words *like* or *as* are used to compare two apparently dissimilar items. The comparison, however, surprises the reader intro a fresh perception by finding an unexpected likeness. In "Blackberry Eating" (p. 615), Galway Kinnell creates such a simile: "the ripest berries / fall almost unbidden to my tongue / as words sometimes do . . ."

SOLILOQUY A *soliloquy* is a long speech expressing the thoughts of a character alone on stage. In William Shakespeare's *Romeo and Juliet* (p. 730), Romeo gives a soliloquy after the servant has fled and Paris has died (Act V, Scene iii, lines 74–120).

See also Monologue.

SONNET A *sonnet* is a fourteen-line lyric poem, usually written in rhymed iambic pentameter. The *English*, or *Shakespearean*, sonnet consists of three quatrains (four-line stanzas) and a couplet (two lines), usually rhyming *abab cdcd efef gg*. The couplet usually comments on the ideas contained in the preceding twelve lines. The sonnet is usually not printed with the stanzas divided, but a reader can see distinct ideas in each. See the English sonnet by William Shakespeare on page 682.

The *Italian*, or *Petrarchan*, sonnet consists of an octave (eight-line stanza) and a sestet (six-line stanza). Often, the octave rhymes *abbaabba* and the sestet rhymes *cdecde*. The octave states a theme or asks a question. The sestet comments on or answers the question.

See also Lyric Poem, Meter, *and* Stanza.

SOUND DEVICES A *sound device* is a technique used by a poet to emphasize the sound relationships among words in order to create musical and emotional effects and emphasize a poem's meaning. These devices include *alliteration, consonance, assonance, onomatopoeia,* and *rhyme*.

SPEAKER The *speaker* is the imaginary voice assumed by the writer of a poem. In many poems, the speaker is not identified by name. When reading a poem, remember that the speaker within the poem may be a person, an animal, a thing, or an abstraction. The speaker in the following stanza by Emily Dickinson is a person who has died:

> Because I could not stop for Death—
>
> He kindly stopped for me—
>
> The Carriage held but just Ourselves—
>
> And Immortality.

STAGE DIRECTIONS *Stage directions* are notes included in a drama to describe how the work is to be performed or staged. These instructions are printed in italics and are not spoken aloud. They are used to describe sets, lighting, sound effects, and the appearance, personalities, and movements of characters.

See also Drama.

STANZA A *stanza* is a repeated grouping of two or more lines in a poem that often share a pattern of rhythm and rhyme. Stanzas are sometimes named according to the number of lines they have—for example, a *couplet*, two lines; a *quatrain*, four lines; a *sestet*, six lines; and an *octave*, eight lines.

STATIC CHARACTER *See* Character.

STYLE *Style* refers to an author's unique way of writing. Elements determining style include diction; tone; characteristic use of figurative language, dialect, or rhythmic devices; and typical grammatical structures and patterns.

See also Diction and Tone.

SURPRISE ENDING A *surprise ending* is a conclusion that violates the expectations of the reader but in a way that is both logical and believable.

O. Henry's "The Gift of the Magi" (p. 246) and Guy de Maupassant's "The Necklace" (p. 294) have surprise endings. Both authors were masters of this form.

SUSPENSE *Suspense* is a feeling of uncertainty about the outcome of events in a literary work. Writers create suspense by raising questions in the minds of their readers.

SYMBOL A *symbol* is anything that stands for something else. In addition to having its own meaning and reality, a symbol also represents abstract ideas. For example, a flag is a piece of cloth, but it also represents the idea of a country. Writers sometimes use conventional symbols like flags. Frequently, however, they create symbols of their own through emphasis or repetition. In James Hurst's "The Scarlet Ibis" (p. 350), for example, the ibis symbolizes the character named Doodle. Both are beautiful and otherworldly.

TALL TALE A *tall tale* is a type of folk tale that contains some or all of these features: humor, hyperbole, far-fetched situations, highly imaginative language, and a hero who performs outrageous feats. Tall tales originated during the development of the American frontier and are a particularly American form of folk tale. "Pecos Bill: The Cyclone" (p. 1114) is an example of a tall tale.

TETRAMETER *See* Meter.

THEME A *theme* is a central message or insight into life revealed through a literary work.

The theme of a literary work may be stated directly or implied. When the theme of a work is implied, readers think about what the work suggests about people or life.

Archetypal themes are those that occur in folklore and literature across the world and throughout history. Ill-fated love, the theme of Romeo and Juliet (p. 730), is an example of such a theme.

TONE The *tone* of a literary work is the writer's attitude toward his or her audience and subject. The tone can often be described by a single adjective, such as *formal* or *informal*, *serious* or *playful*, *bitter* or *ironic*. When O. Henry discusses the young couple in "The Gift of the Magi" (p. 246), he uses a sympathetic tone.

See also Mood.

TRAGEDY A *tragedy* is a work of literature, especially a play, that results in a catastrophe, a disaster or great misfortune, for the main character. In ancient Greek drama, the main character was always a significant person—a king or a hero—and the cause of the tragedy was a tragic flaw, or weakness, in his or her character. In modern drama, the main character can be an ordinary person, and the cause of the tragedy can be some evil in society itself. Tragedy not only arouses fear and pity in the audience, but also, in some cases, conveys a sense of the grandeur and nobility of the human spirit.

Shakespeare's *Romeo and Juliet* (p. 730) is a tragedy. Romeo and Juliet both suffer from the tragic flaw of impulsiveness. This flaw ultimately leads to their deaths.

See also Drama.

TRIMETER *See* Meter.

UNDERSTATEMENT An *understatement* is a figure of speech in which the stated meaning is purposely less than (or "under") what is really meant. It is the opposite of *hyperbole*, which is a deliberate exaggeration.

UNIVERSAL THEME A *universal theme* is a message about life that can be understood by most cultures. Many folk tales and examples of classic literature address universal themes such as the importance of courage, the effects of honesty, or the danger of greed.

VERBAL IRONY *See* Irony.

VILLANELLE A *villanelle* is a nineteen-line lyric poem written in five three-line stanzas and ending in a four-line stanza. It uses two rhymes and repeats two refrain lines that appear initially in the first and third lines of the first stanza. These lines then appear alternately as the third line of subsequent three-line stanzas and, finally, as the last two lines of the poem.

VISUAL ESSAY A *visual essay* is an exploration of a topic that conveys its ideas through visual elements as well as language. Like a standard essay, a visual essay presents an author's views of a single topic. Unlike other essays, however, much of the meaning in a visual essay is conveyed through illustrations or photographs.

VOICE *Voice* is a writer's distinctive "sound" or way of "speaking" on the page. It is related to such elements as word choice, sentence structure, and tone. It is similar to an individual's speech style and can be described in the same way—fast, slow, blunt, meandering, breathless, and so on.

Voice resembles *style*, an author's typical way of writing, but style usually refers to a quality that can be found throughout an author's body of work, while an author's voice may sometimes vary from work to work.

See also *Style*.

TIPS FOR DISCUSSING LITERATURE

As you read and study literature, discussion with other readers can help you understand, enjoy, and develop interpretations of what you read. Use the following tips to practice good speaking and listening skills while participating in group discussions of literature.

Understand the Purpose of Your Discussion

When you discuss literature, your purpose is to broaden your understanding and appreciation of a work by testing your own ideas and hearing the ideas of others. Stay focused on the literature you are discussing and keep your comments relevant to that literature. Starting with one focus question will help to keep your discussion on track.

Communicate Effectively

Effective communication requires thinking before speaking. Plan the points that you want to make and decide how you will express them. Organize these points in logical order and cite details from the work to support your ideas. Jot down informal notes to help keep your ideas focused.

Remember to speak clearly, pronouncing words slowly and carefully so that others can understand your points. Also, keep in mind that some literature touches readers deeply—be aware of the possibility of counterproductive emotional responses and work to control them. Negative emotional responses can also be conveyed through body language, so work to demonstrate respect in your demeanor as well as in your words.

Encourage Everyone to Participate

While some people are comfortable participating in discussions, others are less eager to speak up in groups. However, everyone should work to contribute thoughts and ideas. To encourage the entire group's participation, try the following strategies:

- If you enjoy speaking, avoid monopolizing the conversation. After sharing your ideas, encourage others to share theirs.
- Try different roles. For example, have everyone take turns being the facilitator or host of the discussion.
- Use a prop, such as a book or gavel. Pass the prop around the group, allowing whomever is holding the prop to have the floor.

Make Relevant Contributions

Especially when responding to a short story, a poem, or a novel, avoid simply summarizing the plot. Instead, consider *what* you think might happen next, *why* events take place as they do, or *how* a writer provokes a response in you. Let your ideas inspire deeper thought or discussion about the literature.

Consider Other Ideas and Interpretations

A work of literature can generate a wide variety of responses in different readers—and that can make your discussions exciting. Be open to the idea that many interpretations can be valid. To support your own ideas, point to the events, descriptions, characters, or other literary elements in the work that produced your interpretation. To consider someone else's ideas, decide whether details in the work support the interpretation he or she presents. Be sure to convey your criticism of the ideas of others in a respectful and supportive manner.

Ask Questions and Extend the Contributions of Others

Get in the habit of asking questions to help you clarify your understanding of another reader's ideas. You can also use questions to call attention to possible areas of confusion, to points that are open to debate, or to errors.

In addition, offer elaboration of the points that others make by providing examples and illustrations. To move a discussion forward, pause occasionally to summarize and evaluate tentative conclusions reached by the group members. Then, continue the discussion with a fresh understanding of the material and ideas you have already covered.

Manage Differing Opinions and Views

Each participant brings his or her own personality, experiences, ideas, cultural background, likes and dislikes to the experience of reading, making disagreement almost inevitable. As differences arise, be sensitive to each individual's point of view. Do not personalize disagreements, but keep them focused on the literature or ideas under discussion.

When you meet with a group to discuss literature, use a chart like the one shown to analyze the discussion.

Work Being Discussed:	
Focus Question:	
Your Response:	Another Student's Response:
Supporting Evidence:	Supporting Evidence:
One New Idea That You Considered About the Work During the Discussion:	

LITERARY CRITICISM

Criticism is writing that explores the meaning and techniques of literary works, usually in order to evaluate them. Writing criticism can help you think through your experience of a work of literature and can also help others to deepen their own understanding. All literary criticism shares similar goals:

- **Making Connections** within or between works, or between a work of literature and its context
- **Making Distinctions** or showing differences between elements of a single work or aspects of two or more works
- **Achieving Insights** that were not apparent from a superficial reading
- **Making a Judgment** about the quality or value of a literary work

Critics use various **theories of literary criticism** to understand, appreciate, and evaluate literature. Some theories focus on the context of the work while others focus on the work itself. Sometimes critics combine one or more theories. These charts show a few examples of the many theories of criticism:

Focus on Contexts		Focus on the Work Itself
HUMAN EXPERIENCE	**Mythic Criticism** Explores universal situations, characters, and symbols called archetypes as they appear in a literary work.	**Formal Criticism** Shows how the work reflects characteristics of the genre, or literary type, to which it belongs
CULTURE AND HISTORY	**Historic Criticism** Analyzes how circumstances or ideas of an era influence a work	
AUTHOR'S LIFE	**Biographical Criticism** Explains how the author's life sheds light on the work	

Examples of Literary Theories in Action

- **Mythic Criticism:** discussing how Robert Frost's "The Road Not Taken," p. 661, explores the archetypal situation of choice at a fork in the road
- **Historical Criticism:** showing how American frontier life led to the use of exaggeration in "Pecos Bill: The Cyclone," p. 1114
- **Biographical Criticism:** showing that Edgar Allan Poe's loss of his parents at an early age influenced the theme of "The Raven," p. 639
- **Formal Criticism:** showing how "The Scarlet Ibis," p. 350, displays short-story elements like plot, setting, character, symbol, and theme

Apply It To Your Reading

Choose one selection from this textbook and explore it using two different theories of literary criticism. Write an essay explaining how the unique focus of each theory helped you appreciate different aspects of the selection.

LITERARY MOVEMENTS

Our literary heritage has been shaped by a number of **literary movements**, directions in literature characterized by shared assumptions, beliefs, and practices. This chart shows, in chronological order, some important literary movements. While these movements developed at particular historical moments, all of them may still influence individual writers working today.

Movement	Beliefs and Practices	Examples
Classicism Europe during the Renaissance (c. 1300–1650)	• Looks to classical literature of ancient Greece and Rome as models • Values logic, clarity, balance, and restraint • Prefers "ordered" nature of parks and gardens	the clarity and restraint of Robert Frost's verse ("The Road Not Taken," p.659)
Romanticism Europe during the late 1700s and the early 1800s	• Rebels against Classicism • Values imagination and emotion • Focuses on everyday life	the celebration of the natural world in Rachel Carson's writings ("Silent Spring," p. 153)
Realism Europe and America from the mid–1800s to the 1890s	• Rebels against Romanticism's search for the ideal • Focuses on everyday life	the faithful rendering of Pueblo life in Leslie Marmon Silko's fiction ("The Man to Send Rain Clouds," p. 268)
Naturalism Europe and America during the late 1800s and early 1900s	• Assumes people cannot choose their fate but are shaped by psychological and social forces • Views society as a competitive jungle	the portrayal of characters as victims of social pressures and psychology in Guy de Maupassant's fiction ("The Necklace," p. 294)
Modernism World-wide between 1890 and 1945	• In response to WWI, questions human reason • Focuses on studies of the unconscious and the art of primitive peoples • Experiments with language and form	the experiments with language in E. E. Cummings's poetry ("maggie and milly and molly and may," p. 668)
Post-Modernism World-wide after 1945; still prevalent today	• Believes works of art comment on themselves • Finds inspiration in information technology	the self-commentary in Scott McLoud's work ("Understanding Comics," p. 172)

TIPS FOR IMPROVING READING FLUENCY

When you were younger, you learned to read. Then, you read to expand your experiences or for pure enjoyment. Now, you are expected to read to learn. As you progress in school, you are given more and more material to read. The tips on these pages will help you improve your reading fluency, or your ability to read easily, smoothly, and expressively.

Keeping Your Concentration

One common problem that readers face is the loss of concentration. When you are reading an assignment, you might find yourself rereading the same sentence several times without really understanding it. The first step in changing this behavior is to notice that you do it. Becoming an active, aware reader will help you get the most from your assignments. Practice using these strategies:

- Cover what you have already read with a note card as you go along. Then, you will not be able to reread without noticing that you are doing it.

- Set a purpose for reading beyond just completing the assignment. Then, read actively by pausing to ask yourself questions about the material as you read.

- Use the Reading Strategy instruction and notes that appear with each selection in this textbook.

- Stop reading after a specified period of time (for example, 5 minutes) and summarize what you have read. To help you with this strategy, use the Reading Check questions that appear with each selection in this textbook. Reread to find any answers you do not know.

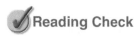

Reading Check

What common problem do many readers face?

Reading Phrases

Fluent readers read phrases rather than individual words. Reading this way will speed up your reading and improve your comprehension. Here are some useful ideas:

- Experts recommend rereading as a strategy to increase fluency. Choose a passage of text that is neither too hard nor too easy. Read the same passage aloud several times until you can read it smoothly. When you can read the passage fluently, pick another passage and keep practicing.

- Read aloud into a tape recorder. Then, listen to the recording, noting your accuracy, pacing, and expression. You can also read aloud and share feedback with a partner.

- Use the *Prentice Hall Listening to Literature* audiotapes or CDs to hear the selections read aloud. Read along silently in your textbook, noticing how the reader uses his or her voice and emphasizes certain words and phrases.

Reading Check

In what ways will reading phrases rather than individual words affect your reading?

Understanding Key Vocabulary

If you do not understand some of the words in an assignment, you may miss out on important concepts. Therefore, it is helpful to keep a dictionary nearby when you are reading. Follow these steps:

- Before you begin reading, scan the text for unfamiliar words or terms. Find out what those words mean before you begin reading.

- Use context—the surrounding words, phrases, and sentences—to help you determine the meanings of unfamiliar words.

- If you are unable to understand the meaning through context, refer to the dictionary.

✓ Reading Check

Why should you look up words you do not know when reading an assignment?

Paying Attention to Punctuation

When you read, pay attention to punctuation. Commas, periods, exclamation points, semicolons, and colons tell you when to pause or stop. They also indicate relationships between groups of words. When you recognize these relationships you will read with greater understanding and expression. Look at the chart below.

Punction Mark	Meaning
comma	brief pause
period	pause at the end of a thought
exclaimation point	pause that indicates emphasis
semicolon	pause between related but distinct thoughts
colon	pause before giving explaination or examples

Using the Reading Fluency Checklist

Use the checklist below each time you read a selection in this textbook. In your Language Arts journal or notebook, note which skills you need to work on and chart your progress each week.

Reading Fluency Checklist

- ☐ Preview the text to check for difficult or unfamiliar words.
- ☐ Practice reading aloud.
- ☐ Read according to punctuation.
- ☐ Break down long sentences into the subject and its meaning.
- ☐ Read groups of words for meaning rather than reading single words.
- ☐ Read with expression (change your tone of voice to add meaning to the word).

Reading is a skill that can be improved with practice. The key to improving your fluency is to read. The more you read, the better your reading will become.

THE MODES OF WRITING

Writing is a process that begins with the exploration of ideas and ends with the presentation of a final draft. Often, the types of writing are grouped into modes according to form and purpose.

NARRATION

Whenever writers tell any type of story, they are using **narration.** Most narratives share certain elements, such as characters, a setting, a sequence of events, and, often, a theme. Following are some types of narration:

Autobiographical Writing Autobiographical writing tells a true story about an important period, experience, or relationship in the writer's life. Effective autobiographical writing includes
- A series of events that involve the writer as the main character
- Details, thoughts, feelings, and insights from the writer's perspective
- A conflict or an event that affects the writer
- A logical organization that tells the story clearly
- Insights that the writer gained from the experience

Types of autobiographical writing include personal narratives, autobiographical sketches, reflective essays, eyewitness accounts, and memoirs.

Short Story A short story is a brief, creative narrative. Most short stories include
- Details that establish the setting in time and place
- A main character who undergoes a change or learns something during the course of the story
- A conflict or a problem to be introduced, developed, and resolved
- A plot, the series of events that make up the action of the story
- A theme or message about life

Types of short stories include realistic stories, fantasies, historical narratives, mysteries, thrillers, science-fiction stories, and adventure stories.

DESCRIPTION

Descriptive writing is writing that creates a vivid picture of a person, place, thing, or event. Most descriptive writing includes
- Sensory details—sights, sounds, smells, tastes, and physical sensations
- Vivid, precise language
- Figurative language or comparisons
- Adjectives and adverbs that paint a word picture
- An organization suited to the subject

Types of descriptive writing include description of ideas, observations, travel brochures, physical descriptions, functional descriptions, remembrances, and character sketches.

PERSUASION

Persuasion is writing or speaking that attempts to convince people to accept a position or take a desired action. Following are some types of persuasion:

Persuasive Essay A persuasive essay presents a position on an issue, urges readers to accept that position, and may encourage a specific action. An effective persuasive essay
- Explores an issue of importance to the writer
- Addresses an issue that is arguable
- Uses facts, examples, statistics, or personal experiences to support a position
- Tries to influence the audience through appeals to the readers' knowledge, experiences, or emotions
- Uses clear organization to present a logical argument

Forms of persuasion include editorials, position papers, persuasive speeches, grant proposals, advertisements, and debates.

Advertisements An advertisement is a planned communication meant to be seen, heard, or read. It attempts to persuade an audience to buy a product or service, accept an idea, or support a cause. Advertisements may appear in printed or broadcast form. An effective advertisement includes
- A memorable slogan to grab the audience's attention
- A call to action
- Persuasive and/or informative text
- Striking visual or aural images
- Informative details about price, location, date, and time

Several common types of advertisements are public-service announcements, billboards, merchandise ads, service ads, and political campaign literature.

EXPOSITION

Exposition is writing that relies on facts to inform or explain. Effective expository writing reflects a well-thought-out organization—one that includes a clear introduction, body, and conclusion. Here are some types of exposition:

Comparison-and-Contrast Essay A comparison-and-contrast essay analyzes the similarities and differences between or among two or more things. An effective comparison-and-contrast essay

- Identifies a purpose for comparison and contrast
- Identifies similarities and differences between or among two or more things, people, places, or ideas
- Gives factual details about the subjects
- Uses an organizational plan suited to the topic and purpose

Cause-and-Effect Essay A cause-and-effect essay examines the relationship between events, explaining how one event or situation causes another. A successful cause-and-effect essay includes

- A discussion of a cause, event, or condition that produces a specific result
- An explanation of an effect, outcome, or result
- Evidence and examples to support the relationship between cause and effect
- A logical organization that makes the explanation clear

Problem-and-Solution Essay A problem-and-solution essay describes a problem and offers one or more solutions to it. It describes a clear set of steps to achieve a result. An effective problem-and-solution essay includes

- A clear statement of the problem, with its causes and effects summarized for the reader
- The most important aspects of the problem
- A proposal of at least one realistic solution
- Facts, statistics, data, or expert testimony to support the solution
- A clear organization that makes the relationship between problem and solution obvious

RESEARCH WRITING

Research writing is based on information gathered from outside sources. A research paper—a focused study of a topic—helps writers explore and connect ideas, make discoveries, and share their findings with an audience. An effective research paper

- Focuses on a specific, narrow topic, which is usually summarized in a thesis statement
- Presents relevant information from a wide variety of sources
- Uses a clear organization that includes an introduction, body, and conclusion
- Includes a bibliography or works-cited list that identifies the sources from which the information was drawn

Other types of writing that depend on accurate and insightful research include multimedia presentations, statistical reports, annotated bibliographies, and experiment journals.

RESPONSE TO LITERATURE

When you write a **response-to-literature essay,** you give yourself the opportunity to discover *what, how,* and *why* a piece of writing affected you. An effective response

- Contains a reaction to a poem, story, essay, or other work of literature
- Analyzes the content of a literary work, its related ideas, or the work's effect on the reader
- Presents a thesis statement to identify the nature of the response
- Focuses on a single aspect of the work or gives a general overview
- Supports opinion with evidence from the work addressed

The following are just a few of the ways you might respond in writing to a literary work: reader's response journals, literary letters, and literary analyses.

WRITING FOR ASSESSMENT

One of the most common types of school **assessment** is the written test. When a test includes an essay, you are expected to write a response that includes

- A clearly stated and well-supported thesis
- Specific information about the topic derived from your reading or from class discussion
- A clear organization

In your school career, you will probably encounter questions that ask you to address each of the following types of writing: explain a process; defend a position; compare, contrast, or categorize; and show cause and effect.

WORKPLACE WRITING

Workplace writing is probably the format you will use most after you finish school. In general, workplace writing is fact-based and meant to communicate specific information in a structured format. Effective workplace writing

- Communicates information concisely
- Includes details that provide necessary information and anticipate potential questions
- Is error-free and neatly presented

Common types of workplace writing include business letters, memorandums, résumés, forms, and applications.

Writing Friendly Letters

A friendly letter is much less formal than a business letter. It is a letter to a friend, a family member, or anyone with whom the writer wants to communicate in a personal, friendly way. Most friendly letters are made up of five parts:

- the heading
- the salutation, or greeting
- the body
- the closing
- the signature

The purpose of a friendly letter is often one of the following:

- to share personal news and feelings
- to send or to answer an invitation
- to express thanks

Model Friendly Letter

In this friendly letter, Betsy thanks her grandparents for a birthday present and gives them some news about her life.

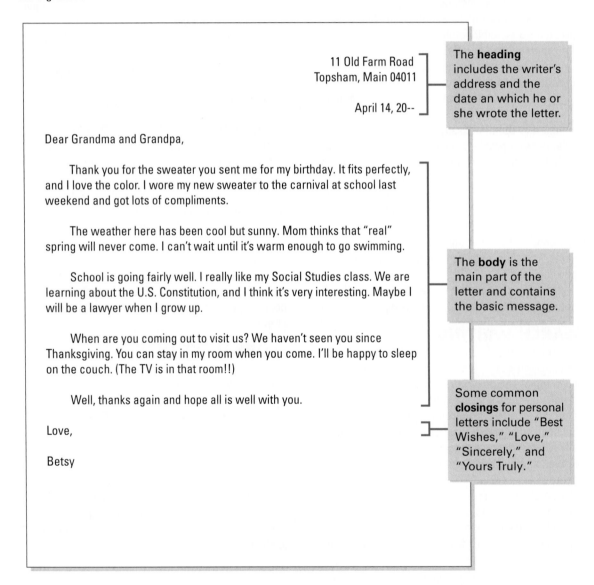

11 Old Farm Road
Topsham, Main 04011

April 14, 20--

The **heading** includes the writer's address and the date an which he or she wrote the letter.

Dear Grandma and Grandpa,

Thank you for the sweater you sent me for my birthday. It fits perfectly, and I love the color. I wore my new sweater to the carnival at school last weekend and got lots of compliments.

The weather here has been cool but sunny. Mom thinks that "real" spring will never come. I can't wait until it's warm enough to go swimming.

School is going fairly well. I really like my Social Studies class. We are learning about the U.S. Constitution, and I think it's very interesting. Maybe I will be a lawyer when I grow up.

When are you coming out to visit us? We haven't seen you since Thanksgiving. You can stay in my room when you come. I'll be happy to sleep on the couch. (The TV is in that room!!)

Well, thanks again and hope all is well with you.

Love,

Betsy

The **body** is the main part of the letter and contains the basic message.

Some common **closings** for personal letters include "Best Wishes," "Love," "Sincerely," and "Yours Truly."

Writing Business Letters

Business letters follow one of several acceptable formats. In **block format** each part of the letter begins at the left margin. A double space is used between paragraphs. In **modified block format,** some parts of the letter are indented to the center of the page. No matter which format is used, all letters in business format have a heading, an inside address, a salutation, or greeting, a body, a closing, and a signature. These parts are shown and annotated on the model business letter below, formatted in modified block style.

Model Business Letter

In this letter, Yolanda Dodson uses modified block format to request information.

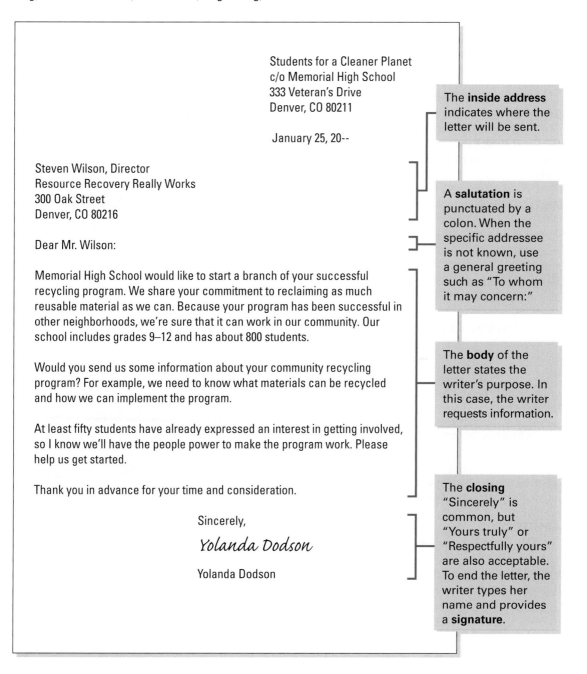

Students for a Cleaner Planet
c/o Memorial High School
333 Veteran's Drive
Denver, CO 80211

January 25, 20--

Steven Wilson, Director
Resource Recovery Really Works
300 Oak Street
Denver, CO 80216

Dear Mr. Wilson:

Memorial High School would like to start a branch of your successful recycling program. We share your commitment to reclaiming as much reusable material as we can. Because your program has been successful in other neighborhoods, we're sure that it can work in our community. Our school includes grades 9–12 and has about 800 students.

Would you send us some information about your community recycling program? For example, we need to know what materials can be recycled and how we can implement the program.

At least fifty students have already expressed an interest in getting involved, so I know we'll have the people power to make the program work. Please help us get started.

Thank you in advance for your time and consideration.

Sincerely,

Yolanda Dodson

Yolanda Dodson

The **inside address** indicates where the letter will be sent.

A **salutation** is punctuated by a colon. When the specific addressee is not known, use a general greeting such as "To whom it may concern:"

The **body** of the letter states the writer's purpose. In this case, the writer requests information.

The **closing** "Sincerely" is common, but "Yours truly" or "Respectfully yours" are also acceptable. To end the letter, the writer types her name and provides a **signature**.

Résumés

A résumé summarizes your educational background, work experiences, relevant skills, and other employment qualifications. It also tells potential employers how to contact you. An effective résumé presents the applicant's name, address, and phone number. It follows an accepted résumé organization, using labels and head-ings to guide readers. A résumé should outline the applicant's educational background, life experiences, and related qualifications using precise and active language.

Model Résumé

With this résumé, James, a college student, hopes to find a full-time job.

James H. McSweeney
1234 Greene Street, Apt. #3
Charlotte, NC 28223
jamesmcswe@email.com

Put contact information such as name, address, telephone number, and e-mail address at the top of the resume.

EDUCATION

University of North Carolina; Charlotte, NC
Bachelor of Science in Administrative Information Management
Expected; June 20 _ _

WORK EXPERIENCE

James uses heads with capital letters to identify each section of his résumé.

P.E.S. Engineering; Charlotte, NC
Summer 2005
Intern
Designed a customized record management system for the engineers; trained in the data entry department.

Gen X Wireless Services; Paramus, NJ
2003–2005 (summers and breaks)
Receivables Management Representative
Handled incoming accounts-receivable call for cellular phone accounts in the New York, New Jersey, and Connecticut markets; trained other representatives.

Entries on résumé should be short and to the point.

Computer Services Department; University of North Carolina, Charlotte, NC
Fall 2004
Computer Lab Technician
Assisted students in the use of software and hardware; responded to user questions and problems.

COMPUTER SKILLS
HTML, XML, Excel, Microsoft Access, and Microsoft Office.

REFERENCES
Furnished on request

USING THE INTERNET

Introduction to the Internet

The Internet is a series of networks that are interconnected all over the world. The Internet allows users to have almost unlimited access to information stored on the networks. Dr. Berners-Lee, a physicist, created the Internet in the 1980s by writing a small computer program that allowed pages to be linked together using key words. The Internet was mostly text-based until 1992, when a computer program called the NCSA Mosaic (National Center for Supercomputing Applications) was created at the University of Illinois. This program was the first Web browser. The development of Web browsers greatly eased the ability of the user to navigate through all the pages stored on the Web. Very soon, the appearance of the Web was altered as well. More appealing visuals were added, and sound, too, was implemented. This change made the Web more user-friendly and more appealing to the general public.

Using the Internet for Research

Key Word Search

Before you begin a search, you should identify your specific topic. To make searching easier, narrow your subject to a key word or a group of key words. These are your search terms, and they should be as specific as possible. For example, if you are looking for the latest concert dates for your favorite musical group, you might use the band's name as a key word. However, if you were to enter the name of the group in the query box of the search engine, you might be presented with thousands of links to information about the group that is unrelated to what you want to know. You might locate such information as band member biographies, the group's history, fan reviews of concerts, and hundreds of sites with related names containing information that is irrelevant to your search. Because you used such a broad key word, you might need to navigate through all that information before you could find a link or subheading for concert dates. In contrast, if you were to type in "Duplex Arena and [band name]," you would have a better chance of locating pages that contain this information.

How to Narrow Your Search

If you have a large group of key words and still do not know which ones to use, write out a list of all the words you are considering. Once you have completed the list, scrutinize it. Then, delete the words that are least important to your search, and highlight those that are most important.

These **key search connectors** can help you fine-tune your search:

AND: Narrows a search by retrieving documents that include both terms. For example: *baseball* AND *playoffs*

OR: Broadens a search by retrieving documents including any of the terms. For example: *play-offs* OR *championships*

NOT: Narrows a search by excluding documents containing certain words. For example: *baseball* NOT *history of*

Tips for an Effective Search

1. Remember that search engines can be case-sensitive. If your first attempt at searching fails, check your search terms for misspellings and try again.

2. If you are entering a group of key words, present them in order from the most important to the least important key word.

3. Avoid opening the link to every single page in your results list. Search engines present pages in descending order of relevancy. The most useful pages will be located at the top of the list. However, read the description of each link before you open the page.

4. Some search engines provide helpful tips for specializing your search. Take the opportunity to learn more about effective searching.

Other Ways to Search

Using Online Reference Sites How you search should be tailored to what you are hoping to find. If you are looking for data and facts, use reference sites before you jump onto a simple search engine. For example, you can find reference sites to provide definitions of words, statistics about almost any subject, biographies, maps, and concise information on many topics. Here are some useful online reference sites:

Online libraries

Online periodicals

Almanacs

Encyclopedias

You can find these sources using subject searches.

Conducting Subject Searches As you prepare to go online, consider your subject and the best way to find information to suit your needs. If you are looking for general information on a topic and you want your search results to be extensive, consider the subject search indexes on most search engines. These indexes, in the form of category and subject lists, often appear on the first page of a search engine. When you click on a specific highlighted word, you will be presented with a new screen containing subcategories of the topic you chose.

Evaluating the Reliability of Internet Resources

Just as you would evaluate the quality, bias, and validity of any other research material you locate, check the source of information you find online. Compare these two sites containing information about the poet and writer Langston Hughes:

Site A is a personal Web site constructed by a college student. It contains no bibliographic information or links to sites that he used. Included on the site are several poems by Langston Hughes and a student essay about the poet's use of symbolism. It has not been updated in more than six months.

Site B is a Web site constructed and maintained by the English Department of a major university. Information on Hughes is presented in a scholarly format, with a bibliography and credits for the writer. The site includes links to other sites and indicates new features that are added weekly.

For your own research, consider the information you find on Site B to be more reliable and accurate than that on Site A. Because it is maintained by experts in their field who are held accountable for their work, the university site will be a better research tool than the student-generated one.

Tips for Evaluating Internet Sources

1. Consider who constructed and who now maintains the Web page. Determine whether this author is a reputable source. Often, the URL endings indicate a source.
   - Sites ending in *.edu* are maintained by educational institutions.
   - Sites ending in *.gov* are maintained by government agencies (federal, state, or local).
   - Sites ending in *.org* are normally maintained by nonprofit organizations and agencies.
   - Sites ending in *.com* are commercially or personally maintained.

2. Skim the official and trademarked Web pages first. It is safe to assume that the information you draw from Web pages of reputable institutions, online encyclopedias, online versions of major daily newspapers, or government-owned sites produce information as reliable as the material you would find in print. In contrast, unbranded sites or those generated by individuals tend to borrow information from other sources without providing documentation. As information travels from one source to another, it could have been muddled, misinterpreted, edited, or revised.

3. You can still find valuable information in the less "official" sites. Check for the writer's credentials, and then consider these factors:
   - Do not be misled by official-looking graphics or presentations.
   - Make sure that the information is updated enough to suit your needs. Many Web pages will indicate how recently they have been updated.
   - If the information is borrowed, notice whether you can trace it back to its original source.

Respecting Copyrighted Material

Because the Internet is a relatively new and quickly growing medium, issues of copyright and ownership arise almost daily. As laws begin to govern the use and reuse of material posted online, they may change the way that people can access or reprint material.

Text, photographs, music, and fine art printed online may not be reproduced without acknowledged permission of the copyright owner.

Citing Sources and Preparing Manuscript

In research writing, cite your sources. In the body of your paper, provide a footnote, an endnote, or a parenthetical citation, identifying the sources of facts, opinions, or quotations. At the end of your paper, provide a bibliography or a works-cited list, a list of all the sources you cite. Follow an established format, such as Modern Language Association (MLA) Style.

Works-Cited List (MLA Style)

A works-cited list must contain accurate information sufficient to enable a reader to locate each source you cite. The basic components of an entry are as follows:

- Name of the author, editor, translator, or group responsible for the work
- Title of the work
- Place and date of publication
- Publisher

For print materials, the information required for a citation generally appears on the copyright and title pages of a work. For the format of works-cited list entries, consult the examples at right and in the chart on page R34.

Parenthetical Citations (MLA Style)

A parenthetical citation briefly identifies the source from which you have taken a specific quotation, factual claim, or opinion. It refers the reader to one of the entries on your works-cited list. A parenthetical citation has the following features:

- It appears in parentheses.
- It identifies the source by the last name of the author, editor, or translator.
- It gives a page reference, identifying the page of the source on which the information cited can be found.

Punctuation A parenthetical citation generally falls outside a closing quotation mark but within the final punctuation of a clause or sentence. For a long quotation set off from the rest of your text, place the citation at the end of the excerpt without any punctuation following.

Special Cases

- If the author is an organization, use the organization's name, in a shortened version if necessary.
- If you cite more than one work by the same author, add the title or a shortened version of the title.

Sample Works-Cited Lists

Carwardine, Mark, Erich Hoyt, R. Ewan Fordyce, and Peter Gill. *The Nature Company Guides: Whales, Dolphins, and Porpoises.* New York: Time-Life Books, 1998.

Whales in Danger. "Discovering Whales." 18 Oct 1999. <http://whales. magna.com.au/DISCOVER>

Neruda, Pablo. *"Ode to Spring." Odes to Opposites.* Trans. Ken Krabbenhoft. Ed. and illus. Ferris Cook. Boston: Little, Brown and Company, 1995.

The Saga of the Volsungs. Trans. Jesse L. Byock. London: Penguin Books, 1990.

List an anonymous work by title

List both the title of the work and the title of the collection in which it is found.

Sample Parenthetical Citations

It make sense that baleen whales such as the blue whale, the bowhead whale, the humpback whale, and the sei whale (to name just a few) grow to immense sizes (Carwardine, Hoyt, and Fordyce 19–21). The blue whale has grooves running from under its chin to partway along the length of its underbelly. As in some other whales, these grooves expand and allow even more food and water to be taken in (Ellis 18–21).

Author's last name

Page numbers where information can be found

MLA Style for Listing Sources

Book with one author	Pyles, T. (1971). *The Origins and Development of the English Language.* (2nd ed.). New York: Harcourt Brace Jovanovich, Inc.
Book with two or three authors	McCrum, R., Cran, W., & MacNeil, R. (1987). *The Story of English.* New York: Penguin Books.
Book with an editor	Truth, S. (1993). *Narrative of Sojourner Truth* (M. Washington, Ed.). New York: Vintage Books.
Book with more than three authors or editors	Donald, R. B., Morrow, B. R., Wargetz, L. G., & Werner, K. (1996). *Writing Clear Eassys.* Upper Saddle River, New Jersey: Prentice-Hall, Inc. [With six or more authors, abbreviate all authors after sixth as "et al."]
Single work from an anthology	Hawthorne, N. (1998) Young Goodman Brown. In E. V. Roberts, & H. E. Jacobs (Eds.), *Literature: An Introduction to Reading and Writing* (pp. 376–385). Upper Saddle River, New Jersey: Prentice-Hall, Inc.
Introduction to a work included in a published edition	Washington, M. (1993). Introduction. In M. WAshington (Ed.), *Narrative of Sojourner Truth* (v–xi). *New York: Vintage Books.*
Signed article in a weekly magazine	Wallace, C. (2000, February 14). A vodacious deal. *Time, 155,* 63. [The volume number appears in italics before the page number.]
Signed article in a monthly magazine	Gustaitis, J. (1998, October). The sticky history of chewing gum. *American History, 33,* 30–38.
Unsigned editorial or story	Selective Silence [Editorial]. (2000, February 11). *Wall Street Journal,* p. A14.
Signed pamphlet	Pearson Education. (2000). *LifeCare* (2nd ed.) [Pamphlet]. New York: Smith, John: Author.
Pamphlet with no author, publisher, or date	*Are You at Risk of Heart Attack?* n.p.n.d. [n.p.n.d. indicates that there is no known publisher or date.]
Filmstrips, slide programs, and videotapes	Stevens, G. (Producer & Director). (1959). *The Diary of Anne Frank.* [Videotape]. United States: Twentieth Century Fox. [If the producer and the director are two different people, list the producer first and then the director, with an ampersand (&) between them.]
Radio or television program transcript	Broderick, D. (Speaker). (1999, May 23). The First Immortal Generation. (R. Williams, Radio Host). *Ockam's Razor.* [Radio Transcript]. New York: National Public Radio.
Internet	National Association of Chewing Gum Manufacturers. (1999). Retrieved December 19th, 1999 from http://www.nacgm.org/consumer/funfacts.html [References to Websites should begin with the author's last name, if available. Indicate the site name and the available path or URL address.]
Newspaper	Thurow, R. (2000, February 11). South Africans who fought for sanctions now scrap for investors. *Wall Street Journal,* pp. A1, A4. [For a multipage article, write only the first page number on which it appears, followed by a plus sign.]
Personal interview	[APA states that, since interviews (and other personal communications) do not provide "recoverable data," they should only be cited in text.]
CD (with multiple publishers)	Simms, James, ed. *Romeo and Juliet.* By William Shakespeare. CD-ROM. Oxford: Attica Cybernetics Ltd.; London: BBC Education; London: HarperCollins Publishers, 1995.
Signed article from an encyclopedia	Askeland, D. R. (1991). Welding. In *World Book Encyclopedia.* (vol. 21 pp. 190–191). Chicago: World Book, Inc.

GUIDE TO RUBRICS

What is a rubric?

A rubric is a tool, often in the form of a chart or a grid, that helps you assess your work. Rubrics are particularly helpful for writing and speaking assignments.

To help you or others assess, or evaluate, your work, a rubric offers several specific criteria to be applied to your work. Then the rubric helps you or an evaluator indicate your range of success or failure according to those specific criteria. Rubrics are often used to evaluate writing for standardized tests.

Using a rubric will save you time, focus your learning, and improve the work you do. When you know what the rubric will be before you begin writing a persuasive essay, for example, you will be aware as you write of specific criteria that are important in that kind of an essay. As you evaluate the essay before giving it to your teacher, you will focus on the specific areas that your teacher wants you to master—or on areas that you know present challenges for you. Instead of searching through your work randomly for any way to improve it or correct its errors, you will have a clear and helpful focus on specific criteria.

How are rubrics constructed?

Rubrics can be constructed in several different ways.

- Your teacher may assign a rubric for a specific assignment.
- Your teacher may direct you to a rubric in your textbook.
- Your teacher and your class may construct a rubric for a particular assignment together.
- You and your classmates may construct a rubric together.
- You may create your own rubric with criteria you want to evaluate in your work.

How will a rubric help me?

A rubric will help you assess your work on a scale. Scales vary from rubric to rubric but usually range from 6 to 1, 5 to 1, or 4 to 1, with 6, 5, or 4 being the highest score and 1 being the lowest. If someone else is using the rubric to assess your work, the rubric will give your evaluator a clear range within which to place your work. If you are using the rubric yourself, it will help you make improvements to your work.

What are the types of rubrics?

- A **holistic rubric** has general criteria that can apply to a variety of assignments. See p. R-37 for an example of a holistic rubric.
- An **analytic rubric** is specific to a particular assignment. The criteria for evaluation address the specific issues important in that assignment. See p. R-36 for examples of analytic rubrics.

Sample Analytic Rubrics

Rubric With a 4-point Scale

The following analytic rubric is an example of a rubric to assess a persuasive essay. It will help you evaluate focus, organization, support/elaboration, and style/convention.

	Focus	Organization	Support/Elaboration	Style/Convention
4	Demonstrates highly effective word choice clearly focused on task.	Uses clear, consistent organization strategy.	Provides convincing, well-elaborated reasons to support the position.	Incorporates transitions; includes very few mechanical errors.
3	Demonstrates good word choice; stays focused on persuasive task.	Uses clear organizational strategy with occasional inconsistencies.	Provides two or more moderately elaborated reasons to support the position.	Incorporates some transitions; includes few mechanical errors.
2	Shows some good word choices; minimally stays focused on persuasive task.	Uses inconsistent organizational strategy; presentation is not logical.	Provides several reasons, but few are elaborated.	Incorporates few transitions; includes many mechanical errors.
1	Shows lack of attention to persuasive task.	Demonstrates lack of organizational strategy.	Provides no specific reasons or does not elaborate.	Does not connect ideas; includes many mechanical errors.

Rubric With a 6-point Scale

The following analytic rubric is an example of a rubric to assess a persuasive essay. It will help you evaluate presentation, position, evidence, and arguments.

	Presentation	Position	Evidence	Arguments
6	Essay clearly and effectively addresses an issue with more than one side.	Essay clearly states a supportable position on the issue.	All evidence is logically organized, well presented, and supports the position.	All reader concerns and counterarguments are effectively addressed.
5	Most of essay addresses an issue that has more than one side.	Essay clearly states a position on the issue.	Most evidence is logically organized, well presented, and supports the position.	Most reader concerns and counterarguments are effectively addressed.
4	Essay adequately addresses issue that has more than one side.	Essay adequately states a position on the issue.	Many parts of evidence support the position; some evidence is out of order.	Many reader concerns and counterarguments are adequately addressed.
3	Essay addresses issue with two sides but does not present second side clearly.	Essay states a position on the issue, but the position is difficult to support.	Some evidence supports the position, but some evidence is out of order.	Some reader concerns and counterarguments are addressed.
2	Essay addresses issue with two sides but does not present second side.	Essay states a position on the issue, but the position is not supportable.	Not much evidence supports the position, and what is included is out of order.	A few reader concerns and counterarguments are addressed.
1	Essay does not addresses issue with more than one side.	Essay does not state a position on the issue.	No evidence supports the position.	No reader concerns or counterarguments are addressed.

Sample Holistic Rubric

Holistic rubrics such as this one are sometimes used to assess writing assignments on standardized tests. Notice that the criteria for evaluation are focus, organization, support, and use of conventions.

Points	Criteria
6 Points	• The writing is strongly focused and shows fresh insight into the writing task. • The writing is marked by a sense of completeness and coherence and is organized with a logical progression of ideas. • A main idea is fully developed, and support is specific and substantial. • A mature command of the language is in evidence, and the writing may employ characteristic creative writing strategies. • Sentence structure is varied, and writing is free of all but purposefully used fragments. • Virtually no errors in writing conventions appear.
5 Points	• The writing is clearly focused on the task. • The writing is well organized and has a logical progression of ideas, though there may be occasional lapses. • A main idea is well developed and supported with relevant details. • Command of the language is mature. • Sentence structure is varied, and the writing is free of fragments, except when used purposefully. • Writing conventions are followed correctly.
4 Points	• The writing is clearly focused on the task, but extraneous material may intrude at times. • A clear organizational pattern is present, though lapses may occur. • A main idea is adequately supported, but development may be uneven. • Sentence structure is generally free of fragments but shows little variation. • Writing conventions are generally followed correctly.
3 Points	• Writing is generally focused on the task, but extraneous material may intrude at times. • An organizational pattern is evident, but writing may lack a logical progression of ideas. • Support for the main idea is generally present but is sometimes illogical. • Sentence structure is generally free of fragments, but there is almost no variation. • The work generally demonstrates a knowledge of writing conventions, with occasional misspellings.
2 Points	• The writing is related to the task but generally lacks focus. • There is little evidence of organizational pattern, and there is little sense of cohesion. • Support for the main idea is generally inadequate, illogical, or absent. • Sentence structure is unvaried, and serious errors may occur. • Errors in writing conventions and spelling are frequent.
1 Point	• The writing may have little connection to the task and is generally unfocused. • There has been little attempt at organization or development. • The paper seems fragmented, with no clear main idea. • Sentence structure is unvaried, and serious errors appear. • Poor word choice and poor command of the language obscure meaning. • Errors in writing conventions and spelling are frequent.
Unscorable	The paper is considered unscorable if • The response is unrelated to the task or is simply a rewording of the prompt. • The response has been copied from a published work. • The student did not write a response. • The response is illegible. • The words in the response are arranged with no meaning. • There is an insufficient amount of writing to score.

STUDENT MODEL

Persuasive Writing

This persuasive letter, which would receive a top score according to a persuasive rubric, is a response to the following writing prompt, or assignment:

With the increased use of technology in the workplace, the skills that high-school graduates must possess have changed. Write a letter to your principal advocating new technology courses that could give high-school graduates a competitive edge.

Dear Principal:

I am writing to alert you to an urgent need in our school's curriculum. We need computer graphics courses!

> The letter begins with an engaging introduction that clearly states the persuasive focus.

Although you would have to find funds to buy the equipment, I've concluded that setting up this course would well be worth it. By adding this course, you would be adding many high paying career options for students. Computer graphics is a type of art, and businesses all around us involve art in some form. You see computer graphics in commercials, movies, news broadcasts, weather broadcasts, architectural design, and business presentations. Workers with computer graphics skills are well paid because they are in such high demand.

You may argue that the school already has computer science classes. Good point! I'm in a computer science class and it is mainly programming. Once we did have an assignment to design a graphic of a pumpkin. You wouldn't believe how much coding it takes to get a simple, animated drawing. In order to get a really creative image with definite lines, shading, lifelike colors, and texture, you need to use computer graphics software designed especially for that purpose. With software, you can make images that move and talk smoothly and environments with realistic colors and lighting. This is the same graphics software that businesses use for commercials, movies, and brochures. Students should be learning how to use this software.

> The author effectively counters an opposing argument to increase the persuasive power of her own argument.

Most importantly, computer graphics is a subject area that allows students to express their creativity. Adding a computer graphics course would have a positive effect on students. Course participants would enjoy doing their assignments, so they would earn good grades and turn in creative work. The energy and enthusiasm they would bring to their projects would catch the attention of the community at large. As a result, they would make the school and the principal look good.

> A positive argument that is well supported enhances the letter's persuasive appeal.

As you can see, adding a computer graphics course could be a very profitable idea for you, the students, and the community. You would be ensuring the success of the students who desire an art or computer career. You would be opening hundreds of different career pathways. Wouldn't it be great to know you were the reason for these students' success? Thanks for your time and consideration.

Sincerely,
Dawn Witherspoon

GRAMMAR, USAGE, AND MECHANICS

Parts of Speech

Nouns

A **noun** names a person, place, or thing. **Common nouns** name any one of a class of people, places, or things. **Proper nouns** name specific people, places, or things.

Common Noun	Proper Noun
city	Washington, D.C.

Exercise A **Distinguishing Between Common and Proper Nouns.** Write the one proper noun in each group, adding the necessary capitalization.

1. planet · · · · · · neptune · · · · · · star
2. jurassic period · · dinosaurs · · · · jaw
3. biology · · · · · · high school · · · · science 9
4. june · · · · · · · · spring · · · · · · month
5. dandelion · · · · · mothers · · · · · · mothers' day

Pronouns

A **pronoun** is a word that stands for a noun or for a word that takes the place of a noun.

A **personal pronoun** refers to (1) the person speaking, (2) the person spoken to, or (3) the person, place, or thing spoken about.

	Singular	Plural
First Person	I, me, my, mine	we, us, our, ours
Second Person	you, your, yours	you, your, yours
Third Person	he, him, his, she, her, hers, it, its	they, them, their, theirs

Exercise B **Identifying and Using Personal Pronouns.** Write the personal pronoun or pronouns in each sentence. Then, write a new sentence, using the same personal pronoun or pronouns.

1. John does his homework before the game.
2. "Dad, can you take Reggie to the baseball game?" Jayne asked.
3. When the bus arrives, it is always late.
4. Patrick asked Sarah if she had his baseball glove.
5. Gregory brought his bat with him.

A **reflexive pronoun** ends in -*self* or -*selves* and adds information to a sentence by pointing back to a noun or pronoun earlier in the sentence.

> As I said these words I busied *myself* among the pile of bones of which I have before spoken.
>
> —"The Cask of Amontillado," p. 61

An **intensive pronoun** ends in -*self* or -*selves* and simply adds emphasis to a noun or a pronoun in the same sentence.

> The best playground, however, was the dark alley *itself*.
>
> —"Rules of the Game," p. 305

Exercise C **Distinguishing Between Reflexive and Intensive Pronouns.** Write the reflexive or intensive pronoun in each sentence. Then, label each reflexive or intensive.

1. Mardi Gras itself has become an event.
2. It was originally intended to allow people to enjoy themselves before a time of fasting.
3. If you yourself have ever attended one, you know it is a week-long celebration.
4. Participants dress themselves in colorful costumes.
5. The mayor himself attends the festivities.

Demonstrative pronouns (*this, these, that,* and *those*) direct attention to a specific person, place, or thing.

> *These* are the juiciest pears I have ever tasted.

A **relative pronoun** begins a subordinate (relative) clause and connects it to another idea in the sentence.

> The poet *who* wrote "Fire and Ice" is Robert Frost.
>
> The poet *whom* I admire is Frost.

An **interrogative pronoun** is used to begin a question. The five interrogative pronouns are: *what, which, who, whom, whose*.

Exercise D **Recognizing Demonstrative, Relative, and Interrogative Pronouns.** Write the pronoun in each sentence. Then, label each demonstrative, reflexive, or interrogative.

1. Mardi Gras is a carnival that is held before Lent.
2. This is the grand finale of a long carnival season.
3. Mardi Gras, which is a French tradition, was introduced to the United States in the 1700s.
4. This is a holiday in a few states.
5. Which of the states has a famous celebration?

An **indefinite pronoun** refers to a person, place, or thing, often without specifying which one.

> *Some* of the flowers were in bloom.
>
> *Everybody* chose something.

GRAMMAR, USAGE, AND MECHANICS

Exercise E Identifying Indefinite Pronouns. Write the indefinite pronoun or pronouns in each sentence.

1. Before 1900, no one moved Ferris wheels from place to place.
2. Eventually, somebody working for the Eli Bridge Company started making portable Ferris wheels.
3. This someone was William E. Sullivan.
4. Many were sold to carnivals that wanted to travel.
5. Now, everyone could enjoy a ride on a Ferris wheel.

Verbs

A **verb** is a word that expresses time while showing an action, a condition, or the fact that something exists.

An **action verb** indicates the action of someone or something.

An action verb is **transitive** if it directs action toward someone or something named in the same sentence.

> Marcos accepted their bouquets . . .
>
> —"Uncle Marcos," p. 133

An action verb is **intransitive** if it does not direct action toward something or someone named in the same sentence.

> "He nodded and smiled a lot."
>
> —"American History," p. 202

Exercise F Recognizing Transitive and Intransitive **Verbs.** Write the action verb in each sentence, and label it transitive or intransitive.

1. The fall of the Shang dynasty occurred about 1000 B.C.
2. The last Shang monarch ruled unjustly.
3. The king of Chou overthrew him.
4. The people of Chou lived on the north-western fringes of the Shang domain.
5. The Chou culture reflected the influence of the Shang civilization.

A **linking verb** is a verb that connects the subject of a sentence with a noun or pronoun that renames or describes the subject. All linking verbs are intransitive.

> Life *is* a broken-winged bird . . .
>
> —"Dreams," p. 567

Exercise G Identifying Linking Verbs. Write each sentence, underlining the linking verb. Then, draw a double-headed arrow to show which words are linked by the verb.

1. The *Apollo 13* mission was successful.
2. It may be the most famous lunar-landing mission.
3. These men were aboard during an explosion on the module.
4. The astronauts felt concerned after sensing the explosion.
5. A minor mid-course correction became the only solution.

A **helping verb** is a verb that can be added to another verb to make a verb phrase.

> Nor *did* I suspect that these experiences could be part of a novel's meaning.

Exercise H Identifying Helping Verbs. Write the helping verb(s) in each sentence.

1. The *Apollo 13* mission may have been the most exciting in history.
2. The mission should have proceeded normally.
3. However, problems would arise from an electrical surge.
4. An electrical surge can cause an explosion and a fire.
5. The crew had quickly moved to the lunar module.

Adjectives

An **adjective** describes a noun or a pronoun or gives a noun or a pronoun a more specific meaning. Adjectives answer these questions:

What kind?	*blue* lamp, *large* tree
Which one?	*this* table, *those* books
How many?	*five* stars, *several* buses
How much?	*less* money, *enough* votes

The articles *the, a,* and *an* are adjectives. *An* is used before a word beginning with a vowel sound.

A noun may sometimes be used as an adjective.

> *diamond* necklace   *summer* vacation

Exercise I Identifying Adjectives and the Words **They Modify.** Identify each adjective in the following sentences. Then, indicate the word each adjective modifies and the question that it answers.

1. Small work boats were sailed extensively for pleasure in early colonial times.
2. The first pleasure schooner was built in 1816.
3. It was built specifically as a large, luxurious yacht.
4. American yacht clubs started around the 1840's.
5. Six members of the New York Yacht Club financed America's first racing yacht.

Adverbs

An **adverb** modifies a verb, an adjective, or another adverb. Adverbs answer the questions *where, when, in what way,* or *to what extent.*

> He could stand *there.* (modifies verb *stand*)
>
> He was *blissfully* happy. (modifies adjective *happy*)
>
> It ended *too* soon. (modifies adverb *soon*)

Exercise J Identifying Adverbs. Identify each adverb and tell which question it answers: *Where? When? In what way?* or *To what extent?*

1. The Maya were very accomplished astronomers.
2. Their primary interest was in carefully observing Zenithal Passages.
3. A special event occurred when the sun crossed directly over the Mayan latitudes.
4. The sun travels annually to its summer solstice point, latitude 23⅛ degrees north.
5. Mayan cities were always located south of this point.

Prepositions

A **preposition** relates a noun or a pronoun that appears with it to another word in the sentence.

> the scene *before* the end   stood *near* me

Exercise K Identifying Prepositions. Write each sentence, replacing the underlined preposition with another preposition that makes sense.

1. Does the basketball season generally come before the football season?
2. The standard length of a basketball court is 94 feet, and the width is 50 feet.
3. A basket attached to a backboard hangs over each end of the court.
4. Her free throw hit the backboard above the basket, and she failed to score.

5. A player can advance the ball only with dribbling or with passing.

Conjunctions

A **conjunction** connects other words or groups of words.

A **coordinating conjunction** connects similar kinds or groups of words.

> mother *and* father   simple *yet* stylish

Correlative conjunctions are used in pairs to connect similar words or groups of words.

> *both* Sue *and* Meg   *neither* he *nor* I

A **subordinating conjunction** connects two complete ideas by placing one idea below the other in rank or importance.

> You would know him *if* you saw him.

Exercise L Identifying Conjunctions. Write the conjunction(s) in each sentence. Then, label each coordinating, correlative, or subordinating. Write none is a sentence contains no conjunction.

1. The term environment refers to the surroundings of either an individual organism or a community or organisms.
2. The word surroundings refers to all living and non-living materials around an organism.
3. An organism is influenced not only by its immediate surroundings but also by physical forces.
4. When we use the word environment, we often think about the adverse effects of human activities.
5. After a ship struck a sandbar, an oil spill occurred.

Interjections

An **interjection** expresses feeling or emotion and functions independently of a sentence.

> "*Oh*, my poor, poor, Mathilde!"
>
> —"The Necklace," p. 294

Exercise M Supplying Interjections. Write each sentence, adding an interjection that conveys the indicated emotion.

1. (disappointment) Look at the garbage left on the ground.
2. (delight) The park certainly is cleaner since the town provided more garbage cans.
3. (happiness) Here comes the recycling truck at last.
4. (pain) I stumbled on that tree root.
5. (annoyance) I missed the trash can.

GRAMMAR, USAGE, AND MECHANICS

Sentences, Phrases, and Clauses

Sentences

A **sentence** is a group of words with a subject and a predicate. Together, these parts express a complete thought.

> I closed my eyes and pondered my next move.
>
> — "Rules of the Game," p. 305

A **fragment** is a group of words that does not express a complete thought.

> The Swan Theater in London

Exercise A **Recognizing Sentence Fragments.** Write *F* if an item below is a fragment and *S* if it is a complete sentence.

1. An array of finely tuned instruments.
2. Will play any instrument in the band.
3. In the concert hall on the stage.
4. That's loud.
5. After you finish reading, I will practice the cello.

A **run-on** is two or more complete sentences run together without punctuation.

Exercise B **Recognizing Run-ons.** On your paper, write *S* if an item is a sentence and *RO* if it is a run-on. Indicate whether each run-on is a fused sentence or a comma splice.

1. Percussion instruments produce sound when struck or shaken, some examples are drums, rattles, and bells.
2. The marimba is a percussion instrument with wooden bars arranged like the keys on a piano, mallets are used to strike the bars and produce sound.
3. If you are near a beach, you can collect driftwood to make your own marimba.
4. Gather several pieces of driftwood test each one for sound quality by striking it in the center.
5. To make the marimba, place the driftwood pieces in order by tone, then attach the pieces side by side over two long support pieces.

A **direct object** is a noun or pronoun that receives the action of a transitive verb.

Exercise C **Recognizing Direct Objects.** Write the direct object in each sentence.

1. A YMCA instructor invented basketball in 1891.
2. In basketball, players put a ball through a basket to make points.
3. The winning team scores the most points.
4. Spectators first watched basketball in the nineteenth century.
5. Most states now hold championships in basketball.

An **indirect object** is a noun or pronoun that appears with a direct object and names the person or thing that something is given to or done for.

Exercise D **Supplying Indirect Objects.** Supply a logical indirect object in each sentence.

1. Pam told _____ the highlights of the basketball game.
2. At the beginning of the game, the center tipped _____ the jump ball.
3. A foul gave _____ a chance to score.
4. In the last 30 seconds of the game, the guard passed _____ the ball and he made a three-pointer.
5. As a result, the home team gave _____ another victory.

The Four Structure of Sentences

These are two kinds of clauses: independent and subordinate. These can be used to form four basic sentence structures: *simple, compound, complex,* and *compound-complex*.

A **simple sentence** consists of a single independent clause.

A **compound sentence** consists of two or more independent clauses.

The clauses in a compound sentence can be joined by a comma and a coordinating conjunction (*and, but, for, not, or, so, yet*) or by a semicolon (;).

A **complex sentence** consists of one independent clause and one or more subordinate clauses.

The independent clause in a complex sentence is often called the *main clause* to distinguish it from the subordinate clause or clauses.

A **compound-complex sentence** consists of two or more independent clauses and one or more subordinate causes.

Exercise E **Identifying the Structure of Sentences.** Identify each sentence as simple, compound, complex, or compound-complex.

1. South Africa is the southernmost country of Africa.
2. It is the most powerful and the wealthiest country of the region.
3. Gold and diamonds are mined in both South African and Namibia, yet it was South Africa where the biggest diamond in the world was found.

4. Although it is not as wealthy as South Africa, Mozambique is the site of the second biggest port in all of Africa.

5. Its capital, Maputo, is the city where the port is located; it is linked by rail with South Africa, Swaziland, and Zimbabwe.

6. Even though most people think of Africa as a desert, Zimbabwe has a hot, tropical climate, so mangoes, passion fruit, pineapples, and avocados grow well.

Phrases

A **phrase** is a group of words, without a subject and a verb, that functions in a sentence as one part of speech.

A **prepositional phrase** is a group of words that includes a preposition and a noun or a pronoun that is the object of the preposition.

> outside my window   below the counter

Exercise F **Identifying Prepositional Phrases.** Write the prepositional phrase or phrases in each sentence. The number at the end of each sentence tells how many prepositional phrases the sentence has.

1. College basketball tournaments came into their own in 1939. (2)

2. Since that time, players have been setting records. (1)

3. Players are often named all-American for outstanding performances. (1)

4. A few players join professional teams after graduation from college. (2)

5. Some teams win medals at international games. (1)

An **adjective phrase** is a prepositional phrase that modifies a noun or a pronoun by telling what *kind* or *which one*.

> The wooden gates *of that lane* stood open.

Exercise G **Identifying Adjective Phrases.** Write each sentence, underlining the adjective phrase or phrases in each. Then, draw an arrow from each phrase to the word it modifies.

1. There are several different kinds of Native American tribes in North America.

2. The culture of each tribe varies.

3. The tribes of western Louisiana and eastern Texas are the Caddo.

4. Farming provided their main source of food.

5. Also important was the annual hunt for buffalo.

An **adverb phrase** is a prepositional phrase that modifies a verb, an adjective, or an adverb by pointing out *where, when, in what way,* or *to what extent.*

> ". . . I could sleep without closing my eyes . . ."
> —"The Most Dangerous Game," p. 215

Exercise H **Identifying Adverb Phrases.** Write each sentence, underlining the adverb phrase or phrases in each. Then, draw an arrow from each phrase to the word it modifies.

1. The Pawnee divided themselves into four different tribes.

2. Most of them lived in earth lodges.

3. One tribe, the Skidi Pawnee, became part of the Grand Pawnee in the early 1800's.

4. Religion was very important to this tribe.

5. In their religion, they paid homage to the morning star.

An **appositive phrase** is a noun or pronoun with modifiers, placed next to a noun or a pronoun to add information and details.

> "It is a very great pleasure and honor to welcome Mr. Sanger Rainsford, *the celebrated hunter*, to my home."
> —"The Most Dangerous Game," p. 215

Exercise I **Identifying Appositive Phrases.** Write the appositive phrase in each sentence. Then, write the word or words each appositive phrase renames.

1. Sugar cane, a plant with a strong stem, was used to make armor for Creek warriors.

2. Clubs, slings, lances, and bows and arrows—the usual weapons or war—were made of cane, rock, and other materials found in the area.

3. A war post, a cane stock painted red and hung with feathers and arrows, signified the start of a war party.

4. Those who wanted to enlist would hit the post as hard as they could with a war club, a piece of cane painted red.

5. Then, warriors would put themselves through a purification rite, a physically strenuous ceremony.

A **participial phrase** is a participle with its modifiers or complements. The entire phrase acts as an adjective.

> "Try the settee," said Holmes, *relapsing into his armchair* . . .
> —"The Red-headed League," p. 1067

GRAMMAR, USAGE, AND MECHANICS

Exercise J **Recognizing Participial Phrases.** Write the participial phrase in each sentence. Then, write the word or word it modifies.

1. Living in the Northwest, the Nootka and other tribes built their lives around fish and wood.
2. Hollowed-out trees were turned into boats.
3. Fishing from these boats, the tribes brought in abundant amounts of salmon and halibut.
4. Hunting whales with great skill, the Nootka tribe of Vancouver Island became well known for its catches.
5. Men, wearing armor carved from wood, had protection when fighting during their battles.

A **gerund phrase** is a gerund with modifiers or a complement, all acting together as a noun.

The baying of the hounds drew nearer, . . .

—"The Most Dangerous Game," p. 215

Exercise K **Identifying Gerund Phrases.** Write the gerund phrases in each sentence, and identify their functions.

1. Pilgrims learned about planting crops from the Wampanoags.
2. Advanced weapons made fighting the Sioux a successful effort for the Chippewa.
3. The Sioux became a tribe that lived by hunting buffalo.
4. Beads brought by the Europeans were used in decorating clothing and other costumes.
5. Trading with Native Americans allowed Europeans to survive.

An **infinitive phrase** is an infinitive (*to* and a verb) with modifiers, complements, or a subject, all acting together as a single part of speech.

I continued, as was my wont, *to smile in his face,* . . .

—"The Cask of Amontillado," p. 61

Exercise L **Writing Sentences with Infinitives.** Write a sentence for each infinitive phrase, using the infinitive phrase as the part of speech indicated.

1. to succeed in school (subject)
2. to call home (direct object)
3. to leave on vacation (adverb modifying adjective *happy*)
4. to travel to another state (predicate noun)
5. to go to the ceremony (appositive)

Clauses

A **clause** is a group of words with a subject and a verb.

An **independent clause** has a subject and a verb and can stand by itself as a complete sentence.

A **subordinate clause** has a subject and a verb but cannot stand by itself as a complete sentence; it can only be part of a sentence.

Exercise M **Identifying Independent and Subordinate Clauses.** Identify each clause as independent if the clause can stand alone or subordinate if the clause cannot stand alone.

1. weavers of this tribe make beautiful cloth
2. each one has a different pattern
3. because one has a different pattern
4. it is called "Gold Dust"
5. when Ghana elected its first president

An **adjective clause** is a subordinate clause that modifies a noun or a pronoun by telling *what kind* or *which one.*

Walter Mitty stopped the car in front of the building *where his wife went to have her hair done.*

—"The Secret Life of Walter Mitty," p. 124

An **adverb clause** modifies a verb, an adjective, an adverb, or a verbal by telling *where, when, in what way, to what extent, under what condition,* or *why.*

The hunter shook his head several times, *as if he was puzzled.*

—"The Most Dangerous Game," p. 215

A **noun clause** is a subordinate clause that acts as a noun.

. . . I discovered *that the intoxication had worn off . . .*

—"The Cask of Amontillado," p. 61

Exercise N **Recognizing Adjective, Adverb, and Noun Clauses.** Write the adjective, adverb, or noun clauses from each sentence. Label each correctly.

1. The Zaire River, which is also known as the Congo, runs almost the whole length of the country.
2. Because it has many tributaries, it is an important source of transportation.
3. The river drains a vast area of rain forests so its levels are always high.
4. The climate of the Democratic Republic of the Congo is hot and humid because it lies on the equator.

5. Besides whatever cooking and cleaning African women do, they also work in the fields and sell crops in the market.

Parallelism involves using similar grammatical structures to express similar ideas. Sentences with parallel structure contain repeated grammatical patterns or repeated types of phrases or clauses within a sentence.

> Marguerite has a great love *for art, for children,* and *for teaching.*

Exercise O **Correcting Faulty Parallelism.** Rewrite the sentences that lack parallel structure. If a sentence needs no revision, write *correct.*

1. As a boy, Frankin taught himself geometry, worked on his writing style, and newspapers.

2. He was a cleverly and creative youth.

3. He became a printer and worked with his brother before going to Philadelphia.

4. Because of his effort, and he was efficient, the British gave him the job of deputy postmaster of the Colonies.

5. Franklin later helped build a hospital, starting a university, and collect money for charities.

The Four Principal Parts of Verbs

Tenses are formed from principal parts and helping verbs.

A verb has four **principal parts**: the present, the present participle, the past, and the past participle.

Exercise A **Writing Sentences With Principal Parts of Verbs.** For each numbered item, write a sentence using the subject and the principal part of the verb indicated. Then, identify the tense of the verb in the sentence you have written.

1. We, past participle of talk

2. Mike, present participle of wait

3. People, present of laugh

4. I, past of stop

5. You, present participle of help

Pronoun Case

The **case** of a pronoun is the form it takes to show its use in a sentence. There are three pronoun cases: nominative, objective, and possessive.

The **nominative case** is used to rename the subject of the sentence. The nominative case pronouns are *I, you, he, she, it, we, you, they.*

> As the subject: *She* is brave.
> Renaming the subject: The leader is *she.*

The **objective case** is used as the direct object, indirect object, or object of the preposition. The objective case pronouns are *me, you, him, her, us, you, them.*

> **As a direct object:** Out manager praised her.
> **As an indirect object:** Give him the new product.
> **As an object of preposition:** The coach gave pointers to me.

The **possessive case** is used to show ownership. The possessive pronouns are *my, you, his, her, its, out, their, mine, yours, his, hers, its, outs, theirs.*

Exercise B **Choosing Pronouns in the Correct Case.** Choose the pronoun that is the correct case to complete each sentence. Identify the case of the pronoun you choose.

1. School fund-raisers taught (we, us) how to sell products to the public.

2. When promoting a product to customers, a salesperson should provide an incentive for (they, them) to buy.

3. (Them, Their) buying often depends on how they react to the seller.

4. This year, my teammates and (I, me) are selling team-spirit banners.

5. Customers know that the sale helps (we, us) earn money for the team.

Subject and Verb Agreement

A singular verb must be used with a singular subject; a plural verb must be used with a plural subject.

> *Reegan is* going home now.
> Many *storms are* the cause of beach erosion.

In a sentence with combined singular and plural subjects, the verb should agree with the subject closest to it.

> Either the *cats* or the *dog is* hungry.
> Neither *Angie* nor her *sisters were* present.

Exercise C **Making Verbs Agree With Their Subjects.** Choose the verb in parentheses that agrees with the subject of each sentence.

1. Before 1940, most Hungarians (was, were) farmers.

2. Today, many people (works, work) in industry.

3. When thinking of the past, my uncle (remembers, remember) the restrictions of Communist party rule.

GRAMMAR, USAGE, AND MECHANICS

4. Since the fall of the communist government, a great change (has, have) occurred.

5. Today, the citizens (elects, elect) their leaders.

Antecedents are the nouns (or the words that take the place of nouns) to which pronouns refer.

A personal pronoun must agree with its antecedent in number and gender. *Number* indicates whether a pronoun is singular or plural.

Some pronouns and nouns also indicate on of three *genders*: masculine, feminine, or neuter.

Use a singular personal pronoun to refer to two or more singular antecedents joined by *or* or *nor*.

Use a plural personal pronoun to refer to two or more antecedents joined by *and*.

Exercise D **Making Personal Pronouns Agree With Their Antecedents.** Write an appropriate personal pronoun to complete each sentence.

1. One computer pioneer is Alan Kay. _____ is noted for _____ role in the development of the laptop computer.

2. Before Kay introduced graphics and animation, _____ had not been seen before on PCs.

3. In the 1970's, the average person did not have a computer in _____ home.

4. However, once the microprocessor was invented, _____ hastened the development of the PC.

5. Today, you and I don't even have to leave home. _____ can access the world through _____ PCs.

Degrees of Comparison

Most adjectives and adverbs have different forms to show degrees of comparison.

The three degrees of comparison are the *positive*, the *comparative*, and the *superlative*.

Use the comparative degree to compare two people, places, or things. Use the superlative degree to compare three or more people, places, or things.

Use *more* or *most* to form the comparative and superlative degrees of all modifiers with three or more syllables.

Memorize the irregular comparative and superlative forms of certain adjectives and adverbs.

The most commonly used irregular modifiers are listed in the following chart. Notice that some modifiers differ only in the positive degree. For instance, the modifiers *bad, badly,* and *ill* all have the same comparative and superlative forms (*worse, worst*).

IRREGULAR MODIFIERS		
Positive	**Comparative**	**Superlative**
bad	worse	worst
badly	worse	worst
far (distance)	farther	farthest
far (extent)	further	furthest
good	better	best
ill	worse	worst
late	later	last or latest
little (amount)	less	least
many	more	most
much	more	most
well	better	best

Exercise E Supplying the Comparative and
Superlative Degrees

Write the appropriate comparative or superlative
degree of the modifier in parentheses.

1. Although Shakespeare died nearly 400 years ago, his
   plays are among those (often) read and performed.
2. Even the (bad) actor will learn to recognize at least
   one Shakespearean character.
3. Shakespeare's popularity as a playwright is
   unequaled by even the (good) modern-day writer.
4. His plays still command some of the (large) number
   of ticket sales.
5. The movie *West Side Story* is one of the (successful)
   modern versions of Shakespeare's *Romeo and Juliet.*

Capitalization and Punctuation

Capitalization

Capitalize the first word of a sentence and also the
first word in a quotation if the quotation is a complete
sentence.

> I said to him, "My dear Fortunato, you are luck-
> ily met."
>
> —"The Cask of Amontillado," p. 61

Capitalize all proper nouns and adjectives.

> O. Henry   Ganges River   Great Wall of China

Capitalize a person's title when it is followed by the
person's name or when it is used in direct address.

> Madame   Dr. Mitty   General Zaroff

Capitalize titles showing family relationships when
they refer to a specific person, unless they are preceded by a possessive noun or pronoun.

> Uncle Marcos   Granddaddy Cain

Capitalize the first word and all other key words in
the titles of books, periodicals, poems, stories, plays,
paintings, and other works of art.

> *Odyssey*   "I Wandered Lonely as a Cloud"

Exercise A Capitalizing Proper Nouns, Proper
Adjectives, and Titles Correctly. Copy the following
sentences onto your paper, adding the missing capitals. Underline any titles that appear in italics.

1. New York City served as the first american capital,
   and president george washington was inaugurated
   there.
2. Throughout history, many influential new yorkers
   have entertained and educated us and helped us
   create a better american way of life.

3. Have you read the short story "rip can winkle,"
   written by Washington Irving, who was born in
   New York city?
4. One of he most celebrated american poets, Walt
   Whitman, spent most of his life in brooklyn.
5. Colin Powell, the son of caribbean immigrants,
   grew up in the south bronx.

Punctuation

End Marks

Use a **period** to end a declarative sentence, an
imperative sentence, an indirect question, and most
abbreviations.

> Mr. Jabez Wilson laughed heavily.
>
> —"The Red-headed League," p. 1067

Use a **question mark** to end a direct question, an
incomplete question, or a statement that is intended
as a question.

> "What do you expect me to do with that?"
>
> —"The Necklace," p. 294

Use an **exclamation mark** after a statement showing strong emotion, an urgent imperative sentence, or
an interjection expressing strong emotion.

> Free at last! Free at last!
> Thank God almighty, we are Free at last!
>
> —"I Have a Dream," p. 494

Exercise B Punctuating the Ends of Sentences. Write
the end mark required in each of the following
sentences.

1. Backpacking is a popular type of hiking
2. Items that are packed must be as lightweight as
   possible
3. For crying out loud, you can't expect a backpacker
   to walk for 50 miles with 200 pounds of equipment
4. By carrying clothes, food, and plenty of water, a
   backpacker can spend many days in remote areas
   where these supplies would normally be unavailable
5. Where Anyplace you want

Commas

Use a **comma** before the coordinating conjunction to
separate two independent clauses in a compound
sentence.

> All at once . . . she came upon a superb dia-
> mond necklace, and her heart started beating
> with overwhelming desire.
>
> —"The Necklace," p. 294

GRAMMAR, USAGE, AND MECHANICS

Use commas to separate three or more words, phrases, or clauses in a series.

> My brothers and I would peer into the medicinal herb shop, watching old Li dole out onto a stiff sheet of white paper the right amount of insect shells, saffron-colored seeds, and pungent leaves for his ailing customers.
>
> —"Rules of the Game," p. 305

Use commas to separate adjectives of equal rank. Do not use commas to separate adjectives that must stay in a specific order.

> The big cottonwood tree stood apart from a small group of winterbare cottonwoods which grew in the wide, sandy arroyo.
>
> —"The Man to Send Rain Clouds," p. 268

> His present turned out to be a box of intricate plastic parts.
>
> —"Rules of the Game," p. 305

Use a comma after an introductory word, phrase, or clause.

> When Marvin was ten years old, his father took him through the long, echoing corridors . . .
>
> —"If I Forget Thee, Oh Earth . . . ," p. 148

Use commas to set off parenthetical and nonessential expressions.

> An evil place can, so to speak, broadcast vibrations of evil.
>
> —"The Most Dangerous Game," p. 215

Use commas with places, dates, and titles.

> Poe was raised in Richmond, Virginia.
>
> On September 1, 1939, World War II began.
>
> Dr. Martin Luther King, Jr., was born in 1929.

Use a comma to set off a direct quotation, to prevent a sentence from being misunderstood, and to indicate the omission of a common verb in a sentence with two or more clauses.

> Michele said, "I'm going to the game tonight."
>
> *Faulty:*   She stifled the sob that rose to her lips and lay motionless.
>
> *Revised:*   She stifled the sob that rose to her lips, and lay motionless.

In the *Odyssey*, the Cyclops may symbolize brutishness; the Sirens, knowledge.

Exercise C **Using Commas Correctly.** Rewrite each sentence, inserting commas where necessary. If the sentence is written correctly, write *correct.*

1. The modern shopping mall was made possible by the automobile the growth of the suburbs and television advertising.

2. Some consist of one long or angled building usually of one story divided into several stores.

3. To get from store to store in an open mall a customer must go outdoors.

4. The enclosed mall is covered by a roof which can be eight stories tall.

5. Malls have become all-purpose entertainment centers where a person may shop or eat or go to the movies.

Semicolons

Use a **semicolon** to join independent clauses that are not already joined by a conjunction.

> The lights of cities sparkle; on nights when there was no moon, it was difficult for me to tell the Earth from the sky. . . .
>
> —"Single Room, Earth View," p. 437

Use a semicolon to join independent clauses separated by either a conjunctive adverb or a transitional expression.

> Edward Way Teale wrote nearly thirty books; moreover, he was also an artist and a naturalist.

Use semicolons to avoid confusion when independent clauses or items in a series already contain commas.

> Unable to afford jewelry, she dressed simply; but she was as wretched as a *déclassée*, for women have neither caste nor breeding—in them beauty, grace, and charm replace pride of birth.
>
> —"The Necklace," p. 294

Exercise D **Using Semicolons Correctly.** Decide where a semicolon is needed in each of the following sentences. Write the word before the semicolon, write the semicolon, and write the words after the semicolon.

1. Astronaut trainees work hard to fill the requirements as a result, they are physically and mentally ready for the arduous tasks that lay before them.

2. Applicants are physically tested and interviewed for a period of one week trainees are selected from those who score the highest.

3. Those applying as pilot astronauts must also complete 1,000 hours in a top-level flight post, such as command pilot in a high-performance jet aircraft following that, they must pass a spaceflight physical.

4. Pilot astronauts must be between 5'4" tall and 6'4" tall payload specialists have no height requirement.

5. To fit the requirements, an astronaut applicant must have the appropriate education, physical health and stature, and experience but, in most cases, an applicant may be of any age.

Colons

Use a **colon** in order to introduce a list of items following an independent clause.

> The authors we are reading include a number of poets: Robert Frost, Lewis Carroll, and Emily Dickinson.

Use a colon to introduce a formal quotation.

> I have a dream that one day this nation will rise up and live out the true meaning of its creed: "We hold these truths to be self-evident; . . ."
> —"I Have a Dream," p. 494

Exercise E **Using Colons Correctly.** Rewrite each item, adding colons where appropriate. Some items may require more than one colon. Write *correct* if an item needs no additional punctuation.

1. August 1, 1998
2. To whom it may concern
3. Meeting Friday, September 8, for Junior Space Camp
4. Place American Hills High School
5. Time 7 00 P.M.

Quotation Marks

A **direct quotation** represents a person's exact speech or thoughts and is enclosed in quotation marks.

> "This great nation will endure as it has endured, will revive and will prosper," said President Franklin D. Roosevelt.
> —"First Inaugural Address," p. 503

An **indirect quotation** reports only the general meaning of what a person said or thought and does not require quotation marks.

> I went up to her, put my arms around her, and said something to her.
> —from *A White House Diary*, p. 99

Always place a comma or a period inside the final quotation mark.

> "There," he said, "there's something for you."
> —"The Necklace," p. 294

Place a question mark or an exclamation mark inside the final quotation mark if the end mark is part of the quotation; if it is not part of the quotation, place it outside the final quotation mark.

> "That pig will devour us, greedily!"
> —"The Golden Kite, the Silver Wind," p. 362

> Have you ever read the poem "Dreams"?

Use single quotation marks for a quotation within a quotation.

> "'But,' said I, 'there would be millions of red-headed men who would apply.'"
> —"The Red-headed League," p. 1067

Use quotation marks around the titles of short written works, episodes in a series, songs, and titles of works mentioned as parts of a collection.

> "I Hear America Singing"   "Pride"

Exercise F **Using Quotation Marks With Other Punctuation Marks.** Copy the following sentences, adding quotation marks and any needed commas, colons, semicolons, or end marks. *Note:* Italics included in some of the sentences are a clue to which text should be in quotations.

1. Solomon was sent away without being admitted to the king, but he was so persistent that the king *had him shut up as a madman*!

2. Nineteenth-century locomotives powered by steam were created by expanding on these basic ideas. *Air expands as it heats. Steam has a lot of power.*

3. Was it really the Marquis of Worcester who first discovered the power of steam from observing *the motion of the lid of a teakettle of boiling water*?

4. Perhaps, but the author of "The First Locomotives" writes *it does seem far more likely that Solomon . . . would be the one to observe the effects of the steam upon the lid of a teakettle.*

Dashes

Use **dashes** to indicate an abrupt change of thought, a dramatic interrupting idea, or a summary statement.

> The streets were lined with people—lots and lots of people—the children all smiling, placards, confetti, people waving from windows.
> —from *A White House Diary*, p. 98

GRAMMAR, USAGE, AND MECHANICS

Exercise G **Using Dashes Correctly.** Rewrite the following sentences, adding dashes where appropriate.

1. Blue and yellow macaws which belong to the parrot family but are not actually called parrots live in South America.

2. Nuts, fruits, seeds, and berries these are the staple foods of the macaw diet.

3. Bonding between the pair is reinforced as the birds preen, they groom each other's feathers.

4. When eggs are laid usually only two at a time the females incubates them.

5. Baby macaws always hatched in pairs are blind and featherless at hatching.

Parentheses

Use **parentheses** to set off asides and explanations only when the material is not essential or when it consists of one or more sentences.

> One last happy moment I had was looking up and seeing Mary Griffith . . . (Mary for many years had been in charge of altering the clothes which I purchased) . . .
>
> —from *A White House Diary*, p. 98

Exercise H **Using Parentheses.** Copy the following sentences, adding the necessary parentheses.

1. The sulphur-crested cockatoo has been kept as a pet I have one since the nineteenth century.

2. Its shrill voice heard mostly early in the morning or when it becomes alarmed can be trained to mimic the human voice.

3. Cockatoos that make the best pets are those that are bred in captivity. They are calmer and easier to train. Buying only birds that are captivity-bred also helps protect the birds of the wild.

4. A cockatoo will use the crest of feather on its head to show strong emotion fear or aggression.

5. When buying a cockatoo, be sure to buy a large cage; cockatoos will grow to be over a foot 18–20 inches long.

Hyphens

Use a **hyphen** with certain numbers, after certain prefixes, with two or more words used as one word, and with a compound modifier coming before a noun.

seventy-six   Post-Modernist

Exercise I **Using Hyphens Properly in Words and to Clarify Sentences.** Rewrite the words that require hyphens. If no hyphen is needed, write *correct*.

1. The all powerful beak of a macaw is hinged to crush tough nuts that other birds are not able to eat.

2. From the top of the body to the tip of the tail, macaws can reach up thirty six inches.

3. Nearly two thirds the length is accounted for in the tail.

4. Cuckoo birds create a coop with other species when raising their young.

5. A female cuckoo looks for an insect eating host species like the one she was raised in.

Apostrophes

Add an **apostrophe** and -*s* to show the possessive case of most singular nouns.

Thurmond's wife   the playwright's craft

Add an apostrophe to show the possessive case of plural nouns ending in -*s* and -*es*.

the sailors' ships   the Wattses' daughter

Add an apostrophe and -*s* to show the possessive case of plural nouns that do not end in -*s* or -*es*.

the children's games   the people's friend

Use an apostrophe in a contraction to indicate the position of the missing letter or letters.

> You'll be lonely at first, they admitted, but you're so nice you'll make friends fast.
>
> —"Checkouts," p. 74

Exercise J **Using Apostrophes With Possessive Nouns.** Copy the underlined nouns, putting them into the possessive form.

1. In India, <u>one</u> personal life tends to be arranged around traditional extended families.

2. When a woman marries, she moves in with her <u>husband</u> family.

3. It is the <u>head of state</u> job to appoint the prime minister.

4. The <u>Council of Ministers</u> appointment is made by the president on the advice of the prime minister.

5. The <u>forests</u> and <u>hills</u> inhabitants are fewer than the cities' inhabitants.

Glossary of Common Usage

among, between

Among is usually used with three or more items. *Between* is generally used with only two items.

> *Among* the poems we read this year, Margaret Walker's "Memory" was my favorite.

> Mark Twain's "The Invalid's Story" includes a humorous encounter *between* the narrator and a character named Thompson.

around

In formal writing, *around* should not be used to mean *approximately* or *about*. These usages are allowable, however, in informal writing or in colloquial dialogue.

> Shakespeare's *Romeo and Juliet* had its first performance in *approximately* 1595.

> Shakespeare was *about* thirty when he wrote this play.

as, because, like, as to

The word *as* has several meanings and can function as several parts of speech. To avoid confusion, use *because* rather than *as* when you want to indicate cause and effect.

> *Because* Cyril was interested in the history of African American poetry, he decided to write his report on Paul Laurence Dunbar.

Do not use the preposition *like* to introduce a clause that requires the conjunction *as*.

> Dorothy Parker conversed *as* she wrote—wittily.

The use of *as to* for *about* is awkward and should be avoided.

> Rosa has an interesting theory *about* E. E. Cummings's unusual typography in his poems.

INDEX OF SKILLS

Page numbers in **boldface** *refer to pages where terms are defined.*

INDEX OF SKILLS

INDEX OF SKILLS

Grammar, Usage, Mechanics

INDEX OF SKILLS

INDEX OF SKILLS

INDEX OF SKILLS

INDEX OF FEATURES

INDEX OF FEATURES

INDEX OF AUTHORS AND TITLES

Nonfiction selections and informational text appears in red. Page numbers in italic text refer to biographical information.

ACKNOWLEDGEMENTS

Harcourt, Inc. "Women" from *Revolutionary Petunias & Other Poems* by Alice Walker. Copyright © 1967 by Alice Walker. "Ithaca" from *The Complete Poems Of Cavafy*. Copyright © 1961 and renewed 1989 by Rae Dalven, reprinted by permission of Harcourt, Inc. "A Lincoln Preface" from *A Lincoln Preface* by Carl Sandburg. Copyright © 1953 by Carl Sandburg and renewed 1981 by Margaret Sandburg, Janet Sandburg, and Helga Sandburg Crile, reprinted by permission of Harcourt, Inc. "The Writer" by Richard Wilbur from *New And Collected Poems*. "Macavity: The Mystery Cat" from *Old Possum's Book Of Practical Cats*. Copyright © 1939 by T. S. Eliot and renewed 1967 by Esme Valerie Eliot. Reprinted by permission of Harcourt, Inc. This material may not be reproduced in any form or by means without the prior written permission of the publisher.

HarperCollins Publishers, Inc. "Summer" from *Brown Angels: An Album Of Pictures And Verse* by Walter Dean Myers. Copyright © 1993 by Walter Dean Myers. "In Country" by Bobbie Ann Mason from *In Country*. Copyright © 1985 by Bobbie Ann Mason. Used by permission of HarperCollins Publishers. All rights reserved.

HarperPerennial "Clear Springs" by Bobbie Ann Mason from *Clear Springs: A Family Story*. Copyright © 1999 by Bobbie Ann Mason. All rights reserved.

The Hartford Courant "Cheerful Gift Becomes a Tradition" by Amy Ash Nixon from *The Hartford Courant, October 23, 2004*.

Harvard University Press "Much Madness is the divinest Sense (#435)" by Emily Dickinson from *The Poems Of Emily Dickinson*. Copyright © 1951, 1955, 1979, 1983, Pres&Fellows Harvard College. Reprinted by permission.

Hawaiian Lifeguard Association "Beach and Ocean Safety Signs" by Staff from *www.aloha.com*. Copyright © 1986, 2001 Hawaiian Life guard Association. All rights (and lefts) reserved.

Heinemann UK "The Girl Who Can" by Ama Ata Aidoo from *Opening Spaces: An Anthology Of Contemporary African Women's Writing*. Preface and collection © Yvonne Vera 1999. Reprinted by permission.

Estate of Helmut Hirnschall "There is a Longing . . ." from *My Heart Soars* by Chief Dan George and Helmut Hirnschall. Copyright © 1974 by Chief Dan George and Helmut Hirnschall. Reprinted by permisssion.

The Barbara Hogenson Agency, Inc. "The Secret Life of Walter Mitty" by James Thurber from *My World-And Welcome To It*. Copyright © 1942 by James Thurber. Copyright © renewed 1970 by Rosemary A. Thurber. Used by arrangement with Rosemary A. Thurber and The Barbara Hogensen Agency. All rights reserved.

Henry Holt and Company, Inc. "Fire and Ice" from *The Poetry Of Robert Frost*, edited by Edward Connery Lathem. Copyright © 1951 by Robert Frost, Copyright © 1923, 1969 by Henry Holt and Company, Inc.

Houghton Mifflin Company "All Watched Over by Machines of Loving Grace" from *The Pill Versus The Springhill Mine Disaster* by Richard Brautigan. Copyright © 1968 by Richard Brautigan. "Blackberry Eating" from *Mortal Acts, Mortal Words* by Galway Kinnell. Copyright © 1980 by Galway Kinnell. "A Fable for tomorrow" from *Silent Spring* by Rachel Carson. Copyright © 1962 by Rachel L. Carson, copyright © renewed 1984 by Roger Christie. All rights reserved. Reprinted by permission of Houghton Mifflin Co. "Siren Song" from *You Are Happy* by Margaret Atwood. Copyright © 1974 by Margaret Atwood.

James R. Hurst "The Scarlet Ibis" by James Hurst, published in the *Atlantic Monthly, July 1960*. Copyright © 1988 by James Hurst. Reprinted by permission of the author.

International Creative Management, Inc. "Single Room, Earth View" by Sally Ride, published in the *April/May 1986 issue of Air & Space/Smithsonian Magazine*, published by The Smithsonian Institution. Copyright © Dr. Sally K. Ride. Published by the Washington Speakers Bure. Reprinted by permission. "Libraries Face Sad Chapter" by Pete Hamill from *www.petehamill.com*.

Japan Publications, Inc. "Dragonfly catcher" and Bearing no flowers" by Chiyojo and "Temple bells die out" by Basho from *One Hundred Famous Haiku* translated by Daniel C. Buchanan. Copyright © 1973 by Japan Publications.

Lyndon B. Johnson Library "A White House Diary" by Ladybird Johnson from *A White House Diary*. Used with permission of the Lyndon B. Johnson Library.

Estate of Dr. Martin Luther King, Jr. "I Have a Dream" by Dr. Martin Luther King, Jr. from *The Words Of Martin Luther King, Jr.* Reprinted by permission.

Adam Kirsch "Chekhov in American" by Adam Kirsch from *The Atlantic Monthly, July 1997, Vol. 280, No. 1, Pages 110–112*. Copyright © 1997 by Adam Kirsch. All rights reserved.

Alfred A. Knopf, Inc. "Dream Deferred" from *The Collected Poems of Langston Hughes* by Langston Hughes. Copyright © 1994 by The Estate of Langston Hughes. "The News" from *Conscientious Objections: Stirring Up Trouble About Language, Technology, And Education*. by Neil Postman. Copyright © 1988 by Neil Postman. "Dreams" from *The Collected Poems of Langston Hughes* by Langston Hughes. Copyright © 1994 by The Estate of Langston Hughes. "Uncle Marcos" by Isabel Allende translated by Magda Bogin from *The House Of The Spirits*. Copyright © 1985 by Alfred A. Knopf, A Division of Random House, Inc. Used by permisson of Alfred A. Knopf, a division of Random House, Inc.

Alfred A. Knopf Children's Books "Pecos Bill: The Cyclone" from *Pecos Bill: Texas Cowpuncher* by Harold W. Felton. Copyright © 1949 by Alfred A. Knopf, a division of Random House, Inc. Copyright renewed 1976 by Harold W. Felton. Used by permission of Alfred A. Knopf Children's Books, a division of Random House, Inc.

Little, Brown and Company, Inc. "Perseus" from *Mythology* by Edith Hamilton. Copyright © 1942 by Edith Hamilton; Copyright © renewed 1969 by Dorian Fielding Reid and Doris Fielding Reid. Reprinted by permission of Little, Brown and Company Inc. "Pyramus and Thisbe" by Edith Hamilton from *Mythology*. Copyright © 1940, 1942 by Edith Hamilton. Copyright renewal © 1969 by Dorian Ffielding Reid and Doris Fielding Reid. Executrix of the will of Edith Hamilton. All rights reserved.

Liveright Publishing Corporation "maggie and milly and molly and may" from *Complete Poems: 1904–1962* by E. E. Cummings, edited by George J. Firmage. Copyright © 1956, 1984, 1991 by the Trustees for the E. E. Cummings Trust. Reprinted by permission of Liveright Publishing Corporation.

Marie-Christine MacAndrew "The Necklace" from *Boule de Suif and Selected Stories* by Guy de Maupassant, translated by Andrew MacAndrew, New York, NAL, 1964, pp. 143-151. Translation copyright © 1964 by Andrew MacAndrew. Used by permission of Marie-Christine MacAndrew.

John McPhee "Arthur Ashe Remembered" by John McPhee, first published in *The New Yorker, March 1, 1993*. Reprinted by permission of the author.

Edna St. Vincent Millay Society "An Ancient Gesture" by Edna St. Vincent Millay. From *Collected Poems*, HarperCollins. Copyright © 1954, 1982 by Norma Millay Ellis. All rights reserved.

Pat Mora "Uncoiling" by Pat Mora from *Daughters Of The Fifth Sun*.

Methuen Publishing Company "The Inspector-General" from *The Sneeze: Plays And Stories* by Anton Chekhov, translated and adapted by Michael Frayn, published by Methuen Drama. Originally from *An Awl in a Sack* by Anton Chekhov, 1885.

National Aeronautics and Space Administration "Space Shuttle Basics" by Staff from *www.nasa.gov*. "Robotics Education Project" by Staff from *http://robotics.arc.nasa.gov*.

The Estate of Charles Neider "The Invalid's Story" by Mark Twain from *The Complete Sketches and Tales of Mark Twain*, edited by Charles Neider. Copyright © 1977 by Charles Neider. Reprinted by permission.

North Carolina Transportation Museum "North Carolina Transportation Museum" by Staff from *North Carolina Transportation Museum*. Used with permission.

Northwestern University Press "Sonnets on Love XIII" by Jean de Sponde from *Sonnets on Love and Death*, translated by David R. Slavitt. Evanston: Northwestern University Press, 2001, p. 29. Used by permission of Northwestern University Press.

Naomi Shihab Nye "Daily" by Naomi Shihab Nye from *Hugging The Jukebox*. Copyright © 1982 by Naomi Shihab Nye. All rights reserved. By permission of the author.

Orchard Books "Checkouts" from *A Couple Of Kooks And Other Stories About Love* by Cynthia Rylant. Published by Orchard Books/Scholastic, Inc. Copyright © 1990 by Cynthia Rylant. Reprinted by permission of Scholastic, Inc.

Oxford University Press, Inc. "The Horses" from *Collected Poems* by Edwin Muir. Copyright © 1960 by Willa Muir. Used by permission of Oxford University Press, Inc. "Siren Song" by Margaret Atwood from *Selected Poems 1966–1984*. Copyright © Margaret Atwood 1990.

Penguin Group (USA), Inc. "Play Hard; Play Together; Play Smart" by Dean Smith and Gerald D. Bell with John Kilgo from *The Carolina Way: Leadership Lessons From A Life In Coaching*. Copyright © 2004 by Dean E. Smith. Used by permission of The Penguin Press, a division of Penguin Group (USA) Inc. "Carry Your Own Skis" by Lian Dolan from *Satellite Sisters' Uncommon Senses*. Copyright © 2001 by Satellite Sisters, LLC. Reprinted by permission "The Only Thing We Have to Fear" from *Nothing to Fear: Lessons in Leadership from FDR* by Alan Axelrod. Copyright © 2003 by Alan Axelrod. Used by permission of Portfolio, an imprint of Penguin Group (USA) Inc.

Playbill Magazine "On Summer" by Lorraine Hansberry, reprinted from *Playbill Magazine, June 1960*. © Playbill, Inc. All rights reserved. Used by permission of Playbill, Inc.

G.P. Putnam's Sons "Rules of the Game" from *The Joy Luck Club* by Amy Tan. Copyright © 1989 by Amy Tan. Used by permission of G.P. Putnam Sons, a division of Penguin Putnam, Inc.

Random House, Inc. "New Directions" from *Wouldn't Take Nothing For My Journey Now* by Maya Angelou. Copyright © 1993 by Maya Angelou. "Blues Ain't No Mockinbird" by Toni Cade Bambara from *GORILLA, MY LOVE*. "Blues Ain't No Mockin Bird" from *Gorilla, My Love* by Toni Cade Bambara. Copyright © 1971, by Toni Cade Bambara. Used by permission of Random House, Inc. "Desiderata" by Elizabeth McCracken from *www.randomhouse.com/boldtype/0397/mccracken/essay.html*. Copyright © 1997 Elizabeth McCracken. "Big Kiss: One Actor's Desperate Attempt to Claw His Way to the Middle" by Henry Alford from *http://www.randomhouse.com/boldtype/0601/alford/exerpt*. "The Giant's House" by Elizabeth McCracken from The Giant's House. Copyright © 1996 by Elizabeth McCracken. All rights reserved.

The Estate of May Swenson "Analysis of Baseball" by May Swenson from *American Sports Poems*. Used by permission of the Literary Estate of May Swenson.

Third Woman Press "Twister Hits Houston" by Sandra Cisneros from *My Wicked Wicked Ways*. Copyright © 1987 by Sandra Cisneros. All rights reserved.

The University of Georgia Press "American History" from *The Latin Deli: Prose and Poetry* by Judith Ortiz Cofer. Copyright © 1992 by Judith Ortiz Cofer. All rights reserved.

University of Pittsburgh Press "Candle Hat" from *Questions About Angels* by Billy Collins. Copyright © 1991. Reprinted by permission of the University of Pittsburgh Press.

University Press of New England "The Talk" from *A Summer Life* by Gary Soto. Copyright © 1990 by University Press of New England.

Viking Penguin, Inc. "Old Man of the Temple" from *Under The Banyan Tree* by R. K. Narayan. Copyright © 1985 by R. K. Narayan. Used by permission of Viking Penguin, a division of Penguin Putnam, Inc.

Vital Speeches of the Day "Glory and Hope" by Nelson Mandela from *Vital Speeches of the Day, June 1, 1994*. Reprinted by permission of Vital Speeches of the Day.

W. W. Norton & Company, Inc. "Alabanza: In Praise of Local 100" from *Alabanza* by Martin Espada. Copyright © 2003 by Martin Espada. "The War Against the Trees" from *The Collected Poems* by Stanley Kunitz. Copyright © 2000 by Stanley Kunitz. Used by permission of W. W. Norton & Company, Inc. Reprinted by permission. All rights reserved.

Wesleyan University Press "Slam, Dunk, & Hook" from *Magic City* by Yusef Komunyakaa. Copyright © 1992 by Yusef Komunyakaa, Wesleyan University Press with University Press of New England. Reprinted by permission of Wesleyan University Press with University Press of New England.

World Book Publishing "Detective Story" by David Geherin from *The World Book Encyclopedia*. Copyright © 2001, World Book, Inc. All rights reserved.

Writer's House, LLC. "Meciendo ("Rocking")" by Gabriela Mistral translated by Doris Dana from *Selected Poems Of Gabriela Mistral*. "Meciendo (Rocking)" by Gabriela Mistral, translated and edited by Doris Dana from *Selected Poems Of Gabriela Mistral*. Copyright © 1961, 1964, 1970, 1971 by Doris Dana. Reprinted by permission of the Joan Daves Agency on behalf of the estate of the author.

The Wylie Agency, Inc. "The Man to Send Rain Clouds" from *Storyteller* by Leslie Marmon Silko. Copyright © 1981 by Leslie Marmon Silko. Reprinted by permission of The Wylie Agency, Inc.

Note: Every effort has been made to locate the copyright owner of material reproduced on this component. Omissions brought to our attention will be corrected in subsequent editions.